FEDERAL & CALIFORNIA EVIDENCE RULES

[STATUTORY SUPPLEMENT]

FEDERAL & CALIFORNIA

EVIDENCE RULES

PRINTED ON FACING PAGES, WITH NOTES, COMMENTS, SELECTED LEGISLATIVE HISTORY, AND COMPARATIVE COMMENTARY

2020-2021 Edition

Thomas J. Leach
Emily Garcia Uhrig

Wolters Kluwer

Published by Wolters Kluwer in New York.

Wolters Kluwer Legal & Regulatory U.S. serves customers worldwide with CCH, Aspen Publishers, and Kluwer Law International products. (www.WKLegaledu.com)

To contact Customer Service, e-mail customer.service@wolterskluwer.com, call 1-800-234-1660, fax 1-800-901-9075, or mail correspondence to:

Wolters Kluwer
Attn: Order Department
PO Box 990
Frederick, MD 21705

Printed in the United States of America.

1 2 3 4 5 6 7 8 9 0

ISBN 978-1-5438-3034-7

About Wolters Kluwer Legal & Regulatory U.S.

Wolters Kluwer Legal & Regulatory U.S. delivers expert content and solutions in the areas of law, corporate compliance, health compliance, reimbursement, and legal education. Its practical solutions help customers successfully navigate the demands of a changing environment to drive their daily activities, enhance decision quality and inspire confident outcomes.

Serving customers worldwide, its legal and regulatory portfolio includes products under the Aspen Publishers, CCH Incorporated, Kluwer Law International, ftwilliam.com and MediRegs names. They are regarded as exceptional and trusted resources for general legal and practice-specific knowledge, compliance and risk management, dynamic workflow solutions, and expert commentary.

SUMMARY OF CONTENTS

FOREWORD

HOW TO USE THIS BOOK

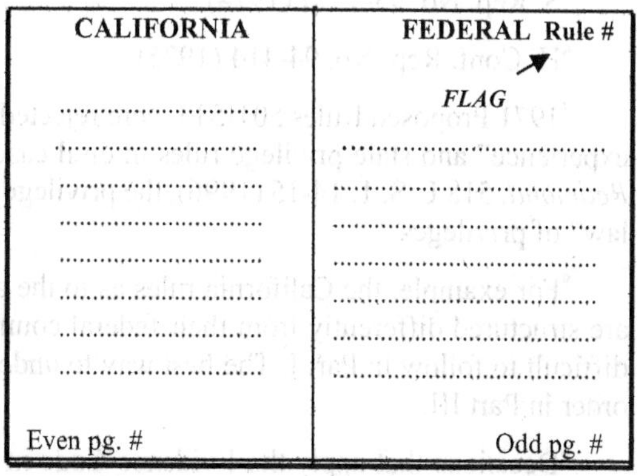

Part I of this book facilitates immediate textual comparisons of the Federal Rules of Evidence (FRE) and corresponding sections of the California Evidence Code (CEC).[1] Each pair of facing pages in Part I shows FRE on the right (odd numbered pages) and CEC on the left (even numbered pages). Comparable provisions are side-by-side. To find a federal rule by number, use the *FLAGS* in the top right corners of the odd-numbered pages. (To find a provision of CEC by section number, use the Table of Contents.) When the text of a rule or section spans more than one page, you must skip every other page to read the entire provision. For example, after reading the first part of FRE 609 on page I-119 you should skip to page I-121 for the continuation.

---

[1]With amendments through June 30, 2020. For citations to sources for amendments, see any of the complete versions of the United States Code and the California Evidence Code.

Part II contains the most important materials for in-depth study of FRE, including: Amendment Alerts, Statutory Notes, Case Notes,[2] Advisory Committee Notes,[3] and excerpts from the legislative process through which FRE were finalized, including House[4] and Senate[5] Judiciary Committee reports, the Conference Committee report,[6] and some of the floor debates in the House and Senate. Part II also includes the deleted provisions of the Proposed Federal Rules of Evidence relating to privileges[7] and the provisions of the Uniform Rules of Evidence relating to privileges.

Part III reproduces CEC in numerical order by sections. That sequence is especially helpful to understanding CEC in places where its structure differs from FRE.[8] Part III also contains interpretive aids, such as Statutory Notes, Amendment Alerts, Case Notes,[9] California Law Revision Commission Comments,[10] and Legislative Committee Comments. While Part I facilitates quick textual comparison of CEC with FRE, Part III enables in-depth study of CEC.

---

[2]Through December 1, 2007, Case Notes include all significant Supreme Court interpretations of FRE, but omitting decisions that apply the Rules in obvious ways. Few court of appeals decisions are included. The selection was aided by Daniel J. Capra, Case Law Divergence from the Federal Rules of Evidence (Federal Judicial Center 2000). For later significant Supreme Court cases, the reader is directed to Prof. Capra's more recent summary: "Case Law Divergence from the Federal Rules of Evidence," in FEDERAL RULES OF EVIDENCE 2013-2014 (West, 2013) or any updates in a more current edition of the same publication.

[3]The original advisory committee notes are taken from Revised Draft of Federal Rules of Evidence, 51 F.R.D. 315 (1971) (hereinafter referred to as "1971 Proposed Rules").

[4]H. Rep. No. 93-650 (1973).

[5]S. Rep. No. 93-1277 (1974).

[6]H. Conf. Rep. No. 94-414 (1975).

[7]1971 Proposed Rules 501-513 were rejected by Congress in favor of "the common law in the light of reason and experience" and state privilege rules in civil cases governed by state law. Fed. R. Evid. 501. According to *Jaffee v. Redmond*, 518 U.S. 1, 14-15 (1996), the privilege provisions of the 1971 Proposed Rules reflect the modern "common law" of privileges.

[8]For example, the California rules as to the admissibility of character evidence (Cal. Evid. Code §§ 1101-1109) are structured differently from their federal counterparts (Fed. R. Evid. 404-406, 413-416). The California rules are difficult to follow in Part I. The best way to understand California's character evidence rules is to read them in Code order in Part III.

[9]Decisions that apply the Evidence Code in obvious ways are excluded. Because of space considerations, very few court of appeals decisions are included.

[10]Undated references to Law Revision Commission Comments are to comments on the bill that was enacted as the Evidence Code in 1965 (Stats. 1965, ch. 299, effective Jan. 1, 1967). They were originally published in 6 CALIF. L. REV. COMM'N, REPORTS, RECOMMENDATIONS, AND STUDIES (1964). Law Revision Commission Comments that say only that the proposed section is consistent with existing California law are omitted. Sources of legislative history of subsequent amendments are cited in a Statutory Note following the affected section. Citations to and detailed information on all amendments may be found in any annotated version of the California codes.

FOREWORD

CHANGES IN THIS 2020-2021 EDITION

A. **Restyled FRE**. Part I continues to show only the "restyled" FRE, effective December 1, 2011. The superseded text of FRE is printed, along with the restyled rules, in Part II. The Evidence Rules Advisory Committee Note describing the purpose and working protocols of the restyling project states:

The Style Project

The Evidence Rules are the fourth set of national procedural rules to be restyled. The restyled Rules of Appellate Procedure took effect in 1998. The restyled Rules of Criminal Procedure took effect in 2002. The restyled Rules of Civil Procedure took effect in 2007. The restyled Rules of Evidence apply the same general drafting guidelines and principles used in restyling the Appellate, Criminal, and Civil Rules.

1. General Guidelines

Guidance in drafting, usage, and style was provided by Bryan Garner, *Guidelines for Drafting and Editing Court Rules,* Administrative Office of the United States Courts (1969) and Bryan Garner, *Dictionary of Modern Legal Usage* (2d ed. 1995). *See also* Joseph Kimble, *Guiding Principles for Restyling the Civil Rules,* in *Preliminary Draft of Proposed Style Revision of the Federal Rules of Civil Procedure,* at page x (Feb. 2005) (available at http://www.uscourts.gov/uscourts/RulesAndPolicies/rules/Prelim_draft_proposed_pt1.pdf); Joseph Kimble, *Lessons in Drafting from the New Federal Rules of Civil Procedure*, 12 Scribes J. Legal Writing 25 (2008-2009). For specific commentary on the Evidence restyling project, see Joseph Kimble, *Drafting Examples from the Proposed New Federal Rules of Evidence*, 88 Mich. B.J. 52 (Aug. 2009); 88 Mich. B.J. 46 (Sept. 2009); 88 Mich. B.J. 54 (Oct. 2009); 88 Mich. B.J. 50 (Nov. 2009).

2. Formatting Changes

Many of the changes in the restyled Evidence Rules result from using format to achieve clearer presentations. The rules are broken down into constituent parts, using progressively indented subparagraphs with headings and substituting vertical for horizontal lists. "Hanging indents" are used throughout. These formatting changes make the structure of the rules graphic and make the restyled rules easier to read and understand even when the words are not changed. Rules 103, 404(b), 606(b), and 612 illustrate the benefits of formatting changes.

3. Changes to Reduce Inconsistent, Ambiguous, Redundant, Repetitive, or Archaic Words

The restyled rules reduce the use of inconsistent terms that say the same thing in different ways. Because different words are presumed to have different meanings, such inconsistencies can result in confusion. The restyled rules reduce inconsistencies by using the same words to express the same meaning. For example, consistent expression is achieved by not switching between "accused" and "defendant" or between "party opponent" and "opposing party" or between the various formulations of civil and criminal action/case/proceeding.

The restyled rules minimize the use of inherently ambiguous words. For example, the word "shall" can mean "must," "may," or something else, depending on context. The potential for confusion is exacerbated by the fact the word "shall" is no longer generally used in spoken or clearly written English. The restyled rules replace "shall" with "must," "may," or "should," depending on which one the context and established interpretation make correct in each rule.

The restyled rules minimize the use of redundant "intensifiers." These are expressions that attempt to add emphasis, but instead state the obvious and create negative implications for other rules. The absence of intensifiers in the restyled rules does not change their substantive meaning. *See, e.g.,* Rule 104(c) (omitting "in all cases"); Rule 602 (omitting "but need not"); Rule 611(b) (omitting "in the exercise of discretion").

The restyled rules also remove words and concepts that are outdated or redundant.

4. Rule Numbers

The restyled rules keep the same numbers to minimize the effect on research. Subdivisions have been rearranged within some rules to achieve greater clarity and simplicity.

5. No Substantive Change

The Committee made special efforts to reject any purported style improvement that might result in a substantive change in the application of a rule. The Committee considered a change to be "substantive" if any of the following conditions were met:

a. Under the existing practice in any circuit, the change could lead to a different result on a question of admissibility (e.g., a change that requires a court to provide either a less or more stringent standard in evaluating the admissibility of particular evidence);

b. Under the existing practice in any circuit, it could lead to a change in the procedure by which an admissibility decision is made (e.g., a change in the time in which an objection must be made, or a change in whether a court must hold a hearing on an admissibility question);

c. The change would restructure a rule in a way that would alter the approach that courts and litigants have used to think about, and argue about, questions of admissibility (e.g., merging Rules 104(a) and 104(b) into a single subdivision); or

d. The amendment would change a "sacred phrase" — one that has become so familiar in practice that to alter it would be unduly disruptive to practice and expectations. Examples in the Evidence Rules include "unfair prejudice" and "truth of the matter asserted."

For space-saving purposes we have not repeated the general Committee Note on each restyled rule, which reads:

> The language of Rule — has been amended as part of the restyling of the Evidence Rules to make them more easily understood and to make style and terminology consistent throughout the rules. These changes are intended to be stylistic only. There is no intent to change any result in any ruling on evidence admissibility.

In the few instances where the Committee added a special note for a particular rule, that note is included. *See, e.g.,* FRE 407-408. For the Reporter's comments on specific issues the Committee faced with certain of the rules, *see* Daniel J. Capra, *Weinstein's Federal Evidence: Restyled Federal Rules of Evidence* (Joseph M. McLaughlin ed., 2d ed. 2011).

Finally, we have not sought to comment on the linguistic differences between the former and the restyled version of the rules, nor on what some commentators opine are substantive differences despite the restyling committee's announced intention to make none.

B. **Comparative Commentary.** In this 2020-2021 edition we continue the 2012 edition's addition of comparative commentary, which stems from the work of co-author Prof. Emily Garcia Uhrig of Pacific McGeorge School of Law. In her Evidence class, Prof. Garcia Uhrig developed a comparative chart lining up FRE and CEC provisions and then summarizing the differences. Prof. Garcia Uhrig graciously contributed her project to the existing version of this volume.

A particular aspect of the comparison between the two codes that deserves attention is the effect on California evidence law of the Proposition 8 initiative ("Prop. 8"), known as the "Victims' Bill of Rights," which California voters passed in June 1982. In relevant part, Prop. 8 amended the California Constitution to include Art. I § 28(d) and (f). Subsection 28(d) provides that, except as provided by statute enacted by two-thirds majority of each house of the state legislature, "relevant evidence shall not be excluded in any criminal proceeding," whether juvenile or adult. But the subsection expressly preserves statutory authority relating to privilege and hearsay, as well as CEC §§ 352, 782, and 1103. Subsection (f) purports to make admissible in criminal proceedings "[a]ny prior felony conviction . . . without limitation for purposes of impeachment." Prop. 8 has no effect on civil proceedings.

Prop. 8 has required California state courts to grapple with the impact of § 28(d) at each juncture where CEC otherwise functions to restrict admissibility of relevant evidence, and with the admissibility of prior conviction evidence to impeach witnesses in light of the apparent internal conflict between subsections (d) and (f), as well as subsection (f)'s further conflict with CEC § 788. In some cases, courts have applied Prop. 8 literally; in others, courts have worked hard to limit its impact. Moreover, many questions still remain unresolved regarding Prop. 8's effects.

We do not attempt through the comparative inserts in this book to provide a comprehensive treatment of this topic.[11] Rather, we summarize throughout where the courts have specifically addressed Prop. 8's impact on CEC and where the impact has been flagged as an open question. Those readers who are confronted with issues of California evidence law in criminal cases are urged to undertake their own full research on the topic.

[11] For an in-depth analysis of the impact of Proposition 8 on CEC, *see* Miguel A. Mendez, The Victims' Bill of Rights – Thirty Years Under Proposition 8, 25 Stan. L. & Pol'y Rev. 379 (2014).

FOREWORD

History of FRE & CEC and Reasons For Comparing Them

The Federal Rules of Evidence have been enormously influential since their enactment in 1975. Other works describe in detail the evolution of those rules,[12] beginning in the early 1960's with a "feasibility and advisability" report to the Judicial Conference of the United States;[13] Chief Justice Earl Warren's appointment of an Advisory Committee on Rules of Evidence in 1965; the Advisory Committee's 1969 "Preliminary Draft,"[14] which was published for comments by the bench and bar; the Advisory Committee's 1971 "Revised Draft";[15] Rules of Evidence promulgated by the Supreme Court in 1973;[16] Congressional action setting aside the Court's rules and taking them on as a legislative project, and bills, hearings and debates in the House of Representatives and Senate of the United States, culminating in the enactment of the Federal Rules of Evidence as Pub. L. 93-595, 88 Stat. 1926, approved January 2, 1975, effective July 1, 1975.

The Federal Rules and a version of the Federal Rules promulgated as the Uniform Rules of Evidence (1974, most recently amended, 1999) have been used as the model for codifying rules of evidence in 43 or 44 states (see note on Connecticut in table above), several territories, and the military.[17]

STATE ADOPTIONS OF EVIDENCE RULES SIMILAR TO THE FEDERAL RULES OF EVIDENCE, WITH EFFECTIVE DATES*

Alabama	January 1, 1996	Nebraska	January 1, 1976
Alaska	August 1, 1979	Nevada†	July 1, 1971
Arizona	September 1, 1977	New Hampshire	July 1, 1985
Arkansas	July 1, 1976	New Jersey	July 1, 1993
Connecticut**	January 1, 2000	New Mexico	July 1, 1973
Colorado	January 1, 1980	North Carolina	July 4, 1984
Delaware	July 1, 1980	North Dakota	February, 15, 1977
Florida	July 1, 1979	Ohio	July 1, 1980
Georgia	January 1, 2013	Oklahoma	May 10, 1978
Hawaii	January 1, 1981	Oregon	January 1, 1983
Idaho	July 1, 1985	Pennsylvania	October 1, 1998
Illinois	January 1, 2011	Rhode Island	October 1, 1987
Indiana	January 1, 1994	South Carolina	September 3, 1995
Iowa	July 1, 1983	South Dakota	July 1, 1978
Kentucky	July 1, 1992	Tennessee	January 1, 1990
Louisiana	January 1, 1989	Texas‡	September 1, 1983
Maine	February 2, 1976	Utah	September 1, 1983
Massachusetts***	Rev. annually	Vermont	April 1, 1983
Maryland	July 1, 1994	Virginia	July 1, 2012
Michigan	March 1, 1978	Washington	April 8, 1979
Minnesota	July 1, 1977	West Virginia	February 1, 1985
Mississippi	January 1, 1976	Wisconsin	January 1, 1974
Montana	July 1, 1977	Wyoming	January 1, 1978

* For details of differences, see State Correlation Tables in Federal Rules of Evidence Service (Callaghan & Co.) (Tables discontinued, 1997).

** Commentators differ on the extent to which Connecticut's Code of Evidence is "similar to" FRE. A comparison by the reader will show where the Code has borrowed extensively from, but also where it has rewritten, omitted, or added to, FRE.

*** "The Massachusetts Guide to Evidence … organizes and states the law of evidence applied in proceedings in the courts of the Commonwealth, as set forth in the Federal and State Constitutions, General Laws, common law, and rules of court….

….

"The Guide follows the arrangement of the law contained in the Federal Rules of Evidence and thus is comprised of eleven articles. Wherever possible, the Guide expresses the principles of Massachusetts evidence law by using the language that appears in the corresponding Federal rules. The Guide is not a set of rules, but rather, as the title suggests, a guide to evidence based on the law as it exists today…. Ultimately, the law of evidence in Massachusetts is what is contained in the authoritative decisions of the Supreme Judicial Court and of the Appeals Court, and the statutes duly enacted by the Legislature."

† Based on 1968 Preliminary Draft of Federal Rules of Evidence.

‡ Civil Rules. Criminal Rules effective three years later.

---

[12] *See, e.g.*, 1 WEINSTEIN'S FEDERAL EVIDENCE xix-xxiii (Joseph M. McLaughlin ed., 2d ed. 1997) (conventional view); 21 CHARLES A. WRIGHT & KENNETH W. GRAHAM, FEDERAL PRACTICE & PROCEDURE: EVIDENCE § 5006 (1977) (critical view).

[13] 30 F.R.D. 737 (1962).

[14] 46 F.R.D. 161 (1969).

[15] 51 F.R.D. 315 (1971).

[16] 56 F.R.D. 183 (1973).

[17] The authors are grateful to Prof. Norman Garland for alerting them to recent additions to the list of states in the table.

FOREWORD

As influential as the Federal Rules have been, there are good reasons for studying them in comparison with the California Evidence Code. An earlier work (developed between 1956 and 1965 and effective January 1, 1967), CEC, like FRE, was the product of extensive scholarly and legislative consideration.[18] CEC is a much more detailed and coherent statement of the law of evidence.[19] In controversial areas, FRE and CEC often disagree, and study of their conflicting provisions illuminates conflicting policies competing for recognition in the law of evidence. Even in areas of agreement, study of the California provision from which a Federal rule was drawn may illuminate the meaning and scope of the Federal rule.

CURRENT AND FUTURE AMENDMENTS

While the general principles of evidence law appear to be stable, the specifics often change. The sources set out below should be consulted for the most current status.

Federal Rules of Evidence

In April 2006, the Evidence Rules Advisory Committee published recommended legislation dealing with inadvertent disclosures of attorney-client communications and limited waivers. The first topic is now covered by Rule 502 (see pp. II-50-55), which became effective December 1, 2008. The proposed rule on limited waivers remains unapproved (see pp. II-55-57).

As of the issue date of this edition, a proposed amendment to Rule 404(b) will become effective December 1, 2020. *See* pp. I-33 and II-23, *infra.*

For continuing updates on Advisory Committee activities, including further amendments under consideration, see postings at https://www.uscourts.gov/rules-policies/records-and-archives-rules-committees/committee-reports.

---

[18] The history is concisely summarized in JACK B. WEINSTEIN ET AL., EVIDENCE RULES, STATUTE & CASE SUPPLEMENT 217 (2004):

> The [California Evidence] Code was enacted after a nine-year period of study and drafting by the California Law Revision Commission. The Commission's mandate pursuant to a legislative resolution was to determine whether and to what extent the Uniform Rules of Evidence [1953] were to be adopted in California. The Commission engaged Professor James H. Chadbourn (then on the faculty at UCLA Law School, later of the Harvard Law School) to prepare a series of studies of the adaptability of the Uniform Rules to California Law.
>
> The Chadbourn studies along with the Commission's tentative recommendations for legislation were published by the Commission between 1962 and 1964 in a series of nine pamphlets, each dealing with a major subject matter area of the law of evidence (reprinted in Volume 6 of the Commission's Reports, Recommendations and Studies (1964)). * * *
>
> The Law Revision Commission prepared most of the Comments to the Code. In a number of instances, however, * * * the Comments were prepared by one of the two state legislative committees that reported out the bill that became the Code. * * *

[19] Compare the treatment of preliminary questions (Fed. R. Evid. 104; Cal. Evid. Code §§ 400-406), judicial notice (Fed. R. Evid. 201; Cal. Evid. Code §§ 450-460), burdens of proof and presumptions (Fed. R. Evid. 301-302; Cal. Evid. Code §§ 500-670), and privileges (Fed. R. Evid. 501; Cal. Evid. Code §§ 900-1070). Some of the coherence of the California Code has been impaired by piecemeal changes since 1967.

California Evidence Code

The California Law Revision Commission, which was a prime mover in the development and adoption of CEC, has not been involved in most of the amendments to the Evidence Code since 1967.[20] For the most part, amendments have originated in the legislature — often at the urging of interest groups. In each legislative session, numerous bills are introduced to add to or amend CEC. "Hot button" political issues of the moment often determine which bills succeed. It is difficult to predict future amendments to the Evidence Code, which are often driven by current politics. Currently pending legislation that pertains to evidentiary matters may be tracked at:

For 2019-2020 Session — http://leginfo.legislature.ca.gov/faces/codes.xhtml, under the "Publications" tab, choose "Table of Statutes Affected."

For 2017-2018 Session — same website, choose "Legislative Index and Table of Sections Affected, Prior Sessions"

For the texts of the added and amended statutes:

For 2019-2020 Session — http://leginfo.legislature.ca.gov/faces/billSearchClient.xhtml?session_year=20192020&house=Both&author=All&lawCode=All

For 2017-2018 Session — http://leginfo.legislature.ca.gov/faces/billSearchClient.xhtml?session_year=20172018&house=Both&author=All&lawCode=All

In 2002, the Law Revision Commission launched a study comparing the California Evidence Code and the Federal Rules of Evidence in order to determine whether any of the California provisions should be revised to achieve greater uniformity with the Federal Rules. The Commission engaged Prof. Miguel Mendez of Stanford Law School to prepare a comprehensive comparison of the California Evidence Code with the Federal Rules and the Uniform Rules. This project, however, was aborted in 2005.

In November 2004, the Law Revision Commission recommended legislation to clarify whether an inadvertent disclosure of privileged information results in a waiver of the privilege. The Commission's recommendation was to amend CEC § 912 to make it clear that only an "intentional disclosure" would result in waiver.[21] The Commission's recommendation was introduced in the California assembly as AB1133 (Harmon) but was not enacted.

---

[20] Its most recent major contribution is the Secondary Evidence Rule, a radical reform of the traditional Best Evidence Rule, enacted in 1998. Cal. Evid. Code §§ 1520-1523.

[21] See Staff Recommendation, available at http://www.clrc.ca.gov/pub/2004/MM04-54.pdf; Law Revision Commission Minutes, available at http://www.clrc.ca.gov/pub/Minutes/Minutes2004-11.pdf.

FOREWORD

GRATITUDE & ACKNOWLEDGMENTS

Prof. Leach: Our late colleague, Prof. David Miller, originated the design and first issues of this volume; his scholarly work and superb attention to detail set the standard to which we continue to aspire. Prof. Daniel J. Capra of Fordham Law School helps keep us abreast of the work of the Advisory Committee on the Federal Rules of Evidence. Barbara Gaal, Chief Deputy Counsel of the California Law Revision Commission, continues kindly to advise us on current developments in California evidence law. My wife, Prof. Cary Bricker, helps me find time for this project and does her best to keep my eye on the big issues, rising above the necessary minutiae. My trial advocacy colleague, Joe Taylor, got me started on learning California evidence law. Special thanks to tireless student researchers at Pacific McGeorge: Michael Youril, Clayton McCarl, and Kirk Wilbur; Mr. McCarl truly deserves the honorific of Executive Editor, as it was he who wrestled the current form of Part I, with interlineated commentary, into submission.

Prof. Garcia Uhrig: My sincerest thanks to the many students who inspired me to undertake — and used and provided invaluable feedback on early versions of — an efficient comparative analysis between FRE and CEC; to research assistants Micah Hauptman, Andrew Ducart, and Rebecca Hause, who assisted in the underlying research; to my colleagues, Jay Leach and the late David Miller; to colleagues Ruth Jones and John Myers for their mentorship; and to my husband Keith and daughter Xochi for their patience and support, which made my participation in this effort possible.

We are solely responsible for the shortcomings of this book. We urge anyone who finds mistakes or has suggestions for improvement to call, write, or e-mail us. Thank you in advance.

Thomas J. Leach
Professor of Law Emeritus
University of the Pacific
McGeorge School of Law
3200 Fifth Avenue
Sacramento, CA 95817
j.leach@pacific.edu
916.715.2348

Emily Garcia Uhrig
Judge, Los Angeles Superior Court
Van Nuys Courthouse – West
14400 Erwin Street Mall
Van Nuys, CA 91401
esuhrig2003@yahoo.com

July 2020

FEDERAL RULES OF EVIDENCE

Rule *Page*

ARTICLE I. GENERAL PROVISIONS

ARTICLE II. JUDICIAL NOTICE

ARTICLE III. PRESUMPTIONS IN CIVIL ACTIONS AND PROCEEDINGS

TABLE OF CONTENTS

ARTICLE IX. AUTHENTICATION AND IDENTIFICATION

ARTICLE X. CONTENTS OF WRITINGS, RECORDINGS AND PHOTOGRAPHS

TABLE OF CONTENTS

Section Page

CALIFORNIA EVIDENCE CODE

DIVISION 1. PRELIMINARY PROVISIONS AND CONSTRUCTION

DIVISION 2. WORDS AND PHRASES DEFINED

DIVISION 3. GENERAL PROVISIONS

Chapter 1. Applicability of Code

Section Page

Chapter 7. Hypnosis of Witness

DIVISION 7. OPINION TESTIMONY AND SCIENTIFIC EVIDENCE

Chapter 1. Expert and Other Opinion Testimony

Article 1. Expert and other Opinion Testimony Generally

Article 2. Value, Damages, and Benefits in Eminent Domain and Inverse Condemnation Cases

Article 3. Opinion Testimony on Particular Subjects

[**Chapter 2. Blood Tests to Determine Paternity.** *Repealed, 1992.* See Family Code §§ 7550-7557]

DIVISION 8. PRIVILEGES

Chapter 1. Definitions

Chapter 2. Applicability of Division

Section *Page*

Article 8.5. Sexual Assault Victim-Counselor Privilege

Article 8.7. Domestic Violence Victim-Counselor Privilege

Article 8.8 Human Trafficking Caseworker-Victim Privilege

Article 9. Official Information and Identity of Informer

Article 10. Political Vote

Article 11. Trade Secret

Chapter 5. Immunity of Newsman from Citation for Contempt

Section Page

DIVISION 9. EVIDENCE AFFECTED OR EXCLUDED BY EXTRINSIC POLICIES

Chapter 1. Evidence of Character, Habit, or Custom

Chapter 2. Mediation

Chapter 3. Other Evidence Affected or Excluded by Extrinsic Policies

TABLE OF CONTENTS

Section *Page*

CALIFORNIA CONSTITUTION, ARTICLE I

CALIFORNIA CODE OF CIVIL PROCEDURE

CALIFORNIA PENAL CODE

PART I

FEDERAL RULES OF EVIDENCE AND CALIFORNIA EVIDENCE CODE ON FACING PAGES

WITH COMPARATIVE COMMENTARY

§ 300. **Applicability of code.** Except as otherwise provided by statute, this code applies in every action before the Supreme Court or a court of appeal or superior court, including proceedings in such actions conducted by a referee, court commissioner, or similar officer, but does not apply in grand jury proceedings. [*Amended 2002.*]

> *Compare FRE 101 and CEC § 300*: FRE do not apply in grand jury proceedings or preliminary examinations. CEC does not apply in grand jury proceedings but does apply in preliminary hearings.

§ 2. **Common law rule construing code abrogated.** The rule of the common law, that statutes in derogation thereof are to be strictly construed, has no application to this code. This code establishes the law of this state respecting the subject to which it relates, and its provisions are to be liberally construed with a view to effecting its objects and promoting justice.

§ 4. **Construction of code.** Unless the provision or context otherwise requires, these preliminary provisions and rules of construction shall govern the construction of this code.

[*The preliminary provisions and rules of construction referred to in § 4 are set forth at p. III-3. Where they have counterparts in FRE, they are also printed opposite those rules.*]

ARTICLE I. GENERAL PROVISIONS

Rule 101. Scope; Definitions

(a) **Scope.** These rules apply to proceedings in United States courts. The specific courts and proceedings to which the rules apply, along with exceptions, are set out in Rule 1101.

(b) **Definitions.** In these rules:

(1) "civil case" means a civil action or proceeding;

(2) "criminal case" includes a criminal proceeding;

(3) "public office" includes a public agency;

(4) "record" includes a memorandum, report, or data compilation;

(5) a "rule prescribed by the Supreme Court" means a rule adopted by the Supreme Court under statutory authority; and

(6) a reference to any kind of written material or any other medium includes electronically stored information.

Rule 102. Purpose

These rules should be construed so as to administer every proceeding fairly, eliminate unjustifiable expense and delay, and promote the development of evidence law, to the end of ascertaining the truth and securing a just determination.

Compare FRE 102 and CEC § 2, 4: CEC abrogates the common-law rule requiring strict interpretation of its terms and endorses a liberal interpretation to effect its objects and promote justice. FRE requires the rules to be construed to secure fairness, economy, and development of evidence law in order to ascertain truth and secure just determinations.

§ 353. **Effect of erroneous admission of evidence.** A verdict or finding shall not be set aside, nor shall the judgment or decision based thereon be reversed, by reason of the erroneous admission of evidence unless:

(a) There appears of record an objection to or a motion to exclude or to strike the evidence that was timely made and so stated as to make clear the specific ground of the objection or motion; and

(b) The court which passes upon the effect of the error or errors is of the opinion that the admitted evidence should have been excluded on the ground stated and that the error or errors complained of resulted in a miscarriage of justice.

§ 354. **Effect of erroneous exclusion of evidence.** A verdict or finding shall not be set aside, nor shall the judgment or decision based thereon be reversed, by reason of the erroneous exclusion of evidence unless the court which passes upon the effect of the error or errors is of the opinion that the error or errors complained of resulted in a miscarriage of justice and it appears of record that:

(a) The substance, purpose, and relevance of the excluded evidence was made known to the court by the questions asked, an offer of proof, or by any other means;

(b) The rulings of the court made compliance with subdivision (a) futile; or

(c) The evidence was sought by questions asked during cross-examination or recross-examination.

[*CEC has no counterpart to FRE 103(d) or (e).*]

§ 310. **Questions of law for court.** (a) All questions of law (including but not limited to questions concerning the construction of statutes and other writings, the admissibility of evidence, and other rules of evidence) are to be decided by the court. Determination of issues of fact preliminary to the admission of evidence are to be decided by the court as provided in Article 2 (commencing with Section 400) of Chapter 4.

(b) Determination of the law of an organization of nations or of the law of a foreign nation or a public entity in a foreign nation is a question of law to be determined in the manner provided in Division 4 (commencing with Section 450).

Rule 103. Rulings on Evidence

(a) **Preserving a Claim of Error.** A party may claim error in a ruling to admit or exclude evidence only if the error affects a substantial right of the party and:

(1) if the ruling admits evidence, a party, on the record:

(A) timely objects or moves to strike; and

(B) states the specific ground, unless it was apparent from the context; or

(2) if the ruling excludes evidence, a party informs the court of its substance by an offer of proof, unless the substance was apparent from the context.

(b) **Not Needing to Renew an Objection or Offer of Proof.** Once the court rules definitively on the record — either before or at trial — a party need not renew an objection or offer of proof to preserve a claim of error for appeal.

(c) **Court's Statement About the Ruling; Directing an Offer of Proof.** The court may make any statement about the character or form of the evidence, the objection made, and the ruling. The court may direct that an offer of proof be made in question-and-answer form.

> *Compare FRE 103(a)-(c) and CEC §§ 353-354*: As a general rule, both FRE and CEC require an objecting party to specify the basis for objection. FRE suspends this requirement where the basis is obvious. CEC has no analogous provision.

(d) **Preventing the Jury from Hearing Inadmissible Evidence.** To the extent practicable, the court must conduct a jury trial so that inadmissible evidence is not suggested to the jury by any means.

(e) **Taking Notice of Plain Error.** A court may take notice of a plain error affecting a substantial right, even if the claim of error was not properly preserved.

[*FRE have no counterpart to CEC § 310.*]

§ 311. Determination of foreign law. If the law of an organization of nations, a foreign nation or a state other than this state, or a public entity in a foreign nation or a state other than this state, is applicable and such law cannot be determined, the court may, as the ends of justice require, either:

(a) Apply the law of this state if the court can do so consistently with the Constitution of the United States and the Constitution of this state; or

(b) Dismiss the action without prejudice or, in the case of a reviewing court, remand the case to the trial court with directions to dismiss the action without prejudice.

§ 312. Jury as trier of fact. Except as otherwise provided by law, where the trial is by jury:

(a) All questions of fact are to be decided by the jury.

(b) Subject to the control of the court, the jury is to determine the effect and value of the evidence addressed to it, including the credibility of witnesses and hearsay declarants.

§ 400. Preliminary fact. As used in this article [§§ 400-406], "preliminary fact" means a fact upon the existence or nonexistence of which depends the admissibility or inadmissibility of evidence. The phrase "the admissibility or inadmissibility of evidence" includes the qualification or disqualification of a person to be a witness and the existence or nonexistence of a privilege.

§ 401. Proffered evidence. As used in this article [§§ 400-406], "proffered evidence" means evidence, the admissibility or inadmissibility of which is dependent upon the existence or nonexistence of a preliminary fact.

§ 405. Determination of foundational and other preliminary facts in other cases. With respect to preliminary fact determinations not governed by Section 403 or 404:

(a) When the existence of a preliminary fact is disputed, the court shall indicate which party has the burden of producing evidence and the burden of proof on the issue as implied by the rule of law under which the question arises. The court shall determine the existence or nonexistence of the preliminary fact and shall admit or exclude the proffered evidence as required by the rule of law under which the question arises.

(b) If a preliminary fact is also a fact in issue in the action:

(1) The jury shall not be informed of the court's determination as to the existence or nonexistence of the preliminary fact.

(2) If the proffered evidence is admitted, the jury shall not be instructed to disregard the evidence if its determination of the fact differs from the court's determination of the preliminary fact.

[*FRE have no counterpart to CEC § 311.*]

[*FRE have no counterpart to CEC § 312.*]

Rule 104. Preliminary Questions

(a) In General. The court must decide any preliminary question about whether a witness is qualified, a privilege exists, or evidence is admissible. In so deciding, the court is not bound by evidence rules, except those on privilege.

Compare FRE 104(a) and CEC § 405: The difference lies primarily in the mechanics, rather than the substance, of each rule. FRE lists the types of preliminary questions that Rule 104(a) governs: qualification of a witness, existence of a privilege, or admissibility of evidence. CEC discusses such preliminary questions at great length in its comments to §§ 403 and 405, although § 405 itself does not contain such a list. Also, FRE and CEC differ as to the type of evidence a court may consider under FRE 104(a) and CEC § 405: under FRE, the court is bound only by privileges law; under CEC, the Code in its entirety applies.

§ 403. Determination of foundational and other preliminary facts where relevancy, personal knowledge, or authenticity is disputed. (a) The proponent of the proffered evidence has the burden of producing evidence as to the existence of the preliminary fact, and the proffered evidence is inadmissible unless the court finds that there is evidence sufficient to sustain a finding of the existence of the preliminary fact, when:

(1) The relevance of the proffered evidence depends on the existence of the preliminary fact;

(2) The preliminary fact is the personal knowledge of a witness concerning the subject matter of his testimony;

(3) The preliminary fact is the authenticity of a writing; or

(4) The proffered evidence is of a statement or other conduct of a particular person and the preliminary fact is whether that person made the statement or so conducted himself.

(b) Subject to Section 702, the court may admit conditionally the proffered evidence under this section, subject to evidence of the preliminary fact being supplied later in the course of the trial.

(c) If the court admits the proffered evidence under this section, the court:

(1) May, and on request shall, instruct the jury to determine whether the preliminary fact exists and to disregard the proffered evidence unless the jury finds that the preliminary fact does exist.

(2) Shall instruct the jury to disregard the proffered evidence if the court subsequently determines that a jury could not reasonably find that the preliminary fact exists.

§ 404. Determination of whether proffered evidence is incriminatory. Whenever the proffered evidence is claimed to be privileged under Section 940, the person claiming the privilege has the burden of showing that the proffered evidence might tend to incriminate him; and the proffered evidence is inadmissible unless it clearly appears to the court that the proffered evidence cannot possibly have a tendency to incriminate the person claiming the privilege.

(b) **Relevance That Depends on a Fact.** When the relevance of evidence depends on whether a fact exists, proof must be introduced sufficient to support a finding that the fact does exist. The court may admit the proposed evidence on the condition that the proof be introduced later.

Compare FRE 104(b) and CEC § 403: As with FRE 104(a) and CEC § 405, the difference is mainly mechanical, not substantive. FRE does not list the specific preliminary facts that trigger conditional relevance analysis. In contrast, CEC lists several preliminary facts requiring such analysis: a witness's personal knowledge, authenticity of a writing, and whether a person made a certain statement or engaged in particular conduct. CEC thus provides greater guidance to courts. In addition, although FRE does not provide for the jury instruction outlined in CEC § 403(c), federal trial practice is to use a similar instruction.

[*FRE have no counterpart to CEC § 404.*]

§ **402. Procedure for determining foundational and other preliminary facts.** (a) When the existence of a preliminary fact is disputed, its existence or nonexistence shall be determined as provided in this article [§§ 400-406].

(b) The court may hear and determine the question of the admissibility of evidence out of the presence or hearing of the jury; but in a criminal action, the court shall hear and determine the question of the admissibility of a confession or admission of the defendant out of the presence and hearing of the jury if any party so requests.

(c) A ruling on the admissibility of evidence implies whatever finding of fact is prerequisite thereto; a separate or formal finding is unnecessary unless required by statute.

[*CEC has no counterpart to FRE 104(d).*]

§ **406. Evidence affecting weight or credibility.** This article [§§ 400-406] does not limit the right of a party to introduce before the trier of fact evidence relevant to weight or credibility.

§ **410. Direct evidence.** As used in this chapter [§§ 410-413], "direct evidence" means evidence that directly proves a fact, without an inference or presumption, and which in itself, if true, conclusively establishes that fact.

§ **411. Direct evidence of one witness sufficient.** Except where additional evidence is required by statute, the direct evidence of one witness who is entitled to full credit is sufficient for proof of any fact.

§ **412. Party having power to produce better evidence.** If weaker and less satisfactory evidence is offered when it was within the power of the party to produce stronger and more satisfactory evidence, the evidence offered should be viewed with distrust.

§ **413. Party's failure to explain or deny evidence.** In determining what inferences to draw from the evidence or facts in the case against a party, the trier of fact may consider, among other things, the party's failure to explain or to deny by his testimony such evidence or facts in the case against him, or his willful suppression of evidence relating thereto, if such be the case.

(c) Conducting a Hearing So That the Jury Cannot Hear It. The court must conduct any hearing on a preliminary question so that the jury cannot hear it if:

(1) the hearing involves the admissibility of a confession;

(2) a defendant in a criminal case is a witness and so requests; or

(3) justice so requires.

(d) Cross-Examining a Defendant in a Criminal Case. By testifying on a preliminary question, a defendant in a criminal case does not become subject to cross-examination on other issues in the case.

(e) Evidence Relevant to Weight and Credibility. This rule does not limit a party's right to introduce before the jury evidence that is relevant to the weight or credibility of other evidence.

[*FRE have no counterpart to CEC §§ 410-413.*]

§ 355. **Limited admissibility.** When evidence is admissible as to one party or for one purpose and is inadmissible as to another party or for another purpose, the court upon request shall restrict the evidence to its proper scope and instruct the jury accordingly.

§ 356. **Entire act, declaration, conversation, or writing may be brought out to elucidate part offered.** Where part of an act, declaration, conversation, or writing is given in evidence by one party, the whole on the same subject may be inquired into by an adverse party; when a letter is read, the answer may be given; and when a detached act, declaration, conversation, or writing is given in evidence, any other act, declaration, conversation, or writing which is necessary to make it understood may also be given in evidence.

Compare FRE 106 and CEC § 356: In the interest of completeness, CEC allows introduction of the whole of writings, recorded statements, and conversations that have been received in part. FRE limits admissibility for completeness to writings and recorded statements, excluding conversations.

§ 450. **Judicial notice may be taken only as authorized by law.** Judicial notice may not be taken of any matter unless authorized or required by law.

§ 451. **Matters which must be judicially noticed.** Judicial notice shall be taken of the following:

(a) The decisional, constitutional, and public statutory law of this state and of the United States and the provisions of any charter described in Section 3, 4, or 5 of Article XI of the California Constitution.

(b) Any matter made a subject of judicial notice by Section 11343.6, 11344.6, or 18576 of the Government Code or by Section 1507 of Title 44 of the United States Code.

(c) Rules of professional conduct for members of the bar adopted pursuant to Section 6076 of the Business and Professions Code and rules of practice and procedure for the courts of this state adopted by the Judicial Council.

(d) Rules of pleading, practice, and procedure prescribed by the United States Supreme Court, such as the Rules of the United States Supreme Court, the Federal Rules of Civil Procedure, the Federal Rules of Criminal Procedure, the Admiralty Rules, the Rules of the Court of Claims, the Rules of the Customs Court, and the General Orders and Forms in Bankruptcy.

(e) The true signification of all English words and phrases and of all legal expressions.

(f) Facts and propositions of generalized knowledge that are so universally known that they cannot reasonably be the subject of dispute. [*Amended 1971, 1972, 1982, 1985, 1986.*]

Rule 105. Limiting Evidence That Is Not Admissible Against Other Parties or for Other Purposes

If the court admits evidence that is admissible against a party or for a purpose — but not against another party or for another purpose — the court, on timely request, must restrict the evidence to its proper scope and instruct the jury accordingly.

Rule 106. Remainder of or Related Writings or Recorded Statements

If a party introduces all or part of a writing or recorded statement, an adverse party may require the introduction, at that time, of any other part — or any other writing or recorded statement — that in fairness ought to be considered at the same time.

ARTICLE II. JUDICIAL NOTICE

Rule 201. Judicial Notice of Adjudicative Facts

(a) **Scope.** This rule governs judicial notice of an adjudicative fact only, not a legislative fact.

(b) **Kinds of Facts That May Be Judicially Noticed.** The court may judicially notice a fact that is not subject to reasonable dispute because it:

(1) is generally known within the trial court's territorial jurisdiction; or

(2) can be accurately and readily determined from sources whose accuracy cannot reasonably be questioned.

Compare FRE 201 and CEC §§ 450-453, 455, 457-458: The most significant difference between FRE and CEC is that FRE covers adjudicative facts only, whereas CEC permits judicial notice of both adjudicative and legal facts. In addition, under FRE, in civil cases the court must instruct the jury to accept the judicially noticed fact as conclusive. In criminal cases, however, the court must instruct the jury that it may, but is not required to, accept a judicially noticed fact as conclusive. Under CEC, the court has discretion to, and upon request by a party must, instruct the jury to accept the judicially noticed fact as conclusive. In criminal cases, California case law, rather than CEC, allows the jury to reject a judicially noticed fact.

§ **452. Matters which may be judicially noticed.** Judicial notice may be taken of the following matters to the extent that they are not embraced within Section 451:

(a) The decisional, constitutional, and statutory law of any state of the United States and the resolutions and private acts of the Congress of the United States and of the Legislature of this state.

(b) Regulations and legislative enactments issued by or under the authority of the United States or any public entity in the United States.

(c) Official acts of the legislative, executive, and judicial departments of the United States and of any state of the United States.

(d) Records of (1) any court of this state or (2) any court of record of the United States or of any state of the United States.

(e) Rules of court of (1) any court of this state or (2) any court of record of the United States or of any state of the United States.

(f) The law of an organization of nations and of foreign nations and public entities in foreign nations.

(g) Facts and propositions that are of such common knowledge within the territorial jurisdiction of the court that they cannot reasonably be the subject of dispute.

(h) Facts and propositions that are not reasonably subject to dispute and are capable of immediate and accurate determination by resort to sources of reasonably indisputable accuracy.

§ **453. Compulsory judicial notice upon request.** The trial court shall take judicial notice of any matter specified in Section 452 if a party requests it and: (a) Gives each adverse party sufficient notice of the request, through the pleadings or otherwise, to enable such adverse party to prepare to meet the request; and

(b) Furnishes the court with sufficient information to enable it to take judicial notice of the matter.

(c) Taking Notice. The court:

(1) may take judicial notice on its own; or

(2) must take judicial notice if a party requests it and the court is supplied with the necessary information.

§ **458. Judicial notice by trial court in subsequent proceedings.** The failure or refusal of the trial court to take judicial notice of a matter, or to instruct the jury with respect to the matter, does not preclude the trial court in subsequent proceedings in the action from taking judicial notice of the matter in accordance with the procedure specified in this division.

§ **459. Judicial notice by reviewing court.** (a) The reviewing court shall take judicial notice of (1) each matter properly noticed by the trial court and (2) each matter that the trial court was required to notice under Section 451 or 453. The reviewing court may take judicial notice of any matter specified in Section 452. The reviewing court may take judicial notice of a matter in a tenor different from that noticed by the trial court.

(b) In determining the propriety of taking judicial notice of a matter, or the tenor thereof, the reviewing court has the same power as the trial court under Section 454.

(c) When taking judicial notice under this section of a matter specified in Section 452 or in subdivision (f) of Section 451 that is of substantial consequence to the determination of the action, the reviewing court shall comply with the provisions of subdivision (a) of Section 455 if the matter was not theretofore judicially noticed in the action.

(d) In determining the propriety of taking judicial notice of a matter specified in Section 452 or in subdivision (f) of Section 451 that is of substantial consequence to the determination of the action, or the tenor thereof, if the reviewing court resorts to any source of information not received in open court or not included in the record of the action, including the advice of persons learned in the subject matter, the reviewing court shall afford each party reasonable opportunity to meet such information before judicial notice of the matter may be taken.

§ **455. Opportunity to present information to court.** With respect to any matter specified in Section 452 or in subdivision (f) of Section 451 that is of substantial consequence to the determination of the action:

(a) If the trial court has been requested to take or has taken or proposes to take judicial notice of such matter, the court shall afford each party reasonable opportunity, before the jury is instructed or before the cause is submitted for decision by the court, to present to the court information relevant to (1) the propriety of taking judicial notice of the matter and (2) the tenor of the matter to be noticed.

(b) If the trial court resorts to any source of information not received in open court, including the advice of persons learned in the subject matter, such information and its source shall be made a part of the record in the action and the court shall afford each party reasonable opportunity to meet such information before judicial notice of the matter may be taken.

§ **452.5. Criminal conviction records; computer-generated records, and electronically digitized copies; admissibility.** (a) The official acts and records specified in subdivisions (c)

(d) Timing. The court may take judicial notice at any stage of the proceeding.

(e) Opportunity to Be Heard. On timely request, a party is entitled to be heard on the propriety of taking judicial notice and the nature of the fact to be noticed. If the court takes judicial notice before notifying a party, the party, on request, is still entitled to be heard.

[*FRE have no counterpart to CEC § 452.5.*]

and (d) of Section 452 include any computer-generated official court records, as specified by the Judicial Council that relate to criminal convictions, when the record is certified by a clerk of the superior court pursuant to Section 69844.5 of the Government Code at the time of computer entry. [*Amended 2016.*]

(b)(1) An official record of conviction certified in accordance with subdivision (a) of Section 1530, or an electronically digitized copy thereof, is admissible under Section 1280 to prove the commission, attempted commission, or solicitation of a criminal offense, prior conviction, service of a prison term, or other act, condition, or event recorded by the record. [*Added 1996. Amended 2002. Amended 2013.*]

(2) For purposes of this subdivision, "electronically digitized copy" means a copy that is made by scanning, photographing, or otherwise exactly reproducing a document, is stored or maintained in a digitized format, and meets either of the following requirements:

(A) The copy bears an electronic signature or watermark unique to the entity responsible for certifying the document.

(B) The copied document is an official record of conviction, certified in accordance with subdivision (a) of Section 1530, that is transmitted by the clerk of the superior court in a manner showing that the copy was prepared and transmitted by that clerk of the superior court. A seal, signature, or other indicia of the court shall constitute adequate showing. [*Added 2013. Amended 2016.*]

§ **454. Information that may be used in taking judicial notice.** (a) In determining the propriety of taking judicial notice of a matter, or the tenor thereof:

(1) Any source of pertinent information, including the advice of persons learned in the subject matter, may be consulted or used, whether or not furnished by a party.

(2) Exclusionary rules of evidence do not apply except for Section 352 and the rules of privilege.

(b) Where the subject of judicial notice is the law of an organization of nations, a foreign nation, or a public entity in a foreign nation and the court resorts to the advice of persons learned in the subject matter, such advice, if not received in open court, shall be in writing.

§ **456. Noting for record denial of request to take judicial notice.** If the trial court denies a request to take judicial notice of any matter, the court shall at the earliest practicable time so advise the parties and indicate for the record that it has denied the request.

§ **457. Instructing jury on matter judicially noticed.** If a matter judicially noticed is a matter which would otherwise have been for determination by the jury, the trial court may, and upon request shall, instruct the jury to accept as a fact the matter so noticed.

[*FRE have no counterpart to CEC § 454.*]

[*FRE have no counterpart to CEC § 456.*]

(f) **Instructing the Jury.** In a civil case, the court must instruct the jury to accept the noticed fact as conclusive. In a criminal case, the court must instruct the jury that it may or may not accept the noticed fact as conclusive.

§ 460. **Appointment of expert by court.** Where the advice of persons learned in the subject matter is required in order to enable the court to take judicial notice of a matter, the court on its own motion or on motion of any party may appoint one or more such persons to provide such advice. If the court determines to appoint such a person, he shall be appointed and compensated in the manner provided in Article 2 (commencing with Section 730) of Chapter 3 of Division 6.

§ 500. **Party who has the burden of proof.** Except as otherwise provided by law, a party has the burden of proof as to each fact the existence or nonexistence of which is essential to the claim for relief or defense that he is asserting.

§ 501. **Criminal actions; statutory assignment of burden of proof; controlling section.** Insofar as any statute, except Section 522, assigns the burden of proof in a criminal action, such statute is subject to Penal Code Section 1096.

§ 502. **Instructions on burden of proof.** The court on all proper occasions shall instruct the jury as to which party bears the burden of proof on each issue and as to whether that burden requires that a party raise a reasonable doubt concerning the existence or nonexistence of a fact or that he establish the existence or nonexistence of a fact by a preponderance of the evidence, by clear and convincing proof, or by proof beyond a reasonable doubt.

§ 520. **Claim that person guilty of crime or wrongdoing.** The party claiming that a person is guilty of crime or wrongdoing has the burden of proof on that issue.

§ 521. **Claim that person did not exercise care.** The party claiming that a person did not exercise a requisite degree of care has the burden of proof on that issue.

§ 522. **Claim that person is or was insane.** The party claiming that any person, including himself, is or was insane has the burden of proof on that issue.

§ 523. **Historic locations of water; claims involving state land patents or grants.** In any action where the state is a party, regardless of who is the moving party, where (a) the boundary of land patented or otherwise granted by the state is in dispute, or (b) the validity of any state patent or grant dated prior to 1950 is in dispute, the state shall have the burden of proof on all issues relating to the historic locations of rivers, streams, and other water bodies and the authority of the state in issuing the patent or grant.

This section is not intended to nor shall it be construed to supersede existing statutes governing disputes where the state is a party and regarding title to real property. [*Added 1994.*]

§ 524. **Burden of proof in cases involving State Board of Equalization; unreasonable search or access to records prohibited; taxpayer defined.** (a) Notwithstanding any other provision of law, in a civil proceeding to which the State Board of Equalization is a party, that board shall have the burden of proof by clear and convincing evidence in sustaining its assertion of a penalty for intent to evade or fraud against a taxpayer, with respect to any factual issue relevant to ascertaining the liability of a taxpayer.

[*FRE have no counterpart to CEC § 460.*]

ARTICLE III. PRESUMPTIONS IN CIVIL CASES

[*FRE have no general provisions on the burden of proof.*]

(b) Nothing in this section shall be construed to override any requirement for a taxpayer to substantiate any item on a return or claim filed with the State Board of Equalization.

(c) Nothing in this section shall subject a taxpayer to unreasonable search or access to records in violation of the United States Constitution, the California Constitution, or any other law.

(d) For purposes of this section, "taxpayer" includes a person on whom fees administered by the State Board of Equalization are imposed. [*Added 2010.*]

§ **550. Party who has the burden of producing evidence.** (a) The burden of producing evidence as to a particular fact is on the party against whom a finding on that fact would be required in the absence of further evidence.

(b) The burden of producing evidence as to a particular fact is initially on the party with the burden of proof as to that fact.

§ **600. Presumption and inference defined.** (a) A presumption is an assumption of fact that the law requires to be made from another fact or group of facts found or otherwise established in the action. A presumption is not evidence.

(b) An inference is a deduction of fact that may logically and reasonably be drawn from another fact or group of facts found or otherwise established in the action.

§ **601. Classification of presumptions.** A presumption is either conclusive or rebuttable. Every rebuttable presumption is either (a) a presumption affecting the burden of producing evidence or (b) a presumption affecting the burden of proof.

§ **602. Statute making one fact prima facie evidence of another fact.** A statute providing that a fact or group of facts is prima facie evidence of another fact establishes a rebuttable presumption.

§ **603. Presumption affecting the burden of producing evidence defined.** A presumption affecting the burden of producing evidence is a presumption established to implement no public policy other than to facilitate the determination of the particular action in which the presumption is applied.

§ **604. Effect of presumption affecting burden of producing evidence.** The effect of a presumption affecting the burden of producing evidence is to require the trier of fact to assume the existence of the presumed fact unless and until evidence is introduced which would support a finding of its nonexistence, in which case the trier of fact shall determine the existence or nonexistence of the presumed fact from the evidence and without regard to the presumption. Nothing in this section shall be construed to prevent the drawing of any inference that may be appropriate.

Rule 301. Presumptions in Civil Cases Generally

In a civil case, unless a federal statute or these rules provide otherwise, the party against whom a presumption is directed has the burden of producing evidence to rebut the presumption. But this rule does not shift the burden of persuasion, which remains on the party who had it originally.

Rule 302. Applying State Law to Presumptions in Civil Cases

In a civil case, state law governs the effect of a presumption regarding a claim or defense for which state law supplies the rule of decision.

Compare FRE 301-302 and CEC §§ 600-607, 620, 630, 660: ***[1]*** CEC recognizes two types of presumptions, each named for the professor who first articulated it. Thayer presumptions are based on the *probability* that if one fact is true (the "basic fact" or "BF"), then another fact is also true (the "presumed fact" or "PF"). Example from CEC's list: one who *possesses* property *owns* it. If the BF is proved by sufficient evidence, then the presumption shifts the burden of production to the opponent of the PF. If the opponent produces no evidence contradicting the PF, then the judge must assume that the PF is true and as a result may withdraw some or all of the issues from the jury, or even direct a verdict against the opponent if the PF is critical to the opponent's entire case. If, on the other hand, the opponent does introduce sufficient evidence to rebut the PF, the presumption disappears and the jury receives no instruction. Morgan presumptions are based on *public policy*, not *probability.* Example from CEC's list: the policy favoring the validity of marriages. If the proponent offers evidence sufficient to support a finding of the BF, then the burden of proof as to the PF is shifted to the opponent.

[*continued on page I-25*]

§ **605. Presumption affecting the burden of proof defined.** A presumption affecting the burden of proof is a presumption established to implement some public policy other than to facilitate the determination of the particular action in which the presumption is applied, such as the policy in favor of establishment of a parent and child relationship, the validity of marriage, the stability of titles to property, or the security of those who entrust themselves or their property to the administration of others. [*Amended 1975.*]

§ **606. Effect of presumption affecting burden of proof.** The effect of a presumption affecting the burden of proof is to impose upon the party against whom it operates the burden of proof as to the nonexistence of the presumed fact.

§ **607. Effect of presumption that establishes an element.** When a presumption affecting the burden of proof operates in a criminal action to establish presumptively any fact that is essential to the defendant's guilt, the presumption operates only if the facts that give rise to the presumption have been found or otherwise established beyond a reasonable doubt and, in such case, the defendant need only raise a reasonable doubt as to the existence of the presumed fact.

§ **620. Conclusive presumptions.** The presumptions established by this article [§§ 622-624], and all other presumptions declared by law to be conclusive, are conclusive presumptions.

> [*Sections 622-624 set forth specific conclusive presumptions. They have no counterparts under FRE.*]

§ **630. Presumptions affecting the burden of producing evidence.** The presumptions established by this article [§§ 631-647], and all other rebuttable presumptions established by law that fall within the criteria of Section 603, are presumptions affecting the burden of producing evidence.

> [*Sections 631-647 set forth specific presumptions affecting the burden of producing evidence. Some have counterparts under FRE, which are printed opposite FRE 901(b) and 902, infra.*]

§ **660. Presumptions affecting the burden of proof.** The presumptions established by this article [§§ 662-670], and all other rebuttable presumptions established by law that fall within the criteria of Section 605, are presumptions affecting the burden of proof.

> [*Sections 662-670 set forth specific presumptions affecting the burden of proof. They have no counterparts under FRE.*]

[*continued from page I-23*]

Then the opponent must satisfy the jury, by the requisite standard of proof, that the PF is not true. Morgan presumptions are thus generally more powerful than Thayer presumptions. FRE 301 largely follows Thayer in that it places on the presumption's opponent the burden of producing evidence to rebut the PF. The burden of proof never shifts; it remains on the proponent throughout the trial. If the proponent offers evidence sufficient to support a finding of the BF, and the opponent offers no evidence contradicting the PF, the court will instruct the jury that it if it finds the BF to be true, it may presume the existence of the PF. If the opponent offers no proof that the PF is untrue, then the court will instruct the jury that it may presume the existence of the PF if it finds the BF to be true. If the opponent of the presumption offers sufficient evidence that the PF is not true, the court retains discretion to instruct the jury that it may infer the PF if it finds the BF to exist. In this way, FRE's presumption differs slightly from a true Thayer presumption, which would prohibit any such instruction where the opponent offers sufficient evidence to rebut the PF.

§ 140. Evidence. "Evidence" means testimony, writings, material objects, or other things presented to the senses that are offered to prove the existence or nonexistence of a fact.

§ 210. Relevant evidence. "Relevant evidence" means evidence, including evidence relevant to the credibility of a witness or hearsay declarant, having any tendency in reason to prove or disprove any disputed fact that is of consequence to the determination of the action.

§ 350. Only relevant evidence admissible. No evidence is admissible except relevant evidence.

§ 351. Admissibility of relevant evidence. Except as otherwise provided by statute, all relevant evidence is admissible.

> *Compare FRE 401-402 and CEC §§ 210, 350, 351*: As interpreted by the courts, FRE and CEC are not substantively different. California courts do not (and practically could not) enforce the "disputed fact" limitation of CEC § 210.

Cal. Const. Art. I § 28(f)(2). Right to Truth-in-Evidence. Except as provided by statute hereafter enacted by a two-thirds vote of the membership in each house of the Legislature, relevant evidence shall not be excluded in any criminal proceeding, including pretrial and post conviction motions and hearings, or in any trial or hearing of a juvenile for a criminal offense, whether heard in juvenile or adult court. Nothing in this section shall affect any existing statutory rule of evidence relating to privilege or hearsay, or Evidence Code, Sections 352, 782 or 1103. Nothing in this section shall affect any existing statutory or constitutional right of the press. [*Added 1982.*]

§ 351.1. Polygraph examinations; results, opinion of examiner or reference; exclusion. (a) Notwithstanding any other provision of law, the results of a polygraph examination, the opinion of a polygraph examiner, or any reference to an offer to take, failure to take, or taking of a polygraph examination, shall not be admitted into evidence in any criminal proceeding, including pretrial and post conviction motions and hearings, or in any trial or hearing of a juvenile for a criminal offense, whether heard in juvenile or adult court, unless all parties stipulate to the admission of such results.

(b) Nothing in this section is intended to exclude from evidence statements made during a polygraph examination which are otherwise admissible. [*Added 1983.*]

> This section was codified by a two-third's majority of the legislature a year after Prop. 8's enactment, avoiding any negating impact of the initiative.

ARTICLE IV. RELEVANCE AND ITS LIMITS

Rule 401. Test for Relevant Evidence

Evidence is relevant if:

(a) it has any tendency to make a fact more or less probable than it would be without the evidence; and

(b) the fact is of consequence in determining the action.

Rule 402. General Admissibility of Relevant Evidence

Relevant evidence is admissible unless any of the following provides otherwise:

- the United States Constitution;
- a federal statute;
- these rules; or
- other rules prescribed by the Supreme Court.

Irrelevant evidence is not admissible.

[*Federal law has no counterpart to Cal. Const. Art. I §28(d).*]

[*FRE have no counterpart to CEC § 351.1.*]

[*Sections 351.2-351.4 have been omitted here, as they have no counterparts in FRE. They are temporary provisions, expiring in 2022, to deal with admissibility of immigration status in light of current (2020) Federal immigration policies. Their text is found in Part III.*]

§ **352. Discretion of court to exclude evidence.** The court in its discretion may exclude evidence if its probative value is substantially outweighed by the probability that its admission will (a) necessitate undue consumption of time or (b) create substantial danger of undue prejudice, of confusing the issues, or of misleading the jury.

§ **352.1. Criminal sex acts; victim's address and telephone number.** In any criminal proceeding under Section 261, 262, or 264.1, subdivision (d) of Section 286, or subdivision (d) of Section 287 of, or former Section 288a of, the Penal Code, or in any criminal proceeding under subdivision (c) of Section 286 or subdivision (c) of Section 287 of, or former Section 288a of, the Penal Code in which the defendant is alleged to have compelled the participation of the victim by force, violence, duress, menace, or threat of great bodily harm, the district attorney may, upon written motion with notice to the defendant or the defendant's attorney, if he or she is represented by an attorney, within a reasonable time prior to any hearing, move to exclude from evidence the current address and telephone number of any victim at the hearing.

The court may order that evidence of the victim's current address and telephone number be excluded from any hearings conducted pursuant to the criminal proceeding if the court finds that the probative value of the evidence is outweighed by the creation of substantial danger to the victim.

Nothing in this section shall abridge or limit the defendant's right to discover or investigate the information. [*Added 1985. Amended 1996, 2018.*]

§ **1101. Evidence of character to prove conduct. (a) General rule.** Except as provided in this section and in Sections 1102, 1103, 1108, and 1109, evidence of a person's character or a trait of his or her character (whether in the form of an opinion, evidence of reputation, or evidence of specific instances of his or her conduct) is inadmissible when offered to prove his or her conduct on a specified occasion. [*Amended 1995, 1996.*]

§ **1104. Character trait for care or skill.** Except as provided in Sections 1102 and 1103, evidence of a trait of a person's character with respect to care or skill is inadmissible to prove the quality of his conduct on a specified occasion.

> *Impact of Prop. 8 on CEC §§ 1101, 1104*: On its face, Prop. 8 appears to repeal CEC §§ 1101 and 1104 as applied in criminal proceedings because those sections restrict the admissibility of "relevant evidence." But in *People v. Ewoldt*, 7 Cal. 4th 380 (1994), the California Supreme Court held that by amending § 1101(b) in 1986 the Legislature re-enacted § 1101 in its entirety. Because the re-enactment satisfied Prop. 8's two-thirds voting requirement for amendments, *Ewoldt* held that the re-enactment supersedes whatever repealing effect Prop. 8 may have had on § 1101. § 1104 adds nothing substantively beyond § 1101. Thus, even if Prop. 8 repealed § 1104 in its entirety, that repeal would have no substantive effect because § 1101 is intact and still in force.

Rule 403. Excluding Relevant Evidence for Prejudice, Confusion, Waste of Time, or Other Reasons

The court may exclude relevant evidence if its probative value is substantially outweighed by a danger of one or more of the following: unfair prejudice, confusing the issues, misleading the jury, undue delay, wasting time, or needlessly presenting cumulative evidence.

[*FRE have no counterpart to CEC § 352.1.*]

Rule 404. Character Evidence; Crimes or Other Acts

(a) Character Evidence.

(1) ***Prohibited Uses.*** Evidence of a person's character or character trait is not admissible to prove that on a particular occasion the person acted in accordance with the character or trait.

§ 1102. Opinion and reputation evidence of character of criminal defendant to prove conduct. In a criminal action, evidence of the defendant's character or a trait of his character in the form of an opinion or evidence of his reputation is not made inadmissible by Section 1101 if such evidence is:

(a) Offered by the defendant to prove his conduct in conformity with such character or trait of character.

(b) Offered by the prosecution to rebut evidence adduced by the defendant under subdivision (a).

§ 1103. Character of crime victim to prove conduct offered by defendant, or by prosecution to rebut. (a) In a criminal action, evidence of the character or a trait of character (in the form of an opinion, evidence of reputation, or evidence of specific instances of conduct) of the victim of the crime for which the defendant is being prosecuted is not made inadmissible by Section 1101 if the evidence is:

(1) Offered by the defendant to prove conduct of the victim in conformity with the character or trait of character.

(2) Offered by the prosecution to rebut evidence adduced by the defendant under paragraph (1).

§ 1103. Evidence of defendant's violent character after evidence of victim's violent character. (b) In a criminal action, evidence of the defendant's character for violence or trait of character for violence (in the form of an opinion, evidence of reputation, or evidence of specific instances of conduct) is not made inadmissible by Section 1101 if the evidence is offered by the prosecution to prove conduct of the defendant in conformity with the character or trait of character and is offered after evidence that the victim had a character for violence or a trait of character tending to show violence has been adduced by the defendant under paragraph (1) of subdivision (a). [*Added 1991.*]

(2) ***Exceptions for a Defendant or Victim in a Criminal Case.*** The following exceptions apply in a criminal case:

(A) a defendant may offer evidence of the defendant's pertinent trait, and if the evidence is admitted, the prosecutor may offer evidence to rebut it;

(B) subject to the limitations in Rule 412, a defendant may offer evidence of an alleged victim's pertinent trait, and if the evidence is admitted, the prosecutor may:

(i) offer evidence to rebut it; and

(ii) offer evidence of the defendant's same trait; and

(C) in a homicide case, the prosecutor may offer evidence of the alleged victim's trait of peacefulness to rebut evidence that the victim was the first aggressor.

Compare FRE 404(a)(2)(A)-(C) and CEC §§ 1102-1103: There is no substantive difference between FRE and CEC on the issue of (i) the *defendant's* right to introduce evidence of his own pertinent character trait, (ii) the prosecutor's right to rebut the same, (iii) the *defendant's* right to offer evidence of a pertinent character trait of the *victim*, and (iv) the prosecutor's right to rebut the same with evidence of the victim's character and with rebuttal evidence of the defendant's character for *violence* where the defendant has offered evidence of the victim's character trait for violence.

However, FRE and CEC differ in the following respects: ***[1]*** In all instances of permitted use of character evidence under CEC § 1103, CEC allows use of specific instances of conduct in addition to opinion and reputation; FRE limits the use of specific instances of conduct as set forth in FRE 405(a). ***[2]*** Under FRE 404(a)(2)(C), the prosecution in a homicide case may offer evidence of the *victim's* character trait for peacefulness to rebut even *non-character* evidence offered by the accused to show that the victim was the first aggressor; in contrast, under CEC § 1103(a) the prosecutor may offer evidence of the victim's character trait for peacefulness only to rebut evidence of the victim's character trait for violence. ***[3]*** Under FRE 404(a)(2)(B)(ii), whenever the defendant offers evidence of any pertinent character trait of the alleged victim, the prosecutor may rebut with evidence of the defendant's same trait; in contrast, CEC limits the prosecutor to rebutting evidence of the alleged victim's character *for violence* with evidence of the defendant's same trait.

§ 1101. Evidence of character to prove conduct. * * * (c) Credibility of witness. Nothing in this section affects the admissibility of evidence offered to support or attack the credibility of a witness.

§ 1101. Evidence of character to prove conduct. * * * (b) Other acts. Nothing in this section prohibits the admission of evidence that a person committed a crime, civil wrong, or other act when relevant to prove some fact (such as motive, opportunity, intent, preparation, plan, knowledge, identity, absence of mistake or accident, or whether a defendant in a prosecution for an unlawful sexual act or attempted unlawful sexual act did not reasonably and in good faith believe that the victim consented) other than his or her disposition to commit such an act.

Compare FRE 404(b) and CEC § 1101(b): ***[1]*** CEC permits "other act" evidence to prove whether a defendant prosecuted for a sex offense reasonably and in good faith believed the victim had consented. FRE 412, rather than FRE 404(b), governs the admissibility of an alleged victim's past consensual sexual conduct on the issue of consent, and is limited, for the most part, to prior sexual conduct *with the defendant*. *See* comparison of FRE 412 and CEC §§ 1103, 1106, *infra*. ***[2]*** FRE contains a notice requirement; CEC does not.

(3) ***Exceptions for a Witness.*** Evidence of a witness's character may be admitted under Rules 607, 608, and 609.

(b) Crimes, Wrongs, or Other Acts.

(1) ***Prohibited Uses.*** Evidence of a crime, wrong, or other act is not admissible to prove a person's character in order to show that on a particular occasion the person acted in accordance with the character.

(2) ***Permitted Uses; Notice in a Criminal Case.*** This evidence may be admissible for another purpose, such as proving motive, opportunity, intent, preparation, plan, knowledge, identity, absence of mistake, or lack of accident. On request by a defendant in a criminal case, the prosecutor must:

(A) provide reasonable notice of the general nature of any such evidence that the prosecutor intends to offer at trial; and

(B) do so before trial — or during trial if the court, for good cause, excuses lack of pretrial notice.

[***Editors' Note:*** *As of the issue date of this edition, the following proposed amendment to FRE 404(b) will become effective December 1, 2020.* See *Part II for the Advisory Committee's Note to the amendment.*]

(b) Other Crimes, Wrongs, or Acts.

(1) ***Prohibited Uses.*** *Evidence of any other crime, wrong, or act is not admissible to prove a person's character in order to show that on a particular occasion the person acted in accordance with the character.*

(2) ***Permitted Uses.*** *This evidence may be admissible for another purpose, such as proving motive, opportunity, intent, preparation, plan, knowledge, identity, absence of mistake, or lack of accident.*

(3) ***Notice in a Criminal Case.*** *In a criminal case, the prosecutor must:*

(A) *provide reasonable notice of any such evidence that the prosecutor intends to offer at trial;*

(B) *articulate in the notice the non-propensity purpose for which the prosecutor intends to offer the evidence and the reasoning that supports the purpose; and*

§ **1100. Manner of proof of character.** Except as otherwise provided by statute, any otherwise admissible evidence (including evidence in the form of an opinion, evidence of reputation, and evidence of specific instances of such person's conduct) is admissible to prove a person's character or a trait of his character.

Compare FRE 405 and CEC § 1100: Where character evidence is permitted under FRE 404(a)(2), then under FRE 405(a) on *direct examination* a party may offer character evidence only in the form of *opinion or reputation*, but on *cross-examination* of a character witness may also inquire into *specific instances of conduct*. In contrast, where character evidence is permitted under CEC §§ 1103, then under CEC § 1100 on direct or cross-examination a party may offer character evidence in the form of opinion, reputation, *or specific instances of conduct*. *See* comparison of FRE 404(a)(2)(A) and CEC §§ 1102, 1103(b), *supra*. *See People v. Felix*, 70 Cal. App. 4th 426, 82 Cal. Rptr. 2d 701 (4th Dist. 1999) (finding that CEC § 1102 is unaffected by Proposition 8's Truth-in-Evidence provision.).

§ **1105. Habit or custom to prove specific behavior.** Any otherwise admissible evidence of habit or custom is admissible to prove conduct on a specified occasion in conformity with the habit or custom.

(C) do so in writing sufficiently ahead of trial to give the defendant a fair opportunity to meet the evidence — or during trial and in any form if the court, for good cause, excuses lack of pretrial notice.]

Rule 405. Methods of Proving Character

(a) **By Reputation or Opinion.** When evidence of a person's character or character trait is admissible, it may be proved by testimony about the person's reputation or by testimony in the form of an opinion. On cross-examination of the character witness, the court may allow an inquiry into relevant specific instances of the person's conduct.

(b) **By Specific Instances of Conduct.** When a person's character or character trait is an essential element of a charge, claim, or defense, the character or trait may also be proved by relevant specific instances of the person's conduct.

Rule 406. Habit; Routine Practice

Evidence of a person's habit or an organization's routine practice may be admitted to prove that on a particular occasion the person or organization acted in accordance with the habit or routine practice. The court may admit this evidence regardless of whether it is corroborated or whether there was an eyewitness.

§ **1151. Subsequent remedial conduct.** When, after the occurrence of an event, remedial or precautionary measures are taken, which, if taken previously, would have tended to make the event less likely to occur, evidence of such subsequent measures is inadmissible to prove negligence or culpable conduct in connection with the event.

Compare FRE 407 and CEC § 1151: CEC does not apply to strict liability cases; FRE does.

Similar Policy-Based Exclusions:

[*Sections 1156-1157.7 regulate both discovery and admissibility of evidence relating to in-hospital staff committees, peer review bodies, and quality assurance committees. Section 1158 regulates inspection of patient records. Section 1159 excludes evidence pertaining to live animal experimentation in product liability actions relating to motor vehicles. Section 1228.1 limits the admissibility of evidence that a parent or guardian has accepted child welfare services. These sections do not have counterparts in FRE.*]

§ **1152. Offer to compromise and the like.** (a) Evidence that a person has, in compromise or from humanitarian motives, furnished or offered or promised to furnish money or any other thing, act, or service to another who has sustained or will sustain or claims that he or she has sustained or will sustain loss or damage, as well as any conduct or statements made in negotiation thereof, is inadmissible to prove his or her liability for the loss or damage or any part of it.

(b) In the event that evidence of an offer to compromise is admitted in an action for breach of the covenant of good faith and fair dealing or violation of subdivision (h) of Section 790.03 of the Insurance Code, then at the request of the party against whom the evidence is admitted, or at the request of the party who made the offer to compromise that was admitted, evidence relating to any other offer or counteroffer to compromise the same or substantially the same claimed loss or damage shall also be admissible for the same purpose as the initial evidence regarding settlement. Other than as may be admitted in an action for breach of the covenant of good faith and fair dealing or violation of subdivision (h) of Section 790.03 of the Insurance Code, evidence of settlement offers shall not be admitted in a motion for a new trial, in any proceeding involving an additur or remittitur, or on appeal.

(c) This section does not affect the admissibility of evidence of any of the following: (1) Partial satisfaction of an asserted claim or demand without questioning its validity when such evidence is offered to prove the validity of the claim. (2) A debtor's payment or promise to pay all or a part of his or her preexisting debt when such evidence is offered to prove the creation of a new duty on his or her part or a revival of his or her preexisting duty. [*Amended 1967, 1987.*]

Rule 407. Subsequent Remedial Measures

When measures are taken that would have made an earlier injury or harm less likely to occur, evidence of the subsequent measures is not admissible to prove:

- negligence;
- culpable conduct;
- a defect in a product or its design; or
- a need for a warning or instruction.

But the court may admit this evidence for another purpose, such as impeachment or — if disputed — proving ownership, control, or the feasibility of precautionary measures.

Rule 408. Compromise Offers and Negotiations

(a) Prohibited Uses. Evidence of the following is not admissible — on behalf of any party — either to prove or disprove the validity or amount of a disputed claim or to impeach by a prior inconsistent statement or a contradiction:

(1) furnishing, promising, or offering — or accepting, promising to accept, or offering to accept — a valuable consideration in compromising or attempting to compromise the claim; and

(2) conduct or a statement made during compromise negotiations about the claim — except when offered in a criminal case and when the negotiations related to a claim by a public office in the exercise of its regulatory, investigative, or enforcement authority.

(b) Exceptions. The court may admit this evidence for another purpose, such as proving a witness's bias or prejudice, negating a contention of undue delay, or proving an effort to obstruct a criminal investigation or prosecution.

Compare FRE 408, 409 and CEC §§ 1152, 1154: *[1]* CEC § 1152, as interpreted, does not apply to criminal cases. Unless an offer to compromise was made with the assistance of a prosecutor, *see* CEC § 1153.5, CEC does not protect against its admission in criminal cases.

[*continued on page I-39*]

§ 1154. Offer to discount a claim. Evidence that a person has accepted or offered or promised to accept a sum of money or any other thing, act, or service in satisfaction of a claim, as well as any conduct or statements made in negotiation thereof, is inadmissible to prove the invalidity of the claim or any part of it.

Mediation:

[*Sections 1115-1129 govern admissibility of statements and other evidence relating to mediation. They have no counterparts in FRE.*]

[*CEC has no counterpart to FRE 409.*]

§ 1160. Admissibility of expressions of sympathy or benevolence; definitions

(a) The portion of statements, writings, or benevolent gestures expressing sympathy or a general sense of benevolence relating to the pain, suffering, or death of a person involved in an accident and made to that person or to the family of that person shall be inadmissible as evidence of an admission of liability in a civil action. A statement of fault, however, which is part of, or in addition to, any of the above shall not be inadmissible pursuant to this section.

(b) For purposes of this section: (1) "Accident" means an occurrence resulting in injury or death to one or more persons which is not the result of willful action by a party. (2) "Benevolent gestures" means actions which convey a sense of compassion or commiseration emanating from humane impulses. (3) "Family" means the spouse, parent, grandparent, stepmother, stepfather, child, grandchild, brother, sister, half brother, half sister, adopted children of parent, or spouse's parents of an injured party. [*Added 2000.*]

§ 1161. Human Trafficking; admissibility of evidence of engagement in commercial sexual act by victim or sexual history of victim.

(a) Evidence that a victim of human trafficking, as defined in Section 236.1 of the Penal Code, has engaged in any commercial sexual act as a result of being a victim of human trafficking is inadmissible to prove the victim's criminal liability for the commercial sexual act.

(b) Evidence of sexual history or history of any commercial sexual act of a victim of human trafficking, as defined in Section 236.1 of the Penal Code, is inadmissible to attack the credibility or impeach the character of the victim in any civil or criminal proceeding. [*Added 2013.*]

§ 1162. Admissibility of evidence of engagement in act of prostitution by victim of felony. Evidence that a victim of, or a witness to, extortion as defined in Section 519 of the Penal Code, stalking as defined in Section 646.9 of the Penal Code, or a violent felony as defined in Section 667.5 of the Penal Code, has engaged in an act of prostitution at or around the time he or she was the victim of or witness to the crime is inadmissible in a separate prosecution of that victim or witness to prove his or her criminal liability for the act of prostitution. [*Added 2018.*]

[*continued from page I-37*]

In contrast, FRE 408 prohibits introduction in any case, civil or criminal, of evidence of conduct or statements made during settlement negotiations regarding the claim at issue, *except* when offered in a criminal case and the negotiations involve a claim by a government office or agency in its exercise of regulatory, investigative, or enforcement authority. Even in such limited circumstances, a court may prohibit introduction of the evidence under FRE 403. ***[2]*** FRE 408 expressly states that its exclusion does not apply to settlement evidence offered for a purpose other than proving liability, *e.g.*, proving a witness's bias or prejudice, negating a contention of undue delay, or proving an effort to obstruct a criminal investigation or prosecution. CEC accomplishes the same result, not through §§ 1152 and 1154, but through § 355's general provision allowing evidence excluded for one purpose to be admitted for another, subject to a limiting instruction.

Rule 409. Offers to Pay Medical and Similar Expenses

Evidence of furnishing, promising to pay, or offering to pay medical, hospital, or similar expenses resulting from an injury is not admissible to prove liability for the injury.

[*FRE have no counterpart to CEC § 1160.*]

[*FRE have no counterpart to CEC § 1161.*]

[*FRE have no counterpart to CEC § 1162.*]

§ 1153. Offer to plead guilty or withdrawn plea of guilty by criminal defendant. Evidence of a plea of guilty, later withdrawn, or of an offer to plead guilty to the crime charged or to any other crime, made by the defendant in a criminal action is inadmissible in any action or in any proceeding of any nature, including proceedings before agencies, commissions, boards, and tribunals.

Compare FRE 410 and CEC § 1153: ***[1]*** FRE limits exclusion to a defendant's statements to a *prosecutor* pursuant to plea negotiations. Thus, for example, statements to a police officer are unprotected. In contrast, CEC protects *all* statements made as part of *bona fide* plea negotiations, including statements to police officers. ***[2]*** FRE excludes evidence regarding plea bargaining for any purpose other than the two exceptions it specifies. Thus, unless the defendant voluntarily waives FRE's protections, *see U.S. v. Mezzanatto*, 513 U.S. 196 (1995), the prosecutor cannot impeach the defendant's trial testimony with prior inconsistent statements made during plea negotiations. In contrast, CEC, as interpreted, permits the use of statements made during plea negotiations to impeach a defendant's trial testimony. See *People v. Crow*, 28 Cal. App. 4th 440 (1994).

Impact of Prop. 8 on CEC §§ 1153, 1153.5: On its face, Prop. 8 seems to remove the exclusionary provisions of CEC §§ 1153 and 1153.5 from application in criminal proceedings. However, no California case has ever so held, presumably because state prosecutors have not pressed the issue due to the critical role these sections play in facilitating plea bargaining.

§ 1153.5. Offer for civil resolution of crimes against property. Evidence of an offer for civil resolution of a criminal matter pursuant to the provisions of Section 33 of the Code of Civil Procedure, or admissions made in the course of or negotiations for the offer shall not be admissible in any action. [*Added 1982.*]

§ 1155. Liability insurance. Evidence that a person was, at the time a harm was suffered by another, insured wholly or partially against loss arising from liability for that harm is inadmissible to prove negligence or other wrongdoing.

Rule 410. Pleas, Plea Discussions, and Related Statements

(a) **Prohibited Uses.** In a civil or criminal case, evidence of the following is not admissible against the defendant who made the plea or participated in the plea discussions:

(1) a guilty plea that was later withdrawn;

(2) a nolo contendere plea;

(3) a statement made during a proceeding on either of those pleas under Federal Rule of Criminal Procedure 11 or a comparable state procedure; or

(4) a statement made during plea discussions with an attorney for the prosecuting authority if the discussions did not result in a guilty plea or they resulted in a later-withdrawn guilty plea.

(b) **Exceptions.** The court may admit a statement described in Rule 410(a)(3) or (4):

(1) in any proceeding in which another statement made during the same plea or plea discussions has been introduced, if in fairness the statements ought to be considered together; or

(2) in a criminal proceeding for perjury or false statement, if the defendant made the statement under oath, on the record, and with counsel present.

[*FRE have no counterpart to CEC § 1153.5.*]

Rule 411. Liability Insurance

Evidence that a person was or was not insured against liability is not admissible to prove whether the person acted negligently or otherwise wrongfully. But the court may admit this evidence for another purpose, such as proving a witness's bias or prejudice or proving agency, ownership, or control.

§ 1103. Evidence of complaining witness' sexual conduct or manner of dress. * * * (c)

(1) Notwithstanding any other provision of this code to the contrary, and except as provided in this subdivision, in any prosecution under Section 261, 262, or 264.1 of the Penal Code or under Section 286, 287, or 289 of, or former Section 288a of, the Penal Code, or for assault with intent to commit, attempt to commit, or conspiracy to commit a crime defined in any of those sections, except where the crime is alleged to have occurred in a local detention facility, as defined in Section 6031.4, or in a state prison, as defined in Section 4504, opinion evidence, reputation evidence, and evidence of specific instances of the complaining witness' sexual conduct, or any of that evidence, is not admissible by the defendant in order to prove consent by the complaining witness.

(2) Notwithstanding paragraph (3), evidence of the manner in which the victim was dressed at the time of the commission of the offense shall not be admissible when offered by either party on the issue of consent in any prosecution for an offense specified in paragraph (1), unless the evidence is determined by the court to be relevant and admissible in the interests of justice. The proponent of the evidence shall make an offer of proof outside the hearing of the jury. The court shall then make its determination and at that time, state the reasons for its ruling on the record. For the purposes of this paragraph, "manner of dress" does not include the condition of the victim's clothing before, during, or after the commission of the offense.

(3) Paragraph (1) shall not be applicable to evidence of the complaining witness' sexual conduct with the defendant.

(4) If the prosecutor introduces evidence, including testimony of a witness, or the complaining witness as a witness gives testimony, and that evidence or testimony relates to the complaining witness' sexual conduct, the defendant may cross-examine the witness who gives the testimony and offer relevant evidence limited specifically to the rebuttal of the evidence introduced by the prosecutor or given by the complaining witness.

(5) Nothing in this subdivision shall be construed to make inadmissible any evidence offered to attack the credibility of the complaining witness as provided in Section 782.

(6) As used in this section, "complaining witness" means the alleged victim of the crime charged, the prosecution of which is subject to this subdivision. [*Added 1974. Amended 1981, 1990, 1996, 1998, 2018.*]

Rule 412. Sex-Offense Cases: The Victim's Sexual Behavior or Predisposition

(a) Prohibited Uses. The following evidence is not admissible in a civil or criminal proceeding involving alleged sexual misconduct:

(1) evidence offered to prove that a victim engaged in other sexual behavior; or

(2) evidence offered to prove a victim's sexual predisposition.

(b) Exceptions.

(1) ***Criminal Cases.*** The court may admit the following evidence in a criminal case:

(A) evidence of specific instances of a victim's sexual behavior, if offered to prove that someone other than the defendant was the source of semen, injury, or other physical evidence;

(B) evidence of specific instances of a victim's sexual behavior with respect to the person accused of the sexual misconduct, if offered by the defendant to prove consent or if offered by the prosecutor; and

(C) evidence whose exclusion would violate the defendant's constitutional rights.

(2) ***Civil Cases.*** In a civil case, the court may admit evidence offered to prove a victim's sexual behavior or sexual predisposition if its probative value substantially outweighs the danger of harm to any victim and of unfair prejudice to any party. The court may admit evidence of a victim's reputation only if the victim has placed it in controversy.

Compare FRE 412 and CEC §§ 1103, 1106: *[1]* FRE allows an *accused* to introduce evidence of the *victim's* sexual conduct (which need not be physical) *with the accused* to prove consent, subject to FRE 403 balancing. FRE also allows evidence of the victim's sexual conduct *with others* to prove that someone other than the accused was the source of semen, injury, or other physical evidence. Similarly, under CEC § 1103(c)(3) an *accused* may introduce evidence of the *victim's prior sexual conduct with the accused* to show consent, subject to § 352 balancing. But the accused may not introduce evidence of *how the victim was dressed* on the occasion at issue unless, after a hearing, the court determines that the evidence is both relevant and admissible in the interests of justice. Moreover, the accused may not introduce evidence of the victim's sexual conduct *with others* except to rebut evidence of such conduct first introduced by the prosecution.

[*continued on page I-45*]

§ 1106. Sexual harassment, sexual assault, or sexual battery cases; opinion or reputation evidence of plaintiff's sexual conduct; inadmissibility; exception; cross-examination. (a) In any civil action alleging conduct which constitutes sexual harassment, sexual assault, or sexual battery, opinion evidence, reputation evidence, and evidence of specific instances of the plaintiff's sexual conduct, or any of that evidence, is not admissible by the defendant in order to prove consent by the plaintiff or the absence of injury to the plaintiff, unless the injury alleged by the plaintiff is in the nature of loss of consortium.

(b) Subdivision (a) does not apply to evidence of the plaintiff's sexual conduct with the alleged perpetrator.

(c) Notwithstanding subdivision (b), in any civil action brought pursuant to Section 1708.5 of the Civil Code involving a minor and adult as described in Section 1708.5.5 of the Civil Code, evidence of the plaintiff minor's sexual conduct with the defendant adult shall not be admissible to prove consent by the plaintiff or the absence of injury to the plaintiff. Such evidence of the plaintiff's sexual conduct may only be introduced to attack the credibility of the plaintiff in accordance with Section 783 or to prove something other than consent by the plaintiff if, upon a hearing of the court out of the presence of the jury, the defendant proves that the probative value of that evidence outweighs the prejudice to the plaintiff consistent with Section 352. [*Added 2014.*]

(d) If the plaintiff introduces evidence, including testimony of a witness, or the plaintiff as a witness gives testimony, and the evidence or testimony relates to the plaintiff's sexual conduct, the defendant may cross-examine the witness who gives the testimony and offer relevant evidence limited specifically to the rebuttal of the evidence introduced by the plaintiff or given by the plaintiff.

(e) This section shall not be construed to make inadmissible any evidence offered to attack the credibility of the plaintiff as provided in Section 783. [*Added 1985. Amended 2016.*]

[*continued from page I-43*]

[2] In a *civil* case, evidence relating to the alleged victim's *"other sexual behavior" or predisposition* is admissible under FRE if the probative value substantially outweighs the risk of harm to any victim and of unfair prejudice to any party. *Cf.* FRE 403. But evidence of the alleged victim's *reputation* is inadmissible unless placed in issue by the victim. Under CEC § 1106, in contrast, evidence of the victim's sexual conduct with others is never admissible in a civil case involving sexual harassment, sexual battery, or sexual assault unless the injury claimed includes loss of consortium. ***[3]*** CEC § 1106 was amended in 2014 to further restrict the use of the victim's sexual conduct as bearing on consent or absence of injury. ***[4]*** FRE requires the proponent of the evidence to give written notice at least 14 days before trial, and the court must hold an *in camera* hearing at which the victim and parties are permitted to attend and be heard. CEC lacks an analogous provision.

(c) Procedure to Determine Admissibility.

(1) ***Motion.*** If a party intends to offer evidence under Rule 412(b), the party must:

(A) file a motion that specifically describes the evidence and states the purpose for which it is to be offered;

(B) do so at least 14 days before trial unless the court, for good cause, sets a different time;

(C) serve the motion on all parties; and

(D) notify the victim or, when appropriate, the victim's guardian or representative.

(2) ***Hearing.*** Before admitting evidence under this rule, the court must conduct an in camera hearing and give the victim and parties a right to attend and be heard. Unless the court orders otherwise, the motion, related materials, and the record of the hearing must be and remain sealed.

(d) Definition of "Victim." In this rule, "victim" includes an alleged victim.

§ 1108. Evidence of another sexual offense by defendant; disclosure; construction of section. (a) In a criminal action in which the defendant is accused of a sexual offense, evidence of the defendant's commission of another sexual offense or offenses is not made inadmissible by Section 1101, if the evidence is not inadmissible pursuant to Section 352.

(b) In an action in which evidence is to be offered under this section, the people shall disclose the evidence to the defendant, including statements of witnesses or a summary of the substance of any testimony that is expected to be offered in compliance with the requirements of Section 1054.7 of the Penal Code.

(c) This section does not limit the admission or consideration of evidence under any other section of this code.

(d) As used in this section, the following definitions shall apply:

(1) "Sexual offense" means a crime under the law of a state or of the United States that involved any of the following:

(A) Any conduct proscribed by subdivision (b) or (c) of Section 236.1, Section 243.4, 261, 261.5, 262, 264.1, 266c, 269, 286, 287, 288, 288.2, 288.5, or 289, or subdivision (b), (c), or (d) of Section 311.2 or Section 311.3, 311.4, 311.10, 311.11, 314, or 647.6, of the Penal Code.

(B) Any conduct proscribed by Section 220 of the Penal Code, except assault with intent to commit mayhem.

(C) Contact, without consent, between any part of the defendant's body or an object and the genitals or anus of another person.

(D) Contact, without consent, between the genitals or anus of the defendant and any part of another person's body.

(E) Deriving sexual pleasure or gratification from the infliction of death, bodily injury, or physical pain on another person.

(F) An attempt or conspiracy to engage in conduct described in this paragraph.

(2) "Consent" shall have the same meaning as provided in Section 261.6 of the Penal Code, except that it does not include consent which is legally ineffective because of the age, mental disorder, or developmental or physical disability of the victim. [*Added 1995. Amended 2001, 2002, 2017, 2018.*]

Compare FRE 413, 414, 415 and CEC § 1108: ***[1]*** CEC's exception to the general ban on character evidence applies only in criminal cases. Thus, CEC has no analogue to FRE 415.

[*continued on page I-48*]

Rule 413. Similar Crimes in Sexual-Assault Cases

(a) **Permitted Uses.** In a criminal case in which a defendant is accused of a sexual assault, the court may admit evidence that the defendant committed any other sexual assault. The evidence may be considered on any matter to which it is relevant.

(b) **Disclosure to the Defendant.** If the prosecutor intends to offer this evidence, the prosecutor must disclose it to the defendant, including witnesses' statements or a summary of the expected testimony. The prosecutor must do so at least 15 days before trial or at a later time that the court allows for good cause.

(c) **Effect on Other Rules.** This rule does not limit the admission or consideration of evidence under any other rule.

(d) **Definition of "Sexual Assault."** In this rule and Rule 415, "sexual assault" means a crime under federal law or under state law (as "state" is defined in 18 U.S.C. § 513) involving:

(1) any conduct prohibited by 18 U.S.C. chapter 109A;

(2) contact, without consent, between any part of the defendant's body — or an object — and another person's genitals or anus;

(3) contact, without consent, between the defendant's genitals or anus and any part of another person's body;

(4) deriving sexual pleasure or gratification from inflicting death, bodily injury, or physical pain on another person; or

(5) an attempt or conspiracy to engage in conduct described in subparagraphs (1)-(4).

Rule 414. Similar Crimes in Child-Molestation Cases

(a) **Permitted Uses.** In a criminal case in which a defendant is accused of child molestation, the court may admit evidence that the defendant committed any other child molestation. The evidence may be considered on any matter to which it is relevant.

(b) **Disclosure.** If the prosecutor intends to offer this evidence, the prosecutor must disclose it to the defendant, including witnesses' statements or a summary of the expected testimony. The prosecutor must do so at least 15 days before trial or at a later time that the court allows for good cause.

(c) **Effect on Other Rules.** This rule does not limit the admission or consideration of evidence under any other rule.

[*continued from page I-46*]

[2] The range of prosecutions in which prior sex offense evidence is admissible under CEC is broader than under FRE 413 and 414. CEC includes not only prior sexual assault and child molestation, but also offenses involving depictions of minors and distribution of pornographic materials depicting minors. ***[3]*** CEC expressly provides for § 352 balancing in determining admissibility of prior sex offense evidence, while FRE is silent on FRE 403's applicability to FRE 413-415. Some federal circuits have read FRE 403 balancing into the FRE 413-415 analysis. *See, e.g., Doe ex rel. Rudy-Glanzer v. Glanzer*, 232 F.3d 1258 (9th Cir. 2000).

(d) Definition of "Child" and "Child Molestation." In this rule and Rule 415:

(1) "child" means a person below the age of 14; and

(2) "child molestation" means a crime under federal law or under state law (as "state" is defined in 18 U.S.C. § 513) involving:

(A) any conduct prohibited by 18 U.S.C. chapter 109A and committed with a child;

(B) any conduct prohibited by 18 U.S.C. chapter 110;

(C) contact between any part of the defendant's body — or an object — and a child's genitals or anus;

(D) contact between the defendant's genitals or anus and any part of a child's body;

(E) deriving sexual pleasure or gratification from inflicting death, bodily injury, or physical pain on a child; or

(F) an attempt or conspiracy to engage in conduct described in subparagraphs (A)-(E).

Rule 415. Similar Acts in Civil Cases Involving Sexual Assault or Child Molestation

(a) Permitted Uses. In a civil case involving a claim for relief based on a party's alleged sexual assault or child molestation, the court may admit evidence that the party committed any other sexual assault or child molestation. The evidence may be considered as provided in Rules 413 and 414.

(b) Disclosure to the Opponent. If a party intends to offer this evidence, the party must disclose it to the party against whom it will be offered, including witnesses' statements or a summary of the expected testimony. The party must do so at least 15 days before trial or at a later time that the court allows for good cause.

(c) Effect on Other Rules. This rule does not limit the admission or consideration of evidence under any other rule.

§ **1109. Evidence of defendant's other acts of domestic violence.** (a)(1) Except as provided in subdivision (e) or (f), in a criminal action in which the defendant is accused of an offense involving domestic violence, evidence of the defendant's commission of other domestic violence is not made inadmissible by Section 1101 if the evidence is not inadmissible pursuant to Section 352.

(2) Except as provided in subdivision (e) or (f), in a criminal action in which the defendant is accused of an offense involving abuse of an elder or dependent person, evidence of the defendant's commission of other abuse of an elder or dependent person is not made inadmissible by Section 1101 if the evidence is not inadmissible pursuant to Section 352.

(b) In an action in which evidence is to be offered under this section, the people shall disclose the evidence to the defendant, including statements of witnesses or a summary of the substance of any testimony that is expected to be offered, in compliance with the provisions of Section 1054. 7 of the Penal Code.

(c) This section shall not be construed to limit or preclude the admission or consideration of evidence under any other statute or case law.

(d) As used in this section, "domestic violence" has the meaning set forth in Section 13700 of the Penal Code. "Abuse of an elder or a dependent person" means physical or sexual abuse, neglect, financial abuse, abandonment, isolation, abduction, or other treatment that results in physical harm, pain, or mental suffering, the deprivation of care by a caregiver, or other deprivation by a custodian or provider of goods or services that are necessary to avoid physical harm or mental suffering. Subject to a hearing conducted pursuant to Section 352, which shall include consideration of any corroboration and remoteness in time, "domestic violence" has the further meaning as set forth in Section 6211 of the Family Code if the act occurred no more than five years before the charged offense.

(e) Evidence of acts occurring more than 10 years before the charged offense is inadmissible under this section, unless the court determines that the admission of this evidence is in the interest of justice.

(f) Evidence of the findings and determinations of administrative agencies regulating the conduct of health facilities licensed under Section 1250 of the Health and Safety Code is inadmissible under this section. [*Added 1996. Amended 1998, 2000, 2004.*]

[*FRE have no counterpart to CEC § 1109.*]

Compare FRE 501 and CEC §§ 911-920. Under FRE, testimonial privileges are generally governed by "the common law—as interpreted by United States courts in the light of reason and experience." Federal courts recognize privileges for confidential communications between attorney-client, husband-wife, and psychotherapist-patient; have rejected privileges for physician-patient and other professional relationships; and recognize various privileges designed to protect governmental functions. Federal courts often seek guidance from the 1971 Proposed Rules. In federal civil cases in which state law provides the rule of decision (typically diversity cases), state privilege law governs. A more detailed comparison of testimonial privileges is beyond the scope of these notes.

§ **911. General rule as to privileges.** Except as otherwise provided by statute:

(a) No person has a privilege to refuse to be a witness.

(b) No person has a privilege to refuse to disclose any matter or to refuse to produce any writing, object, or other thing.

(c) No person has a privilege that another shall not be a witness or shall not disclose any matter or shall not produce any writing, object, or other thing.

§ **900. Application of definitions.** Unless the provision or context otherwise requires, the definitions in this chapter [§§ 900-905] govern the construction of this division [§§ 900-1070]. They do not govern the construction of any other division.

§ **901. Proceeding.** "Proceeding" means any action, hearing, investigation, inquest, or inquiry (whether conducted by a court, administrative agency, hearing officer, arbitrator, legislative body, or any other person authorized by law) in which, pursuant to law, testimony can be compelled to be given.

§ **902. Civil proceeding.** "Civil proceeding" means any proceeding except a criminal proceeding.

§ **903. Criminal proceeding.** "Criminal proceeding" means:

(a) A criminal action; and

(b) A proceeding pursuant to Article 3 (commencing with Section 3060) of Chapter 7 of Division 4 of Title 1 of the Government Code to determine whether a public officer should be removed from office for willful or corrupt misconduct in office.

§ **905. Presiding officer.** "Presiding officer" means the person authorized to rule on a claim of privilege in the proceeding in which the claim is made.

ARTICLE V. PRIVILEGES

Rule 501. Privilege in General

The common law — as interpreted by United States courts in the light of reason and experience — governs a claim of privilege unless any of the following provides otherwise:

- the United States Constitution;
- a federal statute; or
- rules prescribed by the Supreme Court.

But in a civil case, state law governs privilege regarding a claim or defense for which state law supplies the rule of decision.

Editors' Note

The Advisory Committee proposed specific rules on privileges, which were included in the Federal Rules of Evidence promulgated by the Supreme Court in 1973. However, those rules were rejected by Congress in favor of "the common law * * * in the light of reason and experience" and state rules of privilege in civil actions governed by state law. (Rule 501.)

On December 31, 2008, new Rule 502, dealing with limitations on waiver of the attorney-client and work product privileges, became effective. *See infra.*

Although rejected by Congress, the privilege provisions of the 1971 Proposed Rules have been quite influential. They are often cited as evidence of the common law, *see, e.g.*, Jaffee v. Redmond, 518 U.S. 1 (1996). In 1974 they were incorporated with only a few changes into the Uniform Rules of Evidence, on which most state codifications of evidence law have been based.

The Advisory Committee's 1971 Proposed Rules 501-513 are printed for purposes of comparison with the California Evidence Code. The Notes to 1971 Proposed Rules 502-513 in Part II include the original Advisory Committee's Notes as well as detailed comparisons with the Uniform Rules of Evidence (1974, as amended, 1986).

1971 Proposed Rule 501. Privileges Recognized Only as Provided [*Not Enacted*]

Except as otherwise required by the Constitution of the United States or provided by Act of Congress, and except as provided in these rules and in the Rules of Civil and Criminal Procedure, no person has a privilege to:

(a) Refuse to be a witness; or

(b) Refuse to disclose any matter; or

(c) Refuse to produce any object or writing; or

(d) Prevent another from being a witness or disclosing any matter or producing any object or writing.

§ 910. **Applicability of division.** Except as otherwise provided by statute, the provisions of this division [§§ 900-1070] apply in all proceedings. The provisions of any statute making rules of evidence inapplicable in particular proceedings, or limiting the applicability of rules of evidence in particular proceedings, do not make this division inapplicable to such proceedings.

§ 914. **Determination of claim of privilege; limitation on punishment for contempt.** (a) The presiding officer shall determine a claim of privilege in any proceeding in the same manner as a court determines such a claim under Article 2 (commencing with Section 400) of Chapter 4 of Division 3.

(b) No person may be held in contempt for failure to disclose information claimed to be privileged unless he has failed to comply with an order of a court that he disclose such information. This subdivision does not apply to any governmental agency that has constitutional contempt power, nor does it apply to hearings and investigations of the Industrial Accident Commission, nor does it impliedly repeal Chapter 4 (commencing with Section 9400) of Part 1 of Division 2 of Title 2 of the Government Code. If no other statutory procedure is applicable, the procedure prescribed by Section 1991 of the Code of Civil Procedure shall be followed in seeking an order of a court that the person disclose the information claimed to be privileged.

§ 915. **Disclosure of privileged information or attorney work product in ruling on claim of privilege.** (a) Subject to subdivision (b), the presiding officer may not require disclosure of information claimed to be privileged under this division or attorney work product under subdivision (a) of Section 2018.030 of the Code of Civil Procedure in order to rule on the claim of privilege; provided, however, that in any hearing conducted pursuant to subdivision (c) of Section 1524 of the Penal Code in which a claim of privilege is made and the court determines that there is no other feasible means to rule on the validity of the claim other than to require disclosure, the court shall proceed in accordance with subdivision (b).

(b) When a court is ruling on a claim of privilege under Article 9 (commencing with Section 1040) of Chapter 4 (official information and identity of informer) or under Section 1060 (trade secret) or under subdivision (b) of Section 2018.030 of the Code of Civil Procedure (attorney work product) and is unable to do so without requiring disclosure of the information claimed to be privileged, the court may require the person from whom disclosure is sought or the person authorized to claim the privilege, or both, to disclose the information in chambers out of the presence and hearing of all persons except the person authorized to claim the privilege and any other persons as the person authorized to claim the privilege is willing to have present. If the judge determines that the information is privileged, neither the judge nor any other person may ever disclose, without the consent of a person authorized to permit disclosure, what was disclosed in the course of the proceedings in chambers. [*Amended 1979, 2001, 2004, 2005.*]

[*See FRE 1101(c).*]

[*FRE have no counterpart to CEC § 914.*]

[*FRE have no counterpart to CEC § 915.*]

§ 916. Exclusion of privileged information where persons authorized to claim privilege are not present. (a) The presiding officer, on his own motion or on the motion of any party, shall exclude information that is subject to a claim of privilege under this division [§§ 900-1070] if:

(1) The person from whom the information is sought is not a person authorized to claim the privilege; and

(2) There is no party to the proceeding who is a person authorized to claim the privilege.

(b) The presiding officer may not exclude information under this section if:

(1) He is otherwise instructed by a person authorized to permit disclosure; or

(2) The proponent of the evidence establishes that there is no person authorized to claim the privilege in existence.

§ 917. Presumption that certain communications are confidential; privileged character of electronic communications. (a) Whenever a privilege is claimed on the ground that the matter sought to be disclosed is a communication made in confidence in the course of the lawyer-client, lawyer referral service-client, physician-patient, psychotherapist-patient, clergy-penitent, husband-wife, sexual assault victim-counselor, or domestic violence victim-counselor relationship, the communication is presumed to have been made in confidence and the opponent of the claim of privilege has the burden of proof to establish that the communication was not confidential.

(b) A communication between persons in a relationship listed in subdivision (a) does not lose its privileged character for the sole reason that it is communicated by electronic means or because persons involved in the delivery, facilitation, or storage of electronic communication may have access to the content of the communication.

(c) For purposes of this section, "electronic" has the same meaning provided in Section 1633.2 of the Civil Code. [*Amended 2002, 2003, 2004, 2014.*]

§ 920. No implied repeal. Nothing in this division [§§ 900-1070] shall be construed to repeal by implication any other statute relating to privileges.

§ 930. Privilege not to be called as a witness and not to testify. To the extent that such privilege exists under the Constitution of the United States or the State of California, a defendant in a criminal case has a privilege not to be called as a witness and not to testify.

§ 940. Privilege against self-incrimination. To the extent that such privilege exists under the Constitution of the United States or the State of California, a person has a privilege to refuse to disclose any matter that may tend to incriminate him.

[*FRE have no counterpart to CEC § 916.*]

[*FRE have no counterpart to CEC § 917.*]

[*FRE have no counterpart to CEC § 920.*]

[*FRE have no counterpart to CEC § 930. See U.S. Const. Amend. V.*]

[*FRE have no counterpart to CEC § 940. See U.S. Const. Amend. V.*]

§ **1070. Refusal to disclose news source.** (a) A publisher, editor, reporter, or other person connected with or employed upon a newspaper, magazine, or other periodical publication, or by a press association or wire service, or any person who has been so connected or employed, cannot be adjudged in contempt by a judicial, legislative, administrative body, or any other body having the power to issue subpoenas, for refusing to disclose, in any proceeding as defined in Section 901, the source of any information procured while so connected or employed for publication in a newspaper, magazine or other periodical publication, or for refusing to disclose any unpublished information obtained or prepared in gathering, receiving or processing of information for communication to the public.

(b) Nor can a radio or television news reporter or other person connected with or employed by a radio or television station, or any person who has been so connected or employed, be so adjudged in contempt for refusing to disclose the source of any information procured while so connected or employed for news or news commentary purposes on radio or television, or for refusing to disclose any unpublished information obtained or prepared in gathering, receiving or processing of information for communication to the public.

(c) As used in this section, "unpublished information" includes information not disseminated to the public by the person from whom disclosure is sought, whether or not related information has been disseminated and includes, but is not limited to, all notes, outtakes, photographs, tapes or other data of whatever sort not itself disseminated to the public through a medium of communication, whether or not published information based upon or related to such material has been disseminated. [*Amended 1971, 1972, 1974.*]

[*CEC has no counterpart to FRE 502.*]

[FRE have no counterpart to CEC § 1070.]

Rule 502. Attorney-Client Privilege and Work Product; Limitations on Waiver

The following provisions apply, in the circumstances set out, to disclosure of a communication or information covered by the attorney-client privilege or work-product protection.

(a) Disclosure Made in a Federal Proceeding or to a Federal Office or Agency; Scope of a Waiver. When the disclosure is made in a federal proceeding or to a federal office or agency and waives the attorney-client privilege or work-product protection, the waiver extends to an undisclosed communication or information in a federal or state proceeding only if:

(1) the waiver is intentional;

(2) the disclosed and undisclosed communications or information concern the same subject matter; and

(3) they ought in fairness to be considered together.

(b) Inadvertent Disclosure. When made in a federal proceeding or to a federal office or agency, the disclosure does not operate as a waiver in a federal or state proceeding if:

(1) the disclosure is inadvertent;

(2) the holder of the privilege or protection took reasonable steps to prevent disclosure; and

(3) the holder promptly took reasonable steps to rectify the error, including (if applicable) following Federal Rule of Civil Procedure 26(b)(5)(B).

(c) Disclosure Made in a State Proceeding. When the disclosure is made in a state proceeding and is not the subject of a state-court order concerning waiver, the disclosure does not operate as a waiver in a federal proceeding if the disclosure:

(1) would not be a waiver under this rule if it had been made in a federal proceeding; or

(2) is not a waiver under the law of the state where the disclosure occurred.

(d) Controlling Effect of a Court Order. A federal court may order that the privilege or protection is not waived by disclosure connected with the litigation pending before the court – in which event the disclosure is also not a waiver in any other federal or state proceeding.

(e) Controlling Effect of a Party Agreement. An agreement on the effect of disclosure in a federal proceeding is binding only on the parties to the agreement, unless it is incorporated into a court order.

(f) Controlling Effect of this Rule. Notwithstanding Rules 101 and 1101, this rule applies to state proceedings and to federal court-annexed and federal court-mandated arbitration proceedings, in the circumstances set out in the rule. And notwithstanding Rule 501, this rule applies even if state law provides the rule of decision.

(g) Definitions. In this rule:

(1) "attorney-client privilege" means the protection that applicable law provides for confidential attorney-client communications; and

(2) "work-product protection" means the protection that applicable law provides for tangible material (or its intangible equivalent) prepared in anticipation of litigation or for trial.

[*CEC has no counterpart to 1971 Proposed Rule 502 (Not Enacted).*]

§ **951. Client.** As used in this article [§§ 950-962], "client" means a person who, directly or through an authorized representative, consults a lawyer for the purpose of retaining the lawyer or securing legal service or advice from him in his professional capacity, and includes an incompetent (a) who himself so consults the lawyer or (b) whose guardian or conservator so consults the lawyer in behalf of the incompetent.

§ **950. Lawyer.** As used in this article [§§ 950-962], "lawyer" means a person authorized, or reasonably believed by the client to be authorized, to practice law in any state or nation.

§ **952. Confidential communication between client and lawyer.** As used in this article [§§ 950-962], "confidential communication between client and lawyer" means information transmitted between a client and his or her lawyer in the course of that relationship and in confidence by a means which, so far as the client is aware, discloses the information to no third persons other than those who are present to further the interest of the client in the consultation or those to whom disclosure is reasonably necessary for the transmission of the information or the accomplishment of the purpose for which the lawyer is consulted, and includes a legal opinion formed and the advice given by the lawyer in the course of that relationship. [*Amended 1967, 1994, 2002.*]

§ **954. Lawyer-client privilege.** Subject to Section 912 and except as otherwise provided in this article [§§ 950-962], the client, whether or not a party, has a privilege to refuse to disclose, and to prevent another from disclosing, a confidential communication between client and lawyer if the privilege is claimed by:

(a) The holder of the privilege;

(b) A person who is authorized to claim the privilege by the holder of the privilege; or

1971 Proposed Rule 502. Required Reports Privileged by Statute [*Not Enacted*]

A person, corporation, association, or other organization or entity, either public or private, making a return or report required by law to be made has a privilege to refuse to disclose and to prevent any other person from disclosing the return or report, if the law requiring it to be made so provides. A public officer or agency to whom a return or report is required by law to be made has a privilege to refuse to disclose the return or report if the law requiring it to be made so provides. No privilege exists under this rule in actions involving perjury, false statements, fraud in the return or report, or other failure to comply with the law in question.

1971 Proposed Rule 503. Lawyer-Client Privilege [*Not Enacted*]

(a) Definitions. As used in this rule:

(1) A "client" is a person, public officer, or corporation, association, or other organization or entity, either public or private, who is rendered professional legal services by a lawyer, or who consults a lawyer with a view to obtaining professional legal services from him.

(2) A "lawyer" is a person authorized, or reasonably believed by the client to be authorized, to practice law in any state or nation.

(3) A "representative of the lawyer" is one employed to assist the lawyer in the rendition of professional legal services.

(4) A communication is "confidential" if not intended to be disclosed to third persons other than those to whom disclosure is in furtherance of the rendition of professional legal services to the client or those reasonably necessary for the transmission of the communication.

(b) General rule of privilege. A client has a privilege to refuse to disclose and to prevent any other person from disclosing confidential communications made for the purpose of facilitating the rendition of professional legal services to the client, (1) between himself or his representative and his lawyer or his lawyer's representative, or (2) between his lawyer and the lawyer's representative, or (3) by him or his lawyer to a lawyer representing another in a matter of common interest, or (4) between representatives of the client or between the client and a representative of the client, or (5) between lawyers representing the client.

(c) The person who was the lawyer at the time of the confidential communication, but such person may not claim the privilege if there is no holder of the privilege in existence or if he is otherwise instructed by a person authorized to permit disclosure.

The relationship of attorney and client shall exist between a law corporation as defined in Article 10 (commencing with Section 6160) of Chapter 4 of Division 3 of the Business and Professions Code and the persons to whom it renders professional services, as well as between such persons and members of the State Bar employed by such corporation to render services to such persons. The word "persons" as used in this subdivision includes partnerships, corporations, limited liability companies, associations and other groups and entities. [*Amended 1968, 1994, 1996.*]

§ **953. Holder of the privilege.** As used in this article [§§ 950-962], "holder of the privilege" means:

(a) The client, if the client has no guardian or conservator.

(b) (1) A guardian or conservator of the client, if the client has a guardian or conservator, except as provided in paragraph (2).

(2) If the guardian or conservator has an actual or apparent conflict of interest with the client, then the guardian or conservator does not hold the privilege.

(c) The personal representative of the client if the client is dead, including a personal representative appointed pursuant to Section 12252 of the Probate Code.

(d) A successor, assign, trustee in dissolution, or any similar representative of a firm, association, organization, partnership, business trust, corporation, or public entity that is no longer in existence. [*Amended 2009, 2017.*]

§ **955. When lawyer required to claim privilege.** The lawyer who received or made a communication subject to the privilege under this article [§§ 950-962] shall claim the privilege whenever he is present when the communication is sought to be disclosed and is authorized to claim the privilege under subdivision (c) of Section 954.

§ **956. Exception: Crime or fraud.** (a) There is no privilege under this article if the services of the lawyer were sought or obtained to enable or aid anyone to commit or plan to commit a crime or a fraud. [*Amended 2016.*]

(b) This exception to the privilege granted by this article shall not apply to legal services rendered in compliance with state and local laws on medicinal cannabis or adult-use cannabis, and confidential communications provided for the purpose of rendering those services are confidential communications between client and lawyer, as defined in Section 952, provided the lawyer also advises the client on conflicts with respect to federal law. [*Added 2017.*]

§ **957. Exception: Parties claiming through deceased client.** There is no privilege under this article [§§ 950-962] as to a communication relevant to an issue between parties all of whom claim through a deceased client, regardless of whether the claims are by testate or intestate succession, nonprobate transfer, or inter vivos transaction. [*Amended 2009.*]

(c) **Who may claim the privilege.** The privilege may be claimed by the client, his guardian or conservator, the personal representative of a deceased client, or the successor, trustee, or similar representative of a corporation, association, or other organization, whether or not in existence. The person who was the lawyer at the time of the communication may claim the privilege but only on behalf of the client. His authority to do so is presumed in the absence of evidence to the contrary.

(d) **Exceptions.** There is no privilege under this rule:

(1) **Furtherance of crime or fraud.** If the services of the lawyer were sought or obtained to enable or aid anyone to commit or plan to commit what the client knew or reasonably should have known to be a crime or fraud; or

> As of the issue date of this edition, California and Federal law on the legality of marijuana differ; that difference is reflected in the difference between CEC §956(b), added in 2017, and FRE 501 / Proposed Rule 503(c) (which, while not enacted, remains a source of influence for federal-court decisions – *see* Editor's Note at p. I-53, *supra*). Unlike FRE, CEC §956(b) provides a safe harbor for attorney-client communications relating to legal advice on medical and adult-use cannabis (legalized in California January 1, 2018).

(2) **Claimants through same deceased client.** As to a communication relevant to an issue between parties who claim through the same deceased client, regardless of whether the claims are by testate or intestate succession or by inter vivos transaction; or

§ 960. Exception: Intention of deceased client concerning writing affecting property interest. There is no privilege under this article [§§ 950-962] as to a communication relevant to an issue concerning the intention of a client, now deceased, with respect to a deed of conveyance, will, or other writing, executed by the client, purporting to affect an interest in property.

§ 961. Exception: Validity of writing affecting property interest. There is no privilege under this article [§§ 950-962] as to a communication relevant to an issue concerning the validity of a deed of conveyance, will, or other writing, executed by a client, now deceased, purporting to affect an interest in property.

§ 958. Exception: Breach of duty arising out of lawyer-client relationship. There is no privilege under this article [§§ 950-962] as to a communication relevant to an issue of breach, by the lawyer or by the client, of a duty arising out of the lawyer-client relationship.

§ 959. Exception: Lawyer as attesting witness. There is no privilege under this article [§§ 950-962] as to a communication relevant to an issue concerning the intention or competence of a client executing an attested document of which the lawyer is an attesting witness, or concerning the execution or attestation of such a document.

§ 962. Exception: Joint clients. Where two or more clients have retained or consulted a lawyer upon a matter of common interest, none of them, nor the successor in interest of any of them, may claim a privilege under this article [§§ 950-962] as to a communication made in the course of that relationship when such communication is offered in a civil proceeding between one of such clients (or his successor in interest) and another of such clients (or his successor in interest).

§ 956.5. Reasonable belief that disclosure of confidential communication relating to representation of client is necessary to prevent criminal act that lawyer reasonably believes likely to result in death of, or substantial bodily harm to, an individual; exception to privilege. There is no privilege under this article if the lawyer reasonably believes that disclosure of any confidential communication relating to representation of a client is necessary to prevent a criminal act that the lawyer reasonably believes is likely to result in the death of, or substantial bodily harm to, an individual. [*Added 1993. Amended 2003, 2004.*]

[*§§ 965-968, added by amendment in 2013, provide a privilege for confidential communications between a lawyer referral service and its clients. For text, see Part III of this book. The proposed Federal Rules did not recognize such a privilege.*]

§ 1011. Patient. As used in this article [§§ 1010-1027], "patient" means a person who consults a psychotherapist or submits to an examination by a psychotherapist for the purpose of securing a diagnosis or preventive, palliative, or curative treatment of his mental or emotional condition or who submits to an examination of his mental or emotional condition for the purpose of scientific research on mental or emotional problems.

[*The 1971 Proposed Federal Rules had no counterpart to CEC § 961.*]

(3) **Breach of duty by lawyer or client.** As to a communication relevant to an issue of breach of duty by the lawyer to his client or by the client to his lawyer; or

(4) **Document attested by lawyer.** As to a communication relevant to an issue concerning an attested document to which the lawyer is an attesting witness; or

(5) **Joint clients.** As to a communication relevant to a matter of common interest between two or more clients if the communication was made by any of them to a lawyer retained or consulted in common, when offered in an action between any of the clients.

[*The 1971 Proposed Federal Rules had no counterpart to CEC § 956.5.*]

[*The 1971 Proposed Federal Rules had no counterpart to CEC §§ 965-968.*]

1971 Proposed Rule 504. Psychotherapist-Patient Privilege [*Not Enacted*]

(a) Definitions.

(1) A "patient" is a person who consults or is examined or interviewed by a psychotherapist.

§ **1010. Psychotherapist.** As used in this article, "psychotherapist" means a person who is, or is reasonably believed by the patient to be:

(a) A person authorized to practice medicine in any state or nation who devotes, or is reasonably believed by the patient to devote, a substantial portion of his or her time to the practice of psychiatry.

(b) A person licensed as a psychologist under Chapter 6.6 (commencing with Section 2900) of Division 2 of the Business and Professions Code.

(c) A person licensed as a clinical social worker under Chapter 14 (commencing with Section 4991) of Division 2 of the Business and Professions Code, when he or she is engaged in applied psychotherapy of a nonmedical nature.

(d) A person who is serving as a school psychologist and holds a credential authorizing that service issued by the state.

(e) A person licensed as a marriage and family therapist under Chapter 13 (commencing with Section 4980) of Division 2 of the Business and Professions Code.

(f) A person registered as a psychological assistant who is under the supervision of a licensed psychologist or board certified psychiatrist as required by Section 2913 of the Business and Professions Code, or a person registered as an associate marriage and family therapist who is under the supervision of a licensed marriage and family therapist, a licensed clinical social worker, a licensed psychologist, or a licensed physician and surgeon certified in psychiatry, as specified in Section 4980.44 of the Business and Professions Code.

(g) A person registered as an associate clinical social worker who is under supervision as specified in Section 4996.23 of the Business and Professions Code.

(h) A person registered with the Board of Psychology as a registered psychologist who is under the supervision of a licensed psychologist or board certified psychiatrist.

(i) A psychological intern as defined in Section 2911 of the Business and Professions Code who is under the supervision of a licensed psychologist or board certified psychiatrist.

(j) A trainee, as defined in subdivision (c) of Section 4980.03 of the Business and Professions Code, who is fulfilling his or her supervised practicum required by subparagraph (B) of paragraph (1) of subdivision (d) of Section 4980.36 of, or subdivision (c) of Section 4980.37 of, the Business and Professions Code and is supervised by a licensed psychologist, a board certified psychiatrist, a licensed clinical social worker, a licensed marriage and family therapist, or a licensed professional clinical counselor.

(2) A "psychotherapist" is (A) a person authorized to practice medicine in any state or nation, or reasonably believed by the patient so to be, while engaged in the diagnosis or treatment of a mental or emotional condition, including drug addiction, or (B) a person licensed or certified as a psychologist under the laws of any state or nation, while similarly engaged.

(k) A person licensed as a registered nurse pursuant to Chapter 6 (commencing with Section 2700) of Division 2 of the Business and Professions Code, who possesses a master's degree in psychiatric-mental health nursing and is listed as a psychiatric-mental health nurse by the Board of Registered Nursing.

(l) An advanced practice registered nurse who is certified as a clinical nurse specialist pursuant to Article 9 (commencing with Section 2838) of Chapter 6 of Division 2 of the Business and Professions Code and who participates in expert clinical practice in the specialty of psychiatric-mental health nursing.

(m) A person rendering mental health treatment or counseling services as authorized pursuant to Section 6924 of the Family Code.

(n) A person licensed as a professional clinical counselor under Chapter 16 (commencing with Section 4999.10) of Division 2 of the Business and Professions Code.

(o) A person registered as an associate professional clinical counselor who is under the supervision of a licensed professional clinical counselor, a licensed marriage and family therapist, a licensed clinical social worker, a licensed psychologist, or a licensed physician and surgeon certified in psychiatry, as specified in Sections 4999.42 to 4999.48, inclusive, of the Business and Professions Code.

(p) A clinical counselor trainee, as defined in subdivision (g) of Section 4999.12 of the Business and Professions Code, who is fulfilling his or her supervised practicum required by paragraph (3) of subdivision (c) of Section 4999.32 of, or paragraph (3) of subdivision (c) of Section 4999.33 of, the Business and Professions Code, and is supervised by a licensed psychologist, a board-certified psychiatrist, a licensed clinical social worker, a licensed marriage and family therapist, or a licensed professional clinical counselor. [*Amended 1967, 1970, 1972, 1974, 1983, 1987, 1988, 1989. 1990, 1992, 1994, 2001, 2009, 2015, 2016, 2018.*]

§ 1010.5. Privileged communication between patient and educational psychologist. A communication between a patient and an educational psychologist, licensed under Article 5 (commencing with Section 4986) of Chapter 13 of Division 2 of the Business and Professions Code, shall be privileged to the same extent, and subject to the same limitations, as a communication between a patient and a psychotherapist described in subdivisions (c), (d), and (e) of Section 1010. [*Added 1985.*]

§ 1012. Confidential communication between patient and psychotherapist. As used in this article [§§ 1010-1027], "confidential communication between patient and psychotherapist" means information, including information obtained by an examination of the patient, transmitted between a patient and his psychotherapist in the course of that relationship and in confidence by a means which, so far as the patient is aware, discloses the information to no third persons other than those who are present to further the interest of the patient in the consultation, or those to whom disclosure is reasonably necessary for the transmission of the information or the accomplishment of the purpose for which the psychotherapist is consulted, and includes a diagnosis made and the advice given by the psychotherapist in the course of that relationship. [*Amended 1967, 1970.*]

(3) A communication is "confidential" if not intended to be disclosed to third persons other than those present to further the interest of the patient in the consultation, examination, or interview, or persons reasonably necessary for the transmission of the communication, or persons who are participating in the diagnosis and treatment under the direction of the psychotherapist, including members of the patient's family.

§ **1014. Psychotherapist-patient privilege.** Subject to Section 912 and except as otherwise provided in this article [§§ 1010-1027], the patient, whether or not a party, has a privilege to refuse to disclose, and to prevent another from disclosing, a confidential communication between patient and psychotherapist if the privilege is claimed by:

(a) The holder of the privilege.

(b) A person who is authorized to claim the privilege by the holder of the privilege.

(c) The person who was the psychotherapist at the time of the confidential communication,

but the person may not claim the privilege if there is no holder of the privilege in existence or if he or she is otherwise instructed by a person authorized to permit disclosure.

The relationship of a psychotherapist and patient shall exist between a psychological corporation as defined in Article 9 (commencing with Section 2995) of Chapter 6.6 of Division 2 of the Business and Professions Code, a marriage and family therapy corporation as defined in Article 6 (commencing with Section 4987.5) of Chapter 13 of Division 2 of the Business and Professions Code, or a licensed clinical social workers corporation as defined in Article 5 (commencing with Section 4998) of Chapter 14 of Division 2 of the Business and Professions Code, and the patient to whom it renders professional services, as well as between those patients and psychotherapists employed by those corporations to render services to those patients. The word "persons" as used in this subdivision includes partnerships, corporations, limited liability companies, associations and other groups and entities. [*Amended 1969, 1972, 1989, 1990, 1994, 2002.*]

§ **1013. Holder of the privilege.** As used in this article [§§ 1010-1027], "holder of the privilege" means:

(a) The patient when he has no guardian or conservator.

(b) A guardian or conservator of the patient when the patient has a guardian or conservator.

(c) The personal representative of the patient if the patient is dead.

§ **1015. When psychotherapist required to claim privilege.** The psychotherapist who received or made a communication subject to the privilege under this article [§§ 1010-1027] shall claim the privilege whenever he is present when the communication is sought to be disclosed and is authorized to claim the privilege under subdivision (c) of Section 1014.

§ **1024. Exception: Patient dangerous to himself or others.** There is no privilege under this article [§§ 1010-1027] if the psychotherapist has reasonable cause to believe that the patient is in such mental or emotional condition as to be dangerous to himself or to the person or property of another and that disclosure of the communication is necessary to prevent the threatened danger.

(b) General Rule of Privilege. A patient has a privilege to refuse to disclose and to prevent any other person from disclosing confidential communications, made for the purposes of diagnosis or treatment of his mental or emotional condition, including drug addiction, among himself, his psychotherapist, or persons who are participating in the diagnosis or treatment under the direction of the psychotherapist, including members of the patient's family.

(c) Who May Claim the Privilege. The privilege may be claimed by the patient, by his guardian or conservator, or by the personal representative of a deceased patient. The person who was the psychotherapist may claim the privilege but only on behalf of the patient. His authority so to do is presumed in the absence of evidence to the contrary.

(d) Exceptions.

(1) Proceedings for Hospitalization. There is no privilege under this rule for communications relevant to an issue in proceedings to hospitalize the patient for mental illness, if the psychotherapist in the course of diagnosis or treatment has determined that the patient is in need of hospitalization.

§ 1017. Exception: Court-appointed psychotherapist. (a) There is no privilege under this article [§§ 1010-1027] if the psychotherapist is appointed by order of a court to examine the patient, but this exception does not apply where the psychotherapist is appointed by order of the court upon the request of the lawyer for the defendant in a criminal proceeding in order to provide the lawyer with information needed so that he or she may advise the defendant whether to enter or withdraw a plea based on insanity or to present a defense based on his or her mental or emotional condition.

(b) There is no privilege under this article [§§ 1010-1027] if the psychotherapist is appointed by the Board of Prison Terms to examine a patient pursuant to the provisions of Article 4 (commencing with Section 2960) of Chapter 7 of Title 1 of Part 3 of the Penal Code. [*Amended 1967, 1987.*]

§ 1016. Exception: Patient-litigant exception. There is no privilege under this article [§§ 1010-1027] as to a communication relevant to an issue concerning the mental or emotional condition of the patient if such issue has been tendered by:

(a) The patient;

(b) Any party claiming through or under the patient;

(c) Any party claiming as a beneficiary of the patient through a contract to which the patient is or was a party; or

(d) The plaintiff in an action brought under Section 376 or 377 of the Code of Civil Procedure for damages for the injury or death of the patient.

§ 1023. Exception: Proceeding to determine sanity of criminal defendant. There is no privilege under this article [§§ 1010-1027] in a proceeding under Chapter 6 (commencing with Section 1367) of Title 10 of Part 2 of the Penal Code initiated at the request of the defendant in a criminal action to determine his sanity.

§ 1025. Exception: Proceeding to establish competence. There is no privilege under this article [§§ 1010-1027] in a proceeding brought by or on behalf of the patient to establish his competence.

§ 1018. Exception: Crime or tort. There is no privilege under this article [§§ 1010-1027] if the services of the psychotherapist were sought or obtained to enable or aid anyone to commit or plan to commit a crime or a tort or to escape detection or apprehension after the commission of a crime or a tort.

§ 1019. Exception: Parties claiming through deceased patient. There is no privilege under this article [§§ 1010-1027] as to a communication relevant to an issue between parties all of whom claim through a deceased patient, regardless of whether the claims are by testate or intestate succession or by inter vivos transaction.

(2) Examination by Order of Judge. If the judge orders an examination of the mental or emotional condition of the patient, communications made in the course thereof are not privileged under this rule with respect to the particular purpose for which the examination is ordered unless the judge orders otherwise.

(3) Condition an Element of Claim or Defense. There is no privilege under this rule as to communications relevant to an issue of the mental or emotional condition of the patient in any proceeding in which he relies upon the condition as an element of his claim or defense, or, after the patient's death, in any proceeding in which any party relies upon the condition as an element of his claim or defense.

[*The 1971 Proposed Federal Rules had no counterpart to CEC § 1018.*]

[*The 1971 Proposed Federal Rules had no counterpart to CEC § 1019.*]

§ **1020. Exception: Breach of duty arising out of psychotherapist-patient relationship.** There is no privilege under this article [§§ 1010-1027] as to a communication relevant to an issue of breach, by the psychotherapist or by the patient, of a duty arising out of the psychotherapist-patient relationship.

§ **1021. Exception: Intention of deceased patient concerning writing affecting property interest.** There is no privilege under this article [§§ 1010-1027] as to a communication relevant to an issue concerning the intention of a patient, now deceased, with respect to a deed of conveyance, will, or other writing, executed by the patient, purporting to affect an interest in property.

§ **1022. Exception: Validity of writing affecting property interest.** There is no privilege under this article [§§ 1010-1027] as to a communication relevant to an issue concerning the validity of a deed of conveyance, will, or other writing, executed by a patient, now deceased, purporting to affect an interest in property.

§ **1026. Exception: Required report.** There is no privilege under this article [§§ 1010-1027] as to information that the psychotherapist or the patient is required to report to a public employee or as to information required to be recorded in a public office, if such report or record is open to public inspection.

§ **1027. Exception: Child under 16 victim of crime.** There is no privilege under this article [§§ 1010-1027] if all of the following circumstances exist:

(a) The patient is a child under the age of 16.

(b) The psychotherapist has reasonable cause to believe that the patient has been the victim of a crime and that disclosure of the communication is in the best interest of the child. [*Added 1970.*]

Physician-Patient Privilege:

[*Sections 990-1007, provide a privilege for confidential communications between physicians (other than psychotherapists) and patients.*]

Sexual Assault Counselor-Victim Privilege:

[*Sections 1035-1036.2, provide a privilege for confidential communications between sexual assault counselors and victims. The Proposed Federal Rules did not recognize such a privilege.*]

Domestic Violence Counselor-Victim Privilege:

[*Sections 1037-1037.8, provide a privilege for confidential communications between domestic violence counselors and victims. The Proposed Federal Rules did not recognize such a privilege.*]

[*The 1971 Proposed Federal Rules had no counterpart to CEC § 1020.*]

[*The 1971 Proposed Federal Rules had no counterpart to CEC § 1021.*]

[*The 1971 Proposed Federal Rules had no counterpart to CEC § 1022.*]

[*The 1971 Proposed Federal Rules had no counterpart to CEC § 1026.*]

[*The 1971 Proposed Federal Rules had no counterpart to CEC § 1027.*]

[*The 1971 Proposed Rules did not recognize a privilege for confidential communications between physicians (other than psychotherapists) and patients.*]

[*The 1971 Proposed Rules did not recognize a privilege for confidential communications between sexual assault counselors and victims.*]

[*The 1971 Proposed Rules did not recognize a privilege for confidential communications between domestic violence counselors and victims.*]

Human Trafficking Caseworker-Victim Privilege

[*Sections 1038-1038.2.*]

§ **970. Privilege not to testify against spouse.** Except as otherwise provided by statute, a married person has a privilege not to testify against his spouse in any proceeding.

§ **971. Privilege not to be called as a witness against spouse.** Except as otherwise provided by statute, a married person whose spouse is a party to a proceeding has a privilege not to be called as a witness by an adverse party to that proceeding without the prior express consent of the spouse having the privilege under this section unless the party calling the spouse does so in good faith without knowledge of the marital relationship.

§ **972. When privilege not applicable.** A married person does not have a privilege under this article [§§ 970-973] in:

(a) A proceeding brought by or on behalf of one spouse against the other spouse.

(b) A proceeding to commit or otherwise place his or her spouse or his or her spouse's property, or both, under the control of another because of the spouse's alleged mental or physical condition.

(c) A proceeding brought by or on behalf of a spouse to establish his or her competence.

(d) A proceeding under the Juvenile Court Law, Chapter 2 (commencing with Section 200) of Part 1 of Division 2 of the Welfare and Institutions Code.

(e) A criminal proceeding in which one spouse is charged with:

(1) A crime against the person or property of the other spouse or of a child, parent, relative, or cohabitant of either, whether committed before or during marriage.

(2) A crime against the person or property of a third person committed in the course of committing a crime against the person or property of the other spouse, whether committed before or during marriage.

(3) Bigamy.

(4) A crime defined by Section 270 or 270a of the Penal Code.

(f) A proceeding resulting from a criminal act which occurred prior to legal marriage of the spouses to each other regarding knowledge acquired prior to that marriage if prior to the legal marriage the witness spouse was aware that his or her spouse had been arrested for or had been formally charged with the crime or crimes about which the spouse is called to testify.

[*The 1971 Proposed Rules did not recognize a privilege for confidential communications between Human Trafficking Caseworkers and Human Trafficking Victims.*]

1971 Proposed Rule 505. Husband-Wife Privilege [*Not Enacted*]

(a) General rule of privilege. An accused in a criminal proceeding has a privilege to prevent his spouse from testifying against him.

(b) Who may claim the privilege. The privilege may be claimed by the accused or by the spouse on his behalf. The authority of the spouse to do so is presumed in the absence of evidence to the contrary.

(c) Exceptions. There is no privilege under this rule (1) in proceedings in which one spouse is charged with a crime against the person or property of the other or of a child of either, or with a crime against the person or property of a third person committed in the course of committing a crime against the other, or (2) as to matters occurring prior to the marriage, or (3) in proceedings in which a spouse is charged with importing an alien for prostitution or other immoral purpose in violation of 8 U.S.C. § 1328, with transporting a female in interstate commerce for immoral purposes or other offense in violation of 18 U.S.C. §§ 2421-2424, or with violation of other similar statutes.

(g) A proceeding brought against the spouse by a former spouse so long as the property and debts of the marriage have not been adjudicated, or in order to establish, modify, or enforce a child, family or spousal support obligation arising from the marriage to the former spouse; in a proceeding brought against a spouse by the other parent in order to establish, modify, or enforce a child support obligation for a child of a nonmarital relationship of the spouse; or in a proceeding brought against a spouse by the guardian of a child of that spouse in order to establish, modify, or enforce a child support obligation of the spouse. The married person does not have a privilege under this subdivision to refuse to provide information relating to the issues of income, expenses, assets, debts, and employment of either spouse, but may assert the privilege as otherwise provided in this article if other information is requested by the former spouse, guardian, or other parent of the child.

Any person demanding the otherwise privileged information made available by this subdivision, who also has an obligation to support the child for whom an order to establish, modify, or enforce child support is sought, waives his or her marital privilege to the same extent as the spouse as provided in this subdivision. [*Amended 1975, 1982, 1983, 1989.*]

§ **973. Waiver of privilege.** (a) Unless erroneously compelled to do so, a married person who testifies in a proceeding to which his spouse is a party, or who testifies against his spouse in any proceeding, does not have a privilege under this article [§§ 970-973] in the proceeding in which such testimony is given.

(b) There is no privilege under this article [§§ 970-973] in a civil proceeding brought or defended by a married person for the immediate benefit of his spouse or of himself and his spouse.

§ **980. Privilege for confidential marital communications.** Subject to Section 912 and except as otherwise provided in this article, a spouse, or the spouse's guardian or conservator if the spouse has a guardian or conservator, whether or not a party, has a privilege during the marital relationship and afterwards to refuse to disclose, and to prevent another from disclosing, a communication if the spouse claims the privilege and the communication was made in confidence between the spouse and the other spouse while they were married.

§ **981. Exception: Crime or fraud.** There is no privilege under this article [§§ 980-987] if the communication was made, in whole or in part, to enable or aid anyone to commit or plan to commit a crime or a fraud.

§ **982. Exception: Commitment or similar proceedings.** There is no privilege under this article [§§ 980-987] in a proceeding to commit either spouse or otherwise place him or his property, or both, under the control of another because of his alleged mental or physical condition.

§ **983. Exception: Proceeding to establish competence.** There is no privilege under this article [§§ 980-987] in a proceeding brought by or on behalf of either spouse to establish his competence.

[*The 1971 Proposed Federal Rules did not recognize a privilege for confidential marital communications.*]

§ **984. Exception: Proceeding between spouses.** There is no privilege under this article [§§ 980-987] in:

(a) A proceeding brought by or on behalf of one spouse against the other spouse.

(b) A proceeding between a surviving spouse and a person who claims through the deceased spouse, regardless of whether such claim is by testate or intestate succession or by inter vivos transaction.

§ **985. Exception: Certain criminal proceedings.** There is no privilege under this article [§§ 980-987] in a criminal proceeding in which one spouse is charged with:

(a) A crime committed at any time against the person or property of the other spouse or of a child of either.

(b) A crime committed at any time against the person or property of a third person committed in the course of committing a crime against the person or property of the other spouse.

(c) Bigamy.

(d) A crime defined by Section 270 or 270a of the Penal Code. [*Amended 1975.*]

§ **986. Exception: Juvenile court proceeding.** There is no privilege under this article [§§ 980-987] in a proceeding under the Juvenile Court Law, Chapter 2 (commencing with Section 200) of Part 1 of Division 2 of the Welfare and Institutions Code. [*Amended 1982.*]

§ **987. Exception: Communication offered by spouse who is criminal defendant.** There is no privilege under this article [§§ 980-987] in a criminal proceeding in which the communication is offered in evidence by a defendant who is one of the spouses between whom the communication was made.

§ **1030. Member of the clergy.** As used in this article [§§ 1030-1034], "a member of the clergy" means a priest, minister, religious practitioner, or similar functionary of a church or of a religious denomination or religious organization. [*Amended 2002.*]

§ **1031. Penitent.** As used in this article [§§ 1030-1034], "penitent" means a person who has made a penitential communication to a member of the clergy. [*Amended 2002.*]

§ **1032. Penitential communication.** As used in this article [§§ 1030-1034], "penitential communication" means a communication made in confidence, in the presence of no third person so far as the penitent is aware, to a member of the clergy who, in the course of the discipline or practice of the clergy member's church, denomination, or organization, is authorized or accustomed to hear those communications and, under the discipline or tenets of his or her church, denomination, or organization, has a duty to keep those communications secret. [*Amended 2002.*]

§ **1033. Privilege of penitent.** Subject to Section 912, a penitent, whether or not a party, has a privilege to refuse to disclose, and to prevent another from disclosing, a penitential communication if he or she claims the privilege. [*Amended 2002.*]

Proposed Rule 506. Communications to Clergymen [*Not Enacted*]

(a) Definitions. As used in this rule:

(1) A "clergyman" is a minister, priest, rabbi, or other similar functionary of a religious organization, or an individual reasonably believed so to be by the person consulting him.

(2) A communication is "confidential" if made privately and not intended for further disclosure except to other persons present in furtherance of the purpose of the communication.

(b) General rule of privilege. A person has a privilege to refuse to disclose and to prevent another from disclosing a confidential communication by the person to a clergyman in his professional character as spiritual adviser.

(c) Who may claim the privilege. The privilege may be claimed by the person, by his

§ **1034. Privilege of clergy.** Subject to Section 912, a member of the clergy, whether or not a party, has a privilege to refuse to disclose a penitential communication if he or she claims the privilege. [*Amended 2002.*]

§ **1050. Privilege to protect secrecy of vote.** If he claims the privilege, a person has a privilege to refuse to disclose the tenor of his vote at a public election where the voting is by secret ballot unless he voted illegally or he previously made an unprivileged disclosure of the tenor of his vote.

§ **1060. Privilege to protect trade secret.** If he or his agent or employee claims the privilege, the owner of a trade secret has a privilege to refuse to disclose the secret, and to prevent another from disclosing it, if the allowance of the privilege will not tend to conceal fraud or otherwise work injustice.

§ **1061. Procedure for assertion of trade secret privilege.** (a) For purposes of this section, and Sections 1062 and 1063:

(1) "Trade secret" means "trade secret," as defined in subdivision (d) of Section 3426.1 of the Civil Code, or paragraph (9) of subdivision (a) of Section 499c of the Penal Code.

(2) "Article" means "article," as defined in paragraph (2) of subdivision (a) of Section 499c of the Penal Code.

(b) In addition to Section 1062, the following procedure shall apply whenever the owner of a trade secret wishes to assert his or her trade secret privilege, as provided in Section 1060, during a criminal proceeding:

(1) The owner of the trade secret shall file a motion for a protective order, or the people may file the motion on the owner's behalf and with the owner's permission. The motion shall include an affidavit based upon personal knowledge listing the affiant's qualifications to give an opinion concerning the trade secret at issue, identifying, without revealing, the alleged trade secret and articles which disclose the secret, and presenting evidence that the secret qualifies as a trade secret under either subdivision (d) of Section 3426.1 of the Civil Code or paragraph (9) of subdivision (a) of Section 499c of the Penal Code. The motion and affidavit shall be served on all parties in the proceeding.

(2) Any party in the proceeding may oppose the request for the protective order by submitting affidavits based upon the affiant's personal knowledge. The affidavits shall be filed under seal, but shall be provided to the owner of the trade secret and to all parties in the proceeding. Neither the owner of the trade secret nor any party in the proceeding may disclose the affidavit to persons other than to counsel of record without prior court approval.

guardian or conservator, or by his personal representative if he is deceased. The clergyman may claim the privilege on behalf of the person. His authority so to do is presumed in the absence of evidence to the contrary.

1971 Proposed Rule 507. Political Vote [*Not Enacted*]

Every person has a privilege to refuse to disclose the tenor of his vote at a political election conducted by secret ballot unless the vote was cast illegally.

1971 Proposed Rule 508. Trade Secrets [*Not Enacted*]

A person has a privilege, which may be claimed by him or his agent or employee, to refuse to disclose and to prevent other persons from disclosing a trade secret owned by him, if the allowance of the privilege will not tend to conceal fraud or otherwise work injustice. When disclosure is directed, the judge shall take such protective measure as the interests of the holder of the privilege and of the parties and the furtherance of justice may require.

(3) The movant shall, by a preponderance of the evidence, show that the issuance of a protective order is proper. The court may rule on the request without holding an evidentiary hearing. However, in its discretion, the court may choose to hold an in camera evidentiary hearing concerning disputed articles with only the owner of the trade secret, the people's representative, the defendant, and defendant's counsel present. If the court holds such a hearing, the parties' right to examine witnesses shall not be used to obtain discovery, but shall be directed solely toward the question of whether the alleged trade secret qualifies for protection.

(4) If the court finds that a trade secret may be disclosed during any criminal proceeding unless a protective order is issued and that the issuance of a protective order would not conceal a fraud or work an injustice, the court shall issue a protective order limiting the use and dissemination of the trade secret, including, but not limited to, articles disclosing that secret. The protective order may, in the court's discretion, include the following provisions:

(A) That the trade secret may be disseminated only to counsel for the parties, including their associate attorneys, paralegals, and investigators, and to law enforcement officials or clerical officials.

(B) That the defendant may view the secret only in the presence of his or her counsel, or if not in the presence of his or her counsel, at counsel's offices.

(C) That any party seeking to show the trade secret, or articles containing the trade secret, to any person not designated by the protective order shall first obtain court approval to do so:

(i) The court may require that the person receiving the trade secret do so only in the presence of counsel for the party requesting approval.

(ii) The court may require the person receiving the trade secret to sign a copy of the protective order and to agree to be bound by its terms. The order may include a provision recognizing the owner of the trade secret to be a third-party beneficiary of that agreement.

(iii) The court may require a party seeking disclosure to an expert to provide that expert's name, employment history, and any other relevant information to the court for examination. The court shall accept that information under seal, and the information shall not be disclosed by any court except upon termination of the action and upon a showing of good cause to believe the secret has been disseminated by a court-approved expert. The court shall evaluate the expert and determine whether the expert poses a discernible risk of disclosure. The court shall withhold approval if the expert's economic interests place the expert in a competitive position with the victim, unless no other experts are available. The court may interview the expert in camera in aid of its ruling. If the court rejects the expert, it shall state its reasons for doing so on the record and a transcript of those reasons shall be prepared and sealed.

(D) That no articles disclosing the trade secret shall be filed or otherwise made a part of the court record available to the public without approval of the court and prior notice to the owner of the secret. The owner of the secret may give either party permission to accept the notice on the owner's behalf.

(E) Other orders as the court deems necessary to protect the integrity of the trade secret.

(c) A ruling granting or denying a motion for a protective order filed pursuant to subdivision (b) shall not be construed as a determination that the alleged trade secret is or is not a trade secret as defined by subdivision (d) of Section 3426.1 of the Civil Code or paragraph (9) of subdivision (a) of Section 499c of the Penal Code. Such a ruling shall not have any effect on any civil litigation.

(d) This section shall have prospective effect only and shall not operate to invalidate previously entered protective orders. [*Added 1990. Amended 2002.*]

§ 1062. Exclusion of public from criminal proceeding; motion contents; hearing; determination. (a) Notwithstanding any other provision of law, in a criminal case, the court, upon motion of the owner of a trade secret, or upon motion by the People with the consent of the owner, may exclude the public from any portion of a criminal proceeding where the proponent of closure has demonstrated a substantial probability that the trade secret would otherwise be disclosed to the public during that proceeding and a substantial probability that the disclosure would cause serious harm to the owner of the secret, and where the court finds that there is no overriding public interest in an open proceeding. No evidence, however, shall be excluded during a criminal proceeding pursuant to this section if it would conceal a fraud, work an injustice, or deprive the People or the defendant of a fair trial.

(b) The motion made pursuant to subdivision (a) shall identify, without revealing, the trade secrets which would otherwise be disclosed to the public. A showing made pursuant to subdivision (a) shall be made during an in camera hearing with only the owner of the trade secret, the People's representative, the defendant, and defendant's counsel present. A court reporter shall be present during the hearing. Any transcription of the proceedings at the in camera hearing, as well as any articles presented at that hearing, shall be ordered sealed by the court and only a court may allow access to its contents upon a showing of good cause. The court, in ruling upon the motion made pursuant to subdivision (a), may consider testimony presented or affidavits filed in any proceeding held in that action.

(c) If, after the in camera hearing described in subdivision (b), the court determines that exclusion of trade secret information from the public is appropriate, the court shall close only that portion of the criminal proceeding necessary to prevent disclosure of the trade secret. Before granting the motion, however, the court shall find and state for the record that the moving party has met its burden pursuant to subdivision (b), and that the closure of that portion of the proceeding will not deprive the People or the defendant of a fair trial.

(D) That no articles disclosing the trade secret shall be filed or otherwise made a part of the court record available to the public without approval of the court and prior notice to the owner of the secret. The owner of the secret may give either party permission to accept the notice on the owner's behalf.

(E) Other orders as the court deems necessary to protect the integrity of the trade secret.

(c) A ruling granting or denying a motion for a protective order filed pursuant to subdivision (b) shall not be construed as a determination that the alleged trade secret is or is not a trade secret as defined by subdivision (d) of Section 3426.1 of the Civil Code or paragraph (9) of subdivision (a) of Section 499c of the Penal Code. Such a ruling shall not have any effect on any civil litigation.

(d) This section shall have prospective effect only and shall not operate to invalidate previously entered protective orders. [*Added 1990. Amended 2002.*]

§ 1062. Exclusion of public from criminal proceeding; motion; contents; hearing; determination. (a) Notwithstanding any other provision of law, in a criminal case, the court, upon motion of the owner of a trade secret, or upon motion by the People with the consent of the owner, may exclude the public from any portion of a criminal proceeding where the proponent of closure has demonstrated a substantial probability that the trade secret would otherwise be disclosed to the public during that proceeding and a substantial probability that the disclosure would cause serious harm to the owner of the secret, and where the court finds that there is no overriding public interest in an open proceeding. No evidence, however, shall be excluded during a criminal proceeding pursuant to this section if it would conceal a fraud, work an injustice, or deprive the People or the defendant of a fair trial.

(b) The motion made pursuant to subdivision (a) shall identify, without revealing, the trade secrets which would otherwise be disclosed to the public. A showing made pursuant to subdivision (a) shall be made during an in camera hearing with only the owner of the trade secret, the People's representative, the defendant, and defendant's counsel present. A court reporter shall be present during the hearing. Any transcription of the proceedings at the in camera hearing, as well as any articles presented at that hearing, shall be ordered sealed by the court and only a court may allow access to its contents upon a showing of good cause. The court, in ruling upon the motion made pursuant to subdivision (a), may consider testimony presented or affidavits filed in any proceeding held in that action.

(c) If, after the in camera hearing described in subdivision (b), the court determines that exclusion of trade secret information from the public is appropriate, the court shall close only that portion of the criminal proceeding necessary to prevent disclosure of the trade secret. Before granting the motion, however, the court shall find and state for the record that the moving party has met its burden pursuant to subdivision (b), and that the closure of that portion of the proceeding will not deprive the People or the defendant of a fair trial.

(d) The owner of the trade secret, the People, or the defendant may seek relief from a ruling denying or granting closure by petitioning a higher court for extraordinary relief.

(e) Whenever the court closes a portion of a criminal proceeding pursuant to this section, a transcript of that closed proceeding shall be made available to the public as soon as practicable. The court shall redact any information qualifying as a trade secret before making that transcript available.

(f) The court, subject to Section 867 of the Penal Code, may allow witnesses who are bound by a protective order entered in the criminal proceeding protecting trade secrets, pursuant to Section 1061, to remain within the courtroom during the closed portion of the proceeding. [*Added 1990.*]

§ 1063. Sealing of articles protected by protective order; procedures. The following provisions shall govern requests to seal articles which are protected by a protective order entered pursuant to Evidence Code Section 1060 or 1061:

(a) The People shall request sealing of articles reasonably expected to be filed or admitted into evidence as follows:

(1) No less than 10 court days before trial, and no less than five court days before any other criminal proceeding, the People shall file with the court a list of all articles which the People reasonably expect to file with the court, or admit into evidence, under seal at that proceeding. That list shall be available to the public. The People may be relieved from providing timely notice upon showing that exigent circumstances prevent that notice.

(2) The court shall not allow the listed articles to be filed, admitted into evidence, or in any way made a part of the court record otherwise open to the public before holding a hearing to consider any objections to the People's request to seal the articles. The court at that hearing shall allow those objecting to the sealing to state their objections.

(3) After hearing any objections to sealing, the court shall conduct an in camera hearing with only the owner of the trade secret contained within those articles, the People's representative, defendant, and defendant's counsel present. The court shall review the articles sought to be sealed, evaluate objections to sealing, and determine whether the People have satisfied the constitutional standards governing public access to articles which are part of the judicial record. The court may consider testimony presented or affidavits filed in any proceeding held in that action. The People, defendant, and the owner of the trade secret may file affidavits based on the affiant's personal knowledge to be considered at that hearing. Those affidavits are to be sealed and not released to the public, but shall be made available to the parties. The court may rule on the request to seal without taking testimony. If the court takes testimony, examination of witnesses shall not be used to obtain discovery, but shall be directed solely toward whether sealing is appropriate.

(c) If the court finds that the owner has satisfied appropriate constitutional standards with respect to sealing procedures, the court shall seal those articles if and when they are filed, admitted into evidence, or in any way made a part of the court record or otherwise open to the public. The articles shall not be unsealed absent an order of a court upon a showing of good cause. Failure to examine the court file for notice of a request to seal shall not constitute good cause to consider objections to sealing.

(b) The following procedures shall apply to other articles made a part of the court record:

(1) When articles are produced by a person as a trade secret pursuant to Section 1060 or 1061 are filed, admitted into evidence, or in any way made a part of the court record in such a way as to be otherwise open to the public, the People, the defendant, or the owner of a trade secret contained within those articles may request the court to seal those articles.

(2) The request to seal shall be made by written motion filed with the court. It may also be made orally in court at the time the article is to be made a part of the court record. Where the request is made orally, the movant must file within 24 hours a written declaration of that request, including a list of the articles which are the subject of that request. These motions and lists shall be available to the public.

(3) The court shall promptly conduct a hearing as provided in paragraphs (2), (3), and (4) of subdivision (b). The court shall, pending the hearing, seal those articles which are the subject of the request. Where the court agrees to seal the articles conditionally, the court may conduct the hearing at the time the articles are made a part of the court record, but shall reconsider its ruling in light of additional objections made by others within two court days after the written proof of the request to seal is made available to the public.

(4) Any articles sealed pursuant to these hearings shall not be unsealed absent an order of a court upon a showing of good cause. Failure to examine the court file for notice of a request to seal shall not constitute good cause to consider objections to sealing. [[illegible] 1996.]

§ 1040. Privilege for official information. (a) As used in this section, "official information" means information acquired in confidence by a public employee in the course of his or her duty and not open, or officially disclosed, to the public prior to the time the claim of privilege is made.

(b) A public entity has a privilege to refuse to disclose official information, and to prevent another from disclosing official information, if the privilege is claimed by a person authorized by the public entity to do so and either of the following apply:

(1) Disclosure is forbidden by an act of the Congress of the United States or a statute of this state.

(4) If the court finds that the movant has satisfied appropriate constitutional standards with respect to sealing particular articles, the court shall seal those articles if and when they are filed, admitted into evidence, or in any way made a part of the court record otherwise open to the public. The articles shall not be unsealed absent an order of a court upon a showing of good cause. Failure to examine the court file for notice of a request to seal shall not constitute good cause to consider objections to sealing.

(b) The following procedure shall apply to other articles made a part of the court record:

(1) Where any articles protected by a protective order entered pursuant to Section 1060 or 1061 are filed, admitted into evidence, or in any way made a part of the court record in such a way as to be otherwise open to the public, the People, a defendant, or the owner of a trade secret contained within those articles may request the court to seal those articles.

(2) The request to seal shall be made by noticed motion filed with the court. It may also be made orally in court at the time the articles are made a part of the court record. Where the request is made orally, the movant must file within 24 hours a written description of that request, including a list of the articles which are the subject of that request. These motions and lists shall be available to the public.

(3) The court shall promptly conduct hearings as provided in paragraphs (2), (3), and (4) of subdivision (a). The court shall, pending the hearings, seal those articles which are the subject of the request. Where a request to seal is made orally, the court may conduct hearings at the time the articles are made a part of the court record, but shall reconsider its ruling in light of additional objections made by objectors within two court days after the written record of the request to seal is made available to the public.

(4) Any articles sealed pursuant to these hearings shall not be unsealed absent an order of a court upon a showing of good cause. Failure to examine the court file for notice of a request to seal shall not constitute good cause to consider objections to sealing. [*Added 1990.*]

§ **1040. Privilege for official information.** (a) As used in this section, "official information" means information acquired in confidence by a public employee in the course of his or her duty and not open, or officially disclosed, to the public prior to the time the claim of privilege is made.

(b) A public entity has a privilege to refuse to disclose official information, and to prevent another from disclosing official information, if the privilege is claimed by a person authorized by the public entity to do so and either of the following apply:

(1) Disclosure is forbidden by an act of the Congress of the United States or a statute of this state.

1971 Proposed Rule 509. Secrets of State and Other Official Information [*Not Enacted*]

(a) Definitions.

(1) Secret of state. A "secret of state" is a governmental secret relating to the national defense or the international relations of the United States.

(2) Disclosure of the information is against the public interest because there is a necessity for preserving the confidentiality of the information that outweighs the necessity for disclosure in the interest of justice; but no privilege may be claimed under this paragraph if any person authorized to do so has consented that the information be disclosed in the proceeding. In determining whether disclosure of the information is against the public interest, the interest of the public entity as a party in the outcome of the proceeding may not be considered.

(c) Notwithstanding any other law, the Employment Development Department shall disclose to law enforcement agencies, in accordance with subdivision (i) of Section 1095 of the Unemployment Insurance Code, information in its possession relating to any person if an arrest warrant has been issued for the person for commission of a felony. [*Amended 1984, 2015, 2016.*]

§ 1042. Adverse order or finding in certain cases. (a) Except where disclosure is forbidden by an act of the Congress of the United States, if a claim of privilege under this article [§§ 1040-1047] by the state or a public entity in this state is sustained in a criminal proceeding, the presiding officer shall make such order or finding of fact adverse to the public entity bringing the proceeding as is required by law upon any issue in the proceeding to which the privileged information is material.

(b) Notwithstanding subdivision (a), where a search is made pursuant to a warrant valid on its face, the public entity bringing a criminal proceeding is not required to reveal to the defendant official information or the identity of an informer in order to establish the legality of the search or the admissibility of any evidence obtained as a result of it.

(2) Official information. "Official information" is information within the custody or control of a department or agency of the government the disclosure of which is shown to be contrary to the public interest and which consists of: (A) intragovernmental opinions or recommendations submitted for consideration in the performance of decisional or policymaking functions, or (B) subject to the provisions of 18 U.S.C. § 3500, investigatory files compiled for law enforcement purposes and not otherwise available, or (C) information within the custody or control of a governmental department or agency whether initiated within the department or agency or acquired by it in its exercise of its official responsibilities and not otherwise available to the public pursuant to 5 U.S.C. § 552.

(b) General rule of privilege. The government has a privilege to refuse to give evidence and to prevent any person from giving evidence upon a showing of reasonable likelihood of danger that the evidence will disclose a secret of state or official information, as defined in this rule.

(c) Procedures. The privilege for secrets of state may be claimed only by the chief officer of the government agency or department administering the subject matter which the secret information sought concerns, but the privilege for official information may be asserted by any attorney representing the government. The required showing may be made in whole or in part in the form of a written statement. The judge may hear the matter in chambers, but all counsel are entitled to inspect the claim and showing and to be heard thereon, except that, in the case of secrets of state, the judge upon motion of the government, may permit the government to make the required showing in the above form in camera. If the judge sustains the privilege upon a showing in camera, the entire text of the government's statements shall be sealed and preserved in the court's records in the event of appeal. In the case of privilege claimed for official information the court may require examination in camera of the information itself. The judge may take any protective measure which the interests of the government and the furtherance of justice may require.

(d) Notice to government. If the circumstances of the case indicate a substantial possibility that a claim of privilege would be appropriate but has not been made because of oversight or lack of knowledge, the judge shall give or cause notice to be given to the officer entitled to claim the privilege and shall stay further proceedings a reasonable time to afford opportunity to assert a claim of privilege.

(e) Effect of sustaining claim. If a claim of privilege is sustained in a proceeding to which the government is a party and it appears that another party is thereby deprived of material evidence, the judge shall make any further orders which the interests of justice require, including striking the testimony of a witness, declaring a mistrial, finding against the government upon an issue as to which the evidence is relevant, or dismissing the action.

(c) Notwithstanding subdivision (a), in any preliminary hearing, criminal trial, or other criminal proceeding, any otherwise admissible evidence of information communicated to a peace officer by a confidential informant, who is not a material witness to the guilt or innocence of the accused of the offense charged, is admissible on the issue of reasonable cause to make an arrest or search without requiring that the name or identity of the informant be disclosed if the judge or magistrate is satisfied, based upon evidence produced in open court, out of the presence of the jury, that such information was received from a reliable informant and in his discretion does not require such disclosure.

(d) When, in any such criminal proceeding, a party demands disclosure of the identity of the informant on the ground the informant is a material witness on the issue of guilt, the court shall conduct a hearing at which all parties may present evidence on the issue of disclosure. Such hearing shall be conducted outside the presence of the jury, if any. During the hearing, if the privilege provided for in Section 1041 is claimed by a person authorized to do so or if a person who is authorized to claim such privilege refuses to answer any question on the ground that the answer would tend to disclose the identity of the informant, the prosecuting attorney may request that the court hold an in camera hearing. If such a request is made, the court shall hold such a hearing outside the presence of the defendant and his counsel. At the in camera hearing, the prosecution may offer evidence which would tend to disclose or which discloses the identity of the informant to aid the court in its determination whether there is a reasonable possibility that nondisclosure might deprive the defendant of a fair trial. A reporter shall be present at the in camera hearing. Any transcription of the proceedings at the in camera hearing, as well as any physical evidence presented at the hearing, shall be ordered sealed by the court, and only a court may have access to its contents. The court shall not order disclosure, nor strike the testimony of the witness who invokes the privilege, nor dismiss the criminal proceeding, if the party offering the witness refuses to disclose the identity of the informant, unless, based upon the evidence presented at the hearing held in the presence of the defendant and his counsel and the evidence presented at the in camera hearing, the court concludes that there is a reasonable possibility that nondisclosure might deprive the defendant of a fair trial. [*Amended 1965, 1969.*]

Peace or Custodial Officer Personnel Records

[*Sections 1043-1047, contain detailed provisions regulating the discovery and disclosure of peace or custodial officer personnel records and related matters. The Proposed Federal Rules contained no comparable provisions.*]

§ **1041. Privilege for identity of informer.** (a) Except as provided in this section, a public entity has a privilege to refuse to disclose the identity of a person who has furnished information as provided in subdivision (b) purporting to disclose a violation of a law of the United States or of this state or of a public entity in this state, and to prevent another from disclosing the person's identity, if the privilege is claimed by a person authorized by the public entity to do so and either of the following apply:

(1) Disclosure is forbidden by an act of the Congress of the United States or a statute of this state.

1971 Proposed Rule 510. Identity of Informer [*Not Enacted*]

(a) Rule of privilege. The government or a state or subdivision thereof has a privilege to refuse to disclose the identity of a person who has furnished information relating to or assisting in an investigation of a possible violation of law to a law enforcement officer or member of a legislative committee or its staff conducting an investigation.

(2) Disclosure of the identity of the informer is against the public interest because the necessity for preserving the confidentiality of his or her identity outweighs the necessity for disclosure in the interest of justice. The privilege shall not be claimed under this paragraph if a person authorized to do so has consented that the identity of the informer be disclosed in the proceeding. In determining whether disclosure of the identity of the informer is against the public interest, the interest of the public entity as a party in the outcome of the proceeding shall not be considered.

(b) The privilege described in this section applies only if the information is furnished in confidence by the informer to any of the following:

(1) A law enforcement officer.

(2) A representative of an administrative agency charged with the administration or enforcement of the law alleged to be violated.

(3) Any person for the purpose of transmittal to a person listed in paragraph (1) or (2). As used in this paragraph, "person" includes a volunteer or employee of a crime stopper organization.

(c) The privilege described in this section shall not be construed to prevent the informer from disclosing his or her identity.

(d) As used in this section, "crime stopper organization" means a private, nonprofit organization that accepts and expends donations used to reward persons who report to the organization information concerning alleged criminal activity, and forwards the information to the appropriate law enforcement agency. [*Amended 2013.*]

(b) Who may claim. The privilege may be claimed by an appropriate representative of the government, regardless of whether the information was furnished to an officer of the government or of a state or subdivision thereof. The privilege may be claimed by an appropriate representative of a state or subdivision if the information was furnished to an officer thereof, except that in criminal cases the privilege shall not be allowed if the government objects.

(c) Exceptions.

(1) Voluntary disclosure; informer a witness. No privilege exists under this rule if the identity of the informer or his interest in the subject matter of his communication has been disclosed to those who would have cause to resent the communication by a holder of the privilege or by the informer's own action, or if the informer appears as a witness for the government.

(2) Testimony on merits. If it appears from the evidence in the case or from other showing by a party that an informer may be able to give testimony necessary to a fair determination of the issue of guilt or innocence in a criminal case or of a material issue on the merits in a civil case to which the government is a party, and the government invokes the privilege, the judge shall give the government an opportunity to show in camera facts relevant to determining whether the informer can, in fact, supply that testimony. The showing will ordinarily be in the form of affidavits, but the judge may direct that testimony be taken if he finds that the matter cannot be resolved satisfactorily upon affidavit. If the judge finds that there is a reasonable probability that the informer can give the testimony, and the government elects not to disclose his identity, the judge on motion of the defendant in a criminal case shall dismiss the charges to which the testimony would relate, and the judge may do so on his own motion. In civil cases, he may make any order that justice requires. Evidence submitted to the judge shall be sealed and preserved to be made available to the appellate court in the event of an appeal, and the contents shall not otherwise be revealed without consent of the government. All counsel and parties shall be permitted to be present at every stage of proceedings under this subdivision except a showing in camera, at which no counsel or party shall be permitted to be present.

(3) Legality of obtaining evidence. If information from an informer is relied upon to establish the legality of the means by which evidence was obtained and the judge is not satisfied that the information was received from an informer reasonably believed to be reliable or credible, he may require the identity of the informer to be disclosed. The judge shall, on request of the government, direct that the disclosure be made in camera. All counsel and parties concerned with the issue of legality shall be permitted to be present at every stage of proceedings under this subdivision except a disclosure in camera, at which no counsel or party shall be permitted to be present. If disclosure of the identity of the informer is made in camera, the record thereof shall be sealed and preserved to be made available to the appellate court in the event of an appeal, and the contents shall not otherwise be revealed without consent of the government.

§ **912. Waiver of privilege.** (a) Except as otherwise provided in this section, the right of any person to claim a privilege provided by Section 954 (lawyer-client privilege), 966 (lawyer referral service-client privilege), 980 (privilege for confidential marital communications), 994 (physician-patient privilege), 1014 (psychotherapist-patient privilege), 1033 (privilege of penitent), 1034 (privilege of clergy member), 1035.8 (sexual assault counselor-victim privilege), 1037.5 (domestic violence counselor-victim privilege), or 1038 (human trafficking caseworker-victim privilege), is waived with respect to a communication protected by the privilege if any holder of the privilege, without coercion, has disclosed a significant part of the communication or has consented to disclosure made by anyone. Consent to disclosure is manifested by any statement or other conduct of the holder of the privilege indicating consent to the disclosure, including failure to claim the privilege in any proceeding in which the holder has the legal standing and opportunity to claim the privilege.

(b) Where two or more persons are joint holders of a privilege provided by Section 954 (lawyer-client privilege), 966 (lawyer referral service-client privilege), 994 (physician-patient privilege), 1014 (psychotherapist-patient privilege), 1035.8 (sexual assault counselor-victim privilege), 1037.5 (domestic violence counselor- victim privilege), or 1038 (human trafficking caseworker-victim privilege), a waiver of the right of a particular joint holder of the privilege to claim the privilege does not affect the right of another joint holder to claim the privilege. In the case of the privilege provided by Section 980 (privilege for confidential marital communications), a waiver of the right of one spouse to claim the privilege does not affect the right of the other spouse to claim the privilege.

(c) A disclosure that is itself privileged is not a waiver of any privilege.

(d) A disclosure in confidence of a communication that is protected by a privilege provided by Section 954 (lawyer-client privilege), 966 (lawyer referral service-client privilege), 994 (physician-patient privilege), 1014 (psychotherapist-patient privilege), 1035.8 (sexual assault counselor-victim privilege), 1037.5 (domestic violence counselor-victim privilege), or 1038 (human trafficking caseworker-victim privilege), when disclosure is reasonably necessary for the accomplishment of the purpose for which the lawyer, lawyer referral service, physician, psychotherapist, sexual assault counselor, or domestic violence counselor was consulted, is not a waiver of the privilege. [*Amended 1980, 2002, 2004, 2013, 2014.*]

§ **754.5. Privileged statements; deaf or hard of hearing persons; use of interpreter.** Whenever an otherwise valid privilege exists between an individual who is deaf or hard of hearing and another person, that privilege is not waived merely because an interpreter was used to facilitate their communication. [*Added 1990. Amended 1992, 2017.*]

1971 Proposed Rule 511. Waiver of Privilege by Voluntary Disclosure [*Not Enacted*]

A person upon whom these rules confer a privilege against disclosure of the confidential matter or communication waives the privilege if he or his predecessor while holder of the privilege voluntarily discloses or consents to disclosure of any significant part of the matter or communication. This rule does not apply if the disclosure is itself a privileged communication.

§ **919. Admissibility where disclosure erroneously compelled.** (a) Evidence of a statement or other disclosure of privileged information is inadmissible against a holder of the privilege if:

(1) A person authorized to claim the privilege claimed it but nevertheless disclosure erroneously was required to be made; or

(2) The presiding officer did not exclude the privileged information as required by Section 916.

(b) If a person authorized to claim the privilege claimed it, whether in the same or a prior proceeding, but nevertheless disclosure erroneously was required by the presiding officer to be made, neither the failure to refuse to disclose nor the failure to seek review of the order of the presiding officer requiring disclosure indicates consent to the disclosure or constitutes a waiver and, under these circumstances, the disclosure is one made under coercion. [*Amended 1974.*]

§ **918. Effect of error in overruling claim of privilege.** A party may predicate error on a ruling disallowing a claim of privilege only if he is the holder of the privilege, except that a party may predicate error on a ruling disallowing a claim of privilege by his spouse under Section 970 or 971.

§ **913. Comment on, and inferences from, exercise of privilege.** (a) If in the instant proceeding or on a prior occasion a privilege is or was exercised not to testify with respect to any matter, or to refuse to disclose or to prevent another from disclosing any matter, neither the presiding officer nor counsel may comment thereon, no presumption shall arise because of the exercise of the privilege, and the trier of fact may not draw any inference therefrom as to the credibility of the witness or as to any matter at issue in the proceeding.

(b) The court, at the request of a party who may be adversely affected because an unfavorable inference may be drawn by the jury because a privilege has been exercised, shall instruct the jury that no presumption arises because of the exercise of the privilege and that the jury may not draw any inference therefrom as to the credibility of the witness or as to any matter at issue in the proceeding.

1971 Proposed Rule 512. Privileged Matters Disclosed Under Compulsion or Without Opportunity to Claim Privilege [*Not Enacted*]

Evidence of a statement or other disclosure of privileged matter is not admissible against the holder of the privilege if the disclosure was (a) compelled erroneously or (b) made without opportunity to claim the privilege.

1971 Proposed Rule 513. Comment Upon or Inference from Claim of Privilege: Instruction [*Not Enacted*]

(a) **Comment or inference not permitted.** The claim of a privilege, whether in the present proceeding or upon a prior occasion, is not a proper subject of comment by judge or counsel. No inference may be drawn therefrom.

(b) **Claiming privilege without knowledge of jury.** In jury cases, proceedings shall be conducted, to the extent practicable, so as to facilitate the making of claims of privilege without the knowledge of the jury.

(c) **Jury instruction.** Upon request, any party against whom the jury might draw an adverse inference from a claim of privilege is entitled to an instruction that no inference may be drawn therefrom.

§ **700. General rule as to competency.** Except as otherwise provided by statute, every person, irrespective of age, is qualified to be a witness and no person is disqualified to testify to any matter. [*Amended 1985.*]

§ **701. Disqualification of witness.** (a) A person is disqualified to be a witness if he or she is:

(1) Incapable of expressing himself or herself concerning the matter so as to be understood, either directly or through interpretation by one who can understand him; or

(2) Incapable of understanding the duty of a witness to tell the truth.

(b) In any proceeding held outside the presence of a jury, the court may reserve challenges to the competency of a witness until the conclusion of the direct examination of that witness. [*Amended 1985.*]

§ **795. Testimony of hypnosis subject; admissibility; conditions.** (a) The testimony of a witness is not inadmissible in a criminal proceeding by reason of the fact that the witness has previously undergone hypnosis for the purpose of recalling events that are the subject of the witness's testimony, if all of the following conditions are met:

(1) The testimony is limited to those matters that the witness recalled and related prior to the hypnosis.

(2) The substance of the prehypnotic memory was preserved in a writing, audio recording, or video recording prior to the hypnosis.

(3) The hypnosis was conducted in accordance with all of the following procedures:

(A) A written record was made prior to hypnosis documenting the subject's description of the event, and information that was provided to the hypnotist concerning the subject matter of the hypnosis.

(B) The subject gave informed consent to the hypnosis.

(C) The hypnosis session, including the pre- and post-hypnosis interviews, was video recorded for subsequent review.

(D) The hypnosis was performed by a licensed medical doctor, psychologist, licensed clinical social worker, or a licensed marriage and family therapist experienced in the use of hypnosis and independent of and not in the presence of law enforcement, the prosecution, or the defense.

ARTICLE VI. WITNESSES

Rule 601. Competency to Testify in General

Every person is competent to be a witness unless these rules provide otherwise. But in a civil case, state law governs the witness's competency regarding a claim or defense for which state law supplies the rule of decision.

Compare FRE 601 and CEC §§ 700-701: CEC disqualifies a person who is unable to testify understandably or to understand a witness's duty to tell the truth. FRE lacks a similar provision, but does specifically defer to state law to resolve competency issues that arise in civil claims or defenses governed by state law. As to the impact of Prop. 8, on its face the initiative acted to repeal these sections of CEC. However, to date no California appellate court has so held.

[*FRE have no counterpart to CEC § 795.*]

(4) Prior to admission of the testimony, the court holds a hearing pursuant to Section 402 at which the proponent of the evidence proves by clear and convincing evidence that the hypnosis did not so affect the witness as to render the witness's prehypnosis recollection unreliable or to substantially impair the ability to cross-examine the witness concerning the witness's prehypnosis recollection. At the hearing, each side shall have the right to present expert testimony and to cross-examine witnesses.

(b) Nothing in this section shall be construed to limit the ability of a party to attack the credibility of a witness who has undergone hypnosis, or to limit other legal grounds to admit or exclude the testimony of that witness. [*Added 1984, 1987. Amended 1996, 2002, 2009.*]

§ **702. Personal knowledge of witness.** (a) Subject to Section 801, the testimony of a witness concerning a particular matter is inadmissible unless he has personal knowledge of the matter. Against the objection of a party, such personal knowledge must be shown before the witness may testify concerning the matter.

(b) A witness' personal knowledge of a matter may be shown by any otherwise admissible evidence, including his own testimony.

§ **710. Oath required.** Every witness before testifying shall take an oath or make an affirmation or declaration in the form provided by law, except that a child under the age of 10 or a dependent person with a substantial cognitive impairment, in the court's discretion, may be required only to promise to tell the truth. [*Amended 1988, 2004.*]

§ **750. Rules relating to witnesses apply to interpreters and translators.** A person who serves as an interpreter or translator in any action is subject to all the rules of law relating to witnesses.

[*Sections 751-755.5 contain detailed provisions regarding the oath required of interpreters and translators, the qualification and furnishing of interpreters for deaf and hard of hearing persons, and circumstances under which interpreters must be furnished for persons who are not proficient in English. FRE contain no counterparts to these provisions.*]

Rule 602. Need for Personal Knowledge

A witness may testify to a matter only if evidence is introduced sufficient to support a finding that the witness has personal knowledge of the matter. Evidence to prove personal knowledge may consist of the witness's own testimony. This rule does not apply to a witness's expert testimony under Rule 703.

Rule 603. Oath or Affirmation to Testify Truthfully

Before testifying, a witness must give an oath or affirmation to testify truthfully. It must be in a form designed to impress that duty on the witness's conscience.

> *Compare FRE 603 and CEC § 710*: FRE lacks CEC's special dispensation for children under 10 and dependent persons with substantial cognitive impairment, who under CEC are permitted "only to promise to tell the truth," rather than required to take a full oath or affirmation.

Rule 604. Interpreter

An interpreter must be qualified and must give an oath or affirmation to make a true translation.

> *Compare FRE 604 and CEC § 750*: Unlike CEC, FRE requires an interpreter to be qualified as an expert.

§ **703. Judge as witness.** (a) Before the judge presiding at the trial of an action may be called to testify in that trial as a witness, he shall, in proceedings held out of the presence and hearing of the jury, inform the parties of the information he has concerning any fact or matter about which he will be called to testify.

(b) Against the objection of a party, the judge presiding at the trial of an action may not testify in that trial as a witness. Upon such objection, the judge shall declare a mistrial and order the action assigned for trial before another judge.

(c) The calling of the judge presiding at a trial to testify in that trial as a witness shall be deemed a consent to the granting of a motion for mistrial, and an objection to such calling of a judge shall be deemed a motion for mistrial.

(d) In the absence of objection by a party, the judge presiding at the trial of an action may testify in that trial as a witness.

§ **703.5. Judges, arbitrators or mediators as witnesses; subsequent civil proceeding.** No person presiding at any judicial or quasi-judicial proceeding, and no arbitrator or mediator, shall be competent to testify, in any subsequent civil proceeding, as to any statement, conduct, decision, or ruling, occurring at or in conjunction with the prior proceeding, except as to a statement or conduct that could (a) give rise to civil or criminal contempt, (b) constitute a crime, (c) be the subject of investigation by the State Bar or Commission on Judicial Performance, or (d) give rise to disqualification proceedings under paragraph (1) or (6) of subdivision (a) of Section 170.1 of the Code of Civil Procedure. However, this section does not apply to a mediator with regard to any mediation under Chapter 11 (commencing with Section 3160) of Part 2 of Division 8 of the Family Code. [*Added 1979. Amended 1980, 1988, 1990, 1993, 1994.*]

§ **704. Juror as witness.** (a) Before a juror sworn and impaneled in the trial of an action may be called to testify before the jury in that trial as a witness, he shall, in proceedings conducted by the court out of the presence and hearing of the remaining jurors, inform the parties of the information he has concerning any fact or matter about which he will be called to testify.

(b) Against the objection of a party, a juror sworn and impaneled in the trial of an action may not testify before the jury in that trial as a witness. Upon such objection, the court shall declare a mistrial and order the action assigned for trial before another jury.

(c) The calling of a juror to testify before the jury as a witness shall be deemed a consent to the granting of a motion for mistrial, and an objection to such calling of a juror shall be deemed a motion for mistrial.

(d) In the absence of objection by a party, a juror sworn and impaneled in the trial of an action may be compelled to testify in that trial as a witness.

Rule 605. Judge's Competency as a Witness

The presiding judge may not testify as a witness at the trial. A party need not object to preserve the issue.

> *Compare FRE 605 and CEC § 703*: A judge presiding at a trial is prohibited by FRE from testifying at that trial; a party need not object to preserve the issue. CEC allows a presiding judge to testify at trial *if no party objects*. Before testifying, the judge must hold a hearing outside the jury's presence, disclose the substance of the expected testimony, and if a party objects declare a mistrial and transfer the case to another judge.

[*FRE have no counterpart to CEC § 703.5.*]

Rule 606. Juror's Competency as a Witness

(a) **At the Trial.** A juror may not testify as a witness before the other jurors at the trial. If a juror is called to testify, the court must give an adverse party an opportunity to object outside the jury's presence.

> *Compare FRE 606(a) and CEC § 704*: Both FRE and CEC permit an empanelled juror to testify at trial if no party objects. But CEC requires the court first to hold a hearing outside the jury's presence at which the juror-witness must disclose the substance of the expected testimony. If any party objects, the juror may not testify.

§ **1150. Evidence to test a verdict.** (a) Upon an inquiry as to the validity of a verdict, any otherwise admissible evidence may be received as to statements made, or conduct, conditions, or events occurring, either within or without the jury room, of such a character as is likely to have influenced the verdict improperly. No evidence is admissible to show the effect of such statement, conduct, condition, or event upon a juror either in influencing him to assent to or dissent from the verdict or concerning the mental processes by which it was determined.

(b) Nothing in this code affects the law relating to the competence of a juror to give evidence to impeach or support a verdict.

> *Compare FRE 606(b) and CEC § 1150*: Under CEC jurors may testify to objective events that occurred in the jury room, but not to the effect of those events on their deliberative process. FRE is more restrictive, prohibiting jurors from testifying to events occurring during the deliberative process and to the effect of those events on deliberations, but permitting jurors to testify that outside prejudicial information was improperly brought to the jury's attention or that an external influence was improperly brought to bear on a juror. FRE also allows jurors to testify that the reported verdict was the result of a mistake in entering the verdict on the form.

§ **785. Parties may attack or support credibility.** The credibility of a witness may be attacked or supported by any party, including the party calling him.

§ **780. General rule as to credibility.** Except as otherwise provided by statute, the court or jury may consider in determining the credibility of a witness any matter that has any tendency in reason to prove or disprove the truthfulness of his testimony at the hearing, including but not limited to any of the following:

(a) His demeanor while testifying and the manner in which he testifies.

(b) The character of his testimony.

(c) The extent of his capacity to perceive, to recollect, or to communicate any matter about which he testifies.

(d) The extent of his opportunity to perceive any matter about which he testifies.

(e) His character for honesty or veracity or their opposites.

(f) The existence or nonexistence of a bias, interest, or other motive.

(g) A statement previously made by him that is consistent with his testimony at the hearing.

(b) During an Inquiry into the Validity of a Verdict or Indictment.

(1) ***Prohibited Testimony or Other Evidence.*** During an inquiry into the validity of a verdict or indictment, a juror may not testify about any statement made or incident that occurred during the jury's deliberations; the effect of anything on that juror's or another juror's vote; or any juror's mental processes concerning the verdict or indictment. The court may not receive a juror's affidavit or evidence of a juror's statement on these matters.

(2) *Exceptions.* A juror may testify about whether:

(A) extraneous prejudicial information was improperly brought to the jury's attention;

(B) an outside influence was improperly brought to bear on any juror; or

(C) a mistake was made in entering the verdict on the verdict form.

Rule 607. Who May Impeach a Witness

Any party, including the party that called the witness, may attack the witness's credibility.

[*FRE have no counterpart to CEC § 780.*]

(h) A statement made by him that is inconsistent with any part of his testimony at the hearing.

(i) The existence or nonexistence of any fact testified to by him.

(j) His attitude toward the action in which he testifies or toward the giving of testimony.

(k) His admission of untruthfulness.

§ 782. Sexual offenses; evidence of sexual conduct of complaining witness; procedure for admissibility; treatment of resealed affidavits. (a) In any of the circumstances described in subdivision (c), if evidence of sexual conduct of the complaining witness is offered to attack the credibility of the complaining witness under Section 780, the following procedure shall be followed:

(1) A written motion shall be made by the defendant to the court and prosecutor stating that the defense has an offer of proof of the relevancy of evidence of the sexual conduct of the complaining witness proposed to be presented and its relevancy in attacking the credibility of the complaining witness.

(2) The written motion shall be accompanied by an affidavit in which the offer of proof shall be stated. The affidavit shall be filed under seal and only unsealed by the court to determine if the offer of proof is sufficient to order a hearing pursuant to paragraph (3). After that determination, the affidavit shall be resealed by the court.

(3) If the court finds that the offer of proof is sufficient, the court shall order a hearing out of the presence of the jury, if any, and at the hearing allow the questioning of the complaining witness regarding the offer of proof made by the defendant.

(4) At the conclusion of the hearing, if the court finds that evidence proposed to be offered by the defendant regarding the sexual conduct of the complaining witness is relevant pursuant to Section 780, and is not inadmissible pursuant to Section 352, the court may make an order stating what evidence may be introduced by the defendant, and the nature of the questions to be permitted. The defendant may then offer evidence pursuant to the order of the court.

(5) An affidavit resealed by the court pursuant to paragraph (2) shall remain sealed, unless the defendant raises an issue on appeal or collateral review relating to the offer of proof contained in the sealed document. If the defendant raises that issue on appeal, the court shall allow the Attorney General and appellate counsel for the defendant access to the sealed affidavit. If the issue is raised on collateral review, the court shall allow the district attorney and defendant's counsel access to the sealed affidavit. The use of the information contained in the affidavit shall be limited solely to the pending proceeding.

[*FRE have no counterpart to CEC § 782.*]

(b) As used in this section, "complaining witness" means:

(1) The alleged victim of the crime charged, the prosecution of which is subject to this section, pursuant to paragraph (1) of subdivision (c).

(2) An alleged victim offering testimony pursuant to paragraph (2) or paragraph (3) of subdivision (c).

(c) The procedure provided by subdivision (a) shall apply in any of the following circumstances:

(1) In a prosecution under Section 261, 262, 264.1, 286, 287, 288, 288.5, or 289 of, or former Section 288a of, the Penal Code, or for assault with intent to commit, attempt to commit, or conspiracy to commit any crime defined in any of those sections, except if the crime is alleged to have occurred in a local detention facility, as defined in Section 6031.4, or in a state prison, as defined in Section 4504.

(2) When an alleged victim testifies pursuant to subdivision (b) of Section 1101 as a victim of a crime listed in Section 243.4, 261, 261.5, 269, 285, 286, 287, 288, 288.5, 289, 314, or 647.6 of, or former Section 288a of, the Penal Code, except if the crime is alleged to have occurred in a local detention facility, as defined in Section 6031.4 of the Penal Code, or in a state prison, as defined in Section 4504 of the Penal Code.

(3) When an alleged victim of a sexual offense testifies pursuant to Section 1108, except if the crime is alleged to have occurred in a local detention facility, as defined in Section 6031.4 of the Penal Code, or in a state prison, as defined in Section 4504 of the Penal Code.

[*Added 1974. Amended 1981, 1987, 1989, 1996, 2004, 2006, 2018.*]

§ 783. Sexual harassment, sexual assault, or sexual battery cases; admissibility of evidence of plaintiff's sexual conduct; procedure. In any civil action alleging conduct which constitutes sexual harassment, sexual assault, or sexual battery, if evidence of sexual conduct of the plaintiff is offered to attack credibility of the plaintiff under Section 780, the following procedures shall be followed:

(a) A written motion shall be made by the defendant to the court and the plaintiff's attorney stating that the defense has an offer of proof of the relevancy of evidence of the sexual conduct of the plaintiff proposed to be presented.

(b) The written motion shall be accompanied by an affidavit in which the offer of proof shall be stated.

[*FRE have no counterpart to CEC § 783.*]

(c) If the court finds that the offer of proof is sufficient, the court shall order a hearing out of the presence of the jury, if any, and at the hearing allow the questioning of the plaintiff regarding the offer of proof made by the defendant.

(d) At the conclusion of the hearing, if the court finds that evidence proposed to be offered by the defendant regarding the sexual conduct of the plaintiff is relevant pursuant to Section 780, and is not inadmissible pursuant to Section 352, the court may make an order stating what evidence may be introduced by the defendant, and the nature of the questions to be permitted. The defendant may then offer evidence pursuant to the order of the court. [*Added 1985.*]

§ **786. Character evidence generally.** Evidence of traits of his character other than honesty or veracity, or their opposites, is inadmissible to attack or support the credibility of a witness.

§ **790. Good character of witness.** Evidence of the good character of a witness is inadmissible to support his credibility unless evidence of his bad character has been admitted for the purpose of attacking his credibility.

§ **787. Specific instances of conduct.** Subject to Section 788, evidence of specific instances of his conduct relevant only as tending to prove a trait of his character is inadmissible to attack or support the credibility of a witness.

Compare FRE 608 and CEC §§ 786, 787, 790: FRE allow parties in civil and criminal cases, at the court's discretion, to attack or rehabilitate a witness's *character for truthfulness or untruthfulness*. Evidence of other character traits of a witness is inadmissible. On *direct examination*, parties are limited to evidence in the form of *opinion or reputation*. On *cross-examination*, parties may inquire into *specific instances of conduct* relevant to truthfulness or untruthfulness of the witness, or of another witness as to whose character the witness has testified, but extrinsic evidence is prohibited. For civil proceedings, CEC is substantially the same. However, as a result of Prop. 8, there are substantial differences between FRE and CEC in criminal proceedings. Specifically, none of the constraints of CEC §§ 786, 787, and 790 apply in criminal cases. Thus, subject to § 352 balancing, parties may introduce evidence of *any* relevant character trait of a witness in the form of opinion, reputation, or specific instances of conduct; evidence in support of a witness's credibility is admissible even if the witness's credibility has not yet been attacked; and extrinsic evidence of specific instances of conduct is permissible.

Rule 608. A Witness's Character for Truthfulness or Untruthfulness

(a) **Reputation or Opinion Evidence.** A witness's credibility may be attacked or supported by testimony about the witness's reputation for having a character for truthfulness or untruthfulness, or by testimony in the form of an opinion about that character. But evidence of truthful character is admissible only after the witness's character for truthfulness has been attacked.

(b) **Specific Instances of Conduct.** Except for a criminal conviction under Rule 609, extrinsic evidence is not admissible to prove specific instances of a witness's conduct in order to attack or support the witness's character for truthfulness. But the court may, on cross-examination, allow them to be inquired into if they are probative of the character for truthfulness or untruthfulness of:

(1) the witness; or

(2) another witness whose character the witness being cross-examined has testified about.

By testifying on another matter, a witness does not waive any privilege against self-incrimination for testimony that relates only to the witness's character for truthfulness.

§ **788. Conviction of witness for a crime.** For the purpose of attacking the credibility of a witness, it may be shown by the examination of the witness or by the record of the judgment that he has been convicted of a felony unless:

(a) A pardon based on his innocence has been granted to the witness by the jurisdiction in which he was convicted.

(b) A certificate of rehabilitation and pardon has been granted to the witness under the provisions of Chapter 3.5 (commencing with Section 4852.01) of Title 6 of Part 3 of the Penal Code.

(c) The accusatory pleading against the witness has been dismissed under the provisions of Penal Code Section 1203.4, but this exception does not apply to any criminal trial where the witness is being prosecuted for a subsequent offense.

(d) The conviction was under the laws of another jurisdiction and the witness has been relieved of the penalties and disabilities arising from the conviction pursuant to a procedure substantially equivalent to that referred to in subdivision (b) or (c).

Compare FRE 609 and CEC § 788: FRE applies to both civil and criminal cases. CEC § 788 applies in its entirety to civil cases. However, concerning the admissibility of valid prior convictions, in criminal proceedings § 788 has been superseded by Prop. 8. *See People v. Wheeler*, 4 Cal. 4th 289 (1992).

In *civil cases under CEC* and in both *civil and criminal cases under FRE*: *[1]* Any *felony* conviction may be used to impeach a *witness*, subject to discretionary exclusion under FRE 403 and CEC § 352. *See People v.* Beagle, 6 Cal. 3d 441, 492 P.2d 1 (1972) (specifying five circumstances where risk of undue prejudice outweighs the probative value of the conviction under §352). But under FRE, if the witness is the *accused*, the probative value of the prior conviction evidence for purposes of impeachment must outweigh the prejudicial effect to the accused, and a prior conviction for either a *felony or misdemeanor involving a dishonest act or false statement* must be admitted for impeachment (the trial court has no discretion to exclude). *[2]* FRE imposes a ten-year time limit, which can be overcome if the probative value of the prior conviction substantially outweighs the risk of prejudice and the proponent has given reasonable notice. CEC states no time limit, although the age of a conviction may reduce its probative value under CEC § 352. *[3]* CEC includes no provision about prior juvenile adjudications used to impeach a witness, while FRE bans the use of juvenile adjudications to impeach the *accused*, and gives discretion to the court as to *other witnesses* if a similar adult conviction would be admissible. *[4]* Although the details differ, FRE and CEC generally make inadmissible any conviction for which the witness has been pardoned or otherwise relieved of the consequences of the conviction.

[*continued on page I-120*]

Rule 609. Impeachment by Evidence of a Criminal Conviction

(a) **In General.** The following rules apply to attacking a witness's character for truthfulness by evidence of a criminal conviction:

(1) for a crime that, in the convicting jurisdiction, was punishable by death or by imprisonment for more than one year, the evidence:

(A) must be admitted, subject to Rule 403, in a civil case or in a criminal case in which the witness is not a defendant; and

(B) must be admitted in a criminal case in which the witness is a defendant, if the probative value of the evidence outweighs its prejudicial effect to that defendant; and

(2) for any crime regardless of the punishment, the evidence must be admitted if the court can readily determine that establishing the elements of the crime required proving — or the witness's admitting — a dishonest act or false statement.

(b) **Limit on Using the Evidence After 10 Years.** This subdivision (b) applies if more than 10 years have passed since the witness's conviction or release from confinement for it, whichever is later. Evidence of the conviction is admissible only if:

(1) its probative value, supported by specific facts and circumstances, substantially outweighs its prejudicial effect; and

(2) the proponent gives an adverse party reasonable written notice of the intent to use it so that the party has a fair opportunity to contest its use.

(c) **Effect of a Pardon, Annulment, or Certificate of Rehabilitation.** Evidence of a conviction is not admissible if:

(1) the conviction has been the subject of a pardon, annulment, certificate of rehabilitation, or other equivalent procedure based on a finding that the person has been rehabilitated, and the person has not been convicted of a later crime punishable by death or by imprisonment for more than one year; or

(2) the conviction has been the subject of a pardon, annulment, or other equivalent procedure based on a finding of innocence.

[*continued from page I-118*]

In *criminal cases under Prop. 8,* any adult conviction, felony or misdemeanor, may be used to impeach if it survives CEC § 352 and involves a crime of "moral turpitude," *i.e.*, a "readiness to do evil" in that the defendant was aware that the contemplated course of conduct posed a risk of harm to others. *People v. Castro*, 38 Cal. 3d 301 (1985). This analysis focuses only on the elements of the offense and not the particular facts underlying the conviction. *Id.*; *People v. Wheeler*, 4 Cal. 4th 289, 294 (1992). Juvenile adjudications do not constitute "convictions" and thus are inadmissible for impeachment. However, the misconduct underlying a juvenile adjudication may be used to impeach a witness where it manifests moral turpitude. Similarly, Prop. 8 has little to no impact on the general inadmissibility of expunged convictions under CEC § 788 because such convictions are neither "convictions" nor "relevant" within the meaning of Prop. 8. *See People v. Field*, 31 Cal. App. 4th 1778, 1790 (1995). Moreover, any probative value of such convictions would likely be too minor to survive § 352 scrutiny.

Cal. Const. Art. I, § 28(f)(4). Use of Prior Convictions

Any prior felony conviction of any person in any criminal proceeding, whether adult or juvenile, shall subsequently be used without limitation for purposes of impeachment or enhancement of sentence in any criminal proceeding. When a prior felony conviction is an element of any felony offense, it shall be proven to the trier of fact in open court. [*Added by initiative (Prop. 8), 1982.*]

§ **789. Religious belief.** Evidence of his religious belief or lack thereof is inadmissible to attack or support the credibility of a witness.

Compare FRE 610 and CEC § 789: Both FRE and CEC prohibit using evidence of a witness's religious beliefs to attack or support his or her credibility. However, in California criminal proceedings, a literal application of Prop. 8 would repeal CEC's ban to the extent such evidence is probative of a witness's truthfulness. Consistent with other California Supreme Court cases interpreting Prop. 8, the court would likely retain discretion to exclude under CEC § 352.

§ **711. Confrontation.** At the trial of an action, a witness can be heard only in the presence and subject to the examination of all the parties to the action, if they choose to attend and examine.

(d) **Juvenile Adjudications**. Evidence of a juvenile adjudication is admissible under this rule only if:

(1) it is offered in a criminal case;

(2) the adjudication was of a witness other than the defendant;

(3) an adult's conviction for that offense would be admissible to attack the adult's credibility; and

(4) admitting the evidence is necessary to fairly determine guilt or innocence.

(e) **Pendency of an Appeal.** A conviction that satisfies this rule is admissible even if an appeal is pending. Evidence of the pendency is also admissible.

Rule 610. Religious Beliefs or Opinions

Evidence of a witness's religious beliefs or opinions is not admissible to attack or support the witness's credibility.

[*FRE have no counterpart to CEC § 711.*]

§ **320. Power of court to regulate order of proof.** Except as otherwise provided by law, the court in its discretion shall regulate the order of proof.

§ **765. Court to control mode of interrogation.** (a) The court shall exercise reasonable control over the mode of interrogation of a witness so as to make such interrogation as rapid, as distinct, and as effective for the ascertainment of the truth, as may be, and to protect the witness from undue harassment or embarrassment.

(b) With a witness under the age of 14 or a dependent person with a substantial cognitive impairment, the court shall take special care to protect him or her from undue harassment or embarrassment, and to restrict the unnecessary repetition of questions. The court shall also take special care to ensure that questions are stated in a form which is appropriate to the age or cognitive level of the witness. The court may, in the interests of justice, on objection by a party, forbid the asking of a question which is in a form that is not reasonably likely to be understood by a person of the age or cognitive level of the witness. [*Amended 1985, 1986, 2004.*]

§ **766. Responsive answers.** A witness must give responsive answers to questions, and answers that are not responsive shall be stricken on motion of any party.

§ **772. Order of examination.** (a) The examination of a witness shall proceed in the following phases: direct examination, cross-examination, redirect examination, recross-examination, and continuing thereafter by redirect and recross-examination.

(b) Unless for good cause the court otherwise directs, each phase of the examination of a witness must be concluded before the succeeding phase begins.

(c) Subject to subdivision (d), a party may, in the discretion of the court, interrupt his cross-examination, redirect examination, or recross-examination of a witness, in order to examine the witness upon a matter not within the scope of a previous examination of the witness.

(d) If the witness is the defendant in a criminal action, the witness may not, without his consent, be examined under direct examination by another party.

§ **760. Direct examination.** "Direct examination" is the first examination of a witness upon a matter that is not within the scope of a previous examination of the witness.

Rule 611. Mode and Order of Examining Witnesses and Presenting Evidence

(a) Control by the Court; Purposes. The court should exercise reasonable control over the mode and order of examining witnesses and presenting evidence so as to:

(1) make those procedures effective for determining the truth;

(2) avoid wasting time; and

(3) protect witnesses from harassment or undue embarrassment.

> *Compare FRE 611(a) and CEC §§ 320, 765*: Where a witness is under 14 or a dependent person with substantial cognitive impairment, CEC § 765(b) requires the court to take "special care" to protect the witness from undue harassment or embarrassment and to ensure that parties frame questions in an understandable and appropriate form. FRE contains no analogous provision specific to juveniles.

§ **761. Cross-examination.** "Cross-examination" is the examination of a witness by a party other than the direct examiner upon a matter that is within the scope of the direct examination of the witness.

§ **762. Redirect examination.** "Redirect examination" is an examination of a witness by the direct examiner subsequent to the cross-examination of the witness.

§ **763. Recross-examination.** "Recross-examination" is an examination of a witness by a cross-examiner subsequent to a redirect examination of the witness.

§ **773. Cross-examination.** (a) A witness examined by one party may be cross-examined upon any matter within the scope of the direct examination by each other party to the action in such order as the court directs.

(b) The cross-examination of a witness by any party whose interest is not adverse to the party calling him is subject to the same rules that are applicable to the direct examination.

§ **764. Leading question.** A "leading question" is a question that suggests to the witness the answer that the examining party desires.

§ **767. Leading questions.** (a) Except under special circumstances where the interests of justice otherwise require:

(1) A leading question may not be asked of a witness on direct or redirect examination.

(2) A leading question may be asked of a witness on cross-examination or recross-examination.

(b) The court may, in the interests of justice permit a leading question to be asked of a child under 10 years of age or a dependent person with a substantial cognitive impairment in a case involving a prosecution under Section 273a, 273d, 288.5, 368, or any of the acts described in Section 11165.1 or 11165.2 of the Penal Code. [*Amended 1984, 1995, 2004.*]

§ **774. Re-examination.** A witness once examined cannot be reexamined as to the same matter without leave of the court, but he may be reexamined as to any new matter upon which he has been examined by another party to the action. Leave may be granted or withheld in the court's discretion.

(b) Scope of Cross-Examination. Cross-examination should not go beyond the subject matter of the direct examination and matters affecting a witness's credibility. The court may allow inquiry into additional matters as if on direct examination.

Compare FRE 611(b) and CEC §§ 760-763, 772-773: Under FRE, cross-examination should be limited to the subject of direct examination and witness credibility, but the court may allow inquiry into new matters as if on direct examination. CEC contains more detailed instruction: CEC § 772(a) sets forth the order of witness examinations. CEC § 772(b) requires, absent good cause, each stage of examination to conclude before the next begins. CEC § 772(c) allows a party, in the court's discretion, to interrupt any stage of examination to examine a witness outside the scope of the prior examination. CEC § 772(d) prohibits another party in a criminal proceeding from calling the defendant as a witness for direct examination. CEC §§ 760-763 define direct examination, cross-examination, redirect examination, and recross-examination. CEC § 773 provides that, after direct examination, a witness called by one party may be cross-examined by each other party within the scope of the direct examination, but the cross-examination by any party not adverse to the party who called the witness is confined by the rules for direct examination. Notwithstanding the difference in specificity between CEC and FRE, as interpreted by the courts the rules are similar in practice; much of what is specifically controlled under CEC falls within a federal court's "control over the mode . . . of examining witnesses" under FRE 611(a).

(c) Leading Questions. Leading questions should not be used on direct examination except as necessary to develop the witness's testimony. Ordinarily, the court should allow leading questions:

(1) on cross-examination; and

(2) when a party calls a hostile witness, an adverse party, or a witness identified with an adverse party.

Compare FRE 611(c) and CEC §§ 764, 767, 776: FRE instructs that parties should not ask leading questions on direct examination except "as necessary to develop the witness's testimony." Otherwise, leading questions may be used only on cross-examination or in questioning hostile witnesses, adverse parties, or a witness identified with an adverse party. CEC § 767(b) goes further by allowing leading questions in child abuse prosecutions, in the interests of justice, when a witness is a child under 10 or a dependent person with substantial cognitive impairment. As interpreted by the courts and as invited by the Assembly Committee's Comment, CEC § 767 also allows leading questions on direct

[*continued on page I-127*]

§ **776. Examination of adverse party or witness.** (a) A party to the record of any civil action, or a person identified with such a party, may be called and examined as if under cross-examination by any adverse party at any time during the presentation of evidence by the party calling the witness.

(b) A witness examined by a party under this section may be cross-examined by all other parties to the action in such order as the court directs; but, subject to subdivision (e), the witness may be examined only as if under redirect examination by:

(1) In the case of a witness who is a party, his own counsel and counsel for a party who is not adverse to the witness.

(2) In the case of a witness who is not a party, counsel for the party with whom the witness is identified and counsel for a party who is not adverse to the party with whom the witness is identified.

(c) For the purpose of this section, parties represented by the same counsel are deemed to be a single party.

(d) For the purpose of this section, a person is identified with a party if he is:

(1) A person for whose immediate benefit the action is prosecuted or defended by the party.

(2) A director, officer, superintendent, member, agent, employee, or managing agent of the party or of a person specified in paragraph (1), or any public employee of a public entity when such public entity is the party.

(3) A person who was in any of the relationships specified in paragraph (2) at the time of the act or omission giving rise to the cause of action.

(4) A person who was in any of the relationships specified in paragraph (2) at the time he obtained knowledge of the matter concerning which he is sought to be examined under this section.

(e) Paragraph (2) of subdivision (b) does not require counsel for the party with whom the witness is identified and counsel for a party who is not adverse to the party with whom the witness is identified to examine the witness as if under redirect examination if the party who called the witness for examination under this section:

(1) Is also a person identified with the same party with whom the witness is identified.

(2) Is the personal representative, heir, successor, or assignee of a person identified with the same party with whom the witness is identified. [*Amended 1967.*]

[*continued from page I-125*]

examination of experts. CEC § 776 provides for examination of an adverse party or person identified with such a party in civil actions. That section allows cross-examination of the witness by all other parties except those identified with the adverse party, who must conduct a redirect examination. An exception to this constraint applies under § 776(e) if the party who originally called the witness is also a person, or personal representative, heir, successor, or assignee of a person, identified with the same party with whom the witness is identified. Section 776(d) defines in detail "a person ... identified with a party."

The fact that "hostile" is not mentioned in Section 776 does not appear to represent a limitation on the breadth of the permission under the section. *See People v. Spain,* 154 Cal. App. 3d (1984).

§ **778. Recall of witness.** After a witness has been excused from giving further testimony in the action, he cannot be recalled without leave of the court. Leave may be granted or withheld in the court's discretion.

§ **771. Refreshing recollection with a writing.** (a) Subject to subdivision (c), if a witness, either while testifying or prior thereto, uses a writing to refresh his memory with respect to any matter about which he testifies, such writing must be produced at the hearing at the request of an adverse party and, unless the writing is so produced, the testimony of the witness concerning such matter shall be stricken.

(b) If the writing is produced at the hearing, the adverse party may, if he chooses, inspect the writing, cross-examine the witness concerning it, and introduce in evidence such portion of it as may be pertinent to the testimony of the witness.

(c) Production of the writing is excused, and the testimony of the witness shall not be stricken, if the writing:

(1) Is not in the possession or control of the witness or the party who produced his testimony concerning the matter; and

(2) Was not reasonably procurable by such party through the use of the court's process or other available means.

§ **768. Writings.** (a) In examining a witness concerning a writing, it is not necessary to show, read, or disclose to him any part of the writing.

(b) If a writing is shown to a witness, all parties to the action must be given an opportunity to inspect it before any question concerning it may be asked of the witness.

[*FRE have no counterpart to CEC § 778.*]

Rule 612. Writing Used to Refresh a Witness's Memory

(a) **Scope.** This rule gives an adverse party certain options when a witness uses a writing to refresh memory:

(1) while testifying; or

(2) before testifying, if the court decides that justice requires the party to have those options.

(b) **Adverse Party's Options; Deleting Unrelated Matter.** Unless 18 U.S.C. § 3500 provides otherwise in a criminal case, an adverse party is entitled to have the writing produced at the hearing, to inspect it, to cross-examine the witness about it, and to introduce in evidence any portion that relates to the witness's testimony. If the producing party claims that the writing includes unrelated matter, the court must examine the writing in camera, delete any unrelated portion, and order that the rest be delivered to the adverse party. Any portion deleted over objection must be preserved for the record.

(c) **Failure to Produce or Deliver the Writing.** If a writing is not produced or is not delivered as ordered, the court may issue any appropriate order. But if the prosecution does not comply in a criminal case, the court must strike the witness's testimony or — if justice so requires — declare a mistrial.

Compare FRE 612 and CEC §§ 768, 771: Under FRE, an adverse party may require production of a writing that was used to refresh a witness's memory *before* the witness testifies if the court in its discretion finds production necessary in the interests of justice. If such a writing is not produced at the hearing despite a court order to do so, in a civil case the court has discretion to "make any order justice requires"; in a criminal case the court must strike the testimony or, if in its discretion it determines that the interests of justice so require, declare a mistrial. CEC is stricter, requiring the court to strike the testimony at issue in civil and criminal proceedings where, upon request by an adverse party, production of the writing does not occur. Production is excused only where the witness or party presenting the testimony at issue lacks possession or control of the writing and the writing was not "reasonably procurable" by that party through court process or other available means.

§ **769. Inconsistent statement or conduct.** In examining a witness concerning a statement or other conduct by him that is inconsistent with any part of his testimony at the hearing, it is not necessary to disclose to him any information concerning the statement or other conduct.

Compare FRE 613(a) and CEC § 769: Unlike CEC, FRE requires disclosure to any adverse party's counsel of the contents of a witness's prior inconsistent statement used for impeachment.

§ **770. Evidence of inconsistent statement of witness.** Unless the interests of justice otherwise require, extrinsic evidence of a statement made by a witness that is inconsistent with any part of his testimony at the hearing shall be excluded unless:

(a) The witness was so examined while testifying as to give him an opportunity to explain or to deny the statement; or

(b) The witness has not been excused from giving further testimony in the action.

§ **791. Prior consistent statement of witness.** Evidence of a statement previously made by a witness that is consistent with his testimony at the hearing is inadmissible to support his credibility unless it is offered after:

(a) Evidence of a statement made by him that is inconsistent with any part of his testimony at the hearing has been admitted for the purpose of attacking his credibility, and the statement was made before the alleged inconsistent statement; or

(b) An express or implied charge has been made that his testimony at the hearing is recently fabricated or is influenced by bias or other improper motive, and the statement was made before the bias, motive for fabrication, or other improper motive is alleged to have arisen.

As to any impact of Prop. 8, to date no California appellate court has addressed whether the initiative repeals this section.

Rule 613. Witness's Prior Statement

(a) **Showing or Disclosing the Statement During Examination.** When examining a witness about the witness's prior statement, the party need not show it or disclose its contents to the witness. But the party must, on request, show it or disclose its contents to an adverse party's attorney.

(b) **Extrinsic Evidence of a Prior Inconsistent Statement.** Extrinsic evidence of a witness's prior inconsistent statement is admissible only if the witness is given an opportunity to explain or deny the statement and an adverse party is given an opportunity to examine the witness about it, or if justice so requires. This subdivision (b) does not apply to an opposing party's statement under Rule 801(d)(2).

Compare FRE 613(b) and CEC § 770: In criminal proceedings, Prop. 8 appears to repeal CEC's limitations on extrinsic evidence of prior inconsistent statements. To date, however, the California courts have not addressed the issue. CEC § 770 sets forth an exception to the stated limitations where "the interests of justice so require[]." FRE 613(b) contains no such exception

[*FRE have no exact counterpart to CEC § 791. FRE 801(d)(1)(B) defines as not hearsay a prior consistent statement similar to that described in CEC § 791.*]

§ 775. **Court may call witnesses.** The court, on its own motion or on the motion of any party, may call witnesses and interrogate them the same as if they had been produced by a party to the action, and the parties may object to the questions asked and the evidence adduced the same as if such witnesses were called and examined by an adverse party. Such witnesses may be cross-examined by all parties to the action in such order as the court directs.

Compare FRE 614 and CEC § 775: To prevent jury prejudice, FRE allows a party to object to a judge's examination of a witness at the first available opportunity outside the jury's presence, rather than at the time of the court's calling and examining the witness. CEC has no such provision.

§ 777. **Exclusion of witness.** (a) Subject to subdivisions (b) and (c), the court may exclude from the courtroom any witness not at the time under examination so that such witness cannot hear the testimony of other witnesses.

(b) A party to the action cannot be excluded under this section.

(c) If a person other than a natural person is a party to the action, an officer or employee designated by its attorney is entitled to be present.

Compare FRE 615 and CEC § 777: To FRE's and CEC's matching provisions forbidding exclusion from the courtroom of parties or non-natural persons' representatives, FRE adds "a person whose presence is shown by a party to be essential to the presentation of the party's cause" and "a person authorized by statute to be present."

Rule 614. Court's Calling or Examining a Witness

(a) **Calling.** The court may call a witness on its own or at a party's request. Each party is entitled to cross-examine the witness.

(b) **Examining.** The court may examine a witness regardless of who calls the witness.

(c) **Objections.** A party may object to the court's calling or examining a witness either at that time or at the next opportunity when the jury is not present.

Rule 615. Excluding Witnesses

At a party's request, the court must order witnesses excluded so that they cannot hear other witnesses' testimony. Or the court may do so on its own. But this rule does not authorize excluding:

(a) a party who is a natural person;

(b) an officer or employee of a party that is not a natural person, after being designated as the party's representative by its attorney;

(c) a person whose presence a party shows to be essential to presenting the party's claim or defense; or

(d) a person authorized by statute to be present.

§ **800. Opinion testimony by lay witness.** If a witness is not testifying as an expert, his testimony in the form of an opinion is limited to such an opinion as is permitted by law, including but not limited to an opinion that is:

(a) Rationally based on the perception of the witness; and

(b) Helpful to a clear understanding of his testimony.

Compare FRE 701 and CEC § 800: FRE and CEC use the same criteria for admissibility of lay opinion testimony –"rationally based on perception" and "helpful" – but FRE confines lay opinion testimony to opinions or inferences "not based on ... specialized knowledge" within the scope of FRE 702, thus delineating lay and expert testimony more sharply than CEC.

Property Valuation:

[*Sections 810-824 prescribe "special rules of evidence applicable to any action in which the value of property is to be ascertained." They have no counterpart in FRE.*]

§ **720. Qualification as an expert witness.** (a) A person is qualified to testify as an expert if he has special knowledge, skill, experience, training, or education sufficient to qualify him as an expert on the subject to which his testimony relates. Against the objection of a party, such special knowledge, skill, experience, training, or education must be shown before the witness may testify as an expert.

(b) A witness' special knowledge, skill, experience, training, or education may be shown by any otherwise admissible evidence, including his own testimony.

ARTICLE VII. OPINIONS AND EXPERT TESTIMONY

Rule 701. Opinion Testimony by Lay Witnesses

If a witness is not testifying as an expert, testimony in the form of an opinion is limited to one that is:

(a) rationally based on the witness's perception;

(b) helpful to clearly understanding the witness's testimony or to determining a fact in issue; and

(c) not based on scientific, technical, or other specialized knowledge within the scope of Rule 702.

Rule 702. Testimony by Expert Witnesses

A witness who is qualified as an expert by knowledge, skill, experience, training, or education may testify in the form of an opinion or otherwise if:

(a) the expert's scientific, technical, or other specialized knowledge will help the trier of fact to understand the evidence or to determine a fact in issue;

(b) the testimony is based on sufficient facts or data;

(c) the testimony is the product of reliable principles and methods; and

(d) the expert has reliably applied the principles and methods to the facts of the case.

> *Compare FRE 702 and CEC §§ 801/803*: On the general rule of admissibility of expert opinion testimony, there is no substantive difference between FRE and CEC as interpreted by the courts; the requirements are: (a) helpfulness to the jury (b) on a matter of scientific, technical, or specialized knowledge (c) by a qualified expert (d) based on properly applied methods. However, when the court, exercising its gate-keeping function to exclude "junk" science or expertise, must decide whether testimony falls within a cognizable area of expertise, the principles of *Daubert v. Merrell Dow Pharmaceuticals,* 509 U.S. 579 (1993),
> [*continued on page I-137*]

§ **801. Opinion testimony by expert witness.** If a witness is testifying as an expert, his testimony in the form of an opinion is limited to such an opinion as is:

(a) Related to a subject that is sufficiently beyond common experience that the opinion of an expert would assist the trier of fact; and

(b) Based on matter (including his special knowledge, skill, experience, training, and education) perceived by or personally known to the witness or made known to him at or before the hearing, whether or not admissible, that is of a type that reasonably may be relied upon by an expert in forming an opinion upon the subject to which his testimony relates, unless an expert is precluded by law from using such matter as a basis for his opinion.

§ **803. Opinion based on improper matter.** The court may, and upon objection shall, exclude testimony in the form of an opinion that is based in whole or in significant part on matter that is not a proper basis for such an opinion. In such case, the witness may, if there remains a proper basis for his opinion, then state his opinion after excluding from consideration the matter determined to be improper.

§ **804. Opinion based on opinion or statement of another.** (a) If a witness testifying as an expert testifies that his opinion is based in whole or in part upon the opinion or statement of another person, such other person may be called and examined by any adverse party as if under cross-examination concerning the opinion or statement.

(b) This section is not applicable if the person upon whose opinion or statement the expert witness has relied is (1) a party, (2) a person identified with a party within the meaning of subdivision (d) of Section 776, or (3) a witness who has testified in the action concerning the subject matter of the opinion or statement upon which the expert witness has relied.

(c) Nothing in this section makes admissible an expert opinion that is inadmissible because it is based in whole or in part on the opinion or statement of another person.

(d) An expert opinion otherwise admissible is not made inadmissible by this section because it is based on the opinion or statement of a person who is unavailable for examination pursuant to this section.

[*continued from page I-135*]
pervade FRE, while *People v. Kelly*, 17 Cal. 3d 24 (1976), rules CEC. The differences are in both coverage and the applicable test for admissibility. *Kelly* applies only to new scientific techniques bearing an "aura of scientific infallibility" that might mislead the jury, *see People v. Stoll*, 49 Cal. 3d 1136, 1156 (1989), and requires the proponent to show that the technique is generally accepted in the relevant scientific community. *Daubert* and FRE 702 apply to *all* expert testimony, not merely testimony based on science. *See Kumho Tire Co. v. Carmichael*, 526 U.S. 137 (1999). *Daubert* and FRE require that: (a) the testimony be based on sufficient data, (b) the testimony be the product of reliable principles and methods, and (c) those principles and methods have been reliably applied. While *Daubert* allows *Kelly's* "general acceptance in the relevant expert community" to be considered in deciding the issue of "reliable principles and methods," it is only one of a number of exemplifying factors. Under *People v. Harris*, 47 Cal. 3d 1047, 1094-95, 767 P.2d 619 (1989). CEC's limitations on expert testimony are exempt from any effect under Prop. 8.

Rule 703. Bases of an Expert's Opinion Testimony

An expert may base an opinion on facts or data in the case that the expert has been made aware of or personally observed. If experts in the particular field would reasonably rely on those kinds of facts or data in forming an opinion on the subject, they need not be admissible for the opinion to be admitted. But if the facts or data would otherwise be inadmissible, the proponent of the opinion may disclose them to the jury only if their probative value in helping the jury evaluate the opinion substantially outweighs their prejudicial effect.

Compare FRE 703 and CEC §§ 801, 803, 804: Where an expert relies on out-of-court statements from others, both CEC and FRE require that the statements be of a type reasonably relied upon by experts in the particular field of expertise at issue. From here, however, FRE and CEC diverge.

Under FRE, the statements themselves need not be admissible in evidence to be disclosed to the jury as part of the expert's testimony. Rather, out-of-court statements relied upon by an expert may be disclosed to the jury, with a limiting instruction, if the court determines that the probative value outweighs the prejudicial effect. The probative value in question is not the effect of the statements if considered for the truth but rather the assistance the evidence will give to the jury in evaluating the reliability/credibility of the expert's opinion.

But in *Williams v. Illinois,* 567 U.S. 50, 104-10; 125-30 (2012), Justice Thomas in concurrence and Justices Kagan, Scalia, Ginsburg, and Sotomayor in dissent challenged as false logic the admission of out-of-court statements for anything *but* the truth when an expert witness relies upon those statements in forming his or her opinion. Since *Williams* the Court has not revisited the issue.

[*continued on page I-139*]

§ **805. Opinion on ultimate issue.** Testimony in the form of an opinion that is otherwise admissible is not objectionable because it embraces the ultimate issue to be decided by the trier of fact.

§ **870. Opinion as to sanity.** A witness may state his opinion as to the sanity of a person when:

(a) The witness is an intimate acquaintance of the person whose sanity is in question;

(b) The witness was a subscribing witness to a writing, the validity of which is in dispute, signed by the person whose sanity is in question and the opinion relates to the sanity of such person at the time the writing was signed; or

(c) The witness is qualified under Section 800 or 801 to testify in the form of an opinion.

§ **1107. Intimate partner battering and its effects; expert testimony in criminal actions; sufficiency of foundation; abuse and domestic violence; applicability to Penal Code; impact on decisional law.** (a) In a criminal action, expert testimony is admissible by either the prosecution or the defense regarding intimate partner battering and its effects, including the nature and effect of physical, emotional, or mental abuse on the beliefs, perceptions, or behavior of victims of domestic violence, except when offered against a criminal defendant to prove the occurrence of the act or acts of abuse which form the basis of the criminal charge.

[*continued from page I-137*]

Similarly, before 2016, CEC gave the trial court discretion under CEC § 352 to admit any inadmissible hearsay underpinning an expert's opinion as long as its probative value was not substantially outweighed by its prejudicial effect and subject to a limiting instruction, if requested under CEC § 355. But in *People v. Sanchez*, 63 Cal. 4th 665 (2016), echoing Justice Thomas's concurrence and the four Justices in dissent in *Williams*, the California Supreme Court held:

> When any expert relates to the jury case-specific out-of-court statements, and treats the content of those statements as true and accurate to support the expert's opinion, the statements are hearsay. It cannot logically be maintained that the statements are not being admitted for their truth.

63 Cal. 4th 665, 683–86 (2016). Thus, such statements are admissible only where they qualify under one or more CEC hearsay exceptions and, where testimonial, satisfy *Crawford v. Washington*, 541 U.S. 36 (2004). *Id.* at 686.

Finally, CEC § 804 specifically allows the opponent of the evidence to call the hearsay declarant as an adverse witness, with certain exceptions; FRE is silent on the subject in the rules on experts, but FRE 611(a) and (c) support arguments for a similar procedure.

Rule 704. Opinion on an Ultimate Issue

(a) In General — Not Automatically Objectionable. An opinion is not objectionable just because it embraces an ultimate issue.

(b) Exception. In a criminal case, an expert witness must not state an opinion about whether the defendant did or did not have a mental state or condition that constitutes an element of the crime charged or of a defense. Those matters are for the trier of fact alone.

Compare FRE 704(b) and CEC §§ 805, 870: In criminal cases, FRE bars an expert from giving "ultimate issue" testimony as to any mental state or condition constituting a defense to the crime charged. CEC freely allows both lay and expert opinion testimony as to sanity.

[*FRE have no counterpart to CEC § 1107.*]

(b) The foundation shall be sufficient for admission of this expert testimony if the proponent of the evidence establishes its relevancy and the proper qualifications of the expert witness. Expert opinion testimony on intimate partner battering and its effects shall not be considered a new scientific technique whose reliability is unproven.

(c) For purposes of this section, "abuse" is defined in Section 6203 of the Family Code, and "domestic violence" is defined in Section 6211 of the Family Code and may include acts defined in Section 242, subdivision (e) of Section 243, Section 262, 273.5, 273.6, 422, or 653m of the Penal Code.

(d) This section is intended as a rule of evidence only and no substantive change affecting the Penal Code is intended.

(e) This section shall be known, and may be cited, as the Expert Witness Testimony on Intimate Partner Battering and Its Effects Section of the Evidence Code.

(f) The changes in this section that become effective on January 1, 2005, are not intended to impact any existing decisional law regarding this section, and that decisional law should apply equally to this section as it refers to "intimate partner battering and its effects" in place of "battered women's syndrome." [*Added 1991. Amended 1992, 1993, 2004.*]

§ 1107.5. Expert testimony regarding effects of human trafficking on victims. (a) In a criminal action, expert testimony is admissible by either the prosecution or the defense regarding the effects of human trafficking on human trafficking victims, including the nature and effect of physical, emotional, or mental abuse on the beliefs, perceptions, or behavior of human trafficking victims.

(b) The foundation shall be sufficient for admission of this expert testimony if the proponent of the evidence establishes its relevancy and the proper qualifications of the expert witness.

(c) For purposes of this section, "human trafficking victim" is defined as a victim of an offense described in Section 236.1 of the Penal Code.

(d) This section is intended as a rule of evidence only and no substantive change affecting the Penal Code is intended. [*Added 2017.*]

§ 802. Statement of basis of opinion. A witness testifying in the form of an opinion may state on direct examination the reasons for his opinion and the matter (including, in the case of an expert, his special knowledge, skill, experience, training, and education) upon which it is based, unless he is precluded by law from using such reasons or matter as a basis for his opinion. The court in its discretion may require that a witness before testifying in the form of an opinion be first examined concerning the matter upon which his opinion is based.

[*FRE have no counterpart to CEC § 1107.5.*]

Rule 705. Disclosing the Facts or Data Underlying an Expert's Opinion

Unless the court orders otherwise, an expert may state an opinion — and give the reasons for it — without first testifying to the underlying facts or data. But the expert may be required to disclose those facts or data on cross-examination.

Compare FRE 705 and CEC § 802: Under FRE an expert may state an opinion and give reasons for it without first testifying to the underlying facts or data. CEC gives the court discretion to require disclosure of the expert's bases before the opinion. Under both FRE and CEC the expert may be required to disclose the underlying facts and data on cross-examination. CEC also specifies in detail matters that may be covered in cross-examination of an expert.

§ **721. Cross-examination of expert witness.** (a) Subject to subdivision (b), a witness testifying as an expert may be cross-examined to the same extent as any other witness and, in addition, may be fully cross-examined as to (1) his or her qualifications, (2) the subject to which his or her expert testimony relates, and (3) the matter upon which his or her opinion is based and the reasons for his or her opinion.

(b) If a witness testifying as an expert testifies in the form of an opinion, he or she may not be cross-examined in regard to the content or tenor of any scientific, technical, or professional text, treatise, journal, or similar publication unless any of the following occurs:

(1) The witness referred to, considered, or relied upon such publication in arriving at or forming his or her opinion.

(2) The publication has been admitted in evidence.

(3) The publication has been established as a reliable authority by the testimony or admission of the witness or by other expert testimony or by judicial notice.

If admitted, relevant portions of the publication may be read into evidence but may not be received as exhibits. [*Amended 1997.*]

§ **722. Credibility of expert witness.** (a) The fact of the appointment of an expert witness by the court may be revealed to the trier of fact.

(b) The compensation and expenses paid or to be paid to an expert witness by the party calling him is a proper subject of inquiry by any adverse party as relevant to the credibility of the witness and the weight of his testimony.

[FRE have no counterpart to CEC § 721(a).]

[FRE have no exact counterpart to CEC § 721(b). Compare, however, the exception to the hearsay rule for learned treatises, FRE 803(18).]

[FRE's counterpart to CEC § 722(a) is FRE 706(d). FRE has no express counterpart to CEC § 722(b), but the common-law principles of impeachment of witnesses, FRE 401-402, 607 encompass this aspect of cross-examination of expert witnesses.]

§ **730. Appointment of expert by court.** When it appears to the court, at any time before or during the trial of an action, that expert evidence is or may be required by the court or by any party to the action, the court on its own motion or on motion of any party may appoint one or more experts to investigate, to render a report as may be ordered by the court, and to testify as an expert at the trial of the action relative to the fact or matter as to which the expert evidence is or may be required. The court may fix the compensation for these services, if any, rendered by any person appointed under this section, in addition to any service as a witness, at the amount as seems reasonable to the court.

Nothing in this section shall be construed to permit a person to perform any act for which a license is required unless the person holds the appropriate license to lawfully perform that act. [*Added 1979. Amended 1990.*]

§ **732. Calling and examining court-appointed expert.** Any expert appointed by the court under Section 730 may be called and examined by the court or by any party to the action. When such witness is called and examined by the court, the parties have the same right as is expressed in Section 775 to cross-examine the witness and to object to the questions asked and the evidence adduced.

§ **731. Payment of court-appointed expert.** (a)(1) In all criminal actions and juvenile court proceedings, the compensation fixed under Section 730 shall be a charge against the county in which the action or proceeding is pending and shall be paid out of the treasury of that county on order of the court.

(2) Notwithstanding paragraph (1), if the expert is appointed for the court's needs, the compensation shall be a charge against the court. [*Added 2012.*]

(b) In any county in which the superior court so provides, the compensation fixed under Section 730 for medical experts appointed for the court's needs in civil actions shall be a charge against the court. In any county in which the board of supervisors so provides, the compensation fixed under Section 730 for medical experts appointed in civil actions, for purposes other than the court's needs, shall be a charge against and paid out of the treasury of that county on order of the court.

Rule 706. Court-Appointed Expert Witnesses

(a) Appointment Process. On a party's motion or on its own, the court may order the parties to show cause why expert witnesses should not be appointed and may ask the parties to submit nominations. The court may appoint any expert that the parties agree on and any of its own choosing. But the court may only appoint someone who consents to act.

(b) Expert's Role. The court must inform the expert of the expert's duties. The court may do so in writing and have a copy filed with the clerk or may do so orally at a conference in which the parties have an opportunity to participate. The expert:

(1) must advise the parties of any findings the expert makes;

(2) may be deposed by any party;

(3) may be called to testify by the court or any party; and

(4) may be cross-examined by any party, including the party that called the expert.

(c) Compensation. The expert is entitled to a reasonable compensation, as set by the court. The compensation is payable as follows:

(1) in a criminal case or in a civil case involving just compensation under the Fifth Amendment, from any funds that are provided by law; and

(2) in any other civil case, by the parties in the proportion and at the time that the court directs — and the compensation is then charged like other costs.

(d) Disclosing the Appointment to the Jury. The court may authorize disclosure to the jury that the court appointed the expert.

[*CEC's counterpart to FRE 706(d) is CEC § 722(a).*]

(c) Except as otherwise provided in this section, in all civil actions, the compensation fixed under Section 730 shall, in the first instance, be apportioned and charged to the several parties in a proportion as the court may determine and may thereafter be taxed and allowed in like manner as other costs. [*Added 1979.*]

§ 733. **Right to produce other expert evidence.** Nothing contained in this article [§§ 730-733] shall be deemed or construed to prevent any party to any action from producing other expert evidence on the same fact or matter mentioned in Section 730; but, where other expert witnesses are called by a party to the action, their fees shall be paid by the party calling them and only ordinary witness fees shall be taxed as costs in the action.

§ 723. **Limit on number of expert witnesses.** The court may, at any time before or during the trial of an action, limit the number of expert witnesses to be called by any party.

(e) **Parties' Choice of Their Own Experts.** This rule does not limit a party in calling its own experts.

[*FRE have no counterpart to CEC § 723. See, however, FRE 611(a).*]

§ **225. "Statement"** means (a) oral or written verbal expression or (b) nonverbal conduct of a person intended by him as a substitute for oral or written verbal expression.

§ **125. "Conduct"** includes all active and passive behavior, both verbal and nonverbal.

§ **135. "Declarant"** is a person who makes a statement.

§ **145. "The hearing"** means the hearing at which a question under this code arises, and not some earlier or later hearing.

§ **1200. The hearsay rule.** (a) "Hearsay evidence" is evidence of a statement that was made other than by a witness while testifying at the hearing and that is offered to prove the truth of the matter stated. * * *

> *Compare FRE 801-802, CEC 125, 135, 145, 1200, and Prop. 8:* The hearsay rule and definitions of hearsay are substantially similar under FRE and CEC. By its explicit terms, Prop. 8 has no effect on the hearsay rule.

§ **1235. Inconsistent statement.** Evidence of a statement made by a witness is not made inadmissible by the hearsay rule if the statement is inconsistent with his testimony at the hearing and is offered in compliance with Section 770.

ARTICLE VIII. HEARSAY

Rule 801. Definitions That Apply to This Article; Exclusions from Hearsay

(a) **Statement.** "Statement" means a person's oral assertion, written assertion, or nonverbal conduct, if the person intended it as an assertion.

(b) **Declarant.** "Declarant" means the person who made the statement.

(c) **Hearsay.** "Hearsay" means a statement that:

(1) the declarant does not make while testifying at the current trial or hearing; and

(2) a party offers in evidence to prove the truth of the matter asserted in the statement.

(d) **Statements That Are Not Hearsay.** A statement that meets the following conditions is not hearsay:

> *Compare FRE 801(d) and CEC §§ 1220-1227, 1235-1236, 1238*: FRE defines certain prior statements by witnesses and statements by opposing parties as "not hearsay," and thus admissible for their truth as hearsay *exclusions.* In contrast, CEC defines such statements as hearsay, but sets forth *exceptions* to the hearsay rule permitting their admission. Whether defined as an exclusion under FRE or as an exception under CEC, the effect on admissibility is the same.

(1) ***A Declarant-Witness's Prior Statement.*** The declarant testifies and is subject to cross-examination about a prior statement, and the statement:

(A) is inconsistent with the declarant's testimony and was given under penalty of perjury at a trial, hearing, or other proceeding or in a deposition;

> *Compare FRE 801(d)(1)(A) and CEC § 1235*: For admissibility of a witness's *prior inconsistent statement* for the truth, FRE requires the statement to have been "given under penalty of perjury at a trial, hearing, or other proceeding or in a deposition." CEC allows any prior inconsistent statement to be offered for the truth. Thus, out-of-court statements to law enforcement personnel may be admissible as prior inconsistent statements under CEC, but not under FRE. *See also* discussion of FRE 804(b)(1) and CEC § 1294, *infra,* concerning admissibility of an unavailable witness's prior inconsistent statement to impeach the witness's former testimony admitted under CEC § 1291.

§ 791. Prior consistent statement of witness. Evidence of a statement previously made by a witness that is consistent with his testimony at the hearing is inadmissible to support his credibility unless it is offered after:

(a) Evidence of a statement made by him that is inconsistent with any part of his testimony at hearing has been admitted for the purpose of attacking his credibility, and the statement was made before the alleged inconsistent statement; or

(b) An express or implied charge has been made that his testimony at the hearing is recently fabricated or is influenced by bias or other improper motive, and the statement was made before the bias, motive for fabrication, or other improper motive is alleged to have arisen.

§ 1236. Prior consistent statement. Evidence of a statement previously made by a witness is not made inadmissible by the hearsay rule if the statement is consistent with his testimony at the hearing and is offered in compliance with Section 791.

§ 1238. Prior identification. Evidence of a statement previously made by a witness is not made inadmissible by the hearsay rule if the statement would have been admissible if made by him while testifying and: (a) the statement is an identification of a party or another as a person who participated in a crime or other occurrence; (b) the statement was made at a time when the crime or other occurrence was fresh in the witness' memory; and (c) the evidence of the statement is offered after the witness testifies that he made the identification and that it was a true reflection of his opinion at that time.

§ 1220. Admission of party. Evidence of a statement is not made inadmissible by the hearsay rule when offered against the declarant in an action to which he is a party in either his individual or representative capacity, regardless of whether the statement was made in his individual or representative capacity.

Compare FRE 801(d)(2)(A)-(E) and CEC §§ 1220-1222: ***[1]*** To avoid the common misconception that a party-opponent's statement has to "admit" anything to be admissible under this rule, restyled FRE has replaced the misleading term "admission" with the accurate term "statement." CEC's continued use of the term "admission" does not create a difference. CEC's text uses the accurate term "statement." ***[2]*** The similarity between FRE and CEC on the subjects of personal, adoptive, and authorized admissions is broken only by CEC's requirement that the authority of an agent to speak on behalf of the party-opponent be shown by a sufficiency standard, which may be satisfied either before or, in the court's discretion, after the statement has been received. Under FRE, the declarant's authority to speak is a preliminary fact that must be proved to the satisfaction of the court by a preponderance of the evidence pursuant to FRE 104(a) — a more formidable barrier to admissibility than under CEC. *See Bourjaily v. United States, 483 U.S. 171, 175-176 (1987).*

(B) is consistent with the declarant's testimony and is offered:

(i) to rebut an express or implied charge that the declarant recently fabricated it or acted from a recent improper influence or motive in so testifying; or

(ii) to rehabilitate the declarant's credibility as a witness when attacked on another ground; or [*Amended 2014.*]

Compare FRE 801(d)(1)(B) and CEC §§ 791, 1236: Both FRE and CEC allow admission of a *prior consistent statement* for its truth to rebut a charge of recent fabrication, improper influence, or motive where the declarant made the statement before the alleged bias or motive to fabricate or alter testimony is alleged to have arisen. *See Tome v. United States*, 513 U.S. 150 (1995). CEC also allows admission of a prior consistent statement to rehabilitate a witness who has merely been impeached by a prior inconsistent statement, provided the consistent statement was made before the inconsistent one. The 2014 FRE amendment expands the use of prior consistent statements to apply to any situation in which the witness's credibility is attacked, subject to the court's discretion under Rule 403. *See* Advisory Committee Note at p. II-111, *infra*.

(C) identifies a person as someone the declarant perceived earlier.

Compare FRE 801(d)(1)(C) and CEC § 1238: For admissibility of *prior statements of identification,* CEC requires that the proponent of the statement show that the declarant made the statement when the observed event was fresh in the declarant's memory, and that the declarant testify that the statement was a true reflection of his or her opinion at the time it was made. FRE has no such requirement; indeed, under FRE as interpreted a prior statement of identification is admissible even if the witness denies having made it or testifies that it was false.

(2) ***An Opposing Party's Statement.*** The statement is offered against an opposing party and:

(A) was made by the party in an individual or representative capacity;

§ **1204. Hearsay statement offered against criminal defendant.** A statement that is otherwise admissible as hearsay evidence is inadmissible against the defendant in a criminal action if the statement was made, either by the defendant or by another, under such circumstances that it is inadmissible against the defendant under the Constitution of the United States or the State of California.

§ **1221. Adoptive admission.** Evidence of a statement offered against a party is not made inadmissible by the hearsay rule if the statement is one of which the party, with knowledge of the content thereof, has by words or other conduct manifested his adoption or his belief in its truth.

§ **1222. Authorized admission.** Evidence of a statement offered against a party is not made inadmissible by the hearsay rule if:

(a) The statement was made by a person authorized by the party to make a statement or statements for him concerning the subject matter of the statement; and

(b) The evidence is offered either after admission of evidence sufficient to sustain a finding of such authority or, in the court's discretion as to the order of proof, subject to the admission of such evidence.

§ **1224. Statement of declarant whose liability or breach of duty is in issue.** When the liability, obligation, or duty of a party to a civil action is based in whole or in part upon the liability, obligation, or duty of the declarant, or when the claim or right asserted by a party to a civil action is barred or diminished by a breach of duty by the declarant, evidence of a statement made by the declarant is as admissible against the party as it would be if offered against the declarant in an action involving that liability, obligation, duty, or breach of duty.

§ **1225. Statement of declarant whose right or title is in issue.** When a right, title, or interest in any property or claim asserted by a party to a civil action requires a determination that a right, title, or interest exists or existed in the declarant, evidence of a statement made by the declarant during the time the party now claims the declarant was the holder of the right, title, or interest is as admissible against the party as it would be if offered against the declarant in an action involving that right, title, or interest.

§ **1226. Statement of minor child in parent's action for child's injury.** Evidence of a statement by a minor child is not made inadmissible by the hearsay rule if offered against the plaintiff in an action brought under Section 376 of the Code of Civil Procedure for injury to such minor child.

§ **1227. Statement of declarant in action for his wrongful death.** Evidence of a statement by the deceased is not made inadmissible by the hearsay rule if offered against the plaintiff in an action for wrongful death brought under Section 377 of the Code of Civil Procedure.

[*FRE have no counterpart to CEC § 1204; federal law leaves this issue to case rulings on challenges to evidence under the U.S. Constitution.*]

(B) is one the party manifested that it adopted or believed to be true;

(C) was made by a person whom the party authorized to make a statement on the subject;

Compare FRE 801(d)(2)(C) and CEC § 1222: *Authorized statements* under FRE include statements by the declarant *for* the party as well as *to* the party. CEC's language ("statements for him") "is perhaps an ambiguous limitation to statements to third persons." ACN to FRE 801(d)(2)(C). A leading authority on CEC considers this apparent distinction "inadvertent [and] immaterial in most circumstances." *See* Mendez, *Evidence – A Concise Comparison of the Federal Rules with the California Code* (West 2011), at 219.

(D) was made by the party's agent or employee on a matter within the scope of that relationship and while it existed; or

Compare FRE 801(d)(2)(D) and CEC §§ 1224-1227: FRE allows *statements by an opposing party's agent or employee* made "on a matter within the scope of that relationship and while it existed." CEC lacks this broad exception, but does recognize four analogous exceptions: *[1]* CEC § 1224 admits statements by a non-party declarant where a party's asserted civil liability depends on the declarant's conduct. (These may include statements by former employees concerning matters within their former scope of employment; FRE does not permit statements made outside the term of employment.) *[2]* CEC § 1225 admits statements by a non-party declarant whose property rights are also at issue in a civil action involving a property dispute. *[3]* CEC § 1226 admits statements by a minor child in a civil action brought by the parents involving injury to the child. *[4]* CEC § 1227 admits statements of a decedent offered against a plaintiff in a wrongful death action.

§ **1223. Admission of co-conspirator.** Evidence of a statement offered against a party is not made inadmissible by the hearsay rule if:

(a) The statement was made by the declarant while participating in a conspiracy to commit a crime or civil wrong and in furtherance of the objective of that conspiracy;

(b) The statement was made prior to or during the time that the party was participating in that conspiracy; and

(c) The evidence is offered either after admission of evidence sufficient to sustain a finding of the facts specified in subdivisions (a) and (b) or, in the court's discretion as to the order of proof, subject to the admission of such evidence.

§ **1200. The hearsay rule.** * * * (b) Except as provided by law, hearsay evidence is inadmissible.

(c) This section shall be known and may be cited as the hearsay rule.

§ **1205. No implied repeal.** Nothing in this division [§§ 1200-1380] shall be construed to repeal by implication any other statute relating to hearsay evidence.

§ **1241. Contemporaneous statement.** Evidence of a statement is not made inadmissible by the hearsay rule if the statement:

(a) Is offered to explain, qualify, or make understandable conduct of the declarant; and

(b) Was made while the declarant was engaged in such conduct.

(E) was made by the party's co-conspirator during and in furtherance of the conspiracy.

The statement must be considered but does not by itself establish the declarant's authority under (C); the existence or scope of the relationship under (D); or the existence of the conspiracy or participation in it under (E).

Compare FRE 801(d)(2)(E) and CEC § 1223: For *co-conspirator's statements*: ***[1]*** FRE requires the proponent to prove the requisite foundational facts of conspiracy by a preponderance of the evidence. *See* FRE 104(a); *Bourjaily v. United States*, 483 U.S. 171, 175-176 (1987). CEC requires the proponent to prove foundation only by sufficient evidence. ***[2]*** In making the foundational determination under FRE, the court must consider the content of the statement at issue (although the statement alone is not enough), and the court is not bound by the rules of evidence except privileges. Under CEC, the court is limited by the rules of evidence and thus is prohibited from considering the statement at issue in making the determination.

Rule 802. The Rule Against Hearsay

Hearsay is not admissible unless any of the following provides otherwise:

- a federal statute;
- these rules; or
- other rules prescribed by the Supreme Court.

Rule 803. Exceptions to the Rule Against Hearsay — Regardless of Whether the Declarant Is Available as a Witness

The following are not excluded by the rule against hearsay, regardless of whether the declarant is available as a witness:

(1) ***Present Sense Impression.*** A statement describing or explaining an event or condition, made while or immediately after the declarant perceived it.

Compare FRE 803(1) and CEC § 1241: FRE's exception for *present sense impressions* allows statements "*describing or explaining an event or condition*, made while or immediately after the declarant perceived it." CEC's exception is much narrower, allowing only statements offered *to explain the declarant's conduct* made contemporaneously with such conduct.

§ 1240. **Spontaneous statement.** Evidence of a statement is not made inadmissible by the hearsay rule if the statement:

(a) Purports to narrate, describe, or explain an act, condition, or event perceived by the declarant; and

(b) Was made spontaneously while the declarant was under the stress of excitement caused by such perception.

[*See also CEC § 1370's special provision for statements made to a physician, nurse, paramedic, or law enforcement official "purporting to narrate, describe, or explain the infliction or threat of physical injury upon the declarant." FRE have no counterpart.*]

§ 1250. **Statement of declarant's then existing mental or physical state.** (a) Subject to Section 1252, evidence of a statement of the declarant's then existing state of mind, emotion, or physical sensation (including a statement of intent, plan, motive, design, mental feeling, pain, or bodily health) is not made inadmissible by the hearsay rule when:

(1) The evidence is offered to prove the declarant's state of mind, emotion, or physical sensation at that time or at any other time when it is itself an issue in the action; or

(2) The evidence is offered to prove or explain acts or conduct of the declarant.

(b) This section does not make admissible evidence of a statement of memory or belief to prove the fact remembered or believed.

§ 1251. **Statement of declarant's previously existing mental or physical state.** Subject to Section 1252, evidence of a statement of the declarant's state of mind, emotion, or physical sensation (including a statement of intent, plan, motive, design, mental feeling, pain, or bodily health) at a time prior to the statement is not made inadmissible by the hearsay rule if:

(a) The declarant is unavailable as a witness; and

(b) The evidence is offered to prove such prior state of mind, emotion, or physical sensation when it is itself an issue in the action and the evidence is not offered to prove any fact other than such state of mind, emotion, or physical sensation.

§ 1252. **Limitation on admissibility of statement of mental or physical state.** Evidence of a statement is inadmissible under this article [§§ 1250-1253] if the statement was made under circumstances such as to indicate its lack of trustworthiness.

§ 1260. **Statement concerning declarant's will.** (a) Except as provided in subdivision (b), evidence of any of the following statements made by a declarant who is unavailable as a witness is not made inadmissible by the hearsay rule:

(1) That the declarant has or has not made a will or established or amended a revocable trust.

(2) ***Excited Utterance.*** A statement relating to a startling event or condition, made while the declarant was under the stress of excitement that it caused.

Compare FRE 803(2) and CEC §§ 1240, 1370: FRE's exception for *excited utterances* allows statements *"relating to* a startling event or condition, made while the declarant was under the stress of excitement that [the event or condition] caused." CEC limits this exception to statements that *"narrate, describe, or explain"* either such an act, condition, or event (§ 1240) or "the infliction or threat of physical injury on the declarant" (§ 1370). However, California courts interpret CEC consistently with FRE, allowing statements that merely *relate to* such occurrences. *See, e.g., People v. Farmer*, 47 Cal. 3d 888, 904-905 (1989).

(3) ***Then-Existing Mental, Emotional, or Physical Condition.*** A statement of the declarant's then-existing state of mind (such as motive, intent, or plan) or emotional, sensory, or physical condition (such as mental feeling, pain, or bodily health), but not including a statement of memory or belief to prove the fact remembered or believed unless it relates to the validity or terms of the declarant's will.

Compare FRE 803(3) and CEC §§ 1250-1252, 1260: ***[1]*** As written, FRE is broader than CEC, in that FRE's language permits the interpretation that it allows *statements of a declarant's intent* to prove not only the declarant's future conduct but also the future conduct of others, *i.e.*, as a codification in full of the holding of *Mutual Life Ins. Co. v. Hillmon*, 145 U.S. 285 (1892); *see United States v. Houlihan*, 871 F. Supp. 1495 (D. Mass. 1994). By its terms CEC § 1250 allows statements of a declarant's intent to prove only the declarant's conduct. However, California courts have not observed this limitation and have instead followed the *Hillmon* doctrine, allowing statements by a declarant as proof of others' future conduct. *See People v. Han*, 78 Cal. App. 4th 797, 807 (2000). ***[2]*** CEC § 1252 gives the trial judge discretion to exclude *statements of mental or physical state* if the circumstances demonstrate a lack of trustworthiness. FRE does not contain such a limitation. ***[3]*** FRE and the analogous CEC provisions generally prohibit a witness from offering *declarations regarding past state of mind*. However, CEC allows such statements in three instances: ***[a]*** CEC § 1251 allows evidence of a declaration of a past state of mind when that state of mind is itself an issue in the case and the declaration is offered only to prove that mental state, provided the declarant is unavailable to testify. There is no FRE analogue to this provision. ***[b]*** CEC § 1253 allows a witness to offer a past statement made for purposes of medical diagnosis where the declarant was under the age of 12 when he or she described acts or attempted acts of child abuse or neglect and is still a minor at the time of the proceeding. This provision is narrower than FRE 803(4). *See* comparison of FRE 803(4) and CEC § 1253, *infra*. ***[c]*** CEC § 1260 allows a declarant's statement that he or she has or does not have a will or has or has not revoked a will. FRE's similar provision is broader ("relat[ing] to the validity or terms of the declarant's will") and, unlike CEC, does not require the declarant's unavailability.

(2) That the declarant has or has not revoked his or her will, revocable trust, or an amendment to a revocable trust.

(3) That identifies the declarant's will, revocable trust, or an amendment to a revocable trust.

(b) Evidence of a statement is inadmissible under this section if the statement was made under circumstances that indicate its lack of trustworthiness. [*Amended 2009.*]

§ 1261. Statement of decedent offered in action against his estate. (a) Evidence of a statement is not made inadmissible by the hearsay rule when offered in an action upon a claim or demand against the estate of the declarant if the statement was made upon the personal knowledge of the declarant at a time when the matter had been recently perceived by him and while his recollection was clear.

(b) Evidence of a statement is inadmissible under this section if the statement was made under circumstances such as to indicate its lack of trustworthiness.

§ 1253. Statements for purposes of medical diagnosis or treatment; contents of statement; child abuse or neglect; age limitations. Subject to Section 1252, evidence of a statement is not made inadmissible by the hearsay rule if the statement was made for purposes of medical diagnosis or treatment and describes medical history, or past or present symptoms, pain, or sensations, or the inception or general character of the cause or external source thereof insofar as reasonably pertinent to diagnosis or treatment. This section applies only to a statement made by a victim who is a minor at the time of the proceedings, provided the statement was made when the victim was under the age of 12 describing any act, or attempted act, of child abuse or neglect. "Child abuse" and "child neglect," for purposes of this section, have the meanings provided in subdivision (c) of Section 1360. In addition, "child abuse" means any act proscribed by Chapter 5 (commencing with Section 281) of Title 9 of Part 1 of the Penal Code committed against a minor. [*Added 1995.*]

[*See also CEC § 1370's special provision for statements made to a physician, nurse, paramedic, or law enforcement official "purporting to narrate, describe, or explain the infliction or threat of physical injury upon the declarant." FRE have no counterpart.*]

§ 1237. Past recollection recorded. (a) Evidence of a statement previously made by a witness is not made inadmissible by the hearsay rule if the statement would have been admissible if made by him while testifying, the statement concerns a matter as to which the witness has insufficient present recollection to enable him to testify fully and accurately, and the statement is contained in a writing which:

(1) Was made at a time when the fact recorded in the writing actually occurred or was fresh in the witness' memory;

(2) Was made (i) by the witness himself or under his direction or (ii) by some other person for the purpose of recording the witness' statement at the time it was made;

[*FRE have no counterpart to CEC § 1261.*]

(4) ***Statement Made for Medical Diagnosis or Treatment.*** A statement that:

(A) is made for — and is reasonably pertinent to — medical diagnosis or treatment; and

(B) describes medical history; past or present symptoms or sensations; their inception; or their general cause.

Compare FRE 803(4) and CEC §§ 1253, 1370: For *statements made for medical diagnosis or treatment*, FRE applies to any declarant. CEC is limited to either statements by declarants who were under the age of 12 when they described acts or attempted acts of child abuse or neglect and are still minors at the time of the proceeding (§ 1253), or certain statements relating to "the infliction or threat of injury to the declarant" (§ 1370).

(5) ***Recorded Recollection.*** A record that:

(A) is on a matter the witness once knew about but now cannot recall well enough to testify fully and accurately;

(B) was made or adopted by the witness when the matter was fresh in the witness's memory; and

(3) Is offered after the witness testifies that the statement he made was a true statement of such fact; and

(4) Is offered after the writing is authenticated as an accurate record of the statement.

(b) The writing may be read into evidence, but the writing itself may not be received in evidence unless offered by an adverse party.

§ **1270. A business.** As used in this article [§§ 1270-1272], "a business" includes every kind of business, governmental activity, profession, occupation, calling, or operation of institutions, whether carried on for profit or not.

§ **1271. Business record.** Evidence of a writing made as a record of an act, condition, or event is not made inadmissible by the hearsay rule when offered to prove the act, condition, or event if:

(a) The writing was made in the regular course of a business;

(b) The writing was made at or near the time of the act, condition, or event;

(c) The custodian or other qualified witness testifies to its identity and the mode of its preparation; and

(d) The sources of information and method and time of preparation were such as to indicate its trustworthiness.

Compare FRE 803(6) and CEC § 1270-1271: For *business records*: ***[1]*** FRE breaks the concept of "regularity" into two components: the business makes such records in the course of a "regularly conducted activity of [the] business," (803(6)(B)), and does so as "a regular practice of that activity" (803(6)(C)). CEC § 1271 speaks only of writings "made in the regular course of a business"; however, the regularity of the making of the record appears to be subsumed in CEC's overall requirement of a showing of trustworthiness (§ 1271(d)); *see, e.g., Prato-Morrison v. Doe,* 103 Cal. App. 4th 222, 229 n. 6 (2002) (court found lack of trustworthiness because, among other factors, the authenticating witness did "not say she created or maintained such records for *all* of [medical center's] patients ...." [emphasis in original]). ***[2]*** CEC § 1271 places the burden on the proponent to show the record's trustworthiness. FRE places the burden on the opponent to show lack of trustworthiness; the 2014 amendment clarifies this allocation. ***[3]*** Written records that include opinions or diagnoses can be offered under both FRE and CEC § 1271, but the California Supreme Court has interpreted the latter to restrict such opinions or diagnoses to readily observable acts, conditions, or events. *See People v. Reyes,* 12 Cal. 3d 486, 504 (1974). The more thought required to reach an opinion or diagnosis, the more need for cross-examination of the declarant.

(C) accurately reflects the witness's knowledge.

If admitted, the record may be read into evidence but may be received as an exhibit only if offered by an adverse party.

(6) ***Records of a Regularly Conducted Activity.*** A record of an act, event, condition, opinion, or diagnosis if:

(A) the record was made at or near the time by — or from information transmitted by — someone with knowledge;

(B) the record was kept in the course of a regularly conducted activity of a business, organization, occupation, or calling, whether or not for profit;

(C) making the record was a regular practice of that activity;

(D) all these conditions are shown by the testimony of the custodian or another qualified witness, or by a certification that complies with Rule 902(11) or (12) or with a statute permitting certification; and

(E) the opponent does not show that the source of information or the method or circumstances of preparation indicate a lack of trustworthiness. [*Amended 2014.*]

Proof of Business Records by Affidavit:

[*Section 712 allows an affidavit from a nurse or laboratory technologist to be used to prove the technique in taking a blood sample.*]

[*Sections 1560-1566 provide for compliance with a subpoena duces tecum for business records by production of copies of the records accompanied by an affidavit describing the manner of making and maintaining the records, and for admissibility of the records on the basis of the affidavit without a sponsoring witness.*]

[*Section 1567, provides for proof of income and benefits in litigation involving family support by means of a form completed by the employer in compliance with the Family Code.*]

§ **1272. Absence of entry in business records.** Evidence of the absence from the records of a business of a record of an asserted act, condition, or event is not made inadmissible by the hearsay rule when offered to prove the nonoccurrence of the act or event, or the nonexistence of the condition, if:

(a) It was the regular course of that business to make records of all such acts, conditions, or events at or near the time of the act, condition, or event and to preserve them; and

(b) The sources of information and method and time of preparation of the records of that business were such that the absence of a record of an act, condition, or event is a trustworthy indication that the act or event did not occur or the condition did not exist.

[*FRE have no counterpart to CEC § 712.*]

[*FRE 902(11), infra, provides an equivalent procedure to CEC §§ 1560-1566.*]

[*FRE have no counterpart to CEC § 1567.*]

(7) ***Absence of a Record of a Regularly Conducted Activity.*** Evidence that a matter is not included in a record described in paragraph (6) if:

(A) the evidence is admitted to prove that the matter did not occur or exist;

(B) a record was regularly kept for a matter of that kind; and

(C) the opponent does not show that the possible source of the information or other circumstances indicate a lack of trustworthiness. [*Amended 2014.*]

Compare FRE 803(7) and CEC § 1272: For *absence of a matter in a business record,* CEC places the burden on the proponent to show the record's trustworthiness. FRE places the burden on the opponent to show lack of trustworthiness; the 2014 amendment clarifies this allocation.

§ 1280. **Record by public employee.** Evidence of a writing made as a record of an act, condition, or event is not made inadmissible by the hearsay rule when offered in any civil or criminal proceeding to prove the act, condition, or event if all of the following applies:

(a) The writing was made by and within the scope of duty of a public employee.

(b) The writing was made at or near the time of the act, condition, or event.

(c) The sources of information and method and time of preparation were such as to indicate its trustworthiness. [*Amended 1996.*]

§ 452.5. **Criminal conviction records; computer-generated records and electronically digitized copies; admissibility.** (b)(1) An official record of conviction certified in accordance with subdivision (a) of Section 1530, or an electronically digitized copy thereof, is admissible pursuant to Section 1280 to prove the commission, attempted commission, or solicitation of a criminal offense, prior conviction, service of a prison term, or other act, condition, or event recorded by the record. [*Added 1996. Amended 2013.*]

(2) For purposes of this subdivision, "electronically digitized copy" means a copy that is made by scanning, photographing, or otherwise exactly reproducing a document, is stored or maintained in a digitized format, and meets either of the following requirements:

(A) The copy bears an electronic signature or watermark unique to the entity responsible for certifying the document.

(B) The copied document is an official record of conviction, certified in accordance with subdivision (a) of Section 1530, that is transmitted by the clerk of the superior court in a manner showing that the copy was prepared and transmitted by that clerk of the superior court. A seal, signature, or other indicia of the court shall constitute adequate showing. [*Added 2013. Amended 2017.*]

§ 1282. **Finding of presumed death by authorized federal employee.** A written finding of presumed death made by an employee of the United States authorized to make such finding pursuant to the Federal Missing Persons Act (56 Stats. 143, 1092, and P.L. 408, Ch. 371, 2d Sess. 78th Cong.; 50 U.S.C. App. 1001-1016), as enacted or as heretofore or hereafter amended, shall be received in any court, office, or other place in this state as evidence of the death of the person therein found to be dead and of the date, circumstances, and place of his disappearance.

§ 1283. **Record by federal employee that person is missing, captured, or the like.** An official written report or record that a person is missing, missing in action, interned in a foreign country, captured by a hostile force, beleaguered by a hostile force, besieged by a hostile force, or detained in a foreign country against his will, or is dead or is alive, made by an employee of the United States authorized by any law of the United States to make such report or record shall be received in any court, office, or other place in this state as evidence that such person is missing, missing in action, interned in a foreign country, captured by a hostile force, beleaguered by a hostile force, besieged by a hostile force, or detained in a foreign country against his will, or is dead or is alive.

(8) ***Public Records.*** A record or statement of a public office if:

(A) it sets out;

(i) the office's activities;

(ii) a matter observed while under a legal duty to report, but not including, in a criminal case, a matter observed by law-enforcement personnel; or

(iii) in a civil case or against the government in a criminal case, factual findings from a legally authorized investigation; and

(B) the opponent does not show that the source of information or other circumstances indicate a lack of trustworthiness. [*Amended 2014.*]

Compare FRE 803(8) and CEC §§ 1280, 452.5: For *public records*: *[1]* FRE does not allow public records by law enforcement personnel to be offered against the accused in a criminal case. There is no such limitation under CEC § 1280; the accused would have to raise an objection on 6th Amendment confrontation grounds. *[2]* FRE expands the admissibility of public records containing opinions when offered against the government in criminal cases and in civil cases, *see Beech Aircraft Corp. v. Rainey*, 488 U.S. 153 (1988); CEC § 1280 limits admissibility of opinions in public records to acts, conditions, or events. As with CEC § 1271, *supra*, the more thought required behind an opinion, the *greater* the need for cross-examination, and hence the less likelihood the opinion will avoid the hearsay ban. *[3]* CEC places the burden on the proponent to show the record's trustworthiness. FRE places the burden on the opponent to show lack of trustworthiness; the 2014 amendment clarifies this allocation. *[4]* CEC § 1280 requires the record to have been made at or near the time of the event recorded; FRE by its terms does not, but the Advisory Committee Notes to FRE include the timeliness of the investigation in the factors a court should consider when determining whether such a record is trustworthy. *[5]* CEC § 452.5 specifically allows admissibility of *criminal conviction records* under § 1280. Under FRE, admissibility of the actual criminal judgment is governed by FRE 803(22), *infra*. And, although FRE 803(8) is silent on the point, some courts have read "public records" to include other parts of criminal conviction records. *See, e.g., United States v. Weiland*, 420 F.3d 1062, 1074 (9th Cir. 2005).

[*FRE have no counterpart to CEC §§ 1282-1283.*]

§ 1281. **Record of vital statistic.** Evidence of a writing made as a record of a birth, fetal death, death, or marriage is not made inadmissible by the hearsay rule if the maker was required by law to file the writing in a designated public office and the writing was made and filed as required by law.

§ 1284. **Statement of absence of public record.** Evidence of a writing made by the public employee who is the official custodian of the records in a public office, reciting diligent search and failure to find a record, is not made inadmissible by the hearsay rule when offered to prove the absence of a record in that office.

Compare FRE 803(10) and CEC § 1284: For *absence of a public record*, FRE allows testimony or certification to prove that "a matter did not occur or exist, if a public office regularly kept a record or statement for a matter of that kind." CEC allows such evidence only to prove the absence of a record. A 2013 amendment to FRE adds the requirement of "notice-and-demand" in criminal cases where the prosecution intends to rely on use of a certification; CEC has no such provision.

§ 1315. **Church records concerning family history.** Evidence of a statement concerning a person's birth, marriage, divorce, death, parent and child relationship, race, ancestry, relationship by blood or marriage, or other similar fact of family history which is contained in a writing made as a record of a church, religious denomination, or religious society is not made inadmissible by the hearsay rule if:

(a) The statement is contained in a writing made as a record of an act, condition, or event that would be admissible as evidence of such act, condition, or event under Section 1271; and

(b) The statement is of a kind customarily recorded in connection with the act, condition, or event recorded in the writing. [*Amended 1975.*]

§ 1316. **Marriage, baptismal and similar certificates.** Evidence of a statement concerning a person's birth, marriage, divorce, death, parent and child relationship, race, ancestry, relationship by blood or marriage, or other similar fact of family history is not made inadmissible by the hearsay rule if the statement is contained in a certificate that the maker thereof performed a marriage or other ceremony or administered a sacrament and:

(a) The maker was a clergyman, civil officer, or other person authorized to perform the acts reported in the certificate by law or by the rules, regulations, or requirements of a church, religious denomination, or religious society; and

(b) The certificate was issued by the maker at the time and place of the ceremony or sacrament or within a reasonable time thereafter. [*Amended 1975.*]

(9) ***Public Records of Vital Statistics.*** A record of a birth, death, or marriage, if reported to a public office in accordance with a legal duty.

(10) ***Absence of a Public Record.*** Testimony — or a certification under Rule 902 — that a diligent search failed to disclose a public record or statement if:

(A) the testimony or certification is admitted to prove that

(i) the record or statement does not exist; or

(ii) a matter did not occur or exist, if a public office regularly kept a record or statement for a matter of that kind; and

(B) in a criminal case, a prosecutor who intends to offer a certification provides written notice of that intent at least 14 days before trial, and the defendant does not object in writing within 7 days of receiving the notice — unless the court sets a different time for the notice or the objection.

(11) ***Records of Religious Organizations Concerning Personal or Family History.*** A statement of birth, legitimacy, ancestry, marriage, divorce, death, relationship by blood or marriage, or similar facts of personal or family history, contained in a regularly kept record of a religious organization.

> *Compare FRE 803(11) and CEC § 1315*: CEC requires *church records* regarding family or personal history to meet the admissibility standards for business records under CEC § 1271, and the statement therein that a party seeks to admit to be "of a kind customarily recorded in connection with the act, condition, or event recorded in the writing." FRE requires only that such evidence be "contained in a regularly kept record of a religious organization."

(12) ***Certificates of Marriage, Baptism, and Similar Ceremonies.*** A statement of fact contained in a certificate:

(A) made by a person who is authorized by a religious organization or by law to perform the act certified;

(B) attesting that the person performed a marriage or similar ceremony or administered a sacrament; and

(C) purporting to have been issued at the time of the act or within a reasonable time after it.

§ **1312. Entries in family records and the like.** Evidence of entries in family Bibles or other family books or charts, engravings on rings, family portraits, engravings on urns, crypts, or tombstones, and the like, is not made inadmissible by the hearsay rule when offered to prove the birth, marriage, divorce, death, parent and child relationship, race, ancestry, relationship by blood or marriage, or other similar fact of the family history of a member of the family by blood or marriage. [*Amended 1975.*]

[*CEC has no counterpart to FRE 803(14); but see CEC § 1600, which establishes conditions under which the record of a document affecting a property interest is prima facie evidence of the existence, contents, execution, and delivery of the original recorded document.*]

§ **1330. Recitals in writings affecting property.** Evidence of a statement contained in a deed of conveyance or a will or other writing purporting to affect an interest in real or personal property is not made inadmissible by the hearsay rule if:

(a) The matter stated was relevant to the purpose of the writing;

(b) The matter stated would be relevant to an issue as to an interest in the property; and

(c) The dealings with the property since the statement was made have not been inconsistent with the truth of the statement.

§ **1331. Recitals in ancient writings.** Evidence of a statement is not made inadmissible by the hearsay rule if the statement is contained in a writing more than 30 years old and the statement has been since generally acted upon as true by persons having an interest in the matter.

(13) ***Family Records.*** A statement of fact about personal or family history contained in a family record, such as a Bible, genealogy, chart, engraving on a ring, inscription on a portrait, or engraving on an urn or burial marker.

> *Compare FRE 803(13) and CEC § 1312*: CEC includes a non-exhaustive list of the types of *family facts* that may be proved under the exception; FRE does not.

(14) ***Records of Documents That Affect an Interest in Property.*** The record of a document that purports to establish or affect an interest in property if:

(A) the record is admitted to prove the content of the original recorded document, along with its signing and its delivery by each person who purports to have signed it;

(B) the record is kept in a public office; and

(C) a statute authorizes recording documents of that kind in that office.

(15) ***Statements in Documents That Affect an Interest in Property.*** A statement contained in a document that purports to establish or affect an interest in property if the matter stated was relevant to the document's purpose — unless later dealings with the property are inconsistent with the truth of the statement or the purport of the document.

> *Compare FRE 803(15) and CEC § 1330*: For *documents that affect an interest in property,* CEC places the burden on the proponent to establish that subsequent dealings with the property have not been inconsistent with the truth of the statement sought to be admitted. FRE places the burden on the opponent to show inconsistent later dealings.

(16) ***Statements in Ancient Documents.*** A statement in a document that was prepared before January 1, 1998 and whose authenticity is established. [*Amended 2016.*]

> *Compare FRE 803(16) and CEC § 1331*: CEC requires an *"ancient document"* to be more than 30 years old and the statement in it sought to be admitted to have "been since generally acted upon as true by persons having an interest in the matter." FRE requires only that the document be at least 20 years old and that the document's authenticity has been established.

§ **1340. Commercial lists and the like.** Evidence of a statement, other than an opinion, contained in a tabulation, list, directory, register, or other published compilation is not made inadmissible by the hearsay rule if the compilation is generally used and relied upon as accurate in the course of a business as defined in Section 1270.

§ **1341. Publications concerning facts of general notoriety and interest.** Historical works, books of science or art, and published maps or charts, made by persons indifferent between the parties, are not made inadmissible by the hearsay rule when offered to prove facts of general notoriety and interest.

[*See also § 721(b), infra at p. III-42, which regulates the use of learned treatises and similar publications in cross-examination of experts. While this section of the Code does not create an exception further to § 1341 for such publications, it nevertheless may be useful to the practitioner in elucidating uses other than as a hearsay exception.*]

(17) ***Market Reports and Similar Commercial Publications.*** Market quotations, lists, directories, or other compilations that are generally relied on by the public or by persons in particular occupations.

Compare FRE 803(17) and CEC § 1340: For *market reports* and similar documents: ***[1]*** CEC expressly excludes opinions; FRE does not. ***[2]*** FRE expressly includes market quotations; CEC does not. ***[3]*** While reliance "by the public" is not expressly stated by CEC, California courts have construed reliance by a business to include reliance by the public, bringing the definition in line with FRE. *See In re Michael G.*, 19 Cal. App. 4th 1674, 1678 (1993). ***[4]*** FRE's requirement of reliance by persons "in particular occupations" appears to be equivalent to CEC's "reliance in the course of a business."

(18) ***Statements in Learned Treatises, Periodicals, or Pamphlets.*** A statement contained in a treatise, periodical, or pamphlet if:

(A) the statement is called to the attention of an expert witness on cross-examination or relied on by the expert on direct examination; and

(B) the publication is established as a reliable authority by the expert's admission or testimony, by another expert's testimony, or by judicial notice.

If admitted, the statement may be read into evidence but not received as an exhibit.

Compare FRE 803(18) and CEC § 1341: Regarding *learned treatises* and similar publications: ***[1]*** CEC limits admissibility to statements "made by persons who are indifferent between the parties ... offered to prove facts of general notoriety and interest." FRE allows statements from treatises where the expert relies on the treatise on direct examination or the expert is cross-examined regarding it, and where the treatise is established as reliable authority by either expert testimony or judicial notice. ***[2]*** FRE allows the treatise to be read into evidence only, but not received as an exhibit; CEC § 1341 contains no such restriction, though related § 721(b) does.

§ 1313. **Reputation in family concerning family history.** Evidence of reputation among members of a family is not made inadmissible by the hearsay rule if the reputation concerns the birth, marriage, divorce, death, parent and child relationship, race, ancestry, relationship by blood or marriage, or other similar fact of the family history of a member of the family by blood or marriage.

§ 1314. **Reputation in community concerning family history.** Evidence of reputation in a community concerning the date or fact of birth, marriage, divorce, or death of a person resident in the community at the time of the reputation is not made inadmissible by the hearsay rule.

(19) ***Reputation Concerning Personal or Family History.*** A reputation among a person's family by blood, adoption, or marriage — or among a person's associates or in the community — concerning the person's birth, adoption, legitimacy, ancestry, marriage, divorce, death, relationship by blood, adoption, or marriage, or similar facts of personal or family history.

Compare FRE 803(19) and CEC §§ 1313, 1314: ***[1]*** FRE contains one exception for *reputation among family members, associates, or community* regarding a person's "birth, adoption, marriage, divorce, death, legitimacy, relationship by blood, adoption, or marriage, ancestry, or other similar fact of personal or family history." CEC has two exceptions: ***[a]*** § 1313 permits reputation among *family members* concerning birth, marriage, divorce, death, parent and child relationship, race, ancestry, relationship by blood or marriage, or other similar fact of the family history of a member of a family by blood or marriage; ***[b]*** § 1314 concerns reputation within *a community* as to birth, marriage, divorce, or death only. ***[2]*** CEC makes no provision for reputation among associates.

§ **1320. Reputation concerning community history.** Evidence of reputation in a community is not made inadmissible by the hearsay rule if the reputation concerns an event of general history of the community or of the state or nation of which the community is a part and the event was of importance to the community.

§ **1322. Reputation concerning boundary or custom affecting land.** Evidence of reputation in a community is not made inadmissible by the hearsay rule if the reputation concerns boundaries of, or customs affecting, land in the community and the reputation arose before controversy.

§ **1321. Reputation concerning public interest in property.** Evidence of reputation in a community is not made inadmissible by the hearsay rule if the reputation concerns the interest of the public in property in the community and the reputation arose before controversy.

§ **1323. Statement concerning boundary.** Evidence of a statement concerning the boundary of land is not made inadmissible by the hearsay rule if the declarant is unavailable as a witness and had sufficient knowledge of the subject, but evidence of a statement is not admissible under this section if the statement was made under circumstances such as to indicate its lack of trustworthiness.

§ **1324. Reputation concerning character.** Evidence of a person's general reputation with reference to his character or a trait of his character at a relevant time in the community in which he then resided or in a group with which he then habitually associated is not made inadmissible by the hearsay rule.

§ **1300. Judgment of conviction of crime punishable as felony.** Evidence of a final judgment adjudging a person guilty of a crime punishable as a felony is not made inadmissible by the hearsay rule when offered in a civil action to prove any fact essential to the judgment whether or not the judgment was based on a plea of nolo contendere. [*Amended 1982.*]

Compare FRE 803(22) and CEC §§ 1300: ***[1]*** FRE allows evidence of a *judgment of conviction* in both criminal and civil proceedings. However, to avoid Confrontation Clause issues, FRE excludes evidence of a third party's conviction offered against the accused in a criminal case. ***[2]*** CEC applies only to civil proceedings. ***[3]*** CEC allows evidence of felony judgments based on a plea of nolo contendere; FRE does not.

(20) ***Reputation Concerning Boundaries or General History.*** A reputation in a community — arising before the controversy — concerning boundaries of land in the community or customs that affect the land, or concerning general historical events important to that community, state, or nation.

Compare FRE 803(20) and CEC §§ 1320, 1322: As interpreted by the courts, there is no substantive difference between FRE and CEC.

[*FRE have no counterpart to CEC § 1321.*]

[*FRE have no counterpart to CEC § 1323.*]

(21) ***Reputation Concerning Character.*** A reputation among a person's associates or in the community concerning the person's character.

Compare FRE 803(21) and CEC § 1324: CEC emphasizes that "associates" are those with whom one *habitually* associates. FRE does not so qualify the term. Otherwise, the difference in wording between FRE and CEC is immaterial.

(22) ***Judgment of a Previous Conviction.*** Evidence of a final judgment of conviction if:

(A) the judgment was entered after a trial or guilty plea, but not a nolo contendere plea;

(B) the conviction was for a crime punishable by death or by imprisonment for more than a year;

(C) the evidence is admitted to prove any fact essential to the judgment; and

(D) when offered by the prosecutor in a criminal case for a purpose other than impeachment, the judgment was against the defendant.

The pendency of an appeal may be shown but does not affect admissibility.

§ **1301. Judgment against person entitled to indemnity.** Evidence of a final judgment is not made inadmissible by the hearsay rule when offered by the judgment debtor to prove any fact which was essential to the judgment in an action in which he seeks to:

(a) Recover partial or total indemnity or exoneration for money paid or liability incurred because of the judgment;

(b) Enforce a warranty to protect the judgment debtor against the liability determined by the judgment; or

(c) Recover damages for breach of warranty substantially the same as the warranty determined by the judgment to have been breached.

§ **1302. Judgment determining liability of third person.** When the liability, obligation, or duty of a third person is in issue in a civil action, evidence of a final judgment against that person is not made inadmissible by the hearsay rule when offered to prove such liability, obligation, or duty.

[*CEC has no counterpart to FRE 803(23).*]

[*FRE have no counterpart to CEC § 1301.*]

[*FRE have no counterpart to CEC § 1302.*]

(23) ***Judgments Involving Personal, Family, or General History or a Boundary.*** A judgment that is admitted to prove a matter of personal, family, or general history, or boundaries, if the matter:

(A) was essential to the judgment; and

(B) could be proved by evidence of reputation.

(24) **[Other exceptions.]** [Transferred to Rule 807.]

§ **240. "Unavailable as a witness."** (a) Except as otherwise provided in subdivision (b), "unavailable as a witness' means that the declarant is any of the following:

(1) Exempted or precluded on the ground of privilege from testifying concerning the matter to which his or her statement is relevant.

(2) Disqualified from testifying to the matter.

(3) Dead or unable to attend or to testify at the hearing because of then-existing physical or mental illness or infirmity.

(4) Absent from the hearing and the court is unable to compel his or her attendance by its process.

(5) Absent from the hearing and the proponent of his or her statement has exercised reasonable diligence but has been unable to procure his or her attendance by the court's process.

(6) Persistent in refusing to testify concerning the subject matter of the declarant's statement despite having been found in contempt for refusal to testify.

(b) A declarant is not unavailable as a witness if the exemption, preclusion, disqualification, death, inability, or absence of the declarant was brought about by the procurement or wrongdoing of the proponent of his or her statement for the purpose of preventing the declarant from attending or testifying.

(c) Expert testimony which establishes that physical or mental trauma resulting from an alleged crime has caused harm to a witness of sufficient severity that the witness is physically unable to testify or is unable to testify without suffering substantial trauma may constitute a sufficient showing of unavailability pursuant to paragraph (3) of subdivision (a). As used in this section, the term "expert" means a physician and surgeon, including a psychiatrist, or any person described by subdivision (b), (c), or (e) of Section 1010. [*Subdivision (c) added 1988.*]

The introduction of evidence to establish the unavailability of a witness under this subdivision shall not be deemed procurement of unavailability, in absence of proof to the contrary. [*Amended 2010.*]

Rule 804. Exceptions to the Rule Against Hearsay — When the Declarant Is Unavailable as a Witness

(a) **Criteria for Being Unavailable.** A declarant is considered to be unavailable as a witness if the declarant:

(1) is exempted from testifying about the subject matter of the declarant's statement because the court rules that a privilege applies;

(2) refuses to testify about the subject matter despite a court order to do so;

(3) testifies to not remembering the subject matter;

(4) cannot be present or testify at the trial or hearing because of death or a then-existing infirmity, physical illness, or mental illness; or

(5) is absent from the trial or hearing and the statement's proponent has not been able, by process or other reasonable means, to procure:

(A) the declarant's attendance, in the case of a hearsay exception under Rule 804(b)(1) or (5); or

(B) the declarant's attendance or testimony, in the case of a hearsay exception under Rule 804(b)(2), (3), or (4).

But this subdivision (a) does not apply if the statement's proponent procured or wrongfully caused the declarant's unavailability as a witness in order to prevent the declarant from attending or testifying.

Compare FRE 804(a) and CEC § 240: In defining *"unavailability"*: ***[1]*** FRE specifically includes the declarant's *lack of memory*; while CEC does not, the courts have interpreted § 240(a)(3) to include lack of memory that constitutes a "physical or mental illness or infirmity." *People v. Alcala*, 4 Cal. 4th 742, 778-779 (1992). ***[2]*** FRE lists a declarant's *refusal to testify*; CEC does not, but "a witness who is physically available yet refuses to testify, after the court has used all available avenues to coerce such testimony, is unavailable. This is true even though such a witness does not fit neatly into one of the subdivisions of Evidence Code section 240." *People v. Francis*, 200 Cal. App. 3d 579, 587 (1988). ***[3]*** As to declarant's *absence* from the proceedings, FRE 804(a)(5)(B) requires the proponent of the evidence to have attempted to obtain declarant's *attendance or testimony by deposition*, if the hearsay statement is being offered under the exceptions for dying declarations, statements against interest, or statements of personal or family history (FRE 804(b)(2)-(4)); CEC requires only reasonable diligence in attempting to obtain the declarant's *attendance*. ***[4]*** CEC contains a special provision for expert testimony to establish unavailability by reason of physical or mental trauma that is sufficiently severe to cause the declarant to be physically unable to testify or unable to do so "without suffering substantial trauma." FRE does not so specify. Cases and commentators differ on whether FRE 804(a)'s categories are illustrative or exhaustive.

§ **1290. Former testimony.** As used in this article [§§ 1290-1294], "former testimony" means testimony given under oath in:

(a) Another action or in a former hearing or trial of the same action;

(b) A proceeding to determine a controversy conducted by or under the supervision of an agency that has the power to determine such a controversy and is an agency of the United States or a public entity in the United States;

(c) A deposition taken in compliance with law in another action; or

(d) An arbitration proceeding if the evidence of such former testimony is a verbatim transcript thereof.

§ **1291. Former testimony offered against party to former proceeding.** (a) Evidence of former testimony is not made inadmissible by the hearsay rule if the declarant is unavailable as a witness and:

(1) The former testimony is offered against a person who offered it in evidence in his own behalf on the former occasion or against the successor in interest of such person; or

(2) The party against whom the former testimony is offered was a party to the action or proceeding in which the testimony was given and had the right and opportunity to cross-examine the declarant with an interest and motive similar to that which he has at the hearing.

(b) The admissibility of former testimony under this section is subject to the same limitations and objections as though the declarant were testifying at the hearing, except that former testimony offered under this section is not subject to:

(1) Objections to the form of the question which were not made at the time the former testimony was given.

(2) Objections based on competency or privilege which did not exist at the time the former testimony was given.

§ **1292. Former testimony offered against person not a party to former proceeding.** (a) Evidence of former testimony is not made inadmissible by the hearsay rule if:

(1) The declarant is unavailable as a witness;

(2) The former testimony is offered in a civil action; and

(b) The Exceptions. The following are not excluded by the rule against hearsay if the declarant is unavailable as a witness:

(1) ***Former Testimony.*** Testimony that:

(A) was given as a witness at a trial, hearing, or lawful deposition, whether given during the current proceeding or a different one; and

(B) is now offered against a party who had — or, in a civil case, whose predecessor in interest had — an opportunity and similar motive to develop it by direct, cross-, or redirect examination.

> *Compare FRE 804(b)(1) and CEC §§ 1290-1294*: Concerning *"former testimony"*: *[1]* Under FRE, deposition testimony may qualify as "former testimony" regardless of whether obtained in the same or another action. CEC by its terms allows only deposition testimony taken in another action. The California Civil Procedure Code, rather than CEC, governs admissibility of deposition testimony from the same action. *[2]* CEC dictates treatment of objections, competency, and privilege issues arising from the former testimony; FRE leaves those issues to the Federal Rules of Civil Procedure and the court's discretion under FRE 403 and 611. *[3]* When the former testimony is offered in a civil case against a party not a party to the former proceeding, CEC requires only that a party to the former proceeding have had the right, opportunity, and similar motive to cross-examine the declarant. FRE requires that the party to the former proceeding be a "predecessor in interest" to the current party. However, some federal cases threat the definition of "predecessor in interest" loosely rather than requiring strict privity; *see* Case Note at p. II-135, *infra*. *[4]* Unlike FRE, CEC § 1293 provides a special exception for testimony by a minor complaining witness at a preliminary examination. *[5]* Unlike FRE, CEC § 1294 allows admissibility of a declarant's prior inconsistent statement admitted at a preliminary hearing or trial of the same criminal matter pursuant to CEC § 1235, where the declarant is unavailable and the former testimony has been admitted under CEC § 1291. The prior inconsistent statement previously admitted is permitted only in videotape or transcript form. FRE has no analogous provision. *[6]* Where former testimony is introduced against a party to the former proceeding, CEC § 1291(b)(1) precludes the party from making objections not articulated in the prior proceeding. FRE is silent on this point.

(3) The issue is such that the party to the action or proceeding in which the former testimony was given had the right and opportunity to cross-examine the declarant with an interest and motive similar to that which the party against whom the testimony is offered has at the hearing.

(b) The admissibility of former testimony under this section is subject to the same limitations and objections as though the declarant were testifying at the hearing, except that former testimony offered under this section is not subject to objections based on competency or privilege which did not exist at the time the former testimony was given.

§ 1293. Former testimony by minor child complaining witness at preliminary examination. (a) Evidence of former testimony made at a preliminary examination by a minor child who was the complaining witness is not made inadmissible by the hearsay rule if:

(1) The former testimony is offered in a proceeding to declare the minor a dependent child of the court pursuant to Section 300 of the Welfare and Institutions Code.

(2) The issues are such that a defendant in the preliminary examination in which the former testimony was given had the right and opportunity to cross-examine the minor child with an interest and motive similar to that which the parent or guardian against whom the testimony is offered has at the proceeding to declare the minor a dependent child of the court.

(b) The admissibility of former testimony under this section is subject to the same limitations and objections as though the minor child were testifying at the proceeding to declare him or her a dependent child of the court.

(c) The attorney for the parent or guardian against whom the former testimony is offered or, if none, the parent or guardian may make a motion to challenge the admissibility of the former testimony upon a showing that new substantially different issues are present in the proceeding to declare the minor a dependent child than were present in the preliminary examination.

(d) As used in this section, "complaining witness" means the alleged victim of the crime for which a preliminary examination was held.

(e) This section shall apply only to testimony made at a preliminary examination on and after January 1, 1990. [*Added 1989.*]

§ 1294. Unavailable witnesses; prior inconsistent statements; preliminary hearing or prior proceeding. (a) The following evidence of prior inconsistent statements of a witness properly admitted at a conditional examination, preliminary hearing, or trial of the same criminal matter pursuant to Section 1235 is not made inadmissible by the hearsay rule if the witness is unavailable and former testimony of the witness is admitted pursuant to Section 1291:

[*FRE have no counterpart to CEC § 1293; but see Commentary box on preceding page.*]

[*FRE have no counterpart to CEC § 1294; but see Commentary box on preceding page.*]

(1) A video recorded statement introduced at a preliminary hearing or prior proceeding concerning the same criminal matter.

(2) A transcript, containing the statements, of the preliminary hearing or prior proceeding concerning the same criminal matter.

(b) The party against whom the prior inconsistent statements are offered, at his or her option, may examine or cross-examine any person who testified at the preliminary hearing or prior proceeding as to the prior inconsistent statements of the witness.

(c) As used in this section, "conditional examination" has the same meaning as in Chapter 4 (commencing with Section 1335) of Title 10 of Part 2 of the Penal Code. [*Added 1996. Amended 2006, 2017.*]

§ **1242. Dying declaration.** Evidence of a statement made by a dying person respecting the cause and circumstances of his death is not made inadmissible by the hearsay rule if the statement was made upon his personal knowledge and under a sense of immediately impending death.

§ **1230. Declaration against interest.** Evidence of a statement by a declarant having sufficient knowledge of the subject is not made inadmissible by the hearsay rule if the declarant is unavailable as a witness and the statement, when made, was so far contrary to the declarant's pecuniary or proprietary interest, or so far subjected him to the risk of civil or criminal liability, or so far tended to render invalid a claim by him against another, or created such a risk of making him an object of hatred, ridicule, or social disgrace in the community, that a reasonable man in his position would not have made the statement unless he believed it to be true.

> *Compare FRE 804(b)(3) and CEC § 1230*: Concerning *statements against interest*: ***[1]*** Unlike FRE, CEC includes declarations against social interest, *e.g.*, the declarant's interest in a good reputation. ***[2]*** Under FRE, a statement that tends to expose a declarant to criminal liability is not admissible in a criminal case unless corroborating circumstances clearly demonstrate its trustworthiness; CEC contains no such restriction. ***[3]*** The California Supreme Court has construed CEC to include only statements against the interest of the declarant, and not those portions of the statement that are against the interest of others. *See People v. Leach*, 15 Cal. 3d 419 (1975). The U.S. Supreme Court has construed FRE 804(b)(3) similarly, on Confrontation Clause grounds. *See Williamson v. United States*, 512 U.S. 594 (1994).

(2) ***Statement Under the Belief of Imminent Death.*** In a prosecution for homicide or in a civil case, a statement that the declarant, while believing the declarant's death to be imminent, made about its cause or circumstances.

Compare FRE 804(b)(2) and CEC § 1242: Concerning *dying declarations*: ***[1]*** CEC allows admissibility in civil or criminal proceedings; FRE allows admissibility in civil proceedings but limits admissibility in criminal cases to homicide prosecutions. ***[2]*** FRE requires the proponent of a "dying declaration" to demonstrate the declarant's unavailability; CEC does not. ***[3]*** *See also* discussion of FRE 807, *infra*, citing CEC § 1231's special provision for dying declarations in gang-related cases.

(3) ***Statement Against Interest.*** A statement that:

(A) a reasonable person in the declarant's position would have made only if the person believed it to be true because, when made, it was so contrary to the declarant's proprietary or pecuniary interest or had so great a tendency to invalidate the declarant's claim against someone else or to expose the declarant to civil or criminal liability; and

(B) is supported by corroborating circumstances that clearly indicate its trustworthiness, if it is offered in a criminal case as one that tends to expose the declarant to criminal liability.

§ **1310. Statement concerning declarant's own family history.** (a) Subject to subdivision (b), evidence of a statement by a declarant who is unavailable as a witness concerning his own birth, marriage, divorce, a parent and child relationship, relationship by blood or marriage, race, ancestry, or other similar fact of his family history is not made inadmissible by the hearsay rule, even though the declarant had no means of acquiring personal knowledge of the matter declared.

(b) Evidence of a statement is inadmissible under this section if the statement was made under circumstances such as to indicate its lack of trustworthiness. [*Amended 1975.*]

§ **1311. Statement concerning family history of another.** (a) Subject to subdivision (b), evidence of a statement concerning the birth, marriage, divorce, death, parent and child relationship, race, ancestry, relationship by blood or marriage, or other similar fact of the family history of a person other than the declarant is not made inadmissible by the hearsay rule if the declarant is unavailable as a witness and:

(1) The declarant was related to the other by blood or marriage; or

(2) The declarant was otherwise so intimately associated with the other's family as to be likely to have had accurate information concerning the matter declared and made the statement (i) upon information received from the other or from a person related by blood or marriage to the other or (ii) upon repute in the other's family.

(b) Evidence of a statement is inadmissible under this section if the statement was made under circumstances such as to indicate its lack of trustworthiness. [*Amended 1975.*]

§ **1350. Unavailable declarant; hearsay rule.** (a) In a criminal proceeding charging a serious felony, evidence of a statement made by a declarant is not made inadmissible by the hearsay rule if the declarant is unavailable as a witness, and all of the following are true:

(1) There is clear and convincing evidence that the declarant's unavailability was knowingly caused by, aided by, or solicited by the party against whom the statement is offered for the purpose of preventing the arrest or prosecution of the party and is the result of the death by homicide or the kidnapping of the declarant.

(2) There is no evidence that the unavailability of the declarant was caused by, aided by, solicited by, or procured on behalf of, the party who is offering the statement.

(3) The statement has been memorialized in a tape recording made by a law enforcement official, or in a written statement prepared by a law enforcement official and signed by the declarant and notarized in the presence of the law enforcement official, prior to the death or kidnapping of the declarant.

(4) ***Statement of Personal or Family History.*** A statement about:

(A) the declarant's own birth, adoption, legitimacy, ancestry, marriage, divorce, relationship by blood, adoption, or marriage, or similar facts of personal or family history, even though the declarant had no way of acquiring personal knowledge about that fact; or

(B) another person concerning any of these facts, as well as death, if the declarant was related to the person by blood, adoption, or marriage or was so intimately associated with the person's family that the declarant's information is likely to be accurate.

> *Compare FRE 804(b)(4) and CEC § 1310-1311*: Concerning *statements of personal or family history*: ***[1]*** Unlike FRE, CEC expressly gives the court discretion to exclude such a statement if made under circumstances indicating a lack of trustworthiness. ***[2]*** As to family history of another to whom declarant is not related, FRE requires only likelihood of accuracy through intimate association; CEC requires that the declarant made the statement upon information from the other, from a person related to the other, or "upon repute in the other's family." ***[3]*** FRE specifically includes statements concerning legitimacy and relationship by adoption; CEC does not so specify, but does allow "other similar fact[s] of ... family history." ***[4]*** FRE specifically includes relationship by adoption as a foundation for a statement about another's family history; CEC does not, but likely would allow such under the language "otherwise so intimately associated with the other's family ...."

(5) **[Other exceptions.]** [Transferred to Rule 807.]

(6) ***Statement Offered Against a Party That Wrongfully Caused the Declarant's Unavailability.*** A statement offered against a party that wrongfully caused — or acquiesced in wrongfully causing — the declarant's unavailability as a witness, and did so intending that result.

> *Compare FRE 804(b)(6) and CEC § 1350, 1390*: Concerning the exception for *statements offered against a party that wrongfully caused a declarant's unavailability*, the addition of CEC § 1390 in 2010, which applies to proceedings pending as of January 1, 2011, brings CEC and FRE into harmony. However, prior matters under CEC are governed by the more restrictive provisions of § 1350. CEC specifies hearing procedures for determining admissibility; FRE presumably leaves the procedure to the court's discretion under FRE 611 and authority under FRE 104(a).

(4) The statement was made under circumstances which indicate its trustworthiness and was not the result of promise, inducement, threat, or coercion.

(5) The statement is relevant to the issues to be tried.

(6) The statement is corroborated by other evidence which tends to connect the party against whom the statement is offered with the commission of the serious felony with which the party is charged. The corroboration is not sufficient if it merely shows the commission of the offense or the circumstances thereof.

(b) If the prosecution intends to offer a statement pursuant to this section, the prosecution shall serve a written notice upon the defendant at least 10 days prior to the hearing or trial at which the prosecution intends to offer the statement, unless the prosecution shows good cause for the failure to provide that notice. In the event that good cause is shown, the defendant shall be entitled to a reasonable continuance of the hearing or trial.

(c) If the statement is offered during trial, the court's determination shall be made out of the presence of the jury. If the defendant elects to testify at the hearing on a motion brought pursuant to this section, the court shall exclude from the examination every person except the clerk, the court reporter, the bailiff, the prosecutor, the investigating officer, the defendant and his or her counsel, an investigator for the defendant, and the officer having custody of the defendant. Notwithstanding any other provision of law, the defendant's testimony at the hearing shall not be admissible in any other proceeding except the hearing brought on the motion pursuant to this section. If a transcript is made of the defendant's testimony, it shall be sealed and transmitted to the clerk of the court in which the action is pending.

(d) As used in this section, "serious felony" means any of the felonies listed in subdivision (c) of Section 1192.7 of the Penal Code or any violation of Section 11351, 11352, 11378, or 11379 of the Health and Safety Code.

(e) If a statement to be admitted pursuant to this section includes hearsay statements made by anyone other than the declarant who is unavailable pursuant to subdivision (a), those hearsay statements are inadmissible unless they meet the requirements of an exception to the hearsay rule. [*Added 1985, 2001.*]

§ 1390. Statements against parties involved in causing unavailability of declarant witness.

(a) Evidence of a statement is not made inadmissible by the hearsay rule if the statement is offered against a party that has engaged, or aided and abetted, in the wrongdoing that was intended to, and did, procure the unavailability of the declarant as a witness.

(b) (1) The party seeking to introduce a statement pursuant to subdivision (a) shall establish, by a preponderance of the evidence, that the elements of subdivision (a) have been met at a foundational hearing.

[FRE have no counterpart to CEC § 1390.]

(2) The hearsay evidence that is the subject of the foundational hearing is admissible at the foundational hearing. However, a finding that the elements of subdivision (a) have been met shall not be based solely on the unconfronted hearsay statement of the unavailable declarant, and shall be supported by independent corroborative evidence.

(3) The foundational hearing shall be conducted outside the presence of the jury. However, if the hearing is conducted after a jury trial has begun, the judge presiding at the hearing may consider evidence already presented to the jury in deciding whether the elements of subdivision (a) have been met.

(4) In deciding whether or not to admit the statement, the judge may take into account whether it is trustworthy and reliable.

(c) This section shall apply to any civil, criminal, or juvenile case or proceeding initiated or pending as of January 1, 2011.

[*Added 2010. Amended 2015, 2016.*]

§ **1201. Multiple hearsay.** A statement within the scope of an exception to the hearsay rule is not inadmissible on the ground that the evidence of such statement is hearsay evidence if such hearsay evidence consists of one or more statements each of which meets the requirements of an exception to the hearsay rule. [*Amended 1967.*]

§ **1202. Credibility of hearsay declarant.** Evidence of a statement or other conduct by a declarant that is inconsistent with a statement by such declarant received in evidence as hearsay evidence is not inadmissible for the purpose of attacking the credibility of the declarant though he is not given and has not had an opportunity to explain or to deny such inconsistent statement or other conduct. Any other evidence offered to attack or support the credibility of the declarant is admissible if it would have been admissible had the declarant been a witness at the hearing. For the purposes of this section, the deponent of a deposition taken in the action in which it is offered shall be deemed to be a hearsay declarant.

§ **1203. Cross-examination of hearsay declarant.** (a) The declarant of a statement that is admitted as hearsay evidence may be called and examined by any adverse party as if under cross-examination concerning the statement.

(b) This section is not applicable if the declarant is (1) a party, (2) a person identified with a party within the meaning of subdivision (d) of Section 776, or (3) a witness who has testified in the action concerning the subject matter of the statement.

Rule 805. Hearsay Within Hearsay

Hearsay within hearsay is not excluded by the rule against hearsay if each part of the combined statements conforms with an exception to the rule.

Rule 806. Attacking and Supporting the Declarant's Credibility

When a hearsay statement — or a statement described in Rule 801(d)(2)(C), (D), or (E) — has been admitted in evidence, the declarant's credibility may be attacked, and then supported, by any evidence that would be admissible for those purposes if the declarant had testified as a witness. The court may admit evidence of the declarant's inconsistent statement or conduct, regardless of when it occurred or whether the declarant had an opportunity to explain or deny it. If the party against whom the statement was admitted calls the declarant as a witness, the party may examine the declarant on the statement as if on cross-examination.

Compare FRE 806 and CEC §§ 1202-1203: Although structured differently, FRE and CEC have the same general effect: to allow attacks on the credibility of a hearsay declarant and, after such an attack, support of the declarant as if the declarant were on the witness stand.
[*continued on page I-191*]

(c) This section is not applicable if the statement is one described in Article 1 (commencing with Section 1220), Article 3 (commencing with Section 1235), or Article 10 (commencing with Section 1300) of Chapter 2 of this division.

(d) A statement that is otherwise admissible as hearsay evidence is not made inadmissible by this section because the declarant who made the statement is unavailable for examination pursuant to this section.

§ 1203.1. Hearsay offered at preliminary examination; application of § 1203. Section 1203 is not applicable if the hearsay statement is offered at a preliminary examination, as provided in Section 872 of the Penal Code. [*Added by Initiative (Prop. 115), 1990.*]

§ 1228. Admissibility of certain out-of-court statements of minors under the age of 12; establishing elements of certain sexually oriented crimes; notice to defendant. Notwithstanding any other provision of law, for the purpose of establishing the elements of the crime in order to admit as evidence the confession of a person accused of violating Section 261, 264.1, 285, 286, 287, 288, 289, or 647a of, or former Section 288a of, the Penal Code, a court, in its discretion, may determine that a statement of the complaining witness is not made inadmissible by the hearsay rule if it finds all of the following:

(a) The statement was made by a minor child under the age of 12, and the contents of the statement were included in a written report of a law enforcement official or an employee of a county welfare department.

[*continued from page I-189*]

[1] FRE specifically excludes impeachment of an opposing party when that party's own statements or adoptive admissions are admitted under FRE 801(d)(2)(A) or (B). CEC § 1202 does not contain this specific limitation. *[2]* FRE allows any declarant whose statement has been admitted under FRE 806 to be called as a witness and cross-examined by the opposing party. CEC § 1203 places limits on this aspect of the rule: it bars an adverse party from calling as a witness and cross-examining a declarant *[a]* where the declarant is a party, a person identified with a party (as defined in CEC § 776), or has testified concerning the subject matter of the admitted statement, or *[b]* where the hearsay statement is an authorized statement, a statement of a co-conspirator, one of the CEC analogues to agent-employee statements (*see* comparison of FRE 801(d)(2)(D) and CEC §§ 1224-1227, *supra*), a declaration against interest, an inconsistent statement, a prior consistent statement, a past recollection recorded, a statement of identification, or a judgment of conviction. CEC § 1203 also provides that a declarant's unavailability for cross-examination under this section does not make inadmissible an otherwise admissible hearsay statement. *[3]* Both FRE and CEC bar the use of a declarant's inconsistent statement for the truth when the statement is admitted under FRE 806 and CEC § 1202. CEC is explicit on this point; the Law Revision Commission Comment to CEC § 1202 states:

> "Section 1235 provides that evidence of inconsistent statements made by a trial witness may be admitted to prove the truth of the matter stated. No similar exception to the hearsay rule is applicable to a hearsay declarant's inconsistent statements that are admitted under Section 1202. Hence, the hearsay rule prohibits any such statement to prove the truth of the matter stated...."

FRE makes this point only implicitly, in that FRE 806 addresses only methods of impeachment and support of a declarant under the rule, which do not encompass a prior inconsistent statement admitted as substantive proof under FRE 801(d)(1)(A).

[*FRE have no counterpart to CEC § 1203.1.*]

Rule 807. Residual Exception

(a) In General. Under the following conditions, a hearsay statement is not excluded by the rule against hearsay even if the statement is not admissible under a hearsay exception in Rule 803 or 804:

(1) the statement is supported by sufficient guarantees of trustworthiness—after considering the totality of circumstances under which it was made and evidence, if any, corroborating the statement; and

(2) it is more probative on the point for which it is offered than any other evidence that the proponent can obtain through reasonable efforts.

(b) The statement describes the minor child as a victim of sexual abuse.

(c) The statement was made prior to the defendant's confession. The court shall view with caution the testimony of a person recounting hearsay where there is evidence of personal bias or prejudice.

(d) There are no circumstances, such as significant inconsistencies between the confession and the statement concerning material facts establishing any element of the crime or the identification of the defendant, that would render the statement unreliable.

(e) The minor child is found to be unavailable pursuant to paragraph (2) or (3) of subdivision (a) of Section 240 or refuses to testify.

(f) The confession was memorialized in a trustworthy fashion by a law enforcement official.

If the prosecution intends to offer a statement of the complaining witness pursuant to this section, the prosecution shall serve a written notice upon the defendant at least 10 days prior to the hearing or trial at which the prosecution intends to offer the statement.

If the statement is offered during trial, the court's determination shall be made out of the presence of the jury. If the statement is found to be admissible pursuant to this section, it shall be admitted out of the presence of the jury and solely for the purpose of determining the admissibility of the confession of the defendant. [*Added 1984. Amended 1985, 2018.*]

§ 1231. Prior statements of deceased declarant; hearsay exception. Evidence of a prior statement made by a declarant is not made inadmissible by the hearsay rule if the declarant is deceased and the proponent of introducing the statement establishes each of the following:

(a) The statement relates to acts or events relevant to a criminal prosecution under provisions of the California Street Terrorism Enforcement and Prevention Act (Chapter 11 (commencing with Section 186.20) of Title 7 of Part 1 of the Penal Code).

(b) A verbatim transcript, copy, or record of the statement exists. A record may include a statement preserved by means of an audio or video recording or equivalent technology.

(c) The statement relates to acts or events within the personal knowledge of the declarant.

(d) The statement was made under oath or affirmation in an affidavit; or was made at a deposition, preliminary hearing, grand jury hearing, or other proceeding in compliance with law, and was made under penalty of perjury.

(e) The declarant died from other than natural causes.

(b) Notice. The statement is admissible only if the proponent gives an adverse party reasonable notice of the intent to offer the statement including the declarant's name so that the party has a fair opportunity to meet it. The notice must be provided in writing before the trial or hearing—or in any form during the trial or hearing if the court, for good cause, excuses a lack of earlier notice. [*Amended effective December 1, 2019.*]

Compare FRE 807 and CEC §§ 1228, 1231, 1360, 1370, and 1380: CEC contains no equivalent to FRE's residual exception. However, CEC contains several hearsay exceptions, cited here, that include discretionary balancing factors similar to FRE 807. Further, California courts are empowered "to create hearsay exceptions for classes of evidence for which there is a substantial need, and which possess an intrinsic reliability that enable them to surmount constitutional and other objections that generally apply to hearsay evidence." *In re Cindy L.*, 17 Cal. 4th 15, 28 (1997). It would appear that hearsay offered under *Cindy L.* must be in a judicially-recognized "class" of reliable hearsay, rather than admissible because of the needs and circumstances of the individual case as under FRE.

[*FRE have no counterpart to CEC § 1231. See Commentary on FRE 807, supra.*]

(f) The statement was made under circumstances that would indicate its trustworthiness and render the declarant's statement particularly worthy of belief. For purposes of this subdivision, circumstances relevant to the issue of trustworthiness include, but are not limited to, all of the following:

(1) Whether the statement was made in contemplation of a pending or anticipated criminal or civil matter, in which the declarant had an interest, other than as a witness.

(2) Whether the declarant had a bias or motive for fabricating the statement, and the extent of any bias or motive.

(3) Whether the statement is corroborated by evidence other than statements that are admissible only pursuant to this section.

(4) Whether the statement was a statement against the declarant's interest. [*Added 1997.*]

§ **1231.1. Statements made by deceased declarant; admissibility; notice of statement to adverse party.** A statement is admissible pursuant to Section 1231 only if the proponent of the statement makes known to the adverse party the intention to offer the statement and the particulars of the statement sufficiently in advance of the proceedings to provide the adverse party with a fair opportunity to prepare to meet the statement. [*Added 1997.*]

§ **1231.2. Administer and certify oaths.** A peace officer may administer and certify oaths for purposes of this article [§§ 1231-1231.4]. [*Added 1997. Amended 1998.*]

§ **1231.3. Testimony of law enforcement officer; hearsay.** Any law enforcement officer testifying as to any hearsay statement pursuant to this article [§§ 1231-1231.4] shall either have five years of law enforcement experience or have completed a training course certified by the Commission on Peace Officer Standards and Training which includes training in the investigation and reporting of cases and testifying at preliminary hearings and trials. [*Added 1997.*]

§ **1231.4. Cause of death; deceased declarant.** If evidence of a prior statement is introduced pursuant to this article [§§ 1231-1231.4], the jury may not be told that the declarant died from other than natural causes, but shall merely be told that the declarant is unavailable. [*Added 1997.*]

§ **1360. Statements describing an act or attempted act of child abuse or neglect; criminal prosecutions; requirements.** (a) In a criminal prosecution where the victim is a minor, a statement made by the victim when under the age of 12 describing any act of child abuse or neglect performed with or on the child by another, or describing any attempted act of child abuse or neglect with or on the child by another, is not made inadmissible by the hearsay rule if all of the following apply:

[*FRE have no counterpart to CEC § 1360. See Commentary on FRE 807, supra.*]

(1) The statement is not otherwise admissible by statute or court rule.

(2) The court finds, in a hearing conducted outside the presence of the jury, that the time, content, and circumstances of the statement provide sufficient indicia of reliability.

(3) The child either:

(A) Testifies at the proceedings.

(B) Is unavailable as a witness, in which case the statement may be admitted only if there is evidence of the child abuse or neglect that corroborates the statement made by the child.

(b) A statement may not be admitted under this section unless the proponent of the statement makes known to the adverse party the intention to offer the statement and the particulars of the statement sufficiently in advance of the proceedings in order to provide the adverse party with a fair opportunity to prepare to meet the statement.

(c) For purposes of this section, "child abuse" means an act proscribed by Section 273a, 273d, or 288.5 of the Penal Code, or any of the acts described in Section 11165.1 of the Penal Code, and "child neglect" means any of the acts described in Section 11165.2 of the Penal Code. [*Added 1995.*]

§ 1370. Threat of infliction of injury. (a) Evidence of a statement by a declarant is not made inadmissible by the hearsay rule if all of the following conditions are met:

(1) The statement purports to narrate, describe, or explain the infliction or threat of physical injury upon the declarant.

(2) The declarant is unavailable as a witness pursuant to Section 240.

(3) The statement was made at or near the time of the infliction or threat of physical injury. Evidence of statements made more than five years before the filing of the current action or proceeding shall be inadmissible under this section.

(4) The statement was made under circumstances that would indicate its trustworthiness.

(5) The statement was made in writing, was electronically recorded, or made to a physician, nurse, paramedic, or to a law enforcement official.

(b) For purposes of paragraph (4) of subdivision (a), circumstances relevant to the issue of trustworthiness include, but are not limited to, the following:

[*FRE have no counterpart to CEC § 1370. See Commentary on FRE 807, supra.*]

(1) Whether the statement was made in contemplation of pending or anticipated litigation in which the declarant was interested.

(2) Whether the declarant has a bias or motive for fabricating the statement, and the extent of any bias or motive.

(3) Whether the statement is corroborated by evidence other than statements that are admissible only pursuant to this section.

(c) A statement is admissible pursuant to this section only if the proponent of the statement makes known to the adverse party the intention to offer the statement and the particulars of the statement sufficiently in advance of the proceedings in order to provide the adverse party with a fair opportunity to prepare to meet the statement. [*Added 1996. Amended 2000.*]

§ **1380. Elder and dependent adults; statements by victims of abuse.** (a) In a criminal proceeding charging a violation, or attempted violation, of Section 368 of the Penal Code, evidence of a statement made by a declarant is not made inadmissible by the hearsay rule if the declarant is unavailable as a witness, as defined in subdivisions (a) and (b) of Section 240, and all of the following are true:

(1) The party offering the statement has made a showing of particularized guarantees of trustworthiness regarding the statement, the statement was made under circumstances which indicate its trustworthiness, and the statement was not the result of promise, inducement, threat, or coercion. In making its determination, the court may consider only the circumstances that surround the making of the statement and that render the declarant particularly worthy of belief.

(2) There is no evidence that the unavailability of the declarant was caused by, aided by, solicited by, or procured on behalf of, the party who is offering the statement.

(3) The entire statement has been memorialized in a videotape recording made by a law enforcement official, prior to the death or disabling of the declarant.

(4) The statement was made by the victim of the alleged violation.

(5) The statement is supported by corroborative evidence.

(6) The victim of the alleged violation is an individual who meets both of the following requirements:

(A) Was 65 years of age or older or was a dependent adult when the alleged violation or attempted violation occurred.

[*FRE have no counterpart to CEC § 1380. See Commentary on FRE 807, supra.*]

(B) At the time of any criminal proceeding, including, but not limited to, a preliminary hearing or trial, regarding the alleged violation or attempted violation, is either deceased or suffers from the infirmities of aging as manifested by advanced age or organic brain damage, or other physical, mental, or emotional dysfunction, to the extent that the ability of the person to provide adequately for the person's own care or protection is impaired.

(b) If the prosecution intends to offer a statement pursuant to this section, the prosecution shall serve a written notice upon the defendant at least 10 days prior to the hearing or trial at which the prosecution intends to offer the statement, unless the prosecution shows good cause for the failure to provide that notice. In the event that good cause is shown, the defendant shall be entitled to a reasonable continuance of the hearing or trial.

(c) If the statement is offered during trial, the court's determination as to the availability of the victim as a witness shall be made out of the presence of the jury. If the defendant elects to testify at the hearing on a motion brought pursuant to this section, the court shall exclude from the examination every person except the clerk, the court reporter, the bailiff, the prosecutor, the investigating officer, the defendant and his or her counsel, an investigator for the defendant, and the officer having custody of the defendant. Notwithstanding any other provision of law, the defendant's testimony at the hearing shall not be admissible in any other proceeding except the hearing brought on the motion pursuant to this section. If a transcript is made of the defendant's testimony, it shall be sealed and transmitted to the clerk of the court in which the action is pending. [*Added 1999.*]

§ **1400. Authentication defined.** Authentication of a writing means (a) the introduction of evidence sufficient to sustain a finding that it is the writing that the proponent of the evidence claims it is or (b) the establishment of such facts by any other means provided by law.

§ **1401. Authentication required.** (a) Authentication of a writing is required before it may be received in evidence.

(b) Authentication of a writing is required before secondary evidence of its content may be received in evidence.

§ **250. "Writing"** means handwriting, typewriting, printing, photostating, photographing, photocopying, transmitting by electronic mail or facsimile, and every other means of recording upon any tangible thing, any form of communication or representation, including letters, words, pictures, sounds, or symbols, or combinations thereof, and any record thereby created, regardless of the manner in which the record has been stored. [*Amended 2002.*]

§ **1410.5. Graffiti constitutes a writing; admissibility.** (a) For purposes of this chapter [§§ 1400-1454], a writing shall include any graffiti consisting of written words, insignia, symbols, or any other markings which convey a particular meaning.

ARTICLE IX. AUTHENTICATION AND IDENTIFICATION

Rule 901. Authenticating or Identifying Evidence

(a) **In General.** To satisfy the requirement of authenticating or identifying an item of evidence, the proponent must produce evidence sufficient to support a finding that the item is what the proponent claims it is.

Compare FRE 901(a) and CEC §§ 1400-1401: CEC's explicit authentication rules apply only to "writings"; FRE refers broadly to "an item of evidence." This difference diminishes in light of CEC §§ 140 and 210, which strongly imply that every tangible thing offered in evidence must be authenticated in order to be relevant. Both CEC and FRE require only "sufficient evidence" that the offered evidence is what its proponent claims it to be.

[FRE have no counterpart to CEC § 250.]

[FRE have no counterpart to CEC § 1410.5.]

(b) Any writing described in subdivision (a), or any photograph thereof, may be admitted into evidence in an action for vandalism, for the purpose of proving that the writing was made by the defendant.

(c) The admissibility of any fact offered to prove that the writing was made by the defendant shall, upon motion of the defendant, be ruled upon outside the presence of the jury, and is subject to the requirements of Sections 1416, 1417, and 1418. [*Added 1989.*]

§ **1402. Authentication of altered writing.** The party producing a writing as genuine which has been altered, or appears to have been altered, after its execution, in a part material to the question in dispute, must account for the alteration or appearance thereof. He may show that the alteration was made by another, without his concurrence, or was made with the consent of the parties affected by it, or otherwise properly or innocently made, or that the alteration did not change the meaning or language of the instrument. If he does that, he may give the writing in evidence, but not otherwise.

§ **1410. Article not exclusive.** Nothing in this article [§§ 1410-1421] shall be construed to limit the means by which a writing may be authenticated or proved.

§ **1413. Witness to the execution of a writing.** A writing may be authenticated by anyone who saw the writing made or executed, including a subscribing witness.

[*FRE have no counterpart to CEC § 1402.*]

(b) Examples. The following are examples only — not a complete list — of evidence that satisfies the requirement:

Compare FRE 901(b) and CEC §§ 643, 1410, 1413-1421, 1552-1553, 1600: Both FRE and CEC give lists of examples of sufficient authentication for particular types of evidence. Neither list excludes other means of authentication. The lists are similar, except: ***[1]*** Unlike FRE, CEC explicitly provides for authentication by evidence of the opponent's admission of genuineness or reliance. ***[2]*** Unlike CEC, FRE restricts non-expert opinion on handwriting to "familiarity not acquired for purposes of the litigation." ***[3]*** Authentication of a document by age and circumstances requires 30 years under CEC, but only 20 years under FRE. CEC also requires the writing to have been treated as authentic by persons with an interest in the matter. ***[4]*** While both CEC and FRE allow authentication by contents and circumstances, only CEC explicitly includes authentication by evidence of reply. ***[5]*** CEC sets forth detailed rules as to printed representations in computers, video, and other digital media; FRE has no such rules, but does allow authentication by evidence about a process or system that produces accurate results. ***[6]*** Unlike CEC, FRE has explicit provisions for authenticating voices and telephone conversations. ***[7]*** CEC often sets forth more detailed requirements than FRE, *e.g.*, non-expert opinion on handwriting; comparison of handwriting by an expert or the court; authentication by unique contents or circumstances; and public records.

(1) ***Testimony of a Witness with Knowledge.*** Testimony that an item is what it is claimed to be.

§ **1414. Authentication by admission.** A writing may be authenticated by evidence that:

(a) The party against whom it is offered has at any time admitted its authenticity; or

(b) The writing has been acted upon as authentic by the party against whom it is offered.

§ **1415. Authentication by handwriting evidence.** A writing may be authenticated by evidence of the genuineness of the handwriting of the maker.

§ **1416. Proof of handwriting by person familiar therewith.** A witness who is not otherwise qualified to testify as an expert may state his opinion whether a writing is in the handwriting of a supposed writer if the court finds that he has personal knowledge of the handwriting of the supposed writer. Such personal knowledge may be acquired from:

(a) Having seen the supposed writer write;

(b) Having seen a writing purporting to be in the handwriting of the supposed writer and upon which the supposed writer has acted or been charged;

(c) Having received letters in the due course of mail purporting to be from the supposed writer in response to letters duly addressed and mailed by him to the supposed writer; or

(d) Any other means of obtaining personal knowledge of the handwriting of the supposed writer.

§ **1417. Comparison of handwriting by trier of fact.** The genuineness of handwriting, or the lack thereof, may be proved by a comparison made by the trier of fact with handwriting (a) which the court finds was admitted or treated as genuine by the party against whom the evidence is offered or (b) otherwise proved to be genuine to the satisfaction of the court.

§ **1418. Comparison of writing by expert witness.** The genuineness of writing, or the lack thereof, may be proved by a comparison made by an expert witness with writing (a) which the court finds was admitted or treated as genuine by the party against whom the evidence is offered or (b) otherwise proved to be genuine to the satisfaction of the court.

§ **1419. Exemplars when writing is 30 years old.** Where a writing whose genuineness is sought to be proved is more than 30 years old, the comparison under Section 1417 or 1418 may be made with writing purporting to be genuine, and generally respected and acted upon as such, by persons having an interest in knowing whether it is genuine.

§ **1420. Authentication by evidence of reply.** A writing may be authenticated by evidence that the writing was received in response to a communication sent to the person who is claimed by the proponent of the evidence to be the author of the writing.

[*FRE have no counterpart to CEC § 1414.*]

(2) ***Nonexpert Opinion About Handwriting.*** A nonexpert's opinion that handwriting is genuine, based on a familiarity with it that was not acquired for the current litigation.

(3) ***Comparison by an Expert Witness or the Trier of Fact.*** A comparison with an authenticated specimen by an expert witness or the trier of fact.

§ 1421. **Authentication by content.** A writing may be authenticated by evidence that the writing refers to or states matters that are unlikely to be known to anyone other than the person who is claimed by the proponent of the evidence to be the author of the writing.

[*CEC has no counterpart to FRE 901(b)(5)-(6).*]

§ 1600. **Record of document affecting property interest.** (a) The record of an instrument or other document purporting to establish or affect an interest in property is prima facie evidence of the existence and content of the original recorded document and its execution and delivery by each person by whom it purports to have been executed if:

(1) The record is in fact a record of an office of a public entity; and

(2) A statute authorized such a document to be recorded in that office.

(b) The presumption established by this section is a presumption affecting the burden of proof. [*Amended 1967.*]

§ 643. **Authenticity of ancient document.** A deed or will or other writing purporting to create, terminate, or affect an interest in real or personal property is presumed to be authentic if it:

(a) Is at least 30 years old;

(b) Is in such condition as to create no suspicion concerning its authenticity;

(c) Was kept, or if found was found, in a place where such writing, if authentic, would be likely to be kept or found; and

(d) Has been generally acted upon as authentic by persons having an interest in the matter.

(4) ***Distinctive Characteristics and the Like.*** The appearance, contents, substance, internal patterns, or other distinctive characteristics of the item, taken together with all the circumstances.

(5) ***Opinion About a Voice.*** An opinion identifying a person's voice — whether heard firsthand or through mechanical or electronic transmission or recording — based on hearing the voice at any time under circumstances that connect it with the alleged speaker.

(6) ***Evidence About a Telephone Conversation.*** For a telephone conversation, evidence that a call was made to the number assigned at the time to:

(A) a particular person, if circumstances, including self-identification, show that the person answering was the one called; or

(B) a particular business, if the call was made to a business and the call related to business reasonably transacted over the telephone.

(7) ***Evidence About Public Records.*** Evidence that:

(A) a document was recorded or filed in a public office as authorized by law; or

(B) a purported public record or statement is from the office where items of this kind are kept.

(8) ***Evidence About Ancient Documents or Data Compilations.*** For a document or data compilation, evidence that it:

(A) is in a condition that creates no suspicion about its authenticity;

(B) was in a place where, if authentic, it would likely be; and

(C) is at least 20 years old when offered.

[*CEC has no counterpart to FRE 901(b)(9)-(10).*]

§ 1552. Printed representation of computer-generated information. (a) A printed representation of computer information or a computer program is presumed to be an accurate representation of the computer information or computer program that it purports to represent. This presumption is a presumption affecting the burden of producing evidence. If a party to an action introduces evidence that a printed representation of computer information or computer program is inaccurate or unreliable, the party introducing the printed representation into evidence has the burden of proving, by a preponderance of evidence, that the printed representation is an accurate representation of the existence and content of the computer information or computer program that it purports to represent.

(b) Subdivision (a) applies to the printed representation of computer-generated information stored by an automated traffic enforcement system.

(c) Subdivision (a) shall not apply to computer-generated official records certified in accordance with Section 452.5 or 1530. [*Amended 2012.*]

§ 1553. Printed representation of video or digital images. (a) A printed representation of images stored on a video or digital medium is presumed to be an accurate representation of the images it purports to represent. This presumption is a presumption affecting the burden of producing evidence. If a party to an action introduces evidence that a printed representation of images stored on a video or digital medium is inaccurate or unreliable, the party introducing the printed representation into evidence has the burden of proving, by a preponderance of evidence, that the printed representation is an accurate representation of the existence and content of the images that it purports to represent. [*Added 1998. Amended 2012.*]

(b) Subdivision (a) applies to the printed representation of video or photographic images stored by an automated traffic enforcement system. [*Added 2012.*]

§ 1450. Classification of presumptions in article. The presumptions established by this article [§§ 1450-1454] are presumptions affecting the burden of producing evidence.

Compare FRE 902 and CEC §§ 1450 et seq.: FRE recognizes classes of self-authenticating evidence for which no extrinsic evidence of authenticity is required. CEC uses presumptions of authenticity for comparable classes of evidence. Unlike self-authentication, which satisfies the requirement of authentication without more and requires the court to admit the evidence (without, however, precluding evidence of inauthenticity for the jury to weigh), the CEC presumptions are rebuttable and may be overcome by evidence of inauthenticity, which may result in exclusion of the evidence.

(9) ***Evidence About a Process or System.*** Evidence describing a process or system and showing that it produces an accurate result.

(10) ***Methods Provided by a Statute or Rule.*** Any method of authentication or identification allowed by a federal statute or a rule prescribed by the Supreme Court.

[FRE have no counterpart to CEC §§ 1552-1553.]

Rule 902. Evidence That Is Self-Authenticating

The following items of evidence are self-authenticating; they require no extrinsic evidence of authenticity in order to be admitted:

§ **1452. Official seals.** A seal is presumed to be genuine and its use authorized if it purports to be the seal of:

(a) The United States or a department, agency, or public employee of the United States.

(b) A public entity in the United States or a department, agency, or public employee of such public entity.

(c) A nation recognized by the executive power of the United States or a department, agency, or officer of such nation.

(d) A public entity in a nation recognized by the executive power of the United States or a department, agency, or officer of such public entity.

(e) A court of admiralty or maritime jurisdiction.

(f) A notary public within any state of the United States.

§ **1453. Domestic official signatures.** A signature is presumed to be genuine and authorized if it purports to be the signature, affixed in his official capacity, of:

(a) A public employee of the United States.

(b) A public employee of any public entity in the United States.

(c) A notary public within any state of the United States.

(1) ***Domestic Public Documents That Are Sealed and Signed.*** A document that bears:

(A) a seal purporting to be that of the United States; any state, district, commonwealth, territory, or insular possession of the United States; the former Panama Canal Zone; the Trust Territory of the Pacific Islands; a political subdivision of any of these entities; or a department, agency, or officer of any entity named above; and

(B) a signature purporting to be an execution or attestation.

> *Compare FRE 902(1) and CEC § 1452*: ***[1]*** Under FRE a document bearing an official government seal is self-authenticating if it bears "a signature purporting to be an execution or attestation." CEC presumes the authenticity of official seals without any signature requirement. ***[2]*** FRE applies only to domestic entities, while CEC also covers foreign entities recognized by the United States.

(2) ***Domestic Public Documents That Are Not Sealed but Are Signed and Certified.*** A document that bears no seal if:

(A) it bears the signature of an officer or employee of an entity named in Rule 902(1)(A); and

(B) another public officer who has a seal and official duties within that same entity certifies under seal — or its equivalent — that the signer has the official capacity and that the signature is genuine.

> *Compare FRE 902(2) and CEC § 1453*: For unsealed domestic public documents, CEC *presumes* that a domestic official signature is genuine where the signature purports to be an official signature. No sealed certification is required. In contrast, FRE requires a sealed certification by a second officer attesting to the first officer's signature.

§ **1454. Foreign official signatures.** A signature is presumed to be genuine and authorized if it purports to be the signature, affixed in his official capacity, of an officer, or deputy of an officer, of a nation or public entity in a nation recognized by the executive power of the United States and the writing to which the signature is affixed is accompanied by a final statement certifying the genuineness of the signature and the official position of (a) the person who executed the writing or (b) any foreign official who has certified either the genuineness of the signature and official position of the person executing the writing or the genuineness of the signature and official position of another foreign official who has executed a similar certificate in a chain of such certificates beginning with a certificate of the genuineness of the signature and official position of the person executing the writing. The final statement may be made only by a secretary of an embassy or legation, consul general, consul, vice consul, consular agent, or other officer in the foreign service of the United States stationed in the nation, authenticated by the seal of his office.

Compare FRE 902(3) and CEC § 1454: Under both FRE and CEC a document purporting to be signed by an official of a foreign country is self-authenticating (FRE) or presumed to be authentic (CEC) if properly certified at two levels of officialdom. Unlike CEC, FRE allows alternatives to the second certification requirement if all parties have been given "a reasonable opportunity to investigate the document's authenticity and accuracy."

§ **1530. Copy of writing in official custody.** (a) A purported copy of a writing in the custody of a public entity, or of an entry in such a writing, is prima facie evidence of the existence and content of such writing or entry if:

(1) The copy purports to be published by the authority of the nation or state, or public entity therein in which the writing is kept;

(2) The office in which the writing is kept is within the United States or within the Panama Canal Zone, the Trust Territory of the Pacific Islands, or the Ryukyu Islands, and the copy is attested or certified as a correct copy of the writing or entry by a public employee, or a deputy of a public employee, having the legal custody of the writing; or

(3) ***Foreign Public Documents.*** A document that purports to be signed or attested by a person who is authorized by a foreign country's law to do so. The document must be accompanied by a final certification that certifies the genuineness of the signature and official position of the signer or attester — or of any foreign official whose certificate of genuineness relates to the signature or attestation or is in a chain of certificates of genuineness relating to the signature or attestation. The certification may be made by a secretary of a United States embassy or legation; by a consul general, vice consul, or consular agent of the United States; or by a diplomatic or consular official of the foreign country assigned or accredited to the United States. If all parties have been given a reasonable opportunity to investigate the document's authenticity and accuracy, the court may, for good cause, either:

(A) order that it be treated as presumptively authentic without final certification; or

(B) allow it to be evidenced by an attested summary with or without final certification.

(4) ***Certified Copies of Public Records.*** A copy of an official record — or a copy of a document that was recorded or filed in a public office as authorized by law — if the copy is certified as correct by:

(A) the custodian or another person authorized to make the certification; or

(B) a certificate that complies with Rule 902(1), (2), or (3), a federal statute, or a rule prescribed by the Supreme Court.

> *Compare FRE 902(4) and CEC § 1530-1532*: Unlike FRE, CEC sets forth detailed certification requirements that must be satisfied before a public record (including a recorded document) is presumed to be authentic.

(3) The office in which the writing is kept is not within the United States or any other place described in paragraph (2) and the copy is attested as a correct copy of the writing or entry by a person having authority to make attestation. The attestation must be accompanied by a final statement certifying the genuineness of the signature and the official position of (i) the person who attested the copy as a correct copy or (ii) any foreign official who has certified either the genuineness of the signature and official position of the person attesting the copy or the genuineness of the signature and official position of another foreign official who has executed a similar certificate in a chain of such certificates beginning with a certificate of the genuineness of the signature and official position of the person attesting the copy. Except as provided in the next sentence, the final statement may be made only by a secretary of an embassy or legation, consul general, consul, vice consul, or consular agent of the United States, or a diplomatic or consular official of the foreign country assigned or accredited to the United States. Prior to January 1, 1971, the final statement may also be made by a secretary of an embassy or legation, consul general, consul, vice consul, consular agent, or other officer in the foreign service of the United States stationed in the nation in which the writing is kept, authenticated by the seal of his office. If reasonable opportunity has been given to all parties to investigate the authenticity and accuracy of the documents, the court may, for good cause shown, (i) admit an attested copy without the final statement or (ii) permit the writing or entry in foreign custody to be evidenced by an attested summary with or without a final statement.

(b) The presumptions established by this section are presumptions affecting the burden of producing evidence. [*Amended 1970.*]

§ **1531. Certification of copy for evidence.** For the purpose of evidence, whenever a copy of a writing is attested or certified, the attestation or certificate must state in substance that the copy is a correct copy of the original, or of a specified part thereof, as the case may be.

§ **1532. Official record of recorded writing.** (a) The official record of a writing is prima facie evidence of the existence and content of the original recorded writing if:

(1) The record is in fact a record of an office of a public entity; and

(2) A statute authorized such a writing to be recorded in that office.

(b) The presumption established by this section is a presumption affecting the burden of producing evidence.

§ **644. Book purporting to be published by public authority.** A book, purporting to be printed or published by public authority, is presumed to have been so printed or published.

§ **645. Book purporting to contain reports of cases.** A book, purporting to contain reports of cases adjudged in the tribunals of the state or nation where the book is published, is presumed to contain correct reports of such cases.

(5) ***Official Publications.*** A book, pamphlet, or other publication purporting to be issued by a public authority.

[*FRE have no counterpart to CEC § 645. However, FRE's provisions on judicial notice are likely sufficient to ensure no barrier to authentication of reported cases.*]

§ **645.1. Printed materials purporting to be particular newspaper or periodical.** Printed materials, purporting to be a particular newspaper or periodical, are presumed to be that newspaper or periodical if regularly issued at average intervals not exceeding three months. [*Added 1986.*]

[*CEC has no counterpart to FRE 902(7).*]

§ **1451. Acknowledged writings.** A certificate of the acknowledgment of a writing other than a will, or a certificate of the proof of such a writing, is prima facie evidence of the facts recited in the certificate and the genuineness of the signature of each person by whom the writing purports to have been signed if the certificate meets the requirements of Article 3 (commencing with Section 1180) of Chapter 4, Title 4, Part 4, Division 2 of the Civil Code.

[*CEC has no counterpart to FRE 902(9)-(10).*]

[*Sections 1560-1566, at pp. III-162-165, infra, provide for compliance with a subpoena duces tecum for business records by production of copies of the records accompanied by an affidavit describing the manner of making and maintaining the records, and for admissibility of the records on the basis of the affidavit without a sponsoring witness.*]

Compare FRE 902(11) and CEC §§ 1560-1566: While CEC provides more detailed procedures for the authentication of business records by means of affidavit rather than by live witness, the effect and intent are the same.

[*CEC has no counterpart to FRE 902(12)-(14).*]

(6) ***Newspapers and Periodicals.*** Printed material purporting to be a newspaper or periodical.

> *Compare FRE 902(6) and CEC § 645.1*: Unlike FRE, CEC requires that in order to be presumed authentic a newspaper or periodical must be "regularly issued at average intervals not exceeding three months."

(7) ***Trade Inscriptions and the Like.*** An inscription, sign, tag, or label purporting to have been affixed in the course of business and indicating origin, ownership, or control.

(8) ***Acknowledged Documents.*** A document accompanied by a certificate of acknowledgment that is lawfully executed by a notary public or another officer who is authorized to take acknowledgments.

> *Compare FRE 902(8) and CEC § 1451*: CEC does not cover wills in its presumption that acknowledged documents are authentic.

(9) ***Commercial Paper and Related Documents.*** Commercial paper, a signature on it, and related documents, to the extent allowed by general commercial law.

(10) ***Presumptions Under a Federal Statute.*** A signature, document, or anything else that a federal statute declares to be presumptively or prima facie genuine or authentic.

(11) ***Certified Domestic Records of a Regularly Conducted Activity.*** The original or a copy of a domestic record that meets the requirements of Rule 803(6)(A)-(C), as shown by a certification of the custodian or another qualified person that complies with a federal statute or a rule prescribed by the Supreme Court. Before the trial or hearing, the proponent must give an adverse party reasonable written notice of the intent to offer the record — and must make the record and certification available for inspection — so that the party has a fair opportunity to challenge them.

(12) ***Certified Foreign Records of a Regularly Conducted Activity.*** In a civil case, the original or a copy of a foreign record that meets the requirements of Rule 902(11), modified as follows: the certification, rather than complying with a federal statute or Supreme Court rule, must be signed in a manner that, if falsely made, would subject the maker to a criminal penalty in the country where the certification is signed. The proponent must also meet the notice requirements of Rule 902(11).

(13) ***Certified Records Generated by an Electronic Process or System.*** A record generated by an electronic process or system that produces an accurate result, as shown by a certification of a qualified person that complies with the certification requirements of Rule 902(11) or (12). The proponent must also meet the notice requirements of Rule 902(11). [*Added 2016.*]

§ **1411. Subscribing witness' testimony unnecessary.** Except as provided by statute, the testimony of a subscribing witness is not required to authenticate a writing.

§ **1412. Use of other evidence when subscribing witness' testimony required.** If the testimony of a subscribing witness is required by statute to authenticate a writing and the subscribing witness denies or does not recollect the execution of the writing, the writing may be authenticated by other evidence.

§ **250. "Writing"** means handwriting, typewriting, printing, photostating, photographing, photocopying, transmitting by electronic mail or facsimile, and every other means of recording upon any tangible thing, any form of communication or representation, including letters, words, pictures, sounds, or symbols, or combinations thereof, and any record thereby created, regardless of the manner in which the record has been stored. [*Amended 2002.*]

§ **255. "Original"** means the writing itself or any counterpart intended to have the same effect by a person executing or issuing it. An "original" of a photograph includes the negative or any print therefrom. If data are stored in a computer or similar device, any printout or other output readable by sight, shown to reflect the data accurately, is an "original." [*Added 1977.*]

§ **260. A "duplicate"** is a counterpart produced by the same impression as the original, or from the same matrix, or by means of photography, including enlargements and miniatures, or by mechanical or electronic rerecording, or by chemical reproduction, or by other equivalent technique which accurately reproduces the original. [*Added 1977.*]

§ **1520. Content of writing; proof.** The content of a writing may be proved by an otherwise admissible original. [*Added 1998.*]

§ **1521. Secondary evidence rule.** (a) The content of a writing may be proved by otherwise admissible secondary evidence. The court shall exclude secondary evidence of the content of writing if the court determines either of the following:

(1) A genuine dispute exists concerning material terms of the writing and justice requires the exclusion.

(14) ***Certified Data Copied from an Electronic Device, Storage Medium, or File.*** Data copied from an electronic device, storage medium, or file, if authenticated by a process of digital identification, as shown by a certification of a qualified person that complies with the certification requirements of Rule 902(11) or (12). The proponent also must meet the notice requirements of Rule 902(11). [*Added 2016.*]

Rule 903. Subscribing Witness's Testimony

A subscribing witness's testimony is necessary to authenticate a writing only if required by the law of the jurisdiction that governs its validity.

ARTICLE X. CONTENTS OF WRITINGS, RECORDINGS AND PHOTOGRAPHS

Rule 1001. Definitions That Apply to This Article

In this article:

(a) A "writing" consists of letters, words, numbers, or their equivalent set down in any form.

(b) A "recording" consists of letters, words, numbers, or their equivalent recorded in any manner.

(c) A "photograph" means a photographic image or its equivalent stored in any form.

(d) An "original" of a writing or recording means the writing or recording itself or any counterpart intended to have the same effect by the person who executed or issued it. For electronically stored information, "original" means any printout — or other output readable by sight — if it accurately reflects the information. An "original" of a photograph includes the negative or a print from it.

(e) A "duplicate" means a counterpart produced by a mechanical, photographic, chemical, electronic, or other equivalent process or technique that accurately reproduces the original.

Rule 1002. Requirement of the Original

An original writing, recording, or photograph is required in order to prove its content unless these rules or a federal statute provides otherwise.

Rule 1003. Admissibility of Duplicates

A duplicate is admissible to the same extent as the original unless a genuine question is raised about the original's authenticity or the circumstances make it unfair to admit the duplicate.

(2) Admission of the secondary evidence would be unfair.

(b) Nothing in this section makes admissible oral testimony to prove the content of a writing if the testimony is inadmissible under Section 1523 (oral testimony of the content of a writing).

(c) Nothing in this section excuses compliance with Section 1401 (authentication).

(d) This section shall be known as the "Secondary Evidence Rule." [*Added 1998.*]

§ **1522. Additional grounds for exclusion of secondary evidence.** (a) In addition to the grounds for exclusion authorized by Section 1521, in a criminal action the court shall exclude secondary evidence of the content of a writing if the court determines that the original is in the proponent's possession, custody, or control, and the proponent has not made the original reasonably available for inspection at or before trial. This section does not apply to any of the following:

(1) A duplicate as defined in Section 260.

(2) A writing that is not closely related to the controlling issues in the action.

(3) A copy of a writing in the custody of a public entity.

(4) A copy of a writing that is recorded in the public records, if the record or a certified copy of it is made evidence of the writing by statute.

(b) In a criminal action, a request to exclude secondary evidence of the content of a writing, under this section or any other law, shall not be made in the presence of the jury. [*Added 1998.*]

§ **1523. Oral testimony of the content of a writing; admissibility.** (a) Except as otherwise provided by statute, oral testimony is not admissible to prove the content of a writing.

(b) Oral testimony of the content of a writing is not made inadmissible by subdivision (a) if the proponent does not have possession or control of a copy of the writing and the original is lost or has been destroyed without fraudulent intent on the part of the proponent of the evidence.

Compare FRE 1001-1003 and CEC §§ 1520-1522, 1550: As to proving the contents of writings, etc., the main difference between FRE's modernized version of the common-law Best Evidence Rule and CEC's Secondary Evidence Rule is in the preference given to different types of secondary evidence. ***[1]*** FRE is strict about the circumstances under which secondary evidence may be used, but if secondary evidence is allowed no distinction is usually drawn between written evidence and oral testimony as to the contents of the original. In contrast, CEC is liberal in allowing secondary evidence in general but strictly limits the use of oral testimony. ***[2]*** CEC's broad permission to use secondary evidence does not include situations where (1) the material terms of the writing are genuinely disputed and justice requires exclusion, or (2) admission of the secondary evidence would be unfair. CEC § 1521. For a list of considerations underlying "justice" and "unfair," *see Law Revision Commission Comments to CEC 1521* (1998). FRE's analogous provision, FRE 1003, links these issues to the admissibility of duplicates rather than to the admissibility of secondary evidence as a whole. ***[3]*** CEC's liberality is tempered by § 1522 in criminal cases where the proponent has the original but has not made it available for inspection by the opponent. In that case secondary evidence must be excluded unless all four conditions listed in § 1522 are met. FRE has no special provisions for criminal cases. ***[4]*** FRE freely allows a "duplicate" as equivalent to an "original" except as noted in FRE 1003. CEC specifically addresses the admissibility of duplicates only (a) as an exception to CEC § 1522's limitation on secondary evidence in criminal cases, and (b) as to certain public and business records, CEC § 1550, *infra*. However, CEC's general acceptance of secondary evidence appears broad enough to equate to FRE 1003.

Rule 1004. Admissibility of Other Evidence of Content

An original is not required and other evidence of the content of a writing, recording, or photograph is admissible if:

(a) all the originals are lost or destroyed, and not by the proponent acting in bad faith;

(b) an original cannot be obtained by any available judicial process;

(c) the party against whom the original would be offered had control of the original; was at that time put on notice, by pleadings or otherwise, that the original would be a subject of proof at the trial or hearing; and fails to produce it at the trial or hearing; or

(c) Oral testimony of the content of a writing is not made inadmissible by subdivision (a) if the proponent does not have possession or control of the original or a copy of the writing and either of the following conditions is satisfied:

(1) Neither the writing nor a copy of the writing was reasonably procurable by the proponent by use of the court's process or by other available means.

(2) The writing is not closely related to the controlling issues and it would be inexpedient to require its production.

(d) Oral testimony of the content of a writing is not made inadmissible by subdivision (a) if the writing consists of numerous accounts or other writings that cannot be examined in court without great loss of time, and the evidence sought from them is only the general result of the whole. [*Added 1998.*]

Compare FRE 1006 and CEC § 1523(d): FRE`s provision that a summary may be admissible to prove the contents of voluminous writings is similar to CEC`s, which allows oral testimony where numerous accounts cannot be examined without loss of time and where "the evidence sought from them is only the general result of the whole."

[*CEC has no counterpart to FRE 1007.*]

(d) the writing, recording, or photograph is not closely related to a controlling issue.

Compare FRE 1004 and CEC §§ 1521, 1523: ***[1]*** FRE specifies four circumstances in which evidence other than the original is admissible. CEC § 1521(a) subsumes all four categories by allowing the contents of a writing to be proved by otherwise admissible secondary evidence. ***[2]*** CEC 1521(b) excludes oral testimony to prove the contents of a writing except as provided by § 1523, under which there are four circumstances in which oral testimony is allowed to prove the contents of a writing. Those circumstances are substantially the same as those in FRE 1004(a), (b), and (d), with additional allowance for voluminous writings where "the evidence sought from them is only the general result of the whole." *Cf.* FRE 1006, *infra*. ***[3]*** CEC has no provision analogous to FRE 1004(c).

Rule 1005. Copies of Public Records to Prove Content

The proponent may use a copy to prove the content of an official record – or of a document that was recorded or filed in a public office as authorized by law – if these conditions are met: the record or document is otherwise admissible; and the copy is certified as correct in accordance with Rule 902(4) or is testified to be correct by a witness who has compared it with the original. If no such copy can be obtained by reasonable diligence, then the proponent may use other evidence to prove the content.

Compare FRE 1005 and CEC § 1523(c): FRE 1005 is the only provision of FRE creating a preference for written secondary evidence over oral testimony. It allows use of a certified copy of an official record or a recorded writing; it allows other evidence (including oral testimony) only if there is no such copy. Similar results should follow from CEC § 1523(c)(1).

Rule 1006. Summaries to Prove Content

The proponent may use a summary, chart, or calculation to prove the content of voluminous writings, recordings, or photographs that cannot be conveniently examined in court. The proponent must make the originals or duplicates available for examination or copying, or both, by other parties at a reasonable time or place. And the court may order the proponent to produce them in court.

Rule 1007. Testimony or Admission of a Party to Prove Content

The proponent may prove the content of a writing, recording, or photograph by the testimony, deposition, or written statement of the party against whom the evidence is offered. The proponent need not account for the original.

§ **405. Determination of foundational and other preliminary facts in other cases.** With respect to preliminary fact determinations not governed by Section 403 or 404:

(a) When the existence of a preliminary fact is disputed, the court shall indicate which party has the burden of producing evidence and the burden of proof on the issue as implied by the rule of law under which the question arises. The court shall determine the existence or nonexistence of the preliminary fact and shall admit or exclude the proffered evidence as required by the rule of law under which the question arises.

(b) If a preliminary fact is also a fact in issue in the action:

(1) The jury shall not be informed of the court's determination as to the existence or nonexistence of the preliminary fact.

(2) If the proffered evidence is admitted, the jury shall not be instructed to disregard the evidence if its determination of the fact differs from the court's determination of the preliminary fact.

§ **1550. Types of evidence of a writing as admissible as the writing itself.** (a) If made and preserved as a part of the records of a business, as defined in Section 1270, in the regular course of that business, the following types of evidence of a writing are as admissible as the writing itself:

(1) A nonerasable optical image reproduction or any other reproduction of a public record by a trusted system, as defined in Section 12168.7 of the Government Code, if additions, deletions, or changes to the original document are not permitted by the technology.

(2) A photostatic copy or reproduction.

(3) A microfilm, microcard, or miniature photographic copy, reprint, or enlargement.

(4) Any other photographic copy or reproduction, or an enlargement thereof.

(b) The introduction of evidence of a writing pursuant to subdivision (a) does not preclude admission of the original writing if it is still in existence. A court may require the introduction of a hard copy printout of the document. [*Amended 1992, 2002.*]

§ **1550.1. Admissibility of reproductions of files, records, writings, photographs, and fingerprints.** Reproductions of files, records, writings, photographs, fingerprints or other instruments in the official custody of a criminal justice agency that were microphotographed or otherwise reproduced in a manner that conforms with the provisions of Section 11106.1, 11106.2, or 11106.3 of the Penal Code shall be admissible to the same extent and under the same circumstances as the original file, record, writing or other instrument would be admissible. [*Added 2004.*]

Rule 1008. Functions of the Court and Jury

Ordinarily, the court determines whether the proponent has fulfilled the factual conditions for admitting other evidence of the content of a writing, recording, or photograph under Rule 1004 or 1005. But in a jury trial, the jury determines — in accordance with Rule 104(b) — any issue about whether:

(a) an asserted writing, recording, or photograph ever existed;

(b) another one produced at the trial or hearing is the original; or

(c) other evidence of content accurately reflects the content.

Compare FRE 1008 and CEC § 405: CEC's Secondary Evidence Rule contains no specific provision governing the proof of preliminary facts on which admissibility under that rule depends. Presumably the court will apply CEC § 405, which allocates to the court responsibility for deciding all facts on which admissibility depends, except relevance-related facts controlled by CEC § 403. *See Assembly Committee on Judiciary Comment* to § 405, specifically referring to former §§ 1500-1510, the Best Evidence Rule. There is no indication in the *Law Revision Commission Comments* (1998) to the Secondary Evidence Rule that a different regime was intended. Thus, under CEC the court has total authority to decide issues on which the application of the Secondary Evidence Rule depends. A federal court's analogous authority under FRE 104(a), *q.v.*, is diminished by FRE 1008, which allocates to the jury determination of whether a writing ever existed, whether a writing is the original, and whether other evidence of contents accurately reflects the original.

[*See comparison of FRE with CEC § 1550, supra at I-221.*]

[*FRE have no counterpart to CEC § 1550.1.*]

§ **1551. Photographic copies where original destroyed or lost.** A print, whether enlarged or not, from a photographic film (including a photographic plate, microphotographic film, photostatic negative, or similar reproduction) of an original writing destroyed or lost after such film was taken or a reproduction from an electronic recording of video images on magnetic surfaces is admissible as the original writing itself if, at the time of the taking of such film or electronic recording, the person under whose direction and control it was taken attached thereto, or to the sealed container in which it was placed and has been kept, or incorporated in the film or electronic recording, a certification complying with the provisions of Section 1531 and stating the date on which, and the fact that, it was so taken under his direction and control. [*Amended 1969.*]

§ **1601. Proof of content of lost official record affecting property.** (a) Subject to subdivisions (b) and (c), when in any action it is desired to prove the contents of the official record of any writing lost or destroyed by conflagration or other public calamity, after proof of such loss or destruction, the following may, without further proof, be admitted in evidence to prove the contents of such record:

(1) Any abstract of title made and issued and certified as correct prior to such loss or destruction, and purporting to have been prepared and made in the ordinary course of business by any person engaged in the business of preparing and making abstracts of title prior to such loss or destruction; or

(2) Any abstract of title, or of any instrument affecting title, made, issued, and certified as correct by any person engaged in the business of insuring titles or issuing abstracts of title to real estate, whether the same was made, issued, or certified before or after such loss or destruction and whether the same was made from the original records or from abstract and notes, or either, taken from such records in the preparation and upkeeping of its plant in the ordinary course of its business.

(b) No proof of the loss of the original writing is required other than the fact that the original is not known to the party desiring to prove its contents to be in existence.

(c) Any party desiring to use evidence admissible under this section shall give reasonable notice in writing to all other parties to the action who have appeared therein, of his intention to use such evidence at the trial of the action, and shall give all such other parties a reasonable opportunity to inspect the evidence, and also the abstracts, memoranda, or notes from which it was compiled, and to take copies thereof.

§ **1605. Authenticated Spanish title records.** Duplicate copies and authenticated translations of original Spanish title papers relating to land claims in this state, derived from the Spanish or Mexican governments, prepared under the supervision of the Keeper of Archives, authenticated by the Surveyor-General or his successor and by the Keeper of Archives, and filed with a county recorder, in accordance with Chapter 281 of the Statutes of 1865-66, are admissible as evidence with like force and effect as the originals and without proving the execution of such originals. [*Amended 1967.*]

[*FRE have no counterpart to CEC § 1551.*]

[*FRE have no counterpart to CEC § 1601.*]

[*FRE have no counterpart to CEC § 1605.*]

§ **300. Applicability of code.** Except as otherwise provided by statute, this code applies in every action before the Supreme Court or a court of appeal or superior court, including proceedings in such actions conducted by a referee, court commissioner, or similar officer, but does not apply in grand jury proceedings. [*Amended 2002.*]

§ **910. Applicability of division.** Except as otherwise provided by statute, the provisions of this division [§§ 900-1070 relating to privileges] apply in all proceedings. The provisions of any statute making rules of evidence inapplicable in particular proceedings, or limiting the applicability of rules of evidence in particular proceedings, do not make this division inapplicable to such proceedings.

Compare FRE 1101 and CEC § 300, 910: ***[1]*** FRE apply to all types of proceedings in federal trial, appellate, and magistrate courts, including civil, criminal, bankruptcy, admiralty, maritime, and non-summary contempt proceedings. CEC applies in every action before the Supreme Court, a court of appeal, or superior court, including proceedings before referees, court commissioners, and "similar officers." ***[2]*** Unlike CEC, FRE permit the court to determine *preliminary questions* of witness qualification, existence of privilege, or admissibility of evidence without regard to FRE (other than privileges)(*see* discussion of FRE 104(a), *supra*). ***[3]*** Unlike CEC, FRE do not apply to specified miscellaneous proceedings in criminal cases.

[*CEC has no counterpart to FRE 1102.*]

§ **1. Short title.** This code shall be known as the Evidence Code.

ARTICLE XI. MISCELLANEOUS RULES

Rule 1101. Applicability of the Rules

(a) **To Courts and Judges.** These rules apply to proceedings before:

- United States district courts;
- United States bankruptcy and magistrate judges;
- United States courts of appeals;
- the United States Court of Federal Claims; and
- the district courts of Guam, the Virgin Islands, and the Northern Mariana Islands.

(b) **To Cases and Proceedings.** These rules apply in:

- civil cases and proceedings, including bankruptcy, admiralty and maritime cases;
- criminal cases and proceedings; and
- contempt proceedings, except those in which the court may act summarily.

(c) **Rules on Privilege.** The rules on privilege apply to all stages of a case or proceeding.

(d) **Exceptions.** These rules — except for those on privilege — do not apply to the following:

(1) the court's determination, under Rule 104(a), on a preliminary question of fact governing admissibility;

(2) grand-jury proceedings; and

(3) miscellaneous proceedings such as:

- extradition or rendition;
- issuing an arrest warrant, criminal summons, or search warrant;
- a preliminary examination in a criminal case;
- sentencing;
- granting or revoking probation or supervised release; and
- considering whether to release on bail or otherwise.

(e) **Other Statutes and Rules.** A federal statute or a rule prescribed by the Supreme Court may provide for admitting or excluding evidence independently from these rules.

Rule 1102. Amendments

These rules may be amended as provided in 28 U.S.C. § 2072.

Rule 1103. Title

These rules may be cited as the Federal Rules of Evidence.

Part II

FEDERAL RULES OF EVIDENCE AND NOTES

RULES OF EVIDENCE

Restyled 2011

ARTICLE I. GENERAL PROVISIONS

Rule 101. Scope; Definitions

(a) **Scope.** These rules apply to proceedings in United States courts. The specific courts and proceedings to which the rules apply, along with exceptions, are set out in Rule 1101.

(b) **Definitions.** In these rules:

(1) "civil case" means a civil action or proceeding;

(2) "criminal case" includes a criminal proceeding;

(3) "public office" includes a public agency;

(4) "record" includes a memorandum, report, or data compilation;

(5) a "rule prescribed by the Supreme Court" means a rule adopted by the Supreme Court under statutory authority; and

(6) a reference to any kind of written material or any other medium includes electronically stored information.

Committee Note to 2011 Restyled Rule

The language of Rule 101 has been amended, and definitions have been added, as part of the general restyling of the Evidence Rules to make them more easily understood and to make style and terminology consistent throughout the rules. These changes are intended to be stylistic only. There is no intent to change any result in any ruling on evidence admissibility.

The reference to electronically stored information is intended to track the language of Fed. R. Civ. P. 34.

Superseded 2011

ARTICLE I. GENERAL PROVISIONS

Rule 101. Scope

These rules govern proceedings in the courts of the United States and before the United States bankruptcy judges and United States magistrate judges, to the extent and with the exceptions stated in rule 1101. [*Amended 1987, 1993.*]

Advisory Committee's Note

Rule 1101 specifies in detail the courts, proceedings, questions, and stages of proceedings to which the rules apply in whole or in part.

Restyled 2011

Rule 102. Purpose

These rules should be construed so as to administer every proceeding fairly, eliminate unjustifiable expense and delay, and promote the development of evidence law, to the end of ascertaining the truth and securing a just determination.

Superseded 2011

Rule 102. Purpose and Construction

These rules shall be construed to secure fairness in administration, elimination of unjustifiable expense and delay, and promotion of growth and development of the law of evidence to the end that the truth may be ascertained and proceedings justly determined.

Advisory Committee's Note

For similar provisions see Rule 2 of the Federal Rules of Criminal Procedure, Rule 1 of the Federal Rules of Civil Procedure, California Evidence Code § 2, and New Jersey Evidence Rule 5.

Restyled 2011

Rule 103. Rulings on Evidence

(a) Preserving a Claim of Error. A party may claim error in a ruling to admit or exclude evidence only if the error affects a substantial right of the party and:

(1) if the ruling admits evidence, a party, on the record:

(A) timely objects or moves to strike; and

(B) states the specific ground, unless it was apparent from the context; or

(2) if the ruling excludes evidence, a party informs the court of its substance by an offer of proof, unless the substance was apparent from the context.

(b) Not Needing to Renew an Objection or Offer of Proof. Once the court rules definitively on the record — either before or at trial — a party need not renew an objection or offer of proof to preserve a claim of error for appeal.

Superseded 2011

Rule 103. Rulings on Evidence

(a) Effect of erroneous ruling. Error may not be predicated upon a ruling which admits or excludes evidence unless a substantial right of the party is affected, and

(1) Objection. In case the ruling is one admitting evidence, a timely objection or motion to strike appears of record, stating the specific ground of objection, if the specific ground was not apparent from the context; or

(2) Offer of proof. In case the ruling is one excluding evidence, the substance of the evidence was made known to the court by offer or was apparent from the context within which questions were asked.

Once the court makes a definitive ruling on the record admitting or excluding evidence, either at or before trial, a party need not renew an objection or offer of proof to preserve a claim of error for appeal. [*Unnumbered second paragraph added 2000.*]

Case Notes

The degree of precision required by Rule 103 depends on how much leeway the court affords counsel to argue the point. When an objection is sustained, a separate offer of proof is not required if the nature of the proposed testimony is apparent from the question asked. Beech Aircraft Corp. v. Rainey, 488 U.S. 153, 174-175, 109 S.Ct. 439, 452, 102 L.Ed. 2d 445 (1988).

In limine rulings on admissibility of evidence are within a trial court's inherent authority to manage the course of the trial. Luce v. United States, 469 U.S. 38, 41 n.4, 105 S.Ct. 460, 463 n.4, 83 L.Ed. 2d 443 (1984).

Advisory Committee's Note

Subdivision (a) states the law as generally accepted today. Rulings on evidence cannot be assigned as error unless (1) a substantial right is affected, and (2) the nature of the error was called to the attention of the judge, so as to alert him to the proper course of action and enable opposing counsel to take proper corrective measures. The objection and the offer of proof are the techniques for accomplishing these objectives. For similar provisions see Uniform Rules 4 and 5; California Evidence Code §§ 353 and 354; Kansas Code of Civil Procedure §§ 60-404 and 60-405. The rule does not purport to change the law with respect to harmless error. See 28 USC § 2111, F.R.Civ.P. 61, F.R.Crim.P. 52, and decisions construing them. The status of constitutional error as harmless or not is treated in Chapman v. California, 386 U.S. 18, 87 S.Ct. 824, 17 L.Ed.2d 705 (1967), reh. denied id. 987, 87 S.Ct. 1283, 18 L.Ed.2d 241.

Advisory Committee's Note to 2000 Amendment

The amendment applies to all rulings on evidence whether they occur at or before trial, including so-called "in limine" rulings. One of the most difficult questions arising from in limine and other evidentiary rulings is whether a losing party must renew an objection or offer of proof when the evidence is or would be offered at trial, in order to preserve a claim of error on appeal. Courts have taken differing approaches to this question. Some courts have held that a renewal at the time the evidence is to be offered at trial is always required. See, e.g., Collins v. Wayne Corp., 621 F.2d 777 (5th Cir. 1980). Some courts have taken a more flexible approach, holding that renewal is not required if the issue decided is one that (1) was fairly presented to the trial court for an initial ruling, (2) may be decided as a final matter before the evidence is actually offered, and (3) was ruled on definitively by the trial judge, See, e.g., Rosenfeld v. Basquiat, 78 F.3d 84 (2d Cir. 1996) (admissibility of former testimony under the Dead Man's Statute; renewal not required). Other courts have distinguished between objections to evidence, which must be renewed when evidence is offered, and offers of proof, which need not be renewed after a definitive determination is made that the evidence is inadmissible. See, e.g., Fusco v. General Motors Corp., 11 F.3d 259 (1st Cir. 1993). Another court, aware of this Committee's proposed amendment, has adopted its approach. Wilson v. Williams, 182 F. 3d 562 (7th Cir.1999) (en banc). Differing views on this question create uncertainty for litigants and unnecessary work for the appellate courts.

The amendment provides that a claim of error with respect to a definitive ruling is preserved for review when the party has otherwise satisfied the objection or offer of proof requirements of Rule 103(a). When the ruling is definitive, a renewed objection or offer of proof at the time the evidence is to be offered is more a formalism than a necessity. See Fed.R.Civ.P. 46 (formal exceptions unnecessary); Fed.R.Cr.P. 51 (same); United States v. Mejia-Alarcon, 995 F.2d 982, 986 (10th Cir. 1993) ("Requiring a party to renew an objection when the district court has issued a definitive ruling on a matter that can be fairly decided before trial would be in the nature of a formal exception and therefore unnecessary."). On the other hand, when the trial court appears to have reserved its ruling or to have indicated that the ruling is provisional, it makes sense to require the party to bring the issue to the court's attention subsequently. See, e.g., United States v. Vest, 116 F.3d 1179, 1188 (7th Cir. 1997) (where the trial court ruled in limine that testimony from defense witnesses could not be admitted, but allowed the defendant to seek leave at trial to call the witnesses should their testimony turn out to be relevant, the defendant's failure to seek such leave at trial meant that it was "too late to reopen the issue now on appeal"); United States v. Valenti, 60 F.3d 941 (2d Cir. 1995) (failure to proffer evidence at trial waives any claim of error where the trial judge had stated that he would reserve judgment on the in limine motion until he had heard the trial evidence).

The amendment imposes the obligation on counsel to clarify whether an in limine or other evidentiary ruling is definitive when there is doubt on that point. See, e.g., Walden v. Georgia-Pacific Corp., 126 F.3d 506, 520 (3d Cir. 1997) (although "the district court told plaintiffs' counsel not to reargue every ruling, it did not countermand its clear opening statement that all of its rulings were tentative, and counsel never requested clarification, as he might have done.").

Even where the court's ruling is definitive, nothing in the amendment prohibits the court from revisiting its decision when the evidence is to be offered. If the court changes its initial ruling, or if the opposing party violates the terms of the initial ruling, objection must be made when the evidence is offered to preserve the claim of error for appeal. The error, if any, in such a situation occurs only when the evidence is offered and admitted. United States Aviation Underwriters, Inc. v. Olympia Wings, Inc., 896 F.2d 949, 956 (5th Cir. 1990) ("objection is required to preserve error when an opponent, or the court itself, violates a motion in limine that was granted"); United States v. Roenigk, 810 F.2d 809 (8th Cir. 1987) (claim of error was not preserved where the defendant failed to object at trial to secure the benefit of a favorable advance ruling).

A definitive advance ruling is reviewed in light of the facts and circumstances before the trial court at the time of the ruling. If the relevant facts and circumstances change materially after the advance ruling has been made, those facts and circumstances cannot be relied upon on appeal unless they have been brought to the attention of the trial court by way of a renewed, and timely, objection, offer of proof, or motion to strike. See Old Chief v. United States, 519 U.S. 172, 182, n.6 (1997) ("It is important that a reviewing court evaluate the trial court's decision from its perspective when it had to rule and not indulge in review by hindsight."). Similarly, if the court decides in an advance ruling that proffered evidence is admissible subject to the eventual introduction by the proponent of a foundation for the evidence, and that foundation is never provided, the opponent cannot claim error based on the failure to establish the foundation unless the opponent calls that failure to the court's attention by a timely motion to strike or other suitable motion. See Huddleston v. United States, 485 U.S. 681, 690, n.7 (1988) ("It is, of course, not the responsibility of the judge sua sponte to ensure that the foundation evidence is offered; the objector must move to strike the evidence if at the close of the trial the offeror has failed to satisfy the condition.").

Nothing in the amendment is intended to affect the provisions of Fed.R.Civ.P. 72(a) or 28 U.S.C. § 636(b)(1) pertaining to nondispositive pretrial rulings by magistrate judges in proceedings that are not before a magistrate judge by consent of the parties. Fed.R.Civ.P. 72(a) provides that a party who fails to file a written objection to a magistrate judge's nondispositive order within ten days of receiving a copy "may not thereafter assign as error a defect" in the order. 28 U.S.C. § 636(b)(1) provides that any party "may serve and file written objections to such proposed findings and recommendations as provided by rules of court" within ten days of receiving a copy of the order. Several courts have held that a party must comply with this statutory provision in order to preserve a claim of error. See, e.g., Wells v. Shriners Hospital, 109 F.3d 198, 200 (4th Cir. 1997) ("[i]n this circuit, as in others, a party 'may' file objections within ten days or he may not, as he chooses, but he 'shall' do so if he wishes further consideration."). When Fed.R.Civ.P. 72(a) or 28 U.S.C. § 636(b)(1) is operative, its requirement must be satisfied in order for a party to preserve a claim of error on appeal, even where Evidence Rule 103(a) would not require a subsequent objection or offer of proof.

Nothing in the amendment is intended to affect the rule set forth in Luce v. United States, 469 U.S. 38 (1984), and its progeny. The amendment provides that an objection or offer of proof need not be renewed to preserve a claim of error with respect to a definitive pretrial ruling. Luce answers affirmatively a separate question: whether a criminal defendant must testify at trial in order to preserve a claim of error predicated upon a trial court's decision to admit the defendant's prior convictions for impeachment. The Luce principle has been extended by many lower courts to other situations. See United States v. DiMatteo, 759 F.2d 831 (11th Cir. 1985) (applying Luce where the defendant's witness would be impeached with evidence offered under Rule 608). See also United States v. Goldman, 41 F.3d 785, 788 (1st Cir. 1994) ("Although Luce involved impeachment by conviction under Rule 609, the reasons given by the Supreme Court for requiring the defendant to testify apply with full force to the kind of Rule 403 and 404 objections that are advanced by Goldman in this case."); Palmieri v. DeFaria, 88 F.3d 136 (2d Cir. 1996) (where the plaintiff decided to take an adverse judgment rather than challenge an advance ruling by putting on evidence at trial, the in limine ruling would not be reviewed on appeal); United States v. Ortiz, 857 F.2d 900 (2d Cir. 1988) (where uncharged misconduct is ruled admissible if the defendant pursues a certain defense, the defendant must actually pursue that defense at trial in order to preserve a claim of error on appeal); United States v. Bond, 87 F.3d 695 (5th Cir. 1996) (where the trial court rules in limine that the defendant would waive his fifth amendment privilege were he to testify, the defendant must take the stand and testify in order to challenge that ruling on appeal).

The amendment does not purport to answer whether a party who objects to evidence that the court finds admissible in a definitive ruling, and who then offers the evidence to "remove the sting" of its anticipated prejudicial effect, thereby waives the right to appeal the trial court's ruling. See, e.g., United States v. Fisher, 106 F.3d 622 (5th Cir. 1997) (where the trial judge ruled in limine that the government could use a prior conviction to impeach the defendant if he testified, the defendant did not waive his right to appeal by introducing the conviction on direct examination); Judd v. Rodman, 105 F.3d 1339 (11th Cir. 1997) (an objection made in limine is sufficient to preserve a claim of error when the movant, as a matter of trial strategy, presents the objectionable evidence herself on direct examination to minimize its prejudicial effect); Gill v. Thomas, 83 F.3d 537, 540 (1st Cir. 1996) ("by offering the misdemeanor evidence himself, Gill waived his opportunity to object and thus did not preserve the issue for appeal"); United States v. Williams, 939 F.2d 721 (9th Cir. 1991) (objection to impeachment evidence was waived where the defendant was impeached on direct examination).

Restyled 2011

(c) Court's Statement About the Ruling; Directing an Offer of Proof. The court may make any statement about the character or form of the evidence, the objection made, and the ruling. The court may direct that an offer of proof be made in question-and-answer form.

Superseded 2011

(b) Record of offer and ruling. The court may add any other or further statement which shows the character of the evidence, the form in which it was offered, the objection made, and the ruling thereon. It may direct the making of an offer in question and answer form.

Advisory Committee's Note

Subdivision (b). The first sentence is the third sentence of Rule 43(c) of the Federal Rules of Civil Procedure virtually verbatim. Its purpose is to reproduce for an appellate court, insofar as possible, a true reflection of what occurred in the trial court. The second sentence is in part derived from the final sentence of Rule 43(c). It is designed to resolve doubts as to what testimony the witness would have in fact given, and, in nonjury cases, to provide the appellate court with material for a possible final disposition of the case in the event of reversal of a ruling which excluded evidence. See 5 Moore's Federal Practice § 43.11 (2d ed. 1968). Application is made discretionary in view of the practical impossibility of formulating a satisfactory rule in mandatory terms.

Restyled 2011

(d) Preventing the Jury from Hearing Inadmissible Evidence. To the extent practicable, the court must conduct a jury trial so that inadmissible evidence is not suggested to the jury by any means.

Superseded 2011

(c) Hearing of jury. In jury cases, proceedings shall be conducted, to the extent practicable, so as to prevent inadmissible evidence from being suggested to the jury by any means, such as making statements or offers of proof or asking questions in the hearing of the jury.

Advisory Committee's Note

Subdivision (c). This subdivision proceeds on the supposition that a ruling which excludes evidence in a jury case is likely to be a pointless procedure if the excluded evidence nevertheless comes to the attention of the jury. Bruton v. United States, 389 U.S. 818, 88 S.Ct. 126, 19 L.Ed.2d 70 (1968). Rule 43(c) of the Federal Rules of Civil Procedure provides: "The court may require the offer to be made out of the hearing of the jury." In re McConnell, 370 U.S. 230, 82 S.Ct. 1288, 8 L.Ed.2d 434 (1962), left some doubt whether questions on which an offer is based must first be asked in the presence of the jury. The subdivision answers in the negative. The judge can foreclose a particular line of testimony and counsel can protect his record without a series of questions before the jury, designed at best to waste time and at worst "to waft into the jury box" the very matter sought to be excluded.

Restyled 2011

(e) Taking Notice of Plain Error. A court may take notice of a plain error affecting a substantial right, even if the claim of error was not properly preserved.

Superseded 2011

(d) Plain error. Nothing in this rule precludes taking notice of plain errors affecting substantial rights although they were not brought to the attention of the court.

Advisory Committee's Note

Subdivision (d). This wording of the plain error principle is from Rule 52(b) of the Federal Rules of Criminal Procedure. While judicial unwillingness to be constructed by mechanical breakdowns of the adversary system has been more pronounced in criminal cases, there is no scarcity of decisions to the same effect in civil cases. In general, see Campbell, Extent to Which Courts of Review Will Consider Questions Not Properly Raised and Preserved, 7 Wis.L.Rev. 91, 160 (1932); Vestal, Sua Sponte Consideration in Appellate Review, 27 Fordham L.Rev. 477 (1958-59); 64 Harv.L.Rev. 652 (1951). In the nature of things the application of the plain error rule will be more likely with respect to the admission of evidence than to exclusion, since failure to comply with normal requirements of offers of proof is likely to produce a record which simply does not disclose the error.

Restyled 2011

Rule 104. Preliminary Questions

(a) In General. The court must decide any preliminary question about whether a witness is qualified, a privilege exists, or evidence is admissible. In so deciding, the court is not bound by evidence rules, except those on privilege.

Superseded 2011

Rule 104. Preliminary Questions

(a) Questions of admissibility generally. Preliminary questions concerning the qualification of a person to be a witness, the existence of a privilege, or the admissibility of evidence shall be determined by the court, subject to the provisions of subdivision (b). In making its determination it is not bound by the rules of evidence except those with respect to privileges.

Case Notes

Where the admissibility of evidence depends on specific facts required to satisfy a rule of evidence other than relevance, those "preliminary facts" must be proved to the satisfaction of the court. The standard of proof of preliminary facts, which is unrelated to the burden of proof as to the substantive issues in the case, is generally a preponderance of evidence. By declaring that the court is not bound by the rules of evidence (except privileges) in making its determination, Rule 104(a) abolishes the prior rule against "bootstrapping." Therefore, inadmissible hearsay—including the very hearsay whose admissibility is in issue—may be considered in determining the preliminary facts on which admissibility depends. Bourjaily v. United States, 483 U.S. 171, 175-176, 107 S.Ct. 2775, 2778-2779, 97 L.Ed. 2d 144 (1987)

Unlike California Evidence Code § 915(a), Federal Rule 104(a) does not preclude consideration of the information claimed to be privileged in order to determine a claim of privilege. United States v. Zolin, 491 U.S. 554, 566-567, 109 S.Ct. 2619, 2628, 105 L.Ed. 2d 469 (1989).

Advisory Committee's Note

Subdivision (a). The applicability of a particular rule of evidence often depends upon the existence of a condition. Is the alleged expert a qualified physician? Is a witness whose former testimony is offered unavailable? Was a stranger present during a conversation between attorney and client? In each instance the admissibility of evidence will turn upon the answer to the question of the existence of the condition. Accepted practice, incorporated in the rule, places on the judge the responsibility for these determinations. McCormick § 53; Morgan, Basic Problems of Evidence 45-50 (1962).

To the extent that these inquiries are factual, the judge acts as a trier of fact. Often, however, rulings on evidence call for an evaluation in terms of a legally set standard. Thus when a hearsay statement is offered as a declaration against interest, a decision must be made whether it possesses the required against-interest characteristics. These decisions, too, are made by the judge.

In view of these considerations, this subdivision refers to preliminary requirements generally by the broad term "questions," without attempt at specification.

This subdivision is of general application. It must, however, be read as subject to the special provisions for "conditional relevancy" in subdivision (b) and those for confessions in subdivision (d).

If the question is factual in nature, the judge will of necessity receive evidence pro and con on the issue. The rule provides that the rules of evidence in general do not apply to this process. McCormick § 53, p. 123, n. 8, points out that the authorities are "scattered and inconclusive," and observes:

> "Should the exclusionary law of evidence, 'the child of the jury system' in Thayer's phrase, be applied to this hearing before the judge? Sound sense backs the view that it should not, and that the judge should be empowered to hear any relevant evidence, such as affidavits or other reliable hearsay."

This view is reinforced by practical necessity in certain situations. An item, offered and objected to, may itself be considered in ruling on admissibility, though not yet admitted in evidence. Thus, the content of an asserted declaration against interest must be considered in ruling whether it is against interest. Again, common practice calls for considering the testimony of a witness, particularly a child, in determining competency. Another example is the requirement of Rule 602 dealing with personal knowledge. In the case of hearsay, it is enough, if the declarant "so far as appears [has] had an opportunity to observe the fact declared." McCormick, § 10, p. 19.

If concern is felt over the use of affidavits by the judge in preliminary hearings on admissibility, attention is directed to the many important judicial determinations made on the basis of affidavits. Rule 47 of the Federal Rules of Criminal Procedure provides:

> "An application to the court for an order shall be by motion. . . . It may be supported by affidavit."

The Rules of Civil Procedure are more detailed. Rule 43(e), dealing with motions generally, provides:

> "When a motion is based on facts not appearing of record the court may hear the matter on affidavits presented by the respective parties, but the court may direct that the matter be heard wholly or partly on oral testimony or depositions."

Rule 4(g) provides for proof of service by affidavit. Rule 56 provides in detail for the entry of summary judgment based on affidavits. Affidavits may supply the foundation for temporary restraining orders under Rule 65(b).

The study made for the California Law Revision Commission recommended an amendment to Uniform Rule 2 as follows:

"In the determination of the issue aforesaid [preliminary determination], exclusionary rules shall not apply, subject, however, to Rule 45 and any valid claim of privilege." Tentative Recommendation and a Study Relating to the Uniform Rules of Evidence (Article VIII, Hearsay), Cal.Law Revision Comm'n, Rep., Rec. & Studies, 470 (1962).

The proposal was not adopted in the California Evidence Code. The Uniform Rules are likewise silent on the subject. However, New Jersey Evidence Rule 8(1), dealing with preliminary inquiry by the judge, provides:

"In his determination the rules of evidence shall not apply except for Rule 4 [exclusion on grounds of confusion, etc.] or a valid claim of privilege."

Restyled 2011

(b) Relevance That Depends on a Fact. When the relevance of evidence depends on whether a fact exists, proof must be introduced sufficient to support a finding that the fact does exist. The court may admit the proposed evidence on the condition that the proof be introduced later.

Superseded 2011

(b) Relevancy conditioned on fact. When the relevancy of evidence depends upon the fulfillment of a condition of fact, the court shall admit it upon, or subject to, the introduction of evidence sufficient to support a finding of the fulfillment of the condition.

Case Note

Rule 104(b), along with Rule 403, states the appropriate standard for determining the admissibility of other acts evidence under Rule 404(b). Huddleston v. United States, 484 U.S. 681, 108 S.Ct. 1496, 99 L.Ed. 2d 771 (1988).

Advisory Committee's Note

Subdivision (b). In some situations, the relevancy of an item of evidence, in the large sense, depends upon the existence of a particular preliminary fact. Thus when a spoken statement is relied upon to prove notice to X, it is without probative value unless X heard it. Or if a letter purporting to be from Y is relied upon to establish an admission by him, it has no probative value unless Y wrote or authorized it. Relevance in this sense has been labelled "conditional relevancy." Morgan, Basic Problems of Evidence 45-46 (1962). Problems arising in connection with it are to be distinguished from problems of logical relevancy, e.g., evidence in a murder case that accused on the day before purchased a weapon of the kind used in the killing, treated in Rule 401.

If preliminary questions of conditional relevancy were determined solely by the judge, as provided in subdivision (a), the functioning of the jury as a trier of fact would be greatly restricted and in some cases virtually destroyed. These are appropriate questions for juries. Accepted treatment, as provided in the rule, is consistent with that given fact questions generally. The judge makes a preliminary determination whether the foundation evidence is sufficient to support a finding of fulfillment of the condition. If so, the item is admitted. If after all the evidence on the issue is in, pro and con, the jury could reasonably conclude that fulfillment of the condition is not established, the issue is for them. If the evidence is not such as to allow a finding, the judge withdraws the matter from their consideration. Morgan, supra; California Evidence Code § 403; New Jersey Rule 8(2). See also Uniform Rules 19 and 67.

The order of proof here, as generally, is subject to the control of the judge.

Restyled 2011

(c) Conducting a Hearing So That the Jury Cannot Hear It. The court must conduct any hearing on a preliminary question so that the jury cannot hear it if:

(1) the hearing involves the admissibility of a confession;

(2) a defendant in a criminal case is a witness and so requests; or

(3) justice so requires.

Superseded 2011

(c) Hearing of jury. Hearings on the admissibility of confessions shall in all cases be conducted out of the hearing of the jury. Hearings on other preliminary matters shall be so conducted when the interests of justice require, or when an accused is a witness and so requests.

Advisory Committee's Note

Subdivision (c). Preliminary hearings on the admissibility of confessions must be conducted outside the hearing of the jury. See Jackson v. Denno, 378 U.S. 368, 84 S.Ct. 1774, 12 L.Ed.2d 908 (1964). Otherwise, detailed treatment of when preliminary matters should be heard outside the hearing of the jury is not feasible. The procedure is time consuming. Not infrequently the same evidence which is relevant to the issue of establishment of fulfillment of a condition precedent to admissibility is also relevant to weight or credibility, and time is saved by taking foundation proof in the presence of the jury. Much evidence on preliminary questions, though not relevant to jury issues, may be heard by the jury with no adverse effect. A great deal must be left to the discretion of the judge who will act as the interests of justice require.

House Judiciary Committee Report

Rule 104(c) as submitted to the Congress provided that hearings on the admissibility of confessions shall be conducted outside the presence of the jury and hearings on all other preliminary matters should be so conducted when the interests of justice require. The Committee amended the Rule to provide that where an accused is a witness as to a preliminary matter, he has the right, upon his request, to be heard outside the jury's presence. Although recognizing that in some cases duplication of evidence would occur and that the procedure could be subject to abuse, the Committee believed that a proper regard for the right of an accused not to testify generally in the case dictates that he be given an option to testify out of the presence of the jury on preliminary matters.

The Committee construes the second sentence of subdivision (c) as applying to civil actions and proceedings as well as to criminal cases, and on this assumption has left the sentence unamended.

Senate Judiciary Committee Report

Under rule 104(c) the hearing on a preliminary matter may at times be conducted in front of the jury. Should an accused testify in such a hearing, waiving his privilege against self-incrimination as to the preliminary issue, rule 104(d) provides that he will not generally be subject to cross-examination as to any other issue. This rule is not, however, intended to immunize the accused from cross-examination where, in testifying about a preliminary issue, he injects other issues into the hearing. If he could not be cross-examined about any issues gratuitously raised by him beyond the scope of the preliminary matters, injustice might result. Accordingly, in order to prevent any such unjust result, the committee intends the rule to be construed to provide that the accused may subject himself to cross-examination as to issues raised by his own testimony upon a preliminary matter before a jury.

Restyled 2011

(d) Cross-Examining a Defendant in a Criminal Case. By testifying on a preliminary question, a defendant in a criminal case does not become subject to cross-examination on other issues in the case.

Superseded 2011

(d) Testimony by accused. The accused does not, by testifying upon a preliminary matter, become subject to cross-examination as to other issues in the case.

Advisory Committee's Note

Subdivision (d). The limitation upon cross-examination is designed to encourage participation by the accused in the determination of preliminary matters. He may testify concerning them without exposing himself to cross-examination generally. The provision is necessary because of the breadth of cross-examination under Rule 611(b).

The rule does not address itself to questions of the subsequent use of testimony given by an accused at a hearing on a preliminary matter. See Walder v. United States, 347 U.S. 62 (1954); Simmons v. United States, 390 U.S. 377 (1968); Harris v. New York, 401 U.S. 222 (1971).

Restyled 2011

(e) Evidence Relevant to Weight and Credibility. This rule does not limit a party's right to introduce before the jury evidence that is relevant to the weight or credibility of other evidence.

Superseded 2011

(e) Weight and credibility. This rule does not limit the right of a party to introduce before the jury evidence relevant to weight or credibility.

Advisory Committee's Note

Subdivision (e). For similar provisions see Uniform Rule 8; California Evidence Code § 406; Kansas Code of Civil Procedure § 60-408; New Jersey Evidence Rule 8(1).

Restyled 2011

Rule 105. Limiting Evidence That Is Not Admissible Against Other Parties or for Other Purposes

If the court admits evidence that is admissible against a party or for a purpose — but not against another party or for another purpose — the court, on timely request, must restrict the evidence to its proper scope and instruct the jury accordingly.

Superseded 2011

Rule 105. Limited Admissibility

When evidence which is admissible as to one party or for one purpose but not admissible as to another party or for another purpose is admitted, the court, upon request, shall restrict the evidence to its proper scope and instruct the jury accordingly.

Advisory Committee's Note

A close relationship exists between this rule and Rule 403 which requires exclusion when "probative value is substantially outweighed by the danger of unfair prejudice, confusion of the issues, or misleading the jury." The present rule recognizes the practice of admitting evidence for a limited purpose and instructing the jury accordingly. The availability and effectiveness of this practice must be taken into consideration in reaching a decision whether to exclude for unfair prejudice under Rule 403. In Bruton v. United States, 389 U.S. 818, 88 S.Ct. 126, 19 L.Ed.2d 70 (1968), the Court ruled that a limiting instruction did not effectively protect the accused against the prejudicial effect of admitting in evidence the confession of a codefendant which implicated him. The decision does not, however, bar the use of limited admissibility with an instruction where the risk of prejudice is less serious.

Similar provisions are found in Uniform Rule 6; California Evidence Code § 355; Kansas Code of Civil Procedure § 60-406; New Jersey Evidence Rule 6. The wording of the present rule differs, however, in repelling any implication that limiting or curative instructions are sufficient in all situations.

House Judiciary Committee Report

Rule 106 as submitted by the Supreme Court (now Rule 105 in the bill) dealt with the subject of evidence which is admissible as to one party or for one purpose but is not admissible against another party or for another purpose. The Committee adopted this Rule without change on the understanding that it does not affect the authority of a court to order a severance in a multi-defendant case.

Restyled 2011

Rule 106. Remainder of or Related Writings or Recorded Statements

If a party introduces all or part of a writing or recorded statement, an adverse party may require the introduction, at that time, of any other part — or any other writing or recorded statement — that in fairness ought to be considered at the same time.

Superseded 2011

Rule 106. Remainder of or Related Writings or Recorded Statements

When a writing or recorded statement or part thereof is introduced by a party, an adverse party may require the introduction at that time of any other part or any other writing or recorded statement which ought in fairness to be considered contemporaneously with it.

Case Notes

When one party has made use of a portion of a document, and misunderstanding or distortion can be averted only through presentation of another portion, the material required for completeness is *ipso facto* relevant and therefore admissible under Rules 401 and 402, whether or not the precise requirements of Rule 106 are met. Beech Aircraft Corp. v. Rainey, 488 U.S. 153, 172, 109 S.Ct. 439, 451, 102 L.Ed. 2d 445 (1988).

Rule 106 does not make admissible otherwise inadmissible evidence. United States v. Wilkerson, 84 F.3d 692, 696 (4th Cir. 1996). *Contra*, United States v. Sutton, 801 F.2d 1346, 1366-1369 (D.C. Cir. 1986).

Rule 106 does not apply to oral statements. United States v. Wilkerson, *supra. But cf.* United States v. Li, 55 F.3d 325 (7th Cir. 1995) (Rule 611(a) grants the same authority as to oral statements that Rule 106 grants as to written and recorded statements).

Advisory Committee's Note

The rule is an expression of the rule of completeness. McCormick § 56. It is manifested as to depositions in Rule 32(a)(4) of the Federal Rules of Civil Procedure, of which the proposed rule is substantially a restatement.

The rule is based on two considerations. The first is the misleading impression created by taking matters out of context. The second is the inadequacy of repair work when delayed to a point later in the trial. See McCormick § 56; California Evidence Code § 356. The rule does not in any way circumscribe the right of the adversary to develop the matter on cross-examination or as part of his own case.

For practical reasons, the rule is limited to writings and recorded statements and does not apply to conversations.

Restyled 2011

ARTICLE II. JUDICIAL NOTICE

Rule 201. Judicial Notice of Adjudicative Facts

(a) Scope. This rule governs judicial notice of an adjudicative fact only, not a legislative fact.

Superseded 2011

ARTICLE II. JUDICIAL NOTICE

Rule 201. Judicial Notice of Adjudicative Facts

(a) Scope of rule. This rule governs only judicial notice of adjudicative facts.

Advisory Committee's Note

Subdivision (a). This is the only evidence rule on the subject of judicial notice. It deals only with judicial notice of "adjudicative" facts. No rule deals with judicial notice of "legislative" facts. Judicial notice of matters of foreign law is treated in Rule 44.1 of the Federal Rules of Civil Procedure and Rule 26.1 of the Federal Rules of Criminal Procedure.

The omission of any treatment of legislative facts results from fundamental differences between adjudicative facts and legislative facts. Adjudicative facts are simply the facts of the particular case. Legislative facts, on the other hand, are those which have relevance to legal reasoning and the lawmaking process, whether in the formulation of a legal principle or ruling by a judge or court or in the enactment of a legislative body. The terminology was coined by Professor Kenneth Davis in his article An Approach to Problems of Evidence in the Administrative Process, 55 Harv.L.Rev. 364, 404-407 (1942). The following discussion draws extensively upon his writings. In addition, see the same author's Judicial Notice, 55 Colum.L.Rev. 945 (1955); Administrative Law Treatise, ch. 15 (1958); A System of Judicial Notice Based on Fairness and Convenience, in Perspectives of Law 69 (1964).

The usual method of establishing adjudicative facts is through the introduction of evidence, ordinarily consisting of the testimony of witnesses. If particular facts are outside the area of reasonable controversy, this process is dispensed with as unnecessary. A high degree of indisputability is the essential prerequisite.

Legislative facts are quite different. As Professor Davis says:

> "My opinion is that judge-made law would stop growing if judges, in thinking about questions of law and policy, were forbidden to take into account the facts they believe, as distinguished from facts which are 'clearly . . . within the domain of the indisputable.' Facts most needed in thinking about difficult problems of law and policy have a way of being outside the domain of the clearly indisputable." A System of Judicial Notice Based on Fairness and Convenience, supra, at 82.

An illustration is Hawkins v. United States, 358 U.S. 74, 79 S.Ct. 136, 3 L.Ed.2d 125 (1958), in which the Court refused to discard the common law rule that one spouse could not testify against the other, saying, "Adverse testimony given in criminal proceedings would, we think, be likely to destroy almost any marriage." This conclusion has a large intermixture of fact, but the factual aspect is scarcely "indisputable." See Hutchins and Slesinger, Some Observations on the Law of Evidence—Family Relations, 13 Minn.L.Rev. 675 (1929). If the destructive effect of the giving of adverse testimony by a spouse is not indisputable, should the Court have refrained from considering it in the absence of supporting evidence?

> "If the Model Code or the Uniform Rules had been applicable, the Court would have been barred from thinking about the essential factual ingredient of the problems before it, and such a result would be obviously intolerable. What the law needs at its growing points is more, not less, judicial thinking about the factual ingredients of problems of what the law ought to be, and the needed facts are seldom 'clearly' indisputable." Davis, supra, at 83.

Professor Morgan gave the following description of the methodology of determining domestic law:

> "In determining the content or applicability of a rule of domestic law, the judge is unrestricted in his investigation and conclusion. He may reject the propositions of either party or of both parties. He may consult the sources of pertinent data to which they refer, or he may refuse to do so. He may make an independent search for persuasive data or rest content with what he has or what the parties present. . . .[T]he parties do no more than to assist; they control no part of the process." Morgan, Judicial Notice, 57 Harv.L.Rev. 269, 270-271 (1944).

This is the view which should govern judicial access to legislative facts. It renders inappropriate any limitation in the form of indisputability, any formal requirements of notice other than those already inherent in affording opportunity to hear and be heard and exchanging briefs, and any requirement of formal findings at any level. It should, however leave open the possibility of introducing evidence through regular channels in appropriate situations. See Borden's Farm Products Co. v. Baldwin, 293 U.S. 194, 55 S.Ct. 187, 79 L.Ed. 281 (1934), where the cause was remanded for the taking of evidence as to the economic conditions and trade practices underlying the New York Milk Control Law.

Similar considerations govern the judicial use of non-adjudicative facts in ways other than formulating laws and rules. Thayer described them as a part of the judicial reasoning process.

> "In conducting a process of judicial reasoning, as of other reasoning, not a step can be taken without assuming something which has not been proved; and the capacity to do this with competent judgment and efficiency, is imputed to judges and juries as part of their necessary mental outfit." Thayer, Preliminary Treatise on Evidence 279-280 (1898).

As Professor Davis points out, A System of Judicial Notice Based on Fairness and Convenience, in Perspectives of Law 69, 73 (1964), every case involves the use of hundreds or thousands of non-evidence facts. When a witness in an automobile accident case says "car," everyone, judge and jury included, furnishes, from non-evidence sources within himself, the supplementing information that the "car" is an automobile, not a railroad car, that it is self-propelled, probably by an internal combustion engine, that it may be assumed to have four wheels with pneumatic rubber tires, and so on. The judicial process cannot construct every case from scratch, like Descartes creating a world based on the postulate *cogito, ergo sum.* These items could not possibly be introduced into evidence, and no one suggests that they be. Nor are they appropriate subjects for any formalized treatment of judicial notice of facts. See Levin and Levy, Persuading the Jury with Facts Not in Evidence: The Fiction-Science Spectrum, 105 U.Pa.L.Rev. 139 (1956).

Another aspect of what Thayer had in mind is the use of non-evidence facts to appraise or assess the adjudicative facts of the case. Pairs of cases from two jurisdictions illustrate this use and also the difference between non-evidence facts thus used and adjudicative facts. In People v. Strook, 347 Ill. 460, 179 N.E. 821 (1932), venue in Cook County had been held not established by testimony that the crime was committed at 7956 South Chicago Avenue, since judicial notice would not be taken that the address was in Chicago. However, the same court subsequently ruled that venue in Cook County was established by testimony that a crime occurred at 8900 South Anthony Avenue, since notice would be taken of the common practice of omitting the name of the city when speaking of local addresses, and the witness was testifying in Chicago. People v. Pride, 16 Ill.2d 82, 156 N.E.2d 551 (1951). And in Hughes v. Vestal, 264 N.C. 500, 142 S.E.2d 361 (1965), the Supreme Court of North Carolina disapproved the trial judge's admission in evidence of a state-published table of automobile stopping distances on the basis of judicial notice, though the court itself had referred to the same table in an earlier case in a "rhetorical and illustrative" way in determining that the defendant could not have stopped her car in time to avoid striking a child who suddenly appeared in the highway and that a nonsuit was properly granted. Ennis v. Dupree, 262 N.C. 224, 136 S.E.2d 702 (1964). See also Brown v. Hale, 263 N.C. 176, 139 S.E.2d 210 (1964); Clayton v. Rimmer, 262 N.C. 302, 136 S.E.2d 562 (1964). It is apparent that this use of non-evidence facts in evaluating the adjudicative facts of the case is not an appropriate subject for a formalized judicial notice treatment.

In view of these considerations, the regulation of judicial notice of facts by the present rule extends only to adjudicative facts.

What, then, are "adjudicative" facts? Davis refers to them as those "which relate to the parties," or more fully:

"When a court or an agency finds facts concerning the immediate parties—who did what, where, when, how, and with what motive or intent—the court or agency is performing an adjudicative function, and the facts are conveniently called adjudicative facts. . . .

"Stated in other terms, the adjudicative facts are those to which the law is applied in the process of adjudication. They are the facts that normally go to the jury in a jury case. They relate to the parties, their activities, their properties, their businesses." 2 Administrative Law Treatise 353.

Note on Judicial Notice of Law. By rules effective July 1, 1966, the method of invoking the law of a foreign country is covered elsewhere. Rule 44.1 of the Federal Rules of Civil Procedure; Rule 26.1 of the Federal Rules of Criminal Procedure. These two new admirably designed rules are founded upon the assumption that the manner in which law is fed into the judicial process is never a proper concern of the rules of evidence but rather of the rules of procedure. The Advisory Committee on Evidence, believing that this assumption is entirely correct, proposes no evidence rule with respect to judicial notice of law, and suggests that those matters of law which, in addition to foreign-country law, have traditionally been treated as requiring pleading and proof and more recently as the subject of judicial notice be left to the Rules of Civil and Criminal Procedure.

Restyled 2011

(b) Kinds of Facts That May Be Judicially Noticed. The court may judicially notice a fact that is not subject to reasonable dispute because it:

(1) is generally known within the trial court's territorial jurisdiction; or

(2) can be accurately and readily determined from sources whose accuracy cannot reasonably be questioned.

Superseded 2011

(b) Kinds of facts. A judicially noticed fact must be one not subject to reasonable dispute in that it is either (1) generally known within the territorial jurisdiction of the trial court or (2) capable of accurate and ready determination by resort to sources whose accuracy cannot reasonably be questioned.

Advisory Committee's Note

Subdivision (b). With respect to judicial notice of adjudicative facts, the tradition has been one of caution in requiring that the matter be beyond reasonable controversy. This tradition of circumspection appears to be soundly based, and no reason to depart from it is apparent. As Professor Davis says:

"The reason we use trial-type procedure, I think, is that we make the practical judgment, on the basis of experience, that taking evidence, subject to cross-examination and rebuttal, is the best way to resolve controversies involving disputes of adjudicative facts, that is, facts pertaining to the parties. The reason we require a determination on the record is that we think fair procedure in resolving disputes of adjudicative facts calls for giving each party a chance to meet in the appropriate fashion the facts that come to the tribunal's attention, and the appropriate fashion for meeting disputed adjudicative facts includes rebuttal evidence, cross-examination, usually confrontation, and argument (either written or oral or both). The key to a fair trial is opportunity to use the appropriate weapons (rebuttal evidence, cross-examination, and argument) to meet adverse materials that come to the tribunal's attention." A System of Judicial Notice Based on Fairness and Convenience, in Perspectives of Law 69, 93 (1964).

The rule proceeds upon the theory that these considerations call for dispensing with traditional methods of proof only in clear cases. Compare Professor Davis' conclusion that judicial notice should be a matter of convenience, subject to requirements of procedural fairness. Id., 94.

This rule is consistent with Uniform Rule 9(1) and (2) which limit judicial notice of facts to those "so universally known that they cannot reasonably be the subject of dispute," those "so generally known or of such common notoriety within the territorial jurisdiction of the court that they cannot reasonably be the subject of dispute," and those "capable of immediate and accurate determination by resort to easily accessible sources of indisputable accuracy." The traditional textbook treatment has included these general categories (matters of common knowledge, facts capable of verification), McCormick §§ 324, 325, and then has passed on into detailed treatment of such specific topics as facts relating to the personnel and records of the court, Id. § 327, and other governmental facts, Id. § 328. The California draftsmen, with a background of detailed statutory regulation of judicial notice, followed a somewhat similar pattern. California Evidence Code §§ 451, 452. The Uniform Rules, however, were drafted on the theory that these particular matters are included within the general categories and need no specific mention. This approach is followed in the present rule.

The phrase "propositions of generalized knowledge," found in Uniform Rule 9(1) and (2) is not included in the present rule. It was, it is believed, originally included in Model Code Rules 801 and 802 primarily in order to afford some minimum recognition to the right of the judge in his "legislative" capacity (not acting as the trier of fact) to take judicial notice of very limited categories of generalized knowledge. The limitations thus imposed have been discarded herein as undesirable, unworkable, and contrary to existing practice. What is left, then, to be considered, is the status of a "proposition of generalized knowledge" as an "adjudicative" fact to be noticed judicially and communicated by the judge to the jury. Thus viewed, it is considered to be lacking practical significance. While judges use judicial notice of "propositions of generalized knowledge" in a variety of situations: determining the validity and meaning of statutes, formulating common law rules, deciding whether evidence should be admitted, assessing the sufficiency and effect of evidence, all are essentially nonadjudicative in nature. When judicial notice is seen as a significant vehicle for progress in the law, these are the areas involved, particularly in developing fields of scientific knowledge. See McCormick 712. It is not believed that judges now instruct juries as to "propositions of generalized knowledge" derived from encyclopedias or other sources, or that they are likely to do so, or, indeed, that it is desirable that they do so. There is a vast difference between ruling on the basis of judicial notice that radar evidence of speed is admissible and explaining to the jury its principles and degree of accuracy, or between using a table of stopping distances of automobiles at various speeds in a judicial evaluation of testimony and telling the jury its precise application in the case. For cases raising doubt as to the propriety of the use of medical texts by lay triers of fact in passing on disability claims in administrative proceedings, see Sayers v. Gardner, 380 F.2d 940 (6th Cir.1967); Ross v. Gardner, 365 F.2d 554 (6th Cir.1966); Sosna v. Celebrezze, 234 F.Supp. 289 (E.D.Pa.1964); Glendenning v. Ribicoff, 213 F.Supp. 301 (W.D.Mo.1962).

Restyled 2011

(c) Taking Notice. The court:

(1) may take judicial notice on its own; or

(2) must take judicial notice if a party requests it and the court is supplied with the necessary information.

Superseded 2011

(c) When discretionary. A court may take judicial notice, whether requested or not.

(d) When mandatory. A court shall take judicial notice if requested by a party and supplied with the necessary information.

Advisory Committee's Note

Subdivisions (c) and (d). Under subdivision (c) the judge has a discretionary authority to take judicial notice, regardless of whether he is so requested by a party. The taking of judicial notice is mandatory, under subdivision (d), only when a party requests it and the necessary information is supplied. This scheme is believed to reflect existing practice. It is simple and workable. It avoids troublesome distinctions in the many situations in which the process of taking judicial notice is not recognized as such.

Compare Uniform Rule 9 making judicial notice of facts universally known mandatory without request, and making judicial notice of facts generally known in the jurisdiction or capable of determination by resort to accurate sources discretionary in the absence of request but mandatory if request is made and the information furnished. But see Uniform Rule 10(3), which directs the judge to decline to take judicial notice if available information fails to convince him that the matter falls clearly within Uniform Rule 9 or is insufficient to enable him to notice it judicially. Substantially the same approach is found in California Evidence Code §§ 451-453 and in New Jersey Evidence Rule 9. In contrast, the present rule treats alike all adjudicative facts which are subject to judicial notice.

Restyled 2011

(d) Timing. The court may take judicial notice at any stage of the proceeding.

(e) Opportunity to Be Heard. On timely request, a party is entitled to be heard on the propriety of taking judicial notice and the nature of the fact to be noticed. If the court takes judicial notice before notifying a party, the party, on request, is still entitled to be heard.

Superseded 2011

(e) Opportunity to be heard. A party is entitled upon timely request to an opportunity to be heard as to the propriety of taking judicial notice and the tenor of the matter noticed. In the absence of prior notification, the request may be made after judicial notice has been taken.

Advisory Committee's Note

Subdivision (e). Basic considerations of procedural fairness demand an opportunity to be heard on the propriety of taking judicial notice and the tenor of the matter noticed. The rule requires the granting of that opportunity upon request. No formal scheme of giving notice is provided. An adversely affected party may learn in advance that judicial notice is in contemplation, either by virtue of being served with a copy of a request by another party under subdivision (d) that judicial notice be taken, or through an advance indication by the judge. Or he may have no advance notice at all. The likelihood of the latter is enhanced by the frequent failure to recognize judicial notice as such. And in the absence of advance notice, a request made after the fact could not in fairness be considered untimely. See the provision for hearing on timely request in the Administrative Procedure Act, 5 U.S.C. § 556(e). See also Revised Model State Administrative Procedure Act (1961), 9C U.L.A. § 10(4) (Supp.1967).

Superseded 2011

(f) Time of taking notice. Judicial notice may be taken at any stage of the proceeding.

Advisory Committee's Note

Subdivision (f). In accord with the usual view, judicial notice may be taken at any stage of the proceedings, whether in the trial court or on appeal. Uniform Rule 12; California Evidence Code § 459; Kansas Rules of Evidence § 60-412; New Jersey Evidence Rule 12; McCormick § 330, p. 712.

Restyled 2011

(f) Instructing the Jury. In a civil case, the court must instruct the jury to accept the noticed fact as conclusive. In a criminal case, the court must instruct the jury that it may or may not accept the noticed fact as conclusive.

Superseded 2011

(g) Instructing jury. In a civil action or proceeding, the court shall instruct the jury to accept as conclusive any fact judicially noticed. In a criminal case, the court shall instruct the jury that it may, but is not required to, accept as conclusive any fact judicially noticed.

Advisory Committee's Note

Subdivision (g). Much of the controversy about judicial notice has centered upon the question whether evidence should be admitted in disproof of facts of which judicial notice is taken.

The writers have been divided. Favoring admissibility are Thayer, Preliminary Treatise on Evidence 308 (1898); 9 Wigmore § 2567; Davis, A System of Judicial Notice Based on Fairness and Convenience, in Perspectives of Law, 69, 76-77 (1964). Opposing admissibility are Keeffe, Landis and Shaad, Sense and Nonsense about Judicial Notice, 2 Stan.L.Rev. 664, 668 (1950); McNaughton, Judicial Notice—Excerpts Relating to the Morgan-Whitmore Controversy, 14 Vand.L.Rev. 779 (1961); Morgan, Judicial Notice, 57 Harv.L.Rev. 269, 279 (1944); McCormick 710-711. The Model Code and the Uniform Rules are predicated upon indisputability of judicially noticed facts.

The proponents of admitting evidence in disproof have concentrated largely upon legislative facts. Since the present rule deals only with judicial notice of adjudicative facts, arguments directed to legislative facts lose their relevancy.

Within its relatively narrow area of adjudicative facts, the rule contemplates there is to be no evidence before the jury in disproof. The judge instructs the jury to take judicially noticed facts as established. This position is justified by the undesirable effects of the opposite rule in limiting the rebutting party, though not his opponent, to admissible evidence, in defeating the reasons for judicial notice, and in affecting the substantive law to an extent and in ways largely unforeseeable. Ample protection and flexibility are afforded by the broad provision for opportunity to be heard on request, set forth in subdivision (e).

Authority upon the propriety of taking judicial notice against an accused in a criminal case with respect to matters other than venue is relatively meager. Proceeding upon the theory that the right of jury trial does not extend to matters which are beyond reasonable dispute, the rule does not distinguish between criminal and civil cases. People v. Mayes, 113 Cal. 618, 45 P. 860 (1896); Ross v. United States, 374 F.2d 97 (8th Cir.1967). Cf. State v. Main, 94 R.I. 338, 180 A.2d 814 (1962); State v. Lawrence, 120 Utah 323, 234 P.2d 600 (1951).

House Judiciary Committee Report

Rule 201(g) as received from the Supreme Court provided that when judicial notice of a fact is taken, the court shall instruct the jury to accept that fact as established. Being of the view that mandatory instruction to a jury in a criminal case to accept as conclusive any fact judicially noticed is inappropriate because contrary to the spirit of the Sixth Amendment right to a jury trial, the Committee adopted the 1969 Advisory Committee draft of this subsection, allowing a mandatory instruction in civil actions and proceedings and a discretionary instruction in criminal cases.

Restyled 2011

ARTICLE III. PRESUMPTIONS IN CIVIL CASES

Rule 301. Presumptions in Civil Cases Generally

In a civil case, unless a federal statute or these rules provide otherwise, the party against whom a presumption is directed has the burden of producing evidence to rebut the presumption. But this rule does not shift the burden of persuasion, which remains on the party that had it originally.

Superseded 2011

ARTICLE III. PRESUMPTIONS IN CIVIL ACTIONS AND PROCEEDINGS

Rule 301. Presumptions in General in Civil Actions and Proceedings

In all civil actions and proceedings not otherwise provided for by Act of Congress or by these rules, a presumption imposes on the party against whom it is directed the burden of going forward with evidence to rebut or meet the presumption, but does not shift to such party the burden of proof in the sense of the risk of nonpersuasion, which remains throughout the trial upon the party on whom it was originally cast.

Advisory Committee's Note

This rule governs presumptions generally. See Rule 302 for presumptions controlled by state law and Rule 303 [deleted] for those against an accused in a criminal case.

Presumptions governed by this rule are given the effect of placing upon the opposing party the burden of establishing the nonexistence of the presumed fact, once the party invoking the presumption establishes the basic facts giving rise to it. The same considerations of fairness, policy, and probability which dictate the allocation of the burden of the various elements of a case as between the prima facie case of a plaintiff and affirmative defenses also underlie the creation of presumptions. These considerations are not satisfied by giving a lesser effect to presumptions. Morgan and Maguire, Looking Backward and Forward at Evidence, 50 Harv.L.Rev. 909, 913 (1937); Morgan, Instructing the Jury upon Presumptions and Burden of Proof, 47 Harv.L.Rev. 59, 82 (1933); Cleary, Presuming and Pleading: An Essay on Juristic Immaturity, 12 Stan.L.Rev. 5 (1959).

The so-called "bursting bubble" theory, under which a presumption vanishes upon the introduction of evidence which would support a finding of the nonexistence of the presumed fact, even though not believed, is rejected as according presumptions too "slight and evanescent" an effect. Morgan and Maguire, supra, at p. 913.

In the opinion of the Advisory Committee, no constitutional infirmity attends this view of presumptions. In Mobile, J. & K. C. R. Co. v. Turnipseed, 219 U.S. 35, 31 S.Ct. 136, 55 L.Ed. 78 (1910), the Court upheld a Mississippi statute which provided that in actions against railroads proof of injury inflicted by the running of trains should be prima facie evidence of negligence by the railroad. The injury in the case had resulted from a derailment. The opinion made the points (1) that the only effect of the statute was to impose on the railroad the duty of producing some evidence to the contrary, (2) that an inference may be supplied by law if there is a rational connection between the fact proved and the fact presumed, as long as the opposite party is not precluded from presenting his evidence to the contrary, and (3) that considerations of public policy arising from the character of the business justified the application in question. Nineteen years later, in Western & Atlantic R. Co. v. Henderson, 279 U.S. 639, 49 S.Ct. 445, 73 L.Ed. 884 (1929), the Court overturned a Georgia statute making railroads liable for damages done by trains, unless the railroad made it appear that reasonable care had been used, the presumption being against the railroad. The declaration alleged the death of plaintiff's husband from a grade crossing collision, due to specified acts of negligence by defendant. The jury were instructed that proof of the injury raised a presumption of negligence; the burden shifted to the railroad to prove ordinary care; and unless it did so, they should find for plaintiff. The instruction was held erroneous in an opinion stating (1) that there was no rational connection between the mere fact of collision and negligence on the part of anyone, and (2) that the statute was different from that in Turnipseed in imposing a burden upon the railroad. The reader is left in a state of some confusion. Is the difference between a derailment and a grade crossing collision of no significance? Would the Turnipseed presumption have been bad if it had imposed a burden of persuasion on defendant, although that would in nowise have impaired its "rational connection"? If Henderson forbids imposing a burden of persuasion on defendants, what happens to affirmative defenses?

Two factors serve to explain Henderson. The first was that it was common ground that negligence was indispensable to liability. Plaintiff thought so, drafted her complaint accordingly, and relied upon the presumption. But how in logic could the same presumption establish her alternative grounds of negligence that the engineer was so blind he could not see decedent's truck and that he failed to stop after he saw it? Second, take away the basic assumption of no liability without fault, as Turnipseed intimated might be done ("considerations of public policy arising out of the character of the business"), and the structure of the decision in Henderson fails. No question of logic would have arisen if the statute had simply said: a prima facie case of liability is made by proof of injury by a train; lack of negligence is an affirmative defense, to be pleaded and proved as other affirmative defenses. The problem would be one of economic due process only. While it seems likely that the Supreme Court of 1929 would have voted that due process was denied, that result today would be unlikely. See, for example, the shift in the direction of absolute liability in the consumer cases. Prosser, The Assault upon the Citadel (Strict Liability to the Consumer), 69 Yale L.J. 1099 (1960).

Any doubt as to the constitutional permissibility of a presumption imposing a burden of persuasion of the nonexistence of the presumed fact in civil cases is laid at rest by Dick v. New York Life Ins. Co., 359 U.S. 437, 79 S.Ct. 921, 3 L.Ed.2d 935 (1959). The Court unhesitatingly applied the North Dakota rule that the presumption against suicide imposed on defendant the burden of proving that the death of insured, under an accidental death clause, was due to suicide.

> "Proof of coverage and of death by gunshot wound shifts the burden to the insurer to establish that the death of the insured was due to his suicide." 359 U.S. at 443, 79 S.Ct. at 925.
>
> "In a case like this one, North Dakota presumes that death was accidental and places on the insurer the burden of proving that death resulted from suicide." Id. at 446, 79 S.Ct. at 927.

The rational connection requirement survives in criminal cases, Tot v. United States, 319 U.S. 463, 63 S.Ct. 1241, 87 L.Ed. 1519 (1943), because the Court has been unwilling to extend into that area the greater-includes-the-lesser theory of Ferry v. Ramsey, 277 U.S. 88, 48 S.Ct. 443, 72 L.Ed. 796 (1928). In that case the Court sustained a Kansas statute under which bank directors were personally liable for deposits made with their assent and with knowledge of insolvency, and the fact of insolvency was prima facie evidence of assent and knowledge of insolvency. Mr. Justice Holmes pointed out that the state legislature could have made the directors personally liable to depositors in every case. Since the statute imposed a less stringent liability, "the thing to be considered is the result reached, not the possibly inartificial or clumsy way of reaching it." Id. at 94, 48 S.Ct. at 444. Mr. Justice Sutherland dissented: though the state could have created an absolute liability, it did not purport to do so; a rational connection was necessary, but lacking, between the liability created and the prima facie evidence of it; the result might be different if the basis of the presumption were being open for business.

The Sutherland view has prevailed in criminal cases by virtue of the higher standard of notice there required. The fiction that everyone is presumed to know the law is applied to the substantive law of crimes as an alternative to complete unenforceability. But the need does not extend to criminal evidence and procedure, and the fiction does not encompass them. "Rational connection" is not fictional or artificial, and so it is reasonable to suppose that Gainey should have known that his presence at the site of an illicit still could convict him of being connected with (carrying on) the business, United States v. Gainey, 380 U.S. 63, 85 S.Ct. 754, 13 L.Ed.2d 658 (1965), but not that Romano should have known that his presence at a still could convict him of possessing it, United States v. Romano, 382 U.S. 136, 86 S.Ct. 279, 15 L.Ed.2d 210 (1965).

In his dissent in Gainey, Mr. Justice Black put it more artistically:

> "It might be argued, although the Court does not so argue or hold, that Congress if it wished could make presence at a still a crime in itself, and so Congress should be free to create crimes which are called 'possession' and 'carrying on an illegal distillery business' but which are defined in such a way that unexplained presence is sufficient and indisputable evidence in all cases to support conviction for those offenses. See Ferry v. Ramsey, 277 U.S. 88, 48 S.Ct. 443, 72 L.Ed. 796. Assuming for the sake of argument that Congress could make unexplained presence a criminal act, and ignoring also the refusal of this Court in other cases to uphold a statutory presumption on such a theory, see Heiner v. Donnan, 285 U.S. 312, 52 S.Ct. 358, 76 L.Ed. 772, there is no indication here that Congress intended to adopt such a misleading method of draftsmanship, nor in my judgment could the statutory provisions if so construed escape condemnation for vagueness, under the principles applied in Lanzetta v. New Jersey, 306 U.S. 451, 59 S.Ct. 618, 83 L.Ed. 888, and many other cases." 380 U.S. at 84, n. 12, 85 S.Ct. at 766.

And the majority opinion in Romano agreed with him:

> "It may be, of course, that Congress has the power to make presence at an illegal still a punishable crime, but we find no clear indication that it intended to so exercise this power. The crime remains possession, not presence, and with all due deference to the judgment of Congress, the former may not constitutionally be inferred from the latter." 382 U.S. at 144, 86 S.Ct. at 284.

The rule does not spell out the procedural aspects of its application. Questions as to when the evidence warrants submission of a presumption and what instructions are proper under varying states of fact are believed to present no particular difficulties.

House Judiciary Committee Report

Rule 301 as submitted by the Supreme Court provided that in all cases a presumption imposes on the party against whom it is directed the burden of proving that the nonexistence of the presumed fact is more probable than its existence. The Committee limited the scope of Rule 301 to "civil actions and proceedings" to effectuate its decision not to deal with the question of presumptions in criminal cases. (See note on [proposed] Rule 303 in discussion of Rules deleted). With respect to the weight to be given a presumption in a civil case, the Committee agreed with the judgment implicit in the Court's version that the so-called "bursting bubble" theory of presumptions, whereby a presumption vanishes upon the appearance of any contradicting evidence by the other party, gives to presumptions too slight an effect. On the other hand, the Committee believed that the Rule proposed by the Court, whereby a presumption permanently alters the burden of persuasion, no matter how much contradicting evidence is introduced—a view shared by only a few courts—lends too great a force to presumptions. Accordingly, the Committee amended the Rule to adopt an intermediate position under which a presumption does not vanish upon the introduction of contradicting evidence, and does not change the burden of persuasion; instead it is merely deemed sufficient evidence of the fact presumed, to be considered by the jury or other finder of fact.

Senate Judiciary Committee Report

The rule governs presumptions in civil cases generally. Rule 302 provides for presumptions in cases controlled by State law.

As submitted by the Supreme Court, presumptions governed by this rule were given the effect of placing upon the opposing party the burden of establishing the nonexistence of the presumed fact, once the party invoking the presumption established the basic facts giving rise to it.

Instead of imposing a burden of persuasion on the party against whom the presumption is directed, the House adopted a provision which shifted the burden of going forward with the evidence. They further provided that "even though met with contradicting evidence, a presumption is sufficient evidence of the fact presumed, to be considered by the trier of fact." The effect of the amendment is that presumptions are to be treated as evidence.

The committee feels the House amendment is ill-advised. As the joint committees (the Standing Committee on Practice and Procedure of the Judicial Conference and the Advisory Committee on the Rules of Evidence) stated: "Presumptions are not evidence, but ways of dealing with evidence." This treatment requires juries to perform the task of considering "as evidence" facts upon which they have no direct evidence and which may confuse them in performance of their duties. California had a rule much like that contained in the House amendment. It was sharply criticized by Justice Traynor in Speck v. Sarver [20 Cal.2d 585, 128 P.2d 16, 21 (1942)] and was repealed after 93 troublesome years [Cal.Ev.Code 1965 § 600].

Professor McCormick gives a concise and compelling critique of the presumption as evidence rule:

> Another solution, formerly more popular than now, is to instruct the jury that the presumption is "evidence", to be weighed and considered with the testimony in the case. This avoids the danger that the jury may infer that the presumption is conclusive, but it probably means little to the jury, and certainly runs counter to accepted theories of the nature of evidence. [McCormick, Evidence, 669 (1954); Id. 825 (2d ed. 1972)].

For these reasons the committee has deleted that provision of the House-passed rule that treats presumptions as evidence. The effect of the rule as adopted by the committee is to make clear that while evidence of facts giving rise to a presumption shifts the burden of coming forward with evidence to rebut or meet the presumption, it does not shift the burden of persuasion on the existence of the presumed facts. The burden of persuasion remains on the party to whom it is allocated under the rules governing the allocation in the first instance.

The court may instruct the jury that they may infer the existence of the presumed fact from proof of the basic facts giving rise to the presumption. However, it would be inappropriate under this rule to instruct the jury that the inference they are to draw is conclusive.

Conference Committee Report

The House bill provides that a presumption in civil actions and proceedings shifts to the party against whom it is directed the burden of going forward with evidence to meet or rebut it. Even though evidence contradicting the presumption is offered, a presumption is considered sufficient evidence of the presumed fact to be considered by the jury. The Senate amendment provides that a presumption shifts to the party against whom it is directed the burden of going forward with evidence to meet or rebut the presumption, but it does not shift to that party the burden of persuasion on the existence of the presumed fact.

Under the Senate amendment, a presumption is sufficient to get a party past an adverse party's motion to dismiss made at the end of his case-in-chief. If the adverse party offers no evidence contradicting the presumed fact, the court will instruct the jury that if it finds the basic facts, it may presume the existence of the presumed fact. If the adverse party does offer evidence contradicting the presumed fact, the court cannot instruct the jury that it may presume the existence of the presumed fact from proof of the basic facts. The court may, however, instruct the jury that it may infer the existence of the presumed fact from proof of the basic facts.

The conference adopts the Senate amendment.

Restyled 2011

Rule 302. Applying State Law to Presumptions in Civil Cases

In a civil case, state law governs the effect of a presumption regarding a claim or defense for which state law supplies the rule of decision.

Superseded 2011

Rule 302. Applicability of State Law in Civil Actions and Proceedings

In civil actions and proceedings, the effect of a presumption respecting a fact which is an element of a claim or defense as to which State law supplies the rule of decision is determined in accordance with State law.

Advisory Committee's Note

A series of Supreme Court decisions in diversity cases leaves no doubt of the relevance of Erie Railroad Co. v. Tompkins, 304 U.S. 64, 58 S.Ct. 817, 82 L.Ed. 1188 (1938), to questions of burden of proof. These decisions are Cities Service Oil Co. v. Dunlap, 308 U.S. 208, 60 S.Ct. 201, 84 L.Ed. 196 (1939), Palmer v. Hoffman, 318 U.S. 109, 63 S.Ct. 477, 87 L.Ed. 645 (1943), and Dick v. New York Life Ins. Co., 359 U.S. 437, 79 S.Ct. 921, 3 L.Ed.2d 935 (1959). They involved burden of proof, respectively, as to status as bona fide purchaser, contributory negligence, and nonaccidental death (suicide) of an insured. In each instance the state rule was held to be applicable. It does not follow, however, that all presumptions in diversity cases are governed by state law. In each case cited, the burden of proof question had to do with a substantive element of the claim or defense. Application of the state law is called for only when the presumption operates upon such an element. Accordingly the rule does not apply state law when the presumption operates upon a lesser aspect of the case, i.e. "tactical" presumptions.

The situations in which the state law is applied have been tagged for convenience in the preceding discussion as "diversity cases." The designation is not a completely accurate one since Erie applies to any claim or issue having its source in state law, regardless of the basis of federal jurisdiction, and does not apply to a federal claim or issue, even though jurisdiction is based on diversity. Vestal, Erie R.R. v. Tompkins: A Projection, 48 Iowa L.Rev. 248, 257 (1963); Hart and Wechsler, The Federal Courts and the Federal System, 697 (1953); 1A Moore, Federal Practice ¶ 0.305 [3] (2d ed. 1965); Wright, Federal Courts, 217-218 (1963). Hence the rule employs, as appropriately descriptive, the phrase "as to which state law supplies the rule of decision." See A.L.I. Study of the Division of Jurisdiction Between State and Federal Courts, § 2344(c), p. 40, P.F.D. No. 1 (1965).

Restyled 2011

ARTICLE IV. RELEVANCE AND ITS LIMITS

Rule 401. Test for Relevant Evidence

Evidence is relevant if:

(a) it has any tendency to make a fact more or less probable than it would be without the evidence; and

(b) the fact is of consequence in determining the action.

Superseded 2011

ARTICLE IV. RELEVANCY AND ITS LIMITS

Rule 401. Definition of "Relevant Evidence"

"Relevant evidence" means evidence having any tendency to make the existence of any fact that is of consequence to the determination of the action more probable or less probable than it would be without the evidence.

Advisory Committee's Note

Problems of relevancy call for an answer to the question whether an item of evidence, when tested by the processes of legal reasoning, possesses sufficient probative value to justify receiving it in evidence. Thus, assessment of the probative value of evidence that a person purchased a revolver shortly prior to a fatal shooting with which he is charged is a matter of analysis and reasoning.

The variety of relevancy problems is coextensive with the ingenuity of counsel in using circumstantial evidence as a means of proof. An enormous number of cases fall in no set pattern, and this rule is designed as a guide for handling them. On the other hand, some situations recur with sufficient frequency to create patterns susceptible of treatment by specific rules. Rule 404 and those following it are of that variety; they also serve as illustrations of the application of the present rule as limited by the exclusionary principles of Rule 403.

Passing mention should be made of so-called "conditional" relevancy. Morgan, Basic Problems of Evidence 45-46 (1962). In this situation, probative value depends not only upon satisfying the basic requirement of relevancy as described above but also upon the existence of some matter of fact. For example, if evidence of a spoken statement is relied upon to prove notice, probative value is lacking unless the person sought to be charged heard the statement. The problem is one of fact, and the only rules needed are for the purpose of determining the respective functions of judge and jury. See Rules 104(b) and 901. The discussion which follows in the present note is concerned with relevancy generally, not with any particular problem of conditional relevancy.

Relevancy is not an inherent characteristic of any item of evidence but exists only as a relation between an item of evidence and a matter properly provable in the case. Does the item of evidence tend to prove the matter sought to be proved? Whether the relationship exists depends upon principles evolved by experience or science, applied logically to the situation at hand. James, Relevancy, Probability and the Law, 29 Calif.L.Rev. 689, 696, n. 15 (1941), in Selected Writings on Evidence and Trial 610, 615, n. 15 (Fryer ed. 1957). The rule summarizes this relationship as a "tendency to make the existence" of the fact to be proved "more probable or less probable." Compare Uniform Rule 1(2) which states the crux of relevancy as "a tendency in reason," thus perhaps emphasizing unduly the logical process and ignoring the need to draw upon experience or science to validate the general principle upon which relevancy in a particular situation depends.

The standard of probability under the rule is "more . . . probable than it would be without the evidence." Any more stringent requirement is unworkable and unrealistic. As McCormick § 152, p. 317, says, "A brick is not a wall," or, as Falknor, Extrinsic Policies Affecting Admissibility, 10 Rutgers L.Rev. 574, 576 (1956), quotes Professor McBaine, ". . . [I]t is not to be supposed that every witness can make a home run." Dealing with probability in the language of the rule has the added virtue of avoiding confusion between questions of admissibility and questions of the sufficiency of the evidence.

The rule uses the phrase "fact that is of consequence to the determination of the action" to describe the kind of fact to which proof may properly be directed. The language is that of California Evidence Code § 210; it has the advantage of avoiding the loosely used and ambiguous word "material." Tentative Recommendation and a Study Relating to the Uniform Rules of Evidence (Art. I. General Provisions), Cal.Law Revision Comm'n, Rep., Rec. & Studies, 10-11 (1964). The fact to be proved may be ultimate, intermediate, or evidentiary; it matters not, so long as it is of consequence in the determination of the action. Cf. Uniform Rule 1(2) which requires that the evidence relate to a "material" fact.

The fact to which the evidence is directed need not be in dispute. While situations will arise which call for the exclusion of evidence offered to prove a point conceded by the opponent, the ruling should be made on the basis of such considerations as waste of time and undue prejudice (see Rule 403), rather than under any general requirement that evidence is admissible only if directed to matters in dispute. Evidence which is essentially background in nature can scarcely be said to involve disputed matter, yet it is universally offered and admitted as an aid to understanding. Charts, photographs, views of real estate, murder weapons, and many other items of evidence fall in this category. A rule limiting admissibility to evidence directed to a controversial point would invite the exclusion of this helpful evidence, or at least the raising of endless questions over its admission. Cf. California Evidence Code § 210, defining relevant evidence in terms of tendency to prove a disputed fact.

Restyled 2011

Rule 402. General Admissibility of Relevant Evidence

Relevant evidence is admissible unless any of the following provides otherwise:

- the United States Constitution;
- a federal statute;
- these rules; or
- other rules prescribed by the Supreme Court.

Irrelevant evidence is not admissible.

Superseded 2011

Rule 402. Relevant Evidence Generally Admissible; Irrelevant Evidence Inadmissible

All relevant evidence is admissible, except as otherwise provided by the Constitution of the United States, by Act of Congress, by these rules, or by other rules prescribed by the Supreme Court pursuant to statutory authority. Evidence which is not relevant is not admissible.

Case Notes

Evidence of a witness's bias is generally admissible because (1) it is relevant in that it makes the facts to which the witness testified less probable in the eyes of the jury than without the evidence, and (2) the Federal Rules contain no rule dealing specifically with evidence of bias. United States v. Abel, 469 U.S. 45, 50-51, 105 S.Ct. 465, 468, 83 L.Ed. 2d 450 (1984).

When one party has made use of a portion of a document, and misunderstanding or distortion can be averted only through presentation of another portion, the material required for completeness is *ipso facto* relevant and therefore admissible under Rules 401 and 402, whether or not the precise requirements of Rule 106 are met. Beech Aircraft Corp. v. Rainey, 488 U.S. 153, 172, 109 S.Ct. 439, 451, 102 L.Ed. 2d 445 (1988).

Advisory Committee's Note

The provisions that all relevant evidence is admissible, with certain exceptions, and that evidence which is not relevant is not admissible are "a presupposition involved in the very conception of a rational system of evidence." Thayer, Preliminary Treatise on Evidence 264 (1898). They constitute the foundation upon which the structure of admission and exclusion rests. For similar provisions see California Evidence Code §§ 350, 351. Provisions that all relevant evidence is admissible are found in Uniform Rule 7(f); Kansas Code of Civil Procedure § 60-407(f); and New Jersey Evidence Rule 7(f); but the exclusion of evidence which is not relevant is left to implication.

Not all relevant evidence is admissible. The exclusion of relevant evidence occurs in a variety of situations and may be called for by these rules, by the Rules of Civil and Criminal Procedure, by Bankruptcy Rules, by Act of Congress, or by constitutional considerations.

Succeeding rules in the present article, in response to the demands of particular policies, require the exclusion of evidence despite its relevancy. In addition, Article V recognizes a number of privileges; Article VI imposes limitations upon witnesses and the manner of dealing with them; Article VII specifies requirements with respect to opinions and expert testimony; Article VIII excludes hearsay not falling within an exception; Article IX spells out the handling of authentication and identification; and Article X restricts the manner of proving the contents of writings and recordings.The Rules of Civil and Criminal Procedure in some instances require the exclusion of relevant evidence. For example, Rules 30(b) and 32(a)(3) of the Rules of Civil Procedure, by imposing requirements of notice and unavailability of the deponent, place limits on the use of relevant depositions. Similarly, Rule 15 of the Rules of Criminal Procedure restricts the use of depositions in criminal cases, even though relevant. And the effective enforcement of the command, originally statutory and now found in Rule 5(a) of the Rules of Criminal Procedure, that an arrested person be taken without unnecessary delay before a commissioner or other similar officer is held to require the exclusion of statements elicited during detention in violation thereof. Mallory v. United States, 354 U.S. 449, 77 S.Ct. 1356, 1 L.Ed.2d 1479 (1957); 18 U.S.C. § 3501(c).

While congressional enactments in the field of evidence have generally tended to expand admissibility beyond the scope of the common law rules, in some particular situations they have restricted the admissibility of relevant evidence. Most of this legislation has consisted of the formulation of a privilege or of a prohibition against disclosure. 8 U.S.C. § 1202(f), records of refusal of visas or permits to enter United States confidential, subject to discretion of Secretary of State to make available to court upon certification of need; 10 U.S.C. § 3693, replacement certificate of honorable discharge from Army not admissible in evidence; 10 U.S.C. § 8693, same as to Air Force; 11 U.S.C.

§ 25(a)(10), testimony given by bankrupt on his examination not admissible in criminal proceedings against him, except that given in hearing upon objection to discharge; 11 U.S.C. § 205(a), railroad reorganization petition, if dismissed, not admissible in evidence; 11 U.S.C. § 403(a), list of creditors filed with municipal composition plan not an admission; 13 U.S.C. § 9(a), census information confidential, retained copies of reports privileged; 47 U.S.C. § 605, interception and divulgence of wire or radio communications prohibited unless authorized by sender. These statutory provisions would remain undisturbed by the rules.

The rule recognizes but makes no attempt to spell out the constitutional considerations which impose basic limitations upon the admissibility of relevant evidence. Examples are evidence obtained by unlawful search and seizure. Weeks v. United States, 232 U.S. 383, 34 S.Ct. 341, 58 L.Ed. 652 (1914); Katz v. United States, 389 U.S. 347, 88 S.Ct. 507, 19 L.Ed.2d 576 (1967); incriminating statement elicited from an accused in violation of right to counsel. Massiah v. United States, 377 U.S. 201, 84 S.Ct. 1199, 12 L.Ed.2d 246 (1964).

House Judiciary Committee Report

Rule 402 as submitted to the Congress contained the phrase "or by other rules adopted by the Supreme Court". To accommodate the view that the Congress should not appear to acquiesce in the Court's judgment that it has authority under the existing Rules Enabling Acts to promulgate Rules of Evidence, the Committee amended the above phrase to read "or by other rules prescribed by the Supreme Court pursuant to statutory authority" in this and other Rules where the reference appears.

Restyled 2011

Rule 403. Excluding Relevant Evidence for Prejudice, Confusion, Waste of Time, or Other Reasons

The court may exclude relevant evidence if its probative value is substantially outweighed by a danger of one or more of the following: unfair prejudice, confusing the issues, misleading the jury, undue delay, wasting time, or needlessly presenting cumulative evidence.

Superseded 2011

Rule 403. Exclusion of Relevant Evidence on Grounds of Prejudice, Confusion, or Waste of Time

Although relevant, evidence may be excluded if its probative value is substantially outweighed by the danger of unfair prejudice, confusion of the issues, or misleading the jury, or by considerations of undue delay, waste of time, or needless presentation of cumulative evidence.

Case Notes

In a prosecution for unlawful possession of a firearm by one who was previously convicted of a felony, the trial court abused discretion in receiving into evidence the judgment of conviction, which stated the name of the offense for which the defendant was previously convicted, and rejecting the defendant's offer to stipulate that he was previously convicted of a qualifying felony. The probative value and prejudicial tendency of an item of evidence should be evaluated alongside evidentiary alternatives, not in isolation. In general, a stipulation of a fact may not have the same probative value as testimonial evidence of the fact, because a stipulation lacks the "power not only to support conclusions but to sustain the willingness of jurors to draw the inferences, whatever they may be, necessary to reach an honest verdict"; does not "implicate the law's moral underpinnings and a juror's obligation to sit in judgment"; and may fail "to satisfy the jurors' expectations about what proper proof should be." The same considerations do not apply in comparing a stipulation with documentary proof of an objective fact unrelated to the narrative of events constituting the crime. If the documentary proof contains additional information that is irrelevant and prejudicial, then it is an abuse of discretion to receive the documentary proof in the face of the defendant's offer to stipulate. Old Chief v. United States, 519 U.S. 172, 117 S.Ct. 644, 136 L.Ed. 2d 574 (1997) (5-to-4).

Excluding evidence to avoid unfair prejudice or confusion of issues is unnecessary in non-jury trials. See Schultz v. Butcher, 24 F.3d 626, 632 (4th Cir. 1994).

Advisory Committee's Note

The case law recognizes that certain circumstances call for the exclusion of evidence which is of unquestioned relevance. These circumstances entail risks which range all the way from inducing decision on a purely emotional basis, at one extreme, to nothing more harmful than merely wasting time, at the other extreme. Situations in this area call for balancing the probative value of and need for the evidence against the harm likely to result from its admission. Slough, Relevancy Unraveled, 5 Kan.L.Rev. 1, 12-15 (1956); Trautman, Logical or Legal Relevancy—A Conflict in Theory, 5 Van.L.Rev. 385, 392 (1952); McCormick § 152, pp. 319-321. The rules which follow in this Article are concrete applications evolved for particular situations. However, they reflect the policies underlying the present rule, which is designed as a guide for the handling of situations for which no specific rules have been formulated.

Exclusion for risk of unfair prejudice, confusion of issues, misleading the jury, or waste of time, all find ample support in the authorities. "Unfair prejudice" within its context means an undue tendency to suggest decision on an improper basis, commonly, though not necessarily, an emotional one.

The rule does not enumerate surprise as a ground for exclusion, in this respect following Wigmore's view of the common law. 6 Wigmore § 1849. Cf. McCormick § 152, p. 320, n. 29, listing unfair surprise as a ground for exclusion but stating that it is usually "coupled with the danger of prejudice and confusion of issues." While Uniform Rule 45 incorporates surprise as a ground and is followed in Kansas Code of Civil Procedure § 60-445, surprise is not included in California Evidence Code § 352 or New Jersey Rule 4, though both the latter otherwise substantially embody Uniform Rule 45. While it can scarcely be doubted that claims of unfair surprise may still be justified despite procedural requirements of notice and instrumentalities of discovery, the granting of a continuance is a more appropriate remedy than exclusion of the evidence. Tentative Recommendation and a Study Relating to the Uniform Rules of Evidence (Art. VI. Extrinsic Policies Affecting Admissibility), Cal.Law Revision Comm'n, Rep., Rec. & Studies, 612 (1964). Moreover, the impact of a rule excluding evidence on the ground of surprise would be difficult to estimate.

In reaching a decision whether to exclude on grounds of unfair prejudice, consideration should be given to the probable effectiveness or lack of effectiveness of a limiting instruction. See Rule 106 [now 105] and Advisory Committee's Note thereunder. The availability of other means of proof may also be an appropriate factor.

Restyled 2011

Rule 404. Character Evidence; Crimes or Other Acts

(a) Character Evidence.

(1) ***Prohibited Uses.*** Evidence of a person's character or character trait is not admissible to prove that on a particular occasion the person acted in accordance with the character or trait.

(2) ***Exceptions for a Defendant or Victim in a Criminal Case.*** The following exceptions apply in a criminal case:

Superseded 2011

Rule 404. Character Evidence Not Admissible To Prove Conduct; Exceptions; Other Crimes

(a) Character evidence generally. Evidence of a person's character or a trait of character is not admissible for the purpose of proving action in conformity therewith on a particular occasion, except:

Restyled 2011

(A) a defendant may offer evidence of the defendant's pertinent trait, and if the evidence is admitted, the prosecutor may offer evidence to rebut it;

Superseded 2011

(1) Character of accused.—In a criminal case, evidence of a pertinent trait of character offered by an accused, or by the prosecution to rebut the same, or if evidence of a trait of character of the alleged victim of the crime is offered by an accused and admitted under Rule 404(a)(2), evidence of the same trait of character of the accused offered by the prosecution; [*Amended 2000, 2006.*]

Advisory Committee's Note to 2000 Amendment

Rule 404(a)(1) has been amended to provide that when the accused attacks the character of an alleged victim under subdivision (a)(2) of this Rule, the door is opened to an attack on the same character trait of the accused. Current law does not allow the government to introduce negative character evidence as to the accused unless the accused introduces evidence of good character. See, e.g., United States v. Fountain, 768 F.2d 790 (7th Cir. 1985) (when the accused offers proof of self-defense, this permits proof of the alleged victim's character trait for peacefulness, but it does not permit proof of the accused's character trait for violence).

The amendment makes clear that the accused cannot attack the alleged victim's character and yet remain shielded from the disclosure of equally relevant evidence concerning the same character trait of the accused. For example, in a murder case with a claim of self-defense, the accused, to bolster this defense, might offer evidence of the alleged victim's violent disposition. If the government has evidence that the accused has a violent character, but is not allowed to offer this evidence as part of its rebuttal, the jury has only part of the information it needs for an informed assessment of the probabilities as to who was the initial aggressor. This may be the case even if evidence of the accused's prior violent acts is admitted under Rule 404(b), because such evidence can be admitted only for limited purposes and not to show action in conformity with the accused's character on a specific occasion. Thus, the amendment is designed to permit a more balanced presentation of character evidence when an accused chooses to attack the character of the alleged victim.

The amendment does not affect the admissibility of evidence of specific acts of uncharged misconduct offered for a purpose other than proving character under Rule 404(b). Nor does it affect the standards for proof of character by evidence of other sexual behavior or sexual offenses under Rules 412-415. By its placement in Rule 404(a)(1), the amendment covers only proof of character by way of reputation or opinion.

The amendment does not permit proof of the accused's character if the accused merely uses character evidence for a purpose other than to prove the alleged victim's propensity to act in a certain way. See United States v. Burks, 470 F.2d 432, 434-5 (D.C.Cir. 1972) (evidence of the alleged victim's violent character, when known by the accused, was admissible "on the issue of whether or not the defendant reasonably feared he was in danger of imminent great bodily harm"). Finally, the amendment does not permit proof of the accused's character when the accused attacks the alleged victim's character as a witness under Rule 608 or 609.

Advisory Committee's Gap Report* to 2006 Amendment

The Rule has been amended to clarify that in a civil case evidence of a person's character is never admissible to prove that the person acted in conformity with the character trait. The amendment resolves the dispute in the case law over whether the exceptions in subdivisions (a)(1) and (2) permit the circumstantial use of character evidence in civil cases. Compare Carson v. Polley, 689 F.2d 562, 576 (5th Cir. 1982) ("when a central issue in a case is close to one of a criminal nature, the exceptions to the Rule 404(a) ban on character evidence may be invoked"), with SEC v. Towers Financial Corp., 966 F.Supp. 203 (S.D.N.Y. 1997) (relying on the terms "accused" and "prosecution" in Rule 404(a) to conclude that the exceptions in subdivisions (a)(1) and (2) are inapplicable in civil cases). The amendment is consistent with the original intent of the Rule, which was to prohibit the circumstantial use of character evidence in

* For an explanation of "Gap Report," *see* Eileen A. Scallen, *Proceeding with Caution: Making and Amending the Federal Rules of Evidence*, 36 Sw. U. L. Rev. 601, 615 (2008).

cases, even where closely related to criminal charges. See Ginter v. Northwestern Mut. Life Ins. Co., 576 F.Supp. 627, 629-30 (D. Ky.1984) ("It seems beyond peradventure of doubt that the drafters of F.R.Evi. 404(a) explicitly intended that all character evidence, except where 'character is at issue' was to be excluded" in civil cases).

The circumstantial use of character evidence is generally discouraged because it carries serious risks of prejudice, confusion and delay. See Michelson v. United States, 335 U.S. 469, 476 (1948) ("The overriding policy of excluding such evidence, despite its admitted probative value, is the practical experience that its disallowance tends to prevent confusion of issues, unfair surprise and undue prejudice."). In criminal cases, the so-called "mercy rule" permits a criminal defendant to introduce evidence of pertinent character traits of the defendant and the victim. But that is because the accused, whose liberty is at stake, may need "a counterweight against the strong investigative and prosecutorial resources of the government." C. Mueller & L. Kirkpatrick, Evidence: Practice Under the Rules, pp. 264-5 (2d ed. 1999). See also Richard Uviller, Evidence of Character to Prove Conduct: Illusion, Illogic, and Injustice in the Courtroom, 130 U.Pa.L.Rev. 845, 855 (1982) (the rule prohibiting circumstantial use of character evidence "was relaxed to allow the criminal defendant with so much at stake and so little available in the way of conventional proof to have special dispensation to tell the factfinder just what sort of person he really is"). Those concerns do not apply to parties in civil cases.

The amendment also clarifies that evidence otherwise admissible under Rule 404(a)(2) may nonetheless be excluded in a criminal case involving sexual misconduct. In such a case, the admissibility of evidence of the victim's sexual behavior and predisposition is governed by the more stringent provisions of Rule 412.

Restyled 2011

(B) subject to the limitations in Rule 412, a defendant may offer evidence of an alleged crime victim's pertinent trait, and if the evidence is admitted, the prosecutor may:

(i) offer evidence to rebut it; and

(ii) offer evidence of the defendant's same trait; and

(C) in a homicide case, the prosecutor may offer evidence of the alleged victim's trait of peacefulness to rebut evidence that the victim was the first aggressor.

Superseded 2011

(2) Character of alleged victim. Evidence of a pertinent trait of character of the alleged victim of the crime offered by an accused, or by the prosecution to rebut the same, or evidence of a character trait of peacefulness of the alleged victim offered by the prosecution in a homicide case to rebut evidence that the alleged victim was the first aggressor; [*Amended 2000, 2006.*]

Advisory Committee's Note to 2000 Amendment

The term "alleged" is inserted before each reference to "victim" in the Rule, in order to provide consistency with Evidence Rule 412.

Restyled 2011

(3) ***Exceptions for a Witness.*** Evidence of a witness's character may be admitted under Rules 607, 608, and 609.

Superseded 2011

(3) Character of witness. Evidence of the character of a witness, as provided in rules 607, 608, and 609. [*Amended 1991.*]

Restyled 2011- As amended effective December 20, 2020

(b) Other Crimes, Wrongs, or Acts.

(1) Prohibited Uses. Evidence of any other crime, wrong, or act is not admissible to prove a person's character in order to show that on a particular occasion the person acted in accordance with the character.

(2) Permitted Uses. This evidence may be admissible for another purpose, such as proving motive, opportunity, intent, preparation, plan, knowledge, identity, absence of mistake, or lack of accident.

(3) Notice in a Criminal Case. In a criminal case, the prosecutor must:

(A) provide reasonable notice of any such evidence that the prosecutor intends to offer at trial;

(B) articulate in the notice the non-propensity purpose for which the prosecutor intends to offer the evidence and the reasoning that supports the purpose; and

(C) do so in writing sufficiently ahead of trial to give the defendant a fair opportunity to meet the evidence — or during trial and in any form if the court, for good cause, excuses lack of pretrial notice.

Restyled 2011 – superseded by amendment effective December 1, 2020 (*supra*)

(b) Crimes, Wrongs, or Other Acts.

(1) ***Prohibited Uses.*** Evidence of a crime, wrong, or other act is not admissible to prove a person's character in order to show that on a particular occasion the person acted in accordance with the character.

(2) ***Permitted Uses; Notice in a Criminal Case.*** This evidence may be admissible for another purpose, such as proving motive, opportunity, intent, preparation, plan, knowledge, identity, absence of mistake, or lack of accident. On request by a defendant in a criminal case, the prosecutor must:

(A) provide reasonable notice of the general nature of any such evidence that the prosecutor intends to offer at trial; and

(B) do so before trial — or during trial if the court, for good cause, excuses lack of pretrial notice.

Superseded 2011

(b) Other crimes, wrongs, or acts. Evidence of other crimes, wrongs, or acts is not admissible to prove the character of a person in order to show action in conformity therewith. It may, however, be admissible for other purposes, such as proof of motive, opportunity, intent, preparation, plan, knowledge, identity, or absence of mistake or accident, provided that upon request by the accused, the prosecution in a criminal case shall provide reasonable notice in advance of trial, or during trial if the court excuses pretrial notice on good cause shown, of the general nature of any such evidence it intends to introduce at trial. [*Amended 1991, 2006.*]

Case Notes

"Other act" evidence is admissible under Rule 404(b) only if there is sufficient evidence to support a finding that the defendant committed the act under circumstances that make it relevant for a noncharacter purpose. See Rule 104(b). The court does not have to make a finding that the preliminary fact has been proved by a preponderance of the evidence (cf. Rule 104(a)) and does not need to weigh credibility. The danger that other act evidence may be unduly prejudicial should be handled under Rule 403. Huddleston v. United States, 484 U.S. 681, 108 S.Ct. 1496, 99 L.Ed. 2d 771 (1988).

Evidence of prior crimes of which the defendant was previously acquitted may be received under Rule 404(b) without violating either double jeopardy or due process. Dowling v. United States, 493 U.S. 342, 110 S.Ct. 668, 107 L.Ed. 2d 708 (1990).

Advisory Committee's Note

Subdivision (b) deals with a specialized but important application of the general rule excluding circumstantial use of character evidence. Consistently with that rule, evidence of other crimes, wrongs, or acts is not admissible to prove character as a basis for suggesting the inference that conduct on a particular occasion was in conformity with it. However, the evidence may be offered for another purpose, such as proof of motive, opportunity, and so on, which does not fall within the prohibition. In this situation the rule does not require that the evidence be excluded. No mechanical solution is offered. The determination must be made whether the danger of undue prejudice outweighs the probative value of the evidence in view of the availability of other means of proof and other facts appropriate for making decision of this kind under Rule 403. Slough and Knightly, Other Vices, Other Crimes, 41 Iowa L.Rev. 325 (1956).

House Judiciary Committee Report

The second sentence of Rule 404(b) as submitted to the Congress began with the words "This subdivision does not exclude the evidence when offered". The Committee amended this language to read "It may, however, be admissible", the words used in the 1971 Advisory Committee draft, on the ground that this formulation properly placed greater emphasis on admissibility than did the final Court version.

Senate Judiciary Committee Report

This rule provides that evidence of other crimes, wrongs, or acts is not admissible to prove character but may be admissible for other specified purposes such as proof of motive.

Although your committee sees no necessity in amending the rule itself, it anticipates that the use of the discretionary word "may" with respect to the admissibility of evidence of crimes, wrongs, or acts is not intended to confer any arbitrary discretion on the trial judge. Rather, it is anticipated that with respect to permissible uses for such evidence, the trial judge may exclude it only on the basis of those considerations set forth in Rule 403, i.e., prejudice, confusion or waste of time.

Advisory Committee Note to 1991 Amendment

Rule 404(b) has emerged as one of the most cited Rules in the Rules of Evidence. And in many criminal cases evidence of an accused's extrinsic acts is viewed as an important asset in the prosecution's case against an accused. Although there are a few reported decisions on use of such evidence by the defense, see, e.g., United States v. McClure, 546 F.2d 670 (5th Cir.1990) (acts of informant offered in entrapment defense), the overwhelming number of cases involve introduction of that evidence by the prosecution.

The amendment to Rule 404(b) adds a pretrial notice requirement in criminal cases and is intended to reduce surprise and promote early resolution on the issue of admissibility. The notice requirement thus places Rule 404(b) in the mainstream with notice and disclosure provisions in other rules of evidence. See, e.g., Rule 412 (written motion of intent to offer evidence under rule), Rule 609 (written notice of intent to offer conviction older than 10 years), Rule 803(24) and 804(b)(5) (notice of intent to use residual hearsay exceptions).

The Rule expects that counsel for both the defense and the prosecution will submit the necessary request and information in a reasonable and timely fashion. Other than requiring pretrial notice, no specific time limits are stated in recognition that what constitutes a reasonable request or disclosure will depend largely on the circumstances of each case. Compare Fla.Stat.Ann. § 90.404(2)(b) (notice must be given at least 10 days before trial) with Tex.R.Evid. 404(b) (no time limit).

Likewise, no specific form of notice is required. The Committee considered and rejected a requirement that the notice satisfy the particularity requirements normally required of language used in a charging instrument. Cf. Fla.Stat.Ann. § 90.404(2)(b) (written disclosure must describe uncharged misconduct with particularity required of an indictment or information). Instead, the Committee opted for a generalized notice provision which requires the prosecution to apprise the defense of the general nature of the evidence of extrinsic acts. The Committee does not intend that the amendment will supercede [*sic*] other rules of admissibility or disclosure, such as the Jencks Act,
18 U.S.C. § 3500, et seq., nor require the prosecution to disclose directly or indirectly the names and addresses of its witnesses, something it is currently not required to do under Federal Rule of Criminal Procedure 16.

The amendment requires the prosecution to provide notice, regardless of how it intends to use the extrinsic act evidence at trial, i.e., during its case-in-chief, for impeachment, or for possible rebuttal. The court in its discretion may, under the facts, decide that the particular request or notice was not reasonable, either because of the lack of timeliness or completeness. Because the notice requirement serves as condition precedent to admissibility of 404(b) evidence, the offered evidence is inadmissible if the court decides that the notice requirement has not been met.

Nothing in the amendment precludes the court from requiring the government to provide it with an opportunity to rule in limine on 404(b) evidence before it is offered or even mentioned during trial. When ruling in limine, the court may require the government to disclose to it the specifics of such evidence which the court must consider in determining admissibility.

The amendment does not extend to evidence of acts which are "intrinsic" to the charged offense, see United States v. Williams, 900 F.2d 823 (5th Cir.1990) (noting distinction between 404(b) evidence and intrinsic offense evidence). Nor is the amendment intended to redefine what evidence would otherwise be admissible under Rule 404(b). Finally, the Committee does not intend through the amendment to affect the role of the court and the jury in considering such evidence. See United States v. Huddleston, 485 U.S. 681, 108 S.Ct. 1496 (1988).

Advisory Committee's Gap Report* to 2006 Amendment

Nothing in the amendment is intended to affect the scope of Rule 404(b). While Rule 404(b) refers to the "accused," the "prosecution," and a "criminal case," it does so only in the context of a notice requirement. The admissibility standards of Rule 404(b) remain fully applicable to both civil and criminal cases.

---

* See n. * at II-20, *supra*.

Advisory Committee Note to 2020 Amendment

Rule 404(b) has been amended principally to impose additional notice requirements on the prosecution in a criminal case. In addition, clarifications have been made to the text and headings.

The notice provision has been changed in a number of respects:

- The prosecution must not only identify the evidence that it intends to offer pursuant to the rule but also articulate a non-propensity purpose for which the evidence is offered and the basis for concluding that the evidence is relevant in light of this purpose. The earlier requirement that the prosecution provide notice of only the "general nature" of the evidence was understood by some courts to permit the government to satisfy the notice obligation without describing the specific act that the evidence would tend to prove, and without explaining the relevance of the evidence for a non-propensity purpose. This amendment makes clear what notice is required.
- The pretrial notice must be in writing—which requirement is satisfied by notice in electronic form. See Rule 101(b)(6). Requiring the notice to be in writing provides certainty and reduces arguments about whether notice was actually provided. In addition, notice must be provided before trial in such time as to allow the defendant a fair opportunity to meet the evidence, unless the court excuses that requirement upon a showing of good cause. See Rules 609(b), 807, and 902(11). Advance notice of Rule 404(b) evidence is important so that the parties and the court have adequate opportunity to assess the evidence, the purpose for which it is offered, and whether the requirements of Rule 403 have been satisfied, even in cases in which a final determination as to the admissibility of the evidence must await trial.
- The good cause exception applies not only to the timing of the notice as a whole but also to the obligations to articulate a non-propensity purpose and the reasoning supporting that purpose. A good cause exception for the articulation requirements is necessary because in some cases an additional permissible purpose for the evidence may not become clear until just before, or even during, trial.
- Finally, the amendment eliminates the requirement that the defendant must make a request before notice is provided. That requirement is not found in any other notice provision in the Federal Rules of Evidence. It has resulted mostly in boilerplate demands on the one hand, and a trap for the unwary on the other. Moreover, many local rules require the government to provide notice of Rule 404(b) material without regard to whether it has been requested. And in many cases, notice is provided when the government moves in limine for an advance ruling on the admissibility of Rule 404(b) evidence. The request requirement has thus outlived any usefulness it may once have had.

As to the textual clarifications, the word "other" is restored to the location it held before restyling in 2011, to confirm that Rule 404(b) applies to crimes, wrongs and acts "other" than those at issue in the case; and the headings are changed accordingly. No substantive change is intended.

Restyled 2011

Rule 405. Methods of Proving Character

(a) By Reputation or Opinion. When evidence of a person's character or character trait is admissible, it may be proved by testimony about the person's reputation or by testimony in the form of an opinion. On cross-examination of the character witness, the court may allow an inquiry into relevant specific instances of the person's conduct.

(b) By Specific Instances of Conduct. When a person's character or character trait is an essential element of a charge, claim, or defense, the character or trait may also be proved by relevant specific instances of the person's conduct.

Superseded 2011

Rule 405. Methods of Proving Character

(a) Reputation or opinion. In all cases in which evidence of character or a trait of character of a person is admissible, proof may be made by testimony as to reputation or by testimony in the form of an opinion. On cross-examination, inquiry is allowable into relevant specific instances of conduct.

(b) Specific instances of conduct. In cases in which character or a trait of character of a person is an essential element of a charge, claim, or defense, proof may also be made of specific instances of that person's conduct.

Advisory Committee's Note

The rule deals only with allowable methods of proving character, not with the admissibility of character evidence, which is covered in Rule 404.

Of the three methods of proving character provided by the rule, evidence of specific instances of conduct is the most convincing. At the same time it possesses the greatest capacity to arouse prejudice, to confuse, to surprise, and to consume time. Consequently the rule confines the use of evidence of this kind to cases in which character is, in the strict sense, in issue and hence deserving of a searching inquiry. When character is used circumstantially and hence occupies a lesser status in the case, proof may be only by reputation and opinion. These latter methods are also available when character is in issue. This treatment is, with respect to specific instances of conduct and reputation, conventional contemporary common law doctrine. McCormick § 153.

In recognizing opinion as a means of proving character, the rule departs from usual contemporary practice in favor of that of an earlier day. See 7 Wigmore § 1986, pointing out that the earlier practice permitted opinion and arguing strongly for evidence based on personal knowledge and belief as contrasted with "the secondhand, irresponsible product of multiplied guesses and gossip which we term 'reputation'." It seems likely that the persistence of reputation evidence is due to its largely being opinion in disguise. Traditionally character has been regarded primarily in moral overtones of good and bad: chaste, peaceable, truthful, honest. Nevertheless, on occasion nonmoral considerations crop up, as in the case of the incompetent driver, and this seems bound to happen increasingly. If character is defined as the kind of person one is, then account must be taken of varying ways of arriving at the estimate. These may range from the opinion of the employer who has found the man honest to the opinion of the psychiatrist based upon examination and testing. No effective dividing line exists between character and mental capacity, and the latter traditionally has been provable by opinion.

According to the great majority of cases, on cross-examination inquiry is allowable as to whether the reputation witness has heard of particular instances of conduct pertinent to the trait in question. Michelson v. United States, 335 U.S. 469, 69 S.Ct. 213, 93 L.Ed. 168 (1948); Annot., 47 A.L.R.2d 1258. The theory is that, since the reputation witness relates what he has heard, the inquiry tends to shed light on the accuracy of his hearing and reporting. Accordingly, the opinion witness would be asked whether he knew, as well as whether he had heard. The fact is, of course, that these distinctions are of slight if any practical significance, and the second sentence of subdivision (a) eliminates them as a factor in formulating questions. This recognition of the propriety of inquiring into specific instances of conduct does not circumscribe inquiry otherwise into the bases of opinion and reputation testimony.

The express allowance of inquiry into specific instances of conduct on cross-examination in subdivision (a) and the express allowance of it as part of a case in chief when character is actually in issue in subdivision (b) contemplate that testimony of specific instances is not generally permissible on the direct examination of an ordinary opinion witness to character. Similarly as to witnesses to the character of witnesses under Rule 608(b). Opinion testimony on direct in these situations ought in general to correspond to reputation testimony as now given, i.e., be confined to the nature and extent of observation and acquaintance upon which the opinion is based. See Rule 701.

House Judiciary Committee Report

Rule 405(a) as submitted proposed to change existing law by allowing evidence of character in the form of opinion as well as reputation testimony. Fearing, among other reasons, that wholesale allowance of opinion testimony might tend to turn a trial into a swearing contest between conflicting character witnesses, the Committee decided to delete from this Rule, as well as from Rule 608(a) which involves a related problem, reference to opinion testimony.

Conference Committee Report

The Senate makes two language changes in the nature of conforming amendments. The Conference adopts the Senate amendments.

Restyled 2011

Rule 406. Habit; Routine Practice

Evidence of a person's habit or an organization's routine practice may be admitted to prove that on a particular occasion the person or organization acted in accordance with the habit or routine practice. The court may admit this evidence regardless of whether it is corroborated or whether there was an eyewitness.

Superseded 2011

Rule 406. Habit; Routine Practice

Evidence of the habit of a person or of the routine practice of an organization, whether corroborated or not and regardless of the presence of eyewitnesses, is relevant to prove that the conduct of the person or organization on a particular occasion was in conformity with the habit or routine practice.

Advisory Committee's Note

* * * An oft-quoted paragraph, McCormick, § 162, p. 340, describes habit in terms effectively contrasting it with character:

> "Character and habit are close akin. Character is a generalized description of one's disposition, or of one's disposition in respect to a general trait, such as honesty, temperance, or peacefulness. 'Habit,' in modern usage, both lay and psychological, is more specific. It describes one's regular response to a repeated specific situation. If we speak of character for care, we think of the person's tendency to act prudently in all the varying situations of life, in business, family life, in handling automobiles and in walking across the street. A habit, on the other hand, is the person's regular practice of meeting a particular kind of situation with a specific type of conduct, such as the habit of going down a particular stairway two stairs at a time, or of giving the hand-signal for a left turn, or of alighting from railway cars while they are moving. The doing of the habitual acts may become semi-automatic."

Equivalent behavior on the part of a group is designated "routine practice of an organization" in the rule.

Agreement is general that habit evidence is highly persuasive as proof of conduct on a particular occasion. Again quoting McCormick § 162, p. 341:

> "Character may be thought of as the sum of one's habits though doubtless it is more than this. But unquestionably the uniformity of one's response to habit is far greater than the consistency with which one's conduct conforms to character or disposition. Even though character comes in only exceptionally as evidence of an act, surely any sensible man in investigating whether X did a particular act would be greatly helped in his inquiry by evidence as to whether he was in the habit of doing it."

When disagreement has appeared, its focus has been upon the question what constitutes habit, and the reason for this is readily apparent. The extent to which instances must be multiplied and consistency of behavior maintained in order to rise to the status of habit inevitably gives rise to differences of opinion. Lewan, Rationale of Habit Evidence, 16 Syracuse L.Rev. 39, 49 (1964). While adequacy of sampling and uniformity of response are key factors, precise standards for measuring their sufficiency for evidence purposes cannot be formulated.

The rule is consistent with prevailing views. Much evidence is excluded simply because of failure to achieve the status of habit. Thus, evidence of intemperate "habits" is generally excluded when offered as proof of drunkenness in accident cases, Annot., 46 A.L.R.2d 103, and evidence of other assaults is inadmissible to prove the instant one in a civil assault action, Annot., 66 A.L.R.2d 806. In Levin v. United States, 119 U.S.App.D.C. 156, 338 F.2d 265 (1964), testimony as to the religious "habits" of the accused, offered as tending to prove that he was at home observing the Sabbath rather than out obtaining money through larceny by trick, was held properly excluded:

> "It seems apparent to us that an individual's religious practices would not be the type of activities which would lend themselves to the characterization of 'invariable regularity.' [1 Wigmore 520.] Certainly the very volitional basis of the activity raises serious questions as to its invariable nature, and hence its probative value." Id. at 272.

These rulings are not inconsistent with the trend towards admitting evidence of business transactions between one of the parties and a third person as tending to prove that he made the same bargain or proposal in the litigated situation. Slough, Relevancy Unraveled, 6 Kan.L.Rev. 38-41 (1957). Nor are they inconsistent with such cases as Whittemore v. Lockheed Aircraft Corp., 65 Cal.App.2d 737, 151 P.2d 670 (1944), upholding the admission of evidence that plaintiff's intestate had on four other occasions flown planes from defendant's factory for delivery to his employer airline, offered to prove that he was piloting rather than a guest on a plane which crashed and killed all on board while en route for delivery.

A considerable body of authority has required that evidence of the routine practice of an organization be corroborated as a condition precedent to its admission in evidence. Slough, Relevancy Unraveled, 5 Kan.L.Rev. 404, 449 (1957). This requirement is specifically rejected by the rule on the ground that it relates to the sufficiency of the evidence rather than admissibility. A similar position is taken in New Jersey Rule 49. The rule also rejects the requirement of the absence of eyewitnesses, sometimes encountered with respect to admitting habit evidence to prove freedom from contributory negligence in wrongful death cases. For comment critical of the requirements see Frank, J., in Cereste v. New York, N.H. & H.R. Co., 231 F.2d 50 (2d Cir.1956), cert. denied 351 U.S. 951, 76 S.Ct. 848, 100 L.Ed. 1475, 10 Vand.L.Rev. 447 (1957); McCormick § 162, p. 342. The omission of the requirement from the California Evidence Code is said to have effected its elimination. Comment, Cal.Ev.Code § 1105. * * *

Restyled 2011

Rule 407. Subsequent Remedial Measures

When measures are taken that would have made an earlier injury or harm less likely to occur, evidence of the subsequent measures is not admissible to prove:

- negligence;
- culpable conduct;
- a defect in a product or its design; or
- a need for a warning or instruction.

But the court may admit this evidence for another purpose, such as impeachment or — if disputed — proving ownership, control, or the feasibility of precautionary measures.

Committee Note to 2011 Restyled Rule

Rule 407 previously provided that evidence was not excluded if offered for a purpose not explicitly prohibited by the Rule. To improve the language of the Rule, it now provides that the court may admit evidence if offered for a permissible purpose. There is no intent to change the process for admitting evidence covered by the Rule. It remains the case that if offered for an impermissible purpose, it must be excluded, and if offered for a purpose not barred by the Rule, its admissibility remains governed by the general principles of Rules 402, 403, 801, etc.

Superseded 2011

Rule 407. Subsequent Remedial Measures

When, after an injury or harm allegedly caused by an event, measures are taken that, if taken previously, would have made the injury or harm less likely to occur, evidence of the subsequent measures is not admissible to prove negligence, culpable conduct, a defect in a product, a defect in a product's design, or a need for a warning or instruction. This rule does not require the exclusion of evidence of subsequent measures when offered for another purpose, such as proving ownership, control, or feasibility of precautionary measures, if controverted, or impeachment. [*Amended 1997.*]

Case Notes

Rule 407 does not exclude evidence of subsequent remedial measures by someone other than the defendant. TLT-Babcock, Inc. v. Emerson Elec. Co., 33 F.3d 397 (4th Cir. 1994).

Impeachment use of a subsequent remedial measure is not triggered by testimony that a design or condition was "safe"; otherwise, the exception would swallow the rule; but evidence of a subsequent remedial measure may be used to impeach extravagant claims, such as that the design was the safest possible or could not possibly be improved. Wood v. Morbark Indus., 70 F.3d 1201, 1208 (11th Cir. 1995).

Advisory Committee's Note

The rule incorporates conventional doctrine which excludes evidence of subsequent remedial measures as proof of an admission of fault. The rule rests on two grounds. (1) The conduct is not in fact an admission, since the conduct is equally consistent with injury by mere accident or through contributory negligence. Or, as Baron Bramwell put it, the rule rejects the notion that "because the world gets wiser as it gets older, therefore it was foolish before." Hart v. Lancashire & Yorkshire Ry. Co., 21 L.T.R. N.S. 261, 263 (1869). Under a liberal theory of relevancy this ground alone would not support exclusion as the inference is still a possible one. (2) The other, and more impressive, ground for exclusion rests on a social policy of encouraging people to take, or at least not discouraging them from taking, steps in furtherance of added safety. The courts have applied this principle to exclude evidence of subsequent repairs, installation of safety devices, changes in company rules, and discharge of employees, and the language of the present rule is broad enough to encompass all of them. See Falknor, Extrinsic Policies Affecting Admissibility, 10 Rutgers L.Rev. 574, 590 (1956).

The second sentence of the rule directs attention to the limitations of the rule. Exclusion is called for only when the evidence of subsequent remedial measures is offered as proof of negligence or culpable conduct. In effect it rejects the suggested inference that fault is admitted. Other purposes are, however, allowable, including ownership or control, existence of duty, and feasibility of precautionary measures, if controverted, and impeachment. 2 Wigmore § 283; Annot., 64 A.L.R.2d 1296. Two recent federal cases are illustrative. Boeing Airplane Co. v. Brown, 291 F.2d 310 (9th Cir.1961), an action against an airplane manufacturer for using an allegedly defectively designed alternator shaft which caused a plane crash, upheld the admission of evidence of subsequent design modification for the purpose of showing that design changes and safeguards were feasible. And Powers v. J.B. Michael & Co., 329 F.2d 674 (6th Cir.1964), an action against a road contractor for negligent failure to put out warning signs, sustained the admission of evidence that defendant subsequently put out signs to show that the portion of the road in question was under defendant's control. The requirement that the other purpose be controverted calls for automatic exclusion unless a genuine issue be present and allows the opposing party to lay the groundwork for exclusion by making an admission. Otherwise the factors of undue prejudice, confusion of issues, misleading the jury, and waste of time remain for consideration under Rule 403.

For comparable rules, see Uniform Rule 51; California Evidence Code § 1151; Kansas Code of Civil Procedure § 60-451; New Jersey Evidence Rule 51.

Advisory Committee's Note to 1997 Amendment

The amendment to Rule 407 makes two changes in the rule. First, the words "an injury or harm allegedly caused by" were added to clarify that the rule applies only to changes made after the occurrence that produced the damages giving rise to the action. Evidence of measures taken by the defendant prior to the "event" causing "injury or harm" do not fall within the exclusionary scope of Rule 407 even if they occurred after the manufacture or design of the product. See Chase v. General Motors Corp., 856 F.2d 17, 21-22 (4th Cir. 1988).

Second, Rule 407 has been amended to provide that evidence of subsequent remedial measures may not be used to prove "a defect in a product or its design, or that a warning or instruction should have accompanied a product." This amendment adopts the view of a majority of the circuits that have interpreted Rule 407 to apply to products liability actions. See Raymond v. Raymond Corp., 938 F.2d 1518, 1522 (1st Cir. 1991); In re Joint Eastern District and Southern District Asbestos Litigation v. Armstrong World industries, Inc., 995 F.2d 343 (2d Cir. 1993); Cann v. Ford Motor Co., 658 F.2d 54, 60 (2d Cir. 1981), cert. denied, 456 U.S. 960 (1982); Kelly v. Crown Equipment Co., 970 F.2d 1273, 1275 (3d Cir. 1992); Werner v. Upjohn, Inc., 628 F.2d 848 (4th Cir. 1980); cert. denied, 449 U.S. 1080 (1981); Grenada Steel Industries, Inc. v. Alabama Oxygen Co., Inc., 695 F.2d 883 (5th Cir. 1983); Bauman v. Volkswagenwerk Aktiengesellschaft, 621 F.2d 230, 232 (6th Cir. 1980); Flaminio v. Honda Motor Company, Ltd., 733 F.2d 463, 469 (7th Cir. 1984); Gauthier v. AMF, Inc., 788 F.2d 634, 636-37 (9th Cir. 1986).

Although this amendment adopts a uniform federal rule, it should be noted that evidence of subsequent remedial measures may be admissible pursuant to the second sentence of Rule 407. Evidence of subsequent measures that is not barred by Rule 407 may still be subject to exclusion on Rule 403 grounds when the dangers of prejudice or confusion substantially outweigh the probative value of the evidence.

Restyled 2011

Rule 408. Compromise Offers and Negotiations

(a) Prohibited Uses. Evidence of the following is not admissible — on behalf of any party — either to prove or disprove the validity or amount of a disputed claim or to impeach by a prior inconsistent statement or a contradiction:

(1) Furnishing, promising, or offering, or accepting, promising to accept, or offering to accept, a valuable consideration in compromising or attempting to compromise the claim; and

(2) conduct or a statement made during compromise negotiations about the claim — except when offered in a criminal case and when the negotiations related to a claim by a public office in the exercise of its regulatory, investigative, or enforcement authority.

(b) Exceptions. The court may admit this evidence for another purpose, such as proving a witness's bias or prejudice, negating a contention of undue delay, or proving an effort to obstruct a criminal investigation or prosecution.

Committee Note to 2011 Restyled Rule

Rule 408 previously provided that evidence was not excluded if offered for a purpose not explicitly prohibited by the Rule. To improve the language of the Rule, it now provides that the court may admit evidence if offered for a permissible purpose. There is no intent to change the process for admitting evidence covered by the Rule. It remains the case that if offered for an impermissible purpose, it must be excluded, and if offered for a purpose not barred by the Rule, its admissibility remains governed by the general principles of Rules 402, 403, 801, etc.

The Committee deleted the reference to "liability" on the ground that the deletion makes the Rule flow better and easier to read, and because "liability" is covered by the broader term "validity." Courts have not made substantive decisions on the basis of any distinction between validity and liability. No change in current practice or in the coverage of the Rule is intended.

Superseded 2011

Rule 408. Compromise and Offers to Compromise

(a) Prohibited uses.—Evidence of the following is not admissible on behalf of any party, when offered to prove liability for, invalidity of, or amount of a claim that was disputed as to validity or amount, or to impeach through a prior inconsistent statement or contradiction:

(1) furnishing or offering or promising to furnish—or accepting or offering or promising to accept—a valuable consideration in compromising or attempting to compromise the claim; and

(2) conduct or statements made in compromise negotiations regarding the claim, except when offered in a criminal case and the negotiations related to a claim by a public office or agency in the exercise of regulatory, investigative, or enforcement authority.

(b) Permitted uses.—This rule does not require exclusion if the evidence is offered for purposes not prohibited by subdivision (a). Examples of permissible purposes include proving a witness's bias or prejudice; negating a contention of undue delay; and proving an effort to obstruct a criminal investigation or prosecution. [*Amended 2006.*]

Original Advisory Committee's Note

As a matter of general agreement, evidence of an offer to compromise a claim is not receivable in evidence as an admission of, as the case may be, the validity or invalidity of the claim. As with evidence of subsequent remedial measures, dealt with in Rule 407, exclusion may be based on two grounds. (1) The evidence is irrelevant, since the offer may be motivated by a desire for peace rather than from any concession of weakness of position. The validity of this position will vary as the amount of the offer varies in relation to the size of the claim and may also be influenced by other circumstances. (2) A more consistently impressive ground is promotion of the public policy favoring the compromise and settlement of disputes. McCormick §§ 76, 251. While the rule is ordinarily phrased in terms of offers of compromise, it is apparent that a similar attitude must be taken with respect to completed compromises when offered against a party thereto. This latter situation will not, of course, ordinarily occur except when a party to the present litigation has compromised with a third person.

The same policy underlies the provision of Rule 68 of the Federal Rules of Civil Procedure that evidence of an unaccepted offer of judgment is not admissible except in a proceeding to determine costs.

The practical value of the common law rule has been greatly diminished by its inapplicability to admissions of fact, even though made in the course of compromise negotiations, unless hypothetical, stated to be "without prejudice," or so connected with the offer as to be inseparable from it. McCormick § 251, pp. 540-541. An inevitable effect is to inhibit freedom of communication with respect to compromise, even among lawyers. Another effect is the generation of controversy over whether a given statement falls within or without the protected area. These considerations account for the expansion of the rule herewith to include evidence of conduct or statements made in compromise negotiations, as well as the offer or completed compromise itself. For similar provisions see California Evidence Code §§ 1152, 1154.

The policy considerations which underlie the rule do not come into play when the effort is to induce a creditor to settle an admittedly due amount for a lesser sum. McCormick § 251, p. 540. Hence the rule requires that the claim be disputed as to either validity or amount.

The final sentence of the rule serves to point out some limitations upon its applicability. Since the rule excludes only when the purpose is proving the validity or invalidity of the claim or its amount, an offer for another purpose is not within the rule. The illustrative situations mentioned in the rule are supported by the authorities. As to proving bias or prejudice of a witness, see Annot., 161 A.L.R. 395, contra, Fenberg v. Rosenthal, 348 Ill.App. 510, 109 N.E.2d 402 (1952), and negativing a contention of lack of due diligence in presenting a claim, 4 Wigmore § 1061. An effort to "buy off" the prosecution or a prosecuting witness in a criminal case is not within the policy of the rule of exclusion. McCormick § 251, p. 542.

For other rules of similar import, see Uniform Rules 52 and 53; California Evidence Code §§ 1152, 1154; Kansas Code of Civil Procedure §§ 60-452, 60-453; New Jersey Evidence Rules 52 and 53.

House Judiciary Committee Report

Under existing federal law evidence of conduct and statements made in compromise negotiations is admissible in subsequent litigation between the parties. The second sentence of Rule 408 as submitted by the Supreme Court proposed to reverse that doctrine in the interest of further promoting non-judicial settlement of disputes. Some agencies of government expressed the view that the Court formulation was likely to impede rather than assist efforts to achieve settlement of disputes. For one thing, it is not always easy to tell when compromise negotiations begin, and informal dealings end. Also, parties dealing with government agencies would be reluctant to furnish factual information at preliminary meetings; they would wait until "compromise negotiations" began and thus hopefully effect an immunity for themselves with respect to the evidence supplied. In light of these considerations, the Committee recast the Rule so that admissions of liability or opinions given during compromise negotiations continue inadmissible, but evidence of unqualified factual assertions is admissible. The latter aspect of the Rule is drafted, however, so as to preserve other possible objections to the introduction of such evidence. The Committee intends no modification of current law whereby a party may protect himself from future use of his statements by couching them in hypothetical conditional form.

Senate Judiciary Committee Report

This rule as reported makes evidence of settlement or attempted settlement of a disputed claim inadmissible when offered as an admission of liability or the amount of liability. The purpose of this rule is to encourage settlements which would be discouraged if such evidence were admissible.

Under present law, in most jurisdictions, statements of fact made during settlement negotiations, however, are excepted from this ban and are admissible. The only escape from admissibility of statements of fact made in a settlement negotiation is if the declarant or his representative expressly states that the statement is hypothetical in nature or is made without prejudice. Rule 408 as submitted by the Court reversed the traditional rule. It would have brought statements of fact within the ban and made them, as well as an offer of settlement, inadmissible.

The House amended the rule and would continue to make evidence of facts disclosed during compromise negotiations admissible. It thus reverted to the traditional rule. The House committee report states that the committee intends to preserve current law under which a party may protect himself by couching his statements in hypothetical form [See House Report No. 93-650 above]. The real impact of this amendment, however, is to deprive the rule of much of its salutary effect. The exception for factual admissions was believed by the Advisory Committee to hamper free communication between parties and thus to constitute an unjustifiable restraint upon efforts to negotiate settlements—the encouragement of which is the purpose of the rule. Further, by protecting hypothetically phrased statements, it constituted a preference for the sophisticated, and a trap for the unwary.

Three States which had adopted rules of evidence patterned after the proposed rules prescribed by the Supreme Court opted for versions of rule 408 identical with the Supreme Court draft with respect to the inadmissibility of conduct or statements made in compromise negotiations [Nev.Rev.Stats. § 48.105; N.Mex.Stats.Anno. (1973 Supp.) § 20-4-408; West's Wis.Stats.Anno. (1973 Supp.) § 904.08].

For these reasons, the committee has deleted the House amendment and restored the rule to the version submitted by the Supreme Court with one additional amendment. This amendment adds a sentence to insure that evidence, such as documents, is not rendered inadmissible merely because it is presented in the course of compromise negotiations if the evidence is otherwise discoverable. A party should not be able to immunize from admissibility documents otherwise discoverable merely by offering them in a compromise negotiation.

Conference Committee Report

The House bill provides that evidence of admissions of liability or opinions given during compromise negotiations is not admissible, but that evidence of facts disclosed during compromise negotiations is not inadmissible by virtue of having been first disclosed in the compromise negotiations. The Senate amendment provides that evidence of conduct or statements made in compromise negotiations is not admissible. The Senate amendment also provides that the rule does not require the exclusion of any evidence otherwise discoverable merely because it is presented in the course of compromise negotiations.

The House bill was drafted to meet the objection of executive agencies that under the rule as proposed by the Supreme Court, a party could present a fact during compromise negotiations and thereby prevent an opposing party from offering evidence of that fact at trial even though such evidence was obtained from independent sources. The Senate amendment expressly precludes this result.

The Conference adopts the Senate amendment.

Advisory Committee's Note to 2006 Amendment

Rule 408 has been amended to settle some questions in the courts about the scope of the Rule, and to make it easier to read. First, the amendment provides that Rule 408 does not prohibit the introduction in a criminal case of statements or conduct during compromise negotiations regarding a civil dispute by a government regulatory, investigative, or enforcement agency. See, e.g., United States v. Prewitt, 34 F.3d 436, 439 (7th Cir. 1994) (admissions of fault made in compromise of a civil securities enforcement action were admissible against the accused in a subsequent criminal action for mail fraud). Where an individual makes a statement in the presence of government agents, its subsequent admission in a criminal case should not be unexpected. The individual can seek to protect against subsequent disclosure through negotiation and agreement with the civil regulator or an attorney for the government.

Statements made in compromise negotiations of a claim by a government agency may be excluded in criminal cases where the circumstances so warrant under Rule 403. For example, if an individual was unrepresented at the time the statement was made in a civil enforcement proceeding, its probative value in a subsequent criminal case may be minimal. But there is no absolute exclusion imposed by Rule 408.

In contrast, statements made during compromise negotiations of other disputed claims are not admissible in subsequent criminal litigation, when offered to prove liability for, invalidity of, or amount of those claims. When private parties enter into compromise negotiations they cannot protect against the subsequent use of statements in criminal cases by way of private ordering. The inability to guarantee protection against subsequent use could lead to parties refusing to admit fault, even if by doing so they could favorably settle the private matter. Such a chill on settlement negotiations would be contrary to the policy of Rule 408.

The amendment distinguishes statements and conduct (such as a direct admission of fault) made in compromise negotiations of a civil claim by a government agency from an offer or acceptance of a compromise of such a claim. An offer or acceptance of a compromise of any civil claim is excluded under the Rule if offered against the defendant as an admission of fault. In that case, the predicate for the evidence would be that the defendant, by compromising with the government agency, has admitted the validity and amount of the civil claim, and that this admission has sufficient probative value to be considered as evidence of guilt. But unlike a direct statement of fault, an offer or acceptance of a compromise is not very probative of the defendant's guilt. Moreover, admitting such an offer or acceptance could deter a defendant from settling a civil regulatory action, for fear of evidentiary use in a subsequent criminal action. See, e.g., Fishman, Jones on Evidence, Civil and Criminal, § 22:16 at 199, n.83 (7th ed. 2000) ("A target of a potential criminal investigation may be unwilling to settle civil claims against him if by doing so he increases the risk of prosecution and conviction.").

The amendment retains the language of the original rule that bars compromise evidence only when offered as evidence of the "validity," "invalidity," or "amount" of the disputed claim. The intent is to retain the extensive case law finding Rule 408 inapplicable when compromise evidence is offered for a purpose other than to prove the validity, invalidity, or amount of a disputed claim. See, e.g., Athey v. Farmers Ins. Exchange, 234 F.3d 357 (8th Cir. 2000) (evidence of settlement offer by insurer was properly admitted to prove insurer's bad faith); Coakley & Williams v. Structural Concrete Equip., 973 F.2d 349 (4th Cir. 1992) (evidence of settlement is not precluded by Rule 408 where offered to prove a party's intent with respect to the scope of a release); Cates v. Morgan Portable Bldg. Corp., 708 F.2d 683 (7th Cir. 1985) (Rule 408 does not bar evidence of a settlement when offered to prove a breach of the settlement agreement, as the purpose of the evidence is to prove the fact of settlement as opposed to the validity or amount of the underlying claim); Uforma/Shelby Bus. Forms, Inc. v. NLRB, 111 F.3d 1284 (6th Cir. 1997) (threats made in settlement negotiations were admissible; Rule 408 is inapplicable when the claim is based upon a wrong that is committed during the course of settlement negotiations). So for example, Rule 408 is inapplicable if offered to show that a party made fraudulent statements in order to settle a litigation.

The amendment does not affect the case law providing that Rule 408 is inapplicable when evidence of the compromise is offered to prove notice. See, e.g., United States v. Austin, 54 F.3d 394 (7th Cir. 1995) (no error to admit evidence of the defendant's settlement with the FTC, because it was offered to prove that the defendant was on notice that subsequent similar conduct was wrongful); Spell v. McDaniel, 824 F.2d 1380 (4th Cir. 1987) (in a civil rights action alleging that an officer used excessive force, a prior settlement by the City of another brutality claim was properly admitted to prove that the City was on notice of aggressive behavior by police officers).

The amendment prohibits the use of statements made in settlement negotiations when offered to impeach by prior inconsistent statement or through contradiction. Such broad impeachment would tend to swallow the exclusionary rule and would impair the public policy of promoting settlements. See McCormick on Evidence at 186 (5th ed. 1999) ("Use of statements made in compromise negotiations to impeach the testimony of a party, which is not specifically treated in Rule 408, is fraught with danger of misuse of the statements to prove liability, threatens frank interchange of information during negotiations, and generally should not be permitted."). See also EEOC v. Gear Petroleum, Inc., 948 F.2d 1542 (10th Cir.1991) (letter sent as part of settlement negotiation cannot be used to impeach defense witnesses by way of contradiction or prior inconsistent statement; such broad impeachment would undermine the policy of encouraging uninhibited settlement negotiations).

The amendment makes clear that Rule 408 excludes compromise evidence even when a party seeks to admit its own settlement offer or statements made in settlement negotiations. If a party were to reveal its own statement or offer, this could itself reveal the fact that the adversary entered into settlement negotiations. The protections of Rule 408 cannot be waived unilaterally because the Rule, by definition, protects both parties from having the fact of negotiation disclosed to the jury. Moreover, proof of statements and offers made in settlement would often have to be made through the testimony of attorneys, leading to the risks and costs of disqualification. See generally Pierce v. F.R. Tripler & Co., 955 F.2d 820, 828 (2d Cir. 1992) (settlement offers are excluded under Rule 408 even if it is the offeror who seeks to admit them; noting that the "widespread admissibility of the substance of settlement offers could bring with it a rash of motions for disqualification of a party's chosen counsel who would likely become a witness at trial").

The sentence of the Rule referring to evidence "otherwise discoverable" has been deleted as superfluous. See, e.g., Advisory Committee Note to Maine Rule of Evidence 408 (refusing to include the sentence in the Maine version of Rule 408 and noting that the sentence "seems to state what the law would be if it were omitted"); Advisory Committee Note to Wyoming Rule of Evidence 408 (refusing to include the sentence in Wyoming Rule 408 on the ground that it was "superfluous"). The intent of the sentence was to prevent a party from trying to immunize admissible information, such as a pre-existing document, through the pretense of disclosing it during compromise negotiations. See Ramada Development Co. v. Rauch, 644 F.2d 1097 (5th Cir. 1981). But even without the sentence, the Rule cannot be read to protect pre-existing information simply because it was presented to the adversary in compromise negotiations.

Restyled 2011

Rule 409. Offers to Pay Medical and Similar Expenses

Evidence of furnishing, promising to pay, or offering to pay medical, hospital, or similar expenses resulting from an injury is not admissible to prove liability for the injury.

Superseded 2011

Rule 409. Payment of Medical and Similar Expenses

Evidence of furnishing or offering or promising to pay medical, hospital, or similar expenses occasioned by an injury is not admissible to prove liability for the injury.

Advisory Committee's Note

The considerations underlying this rule parallel those underlying Rules 407 and 408, which deal respectively with subsequent remedial measures and offers of compromise. As stated in Annot., 20 A.L.R.2d 291, 293:

"[G]enerally, evidence of payment of medical, hospital, or similar expenses of an injured party by the opposing party, is not admissible, the reason often given being that such payment or offer is usually made from humane impulses and not from an admission of liability, and that to hold otherwise would tend to discourage assistance to the injured person."

Contrary to Rule 408, dealing with offers of compromise, the present rule does not extend to conduct or statements not a part of the act of furnishing or offering or promising to pay. This difference in treatment arises from fundamental differences in nature. Communication is essential if compromises are to be effected, and consequently broad protection of statements is needed. This is not so in cases of payments or offers or promises to pay medical expenses, where factual statements may be expected to be incidental in nature.

For rules on the same subject, but phrased in terms of "humanitarian motives," see Uniform Rule 52; California Evidence Code § 1152; Kansas Code of Civil Procedure § 60-452; New Jersey Evidence Rule 52.

Restyled 2011

Rule 410. Pleas, Plea Discussions, and Related Statements

(a) Prohibited Uses. In a civil or criminal case, evidence of the following is not admissible against the defendant who made the plea or participated in the plea discussions:

(1) a guilty plea that was later withdrawn;

(2) a nolo contendere plea;

(3) a statement made during a proceeding on either of those pleas under Federal Rule of Criminal Procedure 11 or a comparable state procedure; or**(4)** a statement made during plea discussions with an attorney for the prosecuting authority if the discussions did not result in a guilty plea or they resulted in a later-withdrawn guilty plea.

(b) Exceptions. The court may admit a statement described in Rule 410(a)(3) or (4):

(1) in any proceeding in which another statement made during the same plea or plea discussions has been introduced, if in fairness the statements ought to be considered together; or

(2) in a criminal proceeding for perjury or false statement, if the defendant made the statement under oath, on the record, and with counsel present.

Superseded 2011

Rule 410. Inadmissibility of Pleas, Plea Discussions, and Related Statements

Except as otherwise provided in this rule, evidence of the following is not, in any civil or criminal proceeding, admissible against the defendant who made the plea or was a participant in the plea discussions:

(1) a plea of guilty which was later withdrawn;

(2) a plea of nolo contendere;

(3) any statement made in the course of any proceedings under Rule 11 of the Federal Rules of Criminal Procedure or comparable state procedure regarding either of the foregoing pleas; or

(4) any statement made in the course of plea discussions with an attorney for the prosecuting authority which do not result in a plea of guilty or which result in a plea of guilty later withdrawn.

However, such a statement is admissible (i) in any proceeding wherein another statement made in the course of the same plea or plea discussions has been introduced and the statement ought in fairness be considered contemporaneously with it, or (ii) in a criminal proceeding for perjury or false statement if the statement was made by the defendant under oath, on the record and in the presence of counsel. [*Amended 1975, 1980.*]

Case Note

A defendant may waive the exclusionary protection of Rule 410 by knowingly and voluntarily agreeing that statements made during plea negotiations can be used to impeach any contradictory testimony he might give in the event the case goes to trial. United States v. Mezzanatto, 513 U.S. 196, 115 S.Ct. 797, 130 L.Ed. 2d 697 (1995).

Advisory Committee's Note

Withdrawn pleas of guilty were held inadmissible in federal prosecutions in Kercheval v. United States, 274 U.S. 220, 47 S.Ct. 582, 71 L.Ed. 1009 (1927). The Court pointed out that to admit the withdrawn plea would effectively set at naught the allowance of withdrawal and place the accused in a dilemma utterly inconsistent with the decision to award him a trial. The New York Court of Appeals, in People v. Spitaleri, 9 N.Y.2d 168, 212 N.Y.S.2d 53, 173 N.E.2d 35 (1961), reexamined and overturned its earlier decisions which had allowed admission. In addition to the reasons set forth in Kercheval, which was quoted at length, the court pointed out that the effect of admitting the plea was to compel defendant to take the stand by way of explanation and to open the way for the prosecution to call the lawyer who had represented him at the time of entering the plea. State court decisions for and against admissibility are collected in Annot., 86 A.L.R.2d 326.

Pleas of nolo contendere are recognized by Rule 11 of the Rules of Criminal Procedure, although the law of numerous States is to the contrary. The present rule gives effect to the principal traditional characteristic of the nolo plea, i.e. avoiding the admission of guilt which is inherent in pleas of guilty. This position is consistent with the construction of Section 5 of the Clayton Act, 15 U.S.C. § 16(a), recognizing the inconclusive and compromise nature of judgments based on nolo pleas. General Electric Co. v. City of San Antonio, 334 F.2d 480 (5th Cir.1964); Commonwealth Edison Co. v. Allis-Chalmers Mfg. Co., 323 F.2d 412 (7th Cir.1963), cert. denied 376 U.S. 939, 84 S.Ct. 794,

11 L.Ed.2d 659; Armco Steel Corp. v. North Dakota, 376 F.2d 206 (8th Cir.1967); City of Burbank v. General Electric Co., 329 F.2d 825 (9th Cir.1964). See also state court decisions in Annot., 18 A.L.R.2d 1287, 1314.

Exclusion of offers to plead guilty or nolo has as its purpose the promotion of disposition of criminal cases by compromise. As pointed out in McCormick § 251, p. 543:

"Effective criminal law administration in many localities would hardly be possible if a large proportion of the charges were not disposed of by such compromises."

See also People v. Hamilton, 60 Cal.2d 105, 32 Cal.Rptr. 4, 383 P.2d 412 (1963), discussing legislation designed to achieve this result. As with compromise offers generally, Rule 408, free communication is needed, and security against having an offer of compromise or related statement admitted in evidence effectively encourages it.

Limiting the exclusionary rule to use against the accused is consistent with the purpose of the rule, since the possibility of use for or against other persons will not impair the effectiveness of withdrawing pleas or the freedom of discussion which the rule is designed to foster. See A.B.A. Standards Relating to Pleas of Guilty § 2.2 (1968). See also the narrower provisions of New Jersey Evidence Rule 52(2) and the unlimited exclusion provided in California Evidence Code § 1153.

House Judiciary Committee Report

The Committee added the phrase "Except as otherwise provided by Act of Congress" to Rule 410 as submitted by the Court in order to preserve particular congressional policy judgments as to the effect of a plea of guilty or of nolo contendere. See 15 U.S.C. 16(a). The Committee intends that its amendment refers to both present statutes and statutes subsequently enacted.

Senate Judiciary Committee Report

As adopted by the House, rule 410 would make inadmissible pleas of guilty or nolo contendere subsequently withdrawn as well as offers to make such pleas. Such a rule is clearly justified as a means of encouraging pleading. However, the House rule would then go on to render inadmissible for any purpose statements made in connection with these pleas or offers as well.

The committee finds this aspect of the House rule unjustified. Of course, in certain circumstances such statements should be excluded. If, for example, a plea is vitiated because of coercion, statements made in connection with the plea may also have been coerced and should be inadmissible on that basis. In other cases, however, voluntary statements of an accused made in court on the record, in connection with a plea, and determined by a court to be reliable should be admissible even though the plea is subsequently withdrawn. This is particularly true in those cases where, if the House rule were in effect, a defendant would be able to contradict his previous statements and thereby lie with impunity [See Harris v. New York, 401 U.S. 222 (1971)]. To prevent such an injustice, the rule has been modified to permit the use of such statements for the limited purposes of impeachment and in subsequent perjury or false statement prosecutions.

Conference Committee Report

The House bill provides that evidence of a guilty or nolo contendere plea, of an offer of either plea, or of statements made in connection with such pleas or offers of such pleas, is inadmissible in any civil or criminal action, case or proceeding against the person making such plea or offer. The Senate amendment makes the rule inapplicable to a voluntary and reliable statement made in court on the record where the statement is offered in a subsequent prosecution of the declarant for perjury or false statement.

The issues raised by Rule 410 are also raised by proposed Rule 11(e)(6) of the Federal Rules of Criminal Procedure presently pending before Congress. This proposed rule, which deals with the admissibility of pleas of guilty or nolo contendere, offers to make such pleas, and statements made in connection with such pleas, was promulgated by the Supreme Court on April 22, 1974, and in the absence of congressional action will become effective on August 1, 1975. The conferees intend to make no change in the presently-existing case law until that date, leaving the courts free to develop rules in this area on a case-by-case basis.

The Conferees further determined that the issues presented by the use of guilty and nolo contendere pleas, offers of such pleas, and statements made in connection with such pleas or offers, can be explored in greater detail during Congressional consideration of Rule 11(e)(6) of the Federal Rules of Criminal Procedure. The Conferees believe, therefore, that it is best to defer its effective date until August 1, 1975. The Conferees intend that Rule 410 would be superseded by any subsequent Federal Rule of Criminal Procedure or act of Congress with which it is inconsistent, if the Federal Rule of Criminal Procedure or Act of Congress takes effect or becomes law after the date of the enactment of the act establishing the rules of evidence.

The conference adopts the Senate amendment with an amendment that expresses the above intentions.

Advisory Committee's Note to 1980 Amendment

Present rule 410 conforms to rule 11(e)(6) of the Federal Rules of Criminal Procedure. A proposed amendment to rule 11(e)(6) would clarify the circumstances in which pleas, plea discussions and related statements are inadmissible in evidence: see Advisory Committee's Note thereto [set forth below]. The amendment proposed above would make comparable changes in rule 410.

Advisory Committee's Note to 1980 Amendment to Fed.R.Crim.P. 11(e)(6)

The major objective of the amendment to rule 11(e)(6) is to describe more precisely, consistent with the original purpose of the provision, what evidence relating to pleas or plea discussions is inadmissible. The present language is susceptible to interpretation which would make it applicable to a wide variety of statements made under various circumstances other than within the context of those plea discussions authorized by rule 11(e) and intended to be protected by subdivision (e)(6) of the rule. See United States v. Herman, 544 F.2d 791 (5th Cir. 1977), discussed herein.

Fed.R.Ev. 410, as originally adopted by Pub.L. 93-595, provided in part that "evidence of a plea of guilty, later withdrawn, or a plea of nolo contendere, or of an offer to plead guilty or nolo contendere to the crime charged or any other crime, or of statements made in connection with any of the foregoing pleas or offers, is not admissible in any civil or criminal action, case, or proceeding against the person who made the plea or offer." (This rule was adopted with the proviso that it "shall be superseded by any amendment to the Federal Rules of Criminal Procedure which is inconsistent with this rule.") As the Advisory Committee Note explained: "Exclusion of offers to plead guilty or nolo has as its purpose the promotion of disposition of criminal cases by compromise." The amendment of Fed.R.Crim.P. 11, transmitted to Congress by the Supreme Court in April 1974, contained a subdivision (e) (6) essentially identical to the rule 410 language quoted above, as a part of a substantial revision of rule 11. The most significant feature of this revision was the express recognition given to the fact that the "attorney for the government and the attorney for the defendant or the defendant when acting pro se may engage in discussions with a view toward reaching" a plea agreement. Subdivision (e) (6) was intended to encourage such discussions. As noted in H.R. Rep. No. 94-247, 94th Cong., 1st Sess. 7 (1975), the purpose of subdivision (e) (6) is to not "discourage defendants from being completely candid and open during plea negotiations." Similarly, H.R.Rep. No. 94-414, 94th Cong., 1st Sess. 10 (1975), states that "Rule 11e(6) deals with the use of statements made in connection with plea agreements." (Rule 11(e) (6) was thereafter enacted, with the addition of the proviso allowing use of statements in a prosecution for perjury, and with the qualification that the inadmissible statements must also be "relevant to" the inadmissible pleas or offers. Pub.L. 94-64; Fed.R.Ev. 410 was then amended to conform. Pub.L. 94-149.)

While this history shows that the purpose of Fed.R.Ev. 410 and Fed.R.Crim.P. 11(e) (6) is to permit the unrestrained candor which produces effective plea discussions between the "attorney for the government and the attorney for the defendant or the defendant when acting pro se," given visibility and sanction in rule 11(e), a literal reading of the language of these two rules could reasonably lead to the conclusion that a broader rule of inadmissibility obtains. That is, because "statements" are generally inadmissible if "made in connection with, and relevant to" an "offer to plead guilty," it might be thought that an otherwise voluntary admission to law enforcement officials is rendered inadmissible merely because it was made in the hope of obtaining leniency by a plea. Some decisions interpreting rule 11(e)(6) point in this direction. See United States v. Herman, 544 F.2d 791 (5th Cir. 1977) (defendant in custody of two postal inspectors during continuance of removal hearing instigated conversation with them and at some point said he would plead guilty to armed robbery if the murder charge was dropped; one inspector stated they were not "in position" to make any deals in this regard; held, defendant's statement inadmissible under rule 11(e) (6) because the defendant "made the statements during the course of a conversation in which he sought concessions from the government in return for a guilty plea"); United States v. Brooks, 536 F.2d 1137 (6th Cir. 1976) (defendant telephoned postal inspector and offered to plead guilty if he got 2-year maximum; statement inadmissible).

The amendment makes inadmissible statements made "in the course of any proceedings under this rule regarding" either a plea of guilty later withdrawn or a plea of nolo contendere, and also statements "made in the course of plea discussions with an attorney for the government which do not result in a plea of guilty or which result in a plea of guilty later withdrawn." It is not limited to statements by the defendant himself, and thus would cover statements by defense counsel regarding defendant's incriminating admissions to him. It thus fully protects the plea discussion process authorized by rule 11 without attempting to deal with confrontations between suspects and law enforcement agents, which involve problems of quite different dimensions. See, e.g., ALI Model Code of Pre-Arraignment Procedure, art. 140 and § 150.2(8) (Proposed Official Draft, 1975) (latter section requires exclusion if "a law enforcement officer induces any person to make a statement by promising leniency"). This change, it must be emphasized, does not compel the conclusion that statements made to law enforcement agents, especially when the agents purport to have authority to bargain, are inevitably admissible. Rather, the point is that such cases are not covered by the per se rule of 11(e) (6) and thus must be resolved by that body of law dealing with police interrogations.

If there has been a plea of guilty later withdrawn or a plea of nolo contendere, subdivision (e) (6) (C) makes inadmissible statements made "in the course of any proceedings under this rule" regarding such pleas. This includes, for example, admissions by the defendant when he makes his plea in court pursuant to rule 11 and also admissions made to provide the factual basis pursuant to subdivision (f). However, subdivision (e) (6) (C) is not limited to statements made in court. If the court were to defer its decision on a plea agreement pending examination of the presentence report, as authorized by subdivision (e) (2), statements made to the probation officer in connection with the preparation of that report would come within this provision.

This amendment is fully consistent with all recent and major law reform efforts on this subject. ALI Model Code of Pre-Arraignment Procedure § 350.7 (Proposed Official Draft, 1975), and ABA Standards Relating to Pleas of Guilty § 3.4 (Approved Draft, 1968) both provide:

> Unless the defendant subsequently enters a plea of guilty or nolo contendere which is not withdrawn, the fact that the defendant or his counsel and the prosecuting attorney engaged in plea discussions or made a plea agreement should not be received in evidence against or in favor of the defendant in any criminal or civil action or administrative proceedings.

The Commentary to the latter states:

> The above standard is limited to discussions and agreements with the prosecuting attorney. Sometimes defendants will indicate to the police their willingness to bargain, and in such instances these statements are sometimes admitted in court against the defendant. State v. Christian, 245 S.W.2d 895 (Mo.1952). If the police initiate this kind of discussion, this may have some bearing on the admissibility of the defendant's statement. However, the policy considerations relevant to this issue are better dealt with in the context of standards governing in-custody interrogation by the police.

Similarly, Unif.R.Crim.P. 441(d) (Approved Draft, 1974), provides that except under limited circumstances "no discussion between the parties or statement by the defendant or his lawyer under this Rule," i.e., the rule providing "the parties may meet to discuss the possibility of pretrial diversion . . . or of a plea agreement," are admissible. The amendment is likewise consistent with the typical state provision on this subject; see, e.g., Ill.S.Ct. Rule 402(f).

The language of the amendment identifies with more precision than the present language the necessary relationship between the statements and the plea or discussion. See the dispute between the majority and concurring opinions in United States v. Herman, 544 F.2d 791 (5th Cir. 1977), concerning the meanings and effect of the phrases "connection to" and "relevant to" in the present rule. Moreover, by relating the statements to "plea discussions" rather than "an offer to plead," the amendment ensures "that even an attempt to open plea bargaining [is] covered under the same rule of inadmissibility." United States v. Brooks, 536 F.2d 1137 (6th Cir. 1976).

The last sentence of Rule 11(e) (6) is amended to provide a second exception to the general rule of nonadmissibility of the described statements. Under the amendment, such a statement is also admissible "in any proceeding wherein another statement made in the course of the same plea or plea discussions has been introduced and the statement ought in fairness be considered contemporaneously with it." This change is necessary so that, when evidence of statements made in the course of or as a consequence of a certain plea or plea discussions are introduced under circumstances not prohibited by this rule (e.g., not "against" the person who made the plea), other statements relating to the same plea or plea discussions may also be admitted when relevant to the matter at issue. For example, if a defendant upon a motion to dismiss a prosecution on some ground were able to admit certain statements made in aborted plea discussions in his favor, then other relevant statements made in the same plea discussions should be admissible against the defendant in the interest of determining the truth of the matter at issue. The language of the amendment follows closely that in Fed.R.Evid. 106, as the considerations involved are very similar.

The phrase "in any civil or criminal proceeding" has been moved from its present position, following the word "against," for purposes of clarity. An ambiguity presently exists because the word "against" may be read as referring either to the kind of proceeding in which the evidence is offered or the purpose for which it is offered. The change makes it clear that the latter construction is correct. No change is intended with respect to provisions making evidence rules inapplicable in certain situations. See, e.g., Fed.R.Evid. 104(a) and 1101(d).

Unlike ABA Standards Relating to Pleas of Guilty § 3.4 (Approved Draft, 1968), and ALI Model Code of Pre-Arraignment Procedure § 350.7 (Proposed Official Draft, 1975), rule 11(e) (6) does not also provide that the described evidence is inadmissible "in favor of" the defendant. This is not intended to suggest, however, that such evidence will inevitably be admissible in the defendant's favor. Specifically, no disapproval is intended of such decisions as United States v. Verdoorn, 528 F.2d 103 (8th Cir. 1976), holding that the trial judge properly refused to permit the defendants to put into evidence at their trial the fact the prosecution had attempted to plea bargain with them, as "meaningful dialogue between the parties would, as a practical matter, be impossible if either party had to assume the risk that plea offers would be admissible in evidence."

Restyled 2011

Rule 411. Liability Insurance

Evidence that a person was or was not insured against liability is not admissible to prove whether the person acted negligently or otherwise wrongfully. But the court may admit this evidence for another purpose, such as proving a witness's bias or prejudice or proving agency, ownership, or control.

Committee Note to 2011 Restyled Rule

Rule 411 previously provided that evidence was not excluded if offered for a purpose not explicitly prohibited by the Rule. To improve the language of the Rule, it now provides that the court may admit evidence if offered for a permissible purpose. There is no intent to change the process for admitting evidence covered by the Rule. It remains the case that if offered for an impermissible purpose, it must be excluded, and if offered for a purpose not barred by the Rule, its admissibility remains governed by the general principles of Rules 402, 403, 801, etc.

Superseded 2011

Rule 411. Liability Insurance

Evidence that a person was or was not insured against liability is not admissible upon the issue whether the person acted negligently or otherwise wrongfully. This rule does not require the exclusion of evidence of insurance against liability when offered for another purpose, such as proof of agency, ownership, or control, or bias or prejudice of a witness.

Advisory Committee's Note

The courts have with substantial unanimity rejected evidence of liability insurance for the purpose of proving fault, and absence of liability insurance as proof of lack of fault. At best the inference of fault from the fact of insurance coverage is a tenuous one, as is its converse. More important, no doubt, has been the feeling that knowledge of the presence or absence of liability insurance would induce juries to decide cases on improper grounds. McCormick § 168; Annot., 4 A.L.R.2d 761. The rule is drafted in broad terms so as to include contributory negligence or other fault of a plaintiff as well as fault of a defendant.

The second sentence points out the limits of the rule, using well established illustrations. Id.

For similar rules see Uniform Rule 54; California Evidence Code § 1155; Kansas Code of Civil Procedure § 60-454; New Jersey Evidence Rule 54.

Restyled 2011

Rule 412. Sex-Offense Cases: The Victim's Sexual Behavior or Predisposition

(a) Prohibited Uses. The following evidence is not admissible in a civil or criminal proceeding involving alleged sexual misconduct:

(1) evidence offered to prove that a victim engaged in other sexual behavior; or

(2) evidence offered to prove a victim's sexual predisposition.

(b) Exceptions.

(1) ***Criminal Cases.*** The court may admit the following evidence in a criminal case:

(A) evidence of specific instances of a victim's sexual behavior, if offered to prove that someone other than the defendant was the source of semen, injury, or other physical evidence;

(B) evidence of specific instances of a victim's sexual behavior with respect to the person accused of the sexual misconduct, if offered by the defendant to prove consent or if offered by the prosecutor; and

(C) evidence whose exclusion would violate the defendant's constitutional rights.

(2) ***Civil Cases.*** In a civil case, the court may admit evidence offered to prove a victim's sexual behavior or sexual predisposition if its probative value substantially outweighs the danger of harm to any victim and of unfair prejudice to any party. The court may admit evidence of a victim's reputation only if the victim has placed it in controversy.

(c) Procedure to Determine Admissibility.

(1) ***Motion.*** If a party intends to offer evidence under Rule 412(b), the party must:

(A) file a motion that specifically describes the evidence and states the purpose for which it is to be offered;

(B) do so at least 14 days before trial unless the court, for good cause, sets a different time;

(C) serve the motion on all parties; and

(D) notify the victim or, when appropriate, the victim's guardian or representative.

(2) ***Hearing.*** Before admitting evidence under this rule, the court must conduct an in-camera hearing and give the victim and parties a right to attend and be heard. Unless the court orders otherwise, the motion, related materials, and the record of the hearing must be and remain sealed.

(d) Definition of "Victim." In this rule, "victim" includes an alleged victim.

Superseded 2011

Rule 412. Sex Offense Cases; Relevance of Alleged Victim's Past Sexual Behavior or Alleged Sexual Predisposition

(a) Evidence generally inadmissible.—The following evidence is not admissible in any civil or criminal proceeding involving alleged sexual misconduct except as provided in subdivisions (b) and (c):

(1) Evidence offered to prove that any alleged victim engaged in other sexual behavior.

(2) Evidence offered to prove any alleged victim's sexual predisposition.

(b) Exceptions.—

(1) In a criminal case, the following evidence is admissible, if otherwise admissible under these rules

(A) evidence of specific instances of sexual behavior by the alleged victim offered to prove that a person other than the accused was the source of semen, injury or other physical evidence;

(B) evidence of specific instances of sexual behavior by the alleged victim with respect to the person accused of the sexual misconduct offered by the accused to prove consent or by the prosecution; and

(C) evidence the exclusion of which would violate the constitutional rights of the defendant.

(2) In a civil case, evidence offered to prove the sexual behavior or sexual predisposition of any alleged victim is admissible if it is otherwise admissible under these rules and its probative value substantially outweighs the danger of harm to any victim and of unfair prejudice to any party. Evidence of an alleged victim's reputation is admissible only if it has been placed in controversy by the alleged victim.

(c) Procedure to determine admissibility.—

(1) A party intending to offer evidence under subdivision (b) must—

(A) file a written motion at least 14 days before trial specifically describing the evidence and stating the purpose for which it is offered unless the court, for good cause requires a different time for filing or permits filing during trial; and

(B) serve the motion on all parties and notify the alleged victim or, when appropriate, the alleged victim's guardian or representative.

(2) Before admitting evidence under this rule the court must conduct a hearing in camera and afford the victim and parties a right to attend and be heard. The motion, related papers, and the record of the hearing must be sealed and remain under seal unless the court orders otherwise. [*Added 1978. Amended 1988, 1994.*]

Editor's Note

Rule 412 was added to the Federal Rules by legislation enacted in 1978. The intent of that legislation is indicated in the Congressional Discussion, printed below, from 124 Cong. Rec. H1194 (1978).

Rule 412 was substantially revised by legislation enacted in 1994. The Advisory Committee's Notes, printed below, were adopted by the Conference Committee Report recommending passage of the bill, H.R. Conf. Rep. No. 103-711 (1994).

Congressional Discussion of 1978 Enactment

Mr. MANN. * * * Mr. Speaker, for many years in this country, evidentiary rules have permitted the introduction of evidence about a rape victim's prior sexual conduct. Defense lawyers were permitted great latitude in bringing out intimate details about a rape victim's life. Such evidence quite often serves no real purpose and only results in embarrassment to the rape victim and unwarranted public intrusion into her private life.

The evidentiary rules that permit such inquiry have in recent years come under question; and the States have taken the lead to change and modernize their evidentiary rules about evidence of a rape victim's prior sexual behavior. The bill before us similarly seeks to modernize the Federal Evidentiary rules.

The present Federal Rules of Evidence reflect the traditional approach. If a defendant in a rape case raises the defense of consent, that defendant may then offer evidence about the victim's prior sexual behavior. Such evidence may be in the form of opinion evidence, evidence of reputation, or evidence of specific instances of behavior. Rule 404(a)(2) of the Federal Rules of Evidence permits the introduction of evidence of a "pertinent character trait." The advisory committee note to that rule cites, as an example of what the rule covers, the character of a rape victim when the issue is consent. Rule 405 of the Federal Rules of Evidence permits the use of opinion or reputation evidence or the use of evidence of specific behavior to show a character trait.

Thus, Federal evidentiary rules permit a wide ranging inquiry into the private conduct of a rape victim, even though that conduct may have at best a tenuous connection to the offense for which the defendant is being tried.

H.R. 4727 amends the Federal Rules of Evidence to add a new rule, applicable only in criminal cases, to spell out when, and under what conditions, evidence of a rape victim's prior sexual behavior can be admitted. The new rule provides that reputation or opinion evidence about a rape victim's prior sexual behavior is not admissible. The new rule also provides that a court cannot admit evidence of specific instances of a rape victim's prior sexual conduct except in three circumstances.

The first circumstance is where the Constitution requires that the evidence be admitted. This exception is intended to cover those infrequent instances where, because of an unusual chain of circumstances, the general rule of inadmissibility, if followed, would result in denying the defendant a constitutional right.

The second circumstance in which the defendant can offer evidence of specific instances of a rape victim's prior sexual behavior is where the defendant raises the issue of consent and the evidence is of sexual behavior with the defendant. To admit such evidence, however, the court must find that the evidence is relevant and that its probative value outweighs the danger of unfair prejudice.

The third circumstance in which a court can admit evidence of specific instances of a rape victim's prior sexual behavior is where the evidence is of behavior with someone other than the defendant and is offered by the defendant on the issue of whether or not he was the source of semen or injury. Again, such evidence will be admitted only if the court finds that the evidence is relevant and that its probative value outweighs the danger of unfair prejudice.

The new rule further provides that before evidence is admitted under any of these exceptions, there must be an in camera hearing—that is, a proceeding that takes place in the judge's chambers out of the presence of the jury and the general public. At this hearing, the defendant will present the evidence he intends to offer and be able to argue why it should be admitted. The prosecution, of course, will be able to argue against that evidence being admitted.

The purpose of the in camera hearing is twofold. It gives the defendant an opportunity to demonstrate to the court why certain evidence is admissible and ought to be presented to the jury. At the same time, it protects the privacy of the rape victim in those instances when the court finds that evidence is inadmissible. Of course, if the court finds the evidence to be admissible, the evidence will be presented to the jury in open court.

The effect of this legislation, therefore, is to preclude the routine use of evidence of specific instances of a rape victim's prior sexual behavior. Such evidence will be admitted only in clearly and narrowly defined circumstances and only after an in camera hearing. In determining the admissibility of such evidence, the court will consider all of the facts and circumstances surrounding the evidence, such as the amount of time that lapsed between the alleged prior act and the rape charged in the prosecution. The greater the lapse of time, of course, the less likely it is that such evidence will be admitted.

Mr. Speaker, the principal purpose of this legislation is to protect rape victims from the degrading and embarrassing disclosure of intimate details about their private lives. It does so by narrowly circumscribing when such evidence may be admitted. It does not do so, however, by sacrificing any constitutional right possessed by the defendant. The bill before us fairly balances the interests involved—the rape victim's interest in protecting her private life from unwarranted public exposure; the defendant's interest in being able adequately to present a defense by offering relevant and probative evidence; and society's interest in a fair trial, one where unduly prejudicial evidence is not permitted to becloud the issues before the jury.

I urge support of the bill.

Mr. WIGGINS. * * * Mr. Speaker, this legislation addresses itself to a subject that is certainly a proper one for our consideration. Many of us have been troubled for years about the indiscriminate and prejudicial use of testimony with respect to a victim's prior sexual behavior in rape and similar cases. This bill deals with that problem. It is not, in my opinion, Mr. Speaker, a perfect bill in the manner in which it deals with the problem, but my objections are not so fundamental as would lead me to oppose the bill.

I think, Mr. Speaker, that it is unwise to adopt a per se rule absolutely excluding evidence of reputation and opinion with respect to the victim—and this bill does that—but it is difficult for me to foresee the specific case in which such evidence might be admissible. The trouble is this, Mr. Speaker: None of us can foresee perfectly all of the various circumstances under which the propriety of evidence might be before the court. If this bill has a defect, in my view it is because it adopts a per se rule with respect to opinion and reputation evidence.

Alternatively we might have permitted that evidence to be considered in camera as we do other evidence under the bill.

I should note, however, in fairness, having expressed minor reservations, that the bill before the House at this time does improve significantly upon the bill which was presented to our committee.

I will not detail all of those improvements but simply observe that the bill upon which we shall soon vote is a superior product to that which was initially considered by our subcommittee.

Mr. Speaker, I ask my colleagues to vote for this legislation as being, on balance, worthy of their support, and urge its adoption. * * *

Mr. MANN. Mr. Speaker, this legislation has more than 100 cosponsors, but its principal sponsor, as well as its architect is the gentlewoman from New York (Ms. Holtzman). As the drafter of the legislation she will be able to provide additional information about the probable scope and effect of the legislation.

* * *

Ms. HOLTZMAN. Mr. Speaker, I would like to begin first by complimenting the distinguished gentleman from South Carolina (Mr. Mann), the chairman of the subcommittee, for his understanding of the need for corrective legislation in this area and for the fairness with which he has conducted the subcommittee hearings. I would like also to compliment the other members of the subcommittee, including the gentleman from California (Mr. Wiggins).

Too often in this country victims of rape are humiliated and harassed when they report and prosecute the rape. Bullied and cross-examined about their prior sexual experiences, many find the trial almost as degrading as the rape itself. Since rape trials become inquisitions into the victim's morality, not trials of the defendant's innocence or guilt, it is not surprising that it is the least reported crime. It is estimated that as few as one in ten rapes is ever reported.

Mr. Speaker, over 30 States have taken some action to limit the vulnerability of rape victims to such humiliating cross-examination of their past sexual experiences and intimate personal histories. In federal courts, however, it is permissible still to subject rape victims to brutal cross-examination about their past sexual histories. H.R. 4727 would rectify this problem in Federal courts and I hope, also serve as a model to suggest to the remaining states that reform of existing rape laws is important to the equity of our criminal justice system.

H.R. 4727 applies only to criminal rape cases in Federal courts. The bill provides that neither the prosecution nor the defense can introduce any reputation or opinion evidence about the victim's past sexual conduct. It does permit, however, the introduction of specific evidence about the victim's past sexual conduct in three very limited circumstances.

First, this evidence can be introduced if it deals with the victim's past sexual relations with the defendant and is relevant to the issue of whether she consented. Second, when the defendant claims he had no relations with the victim, he can use evidence of the victim's past sexual relations with others if the evidence rebuts the victim's claim that the rape caused certain physical consequences, such as semen or injury. Finally, the evidence can be introduced if it is constitutionally required. This last exception, added in subcommittee, will insure that the defendant's constitutional rights are protected.

Before any such evidence can be introduced, however, the court must determine at a hearing in chambers that the evidence falls within one of the exceptions.

Furthermore, unless constitutionally required, the evidence of specific instances of prior sexual conduct cannot be introduced at all it if would be more prejudicial and inflammatory that probative.

Mr. Speaker, I urge adoption of this bill. It will protect women from both injustice and indignity.

[Thereafter, the bill was passed.]

Advisory Committee's Note to 1994 Amendment

Rule 412 has been revised to diminish some of the confusion engendered by the original rule and to expand the protection afforded alleged victims of sexual misconduct. Rule 412 applies to both civil and criminal proceedings. The rule aims to safeguard the alleged victim against the invasion of privacy, potential embarrassment and sexual stereotyping that is associated with public disclosure of intimate sexual details and the infusion of sexual innuendo into the factfinding process. By affording victims protection in most instances, the rule also encourages victims of sexual misconduct to institute and to participate in legal proceedings against alleged offenders.

Rule 412 seeks to achieve these objectives by barring evidence relating to the alleged victim's sexual behavior or alleged sexual predisposition, whether offered as substantive evidence of for impeachment, except in designated circumstances in which the probative value of the evidence significantly outweighs possible harm to the victim.

The revised rule applies in all cases involving sexual misconduct without regard to whether the alleged victim or person accused is a party to the litigation. Rule 412 extends to "pattern" witnesses in both criminal and civil cases whose testimony about other instances of sexual misconduct by the person accused is otherwise admissible. When the case does not involve alleged sexual misconduct, evidence relating to a third-party witness' alleged sexual activities is not within the ambit of Rule 412. The witness will, however, be protected by other rules such as Rules 404 and 608, as well as Rule 403.

The terminology "alleged victim" is used because there will frequently be a factual dispute as to whether sexual misconduct occurred. It does not connote any requirement that the misconduct be alleged in the pleadings. Rule 412 does not, however, apply unless the person against whom the evidence is offered can reasonably be characterized as a "victim of alleged sexual misconduct." When this is not the case, as for instance in a defamation action involving statements concerning sexual misconduct in which the evidence is offered to show that the alleged defamatory statements were true or did not damage the plaintiff's reputation, neither Rule 404 nor this rule will operate to bar the evidence; Rule 401 and 403 will continue to control. Rule 412 will, however, apply in a Title VII action in which the plaintiff has alleged sexual harassment.

The reference to a person "accused" is also used in a non-technical sense. There is no requirement that there be a criminal charge pending against the person or even that the misconduct would constitute a criminal offense. Evidence offered to prove allegedly false prior claims by the victim is not barred by Rule 412. However, the evidence is subject to the requirements of Rule 404.

Subdivision (a). As amended, Rule 412 bars evidence offered to prove the victim's sexual behavior and alleged sexual predisposition. Evidence, which might otherwise be admissible under Rules 402, 404(b), 405, 607, 608, 609 of some other evidence rule, must be excluded if Rule 412 so requires. The word "other" is used to suggest some flexibility in admitting evidence "intrinsic" to the alleged sexual misconduct. Cf. Committee Note to 1991 amendment to Rule 404(b).

Past sexual behavior connotes all activities that involve actual physical conduct, i.e. sexual intercourse or sexual contact. See, e.g., United States v. Galloway, 937 F.2d 542 (10th Cir. 1991), cert. denied, 113 S.Ct. 418 (1992) (use of contraceptives inadmissible since use implies sexual activity); United States v. One Feather, 702 F.2d 736 (8th Cir. 1983) (birth of an illegitimate child inadmissible); State v. Carmichael, 727 P.2d 918, 925 (Kan. 1986) (evidence of venereal disease inadmissible). In addition, the word "behavior" should be construed to include activities of the mind, such as fantasies of dreams. See 23 C. Wright and K. Graham, Jr., Federal Practice and Procedure, § 5384 at p. 548 (1980) ("While there may be some doubt under statutes that require 'conduct,' it would seem that the language of Rule 412 is broad enough to encompass the behavior of the mind.").

The rule has been amended to also exclude all other evidence relating to an alleged victim of sexual misconduct that is offered to prove a sexual predisposition. This amendment is designed to exclude evidence that does not directly refer to sexual activities or thoughts but that the proponent believes may have a sexual connotation for the fact finder. Admission of such evidence would contravene Rule 412's objectives of shielding the alleged victim from potential embarrassment and safeguarding the victim against stereotypical thinking. Consequently, unless the (b)(2) exception is satisfied, evidence such as that relating to the alleged victim's mode of dress, speech, or life-style will not be admissible.

The introductory phrase in subdivision (a) was deleted because it lacked clarity and contained no explicit reference to the other provisions of the law that were intended to be overridden. The conditional clause, "except as provided in subdivisions (b) and (c)" is intended to make clear that evidence of the types described in subdivision (a) is admissible only under the strictures of those sections.

The reason for extending the rule to all criminal cases is obvious. The strong social policy of protecting a victim's privacy and encouraging victims to come forward to report criminal acts is not confined to cases that involve a charge of sexual assault. The need to protect the victim is equally great when a defendant is charged with kidnapping, and evidence is offered, either to prove motive or as background, that the defendant sexually assaulted the victim.

The reason for extending Rule 412 to civil cases is equally obvious. The need to protect alleged victims against invasions of privacy, potential embarrassment, and unwarranted sexual stereotyping, and the wish to encourage victims to come forward when they have been sexually molested do not disappear because the context has shifted from a criminal prosecution to a claim for damages or injunctive relief. There is a strong social policy in not only punishing those who engage in sexual misconduct, but in also providing relief to the victim. Thus, Rule 412 applies in any civil case in which a person claims to be the victim of sexual misconduct, such as actions for sexual battery or sexual harassment.

Subdivision (b). Subdivision (b) spells out the specific circumstances in which some evidence may be admissible that would otherwise be barred by the general rule expressed in subdivision (a). As amended, Rule 412 will be virtually unchanged in criminal cases, but will provide protection to any person alleged to be a victim of sexual misconduct regardless of the charge actually brought against an accused. A new exception has been added for civil cases.

In a criminal case, evidence may be admitted under subdivision (b)(1) pursuant to three possible exceptions, provided the evidence also satisfies other requirements for admissibility specified in the Federal Rules of Evidence, including Rule 403. Subdivisions (b)(1)(A) and (b)(1)(B) require proof in the form of specific instances of sexual behavior in recognition of the limited probative value and dubious reliability of evidence of reputation or evidence in the form of an opinion.

Under subdivision (b)(1)(A), evidence of specific instances of sexual behavior with persons other than the person whose sexual misconduct is alleged may be admissible if it is offered to prove that another person was the source of semen, injury or other physical evidence. Where the prosecution has directly or indirectly asserted that the physical evidence originated with the accused, the defendant must be afforded an opportunity to prove that another person was responsible. See United States v. Begay, 937 F.2d 515, 523 n. 10 (10th Cir. 1991). Evidence offered for the specific purpose identified in this subdivision may still be excluded if it does not satisfy Rules 401 or 403. See, e.g., United States v. Azure, 845 F.2d 1503, 1505-06 (8th Cir. 1988) (10 year old victim's injuries indicated recent use of force; court excluded evidence of consensual sexual activities with witness who testified at in camera hearing that he had never hurt victim and failed to establish recent activities).

Under the exception in subdivision (b)(1)(B), evidence of specific instances of sexual behavior with respect to the person whose sexual misconduct is alleged is admissible if offered to prove consent, or offered by the prosecution. Admissible pursuant to this exception might be evidence of prior instances of sexual activities between the alleged victim and the accused, as well as statements in which the alleged victim expresses an intent to engage in sexual intercourse with the accused, or voiced sexual fantasies involving that specific accused. In a prosecution for child sexual abuse, for example, evidence of uncharged sexual activity between the accused and the alleged victim offered by the prosecution may be admissible pursuant to Rule 404(b) to show a pattern of behavior. Evidence relating to the victim's alleged sexual predisposition is not admissible pursuant to this exception.

Under subdivision (b)(1)(C), evidence of specific instances of conduct may not be excluded if the result would be to deny a criminal defendant the protections afforded by the Constitution. For example, statements in which the victim has expressed an intent to have sex with the first person encountered on a particular occasion might not be excluded without violating the due process right of a rape defendant seeking to prove consent. Recognition of this basic principle was expressed on subdivision (b)(1) of the original rule. The United States Supreme Court has recognized that in various circumstances a defendant may have a right to introduce evidence otherwise precluded by an evidence rule under the Confrontation Clause. See, e.g., Olden v. Kentucky, 488 U.S. 227 (1988) (defendant in rape cases had right to inquire into alleged victim's cohabitation with another man to show bias).

Subdivision (b)(2) governs the admissibility of otherwise proscribed evidence in civil cases. It employs a balancing test rather than the specific exceptions stated in subdivision (b)(1) in recognition of the difficulty of foreseeing future developments in the law. Greater flexibility is needed to accommodate evolving causes of action such as claims for sexual harassment.

The balancing test requires the proponent of the evidence, whether plaintiff or defendant, to convince the court that the probative value of the proffered evidence "substantially outweighs the danger of harm to any victim and of unfair prejudice of any party." This test for admitting evidence offered to prove sexual behavior or sexual propensity in civil cases differs in three respects from the general rule governing admissibility set forth in Rule 403. First, it reverses that usual procedure spelled out in Rule 403 by shifting the burden to the proponent to demonstrate admissibility rather than making the opponent justify exclusion of the evidence. Second, the standard expressed in subdivision (b)(2) is more stringent than in the original rule; it raises the threshold for admission by requiring that the probative value of the evidence substantially outweigh the specified dangers. Finally, the Rule 412 test puts "harm to the victim" on the scale in addition to prejudice to the parties.

Evidence of reputation may be received in a civil case only if the alleged victim has put his or her reputation into controversy. The victim may do so without making a specific allegation in a pleading. Cf. Fed.R.Civ.P. 35(a).

Subdivision (c). Amended subdivision (c) is more concise and understandable than the subdivision it replaces. The requirement of a motion before trial is continued in the amended rule, as is the provision that a late motion may be permitted for good cause shown. In deciding whether to permit late filing, the court may take into account the conditions previously included in the rule: namely whether the evidence is newly discovered and could not have been obtained earlier through the existence of due diligence, and whether the issue to which such evidence relates has newly arisen in the case. The rule recognizes that in some instances the circumstances that justify an application to introduce evidence otherwise barred by Rule 412 will not become apparent until trial.

The amended rule provides that before admitting evidence that falls within that prohibition of Rule 412(a), the court must hold a hearing in camera at which the alleged victim and any party must be afforded the right to be present and an opportunity to be heard. All papers connected with the motion must be kept and remain under seal during the course of trial and appellate proceedings unless otherwise ordered. This is to assure that the privacy of the alleged victim is preserved in all cases in which the court rules that proffered evidence is not admissible, and in which the hearing refers to matters that are not received, or are received in another form.

The procedures set forth in subdivision (c) do not apply to discovery of a victim's past sexual conduct or predisposition in civil cases, which will be continued to be governed by Fed. R. Civ. P. 26. In order not to undermine the rationale of Rule 412, however, courts should enter appropriate orders pursuant to Fed. R. Civ. P. 26 (c) to protect the victim against unwarranted inquiries and to ensure confidentiality. Courts should presumptively issue protective orders barring discovery unless the party seeking discovery makes a showing that the evidence sought to be discovered would be relevant under the facts and theories of the particular case, and cannot be obtained except through discovery. In an action for sexual harassment, for instance, while some evidence of the alleged victim's sexual behavior and/or predisposition in the workplace may perhaps be relevant, non-work place conduct will usually be irrelevant. Cf. Burns v. McGregor Electronic Industries, Inc., 989 F.2d 959, 962-63 (8th Cir. 1993) (posing for a nude magazine outside work hours is irrelevant to issue of unwelcomeness of sexual advances at work). Confidentiality orders should be presumptively granted as well.

One substantive change made in subdivision (c) is the elimination of the following sentence: "Notwithstanding subdivision (b) of Rule 104, if the relevancy of the evidence which the accused seeks to offer in trial depends upon the fulfillment of a condition of fact, the court, at the hearing in chambers or at a subsequent hearing in chambers scheduled for such purpose, shall accept evidence on the issue of whether such condition of fact is fulfilled and shall determine such issue." On its face, this language would appear to authorize a trial judge to exclude evidence of past sexual conduct between alleged victim and an accused or a defendant in a civil case based upon the judge's belief that such past acts did not occur. Such an authorization raises questions of invasion of the right to a jury trial under the Sixth and Seventh Amendments. See 1 S. Saltzburg & M. Martin, Federal Rules of Evidence Manual, 396-97 (5th ed. 1990).

The Advisory Committee concluded that the amended rule provided adequate protection for all persons claiming to be the victims of sexual misconduct, and that it was inadvisable to continue to include a provision in the rule that has been confusing and that raises substantial constitutional issues.

Restyled 2011

Rule 413. Similar Crimes in Sexual-Assault Cases

(a) Permitted Uses. In a criminal case in which a defendant is accused of a sexual assault, the court may admit evidence that the defendant committed any other sexual assault. The evidence may be considered on any matter to which it is relevant.

(b) Disclosure. If the prosecutor intends to offer this evidence, the prosecutor must disclose it to the defendant, including witnesses' statements or a summary of the expected testimony. The prosecutor must do so at least 15 days before trial or at a later time that the court allows for good cause.

(c) Effect on Other Rules. This rule does not limit the admission or consideration of evidence under any other rule.

(d) Definition of "Sexual Assault." In this rule and Rule 415, "sexual assault" means a crime under federal law or under state law (as "state" is defined in 18 U.S.C. § 513) involving:

(1) any conduct prohibited by 18 U.S.C. chapter 109A;

(2) contact, without consent, between any part of the defendant's body — or an object — and another person's genitals or anus;

(3) contact, without consent, between the defendant's genitals or anus and any part of another person's body;

(4) deriving sexual pleasure or gratification from inflicting death, bodily injury, or physical pain on another person; or

(5) an attempt or conspiracy to engage in conduct described in paragraphs (1)-(4).

Superseded 2011

Rule 413. Evidence of Similar Crimes in Sexual Assault Cases

(a) In a criminal case in which the defendant is accused of an offense of sexual assault, evidence of the defendant's commission of another offense or offenses of sexual assault is admissible, and may be considered for its bearing on any matter to which it is relevant.

(b) In a case in which the Government intends to offer evidence under this rule, the attorney for the Government shall disclose the evidence to the defendant, including statements of witnesses or a summary of the substance of any testimony that is expected to be offered, at least fifteen days before the scheduled date of trial or at such later time as the court may allow for good cause.

(c) This rule shall not be construed to limit the admission or consideration of evidence under any other rule.

(d) For purposes of this rule and Rule 415, "offense of sexual assault" means a crime under Federal law or the law of a State (as defined in section 513 of title 18, United States Code) that involved—

(1) any conduct proscribed by chapter 109A of title 18, United States Code;

(2) contact, without consent, between any part of the defendant's body or an object and the genitals or anus of another person;

(3) contact, without consent, between the genitals or anus of the defendant and any part of another person's body;

(4) deriving sexual pleasure or gratification from the infliction of death, bodily injury, or physical pain on another person; or

(5) an attempt or conspiracy to engage in conduct described in paragraphs (1)-(4). [*Added 1995.*]

Editor's Note

Rules 413 through 415 were added to the Federal Rules in 1994 by an Act of Congress. They were inserted at the Conference Committee stage into a bill that became the Violent Crime Control and Law enforcement Act of 1994, Pub. L. 103-322, 108 Stat. 2136 (1994). The purpose of Rules 413-415, which were contained in § 320935 of the Act, was explained on the House floor by Rep. Susan Molinari (N.Y.), who was their principal sponsor. See Cong.Rec. H8991-92, Aug. 21, 1994.

Section 320935 directed that, before Rules 413-415 went into effect, the Judicial Conference of the United States should "transmit to Congress a report containing recommendations for amending the Federal Rules of Evidence as they affect the admission of evidence of a defendant's prior sexual assault or child molestation crimes in cases involving sexual assault and child molestation." Thereafter, the Congress could either adopt the Judicial Conference's recommendations or, by inaction, allow Rules 413-415 to go into effect. The Judicial Conference transmitted a report to Congress on February 9, 1995. Congress took no action on that report and Rules 413-415 went into effect as enacted, as of July 9, 1995.

Floor Statement of Rep. Susan Molinari

Mr. Speaker, the revised conference bill contains a critical reform that I have long sought to protect the public from crimes of sexual violence—general rules of admissibility in sexual assault and child molestation cases for evidence that the defendant has committed offenses of the same type on other occasions. The enactment of this reform is first and foremost a triumph for the public—for the women who will not be raped and the children who will not be molested because we have strengthened the legal system's tools for bringing the perpetrators of these atrocious crimes to justice.

Senator Dole and I initially proposed this reform in February of 1991 in the Women's Equal Opportunity Act bill, and we later re-introduced it in the Sexual Assault Prevention Act bills of the 102d and 103d Congresses. The proposal also enjoyed the strong support of the Administration in the 102d Congress, and was included in President Bush's violent crime bill of that Congress, S. 635. The Senate passed the proposed rules on Nov. 5, 1993, by a vote of 75 to 19, in a crime bill amendment offered by Senate Dole. This Chamber endorsed the same rules on June 29, 1994, by a vote of 348 to 62, through a motion to instruct conferees that I offered.

The rules in the revised conference bill are substantially identical to our earlier proposals. We have agreed to a temporary deferral of the effective date of the new rules, pending a report by the Judicial Conference, in order to accommodate procedural objections raised by opponents of the reform. However, regardless of what the Judicial Conference may recommend, the new rules will take effect within at most 300 days of the enactment of this legislation, unless repealed or modified by subsequent legislation.

The need for these rules, their precedential support, their interpretation, and the issues and policy questions they raise have been analyzed at length in the legislative history of this proposal. I would direct the Members' attention particularly to two earlier statements:

The first is the portion of the section-by-section analysis accompanying these rules in section 801 of S. 635, which President Bush transmitted to Congress in 1991. That statement appears on pages S 3238 [to] S 3242 of the daily edition of the Congressional Record for March 13, 1991.

The second is the prepared text of an address—entitled "Evidence of Propensity and Probability in Sex Offense Cases and Other Cases"—by Senior Counsel David J. Karp of the Office of Policy Development of the U.S. Department of Justice. Mr. Karp, who is the author of the new evidence rules, presented this statement on behalf of the Justice Department to the Evidence Section of the Association of American Law Schools on January 9, 1993. The statement provided a detailed account of the views of the legislative sponsors and the Administration concerning the proposed reform, and should also be considered an authoritative part of its legislative history.

These earlier statements address the issues raised by this reform in considerable detail. In my present remarks, I will simply emphasize the following essential points:

The new rules will supersede in sex offense cases the restrictive aspects of Federal Rule of Evidence 404(b). In contrast to Rule 404(b)'s general prohibition of evidence of character or propensity, the new rules for sex offense cases authorize admission and consideration of evidence of an uncharged offense for its bearing "on any matter to which it is relevant." This includes the defendant's propensity to commit sexual assault or child molestation offenses, and assessment of the probability or improbability that the defendant has been falsely or mistakenly accused of such an offense.

In other respects, the general standards of the rules of evidence will continue to apply, including the restrictions on hearsay evidence and the court's authority under Evidence Rule 403 to exclude evidence whose probative value is substantially outweighed by its prejudicial effect. Also, the government (or the plaintiff in a civil case) will generally have to disclose to the defendant any evidence that is to be offered under the new rules at least 15 days before trial.

The proposed reform is critical to the protection of the public from rapists and child molesters, and is justified by the distinctive characteristics of the cases it will affect. In child molestation cases, for example, a history of similar acts tends to be exceptionally probative because it shows an unusual disposition of the defendant—a sexual or sadosexual interest in children—that simply does not exist in ordinary people. Moreover, such cases require reliance on child victims whose credibility can readily be attacked in the absence of substantial corroboration. In such cases, there is a compelling public interest in admitting all significant evidence that will illumine the credibility of the charge and any denial by the defense.

Similarly, adult-victim sexual assault cases are distinctive, and often turn on difficult credibility determinations. Alleged consent by the victim is rarely an issue in prosecutions for other violent crimes—the accused mugger does not claim that the victim freely handed over [his] wallet as a gift—but the defendant in a rape case often contends that the victim engaged in consensual sex and then falsely accused him. Knowledge that the defendant has committed rapes on other occasions is frequently critical in assessing the relative plausibility of these claims and accurately deciding cases that would otherwise become unresolvable swearing matches.

The practical effect of the new rules is to put evidence of uncharged offenses in sexual assault and child molestation cases on the same footing as other types of relevant evidence that are not subject to a special exclusionary rule. The presumption is in favor of admission. The underlying legislative judgment is that the evidence admissible pursuant to the proposed rules is typically relevant and probative, and that its probative value is normally not outweighed by any risk of prejudice or other adverse effects.

In line with this judgment, the rules do not impose arbitrary or artificial restrictions on the admissibility of evidence. Evidence of offenses for which the defendant has not previously been prosecuted or convicted will be admissible, as well as evidence of prior convictions. No time limit is imposed on the uncharged offenses for which evidence may be admitted; as a practical matter, evidence of other sex offenses by the defendant is often probative and properly admitted, notwithstanding very substantial lapses of time in relation to the charged offense or offenses. See, e.g., United States v. Hadley, 918 F.2d 848, 850-51 (9th Cir. 1990), cert. dismissed, 113 S.Ct. 486 (1992) (evidence of offenses occurring up to 15 years earlier admitted); State v. Plymate, 345 N.W.2d 327 (Neb.1984) (evidence of defendant's commission of other child molestations more than 20 years earlier admitted).

Finally, the practical efficacy of these rules will depend on faithful execution by judges of the will of Congress in adopting this critical reform. To implement the legislative intent, the courts must liberally construe these rules to provide the basis for a fully informed decision of sexual assault and child molestation cases, including assessment of the defendant's propensities and questions of probability in light of the defendant's past conduct.

Report of the Judicial Conference

I. Introduction

This report is transmitted to Congress in accordance with the Violent Crime Control and Law Enforcement Act of 1994, Pub.L. No. 103-322 (September 13, 1994). Section 320935 of the Act invited the Judicial Conference of the United States within 150 days (February 10, 1995) to submit "a report containing recommendations for amending the Federal Rules of Evidence as they affect the admission of evidence of a defendant's prior sexual assault or child molestation crimes in cases involving sexual assault or child molestation."

Under the Act, new Rules 413, 414, and 415 would be added to the Federal Rules of Evidence. These Rules would admit evidence of a defendant's past similar acts in criminal and civil cases involving a sexual assault or child molestation offense for its bearing on any matter to which it is relevant. The effective date of new Rules 413-415 is contingent in part upon the nature of the recommendations submitted by the Judicial Conference.

After careful study, the Judicial Conference urges Congress to reconsider its decision on the policy questions underlying the new rules for reasons set out in Part III below.

If Congress does not reconsider its decision on the underlying policy questions, the Judicial Conference recommends incorporation of the provisions of new Rules 413-415 as amendments to Rules 404 and 405 of the Federal Rules of Evidence. The amendments would not change the substance of the congressional enactment but would clarify drafting ambiguities and eliminate possible constitutional infirmities.

II. Background

Under the Act, the Judicial Conference was provided 150 days within which to make and submit to Congress alternative recommendations to new Evidence Rules 413-415. Consideration of Rules 413-415 by the Judicial Conference was specifically excepted from the exacting review procedures set forth in the Rules Enabling Act (codified at 28 U.S.C. §§ 2071-2077). Although the Conference acted on these new rules on an expedited basis to meet the Act's deadlines, the review process was thorough.

The new rules would apply to both civil and criminal cases. Accordingly, the Judicial Conference's Advisory Committee on Criminal Rules and the Advisory Committee on Civil Rules reviewed the rules at separate meetings in October 1994. At the same time and in preparation for its consideration of the new rules, the Advisory Committee on Evidence Rules sent out a notice soliciting comment on new Evidence Rules 413, 414, and 415. The notice was sent to the courts, including all federal judges, about 900 evidence law professors, 40 women's rights organizations, and 1,000 other individuals and interested organizations.

III. Discussion

On October 17-18, 1994, the Advisory Committee on Evidence Rules met in Washington, D.C. It considered the public responses, which included 84 written comments, representing 112 individuals, 8 local and 8 national legal organizations. The overwhelming majority of judges, lawyers, law professors, and legal organizations who responded opposed new Evidence Rules 413, 414, and 415. The principal objections expressed were that the rules would permit the admission of unfairly prejudicial evidence and contained numerous drafting problems not intended by their authors.

The Advisory Committee on Evidence Rules submitted its report to the Judicial Conference Committee on Rules of Practice and Procedure (Standing Committee) for review at its January 11-13, 1995 meeting. The committee's report was unanimous except for a dissenting vote by the representative of the Department of Justice. The advisory committee believed that the concerns expressed by Congress and embodied in new Evidence Rules 413, 414, and 415 are already adequately addressed in the existing Federal Rules of Evidence. In particular, Evidence Rule 404(b) now allows the admission of evidence against a criminal defendant of the commission of prior crimes, wrongs, or acts for specified purposes, including to show intent, plan, motive, preparation, identity, knowledge, or absence of mistake or accident.

Furthermore, the new rules, which are not supported by empirical evidence, could diminish significantly the protections that have safeguarded persons accused in criminal cases and parties in civil cases against undue prejudice. These protections form a fundamental part of American jurisprudence and have evolved under long-standing rules and case law. A significant concern identified by the committee was the danger of convicting a criminal defendant for past, as opposed to charged, behavior or for being a bad person.

In addition, the advisory committee concluded that, because prior bad acts would be admissible even though not the subject of a conviction, mini-trials within trials concerning those acts would result when a defendant seeks to rebut such evidence. The committee also noticed that many of the comments received had concluded that the Rules, as drafted, were mandatory—that is, such evidence had to be admitted regardless of other rules of evidence such as the hearsay rule or the Rule 403 balancing test. The committee believed that this position was arguable because Rules 413-415 declare without qualification that such evidence "is admissible." In contrast, the new Rule 412, passed as part of the same legislation, provided that certain evidence "is admissible if it is otherwise admissible under these Rules." Fed.R.Evid. 412(b)(2). If the critics are right, Rules 413-415 free the prosecution from rules that apply to the defendant—including the hearsay rule and Rule 403. If so, serious constitutional questions would arise.

The Advisory Committees on Criminal and Civil Rules unanimously, except for representatives of the Department of Justice, also opposed the new rules. Those committees also concluded that the new rules would permit the introduction of unreliable but highly prejudicial evidence and would complicate trials by causing mini-trials of other alleged wrongs. After the advisory committees reported, the Standing Committee unanimously, again except for the representative of the Department of Justice, agreed with the view of the advisory committees.

It is important to note the highly unusual unanimity of the members of the Standing and Advisory Committees, composed of over 40 judges, practicing lawyers, and academicians, in taking the view that Rules 413-415 are undesirable. Indeed, the only supporters of the Rules were representatives of the Department of Justice.

For these reasons, the Standing Committee recommended that Congress reconsider its decision on the policy questions embodied in new Evidence Rules 413, 414, and 415.

However, if Congress will not reconsider its decision on the policy questions, the Standing Committee recommended that Congress consider an alternative draft recommended by the Advisory Committee on Evidence Rules. That Committee drafted proposed amendments to existing Evidence Rules 404 and 405 that would both correct ambiguities and possible constitutional infirmities identified in new Evidence Rules 413, 414, and 415 yet still effectuate Congressional intent. In particular, the proposed amendments [the "alternative draft"]:

(1) expressly apply the other rules of evidence to evidence offered under the new rules;

(2) expressly allow the party against whom such evidence is offered to use similar evidence in rebuttal;

(3) expressly enumerate the factors to be weighed by a court in making its Rule 403 determination;

(4) render the notice provisions consistent with the provisions in existing Rule 404 regarding criminal cases;

(5) eliminate the special notice provisions of Rules 413-415 in civil cases so that notice will be required as provided in the Federal Rules of Civil Procedure; and

(6) permit reputation or opinion evidence after such evidence is offered by the accused or defendant.

The Standing Committee reviewed the new rules and the alternative recommendations. It concurred with the views of the Evidence Rules Committee and recommended that the Judicial Conference adopt them.

IV. RECOMMENDATIONS

The Judicial Conference concurs with the views of the Standing Committee and urges that Congress reconsider its policy determinations underlying Evidence Rules 413-415. In the alternative, the attached amendments to Evidence Rules 404 and 405 are recommended, in lieu of new Evidence Rules 413, 414, and 415. The alternative amendments to Evidence Rules 404 and 405 are accompanied by the Advisory Committee Notes, which explain them in detail.

ALTERNATIVE DRAFT

Rule 404. Character evidence not admissible to prove conduct; exceptions; other crimes ....

(4) Character in sexual misconduct cases. *Evidence of another act of sexual assault or child molestation, or evidence to rebut such proof or an inference therefrom, if that evidence is otherwise admissible under these rules, in a criminal case in which the accused is charged with sexual assault or child molestation, or in a civil case in which a claim is predicated on a party's alleged commission of sexual assault or child molestation.*

(A) In weighing the probative value of such evidence, the court may, as part of its rule 403 determination, consider:

(i) proximity in time to the charged or predicate misconduct;

(ii) similarity to the charged or predicate misconduct;

(iii) frequency of the other acts;

(iv) surrounding circumstances;

(v) relevant intervening events; and

(vi) other relevant similarities or differences.

(B) In a criminal case in which the prosecution intends to offer evidence under this subdivision, it must disclose the evidence, including statements of witnesses or a summary of the substance of any testimony, at a reasonable time in advance of trial, or during trial if the court excuses pretrial notice on good cause shown.

(C) For purposes of this subdivision:

(i) "sexual assault" means conduct—or an attempt or conspiracy to engage in conduct—of the type proscribed by chapter 109A of title 18, United States Code, or conduct that involved deriving sexual pleasure or gratification from inflicting death, bodily injury, or physical pain on another person irrespective of the age of the victim—regardless of whether that conduct would have subjected the actor to federal jurisdiction.

(ii) "child molestation" means conduct—or an attempt or conspiracy to engage in conduct—of the type proscribed by chapter 110 of title 18, United States Code, or conduct, committed in relation to a child below the age of 14 years, either of the type proscribed by chapter 109A of title 18, United States Code, or that involved deriving sexual pleasure or gratification from inflicting death, bodily injury, or physical pain on another person—regardless of whether that conduct would have subjected the actor to federal jurisdiction.

(b) Other crimes, wrongs, or acts. *Evidence of other crimes, wrongs, or acts is not admissible to prove the character of a person in order to show action in conformity therewith except as provided in subdivision (a)....*

NOTE TO ALTERNATIVE DRAFT RULE 404(A)(4)

The Committee has redrafted Rules 413, 414 and 415 which the Violent Crime Control and Law Enforcement Act of 1994 conditionally added to the Federal Rules of Evidence. [Footnote: Congress provided that the rules would take effect unless within a specified time period the Judicial Conference made recommendations to amend the rules that Congress enacted.] These modifications do not change the substance of the congressional enactment. The changes were made in order to integrate the provisions both substantively and stylistically with the existing Rules of Evidence; to illuminate the intent expressed by the principal drafters of the measure; to clarify drafting ambiguities that might necessitate considerable judicial attention if they remained unresolved; and to eliminate possible constitutional infirmities.

The Committee placed the new provisions in Rule 404 because this rule governs the admissibility of character evidence. The congressional enactment constitutes a new exception to the general rule stated in subdivision (a). The Committee also combined the three separate rules proposed by Congress into one subdivision (a)(4) in accordance with the rules' customary practice of treating criminal and civil issues jointly. An amendment to Rule 405 has been added because the authorization of a new form of character evidence in this rule has an impact on methods of proving character that were not explicitly addressed by Congress. The stylistic changes are self-evident. They are particularly noticeable in the definition section in subdivision (a)(4)(C) in which the Committee eliminated, without any change in meaning, graphic details of sexual acts.

The Committee added language that explicitly provides that evidence under this subdivision must satisfy other rules of evidence such as the hearsay rules in Article VIII and the expert testimony rules in Article VII. Although principal sponsors of the legislation had stated that they intended other evidentiary rules to apply, the Committee believes that the opening phrase of the new subdivision 'if otherwise admissible under these rules' is needed to clarify the relationship between subdivision (a)(4) and other evidentiary provisions.

The Committee also expressly made subdivision (a)(4) subject to Rule 403 balancing in accordance with the repeatedly stated objectives of the legislation's sponsors with which representatives of the Justice Department expressed agreement. Many commentators on Rules 413-415 had objected that Rule 403's applicability was obscured by the actual language employed.

In addition to clarifying the drafters' intent, an explicit reference to Rule 403 may be essential to insulate the rule against constitutional challenge. Constitutional concerns also led the Committee to acknowledge specifically the opposing party's right to offer in rebuttal character evidence that the rules would otherwise bar, including evidence of a third person's prior acts of sexual misconduct offered to prove that the third person rather than the party committed the acts in issue.

In order to minimize the need for extensive and time-consuming judicial interpretation, the Committee listed factors that a court may consider in discharging Rule 403 balancing. Proximity in time is taken into account in a related rule. See Rule 609(b). Similarity, frequency and surrounding circumstances have long been considered by courts in handling other crimes evidence pursuant to Rule 404(b). Relevant intervening events, such as extensive medical treatment of the accused between the time of the prior proffered act and the charged act, may affect the strength of the propensity inference for which the evidence is offered. The final factor—'other relevant similarities or differences'—is added in recognition of the endless variety of circumstances that confront a trial court in rulings on admissibility. Although subdivision (4)(A) explicitly refers to factors that bear on probative value, this enumeration does not eliminate a judge's responsibility to take into account the other factors mentioned in Rule 403 itself—'the danger of unfair prejudice, confusion of the issues, ... misleading the jury, ... undue delay, waste of time, or needless presentation of cumulative evidence.' In addition, the Advisory Committee Note to Rule 403 reminds judges that 'The availability of other means of proof may also be an appropriate factor.'

The Committee altered slightly the notice provision in criminal cases. Providing the trial court with some discretion to excuse pretrial notice was thought preferable to the inflexible 15-day rule provided in Rules 414 and 415. Furthermore, the formulation is identical to that contained in the 1991 amendment to Rule 404(b) so that no confusion will result from having two somewhat different notice provisions in the same rule. The Committee eliminated the notice provision for civil cases stated in Rule 415 because it did not believe that Congress intended to alter the usual time table for disclosure and discovery provided by the Federal Rules of Civil Procedure.

The definition section was simplified with no change in meaning. The reference to 'the law of a State' was eliminated as unnecessarily confusing and restrictive. Conduct committed outside the United States ought equally to be eligible for admission. Evidence offered pursuant to subdivision (a)(4) must relate to a form of conduct proscribed by either chapter 109A or 110 of title 18, United States Code, regardless of whether the actor was subject to federal jurisdiction.

Rule 405. Methods of proving character

*(a) **Reputation or opinion.** In all cases in which evidence of character or a trait of character of a person is admissible, proof may be made by testimony as to reputation or by testimony in the form of an opinion except as provided in subdivision (c) of this rule. On cross-examination, inquiry is allowable into relevant specific instances of conduct.*

*(c) **Proof in sexual misconduct cases.** In a case in which evidence is offered under rule 404(a)(4), proof may be made by specific instances of conduct, testimony as to reputation, or testimony in the form of an opinion, except that the prosecution or claimant may offer reputation or opinion testimony only after the opposing party has offered such testimony.*

NOTE TO ALTERNATIVE DRAFT RULE 405(C)

The addition of a new subdivision (a)(4) to Rule 404 necessitates adding a new subdivision (c) to Rule 405 to govern methods of proof. Congress clearly intended no change in the preexisting law that precludes the prosecution or a claimant from offering reputation or opinion testimony in its case in chief to prove that the opposing party acted in conformity with character. When evidence is admissible pursuant to Rule 404(a)(4), the proponents proof must consist of specific instances of conduct. The opposing party, however, is free to respond with reputation or opinion testimony (including expert testimony if otherwise admissible) as well as evidence of specific instances. In a criminal case, the admissibility of reputation or opinion testimony would, in any event, be authorized by Rule 404(a)(1). The extension to civil cases is essential in order to provide the opponent with an adequate opportunity to refute allegations about a character for sexual misconduct. Once the opposing party offers reputation or opinion testimony, however, the prosecution or claimant may counter using such methods of proof.

Restyled 2011

Rule 414. Similar Crimes in Child-Molestation Cases

(a) **Permitted Uses.** In a criminal case in which a defendant is accused of child molestation, the court may admit evidence that the defendant committed any other child molestation. The evidence may be considered on any matter to which it is relevant.

(b) **Disclosure to the Defendant.** If the prosecutor intends to offer this evidence, the prosecutor must disclose it to the defendant, including witnesses' statements or a summary of the expected testimony. The prosecutor must do so at least 15 days before trial or at a later time that the court allows for good cause.

(c) **Effect on Other Rules.** This rule does not limit the admission or consideration of evidence under any other rule.

(d) **Definition of "Child" and "Child Molestation."** In this rule and Rule 415:

(1) "child" means a person below the age of 14; and

(2) "child molestation" means a crime under federal law or under state law (as "state" is defined in 18 U.S.C. § 513) involving:

(A) any conduct prohibited by 18 U.S.C. chapter 109A and committed with a child;

(B) any conduct prohibited by 18 U.S.C. chapter 110;

(C) contact between any part of the defendant's body — or an object — and a child's genitals or anus;

(D) contact between the defendant's genitals or anus and any part of a child's body;

(E) deriving sexual pleasure or gratification from inflicting death, bodily injury, or physical pain on a child; or

(F) an attempt or conspiracy to engage in conduct described in subparagraphs (A)-(E).

Superseded 2011

Rule 414. Evidence of Similar Crimes in Child Molestation Cases

(a) In a criminal case in which the defendant is accused of an offense of child molestation, evidence of the defendant's commission of another offense or offenses of child molestation is admissible, and may be considered for its bearing on any matter to which it is relevant.

(b) In a case in which the Government intends to offer evidence under this rule, the attorney for the Government shall disclose the evidence to the defendant, including statements of witnesses or a summary of the substance of any testimony that is expected to be offered, at least fifteen days before the scheduled date of trial or at such later time as the court may allow for good cause.

(c) This rule shall not be construed to limit the admission or consideration of evidence under any other rule.

(d) For purposes of this rule and Rule 415, "child" means a person below the age of fourteen, and "offense of child molestation" means a crime under Federal law or the law of a State (as defined in section 513 of title 18, United States Code) that involved—

(1) any conduct proscribed by chapter 109A of title 18, United States Code, that was committed in relation to a child;

(2) any conduct proscribed by chapter 110 of title 18, United States Code;

(3) contact between any part of the defendant's body or an object and the genitals or anus of a child;

(4) contact between the genitals or anus of the defendant and any part of the body of a child;

(5) deriving sexual pleasure or gratification from the infliction of death, bodily injury, or physical pain on a child; or

(6) an attempt or conspiracy to engage in conduct described in paragraphs (1)-(5). [*Added 1995.*]

Editor's Note

See notes to Rule 413.

Restyled 2011

Rule 415. Similar Acts in Civil Cases Involving Sexual Assault or Child Molestation

(a) Permitted Uses. In a civil case involving a claim for relief based on a party's alleged sexual assault or child molestation, the court may admit evidence that the party committed any other sexual assault or child molestation. The evidence may be considered as provided in Rules 413 and 414.

(b) Disclosure to the Opponent. If a party intends to offer this evidence, the party must disclose it to the party against whom it will be offered, including witnesses' statements or a summary of the expected testimony. The party must do so at least 15 days before trial or at a later time that the court allows for good cause.

(c) Effect on Other Rules. This rule does not limit the admission or consideration of evidence under any other rule.

Superseded 2011

Rule 415. Evidence of Similar Acts in Civil Cases Concerning Sexual Assault or Child Molestation

(a) In a civil case in which a claim for damages or other relief is predicated on a party's alleged commission of conduct constituting an offense of sexual assault or child molestation, evidence of that party's commission of another offense or offenses of sexual assault or child molestation is admissible and may be considered as provided in Rule 413 and Rule 414 of these rules.

(b) A party who intends to offer evidence under this Rule shall disclose the evidence to the party against whom it will be offered, including statements of witnesses or a summary of the substance of any testimony that is expected to be offered, at least fifteen days before the scheduled date of trial or at such later time as the court may allow for good cause.

(c) This rule shall not be construed to limit the admission or consideration of evidence under any other rule. [*Added 1995.*]

Editor's Note

See notes to Rule 413.

Restyled 2011

ARTICLE V. PRIVILEGES

Rule 501. Privilege in General

The common law — as interpreted by United States courts in the light of reason and experience — governs a claim of privilege unless any of the following provides otherwise:

- the United States Constitution;
- a federal statute; or
- rules prescribed by the Supreme Court.

But in a civil case, state law governs privilege regarding a claim or defense for which state law supplies the rule of decision.

Superseded 2011

ARTICLE V. PRIVILEGES

Rule 501. General Rule

Except as otherwise required by the Constitution of the United States or provided by Act of Congress or in rules prescribed by the Supreme Court pursuant to statutory authority, the privilege of a witness, person, government, State, or political subdivision thereof shall be governed by the principles of the common law as they may be interpreted by the courts of the United States in the light of reason and experience. However, in civil actions and proceedings, with respect to an element of a claim or defense as to which State law supplies the rule of decision, the privilege of a witness, person, government, State, or political subdivision thereof shall be determined in accordance with State law.

Case Notes

Attorney-Client Privilege: Duration

The privilege for confidential communications between attorney and client survives the death of the client. Swidler & Berlin v. United States, 524 U.S. 399, 118 S.Ct. 2081, 141 L.Ed. 2d 379 (1998).

Attorney-Client Privilege: Corporate Client

A corporation may be a client for purposes of the attorney-client privilege. Corporate management—officers and directors—has the power to assert and waive the privilege on behalf of the corporation. When new management takes over, power to assert and waive the privilege as to communications made by former officers and directors passes to new management. When a corporation is in bankruptcy, the bankruptcy trustee controls the corporation's privilege with respect to pre-bankruptcy communications. Commodities Futures Trading Comm'n v. Weintraub, 471 U.S. 343, 105 S.Ct. 1986, 85 L.Ed. 2d 372 (1985).

The "control group" test for determining who may speak and act on behalf of a corporate client is rejected. The control group test, which includes only officers and agents responsible for directing the corporation's actions in response to legal advice, gives too narrow a scope to the attorney-client privilege. Where communications are made by corporate employees to counsel for the corporation acting as such, at the direction of corporate superiors, in order to secure legal advice for the corporation, and the employees are aware that they are being questioned so that the corporation can obtain legal advice, the communications are within the underlying purposes of the attorney client privilege and are protected against compelled disclosure. Upjohn Co. v. United States, 449 U.S. 383, 101 S.Ct. 677, 66 L.Ed. 2d 584 (1981).

Attorney-Client Privilege: Crime-Fraud Exception

To determine whether an assertedly privileged attorney-client communication falls within the crime-fraud exception, a court may review the communication *in camera*. The opponent of the privilege must first present evidence sufficient to support a reasonable belief that *in camera* review may yield evidence that establishes the exception's applicability. The evidence considered in making this threshold determination need not be independent of the communication in question, and may include any lawfully-obtained evidence that has not been determined to be privileged. United States v. Zolin, 491 U.S. 554, 109 S.Ct. 2619, 105 L.Ed. 2d 469 (1989).

Other Privileges Recognized

Federal law recognizes a privilege for confidential communications between psychotherapist and patient. The psychotherapeutic relationship is socially valuable and depends on confidentiality. Such a privilege is recognized in all states and was recommended by the Advisory Committee that originally drafted the Federal Rules. The privilege extends to the patients of psychiatrists, psychologists, and licensed clinical social workers. The privilege may not be overcome by a showing of need for the evidence. Jaffee v. Redmond, 518 U.S. 1, 116 S.Ct. 1923, 135 L.Ed.2d 337 (1996).

The privilege against adverse spousal testimony may be claimed by the witness spouse, but not by the party spouse. The policy of the privilege—to foster marital harmony—is not served if the witness spouse is willing to testify voluntarily. Voluntariness is not negated by the fact that the witness spouse was granted immunity and promised leniency. Trammel v. United States, 445 U.S. 40, 100 S.Ct. 906 63 L.Ed. 2d 186 (1980).

Other Privileges Not Recognized

Federal law does not recognize a privilege for confidential communications between accountant and client. Couch v. United States, 409 U.S. 322, 335, 93 S.Ct. 611, 619, 34 L.Ed. 2d 548 (1973).

Federal law does not recognize a privilege to prevent the introduction in a federal criminal case of legislative acts of a state legislator. United States v. Gillock, 445 U.S. 360, 100 S.Ct. 1185, 63 L.Ed.2d 454 (1980).

In proceedings to enforce a subpoena by the Equal Employment Opportunity Commission, which is investigating allegations of race and sex discrimination, Federal law does not recognize a privilege against disclosure of peer review materials in connection with the evaluation for tenure of university faculty members. University of Pennsylvania v. EEOC, 493 U.S. 182, 110 S.Ct. 577, 107 L.Ed. 2d 571 (1990).

House Judiciary Committee Report

Article V as submitted to Congress contained thirteen Rules. Nine of those Rules defined specific non-constitutional privileges which the federal courts must recognize (i.e. required reports, lawyer-client, psychotherapist-patient, husband-wife, communications to clergymen, political vote, trade secrets, secrets of state and other official information, and identity of informer.) Another Rule provided that only those privileges set forth in Article V or in some other Act of Congress could be recognized by the federal courts. The three remaining Rules addressed collateral problems as to waiver of privilege by voluntary disclosure, privileged matter disclosed under compulsion or without opportunity to claim privilege, comment upon or inference from a claim of privilege, and jury instruction with regard thereto.

The Committee amended Article V to eliminate all of the Court's specific Rules on privileges. Instead, the Committee, through a single Rule, 501, left the law of privileges in its present state and further provided that privileges shall continue to be developed by the courts of the United States under a uniform standard applicable both in civil and criminal cases. That standard, derived from Rule 26 of the Federal Rules of Criminal Procedure, mandates the application of the principles of the common law as interpreted by the courts of the United States in the light of reason and experience. The words "person, government, State, or political subdivision thereof" were added by the Committee to the lone term "witnesses" used in Rule 26 to make clear that, as under present law, not only witnesses may have privileges. The Committee also included in its amendment a proviso modeled after Rule 302 and similar to language added by the Committee to Rule 601 relating to the competency of witnesses. The proviso is designed to require the application of State privilege law in civil actions and proceedings governed by Erie R. Co. v. Tompkins, 304 U.S. 64 (1938), a result in accord with current federal court decisions. See Republic Gear Co. v. Borg-Warner Corp., 381 F.2d 551, 555-556 n. 2 (2nd Cir.1967). The Committee deemed the proviso to be necessary in the light of the Advisory Committee's view (see its note to Court [proposed] Rule 501) that this result is not mandated under Erie.

The rationale underlying the proviso is that federal law should not supersede that of the States in substantive areas such as privilege absent a compelling reason. The Committee believes that in civil cases in the federal courts where an element of a claim or defense is not grounded upon a federal question, there is no federal interest strong enough to justify departure from State policy. In addition, the Committee considered that the Court's proposed Article V would have promoted forum shopping in some civil actions, depending upon differences in the privilege law applied as among the State and federal courts. The Committee's proviso, on the other hand, under which the federal courts are bound to apply the State's privilege law in actions founded upon a State-created right or defense, removes the incentive to "shop".

Senate Judiciary Committee Report

Article V as submitted to Congress contained 13 rules. Nine of those rules defined specific nonconstitutional privileges which the Federal courts must recognize (i.e., required reports, lawyer-client, psychotherapist-patient, husband-wife, communications to clergymen, political vote, trade secrets, secrets of state and other official information, and identity of informer). Many of these rules contained controversial modifications or restrictions upon common law privileges. As noted supra, the House amended article V to eliminate all of the Court's specific rules on privileges. Through a single rule, 501, the House provided that privileges shall be governed by the principles of the common law as interpreted by the courts of the United States in the light of reason and experience (a standard derived from rule 26 of the Federal Rules of Criminal Procedure) except in the case of an element of a civil claim or defense as to which State law supplies the rule of decision, in which event state privilege law was to govern.

The committee agrees with the main thrust of the House amendment: that a federally developed common law based on modern reason and experience shall apply except where the State nature of the issues renders deference to State privilege law the wiser course, as in the usual diversity case. The committee understands that thrust of the House amendment to require that State privilege law be applied in "diversity" cases (actions on questions of State law between citizens of different States arising under 28 U.S.C. § 1332). The language of the House amendment, however, goes beyond this in some respects, and falls short of it in others: State privilege law applies even in nondiversity, Federal question civil cases, where an issue governed by State substantive law is the object of the evidence (such issues do sometimes arise in such cases); and, in all instances where State privilege law is to be applied, e.g., on proof of a State issue in a diversity case, a close reading reveals that State privilege law is not to be applied unless the matter to be proved is an element of that state claim or defense, as distinguished from a step along the way in the proof of it.

The committee is concerned that the language used in the House amendment could be difficult to apply. It provides that "in civil actions * * * with respect to an element of a claim or defense as to which State law supplies the rule of decision," State law on privilege applies. The question of what is an element of a claim or defense is likely to engender considerable litigation. If the matter in question constitutes an element of a claim, State law supplies the privilege rule; whereas if it is a mere item of proof with respect to a claim, then, even though State law might supply the rule of decision, Federal law on the privilege would apply. Further, disputes will arise as to how the rule should be applied in an antitrust action or in a tax case where the Federal statute is silent as to a particular aspect of the substantive law in question, but Federal cases had incorporated State law by reference to State law. [For a discussion of reference to State substantive law, see note on Federal Incorporation by Reference of State Law, Hart & Wechsler, The Federal Courts and the Federal System, pp. 491-494 (2d ed. 1973).] Is a claim (or defense) based on such a reference a claim or defense as to which federal or State law supplies the rule of decision?

Another problem not entirely avoidable is the complexity or difficulty the rule introduces into the trial of a Federal case containing a combination of Federal and State claims and defenses, e.g. an action involving Federal antitrust and State unfair competition claims. Two different bodies of privilege law would need to be consulted. It may even develop that the same witness-testimony might be relevant on both counts and privileged as to one but not the other. [The problems with the House formulation are discussed in Rothstein, The Proposed Amendments to the Federal Rules of Evidence, 62 Georgetown University Law Journal 125 (1973) at notes 25, 26 and 70-74 and accompanying text.]

The formulation adopted by the House is pregnant with litigious mischief. The committee has, therefore, adopted what we believe will be a clearer and more practical guideline for determining when courts should respect State rules of privilege. Basically, it provides that in criminal and Federal question civil cases, federally evolved rules on privilege should apply since it is Federal policy which is being enforced. [It is also intended that the Federal law of privileges should be applied with respect to pendent State law claims when they arise in a Federal question case.] Conversely, in diversity cases where the litigation in question turns on a substantive question of State law, and is brought in the Federal courts because the parties reside in different States, the committee believes it is clear that State rules of privilege should apply unless the proof is directed at a claim or defense for which Federal law supplies the rule of decision (a situation which would not commonly arise.) [While such a situation might require use of two bodies of privilege law, federal and state, in the same case, nevertheless the occasions on which this would be required are considerably reduced as compared with the House version, and confined to situations where the Federal and State interests are such as to justify application of neither privilege law to the case as a whole. If the rule proposed here results in two conflicting bodies of privilege law applying to the same piece of evidence in the same case, it is contemplated that the rule favoring reception of the evidence should be applied. This policy is based on the present rule 43(a) of the Federal Rules of Civil Procedure which provides: In any case, the statute or rule which favors the reception of the evidence governs and the evidence shall be presented according to the most convenient method prescribed in any of the statutes or rules to which reference is herein made.] It is intended that the State rules of privilege should apply equally in original diversity actions and diversity actions removed under 28 U.S.C. § 1441(b).

Two other comments on the privilege rule should be made. The committee has received a considerable volume of correspondence from psychiatric organizations and psychiatrists concerning the deletion of rule 504 of the rule submitted by the Supreme Court. It should be clearly understood that, in approving this general rule as to privileges, the action of Congress should not be understood as disapproving any recognition of a psychiatrist-patient, or husband-wife, or any other of the enumerated privileges contained in the Supreme Court rules. Rather, our action should be understood as reflecting the view that the recognition of a privilege based on a confidential relationship and other privileges should be determined on a case-by-case basis.

Further, we would understand that the prohibition against spouses testifying against each other is considered a rule of privilege and covered by this rule and not by rule 601 of the competency of witnesses.

Conference Committee Report

Rule 501 deals with the privilege of a witness not to testify. Both the House and Senate bills provide that federal privilege law applies in criminal cases. In civil actions and proceedings, the House bill provides that state privilege law applies "to an element of a claim or defense as to which State law supplies the rule of decision." The Senate bill provides that "in civil actions and proceedings arising under 28 U.S.C. § 1332 or 28 U.S.C. § 1335, or between citizens of different States and removed under 28 U.S.C. § 1441(b) the privilege of a witness, person, government, State or political subdivision thereof is determined in accordance with State law, unless with respect to the particular claim or defense, Federal law supplies the rule of decision."

The wording of the House and Senate bills differs in the treatment of civil actions and proceedings. The rule in the House bill applies to evidence that relates to "an element of a claim or defense." If an item of proof tends to support or defeat a claim or defense, or an element of a claim or defense, and if state law supplies the rule of decision for that claim or defense, then state privilege law applies to that item of proof.

Under the provision in the House bill, therefore, state privilege law will usually apply in diversity cases. There may be diversity cases, however, where a claim or defense is based upon federal law. In such instances, federal privilege law will apply to evidence relevant to the federal claim or defense. See Sola Electric Co. v. Jefferson Electric Co., 317 U.S. 173 (1942).

In nondiversity jurisdiction civil cases, federal privilege law will generally apply. In those situations where a federal court adopts or incorporates state law to fill interstices or gaps in federal statutory phrases, the court generally will apply federal privilege law. As Justice Jackson has said:

> A federal court sitting in a non-diversity case such as this does not sit as a local tribunal. In some cases it may see fit for special reasons to give the law of a particular state highly persuasive or even controlling effect, but in the last analysis its decision turns upon the law of the United States, not that of any state.

D'Oench, Duhme & Co. v. Federal Deposit Insurance Corp., 315 U.S. 447, 471 (1942) (Jackson, J., concurring). When a federal court chooses to absorb state law, it is applying the state law as a matter of federal common law. Thus, state law does not supply the rule of decision (even though the federal court may apply a rule derived from state decisions), and state privilege law would not apply. See C.A. Wright, Federal Courts 251-252 (2d ed. 1970); Holmberg v. Armbrecht, 327 U.S. 392 (1946); DeSylva v. Ballentine, 351 U.S. 570, 581 (1956); 9 Wright & Miller, Federal Rules and Procedure § 2408.

In civil actions and proceedings, where the rule of decision as to a claim or defense or as to an element of a claim or defense is supplied by state law, the House provision requires that state privilege law apply.

The Conference adopts the House provision.

Restyled 2011

Rule 502. Attorney-Client Privilege and Work Product; Limitations on Waiver

The following provisions apply, in the circumstances set out, to disclosure of a communication or information covered by the attorney-client privilege or work-product protection.

(a) Disclosure Made in a Federal Proceeding or to a Federal Office or Agency; Scope of a Waiver. When the disclosure is made in a federal proceeding or to a federal office or agency and waives the attorney-client privilege or work-product protection, the waiver extends to an undisclosed communication or information in a federal or state proceeding only if:

(1) the waiver is intentional;

(2) the disclosed and undisclosed communications or information concern the same subject matter; and

(3) they ought in fairness to be considered together.

(b) Inadvertent Disclosure. When made in a federal proceeding or to a federal office or agency, the disclosure does not operate as a waiver in a federal or state proceeding if:

(1) the disclosure is inadvertent;
(2) the holder of the privilege or protection took reasonable steps to prevent disclosure; and
(3) the holder promptly took reasonable steps to rectify the error, including (if applicable) following Federal Rule of Civil Procedure 26(b)(5)(B).

(c) **Disclosure Made in a State Proceeding.** When the disclosure is made in a state proceeding and is not the subject of a state-court order concerning waiver, the disclosure does not operate as a waiver in a federal proceeding if the disclosure:
(1) would not be a waiver under this rule if it had been made in a federal proceeding; or
(2) is not a waiver under the law of the state where the disclosure occurred.

(d) **Controlling Effect of a Court Order.** A federal court may order that the privilege or protection is not waived by disclosure connected with the litigation pending before the court — in which event the disclosure is also not a waiver in any other federal or state proceeding.

(e) **Controlling Effect of a Party Agreement.** An agreement on the effect of disclosure in a federal proceeding is binding only on the parties to the agreement, unless it is incorporated into a court order.

(f) **Controlling Effect of this Rule.** Notwithstanding Rules 101 and 1101, this rule applies to state proceedings and to federal court-annexed and federal court-mandated arbitration proceedings, in the circumstances set out in the rule. And notwithstanding Rule 501, this rule applies even if state law provides the rule of decision.

(g) **Definitions.** In this rule:
(1) "attorney-client privilege" means the protection that applicable law provides for confidential attorney-client communications; and
(2) "work-product protection" means the protection that applicable law provides for tangible material (or its intangible equivalent) prepared in anticipation of litigation or for trial.

Superseded 2011

Rule 502. Attorney-Client Privilege and Work Product; Limitations on Waiver

The following provisions apply, in the circumstances set out, to disclosure of a communication or information covered by the attorney-client privilege or work-product protection.

(a) Disclosure made in a Federal proceeding or to a Federal office or agency; scope of a waiver.—When the disclosure is made in a Federal proceeding or to a Federal office or agency and waives the attorney-client privilege or work-product protection, the waiver extends to an undisclosed communication or information in a Federal or State proceeding only if:

(1) the waiver is intentional;
(2) the disclosed and undisclosed communications or information concern the same subject matter; and
(3) they ought in fairness to be considered together.

(b) Inadvertent disclosure.—When made in a Federal proceeding or to a Federal office or agency, the disclosure does not operate as a waiver in a Federal or State proceeding if:

(1) the disclosure is inadvertent;
(2) the holder of the privilege or protection took reasonable steps to prevent disclosure; and
(3) the holder promptly took reasonable steps to rectify the error, including (if applicable) following Federal Rule of Civil Procedure 26(b)(5)(B).

(c) Disclosure made in a State proceeding.—When the disclosure is made in a State proceeding and is not the subject of a State-court order concerning waiver, the disclosure does not operate as a waiver in a Federal proceeding if the disclosure:

(1) would not be a waiver under this rule if it had been made in a Federal proceeding; or
(2) is not a waiver under the law of the State where the disclosure occurred.

(d) Controlling effect of a court order.—A Federal court may order that the privilege or protection is not waived by disclosure connected with the litigation pending before the court—in which event the disclosure is also not a waiver in any other Federal or State proceeding.

(e) Controlling effect of a party agreement.—An agreement on the effect of disclosure in a Federal proceeding is binding only on the parties to the agreement, unless it is incorporated into a court order.

(f) Controlling effect of this rule.—Notwithstanding Rules 101 and 1101, this rule applies to State proceedings and to Federal court-annexed and Federal court-mandated arbitration proceedings, in the circumstances set out in the rule. And notwithstanding Rule 501, this rule applies even if State law provides the rule of decision.

(g) Definitions.—In this rule:

(1) "attorney-client privilege" means the protection that applicable law provides for confidential attorney-client communications; and

(2) "work-product protection" means the protection that applicable law provides for tangible material (or its intangible equivalent) prepared in anticipation of litigation or for trial. [*Added 2008.*]

Advisory Committee Notes
Explanatory Note (Revised 11/28/2007)

This new rule has two major purposes:

1) It resolves some longstanding disputes in the courts about the effect of certain disclosures of communications or information protected by the attorney-client privilege or as work product—specifically those disputes involving inadvertent disclosure and subject matter waiver.

2) It responds to the widespread complaint that litigation costs necessary to protect against waiver of attorney-client privilege or work product have become prohibitive due to the concern that any disclosure (however innocent or minimal) will operate as a subject matter waiver of all protected communications or information. This concern is especially troubling in cases involving electronic discovery. *See, e.g., Hopson v. City of Baltimore*, 232 F.R.D. 228, 244 (D.Md. 2005) (electronic discovery may encompass "millions of documents" and to insist upon "record-by-record pre-production privilege review, on pain of subject matter waiver, would impose upon parties costs of production that bear no proportionality to what is at stake in the litigation").

The rule seeks to provide a predictable, uniform set of standards under which parties can determine the consequences of a disclosure of a communication or information covered by the attorney-client privilege or work-product protection. Parties to litigation need to know, for example, that if they exchange privileged information pursuant to a confidentiality order, the court's order will be enforceable. Moreover, if a federal court's confidentiality order is not enforceable in a state court then the burdensome costs of privilege review and retention are unlikely to be reduced.

The rule makes no attempt to alter federal or state law on whether a communication or information is protected under the attorney-client privilege or work-product immunity as an initial matter. Moreover, while establishing some exceptions to waiver, the rule does not purport to supplant applicable waiver doctrine generally.

The rule governs only certain waivers by disclosure. Other common-law waiver doctrines may result in a finding of waiver even where there is no disclosure of privileged information or work product. *See, e.g., Nguyen v. Excel Corp.*, 197 F.3d 200 (5th Cir. 1999) (reliance on an advice of counsel defense waives the privilege with respect to attorney-client communications pertinent to that defense); *Ryers v. Burleson*, 100 F.R.D. 436 (D.D.C. 1983) (allegation of lawyer malpractice constituted a waiver of confidential communications under the circumstances). The rule is not intended to displace or modify federal common law concerning waiver of privilege or work product where no disclosure has been made.

Subdivision (a). The rule provides that a voluntary disclosure in a federal proceeding or to a federal office or agency, if a waiver, generally results in a waiver only of the communication or information disclosed; a subject matter waiver (of either privilege or work product) is reserved for those unusual situations in which fairness requires a further disclosure of related, protected information, in order to prevent a selective and misleading presentation of evidence to the disadvantage of the adversary. *See, e.g., In re United Mine Workers of America Employee Benefit Plans Litig.*, 159 F.R.D. 307, 312 (D.D.C. 1994) (waiver of work product limited to materials actually disclosed, because the party did not deliberately disclose documents in an attempt to gain a tactical advantage). Thus, subject matter waiver is limited to situations in which a party intentionally puts protected information into the litigation in a selective, misleading and unfair manner. It follows that an inadvertent disclosure of protected information can never result in a subject matter waiver. *See* Rule 502(b). The rule rejects the result in *In re Sealed Case*, 877 F.2d 976 (D.C.Cir. 1989), which held that inadvertent disclosure of documents during discovery automatically constituted a subject matter waiver.

The language concerning subject matter waiver—"ought in fairness"—is taken from Rule 106, because the animating principle is the same. Under both Rules, a party that makes a selective, misleading presentation that is unfair to the adversary opens itself to a more complete and accurate presentation.

To assure protection and predictability, the rule provides that if a disclosure is made at the federal level, the federal rule on subject matter waiver governs subsequent state court determinations on the scope of the waiver by that disclosure.

Subdivision (b). Courts are in conflict over whether an inadvertent disclosure of a communication or information protected as privileged or work product constitutes a waiver. A few courts find that a disclosure must be intentional to be a waiver. Most courts find a waiver only if the disclosing party acted carelessly in disclosing the communication or information and failed to request its return in a timely manner. And a few courts hold that any inadvertent disclosure of a communication or information protected under the attorney-client privilege or as work product constitutes a waiver without regard to the protections taken to avoid such a disclosure. *See generally Hopson v. City of Baltimore*, 232 F.R.D. 228 (D.Md. 2005), for a discussion of this case law.

The rule opts for the middle ground: inadvertent disclosure of protected communications or information in connection with a federal proceeding or to a federal office or agency does not constitute a waiver if the holder took reasonable steps to prevent disclosure and also promptly took reasonable steps to rectify the error. This position is in accord with the majority view on whether inadvertent disclosure is a waiver.

Cases such as *Lois Sportswear, U.S.A., Inc. v. Levi Strauss & Co.*, 104 F.R.D. 103, 105 (S.D.N.Y. 1985) and *Hartford Fire Ins. Co. v. Garvey*, 109 F.R.D. 323, 332 (N.D.Cal. 1985), set out a multi-factor test for determining whether inadvertent disclosure is a waiver. The stated factors (none of which is dispositive) are the reasonableness of precautions taken, the time taken to rectify the error, the scope of discovery, the extent of disclosure and the overriding issue of fairness. The rule does not explicitly codify that test, because it is really a set of non-determinative guidelines that vary from case to case. The rule is flexible enough to accommodate any of those listed factors. Other considerations bearing on the reasonableness of a producing party's efforts include the number of documents to be reviewed and the time constraints for production. Depending on the circumstances, a party that uses advanced analytical software applications and linguistic tools in screening for privilege and work product may be found to have taken "reasonable steps" to prevent inadvertent disclosure. The implementation of an efficient system of records management before litigation may also be relevant.

The rule does not require the producing party to engage in a post-production review to determine whether any protected communication or information has been produced by mistake. But the rule does require the producing party to follow up on any obvious indications that a protected communication or information has been produced inadvertently.

The rule applies to inadvertent disclosures made to a federal office or agency, including but not limited to an office or agency that is acting in the course of its regulatory, investigative or enforcement authority. The consequences of waiver, and the concomitant costs of pre-production privilege review, can be as great with respect to disclosures to offices and agencies as they are in litigation.

Subdivision (c). Difficult questions can arise when 1) a disclosure of a communication or information protected by the attorney-client privilege or as work product is made in a state proceeding, 2) the communication or information is offered in a subsequent federal proceeding on the ground that the disclosure waived the privilege or protection, and 3) the state and federal laws are in conflict on the question of waiver. The Committee determined that the proper solution for the federal court is to apply the law that is most protective of privilege and work product. If the state law is more protective (such as where the state law is that an inadvertent disclosure can never be a waiver), the holder of the privilege or protection may well have relied on that law when making the disclosure in the state proceeding. Moreover, applying a more restrictive federal law of waiver could impair the state objective of preserving the privilege or work-product protection for disclosures made in state proceedings. On the other hand, if the federal law is more protective, applying the state law of waiver to determine admissibility in federal court is likely to undermine the federal objective of limiting the costs of production.

The rule does not address the enforceability of a state court confidentiality order in a federal proceeding, as that question is covered both by statutory law and principles of federalism and comity. *See* 28 U.S.C. § 1738 (providing that state judicial proceedings "shall have the same full faith and credit in every court within the United States . . . as they have by law or usage in the courts of such State . . . from which they are taken"). *See also Tucker v. Ohtsu Tire & Rubber Co.*, 191 F.R.D. 495, 499 (D.Md. 2000) (noting that a federal court considering the enforceability of a state confidentiality order is "constrained by principles of comity, courtesy, and . . . federalism"). Thus, a state court order finding no waiver in connection with a disclosure made in a state court proceeding is enforceable under existing law in subsequent federal proceedings.

Subdivision (d). Confidentiality orders are becoming increasingly important in limiting the costs of privilege review and retention, especially in cases involving electronic discovery. But the utility of a confidentiality order in reducing discovery costs is substantially diminished if it provides no protection outside the particular litigation in which the order is entered. Parties are unlikely to be able to reduce the costs of pre-production review for privilege and work product if the consequence of disclosure is that the communications or information could be used by non-parties to the litigation.

There is some dispute on whether a confidentiality order entered in one case is enforceable in other proceedings. *See generally Hopson v. City of Baltimore*, 232 F.R.D. 228 (D.Md. 2005), for a discussion of this case law. The rule provides that when a confidentiality order governing the consequences of disclosure in that case is entered in a federal proceeding, its terms are enforceable against non-parties in any federal or state proceeding. For example, the court order may provide for return of documents without waiver irrespective of the care taken by the disclosing party; the rule contemplates enforcement of "claw-back" and "quick peek" arrangements as a way to avoid the excessive costs of pre-production review for privilege and work product. *See Zubulake v. UBS Warburg LLC*, 216 F.R.D. 280, 290 (S.D.N.Y. 2003) (noting that parties may enter into "so-called 'claw-back' agreements that allow the parties to forego privilege review altogether in favor of an agreement to return inadvertently produced privilege documents"). The rule provides a party with a predictable protection from a court order—predictability that is needed to allow the party to plan in advance to limit the prohibitive costs of privilege and work product review and retention.

Under the rule, a confidentiality order is enforceable whether or not it memorializes an agreement among the parties to the litigation. Party agreement should not be a condition of enforceability of a federal court's order.

Under subdivision (d), a federal court may order that disclosure of privileged or protected information "in connection with" a federal proceeding does not result in waiver. But subdivision (d) does not allow the federal court to enter an order determining the waiver effects of a separate disclosure of the same information in other proceedings, state or federal. If a disclosure has been made in a state proceeding (and is not the subject of a state-court order on waiver), then subdivision (d) is inapplicable. Subdivision (c) would govern the federal court's determination whether the state-court disclosure waived the privilege or protection in the federal proceeding.

Subdivision (e). Subdivision (e) codifies the well-established proposition that parties can enter an agreement to limit the effect of waiver by disclosure between or among them. Of course such an agreement can bind only the parties to the agreement. The rule makes clear that if parties want protection against non-parties from a finding of waiver by disclosure, the agreement must be made part of a court order.

Subdivision (f). The protections against waiver provided by Rule 502 must be applicable when protected communications or information disclosed in federal proceedings are subsequently offered in state proceedings. Otherwise the holders of protected communications and information, and their lawyers, could not rely on the protections provided by the Rule, and the goal of limiting costs in discovery would be substantially undermined. Rule 502(f) is intended to resolve any potential tension between the provisions of Rule 502 that apply to state proceedings and the possible limitations on the applicability of the Federal Rules of Evidence otherwise provided by Rules 101 and 1101.

The rule is intended to apply in all federal court proceedings, including court-annexed and court-ordered arbitrations, without regard to any possible limitations of Rules 101 and 1101. This provision is not intended to raise an inference about the applicability of any other rule of evidence in arbitration proceedings more generally.

The costs of discovery can be equally high for state and federal causes of action, and the rule seeks to limit those costs in all federal proceedings, regardless of whether the claim arises under state or federal law. Accordingly, the rule applies to state law causes of action brought in federal court.

Subdivision (g). The rule's coverage is limited to attorney-client privilege and work product. The operation of waiver by disclosure, as applied to other evidentiary privileges, remains a question of federal common law. Nor does the rule purport to apply to the Fifth Amendment privilege against compelled self-incrimination.

The definition of work product "materials" is intended to include both tangible and intangible information. *See In re Cendant Corp. Sec. Litig.*, 343 F.3d 658, 662 (3d Cir. 2003) ("work product protection extends to both tangible and intangible work product").

Committee Letter

The letter from the Committee on Rules of Practice and Procedure of the Judicial Conference of the United States to the Committee on the Judiciary of the U.S. Senate and House of Representatives, dated September 26, 2007, provided:

On behalf of the Judicial Conference of the United States, I respectfully submit a proposed addition to the Federal Rules of Evidence. The Conference recommends that Congress adopt this proposed rule as Federal Rule of Evidence 502.

The Rule provides for protections against waiver of the attorney-client privilege or work product immunity. The Conference submits this proposal directly to Congress because of the limitations on the rulemaking function of the federal courts in matters dealing with evidentiary privilege. Unlike all other federal rules of procedure prescribed under the Rules Enabling Act, those rules governing evidentiary privilege must by approved by an Act of Congress, 28 U.S.C. § 2074(b).

Description of the Process Leading to the Proposed Rule

The Judicial Conference Rules Committees have long been concerned about the rising costs of litigation, much of which has been caused by the review, required under current law, of every document produced in discovery, in order to determine whether the document contains privileged information. In 2006, the House Judiciary Committee Chair suggested that the Judicial Conference consider proposing a rule dealing with waiver of attorney-client privilege and work product, in order to limit these rising costs. The Judicial Conference was urged to proceed with rulemaking that would:

- protect against the forfeiture of privilege when a disclosure in discovery is the result of an innocent mistake; and
- permit parties, and courts, to protect against the consequences of waiver by permitting disclosures of privileged information between the parties to litigation.

The task of drafting a proposed rule was referred to the Advisory Committee on Evidence Rules (the "Advisory Committee"). The Advisory Committee prepared a draft Rule 502 and invited a select group of judges, lawyers, and academics to testify before the Advisory Committee about the need for the rule, and to suggest any improvements. The Advisory Committee considered all the testimony presented by these experts and redrafted the rule accordingly. At its Spring 2006 meeting, the Advisory Committee approved for release for public comment a proposed Rule 502 that would provide certain exceptions to the federal common law on waiver of privileges and work product. That rule was approved for release for public comment by the Committee on Rules of Practice and Procedure ("the Standing Committee"). The public comment period began in August 2006 and ended February 15, 2007. The Advisory Committee received more that [sic] 70 public comments, and also heard the testimony of more than 20 witnesses at two public hearings. The rule released for public comment was also carefully reviewed by the Standing Committee's Subcommittee on Style. In April 2007, the Advisory Committee issued a revised proposed Rule 502 taking into account the public comment, the views of the Subcommittee on Style, and its own judgment. The revised rule was approved by the Standing Committee and the Judicial Conference. It is enclosed with this letter.In order to inform Congress of the legal issues involved in this rule, the proposed Rule 502 also includes a proposed Committee Note of the kind that accompanies all rules adopted through the Rules Enabling Act. This Committee Note may be incorporated as all or part of the legislative history of the rule if it is adopted by Congress. *See, e.g.*, House Conference Report 103-711 (stating that the "Conferees intend that the Advisory Committee Note on [Evidence] Rule 412, as transmitted by the Judicial Conference of the United States to the Supreme Court on October 25, 1993, applies to Rule 412 as enacted by this section" of the Violent Crime Control and Law Enforcement Act of 1994).

Problems Addressed by the Proposed Rule

In drafting the proposed Rule, the Advisory Committee concluded that the current law on waiver of privilege and work product is responsible in large part for the rising costs of discovery, especially discovery of electronic information. In complex litigation the lawyers spend significant amounts of time and effort to preserve the privilege and work product. The reason is that if a protected document is produced, there is a risk that a court will find a subject matter waiver that will apply not only to the instant case and document but to other cases and documents as well. Moreover, an enormous amount of expense is put into document production in order to protect against inadvertent disclosure of privileged information, because the producing party risks a ruling that even a mistaken disclosure can result in a subject matter waiver. Advisory Committee members also expressed the view that the fear of waiver leads to extravagant claims of privilege. Members concluded that if there were a way to produce documents in discovery without risking subject matter waiver, the discovery process could be made much less expensive. The Advisory Committee noted that the existing law on the effect of inadvertent disclosures and on the scope of waiver is far from consistent or certain. It also noted that agreements between parties with regard to the effect of disclosure on privilege are common, but are unlikely to decrease the costs of discovery due to the ineffectiveness of such agreements as to persons not party to them.

Proposed Rule 502 does not attempt to deal comprehensively with either attorney-client privilege or work-product protection. It also does not purport to cover all issues concerning waiver or forfeiture of either the attorney-client privilege or work-product protection. Rather, it deals primarily with issues involved in the disclosure of protected information in federal court proceedings or to a federal public office or agency. The rule binds state courts only with regard to disclosures made in federal proceedings. It deals with disclosures made in state proceedings only to the extent that the effect of those disclosures becomes an issue in federal litigation. The Rule covers issues of scope of waiver, inadvertent disclosure, and the controlling effect of court orders and agreements.

Rule 502 provides the following protections against waiver of privilege or work product:

- *Limitations on Scope of Waiver.* Subdivision (a) provides that if a waiver is found, it applies only to the information disclosed, unless a broader waiver is made necessary by the holder's intentional and misleading use of privileged or protected communications or information.
- *Protections Against Inadvertent Disclosure.* Subdivision (b) provides that an inadvertent disclosure of privileged or protected communications or information, when made at the federal level, does not operate as a waiver if the holder took reasonable steps to prevent such a disclosure and employed reasonably prompt measures to retrieve the mistakenly disclosed communications or information.
- *Effect on State Proceedings and Disclosures Made in State Courts.* Subdivision (c) provides that 1) if there is a disclosure of privileged or protected communications or information at the federal level, then state courts must honor Rule 502 in subsequent state proceedings; and 2) if there is a disclosure of privileged or protected communications or information in a state proceeding, then admissibility in a subsequent federal proceeding is determined by the law that is most protective against waiver.
- *Orders Protecting Privileged Communications Binding on Non-Parties.* Subdivision (d) provides that if a federal court enters an order providing that a disclosure of privileged or protected communications or information does not constitute a waiver, that order is enforceable against all persons and entities in any federal or state proceeding. This provision allows parties in an action in which such an order is entered to limit their costs of pre-production privilege review.
- *Agreements Protecting Privileged Communications Binding on Parties.* Subdivision (e) provides that parties in a federal proceeding can enter into a confidentiality agreement providing for mutual protection against waiver in that proceeding. While those agreements bind the signatory parties, they are not binding on non-parties unless incorporated into a court order.

Drafting Choices Made by the Advisory Committee

The Advisory Committee made a number of important drafting choices in Rule 502. This section explains those choices.

1) The effect in state proceedings of disclosures initially made in state proceedings. Rule 502 does not apply to a disclosure made in a state proceeding when the disclosed communication or information is subsequently offered in another state proceeding. The first draft of Rule 502 provided for uniform waiver rules in federal and state proceedings, regardless of where the initial disclosure was made. This draft raised the objections of the Conference of State Chief Justices. State judges argued that the Rule as drafted offended principles of federalism and comity, by superseding state law of privilege waiver, even for disclosures that are made initially in state proceedings—and even when the disclosed material is then offered in a state proceeding (the so-called "state-to-state" problem). In response to these objections, the Advisory Committee voted unanimously to scale back the Rule, so that it would not cover the "state-to-state" problem. Under the current proposal state courts are bound by the Federal Rule only when a disclosure is made at the federal level and the disclosed communication or information is later offered in a state proceeding (the so-called "federal-to-state" problem).

During the public comment period on the scaled-back rule, the Advisory Committee received many requests from lawyers and lawyer groups to return to the original draft and provide a uniform rule of privilege waiver that would bind both state and federal courts, for disclosures made in either state or federal proceedings. These comments expressed the concern that if states were not bound by a uniform federal rule on privilege waiver, the protections afforded by Rule 502 would be undermined; parties and their lawyers might not be able to rely on the protections of the Rule, for fear that a state law would find a waiver even though the Federal Rule would not.

The Advisory Committee determined that these comments raised a legitimate concern, but decided not to extend Rule 502 to govern a state court's determination of waiver with respect to disclosures made in state proceedings. The Committee relied on the following considerations:

- Rule 502 is located in the Federal Rules of Evidence, a body of rules determining the admissibility of evidence in federal proceedings. Parties in a state proceeding determining the effect of a disclosure made in that proceeding or in other state courts would be unlikely to look to the Federal Rules of Evidence for the answer.
- In the Advisory Committee's view, Rule 502, as proposed herein, does fulfill its primary goal of reducing the costs of discovery in *federal* proceedings. Rule 502 by its terms governs state courts with regard to the effect of disclosures initially made in federal proceedings or to federal offices or agencies. Parties and their lawyers in federal proceedings can therefore predict the consequences of disclosure by referring to Rule 502; there is no possibility that a state court could find a waiver when Rule 502 would not, when the disclosure is initially made at the federal level.

The Judicial Conference has no position on the merits of separate legislation to cover the problem of waiver of privilege and work product when the disclosure is made at the state level and the consequence is to be determined in a state court.

2) Other applications of Rule 502 to state court proceedings. Although disclosures made in state court proceedings and later offered in state proceedings would not be covered, Rule 502 would have an effect on state court proceedings where the disclosure is initially made in a federal proceeding or to a federal office or agency. Most importantly, state courts in such circumstances would be bound by federal protection orders. The other protections against waiver in Rule 502—against mistaken disclosure and subject matter waiver—would also bind state courts as to disclosures initially made at the federal level. The Rule, as submitted, specifically provides that it applies to state

proceedings under the circumstances set out in the Rule. This protection is needed, otherwise parties could not rely on Rule 502 even as to federal disclosures, for fear that a state court would find waiver even when a federal court would not.

3) Disclosures made in state proceedings and offered in a subsequent federal proceeding. Earlier drafts of proposed Rule 502 did not determine the question of what rule would apply when a disclosure is made in state court and the waiver determination is to be made in a subsequent federal proceeding. Proposed Rule 502 as submitted herein provides that all of the provisions of Rule 502 apply unless the state law of privilege is more protective (less likely to find waiver) than the federal law. The Advisory Committee determined that this solution best preserved federal interests in protecting against waiver, and also provided appropriate respect for state attempts to give greater protection to communications and information covered by the attorney-client privilege or work-product doctrine.

4) Selective waiver. At the suggestion of the House Judiciary Committee Chair, the Advisory Committee considered a rule that would allow persons and entities to cooperate with government agencies without waiving all privileges as to other parties in subsequent litigation. Such a rule is known as a "selective waiver" rule, meaning that disclosure of protected communications or information to the government waives the protection only selectively—to the government—and not to any other person or entity.

The selective waiver provision proved to be very controversial. The Advisory Committee determined that it would not propose adoption of a selective waiver provision; but in light of the request from the House Judiciary Committee, the Advisory Committee did prepare language for a selective waiver provision should Congress decide to proceed. The draft language for a selective waiver provision is available on request.

Conclusion

Proposed Rule 502 is respectfully submitted for consideration by Congress as a rule that will effectively limit the skyrocketing costs of discovery. Members of the Standing Committee, the Advisory Committee, as well as their reporters and consultants, are ready to assist Congress in any way it sees fit.

Advisory Committee's Draft of Cover Letter to Congress on Selective Waiver

The Judicial Conference has respectfully submitted proposed Federal Rule of Evidence 502. As submitted in a separate letter, Proposed Rule 502 governs scope of waiver, inadvertent disclosure and the enforceability of court orders, all with the goal of limiting the costs of privilege review in production of materials during litigation or to federal offices or agencies. Congressman James Sensenbrenner also asked the Advisory Committee on Evidence Rules (the "Advisory Committee") to consider the possibility of proposing a rule that would "allow persons and entities to cooperate with government agencies without waiving all privileges as to other parties in subsequent litigation." Such a rule is known as a "selective waiver" rule, meaning that disclosure of protected communications or information to the government waives the protection only selectively—to the government—and not to any other person or entity. In response to Congressman Sensenbrenner's request, the Advisory Committee prepared a selective waiver provision and it was submitted for public comment. It provided for protection for disclosures made to federal offices or agencies only—but it bound state courts to selective waiver when a disclosure to a federal office or agency was offered in a subsequent state proceeding.

The selective waiver provision proved to be very controversial. The public comment from the legal community (including lawyer groups such as the American Bar Association, Lawyers for Civil Justice, and the American College of Trial Lawyers) was almost uniformly negative. The negative comments can be summarized as follows:

- Lawyers expressed the concern that if selective waiver is enacted, corporate personnel will not communicate confidentially with lawyers for the corporation, for fear that the corporation will be more likely to produce the information to the government and thereby place the individual agents at personal risk.
- Public interest lawyers and lawyers for the plaintiffs bar were concerned that selective waiver will deprive individual plaintiffs of the information necessary to bring meritorious private litigation.
- Selective waiver was criticized as inappropriate in the alleged current environment of what some have called the "culture of waiver." Lawyers expressed the belief that corporations are currently being indicted unless they turn over privileged or protected information; they contended that selective waiver could be expected to increase government demands to produce such information.
- Selective waiver was criticized as unfair, because it allows corporations to waive the privilege to their advantage, without suffering the risks that would ordinarily occur with such a waiver.
- Lawyers emphasized that under the federal common law, every federal circuit court but one has rejected the notion of selective waiver, those courts reasoning 1) that corporations do not need any extra incentive to cooperate, and 2) that selective waiver protection could allow the holder to use the privilege as a sword rather than a shield. Lawyers contended that a doctrine roundly rejected under federal common law should not be enacted by rule.
- Judges of state courts objected that selective waiver raised serious federalism problems, because in order to be effective it would have to bind state courts, and as such it would change the law of privilege in virtually every state, because most of the states do not recognize selective waiver.
- Lawyers argued that selective waiver does not really protect the privilege because nothing prohibits the government agency from publicly disclosing the privileged information.

In sharp contrast, federal agencies and authorities (including the Securities Exchange Commission, the Commodity Futures Trading Commission, and the Department of Justice) expressed strong support for selective waiver. These agencies made the following arguments.

- The agencies doubted that a selective waiver rule will discourage candid conversations between corporate counsel and employees. They noted that even in the current world without selective waiver, employees must already be advised by corporate counsel that the corporation holds the privilege and may choose to waive it, so the agencies concluded that an employee's candor will not be affected by a change in the rules on whether such a waiver is "selective" or not.
- The agencies contended that private parties will in the end benefit from selective waiver, as it will lead to more timely and efficient public investigations.

- The agencies asserted that government practices have not created a "culture of waiver." They also argued that the selective waiver rule addresses only the evidentiary consequences that flow in a later litigation from an earlier disclosure. This is a problem distinct from how often waiver is sought, and is a problem that will exist even if the government never seeks a waiver but companies still provide them, a possibility that even critics acknowledge will continue.
- The protection of selective waiver was asserted to be necessary because corporations are otherwise deterred from cooperating with government investigations, and such cooperation serves the public interest by substantially reducing the cost of those investigations.
- The complaint from private parties about lack of access to information was dismissed on the ground that the information they sought would not even be produced in the absence of selective waiver.
- The agencies noted that even if the government can disclose the information widely, this did not undermine the doctrine of selective waiver; under selective waiver, private parties could not use the information in court, no matter how widely it is distributed in public.
- The agencies found nothing in the federal common law to indicate that legislation on selective waiver would be improper or unjustified.

The Advisory Committee carefully considered and discussed all of the favorable and unfavorable comments on the selective waiver provision. The Advisory Committee finally determined that selective waiver raised questions that were essentially political in nature. Those questions included: 1) Do corporations need selective waiver to cooperate with government investigations? 2) Is there a "culture of waiver" and, if so, how would selective waiver affect that "culture"? These are questions that are difficult if not impossible to determine in the rulemaking process. The Advisory Committee also noted that as a rulemaking matter, selective waiver raised issues different from those addressed in the rest of Rule 502. The basic goal of Rule 502 is to limit the costs of discovery (especially electronic discovery), whereas selective waiver, if implemented, is intended to limit the costs of government investigations, independently of any discovery costs. Thus, the selective waiver provision was outside the central, discovery-related focus of the rest of the rule.

The Advisory Committee determined that it would not include a selective waiver provision as part of proposed Rule 502. The Judicial Conference approves that decision. The Conference recognizes, however, that Congress may be interested in considering separate legislation to enact selective waiver, as evidenced by the Regulatory Relief Act of 2006, which provides that disclosure of privileged information to a banking regulator does not operate as a waiver to private parties.

The Advisory Committee prepared language to assist Congress should it decide to proceed with independent legislation on selective waiver. This suggested language is derived from the Bank Regulatory Act and also incorporates some drafting suggestions received during the public comment period on Rule 502. The draft language includes a Committee Note that explains the drafting choices that were made.

Advisory Committee's Draft of Statutory Language on Selective Waiver (4/13/2007)

(a) Selective waiver. In a federal [or state] proceeding, the disclosure of a communication or information protected by the attorney client privilege or as work product—when made for any purpose to a federal office or agency in the course of any regulatory, investigative, or enforcement process—does not waive the privilege or work-product protection in favor of any person or entity other than a [the] federal office or agency.

(b) Rule of construction.—This rule does not:

1) limit or expand a government office or agency's authority to disclose communications or information to other government offices or agencies or as otherwise authorized or required by law; or

2) limit any protection against waiver provided in any other Act of Congress.

(c) Definitions.—In this Act:

1) "attorney-client privilege" means the protection that applicable law provides for confidential attorney-client communications; and

2) "work-product protection" means the protection that applicable law provides for tangible material or its tangible equivalent, prepared in anticipation of litigation or for trial.

Advisory Committee's Note on Selective Waiver

Courts are in conflict over whether disclosure of privileged or protected communications or information to a government office or agency conducting an investigation of the client constitutes a general waiver of the communications or information disclosed. Most courts have rejected the concept of "selective waiver," holding that waiver of privileged or protected communications or information to a government office or agency constitutes a waiver for all purposes and to all parties. *See, e.g., Westinghouse Electric Corp. v. Republic of the Philippines,* 951 F.2d 1414 (3d Cir. 1991). Other courts have held that selective waiver is enforceable if the disclosure is made subject to a confidentiality agreement with the government office or agency. *See, e.g., Teachers Insurance & Annuity Association of America v. Shamrock Broadcasting Co.,* 521 F. Supp. 638 (S.D.N.Y. 1981). And a few courts have held that disclosure of privileged or protected communications or information to the government does not constitute a general waiver, so that the privilege or protection remains applicable against other parties. *See, e.g., Diversified Industries, Inc. v. Meredith,* 572 F.2d 596 (8th Cir. 1977).

The rule resolves this conflict by providing that disclosure of protected communications or information to a federal office or agency exercising regulatory, investigative or enforcement authority does not constitute a waiver of attorney-client privilege or work product protection as to any person or entity other than a [the] federal public office or agency; that protection of selective waiver applies when the disclosed communication or information is subsequently offered in [either] federal [or state court].

The rule does not purport to affect the disclosure of protected communications or information after receipt by the federal office or agency. The rule does, however, provide protection from waiver in favor of anyone other than federal offices or agencies, regardless of the extent of disclosure of the communications or information by any such office or agency. Even if the communications or information are used in an enforcement proceeding and so become publicly available, the communications or information will continue to be protected as against other persons or entities.

The rule provides that when protected communications or information are disclosed to a "federal office or agency" the disclosure does not operate as a waiver to any person or entity other than a [the] federal office or agency. As such, a disclosure covered by the rule does not operate as a waiver in any congressional investigation or hearing.

The rule is not intended to limit or affect any other Act of Congress that provides for selective waiver protection for disclosures made to government agencies or offices. *See, e.g.,* Financial Services Regulatory Relief Act of 2006, Pub.L.No. 109-351, § 607, 120 Stat. 1966, 1981 (2006).

1971 Proposed Rule 501. Privileges Recognized Only as Provided [*Not Enacted*]

Except as otherwise required by the Constitution of the United States or provided by Act of Congress, and except as provided in these rules and in the Rules of Civil and Criminal Procedure, no person has a privilege to:

(a) Refuse to be a witness; or

(b) Refuse to disclose any matter; or

(c) Refuse to produce any object or writing; or

(d) Prevent another from being a witness or disclosing any matter or producing any object or writing.

Uniform Rules of Evidence

Uniform Rule 501 is identical to Proposed Federal Rule 501, except the introductory clause provides:

Except as otherwise provided by constitution or statute or by these or other rules promulgated by [the Supreme Court of this State], no person has a privilege to: * * *

and in paragraph (d), "record" is substituted for "writing."

Editor's Note

1971 Proposed Rule 501 was the first of thirteen rules on privileges recommended by the Advisory Committee and promulgated by the Supreme Court. Rule 501, as finally adopted, indicates that the proposed privilege rules were rejected by Congress in favor of "the common law * * * in the light of reason and experience" and state rules of privilege in civil actions governed by state law. However, the privilege provisions of the 1971 Proposed Rules have been influential. They are often cited as evidence of the common law, see, e.g., Jaffee v. Redmond, 518 U.S. 1 (1996). In 1974 they were incorporated with only minimal changes into the Uniform Rules of Evidence, on which most state codifications of evidence law have been based.

1971 Proposed Rules 501-513 are printed here along with the original Advisory Committee's Notes. (The original note to 1971 Proposed Rule 501 is omitted.) Each 1971 Proposed Rule is also accompanied by a note indicating any differences between the 1971 Proposed Rule and the Uniform Rules of Evidence (1974, as amended, 1986).

1971 Proposed Rule 502. Required Reports Privileged by Statute [*Not Enacted*]

A person, corporation, association, or other organization or entity, either public or private, making a return or report required by law to be made has a privilege to refuse to disclose and to prevent any other person from disclosing the return or report, if the law requiring it to be made so provides. A public officer or agency to whom a return or report is required by law to be made has a privilege to refuse to disclose the return or report if the law requiring it to be made so provides. No privilege exists under this rule in actions involving perjury, false statements, fraud in the return or report, or other failure to comply with the law in question.

Uniform Rules of Evidence

The Uniform Rules have no privilege for required reports.

Advisory Committee's Note

Statutes which require the making of returns or reports sometimes confer on the reporting party a privilege against disclosure, commonly coupled with a prohibition against disclosure by the officer to whom the report is made. Some of the federal statutes of this kind are mentioned in the Advisory Committee Note to [Proposed] Rule 501, supra. See also the Note to Rule 402, supra. A provision against disclosure may be included in a statute for a variety of reasons, the chief of which are probably assuring the validity of the statute against claims of self-incrimination, honoring the privilege against self-incrimination, and encouraging the furnishing of the required information by assuring privacy.

These statutes, both state and federal, may generally be assumed to embody policies of significant dimension. [Proposed] Rule 501 insulates the federal provisions against disturbance by these rules; the present rule reiterates a result commonly specified in federal statutes and extends its application to state statutes of similar character. Illustrations of the kinds of returns and reports contemplated by the rule appear in the cases, in which a reluctance to compel disclosure is manifested. In re Reid, 155 F. 933 (E.D.Mich.1906), assessor not compelled to produce bankrupt's property tax return in view of statute forbidding disclosure; In re Valecia Condensed Milk Co., 240 F. 310 (7th Cir.1917), secretary of state tax commission not compelled to produce bankrupt's income tax returns in violation of statute; Herman Bros. Pet Supply, Inc. v. N.L.R.B., 360 F.2d 176 (6th Cir.1966), subpoena denied for production of reports to state employment security commission prohibited by statute, in proceeding for back wages. And see the discussion of motor vehicle accident reports in Krizak v. W.C. Brooks & Sons, Inc., 320 F.2d 37, 42-43 (4th Cir.1963). Cf. In re Hines, 69 F.2d 52 (2d Cir.1934).

1971 Proposed Rule 503. Lawyer-Client Privilege [*Not Enacted*]

(a) Definitions. As used in this rule:

(1) A "client" is a person, public officer, or corporation, association, or other organization or entity, either public or private, who is rendered professional legal services by a lawyer, or who consults a lawyer with a view to obtaining professional legal services from him.

(2) A "lawyer" is a person authorized, or reasonably believed by the client to be authorized, to practice law in any state or nation.

(3) A "representative of the lawyer" is one employed to assist the lawyer in the rendition of professional legal services.

(4) A communication is "confidential" if not intended to be disclosed to third persons other than those to whom disclosure is in furtherance of the rendition of professional legal services to the client or those reasonably necessary for the transmission of the communication.

(b) General rule of privilege. A client has a privilege to refuse to disclose and to prevent any other person from disclosing confidential communications made for the purpose of facilitating the rendition of professional legal services to the client, (1) between himself or his representative and his lawyer or his lawyer's representative, or (2) between his lawyer and the lawyer's representative, or (3) by him or his lawyer to a lawyer representing another in a matter of common interest, or (4) between representatives of the client or between the client and a representative of the client, or (5) between lawyers representing the client.

(c) Who may claim the privilege. The privilege may be claimed by the client, his guardian or conservator, the personal representative of a deceased client, or the successor, trustee, or similar representative of a corporation, association, or other organization, whether or not in existence. The person who was the lawyer at the time of the communication may claim the privilege but only on behalf of the client. His authority to do so is presumed in the absence of evidence to the contrary.

(d) Exceptions. There is no privilege under this rule:

(1) Furtherance of crime or fraud. If the services of the lawyer were sought or obtained to enable or aid anyone to commit or plan to commit what the client knew or reasonably should have known to be a crime or fraud; or

(2) Claimants through same deceased client. As to a communication relevant to an issue between parties who claim through the same deceased client, regardless of whether the claims are by testate or intestate succession or by inter vivos transaction; or

(3) Breach of duty by lawyer or client. As to a communication relevant to an issue of breach of duty by the lawyer to his client or by the client to his lawyer; or

(4) Document attested by lawyer. As to a communication relevant to an issue concerning an attested document to which the lawyer is an attesting witness; or

(5) Joint clients. As to a communication relevant to a matter of common interest between two or more clients if the communication was made by any of them to a lawyer retained or consulted in common, when offered in an action between any of the clients.

Uniform Rules of Evidence
(as amended, 1999)

Rule 502. Lawyer-Client Privilege.

(a) Definitions. In this rule:

(1) "Client" means a person for whom a lawyer renders professional legal services or who consults a lawyer with a view to obtaining professional legal services from the lawyer.

(2) A communication is "confidential" if it is not intended to be disclosed to third persons other than those to whom disclosure is made in furtherance of the rendition of professional legal services to the client or those reasonably necessary for the transmission of the communication.

(3) "Lawyer" means a person authorized, or reasonably believed by the client to be authorized, to engage in the practice of law in any State or country.

(4) "Representative of the client" means a person having authority to obtain professional legal services, or to act on legal advice rendered, on behalf of the client or a person who, for the purpose of effectuating legal representation for the client, makes or receives a confidential communication while acting in the scope of employment for the client.

(5) "Representative of the lawyer" means a person employed, or reasonably believed by the client to be employed, by the lawyer to assist the lawyer in rendering professional legal services.

(b) General rule of privilege. A client has a privilege to refuse to disclose and to prevent any other person from disclosing a confidential communication made for the purpose of facilitating the rendition of professional legal services to the client:

(1) between the client or a representative of the client and the client's lawyer or a representative of the lawyer;

(2) between the lawyer and a representative of the lawyer;

(3) by the client or a representative of the client or the client's lawyer or a representative of the lawyer to a lawyer or a representative of a lawyer representing another party in a pending action and concerning a matter of common interest therein;

(4) between representatives of the client or between the client and a representative of the client; or

(5) among lawyers and their representatives representing the same client.

(c) Who may claim privilege. The privilege under this rule may be claimed by the client, the client's guardian or conservator, the personal representative of a deceased client, or the successor, trustee, or similar representative of a corporation, association, or other organization, whether or not in existence. A person who was the lawyer or the lawyer's representative at the time of the communication is presumed to have authority to claim the privilege, but only on behalf of the client.

(d) Exceptions. There is no privilege under this rule:

(1) if the services of the lawyer were sought or obtained to enable or aid anyone to commit or plan to commit what the client knew or reasonably should have known was a crime or fraud;

(2) as to a communication relevant to an issue between parties who claim through the same deceased client, regardless of whether the claims are by testate or intestate succession or by transaction inter vivos;

(3) as to a communication relevant to an issue of breach of duty by a lawyer to the client or by a client to the lawyer;

(4) as to a communication necessary for a lawyer to defend in a legal proceeding an accusation that the lawyer assisted the client in criminal or fraudulent conduct;

(5) as to a communication relevant to an issue concerning an attested document to which the lawyer is an attesting witness;

(6) as to a communication relevant to a matter of common interest between or among two or more clients if the communication was made by any of them to a lawyer retained or consulted in common, when offered in an action between or among any of the clients; or

(7) as to a communication between a public officer or agency and its lawyers unless the communication concerns a pending investigation, claim, or action and the court determines that disclosure will seriously impair the ability of the public officer or agency to act upon the claim or conduct a pending investigation, litigation, or proceeding in the public interest.

Advisory Committee's Note

Subdivision (a). (1) The definition of "client" includes governmental bodies, Connecticut Mutual Life Ins. Co. v. Shields, 18 F.R.D. 448 (S.D.N.Y.1955); People ex rel. Department of Public Works v. Glen Arms Estate, Inc., 230 Cal.App.2d 841, 41 Cal.Rptr. 303 (1965); Rowley v. Ferguson, 48 N.E.2d 243 (Ohio App.1942); and corporations, Radiant Burners, Inc. v. American Gas Assn., 320 F.2d 314 (7th Cir.1963). Contra, Gardner, A Personal Privilege for Communications of Corporate Clients—Paradox or Public Policy, 40 U.Det.L.J. 299, 323, 376 (1963). The definition also extends the status of client to one consulting a lawyer preliminarily with a view to retaining him, even though actual employment does not result. McCormick, § 92, p. 184. The client need not be involved in litigation; the rendition of legal service or advice under any circumstances suffices. 8 Wigmore § 2294 (McNaughton Rev.1961). The services must be professional legal services; purely business or personal matters do not qualify. McCormick § 92, p. 184.

The rule contains no definition of "representative of the client." In the opinion of the Advisory Committee, the matter is better left to resolution by decision on a case-by-case basis. The most restricted position is the "control group" test, limiting the category to persons with authority to seek and act upon legal advice for the client. See, e.g., City of Philadelphia v. Westinghouse Electric Corp., 210 F.Supp. 483 (E.D.Pa.1962), mandamus and prohibition denied sub nom. General Electric Co. v. Kirkpatrick, 312 F.2d 742 (3d Cir.), cert. denied 372 U.S. 943; Garrison v. General Motors Corp., 213 F.Supp. 515 (S.D.Cal.1963); Hogan v. Zletz, 43 F.R.D. 308 (N.D.Okla.1967), aff'd sub nom. Natta v. Hogan, 392 F.2d 686 (10th Cir.1968); Day v. Illinois Power Co., 50 Ill.App.2d 52, 199 N.E.2d 802 (1964). Broader formulations are found in other decisions. See, e.g., United States v. United Shoe Machinery Corp., 89 F.Supp. 357 (D.Mass.1950); Zenith Radio Corp. v. Radio Corp. of America, 121 F.Supp. 792 (D.Del.1954); Harper & Row Publishers, Inc. v. Decker, 423 F.2d 487 (7th Cir.1970), aff'd without opinion by equally divided court 400 U.S. 955 (1971), reh. denied 401 U.S. 950; D.I. Chadbourne, Inc. v. Superior Court, 60 Cal.2d 723, 36 Cal.Rptr. 468, 388 P.2d 700 (1964). Cf. Rucker v. Wabash R. Co., 418 F.2d 146 (7th Cir.1969). See generally, Simon, The Attorney-Client Privilege as Applied to Corporations, 65 Yale L.J. 953, 956-966 (1956); Note, Attorney-Client Privilege for Corporate Clients: The Control Group Test, 84 Harv.L.Rev. 424 (1970).

The status of employees who are used in the process of communicating, as distinguished from those who are parties to the communication, is treated in paragraph (4) of subdivision (a) of the rule.

(2) A "lawyer" is a person licensed to practice law in any state or nation. There is no requirement that the licensing state or nation recognize the attorney-client privilege, thus avoiding excursions into conflict of laws questions. "Lawyer" also includes a person reasonably believed to be a lawyer. For similar provisions, see California Evidence Code § 950.

(3) The definition of "representative of the lawyer" recognizes that the lawyer may, in rendering legal services, utilize the services of assistants in addition to those employed in the process of communicating. Thus the definition includes an expert employed to assist in rendering legal advice. United States v. Kovel, 296 F.2d 918 (2d Cir.1961) (accountant). Cf. Himmelfarb v. United States, 175 F.2d 924 (9th Cir.1949). It also includes an expert employed to assist in the planning and conduct of litigation, though not one employed to testify as a witness. Lalance & Grosjean Mfg. Co. v. Haberman Mfg. Co., 87 F. 563 (S.D.N.Y.1898), and see revised Civil Rule 26(b)(4). The definition does not, however, limit "representative of the lawyer" to experts. Whether his compensation is derived immediately from the lawyer or the client is not material.

(4) The requisite confidentiality of communication is defined in terms of intent. A communication made in public or meant to be relayed to outsiders or which is divulged by the client to third persons can scarcely be considered confidential. McCormick § 95. The intent is inferable from the circumstances. Unless intent to disclose is apparent, the attorney-client communication is confidential. Taking or failing to take precautions may be considered as bearing on intent.

Practicality requires that some disclosure be allowed beyond the immediate circle of lawyer-client and their representatives without impairing confidentiality. Hence the definition allows disclosure to persons "to whom disclosure is in furtherance of the rendition of professional legal services to the client contemplating those in such relation to the client as spouse, parent, business associate, or joint client." Comment, California Evidence Code § 952.

Disclosure may also be made to persons "reasonably necessary for the transmission of the communication," without loss of confidentiality.

Subdivision (b) sets forth the privilege, using the previously defined terms: client, lawyer, representative of the lawyer, and confidential communication.

Substantial authority has in the past allowed the eavesdropper to testify to overheard privileged conversations and has admitted intercepted privileged letters. Today, the evolution of more sophisticated techniques of eavesdropping and interception calls for abandonment of this position. The rule accordingly adopts a policy of protection against these kinds of invasion of the privilege.

The privilege extends to communications (1) between client or his representative and lawyer or his representative, (2) between lawyer and lawyer's representative, (3) by client or his lawyer to a lawyer representing another in a matter of common interest, (4) between representatives of the client or the client and a representative of the client, and (5) between lawyers representing the client. All these communications must be specifically for the purpose of obtaining legal services for the client; otherwise the privilege does not attach.

The third type of communication occurs in the "joint defense" or "pooled information" situation, where different lawyers represent clients who have some interests in common. In Chahoon v. Commonwealth, 62 Va. 822 (1871), the court said that the various clients might have retained one attorney to represent all; hence everything said at a joint conference was privileged, and one of the clients could prevent another from disclosing what the other had himself said. The result seems to be incorrect in overlooking a frequent reason for retaining different attorneys by the various clients, namely actually or potentially conflicting interests in addition to the common interest which brings them together. The needs of these cases seem better to be met by allowing each client a privilege as to his own statements. Thus if all resist disclosure, none will occur. Continental Oil Co. v. United States, 330 F.2d 347 (9th Cir.1964). But, if for reasons of his own, a client wishes to disclose his own statements made at the joint conference, he should be permitted to do so, and the rule is to that effect. The rule does not apply to situations where there is no common interest to be promoted by a joint consultation, and the parties meet on a purely adversary basis. Vance v. State, 190 Tenn. 521, 230 S.W.2d 987 (1950), cert. denied 339 U.S. 988, 70 S.Ct. 1010, 94 L.Ed. 1389. Cf. Hunydee v. United States, 355 F.2d 183 (9th Cir.1965).

Subdivision (c). The privilege is, of course, that of the client, to be claimed by him or by his personal representative. The successor of a dissolved corporate client may claim the privilege. California Evidence Code § 953; New Jersey Evidence Rule 26(1). Contra, Uniform Rule 26(1).

The lawyer may not claim the privilege on his own behalf. However, he may claim it on behalf of the client. It is assumed that the ethics of the profession will require him to do so except under most unusual circumstances. American Bar Association, Canons of Professional Ethics, Canon 37. His authority to make the claim is presumed unless there is evidence to the contrary, as would be the case if the client were now a party to litigation in which the question arose and were represented by other counsel. Ex parte Lipscomb, 111 Tex. 409, 239 S.W. 1101 (1922).

Subdivision (d) in general incorporates well established exceptions.

(1) The privilege does not extend to advice in aid of future wrongdoing. 8 Wigmore § 2298 (McNaughton Rev.1961). The wrongdoing need not be that of the client. The provision that the client knew or reasonably should have known of the criminal or fraudulent nature of the act is designed to protect the client who is erroneously advised that a proposed action is within the law. No preliminary finding that sufficient evidence aside from the communication has been introduced to warrant a finding that the services were sought to enable the commission of a wrong is required. Cf. Clark v. United States, 289 U.S. 1, 15-16, 53 S.Ct. 465, 77 L.Ed. 993 (1933); Uniform Rule 26(2)(a). While any general exploration of what transpired between attorney and client would, of course, be inappropriate, it is wholly feasible, either at the discovery stage or during trial, so to focus the inquiry by specific questions as to avoid any broad inquiry into attorney-client communications. Numerous cases reflect this approach.

(2) Normally the privilege survives the death of the client and may be asserted by his representative. Subdivision (c), supra. When, however, the identity of the person who steps into the client's shoes is in issue, as in a will contest, the identity of the person entitled to

claim the privilege remains undetermined until the conclusion of the litigation. The choice is thus between allowing both sides or neither to assert the privilege, with authority and reason favoring the latter view. McCormick § 98; Uniform Rule 26(2)(b); California Evidence Code § 957; Kansas Code of Civil Procedure § 60-426(b)(2); New Jersey Evidence Rule 26(2)(b).

(3) The exception is required by considerations of fairness and policy when questions arise out of dealings between attorney and client, as in cases of controversy over attorney's fees, claims of inadequacy of representation, or charges of professional misconduct. McCormick § 95; Uniform Rule 26(2)(c); California Evidence Code § 958; Kansas Code of Civil Procedure § 60-426(b)(3); New Jersey Evidence Rule 26(2)(c).

(4) When the lawyer acts as attesting witness, the approval of the client to his so doing may safely be assumed, and waiver of the privilege as to any relevant lawyer-client communications is a proper result. McCormick § 92, p. 184; Uniform Rule 26(2)(d); California Evidence Code § 959; Kansas Code of Civil Procedure § 60-426(b)(d) [*sic*].

1971 Proposed Rule 504. Psychotherapist-Patient Privilege [*Not Enacted*]

(a) Definitions.

(1) A "patient" is a person who consults or is examined or interviewed by a psychotherapist.

(2) A "psychotherapist" is (A) a person authorized to practice medicine in any state or nation, or reasonably believed by the patient so to be, while engaged in the diagnosis or treatment of a mental or emotional condition, including drug addiction, or (B) a person licensed or certified as a psychologist under the laws of any state or nation, while similarly engaged.

(3) A communication is "confidential" if not intended to be disclosed to third persons other than those present to further the interest of the patient in the consultation, examination, or interview, or persons reasonably necessary for the transmission of the communication, or persons who are participating in the diagnosis and treatment under the direction of the psychotherapist, including members of the patient's family.

(b) General Rule of Privilege. A patient has a privilege to refuse to disclose and to prevent any other person from disclosing confidential communications, made for the purposes of diagnosis or treatment of his mental or emotional condition, including drug addiction, among himself, his psychotherapist, or persons who are participating in the diagnosis or treatment under the direction of the psychotherapist, including members of the patient's family.

(c) Who May Claim the Privilege. The privilege may be claimed by the patient, by his guardian or conservator, or by the personal representative of a deceased patient. The person who was the psychotherapist may claim the privilege but only on behalf of the patient. His authority so to do is presumed in the absence of evidence to the contrary.

(d) Exceptions.

(1) Proceedings for Hospitalization. There is no privilege under this rule for communications relevant to an issue in proceedings to hospitalize the patient for mental illness, if the psychotherapist in the course of diagnosis or treatment has determined that the patient is in need of hospitalization.

(2) Examination by Order of Judge. If the judge orders an examination of the mental or emotional condition of the patient, communications made in the course thereof are not privileged under this rule with respect to the particular purpose for which the examination is ordered unless the judge orders otherwise.

(3) Condition an Element of Claim or Defense. There is no privilege under this rule as to communications relevant to an issue of the mental or emotional condition of the patient in any proceeding in which he relies upon the condition as an element of his claim or defense, or, after the patient's death, in any proceeding in which any party relies upon the condition as an element of his claim or defense.

Uniform Rules of Evidence
(as amended, 1999)

Rule 503. [Psychotherapist] [Physician and Psychotherapist] [Physician and Mental-Health Provider] [Mental-Health Provider]-Patient Privilege. (a) Definitions. In this rule:

(1) A communication is "confidential" if it is not intended to be disclosed to third persons, except those present to further the interest of the patient in the consultation, examination, or interview, those reasonably necessary for the transmission of the communication, and persons who are participating in the diagnosis and treatment of the patient under the direction of a [psychotherapist] [physician or psychotherapist] [physician or mental-health provider] [mental-health provider], including members of the patient's family.

[(2) "Mental-health provider" means a person authorized, in any State or country, or reasonably believed by the patient to be authorized, to engage in the diagnosis or treatment of a mental or emotional condition, including addiction to alcohol or drugs.]

[(3) "Patient" means an individual who consults or is examined or interviewed by a [psychotherapist] [physician or psychotherapist] [physician or mental-health provider] [mental-health provider].]

[(4) "Physician" means a person authorized in any State or country, or reasonably believed by the patient to be authorized to practice medicine.]

[(5) "Psychotherapist" means a person authorized in any State or country, or reasonably believed by the patient to be authorized, to practice medicine, while engaged in the diagnosis or treatment of a mental or emotional condition, including addiction to alcohol or drugs, or a person licensed or certified under the laws of any State or country, or reasonably believed by the patient to be licensed or certified, as a psychologist, while similarly engaged.]

(b) General rule of privilege. A patient has a privilege to refuse to disclose and to prevent any other person from disclosing confidential communications made for the purpose of diagnosis or treatment of the patient's [physical,] mental[,] or emotional condition, including addiction to alcohol or drugs, among the patient, the patient's [psychotherapist] [physician or psychotherapist] [physician or mental-health provider] [mental-health provider] and persons, including members of the patient's family, who are participating in the diagnosis or treatment under the direction of the [psychotherapist] [physician or psychotherapist] [physician or mental-health provider] [mental-health provider].

(c) Who may claim the privilege. The privilege under this rule may be claimed by the patient, the patient's guardian or conservator, or the personal representative of a deceased patient. The person who was the [psychotherapist] [physician or psychotherapist] [physician or mental-health provider] [mental-health provider] at the time of the communication is presumed to have authority to claim the privilege, but only on behalf of the patient.

(d) Exceptions. There is no privilege under this rule for a communication:

(1) relevant to an issue in proceedings to hospitalize the patient for mental illness, if the [psychotherapist] [physician or psychotherapist] [physician or mental-health provider] [mental-health provider], in the course of diagnosis or treatment, has determined that the patient is in need of hospitalization;

(2) made in the course of a court-ordered investigation or examination of the [physical,] mental[,] or emotional condition of the patient, whether a party or a witness, with respect to the particular purpose for which the examination is ordered, unless the court orders otherwise;

(3) relevant to an issue of the [physical,] mental[,] or emotional condition of the patient in any proceeding in which the patient relies upon the condition as an element of the patient's claim or defense or, after the patient's death, in any proceeding in which any party relies upon the condition as an element of the party's claim or defense;

(4) if the services of the [psychotherapist] [physician or psychotherapist] [physician or mental-health provider] [mental-health provider] were sought or obtained to enable or aid anyone to commit or plan to commit what the patient knew, or reasonably should have known, was a crime or fraud or mental or physical injury to the patient or another individual;

(5) in which the patient has expressed an intent to engage in conduct likely to result in imminent death or serious bodily injury to the patient or another individual;

(6) relevant to an issue in a proceeding challenging the competency of the [psychotherapist] [physician or psychotherapist] [physician or mental-health provider] [mental-health provider];

(7) relevant to a breach of duty by the [psychotherapist] [physician or psychotherapist] [physician or mental-health provider] [mental-health provider]; or

(8) that is subject to a duty to disclose under [statutory law].

Advisory Committee's Note

The rules contain no provision for a general physician-patient privilege. While many states have by statute created the privilege, the exceptions which have been found necessary in order to obtain information required by the public interest or to avoid fraud are so numerous as to leave little if any basis for the privilege. Among the exclusions from the statutory privilege, the following may be enumerated; communications not made for purposes of diagnosis and treatment; commitment and restoration proceedings; issues as to wills or otherwise between parties claiming by succession from the patient; actions on insurance policies; required reports (venereal diseases, gunshot wounds, child abuse); communications in furtherance of crime or fraud; mental or physical condition put in issue by patient (personal injury cases); malpractice actions; and some or all criminal prosecutions. California, for example, excepts cases in which the patient puts his condition in issue, all criminal proceedings, will and similar contests, malpractice cases, and disciplinary proceedings, as well as certain other situations, thus leaving virtually nothing covered by the privilege. California Evidence Code §§ 990-1007. For other illustrative statutes see Ill.Rev.Stat.1967, c. 51, § 5.1; N.Y.C.P.L.R. § 4504; N.C.Gen.Stat.1953, § 8-53. Moreover, the possibility of compelling gratuitous disclosure by the physician is foreclosed by his standing to raise the question of relevancy. See Note on "Official Information" Privilege following [Proposed] Rule 509, infra.

The doubts attendant upon the general physician-patient privilege are not present when the relationship is that of psychotherapist and patient. While the common law recognized no general physician-patient privilege, it had indicated a disposition to recognize a psychotherapist-patient privilege, Note, Confidential Communications to a Psychotherapist: A New Testimonial Privilege, 47 Nw.U.L.Rev. 384 (1952), when legislatures began moving into the field.

The case for the privilege is convincingly stated in Report No. 45, Group for the Advancement of Psychiatry 92 (1960):

"Among physicians, the psychiatrist has a special need to maintain confidentiality. His capacity to help his patients is completely dependent upon their willingness and ability to talk freely. This makes it difficult if not impossible for him to function without being able to assure his patients of confidentiality and, indeed, privileged communication. Where there may be exceptions to this general rule . . . , there is wide agreement that confidentiality is a sine qua non for successful psychiatric treatment. The relationship may well be likened to that of the priest-penitent or the lawyer-client. Psychiatrists not only explore the very depths of their patients' conscious, but their unconscious feelings and attitudes as well. Therapeutic effectiveness necessitates going beyond a patient's awareness and, in order to do this, it must be possible to communicate freely. A threat to secrecy blocks successful treatment."

A much more extended exposition of the case for the privilege is made in Slovenko, Psychiatry and a Second Look at the Medical Privilege, 6 Wayne L.Rev. 175, 184 (1960), quoted extensively in the careful Tentative Recommendation and Study Relating to the

Uniform Rules of Evidence (Article V. Privileges), Cal.Law Rev.Comm'n, 417 (1964). The conclusion is reached that Wigmore's four conditions needed to justify the existence of a privilege are amply satisfied.

Illustrative statutes are Cal.Evidence Code §§ 1010-1026; Ga.Code § 38-418 (1961 Supp.); Conn.Gen.Stat., § 52-146a (1966 Supp.); Ill.Rev.Stat.1967, c. 51, § 5.2.

While many of the statutes simply place the communications on the same basis as those between attorney and client, 8 Wigmore § 2286, n. 23 (McNaughton Rev.1961), basic differences between the two relationships forbid resorting to attorney-client save as a helpful point of departure. Goldstein and Katz, Psychiatrist-Patient Privilege: The GAP Proposal and the Connecticut Statute, 36 Conn.B.J. 175, 182 (1962).

Subdivision (a). (1) The definition of patient does not include a person submitting to examination for scientific purposes. Cf. Cal.Evidence Code § 1101 [*sic*, 1011]. Attention is directed to 42 U.S.C. 242(a)(2), as amended by the Drug Abuse and Control Act of 1970, P.L. 91-513, authorizing the Secretary of Health, Education, and Welfare to withhold the identity of persons who are the subjects of research on the use and effect of drugs. The rule would leave this provision in full force. See [Proposed] Rule 501.

(2) The definition of psychotherapist embraces a medical doctor while engaged in the diagnosis or treatment of mental or emotional conditions, including drug addiction, in order not to exclude the general practitioner and to avoid the making of needless refined distinctions concerning what is and what is not the practice of psychiatry. The requirement that the psychologist be in fact licensed, and not merely be believed to be so, is believed to be justified by the number of persons, other than psychiatrists, purporting to render psychotherapeutic aid and the variety of their theories. Cal.Law Rev.Comm'n, supra, at pp. 434-437.

The clarification of mental or emotional condition as including drug addiction is consistent with current approaches to drug abuse problems. See, e.g., the definition of "drug dependent person" in 42 U.S.C. 201(q), added by the Drug Abuse Prevention and Control Act of 1970, P.L. 91-513.

(3) Confidential communication is defined in terms conformable with those of the lawyer-client privilege, [Proposed] Rule 503(a)(4), supra, with changes appropriate to the difference in circumstance.

Subdivisions (b) and (c). The lawyer-client rule is drawn upon for the phrasing of the general rule of privilege and the determination of those who may claim it. See [Proposed] Rule 503(b) and (c).

The specific inclusion of communications made for the diagnosis and treatment of drug addiction recognizes the continuing contemporary concern with rehabilitation of drug dependent persons and is designed to implement that policy by encouraging persons in need thereof to seek assistance. The provision is in harmony with Congressional actions in this area. See 42 U.S.C. § 260, providing for voluntary hospitalization of addicts or persons with drug dependence problems and prohibiting use of evidence of admission or treatment in any proceeding against him, and 42 U.S.C. § 3419 providing that in voluntary or involuntary commitment of addicts the results of any hearing, examination, test, or procedure used to determine addiction shall not be used against the patient in any criminal proceeding.

Subdivision (d). The exceptions differ substantially from those of the attorney-client privilege, as a result of the basic differences in the relationships. While it has been argued convincingly that the nature of the psychotherapist-patient relationship demands complete security against legally coerced disclosure in all circumstances, Louisell, The Psychologist in Today's Legal World: Part II, 41 Minn.L.Rev. 731, 746 (1957), the committee of psychiatrists and lawyers who drafted the Connecticut statute concluded that in three instances the need for disclosure was sufficiently great to justify the risk of possible impairment of the relationship. Goldstein and Katz, Psychiatrist-Patient Privilege: The GAP Proposal and the Connecticut Statute, 36 Conn.B.J. 175 (1962). These three exceptions are incorporated in the present rule.

(1) The interests of both patient and public call for a departure from confidentiality in commitment proceedings. Since disclosure is authorized only when the psychotherapist determines that hospitalization is needed, control over disclosure is placed largely in the hands of a person in whom the patient has already manifested confidence. Hence damage to the relationship is unlikely.

(2) In a court ordered examination, the relationship is likely to be an arm's length one, though not necessarily so. In any event, an exception is necessary for the effective utilization of this important and growing procedure. The exception, it will be observed, deals with a court ordered examination rather than with a court appointed psychotherapist. Also, the exception is effective only with respect to the particular purpose for which the examination is ordered. The rule thus conforms with the provisions of 18 U.S.C. § 4244 that no statement made by the accused in the course of an examination into competency to stand trial is admissible on the issue of guilt and of 42 U.S.C. § 3420 that a physician conducting an examination in a drug addiction commitment proceeding is a competent and compellable witness.

(3) By injecting his condition into litigation, the patient must be said to waive the privilege, in fairness and to avoid abuses. Similar considerations prevail after the patient's death.

1971 Proposed Rule 505. Husband-Wife Privilege [*Not Enacted*]

(a) General rule of privilege. An accused in a criminal proceeding has a privilege to prevent his spouse from testifying against him.

(b) Who may claim the privilege. The privilege may be claimed by the accused or by the spouse on his behalf. The authority of the spouse to do so is presumed in the absence of evidence to the contrary.

(c) Exceptions. There is no privilege under this rule (1) in proceedings in which one spouse is charged with a crime against the person or property of the other or of a child of either, or with a crime against the person or property of a third person committed in the course of committing a crime against the other, or (2) as to matters occurring prior to the marriage, or (3) in proceedings in which a spouse is charged with importing an alien for prostitution or other immoral purpose in violation of 8 U.S.C. § 1328, with transporting a female in interstate commerce for immoral purposes or other offense in violation of 18 U.S.C. §§ 2421-2424, or with violation of other similar statutes.

Uniform Rules of Evidence
(as amended, 1999)

Rule 504. Spousal Privilege. (a) Confidential communication. A communication is confidential if it is made privately by an individual to the individual's spouse and is not intended for disclosure to any other person.

(b) Marital communications. An individual has a privilege to refuse to testify and to prevent the individual's spouse or former spouse from testifying as to any confidential communication made by the individual to the spouse during their marriage. The privilege may be waived only by the individual holding the privilege or by the holder's guardian or conservator, or the individual's personal representative if the individual is deceased.

(c) Spousal testimony in criminal proceeding. The spouse of an accused in a criminal proceeding has a privilege to refuse to testify against the accused spouse.

(d) Exceptions. There is no privilege under this rule:

(1) in any civil proceeding in which the spouses are adverse parties;

(2) in any criminal proceeding in which an unrefuted showing is made that the spouses acted jointly in the commission of the crime charged;

(3) in any proceeding in which one spouse is charged with a crime or tort against the person or property of the other, a minor child of either, an individual residing in the household of either, or a third person if the crime or tort is committed in the course of committing a crime or tort against the other spouse, a minor child of either spouse, or an individual residing in the household of either spouse; or

(4) in any other proceeding, in the discretion of the court, if the interests of a minor child of either spouse may be adversely affected by invocation of the privilege.

Advisory Committee's Note

Subdivision (a). Rules of evidence have evolved around the marriage relationship in four respects: (1) incompetency of one spouse to testify for the other; (2) privilege of one spouse not to testify against the other; (3) privilege of one spouse not to have the other testify against him; and (4) privilege against disclosure of confidential communications between spouses, sometimes extended to information learned by virtue of the existence of the relationship. Today these matters are largely governed by statutes.

With the disappearance of the disqualification of parties and interested persons, the basis for spousal incompetency no longer existed, and it, too, virtually disappeared in both civil and criminal actions. Usually reached by statute, this result was reached for federal courts by the process of decision. Funk v. United States, 290 U.S. 371, 54 S.Ct. 212, 78 L.Ed. 369 (1933). These rules contain no recognition of incompetency of one spouse to testify for the other.

While some 10 jurisdictions recognize a privilege not to testify against one's spouse in a criminal case, and a much smaller number do so in civil cases, the great majority recognizes no privilege on the part of the testifying spouse, and this is the position taken by the rule. Compare Wyatt v. United States, 362 U.S. 525, 80 S.Ct. 901, 4 L.Ed.2d 931 (1960), a Mann Act prosecution in which the wife was the victim. The majority opinion held that she could not claim privilege and was compellable to testify. The holding was narrowly based: The Mann Act presupposed that the women with whom it dealt had no independent wills of their own, and this legislative judgment precluded allowing a victim-wife an option whether to testify, lest the policy of the statute be defeated. A vigorous dissent took the view that nothing in the Mann Act required departure from usual doctrine, which was conceived to be one of allowing the injured party to claim or waive privilege.

About 30 jurisdictions recognize a privilege of an accused in a criminal case to prevent his or her spouse from testifying. It is believed to represent the one aspect of marital privilege the continuation of which is warranted. In Hawkins v. United States, 358 U.S. 74, 79 S.Ct. 136, 3 L.Ed.2d 125 (1958) it was sustained. Cf. McCormick § 66; 8 Wigmore § 2228 (McNaughton Rev.1961): Comment, Uniform Rule 23(2).

The rule recognizes no privilege for confidential communications. The traditional justifications for privileges not to testify against a spouse and not to be testified against by one's spouse have been the prevention of marital dissension and the repugnancy of requiring a person to condemn or be condemned by his spouse. 8 Wigmore §§ 2228, 2241 (McNaughton Rev.1961). These considerations bear no relevancy to marital communications. Nor can it be assumed that marital conduct will be affected by a privilege for confidential communications of whose existence the parties in all likelihood are unaware. The other communication privileges, by way of contrast, have as one party a professional person who can be expected to inform the other of the existence of the privilege. Moreover, the relationships from which those privileges arise are essentially and almost exclusively verbal in nature, quite unlike marriage. See Hutchins and Slesinger, Some Observations on the Law of Evidence: Family Relations, 13 Minn.L.Rev. 675 (1929). Cf. McCormick § 90; 8 Wigmore § 2337 (McNaughton Rev.1961). The parties are not spouses if the marriage was a sham, Lutwak v. United States, 344 U.S. 604 (1953), or they have been divorced, Barsky v. United States, 339 F.2d 180 (9th Cir.1964), and therefore the privilege is not applicable.

Subdivision (b). This provision is a counterpart of Rules 503(c), 504(c), and 506(c). Its purpose is to provide a procedure for preventing the taking of the spouse's testimony notably in grand jury proceedings, when the accused is absent and does not know that a situation appropriate for a claim of privilege is presented. If the privilege is not claimed by the spouse, the protection of [Proposed] Rule 512 is available.

Subdivision (c) contains three exceptions to the privilege against spousal testimony in criminal cases.

(1) The need of limitation upon the privilege in order to avoid grave injustice in cases of offenses against the other spouse or a child of either can scarcely be denied. 8 Wigmore § 2239 (McNaughton Rev.1961). The rule therefore disallows any privilege against spousal

testimony in these cases and in this respect is in accord with the result reached in Wyatt v. United States, 362 U.S. 525, 80 S.Ct. 901, 4 L.Ed.2d 931 (1960), a Mann Act prosecution, denying the accused the privilege of excluding his wife's testimony, since she was the woman who was transported for immoral purposes.

(2) The second exception renders the privilege inapplicable as to matters occurring prior to the marriage. This provision eliminates the possibility of suppressing testimony by marrying the witness.

(3) The third exception continues and expands established Congressional policy. In prosecutions for importing aliens for immoral purposes, Congress has specifically denied the accused any privilege not to have his spouse testify against him. 8 U.S.C. § 1328. No provision of this nature is included in the Mann Act, and in Hawkins v. United States, 358 U.S. 74, 79 S.Ct. 136, 3 L.Ed.2d 125 (1958), the conclusion was reached that the common law privilege continued. Consistency requires similar results in the two situations. The rule adopts the Congressional approach, as based upon a more realistic appraisal of the marriage relationship in cases of this kind, in preference to the specific result in Hawkins. Note the common law treatment of pimping and sexual offenses with third persons as exceptions to marital privilege. 8 Wigmore § 2239 (McNaughton Rev.1961).

With respect to bankruptcy proceedings, the smallness of the area of spousal privilege under the rule and the general inapplicability of privileges created by state law render unnecessary any special provision for examination of the spouse of the bankrupt, such as that now contained in section 21(a) of the Bankruptcy Act. 11 U.S.C. § 44(a).

For recent statutes and rules dealing with husband-wife privileges, see California Evidence Code §§ 970-973, 980-987; Kansas Code of Civil Procedure §§ 60-423(b), 60-428; New Jersey Evidence Rules 23(2), 28.

1971 Proposed Rule 506. Communications to Clergymen [*Not Enacted*]

(a) Definitions. As used in this rule:

(1) A "clergyman" is a minister, priest, rabbi, or other similar functionary of a religious organization, or an individual reasonably believed so to be by the person consulting him.

(2) A communication is "confidential" if made privately and not intended for further disclosure except to other persons present in furtherance of the purpose of the communication.

(b) General rule of privilege. A person has a privilege to refuse to disclose and to prevent another from disclosing a confidential communication by the person to a clergyman in his professional character as spiritual adviser.

(c) Who may claim the privilege. The privilege may be claimed by the person, by his guardian or conservator, or by his personal representative if he is deceased. The clergyman may claim the privilege on behalf of the person. His authority so to do is presumed in the absence of evidence to the contrary.

Uniform Rules of Evidence
(as amended, 1999)

Rule 505. Religious Privilege. (a) Definitions. In this rule:

(1) "Cleric" means a minister, priest, rabbi, accredited Christian Science Practitioner, or other similar functionary of a religious organization, or an individual reasonably believed so to be by the individual consulting the cleric.

(2) A communication is "confidential" if it is made privately and not intended for further disclosure except to other persons present in furtherance of the purpose of the communication.

(b) General rule of privilege. An individual has a privilege to refuse to disclose and to prevent another from disclosing a confidential communication by the individual to a cleric in the cleric's professional capacity as spiritual adviser.

(c) Who may claim the privilege. The privilege under this rule may be claimed by an individual or the individual's guardian or conservator, or the individual's personal representative if the individual is deceased. The individual who was the cleric at the time of the communication is presumed to have authority to claim the privilege but only on behalf of the communicant.

Advisory Committee's Note

The considerations which dictate the recognition of privileges generally seem strongly to favor a privilege for confidential communications to clergymen. During the period when most of the common law privileges were taking shape, no clear-cut privilege for communications between priest and penitent emerged. 8 Wigmore § 2394 (McNaughton Rev.1961). The English political climate of the time may well furnish the explanation. In this country, however, the privilege has been recognized by statute in about two-thirds of the states and occasionally by the common law process of decision. Id. § 2395; Mullen v. United States, 105 U.S.App.D.C. 25, 263 F.2d 275 (1959).

Subdivision (a). Paragraph (1) defines a clergyman as a "minister, priest, rabbi, or other similar functionary of a religious organization." The concept is necessarily broader than that inherent in the ministerial exemption for purposes of Selective Service. See United States v. Jackson, 369 F.2d 936 (4th Cir.1966). However, it is not so broad as to include all self-denominated "ministers." A fair construction of the language requires that the person to whom the status is sought to be attached be regularly engaged in activities conforming at least in a general way with those of a Catholic priest, Jewish rabbi, or minister of an established Protestant denomination, though not necessarily on a full-time basis. No further specification seems possible in view of the lack of licensing and certification procedures for clergymen. However, this lack seems to have occasioned no particular difficulties in connection with the solemnization of marriages, which suggests that none may be anticipated here. For similar definitions of "clergyman" see California Evidence Code § 1030; New Jersey Evidence Rule 29.

The "reasonable belief" provision finds support in similar provisions for lawyer-client in [Proposed] Rule 503 and for psychotherapist-patient in [Proposed] Rule 504. A parallel is also found in the recognition of the validity of marriages performed by unauthorized persons if the parties reasonably believed them legally qualified. Harper and Skolnick, Problems of the Family 153 (Rev.Ed.1962).

(2) The definition of "confidential" communication is consistent with the use of the term in [Proposed] Rule 503(a)(5) for lawyer-client and in [Proposed] Rule 504(a)(3) for psychotherapist-patient, suitably adapted to communications to clergymen.

Subdivision (b). The choice between a privilege narrowly restricted to doctrinally required confessions and a privilege broadly applicable to all confidential communications with a clergyman in his professional character as spiritual adviser has been exercised in favor of the latter. Many clergymen now receive training in marriage counseling and the handling of personality problems. Matters of this kind fall readily into the realm of the spirit. The same considerations which underlie the psychotherapist-patient privilege of [Proposed] Rule 504 suggest a broad application of the privilege for communications to clergymen.

State statutes and rules fall in both the narrow and the broad categories. A typical narrow statute proscribes disclosure of "a confession . . . made . . . in the course of discipline enjoined by the church to which he belongs." Ariz.Rev.Stats.Ann.1956, § 12-2233. See also California Evidence Code § 1032; Uniform Rule 29. Illustrative of the broader privilege are statutes applying to "information communicated to him in a confidential manner, properly entrusted to him in his professional capacity, and necessary to enable him to discharge the functions of his office according to the usual course of his practice or discipline, wherein such person so communicating . . . is seeking spiritual counsel and advice," Fla.Stats.Ann.1960, § 90.241, or to any "confidential communication properly entrusted to him in his professional capacity, and necessary and proper to enable him to discharge the functions of his office according to the usual course of practice or discipline," Iowa Code Ann.1950, § 622.10. See also Ill.Rev.Stats.1967, c. 51, § 48.1; Minn.Stats.Ann.1945, § 595.02(3); New Jersey Evidence Rule 29.

Under the privilege as phrased, the communicating person is entitled to prevent disclosure not only by himself but also by the clergyman and by eavesdroppers. For discussion see Advisory Committee Note under lawyer-client privilege, [Proposed] Rule 503(b).

The nature of what may reasonably be considered spiritual advice makes it unnecessary to include in the rule a specific exception for communications in furtherance of crime or fraud, as in [Proposed] Rule 503(d)(1).

Subdivision (c) makes clear that the privilege belongs to the communicating person. However, a prima facie authority on the part of the clergyman to claim the privilege on behalf of the person is recognized. The discipline of the particular church and the discreetness of the clergyman are believed to constitute sufficient safeguards for the absent communicating person. See Advisory Committee Note to the similar provision with respect to attorney-client in [Proposed] Rule 503(c).

1971 Proposed Rule 507. Political Vote [*Not Enacted*]

Every person has a privilege to refuse to disclose the tenor of his vote at a political election conducted by secret ballot unless the vote was cast illegally.

Uniform Rules of Evidence (as amended, 1999)

Rule 506. Political Vote. (a) General rule of privilege. An individual has a privilege to refuse to disclose the tenor of the individual's vote at a political election conducted by secret ballot.

(b) Exceptions. The privilege under subdivision (a) does not apply if the court finds that the vote was cast illegally or determines that disclosure should be compelled pursuant to [the election laws of the State].

Advisory Committee's Note

Secrecy in voting is an essential aspect of effective democratic government, insuring free exercise of the franchise and fairness in elections. Secrecy after the ballot has been cast is as essential as secrecy in the act of voting. Nutting, Freedom of Silence: Constitutional Protection Against Governmental Intrusion in Political Affairs, 47 Mich.L.Rev. 181, 191 (1948). Consequently a privilege has long been recognized on the part of a voter to decline to disclose how he voted. Required disclosure would be the exercise of "a kind of inquisitorial power unknown to the principles of our government and constitution, and might be highly injurious to the suffrages of a free people, as well as tending to create cabals and disturbances between contending parties in popular elections." Johnston v. Charleston, 1 Bay 441, 442 (S.C.1795).

The exception for illegally cast votes is a common one under both statutes and case law, Nutting, supra, at p. 192; 8 Wigmore § 2214, p. 163 (McNaughton Rev.1961). The policy considerations which underlie the privilege are not applicable to the illegal voter. However, nothing in the exception purports to foreclose an illegal voter from invoking the privilege against self-incrimination under appropriate circumstances.

For similar provisions, see Uniform Rule 31; California Evidence Code § 1050; Kansas Code of Civil Procedure § 60-431; New Jersey Evidence Rule 31.

1971 Proposed Rule 508. Trade Secrets [*Not Enacted*]

A person has a privilege, which may be claimed by him or his agent or employee, to refuse to disclose and to prevent other persons from disclosing a trade secret owned by him, if the allowance of the privilege will not tend to conceal fraud or otherwise work injustice. When disclosure is directed, the judge shall take such protective measure as the interests of the holder of the privilege and of the parties and the furtherance of justice may require.

Uniform Rules of Evidence
(as amended, 1999)

Rule 507 is the same as Proposed Federal Rule 508 except that "person" and "person's" are substituted for "him" and "his."

Advisory Committee's Note

While sometimes said not to be a true privilege, a qualified right to protection against disclosure of trade secrets has found ample recognition, and, indeed, a denial of it would be difficult to defend. 8 Wigmore § 2212(3) (McNaughton Rev.1961). And see 4 Moore's Federal Practice ¶¶30.12 and 34.15 (2nd ed. 1963 and Supp.1965) and 2A Barron and Holtzoff, Federal Practice and Procedure § 715.1 (Wright ed. 1961). Congressional policy is reflected in the Securities Exchange Act of 1934, 15 U.S.C. § 78x, and the Public Utility Holding Company Act of 1933, id. § 79v, which deny the Securities and Exchange Commission authority to require disclosure of trade secrets or processes in applications and reports. See also Rule 26(c)(7) of the Rules of Civil Procedure, as revised, mentioned further hereinafter.

Illustrative cases raising trade-secret problems are: E.I. Du Pont de Nemours Powder Co. v. Masland, 244 U.S. 100, 37 S.Ct. 575, 61 L.Ed. 1016 (1917), suit to enjoin former employee from using plaintiff's secret processes, countered by defense that many of the processes were well known to the trade; Segal Lock & Hardware Co. v. FTC, 143 F.2d 935 (2d Cir.1944), question whether expert locksmiths employed by FTC should be required to disclose methods used by them in picking petitioner's "pick-proof" locks; Dobson v. Graham, 49 F. 17 (E.D.Pa.1889), patent infringement suit in which plaintiff sought to elicit from former employees now in the hire of defendant the respects in which defendant's machinery differed from plaintiff's patented machinery; Putney v. Du Bois Co., 240 Mo.App. 1075, 226 S.W.2d 737 (1950), action for injuries allegedly sustained from using defendant's secret formula dishwashing compound. See 8 Wigmore § 2212(3) (McNaughton Rev.1961); Annot., 17 A.L.R.2d 383; 49 Mich.L.Rev. 133 (1950). The need for accommodation between protecting trade secrets, on the one hand, and eliciting facts required for full and fair presentation of a case, on the other hand, is apparent. Whether disclosure should be required depends upon a weighing of the competing interests involved against the background of the total situation, including consideration of such factors as the dangers of abuse, good faith, adequacy of protective measures, and the availability of other means of proof.

The cases furnish examples of the bringing of judicial ingenuity to bear upon the problem of evolving protective measures which achieve a degree of control over disclosure. Perhaps the most common is simply to take testimony in camera. Annot., 62 A.L.R.2d 509. Other possibilities include making disclosure to opposing counsel but not to his client, E.I. Du Pont de Nemours Powder Co. v. Masland, 244 U.S. 100, 37 S.Ct. 575, 61 L.Ed. 1016 (1917); making disclosure only to the judge (hearing examiner), Segal Lock & Hardware Co. v. FTC, 143 F.2d 935 (2d Cir.1944); and placing those present under oath not to make disclosure, Paul v. Sinnott, 217 F.Supp. 84 (W.D.Pa.1963).

Rule 26(c) of the Rules of Civil Procedure, as revised, provides that the judge may make "any order which justice requires to protect a party or person from annoyance, embarrassment, oppression, or undue burden or expense, including one or more of the following: . . . (7) that a trade secret or other confidential research, development, or commercial information not be disclosed or be disclosed only in a designated way . . . ." While the instant evidence rule extends this underlying policy into the trial, the difference in circumstances between discovery stage and trial may well be such as to require a different ruling at the trial.

For other rules recognizing privilege for trade secrets, see Uniform Rule 32; California Evidence Code § 1060; Kansas Code of Civil Procedure § 60-432; New Jersey Evidence Rule 32.

1971 Proposed Rule 509. Secrets of State and Other Official Information [*Not Enacted*]

(a) Definitions.

(1) Secret of state. A "secret of state" is a governmental secret relating to the national defense or the international relations of the United States.

(2) Official information. "Official information" is information within the custody or control of a department or agency of the government the disclosure of which is shown to be contrary to the public interest and which consists of: (A) intragovernmental opinions or recommendations submitted for consideration in the performance of decisional or policymaking functions, or (B) subject to the provisions of 18 U.S.C. § 3500, investigatory files compiled for lawenforcement purposes and not otherwise available, or (C) information within the custody or control of a governmental department or agency whether initiated within the department or agency or acquired by it in its exercise of its official responsibilities and not otherwise available to the public pursuant to 5 U.S.C. § 552.

(b) General rule of privilege. The government has a privilege to refuse to give evidence and to prevent any person from giving evidence upon a showing of reasonable likelihood of danger that the evidence will disclose a secret of state or official information, as defined in this rule.

(c) Procedures. The privilege for secrets of state may be claimed only by the chief officer of the government agency or department administering the subject matter which the secret information sought concerns, but the privilege for official information may be asserted by any attorney representing the government. The required showing may be made in whole or in part in the form of a written statement. The judge may hear the matter in chambers, but all counsel are entitled to inspect the claim and showing and to be heard thereon, except that, in the case of secrets of state, the judge upon motion of the government, may permit the government to make the required showing in the above form in camera. If the judge sustains the privilege upon a showing in camera, the entire text of the government's statements shall be sealed and preserved in the court's records in the event of appeal. In the case of privilege claimed for official information the court may require examination in camera of the information itself. The judge may take any protective measure which the interests of the government and the furtherance of justice may require.

(d) Notice to government. If the circumstances of the case indicate a substantial possibility that a claim of privilege would be appropriate but has not been made because of oversight or lack of knowledge, the judge shall give or cause notice to be given to the officer entitled to claim the privilege and shall stay further proceedings a reasonable time to afford opportunity to assert a claim of privilege.

(e) Effect of sustaining claim. If a claim of privilege is sustained in a proceeding to which the government is a party and it appears that another party is thereby deprived of material evidence, the judge shall make any further orders which the interests of justice require, including striking the testimony of a witness, declaring a mistrial, finding against the government upon an issue as to which the evidence is relevant, or dismissing the action.

Uniform Rules of Evidence
(as amended, 1999)

Rule 508. Secrets of State and Other Official Information; Governmental Privileges. (a) Claim of privilege under law of United States. If the law of the United States creates a governmental privilege that the courts of this State must recognize under the Constitution of the United States, the privilege may be claimed as provided by the law of the United States.

(b) Privileges created by laws of State. No governmental privilege is recognized except as provided in subdivision (a) or created by the constitution, statutes, or rules of this State.

(c) Effect of sustaining claim. If a claim of governmental privilege is sustained and it appears that a party is thereby deprived of material evidence, the court shall make any further orders the interests of justice require, including striking the testimony of a witness, declaring a mistrial, finding upon an issue as to which the evidence is relevant, or dismissing the action.

Advisory Committee's Note

Subdivision (a). (1) The rule embodies the privilege protecting military and state secrets described as "well established in the law of evidence," United States v. Reynolds, 345 U.S. 1, 6, 73 S.Ct. 528, 97 L.Ed. 727 (1953), and as one "the existence of which has never been doubted," 8 Wigmore § 2378, p. 794 (McNaughton Rev.1961).

The use of the term "national defense," without attempt at further elucidation, finds support in the similar usage in statutory provisions relating to the crimes of gathering, transmitting, or losing defense information, and gathering or delivering defense information to aid a foreign government. 18 U.S.C. §§ 793, 794. See also 5 U.S.C. § 1002; 50 U.S.C.App. § 2152(d). In determining whether military or state secrets are involved, due regard will, of course, be given to classification pursuant to executive order.

(2) The rule also recognizes a privilege for specified types of official information and in this respect is designed primarily to resolve questions of the availability to litigants of data in the files of governmental departments and agencies. In view of the lesser danger to the public interest than in cases of military and state secrets, the official information privilege is subject to a generally overriding requirement that disclosure would be contrary to the public interest. It is applicable to three categories of information.

(A) Intergovernmental opinions or recommendations submitted for consideration in the performance of decisional or policy making functions. The policy basis of this aspect of the privilege is found in the desirability of encouraging candor in the exchange of views within the government. Kaiser Aluminum & Chemical Corp. v. United States, 141 Ct.Cl. 38, 157 F.Supp. 939 (1958); Davis v. Braswell Motor Freight Lines, Inc., 363 F.2d 600 (5th Cir.1966); Ackerly v. Ley, 420 F.2d 1336 (D.C.Cir.1969). A privilege of this character is consistent with the Freedom of Information Act, 5 U.S.C. § 552(b)(5), and with the standing of the agency to raise questions of relevancy, though not a party, recognized in such decisions as Boeing Airplane Co. v. Coggeshall, 108 U.S.App.D.C. 106, 280 F.2d 654, 659 (1960) (Renegotiation Board) and Freeman v. Seligson, 132 U.S.App.D.C. 56, 405 F.2d 1326, 1334 (1968) (Secretary of Agriculture).

(B) Investigatory files compiled for law enforcement purposes. This category is expressly made subject to the provisions of the Jencks Act, 18 U.S.C. § 3500, which insulates prior statements or reports of government witnesses in criminal cases against subpoena, discovery, or inspection until the witness has testified on direct examination at the trial but then entitles the defense to its production. Rarely will documents of this nature be relevant until the author has testified and thus placed his credibility in issue. Further protection against discovery of government files in criminal cases is found in Criminal Procedure Rule 16(a) and (b). The breadth of discovery in civil cases, however, goes beyond ordinary bounds of relevancy and raises problems calling for the exercise of judicial control, and in making provision for it the rule implements the Freedom of Information Act, 18 U.S.C. § 552(b)(7).

(C) Information exempted from disclosure under the Freedom of Information Act, 5 U.S.C. § 552. In 1958 the old "housekeeping" statute which had been relied upon as a foundation for departmental regulations curtailing disclosure was amended by adding a provision that it did not authorize withholding information from the public. In 1966 the Congress enacted the Freedom of Information Act for the purpose of making information in the files of departments and agencies, subject to certain specified exceptions, available to the mass media and to the public generally. 5 U.S.C. § 552. These enactments are significant expressions of Congressional policy. The exceptions in the Act are not framed in terms of evidentiary privilege, thus recognizing by clear implication that the needs of litigants may stand on somewhat different footing from those of the public generally. Nevertheless, the exceptions are based on values obviously entitled to weighty consideration in formulating rules of evidentiary privilege. In some instances in these rules, exceptions in the Act have been made the subject of specific privileges, e.g., military and state secrets in the present rule and trade secrets in [Proposed] Rule 508. The purpose of the present provision is to incorporate the remaining exceptions of the Act into the qualified privilege here created, thus subjecting disclosure of the information to judicial determination with respect to the effect of disclosure on the public interest. This approach appears to afford a satisfactory resolution of the problems which may arise.

Subdivision (b). The rule vests the privileges in the government where they properly belong rather than a party or witness. See United States v. Reynolds, supra, p. 7, 73 S.Ct. 528. The showing required as a condition precedent to claiming the privilege represents a compromise between complete judicial control and accepting as final the decision of a departmental officer. See Machin v. Zuckert, 114 U.S.App.D.C. 335, 316 F.2d 336 (1963), rejecting in part a claim of privilege by the Secretary of the Air Force and ordering the furnishing of information for use in private litigation. This approach is consistent with Reynolds.

Subdivision (c). In requiring the claim of privilege for state secrets to be made by the chief departmental officer, the rule again follows Reynolds, insuring consideration by a high-level officer. This provision is justified by the lesser participation by the judge in cases of state secrets. The full participation by the judge in official information cases, on the contrary, warrants allowing the claim of privilege to be made by a government attorney.

Subdivision (d) spells out and emphasizes a power and responsibility on the part of the trial judge. An analogous provision is found in the requirement that the court certify to the Attorney General when the constitutionality of an act of Congress is in question in an action to which the government is not a party. 28 U.S.C. § 2403.

Subdivision (e). If privilege is successfully claimed by the government in litigation to which it is not a party, the effect is simply to make the evidence unavailable, as though a witness had died or claimed the privilege against self-incrimination, and no specification of the consequences is necessary. The rule therefore deals only with the effect of a successful claim of privilege by the government in proceedings to which it is a party. Reference to other types of cases serves to illustrate the variety of situations which may arise and the impossibility of evolving a single formula to be applied automatically to all of them. The privileged materials may be the statement of government witness, [*sic*] as under the Jencks statute, which provides that, if the government elects not to produce the statement, the judge is to strike the testimony of the witness, or that he may declare a mistrial if the interests of justice so require. 18 U.S.C. § 3500(d). Or the privileged materials may disclose a possible basis for applying pressure upon witnesses. United States v. Beekman, 155 F.2d 580 (2d Cir.1946). Or they may bear directly upon a substantive element of a criminal case, requiring dismissal in the event of a successful claim of privilege. United States v. Andolschek, 142 F.2d 503 (2d Cir.1944); and see United States v. Reynolds, 345 U.S. 1, 73 S.Ct. 528, 97 L.Ed. 727 (1953). Or they may relate to an element of a plaintiff's claim against the government, with the decisions indicating unwillingness to allow the government's claim of privilege for secrets of state to be used as an offensive weapon against it. United States v. Reynolds, supra; Republic of China v. National Union Fire Ins. Co., 142 F.Supp. 551 (D.Md.1956).

1971 Proposed Rule 510. Identity of Informer [*Not Enacted*]

(a) Rule of privilege. The government or a state or subdivision thereof has a privilege to refuse to disclose the identity of a person who has furnished information relating to or assisting in an investigation of a possible violation of law to a law enforcement officer or member of a legislative committee or its staff conducting an investigation.

(b) Who may claim. The privilege may be claimed by an appropriate representative of the government, regardless of whether the information was furnished to an officer of the government or of a state or subdivision thereof. The privilege may be claimed by an appropriate representative of a state or subdivision if the information was furnished to an officer thereof, except that in criminal cases the privilege shall not be allowed if the government objects.

(c) Exceptions.

(1) Voluntary disclosure; informer a witness. No privilege exists under this rule if the identity of the informer or his interest in the subject matter of his communication has been disclosed to those who would have cause to resent the communication by a holder of the privilege or by the informer's own action, or if the informer appears as a witness for the government.

(2) Testimony on merits. If it appears from the evidence in the case or from other showing by a party that an informer may be able to give testimony necessary to a fair determination of the issue of guilt or innocence in a criminal case or of a material issue on the merits in a civil case to which the government is a party, and the government invokes the privilege, the judge shall give the government an opportunity to show in camera facts relevant to determining whether the informer can, in fact, supply that testimony. The showing will ordinarily be in the form of affidavits, but the judge may direct that testimony be taken if he finds that the matter cannot be resolved satisfactorily upon affidavit. If the judge finds that there is a reasonable probability that the informer can give the testimony, and the government elects not to disclose his identity, the judge on motion of the defendant in a criminal case shall dismiss the charges to which the testimony would relate, and the judge may do so on his own motion. In civil cases, he may make any order that justice requires. Evidence submitted to the judge shall be sealed and preserved to be made available to the appellate court in the event of an appeal, and the contents shall not otherwise be revealed without consent of the government. All counsel and parties shall be permitted to be present at every stage of proceedings under this subdivision except a showing in camera, at which no counsel or party shall be permitted to be present.

(3) Legality of obtaining evidence. If information from an informer is relied upon to establish the legality of the means by which evidence was obtained and the judge is not satisfied that the information was received from an informer reasonably believed to be reliable or credible, he may require the identity of the informer to be disclosed. The judge shall, on request of the government, direct that the disclosure be made in camera. All counsel and parties concerned with the issue of legality shall be permitted to be present at every stage of proceedings under this subdivision except a disclosure in camera, at which no counsel or party shall be permitted to be present. If disclosure of the identity of the informer is made in camera, the record thereof shall be sealed and preserved to be made available to the appellate court in the event of an appeal, and the contents shall not otherwise be revealed without consent of the government.

Uniform Rules of Evidence
(as amended, 1999)

Rule 509. Identity of Informer. (a) Rule of privilege. The United States or a State has a privilege to refuse to disclose the identity of an individual who has furnished information relating to or assisted in an investigation of a possible violation of a law to a law enforcement officer or member of a legislative committee or its staff conducting an investigation.

(b) Who may claim. The privilege under this rule may be claimed by an appropriate representative of the government to which the information was furnished.

(c) Exceptions. There is no privilege under this rule if the identity of the informer or the informer's interest in the subject matter of the informer's communication has been disclosed by a holder of the privilege or by the informer's own action to persons who would have cause to resent the communication or if the informer appears as a witness for the government.

(d) Procedures. If it appears that an informer may be able to give testimony relevant to an issue in a criminal case, or to a fair determination of a material issue on the merits in a civil case to which the government is a party, and the informed government invokes the privilege, the court shall give the government an opportunity to show in chambers facts relevant to whether the informer can, in fact, supply the testimony. The showing ordinarily will be by affidavit, but the court may direct that testimony be taken if it finds that the matter cannot be resolved satisfactorily upon affidavit. If the court finds there is a reasonable probability that the informer can give the testimony, and the government elects not to disclose the informer's identity, in criminal cases the court on motion of the defendant or on its own motion shall grant appropriate relief, which may include one or more of the following: requiring the prosecuting attorney to comply, granting the defendant additional time or a continuance, relieving the defendant from making disclosures otherwise required of the defendant, prohibiting the prosecuting attorney from introducing specified evidence, and dismissing charges. In civil cases, the court may issue any order the interests of justice require. Evidence submitted to the court must be sealed and preserved to be made available to the appellate court in the event of an appeal, and the contents may not otherwise be revealed without consent of the informed government. All counsel and parties may be present at every stage of a proceeding under this subdivision except a showing in chambers, if the court has determined that no counsel or party may be present.

Advisory Committee's Note

The rule recognizes the use of informers as an important aspect of law enforcement, whether the informer is a citizen who steps forward with information or a paid undercover agent. In either event, the basic importance of anonymity in the effective use of informers is apparent, Bocchicchio v. Curtis Publishing Co., 203 F.Supp. 403 (E.D.Pa.1962), and the privilege of withholding their identity was well established at common law. Roviaro v. United States, 353 U.S. 53, 59, 77 S.Ct. 623, 1 L.Ed.2d 639 (1957); McCormick § 148; 8 Wigmore § 2374 (McNaughton Rev.1961).

Subdivision (a). The public interest in law enforcement requires that the privilege be that of the government, state, or political subdivision, rather than that of the witness. The rule blankets in as an informer anyone who tells a law enforcement officer about a violation of law without regard to whether the officer is one charged with enforcing the particular law. The rule also applies to disclosures to legislative investigating committees and their staffs, and is sufficiently broad to include continuing investigations.

Although the tradition of protecting the identity of informers has evolved in an essentially criminal setting, noncriminal law enforcement situations involving possibilities of reprisal against informers fall within the purview of the considerations out of which the privilege originated. In Mitchell v. Roma, 265 F.2d 633 (3d Cir.1959), the privilege was given effect with respect to persons informing as to violations of the Fair Labor Standards Act, and in Wirtz v. Continental Finance & Loan Co., 326 F.2d 561 (5th Cir.1964), a similar case, the privilege was recognized, although the basis of decision was lack of relevancy to the issues in the case.

Only identity is privileged; communications are not included except to the extent that disclosure would operate also to disclose the informer's identity. The common law was to the same effect. 8 Wigmore § 2374, at p. 765 (McNaughton Rev.1961). See also Roviaro v.

United States, supra, 353 U.S. at p. 60, 77 S.Ct. 623; Bowman Dairy Co. v. United States, 341 U.S. 214, 221, 71 S.Ct. 675, 95 L.Ed. 879 (1951).

The rule does not deal with the question whether presentence reports made under Criminal Procedure Rule 32(c) should be made available to an accused.

Subdivision (b). Normally the "appropriate representative" to make the claim will be counsel. However, it is possible that disclosure of the informer's identity will be sought in proceedings to which the government, state, or subdivision, as the case may be, is not a party. Under these circumstances effective implementation of the privilege requires that other representatives be considered "appropriate." See, for example, Bocchicchio v. Curtis Publishing Co., 203 F.Supp. 403 (E.D.Pa.1962), a civil action for libel, in which a local police officer not represented by counsel successfully claimed the informer privilege.

The privilege may be claimed by a state or subdivision of a state if the information was given to its officer, except that in criminal cases it may not be allowed if the government objects.

Subdivision (c) deals with situations in which the informer privilege either does not apply or is curtailed.

(1) If the identity of the informer is disclosed, nothing further is to be gained from efforts to suppress it. Disclosure may be direct, or the same practical effect may result from action revealing the informer's interest in the subject matter. See, for example, Westinghouse Electric Corp. v. City of Burlington, 122 U.S.App.D.C. 65, 351 F.2d 762 (1965), on remand City of Burlington v. Westinghouse Electric Corp., 246 F.Supp. 839 (D.D.C.1965), which held that the filing of civil antitrust actions destroyed as to plaintiffs the informer privilege claimed by the Attorney General with respect to complaints of criminal antitrust violations. While allowing the privilege in effect to be waived by one not its holder, i.e. the informer himself, is something of a novelty in the law of privilege, if the informer chooses to reveal his identity, further efforts to suppress it are scarcely feasible.

The exception is limited to disclosure to "those who would have cause to resent the communication," in the language of Roviaro v. United States, 353 U.S. 53, 60, 77 S.Ct. 623, 1 L.Ed.2d 639 (1957), since disclosure otherwise, e.g. to another law enforcing agency, is not calculated to undercut the objects of the privilege.

If the informer becomes a witness for the government, the interests of justice in disclosing his status as a source of bias or possible support are believed to outweigh any remnant of interest in nondisclosure which then remains. See Harris v. United States, 371 F.2d 365 (9th Cir.1967), in which the trial judge permitted detailed inquiry into the relationship between the witness and the government. Cf. Attorney General v. Briant, 15 M. & W. 169, 153 Eng.Rep. 808 (Exch.1846). The purpose of the limitation to witnesses for the government is to avoid the possibility of calling persons as witnesses as a means of discovery whether they are informers.

(2) The informer privilege, it was held by the leading case, may not be used in a criminal prosecution to suppress the identity of a witness when the public interest in protecting the flow of information is outweighed by the individual's right to prepare his defense. Roviaro v. United States, supra. The rule extends this balancing to include civil as well as criminal cases and phrases it in terms of "a reasonable probability that the informer may be able to give testimony necessary to a fair determination of the issue of guilt or innocence in a criminal case or of a material issue on the merits in a civil case." Once the privilege is invoked a procedure is provided for determining whether the informer can in fact supply testimony of such nature as to require disclosure of his identity, thus avoiding a "judicial guessing game" on the question. United States v. Day, 384 F.2d 464, 470 (3d Cir.1967). An investigation in camera is calculated to accommodate the conflicting interests involved. The rule also spells out specifically the consequences of a successful claim of the privilege in a criminal case; the wider range of possibilities in civil cases demands more flexibility in treatment. See Advisory Committee Note to [Proposed] Rule 509(e), supra.

(3) One of the acute conflicts between the interest of the public in nondisclosure and the avoidance of unfairness to the accused as a result of nondisclosure arises when information from an informer is relied upon to legitimate a search and seizure by furnishing probable cause for an arrest without a warrant or for the issuance of a warrant for arrest or search. McCray v. Illinois, 386 U.S. 300, 87 S.Ct. 1056, 18 L.Ed.2d 62 (1967), rehearing denied 386 U.S. 1042. A hearing in camera provides an accommodation of these conflicting interests. United States v. Jackson, 384 F.2d 825 (3d Cir.1967). The limited disclosure to the judge avoids any significant impairment of secrecy, while affording the accused a substantial measure of protection against arbitrary police action. The procedure is consistent with McCray and the decisions there discussed.

1971 Proposed Rule 511. Waiver of Privilege by Voluntary Disclosure [*Not Enacted*]

A person upon whom these rules confer a privilege against disclosure of the confidential matter or communication waives the privilege if he or his predecessor while holder of the privilege voluntarily discloses or consents to disclosure of any significant part of the matter or communication. This rule does not apply if the disclosure is itself a privileged communication.

Uniform Rules of Evidence
(as amended, 1999)

Rule 510. Waiver of Privilege. (a) Voluntary disclosure. A person upon whom these rules confer a privilege against disclosure waives the privilege if the person or the person's predecessor, while holder of the privilege, voluntarily discloses or consents to disclosure of any significant part of the privileged matter. This rule does not apply if the disclosure itself is privileged.

(b) Involuntary disclosure. A claim of privilege is not waived by a disclosure that was compelled erroneously or made without an opportunity to claim the privilege.

Advisory Committee's Note

The central purpose of most privileges is the promotion of some interest or relationship by endowing it with a supporting secrecy or confidentiality. It is evident that the privilege should terminate when the holder by his own act destroys this confidentiality. McCormick §§ 87, 97, 106; 8 Wigmore §§ 2242, 2327-2329, 2374, 2389-2390 (McNaughton Rev.1961).

The rule is designed to be read with a view to what it is that the particular privilege protects. For example, the lawyer-client privilege covers only communications, and the fact that a client has discussed a matter with his lawyer does not insulate the client against disclosure of the subject matter discussed, although he is privileged not to disclose the discussion itself. See McCormick § 93. The waiver here provided for is similarly restricted. Therefore a client, merely by disclosing a subject which he had discussed with his attorney, would not waive the applicable privilege; he would have to make disclosure of the communication itself in order to effect a waiver.

By traditional doctrine, waiver is the intentional relinquishment of a known right. Johnson v. Zerbst, 304 U.S. 458, 464, 58 S.Ct. 1019, 82 L.Ed. 1461 (1938). However, in the confidential privilege situations, once confidentiality is destroyed through voluntary disclosure, no subsequent claim of privilege can restore it, and knowledge or lack of knowledge of the existence of the privilege appears to be irrelevant. California Evidence Code § 912; 8 Wigmore § 2327 (McNaughton Rev.1961).

1971 Proposed Rule 512. Privileged Matter Disclosed Under Compulsion or Without Opportunity to Claim Privilege [*Not Enacted*]

Evidence of a statement or other disclosure of privileged matter is not admissible against the holder of the privilege if the disclosure was (a) compelled erroneously or (b) made without opportunity to claim the privilege.

Uniform Rules of Evidence (as amended, 1999)

Compelled disclosures are covered by Rule 510(b), *supra*, following Proposed Federal Rule 511.

Advisory Committee's Note

Ordinarily a privilege is invoked in order to forestall disclosure. However, under some circumstances consideration must be given to the status and effect of a disclosure already made. [Proposed] Rule 511, immediately preceding, gives voluntary disclosure the effect of a waiver, while the present rule covers the effect of disclosure made under compulsion or without opportunity to claim the privilege.

Confidentiality, once destroyed, is not susceptible of restoration, yet some measure of repair may be accomplished by preventing use of the evidence against the holder of the privilege. The remedy of exclusion is therefore made available when the earlier disclosure was compelled erroneously or without opportunity to claim the privilege.

With respect to erroneously compelled disclosure, the argument may be made that the holder should be required in the first instance to assert the privilege, stand his ground, refuse to answer, perhaps incur a judgment of contempt, and exhaust all legal recourse, in order to sustain his privilege. See Fraser v. United States, 145 F.2d 139 (6th Cir.1944), cert. denied 324 U.S. 849, 65 S.Ct. 684, 89 L.Ed. 1409; United States v. Johnson, 76 F.Supp. 538 (M.D.Pa.1947), aff'd 165 F.2d 42 (3d Cir.1947), cert. denied 332 U.S. 852, 68 S.Ct. 355, 92 L.Ed. 422, reh. denied 333 U.S. 834, 68 S.Ct. 457, 92 L.Ed. 1118. However, this exacts of the holder greater fortitude in the face of authority than ordinary individuals are likely to possess, and assumes unrealistically that a judicial remedy is always available. In self-incrimination cases, the writers agree that erroneously compelled disclosures are inadmissible in subsequent criminal prosecution of the holder, Maguire, Evidence of Guilt 66 (1959); McCormick § 127; 8 Wigmore § 2270 (McNaughton Rev.1961), and the principle is equally sound when applied to other privileges. The modest departure from usual principles of res judicata which occurs when the compulsion is judicial is justified by the advantage of having one simple rule, assuring at least one opportunity for judicial supervision in every case.

The second circumstance stated as a basis for exclusion is disclosure made without opportunity to the holder to assert his privilege. Illustrative possibilities are disclosure by an eavesdropper, by the person used in the transmission of a privileged communication, by a family member participating in psychotherapy, or privileged data improperly made available from a computer bank.

1971 Proposed Rule 513. Comment Upon or Inference from Claim of Privilege: Instruction [*Not Enacted*]

(a) Comment or inference not permitted. The claim of a privilege, whether in the present proceeding or upon a prior occasion, is not a proper subject of comment by judge or counsel. No inference may be drawn therefrom.

(b) Claiming privilege without knowledge of jury. In jury cases, proceedings shall be conducted, to the extent practicable, so as to facilitate the making of claims of privilege without the knowledge of the jury.

(c) Jury instruction. Upon request, any party against whom the jury might draw an adverse inference from a claim of privilege is entitled to an instruction that no inference may be drawn therefrom.

Uniform Rules of Evidence (as amended, 1999)

Uniform Rule 511 is substantially the same as 1971 Proposed Federal Rule 513.

Advisory Committee's Note

Subdivision (a). In Griffin v. California, 380 U.S. 609, 614, 85 S.Ct. 1229, 14 L.Ed.2d 106 (1965), the Court pointed out that allowing comment upon the claim of a privilege "cuts down on the privilege by making its assertion costly." Consequently it was held that comment upon the election of the accused not to take the stand infringed upon his privilege against self-incrimination so substantially as to constitute a constitutional violation. While the privileges governed by these rules are not constitutionally based, they are nevertheless founded upon important policies and are entitled to maximum effect. Hence the present subdivision forbids comment upon the exercise of a privilege, in accord with the weight of authority. Courtney v. United States, 390 F.2d 521 (9th Cir.1968); 8

Wigmore §§ 2243, 2322, 2386; Barnhart, Privilege in the Uniform Rules of Evidence, 24 Ohio St.L.J. 131, 137-138 (1963). Cf. McCormick § 80.

Subdivision (b). The value of a privilege may be greatly depreciated by means other than expressly commenting to a jury upon the fact that it was exercised. Thus, the calling of a witness in the presence of the jury and subsequently excusing him after a sidebar conference may effectively convey to the jury the fact that a privilege has been claimed, even though the actual claim has not been made in their hearing. Whether a privilege will be claimed is usually ascertainable in advance and the handling of the entire matter outside the presence of the jury is feasible. Destruction of the privilege by innuendo can and should be avoided. Tallo v. United States, 344 F.2d 467 (1st Cir.1965); Courtney v. United States, 390 F.2d 521 (9th Cir.1968); 6 Wigmore § 1808, pp. 275-276; 6 U.C.L.A.Rev. 455 (1959). This position is in accord cannot be forced to make his election not to testify in the presence of the jury. 8 Wigmore § 2268, p. 407 (McNaughton Rev.1961).

Unanticipated situations are, of course, bound to arise, and much must be left to the discretion of the judge and the professional responsibility of counsel.

Subdivision (c). Opinions will differ as to the effectiveness of a jury instruction not to draw an adverse inference from the making of a claim of privilege. See Bruton v. United States, 389 U.S. 818, 88 S.Ct. 126, 19 L.Ed.2d 70 (1968). Whether an instruction shall be given is left to the sound judgment of counsel for the party against whom the adverse inference may be drawn. The instruction is a matter of right, if requested. This is the result reached in Bruno v. United States, 308 U.S. 287, 60 S.Ct. 198, 84 L.Ed. 257 (1939), holding that an accused is entitled to an instruction under the statute (now 18 U.S.C. § 3481) providing that his failure to testify creates no presumption against him.

The right to the instruction is not impaired by the fact that the claim of privilege is by a witness, rather than by a party, provided an adverse inference against the party may result.

Restyled 2011

ARTICLE VI. WITNESSES

Rule 601. Competency to Testify in General

Every person is competent to be a witness unless these rules provide otherwise. But in a civil case, state law governs the witness's competency regarding a claim or defense for which state law supplies the rule of decision.

Superseded 2011

ARTICLE VI. WITNESSES

Rule 601. General Rule of Competency

Every person is competent to be a witness except as otherwise provided in these rules. However, in civil actions and proceedings, with respect to an element of a claim or defense as to which State law supplies the rule of decision, the competency of a witness shall be determined in accordance with State law.

Advisory Committee's Note

This general ground-clearing eliminates all grounds of incompetency not specifically recognized in the succeeding rules of this Article. Included among the grounds thus abolished are religious belief, conviction of crime, and connection with the litigation as a party or interested person or spouse of a party or interested person. With the exception of the so-called Dead Man's Acts, American jurisdictions generally have ceased to recognize these grounds.

The Dead Man's Acts are surviving traces of the common law disqualification of parties and interested persons. They exist in variety too great to convey conviction of their wisdom and effectiveness. These rules contain no provision of this kind. For the reasoning underlying the decision not to give effect to state statutes in diversity cases, see the Advisory Committee's Note to Rule 501.

No mental or moral qualifications for testifying as a witness are specified. Standards of mental capacity have proved elusive in actual application. A leading commentator observes that few witnesses are disqualified on that ground. Weihofen, Testimonial Competence and Credibility, 34 Geo.Wash.L.Rev. 53 (1965). Discretion is regularly exercised in favor of allowing the testimony. A witness wholly without capacity is difficult to imagine. The question is one particularly suited to the jury as one of weight and credibility, subject to judicial authority to review the sufficiency of the evidence. 2 Wigmore §§ 501, 509. Standards of moral qualification in practice consist essentially of evaluating a person's truthfulness in terms of his own answers about it. Their principal utility is in affording an opportunity on voir dire examination to impress upon the witness his moral duty. This result may, however, be accomplished more directly, and without haggling in terms of legal standards, by the manner of administering the oath or affirmation under Rule 603.

Admissibility of religious belief as a ground of impeachment is treated in Rule 610. Conviction of crime as a ground of impeachment is the subject of Rule 609. Marital relationship is the basis for privilege under Rule 505. Interest in the outcome of litigation and mental capacity are, of course, highly relevant to credibility and require no special treatment to render them admissible along with other matters bearing upon the perception, memory, and narration of witnesses.

House Judiciary Committee Report

Rule 601 as submitted to the Congress provided that "Every person is competent to be a witness except as otherwise provided in these rules." One effect of the Rule as proposed would have been to abolish age, mental capacity, and other grounds recognized in some State jurisdictions as making a person incompetent as a witness. The greatest controversy centered around the Rule's rendering inapplicable in the federal courts the so-called Dead Man's Statutes which exist in some States. Acknowledging that there is substantial disagreement as to the merit of Dead Man's Statutes, the Committee nevertheless believed that where such statutes have been enacted they represent State policy which should not be overturned in the absence of a compelling federal interest. The Committee therefore amended the Rule to make competency in civil actions determinable in accordance with State law with respect to elements of claims or defenses as to which State law supplies the rule of decision. Cf. Courtland v. Walston & Co., Inc., 340 F.Supp. 1076, 1087-1092 (S.D.N.Y.1972).

Senate Judiciary Committee Report

The amendment to rule 601 parallels the treatment accorded Rule 501 discussed immediately above.

Conference Committee Report

Rule 601 deals with competency of witnesses. Both the House and Senate bills provide that federal competency law applies in criminal cases. In civil actions and proceedings, the House bill provides that state competency law applies "to an element of a claim or defense as to which State law supplies the rule of decision." The Senate bill provides that "in civil actions and proceedings arising under 28 U.S.C.
§ 1332 or 28 U.S.C. § 1335, or between citizens of different States and removed under 28 U.S.C. § 1441(b) the competency of a witness, person, government, State or political subdivision thereof is determined in accordance with State law, unless with respect to the particular claim or defense, Federal law supplies the rule of decision."

The wording of the House and Senate bills differs in the treatment of civil actions and proceedings. The rule in the House bill applies to evidence that relates to "an element of a claim or defense." If an item of proof tends to support or defeat a claim or defense, or an element of a claim or defense, and if state law supplies the rule of decision for that claim or defense, then state competency law applies to that item of proof.

For reasons similar to those underlying its action on Rule 501, the Conference adopts the House provision.

Restyled 2011

Rule 602. Need for Personal Knowledge

A witness may testify to a matter only if evidence is introduced sufficient to support a finding that the witness has personal knowledge of the matter. Evidence to prove personal knowledge may consist of the witness's own testimony. This rule does not apply to a witness's expert testimony under Rule 703.

Superseded 2011

Rule 602. Lack of Personal Knowledge

A witness may not testify to a matter unless evidence is introduced sufficient to support a finding that the witness has personal knowledge of the matter. Evidence to prove personal knowledge may, but need not, consist of the witness' own testimony. This rule is subject to the provisions of rule 703, relating to opinion testimony by expert witnesses.

Advisory Committee's Note

". . . [T]he rule requiring that a witness who testifies to a fact which can be perceived by the senses must have had an opportunity to observe, and must have actually observed the fact" is a "most pervasive manifestation" of the common law insistence upon "the most reliable sources of information." McCormick § 10, p. 19. These foundation requirements may, of course, be furnished by the testimony of the witness himself; hence personal knowledge is not an absolute but may consist of what the witness thinks he knows from personal perception. 2 Wigmore § 650. It will be observed that the rule is in fact a specialized application of the provisions of Rule 104(b) on conditional relevancy.

This rule does not govern the situation of a witness who testifies to a hearsay statement as such, if he has personal knowledge of the making of the statement. Rules 801 and 805 would be applicable. This rule would, however, prevent him from testifying to the subject matter of the hearsay statement, as he has no personal knowledge of it.

The reference to Rule 703 is designed to avoid any question of conflict between the present rule and the provisions of that rule allowing an expert to express opinions based on facts of which he does not have personal knowledge.

Restyled 2011

Rule 603. Oath or Affirmation to Testify Truthfully

Before testifying, a witness must give an oath or affirmation to testify truthfully. It must be in a form designed to impress that duty on the witness's conscience.

Superseded 2011

Rule 603. Oath or Affirmation

Before testifying, every witness shall be required to declare that the witness will testify truthfully, by oath or affirmation administered in a form calculated to awaken the witness' conscience and impress the witness' mind with the duty to do so.

Advisory Committee's Note

The rule is designed to afford the flexibility required in dealing with religious adults, atheists, conscientious objectors, mental defectives, and children. Affirmation is simply a solemn undertaking to tell the truth; no special verbal formula is required. As is true generally, affirmation is recognized by federal law. "Oath" includes affirmation, 1 U.S.C. § 1; judges and clerks may administer oaths and affirmations, 28 U.S.C. §§ 459, 953; and affirmations are acceptable in lieu of oaths under Rule 43(d) of the Federal Rules of Civil Procedure. Perjury by a witness is a crime, 18 U.S.C. § 1621.

Restyled 2011

Rule 604. Interpreter

An interpreter must be qualified and must give an oath or affirmation to make a true translation.

Superseded 2011

Rule 604. Interpreters

An interpreter is subject to the provisions of these rules relating to qualification as an expert and the administration of an oath or affirmation to make a true translation.

Advisory Committee's Note

The rule implements Rule 43(f) of the Federal Rules of Civil Procedure and Rule 28(b) of the Federal Rules of Criminal Procedure, both of which contain provisions for the appointment and compensation of interpreters.

Restyled 2011

Rule 605. Judge's Competency as a Witness

The presiding judge may not testify as a witness at the trial. A party need not object to preserve the issue.

Superseded 2011

Rule 605. Competency of Judge as Witness

The judge presiding at the trial may not testify in that trial as a witness. No objection need be made in order to preserve the point.

Advisory Committee's Note

In view of the mandate of 28 U.S.C. § 455 that a judge disqualify himself in "any case in which he . . . is or has been a material witness," the likelihood that the presiding judge in a federal court might be called to testify in the trial over which he is presiding is slight. Nevertheless the possibility is not totally eliminated.

The solution here presented is a broad rule of incompetency, rather than such alternatives as incompetency only as to material matters, leaving the matter to the discretion of the judge, or recognizing no incompetency. The choice is the result of inability to evolve satisfactory answers to questions which arise when the judge abandons the bench for the witness stand. Who rules on objections? Who compels him to answer? Can he rule impartially on the weight and admissibility of his own testimony? Can he be impeached or cross-examined effectively? Can he, in a jury trial, avoid conferring his seal of approval on one side in the eyes of the jury? Can he, in a bench trial, avoid an involvement destructive of impartiality? The rule of general incompetency has substantial support. See Report of the Special Committee on the Propriety of Judges Appearing as Witnesses, 36 A.B.A.J. 630 (1950); cases collected in Annot. 157 A.L.R. 311; McCormick § 68, p. 147; Uniform Rule 42; California Evidence Code § 703; Kansas Code of Civil Procedure § 60-442; New Jersey Evidence Rule 42. Cf. 6 Wigmore § 1909, which advocates leaving the matter to the discretion of the judge, and statutes to that effect collected in Annot. 157 A.L.R. 311.

The rule provides an "automatic" objection. To require an actual objection would confront the opponent with a choice between not objecting, with the result of allowing the testimony, and objecting, with the probable result of excluding the testimony but at the price of continuing the trial before a judge likely to feel that his integrity had been attacked by the objector.

Restyled 2011

Rule 606. Juror's Competency as a Witness

(a) At the Trial. A juror may not testify as a witness before the other jurors at the trial. If a juror is called to testify, the court must give an adverse party an opportunity to object outside the jury's presence.

Superseded 2011

Rule 606. Competency of Juror as Witness

(a) At the trial. A member of the jury may not testify as a witness before that jury in the trial of the case in which the juror is sitting. If the juror is called so to testify, the opposing party shall be afforded an opportunity to object out of the presence of the jury.

Advisory Committee's Note

Subdivision (a). The considerations which bear upon the permissibility of testimony by a juror in the trial in which he is sitting as juror bear an obvious similarity to those evoked when the judge is called as a witness. See Advisory Committee Note to Rule 605. The judge is not, however in this instance so involved as to call for departure from usual principles requiring objection to be made; hence the only provision on objection is that opportunity be afforded for its making out of the presence of the jury. Compare Rule 605.

Restyled 2011

(b) During an Inquiry into the Validity of a Verdict or Indictment.

(1) ***Prohibited Testimony or Other Evidence.*** During an inquiry into the validity of a verdict or indictment, a juror may not testify about any statement made or incident that occurred during the jury's deliberations; the effect of anything on that juror's or another juror's vote; or any juror's mental processes concerning the verdict or indictment. The court may not receive a juror's affidavit or evidence of a juror's statement on these matters.

(2) ***Exceptions.*** A juror may testify about whether:

(A) extraneous prejudicial information was improperly brought to the jury's attention;

(B) an outside influence was improperly brought to bear on any juror; or

(C) a mistake was made in entering the verdict on the verdict form.

Superseded 2011

(b) Inquiry into validity of verdict or indictment. Upon an inquiry into the validity of a verdict or indictment, a juror may not testify as to any matter or statement occurring during the course of the jury's deliberations or to the effect of anything upon that or any other juror's mind or emotions as influencing the juror to assent to or dissent from the verdict or indictment or concerning the juror's mental processes in connection therewith. But a juror may testify about (1) whether extraneous prejudicial information was improperly brought to the jury's attention, (2) whether any outside influence was improperly brought to bear upon any juror, or (3) whether there was a mistake in entering the verdict onto the verdict form. A juror's affidavit or evidence of any statement by the juror may not be received on a matter about which the juror would be precluded from testifying. [*Amended 2006.*]

Case Note

On a motion for a new trial alleging juror misconduct, Rule 606(b) prohibits juror testimony about alcohol and drug use by jurors during the trial. Substance use is not an "outside influence" about which jurors may testify. Tanner v. United States, 483 U.S. 107, 107 S.Ct. 2739, 97 L.Ed. 2d 90 (1987) (5-to-4).

Advisory Committee's Note

Subdivision (b). Whether testimony, affidavits, or statements of jurors should be received for the purpose of invalidating or supporting a verdict or indictment, and if so, under what circumstances, has given rise to substantial differences of opinion. The familiar rubric that a juror may not impeach his own verdict, dating from Lord Mansfield's time, is a gross oversimplification. The values sought to be promoted by excluding the evidence include freedom of deliberation, stability and finality of verdicts, and protection of jurors against annoyance and embarrassment. McDonald v. Pless, 238 U.S. 264, 35 S.Ct. 783, 59 L.Ed. 1300 (1915). On the other hand, simply putting verdicts beyond effective reach can only promote irregularity and injustice. The rule offers an accommodation between these competing considerations.

The mental operations and emotional reactions of jurors in arriving at a given result would, if allowed as a subject of inquiry, place every verdict at the mercy of jurors and invite tampering and harassment. See Grenz v. Werre, 129 N.W.2d 681 (N.D.1964). The authorities are in virtually complete accord in excluding the evidence. Fryer, Note on Disqualification of Witnesses, Selected Writings on Evidence and Trial 345, 347 (Fryer ed. 1957); Maguire, Weinstein, et al., Cases on Evidence 887 (5th ed. 1965); 8 Wigmore § 2349 (McNaughton Rev.1961). As to matters other than mental operations and emotional reactions of jurors, substantial authority refuses to allow a juror to disclose irregularities which occur in the jury room, but allows his testimony as to irregularities occurring outside and allows outsiders to testify as to occurrences both inside and out. 8 Wigmore § 2354 (McNaughton Rev.1961). However, the door of the jury room is not necessarily a satisfactory dividing point, and the Supreme Court has refused to accept it for every situation. Mattox v. United States, 146 U.S. 140, 13 S.Ct. 50, 36 L.Ed. 917 (1892).

Under the federal decisions the central focus has been upon insulation of the manner in which the jury reached its verdict, and this protection extends to each of the components of deliberation, including arguments, statements, discussions, mental and emotional reactions, votes, and any other feature of the process. Thus testimony or affidavits of jurors have been held incompetent to show a compromise verdict. Hyde v. United States, 225 U.S. 347, 382 (1912); a quotient verdict, McDonald v. Pless, 238 U.S. 264 (1915); speculation as to insurance coverage. Holden v. Porter, 405 F.2d 878 (10th Cir.1969); Farmers Coop. Elev. Ass'n v. Strand, 382 F.2d 224, 230 (8th Cir.1967), cert. denied 389 U.S. 1014; misinterpretation of instructions, Farmers Coop. Elev. Ass'n v. Strand, supra; mistake in returning verdict, United States v. Chereton, 309 F.2d 197 (6th Cir.1962); interpretation of guilty plea by one defendant as implicating others, United States v. Crosby, 294 F.2d 928, 949 (2d Cir.1961). The policy does not, however, foreclose testimony by jurors as to prejudicial extraneous information or influences injected into or brought to bear upon the deliberative process. Thus a juror is recognized as competent to testify to statements by the bailiff or the introduction of a prejudicial newspaper account into the jury room, Mattox v. United States, 146 U.S. 140 (1892). See also Parker v. Gladden, 385 U.S. 363 (1966).

This rule does not purport to specify the substantive grounds for setting aside verdicts for irregularity; it deals only with the competency of jurors to testify concerning those grounds. Allowing them to testify as to matters other than their own inner reactions involves no particular hazard to the values sought to be protected. The rule is based upon this conclusion. It makes no attempt to specify the substantive grounds for setting aside verdicts for irregularity.

See also Rule 6(e) of the Federal Rules of Criminal Procedure and 18 U.S.C. § 3500, governing the secrecy of grand jury proceedings. The present rule does not relate to secrecy and disclosure but to the competency of certain witnesses and evidence.

House Judiciary Committee Report

As proposed by the Court, Rule 606(b) limited testimony by a juror in the course of an inquiry into the validity of a verdict or indictment. He could testify as to the influence of extraneous prejudicial information brought to the jury's attention (e.g. a radio newscast or a newspaper account) or an outside influence which improperly had been brought to bear upon a juror (e.g. a threat to the safety of a member of his family), but he could not testify as to other irregularities which occurred in the jury room. Under this formulation a quotient verdict could not be attacked through the testimony of a juror, nor could a juror testify to the drunken condition of a fellow juror which so disabled him that he could not participate in the jury's deliberations.

The 1969 and 1971 Advisory Committee drafts would have permitted a member of the jury to testify concerning these kinds of irregularities in the jury room. The Advisory Committee Note in the 1971 draft stated that "* * * the door of the jury room is not a satisfactory dividing point, and the Supreme Court has refused to accept it." The Advisory Committee further commented that—

> The trend has been to draw the dividing line between testimony as to mental processes, on the one hand, and as to the existence of conditions or occurrences of events calculated improperly to influence the verdict on the other hand, without regard to whether the happening is within or without the jury room. . . . The jurors are the persons who know what really happened. Allowing them to testify as to matters other than their own reactions involves no particular hazard to the values sought to be protected. The rule is based upon this conclusion. It makes no attempt to specify the substantive grounds for setting aside verdicts for irregularity.

Objective jury misconduct may be testified to in California, Florida, Iowa, Kansas, Nebraska, New Jersey, North Dakota, Ohio, Oregon, Tennessee, Texas, and Washington.

Persuaded that the better practice is that provided for in the earlier drafts, the Committee amended subdivision (b) to read as in the text of those drafts.

Senate Judiciary Committee Report

As adopted by the House, this rule would permit the impeachment of verdicts by inquiry into, not the mental processes of the jurors, but what happened in terms of conduct in the jury room. This extension of the ability to impeach a verdict is felt to be unwarranted and ill-advised.

The rule passed by the House embodies a suggestion by the Advisory Committee of the Judicial Conference that is considerably broader than the final version adopted by the Supreme Court, which embodied long-accepted Federal law. Although forbidding the impeachment of verdicts by inquiry into the jurors' mental processes, it deletes from the Supreme Court version the proscription against testimony "as to any matter or statement occurring during the course of the jury's deliberations." This deletion would have the effect of opening verdicts up to challenge on the basis of what happened during the jury's internal deliberations, for example, where a juror alleged that the jury refused to follow the trial judge's instructions or that some of the jurors did not take part in deliberations.

Permitting an individual to attack a jury verdict based upon the jury's internal deliberations has long been recognized as unwise by the Supreme Court. In McDonald v. Pless, the Court stated:

> [L]et it once be established that verdicts solemnly made and publicly returned into court can be attacked and set aside on the testimony of those who took part in their publication and all verdicts could be, and many would be, followed by an inquiry in the hope of

discovering something which might invalidate the finding. Jurors would be harassed and beset by the defeated party in an effort to secure from them evidence of facts which might establish misconduct sufficient to set aside a verdict. If evidence thus secured could be thus used, the result would be to make what was intended to be a private deliberation, the constant subject of public investigation—to the destruction of all frankness and freedom of discussion and conference [238 U.S. 264, at 267 (1914)].

As it stands then, the rule would permit the harassment of former jurors by losing parties as well as the possible exploitation of disgruntled or otherwise badly-motivated ex-jurors.

Public policy requires a finality to litigation. And common fairness requires that absolute privacy be preserved for jurors to engage in the full and free debate necessary to the attainment of just verdicts. Jurors will not be able to function effectively if their deliberations are to be scrutinized in post-trial litigation. In the interest of protecting the jury system and the citizens who make it work, rule 606 should not permit any inquiry into the internal deliberations of the jurors.

Conference Committee Report

Rule 606(b) deals with juror testimony in an inquiry into the validity of a verdict or indictment. The House bill provides that a juror cannot testify about his mental processes or about the effect of anything upon his or another juror's mind as influencing him to assent to or dissent from a verdict or indictment. Thus, the House bill allows a juror to testify about objective matters occurring during the jury's deliberation, such as the misconduct of another juror or the reaching of a quotient verdict. The Senate bill does not permit juror testimony about any matter or statement occurring during the course of the jury's deliberations. The Senate bill does provide, however, that a juror may testify on the question whether extraneous prejudicial information was improperly brought to the jury's attention and on the question whether any outside influence was improperly brought to bear on any juror.

The Conference adopts the Senate amendment. The Conferees believe that jurors should be encouraged to be conscientious in promptly reporting to the court misconduct that occurs during jury deliberations.

Advisory Committee's Note to 2006 Amendments

Rule 606(b) has been amended to provide that juror testimony may be used to prove that the verdict reported was the result of a mistake in entering the verdict on the verdict form. The amendment responds to a divergence between the text of the Rule and the case law that has established an exception for proof of clerical errors. See, e.g., Plummer v. Springfield Term. Ry., 5 F.3d 1, 3 (1st Cir. 1993) ("A number of circuits hold, and we agree, that juror testimony regarding an alleged clerical error, such as announcing a verdict different than that agreed upon, does not challenge the validity of the verdict or the deliberation of mental processes, and therefore is not subject to Rule 606(b)."); Teevee Toons, Inc., v. MP3.Com, Inc., 148 F.Supp.2d 276, 278 (S.D.N.Y. 2001) (noting that Rule 606(b) has been silent regarding inquiries designed to confirm the accuracy of a verdict).

In adopting the exception for proof of mistakes in entering the verdict on the verdict form, the amendment specifically rejects the broader exception, adopted by some courts, permitting the use of juror testimony to prove that the jurors were operating under a misunderstanding about the consequences of the result that they agreed upon. See, e.g., Attridge v. Cencorp Div. of Dover Techs. Int'l, Inc., 836 F.2d 113, 116 (2d Cir. 1987); Eastridge Development Co., v. Halpert Associates, Inc., 853 F.2d 772 (10th Cir. 1988). The broader exception is rejected because an inquiry into whether the jury misunderstood or misapplied an instruction goes to the jurors' mental processes underlying the verdict, rather than the verdict's accuracy in capturing what the jurors had agreed upon. See, e.g. , Karl v. Burlington Northern R.R., 880 F.2d 68, 74 (8th Cir. 1989) (error to receive juror testimony on whether verdict was the result of jurors' misunderstanding of instructions: "The jurors did not state that the figure written by the foreman was different from that which they agreed upon, but indicated that the figure the foreman wrote down was intended to be a net figure, not a gross figure. Receiving such statements violates Rule 606(b) because the testimony relates to how the jury interpreted the court's instructions, and concerns the jurors' 'mental processes,' which is forbidden by the rule."); Robles v. Exxon Corp., 862 F.2d 1201, 1208 (5th Cir. 1989) ("the alleged error here goes to the substance of what the jury was asked to decide, necessarily implicating the jury's mental processes insofar as it questions the jury's understanding of the court's instructions and application of those instructions to the facts of the case"). Thus, the exception established by the amendment is limited to cases such as "where the jury foreperson wrote down, in response to an interrogatory, a number different from that agreed upon by the jury, or mistakenly stated that the defendant was 'guilty' when the jury had actually agreed that the defendant was not guilty." Id.

It should be noted that the possibility of errors in the verdict form will be reduced substantially by polling the jury. Rule 606(b) does not, of course, prevent this precaution. See 8 C. Wigmore, Evidence, § 2350 at 691 (McNaughten ed. 1961) (noting that the reasons for the rule barring juror testimony, "namely, the dangers of uncertainty and of tampering with the jurors to procure testimony, disappear in large part if such investigation as may be desired is made by the judge and takes place before the jurors' discharge and separation") (emphasis in original). Errors that come to light after polling the jury "may be corrected on the spot, or the jury may be sent out to continue deliberations, or, if necessary, a new trial may be ordered." C. Mueller & L. Kirkpatrick, Evidence Under the Rules at 671 (2d ed. 1999) (citing Sincox v. United States, 571 F.2d 876, 878-79 (5th Cir. 1978)).

Restyled 2011

Rule 607. Who May Impeach a Witness

Any party, including the party that called the witness, may attack the witness's credibility.

Superseded 2011

Rule 607. Who May Impeach

The credibility of a witness may be attacked by any party, including the party calling the witness.

Case Notes

Forms of impeachment not specifically covered by the Rules—*e.g.*, bias, contradiction, and mental incapacity—are governed by the general rule that relevant evidence is admissible in the absence of a rule of exclusion, see Rule 402. United States v. Abel, 469 U.S. 45, 50, 105 S.Ct. 465, 468, 83 L.Ed.2d 450 (1984).

The prosecution may not, under the guise of impeachment, call a witness whom it expects to give unfavorable testimony solely for the purpose of eliciting a favorable prior inconsistent statement that is substantively inadmissible because it was not made under oath in a proceeding, see Rule 801(d)(1)(A). United States v. Hogan, 763 F.2d 697, 702 (5th Cir. 1985).

Advisory Committee's Note

The traditional rule against impeaching one's own witness is abandoned as based on false premises. A party does not hold out his witnesses as worthy of belief, since he rarely has a free choice in selecting them. Denial of the right leaves the party at the mercy of the witness and the adversary. If the impeachment is by a prior statement, it is free from hearsay dangers and is excluded from the category of hearsay under Rule 801(d)(1). Ladd, Impeachment of One's Own Witness—New Developments, 4 U.Chi.L.Rev. 69 (1936); McCormick
§ 38; 3 Wigmore §§ 896-918. The substantial inroads into the old rule made over the years by decisions, rules, and statutes are evidence of doubts as to its basic soundness and workability. Cases are collected in 3 Wigmore § 905. Revised Rule 32(a)(1) of the Federal Rules of Civil Procedure allows any party to impeach a witness by means of his deposition, and Rule 43(b) has allowed the calling and impeachment of an adverse party or person identified with him. Illustrative statutes allowing a party to impeach his own witness under varying circumstances are Ill.Rev.Stats.1967, c. 110, § 60; Mass.Laws Annot. 1959, c. 233, § 23; 20 N.M.Stats.Annot. 1953, § 20-2-4; N.Y. CPLR § 4514 (McKinney 1963); 12 Vt.Stats.Annot.1959, §§ 1641a, 1642. Complete judicial rejection of the old rule is found in United States v. Freeman, 302 F.2d 347 (2d Cir.1962). The same result is reached in Uniform Rule 20; California Evidence Code § 785; Kansas Code of Civil Procedure § 60-420. See also New Jersey Evidence Rule 20.

Restyled 2011

Rule 608. A Witness's Character for Truthfulness or Untruthfulness

(a) Reputation or Opinion Evidence. A witness's credibility may be attacked or supported by testimony about the witness's reputation for having a character for truthfulness or untruthfulness, or by testimony in the form of an opinion about that character. But evidence of truthful character is admissible only after the witness's character for truthfulness has been attacked.

Superseded 2011

Rule 608. Evidence of Character and Conduct of Witness

(a) Opinion and reputation evidence of character. The credibility of a witness may be attacked or supported by evidence in the form of opinion or reputation, but subject to these limitations: (1) the evidence may refer only to character for truthfulness or untruthfulness, and (2) evidence of truthful character is admissible only after the character of the witness for truthfulness has been attacked by opinion or reputation evidence or otherwise.

Advisory Committee's Note

Subdivision (a). In Rule 404(a) the general position is taken that character evidence is not admissible for the purpose of proving that the person acted in conformity therewith, subject, however, to several exceptions, one of which is character evidence of a witness as bearing upon his credibility. The present rule develops that exception.

In accordance with the bulk of judicial authority, the inquiry is strictly limited to character for veracity, rather than allowing evidence as to character generally. The result is to sharpen relevancy, to reduce surprise, waste of time, and confusion, and to make the lot of the witness somewhat less unattractive. McCormick § 44.

The use of opinion and reputation evidence as means of proving the character of witnesses is consistent with Rule 405(a). While the modern practice has purported to exclude opinion, witnesses who testify to reputation seem in fact often to be giving their opinions, disguised somewhat misleadingly as reputation. See McCormick § 44. And even under the modern practice, a common relaxation has allowed inquiry as to whether the witnesses would believe the principal witness under oath. United States v. Walker, 313 F.2d 236 (6th Cir.1963), and cases cited therein; McCormick § 44, pp. 94-95, n. 3.

Character evidence in support of credibility is admissible under the rule only after the witness' character has first been attacked, as has been the case at common law. Maguire, Weinstein, et al., Cases on Evidence 295 (5th ed. 1965); McCormick § 49, p. 105; 4 Wigmore § 1104. The enormous needless consumption of time which a contrary practice would entail justifies the limitation. Opinion or reputation that the witness is untruthful specifically qualifies as an attack under the rule, and evidence of misconduct, including conviction of crime, and of corruption also fall within this category. Evidence of bias or interest does not. McCormick § 49; 4 Wigmore §§ 1106, 1107. Whether evidence in the form of contradiction is an attack upon the character of the witness must depend upon the circumstances. McCormick § 49. Cf. 4 Wigmore §§ 1108, 1109.

As to the use of specific instances on direct by an opinion witness, see the Advisory Committee Note to Rule 405, supra.

House Judiciary Committee Report

Rule 608(a) as submitted by the Court permitted attack to be made upon the character for truthfulness or untruthfulness of a witness either by reputation or opinion testimony. For the same reason underlying its decision to eliminate the admissibility of opinion testimony in Rule 405(a), the Committee amended Rule 608(a) to delete the reference to opinion testimony.

Conference Committee Report

The Senate amendment adds the words "opinion or" to conform the first sentence of the rule with the remainder of the rule.

The Conference adopts the Senate amendment.

Restyled 2011

(b) Specific Instances of Conduct. Except for a criminal conviction under Rule 609, extrinsic evidence is not admissible to prove specific instances of a witness's conduct in order to attack or support the witness's character for truthfulness. But the court may, on cross-examination, allow them to be inquired into if they are probative of the character for truthfulness or untruthfulness of:

(1) the witness; or

(2) another witness whose character the witness being cross-examined has testified about.

By testifying on another matter, a witness does not waive any privilege against self-incrimination for testimony that relates only to the witness's character for truthfulness.

Committee Note to 2011 Restyled Rule

The Committee is aware that the Rule's limitation of bad-act impeachment to "cross-examination" is trumped by Rule 607, which allows a party to impeach witnesses on direct examination. Courts have not relied on the term "on cross-examination" to limit impeachment that would otherwise be permissible under Rules 607 and 608. The Committee therefore concluded that no change to the language of the Rule was necessary in the context of a restyling project.

Superseded 2011

(b) Specific instances of conduct. Specific instances of the conduct of a witness, for the purpose of attacking or supporting the witness' character for truthfulness, other than conviction of crime as provided in rule 609, may not be proved by extrinsic evidence. They may, however, in the discretion of the court, if probative of truthfulness or untruthfulness, be inquired into on cross-examination of the witness (1) concerning the witness' character for truthfulness or untruthfulness, or (2) concerning the character for truthfulness or untruthfulness of another witness as to which character the witness being cross-examined has testified.

The giving of testimony, whether by an accused or by any other witness, does not operate as a waiver of the accused's or the witness' privilege against self-incrimination when examined with respect to matters that relate only to character for truthfulness. [*Amended 2003.*]

Case Note

Rule 608(b) regulates the admissibility of specific instances of conduct only when offered to prove a witness's character for veracity. It does not cover evidence offered to prove that a witness is biased. Therefore, extrinsic evidence of specific instances of conduct offered to prove a witness's bias is not precluded by this rule. United States v. Abel, 469 U.S. 45, 55-56, 105 S.Ct. 465, 470-471, 83 L.Ed. 2d 450 (1984).

Advisory Committee's Note

Subdivision (b). In conformity with Rule 405, which forecloses use of evidence of specific incidents as proof in chief of character unless character is an issue in the case, the present rule generally bars evidence of specific instances of conduct of a witness for the purpose of attacking or supporting his credibility. There are, however, two exceptions: (1) specific instances are provable when they have been the subject of criminal conviction, and (2) specific instances may be inquired into on cross-examination of the principal witness or of a witness giving an opinion of his character for truthfulness.

(1) Conviction of crime as a technique of impeachment is treated in detail in Rule 609, and here is merely recognized as an exception to the general rule excluding evidence of specific incidents for impeachment purposes.

(2) Particular instances of conduct, though not the subject of criminal conviction, may be inquired into on cross-examination of the principal witness himself or of a witness who testifies concerning his character for truthfulness. Effective cross-examination demands that some allowance be made for going into matters of this kind, but the possibilities of abuse are substantial. Consequently safeguards are erected in the form of specific requirements that the instances inquired into be probative of truthfulness or its opposite and not remote in time. Also, the overriding protection of Rule 403 requires that probative value not be outweighed by danger of unfair prejudice, confusion of issues, or misleading the jury, and that of Rule 611 bars harassment and undue embarrassment.

The final sentence constitutes a rejection of the doctrine of such cases as People v. Sorge, 301 N.Y. 198, 93 N.E.2d 637 (1950), that any past criminal act relevant to credibility may be inquired into on cross-examination, in apparent disregard of the privilege against self-incrimination. While it is clear that an ordinary witness cannot make a partial disclosure of incriminating matter and then invoke the privilege on cross-examination, no tenable contention can be made that merely by testifying he waives his right to foreclose inquiry on cross-examination into criminal activities for the purpose of attacking his credibility. So to hold would reduce the privilege to a nullity. While it is true that an accused, unlike an ordinary witness, has an option whether to testify, if the option can be exercised only at the price of opening up inquiry as to any and all criminal acts committed during his lifetime, the right to testify could scarcely be said to possess much vitality. In Griffin v. California, 380 U.S. 609, 85 S.Ct. 1229, 14 L.Ed.2d 106 (1965), the Court held that allowing comment on the election of an accused not to testify exacted a constitutionally impermissible price, and so here. While no specific provision in terms confers constitutional status on the right of an accused to take the stand in his own defense, the existence of the right is so completely recognized that a denial of it or substantial infringement upon it would surely be of due process dimensions. See Ferguson v. Georgia, 365 U.S. 570, 81 S.Ct. 756, 5 L.Ed.2d 783 (1961); McCormick § 131; 8 Wigmore § 2276 (McNaughton Rev.1961). In any event, wholly aside from constitutional considerations, the provision represents a sound policy.

House Judiciary Committee Report

The second sentence of Rule 608(b) as submitted by the Court permitted specific instances of misconduct of a witness to be inquired into on cross-examination for the purpose of attacking his credibility, if probative of truthfulness or untruthfulness, "and not remote in time". Such cross-examination could be of the witness himself or of another witness who testifies as to "his" character for truthfulness or untruthfulness.

The Committee amended the Rule to emphasize the discretionary power of the court in permitting such testimony and deleted the reference to remoteness in time as being unnecessary and confusing (remoteness from time of trial or remoteness from the incident involved?). As recast, the Committee amendment also makes clear the antecedent of "his" in the original Court proposal.

Advisory Committee's Note to 2003 Amendment

The Rule [608(b)] has been amended to clarify that the absolute prohibition on extrinsic evidence applies only when the sole reason for proffering that evidence is to attack or support the witness' character for truthfulness. See United States v. Abel, 469 U.S. 45 (1984); United States v. Fusco, 748 F.2d 996 (5th Cir. 1984) (Rule 608(b) limits the use of evidence "designed to show that the witness has done things, unrelated to the suit being tried, that make him more or less believable per se"); Ohio R. Evid. 608(b). On occasion the Rule's use of the overbroad term "credibility" has been read "to bar extrinsic evidence for bias, competency and contradiction impeachment since they too deal with credibility." American Bar Association Section of Litigation, Emerging Problems Under the Federal Rules of Evidence at 161 (3d ed. 1998). The amendment conforms the language of the Rule to its original intent, which was to impose an absolute bar on extrinsic evidence only if the sole purpose for offering the evidence was to prove the witness' character for veracity. See Advisory Committee Note to Rule 608(b) (stating that the Rule is "[i]n conformity with Rule 405, which forecloses use of evidence of specific incidents as proof in chief of character unless character is in issue in the case . . .").

By limiting the application of the Rule to proof of a witness' character for truthfulness, the amendment leaves the admissibility of extrinsic evidence offered for other grounds of impeachment (such as contradiction, prior inconsistent statement, bias and mental capacity) to Rules 402 and 403. See, e.g., United States v. Winchenbach, 197 F.3d 548 (1st Cir. 1999) (admissibility of a prior inconsistent statement offered for impeachment is governed by Rules 402 and 403, not Rule 608(b)); United States v. Tarantino, 846 F.2d 1384 (D.C.Cir. 1988) (admissibility of extrinsic evidence offered to contradict a witness is governed by Rules 402 and 403); United States v. Lindemann, 85 F.3d 1232 (7th Cir. 1996) (admissibility of extrinsic evidence of bias is governed by Rules 402 and 403).

It should be noted that the extrinsic evidence prohibition of Rule 608(b) bars any reference to the consequences that a witness might have suffered as a result of an alleged bad act. For example, Rule 608(b) prohibits counsel from mentioning that a witness was suspended or disciplined for the conduct that is the subject of impeachment, when that conduct is offered only to prove the character of the witness. See United States v. Davis, 183 F.3d 231, 257 n.17 (3d Cir. 1999) (emphasizing that in attacking the defendant's character for truthfulness "the government cannot make reference to Davis's forty-four day suspension or that Internal Affairs found that he lied about" an incident because "[s]uch evidence would not only be hearsay to the extent it contains assertion of fact, it would be inadmissible extrinsic evidence under Rule 608(b)"). See also Stephen A. Saltzburg, Impeaching the Witness: Prior Bad Acts and Extrinsic Evidence, 7 Crim. Just. 28, 31 (Winter 1993) ("Counsel should not be permitted to circumvent the no-extrinsic-evidence provision by tucking a third person's opinion about prior acts into a question asked of the witness who has denied the act.").

For purposes of consistency the term "credibility" has been replaced by the term "character for truthfulness" in the last sentence of subdivision (b). The term "credibility" is also used in subdivision (a). But the Committee found it unnecessary to substitute "character for truthfulness" for "credibility" in Rule 608(a), because subdivision (a)(1) already serves to limit impeachment to proof of such character.

Rules 609(a) and 610 also use the term "credibility" when the intent of those Rules is to regulate impeachment of a witness' character for truthfulness. No inference should be derived from the fact that the Committee proposed an amendment to Rule 608(b) but not to Rules 609 and 610.

Restyled 2011

Rule 609. Impeachment by Evidence of a Criminal Conviction

(a) In General. The following rules apply to attacking a witness's character for truthfulness by evidence of a criminal conviction:

(1) for a crime that, in the convicting jurisdiction, was punishable by death or by imprisonment for more than one year, the evidence:

(A) must be admitted, subject to Rule 403, in a civil case or in a criminal case in which the witness is not a defendant; and

(B) must be admitted in a criminal case in which the witness is a defendant, if the probative value of the evidence outweighs its prejudicial effect to that defendant; and

(2) for any crime regardless of the punishment, the evidence must be admitted if the court can readily determine that establishing the elements of the crime required proving — or the witness's admitting — a dishonest act or false statement.

Superseded 2011

Rule 609. Impeachment by Evidence of Conviction of Crime

(a) General rule.—For the purpose of attacking the character for truthfulness of a witness,

(1) evidence that a witness other than an accused has been convicted of a crime shall be admitted, subject to Rule 403, if the crime was punishable by death or imprisonment in excess of one year under the law under which the witness was convicted, and evidence that an accused has been convicted of such a crime shall be admitted if the court determines that the probative value of admitting this evidence outweighs its prejudicial effect to the accused; and

(2) evidence that any witness has been convicted of a crime shall be admitted regardless of the punishment, if it readily can be determined that establishing the elements of the crime required proof or admission of an act of dishonesty or false statement by the witness. [*Amended 1999, 2006.*]

Case Notes

The defendant must testify at the trial in order to preserve for appellate review a ruling denying the defendant's motion to preclude the use of a prior conviction to impeach his credibility. An *in limine* ruling is subject to change as the case unfolds. To weigh the probative value of the prior conviction against its prejudicial effect on the defendant, the court must know the precise nature of the defendant's testimony, which is impossible if the defendant does not testify. Luce v. United States, 469 U.S. 38, 105 S.Ct. 460, 83 L.Ed. 2d 443 (1984).

A defendant who loses an *in limine* ruling on the admissibility of a prior conviction for impeachment, and who then testifies at trial, may not claim on appeal that admission of the prior conviction was error if the defendant brings out the prior conviction on direct examination. A contrary rule would deny to the prosecution its usual right to decide, after the defendant testifies, whether or not to use the prior conviction. Ohler v. United States, 529 U.S. 753, 120 S.Ct. 1851, 146 L.Ed. 2d 826 (2000) (5-to-4).

Advisory Committee's Note

As a means of impeachment, evidence of conviction of crime is significant only because it stands as proof of the commission of the underlying criminal act. There is little dissent from the general proposition that at least some crimes are relevant to credibility but much disagreement among the cases and commentators about which crimes are usable for this purpose. See McCormick § 43; 2 Wright, Federal Practice and Procedure: Criminal § 416 (1969). The weight of traditional authority has been to allow use of felonies generally, without regard to the nature of the particular offense, and of crimen falsi without regard to the grade of the offense. This is the view accepted by Congress in the 1970 amendment of § 14-305 of the District of Columbia Code, P.L. 91-358, 84 Stat. 473. Uniform Rule 21 and Model Code Rule 106 permit only crimes involving "dishonesty or false statement." Others have thought that the trial judge should have discretion to exclude convictions if the probative value of the evidence of the crime is substantially outweighed by the danger of unfair prejudice. Luck v. United States, 121 U.S.App.D.C. 151, 348 F.2d 763 (1965); McGowan, Impeachment of Criminal Defendants by Prior Convictions, 1970 Law & Soc.Order 1. Whatever may be the merits of those views, this rule is drafted to accord with the Congressional policy manifested in the 1970 legislation.

The proposed rule incorporates certain basic safeguards, in terms applicable to all witnesses but of particular significance to an accused who elects to testify. These protections include the imposition of definite time limitations, giving effect to demonstrated rehabilitation, and generally excluding juvenile adjudications.

Subdivision (a). For purposes of impeachment, crimes are divided into two categories by the rule: (1) those of what is generally regarded as felony grade, without particular regard to the nature of the offense, and (2) those involving dishonesty or false statement, without regard to the grade of the offense. Probable convictions are not limited to violations of federal law. By reason of our constitutional structure, the federal catalog of crimes is far from being a complete one, and resort must be had to the laws of the states for the specification of many crimes. For example, simple theft as compared with theft from interstate commerce. Other instances of borrowing are the Assimilative Crimes Act, making the state law of crimes applicable to the special territorial and maritime jurisdiction of the United States, 18 U.S.C.
§ 13, and the provision of the Judicial Code disqualifying persons as jurors on the grounds of state as well as federal convictions, 28 U.S.C. § 1865. For evaluation of the crime in terms of seriousness, reference is made to the congressional measurement of felony

(subject to imprisonment in excess of one year) rather than adopting state definitions which vary considerably. See 28 U.S.C. § 1865, supra, disqualifying jurors for conviction in state or federal court of crime punishable by imprisonment for more than one year.

House Judiciary Committee Report

Rule 609(a) as submitted by the Court was modeled after Section 133(a) of Public Law 91-358, 14 D.C.Code 305(b)(1), enacted in 1970. The Rule provided that:

For the purpose of attacking the credibility of a witness, evidence that he has been convicted of a crime is admissible but only if the crime (1) was punishable by death or imprisonment in excess of one year under the law under which he was convicted or (2) involved dishonesty or false statement regardless of the punishment.

As reported to the Committee by the Subcommittee, Rule 609(a) was amended to read as follows:

For the purpose of attacking the credibility of a witness, evidence that he has been convicted of a crime is admissible only if the crime (1) was punishable by death or imprisonment in excess of one year, unless the court determines that the danger of unfair prejudice outweighs the probative value of the evidence of the conviction, or (2) involved dishonesty or false statement.

In full committee, the provision was amended to permit attack upon the credibility of a witness by prior conviction only if the prior crime involved dishonesty or false statement. While recognizing that the prevailing doctrine in the federal courts and in most States allows a witness to be impeached by evidence of prior felony convictions without restriction as to type, the Committee was of the view that, because of the danger of unfair prejudice in such practice and the deterrent effect upon an accused who might wish to testify, and even upon a witness who was not the accused, cross-examination by evidence of prior conviction should be limited to those kinds of convictions bearing directly on credibility, i.e., crimes involving dishonesty or false statement.

Senate Judiciary Committee Report

As proposed by the Supreme Court, the rule would allow the use of prior convictions to impeach if the crime was a felony or a misdemeanor if the misdemeanor involved dishonesty or false statement. As modified by the House, the rule would admit prior convictions for impeachment purposes only if the offense, whether felony or misdemeanor, involved dishonesty or false statement.

The committee has adopted a modified version of the House-passed rule. In your committee's view, the danger of unfair prejudice is far greater when the accused, as opposed to other witnesses, testifies, because the jury may be prejudiced not merely on the question of credibility but also on the ultimate question of guilt or innocence. Therefore, with respect to defendants, the committee agreed with the House limitation that only offenses involved false statement or dishonesty may be used. By that phrase, the committee means crimes such as perjury or subornation of perjury, false statement, criminal fraud, embezzlement or false pretense, or any other offense, in the nature of crimen falsi the commission of which involves some element of untruthfulness, deceit or falsification bearing on the accused's propensity to testify truthfully.

With respect to other witnesses, in addition to any prior conviction involving false statement or dishonesty, any other felony may be used to impeach if, and only if, the court finds that the probative value of such evidence outweighs its prejudicial effect against the party offering that witness.

Notwithstanding this provision, proof of any prior offense otherwise admissible under Rule 404 could still be offered for the purposes sanctioned by that rule. Furthermore, the committee intends that notwithstanding this rule, a defendant's misrepresentation regarding the existence or nature of prior convictions may be met by rebuttal evidence, including the record of such prior convictions. Similarly, such records may be offered to rebut representations made by the defendant regarding his attitude toward or willingness to commit a general category of offense, although denials or other representations by the defendant regarding the specific conduct which forms the basis of the charge against him shall not make prior convictions admissible to rebut such statement.

In regard to either type of representation, of course, prior convictions may be offered in rebuttal only if the defendant's statement is made in response to defense counsel's questions or is made gratuitously in the course of cross-examination. Prior convictions may not be offered as rebuttal evidence if the prosecution has sought to circumvent the purpose of this rule by asking questions which elicit such representations from the defendant.

One other clarifying amendment has been added to this subsection, that is, to provide that the admissibility of evidence of a prior conviction is permitted only upon cross-examination of a witness. It is not admissible if a person does not testify. It is to be understood, however, that a court record of a prior conviction is admissible to prove that conviction if the witness has forgotten or denies its existence.

Conference Committee Report

The House bill provides that the credibility of a witness can be attacked by proof of prior conviction of a crime only if the crime involves dishonesty or false statement. The Senate amendment provides that a witness' credibility may be attacked if the crime (1) was punishable by death or imprisonment in excess of one year under the law under which he was convicted or (2) involves dishonesty or false statement, regardless of the punishment.

The Conference adopts the Senate amendment with an amendment. The Conference amendment provides that the credibility of a witness, whether a defendant or someone else, may be attacked by proof of a prior conviction but only if the crime: (1) was punishable by death or imprisonment in excess of one year under the law under which he was convicted and the court determines that the probative value of the conviction outweighs its prejudicial effect to the defendant; or (2) involved dishonesty or false statement regardless of the punishment.

By the phrase "dishonesty and false statement" the Conference means crimes such as perjury or subornation of perjury, false statement, criminal fraud, embezzlement, or false pretense, or any other offense in the nature of crimen falsi, the commission of which involves some element of deceit, untruthfulness, or falsification bearing on the accused's propensity to testify truthfully.

The admission of prior convictions involving dishonesty and false statement is not within the discretion of the Court. Such convictions are peculiarly probative of credibility and, under this rule, are always to be admitted. Thus, judicial discretion granted with respect to the admissibility of other prior convictions is not applicable to those involving dishonesty or false statement.

With regard to the discretionary standard established by paragraph (1) of Rule 609(a), the Conference determined that the prejudicial effect to be weighed against the probative value of the conviction is specifically the prejudicial effect to the defendant. The danger of prejudice to a witness other than the defendant (such as injury to the witness' reputation in his community) was considered and rejected by the Conference as an element to be weighed in determining admissibility. It was the judgment of the Conference that the danger of prejudice to a nondefendant witness is outweighed by the need for the trier of fact to have as much relevant evidence on the issue of credibility as possible. Such evidence should only be excluded where it presents a danger of improperly influencing the outcome of the trial by persuading the trier of fact to convict the defendant on the basis of his prior criminal record.

Advisory Committee's Note to 1990 Amendment to Rule 609(a)

The amendment to Rule 609(a) makes two changes in the rule. The first change removes from the rule the limitation that the conviction may only be elicited during cross-examination, a limitation that virtually every circuit has found to be inapplicable. It is common for witnesses to reveal on direct examination their convictions to "remove the sting" of the impeachment. See e.g., United States v. Bad Cob, 560 F.2d 877 (8th Cir.1977). The amendment does not contemplate that a court will necessarily permit proof of prior convictions through testimony, which might be time-consuming and more prejudicial than proof through a written record. Rules 403 and 611(a) provide sufficient authority for the court to protect against unfair or disruptive methods of proof.

The second change effected by the amendment resolves an ambiguity as to the relationship of Rules 609 and 403 with respect to impeachment of witnesses other than the criminal defendant. See, Green v. Bock Laundry Machine Co., 109 S.Ct. 1981, 490 U.S. 504 (1989). The amendment does not disturb the special balancing test for the criminal defendant who chooses to testify. Thus, the rule recognizes that, in virtually every case in which prior convictions are used to impeach the testifying defendant, the defendant faces a unique risk of prejudice—i.e., the danger that convictions that would be excluded under Fed.R.Evid. 404 will be misused by a jury as propensity evidence despite their introduction solely for impeachment purposes. Although the rule does not forbid all use of convictions to impeach a defendant, it requires that the government show that the probative value of convictions as impeachment evidence outweighs their prejudicial effect.

Prior to the amendment, the rule appeared to give the defendant the benefit of the special balancing test when defense witnesses other than the defendant were called to testify. In practice, however, the concern about unfairness to the defendant is most acute when the defendant's own convictions are offered as evidence. Almost all of the decided cases concern this type of impeachment, and the amendment does not deprive the defendant of any meaningful protection, since Rule 403 now clearly protects against unfair impeachment of any defense witness other than the defendant. There are cases in which a defendant might be prejudiced when a defense witness is impeached. Such cases may arise, for example, when the witness bears a special relationship to the defendant such that the defendant is likely to suffer some spill-over effect from impeachment of the witness.

The amendment also protects other litigants from unfair impeachment of their witnesses. The danger of prejudice from the use of prior convictions is not confined to criminal defendants. Although the danger that prior convictions will be misused as character evidence is particularly acute when the defendant is impeached, the danger exists in other situations as well. The amendment reflects the view that it is desirable to protect all litigants from the unfair use of prior convictions, and that the ordinary balancing test of Rule 403, which provides that evidence shall not be excluded unless its prejudicial effect substantially outweighs its probative value, is appropriate for assessing the admissibility of prior convictions for impeachment of any witness other than a criminal defendant.

The amendment reflects a judgment that decisions interpreting Rule 609(a) as requiring a trial court to admit convictions in civil cases that have little, if anything, to do with credibility reach undesirable results. See, e.g., Diggs v. Lyons, 741 F.2d 577 (3d Cir.1984), cert. denied, 105 S.Ct. 2157 (1985). The amendment provides the same protection against unfair prejudice arising from prior convictions used for impeachment purposes as the rules provide for other evidence. The amendment finds support in decided cases. See, e.g., Petty v. Ideco, 761 F.2d 1146 (5th Cir.1985); Czaka v. Hickman, 703 F.2d 317 (8th Cir.1983).

Fewer decided cases address the question whether Rule 609(a) provides any protection against unduly prejudicial prior convictions used to impeach government witnesses. Some courts have read Rule 609(a) as giving the government no protection for its witnesses. See, e.g., United States v. Thorne, 547 F.2d 56 (8th Cir.1976); United States v. Nevitt, 563 F.2d 406 (9th Cir.1977), cert. denied, 444 U.S. 847 (1979). This approach also is rejected by the amendment. There are cases in which impeachment of government witnesses with prior convictions that have little, if anything, to do with credibility may result in unfair prejudice to the government's interest in a fair trial and unnecessary embarrassment to a witness. Fed.R.Evid. 412 already recognizes this and excluded certain evidence of past sexual behavior in the context of prosecutions for sexual assaults.

The amendment applies the general balancing test of Rule 403 to protect all litigants against unfair impeachment of witnesses. The balancing test protects civil litigants, the government in criminal cases, and the defendant in a criminal case who calls other witnesses. The amendment addresses prior convictions offered under Rule 609, not for other purposes, and does not run afoul, therefore, of Davis v. Alaska, 415 U.S. 308 (1974). Davis involved the use of a prior juvenile adjudication not to prove a past law violation, but to prove bias. The defendant in a criminal case has the right to demonstrate the bias of a witness and to be assured a fair trial, but not to unduly prejudice a trier of fact. See generally Rule 412. In any case in which the trial court believes that confrontation rights require admission of impeachment evidence, obviously the Constitution would take precedence over the rule.

The probability that prior convictions of an ordinary government witness will be unduly prejudicial is low in most criminal cases. Since the behavior of the witness is not the issue in dispute in most cases, there is little chance that the trier of fact will misuse the convictions offered as impeachment evidence as propensity evidence. Thus, trial courts will be skeptical when the government objects to impeachment of its witnesses with prior convictions. Only when the government is able to point to a real danger of prejudice that is sufficient to outweigh substantially the probative value of the conviction for impeachment purposes will the conviction be excluded.

The amendment continues to divide subdivision (a) into subsections (1) and (2) thus facilitating retrieval under current computerized research programs which distinguish the two provisions. The Committee recommended no substantive change in subdivision (a)(2), even though some cases raise a concern about the proper interpretation of the words "dishonesty or false statement." These words were used but not explained in the original Advisory Committee Note accompanying Rule 609. Congress extensively debated the rule, and the Report of the House and Senate Conference Committee states that "[b]y the phrase 'dishonesty and false statement,' the Conference means crimes such as perjury, subornation of perjury, false statement, criminal fraud, embezzlement, or false pretense, or any other offense in the nature of crimen falsi, commission of which involves some element of deceit, untruthfulness, or falsification bearing on the accused's propensity to testify truthfully." The Advisory Committee concluded that the Conference Report provides sufficient guidance to trial courts and that no amendment is necessary, notwithstanding some decisions that take an unduly broad view of "dishonesty," admitting convictions such as for bank robbery or bank larceny. Subsection (a)(2) continues to apply to any witness, including a criminal defendant.

Finally, the Committee determined that it was unnecessary to add to the rule language stating that, when a prior conviction is offered under Rule 609, the trial court is to consider the probative value of the prior conviction for impeachment, not for other purposes. The Committee concluded that the title of the rule, its first sentence, and its placement among the impeachment rules clearly establish that evidence offered under Rule 609 is offered only for purposes of impeachment.

Advisory Committee Note on 2006 Amendments

The amendment provides that Rule 609(a)(2) mandates the admission of evidence of a conviction only when the conviction required the proof of (or in the case of a guilty plea, the admission of) an act of dishonesty or false statement. Evidence of all other convictions is inadmissible under this subsection, irrespective of whether the witness exhibited dishonesty or made a false statement in the process of the commission of the crime of conviction. Thus, evidence that a witness was convicted for a crime of violence, such as murder, is not admissible under Rule 609(a)(2), even if the witness acted deceitfully in the course of committing the crime.

The amendment is meant to give effect to the legislative intent to limit the convictions that are to be automatically admitted under subdivision (a)(2). The Conference Committee provided that by "dishonesty and false statement" it meant "crimes such as perjury, subornation of perjury, false statement, criminal fraud, embezzlement, or false pretense, or any other offense in the nature of crimen falsi, the commission of which involves some element of deceit, untruthfulness, or falsification bearing on the [witness's] propensity to testify truthfully." Historically, offenses classified as crimina falsi have included only those crimes in which the ultimate criminal act was itself an act of deceit. See Green, Deceit and the Classification of Crimes: Federal Rule of Evidence 609(a)(2) and the Origins of Crimen Falsi, 90 J. Crim. L. & Criminology 1087 (2000).

Evidence of crimes in the nature of crimina falsi must be admitted under Rule 609(a)(2), regardless of how such crimes are specifically charged. For example, evidence that a witness was convicted of making a false claim to a federal agent is admissible under this subdivision regardless of whether the crime was charged under a section that expressly references deceit (e.g., 18 U.S.C. § 1001, Material Misrepresentation to the Federal Government) or a section that does not (e.g., 18 U.S.C. § 1503, Obstruction of Justice).

The amendment requires that the proponent have ready proof that the conviction required the factfinder to find, or the defendant to admit, an act of dishonesty or false statement. Ordinarily, the statutory elements of the crime will indicate whether it is one of dishonesty or false statement. Where the deceitful nature of the crime is not apparent from the statute and the face of the judgment—as, for example, where the conviction simply records a finding of guilt for a statutory offense that does not reference deceit expressly—a proponent may offer information such as an indictment, a statement of admitted facts, or jury instructions to show that the factfinder had to find, or the defendant had to admit, an act of dishonesty or false statement in order for the witness to have been convicted. Cf. Taylor v. United States, 495 U.S. 575, 602 (1990) (providing that a trial court may look to a charging instrument or jury instructions to ascertain the nature of a prior offense where the statute is insufficiently clear on its face); Shepard v. United States, 125 S.Ct. 1254 (2005) (the inquiry to determine whether a guilty plea to a crime defined by a nongeneric statute necessarily admitted elements of the generic offense was limited to the charging document's terms, the terms of a plea agreement or transcript of colloquy between judge and defendant in which the factual basis for the plea was confirmed by the defendant, or a comparable judicial record). But the amendment does not contemplate a "mini-trial" in which the court plumbs the record of the previous proceeding to determine whether the crime was in the nature of crimen falsi.

The amendment also substitutes the term "character for truthfulness" for the term "credibility" in the first sentence of the Rule. The limitations of Rule 609 are not applicable if a conviction is admitted for a purpose other than to prove the witness's character for untruthfulness. See, e.g., United States v. Lopez, 979 F.2d 1024 (5th Cir. 1992) (Rule 609 was not applicable where the conviction was offered for purposes of contradiction). The use of the term "credibility" in subdivision (d) is retained, however, as that subdivision is intended to govern the use of a juvenile adjudication for any type of impeachment.

Restyled 2011

(b) Limit on Using the Evidence After 10 Years. This subdivision (b) applies if more than 10 years have passed since the witness's conviction or release from confinement for it, whichever is later. Evidence of the conviction is admissible only if:

(1) its probative value, supported by specific facts and circumstances, substantially outweighs its prejudicial effect; and

(2) the proponent gives an adverse party reasonable written notice of the intent to use it so that the party has a fair opportunity to contest its use.

Superseded 2011

(b) Time limit. Evidence of a conviction under this rule is not admissible if a period of more than ten years has elapsed since the date of the conviction or of the release of the witness from the confinement imposed for that conviction, whichever is the later date, unless the court determines, in the interests of justice, that the probative value of the conviction supported by specific facts and circumstances substantially outweighs its prejudicial effect. However, evidence of a conviction more than 10 years old as calculated herein, is not admissible unless the proponent gives to the adverse party sufficient advance written notice of intent to use such evidence to provide the adverse party with a fair opportunity to contest the use of such evidence.

Advisory Committee's Note

Subdivision (b). Few statutes recognize a time limit on impeachment by evidence of conviction. However, practical considerations of fairness and relevancy demand that some boundary be recognized. See Ladd, Credibility Tests—Current Trends, 89 U.Pa.L.Rev. 166, 176-177 (1940). This portion of the rule is derived from the proposal advanced in Recommendation Proposing in Evidence Code, § 788(5), p. 142, Cal.Law Rev.Comm'n (1965), though not adopted. See California Evidence Code § 788.

House Judiciary Committee Report

Rule 609(b) as submitted by the Court was modeled after Section 133(a) of Public Law 91-358, 14 D.C.Code 305(b)(2)(B), enacted in 1970. The Rule provided:

> Evidence of a conviction under this rule is not admissible if a period of more than ten years has elapsed since the date of the release of the witness from confinement imposed for his most recent conviction, or the expiration of the period of his parole, probation, or sentence granted or imposed with respect to his most recent conviction, whichever is the later date.

Under this formulation, a witness' entire past record of criminal convictions could be used for impeachment (provided the conviction met the standard of subdivision (a)), if the witness had been most recently released from confinement, or the period of his parole or probation had expired, within ten years of the conviction.

The Committee amended the Rule to read in the text of the 1971 Advisory Committee version to provide that upon the expiration of ten years from the date of a conviction of a witness, or of his release from confinement for that offense, that conviction may no longer be used for impeachment. The Committee was of the view that after ten years following a person's release from confinement (or from the date of his conviction) the probative value of the conviction with respect to that person's credibility diminished to a point where it should no longer be admissible.

Senate Judiciary Committee Report

Although convictions over ten years old generally do not have much probative value, there may be exceptional circumstances under which the conviction substantially bears on the credibility of the witness. Rather than exclude all convictions over 10 years old, the committee adopted an amendment in the form of a final clause to the section granting the court discretion to admit convictions over 10 years old, but only upon a determination by the court that the probative value of the conviction supported by specific facts and circumstances, substantially outweighs its prejudicial effect.

It is intended that convictions over 10 years old will be admitted very rarely and only in exceptional circumstances. The rules provide that the decision be supported by specific facts and circumstances thus requiring the court to make specific findings on the record as to the particular facts and circumstances it has considered in determining that the probative value of the conviction substantially outweighs its prejudicial impact. It is expected that, in fairness, the court will give the party against whom the conviction is introduced a full and adequate opportunity to contest its admission.

Conference Committee Report

The House bill provides in subsection (b) that evidence of conviction of a crime may not be used for impeachment purposes under subsection (a) if more than ten years have elapsed since the date of the conviction or the date the witness was released from confinement imposed for the conviction, whichever is later. The Senate amendment permits the use of convictions older than ten years, if the court determines, in the interests of justice, that the probative value of the conviction, supported by specific facts and circumstances, substantially outweighs its prejudicial effect.

The Conference adopts the Senate amendment with an amendment requiring notice by a party that he intends to request that the court allow him to use a conviction older than ten years. The Conferees anticipate that a written notice, in order to give the adversary a fair opportunity to contest the use of the evidence, will ordinarily include such information as the date of the conviction, the jurisdiction, and the offense or statute involved. In order to eliminate the possibility that the flexibility of this provision may impair the ability of a party-opponent to prepare for trial, the Conferees intend that the notice provision operate to avoid surprise.

Restyled 2011

(c) Effect of a Pardon, Annulment, or Certificate of Rehabilitation. Evidence of a conviction is not admissible if:

(1) the conviction has been the subject of a pardon, annulment, certificate of rehabilitation, or other equivalent procedure based on a finding that the person has been rehabilitated, and the person has not been convicted of a later crime punishable by death or by imprisonment for more than one year; or

(2) the conviction has been the subject of a pardon, annulment, or other equivalent procedure based on a finding of innocence.

Superseded 2011

(c) Effect of pardon, annulment, or certificate of rehabilitation. Evidence of a conviction is not admissible under this rule if (1) the conviction has been the subject of a pardon, annulment, certificate of rehabilitation, or other equivalent procedure based on a finding of the rehabilitation of the person convicted, and that person has not been convicted of a subsequent crime which was punishable by death or imprisonment in excess of one year, or (2) the conviction has been the subject of a pardon, annulment, or other equivalent procedure based on a finding of innocence.

Advisory Committee's Note

Subdivision (c). A pardon or its equivalent granted solely for the purpose of restoring civil rights lost by virtue of a conviction has no relevance to an inquiry into character. If, however, the pardon or other proceeding is hinged upon a showing of rehabilitation the situation is otherwise. The result under the rule is to render the conviction inadmissible. The alternative of allowing in evidence both the conviction and the rehabilitation has not been adopted for reasons of policy, economy of time, and difficulties of evaluation.

A similar provision is contained in California Evidence Code § 788. Cf. A.L.I. Model Penal Code, Proposed Official Draft § 306.6(3)(e) (1962), and discussion in A.L.I. Proceedings 310 (1961).

Pardons based on innocence have the effect, of course, of nullifying the conviction ab initio.

House Judiciary Committee Report

Rule 609(c) as submitted by the Court provided in part that evidence of a witness' prior conviction is not admissible to attack his credibility if the conviction was the subject of a pardon, annulment, or other equivalent procedure, based on a showing of rehabilitation, and the witness has not been convicted of a subsequent crime. The Committee amended the Rule to provide that the "subsequent crime" must have been "punishable by death or imprisonment in excess of one year", on the ground that a subsequent conviction of an offense not a felony is insufficient to rebut the finding that the witness has been rehabilitated. The Committee also intends that the words "based on a finding of the rehabilitation of the person convicted" apply not only to "certificate of rehabilitation, or other equivalent procedure", but also to "pardon" and "annulment."

Restyled 2011

(d) Juvenile Adjudications. Evidence of a juvenile adjudication is admissible under this rule only if:

(1) it is offered in a criminal case;

(2) the adjudication was of a witness other than the defendant;

(3) an adult's conviction for that offense would be admissible to attack the adult's credibility; and

(4) admitting the evidence is necessary to fairly determine guilt or innocence.

Superseded 2011

(d) Juvenile adjudications. Evidence of juvenile adjudications is generally not admissible under this rule. The court may, however, in a criminal case allow evidence of a juvenile adjudication of a witness other than the accused if conviction of the offense would be admissible to attack the credibility of an adult and the court is satisfied that admission in evidence is necessary for a fair determination of the issue of guilt or innocence.

Advisory Committee's Note

Subdivision (d). The prevailing view has been that a juvenile adjudication is not usable for impeachment. Thomas v. United States, 74 App.D.C. 167, 121 F.2d 905 (1941); Cotton v. United States, 355 F.2d 480 (10th Cir.1966). This conclusion was based upon a variety of circumstances. By virtue of its informality, frequently diminished quantum of required proof, and other departures from accepted standards for criminal trials under the theory of parens patriae, the juvenile adjudication was considered to lack the precision and general probative value of the criminal conviction. While In re Gault, 387 U.S. 1, 87 S.Ct. 1428, 18 L.Ed.2d 527 (1967), no doubt eliminates these characteristics insofar as objectionable, other obstacles remain. Practical problems of administration are raised by the common provisions in juvenile legislation that records be kept confidential and that they be destroyed after a short time. While Gault was skeptical as to the realities of confidentiality of juvenile records, it also saw no constitutional obstacles to improvement. 387 U.S. at 25, 87 S.Ct. 1428. See also Note, Rights and Rehabilitation in the Juvenile Courts, 67 Colum.L.Rev. 281, 289 (1967). In addition, policy considerations much akin to those which dictate exclusion of adult convictions after rehabilitation has been established strongly suggest a rule of excluding juvenile adjudications. Admittedly, however, the rehabilitative process may in a given case be a demonstrated failure, or the strategic importance of a given witness may be so great as to require the overriding of general policy in the interests of particular justice. See Giles v. Maryland, 386 U.S. 66, 87 S.Ct. 793, 17 L.Ed.2d 737 (1967). Wigmore was outspoken in his condemnation of the disallowance of juvenile adjudications to impeach, especially when the witness is the complainant in a case of molesting a minor. 1 Wigmore § 196; 3 Id. §§ 924a, 980. The rule recognizes discretion in the judge to effect an accommodation among these various factors by departing from the general principle of exclusion. In deference to the general pattern and policy of juvenile statutes, however, no discretion is accorded when the witness is the accused in a criminal case.

Restyled 2011

(e) Pendency of an Appeal. A conviction that satisfies this rule is admissible even if an appeal is pending. Evidence of the pendency is also admissible.

Superseded 2011

(e) Pendency of appeal. The pendency of an appeal therefrom does not render evidence of a conviction inadmissible. Evidence of the pendency of an appeal is admissible.

Advisory Committee's Note

Subdivision (e). The presumption of correctness which ought to attend judicial proceedings supports the position that pendency of an appeal does not preclude use of a conviction for impeachment. United States v. Empire Packing Co., 174 F.2d 16 (7th Cir.1949), cert. denied 337 U.S. 959, 69 S.Ct. 1534, 93 L.Ed. 1758; Bloch v. United States, 226 F.2d 185 (9th Cir.1955), cert. denied 350 U.S. 948, 76 S.Ct. 323, 100 L.Ed. 826 and 353 U.S. 959, 77 S.Ct. 868, 1 L.Ed.2d 910; and see Newman v. United States, 331 F.2d 968 (8th Cir.1964). Contra, Campbell v. United States, 85 U.S.App.D.C. 133, 176 F.2d 45 (1949). The pendency of an appeal is, however, a qualifying circumstance properly considerable.

Restyled 2011

Rule 610. Religious Beliefs or Opinions

Evidence of a witness's religious beliefs or opinions is not admissible to attack or support the witness's credibility.

Superseded 2011

Rule 610. Religious Beliefs or Opinions

Evidence of the beliefs or opinions of a witness on matters of religion is not admissible for the purpose of showing that by reason of their nature the witness' credibility is impaired or enhanced.

Advisory Committee's Note

While the rule forecloses inquiry into the religious beliefs or opinions of a witness for the purpose of showing that his character for truthfulness is affected by their nature, an inquiry for the purpose of showing interest or bias because of them is not within the prohibition. Thus disclosure of affiliation with a church which is a party to the litigation would be allowable under the rule. Cf. Tucker v. Reil, 51 Ariz. 357, 77 P.2d 203 (1938). To the same effect, though less specifically worded, is California Evidence Code § 789. See 3 Wigmore § 936.

Restyled 2011

Rule 611. Mode and Order of Examining Witnesses and Presenting Evidence

(a) Control by the Court; Purposes. The court should exercise reasonable control over the mode and order of examining witnesses and presenting evidence so as to:

(1) make those procedures effective for determining the truth;

(2) avoid wasting time; and

(3) protect witnesses from harassment or undue embarrassment.

Superseded 2011

Rule 611. Mode and Order of Interrogation and Presentation

(a) Control by court. The court shall exercise reasonable control over the mode and order of interrogating witnesses and presenting evidence so as to (1) make the interrogation and presentation effective for the ascertainment of the truth, (2) avoid needless consumption of time, and (3) protect witnesses from harassment or undue embarrassment.

Advisory Committee's Note

Subdivision (a). Spelling out detailed rules to govern the mode and order of interrogating witnesses and presenting evidence is neither desirable nor feasible. The ultimate responsibility for the effective working of the adversary system rests with the judge. The rule sets forth the objectives which he should seek to attain.

Item (1) restates in broad terms the power and obligation of the judge as developed under common law principles. It covers such concerns as whether testimony shall be in the form of a free narrative or responses to specific questions, McCormick § 5, the order of calling witnesses and presenting evidence, 6 Wigmore § 1867, the use of demonstrative evidence, McCormick § 179, and the many other questions arising during the course of a trial which can be solved only by the judge's common sense and fairness in view of the particular circumstances.

Item (2) is addressed to avoidance of needless consumption of time, a matter of daily concern in the disposition of cases. A companion piece is found in the discretion vested in the judge to exclude evidence as a waste of time in Rule 403(b).

Item (3) calls for a judgment under the particular circumstances whether interrogation tactics entail harassment or undue embarrassment. Pertinent circumstances include the importance of the testimony, the nature of the inquiry, its relevance to credibility, waste of time, and confusion. McCormick § 42. In Alford v. United States, 282 U.S. 687, 694, 51 S.Ct. 218, 75 L.Ed. 624 (1931), the Court pointed out that, while the trial judge should protect the witness from questions which "go beyond the bounds of proper cross-examination merely to harass, annoy or humiliate," this protection by no means forecloses efforts to discredit the witness. Reference to the transcript of the prosecutor's cross-examination in Berger v. United States, 295 U.S. 78, 55 S.Ct. 629, 79 L.Ed. 1314 (1935), serves to lay at rest any doubts as to the need for judicial control in this area.

The inquiry into specific instances of conduct of a witness allowed under Rule 608(b) is, of course, subject to this rule.

Restyled 2011

(b) Scope of Cross-Examination. Cross-examination should not go beyond the subject matter of the direct examination and matters affecting a witness's credibility. The court may allow inquiry into additional matters as if on direct examination.

Superseded 2011

(b) Scope of cross-examination. Cross-examination should be limited to the subject matter of the direct examination and matters affecting the credibility of the witness. The court may, in the exercise of discretion, permit inquiry into additional matters as if on direct examination.

Advisory Committee's Note

Subdivision (b). The tradition in the federal courts and in numerous state courts has been to limit the scope of cross-examination to matters testified to on direct, plus matters bearing upon the credibility of the witness. Various reasons have been advanced to justify the rule of limited cross-examination. (1) A party vouches for his own witness but only to the extent of matters elicited on direct. Resurrection Gold Mining Co. v. Fortune Gold Mining Co., 129 F. 668, 675 (8th Cir.1904), quoted in Maguire, Weinstein, et al., Cases on Evidence 277, n. 38 (5th ed. 1965). But the concept of vouching is discredited, and Rule 607 rejects it. (2) A party cannot ask his own witness leading questions. This is a problem properly solved in terms of what is necessary for a proper development of the testimony rather than by a mechanistic formula similar to the vouching concept. See discussion under subdivision (c). (3) A practice of limited cross-examination promotes orderly presentation of the case. Finch v. Weiner, 109 Conn. 616, 145 A. 31 (1929). While this latter reason has merit, the matter is essentially one of the order of presentation and not one in which involvement at the appellate level is likely to prove fruitful. See, for example, Moyer v. Aetna Life Ins. Co., 126 F.2d 141 (3rd Cir.1942); Butler v. New York Central R. Co., 253 F.2d 281 (7th Cir.1958); United States v. Johnson, 285 F.2d 35 (9th Cir.1960); Union Automobile Indemnity Ass'n v. Capitol Indemnity Ins. Co., 310 F.2d 318 (7th Cir.1962). In evaluating these considerations, McCormick says:

"The foregoing considerations favoring the wide-open or restrictive rules may well be thought to be fairly evenly balanced. There is another factor, however, which seems to swing the balance overwhelmingly in favor of the wide-open rule. This is the consideration of economy of time and energy. Obviously, the wide-open rule presents little or no opportunity for dispute in its application. The restrictive practice in all its forms, on the other hand, is productive in many court rooms, of continual bickering over the choice of the numerous variations of the 'scope of the direct' criterion, and of their application to particular cross-questions. These controversies are often reventilated on appeal, and reversals for error in their determination are frequent. Observance of these vague and ambiguous restrictions is a matter of constant and hampering concern to the cross-examiner. If these efforts, delays and misprisions were the necessary incidents to the guarding of substantive rights or the fundamentals of fair trial, they might be worth the cost. As the price of the choice of an obviously debatable regulation of the order of evidence, the sacrifice seems misguided. The American Bar Association's Committee for the Improvement of the Law of Evidence for the year 1937-38 said this:

> 'The rule limiting cross-examination to the precise subject of the direct examination is probably the most frequent rule (except the Opinion rule) leading in the trial practice today to refined and technical quibbles which obstruct the progress of the trial, confuse the jury, and give rise to appeal on technical grounds only. Some of the instances in which Supreme Courts have ordered new trials for the mere transgression of this rule about the order of evidence have been astounding.
> 'We recommend that the rule allowing questions upon any part of the issue known to the witness . . . be adopted. . . .'"
> McCormick, § 27, p. 51. See also 5 Moore's Federal Practice ¶ 43.10 (2nd ed. 1964).

The provision of the second sentence, that the judge may in the interests of justice limit inquiry into new matters on cross-examination, is designed for those situations in which the result otherwise would be confusion, complication, or protraction of the case, not as a matter of rule but as demonstrable in the actual development of the particular case.

The rule does not purport to determine the extent to which an accused who elects to testify thereby waives his privilege against self-incrimination. The question is a constitutional one, rather than a mere matter of administering the trial. Under Simmons v. United States, 390 U.S. 377, 88 S.Ct. 967, 19 L.Ed.2d 1247 (1968), no general waiver occurs when the accused testifies on such preliminary matters as the validity of a search and seizure or the admissibility of a confession. Rule 104(d), supra. When he testifies on the merits, however, can he foreclose inquiry into an aspect or element of the crime by avoiding it on direct? The affirmative answer given in Tucker v. United States, 5 F.2d 818 (8th Cir.1925), is inconsistent with the description of the waiver as extending to "all other relevant facts" in Johnson v. United States, 318 U.S. 189, 195, 63 S.Ct. 549, 87 L.Ed. 704 (1943). See also Brown v. United States, 356 U.S. 148, 78 S.Ct. 622, 2 L.Ed.2d 589 (1958). The situation of an accused who desires to testify on some but not all counts of a multiple-count indictment is one to be approached, in the first instance at least, as a problem of severance under Rule 14 of the Federal Rules of Criminal Procedure. Cross v. United States, 118 U.S.App.D.C. 324, 335 F.2d 987 (1964). Cf. United States v. Baker, 262 F.Supp. 657, 686 (D.D.C.1966). In all events, the extent of the waiver of the privilege against self-incrimination ought not to be determined as a by-product of a rule on scope of cross-examination.

House Judiciary Committee Report

As submitted by the Court, Rule 611(b) provided:

> A witness may be cross-examined on any matter relevant to any issue in the case, including credibility. In the interests of justice, the judge may limit cross-examination with respect to matters not testified to on direct examination.

The Committee amended this provision to return to the rule which prevails in the federal courts and thirty-nine State jurisdictions. As amended, the Rule is in the text of the 1969 Advisory Committee draft. It limits cross-examination to credibility and to matters testified to on direct examination, unless the judge permits more, in which event the cross-examiner must proceed as if on direct examination. This traditional rule facilitates orderly presentation by each party at trial. Further, in light of existing discovery procedures, there appears to be no need to abandon the traditional rule.

Senate Judiciary Committee Report

Rule 611(b) as submitted by the Supreme Court permitted a broad scope of cross-examination: "cross-examination on any matter relevant to any issue in the case" unless the judge, in the interests of justice, limited the scope of cross-examination.

The House narrowed the Rule to the more traditional practice of limiting cross-examination to the subject matter of direct examination (and credibility), but with discretion in the judge to permit inquiry into additional matters in situations where that would aid in the development of the evidence or otherwise facilitate the conduct of the trial.

The committee agrees with the House amendment. Although there are good arguments in support of broad cross-examination from perspectives of developing all relevant evidence, we believe the factors of insuring an orderly and predictable development of the evidence weigh in favor of the narrower rule, especially when discretion is given to the trial judge to permit inquiry into additional matters. The committee expressly approves this discretion and believes it will permit sufficient flexibility allowing a broader scope of cross-examination whenever appropriate.

The House amendment providing broader discretionary cross-examination permitted inquiry into additional matters only as if on direct examination. As a general rule, we concur with this limitation, however, we would understand that this limitation would not preclude the utilization of leading questions if the conditions of subsection (c) of this rule were met, bearing in mind the judge's discretion in any case to limit the scope of cross-examination [see McCormick on Evidence, §§ 24-26 (especially 24) (2d ed. 1972)].

Further, the committee has received correspondence from Federal judges commenting on the applicability of this rule to section 1407 of title 28. It is the committee's judgment that this rule as reported by the House is flexible enough to provide sufficiently broad cross-examination in appropriate situations in multidistrict litigation.

Restyled 2011

(c) Leading Questions. Leading questions should not be used on direct examination except as necessary to develop the witness's testimony. Ordinarily, the court should allow leading questions:

(1) on cross-examination; and

(2) when a party calls a hostile witness, an adverse party, or a witness identified with an adverse party.

Superseded 2011

(c) Leading questions. Leading questions should not be used on the direct examination of a witness except as may be necessary to develop the witness' testimony. Ordinarily leading questions should be permitted on cross-examination. When a party calls a hostile witness, an adverse party, or a witness identified with an adverse party, interrogation may be by leading questions.

Advisory Committee's Note

Subdivision (c). The rule continues the traditional view that the suggestive powers of the leading question are as a general proposition undesirable. Within this tradition, however, numerous exceptions have achieved recognition: The witness who is hostile, unwilling, or biased; the child witness or the adult with communication problems; the witness whose recollection is exhausted; and undisputed preliminary matters. 3 Wigmore §§ 774-778. An almost total unwillingness to reverse for infractions has been manifested by appellate courts. See cases cited in 3 Wigmore § 770. The matter clearly falls within the area of control by the judge over the mode and order of interrogation and presentation and accordingly is phrased in words of suggestion rather than command.

The rule also conforms to tradition in making the use of leading questions on cross-examination a matter of right. The purpose of the qualification "ordinarily" is to furnish a basis for denying the use of leading questions when the cross-examination is cross-examination in form only and not in fact, as for example the "cross-examination" of a party by his own counsel after being called by the opponent (savoring more of re-direct) or of an insured defendant who proves to be friendly to the plaintiff.

The final sentence deals with categories of witnesses automatically regarded and treated as hostile. Rule 43(b) of the Federal Rules of Civil Procedure has included only "an adverse party or an officer, director, or managing agent of a public or private corporation or of a partnership or association which is an adverse party." This limitation virtually to persons whose statements would stand as admissions is believed to be an unduly narrow concept of those who may safely be regarded as hostile without further demonstration. See, for example, Maryland Casualty Co. v. Kador, 225 F.2d 120 (5th Cir.1955), and Degelos v. Fidelity and Casualty Co., 313 F.2d 809 (5th Cir.1963), holding despite the language of Rule 43(b) that an insured fell within it, though not a party in an action under the Louisiana direct action statute. The phrase of the rule, "witness identified with" an adverse party, is designed to enlarge the category of persons thus callable.

House Judiciary Committee Report

The third sentence of Rule 611(c) as submitted by the Court provided that:

> In civil cases, a party is entitled to call an adverse party or witness identified with him and interrogate by leading questions.

The Committee amended this Rule to permit leading questions to be used with respect to any hostile witness, not only an adverse party or person identified with such adverse party. The Committee also substituted the word "When" for the phrase "In civil cases" to reflect the possibility that in criminal cases a defendant may be entitled to call witnesses identified with the government, in which event the Committee believed the defendant should be permitted to inquire with leading questions.

Senate Judiciary Committee Report

As submitted by the Supreme Court, the rule provided: "In civil cases, a party is entitled to call an adverse party or witness identified with him and interrogate by leading questions."

The final sentence of subsection (c) was amended by the House for the purpose of clarifying the fact that a "hostile witness"—that is a witness who is hostile in fact—could be subject to interrogation by leading questions. The rule as submitted by the Supreme Court declared certain witnesses hostile as a matter of law and thus subject to interrogation by leading questions without any showing of hostility in fact. These were adverse parties or witnesses identified with adverse parties. However, the wording of the first sentence of subsection (c) while generally prohibiting the use of leading questions on direct examination, also provides "except as may be necessary to develop his testimony." Further, the first paragraph of the Advisory Committee note explaining the subsection makes clear that they intended that leading questions could be asked of a hostile witness or a witness who was unwilling or biased and even though that witness was not associated with an adverse party. Thus, we question whether the House amendment was necessary.

However, concluding that it was not intended to affect the meaning of the first sentence of the subsection and was intended solely to clarify the fact that leading questions are permissible in the interrogation of a witness, who is hostile in fact, the committee accepts that House amendment.

The final sentence of this subsection was also amended by the House to cover criminal as well as civil cases. The committee accepts this amendment, but notes that it may be difficult in criminal cases to determine when a witness is "identified with an adverse party," and thus the rule should be applied with caution.

Restyled 2011

Rule 612. Writing Used to Refresh a Witness's Memory

(a) Scope. This rule gives an adverse party certain options when a witness uses a writing to refresh memory:

(1) while testifying; or

(2) before testifying, if the court decides that justice requires the party to have those options.

(b) Adverse Party's Options; Deleting Unrelated Matter. Unless 18 U.S.C. § 3500 provides otherwise in a criminal case, an adverse party is entitled to have the writing produced at the hearing, to inspect it, to cross-examine the witness about it, and to introduce in evidence any portion that relates to the witness's testimony. If the producing party claims that the writing includes unrelated matter, the court must examine the writing in camera, delete any unrelated portion, and order that the rest be delivered to the adverse party. Any portion deleted over objection must be preserved for the record.

(c) Failure to Produce or Deliver the Writing. If a writing is not produced or is not delivered as ordered, the court may issue any appropriate order. But if the prosecution does not comply in a criminal case, the court must strike the witness's testimony or — if justice so requires — declare a mistrial.

Superseded 2011

Rule 612. Writing Used to Refresh Memory

Except as otherwise provided in criminal proceedings by section 3500 of title 18, United States Code, if a witness uses a writing to refresh memory for the purpose of testifying, either—

(1) while testifying, or

(2) before testifying, if the court in its discretion determines it is necessary in the interests of justice, an adverse party is entitled to have the writing produced at the hearing, to inspect it, to cross-examine the witness thereon, and to introduce in evidence those portions which relate to the testimony of the witness. If it is claimed that the writing contains matters not related to the subject matter of the testimony the court shall examine the writing in camera, excise any portions not so related, and order delivery of the remainder to the party entitled thereto. Any portion withheld over objections shall be preserved and made available to the appellate court in the event of an appeal. If a writing is not produced or delivered pursuant to order under this rule, the court shall make any order justice requires, except that in criminal cases when the prosecution elects not to comply, the order shall be one striking the testimony or, if the court in its discretion determines that the interests of justice so require, declaring a mistrial.

Advisory Committee's Note

The treatment of writings used to refresh recollection while on the stand is in accord with settled doctrine. McCormick § 9, p. 15. The bulk of the case law has, however, denied the existence of any right to access by the opponent when the writing is used prior to taking the stand, though the judge may have discretion in the matter. Goldman v. United States, 316 U.S. 129, 62 S.Ct. 993, 86 L.Ed. 1322 (1942); Needelman v. United States, 261 F.2d 802 (5th Cir.1958), cert. dismissed 362 U.S. 600, 80 S.Ct. 960, 4 L.Ed.2d 980, rehearing denied 363 U.S. 858, 80 S.Ct. 1606, 4 L.Ed.2d 1739, Annot., 82 A.L.R.2d 473, 562 and 7 A.L.R.3d 181, 247. An increasing group of cases has repudiated the distinction. People v. Scott, 29 Ill.2d 97, 193 N.E.2d 814 (1963); State v. Mucci, 25 N.J. 423, 136 A.2d 761 (1957); State v. Hunt, 25 N.J. 514, 138 A.2d 1 (1958); State v. Deslovers, 40 R.I. 89, 100 A. 64 (1917), and this position is believed to be correct. As Wigmore put it, "the risk of imposition and the need of safeguard is just as great" in both situations. 3 Wigmore § 762, p. 111. To the same effect is McCormick, § 9, p. 17.

The purpose of the phrase "for the purpose of testifying" is to safeguard against using the rule as a pretext for wholesale exploration of an opposing party's files and to insure that access is limited only to those writings which may fairly be said in fact to have an impact upon the testimony of the witness.

The purpose of the rule is the same as that of the Jencks statute, 18 U.S.C. § 3500: to promote the search of credibility and memory. The same sensitivity to disclosure of government files may be involved; hence the rule is expressly made subject to the statute, subdivision (a) of which provides: "In any criminal prosecution brought by the United States, no statement or report in the possession of the United States which was made by a Government witness or prospective Government witness (other than the defendant) shall be the subject of subpena, discovery, or inspection until said witness has testified on direct examination in the trial of the case." Items falling within the purview of the statute are producible only as provided by its terms, Palermo v. United States, 360 U.S. 343, 351 (1959), and disclosure under the rule is limited similarly by the statutory conditions. With this limitation in mind, some differences of application may be noted. The Jencks statute applies only to statements of witnesses; the rule is not so limited. The statute applies only to criminal cases; the rule applies to all cases. The statute applies only to government witnesses; the rule applies to all witnesses. The statute contains no requirement that the statement be consulted for purposes of refreshment before or while testifying; the rule so requires. Since many writings would qualify under either statute or rule, a substantial overlap exists, but the identity of procedures makes this of no importance.

The consequences of nonproduction by the government in a criminal case are those of the Jencks statute, striking the testimony or in exceptional cases a mistrial. 18 U.S.C. § 3500(d). In other cases these alternatives are unduly limited, and such possibilities as contempt, dismissal, finding issues against the offender, and the like are available. See Rule 16(g) of the Federal Rules of Criminal Procedure and Rule 37(b) of the Federal Rules of Civil Procedure for appropriate sanctions.

House Judiciary Committee Report

As submitted to Congress, Rule 612 provided that except as set forth in 18 U.S.C. 3500, if a witness uses a writing to refresh his memory for the purpose of testifying, "either before or while testifying," an adverse party is entitled to have the writing produced at the hearing, to inspect it, to cross-examine the witness on it, and to introduce in evidence those portions relating to the witness' testimony. The Committee amended the Rule so as still to require the production of writings used by a witness while testifying, but to render the production of writings used by a witness to refresh his memory before testifying discretionary with the court in the interests of justice, as is the case under existing federal law. See Goldman v. United States, 316 U.S. 129 (1942). The Committee considered that permitting an adverse party to require the production of writings used before testifying could result in fishing expeditions among a multitude of papers which a witness may have used in preparing for trial.

The Committee intends that nothing in the Rule be construed as barring the assertion of a privilege with respect to writings used by a witness to refresh his memory.

Restyled 2011

Rule 613. Witness's Prior Statement

(a) Showing or Disclosing the Statement During Examining. When examining a witness about the witness's prior statement, a party need not show it or disclose its contents to the witness. But the party must, on request, show it or disclose its contents to an adverse party's attorney.

Superseded 2011

Rule 613. Prior Statements of Witnesses

(a) Examining witness concerning prior statement. In examining a witness concerning a prior statement made by the witness, whether written or not, the statement need not be shown nor its contents disclosed to the witness at that time, but on request the same shall be shown or disclosed to opposing counsel.

Advisory Committee's Note

Subdivision (a). The Queen's Case, 2 Br. & B. 284, 129 Eng.Rep. 976 (1820), laid down the requirement that a cross-examiner, prior to questioning the witness about his own prior statement in writing, must first show it to the witness. Abolished by statute in the country of its origin, the requirement nevertheless gained currency in the United States. The rule abolishes this useless impediment, to cross-examination. Ladd, Some Observations on Credibility: Impeachment of Witnesses, 52 Cornell L.Q. 239, 246-247 (1967); McCormick § 28; 4 Wigmore §§ 1259-1260. Both oral and written statements are included.

The provision for disclosure to counsel is designed to protect against unwarranted insinuations that a statement has been made when the fact is to the contrary.

The rule does not defeat the application of Rule 1002 relating to production of the original when the contents of a writing are sought to be proved. Nor does it defeat the application of Rule 26(b)(3) of the Rules of Civil Procedure, as revised, entitling a person on request to a copy of his own statement, though the operation of the latter may be suspended temporarily.

Restyled 2011

(b) Extrinsic Evidence of a Prior Inconsistent Statement. Extrinsic evidence of a witness's prior inconsistent statement is admissible only if the witness is given an opportunity to explain or deny the statement and an adverse party is given an opportunity to examine the witness about it, or if justice so requires. This subdivision (b) does not apply to an opposing party's statement under Rule 801(d)(2).

Superseded 2011

(b) Extrinsic evidence of prior inconsistent statement of witness. Extrinsic evidence of a prior inconsistent statement by a witness is not admissible unless the witness is afforded an opportunity to explain or deny the same and the opposite party is afforded an opportunity to interrogate the witness thereon, or the interests of justice otherwise require. This provision does not apply to admissions of a party-opponent as defined in rule 801(d)(2).

Advisory Committee's Note

Subdivision (b). The familiar foundation requirement that an impeaching statement first be shown to the witness before it can be proved by extrinsic evidence is preserved but with some modifications. See Ladd, Some Observations on Credibility: Impeachment of Witnesses, 52 Cornell L.Q. 239, 247 (1967). The traditional insistence that the attendance of the witness be directed to the statement on cross-examination is relaxed in favor of simply providing the witness an opportunity to explain and the opposite party an opportunity to examine on the statement, with no specification of any particular time or sequence. Under this procedure, several collusive witnesses can be examined before disclosure of a joint prior inconsistent statement. See Comment to California Evidence Code § 770. Also, dangers of oversight are reduced. See McCormick § 37, p. 68.

In order to allow for such eventualities as the witness becoming unavailable by the time the statement is discovered, a measure of discretion is conferred upon the judge. Similar provisions are found in California Evidence Code § 770 and New Jersey Evidence Rule 22(b).

Under principles of expression [*sic*] unius the rule does not apply to impeachment by evidence of prior inconsistent conduct. The use of inconsistent statements to impeach a hearsay declaration is treated in Rule 806.

Restyled 2011

Rule 614. Court's Calling or Examining a Witness

(a) Calling. The court may call a witness on its own or at a party's request. Each party is entitled to cross-examine the witness.

Superseded 2011

Rule 614. Calling and Interrogation of Witnesses by Court

(a) Calling by court. The court may, on its own motion or at the suggestion of a party, call witnesses, and all parties are entitled to cross-examine witnesses thus called.

Advisory Committee's Note

Subdivision (a). While exercised more frequently in criminal than in civil cases, the authority of the judge to call witnesses is well established. McCormick § 8, p. 14; Maguire, Weinstein, et al., Cases on Evidence 303-304 (5th ed. 1965); 9 Wigmore § 2484. One reason for the practice, the old rule against impeaching one's own witness, no longer exists by virtue of Rule 607, supra. Other reasons remain, however, to justify the continuation of the practice of calling court's witnesses. The right to cross-examine, with all it implies, is assured. The tendency of juries to associate a witness with the party calling him, regardless of technical aspects of vouching, is avoided. And the judge is not imprisoned within the case as made by the parties.

Restyled 2011

(b) Examining. The court may examine a witness regardless of who calls the witness.

Superseded 2011

(b) Interrogation by court. The court may interrogate witnesses, whether called by itself or by a party.

Advisory Committee's Note

Subdivision (b). The authority of the judge to question witnesses is also well established. McCormick § 8, pp. 12-13; Maguire, Weinstein, et al., Cases on Evidence 737-739 (5th ed. 1965); 3 Wigmore § 784. The authority is, of course, abused when the judge abandons his proper role and assumes that of advocate, but the manner in which interrogation should be conducted and the proper extent of its exercise are not susceptible of formulation in a rule. The omission in no sense precludes courts of review from continuing to reverse for abuse.

Restyled 2011

(c) Objections. A party may object to the court's calling or examining a witness either at that time or at the next opportunity when the jury is not present.

Superseded 2011

(c) Objections. Objections to the calling of witnesses by the court or to interrogation by it may be made at the time or at the next available opportunity when the jury is not present.

Advisory Committee's Note

Subdivision (c). The provision relating to objections is designed to relieve counsel of the embarrassment attendant upon objecting to questions by the judge in the presence of the jury, while at the same time assuring that objections are made in apt time to afford the opportunity to take possible corrective measures. Compare the "automatic" objection feature of Rule 605 when the judge is called as a witness.

Restyled 2011

Rule 615. Excluding Witnesses

At a party's request, the court must order witnesses excluded so that they cannot hear other witnesses' testimony. Or the court may do so on its own. But this rule does not authorize excluding:

(a) a party who is a natural person;

(b) an officer or employee of a party that is not a natural person, after being designated as the party's representative by its attorney;

(c) a person whose presence a party shows to be essential to presenting the party's claim or defense; or

(d) a person authorized by statute to be present.

Superseded 2011

Rule 615. Exclusion of Witnesses

At the request of a party the court shall order witnesses excluded so that they cannot hear the testimony of other witnesses, and it may make the order of its own motion. This rule does not authorize exclusion of (1) a party who is a natural person, or (2) an officer or employee of a party which is not a natural person designated as its representative by its attorney, (3) a person whose presence is shown by a party to be essential to the presentation of the party's cause, or (4) a person authorized by statute to be present.

Case Note

While Rule 615 is mandatory within its narrow range, trial courts have discretion to impose other restrictions needed to manage trials in the interests of justice, such as sequestration of witnesses before, during, and after their testimony, ordering witnesses not to discuss the case, and requiring the parties to present witnesses in a certain order. United States v. Sepulveda, 15 F.3d 1161, 1175-1176 (1st Cir. 1993).

Advisory Committee's Note

The efficacy of excluding or sequestering witnesses has long been recognized as a means of discouraging and exposing fabrication, inaccuracy, and collusion. 6 Wigmore §§ 1837-1838. The authority of the judge is admitted, the only question being whether the matter is committed to his discretion or one of right. The rule takes the latter position. No time is specified for making the request.

Several categories of persons are excepted. (1) Exclusion of persons who are parties would raise serious problems of confrontation and due process. Under accepted practice they are not subject to exclusion. 6 Wigmore § 1841. (2) As the equivalent of the right of a natural-person party to be present, a party which is not a natural person is entitled to have a representative present. Most of the cases have involved allowing a police officer who has been in charge of an investigation to remain in court despite the fact that he will be a witness. United States v. Infanzon, 235 F.2d 318, (2d Cir.1956); Portomene v. United States, 221 F.2d 582 (5th Cir.1955); Powell v. United States, 208 F.2d 618 (6th Cir.1953); Jones v. United States, 252 F.Supp. 781 (W.D.Okl.1966). Designation of the representative by the attorney rather than by the client may at first glance appear to be an inversion of the attorney-client relationship, but it may be assumed that the attorney will follow the wishes of the client, and the solution is simple and workable. See California Evidence Code § 777. (3) The category contemplates such persons as an agent who handled the transaction being litigated or an expert needed to advise counsel in the management of the litigation. See 6 Wigmore § 1841, n. 4.

Senate Judiciary Committee Report

Many district courts permit government counsel to have an investigative agent at counsel table throughout the trial although the agent is or may be a witness. The practice is permitted as an exception to the rule of exclusion and compares with the situation defense counsel finds himself in—he always has the client with him to consult during the trial. The investigative agent's presence may be extremely important to government counsel, especially when the case is complex or involves some specialized subject matter. The agent, too, having lived with the case for a long time, may be able to assist in meeting trial surprises where the best-prepared counsel would otherwise have difficulty. Yet, it would not seem the Government could often meet the burden under rule 615 of showing that the agent's presence is essential. Furthermore, it could be dangerous to use the agent as a witness as early in the case as possible, so that he might then help counsel as a nonwitness, since the agent's testimony could be needed in rebuttal. Using another, nonwitness agent from the same investigative agency would not generally meet government counsel's needs.

This problem is solved if it is clear that investigative agents are within the group specified under the second exception made in the rule, for "an officer or employee of a party which is not a natural person designated as its representative by its attorney." It is our understanding that this was the intention of the House committee. It is certainly this committee's construction of the rule.

Restyled 2011

ARTICLE VII. OPINIONS AND EXPERT TESTIMONY

Rule 701. Opinion Testimony by Lay Witnesses

If a witness is not testifying as an expert, testimony in the form of an opinion is limited to one that is:

(a) rationally based on the witness's perception;

(b) helpful to clearly understanding the witness's testimony or to determining a fact in issue; and

(c) not based on scientific, technical, or other specialized knowledge within the scope of Rule 702.

Committee Note to 2011 Restyled Rule

The Committee deleted all reference to an "inference" on the grounds that the deletion made the Rule flow better and easier to read, and because any "inference" is covered by the broader term "opinion." Courts have not made substantive decisions on the basis of any distinction between an opinion and an inference. No change in current practice is intended.

Superseded 2011

ARTICLE VII. OPINIONS AND EXPERT TESTIMONY

Rule 701. Opinion Testimony by Lay Witnesses

If the witness is not testifying as an expert, the witness' testimony in the form of opinions or inferences is limited to those opinions or inferences which are (a) rationally based on the perception of the witness, (b) helpful to a clear understanding of the witness' testimony or the determination of a fact in issue, and (c) not based on scientific, technical, or other specialized knowledge within the scope of Rule 702. [*Clause (c) added 2000.*]

Advisory Committee's Note

The rule retains the traditional objective of putting the trier of fact in possession of an accurate reproduction of the event.

Limitation (a) is the familiar requirement of first-hand knowledge or observation.

Limitation (b) is phrased in terms of requiring testimony to be helpful in resolving issues. Witnesses often find difficulty in expressing themselves in language which is not that of an opinion or conclusion. While the courts have made concessions in certain recurring situations, necessity as a standard for permitting opinions and conclusions has proved too elusive and too unadaptable to particular situations for purposes of satisfactory judicial administration. McCormick § 11. Moreover, the practical impossibility of determining by rule what is a "fact," demonstrated by a century of litigation of the question of what is a fact for purposes of pleading under the Field Code, extends into evidence also. 7 Wigmore § 1919. The rule assumes that the natural characteristics of the adversary system will generally lead to an acceptable result, since the detailed account carries more conviction than the broad assertion, and a lawyer can be expected to display his witness to the best advantage. If he fails to do so, cross-examination and argument will point up the weakness. See Ladd, Expert Testimony, 5 Vand.L.Rev. 414, 415-417 (1952). If, despite these considerations, attempts are made to introduce meaningless assertions which amount to little more than choosing up sides, exclusion for lack of helpfulness is called for by the rule.

The language of the rule is substantially that of Uniform Rule 56(1). Similar provisions are California Evidence Code § 800; Kansas Code of Civil Procedure § 60-456(a); New Jersey Evidence Rule 56(1).

Advisory Committee's Note to 2000 Amendment

Rule 701 has been amended to eliminate the risk that the reliability requirements set forth in Rule 702 will be evaded through the simple expedient of proffering an expert in lay witness clothing. Under the amendment, a witness' testimony must be scrutinized under the rules regulating expert opinion to the extent that the witness is providing testimony based on scientific, technical, or other specialized knowledge within the scope of Rule 702. See generally Asplundh Mfg. Div. v. Benton Harbor Eng'g, 57 F.3d 1190 (3d Cir. 1995). By channeling testimony that is actually expert testimony to Rule 702, the amendment also ensures that a party will not evade the expert witness disclosure requirements set forth in Fed.R.Civ.P. 26 and Fed.R.Crim.P. 16 by simply calling an expert witness in the guise of a layperson. See Joseph. Emerging Expert Issues Under the 1993 Disclosure Amendments to the Federal Rules of Civil Procedure, 164 F.R.D. 97, 108 (1996) (noting that "there is no good reason to allow what is essentially surprise expert testimony" and that "the Court should be vigilant to preclude manipulative conduct designed to thwart the expert disclosure and discovery process"). See also United States v. Figueroa-Lopez, 125 F.3d 1241, 1246 (9th Cir. 1997) (law enforcement agents testifying that the defendant's conduct was consistent with that of a drug trafficker could not testify as lay witnesses: to permit such testimony under Rule 701 "subverts the requirements of Federal Rule of Criminal Procedure 16(a)(1)(E)").

The amendment does not distinguish between expert and lay witnesses, but rather between expert and lay testimony. Certainly it is possible for the same witness to provide both lay and expert testimony in a single case. See, e.g, United States v. Figueroa-Lopez, 125 F.3d 1241, 1246 (9th Cir. 1997) (law enforcement agents could testify that the defendant was acting suspiciously, without being qualified as experts; however, the rules on experts were applicable where the agents testified on the basis of extensive experience that the defendant was using code words to refer to drug quantities and prices). The amendment makes clear that any part of a witness' testimony that is based upon scientific, technical, or other specialized knowledge within the scope of Rule 702 is governed by the standards of Rule 702 and the corresponding disclosure requirements of the Civil and Criminal Rules.

The amendment is not intended to affect the "prototypical example[s] of the type of evidence contemplated by the adoption of Rule 701 relat[ing] to the appearance of persons or things, identity, the manner of conduct, competency of a person, degrees of light or darkness, sound, size, weight, distance, and an endless number of items that cannot be described factually in words apart from inferences." Asplundh Mfg. Div. v. Benton Harbor Eng'g, 57 F.3d 1190, 1196 (3d Cir. 1995).

For example, most courts have permitted the owner or officer of a business to testify to the value or projected profits of the business. without the necessity of qualifying the witness as an accountant, appraiser, or similar expert. See, e.g., Lightning Lube, Inc. v. Witco Corp. 4 F.3d 1153 (3d Cir. 1993) (no abuse of discretion in permitting the plaintiff's owner to give lay opinion testimony as to damages, as it was based on his knowledge and participation in the day-to-day affairs of the business). Such opinion testimony is admitted not because of experience, training or specialized knowledge within the realm of an expert, but because of the particularized knowledge that the witness has by virtue of his or her position in the business. The amendment does not purport to change this analysis. Similarly, courts have permitted lay witnesses to testify that a substance appeared to be a narcotic, so long as a foundation of familiarity with the substance is established. See, e.g., United States v. Westbrook, 896 F.2d 330 (8th Cir. 1990) (two lay witnesses who were heavy amphetamine users were properly permitted to testify that a substance was amphetamine; but it was error to permit another witness to make such an identification where she had no experience with amphetamines). Such testimony is not based on specialized knowledge within the scope of Rule 702, but rather is based upon a layperson's personal knowledge. If, however, that witness were to describe how a narcotic was manufactured, or to describe the intricate workings of a narcotic distribution network, then the witness would have to qualify as an expert under Rule 702. United States v. Figueroa-Lopez, supra.

The amendment incorporates the distinctions set forth in State v. Brown. 836 S.W.2d 530, 549 (1992), a case involving former Tennessee Rule of Evidence 701, a rule that precluded lay witness testimony based on "special knowledge." In Brown, the court declared that the distinction between lay and expert witness testimony is that lay testimony "results from a process of reasoning familiar in everyday life," while expert testimony "results from a process of reasoning which can be mastered only by specialists in the field." The court in Brown noted that a lay witness with experience could testify that a substance appeared to be blood, but that a witness would have to qualify as an expert before he could testify that bruising around the eyes is indicative of skull trauma. That is the kind of distinction made by the amendment to this Rule.

Restyled 2011

Rule 702. Testimony by Expert Witnesses

A witness who is qualified as an expert by knowledge, skill, experience, training, or education may testify in the form of an opinion or otherwise if:

(a) the expert's scientific, technical, or other specialized knowledge will help the trier of fact to understand the evidence or to determine a fact in issue;
(b) the testimony is based on sufficient facts or data;
(c) the testimony is the product of reliable principles and methods; and
(d) the expert has reliably applied the principles and methods to the facts of the case.

Superseded 2011

Rule 702. Testimony by Experts

If scientific, technical, or other specialized knowledge will assist the trier of fact to understand the evidence or to determine a fact in issue, a witness qualified as an expert by knowledge, skill, experience, training, or education, may testify thereto in the form of an opinion or otherwise, if (1) the testimony is based upon sufficient facts or data, (2) the testimony is the product of reliable principles and methods, and (3) the witness has applied the principles and methods reliably to the facts of the case. [*Language after "or otherwise" added 2000.*]

Case Note

Admissibility of evidence to establish fair market value of property is governed by "generally applicable rules of evidence," citing Rules 401-403, 701-705. United States v. 50 Acres of Land, 469 U.S. 24, 36 n.24,105 S.Ct. 451, 458, 83 L.Ed.2d 376 (1984).

Advisory Committee's Note

An intelligent evaluation of facts is often difficult or impossible without the application of some scientific, technical, or other specialized knowledge. The most common source of this knowledge is the expert witness, although there are other techniques for supplying it.

Most of the literature assumes that experts testify only in the form of opinions. The assumption is logically unfounded. The rule accordingly recognizes that an expert on the stand may give a dissertation or exposition of scientific or other principles relevant to the case, leaving the trier of fact to apply them to the facts. Since much of the criticism of expert testimony has centered upon the hypothetical question, it seems wise to recognize that opinions are not indispensable and to encourage the use of expert testimony in non-opinion form when counsel believes the trier can itself draw the requisite inference. The use of opinions is not abolished by the rule, however. It will continue to be permissible for the experts to take the further step of suggesting the inference which should be drawn from applying the specialized knowledge to the facts. See Rules 703 to 705.

Whether the situation is a proper one for the use of expert testimony is to be determined on the basis of assisting the trier. "There is no more certain test for determining when experts may be used than the common sense inquiry whether the untrained layman would be qualified to determine intelligently and to the best possible degree the particular issue without enlightenment from those having a specialized understanding of the subject involved in the dispute." Ladd, Expert Testimony, 5 Vand.L.Rev. 414, 418 (1952). When opinions are excluded, it is because they are unhelpful and therefore superfluous and a waste of time. 7 Wigmore § 1918.

The rule is broadly phrased. The fields of knowledge which may be drawn upon are not limited merely to the "scientific" and "technical" but extend to all "specialized" knowledge. Similarly, the expert is viewed, not in a narrow sense, but as a person qualified by "knowledge, skill, experience, training or education." Thus within the scope of the rule are not only experts in the strictest sense of the word, e.g., physicians, physicists, and architects, but also the large group sometimes called "skilled" witnesses, such as bankers or landowners testifying to land values.

Advisory Committee's Note to 2000 Amendment

Rule 702 has been amended in response to Daubert v. Merrell Dow Pharmaceuticals, Inc., 509 U.S. 579 (1993), and to the many cases applying Daubert, including Kumho Tire Co. v. Carmichael, 119 S.Ct. 1167 (1999). In Daubert the Court charged trial judges with the responsibility of acting as gatekeepers to exclude unreliable expert testimony, and the Court in Kumho clarified that this gatekeeper function applies to all expert testimony, not just testimony based in science. See also Kumho, 119 S.Ct. at 1178 (citing the Committee Note to the proposed amendment to Rule 702, which had been released for public comment before the date of the Kumho decision). The amendment affirms the trial court's role as gatekeeper and provides some general standards that the trial court must use to assess the reliability and helpfulness of proffered expert testimony. Consistently with Kumho, the Rule as amended provides that all types of expert testimony present questions of admissibility for the trial court in deciding whether the evidence is reliable and helpful. Consequently, the admissibility of all expert testimony is governed by the principles of Rule 104(a). Under that Rule, the proponent has the burden of establishing that the pertinent admissibility requirements are met by a preponderance of the evidence. See Bourjaily v. United States, 483 U.S. 171 (1987).

Daubert set forth a non-exclusive checklist for trial courts to use in assessing the reliability of scientific expert testimony. The specific factors explicated by the Daubert Court are (1) whether the expert's technique or theory can be or has been tested—that is, whether the expert's theory can be challenged in some objective sense, or whether it is instead simply a subjective, conclusory approach that cannot reasonably be assessed for reliability; (2) whether the technique or theory has been subject to peer review and publication; (3) the known or potential rate of error of the technique or theory when applied; (4) the existence and maintenance of standards and controls; and (5) whether the technique or theory has been generally accepted in the scientific community. The Court in Kumho held that these factors might also be applicable in assessing the reliability of non-scientific expert testimony, depending upon "the particular circumstances of the particular case at issue." 119 S.Ct. at 1175.

No attempt has been made to "codify" these specific factors. Daubert itself emphasized that the factors were neither exclusive nor dispositive. Other cases have recognized that not all of the specific Daubert factors can apply to every type of expert testimony. In addition to Kumho, 119 S.Ct. at 1175, see Tyus v. Urban Search Management. 102 F.3d 256 (7th Cir. 1996) (noting that the factors mentioned by the Court in Daubert do not neatly apply to expert testimony from a sociologist). See also Kannankeril v. Terminix Int'l. Inc., 128 F.3d 802, 809 (3d Cir. 1997) (holding that lack of peer review or publication was not dispositive where the expert's opinion was supported by "widely accepted scientific knowledge"). The standards set forth in the amendment are broad enough to require consideration of any or all of the specific Daubert factors where appropriate.

Courts both before and after Daubert have found other factors relevant in determining whether expert testimony is sufficiently reliable to be considered by the trier of fact. These factors include:

(1) Whether experts are "proposing to testify about matters growing naturally and directly out of research they have conducted independent of the litigation, or whether they have developed their opinions expressly for purposes of testifying." Daubert v. Merrell Dow Pharmaceuticals, Inc., 43 F.3d 1311. 1317 (9th Cir. 1995).

(2) Whether the expert has unjustifiably extrapolated from an accepted premise to an unfounded conclusion. See General Elec. Co. v. Joiner, 522 U.S. 136, 146 (1997) (noting that in some cases a trial court "may conclude that there is simply too great an analytical gap between the data and the opinion proffered").

(3) Whether the expert has adequately accounted for obvious alternative explanations. See Claar v. Burlington N.R.R., 29 F.3d 499 (9th Cir. 1994) (testimony excluded where the expert failed to consider other obvious causes for the plaintiff's condition). Compare Ambrosini v. Labarraque, 101 F.3d 129 (D.C. Cir. 1996) (the possibility of some uneliminated causes presents a question of weight, so long as the most obvious causes have been considered and reasonably ruled out by the expert).

(4) Whether the expert "is being as careful as he would be in his regular professional work outside his paid litigation consulting." Sheehan v. Daily Racing Form, Inc., 104 F.3d 940, 942 (7th Cir. 1997). See Kumho Tire Co. v. Carmichael, 119 S.Ct. 1167, 1176

(1999) (Daubert requires the trial court to assure itself that the expert "employs in the courtroom the same level of intellectual rigor that characterizes the practice of an expert in the relevant field").

(5) Whether the field of expertise claimed by the expert is known to reach reliable results for the type of opinion the expert would give. See Kumho Tire Co. v. Carmichael, 119 S.Ct.1167, 1175 (1999) (Daubert's general acceptance factor does not "help show that an expert's testimony is reliable where the discipline itself lacks reliability, as for example, do theories grounded in any so-called generally accepted principles of astrology or necromancy."), Moore v. Ashland Chemical, Inc., 151 F.3d 269 (5th Cir. 1998) (en banc) (clinical doctor was properly precluded from testifying to the toxicological cause of the plaintiff's respiratory problem, where the opinion was not sufficiently grounded in scientific methodology); Sterling v. Velsicol Chem. Corp., 855 F.2d 1188 (6th Cir. 1988) (rejecting testimony based on "clinical ecology" as unfounded and unreliable).

All of these factors remain relevant to the determination of the reliability of expert testimony under the Rule as amended. Other factors may also be relevant. See Kumho, 119 S.Ct. 1167, 1176 ("[W]e conclude that the trial judge must have considerable leeway in deciding in a particular case how to go about determining whether particular expert testimony is reliable."). Yet no single factor is necessarily dispositive of the reliability of a particular expert's testimony. See, e.g., Heller v. Shaw Industries, Inc., 167 F.3d 146, 155 (3d Cir. 1999) ("not only must each stage of the expert's testimony be reliable, but each stage must be evaluated practically and flexibly without bright-line exclusionary (or inclusionary) rules."); Daubert v. Merrell Dow Pharmaceuticals, Inc., 43 F.3d 1311, 1317, n.5 (9th Cir. 1995) (noting that some expert disciplines "have the courtroom as a principal theatre of operations" and as to these disciplines "the fact that the expert has developed an expertise principally for purposes of litigation will obviously not be a substantial consideration.").

A review of the case law after Daubert shows that the rejection of expert testimony is the exception rather than the rule. Daubert did not work a "sea change over federal evidence law," and "the trial court's role as gatekeeper is not intended to serve as a replacement for the adversary system." United States v. 14.38 Acres of Land Situated in Leflore County, Mississippi, 80 F.3d 1074, 1078 (5th Cir. 1996). As the Court in Daubert stated: "Vigorous cross-examination, presentation of contrary evidence, and careful instruction on the burden of proof are the traditional and appropriate means of attacking shaky but admissible evidence." 509 U.S. at 595. Likewise, this amendment is not intended to provide an excuse for an automatic challenge to the testimony of every expert. See Kumho Tire Co. v. Carmichael, 119 S.Ct.1167, 1176 (1999) (noting that the trial judge has the discretion "both to avoid unnecessary 'reliability' proceedings in ordinary cases where the reliability of an expert's methods is properly taken for granted, and to require appropriate proceedings in the less usual or more complex cases where cause for questioning the expert's reliability arises.").

When a trial court, applying this amendment, rules that an expert's testimony is reliable, this does not necessarily mean that contradictory expert testimony is unreliable. The amendment is broad enough to permit testimony that is the product of competing principles or methods in the same field of expertise. See, e.g., Heller v. Shaw Industries, Inc., 167 F.3d 146, 160 (3d Cir. 1999) (expert testimony cannot be excluded simply because the expert uses one test rather than another, when both tests are accepted in the field and both reach reliable results). As the court stated in In re Paoli R.R. Yard PCB Litigation, 35 F.3d 717, 744 (3d Cir. 1994), proponents "do not have to demonstrate to the judge by a preponderance of the evidence that the assessments of their experts are correct, they only have to demonstrate by a preponderance of evidence that their opinions are reliable . . . . The evidentiary requirement of reliability is lower than the merits standard of correctness." See also Daubert v. Merrell Dow Pharmaceuticals, Inc., 43 F.3d 1311, 1318 (9th Cir. 1995) (scientific experts might be permitted to testify if they could show that the methods they used were also employed by "a recognized minority of scientists in their field."); Ruiz-Troche v. Pepsi Cola, 161 F.3d 77, 85 (1st Cir. 1998) ("Daubert neither requires nor empowers trial courts to determine which of several competing scientific theories has the best provenance.").

The Court in Daubert declared that the "focus, of course, must be solely on principles and methodology, not on the conclusions they generate." 509 U.S. at 595. Yet as the Court later recognized, "conclusions and methodology are not entirely distinct from one another." General Elec. Co. v. Joiner, 522 U.S. 136, 146 (1997). Under the amendment, as under Daubert, when an expert purports to apply principles and methods in accordance with professional standards, and yet reaches a conclusion that other experts in the field would not reach, the trial court may fairly suspect that the principles and methods have not been faithfully applied. See Lust v. Merrell Dow Pharmaceuticals, Inc., 89 F.3d 594, 598 (9th Cir. 1996). The amendment specifically provides that the trial court must scrutinize not only the principles and methods used by the expert, but also whether those principles and methods have been properly applied to the facts of the case. As the court noted in In re Paoli R.R. Yard PCB Litig., 35 F.3d 717, 745 (3d Cir. 1994), "any step that renders the analysis unreliable . . . renders the expert's testimony inadmissible. This is true whether the step completely changes a reliable methodology or merely misapplies that methodology."

If the expert purports to apply principles and methods to the facts of the case, it is important that this application be conducted reliably. Yet it might also be important in some cases for an expert to educate the fact finder about general principles, without ever attempting to apply these principles to the specific facts of the case. For example, experts might instruct the fact finder on the principles of thermodynamics, or blood clotting, or on how financial markets respond to corporate reports, without ever knowing about or trying to tie their testimony into the facts of the case. The amendment does not alter the venerable practice of using expert testimony to educate the fact finder on general principles. For this kind of generalized testimony, Rule 702 simply requires that: (1) the expert be qualified; (2) the testimony address a subject matter on which the fact finder can be assisted by an expert; (3) the testimony be reliable; and (4) the testimony "fit" the facts of the case.

As stated earlier, the amendment does not distinguish between scientific and other forms of expert testimony. The trial court's gatekeeping function applies to testimony by any expert. See Kumho Tire Co. v. Carmichael, 119 S.Ct. 1167, 1171 (1999) ("We conclude that Daubert's general holding-setting forth the trial judge's general 'gatekeeping' obligation-applies not only to testimony based on 'scientific' knowledge, but also to testimony based on 'technical' and 'other specialized' knowledge."). While the relevant factors for determining reliability will vary from expertise to expertise, the amendment rejects the premise that an expert's testimony should be treated more permissively simply because it is outside the realm of science. An opinion from an expert who is not a scientist should receive the same degree of scrutiny for reliability as an opinion from an expert who purports to be a scientist. See Watkins v. Telsmith, Inc., 121 F.3d 984, 991 (5th Cir. 1997) ("[I]t seems exactly backwards that experts who purport to rely on general engineering principles and practical experience might escape screening by the district court simply by stating that their conclusions were not reached by any particular method or technique."). Some types of expert testimony will be more objectively verifiable, and subject to the expectations of falsifiability, peer review, and publication, than others. Some types of expert testimony will not rely on anything like a scientific method, and so will have to be evaluated by reference to other standard principles attendant to the particular area of expertise. The trial judge in all cases of proffered expert testimony must find that it is properly grounded, well-reasoned, and not speculative before it can be admitted. The expert's testimony must be grounded in an accepted body of learning or experience in the expert's field, and the expert must explain how the conclusion is so grounded. See, e.g., American College of Trial Lawyers, Standards and Procedures for Determining the Admissibility of Expert Testimony after Daubert, 157 F.R.D. 571, 579 (1994) ("[W]hether the testimony concerns economic principles, accounting standards, property valuation or other non-scientific subjects, it should be evaluated by reference to the 'knowledge and experience' of that particular field.").

The amendment requires that the testimony must be the product of reliable principles and methods that are reliably applied to the facts of the case. While the terms "principles" and "methods" may convey a certain impression when applied to scientific knowledge, they remain relevant when applied to testimony based on technical or other specialized knowledge. For example, when a law enforcement agent testifies regarding the use of code words in a drug transaction, the principle used by the agent is that participants in such transactions regularly use code words to conceal the nature of their activities. The method used by the agent is the application of extensive experience to analyze the meaning of the conversations. So long as the principles and methods are reliable and applied reliably to the facts of the case, this type of testimony should be admitted.

Nothing in this amendment is intended to suggest that experience alone-or experience in conjunction with other knowledge, skill, training or education-may not provide a sufficient foundation for expert testimony. To the contrary, the text of Rule 702 expressly contemplates that an expert may be qualified on the basis of experience. In certain fields, experience is the predominant, if not sole, basis for a great deal of reliable expert testimony. See, e.g., United States v. Jones, 107 F.3d 1147 (6th Cir. 1997) (no abuse of discretion in admitting the testimony of a handwriting examiner who had years of practical experience and extensive training, and who explained his methodology in detail); Tassin v. Sears Roebuck, 946 F.Supp. 1241, 1248 (M.D.La. 1996) (design engineer's testimony can be admissible when the expert's opinions "are based on facts, a reasonable investigation, and traditional technical/mechanical expertise, and he provides a reasonable link between the information and procedures he uses and the conclusions he reaches"). See also Kumho Tire Co. v. Carmichael, 119 S.Ct.1167, 1178 (1999) (stating that "no one denies that an expert might draw a conclusion from a set of observations based on extensive and specialized experience.").

If the witness is relying solely or primarily on experience, then the witness must explain how that experience leads to the conclusion reached, why that experience is a sufficient basis for the opinion, and how that experience is reliably applied to the facts. The trial court's gatekeeping function requires more than simply "taking the expert's word for it." See Daubert v. Merrell Dow Pharmaceuticals, Inc., 43 F.3d 1311, 1319 (9th Cir. 1995) ("We've been presented with only the experts' qualifications, their conclusions and their assurances of reliability. Under Daubert, that's not enough."). The more subjective and controversial the expert's inquiry, the more likely the testimony should be excluded as unreliable. See O'Conner v. Commonwealth Edison Co., 13 F.3d 1090 (7th Cir. 1994) (expert testimony based on a completely subjective methodology held properly excluded). See also Kumho Tire Co. v. Carmichael, 119 S.Ct. 1167, 1176 (1999) ("[I]t will at times be useful to ask even of a witness whose expertise is based purely on experience, say, a perfume tester able to distinguish among 140 odors at a sniff, whether his preparation is of a kind that others in the field would recognize as acceptable.").

Subpart (1) of Rule 702 calls for a quantitative rather than qualitative analysis. The amendment requires that expert testimony be based on sufficient underlying "facts or data." The term "data" is intended to encompass the reliable opinions of other experts. See the original Advisory Committee Note to Rule 703. The language "facts or data" is broad enough to allow an expert to rely on hypothetical facts that are supported by the evidence. Id.

When facts are in dispute, experts sometimes reach different conclusions based on competing versions of the facts. The emphasis in the amendment on "sufficient facts or data" is not intended to authorize a trial court to exclude an expert's testimony on the ground that the court believes one version of the facts and not the other.

There has been some confusion over the relationship between Rules 702 and 703. The amendment makes clear that the sufficiency of the basis of an expert's testimony is to be decided under Rule 702. Rule 702 sets forth the overarching requirement of reliability, and an analysis of the sufficiency of the expert's basis cannot be divorced from the ultimate reliability of the expert's opinion. In contrast, the "reasonable reliance" requirement of Rule 703 is a relatively narrow inquiry. When an expert relies on inadmissible information, Rule 703 requires the trial court to determine whether that information is of a type reasonably relied on by other experts in the field. If so, the expert can rely on the information in reaching an opinion. However, the question whether the expert is relying on a sufficient basis of information—whether admissible information or not—is governed by the requirements of Rule 702.

The amendment makes no attempt to set forth procedural requirements for exercising the trial court's gatekeeping function over expert testimony. See Daniel J. Capra, The Daubert Puzzle, 38 Ga.L.Rev. 699, 766 (1998) ("Trial courts should be allowed substantial discretion in dealing with Daubert questions; any attempt to codify procedures will likely give rise to unnecessary changes in practice and create difficult questions for appellate review."). Courts have shown considerable ingenuity and flexibility in considering challenges to expert testimony under Daubert, and it is contemplated that this will continue under the amended Rule. See, e.g., Cortes-Irizarry v. Corporacion Insular, 111 F.3d 184 (1st Cir. 1997) (discussing the application of Daubert in ruling on a motion for summary judgment); In re Paoli R.R. Yard PCB Litig., 35 F.3d 717, 736, 739 (3d Cir. 1994) (discussing the use of in limine hearings); Claar v. Burlington N.R.R., 29 F.3d 499, 502-05 (9th Cir. 1994) (discussing the trial court's technique of ordering experts to submit serial affidavits explaining the reasoning and methods underlying their conclusions).

The amendment continues the practice of the original Rule in referring to a qualified witness as an "expert." This was done to provide continuity and to minimize change. The use of the term "expert" in the Rule does not, however, mean that a jury should actually be informed that a qualified witness is testifying as an "expert." Indeed, there is much to be said for a practice that prohibits the use of the term "expert" by both the parties and the court at trial. Such a practice "ensures that trial courts do not inadvertently put their stamp of authority" on a witness's opinion, and protects against the jury's being "overwhelmed by the so-called 'experts'." Hon. Charles Richey, Proposals to Eliminate the Prejudicial Effect of the Use of the Word "Expert" Under the Federal Rules of Evidence in Criminal and Civil Jury Trials, 154 F.R.D. 537, 559 (1994) (setting forth limiting instructions and a standing order employed to prohibit the use of the term "expert" injury [*sic*] trials)

Restyled 2011

Rule 703. Bases of an Expert's Opinion Testimony

An expert may base an opinion on facts or data in the case that the expert has been made aware of or personally observed. If experts in the particular field would reasonably rely on those kinds of facts or data in forming an opinion on the subject, they need not be admissible for the opinion to be admitted. But if the facts or data would otherwise be inadmissible, the proponent of the opinion may disclose them to the jury only if their probative value in helping the jury evaluate the opinion substantially outweighs their prejudicial effect.

Committee Note to 2011 Restyled Rule

The Committee deleted all reference to an "inference" on the grounds that the deletion made the Rule flow better and easier to read, and because any "inference" is covered by the broader term "opinion." Courts have not made substantive decisions on the basis of any distinction between an opinion and an inference. No change in current practice is intended.

Superseded 2011

Rule 703. Bases of Opinion Testimony by Experts

The facts or data in the particular case upon which an expert bases an opinion or inference may be those perceived by or made known to the expert at or before the hearing. If of a type reasonably relied upon by experts in the particular field in forming opinions or inferences upon the subject, the facts or data need not be admissible in evidence in order for the opinion or inference to be admitted. Facts or data that are otherwise inadmissible shall not be disclosed to the jury by the proponent of the opinion or inference unless the court determines that their probative value in assisting the jury to evaluate the expert's opinion substantially outweighs their prejudicial effect. [*Last sentence and last 10 words of second sentence added 2000.*]

Advisory Committee's Note

Facts or data upon which expert opinions are based may, under the rule, be derived from three possible sources. The first is the firsthand observation of the witness with opinions based thereon traditionally allowed. A treating physician affords an example. Rheingold, The Basis of Medical Testimony, 15 Vand.L.Rev. 473, 489 (1962). Whether he must first relate his observations is treated in Rule 705. The second source, presentation at the trial, also reflects existing practice. The technique may be the familiar hypothetical question or having the expert attend the trial and hear the testimony establishing the facts. Problems of determining what testimony the expert relied upon, when the latter technique is employed and the testimony is in conflict, may be resolved by resort to Rule 705. The third source contemplated by the rule consists of presentation of data to the expert outside of court and other than by his own perception. In this respect the rule is designed to broaden the basis for expert opinions beyond that current in many jurisdictions and to bring the judicial practice into line with the practice of the experts themselves when not in court. Thus a physician in his own practice bases his diagnosis on information from numerous sources and of considerable variety, including statements by patients and relatives, reports and opinions from nurses, technicians and other doctors, hospital records, and X rays. Most of them are admissible in evidence, but only with the expenditure of substantial time in producing and examining various authenticating witnesses. The physician makes life-and-death decisions in reliance upon them. His validation, expertly performed and subject to cross-examination, ought to suffice for judicial purposes. Rheingold, supra, at 531; McCormick § 15. A similar provision is California Evidence Code § 801(b).

The rule also offers a more satisfactory basis for ruling upon the admissibility of public opinion poll evidence. Attention is directed to the validity of the techniques employed rather than to relatively fruitless inquiries whether hearsay is involved. See Judge Feinberg's careful analysis in Zippo Mfg. Co. v. Rogers Imports, Inc., 216 F.Supp. 670 (S.D.N.Y.1963). See also Blum et al., The Art of Opinion Research: A Lawyer's Appraisal of an Emerging Service, 24 U.Chi.L.Rev. 1 (1956); Bonynge Trademark Surveys and Techniques and Their Use in Litigation, 48 A.B.A.J. 329 (1962); Zeisel, The Uniqueness of Survey Evidence, 45 Cornell L.Q. 322 (1960); Annot., 76 A.L.R.2d 919.

If it be feared that enlargement of permissible data may tend to break down the rules of exclusion unduly, notice should be taken that the rule requires that the facts or data "be of a type reasonably relied upon by experts in the particular field." The language would not warrant admitting in evidence the opinion of an "accidentologist" as to the point of impact in an automobile collision based on statements of bystanders since this requirement is not satisfied. See Comment, Cal.Law Rev.Comm'n, Recommendation Proposing an Evidence Code 148-150 (1965).

Advisory Committee's Note to 2000 Amendment

Rule 703 has been amended to emphasize that when an expert reasonably relies on inadmissible information to form an opinion or inference, the underlying information is not admissible simply because the opinion or inference is admitted. Courts have reached different results on how to treat inadmissible information when it is reasonably relied upon by an expert in forming an opinion or drawing an inference. Compare United States v. Rollins, 862 F.2d 1282 (7th Cir. 1988) (admitting, as part of the basis of an FBI agent's expert opinion on the meaning of code language, the hearsay statements of an informant), with United States v. 0.59 Acres of Land. 109 F.3d 1493 (9th Cir. 1997) (error to admit hearsay offered as the basis of an expert opinion, without a limiting instruction). Commentators have also taken differing views. See e.g., Ronald Carlson, Policing the Bases of Modern Expert Testimony, 39 Vand.L.Rev. 577 (1986) (advocating limits on the jury's consideration of otherwise inadmissible evidence used as the basis for an expert opinion); Paul Rice, Inadmissible Evidence as a Basis for Expert Testimony: A Response to Professor Carlson, 40 Vand.L.Rev. 583 (1987) (advocating unrestricted use of information reasonably relied upon by an expert).

When information is reasonably relied upon by an expert and yet is admissible only for the purpose of assisting the jury in evaluating an expert's opinion, a trial court applying this Rule must consider the information's probative value in assisting the jury to weigh the expert's opinion on the one hand, and the risk of prejudice resulting from the jury's potential misuse of the information for substantive purposes on the other. The information may be disclosed to the jury, upon objection, only if the trial court finds that the probative value of the information in assisting the jury to evaluate the expert's opinion substantially outweighs its prejudicial effect. If the otherwise inadmissible information is admitted under this balancing test, the trial judge must give a limiting instruction upon request, informing the jury that the underlying information must not be used for substantive purposes. See Rule 105. In determining the appropriate course, the trial court should consider the probable effectiveness or lack of effectiveness of a limiting instruction under the particular circumstances.

The amendment governs only the disclosure to the jury of information that is reasonably relied on by an expert, when that information is not admissible for substantive purposes. It is not intended to affect the admissibility of an expert's testimony. Nor does the amendment prevent an expert from relying on information that is inadmissible for substantive purposes.

Nothing in this Rule restricts the presentation of underlying expert facts or data when offered by an adverse party. See Rule 705. Of course, an adversary's attack on an expert's basis will often open the door to a proponent's rebuttal with information that was reasonably relied upon by the expert, even if that information would not have been discloseable initially under the balancing test provided by this amendment. Moreover, in some circumstances the proponent might wish to disclose information that is relied upon by the expert in order to "remove the sting" from the opponent's anticipated attack, and thereby prevent the jury from drawing an unfair negative inference. The trial court should take this consideration into account in applying the balancing test provided by this amendment.

This amendment covers facts or data that cannot be admitted for any purpose other than to assist the jury to evaluate the expert's opinion. The balancing test provided in this amendment is not applicable to facts or data that are admissible for any other purpose but have not yet been offered for such a purpose at the time the expert testifies.

The amendment provides a presumption against disclosure to the jury of information used as the basis of an expert's opinion and not admissible for any substantive purpose, when that information is offered by the proponent of the expert. In a multi-party case, where one party proffers an expert whose testimony is also beneficial to other parties, each such party should be deemed a "proponent" within the meaning of the amendment.

Restyled 2011

Rule 704. Opinion on an Ultimate Issue

(a) In General — Not Automatically Objectionable. An opinion is not objectionable just because it embraces an ultimate issue.

(b) Exception. In a criminal case, an expert witness must not state an opinion about whether the defendant did or did not have a mental state or condition that constitutes an element of the crime charged or of a defense those matters are for the trier of fact alone.

Committee Note to 2011 Restyled Rule

The Committee deleted all reference to an "inference" on the grounds that the deletion made the Rule flow better and easier to read, and because any "inference" is covered by the broader term "opinion." Courts have not made substantive decisions on the basis of any distinction between an opinion and an inference. No change in current practice is intended.

Superseded 2011

Rule 704. Opinion on Ultimate Issue

(a) Except as provided in subdivision (b), testimony in the form of an opinion or inference otherwise admissible is not objectionable because it embraces an ultimate issue to be decided by the trier of fact.

(b) No expert witness testifying with respect to the mental state or condition of a defendant in a criminal case may state an opinion or inference as to whether the defendant did or did not have the mental state or condition constituting an element of the crime charged or of a defense thereto. Such ultimate issues are matters for the trier of fact alone. [*Subdivision (b) added 1984.*]

Advisory Committee's Note

The basic approach to opinions, lay and expert, in these rules is to admit them when helpful to the trier of fact. In order to render this approach fully effective and to allay any doubt on the subject, the so-called "ultimate issue" rule is specifically abolished by the instant rule.

The older cases often contained strictures against allowing witnesses to express opinions upon ultimate issues, as a particular aspect of the rule against opinions. The rule was unduly restrictive, difficult of application, and generally served only to deprive the trier of fact of useful information. 7 Wigmore §§ 1920, 1921; McCormick § 12. The basis usually assigned for the rule, to prevent the witness from "usurping the province of the jury," is aptly characterized as "empty rhetoric." 7 Wigmore § 1920, p. 17. Efforts to meet the felt needs of particular situations led to odd verbal circumlocutions which were said not to violate the rule. Thus a witness could express his estimate of the criminal responsibility of an accused in terms of sanity or insanity, but not in terms of ability to tell right from wrong or other more modern standard. And in cases of medical causation, witnesses were sometimes required to couch their opinions in cautious phrases of "might or could," rather than "did," though the result was to deprive many opinions of the positiveness to which they were entitled, accompanied by the hazard of a ruling of insufficiency to support a verdict. In other instances the rule was simply disregarded, and, as concessions to need, opinions were allowed upon such matters as intoxication, speed, handwriting, and value, although more precise coincidence with an ultimate issue would scarcely be possible.

Many modern decisions illustrate the trend to abandon the rule completely. People v. Wilson, 25 Cal.2d 341, 153 P.2d 720 (1944), whether abortion necessary to save life of patient; Clifford-Jacobs Forging Co. v. Industrial Comm., 19 Ill.2d 236, 166 N.E.2d 582 (1960), medical causation; Dowling v. L. H. Shattuck, Inc., 91 N.H. 234, 17 A.2d 529 (1941), proper method of shoring ditch; Schweiger v. Solbeck, 191 Or. 454, 230 P.2d 195 (1951), cause of landslide. In each instance the opinion was allowed.

The abolition of the ultimate issue rule does not lower the bars so as to admit all opinions. Under Rules 701 and 702, opinions must be helpful to the trier of fact, and Rule 403 provides for exclusion of evidence which wastes time. These provisions afford ample assurances against the admission of opinions which would merely tell the jury what result to reach, somewhat in the manner of the oath-helpers of an earlier day. They also stand ready to exclude opinions phrased in terms of inadequately explored legal criteria. Thus the question, "Did T have capacity to make a will?" would be excluded, while the question, "Did T have sufficient mental capacity to know the nature and extent of his property and the natural objects of his bounty and to formulate a rational scheme of distribution?" would be allowed. McCormick § 12.

For similar provisions see Uniform Rule 56(4); California Evidence Code § 805; Kansas Code of Civil Procedure § 60-456(d); New Jersey Evidence Rule 56(3).

Note to Subdivision (b)

Subdivision (b) was added by the Insanity Defense Reform Act of 1984, Pub. L. 98-473. The following explanation is from the Senate Committee Report (S. Rep. 98-225).

The purpose of this amendment is to eliminate the confusing spectacle of competing expert witnesses testifying to directly contradictory conclusions as to the ultimate legal issue to be found by the trier of fact. Under this proposal, expert psychiatric testimony would be limited to presenting and explaining their diagnoses, such as whether the defendant had a severe mental disease or defect and what the characteristics of such a disease or defect, if any, may have been. The basis for this limitation on expert testimony in insanity cases is ably stated by the American Psychiatric Association:

"(I)t is clear that psychiatrists are experts in medicine, not the law. As such, it is clear that the psychiatrist's first obligation and expertise in the courtroom is to 'do psychiatry,' *i.e.*, to present medical information and opinion about the defendant's mental state and motivation and to explain in detail the reason for his medical-psychiatric conclusions. When, however, 'ultimate issue' questions are formulated by the law and put to the expert witness who must then say 'yea' or 'nay,' then the expert witness is required to make a leap in logic. He no longer addresses himself to medical concepts but instead must infer or intuit what is in fact unspeakable, namely, the probable relationship between medical concepts and legal or moral constructs such as free will. These impermissible leaps in logic made by expert witnesses confuse the jury. Juries thus find themselves listening to conclusory and seemingly contradictory psychiatric testimony that defendants are either 'sane' or 'insane' or that they do or do not meet the relevant legal test for insanity. This state of affairs does considerable injustice to psychiatry and, we believe, possibly to criminal defendants. In fact, in many criminal insanity trials both prosecution and defense psychiatrists do agree about the nature and even the extent of mental disorder exhibited by the defendant at the time of the act."

Psychiatrists, of course, must be permitted to testify fully about the defendant's diagnosis, mental state and motivation (in clinical and commonsense terms) at the time of the alleged act so as to permit the jury or judge to reach the ultimate conclusion about which they and only they are expert. Determining whether a criminal defendant was legally insane is a matter for legal fact-finders, not for experts.

Moreover, the rationale for precluding ultimate opinion psychiatric testimony extends beyond the insanity defense to any ultimate mental state of the defendant that is relevant to the legal conclusion sought to be proven. The committee has fashioned its rule 704 provision to reach all such "ultimate" issues, *e.g.*, premeditation in a homicide case, or lack of predisposition in entrapment.

Restyled 2011

Rule 705. Disclosing the Facts or Data Underlying an Expert's Opinion

Unless the court orders otherwise, an expert may state an opinion — and give the reasons for it — without first testifying to the underlying facts or data. But the expert may be required to disclose those facts or data on cross-examination.

Committee Note to 2011 Restyled Rule

The Committee deleted all reference to an "inference" on the grounds that the deletion made the Rule flow better and easier to read, and because any "inference" is covered by the broader term "opinion." Courts have not made substantive decisions on the basis of any distinction between an opinion and an inference. No change in current practice is intended.

Superseded 2011

Rule 705. Disclosure of Facts or Data Underlying Expert Opinion

The expert may testify in terms of opinion or inference and give reasons therefor without first testifying to the underlying facts or data, unless the court requires otherwise. The expert may in any event be required to disclose the underlying facts or data on cross-examination. [*Amended 1993.*]

Advisory Committee's Note

The hypothetical question has been the target of a great deal of criticism as encouraging partisan bias, affording an opportunity for summing up in the middle of the case, and as complex and time consuming. Ladd, Expert Testimony, 5 Vand.L.Rev. 414, 426-427 (1952). While the rule allows counsel to make disclosure of the underlying facts or data as a preliminary to the giving of an expert opinion, if he chooses, the instances in which he is required to do so are reduced. This is true whether the expert bases his opinion on data furnished him at secondhand or observed by him at firsthand.

The elimination of the requirement of preliminary disclosure at the trial of underlying facts or data has a long background of support. In 1937 the Commissioners on Uniform State Laws incorporated a provision to this effect in their Model Expert Testimony Act, which furnished the basis for Uniform Rules 57 and 58. Rule 4515, N.Y. CPLR (McKinney 1963), provides:

> "Unless the court orders otherwise, questions calling for the opinion of an expert witness need not be hypothetical in form, and the witness may state his opinion and reasons without first specifying the data upon which it is based. Upon cross-examination, he may be required to specify the data . . . ."

See also California Evidence Code § 802; Kansas Code of Civil Procedure §§ 60-456, 60-457; New Jersey Evidence Rules 57, 58.

If the objection is made that leaving it to the cross-examiner to bring out the supporting data is essentially unfair, the answer is that he is under no compulsion to bring out any facts or data except those unfavorable to the opinion. The answer assumes that the cross-examiner has the advance knowledge which is essential for effective cross-examination. This advance knowledge has been afforded, though imperfectly, by the traditional foundation requirement. Rule 26(b)(4) of the Rules of Civil Procedure, as revised, provides for substantial discovery in this area, obviating in large measure the obstacles which have been raised in some instances to discovery of findings, underlying data, and even the identity of the experts. Friedenthal Discovery and Use of an Adverse Party's Expert Information, 14 Stan.L.Rev. 455 (1962).

These safeguards are reinforced by the discretionary power of the judge to require preliminary disclosure in any event.

Advisory Committee's Note to 1993 Amendment

This rule, which relates to the manner of presenting testimony at trial, is revised to avoid an arguable conflict with revised Rules 26(a)(2)(B) and 26(e)(1) of the Federal Rules of Civil Procedure or with revised Rule 16 of the Federal Rules of Criminal Procedure, which require disclosure in advance of trial of the basis and reasons for an expert's opinions.

If a serious question is raised under Rule 702 or 703 as to the admissibility of expert testimony, disclosure of the underlying facts or data on which opinions are based may, of course, be needed by the court before deciding whether, and to what extent, the person should be allowed to testify. This rule does not preclude such an inquiry.

Restyled 2011

Rule 706. Court-Appointed Expert Witnesses

(a) **Appointment Process.** On a party's motion or on its own, the court may order the parties to show cause why expert witnesses should not be appointed and may ask the parties to submit nominations. The court may appoint any expert that the parties agree on and any of its own choosing. But the court may only appoint someone who consents to act.

(b) **Expert's Role.** The court must inform the expert of the expert's duties. The court may do so in writing and have a copy filed with the clerk or may do so orally at a conference in which the parties have an opportunity to participate. The expert:

(1) must advise the parties of any findings the expert makes;

(2) may be deposed by any party;

(3) may be called to testify by the court or any party; and

(4) may be cross-examined by any party, including the party that called the expert.

(c) Compensation. The expert is entitled a reasonable compensation, as set by the court. The compensation is payable as follows:

(1) in a criminal case or in a civil case involving just compensation under the Fifth Amendment, from any funds that are provided by law; and

(2) in any other civil case, by the parties in the proportion and at the time that the court directs - and the compensation is then charged like other costs.

(d) Disclosing the Appointment to the Jury. The court may authorize disclosure to the jury that the court appointed the expert.

(e) Parties' Choice of Their Own Experts. This rule does not limit a party in calling its own experts.

Superseded 2011

Rule 706. Court Appointed Experts

(a) Appointment. The court may on its own motion or on the motion of any party enter an order to show cause why expert witnesses should not be appointed, and may request the parties to submit nominations. The court may appoint any expert witnesses agreed upon by the parties, and may appoint expert witnesses of its own selection. An expert witness shall not be appointed by the court unless the witness consents to act. A witness so appointed shall be informed of the witness' duties by the court in writing, a copy of which shall be filed with the clerk, or at a conference in which the parties shall have opportunity to participate. A witness so appointed shall advise the parties of the witness' findings, if any; the witness' deposition may be taken by any party; and the witness may be called to testify by the court or any party. The witness shall be subject to cross-examination by each party, including a party calling the witness.

(b) Compensation. Expert witnesses so appointed are entitled to reasonable compensation in whatever sum the court may allow. The compensation thus fixed is payable from funds which may be provided by law in criminal cases and civil actions and proceedings involving just compensation under the fifth amendment. In other civil actions and proceedings the compensation shall be paid by the parties in such proportion and at such time as the court directs, and thereafter charged in like manner as other costs.

(c) Disclosure of appointment. In the exercise of its discretion, the court may authorize disclosure to the jury of the fact that the court appointed the expert witness.

(d) Parties' experts of own selection. Nothing in this rule limits the parties in calling expert witnesses of their own selection.

Advisory Committee's Note

The practice of shopping for experts, the venality of some experts, and the reluctance of many reputable experts to involve themselves in litigation, have been matters of deep concern. Though the contention is made that court appointed experts acquire an aura of infallibility to which they are not entitled, Levy, Impartial Medical Testimony—Revisited, 34 Temple L.Q. 416 (1961), the trend is increasingly to provide for their use. While experience indicates that actual appointment is a relatively infrequent occurrence, the assumption may be made that the availability of the procedure in itself decreases the need for resorting to it. The ever-present possibility that the judge may appoint an expert in a given case must inevitably exert a sobering effect on the expert witness of a party and upon the person utilizing his services.

The inherent power of a trial judge to appoint an expert of his own choosing is virtually unquestioned. Scott v. Spanjer Bros., Inc., 298 F.2d 928 (2d Cir.1962); Danville Tobacco Assn. v. Bryant-Buckner Associates, Inc., 333 F.2d 202 (4th Cir.1964); Sink, The Unused Power of a Federal Judge to Call His Own Expert Witnesses, 29 S.Cal.L.Rev. 195 (1956); 2 Wigmore § 563, 9 id. § 2484; Annot., 95 A.L.R.2d 383. Hence the problem becomes largely one of detail.

The New York plan is well known and is described in Report by Special Committee of the Association of the Bar of the City of New York: Impartial Medical Testimony (1956). On recommendation of the Section of Judicial Administration, local adoption of an impartial medical plan was endorsed by the American Bar Association. 82 A.B.A.Rep. 184-185 (1957). Descriptions and analyses of plans in effect in various parts of the country are found in Van Dusen, A United States District Judge's View of the Impartial Medical Expert System, 32 F.R.D. 498 (1963); Wick and Kightlinger, Impartial Medical Testimony Under the Federal Civil Rules: A Tale of Three Doctors, 34 Ins. Counsel J. 115 (1967); and numerous articles collected in Klein, Judicial Administration and the Legal Profession 393 (1963). Statutes and rules include California Evidence Code §§ 730-733; Illinois Supreme Court Rule 215(d), Ill.Rev.Stat.1969, c. 110A, § 215(d); Burns Indiana Stats.1956, § 9-1702; Wisconsin Stats.Annot.1958, § 957.27.

In the federal practice, a comprehensive scheme for court appointed experts was initiated with the adoption of Rule 28 of the Federal Rules of Criminal Procedure in 1946. The Judicial Conference of the United States in 1953 considered court appointed experts in civil cases, but only with respect to whether they should be compensated from public funds, a proposal which was rejected. Report of the Judicial Conference of the United States 23 (1953). The present rule expands the practice to include civil cases.

Subdivision (a) is based on Rule 28 of the Federal Rules of Criminal Procedure, with a few changes, mainly in the interest of clarity. Language has been added to provide specifically for the appointment either on motion of a party or on the judge's own motion. A provision subjecting the court appointed expert to deposition procedures has been incorporated. The rule has been revised to make definite the right of any party, including the party calling him, to cross-examine.

Subdivision (b) combines the present provision for compensation in criminal cases with what seems to be a fair and feasible handling of civil cases, originally found in the Model Act and carried from there into Uniform Rule 60. See also California Evidence Code §§ 730-731. The special provision for Fifth Amendment compensation cases is designed to guard against reducing constitutionally guaranteed just compensation by requiring the recipient to pay costs. See Rule 71A(l) of the Rules of Civil Procedure.

Subdivision (c) seems to be essential if the use of court appointed experts is to be fully effective. Uniform Rule 61 so provides.

Subdivision (d) is in essence the last sentence of Rule 28(a) of the Federal Rules of Criminal Procedure.

ARTICLE VIII. HEARSAY

Advisory Committee's Note

INTRODUCTORY NOTE: THE HEARSAY PROBLEM

The factors to be considered in evaluating the testimony of a witness are perception, memory, and narration. Morgan, Hearsay Dangers and the Application of the Hearsay Concept, 62 Harv.L.Rev. 177 (1948), Selected Writings on Evidence and Trial 764, 765 (Fryer ed. 1957); Shientag, Cross-Examination—A Judge's Viewpoint, 3 Record 12 (1948); Strahorn, A Reconsideration of the Hearsay Rule and Admissions, 85 U.Pa.L.Rev. 484, 485 (1937), Selected Writings, supra, 756, 757; Weinstein, Probative Force of Hearsay, 46 Iowa L.Rev. 331 (1961). Sometimes a fourth is added, sincerity, but in fact it seems merely to be an aspect of the three already mentioned.

In order to encourage the witness to do his best with respect to each of these factors, and to expose any inaccuracies which may enter in, the Anglo-American tradition has evolved three conditions under which witnesses will ideally be required to testify: (1) under oath, (2) in the personal presence of the trier of fact, (3) subject to cross-examination.

(1) Standard procedure calls for the swearing of witnesses. While the practice is perhaps less effective than in an earlier time, no disposition to relax the requirement is apparent, other than to allow affirmation by persons with scruples against taking oaths.

(2) The demeanor of the witness traditionally has been believed to furnish trier and opponent with valuable clues. Universal Camera Corp. v. N.L.R.B., 340 U.S. 474, 495-496, 71 S.Ct. 456, 95 L.Ed. 456 (1951); Sahm, Demeanor Evidence: Elusive and Intangible Imponderables, 47 A.B.A.J. 580 (1961), quoting numerous authorities. The witness himself will probably be impressed with the solemnity of the occasion and the possibility of public disgrace. Willingness to falsify may reasonably become more difficult in the presence of the person against whom directed. Rules 26 and 43(a) of the Federal Rules of Criminal and Civil Procedure, respectively, include the general requirement that testimony be taken orally in open court. The Sixth Amendment right of confrontation is a manifestation of these beliefs and attitudes.

(3) Emphasis on the basis of the hearsay rule today tends to center upon the condition of cross-examination. All may not agree with Wigmore that cross-examination is "beyond doubt the greatest legal engine ever invented for the discovery of truth," but all will agree with his statement that it has become a "vital feature" of the Anglo-American system. 5 Wigmore § 1367, p. 29. The belief, or perhaps hope, that cross-examination is effective in exposing imperfections of perception, memory, and narration is fundamental. Morgan, Foreword to Model Code of Evidence 37 (1942).

The logic of the preceding discussion might suggest that no testimony be received unless in full compliance with the three ideal conditions. No one advocates this position. Common sense tells that much evidence which is not given under the three conditions may be inherently superior to much that is. Moreover, when the choice is between evidence which is less than best and no evidence at all, only clear folly would dictate an across-the-board policy of doing without. The problem thus resolves itself into effecting a sensible accommodation between these considerations and the desirability of giving testimony under the ideal conditions.

The solution evolved by the common law has been a general rule excluding hearsay but subject to numerous exceptions under circumstances supposed to furnish guarantees of trustworthiness. Criticisms of this scheme are that it is bulky and complex, fails to screen good from bad hearsay realistically, and inhibits the growth of the law of evidence.

Since no one advocates excluding all hearsay, three possible solutions may be considered: (1) abolish the rule against hearsay and admit all hearsay; (2) admit hearsay possessing sufficient probative force, but with procedural safeguards; (3) revise the present system of class exceptions.

(1) Abolition of the hearsay rule would be the simplest solution. The effect would not be automatically to abolish the giving of testimony under ideal conditions. If the declarant were available, compliance with the ideal conditions would be optional with either party. Thus the proponent could call the declarant as a witness as a form of presentation more impressive than his hearsay statement. Or the opponent could call the declarant to be cross-examined upon his statement. This is the tenor of Uniform Rule 63(1), admitting the hearsay declaration of a person "who is present at the hearing and available for cross-examination." Compare the treatment of declarations of available declarants in Rule 801(d)(1) of the instant rules. If the declarant were unavailable, a rule of free admissibility would make no distinctions in terms of degrees of noncompliance with the ideal conditions and would exact no quid pro quo in the form of assurances of trustworthiness. Rule 503 of the Model Code did exactly that, providing for the admissibility of any hearsay declaration by an unavailable declarant, finding support in the Massachusetts act of 1898, enacted at the instance of Thayer, Mass.Gen.L.1932, c.

233, § 65, and in the English act of 1938, St.1938, c. 28, Evidence. Both are limited to civil cases. The draftsmen of the Uniform Rules chose a less advanced and more conventional position. Comment, Uniform Rule 63. The present Advisory Committee has been unconvinced of the wisdom of abandoning the traditional requirement of some particular assurance of credibility as a condition precedent to admitting the hearsay declaration of an unavailable declarant.

In criminal cases, the Sixth Amendment requirement of confrontation would no doubt move into a large part of the area presently occupied by the hearsay rule in the event of the abolition of the latter. The resultant split between civil and criminal evidence is regarded as an undesirable development.

(2) Abandonment of the system of class exceptions in favor of individual treatment in the setting of the particular case, accompanied by procedural safeguards, has been impressively advocated. Weinstein, The Probative Force of Hearsay, 46 Iowa L.Rev. 331 (1961). Admissibility would be determined by weighing the probative force of the evidence against the possibility of prejudice, waste of time, and the availability of more satisfactory evidence. The bases of the traditional hearsay exceptions would be helpful in assessing probative force. Ladd, The Relationship of the Principles of Exclusionary Rules of Evidence to the Problem of Proof, 18 Minn.L.Rev. 506 (1934). Procedural safeguards would consist of notice of intention to use hearsay, free comment by the judge on the weight of the evidence, and a greater measure of authority in both trial and appellate judges to deal with evidence on the basis of weight. The Advisory Committee has rejected this approach to hearsay as involving too great a measure of judicial discretion, minimizing the predictability of rulings, enhancing the difficulties of preparation for trial, adding a further element to the already over-complicated congeries of pretrial procedures, and requiring substantially different rules for civil and criminal cases. The only way in which the probative force of hearsay differs from the probative force of other testimony is in the absence of oath, demeanor, and cross-examination as aids in determining credibility. For a judge to exclude evidence because he does not believe it has been described as "altogether atypical, extraordinary. * * * " Chadbourn, Bentham and the Hearsay Rule—A Benthamic View of Rule 63(4)(c) of the Uniform Rules of Evidence, 75 Harv.L.Rev. 932, 947 (1962).

(3) The approach to hearsay in these rules is that of the common law, i.e., a general rule excluding hearsay, with exceptions under which evidence is not required to be excluded even though hearsay. The traditional hearsay exceptions are drawn upon for the exceptions, collected under two rules, one dealing with situations where availability of the declarant is regarded as immaterial and the other with those where unavailability is made a condition to the admission of the hearsay statement. Each of the two rules concludes with a provision for hearsay statements not within one of the specified exceptions "but having comparable circumstantial guarantees of trustworthiness." Rules 803(24) and 804(b)(6). This plan is submitted as calculated to encourage growth and development in this area of the law, while conserving the values and experience of the past as a guide to the future.

CONFRONTATION AND DUE PROCESS

Until very recently, decisions invoking the confrontation clause of the Sixth Amendment were surprisingly few, a fact probably explainable by the former inapplicability of the clause to the states and by the hearsay rule's occupancy of much the same ground. The pattern which emerges from the earlier cases invoking the clause is substantially that of the hearsay rule, applied to criminal cases: an accused is entitled to have the witnesses against him testify under oath, in the presence of himself and trier, subject to cross-examination; yet considerations of public policy and necessity require the recognition of such exceptions as dying declarations and former testimony of unavailable witnesses. Mattox v. United States, 156 U.S. 237, 15 S.Ct. 337, 39 L.Ed. 409 (1895); Motes v. United States, 178 U.S. 458, 20 S.Ct. 993, 44 L.Ed. 1150 (1900); Delaney v. United States, 263 U.S. 586, 44 S.Ct. 206, 68 L.Ed. 462 (1924). Beginning with Snyder v. Massachusetts, 291 U.S. 97, 54 S.Ct. 330, 78 L.Ed. 674 (1934), the Court began to speak of confrontation as an aspect of procedural due process, thus extending its applicability to state cases and to federal cases other than criminal. The language of Snyder was that of an elastic concept of hearsay. The deportation case of Bridges v. Wixon, 326 U.S. 135, 65 S.Ct. 1443, 89 L.Ed. 2103 (1945), may be read broadly as imposing a strictly construed right of confrontation in all kinds of cases or narrowly as the product of a failure of the Immigration and Naturalization Service to follow its own rules. In re Oliver, 333 U.S. 257, 68 S.Ct. 499, 92 L.Ed. 682 (1948), ruled that cross-examination was essential to due process in a state contempt proceeding, but in United States v. Nugent, 346 U.S. 1, 73 S.Ct. 991, 97 L.Ed. 1417 (1953), the court held that it was not an essential aspect of a "hearing" for a conscientious objector under the Selective Service Act. Stein v. New York, 346 U.S. 156, 196, 73 S.Ct. 1077, 97 L.Ed. 1522 (1953), disclaimed any purpose to read the hearsay rule into the Fourteenth Amendment, but in Greene v. McElroy, 360 U.S. 474, 79 S.Ct. 1400, 3 L.Ed.2d 1377 (1959), revocation of security clearance without confrontation and cross-examination was held unauthorized, and a similar result was reached in Willner v. Committee on Character, 373 U.S. 96, 83 S.Ct. 1175, 10 L.Ed.2d 224 (1963). Ascertaining the constitutional dimensions of the confrontation-hearsay aggregate against the background of these cases is a matter of some difficulty, yet the general pattern is at least not inconsistent with that of the hearsay rule.

In 1965 the confrontation clause was held applicable to the states. Pointer v. Texas, 380 U.S. 400, 85 S.Ct. 1065, 13 L.Ed.2d 923 (1965). Prosecution use of former testimony given at a preliminary hearing where petitioner was not represented by counsel was a violation of the clause. The same result would have followed under conventional hearsay doctrine read in the light of a constitutional right to counsel, and nothing in the opinion suggests any difference in essential outline between the hearsay rule and the right of confrontation. In the companion case of Douglas v. Alabama, 380 U.S. 415, 85 S.Ct. 1074, 13 L.Ed.2d 934 (1965), however, the result reached by applying the confrontation clause is one reached less readily via the hearsay rule. A confession implicating petitioner was put before the jury by reading it to the witness in portions and asking if he made that statement. The witness refused to answer on grounds of self-incrimination. The result, said the Court, was to deny cross-examination, and hence confrontation. True, it could broadly be said that the confession was a hearsay statement which for all practical purposes was put in evidence. Yet a more easily accepted explanation of the opinion is that its real thrust was in the direction of curbing undesirable prosecutorial behavior, rather than merely applying rules of exclusion, and that the confrontation clause was the means selected to achieve this end. Comparable facts and a like result appeared in Brookhart v. Janis, 384 U.S. 1, 86 S.Ct. 1245, 16 L.Ed.2d 314 (1966).

The pattern suggested in Douglas was developed further and more distinctly in a pair of cases at the end of the 1966 term. United States v. Wade, 388 U.S. 218, 87 S.Ct. 1926, 18 L.Ed.2d 1149 (1967), and Gilbert v. California, 388 U.S. 263, 87 S.Ct. 1951, 18 L.Ed.2d 1178 (1967), hinged upon practices followed in identifying accused persons before trial. This pretrial identification was said to be so decisive an aspect of the case that accused was entitled to have counsel present; a pretrial identification made in the absence of counsel was not itself receivable in evidence and, in addition, might fatally infect a courtroom identification. The presence of counsel at the earlier identification was described as a necessary prerequisite for "a meaningful confrontation at trial." United States v. Wade, supra, 388 U.S. at p. 236, 87 S.Ct. at p. 1937. Wade involved no evidence of the fact of a prior identification and hence was not susceptible of being decided on hearsay grounds. In Gilbert, witnesses did testify to an earlier identification, readily classifiable as hearsay under a fairly strict view of what constitutes hearsay. The Court, however, carefully avoided basing the decision on the hearsay ground, choosing confrontation instead. 388 U.S. 263, 272, n. 3, 87 S.Ct. 1951. See also Parker v. Gladden, 385 U.S. 363, 87 S.Ct. 468, 17 L.Ed.2d 420 (1966), holding that the right of confrontation was violated when the bailiff made prejudicial statements to jurors, and Note, 75 Yale L.J. 1434 (1966).

Under the earlier cases, the confrontation clause may have been little more than a constitutional embodiment of the hearsay rule, even including traditional exceptions but with some room for expanding them along similar lines. But under the recent cases the impact of the clause clearly extends beyond the confines of the hearsay rule. These considerations have led the Advisory Committee to conclude that a hearsay rule can function usefully as an adjunct to the confrontation right in constitutional areas and independently in nonconstitutional areas. In recognition of the separateness of the confrontation clause and the hearsay rule, and to avoid inviting collisions between them or between the hearsay rule and other exclusionary principles, the exceptions set forth in Rules 803 and 804 are stated in terms of exemption from the general exclusionary mandate of the hearsay rule, rather than in positive terms of admissibility. See Uniform Rule 63(1) to (31) and California Evidence Code §§ 1200-1340.

Restyled 2011

Rule 801. Definitions That Apply to This Article; Exclusions from Hearsay

(a) Statement. "Statement" means a person's oral assertion, written assertion, or nonverbal conduct, if the person intended it as an assertion.

Superseded 2011

Rule 801. Definitions

The following definitions apply under this article:

(a) Statement. A "statement" is (1) an oral or written assertion or (2) nonverbal conduct of a person, if it is intended by the person as an assertion.

Advisory Committee's Note

Subdivision (a). The definition of "statement" assumes importance because the term is used in the definition of hearsay in subdivision (c). The effect of the definition of "statement" is to exclude from the operation of the hearsay rule all evidence of conduct, verbal or nonverbal, not intended as an assertion. The key to the definition is that nothing is an assertion unless intended to be one.

It can scarcely be doubted that an assertion made in words is intended by the declarant to be an assertion. Hence verbal assertions readily fall into the category of "statement." Whether nonverbal conduct should be regarded as a statement for purposes of defining hearsay requires further consideration. Some nonverbal conduct, such as the act of pointing to identify a suspect in a lineup, is clearly the equivalent of words, assertive in nature, and to be regarded as a statement. Other nonverbal conduct, however, may be offered as evidence that the person acted as he did because of his belief in the existence of the condition sought to be proved, from which belief the existence of the condition may be inferred. This sequence is, arguably, in effect an assertion of the existence of the condition and hence properly includable within the hearsay concept. See Morgan, Hearsay Dangers and the Application of the Hearsay Concept, 62 Harv.L.Rev. 177, 214, 217 (1948), and the elaboration in Finman, Implied Assertions as Hearsay: Some Criticisms of the Uniform Rules of Evidence, 14 Stan.L.Rev. 682 (1962). Admittedly evidence of this character is untested with respect to the perception, memory, and narration (or their equivalents) of the actor, but the Advisory Committee is of the view that these dangers are minimal in the absence of an intent to assert and do not justify the loss of the evidence on hearsay grounds. No class of evidence is free of the possibility of fabrication, but the likelihood is less with nonverbal than with assertive verbal conduct. The situations giving rise to the nonverbal conduct are such as virtually to eliminate questions of sincerity. Motivation, the nature of the conduct, and the presence or absence of reliance will bear heavily upon the weight to be given the evidence. Falknor, The "Hear-Say" Rule as a "See-Do" Rule: Evidence of Conduct, 33 Rocky Mt.L.Rev. 133 (1961). Similar considerations govern nonassertive verbal conduct and verbal conduct which is assertive but offered as a basis for inferring something other than the matter asserted, also excluded from the definition of hearsay by the language of subdivision (c).

When evidence of conduct is offered on the theory that it is not a statement, and hence not hearsay, a preliminary determination will be required to determine whether an assertion is intended. The rule is so worded as to place the burden upon the party claiming that the intention existed; ambiguous and doubtful cases will be resolved against him and in favor of admissibility. The determination involves no greater difficulty than many other preliminary questions of fact. Maguire, The Hearsay System: Around and Through the Thicket, 14 Vand.L.Rev. 741, 765-767 (1961).

For similar approaches, see Uniform Rule 62(1); California Evidence Code §§ 225, 1200; Kansas Code of Civil Procedure § 60-459(a); New Jersey Evidence Rule 62(1).

Restyled 2011

(b) Declarant. "Declarant" means the person who made the statement.

(c) Hearsay. "Hearsay" means a statement that:

(1) the declarant does not make while testifying at the current trial or hearing; and

(2) a party offers in evidence to prove the truth of the matter asserted in the statement.

Superseded 2011

(b) Declarant. A "declarant" is a person who makes a statement.

(c) Hearsay. "Hearsay" is a statement, other than one made by the declarant while testifying at the trial or hearing, offered in evidence to prove the truth of the matter asserted.

Advisory Committee's Note

Subdivision (c). The definition follows along familiar lines in including only statements offered to prove the truth of the matter asserted. McCormick § 225; 5 Wigmore § 1361, 6 id. § 1766. If the significance of an offered statement lies solely in the fact that it was made, no issue is raised as to the truth of anything asserted, and the statement is not hearsay. Emich Motors Corp. v. General Motors Corp., 181 F.2d 70 (7th Cir.1950), rev'd on other grounds 340 U.S. 558, 71 S.Ct. 408, 95 L.Ed. 534, letters of complaint from customers offered as a reason for cancellation of dealer's franchise, to rebut contention that franchise was revoked for refusal to finance sales through affiliated finance company. The effect is to exclude from hearsay the entire category of "verbal acts" and "verbal parts of an act," in which the statement itself affects the legal rights of the parties or is a circumstance bearing on conduct affecting their rights.

The definition of hearsay must, of course, be read with reference to the definition of statement set forth in subdivision (a).

Testimony given by a witness in the course of court proceedings is excluded since there is compliance with all the ideal conditions for testifying.

Restyled 2011

(d) Statements That Are Not Hearsay. A statement that meets the following conditions is not hearsay:

(1) ***A Declarant-Witness's Prior Statement.*** The declarant testifies and is subject to cross-examination about a prior statement, and the statement:

Superseded 2011

(d) Statements which are not hearsay. A statement is not hearsay if—

(1) Prior statement by witness. The declarant testifies at the trial or hearing and is subject to cross-examination concerning the statement, and the statement is—

Case Note

Admissibility of a prior statement of identification (Rule 801(d)(1)(C)) is not precluded by the witness's inability, due to memory loss, to explain the basis for the prior identification. A witness is "subject to cross-examination" concerning the statement if he is on the stand under oath and responds willingly to questions, and the court does not significantly limit the scope of cross-examination. United States v. Owens. 484 U.S. 554, 108 S.Ct. 838, 98 L.Ed. 2d 951 (1988).

Advisory Committee's Note

Subdivision (d). Several types of statements which would otherwise literally fall within the definition are expressly excluded from it:

(1) Prior statement by witness. Considerable controversy has attended the question whether a prior out-of-court statement by a person now available for cross-examination concerning it, under oath and in the presence of the trier of fact, should be classed as hearsay. If the witness admits on the stand that he made the statement and that it was true, he adopts the statement and there is no hearsay problem. The hearsay problem arises when the witness on the stand denies having made the statement or admits having made it but denies its truth. The argument in favor of treating these latter statements as hearsay is based upon the ground that the conditions of oath, cross-examination, and demeanor observation did not prevail at the time the statement was made and cannot adequately be supplied by the later examination. The logic of the situation is troublesome. So far as concerns the oath, its mere presence has never been regarded as sufficient to remove a statement from the hearsay category, and it receives much less emphasis than cross-examination as a truth-compelling device. While strong expressions are found to the effect that no conviction can be had or important right taken away on the basis of statements not made under fear of prosecution for perjury, Bridges v. Wixon, 326 U.S. 135, 65 S.Ct. 1443, 89 L.Ed. 2103 (1945), the fact is that, of the many common law exceptions to the hearsay rule, only that for reported testimony has required the statement to have been made under oath. Nor is it satisfactorily explained why cross-examination cannot be conducted subsequently with success. The decisions contending most vigorously for its inadequacy in fact demonstrate quite thorough exploration of the weaknesses and doubts attending the earlier statement. State v. Saporen, 205 Minn. 358, 285 N.W. 898 (1939); Ruhala v. Roby, 379 Mich. 102, 150 N.W.2d 146 (1967); People v. Johnson, 68 Cal.2d 646, 68 Cal.Rptr. 599, 441 P.2d 111 (1968). In respect to demeanor, as Judge Learned Hand observed in Di Carlo v. United States, 6 F.2d 364 (2d Cir.1925), when the jury decides that the truth is not what the witness says now, but what he said before, they are still deciding from what they see and hear in court. The bulk of the case law nevertheless has been against allowing prior statements of witnesses to be used generally as substantive evidence. Most of the writers and Uniform Rule 63(1) have taken the opposite position. The position taken by the Advisory Committee in formulating this part of the rule is founded upon an unwillingness to countenance the general use of prior prepared statements as substantive evidence, but with a recognition that particular circumstances call for a contrary result. The judgment is one more of experience than of logic. The rule requires in each instance, as a general safeguard, that the declarant actually testify as a witness, and it then enumerates three situations in which the statement is

excepted from the category of hearsay. Compare Uniform Rule 63(1) which allows any out-of-court statement of a declarant who is present at the trial and available for cross-examination.

Restyled 2011

(A) is inconsistent with the declarant's testimony and was given under penalty of perjury at a trial, hearing, or other proceeding or in a deposition;

Superseded 2011

(A) inconsistent with the declarant's testimony, and was given under oath subject to the penalty of perjury at a trial, hearing, or other proceeding, or in a deposition, or

Advisory Committee's Note

(A) Prior inconsistent statements traditionally have been admissible to impeach but not as substantive evidence. Under the rule they are substantive evidence. As has been said by the California Law Revision Commission with respect to a similar provision:

> "Section 1235 admits inconsistent statements of witnesses because the dangers against which the hearsay rule is designed to protect are largely nonexistent. The declarant is in court and may be examined and cross-examined in regard to his statements and their subject matter. In many cases, the inconsistent statement is more likely to be true than the testimony of the witness at the trial because it was made nearer in time to the matter to which it relates and is less likely to be influenced by the controversy that gave rise to the litigation. The trier of fact has the declarant before it and can observe his demeanor and the nature of his testimony as he denies or tries to explain away the inconsistency. Hence, it is in as good a position to determine the truth or falsity of the prior statement as it is to determine the truth or falsity of the inconsistent testimony given in court. Moreover, Section 1235 will provide a party with desirable protection against the 'turncoat' witness who changes his story on the stand and deprives the party calling him of evidence essential to his case." Comment, California Evidence Code § 1235. See also McCormick § 39.

The Advisory Committee finds these views more convincing than those expressed in People v. Johnson, 68 Cal.2d 646, 68 Cal.Rptr. 599, 441 P.2d 111 (1968). The constitutionality of the Advisory Committee's view was upheld in California v. Green, 399 U.S. 149, 90 S.Ct. 1930, 26 L.Ed.2d 489 (1970). Moreover, the requirement that the statement be inconsistent with the testimony given assures a thorough exploration of both versions while the witness is on the stand and bars any general and indiscriminate use of previously prepared statements.

House Judiciary Committee Report

Present federal law, except in the Second Circuit, permits the use of prior inconsistent statements of a witness for impeachment only. Rule 801(d)(1) as proposed by the Court would have permitted all such statements to be admissible as substantive evidence, an approach followed by a small but growing number of State jurisdictions and recently held constitutional in California v. Green, 399 U.S. 149 (1970). Although there was some support expressed for the Court Rule, based largely on the need to counteract the effect of witness intimidation in criminal cases, the Committee decided to adopt a compromise version of the Rule similar to the position of the Second Circuit. The Rule as amended draws a distinction between types of prior inconsistent statements (other than statements of identification of a person made after perceiving him which are currently admissible, see United States v. Anderson, 406 F.2d 719, 720 (4th Cir.), cert. denied, 395 U.S. 967 (1969)) and allows only those made while the declarant was subject to cross-examination at a trial or hearing or in a deposition, to be admissible for their truth. Compare United States v. DeSisto, 329 F.2d 929 (2nd Cir.), cert. denied, 377 U.S. 979 (1964); United States v. Cunningham, 446 F.2d 194 (2nd Cir.1971) (restricting the admissibility of prior inconsistent statements as substantive evidence to those made under oath in a formal proceeding, but not requiring that there have been an opportunity for cross-examination). The rationale for the Committee's decision is that (1) unlike in most other situations involving unsworn or oral statements, there can be no dispute as to whether the prior statement was made; and (2) the context of a formal proceeding, an oath, and the opportunity for cross-examination provide firm additional assurances of the reliability of the prior statement.

Senate Judiciary Committee Report

Rule 801 defines what is and what is not hearsay for the purpose of admitting a prior statement as substantive evidence. A prior statement of a witness at a trial or hearing which is inconsistent with his testimony is, of course, always admissible for the purpose of impeaching the witness' credibility.

As submitted by the Supreme Court, subdivision (d)(1)(A) made admissible as substantive evidence the prior statement of a witness inconsistent with his present testimony.

The House severely limited the admissibility of prior inconsistent statements by adding a requirement that the prior statement must have been subject to cross-examination, thus precluding even the use of grand jury statements. The requirement that the prior statement must have been subject to cross-examination appears unnecessary since this rule comes into play only when the witness testifies in the present trial. At that time, he is on the stand and can explain an earlier position and be cross-examined as to both. The requirement that the statement be under oath also appears unnecessary. Notwithstanding the absence of an oath contemporaneous with the statement, the witness, when on the stand, qualifying or denying the prior statement, is under oath. In any event, of all the many recognized exceptions to the hearsay rule, only one (former testimony) requires that the out-of-court statement have been made under oath. With respect to the lack of evidence of the demeanor of the witness at the time of the prior statement, it would be difficult to improve upon Judge Learned Hand's observation that when the jury decides that the truth is not what the witness says now but what he said before, they are still deciding from what they see and hear in court. [Di Carlo v. U.S., 6 F.2d 364 (2d Cir.1925).]

The rule as submitted by the Court has positive advantages. The prior statement was made nearer in time to the events, when memory was fresher and intervening influences had not been brought into play. A realistic method is provided for dealing with the turncoat witness who changes his story on the stand. [See Comment, California Evidence Code § 1235; McCormick, Evidence, § 38 (2nd ed. 1972).]

New Jersey, California, and Utah have adopted a rule similar to this one; and Nevada, New Mexico, and Wisconsin have adopted the identical Federal rule.

For all of these reasons, we think the House amendment should be rejected and the rule as submitted by the Supreme Court reinstated. [It would appear that some of the opposition to this Rule is based on a concern that a person could be convicted solely upon evidence admissible under this Rule. The Rule, however, is not addressed to the question of the sufficiency of evidence to send a case to the jury, but merely as to its admissibility. Factual circumstances could well arise where, if this were the sole evidence, dismissal would be appropriate.]

Conference Committee Report

The House bill provides that a statement is not hearsay if the declarant testifies and is subject to cross-examination concerning the statement and if the statement is inconsistent with his testimony and was given under oath subject to cross-examination and subject to the penalty of perjury at a trial or hearing or in a deposition. The Senate amendment drops the requirement that the prior statement be given under oath subject to cross-examination and subject to the penalty of perjury at a trial or hearing or in a deposition.

The Conference adopts the Senate amendment with an amendment, so that the rule now requires that the prior inconsistent statement be given under oath subject to the penalty of perjury at a trial, hearing, or other proceeding, or in a deposition. The rule as adopted covers statements before a grand jury. Prior inconsistent statements may, of course, be used for impeaching the credibility of a witness. When the prior inconsistent statement is one made by a defendant in a criminal case, it is covered by Rule 801(d)(2).

Restyled 2011

(B) is consistent with the declarant's testimony and is offered:

(i) to rebut an express or implied charge that the declarant recently fabricated it or acted from a recent improper influence or motive in so testifying; or

(ii) to rehabilitate the declarant's credibility as a witness when attacked on another ground; or [*Amended 2014.*]

Superseded 2011

(B) consistent with the declarant's testimony and is offered to rebut an express or implied charge against the declarant of recent fabrication or improper influence or motive, or

Case Notes

A prior consistent statement of a witness, offered to rebut a charge of recent fabrication or improper influence or motive is admissible only if the statement was made before the recent fabrication is alleged to have occurred or the improper influence or motive came into being. Prior consistent statements generally carry little rebuttal force, but a consistent statement that predates the motive is a square rebuttal of the charge that the testimony was contrived as a consequence of that motive. Tome v. United States, 513 U.S. 150, 115 S.Ct. 696, 130 L.Ed.2d 574 (1995).

A witness's prior consistent statement may be admitted for the non-hearsay purpose of rehabilitating the witness's credibility even if it is not admissible for its truth under Rule 801(d)(1)(B). *E.g.*, U.S. v. Ellis, 121 F.3d 908, 919-920 (4th Cir. 1997).

Advisory Committee's Note

(B) Prior consistent statements traditionally have been admissible to rebut charges of recent fabrication or improper influence or motive but not as substantive evidence. Under the rule they are substantive evidence. The prior statement is consistent with the testimony given on the stand, and, if the opposite party wishes to open the door for its admission in evidence, no sound reason is apparent why it should not be received generally.

Advisory Committee's Note to 2014 Amendment

Rule 801(d)(l)(B), as originally adopted, provided for substantive use of certain prior consistent statements of a witness subject to cross-examination. As the Advisory Committee noted, "[t]he prior statement is consistent with the testimony given on the stand, and, if the opposite party wishes to open the door for its admission in evidence, no sound reason is apparent why it should not be received generally."

Though the original Rule 801(d)(1)(B) provided for substantive use of certain prior consistent statements, the scope of that Rule was limited. The Rule covered only those consistent statements that were offered to rebut charges of recent fabrication or improper motive or influence. The Rule did not, for example, provide for substantive admissibility of consistent statements that are probative to explain what otherwise appears to be an inconsistency in the witness's testimony. Nor did it cover consistent statements that would be probative to rebut a charge of faulty memory. Thus, the Rule left many prior consistent statements potentially admissible only for the limited purpose of rehabilitating a witness's credibility. The original Rule also led to some conflict in the cases; some courts distinguished between substantive and rehabilitative use for prior consistent statements, while others appeared to hold that prior consistent statements must be admissible under Rule 801(d)(l)(B) or not at all.

The amendment retains the requirement set forth in *Tome v. United States, 513 U.S. 150 (1995):* that under Rule 801(d)(l)(B), a consistent statement offered to rebut a charge of recent fabrication of improper influence or motive must have been made before the alleged fabrication or improper inference or motive arose. The intent of the amendment is to extend substantive effect to consistent statements that rebut other attacks on a witness — such as the charges of inconsistency or faulty memory.

The amendment does not change the traditional and well-accepted limits on bringing prior consistent statements before the factfinder for credibility purposes. It does not allow impermissible bolstering of a witness. As before, prior consistent statements under the amendment may be brought before the factfinder only if they properly rehabilitate a witness whose credibility has been attacked. As before, to be admissible for rehabilitation, a prior consistent statement must satisfy the strictures of Rule 403. As before, the trial court has ample discretion to exclude prior consistent statements that are cumulative accounts of an event. The amendment does not make any consistent statement admissible that was not admissible previously--the only difference is that prior consistent statements otherwise admissible for rehabilitation are now admissible substantively as well.

Restyled 2011

(C) identifies a person as someone the declarant perceived earlier.

Superseded 2011

(C) one of identification of a person made after perceiving the person [*Added 1975*]; or

Advisory Committee's Note

(C) The admission of evidence of identification finds substantial support, although it falls beyond a doubt in the category of prior out-of-court statements. Illustrative are People v. Gould, 54 Cal.2d 621, 7 Cal.Rptr. 273, 354 P.2d 865 (1960); Judy v. State, 218 Md. 168, 146 A.2d 29 (1958); State v. Simmons, 63 Wash.2d 17, 385 P.2d 389 (1963); California Evidence Code § 1238; New Jersey Evidence Rule 63(1)(c); N.Y.Code of Criminal Procedure § 393-b. Further cases are found in 4 Wigmore § 1130. The basis is the generally unsatisfactory and inconclusive nature of courtroom identifications as compared with those made at an earlier time under less suggestive conditions. The Supreme Court considered the admissibility of evidence of prior identification in Gilbert v. California, 388 U.S. 263, 87 S.Ct. 1951, 18 L.Ed.2d 1178 (1967). Exclusion of lineup identification was held to be required because the accused did not then have the assistance of counsel. Significantly, the Court carefully refrained from placing its decision on the ground that testimony as to the making of a prior out-of-court identification ("That's the man") violated either the hearsay rule or the right of confrontation because not made under oath, subject to immediate cross-examination, in the presence of the trier. Instead the Court observed:

"There is a split among the States concerning the admissibility of prior extra-judicial identifications, as independent evidence of identity, both by the witness and third parties present at the prior identification. See 71 ALR2d 449. It has been held that the prior identification is hearsay, and, when admitted through the testimony of the identifier, is merely a prior consistent statement. The recent trend, however, is to admit the prior identification under the exception that admits as substantive evidence a prior communication by a witness who is available for cross-examination at the trial. See 5 ALR2d Later Case Service 1225-1228. . . ." 388 U.S. at 272, n. 3, 87 S.Ct. at 1956.

Senate Judiciary Committee Report

As submitted by the Supreme Court and as passed by the House, subdivision (d)(1)(C) of rule 801 made admissible the prior statement identifying a person made after perceiving him. The committee decided to delete this provision because of the concern that a person could be convicted solely upon evidence admissible under this subdivision.

Conference Committee Report

The House bill provides that a statement is not hearsay if the declarant testifies and is subject to cross-examination concerning the statement and the statement is one of identification of a person made after perceiving him. The Senate amendment eliminated this provision.

The Conference adopts the Senate amendment.

1975 Amendment

House Judiciary Committee Report

(H. Rep. 94-355)

* * * [When the bills that became the Federal Rules of Evidence were in Conference Committee, the Senate strenuously insisted upon its version of Rule 801(d)(1), which omitted subparagraph (C) relating to witnesses' prior statements of identification]; in fact, it was indicated that any compromise that included the House version of the rule would face extended discussion during the Senate debate. In the face of this, the House Conferees agreed to the Senate version of Rule 801(d)(1),

[This bill] * * * seeks to put back into Rule 801(d)(1) the language that was struck at Conference. In other words, the Senate is now acceding to the House version of Rule 801(d)(1).

Rule 801(d)(1)(C), as it is proposed to read, has a precondition to the use of the out-of-court statement of identification. The person who made the statement (the "declarant") must testify at the trial or hearing and must be subject to cross-examination concerning the statement. Even if this precondition is met, the out-of-court statement of identification must still meet constitutional standards. If the precondition is satisfied and the constitutional standards are met, then the out-of-court statement of identification is admissible.

* * *

B. Case Law

There was a split among the authorities as to whether out-of-court statements of identification are admissible. See Annot., 71 A.L.R. 2d 449.

The recent trend, however, is to admit the prior identification under the exception that admits as substantive evidence a prior communication by a witness who is available for cross-examination at trial.

* * * Rule 801(d)(1)(C) * * * is fully consistent with current Federal case law. Federal case law treats such statements as exceptions to the hearsay rule; Rule 801(d)(1)(C) defines them not to be hearsay. The result is the same in either instance—the statement is admissible if the person who made it testifies and is subject to cross-examination.

C. Rationale

Courtroom identification can be very suggestive. The defendant is known to be present and generally sits in a certain location. Out-of-court identifications are generally more reliable. They take place relatively soon after the offense, while the incident is still reasonably fresh in the witness' mind. Out-of-court identifications are particularly important in jurisdictions where there may be a long delay between arrest or indictment and trial. As time goes by, a witness' memory will fade and his identification will become less reliable. An early, out-of-court identification provides fairness to defendants by ensuring accuracy of the identification. At the same time, it aids the government by making sure that delays in the criminal justice system do not lead to cases falling through because the witness can no longer recall the identity of the person he saw commit the crime.

The justification for not admitting out-of-court statements of identification was stated in the Senate Report on the Federal Rules of Evidence bill to be a "concern that a person could be convicted solely upon evidence admitted under this (exception)." * * * The Rule, however, is not addressed to the question of the sufficiency of evidence to send a case to the jury, but merely to its admissibility.

Dissenting Views of Hon. Elizabeth Holtzman

I dissent from the Committee's favorable recommendation of S. 1549.

Eyewitness testimony is notoriously unreliable. As the Supreme Court has stated: 'The vagaries of eyewitness identification are well-known; the annals of criminal law are rife with instances of mistaken identification.' U.S. v. Wade, 388 U.S. 218 (1967).

Nonetheless, S. 1549 would open the doors wide to the admission of all kinds of out-of-court eyewitness identification. The bill creates a new Rule of Evidence for the federal courts. In a departure from current practice, this rule would allow the admission of a prior out-of-court identification made by a witness. The identification could be admitted even if: (1) The witness subsequently retracted it, and (2) the identification were made under highly suggestive circumstances.

* * *

S. 1549 would allow unsworn out-of-court identification testimony to be used as substantive evidence against the defendant. This means that where the defendant has previously been identified by a witness, that identification may be used to convict the defendant—even if the witness subsequently retracts the identification in testimony before the jury. Thus, for example, a witness may have identified a defendant under confusing or highly suggestive circumstances (as after a robbery or in a hospital room), but upon reflection may realize that the identification was mistaken. Under this rule, the earlier, admittedly incorrect, identification could be used to convict the defendant.

In addition, this rule would permit a third party to testify to a witness' out-of-court identification. Thus, a policeman could testify that a witness had identified the defendant at a lineup even though the witness no longer believes the defendant committed the particular crime. * * *

Since the use of such identification testimony raises complex questions, certainly it should not be enacted without careful consideration. Unfortunately, no hearings have been held on this bill either in the Senate or the House. * * * [9]

Restyled 2011

(2) ***An Opposing Party's Statement.*** The statement is offered against an opposing party and:

Committee Note to 2011 Restyled Rule

Statements falling under the hearsay exclusion provided by Rule 801(d)(2) are no longer referred to as "admissions" in the title to the subdivision. The term "admissions" is confusing because not all statements covered by the exclusion are admissions in the colloquial sense - a statement can be within the exclusion even if it "admitted" nothing and was not against the party's interest when made. The term "admissions" also raises confusion in comparison with the Rule 804(b)(3) exception for declarations against interest. No change in application of the exclusion is intended.

Superseded 2011

(2) Admission by party-opponent. The statement is offered against a party and is—

Advisory Committee's Note

Several types of statements which would otherwise literally fall within the definition [of hearsay] are expressly excluded from it: * * *

(2) Admissions. Admissions by a party-opponent are excluded from the category of hearsay on the theory that their admissibility in evidence is the result of the adversary system rather than satisfaction of the conditions of the hearsay rule. Strahorn, A Reconsideration of the Hearsay Rule and Admissions, 85 U.Pa.L.Rev. 484, 564 (1937); Morgan, Basic Problems of Evidence 265 (1962); 4 Wigmore § 1048. No guarantee of trustworthiness is required in the case of an admission. The freedom which admissions have enjoyed from technical demands of searching for an assurance of trustworthiness in some against-interest circumstance, and from the restrictive influences of the opinion rule and the rule requiring firsthand knowledge, when taken with the apparently prevalent satisfaction with the results, calls for generous treatment of this avenue to admissibility.

The rule specifies five categories of statements for which the responsibility of a party is considered sufficient to justify reception in evidence against him.

[9]Although this rule was contained in the new Rules of Evidence as passed by the House, very little attention was paid to it. It was stricken from the final version of the Rules as a result of vigorous objection by Senator Ervin.

Restyled 2011

(A) was made by the party in an individual or representative capacity;

Superseded 2011

(A) the party's own statement, in either an individual or a representative capacity or

Advisory Committee's Note

(A) A party's own statement is the classic example of an admission. If he has a representative capacity and the statement is offered against him in that capacity, no inquiry whether he was acting in the representative capacity in making the statement is required; the statement need only be relevant to represent affairs. To the same effect in California Evidence Code § 1220. Compare Uniform Rule 63(7), requiring a statement to be made in a representative capacity to be admissible against a party in a representative capacity.

Restyled 2011

(B) is one the party manifested that it adopted or believed to be true;

Superseded 2011

(B) a statement of which the party has manifested an adoption or belief in its truth, or

Advisory Committee's Note

(B) Under established principles an admission may be made by adopting or acquiescing in the statement of another. While knowledge of contents would ordinarily be essential, this is not inevitably so: "X is a reliable person and knows what he is talking about." See McCormick § 246, p. 527, n. 15. Adoption or acquiescence may be manifested in any appropriate manner. When silence is relied upon, the theory is that the person would, under the circumstances, protest the statement made in his presence, if untrue. The decision in each case calls for an evaluation in terms of probable human behavior. In civil cases, the results have generally been satisfactory. In criminal cases, however, troublesome questions have been raised by decisions holding that failure to deny is an admission: the inference is a fairly weak one, to begin with; silence may be motivated by advice of counsel or realization that "anything you say may be used against you"; unusual opportunity is afforded to manufacture evidence; and encroachment upon the privilege against self-incrimination seems inescapably to be involved. However, recent decisions of the Supreme Court relating to custodial interrogation and the right to counsel appear to resolve these difficulties. Hence the rule contains no special provisions concerning failure to deny in criminal cases.

Restyled 2011

(C) was made by a person whom the party authorized to make a statement on the subject;

Superseded 2011

(C) a statement by a person authorized by the party to make a statement concerning the subject, or

Advisory Committee's Note

(C) No authority is required for the general proposition that a statement authorized by a party to be made should have the status of an admission by the party. However, the question arises whether only statements to third persons should be so regarded, to the exclusion of statements by the agent to the principal. The rule is phrased broadly so as to encompass both. While it may be argued that the agent authorized to make statements to his principal does not speak for him, Morgan, Basic Problems of Evidence 273 (1962), communication to an outsider has not generally been thought to be an essential characteristic of an admission. Thus a party's books or records are usable against him, without regard to any intent to disclose to third persons. 5 Wigmore § 1557. See also McCormick § 78, pp. 159-161. In accord is New Jersey Evidence Rule 63(8)(a). Cf. Uniform Rule 63(8)(a) and California Evidence Code § 1222 which limit status as an admission in this regard to statements authorized by the party to be made "for" him, which is perhaps an ambiguous limitation to statements to third persons. Falknor, Vicarious Admissions and the Uniform Rules, 14 Vand.L.Rev. 855, 860-861 (1961).

Restyled 2011

(D) was made by the party's agent or employee on a matter within the scope of that relationship and while it existed; or

Superseded 2011

(D) a statement by the party's agent or servant concerning a matter within the scope of the agency or employment, made during the existence of the relationship, or

Advisory Committee's Note

(D) The tradition has been to test the admissibility of statements by agents, as admissions, by applying the usual test of agency. Was the admission made by the agent acting in the scope of his employment? Since few principals employ agents for the purpose of making damaging statements, the usual result was exclusion of the statement. Dissatisfaction with this loss of valuable and helpful evidence has been increasing. A substantial trend favors admitting statements related to a matter within the scope of the agency or employment. Grayson v. Williams, 256 F.2d 61 (10th Cir.1958); Koninklijke Luchtvaart Maatschappij N.V. KLM Royal Dutch Airlines v. Tuller, 110 U.S.App.D.C. 282, 292 F.2d 775, 784 (1961); Martin v. Savage Truck Lines, Inc., 121 F.Supp. 417 (D.D.C.1954), and numerous state court decisions collected in 4 Wigmore, 1964 Supp. pp. 66-73, with comments by the editor that the statements should have been excluded as not within scope of agency. For the traditional view see Northern Oil Co. v. Socony Mobil Oil Co., 347 F.2d 81, 85 (2d Cir.1965) and cases cited therein. Similar provisions are found in Uniform Rule 63(9)(a), Kansas Code of Civil Procedure § 60-460(i)(1), and New Jersey Evidence Rule 63(9)(a).

Restyled 2011

(E) was made by the party's co-conspirator during and in furtherance of the conspiracy.

Superseded 2011

(E) a statement by a coconspirator of a party during the course and in furtherance of the conspiracy.

Case Note

A showing of the declarant's unavailability is not prerequisite to the admissibility of a statement under the co-conspirator exemption. United States v. Inadi, 475 U.S. 387, 106 S.Ct. 1121, 89 L.Ed. 2d 390 (1986).

Advisory Committee's Note

(E) The limitation upon the admissibility of statements of co-conspirators to those made "during the course and in furtherance of the conspiracy" is in the accepted pattern. While the broadened view of agency taken in item (iv) might suggest wider admissibility of statements of co-conspirators, the agency theory of conspiracy is at best a fiction and ought not to serve as a basis for admissibility beyond that already established. See Levie, Hearsay and Conspiracy, 52 Mich.L.Rev. 1159 (1954); Comment, 25 U.Chi.L.Rev. 530 (1958). The rule is consistent with the position of the Supreme Court in denying admissibility to statements made after the objectives of the conspiracy have either failed or been achieved. Krulewitch v. United States, 336 U.S. 440, 69 S.Ct. 716, 93 L.Ed. 790 (1949); Wong Sun v. United States, 371 U.S. 471, 490, 83 S.Ct. 407, 9 L.Ed.2d 441 (1963). For similarly limited provisions see California Evidence Code § 1223 and New Jersey Rule 63(9)(b). Cf. Uniform Rule 63(9)(b).

Senate Judiciary Committee Report

The House approved the long-accepted rule that "a statement by a coconspirator of a party during the course and in furtherance of the conspiracy" is not hearsay as it was submitted by the Supreme Court. While the rule refers to a coconspirator, it is this committee's understanding that the rule is meant to carry forward the universally accepted doctrine that a joint venturer is considered as a coconspirator for the purposes of this rule even though no conspiracy has been charged. United States v. Rinaldi, 393 F.2d 97, 99 (2d Cir.), cert. denied 393 U.S. 913 (1968); United States v. Spencer, 415 F.2d 1301, 1304 (7th Cir. 1969).

Restyled 2011

The statement must be considered but does not by itself establish the declarant's authority under (C); the existence or scope of the relationship under (D); or the existence of the conspiracy or participation in it under (E).

Superseded 2011

The contents of the statement shall be considered but are not alone sufficient to establish the declarant's authority under subdivision (C), the agency or employment relationship and scope thereof under subdivision (D), or the existence of the conspiracy and the participation therein of the declarant and the party against whom the statement is offered under subdivision (E). [*This unnumbered sentence added 1997.*]

Advisory Committee's Note to 1997 Amendment

Rule 801(d)(2) has been amended in order to respond to three issues raised by Bourjaily v. United States, 483 U.S. 171 (1987). First, the amendment codifies the holding in Bourjaily by stating expressly that a court shall consider the contents of a coconspirator's statement in determining "the existence of the conspiracy and the participation therein of the declarant and the party against whom the statement is offered." According to Bourjaily, Rule 104(a) requires these preliminary questions to be established by a preponderance of the evidence.

Second, the amendment resolves an issue on which the Court had reserved decision. It provides that the contents of the declarant's statement do not alone suffice to establish a conspiracy in which the declarant and the defendant participated. The court must consider in addition the circumstances surrounding the statement, such as the identity of the speaker, the context in which the statement was made, or evidence corroborating the contents of the statement in making its determination as to each preliminary question. This amendment is in accordance with existing practice. Every court of appeals that has resolved this issue requires some evidence in addition to the contents of the statement. See, e.g., United States v. Beckham, 968 F.2d 47, 51 (D.C.Cir.1992); United States v. Sepulveda, 15 F.3d 1161, 1181-82 (1st Cir.1993), cert. denied, 114 S.Ct. 2714 (1994); United States v. Daly, 842 F.2d 1380, 1386 (2d Cir.), cert. denied, 488 U.S. 821 (1988); United States v. Clark, 18 F.3d 1337, 1341-42 (6th Cir.), cert. denied, 115 S.Ct. 152 (1994); United States v. Zambrana,

841 F.2d 1320, 1344-45 (7th Cir.1988); United States v. Silverman, 861 F.2d 571, 577 (9th Cir.1988); United States v. Gordon, 844 F.2d 1397, 1402 (9th Cir.1988); United States v. Hernandez, 829 F.2d 988, 993 (10th Cir.1987), cert. denied, 485 U.S. 1013 (1988); United States v. Byrom, 910 F.2d 725, 736 (11th Cir.1990).

Third, the amendment extends the reasoning of Bourjaily to statements offered under subdivisions (C) and (D) of Rule 801(d)(2). In Bourjaily, the Court rejected treating foundational facts pursuant to the law of agency in favor of an evidentiary approach governed by Rule 104(a). The Advisory Committee believes it appropriate to treat analogously preliminary questions relating to the declarant's authority under subdivision (C), and the agency or employment relationship and scope thereof under subdivision (D).

Restyled 2011

Rule 802. The Rule Against Hearsay

Hearsay is not admissible unless any of the following provides otherwise:

- a federal statute;
- these rules; or
- other rules prescribed by the Supreme Court.

Superseded 2011

Rule 802. Hearsay Rule

Hearsay is not admissible except as provided by these rules or by other rules prescribed by the Supreme Court pursuant to statutory authority or by Act of Congress.

Advisory Committee's Note

The provision excepting from the operation of the rule hearsay which is made admissible by other rules adopted by the Supreme Court or by Act of Congress continues the admissibility thereunder of hearsay which would not qualify under these Evidence Rules. The following examples illustrate the working of the exception:

FEDERAL RULES OF CIVIL PROCEDURE

Rule 4(g): proof of service by affidavit.
Rule 32: admissibility of depositions.
Rule 43(e): affidavits when motion based on facts not appearing of record.
Rule 56: affidavits in summary judgment proceedings.
Rule 65(b): showing by affidavit for temporary restraining order.

FEDERAL RULES OF CRIMINAL PROCEDURE

Rule 4(a): affidavits to show grounds for issuing warrants.
Rule 12(b)(4): affidavits to determine issues of fact in connection with motions.

ACTS OF CONGRESS

10 U.S.C. § 7730: affidavits of unavailable witnesses in actions for damages caused by vessel in naval service, or towage or salvage of same, when taking of testimony or bringing of action delayed or stayed on security grounds.
29 U.S.C. § 161(4): affidavit as proof of service in NLRB proceedings.
38 U.S.C. § 5206: affidavit as proof of posting notice of sale of unclaimed property by Veterans Administration.

Restyled 2011

Rule 803. Exceptions to the Rule Against Hearsay — Regardless of Whether the Declarant Is Available as a Witness

The following are not excluded by the rule against hearsay, regardless of whether the declarant is available as a witness:

Superseded 2011

Rule 803. Hearsay Exceptions; Availability of Declarant Immaterial

The following are not excluded by the hearsay rule, even though the declarant is available as a witness:

Advisory Committee's Note

The exceptions are phrased in terms of nonapplication of the hearsay rule, rather than in positive terms of admissibility, in order to repel any implication that other possible grounds for exclusion are eliminated from consideration.

The present rule proceeds upon the theory that under appropriate circumstances a hearsay statement may possess circumstantial guarantees of trustworthiness sufficient to justify nonproduction of the declarant in person at the trial even though he may be available. The theory finds vast support in the many exceptions to the hearsay rule developed by the common law in which unavailability of the declarant is not a relevant factor. The present rule is a synthesis of them, with revision where modern developments and conditions are believed to make that course appropriate.

In a hearsay situation, the declarant is, of course, a witness, and neither this rule nor Rule 804 dispenses with the requirement of firsthand knowledge. It may appear from his statement or be inferable from circumstances. See Rule 602.

Restyled 2011

(1) ***Present Sense Impression.*** A statement describing or explaining an event or condition, made while or immediately after the declarant perceived it.

Superseded 2011

(1) Present sense impression. A statement describing or explaining an event or condition made while the declarant was perceiving the event or condition, or immediately thereafter.

Editor's Note

The notes to Exceptions (1) and (2) are combined together following Exception (2).

Restyled 2011

(2) ***Excited Utterance.*** A statement relating to a startling event or condition, made while the declarant was under the stress of excitement that it caused.

Superseded 2011

(2) Excited utterance. A statement relating to a startling event or condition made while the declarant was under the stress of excitement caused by the event or condition.

Advisory Committee's Note

Exceptions (1) and (2). In considerable measure these two examples overlap, though based on somewhat different theories. The most significant practical difference will lie in the time lapse allowable between event and statement.

The underlying theory of Exception (1) is that substantial contemporaneity of event and statement negate the likelihood of deliberate or conscious misrepresentation. Moreover, if the witness is the declarant, he may be examined on the statement. If the witness is not the declarant, he may be examined as to the circumstances as an aid in evaluating the statement. Morgan, Basic Problems of Evidence 340-341 (1962).

The theory of Exception (2) is simply that circumstances may produce a condition of excitement which temporarily stills the capacity of reflection and produces utterances free of conscious fabrication. 6 Wigmore § 1747, p. 135. Spontaneity is the key factor in each instance, though arrived at by somewhat different routes. Both are needed in order to avoid needless niggling.

While the theory of Exception (2) has been criticized on the ground that excitement impairs accuracy of observation as well as eliminating conscious fabrication, Hutchins and Slesinger, Some Observations on the Law of Evidence: Spontaneous Exclamations, 28 Colum.L.Rev. 432 (1928), it finds support in cases without number. See cases in 6 Wigmore § 1750; Annot. 53 A.L.R.2d 1245 (statements as to cause of or responsibility for motor vehicle accident); Annot., 4 A.L.R.3d 149 (accusatory statements by homicide victims). Since unexciting events are less likely to evoke comment, decisions involving Exception (1) are far less numerous. Illustrative are Tampa Elec. Co. v. Getrost, 151 Fla. 558, 10 So.2d 83 (1942); Houston Oxygen Co. v. Davis, 139 Tex. 1, 161 S.W.2d 474 (1942); and cases cited in McCormick § 273, p. 585, n. 4.

With respect to the *time element*, Exception (1) recognizes that in many, if not most, instances precise contemporaneity is not possible and hence a slight lapse is allowable. Under Exception (2) the standard of measurement is the duration of the state of excitement. "How long can excitement prevail? Obviously there are no pat answers and the character of the transaction or event will largely determine the significance of the time factor." Slough, Spontaneous Statements and State of Mind, 46 Iowa L.Rev. 224, 243 (1961); McCormick § 272, p. 580.

Participation by the declarant is not required: a non-participant may be moved to describe what he perceives, and one may be startled by an event in which he is not an actor. Slough, supra; McCormick, supra; 6 Wigmore § 1755; Annot. 78 A.L.R.2d 300.

Whether *proof of the startling event* may be made by the statement itself is largely an academic question, since in most cases there is present at least circumstantial evidence that something of a startling nature must have occurred. For cases in which the evidence consists of the condition of the declarant (injuries, state of shock), see Insurance Co. v. Mosely, 75 U.S. (8 Wall.) 397, 19 L.Ed. 437 (1869); Wheeler v. United States, 93 U.S. App.D.C. 159, 211 F.2d 19 (1953), cert. denied 347 U.S. 1019, 74 S.Ct. 876, 98 L.Ed. 1140; Wetherbee v. Safety Casualty Co., 219 F.2d 274 (5th Cir.1955); Lampe v. United States, 97 U.S.App.D.C. 160, 229 F.2d 43 (1956). Nevertheless, on occasion the only evidence may be the content of the statement itself, and rulings that it may be sufficient are described as "increasing," Slough, supra at 246, and as the "prevailing practice," McCormick § 272, p. 579. Illustrative are Armour & Co. v. Industrial Commission, 78 Colo. 569, 243 P. 546 (1926); Young v. Stewart, 191 N.C. 297, 131 S.E. 735 (1926). Moreover, under Rule 104(a) the judge is not limited by the hearsay rule in passing upon preliminary questions of fact.

Proof of declarant's perception by his statement presents similar considerations when declarant is identified. People v. Poland, 22 Ill.2d 175, 174 N.E.2d 804 (1961). However, when declarant is an unidentified bystander, the cases indicate hesitancy in upholding the statement alone as sufficient, Garrett v. Howden, 73 N.M. 307, 387 P.2d 874 (1963); Beck v. Dye, 200 Wash. 1, 92 P.2d 1113 (1939), a result which would under appropriate circumstances be consistent with the rule.

Permissible *subject matter* of the statement is limited under Exception (1) to description or explanation of the event or condition, the assumption being that spontaneity, in the absence of a startling event, may extend no farther. In Exception (2), however, the statement need only "relate" to the startling event or condition, thus affording a broader scope of subject matter coverage. 6 Wigmore §§ 1750, 1754. See Sanitary Grocery Co. v. Snead, 67 App.D.C. 129, 90 F.2d 374 (1937), slip-and-fall case sustaining admissibility of clerk's statement. "That has been on the floor for a couple of hours," and Murphy Auto Parts Co., Inc. v. Ball, 101 U.S.App.D.C. 416, 249 F.2d 508 (1957), upholding admission, on issue of driver's agency, of his statement that he had to call on a customer and was in a hurry to get home. Quick, Hearsay, Excitement, Necessity and the Uniform Rules: A Reappraisal of Rule 63(4), 6 Wayne L.Rev. 204, 206-209 (1960).

Similar provisions are found in Uniform Rule 63(4)(a) and (b); California Evidence Code § 1240 (as to Exception (2) only); Kansas Code of Civil Procedure § 60-460(d)(1) and (2); New Jersey Evidence Rule 63(4).

Restyled 2011

(3) ***Then-Existing Mental, Emotional, or Physical Condition.*** A statement of the declarant's then-existing state of mind (such as motive, intent, or plan) or emotional, sensory, or physical condition (such as mental feeling, pain, or bodily health), but not including a statement of memory or belief to prove the fact remembered or believed unless it relates to the validity or terms of the declarant's will.

Superseded 2011

(3) Then existing mental, emotional, or physical condition. A statement of the declarant's then existing state of mind, emotion, sensation, or physical condition (such as intent, plan, motive, design, mental feeling, pain, and bodily health), but not including a statement of memory or belief to prove the fact remembered or believed unless it relates to the execution, revocation, identification, or terms of declarant's will.

Case Note

The conflict between the Advisory Committee Note (Hillmon rule "left undisturbed") and the House Judiciary Committee Report (statements of intent inadmissible to prove "the future conduct of another person") is reflected in a split of authority over the admissibility a statement of intention to meet another person offered to prove that the meeting occurred and that the other person was present. See United States v. Houlihan, 871 F.Supp. 1495 (D. Mass. 1994).

Advisory Committee's Note

Exception (3) is essentially a specialized application of Exception (1), presented separately to enhance its usefulness and accessibility. See McCormick §§ 265, 268.

The exclusion of "statements of memory or belief to prove the fact remembered or believed" is necessary to avoid the virtual destruction of the hearsay rule which would otherwise result from allowing state of mind, provable by a hearsay statement, to serve as the basis for an inference of the happening of the event which produced the state of mind. Shepard v. United States, 290 U.S. 96, 54 S.Ct. 22, 78 L.Ed. 196 (1933); Maguire, The Hillmon Case—Thirty-three Years After, 38 Harv.L.Rev. 709, 719-731 (1925); Hinton, States of Mind and the Hearsay Rule, 1 U.Chi.L.Rev. 394, 421-423 (1934). The rule of Mutual Life Ins. Co. v. Hillmon, 145 U.S. 285, 12 S.Ct. 909, 36 L.Ed. 706 (1892), allowing evidence of intention as tending to prove the doing of the act intended, is, of course, left undisturbed.

The carving out, from the exclusion mentioned in the preceding paragraph, of declarations relating to the execution, revocation, identification, or terms of declarant's will represents and ad hoc judgment which finds ample reinforcement in the decisions, resting on practical grounds of necessity and expediency rather than logic. McCormick § 271, pp. 577-578; Annot. 34 A.L.R.2d 588, 62 A.L.R.2d 855. A similar recognition of the need for and practical value of this kind of evidence is found in California Evidence Code § 1260.

House Judiciary Committee Report

Rule 803(3) was approved in the form submitted by the Court to Congress. However, the Committee intends that the Rule be construed to limit the doctrine of Mutual Life Insurance Co. v. Hillmon, 145 U.S. 285, 295-300 (1892), so as to render statements of intent by a declarant admissible only to prove his future conduct, not the future conduct of another person.

Restyled 2011

(4) ***Statement Made for Medical Diagnosis or Treatment.*** A statement that:

- **(A)** is made for — and is reasonably pertinent to — medical diagnosis or treatment; and
- **(B)** describes medical history; past or present symptoms or sensations; their inception; or their general cause.

Superseded 2011

(4) Statements for purposes of medical diagnosis or treatment. Statements made for purposes of medical diagnosis or treatment and describing medical history, or past or present symptoms, pain, or sensations, or the inception or general character of the cause or external source thereof insofar as reasonably pertinent to diagnosis or treatment.

Advisory Committee's Note

Exception (4). Even those few jurisdictions which have shied away from generally admitting statements of present condition have allowed them if made to a physician for purposes of diagnosis and treatment in view of the patient's strong motivation to be truthful. McCormick § 266, p. 563. The same guarantee of trustworthiness extends to statements of past conditions and medical history, made for purposes of diagnosis or treatment. It also extends to statements as to causation, reasonably pertinent to the same purposes, in accord with the current trend. Shell Oil Co. v. Industrial Commission, 2 Ill.2d 590, 119 N.E.2d 224 (1954); McCormick § 266, p. 564; New Jersey Evidence Rule 63(12)(c). Statements as to fault would not ordinarily qualify under this latter language. Thus a patient's statement that he was struck by an automobile would qualify but not his statement that the car was driven through a red light. Under the exception the statement need not have been made to a physician. Statements to hospital attendants, ambulance drivers, or even members of the family might be included.

Conventional doctrine has excluded from the hearsay exception, as not within its guarantee of truthfulness, statements to a physician consulted only for the purpose of enabling him to testify. While these statements were not admissible as substantive evidence, the expert was allowed to state the basis of his opinion, including statements of this kind. The distinction thus called for was one most unlikely to be made by juries. The rule accordingly rejects the limitation. This position is consistent with the provision of Rule 703 that the facts on which expert testimony is based need not be admissible in evidence if of a kind ordinarily relied upon by experts in the field.

House Judiciary Committee Report

After giving particular attention to the question of physical examination made solely to enable a physician to testify, the Committee approved Rule 803(4) as submitted to Congress, with the understanding that it is not intended in any way to adversely affect present privilege rules or those subsequently adopted.

Senate Judiciary Committee Report

The House approved this rule [Exception 4] as it was submitted by the Supreme Court "with the understanding that it is not intended in any way to adversely affect present privilege rules." We also approve this rule, and we would point out with respect to the question of its relation to privileges, it must be read in conjunction with rule 35 of the Federal Rules of Civil Procedure which provides that whenever the physical or mental condition of a party (plaintiff or defendant) is in controversy, the court may require him to submit to an examination by a physician. It is these examinations which will normally be admitted under this exception.

Restyled 2011

(5) ***Recorded Recollection.*** A record that:

(A) is on a matter the witness once knew about but now cannot recall well enough to testify fully and accurately;

(B) was made or adopted by the witness when the matter was fresh in the witness's memory; and

(C) accurately reflects the witness's knowledge.

If admitted, the record may be read into evidence but may be received as an exhibit only if offered by an adverse party.

Superseded 2011

(5) Recorded recollection. A memorandum or record concerning a matter about which a witness once had knowledge but now has insufficient recollection to enable the witness to testify fully and accurately, shown to have been made or adopted by the witness when the matter was fresh in the witness' memory and to reflect that knowledge correctly. If admitted, the memorandum or record may be read into evidence but may not itself be received as an exhibit unless offered by an adverse party.

Advisory Committee's Note

Exception (5). A hearsay exception for recorded recollection is generally recognized and has been described as having "long been favored by the federal and practically all the state courts that have had occasion to decide the question." United States v. Kelly, 349 F.2d 720, 770 (2d Cir.1965), citing numerous cases and sustaining the exception against a claimed denial of the right of confrontation. Many additional cases are cited in Annot., 82 A.L.R.2d 473, 520. The guarantee of trustworthiness is found in the reliability inherent in a record made while events were still fresh in mind and accurately reflecting them. Owens v. State, 67 Md. 307, 316, 10 A. 210, 212 (1887).

The principal controversy attending the exception has centered, not upon the propriety of the exception itself, but upon the question whether a preliminary requirement of impaired memory on the part of the witness should be imposed. The authorities are divided. If regard be had only to the accuracy of the evidence, admittedly impairment of the memory of the witness adds nothing to it and should not be required. McCormick § 277, p. 593; 3 Wigmore § 738, p. 76; Jordan v. People, 151 Colo. 133, 376 P.2d 699 (1962), cert. denied 373 U.S. 944, 83 S.Ct. 1553, 10 L.Ed.2d 699; Hall v. State, 223 Md. 158, 162 A.2d 751 (1960); State v. Bindhammer, 44 N.J. 372, 209 A.2d 124 (1965). Nevertheless, the absence of the requirement, it is believed, would encourage the use of statements carefully prepared for purposes of litigation under the supervision of attorneys, investigators, or claim adjusters. Hence the example includes a requirement that the witness not have "sufficient recollection to enable him to testify fully and accurately." To the same effect are California Evidence Code § 1237 and New Jersey Rule 63(1)(b), and this has been the position of the federal courts. Vicksburg & Meridian R.R. v. O'Brien, 119 U.S. 99, 7 S.Ct. 118, 30 L.Ed. 299 (1886); Ahern v. Webb, 268 F.2d 45 (10th Cir.1959); and see N.L.R.B. v. Hudson Pulp and Paper Corp., 273 F.2d 660, 665 (5th Cir.1960); N.L.R.B. v. Federal Dairy Co., 297 F.2d 487 (1st Cir.1962). But cf. United States v. Adams, 385 F.2d 548 (2d Cir.1967).

No attempt is made in the exception to spell out the method of establishing the initial knowledge or the contemporaneity and accuracy of the record, leaving them to be dealt with as the circumstances of the particular case might indicate. Multiple person involvement in the process of observing and recording, as in Rathbun v. Brancatella, 93 N.J.L. 222, 107 A. 279 (1919), is entirely consistent with the exception.

Locating the exception at this place in the scheme of the rules is a matter of choice. There were two other possibilities. The first was to regard the statement as one of the group of prior statements of a testifying witness which are excluded entirely from the category of hearsay by Rule 801(d)(1). That category, however, requires that declarant be "subject to cross-examination," as to which the impaired memory aspect of the exception raises doubts. The other possibility was to include the exception among those covered by Rule 804. Since unavailability is required by that rule and lack of memory is listed as a species of unavailability by the definition of the term in Rule 804(a)(3), that treatment at first impression would seem appropriate. The fact is, however, that the unavailability requirement of the exception is of a limited and peculiar nature. Accordingly, the exception is located at this point rather than in the context of a rule where unavailability is conceived of more broadly.

House Judiciary Committee Report

Rule 803(5) as submitted by the Court permitted the reading into evidence of a memorandum or record concerning a matter about which a witness once had knowledge but now has insufficient recollection to enable him to testify accurately and fully, "shown to have been made when the matter was fresh in his memory and to reflect that knowledge correctly." The Committee amended this Rule to add the words "or adopted by the witness" after the phrase "shown to have been made", a treatment consistent with the definition of "statement" in the Jencks Act, 18 U.S.C. 3500. Moreover, it is the Committee's understanding that a memorandum or report, although barred under this Rule, would nonetheless be admissible if it came within another hearsay exception. This last stated principle is deemed applicable to all the hearsay rules.

Senate Judiciary Committee Report

Rule 803(5) as submitted by the Court permitted the reading into evidence of a memorandum or record concerning a matter about which a witness once had knowledge but now has insufficient recollection to enable him to testify accurately and fully, "shown to have been made when the matter was fresh in his memory and to reflect that knowledge correctly." The House amended the rule to add the words "or adopted by the witness" after the phrase "shown to have been made," language parallel to the Jencks Act [18 U.S.C. § 3500].

The committee accepts the House amendment with the understanding and belief that it was not intended to narrow the scope of applicability of the rule. In fact, we understand it to clarify the rule's applicability to a memorandum adopted by the witness as well as one made by him. While the rule as submitted by the Court was silent on the question of who made the memorandum, we view the House amendment as a helpful clarification, noting, however, that the Advisory Committee's note to this rule suggests that the important thing is the accuracy of the memorandum rather than who made it.

The committee does not view the House amendment as precluding admissibility in situations in which multiple participants were involved.

When the verifying witness has not prepared the report, but merely examined it and found it accurate, he has adopted the report, and it is therefore admissible. The rule should also be interpreted to cover other situations involving multiple participants, e.g., employer dictating to secretary, secretary making memorandum at direction of employer, or information being passed along a chain of persons, as in Curtis v. Bradley [65 Conn. 99, 31 Atl. 591 (1894); see, also, Rathbun v. Brancatella, 93 N.J.L. 222, 107 Atl. 279 (1919); see, also, McCormick on Evidence, § 303 (2d ed. 1972)].

The committee also accepts the understanding of the House that a memorandum or report, although barred under this rule, would nonetheless be admissible if it came within another hearsay exception. We consider this principle to be applicable to all the hearsay rules.

Restyled 2011

(6) ***Records of a Regularly Conducted Activity.*** A record of an act, event, condition, opinion, or diagnosis if:

(A) the record was made at or near the time by — or from information transmitted by — someone with knowledge;

(B) the record was kept in the course of a regularly conducted activity of a business, organization, occupation, or calling, whether or not for profit;

(C) making the record was a regular practice of that activity;

(D) all these conditions are shown by the testimony of the custodian or another qualified witness, or by a certification that complies with Rule 902(11) or (12) or with a statute permitting certification; and

(E) the opponent does not show that the source of information or the method or circumstances of preparation indicate a lack of trustworthiness. [*Amended 2014.*]

Superseded 2011

(6) Records of regularly conducted activity. A memorandum, report, record, or data compilation, in any form, of acts, events, conditions, opinions, or diagnoses, made at or near the time by, or from information transmitted by, a person with knowledge, if kept in the course of a regularly conducted business activity, and if it was the regular practice of that business activity to make the memorandum, report, record, or data compilation, all as shown by the testimony of the custodian or other qualified witness, or by certification that complies with Rule 902(11), Rule 902(12), or a statute permitting certification, unless the source of information or the method or circumstances of preparation indicate lack of trustworthiness. The term "business" as used in this paragraph includes business, institution, association, profession, occupation, and calling of every kind, whether or not conducted for profit. [*References to "certification" method added 2000.*]

Advisory Committee's Note

Exception (6) represents an area which has received much attention from those seeking to improve the law of evidence. The Commonwealth Fund Act was the result of a study completed in 1927 by a distinguished committee under the chairmanship of Professor Morgan. Morgan et al., The Law of Evidence: Some Proposals for its Reform 63 (1927). With changes too minor to mention, it was adopted by Congress in 1936 as the rule for federal courts. 28 U.S.C. § 1732. A number of states took similar action. The Commissioners on Uniform State Laws in 1936 promulgated the Uniform Business Records as Evidence Act, 9A U.L.A. 506, which has acquired a substantial following in the states. Model Code Rule 514 and Uniform Rule 63(13) also deal with the subject. Difference of varying degrees of importance exist among these various treatments.

These reform efforts were largely within the context of business and commercial records, as the kind usually encountered, and concentrated considerable attention upon relaxing the requirement of producing as witnesses, or accounting for the nonproduction of, all participants in the process of gathering, transmitting, and recording information which the common law had evolved as a burdensome and crippling aspect of using records of this type. In their areas of primary emphasis on witnesses to be called and the general admissibility of ordinary business and commercial records, the Commonwealth Fund Act and the Uniform Act appear to have worked well. The exception seeks to preserve their advantages.

On the subject of what witnesses must be called, the Commonwealth Fund Act eliminated the common law requirement of calling or accounting for all participants by failing to mention it. United States v. Mortimer, 118 F.2d 266 (2d Cir.1941); La Porte v. United States, 300 F.2d 878 (9th Cir.1962); McCormick § 290, p. 608. Model Code Rule 514 and Uniform Rule 63(13) did likewise. The Uniform Act, however, abolished the common law requirement in express terms, providing that the requisite foundation testimony might be furnished by "the custodian or other qualified witness." Uniform Business Records as Evidence Act, § 2; 9A U.L.A. 506. The exception follows the Uniform Act in this respect.

The element of unusual reliability of business records is said variously to be supplied by systematic checking, by regularity and continuity which produce habits of precision, by actual experience of business in relying upon them, or by a duty to make an accurate record as part of a continuing job or occupation. McCormick §§ 281, 286, 287; Laughlin, Business Entries and the Like, 46 Iowa L.Rev. 276 (1961). The model statutes and rules have sought to capture these factors and to extend their impact by employing the phrase "regular course of business," in conjunction with a definition of "business" far broader than its ordinarily accepted meaning. The result is a tendency unduly to emphasize a requirement of routineness and repetitiveness and an insistence that other types of records be squeezed into the fact patterns which give rise to traditional business records. The rule therefore adopts the phrase "the course of a regularly conducted activity" as capturing the essential basis of the hearsay exception as it has evolved and the essential element which can be abstracted from the various specifications of what is a "business."

Amplification of the kinds of activities producing admissible records has given rise to problems which conventional business records by their nature avoid. They are problems of the source of the recorded information, of entries in opinion form, of motivation, and of involvement as participant in the matters recorded.

Sources of information presented no substantial problem with ordinary business records. All participants, including the observer or participant furnishing the information to be recorded, were acting routinely, under a duty of accuracy, with employer reliance on the result, or in short "in the regular course of business." If, however, the supplier of the information does not act in the regular course, an essential link is broken; the assurance of accuracy does not extend to the information itself, and the fact that it may be recorded with scrupulous accuracy is of no avail. An illustration is the police report incorporating information obtained from a bystander: the officer qualifies as acting in the regular course but the informant does not. The leading case, Johnson v. Lutz, 253 N.Y. 124, 170 N.E. 517 (1930), held that a report thus prepared was inadmissible. Most of the authorities have agreed with the decision. Gencarella v. Fyfe, 171 F.2d 419 (1st Cir.1948); Gordon v. Robinson, 210 F.2d 192 (3d Cir.1954); Standard Oil Co. of California v. Moore, 251 F.2d 188, 214 (9th Cir.1957), cert. denied 356 U.S. 975, 78 S.Ct. 1139, 2 L.Ed.2d 1148; Yates v. Bair Transport, Inc., 249 F.Supp. 681 (S.D.N.Y.1965); Annot., 69 A.L.R.2d 1148. Cf. Hawkins v. Gorea Motor Express, Inc., 360 F.2d 933 (2d Cir.1966); Contra, 5 Wigmore § 1530a, n. 1, pp. 391-392. The point is not dealt with specifically in the Commonwealth Fund Act, the Uniform Act, or Uniform Rule 63(13). However, Model Code Rule 514 contains the requirement "that it was the regular course of that business for one with personal knowledge . . . to make such a memorandum or record or to transmit information thereof to be included in such a memorandum or record . . .." The rule follows this lead in requiring an informant with knowledge acting in the course of the regularly conducted activity.

Entries in the form of opinions were not encountered in traditional business records in view of the purely factual nature of the items recorded, but they are now commonly encountered with respect to medical diagnoses, prognoses, and test results, as well as occasionally in other areas. The Commonwealth Fund Act provided only for records of an "act, transaction, occurrence, or event," while the Uniform Act, Model Code Rule 514, and Uniform Rule 63(13) merely added the ambiguous term "condition." The limited phrasing of the Commonwealth Fund Act, 28 U.S.C. § 1732, may account for the reluctance of some federal decisions to admit diagnostic entries. New York Life Ins. Co. v. Taylor, 79 U.S.App.D.C. 66, 147 F.2d 297 (1945); Lyles v. United States, 103 U.S.App.D.C. 22, 254 F.2d 725 (1957), cert. denied 356 U.S. 961, 78 S.Ct. 997, 2 L.Ed.2d 1067; England v. United States, 174 F.2d 466 (5th Cir.1949); Skogen v. Dow Chemical Co., 375 F.2d 692 (8th Cir.1967). Other federal decisions, however, experienced no difficulty in freely admitting diagnostic entries. Reed v. Order of United Commercial Travelers, 123 F.2d 252 (2d Cir.1941); Buckminster's Estate v. Commissioner of Internal Revenue, 147 F.2d 331 (2d Cir.1944); Medina v. Erickson, 226 F.2d 475 (9th Cir.1955); Thomas v. Hogan, 308 F.2d 355 (4th Cir.1962); Glawe v. Rulon, 284 F.2d 495 (8th Cir.1960). In the state courts, the trend favors admissibility. Borucki v. MacKenzie Bros. Co., 125 Conn. 92, 3 A.2d 224 (1938); Allen v. St. Louis Public Service Co., 365 Mo. 677, 285 S.W.2d 663, 55 A.L.R.2d 1022 (1956); People v. Kohlmeyer, 284 N.Y. 366, 31 N.E.2d 490 (1940); Weis v. Weis, 147 Ohio St. 416, 72 N.E.2d 245 (1947). In order to make clear its adherence to the latter position, the rule specifically includes both diagnoses and opinions, in addition to acts, events, and conditions, as proper subjects of admissible entries.

Problems of the motivation of the informant have been a source of difficulty and disagreement. In Palmer v. Hoffman, 318 U.S. 109, 63 S.Ct. 477, 87 L.Ed. 645 (1943), exclusion of an accident report made by the since deceased engineer, offered by defendant railroad trustees in a grade crossing collision case, was upheld. The report was not "in the regular course of business," not a record of the systematic conduct of the business as a business, said the Court. The report was prepared for use in litigating, not railroading. While the opinion mentions the motivation of the engineer only obliquely, the emphasis on records of routine operations is significant only by virtue of impact on motivation to be accurate. Absence of routineness raises lack of motivation to be accurate. The opinion of the Court of Appeals had gone beyond mere lack of motive to be accurate: the engineer's statement was "dripping with motivations to misrepresent." Hoffman v. Palmer, 129 F.2d 976, 991 (2d Cir.1942). The direct introduction of motivation is a disturbing factor, since absence of motive to misrepresent has not traditionally been a requirement of the rule; that records might be self-serving has not been a ground for exclusion. Laughlin, Business Records and the Like, 46 Iowa L.Rev. 276, 285 (1961). As Judge Clark said in his dissent, "I submit that there is hardly a grocer's account book which could not be excluded on that basis." 129 F.2d at 1002. A physician's evaluation report of a personal injury litigant would appear to be in the routine of his business. If the report is offered by the party at whose instance it was made, however, it has been held inadmissible, Yates v. Bair Transport, Inc., 249 F.Supp. 681 (S.D.N.Y. 1965), otherwise if offered by the opposite party, Korte v. New York, N.H. & H.R. Co., 191 F.2d 86 (2d Cir.1951), cert. denied 342 U.S. 868, 72 S.Ct. 108, 96 L.Ed. 652.

The decisions hinge on motivation and which party is entitled to be concerned about it. Professor McCormick believed that the doctor's report or the accident report were sufficiently routine to justify admissibility. McCormick § 287, p. 604. Yet hesitation must be experienced in admitting everything which is observed and recorded in the course of a regularly conducted activity. Efforts to set a limit are illustrated by Hartzog v. United States, 217 F.2d 706 (4th Cir.1954), error to admit worksheets made by since deceased deputy collector in preparation for the instant income tax evasion prosecution, and United States v. Ware, 247 F.2d 698 (7th Cir.1957), error to admit narcotics agents' records of purchases. See also Exception (8), infra, as to the public record aspects of records of this nature. Some decisions have been satisfied as to motivation of an accident report if made pursuant to statutory duty, United States v. New York Foreign Trade Zone Operators, 304 F.2d 792 (2d Cir.1962); Taylor v. Baltimore & O.R. Co., 344 F.2d 281 (2d Cir.1965), since the report was oriented in a direction other than the litigation which ensued. Cf. Matthews v. United States, 217 F.2d 409 (5th Cir.1954). The formulation of specific terms which would assure satisfactory results in all cases is not possible. Consequently the rule proceeds from the base that records made in the course of a regularly conducted activity will be taken as admissible but subject to authority to exclude if "the sources of information or other circumstances indicate lack of trustworthiness."

Occasional decisions have reached for enhanced accuracy by requiring involvement as a participant in matters reported. Clainos v. United States, 82 U.S.App.D.C. 278, 163 F.2d 593 (1947), error to admit police records of convictions; Standard Oil Co. of California v. Moore, 251 F.2d 188 (9th Cir.1957), cert. denied 356 U.S. 975, 78 S.Ct. 1139, 2 L.Ed.2d 1148, error to admit employees' records of observed business practices of others. The rule includes no requirement of this nature. Wholly acceptable records may involve matters merely observed, e.g. the weather.

The form which the "record" may assume under the rule is described broadly as a "memorandum, report, record, or data compilation, in any form." The expression "data compilation" is used as broadly descriptive of any means of storing information other than the conventional words and figures in written or documentary form. It includes, but is by no means limited to, electronic computer storage. The term is borrowed from revised Rule 34(a) of the Rules of Civil Procedure.

House Judiciary Committee Report

Rule 803(6) as submitted by the Court permitted a record made "in the course of a regularly conducted activity" to be admissible in certain circumstances. The Committee believed there were insufficient guarantees of reliability in records made in the course of activities falling outside the scope of "business" activities as that term is broadly defined in 28 U.S.C. 1732. Moreover, the Committee concluded that the additional requirement of Section 1732 that it must have been the regular practice of a business to make the record is a necessary further assurance of its trustworthiness. The Committee accordingly amended the Rule to incorporate these limitations.

Senate Judiciary Committee Report

Rule 803(6) as submitted by the Supreme Court permitted a record made in the course of a regularly conducted activity to be admissible in certain circumstances. This rule constituted a broadening of the traditional business records hearsay exception which has been long advocated by scholars and judges active in the law of evidence.

The House felt there were insufficient guarantees of reliability of records not within a broadly defined business records exception. We disagree. Even under the House definition of "business" including profession, occupation, and "calling of every kind," the records of many regularly conducted activities will, or may be, excluded from evidence. Under the principle of ejusdem generis, the intent of "calling of every kind" would seem to be related to work-related endeavors—e.g., butcher, baker, artist, etc.

Thus, it appears that the records of many institutions or groups might not be admissible under the House amendments. For example, schools, churches, and hospitals will not normally be considered businesses within the definition. Yet, these are groups which keep financial and other records on a regular basis in a manner similar to business enterprises. We believe these records are of equivalent trustworthiness and should be admitted into evidence.

Three states, which have recently codified their evidence rules, have adopted the Supreme Court version of rule 803(6), providing for admission of memoranda of a "regularly conducted activity." None adopted the words "business activity" used in the House amendment. [See Nev.Rev.Stats. § 15.135; N.Mex.Stats. (1973 Supp.) § 20-4-803(6); West's Wis.Stats.Anno. (1973 Supp.) § 908.03(6).]

Therefore, the committee deleted the word "business" as it appears before the word "activity". The last sentence then is unnecessary and was also deleted.

It is the understanding of the committee that the use of the phrase "person with knowledge" is not intended to imply that the party seeking to introduce the memorandum, report, record, or data compilation must be able to produce, or even identify, the specific individual upon whose first-hand knowledge the memorandum, report, record or data compilation was based. A sufficient foundation for the introduction of such evidence will be laid if the party seeking to introduce the evidence is able to show that it was the regular practice of the activity to base such memorandums, reports, records, or data compilations upon a transmission from a person with knowledge, e.g., in the case of the content of a shipment of goods, upon a report from the company's receiving agent or in the case of a computer printout, upon a report from the company's computer programmer or one who has knowledge of the particular record system. In short, the scope of the phrase "person with knowledge" is meant to be coterminous with the custodian of the evidence or other qualified witness. The committee believes this represents the desired rule in light of the complex nature of modern business organizations.

Conference Committee Report

The House bill provides in subsection (6) that records of a regularly conducted "business" activity qualify for admission into evidence as an exception to the hearsay rule. "Business" is defined as including "business, profession, occupation and calling of every kind." The Senate amendment drops the requirement that the records be those of a "business" activity and eliminates the definition of "business." The Senate amendment provides that records are admissible if they are records of a regularly conducted "activity."

The Conference adopts the House provision that the records must be those of a regularly conducted "business" activity. The Conferees changed the definition of "business" contained in the House provision in order to make it clear that the records of institutions and associations like schools, churches and hospitals are admissible under this provision. The records of public schools and hospitals are also covered by Rule 803(8), which deals with public records and reports.

Advisory Committee's Note to 2000 Amendment

The amendment provides that the foundation requirements of Rule 803(6) can be satisfied under certain circumstances without the expense and inconvenience of producing time-consuming foundation witnesses. Under current law, courts have generally required foundation witnesses to testify. See, e.g., Tongil Co., Ltd. v. Hyundai Merchant Marine Corp., 968 F.2d 999 (9th Cir. 1992) (reversing a judgment based on business records where a qualified person filed an affidavit but did not testify). Protections are provided by the authentication requirements of Rule 902(11) for domestic records, Rule 902(12) for foreign records in civil cases, and 18 U.S.C. § 3505 for foreign records in criminal cases.

Advisory Committee's Note to 2014 Amendment

The Rule has been amended to clarify that if the proponent has established the stated requirements of the exception--regular business with regularly kept record, source with personal knowledge, record made timely, and foundation testimony or certification--then the burden is on the opponent to show that the source of information or the method or circumstances of preparation indicate a lack of trustworthiness. While most courts have imposed that burden on the opponent, some have not. It is appropriate to impose this burden on opponent, as the basic admissibility requirements are sufficient to establish a presumption that the record is reliable.

The opponent, in meeting its burden, is not necessarily required to introduce affirmative evidence of untrustworthiness. For example, the opponent might argue that a record was prepared in anticipationof litigation and is favorable to the preparing party without needing to introduce evidence on the point. A determination of untrustworthiness necessarily depends on the circumstances.

Restyled 2011

(7) ***Absence of a Record of a Regularly Conducted Activity.*** Evidence that a matter is not included in a record described in paragraph (6) if:

(A) the evidence is admitted to prove that the matter did not occur or exist;

(B) a record was regularly kept for a matter of that kind; and

(C) the opponent does not show that the possible source of the information or other circumstances indicate a lack of trustworthiness. [*Amended 2014.*]

Superseded 2011

(7) Absence of entry in records kept in accordance with the provisions of paragraph (6). Evidence that a matter is not included in the memoranda reports, records, or data compilations, in any form, kept in accordance with the provisions of paragraph (6), to prove the nonoccurrence or nonexistence of the matter, if the matter was of a kindof which a memorandum, report, record, or data compilation was regularly made and preserved, unless the sources of information or other circumstances indicate lack of trustworthiness.

Advisory Committee's Note

Exception (7). Failure of a record to mention a matter which would ordinarily be mentioned is satisfactory evidence of its nonexistence. Uniform Rule 63(14), Comment. While probably not hearsay as defined in Rule 801, supra, decisions may be found which class the evidence not only as hearsay but also as not within any exception. In order to set the question at rest in favor of admissibility, it is specifically treated here. McCormick § 289, p. 609; Morgan, Basic Problems of Evidence 314 (1962); 5 Wigmore § 1531; Uniform Rule 63(14); California Evidence Code § 1272; Kansas Code of Civil Procedure § 60-460(n); New Jersey Evidence Rule 63(14).

House Judiciary Committee Report

Rule 803(7) as submitted by the Court concerned the absence of entry in the records of a "regularly conducted activity." The Committee amended this Rule to conform with its action with respect to Rule 803(6).

Advisory Committee's Note to 2014 Amendment

The Rule has been amended to clarify that if the proponent has established the stated requirements of the exception--set forth in Rule 803(6)--then the burden is on the opponent to show that the possible source of the information or other circumstances indicate a lack of trustworthiness. The amendment maintains consistency with the proposed amendment to the trustworthiness clause of Rule 803(6).

Restyled 2011

(8) ***Public Records.*** A record of a public office if:

(A) it sets out:

(i) the office's activities;

(ii) a matter observed while under a legal duty to report, but not including, in a criminal case, a matter observed by law-enforcement personnel; or

(iii) in a civil case or against the government in a criminal case, factual findings from a legally authorized investigation; and

(B) the opponent does not show that the source of information or other circumstances indicate a lack of trustworthiness. [*Amended 2014.*]

Superseded 2011

(8) Public records and reports. Records, reports, statements, or data compilations, in any form, of public

(B) matters observed pursuant to duty imposed by law as to which matters there was a duty to report, excluding, however, in criminal cases matters observed by police officers and other law enforcement personnel, or

(C) in civil actions and proceedings and against the Government in criminal cases, factual findings resulting from an investigation made pursuant to authority granted by law, unless the sources of information or other circumstances indicate lack of trustworthiness.

Case Notes

Statements in the form of opinions or conclusions are within the scope of "(C) * * * factual findings" as long as they are based on factual investigation and satisfy the trustworthiness requirement. Beech Aircraft Corp. v. Rainey, 488 U.S. 153, 161-170, 109 S.Ct. 439, 445-450, 102 L.Ed. 2d 445 (1988).

The exclusionary language of Rule 803(8)(B) does not apply to:

- Police reports offered to exculpate the accused. United States v. Smith, 521 F.2d 957 (D.C. Cir. 1975). *But see* United States v. Sharpe, 193 F.3d 852, 868 (5th Cir. 1999).
- Police reports of ministerial activities prepared under nonadversarial circumstances. United States v. Orozco, 590 F.2d 789 (9th Cir. 1979).

Advisory Committee's Note

Exception (8). Public records are a recognized hearsay exception at common law and have been the subject of statutes without number. McCormick § 291. See, for example, 28 U.S.C. § 1733, the relative narrowness of which is illustrated by its nonapplicability to nonfederal public agencies, thus necessitating resort to the less appropriate business record exception to the hearsay rule. Kay v. United States, 255 F.2d 476 (4th Cir.1958). The rule makes no distinction between federal and nonfederal offices and agencies.

Justification for the exception is the assumption that a public official will perform his duty properly and the unlikelihood that he will remember details independently of the record. Wong Wing Foo v. McGrath, 196 F.2d 120 (9th Cir.1952), and see Chesapeake & Delaware Canal Co. v. United States, 250 U.S. 123, 39 S.Ct. 407, 63 L.Ed. 889 (1919). As to items (a) and (b), further support is found in the reliability factors underlying records of regularly conducted activities generally. See Exception (6), supra.

(a) Cases illustrating the admissibility of records of the office's or agency's own activities are numerous. Chesapeake & Delaware Canal Co. v. United States, 250 U.S. 123, 39 S.Ct. 407, 63 L.Ed. 889 (1919), Treasury records of miscellaneous receipts and disbursements; Howard v. Perrin, 200 U.S. 71, 26 S.Ct. 195, 50 L.Ed. 374 (1906), General Land Office records; Ballew v. United States, 160 U.S. 187, 16 S.Ct. 263, 40 L.Ed. 388 (1895). Pension Office records.

(b) Cases sustaining admissibility of records of matters observed are also numerous. United States v. Van Hook, 284 F.2d 489 (7th Cir.1960), remanded for resentencing 365 U.S. 609, 81 S.Ct. 823, 5 L.Ed.2d 821, letter from induction officer to District Attorney, pursuant to army regulations, stating fact and circumstances of refusal to be inducted; T'Kach v. United States, 242 F.2d 937 (5th Cir.1957), affidavit of White House personnel officer that search of records showed no employment of accused, charged with fraudulently representing himself as an envoy of the President; Minnehaha County v. Kelley, 150 F.2d 356 (8th Cir.1945); Weather Bureau records of rainfall; United States v. Meyer, 113 F.2d 387 (7th Cir.1940), cert. denied 311 U.S. 706, 61 S.Ct. 174, 85 L.Ed. 459, map prepared by government engineer from information furnished by men working under his supervision.

(c) The more controversial area of public records is that of the so-called "evaluative" report. The disagreement among the decisions has been due in part, no doubt, to the variety of situations encountered, as well as to differences in principle. Sustaining admissibility are such cases as United States v. Dumas, 149 U.S. 278, 13 S.Ct. 872, 37 L.Ed. 734 (1893), statement of account certified by Postmaster General in action against postmaster; McCarty v. United States, 185 F.2d 520 (5th Cir.1950), reh. denied 187 F.2d 234, Certificate of Settlement of General Accounting Office showing indebtedness and letter from Army official stating Government had performed, in action on contract to purchase and remove waste food from Army camp; Moran v. Pittsburgh-Des Moines Steel Co., 183 F.2d 467 (3d Cir.1950), report of Bureau of Mines as to cause of gas tank explosion; Petition of W___, 164 F.Supp. 659 (E.D.Pa.1958), report by Immigration and Naturalization Service investigator that petitioner was known in community as wife of man to whom she was not married. To the opposite effect and denying admissibility are Franklin v. Skelly Oil Co., 141 F.2d 568 (10th Cir.1944), State Fire Marshal's report of cause of gas explosion; Lomax Transp. Co. v. United States, 183 F.2d 331 (9th Cir.1950), Certificate of Settlement from General Accounting Office in action for naval supplies lost in warehouse fire; Yung Jin Teung v. Dulles, 229 F.2d 244 (2d Cir.1956), "Status Reports" offered to justify delay in processing passport applications. Police reports have generally been excluded except to the extent to which they incorporate firsthand observations of the officer. Annot., 69 A.L.R.2d 1148. Various kinds of evaluative reports are admissible under federal statutes: 7 U.S.C. § 78, findings of Secretary of Agriculture prima facie evidence of true grade of grain; 7 U.S.C. § 210(f), findings of Secretary of Agriculture prima facie evidence in action for damages against stockyard owner; 7 U.S.C. § 292, order by Secretary of Agriculture prima facie evidence in judicial enforcement proceedings against producers association monopoly; 7 U.S.C. § 1622(h), Department of Agriculture inspection certificates of products shipped in interstate commerce prima facie evidence; 8 U.S.C. §1440(c), separation of alien from military service on conditions other than honorable provable by certificate from department in proceedings to revoke citizenship; 18 U.S.C. § 4245, certificate of Director of Prisons that convicted person has been examined and found probably incompetent at time of trial prima facie evidence in court hearing on competency; 42 U.S.C. § 269(b), bill of health by appropriate official prima facie evidence of vessel's sanitary history and condition and compliance with regulations; 46 U.S.C. § 679, certificate of consul presumptive evidence of refusal of master to transport destitute seamen to United States. While these statutory exceptions to the hearsay rule are left undisturbed, Rule 802, the willingness of Congress to recognize a substantial measure of admissibility for evaluative reports is a helpful guide.

Factors which may be of assistance in passing upon the admissibility of evaluative reports include: (1) the timeliness of the investigation, McCormick, Can the Courts Make Wider Use of Reports of Official Investigations? 42 Iowa L.Rev. 363 (1957); (2) the special skill or experience of the official, id., (3) whether a hearing was held and the level at which conducted, Franklin v. Skelly Oil Co., 141 F.2d 568 (10th Cir.1944); (4) possible motivation problems suggested by Palmer v. Hoffman, 318 U.S. 109, 63 S.Ct. 477, 87 L.Ed. 645 (1943). Others no doubt could be added.

The formulation of an approach which would give appropriate weight to all possible factors in every situation is an obvious impossibility. Hence the rule, as in Exception (6), assumes admissibility in the first instance but with ample provision for escape if sufficient negative factors are present. In one respect, however, the rule with respect to evaluative reports under item (c) is very specific: they are admissible only in civil cases and against the government in criminal cases in view of the almost certain collision with confrontation rights which would result from their use against the accused in a criminal case.

House Judiciary Committee Report

The Committee approved Rule 803(8) without substantive change from the form in which it was submitted by the Court. The Committee intends that the phrase "factual findings" be strictly construed and that evaluations or opinions contained in public reports shall not be admissible under this Rule.

Senate Judiciary Committee Report

The House approved rule 803(8), as submitted by the Supreme Court, with one substantive change. It excluded from the hearsay exception reports containing matters observed by police officers and other law enforcement personnel in criminal cases. Ostensibly, the reason for this exclusion is that observations by police officers at the scene of the crime or the apprehension of the defendant are not as reliable as observations by public officials in other cases because of the adversarial nature of the confrontation between the police and the defendant in criminal cases.

The committee accepts the House's decision to exclude such recorded observations where the police officer is available to testify in court about his observation. However, where he is unavailable as unavailability is defined in rule 804(a)(4) and (a)(5), the report should be admitted as the best available evidence. Accordingly, the committee has amended rule 803(8) to refer to the provision of [proposed] rule 804(b)(5) [deleted], which allows the admission of such reports, records or other statements where the police officer or other law enforcement officer is unavailable because of death, then existing physical or mental illness or infirmity, or not being successfully subject to legal process.

The House Judiciary Committee report contained a statement of intent that "the phrase 'factual findings' in subdivision (c) be strictly construed and that evaluations or opinions contained in public reports shall not be admissible under this rule." The committee takes strong exception to this limiting understanding of the application of the rule. We do not think it reflects an understanding of the intended operation of the rule as explained in the Advisory Committee notes to this subsection. The Advisory Committee notes on subsection (c) of this subdivision point out that various kinds of evaluative reports are now admissible under Federal statutes. 7 U.S.C. § 78, findings of Secretary of Agriculture prima facie evidence of true grade of grain; 42 U.S.C. § 269(b), bill of health by appropriate official prima facie evidence of vessel's sanitary history and condition and compliance with regulations. These statutory exceptions to the hearsay rule are preserved. Rule 802. The willingness of Congress to recognize these and other such evaluative reports provides a helpful guide in determining the kind of reports which are intended to be admissible under this rule. We think the restrictive interpretation of the House overlooks the fact that while the Advisory Committee assumes admissibility in the first instance of evaluative reports, they are not admissible if, as the rule states, "the sources of information or other circumstances indicate lack of trustworthiness."

The Advisory Committee explains the factors to be considered:

> "Factors which may be assistance in passing upon the admissibility of evaluative reports include: (1) the timeliness of the investigation, McCormick, Can the Courts Make Wider Use of Reports of Official Investigations? 42 Iowa L.Rev. 363 (1957); (2) the special skill or experience of the official, id.; (3) whether a hearing was held and the level at which conducted, Franklin v. Skelly Oil Co., 141 F.2d 568 (9th Cir.1944); (4) possible motivation problems suggested by Palmer v. Hoffman, 318 U.S. 109, 63 S.Ct. 477, 87 L.Ed. 645 (1943). Others no doubt could be added."

The committee concludes that the language of the rule together with the explanation provided by the Advisory Committee furnish sufficient guidance on the admissibility of evaluative reports.

Conference Committee Report

The Senate amendment adds language, not contained in the House bill, that refers to another rule that was added by the Senate in another amendment ([proposed] Rule 804(b)(5)—Criminal law enforcement records and reports [deleted]).

In view of its action on [proposed] Rule 804(b)(5) (Criminal law enforcement records and reports) [deleted], the Conference does not adopt the Senate amendment and restores the bill to the House version.

Advisory Committee's Note to 2014 Amendment

The Rule has been amended to clarify that if the proponent has established that the record meets the stated requirements of the exception--prepared by a public office and setting out information as specified in the Rule--then the burden is on the opponent to show that the source of information or other circumstances indicate a lack of trustworthiness. While most courts have imposed that burden on the opponent, some have not. Public records have justifiably carried a presumption of reliability, and it should be up to the opponent to "demonstrate why a timetested and carefully considered presumption is not appropriate." *Ellis v. International Playtex, Inc., 745 F.2d 292, 301 (4th Cir. 1984).* The amendment maintains consistency with the proposed amendment to the trustworthiness clause of Rule 803(6).

The opponent, in meeting its burden, is not necessarily required to introduce affirmative evidence of untrustworthiness. For example, the opponent might argue that a record was prepared in anticipation of litigation and is favorable to the preparing party without needing to introduce evidence on the point. A determination of untrustworthiness necessarily depends on the circumstances.

Restyled 2011

(9) ***Public Records of Vital Statistics.*** A record of a birth, death, or marriage, if reported to a public office in accordance with a legal duty.

Superseded 2011

(9) Records of vital statistics. Records or data compilations, in any form, of births, fetal deaths, deaths, or marriages, if the report thereof was made to a public office pursuant to requirements of law.

Advisory Committee's Note

Exception (9). Records of vital statistics are commonly the subject of particular statutes making them admissible in evidence, Uniform Vital Statistics Act, 9C U.L.A. 350 (1957). The rule is in principle narrower than Uniform Rule 63(16) which includes reports required of persons performing functions authorized by statute, yet in practical effect the two are substantially the same. Comment Uniform Rule 63(16). The exception as drafted is in the pattern of California Evidence Code § 1281.

Restyled 2011, amended 2013

(10) ***Absence of a Public Record.*** Testimony — or a certification under Rule 902 — that a diligent search failed to disclose a public record if:

(A) the testimony or certification is admitted to prove that

(i) the record or statement does not exist; or

(ii) a matter did not occur or exist, if a public office regularly kept a record or statement for a matter of that kind, and

(B) in a criminal case, a prosecutor who intends to offer a certification provides written notice of that intent at least 14 days before trial, and the defendant does not object in writing within 7 days of receiving the notice — unless the court sets a different time for the notice or the objection.

Superseded 2011

(10) Absence of public record or entry. To prove the absence of a record, report, statement, or data compilation, in any form, or the nonoccurrence or nonexistence of a matter of which a record, report, statement, or data compilation, in any form, was regularly made and preserved by a public office or agency, evidence in the form of a certification in accordance with rule 902, or testimony, that diligent search failed to disclose the record, report, statement, or data compilation, or entry.

Advisory Committee's Note

Exception (10). The principle of proving nonoccurrence of an event by evidence of the absence of a record which would regularly be made of its occurrence, developed in Exception (7) with respect to regularly conducted activities, is here extended to public records of the kind mentioned in Exceptions [paragraphs] (8) and (9). 5 Wigmore § 1633(6), p. 519. Some harmless duplication no doubt exists with Exception (7). For instances of federal statutes recognizing this method of proof, see 8 U.S.C. § 1284(b), proof of absence of alien crewman's name from outgoing manifest prima facie evidence of failure to detain or deport, and 42 U.S.C. § 405(c)(3), (4)(B), (4)(C), absence of HEW [Department of Health, Education, and Welfare] record prima facie evidence of no wages or self-employment income.

The rule includes situations in which absence of a record may itself be the ultimate focal point of inquiry, e.g. People v. Love, 310 Ill. 558, 142 N.E. 204 (1923), certificate of Secretary of State admitted to show failure to file documents required by Securities Law, as well as cases where the absence of a record is offered as proof of the nonoccurrence of an event ordinarily recorded.

The refusal of the common law to allow proof by certificate of the lack of a record or entry has no apparent justification, 5 Wigmore § 1678(7), p. 752. The rule takes the opposite position, as to Uniform Rule 63(17); California Evidence Code § 1284; Kansas Code of Civil Procedure § 60-460(c); New Jersey Evidence Rule 63(17). Congress has recognized certification as evidence of the lack of a record. 8 U.S.C. § 1360(d), certificate of Attorney General or other designated officer that no record of Immigration and Naturalization Service of specified nature or entry therein is found, admissible in alien cases.

Committee Note to 2013 Amendment

Rule 803(10) has been amended in response to Melendez-Diaz v. Massachusetts, 557 U.S. 305 (2009). The Melendez-Diaz Court declared that a testimonial certificate could be admitted if the accused is given advance notice and does not timely demand the presence of the official who prepared the certificate. The amendment incorporates, with minor variations, a "notice-and-demand" procedure that was approved by the Melendez-Diaz Court. See Tex. 36 Code Crim. P. Ann., art. 38.41.

Restyled 2011

(11) ***Records of Religious Organizations Concerning Personal or Family History.*** A statement of birth, legitimacy, ancestry, marriage, divorce, death, relationship by blood or marriage, or similar facts of personal or family history, contained in a regularly kept record of a religious organization.

Superseded 2011

(11) Records of religious organizations. Statements of births, marriages, divorces, deaths, legitimacy, ancestry, relationship by blood or marriage, or other similar facts of personal or family history, contained in a regularly kept record of a religious organization.

Advisory Committee's Note

Exception (11). Records of activities of religious organizations are currently recognized as admissible at least to the extent of the business records exception to the hearsay rule, 5 Wigmore § 1523, p. 371, and Exception (6) would be applicable. However, both the business record doctrine and Exception (6) require that the person furnishing the information be one in the business or activity. The result is such decisions as Daily v. Grand Lodge, 311 Ill. 184, 142 N.E. 478 (1924), holding a church record admissible to prove fact, date, and place of baptism, but not age of child except that he had at least been born at the time. In view of the unlikelihood that false information would be furnished on occasions of this kind, the rule contains no requirement that the informant be in the course of the activity. See California Evidence Code § 1315 and Comment.

Restyled 2011

(12) ***Certificates of Marriage, Baptism, and Similar Ceremonies.*** A statement of fact contained in a certificate:

(A) made by a person who is authorized by a religious organization or by law to perform the act certified;

(B) attesting that the person performed a marriage or similar ceremony or administered a sacrament; and

(C) purporting to have been issued at the time of the act or within a reasonable time after it.

Superseded 2011

(12) Marriage, baptismal, and similar certificates. Statements of fact contained in a certificate that the maker performed a marriage or other ceremony or administered a sacrament, made by a clergyman, public official, or other person authorized by the rules or practices of a religious organization or by law to perform the act certified, and purporting to have been issued at the time of the act or within a reasonable time thereafter.

Advisory Committee's Note

Exception (12). The principle of proof by certification is recognized as to public officials in Exceptions (8) and (10), and with respect to authentication in Rule 902. The present exception is a duplication to the extent that it deals with a certificate by a public official, as in the case of a judge who performs a marriage ceremony. The area covered by the rule is, however, substantially larger and extends the certification procedure to clergymen and the like who perform marriages and other ceremonies or administer sacraments. Thus certificates of such matters as baptism or confirmation, as well as marriage, are included. In principle they are as acceptable evidence as certificates of public officers. See 5 Wigmore § 1645, as to marriage certificates. When the person executing the certificate is not a public official, the self-authenticating character of documents purporting to emanate from public officials, see Rule 902, is lacking and proof is required that the person was authorized and did make the certificate. The time element, however, may safely be taken as supplied by the certificate, once authority and authenticity are established, particularly in view of the presumption that a document was executed on the date it bears.

For similar rules, some limited to certificates of marriage, with variations in foundation requirements, see Uniform Rule 63(18); California Evidence Code § 1316; Kansas Code of Civil Procedure § 60-460(p); New Jersey Evidence Rule 63(18).

Restyled 2011

(13) *Family Records.* A statement of fact about personal or family history contained in a family record, such as a Bible, genealogy, chart, engraving on a ring, inscription on a portrait, or engraving on an urn or burial marker.

Superseded 2011

(13) Family records. Statements of fact concerning personal or family history contained in family Bibles, genealogies, charts, engravings on rings, inscriptions on family portraits, engravings on urns, crypts, or tombstones, or the like.

Advisory Committee's Note

Exception (13). Records of family history kept in family Bibles have by long tradition been received in evidence. 5 Wigmore §§ 1495, 1496, citing numerous statutes and decisions. See also Regulations, Social Security Administration, 20 C.F.R. § 404.703(c), recognizing family Bible entries as proof of age in the absence of public or church records. Opinions in the area also include inscriptions on tombstones, publicly displayed pedigrees, and engravings on rings. Wigmore, supra. The rule is substantially identical in coverage with California Evidence Code § 1312.

House Judiciary Committee Report

The Committee approved this Rule in the form submitted by the Court, intending that the phrase "Statements of fact concerning personal or family history" be read to include the specific types of such statements enumerated in Rule 803(11).

Restyled 2011

(14) *Records of Documents That Affect an Interest in Property.* The record of a document that purports to establish or affect an interest in property if:

(A) the record is admitted to prove the content of the original recorded document, along with its signing and its delivery by each person who purports to have signed it;

(B) the record is kept in a public office; and

(C) a statute authorizes recording documents of that kind in that office.

Superseded 2011

(14) Records of documents affecting an interest in property. The record of a document purporting to establish or affect an interest in property, as proof of the content of the original recorded document and its execution and delivery by each person by whom it purports to have been executed, if the record is a record of a public office and an applicable statute authorizes the recording of documents of that kind in that office.

Advisory Committee's Note

Exception (14). The recording of title documents is a purely statutory development. Under any theory of the admissibility of public records, the records would be receivable as evidence of the contents of the recorded document, else the recording process would be reduced to a nullity. When, however, the record is offered for the further purpose of proving execution and delivery, a problem of lack of firsthand knowledge by the recorder, not present as to contents, is presented. This problem is solved, seemingly in all jurisdictions, by qualifying for recording only those documents shown by a specified procedure, either acknowledgement or a form of probate, to have been executed and delivered. 5 Wigmore §§ 1647-1651. Thus what may appear in the rule, at first glance, as endowing the record with an effect independently of local law and inviting difficulties of an Erie nature under Cities Service Oil Co. v. Dunlap, 308 U.S. 208, 60 S.Ct. 201, 84 L.Ed. 196 (1939), is not present, since the local law in fact governs under the example.

Restyled 2011

(15) ***Statements in Documents That Affect an Interest in Property.*** A statement contained in a document that purports to establish or affect an interest in property if the matter stated was relevant to the document's purpose — unless later dealings with the property are inconsistent with the truth of the statement or the purport of the document.

Superseded 2011

(15) Statements in documents affecting an interest in property. A statement contained in a document purporting to establish or affect an interest in property if the matter stated was relevant to the purpose of the document, unless dealings with the property since the document was made have been inconsistent with the truth of the statement or the purport of the document.

Advisory Committee's Note

Exception (15). Dispositive documents often contain recitals of fact. Thus a deed purporting to have been executed by an attorney in fact may recite the existence of the power of attorney, or a deed may recite that the grantors are all the heirs of the last record owner. Under the rule, these recitals are exempted from the hearsay rule. The circumstances under which dispositive documents are executed and the requirement that the recital be germane to the purpose of the document are believed to be adequate guarantees of trustworthiness, particularly in view of the nonapplicability of the rule if dealings with the property have been inconsistent with the document. The age of the document is of no significance, though in practical application the document will most often be an ancient one. See Uniform Rule 63(29), Comment.

Similar provisions are contained in Uniform Rule 63(29); California Evidence Code § 1330; Kansas Code of Civil Procedure § 60-460(aa); New Jersey Evidence Rule 63(29).

Restyled 2011

(16) ***Statements in Ancient Documents.*** A statement in a document that was prepared before January 1, 1998 and whose authenticity is established. [*Amended 2016.*]

Superseded 2011

(16) Statements in ancient documents. Statements in a document in existence twenty years or more the authenticity of which is established.

Advisory Committee's Note

Exception (16). Authenticating a document as ancient, essentially in the pattern of the common law, as provided in Rule 901(b)(8), leaves open as a separate question the admissibility of assertive statements contained therein as against a hearsay objection. 7 Wigmore § 2145a. Wigmore further states that the ancient document technique of authentication is universally conceded to apply to all sorts of documents, including letters, records, contracts, maps, and certificates, in addition to title documents, citing numerous decisions. Id. § 2145. Since most of these items are significant evidentially only insofar as they are assertive, their admission in evidence must be as a hearsay exception. But see 5 id. § 1573, p. 429, referring to recitals in ancient deeds as a "limited" hearsay exception. The former position is believed to be the correct one in reason and authority. As pointed out in McCormick § 298, danger of mistake is minimized by authentication requirements, and age affords assurance that the writing antedates the present controversy. See Dallas County v. Commercial Union Assurance Co., 286 F.2d 388 (5th Cir.1961), upholding admissibility of 58-year-old newspaper story. Cf. Morgan, Basic Problems of Evidence 364 (1962), but see id. 254.

For a similar provision, but with the added requirement that "the statement has since generally been acted upon as true by persons having an interest in the matter," see California Evidence Code § 1331.

Advisory Committee's Note to 2016 Amendment

The ancient documents exception to the rule against hearsay has been limited to statements in documents prepared before January 1, 1998. The Committee has determined that the ancient documents exception should be limited due to the risk that it will be used as a vehicle to admit vast amounts of unreliable electronically stored information (ESI). Given the exponential development and growth of electronic information around the year 1998, the hearsay exception for ancient documents has now become a possible open door for large amounts of unreliable ESI, as no showing of reliability needs to be made to qualify under the exception.

The Committee is aware that in certain cases—such as cases involving latent diseases and environmental damage—parties must rely on hardcopy documents from the past. The ancient documents exception remains available for such cases for documents prepared before 1998. Going forward, it is anticipated that any need to admit old hardcopy documents produced after January 1, 1998 will decrease, because reliable ESI is likely to be available and can be offered under a reliability-based hearsay exception. Rule 803(6) may be used for many of these ESI documents, especially given its flexible standards on which witnesses might be qualified to provide an adequate foundation. And Rule 807 can be used to admit old documents upon a showing of reliability—which will often (though not always) be found by circumstances such as that the document was prepared with no litigation motive in mind, close in time to the relevant events. The limitation of the ancient documents exception is not intended to raise an inference that 20 year-old documents are, as a class, unreliable, or that they should somehow not qualify for admissibility under Rule 807. Finally, many old documents can be admitted for the non-hearsay purpose of proving notice, or as party-opponent statements.

The limitation of the ancient documents hearsay exception is not intended to have any effect on authentication of ancient documents. The possibility of authenticating an old document under Rule 901(b)(8)—or under any ground available for any other document—remains unchanged.

The Committee carefully considered, but ultimately rejected, an amendment that would preserve the ancient documents exception for hardcopy evidence only. A party will often offer hardcopy that is derived from ESI. Moreover, a good deal of old information in hardcopy has been digitized or will be so in the future. Thus, the line between ESI and hardcopy was determined to be one that could not be drawn usefully.

The Committee understands that the choice of a cut-off date has a degree of arbitrariness. But January 1, 1998 is a rational date for treating concerns about old and unreliable ESI. And the date is no more arbitrary than the 20-year cutoff date in the original rule. See Committee Note to Rule 901(b)(8) ("Any time period selected is bound to be arbitrary.").

Under the amendment, a document is "prepared" when the statement proffered was recorded in that document. For example, if a hardcopy document is prepared in 1995, and a party seeks to admit a scanned copy of that document, the date of preparation is 1995 even though the scan was made long after that—the subsequent scan does not alter the document. The relevant point is the date on which the information is recorded, not when the information is prepared for trial. However, if the content of the document is itself altered after the cut-off date, then the hearsay exception will not apply to statements that were added in the alteration.

Changes Made After Publication and Comment

The amendment as issued for public comment would have eliminated the ancient documents exception to the hearsay rule. In response to the public comment, the amendment was changed to limit the coverage of the ancient documents exception to those documents prepared before January 1, 1998.

Restyled 2011

(17) ***Market Reports and Similar Commercial Publications.*** Market quotations, lists, directories, or other compilations that are generally relied on by the public or by persons in particular occupations.

Superseded 2011

(17) Market reports, commercial publications. Market quotations, tabulations, lists, directories, or other published compilations, generally used and relied upon by the public or by persons in particular occupations.

Advisory Committee's Note

Exception (17). Ample authority at common law supported the admission in evidence of items falling in this category. While Wigmore's text is narrowly oriented to lists, etc., prepared for the use of a trade or profession, 6 Wigmore § 1702, authorities are cited which include other kinds of publications, for example, newspaper market reports, telephone directories, and city directories. Id. §§ 1702-1706. The basis of trustworthiness is general reliance by the public or by a particular segment of it, and the motivation of the compiler to foster reliance by being accurate.

For similar provisions, see Uniform Rule 63(30); California Evidence Code § 1340; Kansas Code of Civil Procedure § 60-460(bb); New Jersey Evidence Rule 63(30). Uniform Commercial Code § 2-724 provides for admissibility in evidence of "reports in official publications or trade journals or in newspapers or periodicals of general circulation published as the reports of such [established commodity] market."

Restyled 2011

(18) ***Statements in Learned Treatises, Periodicals, or Pamphlets.*** A statement contained in a treatise, periodical, or pamphlet if:

(A) the statement is called to the attention of an expert witness on cross-examination or relied on by the expert on direct examination; and

(B) the publication is established as a reliable authority by the expert's admission or testimony, by another expert's testimony, or by judicial notice.

If admitted, the statement may be read into evidence but not received as an exhibit.

Superseded 2011

(18) Learned treatises. To the extent called to the attention of an expert witness upon cross-examination or relied upon by the expert witness in direct examination, statements contained in published treatises, periodicals, orpamphlets on a subject of history, medicine, or other science or art, established as a reliable authority by the testimony or admission of the witness or by other expert testimony or by judicial notice. If admitted, the statements may be read into evidence but may not be received as exhibits.

Case Note

A videotaped presentation may be a learned treatise. Costantino v. David M. Herzog, M.D., P.C., 203 F.3d 164, 170-171 (2d Cir. 2000).

Advisory Committee's NoteException (18). The writers have generally favored the admissibility of learned treatises, McCormick § 296, p. 621; Morgan, Basic Problems of Evidence 366 (1962); 6 Wigmore § 1692, with the support of occasional decisions and rules, City of Dothan v. Hardy, 237 Ala. 603, 188 So. 264 (1939); Lewandowski v. Preferred Risk Mut. Ins. Co., 33 Wis.2d 69, 146 N.W.2d 505 (1966), 66 Mich.L.Rev. 183 (1967); Uniform Rule 63(31); Kansas Code of Civil Procedure § 60-460(cc), but the great weight of authority has been that learned treatises are not admissible as substantive evidence though usable in the cross-examination of experts. The foundation of the minority view is that the hearsay objection must be regarded as unimpressive when directed against treatises since a high standard of accuracy is engendered by various factors: the treatise is written primarily and impartially for professionals, subject to scrutiny and exposure for inaccuracy, with the reputation of the writer at stake. 6 Wigmore § 1692. Sound as this position may be with respect to trustworthiness, there is, nevertheless, an additional difficulty in the likelihood that the treatise will be misunderstood and misapplied without expert assistance and supervision. This difficulty is recognized in the cases demonstrating unwillingness to sustain findings relative to disability on the basis of judicially noticed medical texts. Ross v. Gardner, 365 F.2d 554 (6th Cir.1966); Sayers v. Gardner, 380 F.2d 940 (6th Cir.1967); Colwell v. Gardner, 386 F.2d 56 (6th Cir.1967); Glendenning v. Ribicoff, 213 F.Supp. 301 (W.D.-Mo. 1962); Cook v. Celebrezze, 217 F.Supp. 366 (W.D.Mo.1963); Sosna v. Celebrezze, 234 F.Supp. 289 (E.D.Pa.1964); and see McDaniel v. Celebrezze, 331 F.2d 426 (4th Cir.1964). The rule avoids the danger of misunderstanding and misapplication by limiting the use of treatises as substantive evidence to situations in which an expert is on the stand and available to explain and assist in the application of the treatise if desired. The limitation upon receiving the publication itself physically in evidence, contained in the last sentence, is designed, to further this policy.

The relevance of the use of treatises on cross-examination is evident. This use of treatises has been the subject of varied views. The most restrictive position is that the witness must have stated expressly on direct his reliance upon the treatise. A slightly more liberal approach still insists upon reliance but allows it to be developed on cross-examination. Further relaxation dispenses with reliance but requires recognition as an authority by the witness, developable on cross-examination. The greatest liberality is found in decisions allowing use of the treatise on cross-examination when its status as an authority is established by any means. Annot., 60 A.L.R.2d 77. The exception is hinged upon this last position, which is that of the Supreme Court, Reilly v. Pinkus, 338 U.S. 269, 70 S.Ct. 110, 94 L.Ed. 63 (1949), and of recent well considered state court decisions, City of St. Petersburg v. Ferguson, 193 So.2d 648 (Fla.App.1967), cert. denied Fla., 201 So.2d 556; Darling v. Charleston Memorial Community Hospital, 33 Ill.2d 326, 211 N.E.2d 253 (1965); Dabroe v. Rhodes Co., 64 Wash.2d 431, 392 P.2d 317 (1964).

In Reilly v. Pinkus, supra, the Court pointed out that testing of professional knowledge was incomplete without exploration of the witness' knowledge of and attitude toward established treatises in the field. The process works equally well in reverse and furnishes the basis of the rule.

The rule does not require that the witness rely upon or recognize the treatise as authoritative, thus avoiding the possibility that the expert may at the outset block cross-examination by refusing to concede reliance or authoritativeness. Dabroe v. Rhodes Co., supra. Moreover, the rule avoids the unreality of admitting evidence for the purpose of impeachment only, with an instruction to the jury not to consider it otherwise. The parallel to the treatment of prior inconsistent statements will be apparent. See Rules 613(b) and 801(d)(1).

Restyled 2011

(19) ***Reputation Concerning Personal or Family History.*** A reputation among a person's family by blood, adoption, or marriage — or among a person's associates or in the community — concerning the person's birth, adoption, legitimacy, ancestry, marriage, divorce, death, relationship by blood, adoption, or marriage, or similar facts of personal or family history.

(20) ***Reputation Concerning Boundaries or General History.*** A reputation in a community — arising before the controversy — concerning boundaries of land in the community or customs that affect the land, or concerning general historical events important to that community, state, or nation.

(21) ***Reputation Concerning Character.*** A reputation among a person's associates or in the community concerning the person's character.

Superseded 2011

(19) Reputation concerning personal or family history. Reputation among members of a person's family by blood, adoption, or marriage, or among a person's associates, or in the community, concerning a person's birth, adoption, marriage, divorce, death, legitimacy, relationship by blood, adoption, or marriage, ancestry, or other similar fact of personal or family history.

(20) Reputation concerning boundaries or general history. Reputation in a community, arising before the controversy, as to boundaries of or customs affecting lands in the community, and reputation as to events of general history important to the community or State or nation in which located.

(21) Reputation as to character. Reputation of a person's character among associates or in the community.

Advisory Committee's Note

Exceptions (19), (20), and (21). Trustworthiness in reputation evidence is found "when the topic is such that the facts are likely to have been inquired about and that persons having personal knowledge have disclosed facts which have thus been discussed in the community; and thus the community's conclusion, if any has been formed, is likely to be a trustworthy one." 5 Wigmore § 1580, p. 444, and see also
§ 1583. On this common foundation, reputation as to land boundaries, customs, general history, character, and marriage have come to be regarded as admissible. The breadth of the underlying principle suggests the formulation of an equally broad exception, but tradition has in fact been much narrower and more particularized, and this is the pattern of these exceptions in the rule.

Exception (19) is concerned with matters of personal and family history. Marriage is universally conceded to be a proper subject of proof by evidence of reputation in the community. 5 Wigmore § 1602. As to such items as legitimacy, relationship, adoption, birth, and death, the decisions are divided. Id. § 1605. All seem to be susceptible to being the subject of well founded repute. The "world" in which the reputation may exist may be family, associates, or community. This world has proved capable of expanding with changing times from the single uncomplicated neighborhood, in which all activities take place, to the multiple and unrelated worlds of work, religious affiliation, and social activity, in each of which a reputation may be generated. People v. Reeves, 360 Ill. 55, 195 N.E. 443 (1935); State v. Axilrod, 248 Minn. 204, 79 N.W.2d 677 (1956); Mass.Stat.1947, c. 410, M.G.L.A. c. 233 § 21A; 5 Wigmore § 1616. The family has often served as the point of beginning for allowing community reputation. 5 Wigmore § 1488. For comparable provisions see Uniform Rule 63(26), (27)(c); California Evidence Code §§ 1313, 1314; Kansas Code of Civil Procedure § 60-460(x), (y)(3); New Jersey Evidence Rule 63(26), (27)(c).

The first portion of Exception (20) is based upon the general admissibility of evidence of reputation as to land boundaries and land customs, expanded in this country to include private as well as public boundaries. McCormick § 299, p. 625. The reputation is required to antedate the controversy, though not to be ancient. The second portion is likewise supported by authority, id., and is designed to facilitate proof of events when judicial notice is not available. The historical character of the subject matter dispenses with any need that the reputation antedate the controversy with respect to which it is offered. For similar provisions see Uniform Rule 63(27)(a), (b); California Evidence Code §§ 1320-1322; Kansas Code of Civil Procedure § 60-460(y), (1), (2); New Jersey Evidence Rule 63(27)(a), (b).

Exception (21) recognizes the traditional acceptance of reputation evidence as a means of proving human character. McCormick §§ 44, 158. The exception deals only with the hearsay aspect of this kind of evidence. Limitations upon admissibility based on other grounds will be found in Rules 404, relevancy of character evidence generally, and 608, character of witness. The exception is in effect a reiteration, in the context of hearsay, of Rule 405(a). Similar provisions are contained in Uniform Rule 63(28); California Evidence Code § 1324; Kansas Code of Civil Procedure § 60-460(z); New Jersey Evidence Rule 63(28).

Restyled 2011

(22) ***Judgment of a Previous Conviction.*** Evidence of a final judgment of conviction if:

- **(A)** the judgment was entered after a trial or guilty plea, but not a nolo contendere plea;
- **(B)** the conviction was for a crime punishable by death or by imprisonment for more than a year;

(C) the evidence is admitted to prove any fact essential to the judgment; and
(D) when offered by the prosecutor in a criminal case for a purpose other than impeachment, the judgment was against the defendant.

The pendency of an appeal may be shown but does not affect admissibility.

Superseded 2011

(22) Judgment of previous conviction. Evidence of a final judgment, entered after a trial or upon a plea of guilty (but not upon a plea of nolo contendere), adjudging a person guilty of a crime punishable by death or imprisonment in excess of one year, to prove any fact essential to sustain the judgment, but not including, when offered by the Government in a criminal prosecution for purposes other than impeachment, judgments against persons other than the accused. The pendency of an appeal may be shown but does not affect admissibility.

Advisory Committee's Note

Exception (22). When the status of a former judgment is under consideration in subsequent litigation, three possibilities must be noted: (1) the former judgment is conclusive under the doctrine of res judicata, either as a bar or a collateral estoppel; or (2) it is admissible in evidence for what it is worth; or (3) it may be of no effect at all. The first situation does not involve any problem of evidence except in the way that principles of substantive law generally bear upon the relevancy and materiality of evidence. The rule does not deal with the substantive effect of the judgment as a bar or collateral estoppel. When, however, the doctrine of res judicata does not apply to make the judgment either a bar or a collateral estoppel, a choice is presented between the second and third alternatives. The rule adopts the second for judgments of criminal conviction of felony grade. This is the direction of the decisions, Annot., 18 A.L.R.2d 1287, 1299, which manifest an increasing reluctance to reject in toto the validity of the law's factfinding processes outside the confines of res judicata and collateral estoppel. While this may leave a jury with the evidence of conviction but without means to evaluate it, as suggested by Judge Hinton, Note 27 Ill.L.Rev. 195 (1932), it seems safe to assume that the jury will give it substantial effect unless defendant offers a satisfactory explanation, a possibility not foreclosed by the provision. But see North River Ins. Co. v. Militello, 104 Colo. 28, 88 P.2d 567 (1939), in which the jury found for plaintiff on a fire policy despite the introduction of his conviction for arson. For supporting federal decisions see Clark, J., in New York & Cuba Mail S.S. Co. v. Continental Cas. Co., 117 F.2d 404, 411 (2d Cir.1941); Connecticut Fire Ins. Co. v. Farrara, 277 F.2d 388 (8th Cir.1960).

Practical considerations require exclusion of convictions of minor offenses, not because the administration of justice in its lower echelons must be inferior, but because motivation to defend at this level is often minimal or nonexistent. Cope v. Goble, 39 Cal.App.2d 448, 103 P.2d 598 (1940); Jones v. Talbot, 87 Idaho 498, 394 P.2d 316 (1964); Warren v. Marsh, 215 Minn. 615, 11 N.W.2d 528 (1943); Annot., 18 A.L.R.2d 1287, 1295-1297; 16 Brooklyn L.Rev. 286 (1950); 50 Colum.L.Rev. 529 (1950); 35 Cornell L.Q. 872 (1950). Hence the rule includes only convictions of felony grade, measured by federal standards.

Judgments of conviction based upon pleas of nolo contendere are not included. This position is consistent with the treatment of nolo pleas in Rule 410 and the authorities cited in the Advisory Committee's Note in support thereof.

While these rules do not in general purport to resolve constitutional issues, they have in general been drafted with a view to avoiding collision with constitutional principles. Consequently the exception does not include evidence of the conviction of a third person, offered against the accused in a criminal prosecution to prove any fact essential to sustain the judgment of conviction. A contrary position would seem clearly to violate the right of confrontation. Kirby v. United States, 174 U.S. 47, 19 S.Ct. 574, 43 L.Ed. 890 (1899), error to convict of possessing stolen postage stamps with the only evidence of theft being the record of conviction of the thieves. The situation is to be distinguished from cases in which conviction of another person is an element of the crime, e.g. 15 U.S.C. § 902(d), interstate shipment of firearms to a known convicted felon, and, as specifically provided, from impeachment.

For comparable provisions see Uniform Rule 63(20); California Evidence Code § 1300; Kansas Code of Civil Procedure § 60-460(r); New Jersey Evidence Rule 63(20).

Restyled 2011

(23) ***Judgments Involving Personal, Family, or General History or a Boundary.*** A judgment that is admitted to prove a matter of personal, family, or general history, or boundaries, if the matter:
(A) was essential to the judgment; and
(B) could be proved by evidence of reputation.

Superseded 2011

(23) Judgment as to personal, family, or general history, or boundaries. Judgments as proof of matters of personal, family or general history, or boundaries, essential to the judgment, if the same would be provable by evidence of reputation.

Advisory Committee's Note

Exception (23). A hearsay exception in this area was originally justified on the ground that verdicts were evidence of reputation. As trial by jury graduated from the category of neighborhood inquests, this theory lost its validity. It was never valid as to chancery decrees. Nevertheless the rule persisted, though the judges and writers shifted ground and began saying that the judgment or decree was as good evidence as reputation. See City of London v. Clerke, Carth. 181, 90 Eng.Rep. 710(K.B. 1691); Neill v. Duke of Devonshire, 8 App.Cas. 135 (1882). The shift appears to be correct, since the process of inquiry, sifting, and scrutiny which is relied upon to render reputation reliable is present in perhaps greater measure in the process of litigation. While this might suggest a broader area of application, the affinity to reputation is strong, and paragraph (23) goes no further, not even including character.

The leading case in the United States, Patterson v. Gaines, 47 U.S. (6 How.) 550, 599, 12 L.Ed. 553 (1847), follows in the pattern of the English decisions, mentioning as illustrative matters thus provable: manorial rights, public rights of way, immemorial custom, disputed boundary, and pedigree. More recent recognition of the principle is found in Grant Bros. Construction Co. v. United States, 232 U.S. 647, 34 S.Ct. 452, 58 L.Ed. 776 (1914), in action for penalties under Alien Contract Labor Law, decision of board of inquiry of Immigration Service admissible to prove alienage of laborers, as a matter of pedigree; United States v. Mid-Continent Petroleum Corp., 67 F.2d 37 (10th Cir.1933), records of commission enrolling Indians admissible on pedigree; Jung Yen Loy v. Cahill, 81 F.2d 809 (9th Cir.1936), board decisions as to citizenship of plaintiff's father admissible in proceeding for declaration of citizenship. Contra, In re Estate of Cunha, 49 Haw. 273, 414 P.2d 925 (1966).

Restyled 2011

(24) [Other exceptions.] [Transferred to Rule 807.]

Superseded 2011

(24) [*The "residual exception" was transferred to Rule 807 by amendment, 1997.*]

Note to 1997 Amendment

The contents of Rule 803(24) and Rule 804(b)(5) have been combined and transferred to a new Rule 807. This was done to facilitate additions to Rules 803 and 804. No change in meaning is intended. [Editor's Note: The Advisory Committee's Notes and Committee Reports to Rules 803(24) and 804(b)(5) have also been transferred to Rule 807.]

Restyled 2011

Rule 804. Exceptions to the Rule Against Hearsay — When the Declarant Is Unavailable as a Witness

(a) Criteria for Being Unavailable. A declarant is considered to be unavailable as a witness if the declarant:

(1) is exempted from testifying about the subject matter of the declarant's statement because the court rules that a privilege applies;

(2) refuses to testify about the subject matter despite a court order to do so;

(3) testifies to not remembering the subject matter;

(4) cannot be present or testify at the trial or hearing because of death or a then-existing infirmity, physical illness, or mental illness; or

(5) is absent from the trial or hearing and the statement's proponent has not been able, by process or other reasonable means, to procure:

(A) the declarant's attendance, in the case of a hearsay exception under Rule 804(b)(1) or (5); or

(B) the declarant's attendance or testimony, in the case of a hearsay exception under Rule 804(b)(2), (3), or (4).

But this subdivision (a) does not apply if the statement's proponent procured or wrongfully caused the declarant's unavailability as a witness in order to prevent the declarant from attending or testifying.

Superseded 2011

Rule 804. Hearsay Exceptions; Declarant Unavailable

(a) Definition of unavailability. "Unavailability as a witness" includes situations in which the declarant—

(1) is exempted by ruling of the court on the ground of privilege from testifying concerning the subject matter of the declarant's statement; or

(2) persists in refusing to testify concerning the subject matter of the declarant's statement despite an order of the court to do so; or

(3) testifies to a lack of memory of the subject matter of the declarant's statement; or

(4) is unable to be present or to testify at the hearing because of death or then existing physical or mental illness or infirmity; or

(5) is absent from the hearing and the proponent of a statement has been unable to procure the declarant's attendance (or in the case of a hearsay exception under subdivision (b)(2), (3), or (4), the declarant's attendance or testimony) by process or other reasonable means.

A declarant is not unavailable as a witness if exemption, refusal, claim of lack of memory, inability, or absence is due to the procurement or wrongdoing of the proponent of a statement for the purpose of preventing the witness from attending or testifying.

Advisory Committee's Note

As to firsthand knowledge on the part of hearsay declarants, see the introductory portion of the Advisory Committee's Note to Rule 803.

Subdivision (a). The definition of unavailability implements the division of hearsay exceptions into two categories by Rules 803 and 804(b).

At common law the unavailability requirement was evolved in connection with particular hearsay exceptions rather than along general lines. For example, see the separate explications of unavailability in relation to former testimony, declarations against interest, and statements of pedigree, separately developed in McCormick §§ 234, 257, and 297. However, no reason is apparent for making distinctions as to what satisfies unavailability for the different exceptions. The treatment in the rule is therefore uniform although differences in the range of process for witnesses between civil and criminal cases will lead to a less exacting requirement under item (5). See Rule 45(e) of the Federal Rules of Civil Procedure and Rule 17(e) of the Federal Rules of Criminal Procedure.

Five instances of unavailability are specified:

(1) Substantial authority supports the position that exercise of a claim of privilege by the declarant satisfies the requirement of unavailability (usually in connection with former testimony). Wyatt v. State, 35 Ala.App. 147, 46 So.2d 837 (1950); State v. Stewart, 85 Kan. 404, 116 P. 489 (1911); Annot., 45 A.L.R.2d 1354; Uniform Rule 62(7)(a); California Evidence Code § 240(a)(1); Kansas Code of Civil Procedure § 60-459(g)(1). A ruling by the judge is required, which clearly implies that an actual claim of privilege must be made.

(2) A witness is rendered unavailable if he simply refuses to testify concerning the subject matter of his statement despite judicial pressures to do so, a position supported by similar considerations of practicality. Johnson v. People, 152 Colo. 586, 384 P.2d 454 (1963); People v. Pickett, 339 Mich. 294, 63 N.W.2d 681, 45 A.L.R.2d 1341 (1954). Contra, Pleau v. State, 255 Wis. 362, 38 N.W.2d 496 (1949).

(3) The position that a claimed lack of memory by the witness of the subject matter of his statement constitutes unavailability likewise finds support in the cases, though not without dissent. McCormick § 234, p. 494. If the claim is successful, the practical effect is to put the testimony beyond reach, as in the other instances. In this instance, however, it will be noted that the lack of memory must be established by the testimony of the witness himself, which clearly contemplates his production and subjection to cross-examination.

(4) Death and infirmity find general recognition as grounds. McCormick §§ 234, 257, 297; Uniform Rule 62(7)(c); California Evidence Code § 240(a)(3); Kansas Code of Civil Procedure § 60-459(g)(3); New Jersey Evidence Rule 62(6)(c). See also the provisions on use of depositions in Rule 32(a)(3) of the Federal Rules of Civil Procedure and Rule 15(e) of the Federal Rules of Criminal Procedure.

(5) Absence from the hearing coupled with inability to compel attendance by process or other reasonable means also satisfies the requirement. McCormick § 234; Uniform Rule 62(7)(d) and (e); California Evidence Code § 240(a)(4) and (5); Kansas Code of Civil Procedure § 60-459(g)(4) and (5); New Jersey Rule 62(6)(b) and (d). See the discussion of procuring attendance of witnesses who are nonresidents or in custody in Barber v. Page, 390 U.S. 719, 88 S.Ct. 1318, 20 L.Ed.2d 255 (1968).

If the conditions otherwise constituting unavailability result from the procurement or wrongdoing of the proponent of the statement, the requirement is not satisfied. The rule contains no requirement that an attempt be made to take the deposition of a declarant.

House Judiciary Committee Report

Rule 804(a)(3) was approved in the form submitted by the Court. However, the Committee intends no change in existing federal law under which the court may choose to disbelieve the declarant's testimony as to his lack of memory. See United States v. Insana, 423 F.2d 1165, 1169-1170 (2nd Cir.), cert. denied, 400 U.S. 841 (1970).

Rule 804(a)(5) as submitted to the Congress provided, as one type of situation in which a declarant would be deemed "unavailable", that he be "absent from the hearing and the proponent of his statement has been unable to procure his attendance by process or other reasonable means." The Committee amended the Rule to insert after the word "attendance" the parenthetical expression "(or, in the case of a hearsay exception under subdivision (b)(2), (3), or (4), his attendance or testimony)". The amendment is designed primarily to require that an attempt be made to depose a witness (as well as to seek his attendance) as a precondition to the witness being deemed unavailable. The Committee, however, recognized the propriety of an exception to this additional requirement when it is the declarant's former testimony that is sought to be admitted under subdivision (b)(1).

Senate Judiciary Committee Report

Subdivision (a) of rule 804 as submitted by the Supreme Court defined the conditions under which a witness was considered to be unavailable. It was amended in the House.

The purpose of the amendment, according to the report of the House Committee on the Judiciary, is "primarily to require that an attempt be made to depose a witness (as well as to seek his attendance) as a precondition to the witness being unavailable."

Under the House amendment, before a witness is declared unavailable, a party must try to depose a witness (declarant) with respect to dying declarations, declarations against interest, and declarations of pedigree. None of these situations would seem to warrant this needless, impractical and highly restrictive complication. A good case can be made for eliminating the unavailability requirement entirely for declarations against interest cases. [Uniform rule 63(10); Kan.Stat.Anno. 60-460(j); 2A N.J.Stats.Anno. 84-63(10).]

In dying declaration cases, the declarant will usually, though not necessarily, be deceased at the time of trial. Pedigree statements which are admittedly and necessarily based largely on word of mouth are not greatly fortified by a deposition requirement.

Depositions are expensive and time-consuming. In any event, deposition procedures are available to those who wish to resort to them. Moreover, the deposition procedures of the Civil Rules and Criminal Rules are only imperfectly adapted to implementing the amendment. No purpose is served unless the deposition, if taken, may be used in evidence. Under Civil Rule (a)(3) the Criminal Rule 15(e), a deposition, though taken, may not be admissible, and under Criminal Rule 15(a) substantial obstacles exist in the way of even taking a deposition.

For these reasons, the committee deleted the House amendment.

The committee understands that the rule as to unavailability, as explained by the Advisory Committee "contains no requirement that an attempt be made to take the deposition of a declarant." In reflecting the committee's judgment, the statement is accurate insofar as it goes. Where, however, the proponent of the statement, with knowledge of the existence of the statement, fails to confront the declarant with the statement at the taking of the deposition, then the proponent should not, in fairness, be permitted to treat the declarant as "unavailable" simply because the declarant was not amenable to process compelling his attendance at trial. The committee does not consider it necessary to amend the rule to this effect because such a situation abuses, not conforms to, the rule. Fairness would preclude a person from introducing a hearsay statement on a particular issue if the person taking the deposition was aware of the issue at the time of the deposition but failed to depose the unavailable witness on that issue.

Conference Committee Report

Note to Subdivision (a)(5). Subsection (a) defines the term "unavailability as a witness". The House bill provides in subsection (a)(5) that the party who desires to use the statement must be unable to procure the declarant's attendance by process or other reasonable means. In the case of dying declarations, statements against interest and statements of personal or family history, the House bill requires that the proponent must also be unable to procure the declarant's testimony (such as by deposition or interrogatories) by process or other reasonable means. The Senate amendment eliminates this latter provision.

The Conference adopts the provision contained in the House bill.

Restyled 2011

(b) The Exceptions. The following are not excluded by the rule against hearsay if the declarant is unavailable as a witness:

Superseded 2011

(b) Hearsay exceptions. The following are not excluded by the hearsay rule if the declarant is unavailable as a witness:

Advisory Committee's Note

Subdivision (b). Rule 803, supra, is based upon the assumption that a hearsay statement falling within one of its exceptions possesses qualities which justify the conclusion that whether the declarant is available or unavailable is not a relevant factor in determining admissibility. The instant rule proceeds upon a different theory: hearsay which admittedly is not equal in quality to testimony of the declarant on the stand may nevertheless be admitted if the declarant is unavailable and if his statement meets a specified standard. The rule expresses preferences: testimony given on the stand in person is preferred over hearsay, and hearsay, if of the specified quality, is preferred over complete loss of the evidence of the declarant. The exceptions evolved at common law with respect to declarations of unavailable declarants furnish the basis for the exceptions enumerated in the proposal. The term "unavailable" is defined in subdivision (a).

Restyled 2011

(1) *Former Testimony.* Testimony that:

(A) was given as a witness at a trial, hearing, or lawful deposition, whether given during the current proceeding or a different one; and

(B) is now offered against a party who had — or, in a civil case, whose predecessor in interest had — an opportunity and similar motive to develop it by direct, cross-, or redirect examination.

Superseded 2011

(1) Former testimony. Testimony given as a witness at another hearing of the same or a different proceeding, or in a deposition taken in compliance with law in the course of the same or another proceeding, if the party against whom the testimony is now offered, or, in a civil action or proceeding, a predecessor in interest, had an opportunity and similar motive to develop the testimony by direct, cross, or redirect examination.

Case Notes

In a criminal trial, the defense may introduce evidence of an unavailable witness's exculpatory grand jury testimony only upon a showing that the government in fact had a similar motive to develop the witness's testimony. Whether the government had a similar motive cannot be determined as a matter of law. Nor can the motive requirement be ignored in the interests of "fairness." United States v. Salerno, 505 U.S. 317, 112 S.Ct.2503, 120 L.Ed. 2d 255 (1992).

"Predecessor in interest" means a party with a similar motive to develop the testimony and does not require a legal relationship between that party and the party against whom the former testimony is offered. See Lloyd v. American Export Lines, Inc., 580 F.2d 1179, 1185-1187 (3d Cir. 1978). See, generally, Christopher B. Mueller & Laird C. Kirkpatrick, Evidence § 8.69 (2d ed. 2003).

Advisory Committee's Note

Former testimony does not rely upon some set of circumstances to substitute for oath and cross-examination, since both oath and opportunity to cross-examine were present in fact. The only missing one of the ideal conditions for the giving of testimony is the presence of trier and opponent ("demeanor evidence"). This is lacking with all hearsay exceptions. Hence it may be argued that former testimony is the strongest hearsay and should be included under Rule 803, supra. However, opportunity to observe demeanor is what in a large measure confers depth and meaning upon oath and cross-examination. Thus in cases under Rule 803 demeanor lacks the significance which it possesses with respect to testimony. In any event, the tradition, founded in experience, uniformly favors production of the witness if he is available. The exception indicates continuation of the policy. This preference for the presence of the witness is apparent also in rules and statutes on the use of depositions, which deal with substantially the same problem.

Under the exception, the testimony may be offered (1) against the party *against* whom it was previously offered or (2) against the party *by* whom it was previously offered. In each instance the question resolves itself into whether fairness allows imposing, upon the party against whom now offered, the handling of the witness of the earlier occasion. (1) If the party against whom now offered is the one against whom the testimony was offered previously, no unfairness is apparent in requiring him to accept his own prior conduct of cross-examination or decision not to cross-examine. Only demeanor has been lost, and that is inherent in the situation. (2) If the party against whom now offered is the one by whom the testimony was offered previously, a satisfactory answer becomes somewhat more difficult. One possibility is to proceed somewhat along the line of an adoptive admission, i.e. by offering the testimony proponent in effect adopts it. However, this theory savors of discarded concepts of witnesses' belonging to a party, of litigants' ability to pick and choose witnesses, and of vouching for one's own witnesses. Cf. McCormick § 246, pp. 526-527; 4 Wigmore § 1075. A more direct and acceptable approach is simply to recognize direct and redirect examination of one's own witness as the equivalent of cross-examining an opponent's witness. Falknor, Former Testimony and the Uniform Rules: A Comment, 38 N.Y.U.L.Rev. 651, n. 1 (1963); McCormick § 231, p. 483. See also 5 Wigmore § 1389. Allowable techniques for dealing with hostile, double-crossing, forgetful, and mentally deficient witnesses leave no substance to a claim that one could not adequately develop his own witness at the former hearing. An even less appealing argument is presented when failure to develop fully was the result of a deliberate choice.

The common law did not limit the admissibility of former testimony to that given in an earlier trial of the same case, although it did require identity of issues as a means of insuring that the former handling of the witness was the equivalent of what would now be done if the opportunity were presented. Modern decisions reduce the requirement to "substantial" identity. McCormick § 233. Since identity of issues is significant only in that it bears on motive and interest in developing fully the testimony of the witness, expressing the matter in the latter terms is preferable. Id. Testimony given at a preliminary hearing was held in California v. Green, 399 U.S. 149, 90 S.Ct. 1930, 26 L.Ed.2d 489 (1970), to satisfy confrontation requirements in this respect.

As a further assurance of fairness in thrusting upon a party the prior handling of the witness, the common law also insisted upon identity of parties, deviating only to the extent of allowing substitution of successors in a narrowly construed privity. Mutuality as an aspect of identity is now generally discredited, and the requirement of identity of the offering party disappears except as it might affect motive to develop the testimony. Falknor, supra, at 652; McCormick § 232, pp. 487-488. The question remains whether strict identity, or privity, should continue as a requirement with respect to the party against whom offered. The rule departs to the extent of allowing substitution of one with the right and opportunity to develop the testimony with similar motive and interest. This position is supported by modern decisions. McCormick § 232, pp. 489-490; 5 Wigmore § 1388.

Provisions of the same tenor will be found in Uniform Rule 63(3)(b); California Evidence Code §§ 1290-1292; Kansas Code of Civil Procedure § 60-460(c)(2); New Jersey Evidence Rule 63(3). Unlike the rule, the latter three provide either that former testimony is not admissible if the right of confrontation is denied or that it is not admissible if the accused was not a party to the prior hearing. The genesis of these limitations is a caveat in Uniform Rule 63(3) Comment that use of former testimony against an accused may violate his right of confrontation. Mattox v. United States, 156 U.S. 237, 15 S.Ct. 337, 39 L.Ed. 409 (1895), held that the right was not violated by the Government's use, on a retrial of the same case, of testimony given at the first trial by two witnesses since deceased. The decision leaves open the questions (1) whether direct and redirect are equivalent to cross-examination for purposes of confrontation, (2) whether testimony given in a different proceeding is acceptable, and (3) whether the accused must himself have been a party to the earlier proceeding or whether a similarly situated person will serve the purpose. Professor Falknor concluded that, if a dying declaration untested by cross-examination is constitutionally admissible, former testimony tested by the cross-examination of one similarly situated does not offend against confrontation. Falknor, supra, at 659-660. The constitutional acceptability of dying declarations has often been conceded. Mattox v. United States, 156 U.S. 237, 243, 15 S.Ct. 337, 39 L.Ed. 409 (1895); Kirby v. United States, 174 U.S. 47, 61, 19 S.Ct. 574, 43 L.Ed. 890 (1899); Pointer v. Texas, 380 U.S. 400, 407, 85 S.Ct. 1065, 13 L.Ed.2d 923 (1965).

House Judiciary Committee Report

Rule 804(b)(1) as submitted by the Court allowed prior testimony of an unavailable witness to be admissible if the party against whom it is offered or a person "with motive and interest similar" to his had an opportunity to examine the witness. The Committee considered that it is generally unfair to impose upon the party against whom the hearsay evidence is being offered responsibility for the manner in which the witness was previously handled by another party. The sole exception to this, in the Committee's view, is when a party's predecessor in interest in a civil action or proceeding had an opportunity and similar motive to examine the witness. The Committee amended the Rule to reflect these policy determinations.

Senate Judiciary Committee Report

Rule 804(b)(1) as submitted by the Court allowed prior testimony of an unavailable witness to be admissible if the party against whom it is offered or a person "with motive and interest similar" to his had an opportunity to examine the witness.

The House amended the rule to apply only to a party's predecessor in interest. Although the committee recognizes considerable merit to the rule submitted by the Supreme Court, a position which has been advocated by many scholars and judges, we have concluded that the difference between the two versions is not great and we accept the House amendment.

Restyled 2011

(2) ***Statement Under the Belief of Imminent Death.*** In a prosecution for homicide or in a civil case, a statement that the declarant, while believing the declarant's death to be imminent, made about its cause or circumstances.

Superseded 2011

(2) Statement under belief of impending death. In a prosecution for homicide or in a civil action or proceeding, a statement made by a declarant while believing that the declarant's death was imminent, concerning the cause or circumstances of what the declarant believed to be impending death.

Advisory Committee's Note

The exception is the familiar dying declaration of the common law, expanded somewhat beyond its traditionally narrow limits. While the original religious justification for the exception may have lost its conviction for some persons over the years, it can scarcely be doubted that powerful psychological pressures are present. See 5 Wigmore § 1443 and the classic statement of Chief Baron Eyre in Rex v. Woodcock, 1 Leach 500, 502, 168 Eng.Rep. 352, 353 (K.B.1789).

The common law required that the statement be that of the victim, offered in a prosecution for criminal homicide. Thus declarations by victims in prosecutions for other crimes, e.g. a declaration by a rape victim who dies in childbirth, and all declarations in civil cases were outside the scope of the exception. An occasional statute has removed these restrictions, as in Colo.R.S. § 52-1-20, or has expanded the area of offenses to include abortions, 5 Wigmore § 1432, p. 224, n. 4. Kansas by decision extended the exception to civil cases. Thurston v. Fritz, 91 Kan. 468, 138 P. 625 (1914). While the common law exception no doubt originated as a result of the exceptional need for the evidence in homicide cases, the theory of admissibility applies equally in civil cases and in prosecutions for crimes other than homicide. The same considerations suggest abandonment of the limitation to circumstances attending the event in question, yet when the statement deals with matters other than the supposed death, its influence is believed to be sufficiently attenuated to justify the limitation. Unavailability is not limited to death. See subdivision (a) of this rule. Any problem as to declarations phrased in terms of opinion is laid at rest by Rule 701, and continuation of a requirement of firsthand knowledge is assured by Rule 602.

Comparable provisions are found in Uniform Rule 63(5); California Evidence Code § 1242; Kansas Code of Civil Procedure § 60-460(e); New Jersey Evidence Rule 63(5).

House Judiciary Committee Report

Rule 804(b)(3) as submitted by the Court (now Rule 804(b)(2) in the bill) proposed to expand the traditional scope of the dying declaration exception (i.e. a statement of the victim in a homicide case as to the cause or circumstances of his believed imminent death) to allow such statements in all criminal and civil cases. The Committee did not consider dying declarations as among the most reliable forms of hearsay. Consequently, it amended the provision to limit their admissibility in criminal cases to homicide prosecutions, where exceptional need for the evidence is present. This is existing law. At the same time, the Committee approved the expansion to civil actions and proceedings where the stakes do not involve possible imprisonment, although noting that this could lead to forum shopping in some instances.

Restyled 2011

(3) ***Statement Against Interest.*** A statement that:

(A) a reasonable person in the declarant's position would have made only if the person believed it to be true because, when made, it was so contrary to the declarant's proprietary or pecuniary interest or had so great a tendency to invalidate the declarant's claim against someone else or to expose the declarant to civil or criminal liability; and

(B) is supported by corroborating circumstances that clearly indicate its trustworthiness, if it is offered in a criminal case as one that tends to expose the declarant to criminal liability.

Committee Note to 2011 Restyled Rule

No style changes were made to Rule 804(b)(3), because it was already restyled in conjunction with a substantive amendment effective December 1, 2010.

Superseded 2011

(3) Statement against interest — A statement that:

(A) a reasonable person in the declarant's position would have made only if the person believed it to be true because, when made, it was so contrary to the declarant's proprietary or pecuniary interest or had so great a tendency to invalidate the declarant's claim against someone else or to expose the declarant to civil or criminal liability; and

(B) is supported by corroborating circumstances that clearly indicate its trustworthiness, if it is offered in a criminal case as one that tends to expose the declarant to criminal liability. [*Effective Dec. 1, 2010.*]

Case Notes

In applying the exception for declarations against penal interest, a court should separate an extended declaration into simple statements and admit only those statements that are themselves relevant and self-inculpatory. The rule does not allow admission of non-self-inculpatory statements just because they are made within a broader narrative that is generally self-inculpatory. However, the against-interest quality of a statement can only be discerned by its context. A statement implicating another person may be self-serving if designed to shift blame; it may be neutral; or it may be self-inculpatory if a reasonable person in the declarant's position would know, for example, that being linked to the other person implicates the declarant in greater criminality. Williamson v. United States, 512 U.S. 594, 598-605, 114 S.Ct. 2431, 2434-2438, 129 L.Ed. 2d 476 (1994).

Corroborating circumstances are a prerequisite to the admissibility of declarations against penal interest in both civil and criminal cases and without regard to whether they are offered to inculpate or to exculpate the defendant. American Automotive Accessories, Inc. v. Fishman, 175 F.3d 534, 540 (7th Cir. 1999).

Advisory Committee's Note

The circumstantial guaranty of reliability for declarations against interest is the assumption that persons do not make statements which are damaging to themselves unless satisfied for good reason that they are true. Hileman v. Northwest Engineering Co., 346 F.2d 668 (6th Cir.1965). If the statement is that of a party, offered by his opponent, it comes in as an admission, Rule 803(d)(2), and there is no occasion to inquire whether it is against interest, this not being a condition precedent to admissibility of admissions by opponents.

The common law required that the interest declared against be pecuniary or proprietary but within this limitation demonstrated striking ingenuity in discovering an against-interest aspect. Higham v. Ridgway, 10 East 109, 103 Eng.Rep. 717 (K.B.1808); Reg. v. Overseers of Birmingham, 1 B. & S. 763, 121 Eng.Rep. 897 (Q.B.1861); McCormick, § 256, p. 551, nn. 2 and 3.

The exception discards the common law limitation and expands to the full logical limit. One result is to remove doubt as to the admissibility of declarations tending to establish a tort liability against the declarant or to extinguish one which might be asserted by him, in accordance with the trend of the decisions in this country. McCormick § 254, pp. 548-549. Another is to allow statements tending to expose declarant to hatred, ridicule, or disgrace, the motivation here being considered to be as strong as when financial interests are at stake. McCormick § 255, p. 551. And finally, exposure to criminal liability satisfies the against-interest requirement. The refusal of the common law to concede the adequacy of a penal interest was no doubt indefensible in logic, see the dissent of Mr. Justice Holmes in Donnelly v. United States, 228 U.S. 243, 33 S.Ct. 449, 57 L.Ed. 820 (1913), but one senses in the decisions a distrust of evidence of confessions by third persons offered to exculpate the accused arising from suspicions of fabrication either of the fact of the making of the confession or in its contents, enhanced in either instance by the required unavailability of the declarant. Nevertheless, an increasing amount of decisional law recognizes exposure to punishment for crime as a sufficient stake. People v. Spriggs, 60 Cal.2d 868, 36 Cal.Rptr. 841, 389 P.2d 377 (1964); Sutter v. Easterly, 354 Mo. 282, 189 S.W.2d 284 (1945); Band's Refuse Removal, Inc. v. Fairlawn

Borough, 62 N.J.Super. 522, 163 A.2d 465 (1960); Newberry v. Commonwealth, 191 Va. 445, 61 S.E.2d 318 (1950); Annot., 162 A.L.R. 446. The requirement of corroboration is included in the rule in order to effect an accommodation between these competing considerations. When the statement is offered by the accused by way of exculpation, the resulting situation is not adapted to control by rulings as to the weight of the evidence, and hence the provision is cast in terms of a requirement preliminary to admissibility. Cf. Rule 406(a). The requirement of corroboration should be construed in such a manner as to effectuate its purpose of circumventing fabrication.

Ordinarily the third-party confession is thought of in terms of exculpating the accused, but this is by no means always or necessarily the case: it may include statements implicating him, and under the general theory of declarations against interest they would be admissible as related statements. Douglas v. Alabama, 380 U.S. 415, 85 S.Ct. 1074, 13 L.Ed.2d 934 (1965), and Bruton v. United States, 389 U.S. 818, 88 S.Ct. 126, 19 L.Ed.2d 70 (1968), both involved confessions by codefendants which implicated the accused. While the confession was not actually offered in evidence in Douglas, the procedure followed effectively put it before the jury, which the Court ruled to be error. Whether the confession might have been admissible as a declaration against penal interest was not considered or discussed. Bruton assumed the inadmissibility, as against the accused, of the implicating confession of his codefendant, and centered upon the question of the effectiveness of a limiting instruction. These decisions, however, by no means require that all statements implicating another person be excluded from the category of declarations against interest. Whether a statement is in fact against interest must be determined from the circumstances of each case. Thus a statement admitting guilt and implicating another person, made while in custody, may well be motivated by a desire to curry favor with the authorities and hence fail to qualify as against interest. See the dissenting opinion of Mr. Justice White in Bruton. On the other hand, the same words spoken under different circumstances, e.g., to an acquaintance, would have no difficulty in qualifying. The rule does not purport to deal with questions of the right of confrontation.

The balancing of self-serving against dissenting [*sic*, disserving?] aspects of a declaration is discussed in McCormick § 256.

For comparable provisions, see Uniform Rule 63(10); California Evidence Code § 1230; Kansas Code of Civil Procedure § 60-460(j); New Jersey Evidence Rule 63(10).

House Judiciary Committee Report

Rule 804(b)(4) as submitted by the Court (now Rule 804(b)(3) in the bill) provided as follows:

> "Statement against interest.—A statement which was at the time of its making so far contrary to the declarant's pecuniary or proprietary interest or so far tended to subject him to civil or criminal liability or to render invalid a claim by him against another or to make him an object of hatred, ridicule, or disgrace, that a reasonable man in his position would not have made the statement unless he believed it to be true. A statement tending to exculpate the accused is not admissible unless corroborated."

The Committee determined to retain the traditional hearsay exception for statements against pecuniary or proprietary interest. However, it deemed the Court's additional references to statements tending to subject a declarant to civil liability or to render invalid a claim by him against another to be redundant as included within the scope of the reference to statements against pecuniary or proprietary interest. See Gichner v. Antonio Triano Tile and Marble Co., 410 F.2d 238 (D.C.Cir.1968). Those additional references were accordingly deleted.

The Court's Rule also proposed to expand the hearsay limitation from its present federal limitation to include statements subjecting the declarant to criminal liability and statements tending to make him an object of hatred, ridicule, or disgrace. The Committee eliminated the latter category from the subdivision as lacking sufficient guarantees of reliability. See United States v. Dovico, 380 F.2d 325, 327 nn. 2, 4 (2nd Cir.), cert. denied, 389 U.S. 944 (1967). As for statements against penal interest, the Committee shared the view of the Court that some such statements do possess adequate assurances of reliability and should be admissible. It believed, however, as did the Court, that statements of this type tending to exculpate the accused are more suspect and so should have their admissibility conditioned upon some further provision insuring trustworthiness. The proposal in the Court Rule to add a requirement of simple corroboration was, however, deemed ineffective to accomplish this purpose since the accused's own testimony might suffice while not necessarily increasing the reliability of the hearsay statement. The Committee settled upon the language "unless corroborating circumstances clearly indicate the trustworthiness of the statement" as affording a proper standard and degree of discretion. It was contemplated that the result in such cases as Donnelly v. United States, 228 U.S. 243 (1912), where the circumstances plainly indicated reliability, would be changed. The Committee also added to the Rule the final sentence from the 1971 Advisory Committee draft, designed to codify the doctrine of Bruton v. United States, 391 U.S. 123 (1968). The Committee does not intend to affect the existing exception to the Bruton principle where the codefendant takes the stand and is subject to cross-examination, but believed there was no need to make specific provision for this situation in the Rule, since in that event the declarant would not be "unavailable".

Senate Judiciary Committee Report

The rule defines those statements which are considered to be against interest and thus of sufficient trustworthiness to be admissible even though hearsay. With regard to the type of interest declared against, the version submitted by the Supreme Court included inter alia, statements tending to subject a declarant to civil liability or to invalidate a claim by him against another. The House struck these provisions as redundant. In view of the conflicting case law construing pecuniary or proprietary interests narrowly so as to exclude, e.g., tort cases, this deletion could be misconstrued.

Three States which have recently codified their rules of evidence have followed the Supreme Court's version of this rule, i.e., that a statement is against interest if it tends to subject a declarant to civil liability. [Nev.Rev.Stats. § 51.345; N.Mex.Stats. (1973 Supp.) § 20-4-804(4); West's Wis.Stats.Anno. (1973 Supp.) § 908.045(4).]

The committee believes that the reference to statements tending to subject a person to civil liability constitutes a desirable clarification of the scope of the rule. Therefore, we have reinstated the Supreme Court language on this matter.

The Court rule also proposed to expand the hearsay limitation from its present federal limitation to include statements subjecting the declarant to statements tending to make him an object of hatred, ridicule, or disgrace. The House eliminated the latter category from the subdivision as lacking sufficient guarantees of reliability. Although there is considerable support for the admissibility of such statements (all three of the State rules referred to supra, would admit such statements), we accept the deletion by the House.

The House amended this exception to add a sentence making inadmissible a statement or confession offered against the accused in a criminal case, made by a codefendant or other person implicating both himself and the accused. The sentence was added to codify the constitutional principle announced in Bruton v. United States, 391 U.S. 123 (1968). Bruton held that the admission of the extrajudicial hearsay statement of one codefendant inculpating a second codefendant violated the confrontation clause of the sixth amendment.

The committee decided to delete this provision because the basic approach of the rules is to avoid codifying, or attempting to codify, constitutional evidentiary principles, such as the fifth amendment's right against self-incrimination and, here, the sixth amendment's right of confrontation. Codification of a constitutional principle is unnecessary and, where the principle is under development, often unwise. Furthermore, the House provision does not appear to recognize the exceptions to the Bruton rule, e.g. where the codefendant takes the stand and is subject to cross examination; where the accused confessed, see United States v. Mancusi, 404 F.2d 296 (2d Cir.1968), cert. denied 397 U.S. 942 (1907); where the accused was placed at the scene of the crime, see United States v. Zelker, 452 F.2d 1009 (2d Cir.1971). For these reasons, the committee decided to delete this provision.

Conference Committee Report

The Senate amendment to subsection (b)(3) provides that a statement is against interest and not excluded by the hearsay rule when the declarant is unavailable as a witness, if the statement tends to subject a person to civil or criminal liability or renders invalid a claim by him against another. The House bill did not refer specifically to civil liability and to rendering invalid a claim against another. The Senate amendment also deletes from the House bill the provision that subsection (b)(3) does not apply to a statement or confession, made by a codefendant or another, which implicates the accused and the person who made the statement, when that statement or confession is offered against the accused in a criminal case.

The Conference adopts the Senate amendment. The Conferees intend to include within the purview of this rule, statements subjecting a person to civil liability and statements rendering claims invalid. The Conferees agree to delete the provision regarding statements by a codefendant, thereby reflecting the general approach in the Rules of Evidence to avoid attempting to codify constitutional evidentiary principles.

Committee Note to 2010 Amendment

Rule 804(b)(3) has been amended to provide that the corroborating circumstances requirement applies to all declarations against penal interest offered in criminal cases. A number of courts have applied the corroborating circumstances requirement to declarations against penal interest offered by the prosecution, even though the text of the Rule did not so provide. *See, e.g., United States v. Alvarez,* 584 F.2d 694, 701 (5th Cir.1978) ("by transplanting the language governing exculpatory statements onto the analysis for admitting inculpatory hearsay, a unitary standard is derived which offers the most workable basis for applying Rule 804(b)(3)"); *United States v. Shukri,* 207 F.3d 412 (7th Cir. 2000) (requiring corroborating circumstances for against-penal-interest statements offered by the government). A unitary approach to declarations against penal interest assures both the prosecution and the accused that the Rule will not be abused and that only reliable hearsay statements will be admitted under the exception.

All other changes to the structure and wording of the rule are intended to be stylistic only. There is no intent to change any other result in any ruling on evidence admissibility.

The Committee found no need to address the relationship between Rule 804(b)(3) and the Confrontation Clause, because the requirements of this exception assure that declarations admissible under it will not be testimonial.

The amendment does not address the use of the corroborating circumstances for declarations against penal interest offered in civil cases.In assessing whether corroborating circumstances exist, some courts have focused on the credibility of the witness who relates the hearsay statement in court. But the credibility of the witness who relates the statement is not a proper factor for the court to consider in assessing corroborating circumstances. To base admission or exclusion of a hearsay statement on the witness's credibility would usurp the jury's role of determining the credibility of testifying witnesses.

Changes Made After Publication and Comments

The rule, as submitted for public comment, was restyled in accordance with the style conventions of the Style Subcommittee of the Committee on Rules of Practice and Procedure. As restyled, the proposed amendment addresses the style suggestions made in public comments.

The proposed Committee Note was amended to add a short discussion on applying the corroborating circumstances requirement.

Restyled 2011

(4) ***Statement of Personal or Family History.*** A statement about:

(A) the declarant's own birth, adoption, legitimacy, ancestry, marriage, divorce, relationship by blood, adoption, or marriage, or similar facts of personal or family history, even though the declarant had no way of acquiring personal knowledge about that fact; or

(B) another person concerning any of these facts, as well as death, if the declarant was related to the person by blood, adoption, or marriage or was so intimately associated with the person's family that the declarant's information is likely to be accurate.

Superseded 2011

(4) Statement of personal or family history. (A) A statement concerning the declarant's own birth, adoption, marriage, divorce, legitimacy, relationship by blood, adoption, or marriage, ancestry, or other similar fact of personal or family history, even though declarant had no means of acquiring personal knowledge of the matter stated; or (B) a statement concerning the foregoing matters, and death also, of another person, if the declarant was related to the other by blood, adoption, or marriage or was so intimately associated with the other's family as to be likely to have accurate information concerning the matter declared.

Advisory Committee's Note

The general common law requirement that a declaration in this area must have been made ante litem motam has been dropped, as bearing more appropriately on weight than admissibility. See 5 Wigmore § 1483. Item (i) [now (A)] specifically disclaims any need of firsthand knowledge respecting declarant's own personal history. In some instances it is self-evident (marriage) and in others impossible and traditionally not required (date of birth). Item (ii) [now (B)] deals with declarations concerning the history of another person. As at common law, declarant is qualified if related by blood or marriage. 5 Wigmore § 1489. In addition, and contrary to the common law, declarant qualifies by virtue of intimate association with the family. Id., § 1487. The requirement sometimes encountered that when the subject of the statement is the relationship between two other persons the declarant must qualify as to both is omitted. Relationship is reciprocal. Id.,
§ 1491.

For comparable provisions, see Uniform Rule 63(23), (24), (25); California Evidence Code §§ 1310, 1311; Kansas Code of Civil Procedure § 60-460(u), (v), (w); New Jersey Evidence Rules 63-23), 63(24), 63(25).

Restyled 2011

(5) [Other exceptions.] [Transferred to Rule 807.]

Superseded 2011

(5) [The "residual exception" was transferred to Rule 807 by amendment, 1997.]

Advisory Committee's Note to 1997 Amendment

The contents of Rule 803(24) and Rule 804(b)(5) have been combined and transferred to a new Rule 807. This was done to facilitate additions to Rules 803 and 804. No change in meaning is intended.

Restyled 2011

(6) *Statement Offered Against a Party That Wrongfully Caused the Declarant's Unavailability.* A statement offered against a party that wrongfully caused - or acquiesced in wrongfully causing - the declarant's unavailability as a witness, and did so intending that result.

Superseded 2011

(6) Forfeiture by wrongdoing. A statement offered against a party that has engaged or acquiesced in wrongdoing that was intended to, and did, procure the unavailability of the declarant as a witness. [*Added 1997.*]

Advisory Committee's Note to 1997 Amendment

Rule 804(b)(6) has been added to provide that a party forfeits the right to object on hearsay grounds to the admission of a declarant's prior statement when the party's deliberate wrongdoing or acquiescence therein procured the unavailability of the declarant as a witness. This recognizes the need for a prophylactic rule to deal with abhorrent behavior "which strikes at the heart of the system of justice itself." United States v. Mastrangelo, 693 F.2d 269, 273 (2d Cir.1982), cert. denied, 467 U.S. 1204 (1984). The wrongdoing need not consist of a criminal act. The rule applies to all parties, including the government.

Every circuit that has resolved the question has recognized the principle of forfeiture by misconduct, although the tests for determining whether there is a forfeiture have varied. See, e.g., United States v. Aguiar, 975 F.2d 45, 47 (2d Cir.1992); United States v. Potamitis, 739 F.2d 784, 789 (2d Cir.), cert. denied, 469 U.S. 918 (1984); Steele v. Taylor, 684 F.2d 1193, 1199 (6th Cir.1982), cert. denied, 460 U.S. 1053 (1983); United States v. Balano, 618 F.2d 624, 629 (10th Cir.1979), cert. denied, 449 U.S. 840 (1980); United States v. Carlson, 547 F.2d 1346, 1358-59 (8th Cir.), cert. denied, 431 U.S. 914 (1977). The foregoing cases apply a preponderance of the evidence standard. Contra United States v. Thevis, 665 F.2d 616, 631 (5th Cir.) (clear and convincing standard), cert. denied, 459 U.S. 825 (1982). The usual Rule 104(a) preponderance of the evidence standard has been adopted in light of the behavior the new Rule 804(b)(6) seeks to discourage.

Restyled 2011

Rule 805. Hearsay Within Hearsay

Hearsay within hearsay is not excluded by the rule against hearsay if each part of the combined statements conforms with an exception to the rule.

Superseded 2011

Rule 805. Hearsay Within Hearsay

Hearsay included within hearsay is not excluded under the hearsay rule if each part of the combined statements conforms with an exception to the hearsay rule provided in these rules.

Case Note

In determining the admissibility of hearsay within hearsay, an exclusion from the definition of hearsay under Rule 801(d) should be treated the same as an exception to the hearsay rule. United States v. Dotson, 821 F.2d 1034, 1035 (5th Cir.1987).

Advisory Committee's Note

On principle it scarcely seems open to doubt that the hearsay rule should not call for exclusion of a hearsay statement which includes a further hearsay statement when both conform to the requirements of a hearsay exception. Thus a hospital record might contain an entry of the patient's age based on information furnished by his wife. The hospital record would qualify as a regular entry except that the person who furnished the information was not acting in the routine of the business. However, her statement independently qualifies as a statement of pedigree (if she is unavailable) or as a statement made for purposes of diagnosis or treatment, and hence each link in the chain falls under sufficient assurances. Or, further to illustrate, a dying declaration may incorporate a declaration against interest by another declarant. See McCormick § 290, p. 611.

Restyled 2011

Rule 806. Attacking and Supporting the Declarant's Credibility

When a hearsay statement — or a statement described in Rule 801(d)(2)(C), (D), or (E) — has been admitted in evidence, the declarant's credibility may be attacked, and then supported, by any evidence that would be admissible for those purposes if the declarant had testified as a witness. The court may admit evidence of the declarant's inconsistent statement or conduct, regardless of when it occurred or whether the declarant had an opportunity to explain or deny it. If the party against whom the statement was admitted calls the declarant as a witness, the party may examine the declarant on the statement as if on cross-examination.

Superseded 2011

Rule 806. Attacking and Supporting Credibility of Declarant

When a hearsay statement, or a statement defined in Rule 801(d)(2)(C), (D), or (E), has been admitted in evidence, the credibility of the declarant may be attacked, and if attacked may be supported, by any evidence which would be admissible for those purposes if declarant had testified as a witness. Evidence of a statement or conduct by the declarant at any time, inconsistent with the declarant's hearsay statement, is not subject to any requirement that the declarant may have been afforded an opportunity to deny or explain. If the party against whom a hearsay statement has been admitted calls the declarant as a witness, the party is entitled to examine the declarant on the statement as if under cross-examination.

Case Note

Split of authority as to whether the ban on extrinsic evidence of untruthful acts to impeach a witness's credibility, see Rule 608(b), applies to impeachment of a hearsay declarant. *Compare* United States v. Saada, 212 F.3d 210, 220-221 (3d Cir. 2000) (no extrinsic evidence) *with* United States v. Friedman 854 F.2d 535, 570 n.8 (2d Cir. 1988) (extrinsic evidence allowed).

Advisory Committee's Note

The declarant of a hearsay statement which is admitted in evidence is in effect a witness. His credibility should in fairness be subject to impeachment and support as though he had in fact testified. See Rules 608 and 609. There are however, some special aspects of the impeaching of a hearsay declarant which require consideration. These special aspects center upon impeachment by inconsistent statement, arise from factual differences which exist between the use of hearsay and an actual witness and also between various kinds of hearsay, and involve the question of applying to declarants the general rule disallowing evidence of an inconsistent statement to impeach a witness unless he is afforded an opportunity to deny or explain. See Rule 613(b).

The principal difference between using hearsay and an actual witness is that the inconsistent statement will in the case of the witness almost inevitably of necessity in the nature of things be a prior statement, which it is entirely possible and feasible to call to his attention, while in the case of hearsay the inconsistent statement may well be a subsequent one, which practically precludes calling it to the attention of the declarant. The result of insisting upon observation of this impossible requirement in the hearsay situation is to deny the opponent, already barred from cross-examination, any benefit of this important technique of impeachment. The writers favor allowing the subsequent statement. McCormick § 37, p. 69; 3 Wigmore § 1033. The cases, however, are divided. Cases allowing the impeachment include People v. Collup, 27 Cal.2d 829, 167 P.2d 714 (1946); People v. Rosoto, 58 Cal.2d 304, 23 Cal.Rptr. 779, 373 P.2d 867 (1962); Carver v. United States, 164 U.S. 694, 17 S.Ct. 228, 41 L.Ed. 602 (1897). Contra, Mattox v. United States, 156 U.S. 237, 15 S.Ct. 337, 39 L.Ed. 409 (1895); People v. Hines, 284 N.Y. 93, 29 N.E.2d 483 (1940). The force of Mattox, where the hearsay was the former testimony of a deceased witness and the denial of use of a subsequent inconsistent statement was upheld, is much diminished by Carver, where the hearsay was a dying declaration and denial of use of a subsequent inconsistent statement resulted in reversal. The difference in the particular brand of hearsay seems unimportant when the inconsistent statement is a subsequent one. True, the opponent is not totally deprived of cross-examination when the hearsay is former testimony or a deposition but he is deprived of cross-examining on the statement or along lines suggested by it. Mr. Justice Shiras, with two justices joining him, dissented vigorously in Mattox.

When the impeaching statement was made prior to the hearsay statement, differences in the kinds of hearsay appear which arguably may justify differences in treatment. If the hearsay consisted of a simple statement by the witness, e.g. a dying declaration or a declaration against interest, the feasibility of affording him an opportunity to deny or explain encounters the same practical impossibility as where the statement is a subsequent one, just discussed, although here the impossibility arises from the total absence of anything resembling a hearing at which the matter could be put to him. The courts by a large majority have ruled in favor of allowing the statement to be used under these circumstances. McCormick § 37, p. 69; 3 Wigmore § 1033. If, however, the hearsay consists of former testimony or a deposition, the possibility of calling the prior statement to the attention of the witness or deponent is not ruled out, since the opportunity to cross-examine was available. It might thus be concluded that with former testimony or depositions the conventional foundation should be insisted upon. Most of the cases involve depositions, and Wigmore describes them as divided. 3 Wigmore § 1031. Deposition procedures at best are cumbersome and expensive, and to require the laying of the foundation may impose an undue burden. Under the federal practice, there is no way of knowing with certainty at the time of taking a deposition whether it is merely for discovery or will ultimately end up in evidence. With respect to both former testimony and depositions the possibility exists that knowledge of the statement might not be acquired until after the time of the cross-examination. Moreover, the expanded admissibility of former testimony and depositions under Rule 804(b)(1) calls for a correspondingly expanded approach to impeachment. The rule dispenses with the requirement in all hearsay situations, which is readily administered and best calculated to lead to fair results.

Notice should be taken that Rule 26(f) of the Federal Rules of Civil Procedure, as originally submitted by the Advisory Committee, ended with the following:

"... and, without having first called them to the deponent's attention, may show statements contradictory thereto made at any time by the deponent."

This language did not appear in the rule as promulgated in December, 1937. See 4 Moore's Federal Practice ¶¶ 26.01[9], 26.35 (2d ed.1967). In 1951, Nebraska adopted a provision strongly resembling the one stricken from the federal rule:

"Any party may impeach any adverse deponent by self-contradiction without having laid foundation for such impeachment at the time such deposition was taken." R.S.Neb. § 25-1267.07.

For similar provisions, see Uniform Rule 65; California Evidence Code § 1202; Kansas Code of Civil Procedure § 60-462; New Jersey Evidence Rule 65.

The provision for cross-examination of a declarant upon his hearsay statement is a corollary of general principles of cross-examination. A similar provision is found in California Evidence Code § 1203.

Senate Committee Report

Rule 806, as passed by the House and as proposed by the Supreme Court provides that whenever a hearsay statement is admitted, the credibility of the declarant of the statement may be attacked, and if attacked may be supported, by any evidence which would be admissible for those purposes if the declarant had testified as a witness. Rule 801 defines what is a hearsay statement. While statements by a person authorized by a party-opponent to make a statement concerning the subject, by the party-opponent's agent or by a coconspirator of a party—see rule 801(d)(2)(c), (d) and (e) —are traditionally defined as exceptions to the hearsay rule, rule 801 defines such admission by a party-opponent as statements which are not hearsay. Consequently, rule 806 by referring exclusively to the admission of hearsay statements, does not appear to allow the credibility of the declarant to be attacked when the declarant is a coconspirator, agent or authorized spokesman. The committee is of the view that such statements should open the declarant to attacks on his credibility. Indeed, the reason such statements are excluded from the operation of rule 806 is likely attributable to the drafting technique used to codify the hearsay rule, viz. some statements, instead of being referred to as exceptions to the hearsay rule, are defined as statements which are not hearsay. The phrase "or a statement defined inn rule 801(d)(2)(c), (d) and (e)" is added to the rule in order to subject the declarant of such statements, like the declarant of hearsay statements, to attacks on his credibility. [The committee considered it unnecessary to include statements contained in rule 801(d)(2)(A) and (B)—the statement by the party-opponent himself or the statement of which he has manifested his adoption—because the credibility of the party-opponent is always subject to an attack on his credibility.]

Conference Committee Report

The Senate amendment permits an attack upon the credibility of the declarant of a statement if the statement is one by a person authorized by a party-opponent to make a statement concerning the subject, one by an agent of a party-opponent, or one by a coconspirator of the party-opponent, as these statements are defined in Rules 801(d)(2)(C), (D) and (E). The House bill has no such provision.*The Conference adopts the Senate amendment. The Senate amendment conforms the rule to present practice.*

Restyled 2011 – as amended effective December 1, 2019

Rule 807. Residual Exception

(a) **In General.** Under the following conditions, a hearsay statement is not excluded by the rule against hearsay even if the statement is not admissible under a hearsay exception in Rule 803 or 804:

(1) the statement is supported by sufficient guarantees of trustworthiness—after considering the totality of circumstances under which it was made and evidence, if any, corroborating the statement; and

(2) it is more probative on the point for which it is offered than any other evidence that the proponent can obtain through reasonable efforts.

(b) **Notice.** The statement is admissible only if the proponent gives an adverse party reasonable notice of the intent to offer the statement including the declarant's name so that the party has a fair opportunity to meet it. The notice must be provided in writing before the trial or hearing—or in any form during the trial or hearing if the court, for good cause, excuses a lack of earlier notice.

Restyled 2011 – superseded by 2019 amendment (*supra*)

Rule 807. Residual Exception

(a) **In General.** Under the following circumstances, a hearsay statement is not excluded by the rule against hearsay even if the statement is not specifically covered by a hearsay exception in Rule 803 or 804:

(1) the statement has equivalent circumstantial guarantees of trustworthiness;

(2) it is offered as evidence of a material fact;

(3) it is more probative on the point for which it is offered than any other evidence that the proponent can obtain through reasonable efforts; and

(4) admitting it will best serve the purposes of these rules and the interests of justice.

(b) **Notice.** The statement is admissible only if, before the trial or hearing, the proponent gives an adverse party reasonable notice of the intent to offer the statement and its particulars, including the declarant's name and address, so that the party has a fair opportunity to meet it.

Superseded 2011

Rule 807. Residual Exception

A statement not specifically covered by Rule 803 or 804 but having equivalent circumstantial guarantees of trustworthiness, is not excluded by the hearsay rule, if the court determines that (A) the statement is offered as evidence of a material fact; (B) the statement is more probative on the point for which it is offered than any other evidence which the proponent can procure through reasonable efforts; and (C) the general purposes of these rules and the interests of justice will best be served by admission of the statement into evidence. However, a statement may not be admitted under this exception unless the proponent of it makes known to the adverse party sufficiently in advance of the trial or hearing to provide the adverse party with a fair opportunity to prepare to meet it, the proponent's intention to offer the statement and the particulars of it, including the name and address of the declarant. [*Transferred from Rules 803(24) and 804(b)(5), 1997.*]

Case Note

Failure to give pre-trial notice, as required by Rule 807, may be excused in exceptional circumstances. United States v. Baker, 985 F.2d 1248, 1253 n.2 (4th Cir. 1993).

Senate Judiciary Committee Report on Original Rule 803(24)

The proposed Rules of Evidence submitted to Congress contained identical provisions in rules 803 and 804 (which set forth the various hearsay exceptions), admitting any hearsay statement not specifically covered by any of the stated exceptions, if the hearsay statement was found to have "comparable circumstantial guarantees of trustworthiness." The House deleted these provisions (proposed rules 803(24) and 804(b)(6)[(5)]) as injecting "too much uncertainty" into the law of evidence and impairing the ability of practitioners to prepare for trial. The House felt that rule 102, which directs the courts to construe the Rules of Evidence so as to promote growth and development, would permit sufficient flexibility to admit hearsay evidence in appropriate cases under various factual situations that might arise.

We disagree with the total rejection of a residual hearsay exception. While we view rule 102 as being intended to provide for a broader construction and interpretation of these rules, we feel that, without a separate residual provision, the specifically enumerated exceptions could become tortured beyond any reasonable circumstances which they were intended to include (even if broadly construed). Moreover, these exceptions, while they reflect the most typical and well recognized exceptions to the hearsay rule, may not encompass every situation in which the reliability and appropriateness of a particular piece of hearsay evidence make clear that it should be heard and considered by the trier of fact.

The committee believes that there are certain exceptional circumstances where evidence which is found by a court to have guarantees of trustworthiness equivalent to or exceeding the guarantees reflected by the presently listed exceptions, and to have a high degree of probativeness and necessity could properly be admissible.

The case of Dallas County v. Commercial Union Assoc. Co., Ltd., 286 F.2d 388 (5th Cir.1961) illustrates the point. The issue in that case was whether the tower of the county courthouse collapsed because it was struck by lightning (covered by insurance) or because of structural weakness and deterioration of the structure (not covered). Investigation of the structure revealed the presence of charcoal and charred timbers. In order to show that lightning may not have been the cause of the charring, the insurer offered a copy of a local newspaper published over 50 years earlier containing an unsigned article describing a fire in the courthouse while it was under construction. The court found that the newspaper did not qualify for admission as a business record or an ancient document and did not fit within any other recognized hearsay exception. The court concluded, however, that the article was trustworthy because it was inconceivable that a newspaper reporter in a small town would report a fire in the courthouse if none had occurred. See also United States v. Barbati, 284 F.Supp. 409 (E.D.N.Y.1968).

Because exceptional cases like the Dallas County case may arise in the future, the committee has decided to reinstate a residual exception for rules 803 and 804(b).

The committee, however, also agrees with those supporters of the House version who felt that an overly broad residual hearsay exception could emasculate the hearsay rule and the recognized exceptions or vitiate the rationale behind codification of the rules.

Therefore, the committee has adopted a residual exception for rules 803 and 804(b) of much narrower scope and applicability than the Supreme Court version. In order to qualify for admission, a hearsay statement not falling within one of the recognized exceptions would have to satisfy at least four conditions. First, it must have "equivalent circumstantial guarantees of trustworthiness." Second, it must be offered as evidence of a material fact. Third, the court must determine that the statement "is more probative on the point for which it is offered than any other evidence which the proponent can procure through reasonable efforts." This requirement is intended to insure that only statements which have high probative value and necessity may qualify for admission under the residual exceptions. Fourth, the court must determine that "the general purposes of these rules and the interests of justice will best be served by admission of the statement into evidence.It is intended that the residual hearsay exceptions will be used very rarely, and only in exceptional circumstances. The committee does not intend to establish a broad license for trial judges to admit hearsay statements that do not fall within one of the other exceptions contained in rules 803 and 804(b). The residual exceptions are not meant to authorize major judicial revisions of the hearsay rule, including its present exceptions. Such major revisions are best accomplished by legislative action. It is intended that in any case in which evidence is sought to be admitted under these subsections, the trial judge will exercise no less care, reflection and caution than the courts did under the common law in establishing the now-recognized exceptions to the hearsay rule.

In order to establish a well-defined jurisprudence, the special facts and circumstances which, in the court's judgment, indicates that the statement has a sufficiently high degree of trustworthiness and necessity to justify its admission should be stated on the record. It is expected that the court will give the opposing party a full and adequate opportunity to contest the admission of any statement sought to be introduced under these subsections.

Conference Committee Report on Original Rule 803(24)

The Senate amendment adds a new subsection, (24), which makes admissible a hearsay statement not specifically covered by any of the previous twenty-three subsections, if the statement has equivalent circumstantial guarantees of trustworthiness and if the court determines that (A) the statement is offered as evidence of a material fact; (B) the statement is more probative on the point for which it is offered than any other evidence the proponent can procure through reasonable efforts; and (C) the general purposes of these rules and the interests of justice will best be served by admission of the statement into evidence.

The House bill eliminated a similar, but broader, provision because of the conviction that such a provision injected too much uncertainty into the law of evidence regarding hearsay and impaired the ability of a litigant to prepare adequately for trial.

The Conference adopts the Senate amendment with an amendment that provides that a party intending to request the court to use a statement under this provision must notify any adverse party of this intention as well as of the particulars of the statement, including the name and address of the declarant. This notice must be given sufficiently in advance of the trial or hearing to provide any adverse party with a fair opportunity to prepare to contest the use of the statement.

Advisory Committee's Note to 1997 Amendment

The contents of Rule 803(24) and Rule 804(b)(5) have been combined and transferred to a new Rule 807. This was done to facilitate additions to Rules 803 and 804. No change in meaning is intended.

Advisory Committee's Note to 2019 Amendment

Committee Note Rule 807 has been amended to fix a number of problems that the courts have encountered in applying it.

Courts have had difficulty with the requirement that the proffered hearsay carry "equivalent" circumstantial guarantees of trustworthiness. The "equivalence" standard is difficult to apply, given the different types of guarantees of reliability, of varying strength, found among the categorical exceptions (as well as the fact that some hearsay exceptions, e.g., Rule 804(b)(6), are not based on reliability at all). The "equivalence" standard" has not served to guide a court's discretion to admit hearsay, because the court is free to choose among a spectrum of exceptions for comparison. Moreover, experience has shown that some statements offered as residual hearsay cannot be compared usefully to any of the categorical exceptions and yet might well be trustworthy. Thus the requirement of an equivalence analysis has been eliminated. Under the amendment, the court should proceed directly to a determination of whether the hearsay is supported by guarantees of trustworthiness. See Rule 104(a). As with any hearsay statement offered under an exception, the court's threshold finding that admissibility requirements are met merely means that the jury may consider the statement and not that it must assume the statement to be true.

The amendment specifically requires the court to consider corroborating evidence in the trustworthiness enquiry. Most courts have required the consideration of corroborating evidence, though some courts have disagreed. The rule now provides for a uniform approach, and recognizes that the existence or absence of corroboration is relevant to, but not dispositive of, whether a statement should be admissible under this exception. Of course, the court must consider not only the existence of corroborating evidence but also the strength and quality of that evidence.

The amendment does not alter the case law prohibiting parties from proceeding directly to the residual exception, without considering admissibility of the hearsay under Rules 803 and 804. A court is not required to make a finding that no other hearsay exception is applicable. But the opponent cannot seek admission under Rule 807 if it is apparent that the hearsay could be admitted under another exception.

The rule in its current form applies to hearsay "not specifically covered" by a Rule 803 or 804 exception. The amendment makes the rule applicable to hearsay "not admissible under" those exceptions. This clarifies that a court assessing guarantees of trustworthiness may consider whether the statement is a "near-miss" of one of the Rule 803 or 804 exceptions. If the court employs a "near-miss" analysis it should—in addition to evaluating all relevant guarantees of trustworthiness—take into account the reasons that the hearsay misses the admissibility requirements of the standard exception.

In deciding whether the statement is supported by sufficient guarantees of trustworthiness, the court should not consider the credibility of any witness who relates the declarant's hearsay statement in court. The credibility of an in-court witness does not present a hearsay question. To base admission or exclusion of a hearsay statement on the witness's credibility would usurp the jury's role of determining the credibility of testifying witnesses. The rule provides that the focus for trustworthiness is on circumstantial guarantees surrounding the making of the statement itself, as well as any independent evidence corroborating the statement. The credibility of the witness relating the statement is not a part of either enquiry.

Of course, even if the court finds sufficient guarantees of trustworthiness, the independent requirements of the Confrontation Clause must be satisfied if the hearsay statement is offered against a defendant in a criminal case.

The Committee decided to retain the requirement that the proponent must show that the hearsay statement is more probative than any other evidence that the proponent can reasonably obtain. This necessity requirement will continue to serve to prevent the residual exception from being used as a device to erode the categorical exceptions.

The requirements that residual hearsay must be evidence of a material fact and that its admission will best serve the purposes of these rules and the interests of justice have been deleted. These requirements have proved to be superfluous in that they are already found in other rules. See Rules 102, 401. The notice provision has been amended to make four changes in the operation of the rule:

- First, the amendment requires the proponent to disclose the "substance" of the statement. This term is intended to require a description that is sufficiently specific under the circumstances to allow the opponent a fair opportunity to meet the evidence. See Rule 103(a)(2) (requiring the party making an offer of proof to inform the court of the "substance" of the evidence).

- Second, the prior requirement that the declarant's address must be disclosed has been deleted. That requirement was nonsensical when the declarant was unavailable, and unnecessary in the many cases in which the declarant's address was known or easily obtainable. If prior disclosure of the declarant's address is critical and cannot be obtained by the opponent through other means, then the opponent can seek relief from the court.

- Third, the amendment requires that the pretrial notice be in writing—which is satisfied by notice in electronic form. See Rule 101(b)(6). Requiring the notice to be in writing provides certainty and reduces arguments about whether notice was actually provided.

- Finally, the pretrial notice provision has been amended to provide for a good cause exception. Most courts have applied a good cause exception under Rule 807 even though the rule in its current form does not provide for it, while some courts have read the rule as it was written. Experience under the residual exception has shown that a good cause exception is necessary in certain limited situations. For example, the proponent may not become aware of the existence of the hearsay statement until after the trial begins; or the proponent may plan to call a witness who without warning becomes unavailable during trial, and the proponent might then need to resort to residual hearsay.

The rule retains the requirement that the opponent receive notice in a way that provides a fair opportunity to meet the evidence. When notice is provided during trial after a finding of good cause, the court may need to consider protective measures, such as a continuance, to assure that the opponent is not prejudiced.

Restyled 2011

ARTICLE IX. AUTHENTICATION AND IDENTIFICATION

Rule 901. Authenticating or Identifying Evidence

(a) In General. To satisfy the requirement of authenticating or identifying an item of evidence, the proponent must produce evidence sufficient to support a finding that the item is what the proponent claims it is.

Superseded 2011

ARTICLE IX. AUTHENTICATION AND IDENTIFICATION

Rule 901. Requirement of Authentication or Identification

(a) General provision. The requirement of authentication or identification as a condition precedent to admissibility is satisfied by evidence sufficient to support a finding that the matter in question is what its proponent claims.

Advisory Committee's Note

Subdivision (a). Authentication and identification represent a special aspect of relevancy. Michael and Adler, Real Proof, 5 Vand.L.Rev. 344, 362 (1952); McCormick §§ 179, 185; Morgan, Basic Problems of Evidence 378 (1962). Thus a telephone conversation may be irrelevant because on an unrelated topic or because the speaker is not identified. The latter aspect is the one here involved. Wigmore describes the need for authentication as "an inherent logical necessity." 7 Wigmore § 2129, p. 564.

This requirement of showing authenticity or identity falls in the category of relevancy dependent upon fulfillment of a condition of fact and is governed by the procedure set forth in Rule 104(b).

The common law approach to authentication of documents has been criticized as an "attitude of agnosticism," McCormick, Cases on Evidence 388, n. 4 (3rd ed. 1956), as one which "departs sharply from men's customs in ordinary affairs," and as presenting only a slight obstacle to the introduction of forgeries in comparison to the time and expense devoted to proving genuine writings which correctly show their origin on their face, McCormick § 185, pp. 395, 396. Today, such available procedures as requests to admit and pretrial conference afford the means of eliminating much of the need for authentication or identification. Also, significant inroads upon the traditional insistence on authentication and identification have been made by accepting as at least prima facie genuine items of the kind treated in Rule 902, infra. However, the need for suitable methods of proof still remains, since criminal cases pose their own obstacles to the use of preliminary procedures, unforeseen contingencies may arise, and cases of genuine controversy will still occur.

Restyled 2011

(b) Examples. The following are examples only — not a complete list — of evidence that satisfies the requirement:

Superseded 2011

(b) Illustrations. By way of illustration only, and not by way of limitation, the following are examples of authentication or identification conforming with the requirements of this rule:

Advisory Committee's Note

Subdivision (b). The treatment of authentication and identification draws largely upon the experience embodied in the common law and in statutes to furnish illustrative applications of the general principle set forth in subdivision (a). The examples are not intended as an exclusive enumeration of allowable methods but are meant to guide and suggest, leaving room for growth and development in this area of the law.

The examples relate for the most part to documents, with some attention given to voice communications and computer printouts. As Wigmore noted, no special rules have been developed for authenticating chattels. Wigmore, Code of Evidence § 2086 (3rd ed. 1942).

It should be observed that compliance with requirements of authentication or identification by no means assures admission of an item into evidence, as other bars, hearsay for example, may remain.

Restyled 2011

(1) ***Testimony of a Witness with Knowledge.*** Testimony that an item is what it is claimed to be.

Superseded 2011

(1) Testimony of witness with knowledge. Testimony that a matter is what it is claimed to be.

Advisory Committee's Note

Example (1) contemplates a broad spectrum ranging from testimony of a witness who was present at the signing of a document to testimony establishing narcotics as taken from an accused and accounting for custody through the period until trial, including laboratory analysis. See California Evidence Code § 1413, eyewitness to signing.

Restyled 2011

(2) *Nonexpert Opinion About Handwriting.* A nonexpert's opinion that handwriting is genuine, based on a familiarity with it that was not acquired for the current litigation.

Superseded 2011

(2) Nonexpert opinion on handwriting. Nonexpert opinion as to the genuineness of handwriting, based upon familiarity not acquired for purposes of the litigation.

Advisory Committee's Note

Example (2) states conventional doctrine as to lay identification of handwriting, which recognizes that a sufficient familiarity with the handwriting of another person may be acquired by seeing him write, by exchanging correspondence, or by other means, to afford a basis for identifying it on subsequent occasions. McCormick § 189. See also California Evidence Code § 1416. Testimony based upon familiarity acquired for purposes of the litigation is reserved to the expert under the example which follows.

Restyled 2011

(3) *Comparison by an Expert Witness or the Trier of Fact.* A comparison with an authenticated specimen by an expert witness or the trier of fact.

Superseded 2011

(3) Comparison by trier or expert witness. Comparison by the trier of fact or by expert witnesses with specimens which have been authenticated.

Advisory Committee's Note

Example (3). The history of common law restrictions upon the technique of proving or disproving the genuineness of a disputed specimen of handwriting through comparison with a genuine specimen, by either the testimony of expert witnesses or direct viewing by the triers themselves, is detailed in 7 Wigmore §§ 1991-1994. In breaking away, the English Common Law Procedure Act of 1854, 17 and 18 Vict., c. 125, § 27, cautiously allowed expert or trier to use exemplars "proved to the satisfaction of the judge to be genuine" for purposes of comparison. The language found its way into numerous statutes in this country, e.g., California Evidence Code §§ 1417, 1418. While explainable as a measure of prudence in the process of breaking with precedent in the handwriting situation, the reservation to the judge of the question of the genuineness of exemplars and the imposition of an unusually high standard of persuasion are at variance with the general treatment of relevancy which depends upon fulfillment of a condition of fact. Rule 104(b). No similar attitude is found in other comparison situations, e.g., ballistics comparison by jury, as in Evans v. Commonwealth, 230 Ky. 411, 19 S.W.2d 1091 (1929), or by experts, Annot., 26 A.L.R.2d 892, and no reason appears for its continued existence in handwriting cases. Consequently Example (3) sets no higher standard for handwriting specimens and treats all comparison situations alike, to be governed by Rule 104(b). This approach is consistent with 28 U.S.C. § 1731: "The admitted or proved handwriting of any person shall be admissible, for purposes of comparison, to determine genuineness of other handwriting attributed to such person."

Precedent supports the acceptance of visual comparison as sufficiently satisfying preliminary authentication requirements for admission in evidence. Brandon v. Collins, 267 F.2d 731 (2d Cir.1959); Wausau Sulphate Fibre Co. v. Commissioner of Internal Revenue, 61 F.2d 879 (7th Cir.1932); Desimone v. United States, 227 F.2d 864 (9th Cir.1955).

Restyled 2011

(4) ***Distinctive Characteristics and the Like.*** The appearance, contents, substance, internal patterns, or other distinctive characteristics of the item, taken together with all the circumstances.

Superseded 2011

(4) Distinctive characteristics and the like. Appearance, contents, substance, internal patterns, or other distinctive characteristics, taken in conjunction with circumstances.

Advisory Committee's Note

Example (4). The characteristics of the offered item itself, considered in the light of circumstances, afford authentication techniques in great variety. Thus a document or telephone conversation may be shown to have emanated from a particular person by virtue of its disclosing knowledge of facts known peculiarly to him; Globe Automatic Sprinkler Co. v. Braniff, 89 Okl. 105, 214 P. 127 (1923); California Evidence Code § 1421; similarly, a letter may be authenticated by content and circumstances indicating it was in reply to a duly authenticated one. McCormick § 192; California Evidence Code § 1420. Language patterns may indicate authenticity or its opposite. Magnuson v. State, 187 Wis. 122, 203 N.W. 749 (1925); Arens and Meadow, Psycholinguistics and the Confession Dilemma, 56 Colum.L.Rev. 19 (1956).

Restyled 2011

(5) ***Opinion About a Voice.*** An opinion identifying a person's voice — whether heard firsthand or through mechanical or electronic transmission or recording — based on hearing the voice at any time under circumstances that connect it with the alleged speaker.

Superseded 2011

(5) Voice identification. Identification of a voice, whether heard firsthand or through mechanical or electronic transmission or recording, by opinion based upon hearing the voice at any time under circumstances connecting it with the alleged speaker.

Advisory Committee's Note

Example (5). Since aural voice identification is not a subject of expert testimony, the requisite familiarity may be acquired either before or after the particular speaking which is the subject of the identification, in this respect resembling visual identification of a person rather than identification of handwriting. Cf. Example (2), supra, People v. Nichols, 378 Ill. 487, 38 N.E.2d 766 (1942); McGuire v. State, 200 Md. 601, 92 A.2d 582 (1952); State v. McGee, 336 Mo. 1082, 83 S.W.2d 98 (1935).

Restyled 2011

(6) ***Evidence About a Telephone Conversation.*** For a telephone conversation, evidence that a call was made to the number assigned at the time to:

(A) a particular person, if circumstances, including self-identification, show that the person answering was the one called; or

(B) a particular business, if the call was made to a business and the call related to business reasonably transacted over the telephone.

Superseded 2011

(6) Telephone conversations. Telephone conversations, by evidence that a call was made to the number assigned at the time by the telephone company to a particular person or business, if (A) in the case of a person, circumstances, including self-identification, show the person answering to be the one called, or (B) in the case of a business, the call was made to a place of business and the conversation related to business reasonably transacted over the telephone.

Advisory Committee's Note

Example (6). The cases are in agreement that a mere assertion of his identity by a person talking on the telephone is not sufficient evidence of the authenticity of the conversation and that additional evidence of his identity is required. The additional evidence need not fall in any set pattern. Thus the content of his statements or the reply technique, under Example (4), supra, or voice identification under Example (5), may furnish the necessary foundation. Outgoing calls made by the witness involve additional factors bearing upon authenticity. The calling of a number assigned by the telephone company reasonably supports the assumption that the listing is correct and that the number is the one reached. If the number is that of a place of business, the mass of authority allows an ensuing conversation if it relates to business reasonably transacted over the telephone, on the theory that the maintenance of the telephone connection is an invitation to do business without further identification. Matton v. Hoover Co., 350 Mo. 506, 166 S.W.2d 557 (1942); City of Pawhuska v. Crutchfield, 147 Okl. 4, 293 P. 1095 (1930); Zurich General Acc. & Liability Ins. Co. v. Baum, 159 Va. 404, 165 S.E. 518 (1932). Otherwise, some additional circumstance of identification of the speaker is required. The authorities divide on the question whether the self-identifying statement of the person answering suffices. Example (6) answers in the affirmative on the assumption that usual conduct respecting telephone calls furnish adequate assurances of regularity, bearing in mind that the entire matter is open to exploration before the trier of fact. In general, see McCormick § 193; 7 Wigmore § 2155; Annot., 71 A.L.R. 5, 105 id. 326.

Restyled 2011

(7) ***Evidence About Public Records.*** Evidence that:

(A) a document was recorded or filed in a public office as authorized by law; or

(B) a purported public record or statement is from the office where items of this kind are kept.

Superseded 2011

(7) Public records or reports. Evidence that a writing authorized by law to be recorded or filed and in fact recorded or filed in a public office, or a purported public record, report, statement, or data compilation, in any form, is from the public office where items of this nature are kept.

Advisory Committee's Note

Example (7). Public records are regularly authenticated by proof of custody, without more. McCormick § 191; 7 Wigmore §§ 2158, 2159. The example extends the principle to include data stored in computers and similar methods, of which increasing use in the public records area may be expected. See California Evidence Code §§ 1532, 1600.

Restyled 2011

(8) ***Evidence About Ancient Documents or Data Compilations.*** For a document or data compilation, evidence that it:

(A) is in a condition that creates no suspicion about its authenticity;

(B) was in a place where, if authentic, it would likely be; and

(C) is at least 20 years old when offered.

Superseded 2011

(8) Ancient documents or data compilation. Evidence that a document or data compilation, in any form, (A) is in such condition as to create no suspicion concerning its authenticity, (B) was in a place where it, if authentic, would likely be, and (C) has been in existence 20 years or more at the time it is offered.

Advisory Committee's Note

Example (8). The familiar ancient document rule of the common law is extended to include data stored electronically or by other similar means. Since the importance of appearance diminishes in this situation, the importance of custody or place where found increases correspondingly. This expansion is necessary in view of the widespread use of methods of storing data in forms other than conventional written records.

Any time period selected is bound to be arbitrary. The common law period of 30 years is here reduced to 20 years, with some shift of emphasis from the probable unavailability of witnesses to the unlikeliness of a still viable fraud after the lapse of time. The shorter period is specified in the English Evidence Act of 1938, 1 & 2 Geo. 6, c. 28, and in Oregon R.S.1963, § 41.360(34). See also the numerous statutes prescribing periods of less than 30 years in the case of recorded documents. 7 Wigmore § 2143.

The application of Example (8) is not subject to any limitation to title documents or to any requirement that possession, in the case of a title document, has been consistent with the document. See McCormick § 190.

Restyled 2011

(9) ***Evidence About a Process or System.*** Evidence describing a process or system and showing that it produces an accurate result.

Superseded 2011

(9) Process or system. Evidence describing a process or system used to produce a result and showing that the process or system produces an accurate result.

Advisory Committee's Note

Example (9) is designed for situations in which the accuracy of a result is dependent upon a process or system which produces it. X rays afford a familiar instance. Among more recent developments is the computer, as to which see Transport Indemnity Co. v. Seib, 178 Neb. 253, 132 N.W.2d 871 (1965); State v. Veres, 7 Ariz.App. 117, 436 P.2d 629 (1968); Merrick v. United States Rubber Co., 7 Ariz.App. 433, 440 P.2d 314 (1968); Freed, Computer Print-Outs as Evidence, 16 Am.Jur.Proof of Facts 273; Symposium, Law and Computers in the Mid-Sixties, ALI-ABA (1966); 37 Albany L.Rev. 61 (1967). Example (9) does not, of course, foreclose taking judicial notice of the accuracy of the process or system.

Restyled 2011

(10) ***Methods Provided by a Statute or Rule.*** Any method of authentication or identification allowed by a federal statute or a rule prescribed by the Supreme Court.

Superseded 2011

(10) Methods provided by statute or rule. Any method of authentication or identification provided by Act of Congress or by other rules prescribed by the Supreme Court pursuant to statutory authority.

Advisory Committee's Note

Example (10). The example makes clear that methods of authentication provided by Act of Congress and by the Rules of Civil and Criminal Procedure or by Bankruptcy Rules are not intended to be superseded. Illustrative are the provisions for authentication of official records in Civil Procedure Rule 44 and Criminal Procedure Rule 27, for authentication of records of proceedings by court reporters in 28 U.S.C. § 753(b) and Civil Procedure Rule 80(c), and for authentication of depositions in Civil Procedure Rule 30(f).

Restyled 2011

Rule 902. Evidence That Is Self-Authenticating

The following items of evidence are self-authenticating; they require no extrinsic evidence of authenticity in order to be admitted:

Superseded 2011

Rule 902. Self-authentication

Extrinsic evidence of authenticity as a condition precedent to admissibility is not required with respect to the following:

Advisory Committee's Note

Case law and statutes have, over the years, developed a substantial body of instances in which authenticity is taken as sufficiently established for purposes of admissibility without extrinsic evidence to that effect, sometimes for reasons of policy but perhaps more often because practical considerations reduce the possibility of unauthenticity to a very small dimension. The present rule collects and incorporates these situations, in some instances expanding them to occupy a larger area which their underlying considerations justify. In no instance is the opposite party foreclosed from disputing authenticity.

Restyled 2011

(1) ***Domestic Public Documents That Are Sealed and Signed.*** A document that bears:

(A) a seal purporting to be that of the United States; any state, district, commonwealth, territory, or insular possession of the United States; the former Panama Canal Zone; the Trust Territory of the Pacific Islands; a political subdivision of any of these entities; or a department, agency, or officer of any entity named above.

(B) a signature purporting to be an execution or attestation.

Superseded 2011

(1) Domestic public documents under seal. A document bearing a seal purporting to be that of the United States, or of any State, district, Commonwealth, territory, or insular possession thereof, or the Panama Canal Zone, or the Trust Territory of the Pacific Islands, or of a political subdivision, department, officer, or agency thereof, and a signature purporting to be an attestation or execution.

Advisory Committee's Note

Paragraph (1). The acceptance of documents bearing a public seal and signature, most often encountered in practice in the form of acknowledgments or certificates authenticating copies of public records, is actually of broad application. Whether theoretically based in whole or in part upon judicial notice, the practical underlying considerations are that forgery is a crime and detection is fairly easy and certain. 7 Wigmore § 2161, p. 638; California Evidence Code § 1452. More than 50 provisions for judicial notice of official seals are contained in the United States Code.

Restyled 2011

(2) ***Domestic Public Documents That Are Not Sealed but Are Signed and Certified.*** A document that bears no seal if:

(A) it bears the signature of an officer or employee of an entity named in Rule 902(1)(A); and

(B) another public officer who has a seal and official duties within that same entity certifies under seal — or its equivalent — that the signer has the official capacity and that the signature is genuine.

Superseded 2011

(2) Domestic public documents not under seal. A document purporting to bear the signature in the official capacity of an officer or employee of any entity included in paragraph (1) hereof, having no seal, if a public officer having a seal and having official duties in the district or political subdivision of the officer or employee certifies under seal that the signer has the official capacity and that the signature is genuine.

Advisory Committee's Note

Paragraph (2). While statutes are found which raise a presumption of genuineness of purported official signatures in the absence of an official seal, 7 Wigmore § 2167; California Evidence Code § 1453, the greater ease of effecting a forgery under these circumstances is apparent. Hence this paragraph of the rule calls for authentication by an officer who has a seal. Notarial acts by members of the armed forces and other special situations are covered in paragraph (10).

Restyled 2011

(3) ***Foreign Public Documents.*** A document that purports to be signed or attested by a person who is authorized by a foreign country's law to do so. The document must be accompanied by a final certification that certifies the genuineness of the signature and official position of the signer or attester — or of any foreign official whose certificate of genuineness relates to the signature or attestation or is in a chain of certificates of genuineness relating to the signature or attestation. The certification may be made by a secretary of a United States embassy or legation; by a consul general, vice consul, or consular agent of the United States; or by a diplomatic or consular official of the foreign country assigned or accredited to the United States. If all parties have been given a reasonable opportunity to investigate the document's authenticity and accuracy, the court may, for good cause, either:

(A) order that it be treated as presumptively authentic without final certification; or

(B) allow it to be evidenced by an attested summary with or without final certification.

Superseded 2011

(3) Foreign public documents. A document purporting to be executed or attested in an official capacity by a person authorized by the laws of a foreign country to make the execution or attestation, and accompanied by a final certification as to the genuineness of the signature and official position (A) of the executing or attesting person, or (B) of any foreign official whose certificate of genuineness of signature and official position relates to the execution or attestation or is in a chain of certificates of genuineness of signature and official position relating to the execution or attestation. A final certification may be made by a secretary of an embassy or legation, consul general, consul, vice consul, or consular agent of the United States, or a diplomatic or consular official of the foreign country assigned or accredited to the United States. If reasonable opportunity has been given to all parties to investigate the authenticity and accuracy of official documents, the court may, for good cause shown, order that they be treated as presumptively authentic without final certification or permit them to be evidenced by an attested summary with or without final certification.

Advisory Committee's Note

Paragraph (3) provides a method for extending the presumption of authenticity to foreign official documents by a procedure of certification. It is derived from Rule 44(a)(2) of the Rules of Civil Procedure but is broader in applying to public documents rather than being limited to public records.

Restyled 2011

(4) ***Certified Copies of Public Records.*** A copy of an official record — or a copy of a document that was recorded or filed in a public office as authorized by law — if the copy is certified as correct by:

(A) the custodian or another person authorized to make the certification; or

(B) a certificate that complies with Rule 902(1), (2), or (3), a federal statute, or a rule prescribed by the Supreme Court.

Superseded 2011

(4) Certified copies of public records. A copy of an official record or report or entry therein, or of a document authorized by law to be recorded or filed and actually recorded or filed in a public office, including data compilations in any form, certified as correct by the custodian or other person authorized to make the certification, by certificate complying with paragraph (1), (2), or (3) of this rule or complying with any Act of Congress or rule prescribed by the Supreme Court pursuant to statutory authority.

Advisory Committee's Note

Paragraph (4). The common law and innumerable statutes have recognized the procedure of authenticating copies of public records by certificate. The certificate qualifies as a public document, receivable as authentic when in conformity with paragraph (1), (2), or (3). Rule 44(a) of the Rules of Civil Procedure and Rule 27 of the Rules of Criminal Procedure have provided authentication procedures of this nature for both domestic and foreign public records. It will be observed that the certification procedure here provided extends only to public records, reports, and recorded documents, all including data compilations, and does not apply to public documents generally. Hence documents provable when presented in original form under paragraphs (1), (2), or (3) may not be provable by certified copy under paragraph (4).

Restyled 2011

(5) ***Official Publications.*** A book, pamphlet, or other publication purporting to be issued by a public authority.

Superseded 2011

(5) **Official publications.** Books, pamphlets, or other publications purporting to be issued by public authority.

Advisory Committee's Note

Paragraph (5). Dispensing with preliminary proof of the genuineness of purportedly official publications, most commonly encountered in connection with statutes, court reports, rules, and regulations, has been greatly enlarged by statutes and decisions. 5 Wigmore § 1684. Paragraph (5), it will be noted, does not confer admissibility upon all official publications; it merely provides a means whereby their authenticity may be taken as established for purposes of admissibility. Rule 44(a) of the Rules of Civil Procedure has been to the same effect.

Restyled 2011

(6) ***Newspapers and Periodicals.*** Printed material purporting to be a newspaper or periodical.

Superseded 2011

(6) **Newspapers and periodicals.** Printed materials purporting to be newspapers or periodicals.

Advisory Committee's Note

Paragraph (6). The likelihood of forgery of newspapers or periodicals is slight indeed. Hence no danger is apparent in receiving them. Establishing the authenticity of the publication may, of course, leave still open questions of authority and responsibility for items therein contained. See 7 Wigmore § 2150. Cf. 39 U.S.C. § 4005(b), public advertisement prima facie evidence of agency of person named, in postal fraud order proceeding; Canadian Uniform Evidence Act, Draft of 1936, printed copy of newspaper prima facie evidence that notices or advertisements were authorized.

Restyled 2011

(7) ***Trade Inscriptions and the Like.*** An inscription, sign, tag, or label purporting to have been affixed in the course of business and indicating origin, ownership, or control.

Superseded 2011

(7) **Trade inscriptions and the like.** Inscriptions, signs, tags, or labels purporting to have been affixed in the course of business and indicating ownership, control, or origin.

Advisory Committee's Note

Paragraph (7). Several factors justify dispensing with preliminary proof of genuineness of commercial and mercantile labels and the like. The risk of forgery is minimal. Trademark infringement involves serious penalties. Great efforts are devoted to inducing the public to buy in reliance on brand names, and substantial protection is given them. Hence the fairness of this treatment finds recognition in the cases. Curtiss Candy Co. v. Johnson, 163 Miss. 426, 141 So. 762 (1932), Baby Ruth candy bar; Doyle v. Continental Baking Co., 262 Mass. 516, 160 N.E. 325 (1928), loaf of bread; Weiner v. Mager & Throne, Inc., 167 Misc. 338, 3 N.Y.S.2d 918 (1938), same. And see

W.Va.Code 1966, § 47-3-5, trademark on bottle prima facie evidence of ownership. Contra, Keegan v. Green Giant Co., 150 Me. 283, 110 A.2d 599 (1954); Murphy v. Campbell Soup Co., 62 F.2d 564 (1st Cir.1933). Cattle brands have received similar acceptance in the western states. Rev.Code Mont.1947, § 46-606, State v. Wolfley, 75 Kan. 406, 89 P. 1046 (1907); Annot., 11 L.R.A.(N.S.) 87. Inscriptions on trains and vehicles are held to be prima facie evidence of ownership or control. Pittsburgh, Ft. W. & C. Ry. v. Callaghan, 157 Ill. 406, 41 N.E. 909 (1895); 9 Wigmore § 2510a. See also the provision of 19 U.S.C. § 1615(2) that marks, labels, brands, or stamps indicating foreign origin are prima facie evidence of foreign origin of merchandise.

Restyled 2011

(8) ***Acknowledged Documents.*** A document accompanied by a certificate of acknowledgment that is lawfully executed by a notary public or another officer who is authorized to take acknowledgments.

Superseded 2011

(8) Acknowledged documents. Documents accompanied by a certificate of acknowledgment executed in the manner provided by law by a notary public or other officer authorized by law to take acknowledgments.

Advisory Committee's Note

Paragraph (8). In virtually every state, acknowledged title documents are receivable in evidence without further proof. Statutes are collected in 5 Wigmore § 1676. If this authentication suffices for documents of the importance of those affecting titles, logic scarcely permits denying this method when other kinds of documents are involved. Instances of broadly inclusive statutes are California Evidence Code § 1451 and N.Y.CPLR 4538, McKinney's Consol.Laws 1963.

House Judiciary Committee Report

Rule 902(8) as submitted by the Court referred to certificates of acknowledgment "under the hand and seal of" a notary public or other officer authorized by law to take acknowledgments. The Committee amended the Rule to eliminate the requirement, believed to be inconsistent with the law in some States, that a notary public must affix a seal to a document acknowledged before him. As amended the Rule merely requires that the document be executed in the manner prescribed by State law.

Restyled 2011

(9) ***Commercial Paper and Related Documents.*** Commercial paper, a signature on it, and related documents, to the extent allowed by general commercial law.

Superseded 2011

(9) Commercial paper and related documents. Commercial paper, signatures thereon, and documents relating thereto to the extent provided by general commercial law.

Advisory Committee's Note

Paragraph (9). Issues of the authenticity of commercial paper in federal courts will usually arise in diversity cases, will involve an element of a cause of action or defense, and with respect to presumptions and burden of proof will be controlled by Erie Railroad Co. v. Tompkins, 304 U.S. 64, 58 S.Ct. 817, 82 L.Ed. 1188 (1938). Rule 302, supra. There may, however, be questions of authenticity involving lesser segments of a case or the case may be one governed by federal common law. Clearfield Trust Co. v. United States, 318 U.S. 363, 63 S.Ct. 573, 87 L.Ed. 838 (1943). Cf. United States v. Yazell, 382 U.S. 341, 86 S.Ct. 500, 15 L.Ed.2d 404 (1966). In these situations, resort to the useful authentication provisions of the Uniform Commercial Code is provided for. While the phrasing is in terms of "general commercial law," in order to avoid the potential complications inherent in borrowing local statutes, today one would have difficulty in determining the general commercial law without referring to the Code. See Williams v. Walker-Thomas Furniture Co., 121 U.S.App.D.C. 315, 350 F.2d 445 (1965). Pertinent Code provisions are sections 1-202, 3-307, and 3-510, dealing with third-party documents, signatures on negotiable instruments, protests, and statements of dishonor.

House Judiciary Committee Report

The Committee approved Rule 902(9) as submitted by the Court. With respect to the meaning of the phrase "general commercial law", the Committee intends that the Uniform Commercial Code, which has been adopted in virtually every State, will be followed generally, but that federal commercial law will apply where federal commercial paper is involved. See Clearfield Trust Co. v. United States, 318 U.S. 363 (1943). Further, in those instances in which the issues are governed by Erie R. Co. v. Tompkins, 304 U.S. 64 (1938), State law will apply irrespective of whether it is the Uniform Commercial Code.

Restyled 2011

(10) ***Presumptions Under a Federal Statute.*** A signature, document, or anything else that a federal statute declares to be presumptively or prima facie genuine or authentic.

Superseded 2011

(10) Presumptions under Acts of Congress. Any signature, document, or other matter declared by Act of Congress to be presumptively or prima facie genuine or authentic.

Advisory Committee's Note

Paragraph (10). The paragraph continues in effect dispensations with preliminary proof of genuineness provided in various Acts of Congress. See, for example, 10 U.S.C. § 936, signature, without seal, together with title, prima facie evidence of authenticity of acts of certain military personnel who are given notarial powers; 15 U.S.C. § 77f(a), signature on SEC registration presumed genuine; 26 U.S.C. § 6064, signature to tax return prima facie genuine.

Restyled 2011

(11) *Certified Domestic Records of a Regularly Conducted Activity.* The original or a copy of a domestic record that meets the requirements of Rule 803(6)(A)-(C), as shown by a certification of the custodian or another qualified person that complies with a federal statute or a rule prescribed by the Supreme Court. Before the trial or hearing, the proponent must give an adverse party reasonable written notice of the intent to offer the record — and must make the record and certification available for inspection — so that the party has a fair opportunity to challenge them.

Superseded 2011

(11) Certified Domestic Records of Regularly Conducted Activity. The original or a duplicate of a domestic record of regularly conducted activity that would be admissible under Rule 803(6) if accompanied by a written declaration of its custodian or other qualified person, in a manner complying with any Act of Congress or rule prescribed by the Supreme Court pursuant to statutory authority, certifying that the record—

(A) was made at or near the time of the occurrence of the matters set forth by, or from information transmitted by, a person with knowledge of those matters;

(B) was kept in the course of the regularly conducted activity; and

(C) was made by the regularly conducted activity as a regular practice.

A party intending to offer a record into evidence under this paragraph must provide written notice of that intention to all adverse parties, and must make the record and declaration available for inspection sufficiently in advance of their offer into evidence to provide an adverse party with a fair opportunity to challenge them.

Editor's Note

See note following Rule 902(12).

Restyled 2011

(12) *Certified Foreign Records of a Regularly Conducted Activity.* In a civil case, the original or a copy of a foreign record that meets the requirements of Rule 902(11), modified as follows: the certification, rather than complying with a federal statute or Supreme Court rule, must be signed in a manner that, if falsely made, would subject the maker to a criminal penalty in the country where the certification is signed. The proponent must also meet the notice requirements of Rule 902(11).

Superseded 2011

(12) Certified Foreign Records of Regularly Conducted Activity. In a civil case, the original or a duplicate of a foreign record of regularly conducted activity that would be admissible under Rule 803(6) if accompanied by a written declaration by its custodian or other qualified person certifying that the record—

(A) was made at or near the time of the occurrence of the matters set forth by, or from information transmitted by, a person with knowledge of those matters;

(B) was kept in the course of the regularly conducted activity; and

(C) was made by the regularly conducted activity as a regular practice.

The declaration must be signed in a manner that, if falsely made, would subject the maker to criminal penalty under the laws of the country where the declaration is signed. A party intending to offer a record into evidence under this paragraph must provide written notice of that intention to all adverse parties, and must make the record and declaration available for inspection sufficiently in advance of their offer into evidence to provide an adverse party with a fair opportunity to challenge them. [*Paragraphs 11 and 12 added 2000.*]

Advisory Committee's Note to 2000 Amendment

The amendment adds two new paragraphs to the rule on self-authentication. It sets forth a procedure by which parties can authenticate certain records of regularly conducted activity, other than through the testimony of a foundation witness. See the amendment to Rule 803(6). 18 U.S.C. § 3505 currently provides a means for certifying foreign records of regularly conducted activity in criminal cases, and this amendment is intended to establish a similar procedure for domestic records, and for foreign records offered in civil cases.

A declaration that satisfies 28 U.S.C. § 1746 would satisfy the declaration requirement of Rule 902(11), as would any comparable certification under oath.

The notice requirement in Rules 902(11) and (12) is intended to give the opponent of the evidence a full opportunity to test the adequacy of the foundation set forth in the declaration.

Restyled 2011

(13) ***Certified Records Generated by an Electronic Process or System.*** A record generated by an electronic process or system that produces an accurate result, as shown by a certification of a qualified person that complies with the certification requirements of Rule 902(11) or (12). The proponent must also meet the notice requirements of Rule 902(11). *[Added 2016.]*

Advisory Committee's Note to 2016 Amendment

The amendment sets forth a procedure by which parties can authenticate certain electronic evidence other than through the testimony of a foundation witness. As with the provisions on business records in Rules 902(11) and (12), the Committee has found that the expense and inconvenience of producing a witness to authenticate an item of electronic evidence is often unnecessary. It is often the case that a party goes to the expense of producing an authentication witness and then the adversary either stipulates authenticity before the witness is called or fails to challenge the authentication testimony once it is presented. The amendment provides a procedure under which the parties can determine in advance of trial whether a real challenge to authenticity will be made, and can then plan accordingly.

Nothing in the amendment is intended to limit a party from establishing authenticity of electronic evidence on any ground provided in these Rules, including through judicial notice where appropriate.

A proponent establishing authenticity under this Rule must present a certification containing information that would be sufficient to establish authenticity were that information provided by a witness at trial. If the certification provides information that would be insufficient to authenticate the record if the certifying person testified, then authenticity is not established under this Rule. The Rule specifically allows the authenticity foundation that satisfies Rule 901(b)(9) to be established by a certification rather than the testimony of a live witness.

The reference to the "certification requirements of Rule 902(11) or (12)" is only to the procedural requirements for a valid certification. There is no intent to require, or permit, a certification under this rule to prove the requirements of Rule 803(6). Rule 902(13) is solely limited to authentication and any attempt to satisfy a hearsay exception must be made independently.

A certification under this Rule can establish only that the proffered item has satisfied the admissibility requirements for authenticity. The opponent remains free to object to admissibility of the proffered item on other grounds—including hearsay, relevance, or in criminal cases the right to confrontation. For example, assume that a plaintiff in a defamation case offers what purports to be a printout of a webpage on which a defamatory statement was made. Plaintiff offers a certification under this Rule in which a qualified person describes the process by which the webpage was retrieved. Even if that certification sufficiently establishes that the webpage is authentic, defendant remains free to object that the statement on the webpage was not placed there by defendant. Similarly, a certification authenticating a computer output, such as a spreadsheet, does not preclude an objection that the information produced is unreliable—the authentication establishes only that the output came from the computer.

A challenge to the authenticity of electronic evidence may require technical information about the system or process at issue, including possibly retaining a forensic technical expert; such factors will effect whether the opponent has a fair opportunity to challenge the evidence given the notice provided.

The reference to Rule 902(12) is intended to cover certifications that are made in a foreign country.

Changes Made After Publication and Comment

Minor adjustments were made to the Committee Note to clarify the meaning of the certification requirement and to emphasize the importance of reasonable notice.

Restyled 2011

(14) ***Certified Data Copied from an Electronic Device, Storage Medium, or File.*** Data copied from an electronic device, storage medium, or file, if authenticated by a process of digital identification, as shown by a certification of a qualified person that complies with the certification requirements of Rule 902(11) or (12). The proponent also must meet the notice requirements of Rule 902(11). *[Added 2016.]*

Advisory Committee Note to 2016 Amendment

The amendment sets forth a procedure by which parties can authenticate data copied from an electronic device, storage medium, or an electronic file, other than through the testimony of a foundation witness. As with the provisions on business records in Rules 902(11) and (12), the Committee has found that the expense and inconvenience of producing an authenticating witness for this evidence is often unnecessary. It is often the case that a party goes to the expense of producing an authentication witness, and then the adversary either stipulates authenticity before the witness is called or fails to challenge the authentication testimony once it is presented. The amendment provides a procedure in which the parties can determine in advance of trial whether a real challenge to authenticity will be made, and can then plan accordingly.

Today, data copied from electronic devices, storage media, and electronic files are ordinarily authenticated by "hash value." A hash value is a number that is often represented as a sequence of characters and is produced by an algorithm based upon the digital contents of a drive, medium, or file. If the hash values for the original and copy are different, then the copy is not identical to the original. If the hash values for the original and copy are the same, it is highly improbable that the original and copy are not identical. Thus, identical hash values for the original and copy reliably attest to the fact that they are exact duplicates. This amendment allows self-authentication by a certification of a qualified person that she checked the hash value of the proffered item and that it was identical to the original. The rule is flexible enough to allow certifications through processes other than comparison of hash value, including by other reliable means of identification provided by future technology.

Nothing in the amendment is intended to limit a party from establishing authenticity of electronic evidence on any ground provided in these Rules, including through judicial notice where appropriate.

A proponent establishing authenticity under this Rule must present a certification containing information that would be sufficient to establish authenticity were that information provided by a witness at trial. If the certification provides information that would be insufficient to authenticate the record if the certifying person testified, then authenticity is not established under this Rule.

The reference to the "certification requirements of Rule 902(11) or (12)" is only to the procedural requirements for a valid certification. There is no intent to require, or permit, a certification under this rule to prove the requirements of Rule 803(6). Rule 902(14) is solely limited to authentication and any attempt to satisfy a hearsay exception must be made independently.

A certification under this Rule can only establish that the proffered item is authentic. The opponent remains free to object to admissibility of the proffered item on other grounds—including hearsay, relevance, or in criminal cases the right to confrontation. For example, in a criminal case in which data copied from a hard drive is proffered, the defendant can still challenge hearsay found in the hard drive, and can still challenge whether the information on the hard drive was placed there by the defendant.

A challenge to the authenticity of electronic evidence may require technical information about the system or process at issue, including possibly retaining a forensic technical expert; such factors will effect whether the opponent has a fair opportunity to challenge the evidence given the notice provided.

The reference to Rule 902(12) is intended to cover certifications that are made in a foreign country.

Restyled 2011

Rule 903. Subscribing Witness's Testimony

A subscribing witness's testimony is necessary to authenticate a writing only if required by the law of the jurisdiction that governs its validity.

Superseded 2011

Rule 903. Subscribing Witness' Testimony Unnecessary

The testimony of a subscribing witness is not necessary to authenticate a writing unless required by the laws of the jurisdiction whose laws govern the validity of the writing.

Advisory Committee's Note

The common law required that attesting witnesses be produced or accounted for. Today the requirement has generally been abolished except with respect to documents which must be attested to be valid, e.g. wills in some states. McCormick § 188. Uniform Rule 71; California Evidence Code § 1411; Kansas Code of Civil Procedure § 60-468; New Jersey Evidence Rule 71; New York CPLR Rule 4537.

ARTICLE X. CONTENTS OF WRITINGS, RECORDINGS AND PHOTOGRAPHS

Advisory Committee's Note

In an earlier day, when discovery and other related procedures were strictly limited, the misleading named "best evidence rule" afforded substantial guarantees against inaccuracies and fraud by its insistence upon production or original documents. The great enlargement of the scope of discovery and related procedures in recent times has measurably reduced the need for the rule. Nevertheless important areas of usefulness persist: discovery of documents outside the jurisdiction may require substantial outlay of time and money; the unanticipated document may not practically be discoverable; criminal cases have built-in limitations on discovery. Cleary and Strong, The Best Evidence Rule: An Evaluation in Context, 51 Iowa L.Rev. 825 (1966).

Restyled 2011

Rule 1001. Definitions That Apply to This Article

In this article:

(a) A "writing" consists of letters, words, numbers, or their equivalent set down in any form.

(b) A "recording" consists of letters, words, numbers, or their equivalent recorded in any manner.

Superseded 2011

Rule 1001. Definitions

For purposes of this article the following definitions are applicable:

(1) Writings and recordings. "Writings" and "recordings" consist of letters, words, or numbers, or their equivalent, set down by handwriting, typewriting, printing, photostating, photographing, magnetic impulse, mechanical or electronic recording, or other form of data compilation.

Advisory Committee's Note

Paragraph (1). Traditionally the rule requiring the original centered upon accumulations of data and expressions affecting legal relations set forth in words and figures. this meant that the rule was one essentially related to writings. Present day techniques have expanded methods of storing data, yet the essential form which the information ultimately assumes for usable purposes is words and figures. Hence the considerations underlying the rule dictate its expansion to include computers, photographic systems, and other modern developments.

Restyled 2011

(c) A "photograph" means a photographic image or its equivalent stored in any form.

Superseded 2011

(2) Photographs. "Photographs" include still photographs, X-ray films, video tapes, and motion pictures.

House Judiciary Committee Report

The Committee amended this Rule expressly to include "video tapes" in the definition of "photographs."

Restyled 2011

(d) An "original" of a writing or recording means the writing or recording itself or any counterpart intended to have the same effect by the person who executed or issued it. For electronically stored information, "original" means any printout — or other output readable by sight — if it accurately reflects the information. An "original" of a photograph includes the negative or a print from it.

Superseded 2011

(3) Original. An "original" of a writing or recording is the writing or recording itself or any counterpart intended to have the same effect by a person executing or issuing it. An "original" of a photograph includes the negative or any print therefrom. If data are stored in a computer or similar device, any printout or other output readable by sight, shown to reflect the data accurately, is an "original".

Advisory Committee's Note

Paragraph (3). In most instances, what is an original will be self-evident and further refinement will be unnecessary. However, in some instances particularized definition is required. A carbon copy of a contract executed in duplicate becomes an original, as does a sales ticket carbon copy given to a customer. While strictly speaking the original of a photograph might be thought to be only the negative, practicality and common usage require that any print from the negative be regarded as an original. Similarly, practicality and usage confer the status of original upon any computer printout. Transport Indemnity Co. v. Seib, 178 Neb. 253, 132 N.W.2d 871 (1965).

Restyled 2011

(e) A "duplicate" means a counterpart produced by a mechanical, photographic, chemical, electronic, or other equivalent process or technique that accurately reproduces the original.

Superseded 2011

(4) Duplicate. A "duplicate" is a counterpart produced by the same impression as the original, or from the same matrix, or by means of photography, including enlargements and miniatures, or by mechanical or electronic re-recording, or by chemical reproduction, or by other equivalent techniques which accurately reproduces the original.

Advisory Committee's Note

Paragraph (4). The definition describes "copies" produced by methods possessing an accuracy which virtually eliminates the possibility of error. Copies thus produced are given the status of originals in large measure by Rule 1003, infra. Copies subsequently produced manually, whether handwritten or typed, are not within the definition. It should be noted that what is an original for some purposes may be a duplicate for others. Thus a bank's microfilm record of checks cleared is the original as a record. However, a print offered as a copy of a check whose contents are in controversy is a duplicate. This result is substantially consistent with 28 U.S.C. § 1732(b). Compare 26 U.S.C. § 7513(c), giving full status as originals to photographic reproductions of tax returns and other documents, made by authority of the Secretary of the Treasury, and 44 U.S.C. § 399(a), giving original status to photographic copies in the National Archives.

Restyled 2011

Rule 1002. Requirement of the Original

An original writing, recording, or photograph is required in order to prove its content unless these rules or a federal statute provides otherwise.

Superseded 2011

Rule 1002. Requirement of Original

To prove the content of a writing, recording, or photograph, the original writing, recording, or photograph is required, except as otherwise provided in these rules or by Act of Congress.

Advisory Committee's Note

The rule is the familiar one requiring production of the original of a document to prove its contents, expanded to include writings, recordings, and photographs, as defined in Rule 1001(1) and (2), supra.

Application of the rule requires a resolution of the question whether contents are sought to be proved. Thus an event may be proved by nondocumentary evidence, even though a written record of it was made. If, however, the event is sought to be proved by the written record, the rule applies. For example, payment may be proved without producing the written receipt which was given. Earnings may be proved without producing books of account in which they are entered. McCormick § 198; 4 Wigmore § 1245. Nor does the rule apply to testimony that books or records have been examined and found not to contain any reference to a designated matter.

The assumption should not be made that the rule will come into operation on every occasion when use is made of a photograph in evidence. On the contrary, the rule will seldom apply to ordinary photographs. In most instances a party wishes to introduce the item and the question raised is the propriety of receiving it in evidence. Cases in which an offer is made of the testimony of a witness as to what he saw in a photograph or motion picture, without producing the same, are most unusual. The usual course is for a witness on the stand to identify the photograph or motion picture as a correct representation of events which he saw or of a scene with which he is familiar. In fact he adopts the picture as his testimony, or, in common parlance, uses the picture to illustrate his testimony. Under these circumstances, no effort is made to prove the contents of the picture, and the rule is inapplicable. Paradis, The Celluloid Witness, 37 U.Colo.L.Rev. 235, 249-251 (1965).

On occasion, however, situations arise in which contents are sought to be proved. Copyright, defamation, and invasion of privacy by photograph or motion picture falls in this category. Similarly as to situations in which the picture is offered as having independent probative value, e.g. automatic photograph of bank robber. See People v. Doggett, 83 Cal.App.2d 405, 188 P.2d 792 (1948), photograph of defendants engaged in indecent act; Mouser and Philbin, Photographic Evidence—Is There a Recognized Basis for Admissibility? 8 Hastings L.J. 310 (1957). The most commonly encountered of this latter group is of course, the X ray, with substantial authority calling for production of the original. Daniels v. Iowa City, 191 Iowa 811, 183 N.W. 415 (1921); Cellamare v. Third Acc. Transit Corp., 273 App.Div. 260, 77 N.Y.S.2d 91 (1948); Patrick & Tilman v. Matkin, 154 Okl. 232, 7 P.2d 414 (1932); Mendoza v. Rivera, 78 P.R.R. 569 (1955).

It should be noted, however, that Rule 703, supra, allows an expert to give an opinion based on matters not in evidence, and the present rule must be read as being limited accordingly in its application. Hospital records which may be admitted as business records under Rule 803(6) commonly contain reports interpreting X-rays by the staff radiologist, who qualifies as an expert, and these reports need not be excluded from the records by the instant rule.

The reference to Acts of Congress is made in view of such statutory provisions as 26 U.S.C. § 7513, photographic reproductions of tax returns and documents, made by authority of the Secretary of the Treasury, treated as originals, and 44 U.S.C. § 399(a), photographic copies in National Archives treated as originals.

Restyled 2011

Rule 1003. Admissibility of Duplicates

A duplicate is admissible to the same extent as the original unless a genuine question is raised about the original's authenticity or the circumstances make it unfair to admit the duplicate.

Superseded 2011

Rule 1003. Admissibility of Duplicates

A duplicate is admissible to the same extent as an original unless (1) a genuine question is raised as to the authenticity of the original or (2) in the circumstances it would be unfair to admit the duplicate in lieu of the original.

Advisory Committee's Note

When the only concern is with getting the words or other contents before the court with accuracy and precision, then a counterpart serves equally as well as the original, if the counterpart is the product of a method which insures accuracy and genuineness. By definition in Rule 1001(4), supra, a "duplicate" possesses this character.

Therefore, if no genuine issue exists as to authenticity and no other reason exists for requiring the original, a duplicate is admissible under the rule. This position finds support in the decisions, Myrick v. United States, 332 F.2d 279 (5th Cir.1964), no error in admitting photostatic copies of checks instead of original microfilm in absence of suggestion to trial judge that photostats were incorrect; Johns v. United States, 323 F.2d 421 (5th Cir.1963), not error to admit concededly accurate tape recording made from original wire recording; Sauget v. Johnston, 315 F.2d 816 (9th Cir.1963), not error to admit copy of agreement when opponent had original and did not on appeal claim any discrepancy. Other reasons for acquiring the original may be present when only a part of the original is reproduced and the remainder is needed for cross-examination or may disclose matters qualifying the part offered or otherwise useful to the opposing party. United States v. Alexander, 326 F.2d 736 (4th Cir.1964). And see Toho Bussan Kaisha, Ltd. v. American President Lines, Ltd., 265 F.2d 418, 76 A.L.R.2d 1344 (2d Cir.1959).

House Judiciary Committee Report

The Committee approved this Rule in the form submitted by the Court, with the expectation that the courts would be liberal in deciding that a "genuine question is raised as to the authenticity of the original."

Restyled 2011

Rule 1004. Admissibility of Other Evidence of Content

An original is not required and other evidence of the content of a writing, recording, or photograph is admissible if:

Superseded 2011

Rule 1004. Admissibility of Other Evidence of Contents

The original is not required, and other evidence of the contents of a writing, recording, or photograph is admissible if—

Advisory Committee's Note

Basically the rule requiring the production of the original as proof of contents has developed as a rule of preference: if failure to produce the original is satisfactorily explained, secondary evidence is admissible. The instant rule specifies the circumstances under which production of the original is excused.

The rule recognizes no "degrees" of secondary evidence. While strict logic might call for extending the principle of preference beyond simply preferring the original, the formulation of a hierarchy of preferences and a procedure for making it effective is believed to involve unwarranted complexities. Most, if not all, that would be accomplished by an extended scheme of preferences will, in any event, be achieved through the normal motivation of a party to present the most convincing evidence possible and the arguments and procedures available to his opponent if he does not. Compare McCormick § 207.

Restyled 2011

(a) all the originals are lost or destroyed, and not by the proponent acting in bad faith;

Superseded 2011

(1) **Originals lost or destroyed.** All originals are lost or have been destroyed, unless the proponent lost or destroyed them in bad faith; or

Advisory Committee's Note

Paragraph (1). Loss or destruction of the original, unless due to bad faith of the proponent, is a satisfactory explanation of nonproduction. McCormick § 201.

House Judiciary Committee Report

The Committee approved Rule 1004(1) in the form submitted to Congress. However, the Committee intends that loss or destruction of an original by another person at the instigation of the proponent should be considered as tantamount to loss or destruction in bad faith by the proponent himself.

Restyled 2011

(b) an original cannot be obtained by any available judicial process;

Superseded 2011

(2) Original not obtainable. No original can be obtained by any available judicial process or procedure; or

Advisory Committee's Note

Paragraph (2). When the original is in the possession of a third person, inability to procure it from him by resort to process or other judicial procedure is a sufficient explanation of nonproduction. Judicial procedure includes subpoena duces tecum as an incident to the taking of a deposition in another jurisdiction. No further showing is required. See McCormick § 202.

Restyled 2011

(c) the party against whom the original would be offered had control of the original; was at that time put on notice, by pleadings or otherwise, that the original would be a subject of proof at the trial or hearing; and fails to produce it at the trial or hearing; or

Superseded 2011

(3) Original in possession of opponent. At a time when an original was under the control of the party against whom offered, that party was put on notice, by the pleadings or otherwise, that the contents would be a subject of proof at the hearing, and that party does not produce the original at the hearing; or

Advisory Committee's Note

Paragraph (3). A party who has an original in his control has no need for the protection of the rule if put on notice that proof of contents will be made. He can ward off secondary evidence by offering the original. The notice procedure here provided is not to be confused with orders to produce or other discovery procedures, as the purpose of the procedure under this rule is to afford the opposite party an opportunity to produce the original, not to compel him to do so. McCormick § 203.

Restyled 2011

(d) the writing, recording, or photograph is not closely related to a controlling issue.

Superseded 2011

(4) Collateral matters. The writing, recording, or photograph is not closely related to a controlling issue.

Advisory Committee's Note

Paragraph (4). While difficult to define with precision, situations arise in which no good purpose is served by production of the original. Examples are the newspaper in an action for the price of publishing defendant's advertisement, Foster-Holcomb Investment Co. v. Little Rock Publishing Co., 151 Ark. 449, 236 S.W. 597 (1922), and the streetcar transfer of plaintiff claiming status as a passenger, Chicago City Ry. Co. v. Carroll, 206 Ill. 318, 68 N.E. 1087 (1903). Numerous cases are collected in McCormick § 200, p. 412, n. 1.

Restyled 2011

Rule 1005. Copies of Public Records to Prove Content

The proponent may use a copy to prove the content of an official record — or of a document that was recorded or filed in a public office as authorized by law — if these conditions are met: the record or document is otherwise admissible; and the copy is certified as correct in accordance with Rule 902(4) or is testified to be correct by a witness who has compared it with the original. If no such copy can be obtained by reasonable diligence, then the proponent may use other evidence to prove the content.

Superseded 2011

Rule 1005. Public Records

The contents of an official record, or of a document authorized to be recorded or filed and actually recorded or filed, including data compilations in any form, if otherwise admissible, may be proved by copy, certified as correct in accordance with rule 902 or testified to be correct by a witness who has compared it with the original. If a copy which complies with the foregoing cannot be obtained by the exercise of reasonable diligence, then other evidence of the contents may be given.

Advisory Committee's Note

Public records call for somewhat different treatment. Removing them from their usual place of keeping would be attended by serious inconvenience to the public and to the custodian. As a consequence judicial decisions and statutes commonly hold that no explanation need be given for failure to produce the original of a public record. McCormick § 204; 4 Wigmore §§ 1215-1228. This blanket dispensation from producing or accounting for the original would open the door to the introduction of every kind of secondary evidence of contents of public records were it not for the preference given certified or compared copies. Recognition of degrees of secondary evidence in this situation is an appropriate quid pro quo for not applying the requirement of producing the original.

The provisions of 28 U.S.C. § 1733(b) apply only to departments or agencies of the United States. The rule, however, applies to public records generally and is comparable in scope in this respect to Rule 44(a) of the Rules of Civil Procedure.

Rule 1006. Summaries to Prove Content

The proponent may use a summary, chart, or calculation to prove the content of voluminous writings, recordings, or photographs that cannot be conveniently examined in court. The proponent must make the originals or duplicates available for examination or copying, or both, by other parties at a reasonable time or place. And the court may order the proponent to produce them in court.

Superseded 2011

Rule 1006. Summaries

The contents of voluminous writings, recordings, or photographs which cannot conveniently be examined in court may be presented in the form of a chart, summary, or calculation. The originals, or duplicates, shall be made available for examination or copying, or both, by other parties at reasonable time and place. The court may order that they be produced in court.

Advisory Committee's Note

The admission of summaries of voluminous books, records, or documents offers the only practicable means of making their contents available to judge and jury. The rule recognizes this practice, with appropriate safeguards. 4 Wigmore § 1230.

Restyled 2011

Rule 1007. Testimony or Statement of a Party to Prove Content

The proponent may prove the content of a writing, recording, or photograph by the testimony, deposition, or written statement of the party against whom the evidence is offered. The proponent need not account for the original.

Superseded 2011

Rule 1007. Testimony or Written Admission of Party

Contents of writings, recordings, or photographs may be proved by the testimony or deposition of the party against whom offered or by that party's written admission, without accounting for the nonproduction of the original.

Advisory Committee's Note

While the parent case, Slatterie v. Pooley, 6 M. & W. 664, 151 Eng.Rep. 579 (Exch.1840), allows proof of contents by evidence of an oral admission by the party against whom offered, without accounting for nonproduction of the original, the risk of inaccuracy is substantial and the decision is at odds with the purpose of the rule giving preference to the original. See 4 Wigmore § 1255. The instant rule follows Professor McCormick's suggestion of limiting this use of admissions to those made in the course of giving testimony or in writing. McCormick § 208, p. 424. The limitation, of course, does not call for excluding evidence of an oral admission when nonproduction of the original has been accounted for and secondary evidence generally has become admissible. Rule 1004, supra.

A similar provision is contained in New Jersey Evidence Rule 70(1)(h).

Restyled 2011

Rule 1008. Functions of the Court and Jury

Ordinarily, the court determines whether the proponent has fulfilled the factual conditions for admitting other evidence of the content of a writing, recording, or photograph under Rule 1004 or 1005. But in a jury trial, the jury determines — in accordance with Rule 104(b) — any issue about whether:

(a) an asserted writing, recording, or photograph ever existed;

(b) another one produced at the trial or hearing is the original; or

(c) other evidence of content accurately reflects the content.

Superseded 2011

Rule 1008. Functions of Court and Jury

When the admissibility of other evidence of contents of writings, recordings, or photographs under these rules depends upon the fulfillment of a condition of fact, the question whether the condition has been fulfilled is ordinarily for the court to determine in accordance with the provisions of rule 104. However, when an issue is raised (a) whether the asserted writing ever existed, or (b) whether another writing, recording, or photograph produced at the trial is the original, or (c) whether other evidence of contents correctly reflects the contents, the issue is for the trier of fact to determine as in the case of other issues of fact.

Advisory Committee's Note

Most preliminary questions of fact in connection with applying the rule preferring the original as evidence of contents are for the judge, under the general principles announced in Rule 104, supra. Thus, the question whether the loss of the originals has been established, or of the fulfillment of other conditions specified in Rule 1004, supra, is for the judge. However, questions may arise which go beyond the mere administration of the rule preferring the original and into the merits of the controversy. For example, plaintiff offers secondary evidence of the contents of an alleged contract, after first introducing evidence of loss of the original, and defendant counters with evidence that no such contract was ever executed. If the judge decides that the contract was never executed and excludes the secondary evidence, the case is at an end without ever going to the jury on a central issue. Levin, Authentication and Content of Writings, 10 Rutgers L.Rev. 632, 644 (1956). The latter portion of the instant rule is designed to insure treatment of these situations as raising jury questions. The decision is not one for uncontrolled discretion of the jury but is subject to the control exercised generally by the judge over jury determinations. See Rule 104(b), supra.

For similar provisions, see Uniform Rule 70(2); Kansas Code of Civil Procedure § 60-467(b); New Jersey Evidence Rule 70(2), (3).

Restyled 2011

ARTICLE XI. MISCELLANEOUS RULES

Rule 1101. Applicability of the Rules

(a) To Courts and Judges. These rules apply to proceedings before:

- United States district courts;
- United States bankruptcy courts and magistrate judges;
- United States courts of appeals;
- the United States Court of Federal Claims; and
- the district courts of Guam, the Virgin Islands, and Northern Mariana Islands.

Superseded 2011

ARTICLE XI. MISCELLANEOUS RULES

Rule 1101. Applicability of Rules

(a) Courts and judges. These rules apply to the United States district courts, the District Court of Guam, the District Court of the Virgin Islands, the District Court for the Northern Mariana Islands, the United States courts of appeals, the United States Claims Court, and to United States bankruptcy judges and United States magistrate judges, in the actions, cases, and proceedings and to the extent hereinafter set forth. The terms "judge" and "court" in these rules include United States bankruptcy judges and United States magistrate judges.

Advisory Committee's Note

Subdivision (a). The various enabling acts contain differences in phraseology in their descriptions of the courts over which the Supreme Court's power to make rules of practice and procedure extends. The act concerning civil actions, as amended in 1966, refers to "the district courts . . . of the United States in civil actions, including admiralty and maritime cases. . . ." 28 U.S.C. § 2072, Pub.L. 89-773, § 1, 80 Stat. 1323. The bankruptcy authorization is for rules of practice and procedure "under the Bankruptcy Act." 28 U.S.C. § 2075, Pub.L. 88-623, § 1, 78 Stat. 1001. The Bankruptcy Act in turn creates bankruptcy courts of "the United States district courts and the district courts of the Territories and possessions to which this title is or may hereafter be applicable." 11 U.S.C. §§ 1(10), 11(a). The provision as to criminal rules up to and including verdicts applies to "criminal cases and proceedings to punish for criminal contempt of court in the United States district courts, in the district courts for the districts of the Canal Zone and Virgin Islands, in the Supreme Court of Puerto Rico, and in proceedings before United States magistrates." 18 U.S.C. § 3771.

These various provisions do not in terms describe the same courts. In congressional usage the phrase "district courts of the United States," without further qualification, traditionally has included the district courts established by Congress in the states under Article III of the Constitution, which are "constitutional" courts, and has not included the territorial courts created under Article IV, Section 3, clause 2, which are "legislative" courts. Hornbuckle v. Toombs, 85 U.S. 648, 21 L.Ed. 966 (1873). However, any doubt as to the inclusion of the District Court for the District of Columbia in the phrase is laid at rest by the provisions of the Judicial Code constituting the judicial districts, 28 U.S.C. § 81 et seq., creating district courts therein, id. § 132, and specifically providing that the term "district court of the United States" means the court so constituted. Id. § 451. The District of Columbia is included. Id. § 88. Moreover, when these provisions were enacted, reference to the District of Columbia was deleted from the original civil rules enabling act. 28 U.S.C. § 2072. Likewise Puerto Rico is made a district, with a district court, and included in the term. Id. § 119. The question is simply one of the extent of the authority conferred by Congress. With respect to civil rules it seems clearly to include the district courts in the states, the District Court for the District of Columbia, and the District Court for the District of Puerto Rico.

The bankruptcy coverage is broader. The bankruptcy courts include "the United States district courts," which includes those enumerated above. Bankruptcy courts also include "the district courts of the Territories and possessions to which this title is or may hereafter be applicable." 11 U.S.C. §§ 1(10), 11(a). These courts include the district courts of Guam and the Virgin Islands. 48 U.S.C. §§ 1424(b), 1615. Professor Moore points out that whether the District Court for the District of the Canal Zone is a court of bankruptcy "is not free from doubt in view of the fact that no other statute expressly or inferentially provides for the applicability of the Bankruptcy Act in the Zone." He further observes that while there seems to be little doubt that the Zone is a territory or possession within the meaning of the Bankruptcy Act, 11 U.S.C. § 1(10), it must be noted that the appendix to the Canal Zone Code of 1934 did not list the Act among the laws of the United States applicable to the Zone. 1 Moore's Collier on Bankruptcy ¶ 1.10, pp. 67, 72, n. 25 (14th ed. 1967). The Code of 1962 confers on the district court jurisdiction of:

> "(4) actions and proceedings involving laws of the United States applicable to the Canal Zone; and
>
> "(5) other matters and proceedings wherein jurisdiction is conferred by this Code or any other law." Canal Zone Code, 1962, Title 3, § 141.

Admiralty jurisdiction is expressly conferred. Id. § 142. General powers are conferred on the district court, "if the course of proceeding is not specifically prescribed by this Code, by the statute, or by applicable rule of the Supreme Court of the United States . . ." Id. § 279. Neither these provisions nor § 1(10) of the Bankruptcy Act ("district courts of the Territories and possessions to which this title is or may hereafter be applicable") furnishes a satisfactory answer as to the status of the District Court for the District of the Canal Zone as a court of bankruptcy. However, the fact is that this court exercises no bankruptcy jurisdiction in practice.

The criminal rules enabling act specified United States district courts, district courts for the districts of the Canal Zone and the Virgin Islands, the Supreme Court of the Commonwealth of Puerto Rico, and proceedings before United States commissioners. Aside from the addition of commissioners, now magistrates, this scheme differs from the bankruptcy pattern in that it makes no mention of the District Court of Guam but by specific mention removes the Canal Zone from the doubtful list.

The further difference in including the Supreme Court of the Commonwealth of Puerto Rico seems not to be significant for present purposes, since the Supreme Court of the Commonwealth of Puerto Rico is an appellate court. The Rules of Criminal Procedure have not been made applicable to it, as being unneeded and inappropriate, Rule 54(a) of the Federal Rules of Criminal Procedure, and the same approach is indicated with respect to rules of evidence.

If one were to stop at this point and frame a rule governing the applicability of the proposed rules of evidence in terms of the authority conferred by the three enabling acts, an irregular pattern would emerge as follows:

Civil actions, including admiralty and maritime cases—district courts in the states, District of Columbia, and Puerto Rico.

Bankruptcy—same as civil actions, plus Guam and Virgin Islands.

Criminal cases—same as civil actions, plus Canal Zone and Virgin Islands (but not Guam).

This irregular pattern need not, however, be accepted. Originally the Advisory Committee on the Rules of Civil Procedure took the position that, although the phrase "district courts of the United States" did not include territorial courts, provisions in the organic laws of Puerto Rico and Hawaii would make the rules applicable to the district courts thereof, though this would not be so as to Alaska, the Virgin Islands, or the Canal Zone, whose organic acts contained no corresponding provisions. At the suggestion of the Court, however, the Advisory Committee struck from its notes a statement to the above effect. 2 Moore's Federal Practice ¶ 1.07 (2nd ed. 1967); 1 Barron and Holtzoff, Federal Practice and Procedure § 121 (Wright ed. 1960). Congress thereafter by various enactments provided that the rules and future amendments thereto should apply to the district courts of Hawaii, 53 Stat. 841 (1939), Puerto Rico, 54 Stat. 22 (1940), Alaska, 63 Stat. 445 (1949), Guam, 64 Stat. 384-390 (1950), and the Virgin Islands, 68 Stat. 497, 507 (1954). The original enabling act for rules of criminal procedure specifically mentioned the district courts of the Canal Zone and the Virgin Islands. The Commonwealth of Puerto Rico was blanketed in by creating its court a "district court of the United States" as previously described. Although Guam is not mentioned in either the enabling act or in the expanded definition of "district court of the United States," the Supreme Court in 1956 amended Rule 54(a) to state that the Rules of Criminal Procedure are applicable in Guam. The Court took this step following the enactment of legislation by Congress in 1950 that rules theretofore or thereafter promulgated by the Court in civil cases, admiralty, criminal cases and bankruptcy should apply to the District Court of Guam, 48 U.S.C. § 1424(b), and two Ninth Circuit decisions upholding the applicability of the Rules of Criminal Procedure to Guam. Pugh v. United States, 212 F.2d 761 (9th Cir.1954); Hatchett v. Guam, 212 F.2d 767 (9th Cir.1954); Orfield, The Scope of the Federal Rules of Criminal Procedure, 38 U. of Det.L.J. 173, 187 (1960).

From this history, the reasonable conclusion is that Congressional enactment of a provision that rules and future amendments shall apply in the courts of a territory or possession is the equivalent of mention in an enabling act and that a rule on scope and applicability may properly be drafted accordingly. Therefore the pattern set by Rule 54 of the Federal Rules of Criminal Procedure is here followed.

The substitution of magistrates in lieu of commissioners is made in pursuance of the Federal Magistrates Act, P.L. 90-578, approved October 17, 1968, 82 Stat. 1107.

House Judiciary Committee Report

Subdivision (a) as submitted to the Congress, in stating the courts and judges to which the Rules of Evidence apply, omitted the Court of Claims and commissioners of that Court. At the request of the Court of Claims, the Committee amended the Rule to include the Court and its commissioners within the purview of the Rules.

Restyled 2011

(b) To Cases and Proceedings. These rules apply in:

- civil cases and proceedings, including bankruptcy, admirality, and maritime cases;
- criminal cases and proceedings; and
- contempt proceedings, except those in which the court may act summarily.

Superseded 2011

(b) Proceedings generally. These rules apply generally to civil actions and proceedings, including admiralty and maritime cases, to criminal cases and proceedings, to contempt proceedings except those in which the court may act summarily, and to proceedings and cases under title 11, United States Code.

Advisory Committee's Note

Subdivision (b) is a combination of the language of the enabling acts, supra, with respect to the kinds of proceedings in which the making of rules is authorized. It is subject to the qualifications expressed in the subdivisions which follow.

House Judiciary Committee Report

Subdivision (b) was amended merely to substitute positive law citations for those which were not.

Restyled 2011

(c) Rules on Privilege. The rules on privilege apply to all stages of a case or proceeding.

Superseded 2011

(c) Rule of privilege. The rule with respect to privileges applies at all stages of all actions, cases, and proceedings.

Advisory Committee's Note

Subdivision (c), singling out the rules of privilege for special treatment, is made necessary by the limited applicability of the remaining rules.

Restyled 2011

(d) Exceptions. These rules — except for those on privilege — do not apply to the following:

Superseded 2011

(d) Rules inapplicable. The rules (other than with respect to privileges) do not apply in the following situations:

Advisory Committee's Note

Subdivision (d). The rule is not intended as an expression as to when due process or other constitutional provisions may require an evidentiary hearing.

Restyled 2011

(1) the court's determination, under Rule 104(a), on a preliminary question of fact governing admissibility;

Superseded 2011

(1) Preliminary questions of fact. The determination of questions of fact preliminary to admissibility of evidence when the issue is to be determined by the court under rule 104.

Advisory Committee's Note

Paragraph (1) restates, for convenience, the provisions of the second sentence of Rule 104(a), supra. See Advisory Committee's Note to that rule.

Restyled 2011

(2) grand-jury proceedings; and

Superseded 2011

(2) Grand jury. Proceedings before grand juries.

Advisory Committee's Note

(2) While some states have statutory requirements that indictments be based on "legal evidence," and there is some case law to the effect that the rules of evidence apply to grand jury proceedings, 1 Wigmore § 4(5), the Supreme Court has not accepted this view. In Costello v. United States, 350 U.S. 359, 76 S.Ct. 406, 100 L.Ed. 397 (1965), the Court refused to allow an indictment to be attacked, for either constitutional or policy reasons, on the ground that only hearsay evidence was presented.

> "It would run counter to the whole history of the grand jury institution, in which laymen conduct their inquiries unfettered by technical rules. Neither justice nor the concept of a fair trial requires such a change." Id. at 364.

The rule as drafted does not deal with the evidence required to support an indictment.

(3) miscellaneous proceedings such as:
- extradition or rendition;
- issuing an arrest warrant, criminal summons, or search warrant;
- a preliminary examination in a criminal case;
- sentencing;
- granting or revoking probation or supervised release; and
- considering whether to release on bail or otherwise.

Superseded 2011

(3) Miscellaneous proceedings. Proceedings for extradition or rendition; preliminary examinations in criminal cases; sentencing, or granting or revoking probation; issuance of warrants for arrest, criminal summonses, and search warrants; and proceedings with respect to release on bail or otherwise.

Advisory Committee's Note

(3) The rule exempts preliminary examinations in criminal cases. Authority as to the applicability of the rules of evidence to preliminary examinations has been meager and conflicting. Goldstein, The State and the Accused: Balance of Advantage in Criminal Procedure, 69 Yale L.J. 1149, 1168, n. 53 (1960); Comment, Preliminary Hearings on Indictable Offenses in Philadelphia, 106 U. of Pa.L.Rev. 589, 592-593 (1958). Hearsay testimony is, however, customarily received in such examinations. Thus in a Dyer Act case, for example, an affidavit may properly be used in a preliminary examination to prove ownership of the stolen vehicle, thus saving the victim of the crime the hardship of having to travel twice to a distant district for the sole purpose of testifying as to ownership. It is believed that the extent of the applicability of the Rules of Evidence to preliminary examinations should be appropriately dealt with by the Federal Rules of Criminal Procedure which regulate those proceedings.

Extradition and rendition proceedings are governed in detail by statute. 18 U.S.C. §§ 3181-3195. They are essentially administrative in character. Traditionally the rules of evidence have not applied. 1 Wigmore § 4(6). Extradition proceedings are accepted from the operation of the Rules of Criminal Procedure. Rule 54(b)(5) of Federal Rules of Criminal Procedure.

The rules of evidence have not been regarded as applicable to sentencing or probation proceedings, where great reliance is placed upon the presentence investigation and report. Rule 32(c) of the Federal Rules of Criminal Procedure requires a presentence investigation and report in every case unless the court otherwise directs. In Williams v. New York, 337 U.S. 241, 69 S.Ct. 1079, 93 L.Ed. 1337 (1949), in which the judge overruled a jury recommendation of life imprisonment and imposed a death sentence, the Court said that due process does not require confrontation or cross-examination in sentencing or passing on probation, and that the judge has broad discretion as to the sources and types of information relied upon. Compare the recommendation that the substance of all derogatory information be disclosed to the defendant, in A.B.A. Project on Minimum Standards for Criminal Justice, Sentencing Alternatives and Procedures § 4.4, Tentative Draft (1967, Sobeloff, Chm.). Williams was adhered to in Specht v. Patterson, 386 U.S. 605, 87 S.Ct. 1209, 18 L.Ed.2d 326 (1967), but not extended to a proceeding under the Colorado Sex Offenders Act, which was said to be a new charge leading in effect to punishment, more like the recidivist statutes where opportunity must be given to be heard on the habitual criminal issue.

Warrants for arrest, criminal summonses, and search warrants are issued upon complaint or affidavit showing probable cause. Rules 4(a) and 41(c) of the Federal Rules of Criminal Procedure. The nature of the proceedings makes application of the formal rules of evidence inappropriate and impracticable.

Criminal contempts are punishable summarily if the judge certifies that he saw or heard the contempt and that it was committed in the presence of the court. Rule 42(a) of the Federal Rules of Criminal Procedure. The circumstances which preclude application of the rules of evidence in this situation are not present, however, in other cases of criminal contempt.

Proceedings with respect to release on bail or otherwise do not call for application of the rules of evidence. The governing statute specifically provides:

> "Information stated in, or offered in connection with, any order entered pursuant to this section need not conform to the rules pertaining to the admissibility of evidence in a court of law." 18 U.S.C.A. § 3146(f).

This provision is consistent with the type of inquiry contemplated in A.B.A. Project on Minimum Standards for Criminal Justice, Standards Relating to Pretrial Release, § 4.5(b), (c), p. 16 (1968). The references to the weight of the evidence against the accused, in Rule 46(a)(1), (c) of the Federal Rules of Criminal Procedure and in 18 U.S.C.A. § 3146(b), as a factor to be considered, clearly do not have in view evidence introduced at a hearing under the rules of evidence.

The rule does not exempt habeas corpus proceedings. The Supreme Court held in Walker v. Johnston, 312 U.S. 275, 61 S.Ct. 574, 85 L.Ed. 830 (1941), that the practice of disposing of matters of fact on affidavit, which prevailed in some circuits, did not "satisfy the command of the statute that the judge shall proceed 'to determine the facts of the case, by hearing the testimony and arguments.'" This view accords with the emphasis in Townsend v. Sain, 372 U.S. 293, 83 S.Ct. 745, 9 L.Ed.2d 770 (1963), upon trial-type proceedings, id. 311, 83 S.Ct. 745, with demeanor evidence as a significant factor, id. 322, 83 S.Ct. 745, in applications by state prisoners aggrieved by unconstitutional detentions. Hence subdivision (3) applies the rules to habeas corpus proceedings to the extent not inconsistent with the statute.

Restyled 2011

(e) Other Statutes and Rules. A federal statute or a rule prescribed by the Supreme Court may provide for admitting or excluding evidence independently from these rules.

Superseded 2011

(e) Rules applicable in part. In the following proceedings these rules apply to the extent that matters of evidence are not provided for in the statutes which govern procedure therein or in other rules prescribed by the Supreme Court pursuant to statutory authority: the trial of misdemeanors and other petty offenses before United States magistrate judges; review of agency actions when the facts are subject to trial de novo under section 706(2)(F) of title 5, United States Code; review of orders of the Secretary of Agriculture under section 2 of the Act entitled "An Act to authorize association of producers of agricultural products" approved February 18, 1922 (7 U.S.C. 292), and under sections 6 and 7(c) of the Perishable Agricultural Commodities Act, 1930 (7 U.S.C. 499f, 499g(c)); naturalization and revocation of naturalization under sections 310-318 of the Immigration and Nationality Act (8 U.S.C. 1421-1429); prize proceedings in admiralty under sections 7651-7681 of title 10, United States Code; review of orders of the Secretary of the Interior under section 2 of the Act entitled "An Act authorizing associations of producers of aquatic products" approved June 25, 1934 (15 U.S.C. 522); review of orders of petroleum control boards under section 5 of the Act entitled "An Act to regulate interstate and foreign commerce in petroleum and its products by prohibiting the shipment in such commerce of petroleum and its products produced in violation of State law, and for other purposes", approved February 22, 1935 (15 U.S.C. 715d); actions for fines, penalties, or forfeitures under part V of title IV of the Tariff Act of 1930 (19 U.S.C. 1581-1624), or under the Anti-SmugglingAct (19 U.S.C. 1701-1711); criminal libel for condemnation, exclusion of imports, or other proceedings under the Federal Food, Drug, and Cosmetic Act (21 U.S.C. 301-392); disputes between seamen under sections 4079, 4080, and 4081 of the Revised Statutes (22 U.S.C. 256-258); habeas corpus under sections 2241-2254 of title 28, United States Code; motions to vacate, set aside or correct sentence under section 2255 of title 28, United States Code; actions for penalties for refusal to transport destitute seamen under section 4578 of the Revised Statutes (46 U.S.C. 679); actions against the United States under the Act entitled "An Act authorizing suits against the United States in admiralty for damage caused by and salvage service rendered to public vessels belonging to the United States, and for other purposes", approved March 3, 1925 (46 U.S.C. 781-790), as implemented by section 7730 of title 10, United States Code. [*Amended 1975, 1978, 1982, 1987, 1988, 1993.*]

Advisory Committee's Note

Subdivision (e). In a substantial number of special proceedings, ad hoc evaluation has resulted in the promulgation of particularized evidentiary provisions, by Act of Congress or by rule adopted by the Supreme Court. Well adapted to the particular proceedings, though not apt candidates for inclusion in a set of general rules, they are left undisturbed. Otherwise, however, the rules of evidence are applicable to the proceedings enumerated in the subdivision.

Restyled 2011

Rule 1102. Amendments

These rules may be amended as provided in 28 U.S.C. § 2072.

Superseded 2011

Rule 1102. Amendments

Amendments to the Federal Rules of Evidence may be made as provided in section 2072 of title 28 of the United States Code.

Statutory Note

28 U.S.C. § 2072 provides:

(a) The Supreme Court shall have the power to prescribe general rules of practice and procedure and rules of evidence for cases in the United States district courts (including proceedings before magistrates thereof) and courts of appeals.

(b) Such rules shall not abridge, enlarge or modify any substantive right. All laws in conflict with such rules shall be of no further force or effect after such rules have taken effect.

(c) Such rules may define when a ruling of a district court is final for the purposes of appeal under section 1291 of this title.

28 U.S.C. § 2073 provides:

(a) (1) The Judicial Conference shall prescribe and publish the procedures for the consideration of proposed rules under this section.

(2) The Judicial Conference may authorize the appointment of committees to assist the Conference by recommending rules to be prescribed under sections 2072 and 2075 of this title. Each such committee shall consist of members of the bench and the professional bar, and trial and appellate judges.

(b) The Judicial Conference shall authorize the appointment of a standing committee on rules of practice, procedure, and evidence under subsection (a) of this section. Such standing committee shall review each recommendation of any other committees so appointed and recommend to the Judicial Conference rules of practice, procedure, and evidence and such changes in rules proposed by a committee appointed under subsection (a)(2) of this section as may be necessary to maintain consistency and otherwise promote the interest of justice.

(c) (1) Each meeting for the transaction of business under this chapter by any committee appointed under this section shall be open to the public, except when the committee so meeting, in open session and with a majority present, determines that it is in the public interest that all or part of the remainder of the meeting on that day shall be closed to the public, and states the reason for so closing the meeting. Minutes of each meeting for the transaction of business under this chapter shall be maintained by the committee and made available to the public, except that any portion of such minutes, relating to a closed meeting and made available to the public, may contain such deletions as may be necessary to avoid frustrating the purposes of closing the meeting.

(2) Any meeting for the transaction of business under this chapter, by a committee appointed under this section, shall be preceded by sufficient notice to enable all interested persons to attend.

(d) In making a recommendation under this section or under section 2072 or 2075, the body making that recommendation shall provide a proposed rule, an explanatory note on the rule, and a written report explaining the body's action, including any minority or other separate views.

(e) Failure to comply with this section does not invalidate a rule prescribed under section 2072 or 2075 of this title.

28 U.S.C. § 2074 provides:

(a) The Supreme Court shall transmit to the Congress not later than May 1 of the year in which a rule prescribed undersection 2072 is to become effective a copy of the proposed rule. Such rule shall take effect no earlier than December 1 of the year in which such rule is so transmitted unless otherwise provided by law. The Supreme Court may fix the extent such rule shall apply to proceedings then pending, except that the Supreme Court shall not require the application of such rule to further proceedings then pending to the extent that, in the opinion of the court in which such proceedings are pending, the application of such rule in such proceedings would not be feasible or would work injustice, in which event the former rule applies.

(b) Any such rule creating, abolishing, or modifying an evidentiary privilege shall have no force or effect unless approved by Act of Congress.

Restyled 2011

Rule 1103. Title

These rules may be cited as the Federal Rules of Evidence.

Superseded 2011

Rule 1103. Title

These rules may be known and cited as the Federal Rules of Evidence.

Part III

CALIFORNIA EVIDENCE CODE AND NOTES

EVIDENCE CODE

DIVISION 1. PRELIMINARY PROVISIONS AND CONSTRUCTION

§ 1. **Short title.** This code shall be known as the Evidence Code.

§ 2. **Common law rule construing code abrogated.** The rule of the common law, that statutes in derogation thereof are to be strictly construed, has no application to this code. This code establishes the law of this state respecting the subject to which it relates, and its provisions are to be liberally construed with a view to effecting its objects and promoting justice.

§ 3. **Severability.** If any provision or clause of this code or application thereof to any person or circumstances is held invalid, such invalidity shall not affect other provisions or applications of the code which can be given effect without the invalid provision or application, and to this end the provisions of this code are declared to be severable.

§ 4. **Construction of code.** Unless the provision or context otherwise requires, these preliminary provisions and rules of construction shall govern the construction of this code.

§ 5. **Effect of headings.** Division, chapter, article, and section headings do not in any manner affect the scope, meaning, or intent of the provisions of this code.

§ 6. **References to statutes.** Whenever any reference is made to any portion of this code or of any other statute, such reference shall apply to all amendments and additions heretofore or hereafter made.

§ 7. **"Division," "chapter," "article," "section," "subdivision," and "paragraph."** Unless otherwise expressly stated:

(a) "Division" means a division of this code.

(b) "Chapter" means a chapter of the division in which that term occurs.

(c) "Article" means an article of the chapter in which that term occurs.

(d) "Section" means a section of this code.

(e) "Subdivision" means a subdivision of the section in which that term occurs.

(f) "Paragraph" means a paragraph of the subdivision in which that term occurs.

§ 8. **Construction of tenses.** The present tense includes the past and future tenses; and the future, the present.

§ 9. **Construction of genders.** The masculine gender includes the feminine and neuter.

§ 10. **Construction of singular and plural.** The singular number includes the plural; and the plural, the singular.

§ 11. **"Shall" and "may."** "Shall" is mandatory and "may" is permissive.

§ 12. **Code effective January 1, 1967.** (a) This code shall become operative on January 1, 1967, and shall govern proceedings in actions brought on or after that date and, except as provided in subdivision (b), further proceedings in actions pending on that date.

(b) Subject to subdivision (c), a trial commenced before January 1, 1967, shall not be governed by this code. For the purpose of this subdivision:

(1) A trial is commenced when the first witness is sworn or the first exhibit is admitted into evidence and is terminated when the issue upon which such evidence is received is submitted to the trier of fact. A new trial, or a separate trial of a different issue, commenced on or after January 1, 1967, shall be governed by this code.

(2) If an appeal is taken from a ruling made at a trial commenced before January 1, 1967, the appellate court shall apply the law applicable at the time of the commencement of the trial.

(c) The provisions of Division 8 (commencing with Section 900) relating to privileges shall govern any claim of privilege made after December 31, 1966.

DIVISION 2. WORDS AND PHRASES DEFINED

§ 100. **Application of definitions.** Unless the provision or context otherwise requires, these definitions [§§ 105-260] govern the construction of this code.

§ 105. "Action" includes a civil action and a criminal action.

§ 110. "Burden of producing evidence" means the obligation of a party to introduce evidence sufficient to avoid a ruling against him on the issue.

Assembly Committee on Judiciary Comment

The phrases defined in Sections 110 and 115 provide a convenient means for distinguishing between the burden of proving a fact and the burden of going forward with the evidence. They recognize a distinction that is well established in California. Witkin, California Evidence §§ 53-60 (1958). The practical effect of the distinction is discussed in the Comments to Division 5 (commencing with Section 500), especially in the Comments to Sections 500 and 550.

§ 115. "Burden of proof" means the obligation of a party to establish by evidence a requisite degree of belief concerning a fact in the mind of the trier of fact or the court. The burden of proof may require a party to raise a reasonable doubt concerning the existence or nonexistence of a fact or that he establish the existence or nonexistence of a fact by a preponderance of the evidence, by clear and convincing proof, or by proof beyond a reasonable doubt. Except as otherwise provided by law, the burden of proof requires proof by a preponderance of the evidence.

Assembly Committee on Judiciary Comment

See the Comment to Section 110.

After stating the general definition of "burden of proof," the first paragraph of Section 115 gives examples of specific burdens that may be imposed by statutory or decisional law. The list of examples is not exclusive, and in some cases the law may prescribe some other burden of proof. For example, under Penal Code Section 872, the prosecution's burden of proof at a preliminary hearing is to establish "sufficient cause"—i.e., a "strong suspicion"—of the accused's guilt. Garabedian v. Superior Court, 59 Cal.2d 124, 28 Cal.Rptr. 318, 378 P.2d 590 (1963); Rogers v. Superior Court, 46 Cal.2d 3, 291 P.2d 929 (1955).

The second paragraph of Section 115 makes it clear that "burden of proof" refers to the burden of proving the fact in question by a preponderance of the evidence unless a heavier or lesser burden of proof is specifically required in a particular case by constitutional, statutory, or decisional law. See the definition of "law" in Evidence Code § 160.

§ 120. "Civil action" includes civil proceedings.

§ 125. "Conduct" includes all active and passive behavior, both verbal and nonverbal.

§ 130. "Criminal action" includes criminal proceedings.

§ 135. "Declarant" is a person who makes a statement.

Law Revision Commission Comment

Ordinarily, the word "declarant" is used in the Evidence Code to refer to a person who makes a hearsay statement as distinguished from the witness who testifies to the content of the statement. See Evidence Code § 1200 and the Comment thereto.

§ 140. "Evidence" means testimony, writings, material objects, or other things presented to the senses that are offered to prove the existence or nonexistence of a fact.

Law Revision Commission Comment

"Evidence" is defined broadly to include the testimony of witnesses, tangible objects, sights (such as a jury view or the appearance of a person exhibited to a jury), sounds (such as the sound of a voice demonstrated for a jury), and any other thing that may be presented as a basis of proof. The definition includes anything offered in evidence whether or not it is technically inadmissible and whether or not it is received. For example, Division 10 (commencing with Section 1200) uses "evidence" to refer to hearsay which may be excluded as inadmissible but which may be admitted if no proper objection is made. Thus, when inadmissible hearsay or opinion testimony is admitted without objection, this definition makes it clear that it constitutes evidence that may be considered by the trier of fact.

Section 140 is a better statement of existing law than Code of Civil Procedure Section 1823, which is superseded by Section 140. Although Section 1823 by its terms restricts "judicial evidence" to that "sanctioned by law," the general principle is well established that matter which is technically inadmissible under an exclusionary rule is nonetheless evidence and may be considered in support of a judgment if it is offered and received in evidence without proper objection or motion to strike. E.g., People v. Alexander, 212 Cal.App.2d 84, 98, 27 Cal.Rptr. 720, 727 (1963) ("illustrations of this principle are numerous and cover a wide range of evidentiary topics such as incompetent hearsay, secondary evidence violating the best evidence rule, inadmissible opinions, lack of foundation, incompetent, privileged or unqualified witnesses, and violations of the parol evidence rule"). See Witkin, California Evidence §§ 723-724 (1958).

Under this definition, a presumption is not evidence. See also Evidence Code § 600 and the Comment thereto.

§ 145. "The hearing" means the hearing at which a question under this code arises, and not some earlier or later hearing.

Law Revision Commission Comment

"The hearing" is defined to mean the hearing at which the particular question under the Evidence Code arises, and, unless a particular provision or its context otherwise indicates, not some earlier or later hearing. This definition is much broader than would be a reference to the trial itself; the definition includes, for example, preliminary hearings and post-trial proceedings.

§ 150. "Hearsay evidence" is defined in Section 1200.

Law Revision Commission Comment

Because of its special significance to Division 10, the substantive definition of "hearsay evidence" is contained in Section 1200. See the Comment to Section 1200.

§ 160. "Law" includes constitutional, statutory, and decisional law.

Law Revision Commission Comment

This definition makes it clear that a reference to "law" includes the law established by judicial decisions as well as by constitutional and statutory provisions.

§ 165. "Oath" includes affirmation or declaration under penalty of perjury.

§ 170. "Perceive" means to acquire knowledge through one's senses.

§ 175. "Person" includes a natural person, firm, association, organization, partnership, business trust, corporation, limited liability company, or public entity.

§ 177. "Dependent person" means a person, regardless of whether the person lives independently, who has a physical or mental impairment that substantially restricts his or her ability to carry out normal activities or to protect his or her rights, including, but not limited to, persons who have physical or developmental disabilities or whose physical or mental abilities have significantly diminished because of age. "Dependent person" includes any person who is admitted as an inpatient to a 24-hour health facility, as defined in Sections 1250, 1250.2, and 1250.3 of the Health and Safety Code. [*Added 2004. Amended 2018.*]

Statutory Note

The bill that added § 170 also amended §§ 710, 765, 767, and 1109, and declared "the intent of the Legislature to enact legislation protecting the rights of developmentally disabled persons and other dependent persons who are witnesses in criminal cases and ensuring that they are given equal access to the criminal justice system."

§ 180. "Personal property" includes money, goods, chattels, things in action, and evidences of debt.

§ 185. "Property" includes both real and personal property.

§ 190. "Proof" is the establishment by evidence of a requisite degree of belief concerning a fact in the mind of the trier of fact or the court.

Law Revision Commission Comment

This definition is more accurate than the definition of "proof" in Code of Civil Procedure Section 1824, which is superseded by Section 190. The disjunctive reference to "the trier of fact or the court" is needed because, even when the jury is the trier of fact, the court is required to determine preliminary questions of fact on the basis of proof.

§ 195. "Public employee" means an officer, agent, or employee of a public entity.

Law Revision Commission Comment

This definition specifically includes public officers and agents, thereby eliminating any distinction between employees and officers and making it unnecessary to repeat the phrase "officer, agent, or employee" in numerous code sections.

§ 200. "Public entity" includes a nation, state, county, city and county, city, district, public authority, public agency, or any other political subdivision or public corporation, whether foreign or domestic.

Law Revision Commission Comment

The broad definition of "public entity" includes every form of public authority, both foreign and domestic. Occasionally, "public entity" is used in the Evidence Code with limiting language to refer specifically to entities within this State or the United States. E.g., Evidence Code § 452(b). Cf. Evidence Code § 452(f).

§ 205. "Real property" includes lands, tenements, and hereditaments.

§ 210. "Relevant evidence" means evidence, including evidence relevant to the credibility of a witness or hearsay declarant, having any tendency in reason to prove or disprove any disputed fact that is of consequence to the determination of the action.

Law Revision Commission Comment

* * *[U]nder Section 210, "relevant evidence" includes not only evidence of the ultimate facts actually in dispute but also evidence of other facts from which such ultimate facts may be presumed or inferred. * * * In addition, Section 210 makes it clear that evidence relating to the credibility of witnesses and hearsay declarants is "relevant evidence." * * *

§ 215. "Spouse" includes "registered domestic partner,: as required by Section 297.5 of the Family Code. [*Added 2016.*]

§ 220. "State" means the State of California, unless applied to the different parts of the United States. In the latter case, it includes any state, district, commonwealth, territory, or insular possession of the United States.

§ 225. "Statement" means (a) oral or written verbal expression or (b) nonverbal conduct of a person intended by him as a substitute for oral or written verbal expression.

Law Revision Commission Comment

The significance of this definition is explained in the Comment to Evidence Code Section 1200.

§ 230. "Statute" includes a treaty and a constitutional provision.

Law Revision Commission Comment

In the Evidence Code, "statute" includes a constitutional provision. Thus, for example, when a particular section in subject to any exceptions "otherwise provided by statute," exceptions provided by the Constitution also are applicable.

§ 235. "Trier of fact" includes (a) the jury and (b) the court when the court is trying an issue of fact other than one relating to the admissibility of evidence.

Law Revision Commission Comment

"Trier of fact" is defined to include not only the jury but also the court when it is trying an issue of fact without a jury. The definition is not exclusive; a referee, court commissioner, or other officer conducting proceedings governed by the Evidence Code may be a trier of fact. See Evidence Code § 300.

§ 240. "Unavailable as a witness." (a) Except as otherwise provided in subdivision (b), "unavailable as a witness" means that the declarant is any of the following:

(1) Exempted or precluded on the ground of privilege from testifying concerning the matter to which his or her statement is relevant.

(2) Disqualified from testifying to the matter.

(3) Dead or unable to attend or to testify at the hearing because of then-existing physical or mental illness or infirmity.

(4) Absent from the hearing and the court is unable to compel his or her attendance by its process.

(5) Absent from the hearing and the proponent of his or her statement has exercised reasonable diligence but has been unable to procure his or her attendance by the court's process.

(6) Persistent in refusing to testify concerning the subject matter of the declarant's statement despite having been found in contempt for refusal to testify.

(b) A declarant is not unavailable as a witness if the exemption, preclusion, disqualification, death, inability, or absence of the declarant was brought about by the procurement or wrongdoing of the proponent of his or her statement for the purpose of preventing the declarant from attending or testifying.

(c) Expert testimony that establishes that physical or mental trauma resulting from an alleged crime has caused harm to a witness of sufficient severity that the witness is physically unable to testify or is unable to testify without suffering substantial trauma may constitute a sufficient showing of unavailability pursuant to paragraph (3) of subdivision (a). As used in this section, the term "expert" means a physician and surgeon, including a

psychiatrist, or any person described by subdivision (b), (c), or (e) of Section 1010.

The introduction of evidence to establish the unavailability of a witness under this subdivision shall not be deemed procurement of unavailability, in absence of proof to the contrary. [*Amended 2010.*]

Note on Proposed Amendment

The Law Revision Commission tentatively decided in March 2003 to recommend adding to § 240 refusal to testify despite a court order to do so and lack of memory.

Case Notes

Section 240 does not state the exclusive circumstances under which a witness may be deemed legally unavailable for purposes of § 1291. People v. Reed, 13 Cal. 4th 217, 226-229, 52 Cal. Rptr. 106, 112-114, 914 P.2d 184, 190-192 (1996) (for sentence enhancement purposes, proof of "serious" nature of prior felony was confined to the record of prior proceedings; since witnesses who testified at prior preliminary hearing were thus "legally disqualified" from testifying in current proceedings, preliminary hearing transcript was admissible as former testimony under § 1291).

Witness who refuses to testify because of fear for the safety of his person and that of his family is unavailable on the grounds of "mental infirmity." People v. Rojas, 15 Cal. 3d 540, 550-552, 125 Cal. Rptr. 357, 363-364, 542 P.2d 229, 235-236 (1975).

Expert testimony is not required to support a trial court finding that a witness's inability to remember the events to which she had previously testified was the result of "mental illness or infirmity." People v. Alcala, 4 Cal. 4th 742, 777-782, 15 Cal. Rptr. 2d 432, 452-455, 842 P.2d 1192, 1212-1215 (1992, modified, 1993).

A witness's occasional memory lapses while testifying at trial do not support a finding of unavailability, and thus do not support admissibility at trial of the witness's preliminary hearing testimony under the former testimony exception to the hearsay rule. People v. Price, 1 Cal. 4th 324, 415, 3 Cal. Rptr. 2d 106, 156, 821 P.2d 610, 660 (1992).

Assembly Committee on Judiciary Comment

Usually, the phrase "unavailable as a witness" is used in the Evidence Code to state the condition that must be met whenever the admissibility of hearsay evidence is dependent upon the declarant's present unavailability to testify. See, e.g., Evidence Code §§ 1230, 1251, 1291, 1292, 1310, 1311, 1323. See also Code Civ.Proc. § 2016(d)(3) and Penal Code §§ 1345 and 1362, relating to depositions.

"Unavailable as a witness" includes, in addition to cases where the declarant is physically unavailable (i.e., dead, insane, or beyond the reach of the court's process), situations in which the declarant is legally unavailable (i.e., prevented from testifying by a claim of privilege or disqualified from testifying). Of course, if the declaration made out of court is itself privileged, the fact that the declarant is unavailable to testify at the hearing on the ground of privilege does not make the declaration admissible. The exceptions to the hearsay rule that are set forth in Division 10 (commencing with Section 1200) of the Evidence Code do not declare that the evidence described is necessarily admissible. They merely declare that such evidence is not inadmissible under the hearsay rule. If there is some other rule of law—such as privilege—which makes the evidence inadmissible, the court is not authorized to admit the evidence merely because it falls within an exception to the hearsay rule. Accordingly, the hearsay exceptions permit the introduction of evidence where the declarant is unavailable because of privilege only if the declaration itself is not privileged or is not inadmissible for some other reason.

Subdivision (b) is designed to establish safeguards against sharp practices and, in the words of the Commissioners on Uniform State Laws, to assure "that unavailability is honest and not planned in order to gain an advantage." Uniform Rules of Evidence, Rule 62 Comment. Under this subdivision, a party may not arrange a declarant's disappearance in order to use the declarant's out-of-court statement. Moreover, if the out-of-court statement is that of the party himself, he may not create "unavailability" under this section by invoking a privilege not to testify.

Section 240 substitutes a uniform standard for the varying standards of unavailability provided by the superseded Code of Civil Procedure sections providing hearsay exceptions. * * * The conditions constituting unavailability under these superseded sections vary from exception to exception without apparent reason. Under some of these sections, the evidence is admissible if the declarant is dead; under others, the evidence is admissible if the declarant is dead or insane; under still others, the evidence is admissible if the declarant is absent from the jurisdiction. Despite the express language of these superseded sections, Section 240 may, to a considerable extent, restate existing law. Compare People v. Spriggs, 60 Cal.2d 868, 875, 36 Cal.Rptr. 841, 845, 389 P.2d 377, 381 (1964) (generally consistent with Section 240), with the older cases, some but not all of which are inconsistent with the Spriggs case and with Section 240. See the cases cited in Tentative Recommendation and a Study Relating to the Uniform Rules of Evidence (Article VIII. Hearsay Evidence), 6 Cal.Law Revision Comm'n, Rep., Rec. & Studies Appendix at 411 note 7 (1964).

§ 250. "Writing" means handwriting, typewriting, printing, photostating, photographing, photocopying, transmitting by electronic mail or facsimile, and every other means of recording upon any tangible thing, any form of communication or representation, including letters, words, pictures, sounds, or symbols, or combinations thereof, and any record thereby created, regardless of the manner in which the record has been stored. [*Amended 2002.*]

Law Revision Commission Comment

"Writing" is defined very broadly to include all forms of tangible expression, including pictures and sound recordings.

§ 255. "Original" means the writing itself or any counterpart intended to have the same effect by a person executing or issuing it. An "original" of a photograph includes the negative or any print therefrom. If data are stored in a computer or similar device, any printout or other output readable by sight, shown to reflect the data accurately, is an "original." [*Added 1977.*]

§ 260. A "duplicate" is a counterpart produced by the same impression as the original, or from the same matrix, or by means of photography, including enlargements and miniatures, or by mechanical or electronic rerecording, or by chemical reproduction, or by other equivalent technique which accurately reproduces the original. [*Added 1977.*]

DIVISION 3. GENERAL PROVISIONS

Chapter 1. Applicability of Code

§ 300. Applicability of code. Except as otherwise provided by statute, this code applies in every action before the Supreme Court or a court of appeal or superior court, including proceedings in such actions conducted by a referee, court commissioner, or similar officer, but does not apply in grand jury proceedings. [*Amended 2002.*]

Law Revision Commission Comment

Section 300 makes the Evidence Code applicable to all proceedings conducted by California courts except those court proceedings to which it is made inapplicable by statute. The provisions of the code do not apply in administrative proceedings, legislative hearings, or any other proceedings unless some statute so provides or the agency concerned chooses to apply them.

Various code sectionsCin the Evidence Code as well as in other codesCmake the provisions of the Evidence Code applicable to a certain extent in proceedings other than court proceedings. E.g., Govt.Code § 11513 (a finding in a proceeding conducted under the Administrative Procedure Act may not be based on hearsay evidence unless the evidence would be admissible over objection in a civil action); Penal Code § 939.6 (a grand jury, in investigating a charge, may receive only evidence admissible over objection in a criminal action); Evidence Code § 910 (provisions of the Evidence Code relating to privileges are applicable in all proceedings of every kind in which testimony can be compelled to be given); and Evidence Code § 1566 (Sections 1560-1565 are applicable in nonjudicial proceedings).

Section 300 does not affect any other statute relaxing rules of evidence for specified purposes. See, e.g., Code Civ.Proc. § 117g (judge of small claims court may make informal investigation either in or out of court), § 1768 (hearing of conciliation proceeding to be conducted informally), § 2016(b) (inadmissibility of testimony at trial is not ground for objection to testimony sought from a deponent, provided that such testimony is reasonably calculated to lead to the discovery of admissible evidence); Penal Code § 1203 (judge must consider probation officer's investigative report on question of probation); Welf. & Inst. Code § 706 (juvenile court must consider probation officer's social study in determining disposition to be made of ward or dependent child).

Chapter 2. Province of Court and Jury

§ 310. Questions of law for court. (a) All questions of law (including but not limited to questions concerning the construction of statutes and other writings, the admissibility of evidence, and other rules of evidence) are to be decided by the court. Determination of issues of fact preliminary to the admission of evidence are to be decided by the court as provided in Article 2 (commencing with Section 400) of Chapter 4.

(b) Determination of the law of an organization of nations or of the law of a foreign nation or a public entity in a foreign nation is a question of law to be determined in the manner provided in Division 4 (commencing with Section 450).

Assembly Committee on Judiciary Comment

* * * Section 310 refers specifically to the law of organizations of nations in order to make certain that the law of supranational organizations that have lawmaking authority—such as the European Economic Community—is to be determined as other foreign law is determined. * * * Of course, the Evidence Code does not require California courts to give the force of law to anything that does not have the force of law. The Evidence Code merely prescribes the procedure for determining the existing foreign law.

The judicial notice provisions of the Evidence Code have no effect on which party has the burden of establishing the applicable foreign law under Probate Code Section 259 (relating to the right of nonresident aliens to inherit). The applicable foreign law is, however, to be determined in accordance with the judicial notice provisions of the Evidence Code. Estate of Gogabashvele, 195 Cal.App.2d 503, 16 Cal.Rptr. 77 (1961).

§ 311. Determination of foreign law. If the law of an organization of nations, a foreign nation or a state other than this state, or a public entity in a foreign nation or a state other than this state, is applicable and such law cannot be determined, the court may, as the ends of justice require, either:

(a) Apply the law of this state if the court can do so consistently with the Constitution of the United States and the Constitution of this state; or

(b) Dismiss the action without prejudice or, in the case of a reviewing court, remand the case to the trial court with directions to dismiss the action without prejudice.

Assembly Committee on Judiciary Comment

Insofar as it relates to the law of foreign nations, Section 311 restates the substance of and supersedes the last paragraph of Section 1875 of the Code of Civil Procedure. * * *

The last paragraph of Section 1875, which Section 311 supersedes, applies, "if the court is unable to determine" the applicable foreign law. Instead, Section 311 comes into operation if the applicable out-of-state law "cannot be determined." This revised language emphasizes that every effort should be made by the court to determine the applicable law before the case is otherwise disposed of under Section 311.

The reason why the court cannot determine the applicable foreign or sister-state law may be that the parties have not provided the court with sufficient information to make such determination. In such a case, the court may, of course, grant the parties additional time within which to obtain such information and make it available to the court. If they fail to obtain such information and the court is not satisfied that they made a reasonable effort to do so, the court may dismiss the action without prejudice. On the other hand, where counsel have made a reasonable effort and when all sources of information as to the applicable foreign or sister-state law are exhausted and the court cannot determine it, the court may either apply California law, within constitutional limits, or dismiss the action without prejudice.

§ 312. Jury as trier of fact. Except as otherwise provided by law, where the trial is by jury:

(a) All questions of fact are to be decided by the jury.

(b) Subject to the control of the court, the jury is to determine the effect and value of the evidence addressed to it, including the credibility of witnesses and hearsay declarants.

Chapter 3. Order of Proof

§ 320. Power of court to regulate order of proof. Except as otherwise provided by law, the court in its discretion shall regulate the order of proof.

Law Revision Commission Comment

* * *

Directions of the trial judge which control the order of proof should be distinguished from those which actually exclude evidence. Obviously, it is not permissible, through repeated directions of the order of proof, to prevent a party from presenting relevant evidence on a disputed fact. Foster v. Keating, 120 Cal.App.2d 435, 261 P.2d 529 (1953); California Civil Procedure During Trial, Parrish, Order of Proof, 205, 210 (Cal.Cont.Ed.Bar 1960). See also Murry v. Manley, 170 Cal.App.2d 364, 338 P.2d 976 (1959).

Chapter 4. Admitting and Excluding Evidence

Article 1. General Provisions

§ 350. Only relevant evidence admissible. No evidence is admissible except relevant evidence.

§ 351. Admissibility of relevant evidence. Except as otherwise provided by statute, all relevant evidence is admissible.

Law Revision Commission Comment

Section 351 abolishes all limitations on the admissibility of relevant evidence except those that are based on a statute, including a constitutional provision. See Evidence Code § 230. The Evidence Code contains a number of provisions that exclude relevant evidence either for reasons of public policy or because the evidence is too unreliable to be presented to the trier of fact. See, e.g., Evidence Code § 352 (cumulative, unduly prejudicial, etc. evidence), §§ 900-1070 (privileges), §§ 1100-1156 (extrinsic policies), § 1200 (hearsay). Other codes also contain provisions that may in some cases result in the exclusion of relevant evidence. See, e.g., Civil Code §§ 79.06, 79.09, 227; Code Civ.Proc. § 1747; Educ.Code § 14026; Fin.Code § 8754; Fish & Game Code § 7923; Govt.Code §§ 15619, 18573, 18934, 18952, 20134, 31532; Health & Saf.Code §§ 211.5, 410; Ins.Code §§ 735, 855, 10381.5; Labor Code § 6319; Penal Code §§ 290, 938.1, 3046, 3107, 11105; Pub.Res.Code § 3234; Rev. & Tax.Code §§ 16563, 19282-19289; Unempl.Ins.Code §§ 1094, 2111, 2714; Vehicle Code §§ 1808, 16005, 20012-20015, 40803, 40804, 40832, 40833; Water Code § 12516; Welf. & Inst.Code §§ 118, 827.

§ 351.1. Polygraph examinations; results, opinion of examiner or reference; exclusion.

(a) Notwithstanding any other provision of law, the results of a polygraph examination, the opinion of a polygraph examiner, or any reference to an offer to take, failure to take, or taking of a polygraph examination, shall not be admitted into evidence in any criminal proceeding, including pretrial and post conviction motions and hearings, or in any trial or hearing of a juvenile for a criminal offense, whether heard in juvenile or adult court, unless all parties stipulate to the admission of such results.

(b) Nothing in this section is intended to exclude from evidence statements made during a polygraph examination which are otherwise admissible. [*Added 1983.*]

Case Note

Even if the results of a particular polygraph examination could be shown to satisfy the *Frye/Kelly* test (see § 720, *infra*), they would be inadmissible because of the categorical exclusion imposed by this section. People v. Wilkinson, 33 Cal. 4th 821, 16 Cal. Rptr 3d 420, 94 P.3d 551 (2004).

§ 351.2. Evidence of immigration status – personal injury or wrongful death. (a) In a civil action for personal injury or wrongful death, evidence of a person's immigration status shall not be admitted into evidence, nor shall discovery into a person's immigration status be permitted.

(b) This section does not affect the standards of relevance, admissibility, or discovery prescribed by Section 3339 of the Civil Code, Section 7285 of the Government Code, Section 24000 of the Health and Safety Code, and Section 1171.5 of the Labor Code. [*Added 2017.*]

§ 351.3. Evidence of immigration status – civil cases generally. (a) In a civil action not governed by Section 351.2, evidence of a person's immigration status shall not be disclosed in open court by a party or his or her attorney unless the judge presiding over the matter first determines that the evidence is admissible in an in camera hearing requested by the party seeking disclosure of the person's immigration status.

(b) This section does not do any of the following:

(1) Apply to cases in which a person's immigration status is necessary to prove an element of a claim or an affirmative defense.

(2) Impact otherwise applicable laws governing the relevance of immigration status to liability or the standards applicable to inquiries regarding immigration status in discovery or proceedings in a civil action, including Section 3339 of the Civil Code, Section 7285 of the Government Code, Section 24000 of the Health and Safety Code, and Section 1171.5 of the Labor Code.

(3) Prohibit a person or his or her attorney from voluntarily revealing his or her immigration status to the court.

(c) This section shall remain in effect only until January 1, 2022, and as of that date is repealed.
[*Added effective May 17, 2018. Repealed as of January 1, 2022, by its own provisions.*]

§ 351.4. Evidence of immigration status – criminal cases. (a) In a criminal action, evidence of a person's immigration status shall not be disclosed in open court by a party or his or her attorney unless the judge presiding over the matter first determines that the evidence is admissible in an in camera hearing requested by the party seeking disclosure of the person's immigration status.

(b) This section does not do any of the following:

(1) Apply to cases in which a person's immigration status is necessary to prove an element of an offense or an affirmative defense.

(2) Limit discovery in a criminal action.

(3) Prohibit a person or his or her attorney from voluntarily revealing his or her immigration status to

(c) This section shall remain in effect only until January 1, 2022, and as of that date is repealed. [*Added effective May 17, 2018. Repealed as of January 1, 2022, by its own provisions.*]

§ 352. Discretion of court to exclude evidence. The court in its discretion may exclude evidence if its probative value is substantially outweighed by the probability that its admission will (a) necessitate undue consumption of time or (b) create substantial danger of undue prejudice, of confusing the issues, or of misleading the jury.

Case Notes

Doubts about witness's credibility are not a sufficient basis to exclude testimony. People v. Cudjo, 6 Cal. 4th 585, 610, 25 Cal. Rptr. 2d 390, 405-406, 863 P.2d 635, 650-651 (1993).

Fact that a witness, in prior testimony in the same proceedings, directly contradicted himself on the point of his testimony is not a legitimate basis for excluding his testimony. Vulnerability to impeachment does not render evidence irrelevant or unduly prejudicial. People v. Alcala, 4 Cal. 4th 742, 790, 15 Cal. Rptr. 2d 432, 461, 842 P.2d 1192, 1221 (1992, modified, 1993).

Evidence of poverty or indebtedness is generally inadmissible to establish a motive to commit robbery because the probative value of such evidence is outweighed by the risk of unfair prejudice to the defendant, but such evidence may be admissible to refute a defendant's claim that he did not commit the robbery because he did not need the money. People v. Wilson, 3 Cal. 4th 926, 938-939, 13 Cal. Rptr. 2d 259, 266, 838 P.2d 1212, 1219 (1992).

§ 352.1. Criminal sex acts; victim's address and telephone number. In any criminal proceeding under Section 261, 262, or 264.1, subdivision (d) of Section 286, or subdivision (d) of Section 287 of, or former Section 288a of, the Penal Code, or in any criminal proceeding under subdivision (c) of Section 286 or subdivision (c) of Section 287 of, or former Section 288a of, the Penal Code in which the defendant is alleged to have compelled the participation of the victim by force, violence, duress, menace, or threat of great bodily harm, the district attorney may, upon written motion with notice to the defendant or the defendant's attorney, if he or she is represented by an attorney, within a reasonable time prior to any hearing, move to exclude from evidence the current address and telephone number of any victim at the hearing.

The court may order that evidence of the victim's current address and telephone number be excluded from any hearings conducted pursuant to the criminal proceeding if the court finds that the probative value of the evidence is outweighed by the creation of substantial danger to the victim.

Nothing in this section shall abridge or limit the defendant's right to discover or investigate the information. [*Added 1985. Amended 1996, 2018.*]

§ 353. Effect of erroneous admission of evidence. A verdict or finding shall not be set aside, nor shall the judgment or decision based thereon be reversed, by reason of the erroneous admission of evidence unless:

(a) There appears of record an objection to or a motion to exclude or to strike the evidence that was timely made and so stated as to make clear the specific ground of the objection or motion; and

(b) The court which passes upon the effect of the error or errors is of the opinion that the admitted evidence should have been excluded on the ground stated and that the error or errors complained of resulted in a miscarriage of justice.

Assembly Committee on Judiciary Comment

* * * Section 353 does not specify the form in which an objection must be made; hence, the use of a continuing objection to a line of questioning would be proper under Section 353 just as it is under existing law. See Witkin, California Evidence § 708 (1958).

* * * Section 353 is, of course, subject to the constitutional requirement that a judgment must be reversed if an error has resulted in a denial of due process of law. People v. Matteson, 61 Cal.2d 466, 39 Cal.Rptr. 1, 393 P.2d 161 (1964).

§ 354. Effect of erroneous exclusion of evidence. A verdict or finding shall not be set aside, nor shall the judgment or decision based thereon be reversed, by reason of the erroneous exclusion of evidence unless the court which passes upon the effect of the error or errors is of the opinion that the error or errors complained of resulted in a miscarriage of justice and it appears of record that:

(a) The substance, purpose, and relevance of the excluded evidence was made known to the court by the questions asked, an offer of proof, or by any other means;

(b) The rulings of the court made compliance with subdivision (a) futile; or

(c) The evidence was sought by questions asked during cross-examination or recross-examination.

Law Revision Commission Comment

Section 354, like Section 353, reiterates the requirement of the California Constitution that a judgment may not be reversed, nor may a new trial be granted, because of an error unless the error is prejudicial. Cal.Const., Art. VI, § 4 2.

The provisions of Section 354 that require an offer of proof or other disclosure of the evidence improperly excluded reflect existing law. See Witkin, California Evidence § 713 (1958). The exceptions to this requirement that are stated in Section 354 also reflect existing law. Thus, an offer of proof is unnecessary where the judge has limited the issues so that an offer to prove matters related to excluded issues would be futile. Lawless v. Calaway, 24 Cal.2d 81, 91, 147 P.2d 604, 609 (1944). An offer of proof is also unnecessary when an objection is improperly sustained to a question on cross-examination. Tossman v. Newman, 37 Cal.2d 522, 525-526, 233 P.2d 1, 3 (1951) ("no offer of proof is necessary in order to obtain a review of rulings on cross-examination"); People v. Jones, 160 Cal. 358, 117 Pac. 176 (1911).

§ 355. Limited admissibility. When evidence is admissible as to one party or for one purpose and is inadmissible as to another party or for another purpose, the court upon request shall restrict the evidence to its proper scope and instruct the jury accordingly.

Case Note

Where the admissible purpose of evidence is of modest value and the inadmissible purpose is extremely prejudicial, a limiting instruction may not remedy the problem, and exclusion under § 352 may be required. People v. Coleman, 38 Cal.3d 69, 81-86, 211 Cal. Rptr. 102, 108-112, 695 P.2d 189, 195-199 (1985).

Law Revision Commission Comment

Section 355 codifies existing law which requires the court to instruct the jury as to the limited purpose for which evidence may be considered when such evidence is admissible for one purpose and inadmissible for another. See Adkins v. Brett, 184 Cal. 252, 193 Pac. 251 (1920).

Under Section 352, as under existing law, the judge is permitted to exclude such evidence if he deems it so prejudicial that a limiting instruction would not protect a party adequately and the matter in question can be proved sufficiently by other evidence. See discussion in Adkins v. Brett, 184 Cal. 252, 258, 193 Pac. 251, 254 (1920); Tentative Recommendation and a Study Relating to the Uniform Rules of Evidence (Article VI. Extrinsic Policies Affecting Admissibility), 6 Cal.Law Revision Comm'n, Rep., Rec. & Studies 601, 612, 639-640 (1964).

§ 356. Entire act, declaration, conversation, or writing may be brought out to elucidate part offered. Where part of an act, declaration, conversation, or writing is given in evidence by one party, the whole on the same subject may be inquired into by an adverse party; when a letter is read, the answer may be given; and when a detached act, declaration, conversation, or writing is given in evidence, any other act, declaration, conversation, or writing which is necessary to make it understood may also be given in evidence.

Assembly Committee on Judiciary Comment

* * * The rule stated in Section 356 * * * only makes admissible such parts of an act, declaration, conversation, or writing as are relevant to the part thereof previously given in evidence. See, e.g., Witt v. Jackson, 57 Cal.2d 57, 67, 17 Cal.Rptr. 369, 374, 366 P.2d 641, 646 (1961) (the rule "is necessarily subject to the qualification that the court may exclude those portions of the conversation not relevant to the items thereof which have been introduced"). See also Evidence Code § 350.

Article 2. Preliminary Determinations on Admissibility of Evidence

§ 400. Preliminary fact. As used in this article [§§ 400-406], "preliminary fact" means a fact upon the existence or nonexistence of which depends the admissibility or inadmissibility of evidence. The phrase "the admissibility or inadmissibility of evidence" includes the qualification or disqualification of a person to be a witness and the existence or nonexistence of a privilege.

Law Revision Commission Comment

"Preliminary fact" is defined to distinguish those facts upon which the admissibility of evidence depends from those facts sought to be proved by that evidence.

§ 401. Proffered evidence. As used in this article [§§ 400-406], "proffered evidence" means evidence, the admissibility or inadmissibility of which is dependent upon the existence or nonexistence of a preliminary fact.

Law Revision Commission Comment

"Proffered evidence" is defined to avoid confusion between evidence whose admissibility is in question and evidence offered on the preliminary fact issue. "Proffered evidence" includes such matters as the testimony to be elicited from a witness who is claimed to be disqualified, testimony or tangible evidence claimed to be privileged, and any other evidence to which objection is made.

§ 402. Procedure for determining foundational and other preliminary facts. (a) When the existence of a preliminary fact is disputed, its existence or nonexistence shall be determined as provided in this article [§§ 400-406].

(b) The court may hear and determine the question of the admissibility of evidence out of the presence or hearing of the jury; but in a criminal action, the court shall hear and determine the question of the admissibility of a confession or admission of the defendant out of the presence and hearing of the jury if any party so requests.

(c) A ruling on the admissibility of evidence implies whatever finding of fact is prerequisite thereto; a separate or formal finding is unnecessary unless required by statute.

Note on Proposed Amendment

The Law Revision Commission tentatively decided in September 2004 to recommend that § 402(b) be amended to require that in a criminal action a hearing on the admissibility of a confession or admission by the defendant be held out of the presence and hearing of the jury, whether or not requested.

Assembly Committee on Judiciary Comment

Under Section 310, the court must decide preliminary questions of fact upon which the admissibility of evidence depends. Section 402 prescribes certain procedures that must be observed by the court when making such preliminary determinations.

Subdivision (a). Subdivision (a) requires the judge to observe the procedures specified in Article 2 (commencing with Section 400) when he is determining disputed factual questions preliminary to the admission or exclusion of evidence. The provisions of Article 2 are designed to distinguish clearly between (1) those situations where the judge must be persuaded of the existence of the preliminary fact upon which admissibility depends and (2) those situations where the judge must admit the proffered evidence merely upon the introduction of evidence sufficient to sustain a finding of the preliminary fact. Under the Evidence Code, as under existing law, the judge determines some preliminary fact questions on the basis of all of the evidence presented to him by both parties, resolving any conflicts in that evidence. Evidence Code § 405. See, e.g., People v. Glab, 13 Cal.App.2d 528, 57 P.2d 588 (1936) (judge considered conflicting evidence and decided that a proposed witness was not married to the defendant and, therefore, was competent to testify). See also Fairbank v. Hughson, 58 Cal. 314 (1881) (error to permit jury to determine whether witness was an expert). On the other hand, the judge does not always resolve conflicts in the evidence submitted on preliminary fact questions; in some cases, the proffered evidence must be admitted if there is evidence sufficient to sustain a finding of the preliminary fact. Evidence Code § 403. See, e.g., Reed v. Clark, 47 Cal. 194, 200 (1873); Verzan v. McGregor, 23 Cal. 339 (1863).

Subdivision (b). Subdivision (b) requires the judge, on request, to determine the admissibility of a confession or admission of a criminal defendant out of the presence and hearing of the jury. Under existing law, whether the preliminary hearing is held out of the presence of the jury is left to the judge's discretion. People v. Gonzales, 24 Cal.2d 870, 151 P.2d 251 (1944); People v. Nelson, 90 Cal.App. 27, 31, 265 Pac. 366, 367 (1928). The existing procedure permits the jury to hear evidence that may be extremely prejudicial. For example, in People v. Black, 73 Cal.App. 13, 238 Pac. 374 (1925), the alleged coercion consisted of threats to send the defendants to New Mexico to be prosecuted for murder. Subdivision (b) prevents this kind of prejudice. Nothing in subdivision (b) precludes a defendant from presenting to the jury evidence attacking the credibility of a confession that is admitted (Evidence Code § 406), and such evidence may include some of the same matters presented to the judge during the preliminary hearing.

Subdivision (c). Subdivision (c) codifies existing law. Wilcox v. Berry, 32 Cal.2d 189, 195 P.2d 414 (1948) (where evidence is properly received, the ground of the court's ruling is immaterial); City & County of San Francisco v. Western Air Lines, Inc., 204 Cal.App.2d 105, 22 Cal.Rptr. 216 (1962) (where evidence is excluded, the ruling will be upheld if any ground exists for the exclusion).

§ 403. Determination of foundational and other preliminary facts where relevancy, personal. knowledge, or authenticity is disputed. (a) The proponent of the proffered evidence has the burden of producing evidence as to the existence of the preliminary fact, and the proffered evidence is inadmissible unless the court finds that there is evidence sufficient to sustain a finding of the existence of the preliminary fact, when:

(1) The relevance of the proffered evidence depends on the existence of the preliminary fact;

(2) The preliminary fact is the personal knowledge of a witness concerning the subject matter of his testimony;

(3) The preliminary fact is the authenticity of a writing; or

(4) The proffered evidence is of a statement or other conduct of a particular person and the preliminary fact is whether that person made the statement or so conducted himself.

(b) Subject to Section 702, the court may admit conditionally the proffered evidence under this section, subject to evidence of the preliminary fact being supplied later in the course of the trial.

(c) If the court admits the proffered evidence under this section, the court:

(1) May, and on request shall, instruct the jury to determine whether the preliminary fact exists and to disregard the proffered evidence unless the jury finds that the preliminary fact does exist.

(2) Shall instruct the jury to disregard the proffered evidence if the court subsequently determines that a jury could not reasonably find that the preliminary fact exists.

Assembly Committee on Judiciary Comment

As indicated in the Comment to Section 402, the judge does not determine in all instances whether a preliminary fact exists or does not exist. At times, the judge must admit the proffered evidence if there is evidence sufficient to sustain a finding of the preliminary fact, and the jury must finally decide whether the preliminary fact exists. See, e.g., Verzan v. McGregor, 23 Cal. 339 (1863). Section 403 covers those situations in which the judge is required to admit the proffered evidence upon the introduction of evidence sufficient to sustain a finding of the preliminary fact.

Subdivision (a)

Some writers have attempted to distinguish the kinds of questions to be decided under the standard prescribed in Section 403 from the kinds of questions to be decided under the standard described in Section 405 on the ground that the former questions involve the relevancy of the proffered evidence while the latter questions involve the competency of evidence that is relevant. Maguire & Epstein, Preliminary Questions of Fact in Determining the Admissibility of Evidence, 40 Harv.L.Rev. 392 (1927); Morgan, Functions of Judge and Jury in the Determination of Preliminary Questions of Fact, 43 Harv.L.Rev. 165 (1929). It is difficult, however, to distinguish all preliminary fact questions upon this principle. And eminent legal authorities sometimes differ over whether a particular preliminary fact question is one of relevancy or competency. For example, Wigmore classifies admissions with questions of relevancy (4 Wigmore, Evidence 1 (3d ed. 1940)) while Morgan classifies admissions with questions of competency to be decided under the standard prescribed in Section 405 (Morgan, Basic Problems of Evidence 244 (1957)).

To eliminate uncertainties of classification, subdivision (a) lists the kinds of preliminary fact questions that are to be determined under the standard prescribed in Section 403. And to eliminate any uncertainties that are not resolved by this listing, various Evidence Code sections state specifically that admissibility depends on "evidence sufficient to sustain a finding" of certain facts. See, e.g., Evidence Code §§ 1222, 1223, 1400.

The preliminary fact questions listed in subdivision (a), or identified elsewhere as matters to be determined under the Section 403 standard, are not finally decided by the judge because they have been traditionally regarded as jury questions. The questions involve the credibility of testimony or the probative value of evidence that is admitted on the ultimate issues. It is the jury's function to determine the effect and value of the evidence addressed to it. Evidence Code § 312. Hence, the judge's function on questions of this sort is merely to determine whether there is evidence sufficient to permit a jury to decide the question. The "question of admissibility . . . merges imperceptibly into the weight of the evidence, if admitted." Di Carlo v. United States, 6 F.2d 364, 367 (2d Cir.1925). If the judge finally determined the existence or nonexistence of the preliminary fact, he would deprive a party of a jury decision on a question that the party has a right to have decided by the jury.

For example, if the question of A's title to land is in issue, A may seek to prove his title by a deed from former owner O. Section 1401 requires that the deed be authenticated, and the judge, under Section 403, must rule on the question of authentication. If A introduces evidence sufficient to sustain a finding of the genuineness of the deed, the judge is required to admit it. If the rule were otherwise and the judge, on the basis of the adverse party's evidence, were permitted to decide that the deed was spurious and not admissible, the judge would be resolving the basic factual issue in the case and A would be deprived of a jury finding on the issue, even though he is entitled to a jury decision and even though he has introduced evidence sufficient to warrant a jury finding in his favor.

Illustrative of the preliminary fact questions that should be decided under Section 403 are the following:

Section 350—Relevancy. Under existing law, as under Section 403, if the relevancy of proffered evidence depends on the existence of some preliminary fact, the evidence is admissible if there is evidence sufficient to warrant a jury finding of the preliminary fact. Reed v. Clark, 47 Cal. 194, 200 (1873). Thus, for example, if P sues D upon an alleged agreement, evidence of negotiations with A is inadmissible because irrelevant unless A is shown to be D's agent; but the evidence of the negotiations with A is admissible if there is evidence sufficient to sustain a finding of the agency. Brown v. Spencer, 163 Cal. 589, 126 Pac. 493 (1912). The same rule is applicable when a person is charged with criminal responsibility for the acts of another because they are conspirators. See discussion in People v. Steccone, 36 Cal.2d 234, 238, 223 P.2d 17, 19 (1950).

Section 702—Requirement of personal knowledge. Evidence sufficient to sustain a finding of a witness' personal knowledge seems to be sufficient under the existing California practice. See, e.g., People v. Avery, 35 Cal.2d 487, 492, 218 P.2d 527, 530 (1950) ("Bolton testified that he observed the incident about which he testified. His testimony, therefore, was not incompetent under section 1845 of the Code of Civil Procedure."); People v. McCarthy, 14 Cal.App. 148, 151, 111 Pac. 274, 275 (1910). See also Tentative Recommendation and a Study Relating to the Uniform Rules of Evidence (Article IV. Witnesses), 6 Cal.Law Revision Comm'n, Rep., Rec. & Studies 701, 711-713 (1964).

Section 788—Conviction of a crime when offered to attack credibility. In this situation, the preliminary fact issue to be decided under Section 403 is whether the witness is actually the person who was convicted. This involves the relevancy of the evidence (since, obviously, the conviction of another does not affect the witness' credibility) and should be a question to be resolved by the jury. The judge should not be able to decide finally that it was the witness who was convicted and, thus, to prevent a contest on that issue before the jury. The existing law is uncertain in this regard; however, it seems likely that any evidence sufficient to identify the witness as the person convicted is sufficient to warrant admission of the conviction. See People v. Theodore, 121 Cal.App.2d 17, 28, 262 P.2d 630, 637 (1953) (relying on presumption of identity of person from identity of name).

Section 800—Requirement that lay opinion be based on personal perception. The requirement specified in Section 800 is merely a specific application of the personal knowledge requirement in Section 702. See the discussion of Section 702 in this Comment, supra.

Sections 1200-1341—Identity of hearsay declarant. For most hearsay evidence, admissibility depends upon two preliminary determinations: (1) Did the declarant actually make the statement as claimed by the proponent of the evidence? (2) Does the statement meet certain standards of trustworthiness required by some exception to the hearsay rule?

The first determination involves the relevancy of the evidence. For example, if the issue is the state of mind of X, a person's statement as to his state of mind has no tendency to prove X's state of mind unless the declarant was X. Relevancy depends on the fact that X made the statement. Accordingly, if otherwise competent, a hearsay statement is admitted upon evidence sufficient to sustain a finding that the claimed declarant made the statement.

The second determination involves the competency of the evidence. Unless the evidence meets the requisite standards of an exception to the hearsay rule, it must be kept from the trier of fact despite its relevancy either because it is too unreliable or because public policy requires its suppression. For example, if an admission was in fact made by a defendant to a criminal action, the admission is relevant. But public policy requires that the admission be held inadmissible if it was not given voluntarily.

The admissibility of some hearsay declarations is dependent solely upon the determination that a particular declarant made the statement. Some of these exceptions to the hearsay rule—such as inconsistent statements of trial witnesses and admissions—are mentioned specifically below. Since the only preliminary fact to be determined in regard to these declarations involves the relevancy of the evidence, they should be admitted upon the introduction of evidence sufficient to sustain a finding of the preliminary fact.

When the admissibility of hearsay depends both upon a determination that a particular declarant made the statement and upon a determination that the requisite standards of a hearsay exception have been met, the former determination is to be made upon evidence sufficient to sustain a finding of the preliminary fact. Paragraph (4) is included in subdivision (a) to make this clear.

Section 1220—Admissions of a party. The only preliminary fact that is subject to dispute is the identity of the declarant. Under Section 403(a)(4), an admission is admissible upon the introduction of evidence sufficient to sustain a finding that the party made the statement. Existing law appears to be in accord. Eastman v. Means, 75 Cal.App. 537, 242 Pac. 1089 (1925).

An admission is not admissible in a criminal case unless it was given voluntarily. The voluntariness of an admission by a criminal defendant is determined under Section 405, not Section 403.

Sections 1221, 1222—Authorized and adoptive admissions. Under existing law, both authorized admissions (by an agent of a party) and adoptive admissions are admitted upon the introduction of evidence sufficient to sustain a finding of the foundational fact. Sample v. Round Mountain Citrus Farm Co., 29 Cal.App. 547, 156 Pac. 983 (1916) (authorized admission); Southers v. Savage, 191 Cal.App.2d 100, 12 Cal.Rptr. 470 (1961) (adoptive admission).

Section 1223—Admission of co-conspirator. The admission of a co-conspirator is another form of an authorized admission. Hence, the proffered evidence is admissible upon the introduction of evidence sufficient to sustain a finding of the conspiracy. Existing law is in accord. People v. Robinson, 43 Cal.2d 132, 137, 271 P.2d 865, 868 (1954).

Sections 1224-1227—Admission of third person whose liability, breach of duty, or right is in issue. The only preliminary fact subject to dispute is the identity of the declarant; and the preliminary showing required in regard to this class of admissions is the same as if the declarant were being sued directly. Any evidence of the making of the statement by the claimed declarant is sufficient to warrant its admission. Existing law is in accord. See Langley v. Zurich General Acc. & Liab. Ins. Co., 219 Cal. 101, 25 P.2d 418 (1933). Although Sections 1226 and 1227 are new to California law, the same principles should be applicable.

Sections 1235, 1236—Previous statements of witnesses. Prior inconsistent statements and prior consistent statements made before bias or other improper motive arose are dealt with in Sections 1235 and 1236. In each case, the evidence is relevant and probative if the witnesses to the statements are credible. The credibility of the witnesses testifying to these statements should be decided finally by the jury. Moreover, the only preliminary fact subject to dispute insofar as alleged inconsistent statements are concerned is the identity of the declarant. Hence, evidence is admitted under these sections upon the introduction of evidence sufficient to sustain a finding of the preliminary fact. The existing practice seems to be consistent with Section 403. See Schneider v. Market Street Ry., 134 Cal. 482, 492, 66 Pac. 734, 738 (1901) ("Whether the [prior inconsistent] statements made to Glassman and Hubbell were made by Meley, or by some other man, was a question for the jury. Both witnesses testified that they were made by him."); People v. Neely, 163 Cal.App.2d 289, 312, 329 P.2d 357, 371 (1958) (two prior consistent statements held admissible because the "jury could properly infer . . . the motive to fabricate did arise after the making of the two statements").

Sections 1400-1402—Authentication of writings. Under existing law, an otherwise competent writing is admissible upon the introduction of evidence sufficient to sustain a finding of the authenticity of the writing. Verzan v. McGregor, 23 Cal. 339 (1863). Section 403(a)(3) retains this existing law.

Sections 1410-1421—Means of authenticating writings. Sections 1410 through 1421 merely state several ways in which the requirements of Sections 1400 through 1402 may be met. Hence, to the extent that Sections 1410 through 1421 specify facts that may be shown to authenticate writings, the same principles apply: In each case, the judge must decide whether the evidence offered is sufficient to sustain a finding of the authenticity of the proffered writing and admit the writing if there is such evidence. Care should be exercised, however, to distinguish those cases where the disputed preliminary fact is the authenticity of an exemplar with which the proffered writing is to be compared (Evidence Code §§ 1417-1419) or the qualification of a witness to give an opinion concerning the authenticity of a writing (Evidence Code §§ 1416, 1418); the judge is required to determine such questions under the provisions of Section 405.

Subdivision (b)

Subdivision (b) restates the apparent meaning of Section 1834 of the Code of Civil Procedure. Under this subdivision, the judge may receive evidence that is conditionally admissible under Section 403, subject to the presentation of evidence of the preliminary fact later in the course of the trial. See Brea v. McGlashan, 3 Cal.App.2d 454, 465, 39 P.2d 877, 882 (1934).

Subdivision (c)

Subdivision (c) relates to the instructions to be given the jury when evidence is admitted whose admissibility depends on the existence of a preliminary fact determined under Section 403. When such evidence is admitted, the jury is required to make the ultimate determination of the existence of the preliminary fact. Unless the jury is persuaded that the preliminary fact exists, it is not permitted to consider the evidence.

For example, if P offers evidence of his negotiations with A in his contract action against D, the judge must admit the evidence if there is other evidence sufficient to sustain a finding that A was D's agent. If the jury is not persuaded that A was in fact D's agent, then it is not permitted to consider the evidence of the negotiations with A in determining D's liability.

Frequently, the jury's duty to disregard conditionally admissible evidence when it is not persuaded of the existence of the preliminary fact on which relevancy is conditioned is so clear that an instruction to this effect is unnecessary. For example, if the disputed preliminary fact is the authenticity of a deed, it hardly seems necessary to instruct the jury to disregard the deed if it should find that the deed is not genuine. No rational jury could find the deed to be spurious and, yet, to be still effective to transfer title from the purported grantor.

At times, however, it is not quite so clear that conditionally admissible evidence should be disregarded unless the preliminary fact is found to exist. In such cases, the jury should be appropriately instructed. For example, the theory upon which agent's and co-conspirator's statements are admissible is that the party is vicariously responsible for the acts and statements of agents and co-conspirators within the scope of the agency or conspiracy. Yet, it is not always clear that statements made by a purported agent or co-conspirator should be disregarded if not made in furtherance of the agency or conspiracy. Hence, the jury should be instructed to disregard such statements unless it is persuaded that the statements were made within the scope of the agency or conspiracy. People v. Geiger, 49 Cal. 643, 649 (1875); People v. Talbott, 65 Cal.App.2d 654, 663, 151 P.2d 317, 322 (1944). Subdivision (c), therefore, permits the judge in any case to instruct the jury to disregard conditionally admissible evidence unless it is persuaded of the existence of the preliminary fact; further, subdivision (c) requires the judge to give such an instruction whenever he is requested by a party to do so.

§ 404. Determination of whether proffered evidence is incriminatory. Whenever the proffered evidence is claimed to be privileged under Section 940, the person claiming the privilege has the burden of showing that the proffered evidence might tend to incriminate him; and the proffered evidence is inadmissible unless it clearly appears to the court that the proffered evidence cannot possibly have a tendency to incriminate the person claiming the privilege.

Law Revision Commission Comment

Section 404 provides a special procedure to be followed by the judge when an objection is made in reliance upon the privilege against self-incrimination. Under Section 404, the objecting party has the burden of showing that the testimony sought might incriminate him. However, the party is not required to produce evidence as such. In addition to considering evidence, the judge must consider the matters disclosed in argument, the implications of the question, the setting in which it is asked, the applicable statute of limitations, and all other relevant factors. See Cohen v. Superior Court, 173 Cal.App.2d 61, 70, 343 P.2d 286, 291 (1959). Nonetheless, the burden is on the objector to present to the judge information of this sort sufficient to indicate that the proffered evidence might incriminate him. If he presents information of this sort, Section 404 requires the judge to sustain the claim of privilege unless it clearly appears that the proffered evidence cannot possibly have a tendency to incriminate the person claiming the privilege.

Section 404 is consistent with existing law: The party claiming the privilege "has the burden of showing that the testimony which was being required might be used in a prosecution to help establish his guilt"; the court may require testimony to be given only if it clearly appears to the court that the claim of privilege is mistaken and that any answer "'cannot possibly'" have a tendency to incriminate the witness. Cohen v. Superior Court, 173 Cal.App.2d 61, 68, 70-72, 343 P.2d 286, 290, 291-292 (1959).

§ 405. Determination of foundational and other preliminary facts in other cases. With respect to preliminary fact determinations not governed by Section 403 or 404:

(a) When the existence of a preliminary fact is disputed, the court shall indicate which party has the burden of producing evidence and the burden of proof on the issue as implied by the rule of law under which the question arises. The court shall determine the existence or nonexistence of the preliminary fact and shall admit or exclude the proffered evidence as required by the rule of law under which the question arises.

(b) If a preliminary fact is also a fact in issue in the action:

(1) The jury shall not be informed of the court's determination as to the existence or nonexistence of the preliminary fact.

(2) If the proffered evidence is admitted, the jury shall not be instructed to disregard the evidence if its determination of the fact differs from the court's determination of the preliminary fact.

Note on Proposed Amendment

The Law Revision Commission tentatively decided in September 2004 to recommend that § 405 be amended to conform to FRE 104(a), so that, in making its determination of a preliminary fact other than one relating to relevance, the court is not bound by the rules of evidence except those relating to privilege.

Case Note

When the existence of a preliminary fact is disputed, it is for the court, not the jury, to determine the existence or nonexistence of the preliminary fact, and the issue should not be submitted to the jury for redetermination. People v. Alcala, 4 Cal. 4th 742, 787, 15 Cal. Rptr. 2d 432, 458, 842 P.2d 1192, 1218 (1992, modified, 1993).

Assembly Committee on Judiciary Comment

Section 405 requires the judge to determine the existence or nonexistence of disputed preliminary facts except in certain situations covered by Sections 403 and 404. Section 405 deals with evidentiary rules designed to withhold evidence from the jury because it is too unreliable to be evaluated properly or because public policy requires its exclusion.

Under Section 405, the judge first indicates to the parties who has the burden of proof and the burden of producing evidence on the disputed issue as implied by the rule of law under which the question arises. For example, Section 1200 indicates that the burden of proof is usually on the proponent of the evidence to show that the proffered evidence is within a hearsay exception. Thus, if the disputed preliminary fact is whether the proffered statement was spontaneous, as required by Section 1240, the proponent would have the burden of persuading the judge as to the spontaneity of the statement. On the other hand, the privilege rules usually place the burden of proof on the objecting party to show that a privilege is applicable. Thus, if the disputed preliminary fact is whether a person is married to a party and, hence, whether their confidential communications are privileged under Section 980, the burden of proof is on the party asserting the privilege to persuade the judge of the existence of the marriage.

After the judge has indicated to the parties who has the burden of proof and the burden of producing evidence, the parties submit their evidence on the preliminary issue to the judge. If the judge is persuaded by the party with the burden of proof, he finds in favor of that party in regard to the preliminary fact and either admits or excludes the proffered evidence as required by the rule of law under which the question arises. Otherwise, he finds against that party on the preliminary fact and either admits or excludes the proffered evidence as required by such finding.

* * *

Examples of preliminary fact issues to be decided under Section 405

Illustrative of the preliminary fact questions that should be decided under Section 405 are the following:

Section 701—Disqualification of a witness for lack of mental capacity. Under existing law, as under this code, the party objecting to a proffered witness has the burden of proving the witness' lack of capacity. People v. Craig, 111 Cal. 460, 469, 44 Pac. 186, 188 (1896); People v. Tyree, 21 Cal.App. 701, 706, 132 Pac. 784, 786 (1913) (disapproved) on other grounds in People v. McCaughan, 49 Cal.2d 409, 420, 317 P.2d 974, 981 (1957)).

Section 720—Qualifications of an expert witness. Under Section 720, as under existing law, the proponent must persuade the judge that his expert is qualified, and it is error for the judge to submit the qualifications of the expert to the jury. Fairbank v. Hughson, 58 Cal. 314 (1881); Eble v. Peluso, 80 Cal.App.2d 154, 181 P.2d 680 (1947).

Section 788—Conviction of a crime when offered to attack credibility. If the disputed preliminary fact is whether a pardon or some similar relief has been granted to a witness convicted of a crime, the judge's determination is made under Section 405. Cf. Comment to Section 403.

Section 870—Opinion evidence on sanity. Whether a witness is sufficiently acquainted with a person whose sanity is in question to be qualified to express an opinion on the matter involves, in effect, the expertise of the witness on that limited subject. The witness' qualifications to express such an opinion, therefore, are to be determined by the judge under Section 405 just as the qualifications of other experts are decided by the judge. See the discussion of Section 720 in this Comment, supra. Under existing law, too, determination of whether a witness is an "intimate acquaintance" is a question addressed to the court. Estate of Budan, 156 Cal. 230, 104 Pac. 442 (1909).

Sections 900-1070—Privileges. Under this code, as under existing law, the party claiming a privilege has the burden of proof on the preliminary facts. San Diego Professional Ass'n v. Superior Court, 58 Cal.2d 194, 199, 23 Cal.Rptr. 384, 387, 373 P.2d 448, 451 (1962) ("The burden of establishing that a particular matter is privileged is on the party asserting that privilege."); Chronicle Publishing Co. v. Superior Court, 54 Cal.2d 548, 565, 7 Cal.Rptr. 109, 117, 354 P.2d 637, 645 (1960). The proponent of the proffered evidence, however, has the burden of proof upon any preliminary fact necessary to show that an exception to the privilege is applicable. But see Abbott v. Superior Court, 78 Cal.App.2d 19, 21, 177 P.2d 317, 318 (1947) (suggesting that a prima facie showing by the proponent is sufficient where the issue is whether a communication between attorney and client was made in contemplation of crime).

Sections 1152, 1154—Admissions made during compromise negotiations. With respect to admissions made during compromise negotiations, the disputed preliminary fact to be decided by the judge is whether the admission occurred during compromise negotiations or at some other time. This code places the burden on the objecting party to satisfy the judge that the admission occurred during such negotiations.

Sections 1200-1341—Hearsay evidence. When hearsay evidence is offered, two preliminary fact questions may be raised. The first question relates to the authenticity of the proffered declarationCwas the statement actually made by the person alleged to have made it? The second question relates to the existence of those circumstances that make the hearsay sufficiently trustworthy to be received in evidence—e.g., was the declaration spontaneous, the confession voluntary, the business record trustworthy? Under this code, questions relating to the authenticity of the proffered declaration are decided under Section 403. See the Comment to Section 403. But other preliminary fact questions are decided under Section 405.

For example, the court must decide whether a statement offered as a dying declaration was made under a sense of impending death, and the proponent of the evidence has the burden of proof on this issue. People v. Keelin, 136 Cal.App.2d 860, 873, 289 P.2d 520, 528 (1955); People v. Pollock, 31 Cal.App.2d 747, 753-754, 89 P.2d 128, 131 (1939). Under this code, the proponent of a hearsay declaration has the burden of proof on the unavailability of the declarant as a witness under Section 1291 or 1310; but the party objecting to the evidence has the burden of proving that the unavailability of the declarant was procured by the proponent in order to prevent the declarant from testifying. See Evidence Code § 240.

Section 1416—Opinion evidence on handwriting. Whether a witness is sufficiently acquainted with the handwriting of a person to give an opinion on whether a questioned writing is in that person's handwriting involves, in effect, the expertise of the witness on the limited subject of the supposed writer's handwriting. The witness' qualifications to express such an opinion, therefore, are to be determined by the judge under Section 405 just as the qualifications of other experts are decided by the judge. See the discussion of Section 720 in this Comment, supra.

Sections 1417-1419—Comparison of writing with exemplar. Under Sections 1417 through 1419, as under existing law, the judge must be satisfied that a writing is genuine before he may admit it for comparison with other writings whose authenticity is in dispute. People v. Creegan, 121 Cal. 554, 53 Pac. 1082 (1898); Marshall v. Hancock, 80 Cal. 82, 22 Pac. 61 (1889).

Sections 1500-1510—Best evidence rule. Under Section 405, as under existing law, the trial judge is required to determine the preliminary fact necessary to warrant reception of secondary evidence of a writing, and the burden of proof on the issue is on the proponent of the secondary evidence. Cotton v. Hudson, 42 Cal.App.2d 812, 110 P.2d 70 (1941).

Sections 1550, 1551—Photographic copy of writing. Sections 1550 and 1551 are special exceptions to the best evidence rule; hence, Section 405 governs the determination of any disputed preliminary fact under these sections just as it governs the determination of disputed preliminary facts under Sections 1500 through 1510. See the discussion of Sections 1550-1510 in this Comment, supra.

Function of court and jury under Section 405

When preliminary fact question is also an issue involved in merits of case. In some cases, a factual issue to be decided by the judge under Section 405 will coincide with an issue involved in the merits of the case. For example, in People v. MacDonald, 24 Cal.App.2d 702, 76 P.2d 121 (1938), the defendant in an incest prosecution objected to the testimony of the prosecutrix on the ground that she was his wife. The judge, in ruling on the objection, had to determine whether the prosecutrix was also the defendant's daughter and, hence, whether their marriage was incestuous and void. In such a case, it would be prejudicial to the parties for the judge to inform the jury how he had decided the same factual question that it must decide in determining the merits of the case. Subdivision (b), therefore, prohibits a judge from informing the jury how he decided a question under Section 405 that the jury must ultimately resolve on the merits.

The judge is also prohibited from instructing the jury to disregard evidence that has been admitted if the jury's determination of a fact in deciding the merits differs from the judge's determination of the same fact under Section 405. The rules of admissibility being applied by the judge under Section 405 are designed to withhold evidence from the jury because it is too unreliable to be evaluated properly or because public policy requires its exclusion. The policies underlying these rules are served only by the exclusion of the evidence. No valid public or evidentiary purpose is served by submitting the admissibility question again to the jury. For example, the interspousal testimonial privilege involved in People v. MacDonald, 24 Cal.App.2d 702, 76 P.2d 121 (1938), exists to preclude a spouse from being involuntarily compelled to testify against the other spouse. The privilege serves its purpose only if the spouse does not testify. The harm the privilege is designed to prevent has occurred if the spouse testifies. Therefore, subdivision (b) provides for the finality of the judge's rulings on admissibility under Section 405 even in those cases where the factual questions decided by the judge coincide with the factual questions ultimately to be resolved by the jury.

Of course, Section 405 has no effect on the constitutional right of the judge to comment on the evidence and on the testimony and credibility of witnesses. See Cal.Const., Art. I, § 13, and Art. VI, § 19.

Confessions, dying declarations, and spontaneous statements. Although Section 405 is generally consistent with existing law, it will, however, substantially change the law relating to confessions, dying declarations, and spontaneous statements. Under existing law, the judge considers all of the evidence and decides whether evidence of this sort is admissible, as indicated in Section 405. But if he decides the proffered evidence is admissible, he submits the preliminary question to the jury for a final determination whether the confession was voluntary, whether the dying declaration was made in realization of impending doom, or whether the spontaneous statement was in fact spontaneous; and the jury is instructed to disregard the statement if it does not believe that the condition of admissibility has been satisfied. People v. Baldwin, 42 Cal.2d 858, 866-867, 270 P.2d 1028, 1033-1034 (1954) (confessionCsee the court's instruction, id. at 866, 270 P.2d at 1033); People v. Gonzales, 24 Cal.2d 870, 876-877, 151 P.2d 251, 254 (1944) (confession); People v. Singh, 182 Cal. 457, 476, 188 Pac. 987, 995 (1920) (dying declaration); People v. Keelin, 136 Cal.App.2d 860, 871, 289 P.2d 520, 527 (1955) (spontaneous declaration).

Under Section 405, the judge's rulings on these questions are final; the jury does not have an opportunity to redetermine the issue.

Section 405 will have no effect on the admissibility of confessions where the uncontradicted evidence shows that the confession was not voluntary. Under existing law, as under the Evidence Code, such a confession may not be admitted for consideration by the jury. People v. Trout, 54 Cal.2d 576, 6 Cal.Rptr. 759, 354 P.2d 231 (1960); People v. Jones, 24 Cal.2d 601, 150 P.2d 801 (1944). Section 405 will also have no effect on the admissibility of confessions in those instances where, despite a conflict in the evidence, the court is persuaded that the confession was not voluntary; for, under existing law (as under the Evidence Code), "if the court concludes that the confession was not free and voluntary it . . . is in duty bound to withhold it from the jury's consideration." People v. Gonzales, 24 Cal.2d 870, 876, 151 P.2d 251, 254 (1944).

Hence, Section 405 changes the law relating to confessions only where there is a substantial conflict in the evidence over voluntariness and the court is not persuaded that the confession was involuntary. Under existing law, a court that is in doubt may "pass the buck" concerning such a confession to the jury when there is a difficult factual question to resolve; for "if there is evidence that the confession was free and voluntary, it is within the court's discretion to permit it to be read to the jury, and to submit to the jury for its determination the question whether under all the circumstances the confession was made freely and voluntarily." People v. Gonzales, 24 Cal.2d 870, 876, 151 P.2d 251, 254 (1944). Under the Evidence Code, however, the court is required to withhold a confession from the jury unless the court is persuaded that the confession was made freely and voluntarily. The court has no "discretion" to avoid difficult decisions by shifting the responsibility to the jury. If the court is in doubt, if the prosecution has not persuaded it of the voluntary nature of the confession, Section 405 requires the court to exclude the confession. Thus, Section 405 makes the procedure for determining the admissibility of a confession the same as the procedure for determining the admissibility of physical evidence claimed to have been seized in violation of constitutional guarantees. See People v. Gorg, 45 Cal.2d 776, 291 P.2d 469 (1955); People v. Chavez, 208 Cal.App.2d 248, 24 Cal.Rptr. 895 (1962).

The existing law is based on the belief that a jury, in determining the defendant's guilt or innocence, can and will refuse to consider a confession that it has determined was involuntary even though it believes that the confession is true. Section 405, on the other hand, proceeds upon the belief that it is unrealistic to expect a jury to perform such a feat. Corroborating facts stated in a confession cannot but assist the jury in resolving other conflicts in the evidence. The question of voluntariness will inevitably become merged with the question of guilt and the truth of the confession; and, as a result of this merger, the admitted confession will inevitably be considered on the issue of guilt. The defendant will receive a greater degree of protection if the court is deprived of the power to shift its fact-determining responsibility to the jury and is required to exclude a confession whenever it is not persuaded that the confession was voluntary.

The foregoing discussion has focused on confessions because the case law is well developed there. But the "second crack" doctrine is equally unsatisfactory when applied to dying declarations and spontaneous statements. Hence, Section 405 requires the court to rule finally on the admissibility of these statements as well.

Of course, Section 405 does not prevent the presentation of any evidence to the jury that is relevant to the reliability of the hearsay statement. See Evidence Code § 406. Thus, a party may present evidence of the circumstances under which a confession, dying declaration, or spontaneous statement was made where such evidence is relevant to the credibility of the statement, even though such evidence may duplicate to some degree the evidence presented to the court on the issue of admissibility. But the jury's sole concern is the truth or falsity of the facts stated, not the admissibility of the statement.

§ 406. Evidence affecting weight or credibility. This article [§§ 400-406] does not limit the right of a party to introduce before the trier of fact evidence relevant to weight or credibility.

Law Revision Commission Comment

Other sections in this article provide that the judge determines whether proffered evidence is admissible, i.e., whether it may be considered by the trier of fact. Section 406 simply makes it clear that the judge's decision on a question of admissibility does not preclude the parties from introducing before the trier of fact evidence relevant to weight and credibility.

Chapter 5. Weight of Evidence Generally

§ 410. Direct evidence. As used in this chapter [§§ 410-413], "direct evidence" means evidence that directly proves a fact, without an inference or presumption, and which in itself, if true, conclusively establishes that fact.

§ 411. Direct evidence of one witness sufficient. Except where additional evidence is required by statute, the direct evidence of one witness who is entitled to full credit is sufficient for proof of any fact.

Law Revision Commission Comment

Section 411 restates the substance of and supersedes Section 1844 of the Code of Civil Procedure. The phrase "except where additional evidence is required by statute" has been substituted for the phrase "except perjury and treason" in Section 1844 because the "perjury and treason" exception to Section 1844 is too limited: Corroboration is required by Section 20 of Article I of the California Constitution (treason) and by Penal Code Sections 653f (solicitation to commit felonies), 1103a (perjury), 1108 (abortion and prostitution cases), 1110 (obtaining property by oral false pretenses), and 1111 (testimony of accomplices); in addition, Civil Code Section 130 provides that divorces cannot be granted on the uncorroborated testimony of the parties.

§ 412. Party having power to produce better evidence. If weaker and less satisfactory evidence is offered when it was within the power of the party to produce stronger and more satisfactory evidence, the evidence offered should be viewed with distrust.

Law Revision Commission Comment

* * * Evidence Code Section 913 provides that "no presumption shall arise because of the exercise of [a] privilege, and the trier of fact may not draw any inference therefrom," and the trial judge is required to give such an instruction if he is requested to do so. However, there is no inconsistency between Section 913 and Sections 412 and 413. Section 913 deals only with the inferences that may be drawn from the exercise of a privilege; it does not purport to deal with the inferences that may be drawn from the evidence in the case. Sections 412 and 413, on the other hand, deal with the inferences to be drawn from the evidence in the case; and the fact that a privilege has been relied on is irrelevant to the application of these sections. Cf. People v. Adamson, 27 Cal.2d 478, 165 P.2d 3 (1946).

§ 413. Party's failure to explain or deny evidence. In determining what inferences to draw from the evidence or facts in the case against a party, the trier of fact may consider, among other things, the party's failure to explain or to deny by his testimony such evidence or facts in the case against him, or his willful suppression of evidence relating thereto, if such be the case.

DIVISION 4. JUDICIAL NOTICE

§ 450. Judicial notice may be taken only as authorized by law. Judicial notice may not be taken of any matter unless authorized or required by law.

Law Revision Commission Comment

Section 450 provides that judicial notice may not be taken of any matter unless authorized or required by law. See Evidence Code § 160, defining "law." Sections 451 and 452 state a number of matters which must or may be judicially noticed. Judicial notice of other matters is authorized or required by other statutes or by decisional law. E.g., Civil Code § 53; Corp.Code § 6602. * * *

Under the Evidence Code, as under existing law, courts may consider whatever materials are appropriate in construing statutes, determining constitutional issues, and formulating rules of law. That a court may consider legislative history, discussions by learned writers in treatises and law reviews, materials that contain controversial economic and social facts or findings or that indicate contemporary opinion, and similar materials is inherent in the requirement that it take judicial notice of the law. In many cases, the meaning and validity of statutes, the precise nature of a common law rule, or the correct interpretation of a constitutional provision can be determined only with the help of such extrinsic aids. Cf. People v. Sterling Refining Co., 86 Cal.App. 558, 564, 261 Pac. 1080, 1083 (1927) (statutory authority to notice "public and private acts" of legislature held to authorize examination of legislative history of certain acts). See also Perez v. Sharp, 32 Cal.2d 711, 198 P.2d 17 (1948) (texts and authorities used by court in opinions determining constitutionality of statute prohibiting interracial marriages). Section 450 will neither broaden nor limit the extent to which a court may resort to extrinsic aids in determining the rules of law that it is required to notice. Nor will Section 450 broaden or limit the extent to which a court may take judicial notice of any other matter not specified in Section 451 or 452.

§ 451. Matters which must be judicially noticed. Judicial notice shall be taken of the following:

(a) The decisional, constitutional, and public statutory law of this state and of the United States and the provisions of any charter described in Section 3, 4, or 5 of Article XI of the California Constitution.

(b) Any matter made a subject of judicial notice by Section 11343.6, 11344.6, or 18576 of the Government Code or by Section 1507 of Title 44 of the United States Code.

(c) Rules of professional conduct for members of the bar adopted pursuant to Section 6076 of the Business and Professions Code and rules of practice and procedure for the courts of this state adopted by the Judicial Council.

(d) Rules of pleading, practice, and procedure prescribed by the United States Supreme Court, such as the Rules of the United States Supreme Court, the Federal Rules of Civil Procedure, the Federal Rules of Criminal Procedure, the Admiralty Rules, the Rules of the Court of Claims, the Rules of the Customs Court, and the General Orders and Forms in Bankruptcy.

(e) The true signification of all English words and phrases and of all legal expressions.

(f) Facts and propositions of generalized knowledge that are so universally known that they cannot reasonably be the subject of dispute. [*Amended 1971, 1972, 1982, 1985, 1986.*]

Assembly Committee on Judiciary Comment

Judicial notice of the matters specified in Section 451 is mandatory, whether or not the court is requested to notice them. Although the court errs if it fails to take judicial notice of the matters specified in this section, such error is not necessarily reversible error. Depending upon the circumstances, the appellate court may hold that the error was "invited" (and, hence, is not reversible error) or that points not urged in the trial court may not be advanced on appeal. These and similar principles of appellate practice are not abrogated by this section.

Section 451 includes matters both of law and of fact. The matters specified in subdivisions (a), (b), (c), and (d) are all matters that, broadly speaking, can be considered as a part of the "law" applicable to the particular case. The court can reasonably be expected to discover and apply this law even if the parties fail to provide the court with references to the pertinent cases, statutes, regulations and rules. Other matters that also might properly be considered as a part of the law applicable to the case (such as the law of foreign nations and certain regulations and ordinances) are included under Section 452, rather than under Section 451, primarily because of the difficulty of ascertaining such matters. Subdivision (e) of Section 451 requires the court to judicially notice "the true signification of all English words and phrases and of all legal expressions." These are facts that must be judicially noticed in order to conduct meaningful proceedings. Similarly, subdivision (f) of Section 451 covers "universally known" facts.

Listed below are the matters that must be judicially noticed under Section 451.

California and federal law. The decisional, constitutional, and public statutory law of California and of the United States must be judicially noticed under subdivision (a). This requirement states existing law as found in subdivision 3 of Code of Civil Procedure Section 1875 (superseded by the Evidence Code).

Charter provisions of California cities and counties. Judicial notice must be taken under subdivision (a) of the provisions of charters adopted pursuant to Section 7 ½ or 8 of Article XI of the California Constitution. Notice of these provisions is mandatory under the State Constitution. Cal.Const., Art. XI, § 7 ½ (county charter), § 8 (charter of city or city and county).

Regulations of California and federal agencies. Judicial notice must be taken under subdivision (b) of the rules, regulations, orders, and standards of general application adopted by California state agencies and filed with the Secretary of State or printed in the California Administrative Code or the California Administrative Register. This is existing law as found in Government Code Sections 11383 and 11384. Under subdivision (b), judicial notice must also be taken of the rules of the State Personnel Board. This, too, is existing law under Government Code Section 18576.

Subdivision (b) also requires California courts to judicially notice documents published in the Federal Register (such as (1) presidential proclamations and executive orders having general applicability and legal effect and (2) orders, regulations, rules, certificates, codes of fair competition, licenses, notices, and similar instruments, having general applicability and legal effect, that are issued, prescribed, or promulgated by federal agencies). There is no clear holding that this is existing California law. Although Section 307 of Title 44 of the United States Code provides that the "contents of the Federal Register shall be judicially noticed," it is not clear that this requires notice by state courts. See Broadway Fed. etc. Loan Ass'n v. Howard, 133 Cal.App.2d 382, 386 note 4, 285 P.2d 61, 64 note 4 (1955) (referring to 44 U.S.C.A. §§ 301-314). Compare Note, 59 Harv.L.Rev. 1137, 1141 (1946) (doubt expressed that notice is required), with Knowlton, Judicial Notice, 10 Rutgers L.Rev. 501, 504 (1956) ("it would seem that this provision is binding upon the state courts"). Livermore v. Beal, 18 Cal.App.2d 535, 542-543, 64 P.2d 987, 992 (1937), suggests that California courts are required to judicially notice pertinent federal official action, and California courts have judicially noticed the contents of various proclamations, orders, and regulations of federal agencies. E.g., Pacific Solvents Co. v. Superior Court, 88 Cal.App.2d 953, 955, 199 P.2d 740, 741 (1948) (orders and regulations); People v. Mason, 72 Cal.App.2d 699, 706-707, 165 P.2d 481, 485 (1946) (presidential and executive proclamations) (disapproved on other grounds in People v. Friend, 50 Cal.2d 570, 578, 327 P.2d 97, 102 (1958)); Downer v. Grizzly Livestock & Land Co., 6 Cal.App.2d 39, 42, 43 P.2d 843, 845 (1935) (rules and regulations). Section 451 makes the California law clear.

Rules of court. Judicial notice of the California Rules of Court is required under subdivision (c). These rules, adopted by the Judicial Council, are as binding on the parties as procedural statutes. Cantillon v. Superior Court, 150 Cal.App.2d 184, 309 P.2d 890 (1957). See Albermont Petroleum, Ltd. v. Cunningham, 186 Cal.App.2d 84, 9 Cal.Rptr. 405 (1960). Likewise, the rules of pleading, practice, and procedure promulgated by the United States Supreme Court are required to be judicially noticed under subdivision (d).

The rules of the California and federal courts which are required to be judicially noticed under subdivisions (c) and (d) are, or should be, familiar to the court or easily discoverable from materials readily available to the court. However, this may not be true of the court rules of sister states or other jurisdictions nor, for example, of the rules of the various United States Courts of Appeals or local rules of a particular superior court. See Albermont Petroleum, Ltd. v. Cunningham, 186 Cal.App.2d 84, 9 Cal.Rptr. 405 (1960). Judicial notice of these rules is permitted under subdivision (e) of Section 452 but is not required unless there is compliance with the provisions of Section 453.

State Bar Rules of Professional Conduct. The Rules of Professional Conduct of the State Bar of California are, in effect, rules of the Supreme Court, for they must be approved by that court. Barton v. State Bar, 209 Cal. 677, 289 Pac. 818 (1930). Subdivision (c), therefore, requires the court to take judicial notice of these rules to the same extent that it takes notice of other rules of court.

Words, phrases, and legal expressions. Subdivision (e) requires the court to take judicial notice of "the true signification of all English words and phrases and of all legal expressions." This restates the same matter covered in subdivision 1 of Code of Civil Procedure Section 1875. Under existing law, however, it is not clear that judicial notice of these matters is mandatory.

"Universally known" facts. Subdivision (f) requires the court to take judicial notice of indisputable facts and propositions universally known. "Universally known" does not mean that every man on the street has knowledge of such facts. A fact known among persons of reasonable and average intelligence and knowledge will satisfy the "universally known" requirement. Cf. People v. Tossetti, 107 Cal.App. 7, 12, 289 Pac. 881, 883 (1930).

Subdivision (f) should be contrasted with subdivisions (g) and (h) of Section 452, which provide for judicial notice of indisputable facts and propositions that are matters of common knowledge or are capable of immediate and accurate determination by resort to sources of reasonably indisputable accuracy. Subdivisions (g) and (h) permit notice of facts and propositions that are indisputable but are not "universally" known.

Judicial notice does not apply to facts merely because they are known to the judge to be indisputable. The facts must fulfill the requirements of subdivision (f) of Section 451 or subdivision (g) or (h) of Section 452. If a judge happens to know a fact that is not widely enough known to be subject to judicial notice under this division, he may not "notice" it.

It is clear under existing law that the court may judicially notice the matters specified in subdivision (f); it is doubtful, however, that the court must notice them. See Varcoe v. Lee, 180 Cal. 338, 347, 181 Pac. 223, 227 (1919) (dictum). Since subdivision (f) covers universally known facts, the parties ordinarily will expect the court to take judicial notice of them; the court should not be permitted to ignore such facts merely because the parties fail to make a formal request for judicial notice.

§ 452. Matters which may be judicially noticed. Judicial notice may be taken of the following matters to the extent that they are not embraced within Section 451:

(a) The decisional, constitutional, and statutory law of any state of the United States and the resolutions and private acts of the Congress of the United States and of the Legislature of this state.

(b) Regulations and legislative enactments issued by or under the authority of the United States or any public entity in the United States.

(c) Official acts of the legislative, executive, and judicial departments of the United States and of any state of the United States.

(d) Records of (1) any court of this state or (2) any court of record of the United States or of any state of the United States.

(e) Rules of court of (1) any court of this state or (2) any court of record of the United States or of any state of the United States.

(f) The law of an organization of nations and of foreign nations and public entities in foreign nations.

(g) Facts and propositions that are of such common knowledge within the territorial jurisdiction of the court that they cannot reasonably be the subject of dispute.

(h) Facts and propositions that are not reasonably subject to dispute and are capable of immediate and accurate determination by resort to sources of reasonably indisputable accuracy.

Statutory Note

See Penal Code § 963 (judicial notice of private statutes and county and municipal ordinances).

Assembly Committee on Judiciary Comment

Section 452 includes matters both of law and of fact. The court may take judicial notice of these matters, even when not requested to do so; it is required to notice them if a party requests it and satisfies the requirements of Section 453.

The matters of law included under Section 452 may be neither known to the court nor easily discoverable by it because the sources of information are not readily available. However, if a party requests it and furnishes the court with "sufficient information" for it to take judicial notice, the court must do so if proper notice has been given to each adverse party. See Evidence Code § 453. Thus, judicial notice of these matters of law is mandatory only if counsel adequately discharges his responsibility for informing the court as to the law applicable to the case. The simplified process of judicial notice can then be applied to all of the law applicable to the case, including such law as ordinances and the law of foreign nations.

Although Section 452 extends the process of judicial notice to some matters of law which the courts do not judicially notice under existing law, the wider scope of such notice is balanced by the assurance that the matter need not be judicially noticed unless adequate information to support its truth is furnished to the court. Under Section 453, this burden falls upon the party requesting that judicial notice be taken. In addition, the parties are entitled under Section 455 to a reasonable opportunity to present information to the court as to the propriety of taking judicial notice and as to the tenor of the matter to be noticed.

Listed below are the matters that may be judicially noticed under Section 452 (and must be noticed if the conditions specified in Section 453 are met).

Law of sister states. Subdivision (a) provides for judicial notice of the decisional, constitutional, and statutory law in force in sister states. California courts now take judicial notice of the law of sister states under subdivision 3 of Section 1875 of the Code of Civil Procedure. However, Section 1875 seems to preclude notice of sister-state law as interpreted by the intermediate-appellate courts of sister states, whereas Section 452 permits notice of relevant decisions of all sister-state courts. If this be an extension of existing law, it is a desirable one, for the courts of sister states generally can be considered as responsive to the need for properly determining the law as are equivalent courts in California. The existing law also is not clear as to whether a request for judicial notice of sister-state law is required and whether judicial notice is mandatory. On the necessity for a request for judicial notice, see Comment, 24 Cal.L.Rev. 311, 316 (1936). On whether judicial notice is mandatory, see In re Bartges, 44 Cal.2d 241, 282 P.2d 47 (1955), and the opinion of the Supreme Court in denying a hearing in Estate of Moore, 7 Cal.App.2d 722, 726, 48 P.2d 28, 29 (1935).

Law of territories and possessions of the United States. Subdivision (a) also provides for judicial notice of the decisional, constitutional, and statutory law in force in the territories and possessions of the United States. See the broad definition of "state" in Evidence Code § 220. It is not clear under existing California law whether this law is treated as sister-state law or foreign law. See Witkin, California Evidence § 45 (1958).

Resolutions and private acts. Subdivision (a) provides for judicial notice of resolutions and private acts of the Congress of the United States and of the legislature of any state, territory, or possession of the United States. See the broad definition of "state" in Evidence Code § 220.

The California law on this matter is not clear. Our courts are authorized by subdivision 3 of Code of Civil Procedure Section 1875 to take judicial notice of private statutes of this State and the United States, and they probably would take judicial notice of resolutions of this State and the United States under the same subdivision. It is not clear whether such notice is compulsory. It may be that judicial notice of a private act pleaded in a criminal action pursuant to Penal Code Section 963 is mandatory, whereas judicial notice of the same private act may be discretionary when pleaded in a civil action pursuant to Section 459 of the Code of Civil Procedure.

Although no case in point has been found, California courts probably would not take judicial notice of a resolution or private act of a sister state or territory or possession of the United States. Although Section 1875 is not the exclusive list of the matters that will be judicially noticed, the courts did not take judicial notice of a private statute prior to the enactment of Section 1875. Ellis v. Eastman, 32 Cal. 447 (1867).

Regulations, ordinances, and similar legislative enactments. Subdivision (b) provides for judicial notice of regulations and legislative enactments, adopted by or under the authority of the United States or of any state, territory, or possession of the United States, including public entities therein. See the broad definition of "public entity" in Evidence Code § 200. The words "regulations and legislative enactments" include such matters as "ordinances" and other similar legislative enactments. Not all public entities legislate by ordinance.

This subdivision changes existing law. Under existing law, municipal courts take judicial notice of ordinances in force within their jurisdiction. People v. Cowles, 142 Cal.App.2d Supp. 865, 867, 298 P.2d 732, 733-734 (1956); People v. Crittenden, 93 Cal.App.2d Supp. 871, 877, 209 P.2d 161, 165 (1949). In addition, an ordinance pleaded in a criminal action pursuant to Penal Code Section 963 must be judicially noticed. On the other hand, neither the superior court nor a district court of appeal will take judicial notice in a civil action of municipal or county ordinances. Thompson v. Guyer-Hays, 207 Cal.App.2d 366, 24 Cal.Rptr. 461 (1962); County of Los Angeles v. Bartlett, 203 Cal.App.2d 523, 21 Cal.Rptr. 776 (1962); Becerra v. Hochberg, 193 Cal.App.2d 431, 14 Cal.Rptr. 101 (1961). It seems safe to assume that ordinances of sister states and of territories and possessions of the United States would not be judicially noticed under existing law.

Judicial notice of certain regulations of California and federal agencies is mandatory under subdivision (b) of Section 451. Subdivision (b) of Section 452 provides for judicial notice of California and federal regulations that are not included under subdivision (b) of Section 451 and, also, for judicial notice of regulations of other states and territories and possessions of the United States.

Both California and federal regulations have been judicially noticed under subdivision 3 of Code of Civil Procedure Section 1875. 18 Cal.Jur.2d Evidence § 24. Although no case in point has been found, it is unlikely that regulations of other states or of territories or possessions of the United States would be judicially noticed under existing law.

Official acts of the legislative, executive, and judicial departments. Subdivision (c) provides for judicial notice of the official acts of the legislative, executive, and judicial departments of the United States and any state, territory, or possession of the United States. See the broad definition of "state" in Evidence Code § 220. Subdivision (c) states existing law as found in subdivision 3 of Code of Civil Procedure Section 1875. Under this provision, the California courts have taken judicial notice of a wide variety of administrative and executive acts, such as proceedings and reports of the House Committee on Un-American Activities, records of the State Board of Education, and records of a county planning commission. See Witkin, California Evidence § 49 (1958), and 1963 Supplement thereto.

Court records and rules of court. Subdivisions (d) and (e) provide for judicial notice of the court records and rules of court of (1) any court of this State or (2) any court of record of the United States or of any state, territory, or possession of the United States. See the broad definition of "state" in Evidence Code § 220. So far as court records are concerned, subdivision (d) states existing law. Flores v. Arroyo, 56 Cal.2d 492, 15 Cal.Rptr. 87, 364 P.2d 263 (1961). While the provisions of subdivision (c) of Section 452 are broad enough to include court records, specific mention of these records in subdivision (d) is desirable in order to eliminate any uncertainty in the law on this point. See the Flores case, supra.

Subdivision (e) may change existing law so far as judicial notice of rules of court is concerned, but the provision is consistent with the modern philosophy of judicial notice as indicated by the holding in Flores v. Arroyo, supra. To the extent that subdivision (e) overlaps with subdivisions (c) and (d) of Section 451, notice is, of course, mandatory under Section 451.

Foreign law. Subdivision (f) provides for judicial notice of the law of organizations of nations, foreign nations, and public entities in foreign nations. See the broad definition of "public entity" in Evidence Code § 200. Subdivision (f) should be read in connection with Sections 310, 311, 453, and 454. These provisions retain the substance of the existing law which was enacted in 1957 upon recommendation of the California Law Revision Commission. Code Civ.Proc. § 1875. See 1 Cal.Law Revision Comm'n. Rep., Rec. & Studies, Recommendation and Study Relating to Judicial Notice of the Law of Foreign Countries at I-1 (1957).

Subdivision (f) refers to "the law" of organizations of nations, foreign nations, and public entities in foreign nations. This makes all law, in whatever form, subject to judicial notice.

Matters of "common knowledge" and verifiable facts. Subdivision (g) provides for judicial notice of matters of common knowledge within the court's territorial jurisdiction that are not subject to dispute. "Territorial jurisdiction," in this context, refers to the county in which a superior court is located or the judicial district in which a municipal or justice court is located. The fact of which notice is taken need not be something physically located within the court's territorial jurisdiction, but common knowledge of the fact must exist within the court's territorial jurisdiction. Subdivision (g) reflects existing case law. Varcoe v. Lee, 180 Cal. 338, 181 Pac. 223 (1919); 18 Cal.Jur.2d Evidence § 19 at 439-440. The California courts have taken judicial notice of a wide variety of matters of common knowledge. Witkin, California Evidence §§ 50-52 (1958).

Subdivision (h) provides for judicial notice of indisputable facts immediately ascertainable by reference to sources of reasonably indisputable accuracy. In other words, the facts need not be actually known if they are readily ascertainable and indisputable. Sources of "reasonably indisputable accuracy" include not only treatises, encyclopedias, almanacs, and the like, but also persons learned in the subject matter. This would not mean that reference works would be received in evidence or sent to the jury room. Their use would be limited to consultation by the judge and the parties for the purposes of determining whether or not to take judicial notice and determining the tenor of the matter to be noticed.

Subdivisions (g) and (h) include, for example, facts which are accepted as established by experts and specialists in the natural, physical, and social sciences, if those facts are of such wide acceptance that to submit them to the jury would be to risk irrational findings. These subdivisions include such matters listed in Code of Civil Procedure Section 1875 as the "geographical divisions and political history of the world." To the extent that subdivisions (g) and (h) overlap subdivision (f) of Section 451, notice is, of course, mandatory under Section 451.

The matters covered by subdivisions (g) and (h) are included in Section 452, rather than Section 451, because it seems reasonable to put the burden on the parties to bring adequate information before the court if judicial notice of these matters is to be mandatory. See Evidence Code § 453 and the Comment thereto.

Under existing law, courts take judicial notice of the matters that are included under subdivisions (g) and (h), either pursuant to Section 1875 of the Code of Civil Procedure or because such matters are matters of common knowledge which are certain and indisputable. Witkin, California Evidence §§ 50-52 (1958). Notice of these matters probably is not compulsory under existing law. C.C.P. § 1875, enacted 1872, amended by Stats.1927, c. 62, p. 110; Stats.1957, c. 249, p. 902, § 1.

§ 452.5. Criminal conviction records; computer-generated records and electronically digitized copies; admissibility. (a) The official acts and records specified in subdivisions (c) and (d) of Section 452 include any computer-generated official court records, as specified by the Judicial Council that relate to criminal convictions, when the record is certified by a clerk of the superior court pursuant to Section 69844.5 of the Government Code at the time of computer entry.

(b)(1) An official record of conviction certified in accordance with subdivision (a) of Section 1530, or an electronically digitized copy thereof, is admissible under Section 1280 to prove the commission, attempted commission, or solicitation of a criminal offense, prior conviction, service of a prison term, or other act, condition, or event recorded by the record. [*Added 1996. Amended 2002. Amended 2013.*]

(2.) For purposes of this subdivision, "electronically digitized copy" means a copy that is made by scanning, photographing, or otherwise exactly reproducing a document, is stored or maintained in a digitized format, and meets either of the following requirements:

(A) The copy bears an electronic signature or watermark unique to the entity responsible for certifying the document.

(B) The copied document is an official record of conviction, certified in accordance with subdivision (a) of Section 1530, that is transmitted by the clerk of the superior court in a manner showing that the copy was prepared and transmitted by that clerk of the superior court. A seal, signature, or other indicia of the court shall constitute adequate showing. [*Added 2013. Amended 2017.*]

Note on Proposed Amendment

The Law Revision Commission tentatively decided in June 2004 to recommend that the uses that may be made of a certified record of conviction should be subject to the limitations of § 1300.

Statutory Note

Section 2 of Stats. 1996, c. 642, which added § 452.5, declared:

It is the intent of the Legislature to simplify recordkeeping and admission in evidence of records of criminal convictions by establishing a central computer data base of that data, and by authorizing admission in evidence of this computer data. It is anticipated that this will result in considerable savings of time and money by state and county courts and agencies while improving or maintaining the accuracy of the records.

Penal Code § 969b provides:

For the purpose of establishing prima facie evidence of the fact that a person being tried for a crime or public offense under the laws of this State has been convicted of an act punishable by imprisonment in a state prison, county jail or city jail of this State, and has served a term therefor in any penal institution, or has been convicted of an act in any other state, which would be punishable as a crime in this State, and has served a term therefor in any state penitentiary, reformatory, county jail or city jail, or has been convicted of an act declared to be a crime by any act or law of the United States, and has served a term therefor in any penal institution, the records or copies of records of any state penitentiary, reformatory, county jail, city jail, or federal penitentiary in which such person has been imprisoned, when such records or copies thereof have been certified by the official custodian of such records, may be introduced as such evidence. [*Added 1931. Amended 1949.*]

Case Note

Penal Code § 969b is essentially a hearsay exception that allows certified copies of certain records to be used for the truth of the matters asserted in those records. Section 969b is permissive. It does not restrict other forms of proof to establish the fact of previous imprisonment. Thus, computer-generated records from the California Law Enforcement Telecommunications System (CLETS) may be admissible under § 1280. People v. Martinez, 22 Cal. 4th 106, 116-119, 91 Cal. Rptr. 2d 687, 694-697, 900 P.2d 563, 570-573 (2000).

§ 453. Compulsory judicial notice upon request. The trial court shall take judicial notice of any matter specified in Section 452 if a party requests it and: (a) Gives each adverse party sufficient notice of the request, through the pleadings or otherwise, to enable such adverse party to prepare to meet the request; and

(b) Furnishes the court with sufficient information to enable it to take judicial notice of the matter.

Law Revision Commission Comment

Section 453 provides that the court must take judicial notice of any matter specified in Section 452 if a party requests that such notice be taken, furnishes the court with sufficient information to enable it to take judicial notice of the matter, and gives each adverse party sufficient notice of the request to prepare to meet it.

Section 453 is intended as a safeguard and not as a rigid limitation on the court's power to take judicial notice. The section does not affect the discretionary power of the court to take judicial notice under Section 452 where the party requesting that judicial notice be taken fails to give the requisite notice to each adverse party or fails to furnish sufficient information as to the propriety of taking judicial notice or as to the tenor of the matter to be noticed. Hence, when he considers it appropriate, the judge may take judicial notice under Section 452 and may consult and use any source of pertinent information, whether or not furnished by the parties. However, where the matter noticed under Section 452 is one that is of substantial consequence to the action—even though the court may take judicial notice under Section 452 when the requirements of Section 453 have not been satisfied—the party adversely affected must be given a reasonable opportunity to present information as to the propriety of taking judicial notice and as to the tenor of the matter to be noticed. See Evidence Code § 455 and the Comment thereto.

The "notice" requirement. The party requesting the court to judicially notice a matter under Section 453 must give each adverse party sufficient notice, through the pleadings or otherwise, to enable him to prepare to meet the request. In cases where the notice given does not satisfy this requirement, the court may decline to take judicial notice. A somewhat similar notice to the adverse parties is required under subdivision 4 of Section 1875 of the Code of Civil Procedure when a request for judicial notice of the law of a foreign country is made. Section 453 broadens this existing requirement to cover all matters specified in Section 452.

The notice requirement is an important one since judicial notice is binding on the jury under Section 457. Accordingly, the adverse parties should be given ample notice so that they will have an opportunity to prepare to oppose the taking of judicial notice and to obtain information relevant to the tenor of the matter to be noticed.

Since Section 452 relates to a wide variety of facts and law, the notice requirement should be administered with flexibility in order to insure that the policy behind the judicial notice rules is properly implemented. In many cases, it will be reasonable to expect the notice to be given at or before the time of the pretrial conference. In other cases, matters of fact or law of which the court should take judicial notice may come up at the trial. Section 453 merely requires reasonable notice, and the reasonableness of the notice given will depend upon the circumstances of the particular case.

The "sufficient information" requirement. Under Section 453, the court is not required to resort to any sources of information not provided by the parties. If the party requesting that judicial notice be taken under Section 453 fails to provide the court with "sufficient information," the judge may decline to take judicial notice. For example, if the party requests the court to take judicial notice of the specific gravity of gold, the party requesting that notice be taken must furnish the judge with definitive information as to the specific gravity of gold. The judge is not required to undertake the necessary research to determine the fact, though, of course, he is not precluded from doing such research if he so desires.

Section 453 does not define "sufficient information"; this will necessarily vary from case to case. While the parties will understandably use the best evidence they can produce under the circumstances, mechanical requirements that are ill-suited to the individual case should be avoided. The court justifiably might require that the party requesting that judicial notice be taken provide expert testimony to clarify especially difficult problems.

Burden on party requesting that judicial notice be taken. Where a request is made to take judicial notice under Section 453, the court may decline to take judicial notice unless the party requesting that notice be taken persuades the judge that the matter is one that properly may be noticed under Section 452 and also persuades the judge as to tenor of the matter to be noticed. The degree of the judge's persuasion regarding a particular matter is determined by the subdivision of Section 452 which authorizes judicial notice of the matter. For example, if the matter is claimed to be a fact of common knowledge under paragraph (g) of Section 452, the party must persuade the judge that the fact is of such common knowledge within the territorial jurisdiction of the court that it cannot reasonably be subject to dispute, i.e., that no reasonable person having the same information as is available to the judge could rationally disbelieve the fact. On the other hand, if the matter to be noticed is a city ordinance under paragraph (b) of Section 452, the party must persuade the judge that a valid ordinance exists and also as to its tenor; but the judge need not believe that no reasonable person could conclude otherwise.

Without regard to the evidence supplied by the party requesting that judicial notice be taken, the judge's determination to take judicial notice of a matter specified in Section 452 will be upheld on appeal if the matter was properly noticed. The reviewing court may resort to any information, whether or not available at the trial, in order to sustain the proper taking of judicial notice. See Evidence Code § 459. On the other hand, even though a party requested that judicial notice be taken under Section 453 and gave notice to each adverse party in compliance with subdivision (a) of Section 453, the decision of the judge not to take judicial notice will be upheld on appeal unless the reviewing court determines that the party furnished information to the judge that was so persuasive that no reasonable judge would have refused to take judicial notice of the matter.

§ 454. Information that may be used in taking judicial notice. (a) In determining the propriety of taking judicial notice of a matter, or the tenor thereof:

(1) Any source of pertinent information, including the advice of persons learned in the subject matter, may be consulted or used, whether or not furnished by a party.

(2) Exclusionary rules of evidence do not apply except for Section 352 and the rules of privilege.

(b) Where the subject of judicial notice is the law of an organization of nations, a foreign nation, or a public entity in a foreign nation and the court resorts to the advice of persons learned in the subject matter, such advice, if not received in open court, shall be in writing.

Assembly Committee on Judiciary Comment

Since one of the purposes of judicial notice is to simplify the process of proofmaking, the judge should be given considerable latitude in deciding what sources are trustworthy. This section permits the court to use any source of pertinent information, including the advice of persons learned in the subject matter. * * *

§ 455. Opportunity to present information to court. With respect to any matter specified in Section 452 or in subdivision (f) of Section 451 that is of substantial consequence to the determination of the action:

(a) If the trial court has been requested to take or has taken or proposes to take judicial notice of such matter, the court shall afford each party reasonable opportunity, before the jury is instructed or before the cause is submitted for decision by the court, to present to the court information relevant to (1) the propriety of taking judicial notice of the matter and (2) the tenor of the matter to be noticed.

(b) If the trial court resorts to any source of information not received in open court, including the advice of persons learned in the subject matter, such information and its source shall be made a part of the record in the action and the court shall afford each party reasonable opportunity to meet such information before judicial notice of the matter may be taken.

Law Revision Commission Comment

Section 455 provides procedural safeguards designed to afford the parties reasonable opportunity to be heard both as to the propriety of taking judicial notice of a matter and as to the tenor of the matter to be noticed.

Subdivision (a). This subdivision guarantees to the parties a reasonable opportunity to present information to the court as to the propriety of taking judicial notice and as to the tenor of the matter to be noticed. In a jury case, the subdivision provides the parties with an opportunity to present their information to the judge before a jury instruction based on a matter judicially noticed is given. Where the matter subject to judicial notice relates to a cause tried by the court, the subdivision guarantees the parties an opportunity to dispute the taking of judicial notice of the matter before the cause is submitted for decision. If the judge does not discover that a matter should be judicially noticed until after the cause is submitted for decision, he may, of course, order the cause to be reopened for the purpose of permitting the parties to provide him with information concerning the matter.

Subdivision (a) is limited in its application to those matters specified in subdivision (f) of Section 451 or in Section 452 that are of substantial consequence to the determination of the action, for it would not be practicable to make the subdivision applicable to the other matters listed in Section 451 or to matters that are of inconsequential significance.

What constitutes a "reasonable opportunity" to "present . . . information" will depend upon the complexity of the matter and its importance to the case. For example, in a case where there is no dispute as to the existence and validity of a city ordinance, no formal hearing would be necessary to determine the propriety of taking judicial notice of the ordinance and of its tenor. But, where there is a complex question as to the tenor of foreign law applicable to the case, the granting of a hearing under subdivision (a) would be mandatory. The New York courts have so construed their judicial notice statute, saying that an opportunity for a litigant to know what the deciding tribunal is considering and to be heard with respect to both law and fact is guaranteed by due process of law. Arams v. Arams, 182 Misc. 328, 182 Misc. 336, 45 N.Y.S.2d 251 (Sup.Ct. 1943).

Subdivision (b). If the court resorts to sources of information not previously known to the parties, this subdivision requires that such information and its source be made a part of the record when it relates to taking judicial notice of a matter specified in subdivision (f) of Section

451 or in Section 452 that is of substantial consequence to the determination of the action. This requirement is based on a somewhat similar requirement found in Code of Civil Procedure Section 1875 regarding the law of a foreign nation. Making the information and its source a part of the record assures its availability for examination by the parties and by a reviewing court. In addition, subdivision (b) requires the court to give the parties a reasonable opportunity to meet such additional information before judicial notice of the matter may be taken.

§ 456. Noting for record denial of request to take judicial notice. If the trial court denies a request to take judicial notice of any matter, the court shall at the earliest practicable time so advise the parties and indicate for the record that it has denied the request.

Law Revision Commission Comment

Section 456 requires the judge to advise the parties and indicate for the record at the earliest practicable time any denial of a request to take judicial notice of a matter. The requirement is imposed in order to provide the parties with an adequate opportunity to submit evidence on any matter as to which judicial notice was anticipated but not taken. No comparable requirement is found in existing law. Compare Evidence Code § 455 and the Comment thereto.

§ 457. Instructing jury on matter judicially noticed. If a matter judicially noticed is a matter which would otherwise have been for determination by the jury, the trial court may, and upon request shall, instruct the jury to accept as a fact the matter so noticed.

Law Revision Commission Comment

Section 457 makes matters judicially noticed binding on the jury and thereby eliminates any possibility of presenting to the jury evidence disputing the fact as noticed by the court. The section is limited to instruction on a matter that would otherwise have been for determination by the jury; instruction of juries on matters of law is not a matter of evidence and is covered by the general provisions of law governing instruction of juries. * * *

§ 458. Judicial notice by trial court in subsequent proceedings. The failure or refusal of the trial court to take judicial notice of a matter, or to instruct the jury with respect to the matter, does not preclude the trial court in subsequent proceedings in the action from taking judicial notice of the matter in accordance with the procedure specified in this division.

Law Revision Commission Comment

This section provides that the failure or even the refusal of the court to take judicial notice of a matter at the trial does not bar the trial judge, or another trial judge, from taking judicial notice of that matter in a subsequent proceeding, such as a hearing on a motion for new trial or the like.

§ 459. Judicial notice by reviewing court. (a) The reviewing court shall take judicial notice of (1) each matter properly noticed by the trial court and (2) each matter that the trial court was required to notice under Section 451 or 453. The reviewing court may take judicial notice of any matter specified in Section 452. The reviewing court may take judicial notice of a matter in a tenor different from that noticed by the trial court.

(b) In determining the propriety of taking judicial notice of a matter, or the tenor thereof, the reviewing court has the same power as the trial court under Section 454.

(c) When taking judicial notice under this section of a matter specified in Section 452 or in subdivision (f) of Section 451 that is of substantial consequence to the determination of the action, the reviewing court shall comply with the provisions of subdivision (a) of Section 455 if the matter was not theretofore judicially noticed in the action.

(d) In determining the propriety of taking judicial notice of a matter specified in Section 452 or in subdivision (f) of Section 451 that is of substantial consequence to the determination of the action, or the tenor thereof, if the reviewing court resorts to any source of information not received in open court or not included in the record of the action, including the advice of persons learned in the subject matter, the reviewing court shall afford each party reasonable opportunity to meet such information before judicial notice of the matter may be taken.

Law Revision Commission Comment

Section 459 sets forth a separate set of rules for the taking of judicial notice by a reviewing court.

Subdivision (a). Subdivision (a) requires that a reviewing court take judicial notice of any matter that the trial court properly noticed or was obliged to notice. This means that the matters specified in Section 451 must be judicially noticed by the reviewing court even though the trial court failed to take judicial notice of such matters. A matter specified in Section 452 also must be judicially noticed by the reviewing court if such matter was properly noticed by the trial court in the exercise of its discretion or an appropriate request was made at the trial level and the party making the request satisfied the conditions specified in Section 453. However, if the trial court erred, the reviewing court is not bound by the tenor of the notice taken by the trial court.

Having taken judicial notice of such a matter, the reviewing court may or may not apply it in the particular case on appeal. The effect to be given to matters judicially noticed on appeal, where the question has not been raised below, depends on factors that are not evidentiary in character and are not mentioned in this code. For example, the appellate court is required to notice the matters of law mentioned in Section 451, but it may hold that an error which the appellant has "invited" is not reversible error or that points not urged in the trial court may not be advanced on appeal, and refuse, therefore, to apply the law to the pending case. These principles do not mean that the appellate court does not take judicial notice of the applicable law; they merely mean that, for reasons of policy governing appellate review, the appellate court may refuse to apply the law to the case before it.

In addition to requiring the reviewing court to judicially notice those matters which the trial court properly noticed or was required to notice, the subdivision also provides authority for the reviewing court to exercise the same discretionary power to take judicial notice as is possessed by the trial court.

Subdivision (b). The reviewing court may consult any source of pertinent information for the purpose of determining the propriety of taking judicial notice or the tenor of the matter to be noticed. This includes, of course, the power to consult such sources for the purpose of sustaining or reversing the taking of judicial notice by the trial court. As to the rights of the parties when the reviewing court consults such materials, see subdivision (d) and the Comment thereto.

Subdivision (c). This subdivision provides the parties with the same procedural protection when judicial notice is taken by the reviewing court as is provided by Section 455(a).

Subdivision (d). This subdivision assures the parties the same procedural safeguard at the appellate level that they have in the trial court: If the appellate court resorts to sources of information not included in the record in the action or proceeding, or not received in open court at the appellate level, either to sustain the tenor of the notice taken by the trial court or to notice a matter in a tenor different from that noticed by the trial court, the parties must be given a reasonable opportunity to meet such additional information before judicial notice of the matter may be taken. See Evidence Code § 455(b) and the Comment thereto.

§ 460. Appointment of expert by court. Where the advice of persons learned in the subject matter is required in order to enable the court to take judicial notice of a matter, the court on its own motion or on motion of any party may appoint one or more such persons to provide such advice. If the court determines to appoint such a person, he shall be appointed and compensated in the manner provided in Article 2 (commencing with Section 730) of Chapter 3 of Division 6.

Assembly Committee on Judiciary Comment

Section 460 makes it clear that a court may appoint experts on matters that are subject to judicial notice when the advice of such persons is required in order to enable the court to take such notice. Such persons are to be appointed and compensated in the same manner as expert witnesses are appointed and compensated under the provisions of Evidence Code Sections 730-733. In the normal case, the parties may be expected to produce the advice of experts if it is needed. Section 460, however, enables the court to appoint experts in those cases where the advice of an expert not identified with a party seems desirable.

DIVISION 5. BURDEN OF PROOF; BURDEN OF PRODUCING EVIDENCE; PRESUMPTIONS AND INFERENCES

Chapter 1. Burden of Proof

Article 1. General

§ 500. Party who has the burden of proof. Except as otherwise provided by law, a party has the burden of proof as to each fact the existence or nonexistence of which is essential to the claim for relief or defense that he is asserting.

Case Note

For a general discussion of allocation of the burden of persuasion, see Samuels v. Mix, 22 Cal. 4th 1, 91 Cal. Rptr. 273, 989 P.2d 701 (1999) (defendant-attorney bears burden of proving when plaintiff-client discovered or should have discovered facts constituting alleged malpractice for purposes of one-year-from-discovery statute of limitations).

Law Revision Commission Comment

As used in Section 500, the burden of proof means the obligation of a party to produce a particular state of conviction in the mind of the trier of fact as to the existence or nonexistence of a fact. See Evidence Code §§ 115, 190. If this requisite degree of conviction is not achieved as to the existence of a particular fact, the trier of fact must assume that the fact does not exist. Morgan, Basic Problems of Evidence 19 (1957); 9 Wigmore, Evidence § 2485 (3d ed. 1940). Usually, the burden of proof requires a party to convince the trier of fact that the existence of a particular fact is more probable than its nonexistence—a degree of proof usually described as proof by a preponderance of the evidence. Evidence Code § 115; Witkin, California Evidence § 59 (1958). However, in some instances, the burden of proof requires a party to produce a substantially greater degree of belief in the mind of the trier of fact concerning the existence of the fact—a burden usually described by stating that the party must introduce clear and convincing proof (Witkin, California Evidence § 60 (1958)) or, with respect to the prosecution in a criminal case, proof beyond a reasonable doubt (Penal Code § 1096).

The defendant in a criminal case sometimes has the burden of proof in regard to a fact essential to negate his guilt. However, in such cases, he usually is not required to persuade that trier of fact as to the existence of such fact; he is merely required to raise a reasonable doubt in the mind of the trier of fact as to his guilty. Evidence Code § 501; People v. Bushton, 80 Cal. 160, 22 Pac. 127 (1889). If the defendant produces no evidence concerning the fact, there is no issue on the matter to be decided by the jury; hence, the jury may be instructed that the nonexistence of the fact must be assumed. See, e.g., People v. Harmon, 89 Cal.App.2d 55, 58, 200 P.2d 32, 34 (1948) (prosecution for narcotics possession; jury instructed "that the burden of proof is upon the defendant that he possessed a written prescription and that in the absence of such evidence it must be assumed that he had no such prescription"). See also People v. Boo Doo Hong, 122 Cal. 606, 607, 55 Pac. 402, 403 (1898).

Section 1981 of the Code of Civil Procedure (superseded by Evidence Code Section 500) provides that the party holding the affirmative of the issue must produce the evidence to prove it and that the burden of proof lies on the party who would be defeated if no evidence were given on either side. This section has been criticized as establishing a meaningless standard:

The "affirmative of the issue" lacks any substantial objective meaning, and the allocation of the burden actually requires the application of several rules of practice and policy, not entirely consistent and not wholly reliable. [Witkin, California Evidence § 56 at 72-73 (1958).]

That the burden is on the party having the affirmative [or] that a party is not required to prove a negative . . . is no more than a play on words, since practically any proposition may be stated in either affirmative or negative form. Thus a plaintiff's exercise of ordinary care equals absence of contributory negligence, in the minority of jurisdictions which place this element in plaintiff's case. In any event, the proposition seems simply not to be so. [Cleary, Presuming and Pleading: An Essay on Juristic Immaturity, 12 Stan.L.Rev. 5, 11 (1959).]

"The basic rule, which covers most situations, is that whatever facts a party must affirmatively plead he also has the burden of proving." Witkin, California Evidence § 56 at 73 (1958). Section 500 follows this basic rule. However, Section 500 is broader, applying to issues not necessarily raised in the pleadings.

Under Section 500, the burden of proof as to a particular fact is normally on the party to whose case the fact is essential. "[W]hen a party seeks relief the burden is upon him to prove his case, and he cannot depend wholly upon the failure of the defendant to prove his defenses." Cal. Employment Comm'n v. Malm, 59 Cal.App.2d 322, 323, 138 P.2d 744, 745 (1943). And, "as a general rule, the burden is on the defendant to prove new matter alleged as a defense . . ., even though it requires the proof of a negative." Wilson v. California Cent. R.R., 94 Cal. 166, 172, 29 Pac. 861, 864 (1892).

Section 500 does not attempt to indicate what facts may be essential to a particular party's claim for relief or defense. The facts that must be shown to establish a cause of action or a defense are determined by the substantive law, not the law of evidence.

The general rule allocating the burden of proof applies "except as otherwise provided by law." The exception is included in recognition of the fact that the burden of proof is sometimes allocated in a manner that is at variance with the general rule. In determining whether the normal allocation of the burden of proof should be altered, the courts consider a number of factors: the knowledge of the parties concerning the particular fact, the availability of the evidence to the parties, the most desirable result in terms of public policy in the absence of proof of the particular fact, and the probability of the existence or nonexistence of the fact. In determining the incidence of the burden of proof, "the truth is that there is not and cannot be any one general solvent for all cases. It is merely a question of policy and fairness based on experience in the different situations." 9 Wigmore, Evidence § 2486 at 275 (3d ed. 1940).

Under existing California law, certain matters have been called "presumptions" even though they do not fall within the definition contained in Code of Civil Procedure Section 1959 (superseded by Evidence Code Section 600). Both Section 1959 and Evidence Code Section 600 define a presumption to be an assumption or conclusion of fact that the law requires to be drawn from the proof or establishment of some other fact. Despite the statutory definition, subdivisions 1 and 4 of Code of Civil Procedure Section 1963 (superseded by Sections 520 and 521 of the Evidence Code) provide presumptions that a person is innocent of crime or wrong and that a person exercises ordinary care for his own concerns. Similarly, some cases refer to a presumption of sanity. It is apparent that these so-called presumptions do not arise from the establishment or proof of a fact in the action. In fact, they are not presumptions at all but are preliminary allocations of the burden of proof in regard to the particular issue. This preliminary allocation of the burden of proof may be satisfied in particular cases by proof of a fact giving rise to a presumption that does affect the burden of proof. For example, the initial burden of proving negligence may be satisfied in a particular case by proof that undamaged goods were delivered to a bailee and that such goods were lost or damaged while in the bailee's possession. Upon such proof, the bailee would have the burden of proof as to his lack of negligence. George v. Begins Van & Storage Co., 33 Cal.2d 834, 205 P.2d 1037 (1949). Cf. Com. Code § 7403.

Because the assumptions referred to above do not meet the definition of a presumption contained in Section 600, they are not continued in this code as presumptions. Instead, they appear in the next article in several sections allocating the burden of proof on specific issues. See Article 2 (Sections 520-522).

§ 501. Criminal actions; statutory assignment of burden of proof; controlling section. Insofar as any statute, except Section 522, assigns the burden of proof in a criminal action, such statute is subject to Penal Code Section 1096.

Law Revision Commission Comment

A statute assigning the burden of proof may require the party to whom the burden is assigned to raise a reasonable doubt in the mind of the trier of fact or to persuade the trier of fact by a preponderance of evidence, by clear and convincing proof, or by proof beyond a reasonable doubt. See Evidence Code § 115.

Sections 520-522 (Which assign the burden of proof on specific issues) may, at times, assign the burden of proof to the defendant in a criminal action. Elsewhere in the codes are other sections that either specifically allocate the burden of proof to the defendant in a criminal action or have been construed to allocate the burden of proof to the defense. For example, Health and Safety Code Section 11721 provides specifically that, in a prosecution for the use of narcotics, it is the burden of the defense to show that the narcotics were administered by or under the direction of a person licensed to prescribe and administer narcotics. Health and Safety Code Section 11500, on the other hand, prohibits the possession of narcotics but provides an exception for narcotics possessed pursuant to a prescription. The courts have construed this section to place the burden of proof on the defense to show that the exception applies and that the narcotics were possessed pursuant to a prescription. People v. Marschalk, 206 Cal.App.2d 346, 23 Cal.Rptr. 743 (1962); People v. Bill, 140 Cal.App. 389, 392-394, 35 P.2d 645, 647-648 (1934).

Section 501 is intended to make it clear that the statutory allocations of the burden of proof appearing in this chapter and elsewhere in the codes are subject to Penal Code Section 1096, which requires that a criminal defendant be proved guilty beyond a reasonable doubt, i.e., that the statutory allocations do not (except on the issue of insanity) require the defendant to persuade the trier of fact of his innocence. Under Evidence Code Section 522, as under existing law, the defendant must prove his insanity by a preponderance of the evidence. People v. Daugherty, 40 Cal.2d 876, 256 P.2d 911 (1953). However, where a statute allocates the burden of proof to the defendant on any other issue relating to the defendant's guilt, the defendant's burden, as under existing law, is merely to raise a reasonable doubt as to his guilt. People v. Bushton, 80 Cal. 160, 22 Pac. 127 (1889). Section 501 also makes it clear that, when a statute assigns the burden of proof to the prosecution in a criminal action, the prosecution must discharge that burden by proof beyond a reasonable doubt.

§ 502. Instructions on burden of proof. The court on all proper occasions shall instruct the jury as to which party bears the burden of proof on each issue and as to whether that burden requires that a party raise a reasonable doubt concerning the existence or nonexistence of a fact or that he establish the existence or nonexistence of a fact by a preponderance of the evidence, by clear and convincing proof, or by proof beyond a reasonable doubt.

Article 2. Burden of Proof on Specific Issues

§ 520. Claim that person guilty of crime or wrongdoing. The party claiming that a person is guilty of crime or wrongdoing has the burden of proof on that issue.

§ 521. Claim that person did not exercise care. The party claiming that a person did not exercise a requisite degree of care has the burden of proof on that issue.

Law Revision Commission Comment

Section 521 supersedes the presumption in subdivision 4 of Code of Civil Procedure Section 1963. Under existing law, the presumption is considered "evidence"; while under the Evidence Code, it is not. See Evidence Code § 600 and the Comment thereto.

§ 522. Claim that person is or was insane. The party claiming that any person, including himself, is or was insane has the burden of proof on that issue.

Law Revision Commission Comment

Section 522 codifies an allocation of the burden of proof that is frequently referred to in the cases as a presumption. See, e.g., People v. Daugherty, 40 Cal.2d 876, 899, 256 P.2d 911, 925-926 (1953).

§ 523. Historic locations of water; claims involving state land patents or grants. In any action where the state is a party, regardless of who is the moving party, where (a) the boundary of land patented or otherwise granted by the state is in dispute, or (b) the validity of any state patent or grant dated prior to 1950 is in dispute, the state shall have the burden of proof on all issues relating to the historic locations of rivers, streams, and other water bodies and the authority of the state in issuing the patent or grant.

This section is not intended to nor shall it be construed to supersede existing statutes governing disputes where the state is a party and regarding title to real property. [*Added 1994.*]

§ 524. Burden of proof in cases involving State Board of Equalization; unreasonable search or access to records prohibited; taxpayer defined. (a) Notwithstanding any other provision of law, in a civil proceeding to which the State Board of Equalization is a party, that board shall have the burden of proof by clear and convincing evidence in sustaining its assertion of a penalty for intent to evade or fraud against a taxpayer, with respect to any factual issue relevant to ascertaining the liability of a taxpayer.

(b) Nothing in this section shall be construed to override any requirement for a taxpayer to substantiate any item on a return or claim filed with the State Board of Equalization.

(c) Nothing in this section shall subject a taxpayer to unreasonable search or access to records in violation of the United States Constitution, the California Constitution, or any other law.

(d) For purposes of this section, "taxpayer" includes a person on whom fees administered by the State Board of Equalization are imposed. [*Added 2010.*]

Chapter 2. Burden of Producing Evidence

§ 550. Party who has the burden of producing evidence. (a) The burden of producing evidence as to a particular fact is on the party against whom a finding on that fact would be required in the absence of further evidence.

(b) The burden of producing evidence as to a particular fact is initially on the party with the burden of proof as to that fact.

Law Revision Commission Comment

Section 550 deals with the allocation of the burden of producing evidence. At the outset of the case, this burden will coincide with the burden of proof. 9 Wigmore, Evidence § 2487 at 279 (3d ed. 1940). However, during the course of the trial, the burden may shift from one party to another, irrespective of the incidence of the burden of proof. For example, if the party with the initial burden of producing evidence establishes a fact giving rise to a presumption, the burden of producing evidence will shift to the other party, whether or not the presumption is one that affects the burden of proof. In addition, a party may introduce evidence of such overwhelming probative force that no person could reasonably disbelieve it in the absence of countervailing evidence, in which case the burden of producing evidence would shift to the opposing party to produce some evidence. These principles are in accord with well-settled California law. See Discussion in Witkin, California Evidence §§ 53-56 (1958). See also 9 Wigmore, Evidence § 2487 (3d ed. 1940).

Chapter 3. Presumptions and Inferences

Article 1. General

§ 600. Presumption and inference defined. (a) A presumption is an assumption of fact that the law requires to be made from another fact or group of facts found or otherwise established in the action. A presumption is not evidence.

(b) An inference is a deduction of fact that may logically and reasonably be drawn from another fact or group of facts found or otherwise established in the action.

Assembly Committee on Judiciary Comment

The definition of a presumption in Section 600 is substantially the same as that contained in Code of Civil Procedure Section 1959: "A presumption is a deduction which the law expressly directs to be made from particular facts." Section 600 was derived from Rule 13 of the Uniform Rules of Evidence and supersedes Code of Civil Procedure Section 1959.

The second sentence of subdivision (a) may be unnecessary in light of the definition of "evidence" in Section 140— "testimony, writings, material objects, or other things presented to the senses that are offered to prove the existence or nonexistence of a fact." Presumptions, then, are not "evidence" but are conclusions that the law requires to be drawn (in the absence of a sufficient contrary showing) when some other fact is proved or otherwise established in the action.

Nonetheless, the second sentence has been added here to repudiate specifically the rule of Smellie v. Southern Pac. Co., 212 Cal. 540, 299 Pac. 529 (1931). That case held that a presumption is evidence that must be weighed against conflicting evidence; and in Scott v. Burke, 39 Cal.2d 388, 247 P.2d 313 (1952), the Supreme Court held that conflicting presumptions must be weighed against each other. These decisions require the jury to perform an intellectually impossible task. The jury is required to weigh the testimony of witnesses and other evidence as to the circumstances of a particular event against the fact that the law requires an opposing conclusion in the absence of contrary evidence and to determine which "evidence" is of greater probative force. Or else, the jury is required to accept the fact that the law requires two opposing conclusions and to determine which required conclusion is of greater probative force.

Moreover, the doctrine that a presumption is evidence imposes upon the party with the burden of proof a much higher burden of proof than is warranted. For example, if a party with the burden of proof has a presumption invoked against him and if the presumption remains in the case as evidence even though the jury believes that he has produced a preponderance of the evidence, the effect is that he must produce some additional but unascertainable quantum of proof in order to dispel the effect of the presumption. See Scott v. Burke, 39 Cal.2d 388, 405-406, 247 P.2d 313, 323-324 (1952) (dissenting opinion). The doctrine that a presumption is evidence gives no guidance to the jury or to the parties as to the amount of this additional proof. The most that should be expected of a party in a civil case is that he prove his case by a preponderance of the evidence (unless some specific presumption or rule of law requires proof of a particular issue by clear and convincing evidence). The most that should be expected of the prosecution in a criminal case is that it establish the defendant's guilt beyond a reasonable doubt. To require some additional quantum of proof, unspecified and uncertain in amount, to dispel a presumption which persists as evidence in the case unfairly weights the scales of justice against the party with the burden of proof.

To avoid the confusion engendered by the doctrine that a presumption is evidence, this code describes "evidence" as the matters presented in judicial proceedings and uses presumptions solely as devices to aid in determining the facts from the evidence presented.

The definition of "inference" in subdivision (b) restates in substance the definition contained in Code of Civil Procedure Sections 1958 and 1960. Under the Evidence Code, an inference is not itself evidence; it is the result of reasoning from evidence.

In the sections that follow, the Evidence Code classifies presumptions and lists a number of specific presumptions. Some presumptions that have been listed in the Code of Civil Procedure have not been listed as presumptions in the Evidence Code. But the fact that a statutory presumption has been repealed will not preclude the drawing of any appropriate inferences from the facts that would have given rise to the presumption. And, in appropriate cases, the court may instruct the jury on the propriety of drawing particular inferences.

§ 601. Classification of presumptions. A presumption is either conclusive or rebuttable. Every rebuttable presumption is either (a) a presumption affecting the burden of producing evidence or (b) a presumption affecting the burden of proof.

Law Revision Commission Comment

Under existing law, some presumptions are conclusive. The court or jury is required to find the existence of the presumed fact regardless of the strength of the opposing evidence. The conclusive presumptions are specified in Section 1962 of the Code of Civil Procedure (superseded by Article 2 (Sections 620-624) of this chapter).

Under existing law, too, all presumptions that are not conclusive are rebuttable presumptions. Code Civ.Proc. § 1961 (superseded by Evidence Code § 601). However, the existing statutes make no attempt to classify the rebuttable presumptions.

For several decades, courts and legal scholars have wrangled over the purpose and function of presumptions. The view espoused by Professors Thayer (Thayer, Preliminary Treatise on Evidence 313-352 (1898)) and Wigmore (9 Wigmore, Evidence §§ 2485-2491 (3d ed. 1940)), accepted by most courts (see Morgan, Presumptions, 10 Rutgers L.Rev. 512, 516 (1956)), and adopted by the American Law Institute's Model Code of

Evidence, is that a presumption is a preliminary assumption of fact that disappears from the case upon the introduction of evidence sufficient to sustain a finding of the nonexistence of the presumed fact. In Professor Thayer's view, a presumption merely reflects the judicial determination that the same conclusionary fact exists so frequently when the preliminary fact exists that, once the preliminary fact is established, proof of the conclusionary fact may be dispensed with unless there is actually some contrary evidence:

> Many facts and groups of facts often recur, and when a body of men with a continuous tradition has carried on for some length of time this process of reasoning upon facts that often repeat themselves, they cut short the process and lay down a rule. To such facts they affix, by a general declaration, the character and operation which common experience has assigned to them. [Thayer, Preliminary Treatise on Evidence 326 (1898).]

Professors Morgan and McCormick argue that a presumption should shift the burden of proof to the adverse party. Morgan, Some Problems of Proof 81 (1956); McCormick, Evidence § 317 at 671-672 (1954). They believe that presumptions are created for reasons of policy and argue that, if the policy underlying a presumption is of sufficient weight to require a finding of the presumed fact when there is no contrary evidence, it should be of sufficient weight to require a finding when the mind of the trier of fact is in equilibrium, and, a fortiori, it should be of sufficient weight to require a finding if the trier of fact does not believe the contrary evidence.

The classification of presumptions in the Evidence Code is based on a third view suggested by Professor Bohlen in 1920. Bohlen, The Effect of Rebuttable Presumptions of Law Upon the Burden of Proof, 68 U.Pa.L.Rev. 307 (1920). Underlying the presumptions provisions of the Evidence Code is the conclusion that the Thayer view is correct as to some presumptions, but that the Morgan view is right as to others. The fact is that presumptions are created for a variety of reasons, and no single theory or rationale of presumptions can deal adequately with all of them. Hence, the Evidence Code classifies all rebuttable presumptions as either (1) presumptions affecting the burden of producing evidence (essentially Thayer presumptions), or (2) presumptions affecting the burden of proof (essentially Morgan presumptions).

Sections 603 and 605 set forth the criteria by which the two classes of rebuttable presumptions may be distinguished, and Sections 604, 606, and 607 prescribe their effect. Articles 3 and 4 (Sections 630-668) classify many presumptions found in California law; but many other presumptions, both statutory and common law, must await classification by the courts in accordance with the criteria contained in Sections 603 and 605.

The classification scheme contained in the Evidence Code follows a distinction that appears in the California cases. Thus, for example, the courts have at times held that presumptions do not affect the burden of proof. Estate of Eakle, 33 Cal.App.2d 379, 91 P.2d 954 (1939) (presumption of undue influence); Valentine v. Provident Mut. Life Ins. Co., 12 Cal.App.2d 616, 55 P.2d 1243 (1936) (presumption of death from seven years' absence). And at other times the courts have held that certain presumptions do affect the burden of proof. Estate of Nickson, 187 Cal. 603, 203 Pac. 106 (1921) ("clear and convincing proof" required to overcome presumption of community property); Estate of Walker, 180 Cal. 478, 181 Pac. 792 (1919) ("clear and satisfactory proof" required to overcome presumption of legitimacy). The cases have not, however, explicitly recognized the distinction, nor have they applied it consistently. Compare Estate of Eakle, supra (presumption of undue influence does not affect burden of proof), with Estate of Witt, 198 Cal. 407, 245 Pac. 197 (1926) (presumption of undue influence must be overcome with "the clearest and most satisfactory evidence"). The Evidence Code clarifies the law relating to presumptions by identifying the distinguishing factors, and it provides a measure of certainty by classifying a number of specific presumptions.

§ 602. Statute making one fact prima facie evidence of another fact. A statute providing that a fact or group of facts is prima facie evidence of another fact establishes a rebuttable presumption.

Law Revision Commission Comment

Section 602 indicates the construction to be given to the large number of statutes scattered through the codes that state that one fact or group of facts is prima facie evidence of another fact. See, e.g., Agric.Code § 18, Com.Code § 1202, Rev. & Tax.Code § 6714. In some instances, these statutes have been enacted for reasons of public policy that require them to be treated as presumptions affecting the burden of proof. See People v. Schwartz, 31 Cal.2d 59, 63, 187 P.2d 12, 14 (1947); People v. Mahoney, 13 Cal.2d 729, 732-733, 91 P.2d 1029, 1030-1031 (1939). It seems likely, however, that in many instances such statutes are not intended to affect the burden of proof but only the burden of producing evidence. Section 602 provides that these statutes are to be regarded as rebuttable presumptions. Hence, unless some specific language applicable to the particular statute in question indicates whether it affects the burden of proof or only the burden of producing evidence, the courts will be required to classify these statutes as presumptions affecting the burden of proof or the burden of producing evidence in accordance with the criteria set forth in Sections 603 and 605.

§ 603. Presumption affecting the burden of producing evidence defined. A presumption affecting the burden of producing evidence is a presumption established to implement no public policy other than to facilitate the determination of the particular action in which the presumption is applied.

Law Revision Commission Comment

Sections 603 and 605 set forth the criteria for determining whether a particular presumption is a presumption affecting the burden of producing evidence or a presumption affecting the burden of proof. Many presumptions are classified in Articles 3 and 4 (Sections 630-668) of this chapter. In the absence of specific statutory classification, the courts may determine whether a presumption is a presumption affecting the burden of producing evidence or a presumption affecting the burden of proof by applying the standards contained in Sections 603 and 605.

Section 603 describes those presumptions that are not based on any public policy extrinsic to the action in which they are invoked. These presumptions are designed to dispense with unnecessary proof of facts that are likely to be true if not disputed. Typically, such presumptions are based on an underlying logical inference. In some cases, the presumed fact is so likely to be true and so little likely to be disputed that the law requires it to be assumed in the absence of contrary evidence. In other cases, evidence of the nonexistence of the presumed fact, if there is any, is so much more readily available to the party against whom the presumption operates that he is not permitted to argue that the presumed fact does not exist unless he is willing to produce such evidence. In still other cases, there may be no direct evidence of the existence or nonexistence of the presumed fact; but, because the case must be decided, the law requires a determination that the presumed fact exists in light of common experience indicating that it usually exists in such cases. Cf. Bohlen, Studies in the Law of Torts 644 (1926). Typical of such presumptions are the presumption that a mailed letter was received (Section 641) and presumptions relating to the authenticity of documents (Sections 643-645).

The presumptions described in Section 603 are not expressions of policy; they are expressions of experience. They are intended solely to eliminate the need for the trier of fact to reason from the proven or established fact to the presumed fact and to forestall argument over the existence of the presumed fact when there is no evidence tending to prove the nonexistence of the presumed fact.

§ 604. Effect of presumption affecting burden of producing evidence. The effect of a presumption affecting the burden of producing evidence is to require the trier of fact to assume the existence of the presumed fact unless and until evidence is introduced which would support a finding of its nonexistence, in which case the trier of fact shall determine the existence or nonexistence of the presumed fact from the evidence and without regard to the presumption. Nothing in this section shall be construed to prevent the drawing of any inference that may be appropriate.

Assembly Committee on Judiciary Comment

Section 604 describes the manner in which a presumption affecting the burden of producing evidence operates. Such a presumption is merely a preliminary assumption in the absence of contrary evidence, i.e., evidence sufficient to sustain a finding of the nonexistence of the presumed fact. If contrary evidence is introduced, the trier of fact must weigh the inferences arising from the facts that gave rise to the presumption against the contrary evidence and resolve the conflict. For example, if a party proves that a letter was mailed, the trier of fact is required to find that the letter was received in the absence of any believable contrary evidence. However, if the adverse party denies receipt, the presumption is gone from the case. The trier of fact must then weigh the denial of receipt against the inference of receipt arising from proof of mailing and decide whether or not the letter was received.

If a presumption affecting the burden of producing evidence is relied on, the judge must determine whether there is evidence sufficient to sustain a finding of the nonexistence of the presumed fact. If there is such evidence, the presumption disappears and the judge need say nothing about it in his instructions. If there is not evidence sufficient to sustain a finding of the nonexistence of the presumed fact, the judge should instruct the jury concerning the presumption. If the basic fact from which the presumption arises is established (by the pleadings, by stipulation, by judicial notice, etc.) so that the existence of the basic fact is not a question of fact for the jury, the jury should be instructed that the presumed fact is also established. If the basic fact is a question of fact for the jury, the judge should charge the jury that, if it finds the basic fact, the jury must also find the presumed fact. Morgan, Basic Problems of Evidence 36-38 (1957).

Of course, in a criminal case, the jury has the power to disregard the judge's instructions and find a defendant guilty of a lesser crime than that shown by the evidence or acquit a defendant despite the facts established by the undisputed evidence. Cf. People v. Powell, 34 Cal.2d 196, 208 P.2d 974 (1949); Pike, What Is Second Degree Murder in California?, 9 So.Cal.L.Rev. 112, 128-132 (1936). Nonetheless, the jury should be instructed on the rules of law applicable, including those rules of law called presumptions. The fact that the jury may choose to disregard the applicable rules of law should not affect the nature of the instructions given. See People v. Lem You, 97 Cal. 224, 32 Pac. 11 (1893); People v. Macken, 32 Cal.App.2d 31, 89 P.2d 173 (1939).

§ 605. Presumption affecting the burden of proof defined. A presumption affecting the burden of proof is a presumption established to implement some public policy other than to facilitate the determination of the particular action in which the presumption is applied, such as the policy in favor of establishment of a parent and child relationship, the validity of marriage, the stability of titles to property, or the security of those who entrust themselves or their property to the administration of others. [*Amended 1975.*]

Law Revision Commission Comment

Section 605 describes a presumption affecting the burden of proof. Such presumptions are established in order to carry out or to effectuate some public policy other than or in addition to the policy of facilitating the trial of actions.

Frequently, presumptions affecting the burden of proof are designed to facilitate determination of the action in which they are applied. Superficially, therefore, such presumptions may appear merely to be presumptions affecting the burden of producing evidence. What makes a presumption one affecting the burden of proof is the fact that there is always some further reason of policy for the establishment of the presumption. It is the existence of this further basis in policy that distinguishes a presumption affecting the burden of proof from a presumption affecting the burden of producing evidence. For example, the presumption of death from seven years' absence (Section 667) exists in part to facilitate the disposition of actions by supplying a rule of thumb to govern certain cases in which there is likely to be no direct evidence of the presumed fact. But the policy in favor of distributing estates, of settling titles, and of permitting life to proceed normally at some time prior to the expiration of the absentee's normal life expectancy (perhaps 30 or 40 years) that underlies the presumption indicates that it should be a presumption affecting the burden of proof.

Frequently, too, a presumption affecting the burden of proof will have an underlying basis in probability and logical inference. For example, the presumption of the validity of a ceremonial marriage may be based in part on the probability that most marriages are valid. However, an underlying logical inference is not essential. In fact, the lack of an underlying inference is a strong indication that the presumption affects the burden of proof. Only the needs of public policy can justify the direction of a particular assumption that is not warranted by the application of probability and common experience to the known facts. Thus, the total lack of any inference underlying the presumption of the negligence of an employer that arises from his failure to secure the payment of workmen's compensation (Labor Code § 3708) is a clear indication that the presumption is based on public policy and affects the burden of proof. Similarly, the fact that the presumption of death from seven years' absence may conflict directly with the logical inference that life continues for its normal expectancy is an indication that the presumption is based on public policy and, hence, affects the burden of proof.

§ 606. Effect of presumption affecting burden of proof. The effect of a presumption affecting the burden of proof is to impose upon the party against whom it operates the burden of proof as to the nonexistence of the presumed fact.

Assembly Committee on Judiciary Comment

Section 606 describes the manner in which a presumption affecting the burden of proof operates. In the ordinary case, the party against whom it is invoked will have the burden of proving the nonexistence of the presumed fact by a preponderance of the evidence. Certain presumptions affecting the burden of proof may be overcome only by clear and convincing proof. When such a presumption is relied on, the party against whom the presumption operates will have a heavier burden of proof and will be required to persuade the trier of fact of the nonexistence of the presumed fact by proof "sufficiently strong to command the unhesitating assent of every reasonable mind." Sheehan v. Sullivan, 126 Cal. 189, 193, 58 Pac. 543, 544 (1899).

If the party against whom the presumption operates already has the same burden of proof as to the nonexistence of the presumed fact that is assigned by the presumption, the presumption can have no effect on the case and no instruction in regard to the presumption should be given. See Speck v. Sarver, 20 Cal.2d 585, 590, 128 P.2d 16, 19 (1942) (dissenting opinion by Traynor, J.); Morgan, Instructing the Jury Upon Presumptions and Burden of Proof, 47 Harv.L.Rev. 59, 69 (1933). If the evidence is not sufficient to sustain a finding of the nonexistence of the presumed fact, the judge's instructions will be the same as if the presumption were merely a presumption affecting the burden of producing evidence. See the Comment to Section 604. If there is evidence of the nonexistence of the presumed fact, the judge should instruct the jury on the manner in which the presumption affects the factfinding process. If the basic fact from which the presumption arises is so established that the existence of the basic fact is not a question of fact for the jury (as, for example, by the pleadings, by judicial notice, or by stipulation of the parties), the judge should instruct the jury that the existence of the presumed fact is to be assumed until the jury is persuaded to the contrary by the requisite degree of proof (proof by a preponderance of the evidence, clear and convincing proof, etc.). See McCormick, Evidence § 317 at 672 (1954). If the basic fact is a question of fact for the jury, the judge should instruct the jury that, if it finds the basic fact, it must also find the presumed fact unless persuaded of the nonexistence of the presumed fact by the requisite degree of proof. Morgan, Basic Problems of Evidence 38 (1957).

In a criminal case, a presumption affecting the burden of proof may be relied upon by the prosecution to establish an element of the crime with which the defendant is charged. The effect of the presumption on the factfinding process and the nature of the instructions in such a case are described in Section 607 and the Comment thereto. On other issues, a presumption affecting the burden of proof will have the same effect in a criminal case as it does in a civil case, and the instructions will be the same.

§ 607. Effect of presumption that establishes an element. When a presumption affecting the burden of proof operates in a criminal action to establish presumptively any fact that is essential to the defendant's guilt, the presumption operates only if the facts that give rise to the presumption have been found or otherwise established beyond a reasonable doubt and, in such case, the defendant need only raise a reasonable doubt as to the existence of the presumed fact.

Assembly Committee on Judiciary Comment

If a presumption affecting the burden of proof is relied upon by the prosecution in a criminal case to establish a fact essential to the defendant's guilt, the defendant will not be required to overcome the presumption by clear and convincing evidence or even by a preponderance of the evidence; the defendant will be required merely to raise a reasonable doubt as to the existence of the presumed fact. This is the effect of a presumption in a criminal case under existing law. People v. Hardy, 33 Cal.2d 52, 198 P.2d 865 (1948); People v. Scott, 24 Cal.2d 774, 151 P.2d 517 (1944); People v. Agnew, 16 Cal.2d 655, 107 P.2d 601 (1940).

Instructions in criminal cases on presumptions affecting the burden of proof will be similar to the instructions given on presumptions and on issues where the defendant has the burden of proof under existing law. Where no evidence has been introduced to show the nonexistence of the presumed fact, the court should instruct the jury that, if it finds beyond a reasonable doubt the facts giving rise to the presumption, it should also find the presumed fact. Where some evidence of the nonexistence of the presumed fact has been introduced, the court should instruct the jury that, if it finds beyond a reasonable doubt the facts giving rise to the presumption, it should also find the presumed fact unless the contrary evidence has raised a reasonable doubt as to the existence of the presumed fact. Cf. People v. Hardy, 33 Cal.2d 52, 63-64, 198 P.2d 865, 871-872 (1948); People v. Agnew, 16 Cal.2d 655, 661-667, 107 P.2d 601, 603-607 (1940); People v. Martina, 140 Cal.App.2d 17, 25, 294 P.2d 1015, 1019 (1956). The judge must be careful to specify that a presumption is rebutted by any evidence that raises a reasonable doubt as to the presumed fact. In the absence of this qualification, the jury may be led to believe that the defendant has the burden of disproof of the presumed fact by a preponderance of the evidence and the instruction will be erroneous. People v. Agnew, 16 Cal.2d 655, 107 P.2d 601 (1940). Cf. People v. Hardy, 33 Cal.2d 52, 198 P.2d 865 (1948).

Of course, in a criminal case, the jury may choose to disregard the instructions relating to presumptions. But this should not affect the duty of the court to instruct the jury on the rules of law, including presumptions, applicable to the case. See the Comment to Section 604.

Section 607 does not apply to the "presumption" of sanity. Under the Evidence Code, the burden of proof on the issue of sanity is allocated by Section 522, and there is no "presumption" of sanity. See Evidence Code § 522 and the Comment thereto. Hence, notwithstanding the provisions of Section 607, a defendant who pleads insanity has the burden of proving by a preponderance of the evidence that he was insane. See the Comment to Section 501.

Article 2. Conclusive Presumptions

§ 620. Conclusive presumptions. The presumptions established by this article [§§ 622-624], and all other presumptions declared by law to be conclusive, are conclusive presumptions.

Law Revision Commission Comment

This article supersedes and continues in effect without substantive change the provisions of subdivisions 2, 3, 4, and 5 of Section 1962 of the Code of Civil Procedure. Other statutes not listed in this article also provide conclusive presumptions. See, e.g., Civil Code § 3440. There may also be a few nonstatutory conclusive presumptions. See Witkin, California Evidence § 63 (1958).

Conclusive presumptions are not evidentiary rules so much as they are rules of substantive law. Hence, the Commission has not recommended any substantive revision of the conclusive presumptions contained in this article.

§ 622. Facts recited in written instrument. The facts recited in a written instrument are conclusively presumed to be true as between the parties thereto, or their successors in interest; but this rule does not apply to the recital of a consideration.

§ 623. Estoppel by own statement or conduct. Whenever a party has, by his own statement or conduct, intentionally and deliberately led another to believe a particular thing true and to act upon such belief, he is not, in any litigation arising out of such statement or conduct, permitted to contradict it.

§ 624. Estoppel of tenant to deny title of landlord. A tenant is not permitted to deny the title of his landlord at the time of the commencement of the relation.

Article 3. Presumptions Affecting the Burden of Producing Evidence

Law Revision Commission Comment

Article 3 sets forth a list of presumptions, recognized in existing law, that are classified here as presumptions affecting the burden of producing evidence. The list is not exhaustive. Other presumptions affecting the burden of producing evidence may be found in other codes. Others will be found in the common law. Specific statutes will classify some of these, but some must await classification by the courts. The list here, however, will eliminate any uncertainty as to the proper classification for the presumptions in this article.

§ 630. Presumptions affecting the burden of producing evidence. The presumptions established by this article [§§ 631-647], and all other rebuttable presumptions established by law that fall within the criteria of Section 603, are presumptions affecting the burden of producing evidence.

§ 631. Money delivered by one to another. Money delivered by one to another is presumed to have been due to the latter.

§ 632. Thing delivered by one to another. A thing delivered by one to another is presumed to have belonged to the latter.

§ 633. Obligation delivered up to the debtor. An obligation delivered up to the debtor is presumed to have been paid.

§ 634. Person in possession of order on himself. A person in possession of an order on himself for the payment of money, or delivery of a thing, is presumed to have paid the money or delivered the thing accordingly.

§ 635. Obligation possessed by creditor. An obligation possessed by the creditor is presumed not to have been paid.

§ 636. Payment of earlier rent or installments. The payment of earlier rent or installments is presumed from a receipt for later rent or installments.

§ 637. Ownership of things possessed. The things which a person possesses are presumed to be owned by him.

§ 638. Ownership of property by person who exercises acts of ownership. A person who exercises acts of ownership over property is presumed to be the owner of it.

§ 639. Judgment correctly determines rights of parties. A judgment, when not conclusive, is presumed to correctly determine or set forth the rights of the parties, but there is no presumption that the facts essential to the judgment have been correctly determined.

Law Revision Commission Comment

* * * The presumption involved here is that the judgment correctly determines that one party owes another money, or that the parties are divorced, or their marriage has been annulled, or any similar rights of the parties. The presumption does not apply to the facts underlying the judgment. For example, a judgment of annulment is presumed to determine correctly that the marriage is void. Clark v. City of Los Angeles, 187 Cal.App.2d 792, 9 Cal.Rptr. 913 (1960). However, the judgment may not be used to establish presumptively that one of the parties was guilty of fraud as against some third party who is not bound by the judgment.

In a few cases, a judgment may be used as evidence of the facts necessarily determined by the judgment. See, e.g., Evidence Code §§ 1300-1302. But, even in those cases, the judgments do not presumptively establish the facts determined; they are merely evidence.

§ 640. Writing truly dated. A writing is presumed to have been truly dated.

§ 641. Letter received in ordinary course of mail. A letter correctly addressed and properly mailed is presumed to have been received in the ordinary course of mail.

§ 642. Conveyance by person having duty to convey real property. A trustee or other person, whose duty it was to convey real property to a particular person, is presumed to have actually conveyed to him when such presumption is necessary to perfect title of such person or his successor in interest.

§ 643. Authenticity of ancient document. A deed or will or other writing purporting to create, terminate, or affect an interest in real or personal property is presumed to be authentic if it:

(a) Is at least 30 years old;

(b) Is in such condition as to create no suspicion concerning its authenticity;

(c) Was kept, or if found was found, in a place where such writing, if authentic, would be likely to be kept or found; and

(d) Has been generally acted upon as authentic by persons having an interest in the matter.

Law Revision Commission Comment

Section 643 restates and supersedes the presumption found in subdivision 34 of Code of Civil Procedure Section 1963. Although the statement of the ancient documents rule in Section 1963 requires the document to have been acted upon as if genuine before the presumption applies, some recent cases have not insisted upon this requirement. Estate of Nidever, 181 Cal.App.2d 367, 5 Cal.Rptr. 343 (1960); Kirkpatrick v. Tapo Oil Co., 144 Cal.App.2d 404, 301 P.2d 274 (1956). The requirement that the document be acted upon as genuine is, in substance, a requirement of the possession of property by those persons who would be entitled to such possession under the document if it were genuine. See 7 Wigmore, Evidence ss 2141, 2146 (3d ed. 1940); Tentative Recommendation and a Study Relating to the Uniform Rules of Evidence (Article IX. Authentication and Content of Writings), 6 Cal. Law Revision Comm'n, Rep., Rec. & Studies 101, 135-137 (1964). Giving the ancient documents rule a presumptive effect—i.e., requiring a finding of the authenticity of an ancient document—seems justified when it is a dispositive instrument and the persons interested in the matter have acted upon the instrument for a period of at least 30 years as if it were genuine. Evidence which is not of this strength may be sufficient in particular cases to warrant an inference of genuineness and thus justify the admission of the document into evidence, but the presumption should be confined to those cases where the evidence of genuineness is not likely to be disputed. See 7 Wigmore, Evidence § 2146 (3d ed. 1940). Accordingly, Section 643 limits the presumptive application of the ancient documents rule to dispositive instruments.

§ 644. Book purporting to be published by public authority. A book, purporting to be printed or published by public authority, is presumed to have been so printed or published.

§ 645. Book purporting to contain reports of cases. A book, purporting to contain reports of cases adjudged in the tribunals of the state or nation where the book is published, is presumed to contain correct reports of such cases.

§ 645.1. Printed materials purporting to be particular newspaper or periodical. Printed materials, purporting to be a particular newspaper or periodical, are presumed to be that newspaper or periodical if regularly issued at average intervals not exceeding three months. [*Added 1986.*]

§ 646. Res ipsa loquitur; instruction. (a) As used in this section, "defendant" includes any party against whom the res ipsa loquitur presumption operates.

(b) The judicial doctrine of res ipsa loquitur is a presumption affecting the burden of producing evidence.

(c) If the evidence, or facts otherwise established, would support a res ipsa loquitur presumption and the defendant has introduced evidence which would support a finding that he was not negligent or that any negligence on his part was not a proximate cause of the occurrence, the court may, and upon request shall, instruct the jury to the effect that:

(1) If the facts which would give rise to a res ipsa loquitur presumption are found or otherwise established, the jury may draw the inference from such facts that a proximate cause of the occurrence was some negligent conduct on the part of the defendant; and

(2) The jury shall not find that a proximate cause of the occurrence was some negligent conduct on the part of the defendant unless the jury believes, after weighing all the evidence in the case and drawing such inferences therefrom as the jury believes are warranted, that it is more probable than not that the occurrence was caused by some negligent conduct on the part of the defendant. [*Added 1970.*]

Law Revision Commission Comment - 1970 Addition

Section 646 is designed to clarify the manner in which the doctrine of res ipsa loquitur functions under the provisions of the Evidence Code relating to presumptions.

The doctrine of res ipsa loquitur, as developed by the California courts, is applicable in an action to recover damages for negligence when the plaintiff establishes three conditions:

First, that it is the kind of [accident] [injury] which ordinarily does not occur in the absence of someone's negligence;

Second, that it was caused by an agency or instrumentality in the exclusive control of the defendant [originally, and which was not mishandled or otherwise changed after defendant relinquished control]; and

Third, that the [accident] [injury] was not due to any voluntary action or contribution on the part of the plaintiff which was the responsible cause of his injury [BAJI (5th ed.1969) No. 4.00 (brackets in original).]

This section provides that the doctrine of res ipsa loquitur is a presumption affecting the burden of producing evidence. Therefore, when the plaintiff has established the three conditions that give rise to the doctrine, the jury is required to find that the accident resulted from the defendant's negligence unless the defendant comes forward with evidence that would support a contrary finding. EVIDENCE CODE 604. If evidence is produced that would support a finding that the defendant was not negligent or that any negligence on his part was not a proximate cause of the accident, the presumptive effect of the doctrine vanishes. However, the jury may still be able to draw an inference that the accident was caused by the defendant's lack of due care from the facts that gave rise to the presumption. See EVIDENCE CODE § 604 and the Comment thereto. In rare cases, the defendant may produce such conclusive evidence that the inference of negligence is dispelled as a matter of law. See, e.g., Leonard v. Watsonville Community Hosp., 47 Cal.2d 509, 305 P.2d 36 (1956). But, except in such a case, the facts giving rise to the doctrine will support an inference of negligence even after its presumptive effect has disappeared.

To assist the jury in the performance of its factfinding function, the court may instruct that the facts that give rise to res ipsa loquitur are themselves circumstantial evidence from which the jury can infer that the accident resulted from the defendant's failure to exercise due care. This section requires the court to give such an instruction when a party so requests. Whether the jury should so find will depend on whether the jury believes that the probative force of the circumstantial and other evidence of the defendant's negligence exceeds the probative force of the contrary evidence and, therefore, that it is more probable than not that the accident resulted from the defendant's negligence.

At times the doctrine of res ipsa loquitur will coincide in a particular case with another presumption or with another rule of law that requires the defendant to discharge the burden of proof on the issue. See Prosser, Res Ipsa Loquitur in California, 37 Cal.L.Rev. 183 (1949). In such cases the defendant will have the burden of proof on issues where res ipsa loquitur appears to apply. But because of the allocation of the burden of proof to the defendant, the doctrine of res ipsa loquitur will serve no function in the disposition of the case. However, the facts that would give rise to the doctrine may nevertheless be used as circumstantial evidence tending to rebut the evidence produced by the party with the burden of proof.

For example, a bailee who has received undamaged goods and returns damaged goods has the burden of proving that the damage was not caused by his negligence unless the damage resulted from a fire. See discussion in Redfoot v. J. T. Jenkins Co., 138 Cal.App.2d 108, 112, 291 P.2d 134, 135 (1955). See Com. Code § 7403(1) (b). When the defendant has produced evidence of his exercise of care in regard to the bailed goods, the facts that would give rise to the doctrine of res ipsa loquitur may be weighed against the evidence produced by the defendant in determining whether it is more likely than not that the goods were damaged without fault on the part of the bailee. But because the bailee has both the burden of producing evidence and the burden of proving that the damage was not caused by his negligence, the presumption of negligence arising from res ipsa loquitur cannot have any effect on the proceeding.

Effect of the Failure of the Plaintiff to Establish All the Preliminary Facts That Give Rise to the Presumption.

The fact that the plaintiff fails to establish all of the facts giving rise to the res ipsa presumption does not necessarily mean that he has not produced sufficient evidence of negligence to sustain a jury finding in his favor. The requirements of res ipsa loquitur are merely those that must be met to give rise to a compelled conclusion (or presumption) of negligence in the absence of contrary evidence. An inference of negligence may well be warranted from all of the evidence in the case even though the plaintiff fails to establish all the elements of res ipsa loquitur. See Prosser, Res Ipsa Loquitur: A Reply to Professor Carpenter, 10 So.Cal.L.Rev. 459 (1937). In appropriate cases, therefore, the jury may be instructed that, even though it does not find that the facts giving rise to the presumption have been proved by a preponderance of the evidence, it may nevertheless find the defendant negligent if it concludes from a consideration of all the evidence that it is more probable than not that the defendant was negligent. Such an instruction would be appropriate, for example, in a case where there was evidence of the defendant's negligence apart from the evidence going to the elements of the res ipsa loquitur doctrine.

Examples of Operation of Res Ipsa Loquitur Presumption.

The doctrine of res ipsa loquitur may be applicable to a case under four varying sets of circumstances:

(1) Where the facts giving rise to the doctrine are established as a matter of law (by the pleadings by stipulation, by pretrial order, or by some other means) and there is no evidence sufficient to sustain a finding either that the accident resulted from some cause other than the defendant's negligence or that he exercised due care in all possible respects wherein he might have been negligent.

(2) Where the facts giving rise to the doctrine are established as a matter of law, but the defendant has introduced evidence sufficient to sustain a finding either of his due care or of some cause for the accident other than his negligence.

(3) Where the defendant introduces evidence tending to show the nonexistence of the essential conditions of the doctrine but does not introduce evidence to rebut the presumption.

(4) Where the defendant introduces evidence to contest both the conditions of the doctrine and the conclusion that his negligence caused the accident.

Set forth below is an explanation of the manner in which this section functions in each of these situations.

Basic facts established as a matter of law; no rebuttal evidence. If the basic facts that give rise to the presumption are established as a matter of law (by the pleadings, by stipulation, by pretrial order, etc.), the presumption requires that the jury find that the defendant's negligence was the proximate cause of the accident unless evidence is introduced sufficient to sustain a finding either that the accident resulted from some cause other than the defendant's negligence or that he exercised due care in all possible respects wherein he might have been negligent. When the defendant fails to introduce such evidence, the court must simply instruct the jury that it is required to find that the accident was caused by the defendant's negligence.

For example, if a plaintiff automobile passenger sues the driver for injuries sustained in an accident, the defendant may determine not to contest the fact that the accident was of a type that ordinarily does not occur unless the driver was negligent. Moreover, the defendant may introduce no evidence that he exercised due care in the driving of the automobile. Instead, the defendant may rest his defense solely on the ground that the plaintiff was a guest and not a paying passenger. In this case, the court should instruct the jury that it must assume that the defendant was negligent. Cf. Phillips v. Noble, 50 Cal.2d 163, 323 P.2d 385 (1958); Fiske v. Wilkie, 67 Cal.App.2d 440, 154 P.2d 725 (1945).

Basic facts established as matter of law; evidence introduced to rebut presumption. Where the facts giving rise to the doctrine are established as a matter of law but the defendant has introduced evidence sufficient to sustain a finding either of his due care or of a cause for the accident other than his negligence, the presumptive effect of the doctrine vanishes. Except in those rare cases where the inference is dispelled as a matter of law, the court may instruct the jury that it may infer from the established facts that negligence on the part of the defendant was a proximate cause of the accident. The court is required to give such an instruction when requested. The instruction should make it clear, however, that the jury should not find that a proximate cause of the occurrence was some negligent conduct on the part of the defendant unless the jury believes, after weighing all the evidence in the case, that it is more probable than not that the accident was caused by the defendant's negligence.

Basic facts contested; no rebuttal evidence. The defendant may attack only the elements of the doctrine. His purpose in doing so would be to prevent the application of the doctrine. In this situation, the court cannot determine whether the doctrine is applicable or not because the basic facts that give rise to the doctrine must be determined by the jury. Therefore, the court must give an instruction on what has become known as conditional res ipsa loquitur.

Where the basic facts contested by evidence, but there is no rebuttal evidence, the court should instruct the jury that, if it finds that the basic facts have been established by a preponderance of the evidence, then it must also find that the accident was caused by some negligent conduct on the part of the defendant.

Basic facts contested; evidence introduced to rebut presumption. The defendant may introduce evidence that both attacks the basic facts that underlie the doctrine of res ipsa loquitur and tends to show that the accident was not caused by his failure to exercise due care. Because of the evidence contesting the presumed conclusion of negligence, the presumptive effect of the doctrine vanishes, and the greatest effect the doctrine can have in the case is to support an inference that the accident resulted from the defendant's negligence.

In this situation, the court should instruct the jury that, if it finds that the basic facts have been established by a preponderance of the evidence, then it may infer from those facts that the accident was caused because the defendant was negligent. But the court shall also instruct the jury that it should not find that a proximate cause of the accident was some negligent conduct on the part of the defendant unless it believes, after weighing all of the evidence, that it is more probable than not that the defendant was negligent and that the accident resulted from his negligence. Other Appropriate Instructions.

The jury instructions referred to in Section 646 do not preclude the judge from giving the jury any additional instructions on res ipsa loquitur that are appropriate to the particular case. [9 Cal. L. Rev. Comm. Reports 137 (1970).]

§ 647. Return of process served by registered process server. The return of a process server registered pursuant to Chapter 16 (commencing with Section 22350) of Division 8 of the Business and Professions Code upon process or notice establishes a presumption, affecting the burden of producing evidence, of the facts stated in the return. [*Added 1978.*]

Article 4. Presumptions Affecting the Burden of Proof

§ 660. Presumptions affecting the burden of proof. The presumptions established by this article [§§ 662-670], and all other rebuttable presumptions established by law that fall within the criteria of Section 605, are presumptions affecting the burden of proof.

Law Revision Commission Comment

In some cases it may be difficult to determine whether a particular presumption is a presumption affecting the burden of proof or a presumption affecting the burden of producing evidence. To avoid uncertainty, it is desirable to classify as many presumptions as possible. Article 4 (§§ 660-668), therefore, lists several presumptions that are to be regarded as presumptions affecting the burden of proof. The list is not exclusive. Other statutory and common law presumptions that affect the burden of proof must await classification by the courts.

§ 662. Owner of legal title to property is owner of beneficial title. The owner of the legal title to property is presumed to be the owner of the full beneficial title. This presumption may be rebutted only by clear and convincing proof.

§ 663. Ceremonial marriage. A ceremonial marriage is presumed to be valid.

§ 664. Official duty regularly performed. It is presumed that official duty has been regularly performed. This presumption does not apply on an issue as to the lawfulness of an arrest if it is found or otherwise established that the arrest was made without a warrant.

§ 665. Ordinary consequences of voluntary act. A person is presumed to intend the ordinary consequences of his voluntary act. This presumption is inapplicable in a criminal action to establish the specific intent of the defendant where specific intent is an element of the crime charged.

§ 666. Judicial action in lawful exercise of jurisdiction. Any court of this state or the United States, or any court of general jurisdiction in any other state or nation, or any judge of such a court, acting as such, is presumed to have acted in the lawful exercise of its jurisdiction. This presumption applies only when the act of the court or judge is under collateral attack.

Assembly Committee on Judiciary Comment

Section 666 restates and supersedes the presumption in subdivision 16 of Code of Civil Procedure Section 1963. Under existing law, the presumption applies only to courts of general jurisdiction; the presumption has been held inapplicable to a superior court in California when acting in a special or limited jurisdiction. Estate of Sharon, 179 Cal. 447, 177 Pac. 283 (1918). The presumption also has been held inapplicable to courts of inferior jurisdiction. Santos v. Dondero, 11 Cal.App.2d 720, 54 P.2d 764 (1936). There is no reason to perpetuate this distinction insofar as the courts of California and of the United States are concerned. California's municipal and justice courts are served by able and conscientious judges and are no more likely to act beyond their jurisdiction than are the superior courts. Moreover, there is no reason to suppose that a superior court or a federal court is less respectful of its jurisdiction when acting in a limited capacity (for example, as a juvenile court) than it is when acting in any other capacity. Section 666, therefore, applies to any court or judge of any court of California or of the United States. So far as other states are concerned, the distinction is still applicable, and the presumption applies only to courts of general jurisdiction.

Under Section 666, as under existing law, the presumption applies only when the act of the court or judge is under collateral attack. See City of Los Angeles v. Glassell, 203 Cal. 44, 262 Pac. 1084 (1928).

§ 667. Death of person not heard from in five years. A person not heard from in five years is presumed to be dead. [*Amended 1983.*]

Law Revision Commission Comment - 1983 Amendment

Section 667 is amended to adopt a five-year missing period. This period is consistent with Probate Code Section 1301 (administration of estates of persons missing five years) and Civil Code Sections 4401(2), 4425(b) (five-year absence in bigamy situations). Except for the change in the duration of the missing period from seven to five years, the amendment of Section 667 has no effect on the case law interpreting this section. [16 Cal.L.Rev.Comm. Reports 105 (1982).]

§ 668. Unlawful intent. An unlawful intent is presumed from the doing of an unlawful act. This presumption is inapplicable in a criminal action to establish the specific intent of the defendant where specific intent is an element of the crime charged.

§ 669. Due care; failure to exercise. (a) The failure of a person to exercise due care is presumed if:

(1) He violated a statute, ordinance, or regulation of a public entity;

(2) The violation proximately caused death or injury to person or property;

(3) The death or injury resulted from an occurrence of the nature which the statute, ordinance, or regulation was designed to prevent; and

(4) The person suffering the death or the injury to his person or property was one of the class of persons for whose protection the statute, ordinance, or regulation was adopted.

(b) This presumption may be rebutted by proof that:

(1) The person violating the statute, ordinance, or regulation did what might reasonably be expected of a person of ordinary prudence, acting under similar circumstances, who desired to comply with the law; or

(2) The person violating the statute, ordinance, or regulation was a child and exercised the degree of care ordinarily exercised by persons of his maturity, intelligence, and capacity under similar circumstances, but the presumption may not be rebutted by such proof if the violation occurred in the course of an activity normally engaged in only by adults and requiring adult qualifications. [*Added 1967.*]

Law Revision Commission Comment - 1967 Addition

Section 669 codifies a common law presumption that is frequently applied in the California cases. See Alarid v. Vanier, 50 Cal.2d 617, 327 P.2d 897 (1958). The presumption may be used to establish a plaintiff's contributory negligence as well as a defendant's negligence. Nevis v. Pacific Gas & Elec. Co., 43 Cal.2d 626, 275 P.2d 761 (1954).

Effect of Presumption

If the conditions listed in subdivision (a) are established, a presumption of negligence arises which may be rebutted by proof of the facts specified in subdivision (b). The presumption is one of simple negligence only, not gross negligence. Taylor v. Cockrell, 116 Cal.App. 596, 3 P.2d 16 (1931).

Section 669 appears in Article 4 (beginning with Section 660), Chapter 3, of Division 5 of the Evidence Code and, therefore, is a presumption affecting the burden of proof. Evidence Code § 660. Thus, if it is established that a person violated a statute under the conditions specified in subdivision (a), the opponent of the presumption is required to prove to the trier of fact that it is more probable than not that the violation of the statute was reasonable and justifiable under the circumstances. See Evidence Code § 606 and the Comment thereto. Since the ultimate question is whether the opponent of the presumption was negligent rather than whether he violated the statute, proof of justification or excuse under subdivision (b) negates the existence of negligence instead of merely establishing an excuse for negligent conduct. Therefore, if the presumption is rebutted by proof of justification or excuse under subdivision (b), the trier of fact is required to find that the violation of the statute was not negligent.

Violations by children. Section 669 applies to the violation of a statute, ordinance, or regulation by a child as well as by an adult. But in the case of a violation by a child, the presumption may be rebutted by a showing that the child, in spite of the violation, exercised the care that children of his maturity, intelligence, and capacity ordinarily exercise under similar circumstances. Daun v. Truax, 56 Cal.2d 647, 16 Cal.Rptr. 351, 365 P.2d 407 (1961). However, if a child engages in an activity normally engaged in only by adults and requiring adult qualifications, the "reasonable" behavior he must show to establish justification or excuse under subdivision (b) must meet the standard of conduct established primarily for adults. Cf. Prichard v. Veterans Cab Co., 63 Cal.2d 727, 47 Cal.Rptr. 904, 408 P.2d 360 (1965) (minor operating a motorcycle).

Failure to establish conditions of presumption. Even though a party fails to establish that a violation occurred or that a proven violation meets all the requirements of subdivision (a), it is still possible for the party to recover by proving negligence apart from any statutory violation. Nunneley v. Edgar Hotel, 36 Cal.2d 493, 225 P.2d 497 (1950) (plaintiff permitted to recover even though her injury was not of the type to be prevented by statute).

Functions of Judge and Jury

If a case is tried without a jury, the judge is responsible for deciding both questions of law and questions of fact arising under Section 669. However, in a case tried by a jury, there is an allocation between the judge and jury of the responsibility for determining the existence or nonexistence of the elements underlying the presumption and the existence of excuse or justification.

Subdivision (a), paragraph (3) and (4). Whether the death or injury involved in an action resulted from an occurrence of the nature which the statute, ordinance, or regulation was designed to prevent (paragraph (3) of subdivision (a)) and whether the plaintiff was one of the class of persons for whose protection the statute, ordinance, or regulation was adopted (paragraph (4) of subdivision (a)) are questions of law. Nunneley v. Edgar Hotel, 36 Cal.2d 493, 225 P.2d 497 (1950) (statute requiring parapet of particular height at roofline of vent shaft designed to protect against walking into shaft, not against falling into shaft while sitting on parapet). If a party were relying solely on the violation of a statute to establish the other party's negligence or contributory negligence, his opponent would be entitled to a directed verdict on the issue if the judge failed to find either of the above elements of the presumption. See Nunneley v. Edgar Hotel, 36 Cal.2d 493, 225 P.2d 497 (1950) (by implication).

Subdivision (a), paragraphs (1) and (2). Whether or not a party to an action has violated a statute, ordinance, or regulation (paragraph (1) of subdivision (a)) is generally a question of fact. However, if a party admits the violation or if the evidence of the violation is undisputed, it is appropriate for the judge to instruct the jury that a violation of the statute, ordinance, or regulation has been established as a matter of law. Alarid v. Vanier, 50 Cal.2d 617, 327 P.2d 897 (1958) (undisputed evidence of driving with faulty brakes).

The question of whether the violation has proximately caused or contributed to the plaintiff's death or injury (paragraph (2) of subdivision (a)) is normally a question for the jury. Satterlee v. Orange Glenn School Dist., 29 Cal.2d 581, 177 P.2d 279 (1947). However, the existence or nonexistence of proximate cause becomes a question of law to be decided by the judge if reasonable men can draw but one inference from the facts. Satterlee v. Orange Glenn School Dist., 29 Cal.2d 581, 177 P.2d 279 (1947). See also Alarid v. Vanier, 50 Cal.2d 617, 327 P.2d 897 (1958) (defendant's admission establishes proximate cause); Moon v. Payne, 97 Cal.App.2d 717, 218 P.2d 550 (1950) (failure to obtain permit to burn weeds not proximate cause of child's burns).

Subdivision (b). Normally, the question of justification or excuse is a jury question. Fuentes v. Panella, 120 Cal.App.2d 175, 260 P.2d 853 (1953). The jury should be instructed on the issue of justification or excuse whether the excuse or justification appears from the circumstances surrounding the violation itself or appears from evidence offered specifically to show justification. Fuentes v. Panella, 120 Cal.App.2d 175, 260 P.2d 853 (1953) (instruction on justification proper in light of conflicting testimony concerning violation itself and surrounding circumstances). However, an instruction on the issue of excuse or justification should not be given if there is no evidence that would sustain a finding by the jury that the violation was excused. McCaughan v. Hansen Pac. Lumber Co., 176 Cal.App.2d 827, 833-834, 1 Cal.Rptr. 796, 800 (1959) (evidence went to contributory negligence, not to excuse); Fuentes v. Panella, 120 Cal.App.2d 175, 260 P.2d 853 (1953) (dictum). [8 Cal.L.Rev.Comm. Reports 101 (1967).]

§ 669.1. Standards of conduct for public employees; presumption of failure to exercise due care. A rule, policy, manual, or guideline of state or local government setting forth standards of conduct or guidelines for its employees in the conduct of their public employment shall not be considered a statute, ordinance, or regulation of that public entity within the meaning of Section 669, unless the rule, manual, policy, or guideline has been formally adopted as a statute, as an ordinance of a local governmental entity in this state empowered to adopt ordinances, or as a regulation by an agency of the state pursuant to the Administrative Procedure Act (Chapter 3.5 (commencing with Section 11340) of Division 3 of Title 2 of the Government Code), or by an agency of the United States government pursuant to the federal Administrative Procedure Act (Chapter 5 (commencing with Section 5001) of Title 5 of the United States Code). This section affects only the presumption set forth in

Section 669, and is not otherwise intended to affect the admissibility or inadmissibility of the rule, policy, manual, or guideline under other provisions of law. [*Added 1987.*]

§ 669.5. Ordinances limiting building permits or development of buildable lots for residential purposes; impact on supply of residential units; actions challenging validity. (a) Any ordinance enacted by the governing body of a city, county, or city and county which (1) directly limits, by number, the building permits that may be issued for residential construction or the buildable lots which may be developed for residential purposes, or (2) changes the standards of residential development on vacant land so that the governing body's zoning is rendered in violation of Section 65913.1 of the Government Code is presumed to have an impact on the supply of residential units available in an area which includes territory outside the jurisdiction of the city, county, or city and county.

(b) With respect to any action which challenges the validity of an ordinance specified in subdivision (a) the city, county, or city and county enacting the ordinance shall bear the burden of proof that the ordinance is necessary for the protection of the public health, safety, or welfare of the population of the city, county, or city and county.

(c) This section does not apply to state and federal building code requirements or local ordinances which (1) impose a moratorium, to protect the public health and safety, on residential construction for a specified period of time, if, under the terms of the ordinance, the moratorium will cease when the public health or safety is no longer jeopardized by the construction, (2) create agricultural preserves under Chapter 7 (commencing with Section 51200) of Part 1 of Division 1 of Title 5 of the Government Code, or (3) restrict the number of buildable parcels or designate lands within a zone for nonresidential uses in order to protect agricultural uses as defined in subdivision (b) of Section 51201 of the Government Code or open-space land as defined in subdivision (h) of Section 65560 of the Government Code.

(d) This section shall not apply to a voter approved ordinance adopted by referendum or initiative prior to the effective date of this section which (1) requires the city, county, or city and county to establish a population growth limit which represents its fair share of each year's statewide population growth, or (2) which sets a growth rate of no more than the average population growth rate experienced by the state as a whole. Paragraph (2) of subdivision (a) does not apply to a voter-approved ordinance adopted by referendum or initiative which exempts housing affordable to persons and families of low or moderate income, as defined in Section 50093 of the Health and Safety Code, or which otherwise provides low- and moderate-income housing sites equivalent to such an exemption. [*Added 1980. Amended 1988, 2017.*]

§ 670. Payments by check. (a) In any dispute concerning payment by means of a check, a copy of the check produced in accordance with Section 1550 of the Evidence Code, together with the original bank statement that reflects payment of the check by the bank on which it was drawn or a copy thereof produced in the same manner, creates a presumption that the check has been paid.

(b) As used in this section:

(1) "Bank" means any person engaged in the business of banking and includes, in addition to a commercial bank, a savings and loan association, savings bank, or credit union.

(2) "Check" means a draft, other than a documentary draft, payable on demand and drawn on a bank, even though it is described by another term, such as "share draft" or "negotiable order of withdrawal." [*Added 1992. Amended 2001.*]

DIVISION 6. WITNESSES

Chapter 1. Competency

§ 700. General rule as to competency. Except as otherwise provided by statute, every person, irrespective of age, is qualified to be a witness and no person is disqualified to testify to any matter. [*Amended 1985.*]

Statutory Note

The 1985 amendment added "irrespective of age."

Law Revision Commission Comment

Section 700 makes it clear that all grounds for disqualification of witnesses must be based on statute. There can be no nonstatutory grounds for disqualification.

Just as Code of Civil Procedure Section 1879 is limited by various statutory restrictions on the competency of witnesses, the broad rule stated in Section 700 is also substantially qualified by statutory restrictions appearing in the Evidence Code and in other California codes. See, e.g., Evidence Code § 701 (mental or physical capacity to be a witness), § 702 (requirement of personal knowledge), § 703 (judge as a witness), § 704 (juror as a witness), §§ 900-1070 (privileges), § 1150 (continuing existing law limiting use of juror's evidence concerning jury misconduct); Vehicle Code § 40804 (speed trap evidence).

§ 701. Disqualification of witness. (a) A person is disqualified to be a witness if he or she is:

(1) Incapable of expressing himself or herself concerning the matter so as to be understood, either directly or through interpretation by one who can understand him; or

(2) Incapable of understanding the duty of a witness to tell the truth.

(b) In any proceeding held outside the presence of a jury, the court may reserve challenges to the competency of a witness until the conclusion of the direct examination of that witness. [*Amended 1985.*]

Statutory Note

The 1985 amendment added subdivision (b).

Case Note

If a hearsay declarant was incompetent to testify when making the out-of-court statement, evidence of the statement may not be admitted under an exception to the hearsay rule unless the exception is based on the inherent reliability and trustworthiness of a class of out-of-court statements, such as excited utterances. In re Cindy L., 17 Cal. 4th 15, 31-36, 69 Cal. Rptr. 2d 803, 813-817, 947 P.2d 1340, 1350-1354 (1997) (judicially recognizing and applying "child dependency" exception).

Law Revision Commission Comment

Under existing law, the competency of a person to be a witness is a question to be determined by the court and depends upon his capacity to understand the oath and to perceive, recollect, and communicate that which he is offered to relate. "Whether he did perceive accurately, does recollect, and is communicating accurately and truthfully are questions of credibility to be resolved by the trier of fact." People v. McCaughan, 49 Cal.2d 409, 420, 317 P.2d 974, 981 (1957).

Under the Evidence Code, too, the competency of a person to be a witness is a question to be determined by the court. See Evidence Code § 405 and the Comment thereto. However, Section 701 requires the court to determine only the prospective witness' capacity to communicate and his understanding of the duty to tell the truth. The missing qualifications—the capacity to perceive and to recollect—are determined in a different manner. Because a witness, qualified under Section 701, must have personal knowledge of the facts to which he testifies (Section 702), he must, of course, have the capacity to perceive and to recollect those facts. But the court may exclude the testimony of a witness for lack of personal knowledge only if no jury could reasonably find that he has such knowledge. See Evidence Code § 403 and the Comment thereto. Thus, the Evidence Code has made a person's capacity to perceive and to recollect a condition for the admission of his testimony concerning a particular matter instead of a condition for his competency to be a witness. And, under the Evidence Code, if there is evidence that the witness has those capacities, the determination whether he in fact perceived and does recollect is left to the trier of fact. See Evidence Code §§ 403 and 702 and the Comments thereto.

Although Section 701 modifies the existing law with respect to determining the competency of witnesses, it seems unlikely that the change will have much practical significance. Theoretically, Section 701 may permit children and persons suffering from mental impairment to testify in some instances where they are now disqualified from testifying; in practice, however, the California courts have permitted children of very tender years and persons with mental impairment to testify. See Witkin, California Evidence §§ 389, 390 (1958). See also Bradburn v. Peacock, 135 Cal.App.2d 161, 164-165, 286 P.2d 972, 974 (1955) (reversible error to preclude a child from testifying without conducting a voir dire examination to determine his competency: "We cannot say that *no* child of 3 years and 3 months is capable of receiving just impressions of the facts that a man whom he knows in a truck which he knows ran over his little sister. Nor can we say that *no* child of 3 years and 3 months would remember such facts and be able to relate them truly at the age of 5." (Emphasis in original.)); People v. McCaughan, 49 Cal.2d 409, 317 P.2d 974 (1957) (indicating that committed mental patients may be competent witnesses). For further discussion, see Tentative Recommendation and a Study Relating to the Uniform Rules of Evidence (Article IV. Witnesses), 6 Cal. Law Revision Comm'n, Rep., Rec. & Studies 701, 709-710 (1964).

§ 702. Personal knowledge of witness. (a) Subject to Section 801, the testimony of a witness concerning a particular matter is inadmissible unless he has personal knowledge of the matter. Against the objection of a party, such personal knowledge must be shown before the witness may testify concerning the matter.

(b) A witness' personal knowledge of a matter may be shown by any otherwise admissible evidence, including his own testimony.

Case Note

Court must be satisfied by preponderance of evidence that a witness is capable of expressing himself concerning the matter and capable of understanding the duty to tell the truth (§ 701). In contrast, court can exclude testimony for lack of personal knowledge only if no jury could reasonably find that the witness has such knowledge (§ 702). A witness whose testimony is challenged as being based on insane delusions must be allowed to testify if there is evidence from which a rational trier of fact could find that the witness accurately perceived and recollected the testimonial events. A finding that the witness was deluded as to a part of her testimony did not bar testimony that was internally consistent and corroborated in important details. People v. Anderson, 25 Cal. 4th 543, 571-574, 106 Cal. Rptr. 2d 575, 598-600, 22 P.3d 347, 366-368 (2001).

Law Revision Commission Comment

Section 702 states the general requirement that a witness must have personal knowledge of the facts to which he testifies. "Personal knowledge" means a present recollection of an impression derived from the exercise of the witness' own senses. 2 Wigmore, Evidence § 657 at 762 (3d ed. 1940). Cf. Evidence Code § 170, defining "perceive." Section 702 restates the substance of and supersedes Code of Civil Procedure Section 1845.

Except to the extent that experts may give opinion testimony not based on personal knowledge (see Evidence Code § 801), the requirement of Section 702 is applicable to all witnesses, whether expert or not. Certain additional qualifications that an expert witness must possess are set forth in Article 1 (commencing with Section 720) of Chapter 3.

Under existing law, as under Section 702, an objection must be made to the testimony of a witness who does not have personal knowledge; but, if there is no reasonable opportunity to object before the testimony is given, a motion to strike is appropriate after lack of knowledge has been shown. Fildew v. Shattuck & Nimmo Warehouse Co., 39 Cal.App. 42, 46, 177 Pac. 866, 867 (1918) (objection to question properly sustained when foundational showing of personal knowledge was not made); Sneed v. Marysville Gas & Elec. Co., 149 Cal. 704, 709, 87 Pac. 376, 378 (1906) (error to overrule motion to strike testimony after lack of knowledge shown on cross-examination); Parker v. Smith, 4 Cal. 105 (1854) (testimony properly stricken by court when lack of knowledge shown on cross-examination).

If a timely objection is made that a witness lacks personal knowledge, the court may not receive his testimony subject to the condition that evidence of personal knowledge be supplied later in the trial. Section 702 thus limits the ordinary power of the court with respect to the order of proof. See Evidence Code § 403(b). See also Evidence Code § 320.

§ 703. Judge as witness. (a) Before the judge presiding at the trial of an action may be called to testify in that trial as a witness, he shall, in proceedings held out of the presence and hearing of the jury, inform the parties of the information he has concerning any fact or matter about which he will be called to testify.

(b) Against the objection of a party, the judge presiding at the trial of an action may not testify in that trial as a witness. Upon such objection, the judge shall declare a mistrial and order the action assigned for trial before another judge.

(c) The calling of the judge presiding at a trial to testify in that trial as a witness shall be deemed a consent to the granting of a motion for mistrial, and an objection to such calling of a judge shall be deemed a motion for mistrial.

(d) In the absence of objection by a party, the judge presiding at the trial of an action may testify in that trial as a witness.

Assembly Committee on Judiciary Comment

Under existing law, a judge may be called as a witness even if a party objects, but the judge in his discretion may order the trial to be postponed or suspended and to take place before another judge. Code Civ.Proc. § 1883 (superseded by Evidence Code §§ 703 and 704). But see People v. Connors, 77 Cal.App. 438, 450-457, 246 Pac. 1072, 1076-1079 (1926) (dictum) (abuse of discretion for the presiding judge to testify to important and necessary facts).

Section 703, however, precludes the judge from testifying if a party objects. Before the judge may be called to testify in a civil or criminal action, he must disclose to the parties out of the presence and hearing of the jury the information he has concerning the case. After such disclosure, if no party objects, the judge is permitted—but not required—to testify.

Section 703 is based on the fact that examination and cross-examination of a judge-witness may be embarrassing and prejudicial to a party. By testifying as a witness for one party a judge appears in a partisan attitude before the jury. Objections to questions and to his testimony must be ruled on by the witness himself. The extent of cross-examination and the introduction of impeaching and rebuttal evidence may be limited by the fear of appearing to attack the judge personally. For these and other reasons, Section 703 is preferable to Code of Civil Procedure Section 1883.

Subdivision (c) is designed to prevent a plea of double jeopardy by a defendant who either calls or objects to the calling of the judge to testify. Under subdivision (c), the defendant will, in effect, have consented to the mistrial and thus waived any objection to a retrial. See Witkin, California Crimes § 193 (1963).

§ 703.5. Judges, arbitrators or mediators as witnesses; subsequent civil proceeding. No person presiding at any judicial or quasi-judicial proceeding, and no arbitrator or mediator, shall be competent to testify, in any subsequent civil proceeding, as to any statement, conduct, decision, or ruling, occurring at or in conjunction with the prior proceeding, except as to a statement or conduct that could (a) give rise to civil or criminal contempt, (b) constitute a crime, (c) be the subject of investigation by the State Bar or Commission on Judicial Performance, or (d) give rise to disqualification proceedings under paragraph (1) or (6) of subdivision (a) of Section 170.1 of the Code of Civil Procedure. However, this section does not apply to a mediator with regard to any mediation under Chapter 11 (commencing with Section 3160) of Part 2 of Division 8 of the Family Code. [*Added 1979. Amended 1980, 1988, 1990, 1993, 1994.*]

§ 704. Juror as witness. (a) Before a juror sworn and impaneled in the trial of an action may be called to testify before the jury in that trial as a witness, he shall, in proceedings conducted by the court out of the presence and hearing of the remaining jurors, inform the parties of the information he has concerning any fact or matter about which he will be called to testify.

(b) Against the objection of a party, a juror sworn and impaneled in the trial of an action may not testify before the jury in that trial as a witness. Upon such objection, the court shall declare a mistrial and order the action assigned for trial before another jury.

(c) The calling of a juror to testify before the jury as a witness shall be deemed a consent to the granting of a motion for mistrial, and an objection to such calling of a juror shall be deemed a motion for mistrial.

(d) In the absence of objection by a party, a juror sworn and impaneled in the trial of an action may be compelled to testify in that trial as a witness.

Assembly Committee on Judiciary Comment

Under existing law, a juror may be called as a witness even if a party objects, but the judge in his discretion may order the trial to be postponed or suspended and to take place before another jury. Code Civ.Proc. § 1883 (superseded by Evidence Code §§ 703 and 704). Section 704, on the other hand, prevents a juror from testifying before the jury if any party objects.

A juror-witness is in an anomalous position. He manifestly cannot weigh his own testimony impartially. A party affected adversely by the juror's testimony is placed in an embarrassing position. He cannot freely cross-examine or impeach the juror for fear of antagonizing the juror—and perhaps his fellow jurors as well. And, if he does not attack the juror's testimony, the other jurors may give his testimony undue weight. For these and other reasons, Section 704 forbids jurors to testify over the objection of any party.

Before a juror may be called to testify before the jury in a civil or criminal action, he is required to disclose to the parties out of the presence and hearing of the remaining jurors the information he has concerning the case. After such disclosure, if no party objects, the juror is required to testify. If a party objects, the objection is deemed a motion for mistrial and the judge is required to declare a mistrial and order the action assigned for trial before another jury.

Section 704 is concerned only with the problem of a juror who is called to testify before the jury. Section 704 does not deal with voir dire examinations of jurors, with testimony of jurors in post-verdict proceedings (such as on motions for new trial), or with the testimony of jurors on any other matter that is to be decided by the court. Cf. Evidence Code § 1150 and the Comment thereto.

Subdivision (c) is designed to prevent a plea of double jeopardy by a defendant who either calls or objects to the calling of the juror to testify. Under subdivision (c), the defendant will, in effect, have consented to the mistrial and thus waived any objection to a retrial. See Witkin, California Crimes § 193 (1963).

Chapter 2. Oath and Confrontation

§ 710. Oath required. Every witness before testifying shall take an oath or make an affirmation or declaration in the form provided by law, except that a child under the age of 10 or a dependent person with a substantial cognitive impairment, in the court's discretion, may be required only to promise to tell the truth. [*Amended 1988, 2004.*]

Statutory Note

The 1988 amendment added the exception for children under 10. The 2004 amendment inserted "or a dependent person with a substantial cognitive impairment."

§ 711. Confrontation. At the trial of an action, a witness can be heard only in the presence and subject to the examination of all the parties to the action, if they choose to attend and examine.

§ 712. Blood samples; technique in taking; affidavits in criminal actions; service; objections. Notwithstanding Sections 711 and 1200, at the trial of a criminal action, evidence of the technique used in taking blood samples may be given by a registered nurse, licensed vocational nurse, or licensed clinical laboratory technologist or clinical laboratory bioanalyst, by means of an affidavit. The affidavit shall be admissible, provided the party offering the affidavit as evidence has served all other parties to the action, or their counsel, with a copy of the affidavit no less than 10 days prior to trial. Nothing in this section shall preclude any party or his counsel from objecting to the introduction of the affidavit at any time, and requiring the attendance of the affiant, or compelling attendance by subpoena. [*Added 1978.*]

Chapter 3. Expert Witnesses

Article 1. Expert Witnesses Generally

§ 720. Qualification as an expert witness. (a) A person is qualified to testify as an expert if he has special knowledge, skill, experience, training, or education sufficient to qualify him as an expert on the subject to which his testimony relates. Against the objection of a party, such special knowledge, skill, experience, training, or education must be shown before the witness may testify as an expert.

(b) A witness' special knowledge, skill, experience, training, or education may be shown by any otherwise admissible evidence, including his own testimony.

Case Note

Rejecting Daubert v. Merrell Dow Pharmaceuticals, Inc., 509 U.S. 579, 113 S.Ct. 2786, 125 L.Ed. 2d 469 (1993), California continues to adhere to the Kelly/Frye general acceptance test for the admissibility of expert testimony based on new scientific techniques. People v. Leahy, 8 Cal. 4th 587, 598, 34 Cal. Rptr. 2d 663, 669, 882 P.2d 321, 327 (1994).

Law Revision Commission Comment

* * * The judge must be satisfied that the proposed witness is an expert. People v. Haeussler, 41 Cal.2d 252, 260 P.2d 8 (1953); Pfingsten v. Westenhaver, 39 Cal.2d 12, 244 P.2d 395 (1952); Bossert v. Southern Pac. Co., 172 Cal. 504, 157 Pac. 597 (1916); People v. Pacific Gas & Elec. Co., 27 Cal.App.2d 725, 81 P.2d 584 (1938).

Against the objection of a party, the special qualifications of the proposed witness must be shown as a prerequisite to his testimony as an expert. With the consent of the parties, the judge may receive a witness' testimony conditionally, subject to the necessary foundation being supplied later in the trial. See Evidence Code § 320. Unless the foundation is subsequently supplied, however, the judge should grant a motion to strike or should order the testimony stricken from the record on his own motion.

The judge's determination that a witness qualifies as an expert witness is binding on the trier of fact, but the trier of fact may consider the witness' qualifications as an expert in determining the weight to be given his testimony. Pfingsten v. Westenhaver, 39 Cal.2d 12, 244 P.2d 395 (1952); Howland v. Oakland Consol. St. Ry., 110 Cal. 513, 42 Pac. 983 (1895); Estate of Johnson, 100 Cal.App.2d 73, 223 P.2d 105 (1950). See Evidence Code §§ 405 and 406 and the Comments thereto.

§ 721. Cross-examination of expert witness. (a) Subject to subdivision (b), a witness testifying as an expert may be cross-examined to the same extent as any other witness and, in addition, may be fully cross-examined as to (1) his or her qualifications, (2) the subject to which his or her expert testimony relates, and (3) the matter upon which his or her opinion is based and the reasons for his or her opinion.

(b) If a witness testifying as an expert testifies in the form of an opinion, he or she may not be cross-examined in regard to the content or tenor of any scientific, technical, or professional text, treatise, journal, or similar publication unless any of the following occurs:

(1) The witness referred to, considered, or relied upon such publication in arriving at or forming his or her opinion.

(2) The publication has been admitted in evidence.

(3) The publication has been established as a reliable authority by the testimony or admission of the witness or by other expert testimony or by judicial notice.

If admitted, relevant portions of the publication may be read into evidence but may not be received as exhibits. [*Amended 1997.*]

Statutory Note

The 1997 amendment added paragraph (b) (3) and the last paragraph.

Law Revision Commission Comment

Under Section 721, a witness who testifies as an expert may, of course, be cross-examined to the same extent as any other witness. See Chapter 5 (commencing with Section 760). But, under subdivision (a) of Section 721, as under existing law, the expert witness is also subject to a somewhat broader cross-examination: "Once an expert offers his opinion, however, he exposes himself to the kind of inquiry which ordinarily would have no place in the cross-examination of a factual witness. The expert invites investigation into the extent of his knowledge, the reasons for his opinion including facts and other matters upon which it is based (Code Civ.Proc., § 1872), and which he took into consideration; and he may be 'subjected to the most rigid cross examination' concerning his qualifications, and his opinion and its sources [citation omitted]." Hope v. Arrowhead & Puritas Waters, Inc., 174 Cal.App.2d 222, 230, 344 P.2d 428, 433 (1959). The cross-examination rule stated in subdivision (a) is based in part on the last clause of Code of Civil Procedure Section 1872.

Subdivision (b) clarifies a matter concerning which there is considerable confusion in the California decisions. It is at least clear under existing law that an expert witness may be cross-examined in regard to those books on which he relied in forming or arriving at his opinion. Lewis v. Johnson, 12 Cal.2d 558, 86 P.2d 99 (1939); People v. Hooper, 10 Cal.App.2d 332, 51 P.2d 1131 (1935). Dicta in some decisions indicate that the cross-examiner is strictly limited to the books relied on by the expert witness. See, e.g., Baily v. Kreutzmann, 141 Cal. 519, 75 Pac. 104 (1904). Other cases, however, suggest that an expert witness may be cross-examined in regard to any book of the same character as the books on which he relied in forming his opinion. Griffith v. Los Angeles Pac. Co., 14 Cal.App. 145, 111 Pac. 107 (1910). See Salgo v. Leland Stanford etc. Bd. Trustees, 154 Cal.App.2d 560, 317 P.2d 170 (1957); Gluckstein v. Lipsett, 93 Cal.App.2d 391, 209 P.2d 98 (1949) (reviewing California authorities). (Possibly, the cross-examiner is restricted under this view to the use of such books as "are not in harmony with the testimony of the witness." Griffith v. Los Angeles Pac. Co., supra.) Language in several earlier cases indicated that the cross-examiner could use books to test the competency of an expert witness, whether or not the expert relied on books in forming his opinion. Fisher v. Southern Pac. R.R., 89 Cal. 399, 26 Pac. 894 (1891); People v. Hooper, 10 Cal.App.2d 332, 51 P.2d 1131 (1935). More recent decisions indicate, however, that the opinion of an expert witness must be based either generally or specifically on books before the expert can be cross-examined concerning them. Lewis v. Johnson, 12 Cal.2d 558, 86 P.2d 99 (1939); Salgo v. Leland Stanford etc. Bd. Trustees, 154 Cal.App.2d 560, 317 P.2d 170 (1957); Gluckstein v. Lipsett, 93 Cal.App.2d 391, 209 P.2d 98 (1949). The conflicting California cases are gathered in Annot., 60 A.L.R.2d 77 (1958).

If an expert witness has relied on a particular publication in forming his opinion, it is necessary to permit cross-examination in regard to that publication in order to show whether the expert correctly read, interpreted, and applied the portions he relied on. Similarly, it is important to permit an expert witness to be cross-examined concerning those publications referred to or considered by him even though not specifically relied on by him in forming his opinion. An expert's reasons for not relying on particular publications that were referred to or considered by him while forming his opinion may reveal important information bearing upon the credibility of his testimony. However, a rule permitting cross-examination on technical treatises not considered by the expert witness would permit the cross-examiner to utilize this opportunity not for its ostensible purpose—to test the expert's opinion—but to bring before the trier of fact the opinions of absentee authors without the safeguard of cross-examination. Although the court would be required upon request to caution the jury that the statements read are not to be considered evidence of the truth of the propositions stated, there is a danger that at least some jurors might rely on the author's statements for this purpose. Yet, the statements in the text might be based on inadequate background research, might be subject to unexpressed qualifications that would be applicable to the case before the court, or might be unreliable for some other reason that could be revealed if the author were subject to cross-examination. Therefore, subdivision (b) does not permit cross-examination of an expert witness on scientific, technical, or professional works not referred to, considered, or relied on by him.

If a particular publication has already been admitted in evidence, however, the reason for subdivision (b) —to prevent inadmissible evidence from being brought before the jury—is inapplicable. Hence, the subdivision permits an expert witness to be examined concerning such a publication without regard to whether he referred to, considered, or relied on it in forming his opinion. Cf. Laird v. T. W. Mather, Inc., 51 Cal.2d 210, 331 P.2d 617 (1958).

The rule stated in subdivision (b) thus provides a fair and workable solution to this conflict of competing interests with respect to the permissible use of scientific, technical, or professional publications by the cross-examiner.

§ 722. Credibility of expert witness. (a) The fact of the appointment of an expert witness by the court may be revealed to the trier of fact.

(b) The compensation and expenses paid or to be paid to an expert witness by the party calling him is a proper subject of inquiry by any adverse party as relevant to the credibility of the witness and the weight of his testimony.

Law Revision Commission Comment

* * * [T]he rule enunciated in Section 722 is a desirable rule. The tendency of some experts to become advocates for the party employing them has been recognized. 2 Wigmore, Evidence § 563 (3d ed. 1940); Friedenthal, Discovery and Use of an Adverse Party's Expert Information, 14 Stan.L.Rev. 455, 485-486 (1962). The jury can better appraise the extent to which bias may have influenced an expert's opinion if it is informed of the amount of his fee—and, hence, the extent of his possible feeling of obligation to the party calling him.

§ 723. Limit on number of expert witnesses. The court may, at any time before or during the trial of an action, limit the number of expert witnesses to be called by any party.

Article 2. Appointment of Expert Witness by Court

§ 730. Appointment of expert by court. When it appears to the court, at any time before or during the trial of an action, that expert evidence is or may be required by the court or by any party to the action, the court on its own motion or on motion of any party may appoint one or more experts to investigate, to render a report as may be ordered by the court, and to testify as an expert at the trial of the action relative to the fact or matter as to which the expert evidence is or may be required. The court may fix the compensation for these services, if any, rendered by any person appointed under this section, in addition to any service as a witness, at the amount as seems reasonable to the court.

Nothing in this section shall be construed to permit a person to perform any act for which a license is required unless the person holds the appropriate license to lawfully perform that act.
[*Added 1979. Amended 1990.*]

Statutory Note

The 1990 amendment added the second paragraph.

§ 731. Payment of court-appointed expert. (a)(1) In all criminal actions and juvenile court proceedings, the compensation fixed under Section 730 shall be a charge against the county in which such action or proceeding is pending and shall be paid out of the treasury of such county on order of the court.

(2) Notwithstanding paragraph (1), if the expert is appointed for the court's needs, the compensation shall be a charge against the court.

(b) In any county in which the superior court so provides, the compensation fixed under section 730 for medical experts appointed for the courts needs in civil actions shall be a charge against the court. In any county in which the board of supervisors so provides, the compensation fixed under Section 730 for medical experts appointed in civil actions, for purposes other than the court's needs, shall be a charge against and paid out of the treasury of that county on order of the court.

(c) Except as otherwise provided in this section, in all civil actions, the compensation fixed under Section 730 shall, in the first instance, be apportioned and charged to the several parties in such proportion as the court may determine and may thereafter be taxed and allowed in like manner as other costs. [*Added 1979. Amended 2012.*]

Law Review Commission Comment – 2012 Amendment

Subdivisions (a) and (b) of Section 731 are amended to reflect the enactment of the Lockyer-Isenberg Trial Court Funding Act, 1997 Cal. Stat. ch. 850 (see generally Gov't Code §§ 77000-77655). See, e.g., Gov't Code §§ 77001 (local trial court management), 77003 ("court operations" defined), 77200 (state funding of "court operations"); see also Cal. R. Ct. 10.810(d), Functions 4 (court interpreters) & 10 (referring to "court-appointed expert witness fees (for the court's needs)").

Subdivisions (a), (b), and (c) are also amended to make stylistic revisions. [39 Cal.L.Rev.Comm. Reports 109 (2009)].

§ 732. Calling and examining court-appointed expert. Any expert appointed by the court under Section 730 may be called and examined by the court or by any party to the action. When such witness is called and examined by the court, the parties have the same right as is expressed in Section 775 to cross-examine the witness and to object to the questions asked and the evidence adduced.

§ 733. Right to produce other expert evidence. Nothing contained in this article [§§ 730-733] shall be deemed or construed to prevent any party to any action from producing other expert evidence on the same fact or matter mentioned in Section 730; but, where other expert witnesses are called by a party to the action, their fees shall be paid by the party calling them and only ordinary witness fees shall be taxed as costs in the action.

Chapter 4. Interpreters and Translators

§ 750. Rules relating to witnesses apply to interpreters and translators. A person who serves as an interpreter or translator in any action is subject to all the rules of law relating to witnesses.

§ 751. Oath required of interpreters and translators. (a) An interpreter shall take an oath that he or she will make a true interpretation to the witness in a language that the witness understands and that he or she will make a true interpretation of the witness' answers to questions to counsel, court, or jury, in the English language, with his or her best skill and judgment.

(b) In any proceeding in which a deaf or hard-of-hearing person is testifying under oath, the interpreter certified pursuant to subdivision (f) of Section 754 shall advise the court whenever he or she is unable to comply with his or her oath taken pursuant to subdivision (a).

(c) A translator shall take an oath that he or she will make a true translation in the English language of any writing he or she is to decipher or translate.

(d) An interpreter regularly employed by the court and certified or registered in accordance with Article 4 (commencing with Section 68560) of Chapter 2 of Title 8 of the Government Code, or a translator regularly employed by the court, may file an oath as prescribed by this section with the clerk of the court. The filed oath shall serve for all subsequent court proceedings until the appointment is revoked by the court. [*Amended 1984, 1990, 1997.*]

§ 752. Interpreters for witnesses; compensation. (a) When a witness is incapable of understanding the English language or is incapable of expressing himself or herself in the English language so as to be understood directly by counsel, court, and jury, an interpreter whom the witness can understand and who can understand the witness shall be sworn to interpret for the witness.

(b) The record shall identify the interpreter, who may be appointed and compensated as provided in Article 2 (commencing with Section 730) of Chapter 3, with that compensation charged as follows:

(1) In all criminal actions and juvenile court proceedings, the compensation for an interpreter under this section shall be a charge against the court.

(2) In all civil actions, the compensation for an interpreter under this section shall, in the first instance, be apportioned and charged to the several parties in a proportion as the court may determine and may thereafter be taxed and allowed in a like manner as other costs. [*Added 2012. Amended 2012.*]

Law Revision Commission Comments

***Section 752 restates the substance of and supersedes Section 1884 of the Code of Civil Procedure. It is drawn broadly enough to authorize the use of an interpreter for a person whose inability to be understood directly stems from physical disability as well as from lack of understanding of the English language. See discussion in People v. Walker, 69 Cal.App. 475, 231 Pac. 572 (1924). Under Section 752, as under existing law, whether an interpreter should be appointed is largely within the discretion of the trial judge. People v. Holtzclaw, 76 Cal.App. 168, 243 Pac. 894 (1926).

Subdivision (b) of Section 752 substitutes for the detailed language in Code of Civil Procedure Section 1884 a reference to the general authority of a court to appoint expert witnesses, since interpreters are treated as expert witnesses and subject to the same rules of competency and examination as are experts generally. The existing procedure provided by Code of Civil Procedure Section 1884 does not insure that an interpreter who is required to testify will be paid reasonable compensation for his services. Section 752 corrects this deficiency in the existing law. [7 Cal.L.Rev.Comm. Reports 1 (1965)].

2012 Amendment

Subdivision (a) of Section 752 is amended to make stylistic revisions.

Subdivision (b) is amended to reflect enactment of the Lockyer-Isenberg Trial Court Funding Act, 1997 Cal. Stat. ch. 850 (see generally Gov't Code §§ 77000-77655). See, e.g., Gov't Code §§ 77001 (local trial court management), 77003 ("court operations" defined), 77200 (state funding of "court operations"); see also Cal. R. Ct. 10.810(d), Function 4 (court interpreters).

Subdivision (b) is also amended to make a stylistic revision.

The purpose of the revisions in the act that amended this section is to remove material made obsolete by trial court restructuring. See Gov't Code § 71674. The act should not be construed as a re-evaluation of the extent to which interpretation or translation should be provided in court proceedings, or who should bear the expense of interpretation or translation. [39 Cal.L.Rev.Comm. Reports 109 (2009)].

§ 753. Translators of writings; compensation. (a) When the written characters in a writing offered in evidence are incapable of being deciphered or understood directly, a translator who can decipher the characters or understand the language shall be sworn to decipher or translate the writing.

(b) The record shall identify the translator, who may be appointed and compensated as provided in Article 2 (commencing with Section 730) of Chapter 3, with that compensation charged as follows:

(1) In all criminal actions and juvenile court proceedings, the compensation for a translator under this section shall be a charge against the court.

(2) In all civil actions the compensation for a translator under this section shall, in the first instance, be apportioned and charged to the several parties in a proportion as the court may determine and may thereafter be taxed and allowed in like manner as other costs. [*Amended 2012.*]

Law Revision Commission Comments

***Section 753 restates the substance of and supersedes Section 1863 of the Code of Civil Procedure, but the language of Section 753 is new. The same principles that require the appointment of an interpreter for a witness who is incapable of expressing himself so as to be understood directly apply with equal force to documentary evidence. See Evidence Code § 752 and the Comment thereto. [7 Cal.L.Rev.Comm. Reports 1 (1965)].

2012 Amendment

Subdivision (b) is amended to reflect enactment of the Lockyer-Isenberg Trial Court Funding Act, 1997 Cal. Stat. ch. 850 (see generally Gov't Code §§ 77000-77655). See, e.g., Gov't Code §§ 77001 (local trial court management), 77003 ("court operations" defined), 77200 (state funding of "court operations"); see also Cal. R. Ct. 10.810(d), Function 4 (court interpreters).

Subdivision (b) is also amended to make a stylistic revision.

The purpose of the revisions in the act that amended this section is to remove material made obsolete by trial court restructuring. See Gov't Code § 71674. The act should not be construed as a re-evaluation of the extent to which interpretation or translation should be provided in court proceedings, or who should bear the expense of interpretation or translation. [39 Cal.L.Rev.Comm. Reports 109 (2009)].

§ 754. Deaf or hearing impaired persons; interpreters; qualifications; guidelines; compensation; questioning; use of statements. (a) As used in this section, "individual who is deaf or hard of hearing " means an individual with a hearing loss so great as to prevent his or her understanding language spoken in a normal tone, but does not include an individual who is hard of hearing provided with, and able to fully participate in the proceedings through the use of, an assistive listening system or computer-aided transcription equipment provided pursuant to Section 54.8 of the Civil Code.

(b) In a civil or criminal action, including an action involving a traffic or other infraction, a small claims court proceeding, a juvenile court proceeding, a family court proceeding or service, or a proceeding to determine the mental competency of a person, in a court-ordered or court-provided alternative dispute resolution, including mediation and arbitration, or in an administrative hearing, where a party or witness is an individual who is deaf or hard of hearing and the individual who is deaf or hard of hearing is present and participating, the proceedings shall be interpreted in a language that the individual who is deaf or hearing impaired understands by a qualified interpreter appointed by the court or other appointing authority, or as agreed upon.

(c) For purposes of this section, "appointing authority" means a court, department, board, commission, agency, licensing or legislative body, or other body for proceedings requiring a qualified interpreter.

(d) For the purposes of this section, "interpreter" includes, but is not limited to, an oral interpreter, a sign language interpreter, or a deaf-blind interpreter, depending upon the needs of the individual who is deaf or hard of hearing.

(e) For purposes of this section, "intermediary interpreter" means an individual who is deaf or hard of hearing, or a hearing individual who is able to assist in providing an accurate interpretation between spoken English and sign language or between variants of sign language or between American Sign Language and other foreign languages by acting as an intermediary between the individual who is deaf or hard of hearing and the qualified interpreter.

(f) For purposes of this section, "qualified interpreter" means an interpreter who has been certified as competent to interpret court proceedings by a testing organization, agency, or educational institution approved by the Judicial Council as qualified to administer tests to court interpreters for individuals who are deaf or hard of hearing.

(g) In the event that the appointed interpreter is not familiar with the use of particular signs by the individual who is deaf or hard of hearing or his or her particular variant of sign language, the court or other appointing authority shall, in consultation with the individual who is deaf or hard of hearing or his or her representative, appoint an intermediary interpreter.

(h) Prior to July 1, 1992, the Judicial Council shall conduct a study to establish the guidelines pursuant to which it shall determine which testing organizations, agencies, or educational institutions will be approved to administer tests for certification of court interpreters for individuals who are deaf or hard of hearing. It is the intent of the Legislature that the study obtain the widest possible input from the public, including, but not limited to, educational institutions, the judiciary, linguists, members of the State Bar, court interpreters, members of professional interpreting organizations, and members of the deaf and hearing-impaired communities. After obtaining public comment and completing its study, the Judicial Council shall publish these guidelines. By January 1, 1997, the Judicial Council shall approve one or more entities to administer testing for court interpreters for individuals who are deaf or hard of hearing. Testing entities may include educational institutions, testing organizations, joint powers agencies, or public agencies.

Commencing July 1, 1997, court interpreters for individuals who are deaf or hard of hearing shall meet the qualifications specified in subdivision (f).

(i) Persons appointed to serve as interpreters under this section shall be paid, in addition to actual travel costs, the prevailing rate paid to persons employed by the court to provide other interpreter services unless such service is considered to be a part of the person's regular duties as an employee of the state, county, or other political subdivision of the state. Except as provided in subdivision (j), payment of the interpreter's fee shall be a charge against the court. Payment of the interpreter's fee in administrative proceedings shall be a charge against the appointing board or authority.

(j) Whenever a peace officer or any other person having a law enforcement or prosecutorial function in any criminal or quasi-criminal investigation or non-court proceeding questions or otherwise interviews an alleged victim or witness who demonstrates or alleges deafness or hearing impairment, a good faith effort to secure the services of an interpreter shall be made, without any unnecessary delay unless either the individual who is deaf or hard of hearing affirmatively indicates that he or she does not need or cannot use an interpreter, or an interpreter is not otherwise required by Title II of the Americans with Disabilities Act of 1990 (Public Law 101-336) and federal regulations adopted thereunder. Payment of the interpreter's fee shall be a charge against the county, or other political subdivision of the state, in which the action is pending.

(k) No statement, written or oral, made by an individual who the court finds is deaf or hard of hearing in reply to a question of a peace officer, or any other person having a law enforcement or prosecutorial function in any criminal or quasi-criminal investigation or proceeding, may be used against that individual who is deaf or hard of hearing unless the question was accurately interpreted and the statement was made knowingly, voluntarily, and intelligently and was accurately interpreted, or the court makes special findings that either the individual could not have used an interpreter or an interpreter was not otherwise required by Title II of the Americans with Disabilities Act of 1990 (Public Law 101-336) and federal regulations adopted thereunder and that the statement was made knowingly, voluntarily, and intelligently.

(l) In obtaining services of an interpreter for purposes of subdivision (j) or (k), priority shall be given to first obtaining a qualified interpreter.

(m) Nothing in subdivision (j) or (k) shall be deemed to supersede the requirement of subdivision (b) for use of a qualified interpreter for individuals who are deaf or hard of hearing participating as parties or witnesses in a trial or hearing.

(n) In any action or proceeding in which an individual who is deaf or hard of hearing is a participant, the appointing authority shall not commence proceedings until the appointed interpreter is in full view of and spatially situated to assure proper communication with the participating individual who is deaf or hard of hearing.

(o) Each superior court shall maintain a current roster of qualified interpreters certified pursuant to subdivision (f). [*Amended 1977, 1984, 1989, 1990, 1991, 1992, 1995, 1997, 2012, 2017.*]

Law Review Commission Comments

Section 754 restates the substance of and supersedes Section 1885 of the Code of Civil Procedure. Subdivision (c) of Section 1885 is not continued in Section 754 but is restated in substance in Section 751.

The phrase "with or without a hearing aid" has been deleted from the definition of "deaf person" as unnecessary. The court's inquiry should be directed towards the ability of the person to hear; the court should not be concerned with the means by which he might be enabled to hear. [7 Cal.L.Rev.Comm. Reports 1 (1965)].

2012 Amendment

Subdivisions (i) and (j) of Section 754 are amended to reflect enactment of the Lockyer-Isenberg Trial Court Funding Act, 1997 Cal. Stat. ch. 850 (see generally Gov't Code §§ 77000-77655). See, e.g., Gov't Code §§ 77003 ("court operations" defined), 77200 (state funding of "court operations"); see also Cal. R. Ct. 10.810(d), Function 4 (court interpreters). [39 Cal.L.Rev.Comm. Reports 157 (2009)].

§ 754.5. Privileged statements; deaf or hard of hearing persons; use of interpreter. Whenever an otherwise valid privilege exists between an individual who is deaf or hard of hearing and another person, that privilege is not waived merely because an interpreter was used to facilitate their communication. [*Added 1990. Amended 1992, 2017.*]

§ 755.5. Medical examinations; parties not proficient in English language; interpreters; fees; admissibility of record. (a) During any medical examination, requested by an insurer or by the defendant, of a person who is a party to a civil action and who does not proficiently speak or understand the English language, conducted for the purpose of determining damages in a civil action, an interpreter shall be present to interpret the examination in a language that the person understands. The interpreter shall be certified pursuant to Article 8 (commencing with Section 11435.05) of Chapter 4.5 of Part 1 of Division 3 of Title 2 of the Government Code.

(b) The fees of interpreters used under subdivision (a) shall be paid by the insurer or defendant requesting the medical examination.

(c) The record of, or testimony concerning, any medical examination conducted in violation of subdivision (a) shall be inadmissible in the civil action for which it was conducted or any other civil action.

(d) This section does not prohibit the presence of any other person to assist a party.

(e) In the event that interpreters certified pursuant to Article 8 (commencing with Section 11435.05) of Chapter 4.5 of Part 1 of Division 3 of Title 2 of the Government Code cannot be present at the medical examination, upon stipulation of the parties the requester specified in subdivision (a) shall have the discretionary authority to provisionally qualify and use other interpreters. [*Added 1992. Amended 1995, 1997.*]

§ 756. Reimbursement to courts for court interpreter services in civil actions and proceedings. (a) To the extent required by other state or federal laws, the Judicial Council shall reimburse courts for court interpreter services provided in civil actions and proceedings to any party who is present in court and who does not proficiently speak or understand the English language for the purpose of interpreting the proceedings in a language the party understands, and assisting communications between the party, his or her attorney, and the court.

(b) If sufficient funds are not appropriated to provide an interpreter to every party that meets the standard of eligibility, court interpreter services in civil cases reimbursed by the Judicial Council, pursuant to subdivision (a), shall be prioritized by case type by each court in the following order:

(1) Actions and proceedings under Division 10 (commencing with Section 6200) of the Family Code, actions or proceedings under the Uniform Parentage Act (Part 3 (commencing with Section 7600) of Division 12 of the Family Code) in which a protective order has been granted or is being sought pursuant to Section 6221 of the Family Code, and actions and proceedings for dissolution or nullity of marriage or legal separation of the parties in which a protective order has been granted or is being sought pursuant to Section 6221 of the Family Code; actions and proceedings under subdivision (y) of Section 527.6 of the Code of Civil Procedure; and actions and proceedings for physical abuse or neglect under the Elder Abuse and Dependent Adult Civil Protection Act (Chapter 11 (commencing with Section 15600) of Part 3 of Division 9 of the Welfare and Institutions Code).

(2) Actions and proceedings relating to unlawful detainer.

(3) Actions and proceedings to terminate parental rights.

(4) Actions and proceedings relating to conservatorship or guardianship, including the appointment or termination of a probate guardian or conservator.

(5) Actions and proceedings by a parent to obtain sole legal or physical custody of a child or rights to visitation.

(6) All other actions and proceedings under Section 527.6 of the Code of Civil Procedure or the Elder Abuse and Dependent Adult Civil Protection Act (Chapter 11 (commencing with Section 15600) of Part 3 of Division 9 of the Welfare and Institutions Code).

(7) All other actions and proceedings related to family law.

(8) All other civil actions or proceedings.

(c) (1) If funds are not available to provide an interpreter to every party that meets the standard of eligibility, preference shall be given for parties proceeding in forma pauperis pursuant to Section 68631 of the Government Code in any civil action or proceeding described in paragraph (3), (4), (5), (6), (7), or (8) of subdivision (b).

(2) Courts may provide an interpreter to a party outside the priority order listed in subdivision (b) when a qualified interpreter is present and available at the court location and no higher priority action that meets the standard of eligibility described in subdivision (a) is taking place at that location during the period of time for which the interpreter has already been compensated.

(d) A party shall not be charged a fee for the provision of a court interpreter.

(e) In seeking reimbursement for court interpreter services, the court shall identify to the Judicial Council the case types for which the interpretation to be reimbursed was provided. Courts shall regularly certify that in providing the interpreter services, they have complied with the priorities and preferences set forth in subdivisions (b) and (c), which shall be subject to review by the Judicial Council

(f) This section shall not be construed to alter, limit, or negate any right to an interpreter in a civil action or proceeding otherwise provided by state or federal law, or the right to an interpreter in criminal, traffic, or other infraction, juvenile, or mental competency actions or proceedings.

(g) This section shall not result in a reduction in staffing or compromise the quality of interpreting services in criminal, juvenile, or other types of matters in which interpreters are provided. [*Added 2014.*]

§ 757. Pursuant to this chapter, other applicable law, and existing Judicial Council policy, including the policy adopted on January 23, 2014, existing authority to provide interpreters in civil court includes the authority to provide an interpreter in a proceeding in which a petitioner requests an order from the superior court to make the findings regarding special immigrant juvenile status pursuant to Section 1101(a)(27)(J) of Title 8 of the United States Code. [*Added 2014. Amended 2019.*]

Chapter 5. Method and Scope of Examination

Article 1. Definitions

§ 760. Direct examination. "Direct examination" is the first examination of a witness upon a matter that is not within the scope of a previous examination of the witness.

Law Revision Commission Comment

Section 760 restates the substance of and supersedes the first clause of Code of Civil Procedure Section 2045 and the last clause of Code of Civil Procedure Section 2048. Under Section 760, an examination of a witness called by another party is direct examination if the examination relates to a matter that is not within the scope of the previous examination of the witness.

§ 761. Cross-examination. "Cross-examination" is the examination of a witness by a party other than the direct examiner upon a matter that is within the scope of the direct examination of the witness.

Law Revision Commission Comment

Section 761 restates the substance of and supersedes the definition of "cross-examination" found in Section 2045 of the Code of Civil Procedure. In accordance with existing law, it limits cross-examination of a witness to the scope of the witness' direct examination. See generally Witkin, California Evidence §§ 622-638 (1958).

Section 761, together with Section 773, retains the cross-examination rule now applicable to a defendant in a criminal action who testifies as a witness in that action. See People v. McCarthy, 88 Cal.App.2d 883, 200 P.2d 69 (1948). See also People v. Arrighini, 122 Cal. 121, 54 Pac. 591 (1898); People v. O'Brien, 66 Cal. 602, 6 Pac. 695 (1885); Witkin, California Evidence § 629 (1958). See also Evidence Code § 772(d).

§ 762. Redirect examination. "Redirect examination" is an examination of a witness by the direct examiner subsequent to the cross-examination of the witness.

Law Revision Commission Comment

"Redirect examination" and "recross-examination" are not defined in existing statutes, but the terms are recognized in practice. See Witkin, California Evidence §§ 697, 698 (1958). The scope of redirect and recross-examination is limited by Section 774.

The definition of "redirect examination" embraces not only the examination immediately following cross-examination of the witness but also any subsequent re-examination of the witness by the direct examiner.

§ 763. Recross-examination. "Recross-examination" is an examination of a witness by a cross-examiner subsequent to a redirect examination of the witness.

Law Revision Commission Comment

See the Comment to Section 762. The definition of "recross-examination" embraces not only the examination immediately following the first redirect examination of the witness but also any subsequent re-examination of the witness by a cross-examiner.

§ 764. Leading question. A "leading question" is a question that suggests to the witness the answer that the examining party desires.

Article 2. Examination of Witnesses

§ 765. Court to control mode of interrogation. (a) The court shall exercise reasonable control over the mode of interrogation of a witness so as to make such interrogation as rapid, as distinct, and as effective for the ascertainment of the truth, as may be, and to protect the witness from undue harassment or embarrassment.

(b) With a witness under the age of 14 or a dependent person with a substantial cognitive impairment, the court shall take special care to protect him or her from undue harassment or embarrassment, and to restrict the unnecessary repetition of questions. The court shall also take special care to ensure that questions are stated in a form which is appropriate to the age or cognitive level of the witness. The court may, in the interests of justice, on objection by a party, forbid the asking of a question which is in a form that is not reasonably likely to be understood by a person of the age or cognitive level of the witness. [*Amended 1985, 1986, 2004.*]

Statutory Note

The 1985 amendment added the first sentence of subdivision (b). The 1986 amendment added the second and third sentences of subdivision (b). The 2004 amendment added "dependent person with a substantial cognitive impairment" to the first sentence of subdivision (b) and references to "cognitive level" in the second and third sentences of subdivision (b).

Law Revision Commission Comment

Section 765 restates the substance of and supersedes Section 2044 of the Code of Civil Procedure. As to the latitude permitted the judge in controlling the examination of witnesses under existing law, which is continued in effect by Section 765, see Commercial Union Assur. Co. v. Pacific Gas & Elec. Co., 220 Cal. 515, 31 P.2d 793 (1934). See also People v. Davis, 6 Cal.App. 229, 91 Pac. 810 (1907).

§ 766. Responsive answers. A witness must give responsive answers to questions, and answers that are not responsive shall be stricken on motion of any party.

§ 767. Leading questions. (a) Except under special circumstances where the interests of justice otherwise require:

(1) A leading question may not be asked of a witness on direct or redirect examination.

(2) A leading question may be asked of a witness on cross-examination or recross-examination.

(b) The court may, in the interests of justice permit a leading question to be asked of a child under 10 years of age or a dependent person with a substantial cognitive impairment in a case involving a prosecution under Section 273a, 273d, 288.5, 368, or any of the acts described in Section 11165.1 or 11165.2 of the Penal Code. [*Amended 1984, 1995, 2004.*]

Statutory Note

The 1984 amendment added subdivision (b) as to children under 10 years of age. The 2004 amendment added in (b) "or a dependent person with substantial cognitive impairment" and expanded the list of offenses to which this subdivision applies.

Assembly Committee on Judiciary Comment

* * * The exception stated at the beginning of the section continues the present law that permits leading questions on direct examination where there is little danger of improper suggestion or where such questions are necessary to obtain relevant evidence. This would permit leading questions on direct examination for preliminary matters, refreshing recollection, and examining handicapped witnesses, expert witnesses, and hostile witnesses. See Witkin, California Evidence §§ 591, 592 (1958); 3 Wigmore, Evidence § 769 et seq. (3d ed. 1940). The court may also forbid the asking of leading questions on cross-examination where the witness is biased in favor of the cross-examiner and would be unduly susceptible to the influence of questions that suggested the desired answer. See 3 Wigmore, Evidence § 773 (3d ed. 1940).

§ 768. Writings. (a) In examining a witness concerning a writing, it is not necessary to show, read, or disclose to him any part of the writing.

(b) If a writing is shown to a witness, all parties to the action must be given an opportunity to inspect it before any question concerning it may be asked of the witness.

Assembly Committee on Judiciary Comment

Existing law apparently does not require that a writing (other than one containing prior inconsistent statements used for impeachment purposes) be shown to a witness before he can be examined concerning it. Section 2054 of the Code of Civil Procedure, which seems to so require, actually requires only that the adverse party be given an opportunity to inspect any writing that is actually shown to a witness before the witness can be examined concerning the writing. See People v. Briggs, 58 Cal.2d 385, 413, 24 Cal.Rptr. 417, 435, 374 P.2d 257, 275 (1962); People v. Keyes, 103 Cal.App. 624, 284 Pac. 1096 (1930) (hearing denied); People v. De Angelli, 34 Cal.App. 716, 168 Pac. 699 (1917). Section 768 clarifies whatever doubt may exist in this regard by declaring that such a writing need not be shown to the witness before he can be examined concerning it. Of course, the best evidence rule may in some cases preclude eliciting testimony concerning the content of a writing. See Evidence Code § 1500 and the Comment thereto.

Insofar as Section 768 relates to prior inconsistent statements that are in writing, see the Comment to Section 769.

Subdivision (b) of Section 768 preserves the right of the adverse party to inspect a writing that is actually shown to a witness before the witness can be examined concerning it. As indicated above, this preserves the existing requirement declared in Code of Civil Procedure Section 2054. However, the right of inspection has been extended to all parties to the action.

§ 769. Inconsistent statement or conduct. In examining a witness concerning a statement or other conduct by him that is inconsistent with any part of his testimony at the hearing, it is not necessary to disclose to him any information concerning the statement or other conduct.

Assembly Committee on Judiciary Comment

Section 769 is consistent with the existing California law regarding the examination of a witness concerning prior inconsistent oral statements. Under existing law, a party need not disclose to a witness any information concerning a prior inconsistent oral statement of the witness before asking him questions about the statement. People v. Kidd, 56 Cal.2d 759, 765, 16 Cal.Rptr. 793, 796-797, 366 P.2d 49, 52-53 (1961); People v. Campos, 10 Cal.App.2d 310, 317, 52 P.2d 251, 254 (1935). However, if a witness' prior inconsistent statements are in writing or, as in the case of former oral testimony, have been reduced to writing, "they must be shown to the witness before any question is put to him concerning them." Code Civ.Proc. § 2052 (superseded by Evidence Code § 768); Umemoto v. McDonald, 6 Cal.2d 587, 592, 58 P.2d 1274, 1276 (1936).

Section 769 eliminates the distinction made in existing law between oral and written statements and permits a witness to be asked questions concerning a prior inconsistent statement, whether written or oral, even though no disclosure is made to him concerning the prior statement. (Whether a foundational showing is required before other evidence of the prior statement may be admitted is not covered in Section 769; the prerequisites for the admission of such evidence are set forth in Section 770.) The disclosure of inconsistent written statements that is required under existing law limits the effectiveness of cross-examination by removing the element of surprise. The forewarning gives the dishonest witness the opportunity to reshape his testimony in conformity with the prior statement. The existing rule is based on an English common law rule that has been abandoned in England for 100 years. See McCormick, Evidence § 28 at 53 (1954).

§ 770. Evidence of inconsistent statement of witness. Unless the interests of justice otherwise require, extrinsic evidence of a statement made by a witness that is inconsistent with any part of his testimony at the hearing shall be excluded unless:

(a) The witness was so examined while testifying as to give him an opportunity to explain or to deny the statement; or

(b) The witness has not been excused from giving further testimony in the action.

Note on Proposed Amendment

The Law Revision Commission tentatively decided in March 2003 to recommend no change to § 770.

Law Revision Commission Comment

Under Section 2052 of the Code of Civil Procedure, extrinsic evidence of a witness' inconsistent statement may be admitted only if the witness was given the opportunity, while testifying, to explain or deny the contradictory statement. Permitting a witness to explain or deny an alleged inconsistent statement is desirable, but there is no compelling reason to provide the opportunity for explanation before the inconsistent statement is introduced in evidence. Accordingly, unless the interests of justice otherwise require, Section 770 permits the judge to exclude evidence of an inconsistent statement only if the witness during his examination was not given an opportunity to explain or deny the statement and he has been unconditionally excused and is not subject to being recalled as a witness. Among other things, Section 770 will permit more effective cross-examination and impeachment of several collusive witnesses, since there need be no disclosure of prior inconsistency before all such witnesses have been examined.

Where the interests of justice require it, the court may permit extrinsic evidence of an inconsistent statement to be admitted even though the witness has been excused and has had no opportunity to explain or deny the statement. An absolute rule forbidding introduction of such evidence where the specified conditions are not met may cause hardship in some cases. For example, the party seeking to introduce the statement may not have learned of its existence until after the witness has left the court and is no longer available to testify. For the foundational requirements for the admission of a hearsay declarant's inconsistent statement, see Evidence Code § 1202 and the Comment thereto.

§ 771. Refreshing recollection with a writing. (a) Subject to subdivision (c), if a witness, either while testifying or prior thereto, uses a writing to refresh his memory with respect to any matter about which he testifies, such writing must be produced at the hearing at the request of an adverse party and, unless the writing is so produced, the testimony of the witness concerning such matter shall be stricken.

(b) If the writing is produced at the hearing, the adverse party may, if he chooses, inspect the writing, cross-examine the witness concerning it, and introduce in evidence such portion of it as may be pertinent to the testimony of the witness.

(c) Production of the writing is excused, and the testimony of the witness shall not be stricken, if the writing:

(1) Is not in the possession or control of the witness or the party who produced his testimony concerning the matter; and

(2) Was not reasonably procurable by such party through the use of the court's process or other available means.

Note on Proposed Amendment

The Law Revision Commission tentatively decided in March 2003 to recommend no change to § 771.

Assembly Committee on Judiciary Comment

Section 771 grants to an adverse party the right to inspect any writing used to refresh a witness' recollection, whether the writing is used by the witness while testifying or prior thereto. The right of inspection granted by Section 771 may be broader than the similar right of inspection granted by Section 2047 of the Code of Civil Procedure, for Section 2047 has been interpreted by the courts to grant a right of inspection of only those writings used by the witness while he is testifying. People v. Gallardo, 41 Cal.2d 57, 257 P.2d 29 (1953); People v. Grayson, 172 Cal.App.2d 372, 341 P.2d 820 (1959); Smith v. Smith, 135 Cal.App.2d 100, 286 P.2d 1009 (1955). In a criminal case, however, the defendant can compel the prosecution to produce any written statement of a prosecution witness relating to matters covered in the witness' testimony. People v. Estrada, 54 Cal.2d 713, 7 Cal.Rptr. 897, 355 P.2d 641 (1960). The extent to which the public policy reflected in criminal discovery practice overrides the restrictive interpretation of Code of Civil Procedure Section 2047 is not clear. See Witkin, California Evidence § 602 (Supp. 1963). In any event, Section 771 follows the lead of the criminal cases, such as People v. Silberstein, 159 Cal.App.2d Supp. 848, 323 P.2d 591 (1958) (defendant entitled to inspect police report used by police officer to refresh his recollection before testifying), and grants a right of inspection without regard to when the writing is used to refresh recollection. If a witness' testimony depends upon the use of a writing to refresh his recollection, the adverse party's right to inspect the writing should not be made to depend upon the happenstance of when the writing is used.

Subdivision (b) gives an adverse party the right to introduce the refreshing memorandum into evidence. An adverse party has a similar right under Code of Civil Procedure Section 2047, which is superseded by this section. This right is not unlimited, however. Only those parts of the refreshing memorandum that are pertinent to the testimony given by the witness are admissible under this rule. Cf. People v. Silberstein, 159 Cal.App.2d Supp. 848, 851-852, 323 P.2d 591, 593 (1958) ("the right to inspect [a refreshing writing] cannot be denied although its admission in evidence may be refused if . . . its contents are immaterial"); Dragash v. Western Pac. R.R., 161 Cal.App.2d 233, 326 P.2d 649 (1958). See also Evidence Code § 356 and the Comment thereto.

Subdivision (c) excuses the nonproduction of the memory-refreshing writing where the writing cannot be produced through no fault of the witness or the party eliciting his testimony concerning the matter. The rule is analogous to the rule announced in People v. Parham, 60 Cal.2d 378, 33 Cal.Rptr. 497, 384 P.2d 1001 (1963), which affirmed an order denying defendant's motion to strike certain witnesses' testimony where the witnesses' prior statements were withheld by the Federal Bureau of Investigation.

It should be noted that there is no restriction in the Evidence Code on the means that may be used to refresh recollection. Thus, the limitations on the types of writings that may be used as recorded memory under Section 1237 do not limit the types of writings that may be used to refresh recollection under Section 771.

§ 772. Order of examination. (a) The examination of a witness shall proceed in the following phases: direct examination, cross-examination, redirect examination, recross-examination, and continuing thereafter by redirect and recross-examination.

(b) Unless for good cause the court otherwise directs, each phase of the examination of a witness must be concluded before the succeeding phase begins.

(c) Subject to subdivision (d), a party may, in the discretion of the court, interrupt his cross-examination, redirect examination, or recross-examination of a witness, in order to examine the witness upon a matter not within the scope of a previous examination of the witness.

(d) If the witness is the defendant in a criminal action, the witness may not, without his consent, be examined under direct examination by another party.

Assembly Committee on Judiciary Comment

* * * Under subdivision (c), as under existing law, a party examining a witness under cross-examination, redirect examination, or recross-examination may go beyond the scope of the initial direct examination if the court permits. See Code Civ.Proc. §§ 2048 (last clause), 2050; Witkin, California Evidence §§ 627, 697 (1958). Under the definition in Section 760, such an extended examination is direct examination. Cf. Code Civ.Proc. § 2048 ("such examination is to be subject to the same rules as a direct examination"). Such direct examination may, however, be subject to the rules applicable to a cross-examination by virtue of the provisions of Section 776, 804, or 1203. * * *

§ 773. Cross-examination. (a) A witness examined by one party may be cross-examined upon any matter within the scope of the direct examination by each other party to the action in such order as the court directs.

(b) The cross-examination of a witness by any party whose interest is not adverse to the party calling him is subject to the same rules that are applicable to the direct examination.

Law Revision Commission Comment

Subdivision (a) restates the substance of Sections 2045 (part) and 2048 of the Code of Civil Procedure and Section 1323 of the Penal Code.

Subdivision (b) is based on the holding in Atchison, T. & S.F. Ry. v. Southern Pac. Co., 13 Cal.App.2d 505, 57 P.2d 575 (1936). That case held that a party not adverse to the direct examiner of a witness did not have the right to cross-examine the witness. Under subdivision (a), such a party would have the right to cross-examine the witness upon any matter within the scope of the direct examination, but he would be prohibited by Section 767 from asking leading questions during such examination. If the witness testifies on direct examination to matters that are, in fact, antagonistic to a party's position, he may be permitted to cross-examine with leading questions even though from a technical point of view the interest of the cross-examiner is not adverse to that of the direct examiner. Cf. McCarthy v. Mobile Cranes, Inc., 199 Cal.App.2d 500, 18 Cal.Rptr. 750 (1962).

§ 774. Re-examination. A witness once examined cannot be reexamined as to the same matter without leave of the court, but he may be reexamined as to any new matter upon which he has been examined by another party to the action. Leave may be granted or withheld in the court's discretion.

§ 775. Court may call witnesses. The court, on its own motion or on the motion of any party, may call witnesses and interrogate them the same as if they had been produced by a party to the action, and the parties may object to the questions asked and the evidence adduced the same as if such witnesses were called and examined by an adverse party. Such witnesses may be cross-examined by all parties to the action in such order as the court directs.

Assembly Committee on Judiciary Comment

* * * Of course, the judge would be guilty of misconduct were he to show partiality or bias in calling and interrogating witnesses. See 2 Witkin, California Procedure, Trial §§ 14-17 (1954).

§ 776. Examination of adverse party or witness. (a) A party to the record of any civil action, or a person identified with such a party, may be called and examined as if under cross-examination by any adverse party at any time during the presentation of evidence by the party calling the witness.

(b) A witness examined by a party under this section may be cross-examined by all other parties to the action in such order as the court directs; but, subject to subdivision (e), the witness may be examined only as if under redirect examination by:

(1) In the case of a witness who is a party, his own counsel and counsel for a party who is not adverse to the witness.

(2) In the case of a witness who is not a party, counsel for the party with whom the witness is identified and counsel for a party who is not adverse to the party with whom the witness is identified.

(c) For the purpose of this section, parties represented by the same counsel are deemed to be a single party.

(d) For the purpose of this section, a person is identified with a party if he is:

(1) A person for whose immediate benefit the action is prosecuted or defended by the party.

(2) A director, officer, superintendent, member, agent, employee, or managing agent of the party or of a person specified in paragraph (1), or any public employee of a public entity when such public entity is the party.

(3) A person who was in any of the relationships specified in paragraph (2) at the time of the act or omission giving rise to the cause of action.

(4) A person who was in any of the relationships specified in paragraph (2) at the time he obtained knowledge of the matter concerning which he is sought to be examined under this section.

(e) Paragraph (2) of subdivision (b) does not require counsel for the party with whom the witness is identified and counsel for a party who is not adverse to the party with whom the witness is identified to examine the witness as if under redirect examination if the party who called the witness for examination under this section:

(1) Is also a person identified with the same party with whom the witness is identified.

(2) Is the personal representative, heir, successor, or assignee of a person identified with the same party with whom the witness is identified. [*Amended 1967.*]

Law Revision Commission Comment

Section 776 restates the substance of Code of Civil Procedure Section 2055 as it has been interpreted by the courts. See Witkin, California Evidence §§ 607-613 (1958), and pertinent cases cited and discussed therein.

Subdivision (a). Subdivision (a) restates the provisions of Section 2055 that permit a party to call and examine as if under cross-examination an adverse party and certain adverse witnesses. However, Section 776 substitutes the phrase "or a person identified with such a party" for the confusing enumeration of persons listed in the first sentence of Section 2055. This phrase is defined in subdivision (d) of Section 776 to include all of the persons presently named in Section 2055. See the Comment to subdivision (d), infra.

Subdivision (b). Subdivision (b) is based in part on similar provisions contained in Code of Civil Procedure Section 2055. Unlike Section 2055, however, this subdivision is drafted in recognition of the problems involved in multiple party litigation. Thus, the introductory portion of subdivision (b) states the general rule that a witness examined under this section may be cross-examined by all other parties to the action in such order as the court directs. For example, a party whose interest in the action is identical with that of the party who called the witness for examination under this section has a right to cross-examine the witness fully because he, too, has the right to call the witness for examination under this section. Similarly, a party whose interest in the action is adverse to the party who calls the witness for examination under this section has the right to cross-examine the witness fully unless he is identified with the witness as described in paragraphs (1) and (2) of this subdivision. Paragraphs (1) and (2) restrict the nature of the cross-examination permitted of a witness by a party with whom the witness is identified and by parties whose interest in the action is not adverse to the party with whom the witness is identified. These parties are limited to examination of the witness as if under redirect examination. In essence, this means that leading questions cannot be asked of the witness by these parties. See Evidence Code § 767. Although the examination must proceed as if it were a redirect examination, under Section 761 it is in fact a cross-examination and limited to the scope of the direct. See also Evidence Code §§ 760, 773.

Subdivision (c). Subdivision (c) codifies a principle that has been recognized in the California cases even though not explicitly stated in Code of Civil Procedure Section 2055. See Gates v. Pendleton, 71 Cal.App. 752, 236 Pac. 365 (1925); Goehring v. Rogers, 67 Cal.App. 260, 227 Pac. 689 (1924).

Subdivision (d). Subdivision (d) lists the classes of persons who are "identified with a party" as that phrase and variations of it are used in subdivisions (a) and (b) of Section 776. The persons named in paragraphs (1) and (2) are those described in the first sentence of Code of Civil Procedure Section 2055 as being subject to examination pursuant to the section because of a particular relationship to a party. See the definitions of "person," "public employee," and "public entity" in Evidence Code §§ 175, 195, and 200, respectively. In addition, paragraph (3) of this subdivision describes persons who were in any of the requisite relationships at the time of the act or omission giving rise to the cause of action. This states existing case law. Scott v. Del Monte Properties, Inc., 140 Cal.App.2d 756, 295 P.2d 947 (1956); Wells v. Lloyd, 35 Cal.App.2d 6, 94 P.2d 373 (1939). Similarly, paragraph (4) extends this principle to include any person who obtained relevant knowledge as a result of such a relationship but who does not fit the precise descriptions contained in paragraphs (1) through (3). For example, a person whose employment by a party began after the cause of action arose and terminated prior to the time of his examination at the trial would be included in the description contained in paragraph (4) if he obtained relevant knowledge of the incident as a result of his employment. It is not clear whether this states existing law, for no California decision has been found that decides this question. The paragraph is necessary, however, to preclude a party from preventing examination of his employee pursuant to this section by the simple expedient of discharging the employee prior to trial and reinstating him afterwards. Cf. Wells v. Lloyd, 35 Cal.App.2d 6, 12, 94 P.2d 373, 376-377 (1939).

Law Revision Commission Comment - 1967 Amendment

Section 776 permits a party calling as a witness an employee of (or someone similarly identified in interest with) an adverse party to examine the witness as if under cross-examination, i.e., to use leading questions in his examination. Section 776 requires the party whose employee was thus called and examined to examine the witness as if under redirect examination, i.e., to refrain from the use of leading questions. If a party is able to persuade the court that the usual rule prescribed by Section 776 is not in the interest of justice in a particular case, the court may enlarge or restrict the right to use leading questions as provided in Section 767.

These rules are based on the premise that ordinarily such a witness will have a feeling of identification in the lawsuit with his employer rather than with the other party to the action.

Subdivision (b) has been amended, and subdivision (e) has been added because the premise upon which Section 776 is based does not necessarily apply when the party calling the witness is also closely identified with the adverse party; hence, the adverse party should be entitled to the usual rights of a cross-examiner when he examines the witness. For example, when an employee sues his employer and calls a co-employee as a witness, there is no reason to assume that the witness will be adverse to the employee-party and in sympathy with the employer-party. The reverse may be the case. The amendment to Section 776 will permit an employer, as a general rule, to use leading questions in his cross-examination of an employee-witness who has been called to testify under Section 776 by a co-employee. However, if the party calling the witness can satisfy the court that the witness is in fact identified in interest with the employer or for some other reason is amenable to suggestive questioning by the employer, the court may limit the employer's use of leading questions during his examination of the witness pursuant to Section 767. See J. & B. Motors, Inc. v. Margolis, 75 Ariz. 392, 257 P.2d 588 (1953). [8 Cal.L.Rev.Comm. Reports 101 (1967).]

§ 777. Exclusion of witness. (a) Subject to subdivisions (b) and (c), the court may exclude from the courtroom any witness not at the time under examination so that such witness cannot hear the testimony of other witnesses.

(b) A party to the action cannot be excluded under this section.

(c) If a person other than a natural person is a party to the action, an officer or employee designated by its attorney is entitled to be present.

§ 778. Recall of witness. After a witness has been excused from giving further testimony in the action, he cannot be recalled without leave of the court. Leave may be granted or withheld in the court's discretion.

Chapter 6. Credibility of Witnesses

Article 1. Credibility Generally

§ 780. General rule as to credibility. Except as otherwise provided by statute, the court or jury may consider in determining the credibility of a witness any matter that has any tendency in reason to prove or disprove the truthfulness of his testimony at the hearing, including but not limited to any of the following:

(a) His demeanor while testifying and the manner in which he testifies.

(b) The character of his testimony.

(c) The extent of his capacity to perceive, to recollect, or to communicate any matter about which he testifies.

(d) The extent of his opportunity to perceive any matter about which he testifies.

(e) His character for honesty or veracity or their opposites.

(f) The existence or nonexistence of a bias, interest, or other motive.

(g) A statement previously made by him that is consistent with his testimony at the hearing.

(h) A statement made by him that is inconsistent with any part of his testimony at the hearing.

(i) The existence or nonexistence of any fact testified to by him.

(j) His attitude toward the action in which he testifies or toward the giving of testimony.

(k) His admission of untruthfulness.

Law Revision Commission Comment

* * * Section 780 is a general catalog of those matters that have any tendency in reason to affect the credibility of a witness. So far as the admissibility of evidence relating to credibility is concerned, Section 780 is technically unnecessary because Section 351 declares that "all relevant evidence is admissible." However, this section makes it clear that matters that may not be "evidence" in a technical sense can affect the credibility of a witness, and it provides a convenient list of the most common factors that bear on the question of credibility. See Davis v. Judson, 159 Cal. 121, 128, 113 Pac. 147, 150 (1910); La Jolla Casa de Manana v. Hopkins, 98 Cal.App.2d 339, 346, 219 P.2d 871, 876 (1950). See generally Witkin, California Evidence §§ 480-485 (1958). Limitations on the admissibility of evidence offered to attack or support the credibility of a witness are stated in Article 2 (commencing with Section 785).

There is no specific limitation in the Evidence Code on the use of impeaching evidence on the ground that it is "collateral". The so-called "collateral matter" limitation on attacking the credibility of a witness excludes evidence relevant to credibility unless such evidence is independently relevant to the issue being tried. It is based on the sensible notion that trials should be confined to settling those disputes between the parties upon which their rights in the litigation depend. Under existing law, this "collateral matter" doctrine has been treated as an inflexible rule excluding evidence relevant to the credibility of the witness. See, e.g., People v. Wells, 33 Cal.2d 330, 340, 202 P.2d 53, 59 (1949), and cases cited therein.

The effect of Section 780 (together with Section 351) is to eliminate this inflexible rule of exclusion. This is not to say that all evidence of a collateral nature offered to attack the credibility of a witness would be admissible. Under Section 352, the court has substantial discretion to exclude collateral evidence. The effect of Section 780, therefore, is to change the present somewhat inflexible rule of exclusion to a rule of discretion to be exercised by the trial judge.

There is no limitation in the Evidence Code on the use of opinion evidence to prove the character of a witness for honesty, veracity, or the lack thereof. Hence, under Sections 780 and 1100, such evidence is admissible. This represents a change in the present law. See People v. Methvin, 53 Cal. 68 (1878). However, the opinion evidence that may be offered by those persons intimately familiar with the witness is likely to be of more probative value than the generally admissible evidence of reputation. See 7 Wigmore, Evidence § 1986 (3d ed. 1940).

§ 782. Sexual offenses; evidence of sexual conduct of complaining witness; procedure for admissibility; treatment of resealed affidavits. (a) In any of the circumstances described in subdivision (c), if evidence of sexual conduct of the complaining witness is offered to attack the credibility of the complaining witness under Section 780, the following procedure shall be followed:

(1) A written motion shall be made by the defendant to the court and prosecutor stating that the defense has an offer of proof of the relevancy of evidence of the sexual conduct of the complaining witness proposed to be presented and its relevancy in attacking the creditability of the complaining witness.

(2) The written motion shall be accompanied by an affidavit in which the offer of proof shall be stated. The affidavit shall be filed under seal and only unsealed by the court to determine if the offer of proof is sufficient to order a hearing pursuant to paragraph (3). After that determination, the affidavit shall be resealed by the court.

(3) If the court finds that the offer of proof is sufficient, the court shall order a hearing out of the presence of the jury, if any, and at the hearing allow the questioning of the complaining witness regarding the offer of proof made by the defendant.

(4) At the conclusion of the hearing, if the court finds that evidence proposed to be offered by the defendant regarding the sexual conduct of the complaining witness is relevant pursuant to Section 780, and is not inadmissible pursuant to Section 352, the court may make an order stating what evidence may be introduced by the defendant, and the nature of the questions to be permitted. The defendant may then offer evidence pursuant to the order of the court.

(5) An affidavit resealed by the court pursuant to paragraph (2) shall remain sealed, unless the defendant raises an issue on appeal or collateral review relating to the offer of proof contained in the sealed document. If the defendant raises that issue on appeal, the court shall allow the Attorney General and appellate counsel for the defendant access to the sealed affidavit. If the issue is raised on collateral review, the court shall allow the district attorney and defendant's counsel access to the sealed affidavit. The use of the information contained in the affidavit shall be limited solely to the pending proceeding.

(b) As used in this section, "complaining witness" means:

(1) The alleged victim of the crime charged, the prosecution of which is subject to this section, pursuant to paragraph (1) of subdivision (c).

(2) An alleged victim offering testimony pursuant to paragraph (2) or paragraph (3) of subdivision (c).

(c) The procedure provided by subdivision (a) shall apply in any of the following circumstances:

(1) In a prosecution under Section 261, 262, 264.1, 286, 287, 288, 288.5, or 289 of, or former Section 288a of, the Penal Code, or for assault with intent to commit, attempt to commit, or conspiracy to commit any crime defined in any of those sections, except if the crime is alleged to have occurred in a local detention facility, as defined in Section 6031.4, or in a state prison, as defined in Section 4504.

(2) When an alleged victim testifies pursuant to subdivision (b) of Section 1101 as a victim of a crime listed in under Section 243.4, 261, 261.5, 269, 285, 286, 287, 288, 288.5, 289, 314, or 647.6 of, or former Section 288a of, the Penal Code, except if the crime is alleged to have occurred in a local detention facility, as defined in Section 6031.4 of the Penal Code, or in a state prison, as defined in Section 4504 of the Penal Code.

(3) When an alleged victim of a sexual offense testifies pursuant to Section 1108, except if the crime is alleged to have occurred in a local detention facility, as defined in Section 6031.4 of the Penal Code, or in a state prison, as defined in Section 4504 of the Penal Code.

[*Added 1974. Amended 1981, 1987, 1989, 1996, 2004, 2006, 2018.*]

Statutory Note

The 1981, 1987. 1989, and 1996 amendments expanded the list of crimes in subdivision (a). The 2004 amendment added provisions for sealing, unsealing, and resealing the affidavit. The 2006 amendment rewrote the introductory paragraph, rewrote subdivision (b) and clarified use of sealed affidavits in subsequent proceedings.

Legislative Note

Section 1 of the bill containing the 1989 Amendment stated:

"Section 1. (a) The Legislature finds and declares that because of the court's decision in People v. Van Hoek, 200 Cal.App.3d 811, there is an immediate need for additional statutory protection for the most vulnerable among our children, those of tender years, some of whom are being subjected to continuing sexual abuse by those commonly referred to as 'resident child molesters.' These molesters reside with, or have recurring access to, a child and repeatedly molest the child over a prolonged period of time but the child, because of age or the frequency of the molestations, or both, often is unable to distinguish one incident from another in terms of time, place, or other particulars, and as a consequence prosecutors are unable to provide the specificity of charges necessary to overcome the constitutional due process problems raised in the Van Hoek case within the framework of existing statutory law. As a consequence, some of our most vulnerable children continue to be at risk and some of our worst offenders continue to go unpunished.

"(b) It is the intent of the Legislature in enacting this act to provide additional protection for children subjected to continuing sexual abuse and certain punishment for persons referred to as 'resident child molesters' by establishing a new crime of continuing sexual abuse of a child under circumstances where there have been repeated acts of molestation over a period of time, and the perpetrator either resides with or has recurring access to the child. It is the further intent of the Legislature that the penalty for this crime shall be greater than the maximum penalty under existing law for any single felony sex offense."

§ 782.1. Disorderly, lewd, or dissolute conduct; prostitution; admissibility of evidence of possession of condoms; procedure for admissibility. The possession of a condom is not admissible as evidence in the prosecution of a violation of Section 372 of, subdivision (a) or (b) of Section 647 of, or Section 653.22 of, the Penal Code, if the offense is related to prostitution. [*Added 2014. Amended 2019.*]

§ 783. Sexual harassment, sexual assault, or sexual battery cases; admissibility of evidence of plaintiff's sexual conduct; procedure. In any civil action alleging conduct which constitutes sexual harassment, sexual assault, or sexual battery, if evidence of sexual conduct of the plaintiff is offered to attack credibility of the plaintiff under Section 780, the following procedures shall be followed:

(a) A written motion shall be made by the defendant to the court and the plaintiff's attorney stating that the defense has an offer of proof of the relevancy of evidence of the sexual conduct of the plaintiff proposed to be presented.

(b) The written motion shall be accompanied by an affidavit in which the offer of proof shall be stated.

(c) If the court finds that the offer of proof is sufficient, the court shall order a hearing out of the presence of the jury, if any, and at the hearing allow the questioning of the plaintiff regarding the offer of proof made by the defendant.

(d) At the conclusion of the hearing, if the court finds that evidence proposed to be offered by the defendant regarding the sexual conduct of the plaintiff is relevant pursuant to Section 780, and is not inadmissible pursuant to Section 352, the court may make an order stating what evidence may be introduced by the defendant, and the nature of the questions to be permitted. The defendant may then offer evidence pursuant to the order of the court. [*Added 1985.*]

Statutory Note

Section 1 of Stats.1985, c. 1328, which added § 783, declared:

The Legislature finds and declares that it is the existing policy of the State of California to ensure that the causes of action for claims of sexual harassment, sexual assault, or sexual battery are given proper meaning. The discovery of sexual aspects of complainant's lives, as well as those of their past and current friends and acquaintances, has the clear potential to discourage complaints and to annoy and harass litigants. That annoyance and discomfort, as a result of defendant or respondent inquiries, is unnecessary and deplorable. Without protection against it, individuals whose intimate lives are unjustifiably and offensively intruded upon might face the 'Catch-22' of invoking their remedy only at the risk of enduring further intrusions into details of their personal lives in discovery, and in open quasi-judicial or judicial proceedings.

The Legislature is mindful that a similar state of affairs once confronted victims in criminal prosecutions for rape, who often ran the risk of finding their own moral characters on trial during the prosecution of their assailants. The Legislature has taken measures to curb those abuses in rape proceedings. It is the intent of the Legislature to take similar measures in sexual harassment, sexual assault, or sexual battery cases.

The Legislature concludes that the use of evidence of a complainant's sexual behavior is more often harassing and intimidating than genuinely probative, and the potential for prejudice outweighs whatever probative value that evidence may have. Absent extraordinary circumstances, inquiry into those areas should not be permitted, either in discovery or at trial.

Article 2. Attacking or Supporting Credibility

§ 785. Parties may attack or support credibility. The credibility of a witness may be attacked or supported by any party, including the party calling him.

Law Revision Commission Comment

Section 785 eliminates the present restriction on attacking the credibility of one's own witness. Under the existing law, a party is precluded from attacking the credibility of his own witness unless he has been surprised and damaged by the witness' testimony. Code Civ.Proc. §§ 2049, 2052 (superseded by Evidence Code §§ 768, 769, 770, 785); People v. LeBeau, 39 Cal.2d 146, 148, 245 P.2d 302, 303 (1952). In large part, the present law rests upon the theory that a party producing a witness is bound by his testimony. See discussion in Smellie v. Southern Pac. Co., 212 Cal. 540, 555-556, 299 Pac. 529, 535 (1931). This theory has long been abandoned in several jurisdictions where the practical exigencies of litigation have been recognized. See McCormick, Evidence § 38 (1954). A party has no actual control over a person who witnesses an event and is required to testify to aid the trier of fact in its function of determining the truth. Hence, a party should not be "bound" by the testimony of a witness produced by him and should be permitted to attack the credibility of the witness without anachronistic limitations. Denial of the right to attack credibility may often work a hardship on a party where by necessity he must call a hostile witness. Expanded opportunity for testing credibility is in keeping with the interest of providing a forum for full and free disclosure. In regard to attacking the credibility of a "necessary" witness, see generally People v. McFarlane, 134 Cal. 618, 66 Pac. 865 (1901); Anthony v. Hobbie, 85 Cal.App.2d 798, 803-804, 193 P.2d 748, 751 (1948); First Nat'l Bank v. De Moulin, 56 Cal.App. 313, 321, 205 Pac. 92, 96 (1922).

§ 786. Character evidence generally. Evidence of traits of his character other than honesty or veracity, or their opposites, is inadmissible to attack or support the credibility of a witness.

Case Note

This section does not apply in criminal proceedings because of Cal. Const. art. I, § 28(d) [p. 478, *infra*]. People v. Harris, 47 Cal. 3d 1047, 1080-1083, 255 Cal. Rptr. 352, 373-374, 767 P.2d 619, 640-641 (1989).

Law Revision Commission Comment

Section 786 limits evidence relating to the character of a witness to the character traits necessarily involved in a proper determination of credibility. Other character traits are not sufficiently probative of a witness' honesty or veracity to warrant their consideration on the issue of credibility.

§ 787. Specific instances of conduct. Subject to Section 788, evidence of specific instances of his conduct relevant only as tending to prove a trait of his character is inadmissible to attack or support the credibility of a witness.

Case Notes

This section does not apply in criminal proceedings because of Cal. Const. art. I, § 28(d) [p. 478, *infra*]. People v. Harris, 47 Cal. 3d 1047, 1080-1083, 255 Cal. Rptr. 352, 373-374, 767 P.2d 619, 640-641 (1989).

Inadmissibility of misdemeanor convictions to impeach witness credibility, pursuant to §§ 787-788, was abrogated by Cal. Const. art. I, § 28(d), p. 478, as long as the misdemeanor involves moral turpitude, which is the minimum requirement for relevance. However, a misdemeanor judgment of conviction is hearsay to prove commission of the underlying conduct, and there is no applicable exception to the hearsay rule. (Section 1300, p. 455, covers only felony convictions.) Nonhearsay proof of the underlying criminal conduct may be admissible if the probative value for impeachment is not outweighed in the particular case by the danger of unfair prejudice, undue consumption of time, etc., see § 352. People v. Wheeler, 4 Cal. 4th 284, 14 Cal. Rptr. 2d 418, 841 P.2d 938 (1993).

Law Revision Commission Comment

Under Section 787, as under existing law, evidence of specific instances of a witness' conduct is inadmissible to prove a trait of his character for the purpose of attacking or supporting his credibility. See Sharon v. Sharon, 79 Cal. 633, 673-674, 22 Pac. 26, 38 (1889); Code Civ.Proc. § 2051 (superseded by Section 787 and several other sections in Chapter 6). Section 787 is subject, however, to Section 788, which permits certain kinds of criminal convictions to be used for the purpose of attacking a witness' credibility.

§ 788. Conviction of witness for a crime. For the purpose of attacking the credibility of a witness, it may be shown by the examination of the witness or by the record of the judgment that he has been convicted of a felony unless:

(a) A pardon based on his innocence has been granted to the witness by the jurisdiction in which he was convicted.

(b) A certificate of rehabilitation and pardon has been granted to the witness under the provisions of Chapter 3.5 (commencing with Section 4852.01) of Title 6 of Part 3 of the Penal Code.

(c) The accusatory pleading against the witness has been dismissed under the provisions of Penal Code Section 1203.4, but this exception does not apply to any criminal trial where the witness is being prosecuted for a subsequent offense.

(d) The conviction was under the laws of another jurisdiction and the witness has been relieved of the penalties and disabilities arising from the conviction pursuant to a procedure substantially equivalent to that referred to in subdivision (b) or (c).

Case Notes

See case notes under Cal. Const. art. I, § 28(f), p. 478.

Senate Committee on Judiciary Comment

Under Section 787, evidence of specific instances of a witness' conduct is inadmissible for the purpose of attacking or supporting his credibility. Section 788 states an exception to this general rule where the evidence of the witness' misconduct consists of his conviction of a felony. A judgment of conviction that is offered to prove that the person adjudged guilty committed the crime is hearsay. See Evidence Code §§ 1200 and 1300 and the Comments thereto. But the hearsay objection to the evidence specified in Section 788 is overcome by the declaration in the section that such evidence "may be shown" for the purpose of attacking a witness' credibility.

Section 788 is based on Section 2051 of the Code of Civil Procedure. Under Section 788, as under Section 2051, only the testimony of the witness himself or the record of the judgment of conviction may be used to prove the fact of conviction. As Section 788 is, in substance, a recodification of the existing law, it will have no effect on the case-developed rules limiting the circumstances under which a witness may be asked whether he was convicted of a felony. See People v. Perez, 58 Cal.2d 229, 23 Cal.Rptr. 569, 373 P.2d 617 (1962); People v. Darnold, 219 Cal.App.2d 561, 33 Cal.Rptr. 369 (1963).

Subdivision (a) prohibits the use of a conviction to attack the credibility of a witness if a pardon has been granted to the witness on the ground that he was innocent and was erroneously convicted. Subdivision (a) changes the existing California law. Under the existing law, the conviction is admissible to attack credibility, and the pardon—even though based on innocence—is admissible merely to mitigate the effect of the conviction. People v. Hardwick, 204 Cal. 582, 269 Pac. 427 (1928).

Subdivision (b) recodifies the provision of Section 2051 that prohibits the use of a conviction to attack credibility if a pardon has been granted upon the basis of a certificate of rehabilitation. See also Code Civ.Proc. § 2065.

Subdivision (c) recodifies the existing law that prohibits the use of a conviction to attack the credibility of a witness if the conviction has been set aside under Penal Code Section 1203.4. See People v. Mackey, 58 Cal.App. 123, 208 Pac. 135 (1922). The exception that permits the use of such a conviction to attack the credibility of a criminal defendant who testifies as a witness also reflects existing law. See People v. James, 40 Cal.App.2d 740, 105 P.2d 947 (1940).

Subdivision (d) merely provides that a witness who has been relieved of the penalties and disabilities of a prior conviction under the laws of another jurisdiction will be subject to attacks on his credibility under the same conditions that would be applicable if such relief had been granted him under the laws of California.

§ 789. Religious belief. Evidence of his religious belief or lack thereof is inadmissible to attack or support the credibility of a witness.

§ 790. Good character of witness. Evidence of the good character of a witness is inadmissible to support his credibility unless evidence of his bad character has been admitted for the purpose of attacking his credibility.

Case Note

This section does not apply in criminal proceedings because of Cal. Const. art. I, § 28(d), p. 478. People v. Harris, 47 Cal. 3d 1047, 1080-1083, 255 Cal. Rptr. 352, 373-374, 767 P.2d 619, 641-641 (1989).

Law Revision Commission Comment

Section 790 restates without substantive change a rule that is well recognized by statutory and case law in California. Code Civ.Proc. § 2053 (superseded by Evidence Code §§ 790, 1101); People v. Bush, 65 Cal. 129, 131, 3 Pac. 590, 591 (1884). Unless the credibility of a witness is put in issue by an attack impugning his character for honesty or veracity (see Section 786), evidence of the witness' good character admitted merely to support his credibility introduces collateral material that is unnecessary to a proper determination of any legitimate issue in the action. See People v. Sweeney, 55 Cal.2d 27, 38-39, 9 Cal.Rptr. 793, 799, 357 P.2d 1049, 1055 (1960).

§ 791. Prior consistent statement of witness. Evidence of a statement previously made by a witness that is consistent with his testimony at the hearing is inadmissible to support his credibility unless it is offered after:

(a) Evidence of a statement made by him that is inconsistent with any part of his testimony at the hearing has been admitted for the purpose of attacking his credibility, and the statement was made before the alleged inconsistent statement; or

(b) An express or implied charge has been made that his testimony at the hearing is recently fabricated or is influenced by bias or other improper motive, and the statement was made before the bias, motive for fabrication, or other improper motive is alleged to have arisen.

Law Revision Commission Comment

Section 791 sets forth the conditions for admitting a witness' prior consistent statements for the purpose of supporting his credibility as a witness. For a discussion of the effect to be given to the evidence admitted under this section, see Evidence Code § 1236 and the Comment thereto.

Subdivision (a). Subdivision (a) permits the introduction of a witness' prior consistent statement if evidence of an inconsistent statement of the witness has been admitted for the purpose of attacking his credibility and if the consistent statement was made before the alleged inconsistent statement.

Under existing California law, evidence of a prior consistent statement is admissible to rebut a charge of bias, interest, recent fabrication, or other improper motive. See the Comment to subdivision (b), infra. Existing law may preclude admission of a prior consistent statement to rehabilitate a witness where only a prior inconsistent statement has been admitted for the purpose of attacking his credibility. See People v. Doyell, 48 Cal. 85, 90-91 (1874). However, recent cases indicate that the offering of a prior inconsistent statement necessarily is an implied charge that the witness has fabricated his testimony since the time the inconsistent statement was made and justifies the admission of a consistent statement made prior to the alleged inconsistent statement. People v. Bias, 170 Cal.App.2d 502, 511-512, 339 P.2d 204, 210-211 (1959). Subdivision (a) makes it clear that evidence of a previous consistent statement is admissible under these circumstances to show that no such fabrication took place. Subdivision (a), thus, is no more than a logical extension of the general rule that evidence of a prior consistent statement is admissible to rehabilitate a witness following an express or implied charge of recent fabrication.

Subdivision (b). This subdivision codifies existing law. See People v. Kynette, 15 Cal.2d 731, 104 P.2d 794 (1940) (overruled on other grounds in People v. Snyder, 50 Cal.2d 190, 197, 324 P.2d 1, 6 (1958)). Of course, if the consistent statement was made after the time the improper motive is alleged to have arisen, the logical thrust of the evidence is lost and the statement is inadmissible. See People v. Doetschman, 69 Cal.App.2d 486, 159 P.2d 418 (1945).

Chapter 7. Hypnosis of Witness

§ 795. Testimony of hypnosis subject; admissibility; conditions. (a) The testimony of a witness is not inadmissible in a criminal proceeding by reason of the fact that the witness has previously undergone hypnosis for the purpose of recalling events that are the subject of the witness's testimony, if all of the following conditions are met:

(1) The testimony is limited to those matters that the witness recalled and related prior to the hypnosis.

(2) The substance of the prehypnotic memory was preserved in a writing, audio recording, or video recording prior to the hypnosis.

(3) The hypnosis was conducted in accordance with all of the following procedures:

(A) A written record was made prior to hypnosis documenting the subject's description of the event, and information that was provided to the hypnotist concerning the subject matter of the hypnosis.

(B) The subject gave informed consent to the hypnosis.

(C) The hypnosis session, including the pre- and post-hypnosis interviews, was video recorded for subsequent review.

(D) The hypnosis was performed by a licensed medical doctor, psychologist, licensed clinical social worker, or a licensed marriage and family therapist experienced in the use of hypnosis and independent of and not in the presence of law enforcement, the prosecution, or the defense.

(4) Prior to admission of the testimony, the court holds a hearing pursuant to Section 402 at which the proponent of the evidence proves by clear and convincing evidence that the hypnosis did not so affect the witness as to render the witness's prehypnosis recollection unreliable or to substantially impair the ability to cross-examine the witness concerning the witness's prehypnosis recollection. At the hearing, each side shall have the right to present expert testimony and to cross-examine witnesses.

(b) Nothing in this section shall be construed to limit the ability of a party to attack the credibility of a witness who has undergone hypnosis, or to limit other legal grounds to admit or exclude the testimony of that witness. [*Added 1984. Amended 1987, 1996, 2002, 2009.*]

DIVISION 7. OPINION TESTIMONY AND SCIENTIFIC EVIDENCE

Law Revision Commission Comment

Two matters concerning the terminology used in this division [§§ 800-870] should be noted: (1) The word "opinion" is used to include all opinions, inferences, conclusions, and other subjective statements made by a witness. (2) The word "matter" is used to encompass facts, data, and such matters as a witness' knowledge, experience, and other intangibles upon which an opinion may be based. Thus, every conceivable basis for an opinion is included within this term.

Chapter 1. Expert and Other Opinion Testimony

Article 1. Expert and other Opinion Testimony Generally

§ 800. Opinion testimony by lay witness. If a witness is not testifying as an expert, his testimony in the form of an opinion is limited to such an opinion as is permitted by law, including but not limited to an opinion that is:

(a) Rationally based on the perception of the witness; and
(b) Helpful to a clear understanding of his testimony.

Case Note

Lay opinion testimony that the defendant is not a "sexual deviant" is admissible if based on relevant facts personally observed by the witness. In child molestation prosecution, defendant's behavior with children is relevant; with adults, irrelevant. People v. McAlpin, 53 Cal. 3d 1289, 1305-1309, 283 Cal. Rptr. 382, 391-394, 812 P.2d 563, 572-575 (1991).

Law Revision Commission Comment

* * * Section 800 does not make inadmissible an opinion that is admissible under existing law, even though the requirements of subdivisions (a) and (b) are not satisfied. Thus, the section does not affect the existing rule that a nonexpert witness may give his opinion as to the value of his property or the value of his own services. See Witkin, California Evidence § 179 (1958). The words "such an opinion as is permitted by law" in Section 800 make this clear.

§ 801. Opinion testimony by expert witness. If a witness is testifying as an expert, his testimony in the form of an opinion is limited to such an opinion as is:

(a) Related to a subject that is sufficiently beyond common experience that the opinion of an expert would assist the trier of fact; and

(b) Based on matter (including his special knowledge, skill, experience, training, and education) perceived by or personally known to the witness or made known to him at or before the hearing, whether or not admissible, that is of a type that reasonably may be relied upon by an expert in forming an opinion upon the subject to which his testimony relates, unless an expert is precluded by law from using such matter as a basis for his opinion.

Case Notes

When an expert relies on privileged material, a court may exclude the expert's testimony or report as necessary to enforce the privilege. Fox v. Kramer, 22 Cal. 4th 531, 541, 93 Cal. Rptr. 2d 497, 503, 994 P.2d 343, 349 (2000).

Rejecting Daubert v. Merrell Dow Pharmaceuticals, Inc., 509 U.S. 579, 113 S.Ct. 2786, 125 L.Ed. 2d 469 (1993), California continues to use the Kelly/Frye general acceptance test for determining the admissibility of expert testimony based on new scientific techniques. People v. Leahy, 8 Cal. 4th 587, 598, 34 Cal. Rptr. 2d 663, 669, 882 P.2d 321, 327 (1994).

Evidence that the accused matches a "profile"—a collection of conduct and characteristics commonly displayed by persons who commit a certain type of crime—is inherently prejudicial and generally inadmissible. People v. Robbie, 92 Cal. App. 4th 1075, 112 Cal. Rptr. 2d 479 (Ct. App. 1st Dist. 2001).

Expert testimony about the behavior of a victim of domestic violence may be admissible under § 801 even if it is not admissible under § 1107. People v. Brown, 33 Cal.4th 892, 16 Cal.Rptr.3d 447, 94 P.3d 574 (2004).

Law Revision Commission Comment

Section 801 deals with opinion testimony of a witness testifying as an expert; it sets the standard for admissibility of such testimony.

Subdivision (a), which states when an expert may give his opinion upon a subject that is within the scope of his expertise, codifies the existing rule that expert opinion is limited to those subjects that are beyond the competence of persons of common experience, training, and education. People v. Cole, 47 Cal.2d 99, 103, 301 P.2d 854, 856 (1956). For examples of the variety of subjects upon which expert testimony is admitted, see Witkin, California Evidence §§ 190-195 (1958).

Subdivision (b) states a general rule in regard to the permissible bases upon which the opinion of an expert may be founded. The California courts have made it clear that the nature of the matter upon which an expert may base his opinion varies from case to case. In some fields of expert knowledge, an expert may rely on statements made by and information received from other persons; in some other fields of expert knowledge, an expert may not do so. For example, a physician may rely on statements made to him by the patient concerning the history of his condition. People v. Wilson, 25 Cal.2d 341, 153 P.2d 720 (1944). A physician may also rely on reports and opinions of other physicians. Kelley v. Bailey, 189 Cal.App.2d 728, 11 Cal.Rptr. 448 (1961); Hope v. Arrowhead & Puritas Waters, Inc., 174 Cal.App.2d 222, 344 P.2d 428 (1959). An expert on the valuation of real or personal property, too, may rely on inquiries made of others, commercial reports, market quotations, and relevant sales known to the witness. Betts v. Southern Cal. Fruit Exchange, 144 Cal. 402, 77 Pac. 993 (1904); Hammond Lumber Co. v. County of Los Angeles, 104 Cal.App. 235, 285 Pac. 896 (1930); Glantz v. Freedman, 100 Cal.App. 611, 280 Pac. 704 (1929). On the other hand, an expert on automobile accidents may not rely on extrajudicial statements of others as a partial basis for an opinion as to the point of impact, whether or not the statements would be admissible evidence. Hodges v. Severns, 201 Cal.App.2d 99, 20 Cal.Rptr. 129 (1962); Ribble v. Cook, 111 Cal.App.2d 903, 245 P.2d 593 (1952). See also Behr v. County of Santa Cruz, 172 Cal.App.2d 697, 342 P.2d 987 (1959) (report of fire ranger as to cause of fire held inadmissible because it was based primarily upon statements made to him by other persons).

Likewise, under existing law, irrelevant or speculative matters are not a proper basis for an expert's opinion. See Roscoe Moss Co. v. Jenkins, 55 Cal.App.2d 369, 130 P.2d 477 (1942) (expert may not base opinion upon a comparison if the matters compared are not reasonably comparable); People v. Luis, 158 Cal. 185, 110 Pac. 580 (1910) (physician may not base opinion as to person's feeblemindedness merely upon the person's exterior appearance); Long v. Cal.-Western States Life Ins. Co., 43 Cal.2d 871, 279 P.2d 43 (1955) (speculative or conjectural data); Eisenmayer v. Leonardt, 148 Cal. 596, 84 Pac. 43 (1906) (speculative or conjectural data). Compare People v. Wochnick, 98 Cal.App.2d 124, 219 P.2d 70 (1950) (expert may not give opinion as to the truth or falsity of certain statements on basis of lie detector test), with People v. Jones, 42 Cal.2d 219, 266 P.2d 38 (1954) (psychiatrist may consider an examination given under the influence of sodium pentothal—the so-called "truth serum"—in forming an opinion as to the mental state of the person examined).

The variation in the permissible bases of expert opinion is unavoidable in light of the wide variety of subjects upon which such opinion can be offered. In regard to some matters of expert opinion, an expert must, if he is going to give an opinion that will be helpful to the jury, rely on reports, statements, and other information that might not be admissible evidence. A physician in many instances cannot make a diagnosis without relying on the case history recited by the patient or on reports from various technicians or other physicians. Similarly, an appraiser must rely on reports of sales and other market data if he is to give an opinion that will be of value to the jury. In the usual case where a physician's or an appraiser's opinion is required, the adverse party also will have its expert who will be able to check the data relied upon by the adverse expert. On the other hand, a police officer can analyze skid marks, debris, and the condition of vehicles that have been involved in an accident without relying on the statements of bystanders; and it seems likely that the jury would be as able to evaluate the statements of others in the light of the physical facts, as interpreted by the officer, as would the officer himself. It is apparent that the extent to which an expert may base his opinion upon the statements of others is far from clear. It is at least clear, however, that it is permitted in a number of instances. See Young v. Bates Valve Bag Corp., 52 Cal.App.2d 86, 96-97, 125 P.2d 840, 846 (1942), and cases therein cited. Cf. People v. Alexander, 212 Cal.App.2d 84, 27 Cal.Rptr. 720 (1963).

It is not practical to formulate a detailed statutory rule that lists all of the matters upon which an expert may properly base his opinion, for it would be necessary to prescribe specific rules applicable to each field of expertise. This is clearly impossible; the subjects upon which expert opinion may be received are too numerous to make statutory prescription of applicable rules a feasible venture. It is possible, however, to formulate a general rule that specifies the minimum requisites that must be met in every case, leaving to the courts the task of determining particular detail within this general framework. This standard is expressed in subdivision (b) which states a general rule that is applicable whenever expert opinion is offered on a given subject.

Under subdivision (b), the matter upon which an expert's opinion is based must meet each of three separate but related tests. First, the matter must be perceived by or personally known to the witness or must be made known to him at or before the hearing at which the opinion is expressed. This requirement assures the expert's acquaintance with the facts of a particular case either by his personal perception or observation or by means of assuming facts not personally known to the witness. Second, and without regard to the means by which an expert familiarizes himself with the matter upon which his opinion is based, the matter relied upon by the expert in forming his opinion must be of a type that reasonably may be relied upon by experts in forming an opinion upon the subject to which his testimony relates. In large measure, this assures the reliability and trustworthiness of the information used by experts in forming their opinions. Third, an expert may not base his opinion upon any matter that is declared by the constitutional, statutory, or decisional law of this State to be an improper basis for an opinion. For example, the statements of bystanders as to the cause of a fire may be considered reliable for some purposes by an investigator of the fire, particularly when coupled with physical evidence found at the scene, but the courts have determined this to be an improper basis for an opinion since the trier of fact is as capable as the expert of evaluating such statements in light of the physical facts as interpreted by the expert. Behr v. County of Santa Cruz, 172 Cal.App.2d 697, 342 P.2d 987 (1959).

The rule stated in subdivision (b) thus permits an expert to base his opinion upon reliable matter, whether or not admissible, of a type that may reasonably be used in forming an opinion upon the subject to which his expert testimony relates. In addition, it provides assurance that the courts and the Legislature are free to continue to develop specific rules regarding the proper bases for particular kinds of expert opinion in specific fields. See, e.g., 3 Cal.Law Revision Comm'n, Rep., Rec. & Studies, Recommendation and Study Relating to Evidence in Eminent Domain Proceedings at A-1 (1961), Subdivision (b) thus provides a sensible standard of admissibility while, at the same time, it continues in effect the discretionary power of the courts to regulate abuses, thereby retaining in large measure the existing California law.

§ 802. Statement of basis of opinion. A witness testifying in the form of an opinion may state on direct examination the reasons for his opinion and the matter (including, in the case of an expert, his special knowledge, skill, experience, training, and education) upon which it is based, unless he is precluded by law from using such reasons or matter as a basis for his opinion. The court in its discretion may require that a witness before testifying in the form of an opinion be first examined concerning the matter upon which his opinion is based.

Law Revision Commission Comment

* * * Although Section 802 * * * provides that a witness may state the basis for his opinion on direct examination, it is clear that, in some cases, a witness is required to do so in order to show that his opinion is applicable to the action before the court. Under existing law, where a witness testifies in the form of opinion not based upon his personal observation, the assumed facts upon which his opinion is based must be stated in order to show that the witness has some basis for forming an intelligent opinion and to permit the trier of fact to determine the applicability of the opinion in light of the existence or nonexistence of such facts. Eisenmayer v. Leonardt, 148 Cal. 596, 84 Pac. 43 (1906); Lemley v. Doak Gas Engine Co., 40 Cal.App. 146, 180 Pac. 671 (1919) (hearing denied). Evidence Code Section 802 will not affect the rule set forth in these cases, for it is based essentially on the requirement that all evidence must be shown to be applicable—or relevant—to the action. Evidence Code §§ 350, 403. But under Section 802, as under existing law, a witness testifying from his personal observation of the facts upon which his opinion is based need not be examined concerning such facts before testifying in the form of opinion; his personal observation is a sufficient basis upon which to found his opinion. Lumbermen's Mut. Cas. Co. v. Industrial Acc. Comm'n, 29 Cal.2d 492, 175 P.2d 823 (1946); Hart v. Olson, 68 Cal.App.2d 657, 157 P.2d 385 (1945); Lemley v. Doak Gas Engine Co., supra. However, the court may require a witness to state the facts observed before stating his opinion. In this respect Section 802 codifies the existing rule concerning lay witnesses and, although the existing law is unclear, probably states the existing rule as to expert witnesses. See Tentative Recommendation and a Study Relating to the Uniform Rules of Evidence (Article VII. Expert and Other Opinion Testimony), 6 Cal.Law Revision Comm'n, Rep., Rec. & Studies 901, 934 (lay witness), 939 (expert witness) (1964).

§ 803. Opinion based on improper matter. The court may, and upon objection shall, exclude testimony in the form of an opinion that is based in whole or in significant part on matter that is not a proper basis for such an opinion. In such case, the witness may, if there remains a proper basis for his opinion, then state his opinion after excluding from consideration the matter determined to be improper.

Law Revision Commission Comment

Under Section 803, as under existing law, an opinion may be held inadmissible or may be stricken if it is based wholly or in substantial part upon improper considerations. Whether or not the opinion should be held inadmissible or stricken will depend in a particular case on the extent to which the improper considerations have influenced the opinion. "The question is addressed to the discretion of the trial court." People v. Lipari, 213 Cal.App.2d 485, 493, 28 Cal.Rptr. 808, 813-814 (1963). See discussion in City of Gilroy v. Filice, 221 Cal.App.2d 259, 271-272, 34 Cal.Rptr. 368, 375-376 (1963), and cases cited therein. If a witness' opinion is stricken because of reliance upon improper considerations, the second sentence of Section 803 assures the witness the opportunity to express his opinion after excluding from his consideration the matter determined to be improper.

§ 804. Opinion based on opinion or statement of another. (a) If a witness testifying as an expert testifies that his opinion is based in whole or in part upon the opinion or statement of another person, such other person may be called and examined by any adverse party as if under cross-examination concerning the opinion or statement.

(b) This section is not applicable if the person upon whose opinion or statement the expert witness has relied is (1) a party, (2) a person identified with a party within the meaning of subdivision (d) of Section 776, or (3) a witness who has testified in the action concerning the subject matter of the opinion or statement upon which the expert witness has relied.

(c) Nothing in this section makes admissible an expert opinion that is inadmissible because it is based in whole or in part on the opinion or statement of another person.

(d) An expert opinion otherwise admissible is not made inadmissible by this section because it is based on the opinion or statement of a person who is unavailable for examination pursuant to this section.

Statutory Note

See Penal Code § 1347.5 (person with a disability may not be compelled to testify at hearing on motion for accommodations to facilitate testimony by such person in certain criminal prosecutions).

Law Revision Commission Comment

Section 804 is designed to provide protection to a party who is confronted with an expert witness who relies on the opinion or statement of some other person. (See the Comment to Section 801 for examples of opinions that may be based on the statements and opinions of others.) In such a situation, a party may find that cross-examination of the witness will not reveal the weakness in his opinion, for the crucial parts are based on the observations or opinions of someone else. Under existing law, if that other person is called as a witness, he is the witness of the party calling him and, therefore, that party may not subject him to cross-examination.

The existing law operates unfairly, for it unnecessarily restricts meaningful cross-examination. Hence, Section 804 permits a party to extend his cross-examination into the underlying bases of the opinion testimony introduced against him by calling the authors of opinions and statements relied on by adverse witnesses and examining them as if under cross-examination concerning the subject matter of their opinions and statements. See the Comment to Evidence Code § 1203.

§ 805. Opinion on ultimate issue. Testimony in the form of an opinion that is otherwise admissible is not objectionable because it embraces the ultimate issue to be decided by the trier of fact.

Law Revision Commission Comment

Although several older cases indicated that an opinion could not be received on an ultimate issue, more recent cases have repudiated this rule. Hence, this section is declarative of existing law. People v. Wilson, 25 Cal.2d 341, 349-350, 153 P.2d 720, 725 (1944); Wells Truckways, Ltd. v. Cebrian, 122 Cal.App.2d 666, 265 P.2d 557 (1954); People v. King, 104 Cal.App.2d 298, 231 P.2d 156 (1951).

Article 2. Value, Damages, and Benefits in Eminent Domain and Inverse Condemnation Cases

§ 810. Application of article. (a) Except where another rule is provided by statute, this article [§§ 810-824] provides special rules of evidence applicable to any action in which the value of property is to be ascertained.

(b) This article [§§ 810-824] does not govern ad valorem property tax assessment or equalization proceedings. [*Added 1965. Amended 1978, 1980.*]

§ 811. Value of property. As used in this article [§§ 810-824], "value of property" means market value of any of the following:

(a) Real property or any interest therein.

(b) Real property or any interest therein and tangible personal property valued as a unit.

[*Amended 1975, 1978, 1980.*]

Law Revision Commission Comment - 1975 Amendment

* * * Section 811 makes clear that this article as applied to eminent domain proceedings governs only evidence relating to the determination of property value and damages and benefits to the remainder. This article does not govern evidence relating to the determination of loss of goodwill (Code Civ.Proc. § 1263.510).

The evidence admissible to prove loss of goodwill is governed by the general provisions of the Evidence Code. Hence, nothing in this article should be deemed a limitation on the admissibility of evidence to prove loss of goodwill if such evidence is otherwise admissible. [12 Cal.L.Rev.Comm. Reports 1601 (1975).]

Senate Committee Comment - 1978 Amendment

Section 811 is amended to make clear the limited application of this article. This article applies only where market value of real property, an interest in real property (e.g., a leasehold), or tangible personal property is to be determined, whether for computing damages and benefits or otherwise. This article does not apply to the valuation of intangible personal property that is not an interest in real property, such as goodwill of a business; valuation of such property is governed by the rules of evidence otherwise applicable. However, nothing in this article precludes a court from using the rules prescribed in this article in valuation proceedings to which the article is not made applicable, where the court determines that the rules prescribed are appropriate. See Comment to Section 810.

Senate Committee Comment - 1980 Amendment

Subdivision (b) of Section 811 is amended to include personal property only when valued together with real property. The effect of this amendment is to limit the scope of the evidence of market value provisions to actions involving real property or real and personal property combined. See Section 810 (article provides rules applicable to action in which "value of property" to be ascertained). Actions involving personal property alone are governed by general law, including the general rules of evidence prescribed in this code, although where appropriate the court may look to the special rules prescribed in this article.

§ 812. Market value; interpretation of meaning. This article [§§ 810-824] is not intended to alter or change the existing substantive law, whether statutory or decisional, interpreting the meaning of "market value," whether denominated "fair market value" or otherwise. [*Amended 1975, 1976, 1978.*]

§ 813. Value of property; authorized opinions; view of property; admissible evidence. (a) The value of property may be shown only by the opinions of any of the following:

(1) Witnesses qualified to express such opinions.

(2) The owner or the spouse of the owner of the property or property interest being valued.

(3) An officer, regular employee, or partner designated by a corporation, partnership, or unincorporated association that is the owner of the property or property interest being valued, if the designee is knowledgeable as to the value of the property or property interest.

(b) Nothing in this section prohibits a view of the property being valued or the admission of any other admissible evidence (including but not limited to evidence as to the nature and condition of the property and, in an eminent domain proceeding, the character of the improvement proposed to be constructed by the plaintiff) for the limited purpose of enabling the court, jury, or referee to understand and weigh the testimony given under subdivision (a); and such evidence, except evidence of the character of the improvement proposed to be constructed by the plaintiff in an eminent domain proceeding, is subject to impeachment and rebuttal.

(c) For the purposes of subdivision (a), "owner of the property or property interest being valued" includes, but is not limited to, the following persons:

(1) A person entitled to possession of the property.

(2) Either party in an action or proceeding to determine the ownership of the property between the parties if the court determines that it would not be in the interest of efficient administration of justice to determine the issue of ownership prior to the admission of the opinion of the party. [*Amended 1978, 1980.*]

Law Revision Commission Comment - 1978 Amendment

Paragraph (3) is added to Section 813(a) to make clear that, where a corporation, partnership, or unincorporated association owns property being valued, a designated officer, regular employee, or partner who is knowledgeable as to the value of the property may testify to an opinion of its value as an owner, notwithstanding any contrary implications in City of Pleasant Hill v. First Baptist Church, 1 Cal.App.3d 384, 82 Cal.Rptr. 1 (1969). The designee may be knowledgeable as to the value of the property as a result of being instrumental in its acquisition or management or as a result of being knowledgeable as to its character and use; the designee need not qualify as a general valuation expert. Compare Section 720 (qualification as an expert witness). Nothing in Section 813 affects the authority of the court to limit the number of expert witnesses to be called by any party (see Section 723) or to limit cumulative evidence (see Section 352).

The phrase "value of property," as used in this section, is defined in Section 811. [14 Cal.L.Rev.Comm. Reports 105 (1978).]

Senate Committee Comment - 1980 Amendment

Paragraph (2) of Section 813(a) is amended by make clear that either spouse may testify as to the value of community property since both spouses are the owners. In addition, paragraph (2) authorizes either spouse to testify as to the value of the separate property of the other spouse as well as to his or her own separate property. This authority may be useful in cases under the Family Law Act where the character of the property is in dispute as well as in other cases requiring valuation where the nonowning spouse may be a more competent valuation witness than the owning spouse.

Subdivision (c) of Section 813 is amended to make clear that a person claiming to be an owner may testify as an owner in litigation over title. Such litigation may arise, for example, between a buyer and seller concerning title to and value of real property under a contract of sale, or between a landlord and tenant concerning characterization and value of property as trade fixtures.

§ 814. Matter upon which opinion must be based. The opinion of a witness as to the value of property is limited to such an opinion as is based on matter perceived by or personally known to the witness or made known to the witness at or before the hearing, whether or not admissible, that is of a type that reasonably may be relied upon by an expert in forming an opinion as to the value of property, including but not limited to the matters listed in Sections 815 to 821, inclusive, unless a witness is precluded by law from using such matter as a basis for an opinion. [*Amended 1975, 1976, 1980.*]

Senate Committee Comment - 1975 Amendment

Section 814 is amended to delete the listing of particular matters constituting fair market value that an expert may rely on in forming an opinion as to the value of property. This listing is unnecessary. See Code Civ.Proc. § 1263.320 (fair market value).
It should be noted that the definition of fair market value contained in Section 1263.320(a) omits the phrase "in the open market" since there may be no open market for some types of special purpose properties such as schools, churches, cemeteries, parks, utilities, and similar properties. The fair market value of these properties is covered by Section 1263.320(b). Within the limits of this article, fair market value may be determined by reference to matters of a type that reasonably may be relied upon by an expert in forming an opinion as to the value of property including, but not limited to, (1) the market data (or comparable sales approach) (2) the income (or capitalization) method, and (3) the cost analysis (or production less depreciation) formula. See the Comment to Section 1263.320.

Senate Committee Comment - 1980 Amendment

Section 814 is amended to make technical changes. While the value of property may be determined by reference to matters listed in Sections 815 to 821 where appropriate, an opinion as to value may also be based on any other matter that satisfies the general requirements of Section 814. See, e.g., City of Los Angeles v. Retlaw Enterprises, Inc., 16 Cal.3d 473, 486 n. 8, 546 P.2d 1380, 1388 n. 8, 128 Cal.Rptr. 436, 444 n. 8 (1976) (price trend data admissible); People ex rel. Dep't of Transp. v. Southern Pac. Transp. Co., 84 Cal.App.3d 315, 325, 148 Cal.Rptr. 535, 541 (1978) (replacement cost of land as opposed to improvements admissible); South Bay Irr. Dist. v. California-American Water Co., 61 Cal.App.3d 944, 980, 133 Cal.Rptr. 166, 191 (1976), (capitalization based on nonrental income admissible); Redevelopment Agency v. Del-Camp Inv., Inc., 38 Cal.App.3d 836, 842, 113 Cal.Rptr. 762, 766-67 (1974) (capitalization based on gross rentals admissible); People ex rel. Dep't of Pub. Works v. Home Trust Inv. Co., 8 Cal.App.3d 1022, 1026, 87 Cal.Rptr. 722, 724 (1970) (noncomparable sales admissible in appropriate circumstances).

§ 815. Sales of subject property. When relevant to the determination of the value of property, a witness may take into account as a basis for an opinion the price and other terms and circumstances of any sale or contract to sell and purchase which included the property or property interest being valued or any part thereof if the sale or contract was freely made in good faith within a reasonable time before or after the date of valuation, except that in an eminent domain proceeding where the sale or contract to sell and purchase includes only the property or property interest being taken or a part thereof, such sale or contract to sell and purchase may not be taken into account if it occurs after the filing of the lis pendens. [*Amended 1978.*]

§ 816. Comparable sales. When relevant to the determination of the value of property, a witness may take into account as a basis for his opinion the price and other terms and circumstances of any sale or contract to sell and purchase comparable property if the sale or contract was freely made in good faith within a reasonable time before or after the date of valuation. In order to be considered comparable, the sale or contract must have been made sufficiently near in time to the date of valuation, and the property sold must be located sufficiently near the property being valued, and must be sufficiently alike in respect to character, size, situation, usability, and improvements, to make it clear that the property sold and the property being valued are comparable in value and that the price realized for the property sold may fairly be considered as shedding light on the value of the property being valued.

§ 817. Leases of subject property. (a) Subject to subdivision (b), when relevant to the determination of the value of property, a witness may take into account as a basis for an opinion the rent reserved and other terms and circumstances of any lease which included the property or property interest being valued or any part thereof which was in effect within a reasonable time before or after the date of valuation, except that in an eminent domain proceeding where the lease includes only the property or property interest being taken or a part thereof, such lease may not be taken into account in the determination of the value of property if it is entered into after the filing of the lis pendens.

(b) A witness may take into account a lease providing for a rental fixed by a percentage or other measurable portion of gross sales or gross income from a business conducted on the leased property only for the purpose of arriving at an opinion as to the reasonable net rental value attributable to the property or property interest being valued as provided in Section 819 or determining the value of a leasehold interest. [*Amended 1978.*]

Law Revision Commission Comment - 1978 Amendment

Subdivision (a) of Section 817 is amended to add the limitation that a lease of the subject property is not a proper basis for an opinion of value of the property after the filing of the lis pendens in an eminent domain proceeding. This is comparable to a provision of Section 815 (sale of subject property). Nothing in subdivision (a) should be construed to limit the use of leases created after filing of the lis pendens to show damages to the property, such as those authorized by Klopping v. City of Whittier, 8 Cal.3d 39, 500 P.2d 1345, 104 Cal.Rptr. 1 (1972).

Subdivision (b) limits the extent to which a witness may take into account a lease based on gross sales or gross income of a business conducted on the property. This limitation applies only to valuation of the real property or an interest therein, or of tangible personal property, and does not apply to the determination of loss of goodwill. See Section 811 and Comment thereto; Code Civ.Proc. § 1263.510 and Comment thereto.

The phrase "value of property," as used in this section, is defined in Section 811. [14 Cal.L.Rev.Comm. Reports 105 (1978).]

§ 818. Comparable leases. For the purpose of determining the capitalized value of the reasonable net rental value attributable to the property or property interest being valued as provided in Section 819 or determining the value of a leasehold interest, a witness may take into account as a basis for his opinion the rent reserved and other terms and circumstances of any lease of comparable property if the lease was freely made in good faith within a reasonable time before or after the date of valuation.

§819. Capitalization of income. When relevant to the determination of the value of property, a witness may take into account as a basis for his opinion the capitalized value of the reasonable net rental value attributable to the land and existing improvements thereon (as distinguished from the capitalized value of the income or profits attributable to the business conducted thereon).

§ 820. Reproduction cost. When relevant to the determination of the value of property, a witness may take into account as a basis for his opinion the value of the property or property interest being valued as indicated by the value of the land together with the cost of replacing or reproducing the existing improvements thereon, if the improvements enhance the value of the property or property interest for its highest and best use, less whatever depreciation or obsolescence the improvements have suffered.

§ 821. Conditions in general vicinity of subject property. When relevant to the determination of the value of property, a witness may take into account as a basis for his opinion the nature of the improvements on properties in the general vicinity of the property or property interest being valued and the character of the existing uses being made of such properties.

§ 822. Matter upon which opinion may not be based. (a) In an eminent domain or inverse condemnation proceeding, notwithstanding the provisions of Sections 814 to 821, inclusive, the following matter is inadmissible as evidence and shall not be taken into account as a basis for an opinion as to the value of property:

(1) The price or other terms and circumstances of an acquisition of property or a property interest if the acquisition was for a public use for which the property could have been taken by eminent domain.

The price or other terms and circumstances shall not be excluded pursuant to this paragraph if the proceeding relates to the valuation of all or part of a water system as defined in Section 240 of the Public Utilities Code.

(2) The price at which an offer or option to purchase or lease the property or property interest being valued or any other property was made, or the price at which the property or interest was optioned, offered, or listed for sale or lease, except that an option, offer, or listing may be introduced by a party as an admission of another party to the proceeding; but nothing in this subdivision permits an admission to be used as direct evidence upon any matter that may be shown only by opinion evidence under Section 813.

(3) The value of any property or property interest as assessed for taxation purposes or the amount of taxes which may be due on the property, but nothing in this subdivision prohibits the consideration of actual or estimated taxes for the purpose of determining the reasonable net rental value attributable to the property or property interest being valued.

(4) An opinion as to the value of any property or property interest other than that being valued.

(5) The influence upon the value of the property or property interest being valued of any noncompensable items of value, damage, or injury.

(6) The capitalized value of the income or rental from any property or property interest other than that being valued.

(b) In an action other than an eminent domain or inverse condemnation proceeding, the matters listed in subdivision (a) are not admissible as evidence, and may not be taken into account as a basis for an opinion as to the value of property, except to the extent permitted under the rules of law otherwise applicable. [*Amended 1978, 1980, 1986, 1987, 2000.*]

Law Revision Commission Comment - 1978 Amendment

Subdivision (c) of Section 822 is amended to incorporate a provision formerly found in Revenue and Taxation Code Section 4986(b). Unlike the former provision, subdivision (c) does not provide for a mistrial for mention of the amount of taxes which may be due. Whether such mention is grounds for a mistrial is governed by the general principles of court discretion to declare a mistrial when evidence has been presented which is inadmissible, highly prejudicial, and cannot be corrected by an admonition to the jury.

Subdivision (d) does not prohibit a witness from testifying to adjustments made in sales of comparable property used as a basis for an opinion. Merced Irrigation Dist. v. Woolstenhulme, 4 Cal.3d 478, 501-03, 483 P.2d 1, 16-17, 93 Cal.Rptr. 833, 848-49 (1971).

Section 822 does not prohibit cross-examination of a witness on any matter precluded from admission as evidence if such cross-examination is for the limited purpose of determining whether a witness based an opinion in whole or in part on matter that is not a proper basis for an opinion; such cross-examination may not, however, serve as a means of placing improper matters before the trier of fact. See Evid. Code §§ 721, 802, 803.

The phrase "value of property," as used in this section, is defined in Section 811. [14 Cal.L.Rev.Comm. Reports 105 (1978).]

Senate Committee Comment - 1980 Amendment

Section 822 is amended to limit the application of subdivision (a) to eminent domain and inverse condemnation cases despite the general expansion of this article to cover real property valuation cases generally. See Sections 810 and 811 and Comments thereto. The introductory portion of subdivision (a) is also amended to make clear that subdivision (a) regulates only the bases for an opinion of value admissible in evidence; it does not purport to prescribe rules or regulations governing the practice of the appraisal profession outside of expert testimony in a case.

Subdivision (b) is added to make clear that the exclusion of the matters listed in subdivision (a) in eminent domain and inverse condemnation cases does not imply that those matters are admissible in other cases. The rules governing admissibility in other cases of matters listed in subdivision (a) are found in Section 814 and in the general Evidence Code rules relating to relevance, prejudice, and the like.

Law Revision Commission Comment - 2000 Amendment

Subdivision (a)(1) of Section 822 is amended to delete the special exception relating to property appropriated to public use, in reliance on general evidentiary principles. See, e.g., Section 823 ("Notwithstanding any other provision of this article, the value of property for which there is no relevant, comparable market may be determined by any method of valuation that is just and equitable."); see also Code Civ. Proc. § 1263.320(b) (fair market value). Thus, evidence of an acquisition that is otherwise inadmissible under subdivision (a)(1) may, in an appropriate case, be admissible under Section 823 if a private market is lacking, e.g., the acquisition involves a special purpose property such as a school, church, cemetery, park, utility corridor, or similar property.

The new exception added to subdivision (a)(1) is intended to apply in an eminent domain or inverse condemnation proceeding that relates to a public agency's acquisition or taking of all or any part of a water system owned by a water company.

Subdivision (c) is deleted as obsolete.

§ 823. Property with no relevant, comparable market. Notwithstanding any other provision of this article [§§ 810-824], the value of property for which there is no relevant, comparable market may be determined by any method of valuation that is just and equitable. [*Added 1980. Amended 1992.*]

Senate Committee Comment - 1980 Addition

Section 823 is drawn from Code of Civil Procedure Section 1263.320(b) (fair market value in eminent domain proceeding of property for which there is no relevant market). Section 823 is included because there may be no relevant market for some types of special purpose properties such as schools, churches, cemeteries, parks, utilities, and similar properties. See Code Civ.Proc. § 1263.320(b) and Comment thereto.

§ 824. Nonprofit, special use property. (a) Notwithstanding any other provision of this article [§§ 810-824], a just and equitable method of determining the value of nonprofit, special use property, as defined by Section 1235.155 of the Code of Civil Procedure, for which there is no relevant, comparable market, is the cost of purchasing land and the reasonable cost of making it suitable for the conduct of the same nonprofit, special use, together with the cost of constructing similar improvements. The method for determining compensation for improvements shall be as set forth in subdivision (b).

(b) Notwithstanding any other provision of this article [§§ 810-824], a witness providing opinion testimony on the value of nonprofit, special use property, as defined by Section 1235.155 of the Code of Civil Procedure, for which there is no relevant, comparable market, shall base his or her opinion on the value of reproducing the improvements without taking into consideration any depreciation or obsolescence of the improvements.

(c) This section does not apply to actions or proceedings commenced by a public entity or public utility to acquire real property or any interest in real property for the use of water, sewer, electricity, telephone, natural gas, or flood control facilities or rights-of-way where those acquisitions neither require removal or destruction of existing improvements, nor render the property unfit for the owner's present or proposed use. [*Added 1992.*]

Article 3. Opinion Testimony on Particular Subjects

§ 870. Opinion as to sanity. A witness may state his opinion as to the sanity of a person when:

(a) The witness is an intimate acquaintance of the person whose sanity is in question;

(b) The witness was a subscribing witness to a writing, the validity of which is in dispute, signed by the person whose sanity is in question and the opinion relates to the sanity of such person at the time the writing was signed; or

(c) The witness is qualified under Section 800 or 801 to testify in the form of an opinion.

Law Revision Commission Comment

Subdivisions (a) and (b) restate the substance of and supersede subdivision 10 of Section 1870 of the Code of Civil Procedure. Subdivision (c) merely makes it clear that a witness who meets the requirements of Section 800 or Section 801 is qualified to testify in the form of an opinion as to the sanity of a person. Section 870 does not disturb the present rule that permits a witness to testify to a person's rational or irrational appearance or conduct, even though the witness is not qualified under Section 870 to express an opinion on the person's sanity. See Pfingst v. Goetting, 96 Cal.App.2d 293, 215 P.2d 93 (1950).

[Former Chapter 2. Blood Tests to Determine Paternity]

[*Repealed 1992.* See Family Code §§ 7550-7557.]

DIVISION 8. PRIVILEGES

Chapter 1. Definitions

§ 900. Application of definitions. Unless the provision or context otherwise requires, the definitions in this chapter [§§ 900-905] govern the construction of this division [§§ 900-1070]. They do not govern the construction of any other division.

Law Revision Commission Comment

Section 900 makes it clear that the definitions in Sections 901 through 905 apply only to Division 8 (Privileges) and that these definitions are not applicable where the context or language of a particular section in Division 8 requires that a word or phrase used in that section be given a different meaning. The definitions contained in Division 2 (commencing with Section 100) apply to the entire code, including Division 8. Definitions applicable only to a particular article are found in that article.

§ 901. Proceeding. "Proceeding" means any action, hearing, investigation, inquest, or inquiry (whether conducted by a court, administrative agency, hearing officer, arbitrator, legislative body, or any other person authorized by law) in which, pursuant to law, testimony can be compelled to be given.

Law Revision Commission Comment

"Proceeding" is defined to mean all proceedings of whatever kind in which testimony can be compelled by law be to given. It includes civil and criminal actions and proceedings, administrative proceedings, legislative hearings, grand jury proceedings, coroners' inquests, arbitration proceedings, and any other kind of proceeding in which a person can be compelled by law to appear and give evidence. This broad definition is necessary in order that Division 8 may be made applicable to all situations where a person can be compelled to testify. The reasons for giving this broad scope to Division 8 are stated in the Comment to Section 910.

§ 902. Civil proceeding. "Civil proceeding" means any proceeding except a criminal proceeding.

Law Revision Commission Comment

"Civil proceeding" includes not only a civil action or proceeding, but also any nonjudicial proceeding in which, pursuant to law, testimony can be compelled to be given. See Evidence Code §§ 901 and 903.

§ 903. Criminal proceeding. "Criminal proceeding" means:

(a) A criminal action; and

(b) A proceeding pursuant to Article 3 (commencing with Section 3060) of Chapter 7 of Division 4 of Title 1 of the Government Code to determine whether a public officer should be removed from office for willful or corrupt misconduct in office.

Law Revision Commission Comment

This division treats a proceeding by accusation for the removal of a public officer under Government Code Sections 3060-3073 the same as a criminal action. Proceedings by accusation and criminal actions are so nearly alike in their basic nature that, so far as privileges are concerned, this similar treatment is justified.

§ 905. Presiding officer. "Presiding officer" means the person authorized to rule on a claim of privilege in the proceeding in which the claim is made.

Law Revision Commission Comment

"Presiding officer" is defined so that reference may be made in Division 8 to the person who makes rulings on questions of privilege in nonjudicial proceedings. The term includes arbitrators, hearing officers, referees, and any other person who is authorized to make rulings on claims of privilege. It, of course, includes the judge or other person presiding in a judicial proceeding.

Chapter 2. Applicability of Division

§ 910. Applicability of division. Except as otherwise provided by statute, the provisions of this division [§§ 900-1070] apply in all proceedings. The provisions of any statute making rules of evidence inapplicable in particular proceedings, or limiting the applicability of rules of evidence in particular proceedings, do not make this division inapplicable to such proceedings.

Law Revision Commission Comment

Most rules of evidence are designed for use in courts. Generally, their purpose is to keep unreliable or prejudicial evidence from being presented to the trier of fact. Privileges are granted, however, for reasons of policy unrelated to the reliability of the information involved. A privilege is granted because it is considered more important to keep certain information confidential than it is to require disclosure of all the information relevant to the issues in a pending proceeding. Thus, for example, to protect the attorney-client relationship, it is necessary to prevent disclosure of confidential communications made in the course of that relationship.

If confidentiality is to be protected effectively by a privilege, the privilege must be recognized in proceedings other than judicial proceedings. The protection afforded by a privilege would be insufficient if a court were the only place where the privilege could be invoked. Every officer with power to issue subpoenas for investigative purposes, every administrative agency, every local governing board, and many more persons could pry into the protected information if the privilege rules were applicable only in judicial proceedings.

Therefore, the policy underlying the privilege rules requires their recognition in all proceedings of any nature in which testimony can be compelled by law to be given. Section 910 makes the privilege rules applicable to all such proceedings. In this respect, it follows the precedent set in New Jersey when privilege rules, based in part on the Uniform Rules of Evidence, were enacted. See N.J.Laws 1960, Ch. 52, p. 452 (N.J.Rev.Stat. §§ 2A:84A-1 to 2A:84A-49).

Statutes that relax the rules of evidence in particular proceedings do not have the effect of making privileges inapplicable in such proceedings. For example, Labor Code Section 5708, which provides that the officer conducting an Industrial Accident Commission proceeding "shall not be bound by the common law or statutory rules of evidence," does not make privileges inapplicable in such proceedings. Thus, the lawyer-client privilege must be recognized in an Industrial Accident Commission proceeding. On the other hand, Division 8 and other statutes provide exceptions to particular privileges for particular types of proceedings. e.g., Evidence Code § 998 (physician-patient privilege inapplicable in criminal proceeding); Labor Code §§ 4055, 6407, 6408 (testimony by physician and certain reports of physicians admissible as evidence in Industrial Accident Commission proceedings). * * *

Chapter 3. General Provisions Relating to Privileges

§ 911. General rule as to privileges. Except as otherwise provided by statute:

(a) No person has a privilege to refuse to be a witness.

(b) No person has a privilege to refuse to disclose any matter or to refuse to produce any writing, object, or other thing.

(c) No person has a privilege that another shall not be a witness or shall not disclose any matter or shall not produce any writing, object, or other thing.

Case Note

By enacting the Evidence Code, the legislature supplanted any privileges previously available at common law, and courts are no longer free to modify existing privileges or to create new privileges. Pitchess v Superior Court, 11 Cal. 3d 531, 539-540, 113 Cal. Rptr. 897, 903, 522 P.2d 305, 311 (1974); see People v. Gionis, 9 Cal. 4th 1196, 1206, 40 Cal. Rptr. 2d 456, 461, 892 P.2d 1199, 1204 (1995) (dictum).

Law Revision Commission Comment

This section codifies the existing law that privileges are not recognized in the absence of statute. See Chronicle Pub. Co. v. Superior Court, 54 Cal.2d 548, 565, 7 Cal.Rptr. 109, 117, 354 P.2d 637, 645 (1960); Tatkin v. Superior Court, 160 Cal.App.2d 745, 753, 326 P.2d 201, 205-206 (1958); Whitlow v. Superior Court, 87 Cal.App.2d 175, 196 P.2d 590 (1948). See also 8 Wigmore, Evidence § 2286 (McNaughton rev. 1961); Witkin, California Evidence § 396 at 446 (1958). This is one of the few instances where the Evidence Code precludes the courts from elaborating upon the statutory scheme. Even with respect to privileges, however, the courts to a limited extent are permitted to develop the details of declared principles. See, e.g., Section 1060 (trade secret).

§912. Waiver of privilege. (a) Except as otherwise provided in this section, the right of any person to claim a privilege provided by Section 954 (lawyer-client privilege), 966 (lawyer referral service-client privilege), 980 (privilege for confidential marital communications), 994 (physician-patient privilege), 1014 (psychotherapist-patient privilege), 1033 (privilege of penitent), 1034 (privilege of clergy member), 1035.8 (sexual assault counselor-victim privilege), 1037.5 (domestic violence counselor-victim privilege), or 1038 (human trafficking caseworker-victim privilege), is waived with respect to a communication protected by the privilege if any holder of the privilege, without coercion, has disclosed a significant part of the communication or has consented to disclosure made by anyone. Consent to disclosure is manifested by any statement or other conduct of the holder of the privilege indicating consent to the disclosure, including failure to claim the privilege in any proceeding in which the holder has the legal standing and opportunity to claim the privilege.
(b) Where two or more persons are joint holders of a privilege provided by Section 954 (lawyer-client privilege), 966 (lawyer referral service-client privilege), 994 (physician-patient privilege), 1014 (psychotherapist-patient privilege), 1035.8 (sexual assault counselor-victim privilege), 1037.5 (domestic violence counselor- victim privilege), or 1038 (human trafficking caseworker-victim privilege), a waiver of the right of a particular joint holder of the privilege to claim the privilege does not affect the right of another joint holder to claim the privilege. In the case of the privilege provided by Section 980 (privilege for confidential

marital communications), a waiver of the right of one spouse to claim the privilege does not affect the right of the other spouse to claim the privilege.
(c) A disclosure that is itself privileged is not a waiver of any privilege.
(d) A disclosure in confidence of a communication that is protected by a privilege provided by Section 954 (lawyer-client privilege), 966 (lawyer referral service-client privilege), 994 (physician-patient privilege), 1014 (psychotherapist-patient privilege), 1035.8 (sexual assault counselor-victim privilege), 1037.5 (domestic violence counselor-victim privilege), or 1038 (human trafficking caseworker-victim privilege), when disclosure is reasonably necessary for the accomplishment of the purpose for which the lawyer, lawyer referral service, physician, psychotherapist, sexual assault counselor, or domestic violence counselor was consulted, is not a waiver of the privilege. [*Amended 1980, 2002, 2004, 2013, 2014.*]

Case Note

Disclosure of facts of consultation with attorney and of reliance on attorney's conclusion did not constitute either a common-law or statutory waiver of the attorney-client privilege. Southern Cal. Gas Co. v. Public Util. Comm'n, 50 Cal. 3d 31, 265 Cal. Rptr. 801, 784 P.2d 1373 (1990).

Senate Committee on Judiciary Comment

This section covers in some detail the matter of waiver of those privileges that protect confidential communications.

Subdivision (a). Subdivision (a) states the general rule with respect to the manner in which a privilege is waived. Failure to claim the privilege where the holder of the privilege has the legal standing and the opportunity to claim the privilege constitutes a waiver. * * *

Subdivision (b). A waiver of the privilege by a joint holder of the privilege does not operate to waive the privilege for any of the other joint holders of the privilege. * * *

Subdivision (c). A privilege is not waived when a revelation of the privileged matter takes place in another privileged communication. Thus, for example, a person does not waive his lawyer-client privilege by telling his wife in confidence what it was that he told his attorney. Nor does a person waive the marital communication privilege by telling his attorney in confidence in the course of the attorney-client relationship what it was that he told his wife. And a person does not waive the lawyer-client privilege as to a communication by relating it to another attorney in the course of a separate relationship. A privileged communication should not cease to be privileged merely because it has been related in the course of another privileged communication. The theory underlying the concept of waiver is that the holder of the privilege has abandoned the secrecy to which he is entitled under the privilege. Where the revelation of the privileged matter takes place in another privileged communication, there has not been such an abandonment. Of course, this rule does not apply unless the revelation was within the scope of the relationship in which it was made; a client consulting his lawyer on a contract matter who blurts out that he told his doctor that he had a venereal disease has waived the privilege, even though he intended the revelation to be confidential, because the revelation was not necessary to the contract business at hand.

Subdivision (d). Subdivision (d) is designed to maintain the confidentiality of communications in certain situations where the communications are disclosed to others in the course of accomplishing the purpose for which the lawyer, physician, or psychotherapist was consulted. For example, where a confidential communication from a client is related by his attorney to a physician, appraiser, or other expert in order to obtain that person's assistance so that the attorney will better be able to advise his client, the disclosure is not a waiver of the privilege, even though the disclosure is made with the client's knowledge and consent. Nor would a physician's or psychotherapist's keeping of confidential records necessary to diagnose or treat a patient, such as confidential hospital records, be a waiver of the privilege, even though other authorized persons have access to the records. Similarly, the patient's presentation of a physician's prescription to a registered pharmacist would not constitute a waiver of the physician-patient privilege because such disclosure is reasonably necessary for the accomplishment of the purpose for which the physician is consulted. See also Evidence Code § 992. Communications such as these, when made in confidence, should not operate to destroy the privilege even when they are made with the consent of the client or patient. Here, again, the privilege holder has not evidenced any abandonment of secrecy. Hence, he should be entitled to maintain the confidential nature of his communications to his attorney or physician despite the necessary further disclosure.

Subdivision (d) may change California law. Green v. Superior Court, 220 Cal.App.2d 121, 33 Cal.Rptr. 604 (1963) (hearing denied), held that the physician-patient privilege did not provide protection against disclosure by a pharmacist of information concerning the nature of drugs dispensed upon prescription. See also Himmelfarb v. United States, 175 F.2d 924 (9th Cir.1949) (applying the California law of privileges and holding that a lawyer's revelation to an accountant of a client's communication to the lawyer waived the client's privilege if such revelation was authorized by the client).

Law Revision Comment - 2002 Amendment

Section 912 is amended to make clear that it applies to the privilege for confidential communications between a domestic violence victim and counselor, which did not exist when the statute was originally enacted in 1965. See Sections 1037-1037.7 (domestic violence victim).

§ 913. Comment on, and inferences from, exercise of privilege. (a) If in the instant proceeding or on a prior occasion a privilege is or was exercised not to testify with respect to any matter, or to refuse to disclose or to prevent another from disclosing any matter, neither the presiding officer nor counsel may comment thereon, no presumption shall arise because of the exercise of the privilege, and the trier of fact may not draw any inference therefrom as to the credibility of the witness or as to any matter at issue in the proceeding.

(b) The court, at the request of a party who may be adversely affected because an unfavorable inference may be drawn by the jury because a privilege has been exercised, shall instruct the jury that no presumption arises because of the exercise of the privilege and that the jury may not draw any inference therefrom as to the credibility of the witness or as to any matter at issue in the proceeding.

Case Note

To support defense theory that X committed the crime with which the defendant was charged, the defense called X to testify, but X refused on grounds of self-incrimination. Held, this section precludes X from being required to invoke the privilege in the presence of the jury and, as so applied, does not deprive the defendant of a fair trial. An inference of guilt from invocation of the privilege is entirely speculative. People v. Mincey, 2 Cal. 4th 408, 440-442, 6 Cal. Rptr. 2d 822, 841-843, 827 P.2d 388, 407-409 (1992).

This section applies equally in civil and criminal cases. People v. Holloway, 33 Cal. 4th 96, 14 Cal. Rptr. 212, 91 P3d 64 (2004).

Assembly Committee on Judiciary Comment

Section 913 prohibits any comment on the exercise of a privilege and provides that the trier of fact may not draw any inference therefrom. Except as noted below, this probably states existing law. See People v. Wilkes, 44 Cal.2d 679, 284 P.2d 481 (1955). In addition, the court is required, upon request of a party who may be adversely affected, to instruct the jury that no presumption arises and that no inference is to be drawn from the exercise of a privilege. If comment could be made on the exercise of a privilege and adverse inferences drawn therefrom, a litigant would be under great pressure to forgo his claim of privilege and the protection sought to be afforded by the privilege would be largely negated. Moreover, the inferences which might be drawn would, in many instances, be quite unwarranted.

It should be noted that Section 913 deals only with comment upon, and the drawing of adverse inferences from, the exercise of a privilege. Section 913 does not purport to deal with the inferences that may be drawn from, or the comment that may be made upon, the evidence in the case.

Section 13 of Article I of the California Constitution provides that, in a criminal case, the failure of the defendant to explain or to deny by his testimony the evidence in the case against him may be commented upon. The courts, in reliance on this provision, have held that the failure of a party in either a civil or criminal case to explain or to deny the evidence against him may be considered in determining what inferences should be drawn from that evidence. People v. Adamson, 27 Cal.2d 478, 165 P.2d 3 (1946); Fross v. Wotton, 3 Cal.2d 384, 44 P.2d 350 (1935). However, the cases have emphasized that this right of comment and consideration does not extend in criminal cases to the drawing of inferences from the claim of privilege itself. Inferences may be drawn only from the evidence in the case and the defendant's failure to explain or deny such evidence. People v. Ashley, 42 Cal.2d 246, 267 P.2d 271 (1954); People v. Adamson, supra, 27 Cal.2d 478, 165 P.2d 3 (1946). Section 413 of the Evidence Code expresses the principle underlying this constitutional provision; nothing in Section 913 affects the application of Section 413 in either criminal or civil cases. See the Comment to Evidence Code § 413. Thus, for example, it is perfectly proper under the Evidence Code for counsel to point out that the evidence against the other party is uncontradicted.

Section 913 may modify existing California law as it applies in civil cases. In Nelson v. Southern Pacific Co., 8 Cal.2d 648, 67 P.2d 682 (1937), the Supreme Court held that evidence of a person's exercise of the privilege against self-incrimination in a prior proceeding may be shown for impeachment purposes if he testifies in a self-exculpatory manner in a subsequent proceeding. The Supreme Court within recent years has overruled statements in certain criminal cases declaring a similar rule. People v. Snyder, 50 Cal.2d 190, 197, 324 P.2d 1, 6 (1958) (overruling or disapproving several cases there cited). See also People v. Sharer, 61 Cal.2d 869, 40 Cal.Rptr. 851, 395 P.2d 899 (1964). Section 913 will, in effect, overrule the holding in the Nelson case, for it declares that no inference may be drawn from an exercise of a privilege either on the issue of credibility or on any other issue, whether the privilege was exercised in the instant proceeding or on a prior occasion. The status of the rule in the Nelson case has been in doubt because of the recent holdings in criminal cases; Section 913 eliminates any remaining basis for applying a different rule in civil cases.

There is some language in Fross v. Wotton, 3 Cal.2d 384, 44 P.2d 350 (1935), that indicates that unfavorable inferences may be drawn in a civil case from a party's claim of the privilege against self-incrimination during the case itself. Such language was unnecessary to that decision; but, if it does indicate California law, that law is changed by Evidence Code Sections 413 and 913. Under these sections, it is clear that, in civil cases as well as criminal cases, inferences may be drawn only from the evidence in the case, not from the claim of privilege.

§ 914. Determination of claim of privilege; limitation on punishment for contempt. (a) The presiding officer shall determine a claim of privilege in any proceeding in the same manner as a court determines such a claim under Article 2 (commencing with Section 400) of Chapter 4 of Division 3.

(b) No person may be held in contempt for failure to disclose information claimed to be privileged unless he has failed to comply with an order of a court that he disclose such information. This subdivision does not apply to any governmental agency that has constitutional contempt power, nor does it apply to hearings and investigations of the Industrial Accident Commission, nor does it impliedly repeal Chapter 4 (commencing with Section 9400) of Part 1 of Division 2 of Title 2 of the Government Code. If no other statutory procedure is applicable, the procedure prescribed by Section 1991 of the Code of Civil Procedure shall be followed in seeking an order of a court that the person disclose the information claimed to be privileged.

Assembly Committee on Judiciary Comment

Subdivision (a) makes the general provisions concerning preliminary determinations on admissibility of evidence (Sections 400-406) applicable when a presiding officer who is not a judge is called upon to determine whether or not a privilege exists. Subdivision (a) is necessary because Sections 400-406, by their terms, apply only to determinations by a court.

Subdivision (b) is needed to protect persons claiming privileges in nonjudicial proceedings. Because such proceedings are often conducted by persons untrained in law, it is desirable to have a judicial determination of whether a person is required to disclose information claimed to be privileged before he can be held in contempt for failing to disclose such information. What is contemplated is that, if a claim of privilege is made in a nonjudicial proceeding and is overruled, application must be made to a court for an order compelling the witness to answer. Only if such order is made and is disobeyed may a witness be held in contempt. That the determination of privilege in a judicial proceeding is a question for the judge is well-established California law. See, e.g., Holm v. Superior Court, 42 Cal.2d 500, 507, 267 P.2d 1025, 1029 (1954).

Subdivision (b), of course, does not apply to any bodyCsuch as the Public Utilities CommissionCthat has constitutional power to impose punishment for contempt. See, e.g., Cal.Const., Art. XII, § 22. Nor does this subdivision apply to witnesses before the State Legislature or its committees. See Govt.Code §§ 9400-9414. Likewise, subdivision (b) does not apply to hearings and investigations of the State Industrial Accident Commission.

§ 915. Disclosure of privileged information or attorney work product in ruling on claim of privilege. (a) Subject to subdivision (b), the presiding officer may not require disclosure of information claimed to be privileged under this division or attorney work product under subdivision (a) of Section 2018.030 of the Code of Civil Procedure in order to rule on the claim of privilege; provided, however, that in any hearing conducted pursuant to subdivision (c) of Section 1524 of the Penal Code in which a claim of privilege is made and the court determines that there is no other feasible means to rule on the validity of the claim other than to require disclosure, the court shall proceed in accordance with subdivision (b).

(b) When a court is ruling on a claim of privilege under Article 9 (commencing with Section 1040) of Chapter 4 (official information and identity of informer) or under Section 1060 (trade secret) or under subdivision (b) of Section 2018.030 of the Code of Civil Procedure (attorney work product) and is unable to do so without requiring disclosure of the information claimed to be privileged, the court may require the person from whom disclosure is sought or the person authorized to claim the privilege, or both, to disclose the information in chambers out of the presence and hearing of all persons except the person authorized to claim the privilege and any other persons as the person authorized to claim the privilege is willing to have present. If the judge determines that the information is privileged, neither the judge nor any other person may ever disclose, without the consent of a person authorized to permit disclosure, what was disclosed in the course of the proceedings in chambers. [*Amended, 1979, 2001, 2004, 2005.*]

Statutory Note

The 1979 amendment added the proviso at the end of subdivision (a), relating to search warrants for documents possessed or controlled by lawyers, physicians, psychotherapists, and clergy, pursuant to Penal Code § 1524(c). The 2001 amendment added attorney work product.

Law Revision Commission Comment

Subdivision (a) states the general rule that revelation of the information asserted to be privileged may not be compelled in order to determine whether or not it is privileged. This codifies existing law. See Collette v. Sarrasin, 184 Cal. 283, 288-289, 193 Pac. 571, 573 (1920); People v. Glen Arms Estate, Inc., 230 Cal.App.2d 841, 846 note 1, 41 Cal.Rptr. 303, 305 note 1 (1964).

Subdivision (b) provides an exception to this general rule for information claimed to be privileged under Section 1040 (official information), Section 1041 (identity of an informer), or Section 1060 (trade secret). These privileges exist only if the interest in maintaining the secrecy of the information outweighs the interest in seeing that justice is done in the particular case. In at least some cases, it will be necessary for the judge to examine the information claimed to be privileged in order to balance these competing considerations intelligently. See People v. Glen Arms Estate, Inc., 230 Cal.App.2d 841, 846 note 1, 41 Cal.Rptr. 303, 305 note 1 (1964), and the cases cited in 8 Wigmore, Evidence § 2379 at 812 note 6 (McNaughton rev. 1961). And see United States v. Reynolds, 345 U.S. 1, 7-11 (1953), and pertinent discussion thereof in 8 Wigmore, Evidence § 2379 (McNaughton rev. 1961). Even in these cases, Section 915 undertakes to give adequate protection to the person claiming the privilege by providing that the information be disclosed in confidence to the judge and requiring that it be kept in confidence if it is found to be privileged.

The exception in subdivision (b) applies only when a court is ruling on the claim of privilege. Thus, in view of subdivision (a), disclosure of the information cannot be required, for example, in an administrative proceeding.

§ 916. Exclusion of privileged information where persons authorized to claim privilege are not present.

(a) The presiding officer, on his own motion or on the motion of any party, shall exclude information that is subject to a claim of privilege under this division [§§ 900-1070] if:

(1) The person from whom the information is sought is not a person authorized to claim the privilege; and

(2) There is no party to the proceeding who is a person authorized to claim the privilege.

(b) The presiding officer may not exclude information under this section if:

(1) He is otherwise instructed by a person authorized to permit disclosure; or

(2) The proponent of the evidence establishes that there is no person authorized to claim the privilege in existence.

Assembly Committee on Judiciary Comment

Section 916 is needed to protect the holder of a privilege when he is not available to protect his own interest. For example, a third party—perhaps the lawyer's secretary—may have been present when a confidential communication to a lawyer was made. In the absence of both the holder himself and the lawyer, the secretary could be compelled to testify concerning the communication if there were no provision such as Section 916 which requires the presiding officer to recognize the privilege.

Section 916 is designed to protect only privileged information that the holder of the privilege could protect by claiming the privilege at the hearing. It is not designed to protect unprivileged information. For example, if the statement offered in evidence is a declaration against the penal interest of the declarant, Section 916 does not authorize the presiding officer to exclude the evidence on the ground of the declarant's privilege against self-incrimination. If the declarant were present, his self-incrimination privilege would merely preclude his giving self-incriminating testimony at the hearing; it could not be asserted to prevent the disclosure of previously made self-incriminating statements.

The erroneous exclusion of information pursuant to Section 916 on the ground that it is privileged might amount to prejudicial error. On the other hand, the erroneous failure to exclude information pursuant to Section 916 could not amount to prejudicial error. See Evidence Code § 918.

* * *

§ 917. Presumption that certain communications are confidential; privileged character of electronic communications. (a) If a privilege is claimed on the ground that the matter sought to be disclosed is a communication made in confidence in the course of the lawyer-client, lawyer referral service-client, physician-patient, psychotherapist-patient, clergy-penitent, husband-wife, sexual assault counselor-victim, or domestic violence counselor-victim relationship, the communication is presumed to have been made in confidence and the opponent of the claim of privilege has the burden of proof to establish that the communication was not confidential.

(b) A communication between persons in a relationship listed in subdivision (a) does not lose its privileged character for the sole reason that it is communicated by electronic means or because persons involved in the delivery, facilitation, or storage of electronic communication may have access to the content of the communication.

(c) For purposes of this section, "electronic" has the same meaning provided in Section 1633.2 of the Civil Code. [*Amended 2002, 2003, 2004, 2006, 2014.*]

Assembly Committee on Judiciary Comment

A number of sections provide privileges for communications made "in confidence" in the course of certain relationships. Although there appear to have been no cases involving the question in California, the general rule elsewhere is that a communication made in the course of such a relationship is presumed to be confidential and the party objecting to the claim of privilege has the burden of showing that it was not. See generally, with respect to the marital communication privilege, 8 Wigmore, Evidence § 2336 (McNaughton rev. 1961). See also Blau v. United States, 340 U.S. 332, 333-335 (1951) (holding that marital communications are presumed to be confidential). In adopting by statute a revised version of the privileges article of the Uniform Rules of Evidence, New Jersey included such a provision in its statement of the lawyer-client privilege. N.J.Rev.Stat. § 2A:84A-20(3), added by N.J.Laws 1960, Ch. 52, p. 452.

If the privilege claimant were required to show that the communication was made in confidence, he would be compelled, in many cases, to reveal the subject matter of the communication in order to establish his right to the privilege. Hence, Section 917 is included to establish a presumption of confidentiality, if this is not already the existing law in California. See Sharon v. Sharon, 79 Cal. 633, 678, 22 Pac. 26, 40 (1889) (attorney-client privilege); Hager v. Shindler, 29 Cal. 47, 63 (1865) ("Prima facie, all communications made by a client to his attorney or counsel [in the course of that relationship] must be regarded as confidential.").

To overcome the presumption, the proponent of the evidence must persuade the presiding officer that the communication was not made in confidence. Of course, if the facts show that the communication was not intended to be kept in confidence, the communication is not privileged. See Solon v. Lichtenstein, 39 Cal.2d 75, 244 P.2d 907 (1952). And the fact that the communication was made under circumstances where others could easily overhear is a strong indication that the communication was not intended to be confidential and is, therefore, unprivileged. See Sharon v. Sharon, 79 Cal. 633, 677, 22 Pac. 26, 39 (1889); People v. Castiel, 153 Cal.App.2d 653, 315 P.2d 79 (1957).

Law Revision Commission Comment - 2002 Amendment

Subdivision (a) of Section 917 is amended to make clear that it also applies to confidential communication privileges created after its original enactment in 1965. See Sections 1035-1036.2 (sexual assault victim), 1037-1037.7 (domestic violence victim). The presumption set forth in subdivision (a) applies regardless of how a communication is transmitted. In each instance, the opponent of the claim of privilege has the burden of proof to establish that the communication was not confidential.

Subdivision (b) is drawn from New York law (N.Y. C.P.L.R. 4548 (McKinney 2001)) and from language formerly found in Section 952 relating to confidentiality of an electronic communication between a client and a lawyer. For waiver of privileges, see Section 912 & Comment.

Under subdivision (c), the definition of "electronic" is broad, including any "intangible media which are technologically capable of storing, transmitting and reproducing information in human perceivable form." Unif. Electronic Transactions Act, § 2 comment (1999) (enacted as Civ. Code § 1633.2).

For discussion of ethical considerations where a lawyer communicates with a client by electronic means, see Bus. & Prof. Code § 6068(e) (attorney has duty to "maintain inviolate the confidence, and at every peril to himself or herself to preserve the secrets, of his or her client"); ABA Standing Committee on Ethics & Professional Responsibility, Formal Op. 99-413 ("Protecting the Confidentiality of Unencrypted E-Mail"); ABA Standing Committee on Ethics & Professional Responsibility, Formal Op. 92-368 ("Inadvertent Disclosure of Confidential Materials").

For examples of provisions on the admissibility of electronic communications, see Evid. Code §§ 1521 & Comment (Secondary Evidence Rule), 1552 (printed representation of computer information or computer program), 1553 (printed representation of images stored on video or digital medium); Civ. Code § 1633.13 ("In a proceeding, evidence of a record or signature may not be excluded solely because it is in electronic form."). See also People v. Martinez, 22 Cal. 4th 106, 990 P.2d 563, 91 Cal. Rptr. 2d 687 (2000); People v. Hernandez, 55 Cal. App. 4th 225, 63 Cal. Rptr. 2d 769 (1997); Aguimatang v. California State Lottery, 234 Cal. App. 3d 769, 286 Cal. Rptr. 57 (1991); People v. Lugashi, 205 Cal. App. 3d 632, 252 Cal. Rptr. 434 (1988).

§ 918. Effect of error in overruling claim of privilege. A party may predicate error on a ruling disallowing a claim of privilege only if he is the holder of the privilege, except that a party may predicate error on a ruling disallowing a claim of privilege by his spouse under Section 970 or 971.

§ 919. Admissibility where disclosure erroneously compelled. (a) Evidence of a statement or other disclosure of privileged information is inadmissible against a holder of the privilege if:

(1) A person authorized to claim the privilege claimed it but nevertheless disclosure erroneously was required to be made; or

(2) The presiding officer did not exclude the privileged information as required by Section 916.

(b) If a person authorized to claim the privilege claimed it, whether in the same or a prior proceeding, but nevertheless disclosure erroneously was required by the presiding officer to be made, neither the failure to refuse to disclose nor the failure to seek review of the order of the presiding officer requiring disclosure indicates consent to the disclosure or constitutes a waiver and, under these circumstances, the disclosure is one made under coercion. [*Amended 1974.*]

Law Revision Commission Comment

Section 919 protects a holder of a privilege from the detriment he would otherwise suffer in a later proceeding when, in a prior proceeding, the presiding officer erroneously overruled a claim of privilege and compelled revelation of the privileged information. Although Section 912 provides that such a coerced disclosure does not waive a privilege, it does not provide specifically that evidence of the prior disclosure is inadmissible; Section 919 assures the inadmissibility of such evidence in the subsequent proceeding. * * *

Law Revision Commission Comment - 1974 Amendment

Subdivision (b) has been added to Section 919 to make clear that, after disclosure of privileged information has been erroneously required to be made by order of a trial court or other presiding officer, neither the failure to refuse to disclose nor the failure to challenge the order (by, for example, a petition for a writ of habeas corpus or other special writ or by an appeal from a contempt order) amounts to a waiver and the disclosure is one made under coercion for the purposes of Sections 912(a) and 919(a) (1). See Section 905 (defining "presiding officer"). The addition of subdivision (b) will preclude any possibility of a contrary interpretation of Sections 912 and 919 based on the language found in Markwell v. Sykes, 173 Cal.App.2d 642, 649-650, 343 P.2d 769, 773-774 (1959). See Recommendation Relating to Erroneously Ordered Disclosure of Privileged Information, 11 Cal.L. Revision Comm'n Reports 1163 (1973).

The phrase "whether in the same or a prior proceeding" has been included in subdivision (b) to avoid any implication that might be drawn from the original Law Revision Commission Comment to Section 919 that subdivision (a) (1) applies only where the privilege was claimed in a prior proceeding. The protection afforded by Section 919, of course, also applies where a claim of privilege is made at an earlier stage in the same proceeding and the presiding officer erroneously overruled the claim and ordered disclosure of the privileged information to be made. [11 Cal.L.Rev.Comm. Reports 1163 (1974).]

§ 920. No implied repeal. Nothing in this division [§§ 900-1070] shall be construed to repeal by implication any other statute relating to privileges.

Law Revision Commission Comment

Some of the statutes relating to privileges are found in other codes and are continued in force. See, e.g., Penal Code §§ 266h and 266i (making the marital communications privilege inapplicable in prosecutions for pimping and pandering respectively). Section 920 assures that nothing in this division makes privileged any information declared by statute to be unprivileged or makes unprivileged any information declared by statute to be privileged.

Chapter 4. Particular Privileges

Article 1. Privilege of Defendant in Criminal Case

§ 930. Privilege not to be called as a witness and not to testify. To the extent that such privilege exists under the Constitution of the United States or the State of California, a defendant in a criminal case has a privilege not to be called as a witness and not to testify.

Law Revision Commission Comment

Section 930 recognizes that the defendant in a criminal case has a constitutional privilege not to be called as a witness and not to testify. Cal.Const., Art. I, § 13. See Killpatrick v. Superior Court, 153 Cal.App.2d 146, 314 P.2d 164 (1957); People v. Talle, 111 Cal.App.2d 650, 245 P.2d 633 (1952). Section 930 also recognizes that the defendant may have a similar privilege under the United States Constitution. See Malloy v. Hogan, 378 U.S. 1 (1964).

Article 2. Privilege Against Self-Incrimination

§ 940. Privilege against self-incrimination. To the extent that such privilege exists under the Constitution of the United States or the State of California, a person has a privilege to refuse to disclose any matter that may tend to incriminate him.

Law Revision Commission Comment

Section 940 recognizes the privilege (derived from the California and United States Constitutions) of a person to refuse, when testifying, to give information that might tend to incriminate him. See Fross v. Wotton, 3 Cal.2d 384, 44 P.2d 350 (1935); In re Leavitt, 174 Cal.App.2d 535, 345 P.2d 75 (1959). This privilege should be distinguished from the privilege stated in Section 930 (privilege of defendant in a criminal case to refuse to testify at all).

Section 940 does not determine the scope of the privilege against self-incrimination; the scope of the privilege is determined by the pertinent provisions of the California and United States Constitutions as interpreted by the courts. See Cal.Const., Art. I, § 13. See also Malloy v. Hogan, 378 U.S. 1 (1964). Nor does Section 940 prescribe the exceptions to the privilege or indicate when it has been waived. This, too, is determined by the cases interpreting the pertinent provisions of the California and United States Constitutions. For a statement of the scope of the constitutional privilege and some of its exceptions, see Tentative Recommendation and a Study Relating to the Uniform Rules of Evidence (Article V. Privileges), 6 Cal.Law Revision Comm'n, Rep., Rec. & Studies 201, 215-218, 343-377 (1964).

Article 3. Lawyer-Client Privilege

§ 950. Lawyer. As used in this article [§§ 950-962], "lawyer" means a person authorized, or reasonably believed by the client to be authorized, to practice law in any state or nation.

Law Revision Commission Comment

"Lawyer" is defined to include a person "reasonably believed by the client to be authorized" to practice law. Since the privilege is intended to encourage full disclosure, the client's reasonable belief that the person he is consulting is an attorney is sufficient to justify application of the privilege. See 8 Wigmore, Evidence § 2302 (McNaughton rev. 1961), and cases there cited in note 1. See also McCormick, Evidence § 92 (1954). There is no requirement that the lawyer be licensed to practice in a jurisdiction that recognizes the lawyer-client privilege. Legal transactions frequently cross state and national boundaries and require consultation with attorneys from many different jurisdictions. When a California resident travels outside the State and has occasion to consult a lawyer during such travel, or when a lawyer from another state or nation participates in a transaction involving a California client, the client should be entitled to assume that his communications will be given as much protection as they would be if he consulted a California lawyer in California. A client should not be forced to inquire about the jurisdictions where the lawyer is authorized to practice and whether such jurisdictions recognize the lawyer-client privilege before he may safely communicate with the lawyer.

§ 951. Client. As used in this article [§§ 950-962], "client" means a person who, directly or through an authorized representative, consults a lawyer for the purpose of retaining the lawyer or securing legal service or advice from him in his professional capacity, and includes an incompetent (a) who himself so consults the lawyer or (b) whose guardian or conservator so consults the lawyer in behalf of the incompetent.

Case Note

The privilege protects confidential communications during initial consultation with a lawyer, whether or not the lawyer is subsequently retained. Client must seek advice from the lawyer "in his professional capacity," rather than in his capacity as a friend or business associate. Lawyer's explicit statement that he was unwilling to represent the client leads to inference that subsequent incriminating disclosures were made to the lawyer as a friend rather than in his professional capacity. People v. Gionis, 9 Cal. 4th 1196, 1208-1212, 40 Cal. Rptr. 2d 456, 462-465, 892 P.2d 1199, 1205-1208 (1995).

See also Case Notes to §§ 952, 954.

Law Revision Commission Comment

Under Section 951, public entities have a privilege insofar as communications made in the course of the lawyer-client relationship are concerned. This codifies existing law. See Holm v. Superior Court, 42 Cal.2d 500, 267 P.2d 1025 (1954). Likewise, such unincorporated organizations as labor unions, social clubs, and fraternal societies have a lawyer-client privilege when the organization (rather than its individual members) is the client. See Evidence Code § 175 (defining "person") and § 200 (defining "public entity").

§ 952. Confidential communication between client and lawyer. As used in this article [§§ 950-962], "confidential communication between client and lawyer" means information transmitted between a client and his or her lawyer in the course of that relationship and in confidence by a means which, so far as the client is aware, discloses the information to no third persons other than those who are present to further the interest of the client in the consultation or those to whom disclosure is reasonably necessary for the transmission of the information or the accomplishment of the purpose for which the lawyer is consulted, and includes a legal opinion formed and the advice given by the lawyer in the course of that relationship. [*Amended 1967, 1994, 2002.*]

Statutory Notes

See Bus. & Prof. Code § 6149 (confidentiality of written fee contract). The 1967 amendment added at the beginning of the last clause the reference to "a legal opinion." The 1994 amendment added a sentence concerning electronic communication. The 2002 amendment repealed the 1994 amendment as redundant with amended § 917.

Case Note

Privilege for communications between corporate employee and corporation's attorney is determined by whether employee is a natural person to speak for the corporation; factors listed. D.I. Chadbourne, Inc. v. Superior Court, 60 Cal. 2d 723, 36 Cal. Rptr 468, 388 P.2d 700 (1964).

Law Revision Commission Comment

* * * Confidential communications * * * include those made to third parties—such as the lawyer's secretary, a physician, or similar expert—for the purpose of transmitting such information to the lawyer because they are "reasonably necessary for the transmission of the information." * * *

A lawyer at times may desire to have a client reveal information to an expert consultant in order that the lawyer may adequately advise his client. The inclusion of the words "or the accomplishment of the purpose for which the lawyer is consulted" assures that these communications, too, are within the scope of the privilege. This part of the definition may change existing law. Himmelfarb v. United States, 175 F.2d 924, 938-939 (9th Cir.1949), applying California law, held that the presence of an accountant during a lawyer-client consultation destroyed the privilege, but no California case directly in point has been found. Of course, if the expert consultant is acting merely as a conduit for communications from the client to the attorney, the doctrine of City & County of San Francisco v. Superior Court, supra, applies and the communication would be privileged under existing law as well as under this section. See also Evidence Code § 912(d) and the Comment thereto.

The words "other than those who are present to further the interest of the client in the consultation" indicate that a communication to a lawyer is nonetheless confidential even though it is made in the presence of another person—such as a spouse, parent, business associate, or joint client—who is present to further the interest of the client in the consultation. These words refer, too, to another person and his attorney who may meet with the client and his attorney in regard to a matter of joint concern. This may change existing law, for the presence of a third person sometimes has been held to destroy the confidential character of the consultation, even where the third person was present because of his concern for the welfare of the client. See Attorney-Client Privilege in California, 10 Stan.L.Rev. 297, 308 (1958), and authorities there cited in notes 67-71. See also Himmelfarb v. United States, supra.

Law Revision Commission Comment - 1967 Amendment

The express inclusion of "a legal opinion" in the last clause will preclude a possible construction of this section that would leave the attorney's uncommunicated legal opinion—which includes his impressions and conclusions—unprotected by the privilege. Such a construction would virtually destroy the privilege. [8 Cal.L.Rev.Comm. Reports 101 (1967).]

Law Revision Commission Comment - 2002 Amendment

Section 952 is amended to delete the last sentence concerning confidentiality of electronic communications, because this rule is generalized in Section 917(b)-(c) applicable to all confidential communication privileges.

§ 953. Holder of the privilege. As used in this article [§§ 950-962], "holder of the privilege" means:

(a) The client, if the client has no guardian or conservator.

(b) (1) A guardian or conservator of the client, if the client has a guardian or conservator, except as provided in paragraph (2).

(2) If the guardian or conservator has an actual or apparent conflict of interest with the client, then the guardian or conservator does not hold the privilege.

(c) The personal representative of the client if the client is dead, including a personal representative appointed pursuant to Section 12252 of the Probate Code.

(d) A successor, assign, trustee in dissolution, or any similar representative of a firm, association, organization, partnership, business trust, corporation, or public entity that is no longer in existence. [*Amended 2009 & 2018.*]

Case Note

When a client dies, the client's privilege for confidential communications with a lawyer is transferred to the client's personal representative. The privilege terminates when the client's estate is wound up, the personal representative is finally discharged, and there is no longer a holder of the privilege in existence. HLC Properties, Ltd. v. Superior Ct., 35 Cal. 4th 54, 24 Cal. Rptr 3d 199, 105 P.3d 560 (2005).

Law Revision Commission Comment

Under subdivisions (a) and (b), the guardian of a client is the holder of the privilege if the client has a guardian, and the client becomes the holder of the privilege when he no longer has a guardian. For example, if an underage client or his guardian consults a lawyer, the guardian is the holder of the privilege under subdivision (b) until the guardianship is terminated; thereafter, the client himself is the holder of the privilege. * * *

Under subdivision (c), the personal representative of a client is the holder of the privilege when the client is dead. He may either claim or waive the privilege on behalf of the deceased client. This may be a change in California law. Under existing law, it seems probable that the privilege survives the death of the client and that no one can waive it after the client's death. See Collette v. Sarrasin, 184 Cal. 283, 289, 193 Pac. 571, 573 (1920). Hence, the privilege apparently is recognized even when it would be clearly to the interest of the estate of the deceased client to waive it. Under Section 953, however, the personal representative of a deceased client may waive the privilege. The purpose underlying the privilegeCto provide a client with the assurance of confidentialityCdoes not require the recognition of the privilege when to do so is detrimental to his interest or to the interests of his estate.

§ 954. Lawyer-client privilege. Subject to Section 912 and except as otherwise provided in this article [§§ 950-962], the client, whether or not a party, has a privilege to refuse to disclose, and to prevent another from disclosing, a confidential communication between client and lawyer if the privilege is claimed by:

(a) The holder of the privilege;

(b) A person who is authorized to claim the privilege by the holder of the privilege; or

(c) The person who was the lawyer at the time of the confidential communication, but such person may not claim the privilege if there is no holder of the privilege in existence or if he is otherwise instructed by a person authorized to permit disclosure.

The relationship of attorney and client shall exist between a law corporation as defined in Article 10 (commencing with Section 6160) of Chapter 4 of Division 3 of the Business and Professions Code and the persons to whom it renders professional services, as well as between such persons and members of the State Bar employed by such corporation to render services to such persons. The word "persons" as used in this subdivision includes partnerships, corporations, limited liability companies, associations and other groups and entities. [*Amended 1968, 1994, 1996.*]

Statutory Note

See Welfare. & Inst. Code § 15637 (requirement to report elder abuse does not require violation of attorney's duty of confidentiality).

Case Note

City attorney's legal memorandum, distributed to members of city council, was privileged as confidential attorney-client communication. Public Records Act exemption from disclosure of records pertaining to pending litigation does not create implied exception to attorney-client privilege for communications not relating to pending litigation. Brown Act open meeting requirements do not abrogate the privilege for clients that are public entities. Roberts v. City of Palmdale, 5 Cal. 4th 363, 20 Cal. Rptr. 330, 853 P.2d 496 (1993). Privileged communications between a trustee and the trustee's attorney are not discoverable by the trust beneficiaries because there is no statutory exception by which the trustee's fiduciary duties take precedence over its privilege as the client of an attorney. Wells Fargo Bank, N.A. v. Superior Court, 22 Cal. 4th 201, 91 Cal. Rptr. 716, 990 P.2d 591 (2000).

Law Revision Commission Comment

Section 954 is the basic statement of the lawyer-client privilege. Exceptions to this privilege are stated in Sections 956-962.

Persons entitled to claim the privilege. The persons entitled to claim the privilege are specified in subdivisions (a), (b), and (c). See Evidence Code § 953 for the definition of "holder of the privilege."

Eavesdroppers. Under Section 954, the lawyer-client privilege can be asserted to prevent anyone from testifying to a confidential communication. Thus, clients are protected against the risk of disclosure by eavesdroppers and other wrongful interceptors of confidential communications between lawyer and client. Probably no such protection was provided prior to the enactment of Penal Code Sections 653i and 653j. See People v. Castiel, 153 Cal.App.2d 653, 315 P.2d 79 (1957). See also Attorney-Client Privilege in California, 10 Stan.L.Rev. 297, 310-312 (1958), and cases there cited in note 84.

Penal Code Section 653j makes evidence obtained by electronic eavesdropping or recording in violation of the section inadmissible in "any judicial, administrative, legislative, or other proceeding." The section also provides a criminal penalty and contains definitions and exceptions. Penal Code Section 653i makes it a felony to eavesdrop by an electronic or other device upon a conversation between a person in custody of a public officer or on public property and that person's lawyer, religious advisor, or physician.

Section 954 is consistent with Penal Code Sections 653i and 653j but provides broader protection, for it protects against disclosure of confidential communications by anyone who obtained knowledge of the communication without the client's consent. See also Evidence Code § 912 (when disclosure with client's consent constitutes a waiver of the privilege). The use of the privilege to prevent testimony by eavesdroppers and those to whom the communication was wrongfully disclosed does not, however, affect the rule that the making of the communication under circumstances where others could easily overhear it is evidence that the client did not intend the communication to be confidential. See Sharon v. Sharon, 79 Cal. 633, 677, 22 Pac. 26, 39 (1889).

Termination of privilege. The privilege may be claimed by a person listed in Section 954, or the privileged information excluded by the presiding officer under Section 916, only if there is a holder of the privilege in existence. Hence, the privilege ceases to exist when the client's estate is finally distributed and his personal representative is discharged. This is apparently a change in California law. Under the existing law, it seems likely that the privilege continues to exist indefinitely after the client's death and that no one has authority to waive the privilege. See Collette v. Sarrasin, 184 Cal. 283, 193 Pac. 571 (1920). See generally Paley v. Superior Court, 137 Cal.App.2d 450, 290 P.2d 617 (1955), and discussion of the analogous situation in connection with the physician-patient privilege in Tentative Recommendation and a Study Relating to the Uniform Rules of Evidence (Article V. Privileges), 6 Cal.Law Revision Comm'n, Rep., Rec. & Studies 201, 408-410 (1964). Although there is good reason for maintaining the privilege while the estate is being administered—particularly if the estate is involved in litigation—there is little reason to preserve secrecy at the expense of excluding relevant evidence after the estate is wound up and the representative is discharged.

§ 955. When lawyer required to claim privilege. The lawyer who received or made a communication subject to the privilege under this article [§§ 950-962] shall claim the privilege whenever he is present when the communication is sought to be disclosed and is authorized to claim the privilege under subdivision (c) of Section 954.

§ 956. Exception: Crime or fraud. (a) There is no privilege under this article if the services of the lawyer were sought or obtained to enable or aid anyone to commit or plan to commit a crime or a fraud. [*Amended 2016.*]

(b) This exception to the privilege granted by this article shall not apply to legal services rendered in compliance with state and local laws on medicinal cannabis or adult-use cannabis, and confidential communications provided for the purpose of rendering those services are confidential communications between client and lawyer, as defined in Section 952, provided the lawyer also advises the client on conflicts with respect to federal law. [*Added 2017.*]

§ 956.5. Reasonable belief that disclosure of confidential communication relating to representation of client is necessary to prevent criminal act that lawyer reasonably believes likely to result in death of, or substantial bodily harm to, an individual; exception to privilege. There is no privilege under this article if the lawyer reasonably believes that disclosure of any confidential communication relating to representation of a client is necessary to prevent a criminal act that the lawyer reasonably believes is likely to result in the death of, or substantial bodily harm to, an individual. [*Added 1993. Amended 2003, 2004.*]

Statutory Note

The 2003 amendment substituted "a criminal act that the lawyer reasonably believes is likely to result in death of, or substantial bodily harm to, an individual" for "the client from committing a criminal act that the lawyer believes is likely to result in death or substantial bodily harm."

§957. Exception: Parties claiming through deceased client. There is no privilege under this article [§§ 950-962] as to a communication relevant to an issue between parties all of whom claim through a deceased client, regardless of whether the claims are by testate or intestate succession, nonprobate transfer, or inter vivos transaction. [*Amended 2009.*]

Law Revision Commission Comment

The lawyer-client privilege does not apply to a communication relevant to an issue between parties all of whom claim through a deceased client. Under existing law, all must claim through the client by testate or intestate succession in order for this exception to be applicable; a claim by inter vivos transaction apparently is not within the exception. Paley v. Superior Court, 137 Cal.App.2d 450, 457-460, 290 P.2d 617, 621-623 (1955). Section 957 extends this exception to include inter vivos transactions.

The traditional exception for litigation between claimants by testate or intestate succession is based on the theory that claimants in privity with the estate claim through the client, not adversely, and the deceased client presumably would want his communications disclosed in litigation between such claimants so that his desires in regard to the disposition of his estate might be correctly ascertained and carried out. This rationale is equally applicable where one or more of the parties is claiming by inter vivos transaction as, for example, in an action between a party who claims under a deed (executed by a client in full possession of his faculties) and a party who claims under a will executed while the client's mental stability was dubious. See the discussion in Tentative Recommendation and a Study Relating to the Uniform Rules of Evidence (Article V. Privileges), 6 Cal.Law Revision Comm'n, Rep., Rec. & Studies 201, 392-396 (1964).

§ 958. Exception: Breach of duty arising out of lawyer-client relationship. There is no privilege under this article [§§ 950-962] as to a communication relevant to an issue of breach, by the lawyer or by the client, of a duty arising out of the lawyer-client relationship.

Statutory Note

See Bus. & Prof. Code § 6202 (disclosure of relevant communications in connection with arbitration of attorney's fees and related proceedings).

Law Revision Commission Comment

* * * It would be unjust to permit a client either to accuse his attorney of a breach of duty and to invoke the privilege to prevent the attorney from bringing forth evidence in defense of the charge or to refuse to pay his attorney's fee and invoke the privilege to defeat the attorney's claim. Thus, for example, if the defendant in a criminal action claims that his lawyer did not provide him with an adequate defense, communications between the lawyer and client relevant to that issue are not privileged. See People v. Tucker, 61 Cal.2d 828, 40 Cal.Rptr. 609, 395 P.2d 449 (1964). The duty involved must, of course, be one arising out of the lawyer-client relationship, e.g., the duty of the lawyer to exercise reasonable diligence on behalf of his client, the duty of the lawyer to care faithfully and account for his client's property, or the client's duty to pay for the lawyer's services.

§ 959. Exception: Lawyer as attesting witness. There is no privilege under this article [§§ 950-962] as to a communication relevant to an issue concerning the intention or competence of a client executing an attested document of which the lawyer is an attesting witness, or concerning the execution or attestation of such a document.

Law Revision Commission Comment

This exception relates to the type of communication about which an attesting witness would testify. The mere fact that an attorney acts as an attesting witness should not destroy the lawyer-client privilege as to all statements made concerning the document attested; but the privilege should not prohibit the lawyer from performing the duties expected of an attesting witness. Under existing law, the attesting witness exception is broader, having been used as a device to obtain information which the lawyer who is an attesting witness received in his capacity as a lawyer rather than as an attesting witness. See In re Mullin, 110 Cal. 252, 42 Pac. 645 (1895).

§ 960. Exception: Intention of deceased client concerning writing affecting property interest. There is no privilege under this article [§§ 950-962] as to a communication relevant to an issue concerning the intention of a client, now deceased, with respect to a deed of conveyance, will, or other writing, executed by the client, purporting to affect an interest in property.

Law Revision Commission Comment

Although the attesting witness exception stated in Section 959 is limited to information of the kind to which one would expect an attesting witness to testify, there is merit to having an exception that applies to all dispositive instruments. A client ordinarily would desire his lawyer to communicate his true intention with regard to a dispositive instrument if the instrument itself leaves the matter in doubt and the client is deceased. Likewise, the client ordinarily would desire his attorney to testify to communications relevant to the validity of such instruments after the client dies. Accordingly, two additional exceptionsCSections 960 and 961Care provided for this purpose. * * *

§ 961. Exception: Validity of writing affecting property interest. There is no privilege under this article [§§ 950-962] as to a communication relevant to an issue concerning the validity of a deed of conveyance, will, or other writing, executed by a client, now deceased, purporting to affect an interest in property.

§ 962. Exception: Joint clients. Where two or more clients have retained or consulted a lawyer upon a matter of common interest, none of them, nor the successor in interest of any of them, may claim a privilege under this article [§§ 950-962] as to a communication made in the course of that relationship when such communication is offered in a civil proceeding between one of such clients (or his successor in interest) and another of such clients (or his successor in interest).

Case Note

Where, under an insurance policy, insurer selects attorney to represent the insured against an action covered by the policy, the insured and the insurer are not joint clients; thus, in subsequent litigation between insured and insurer, insurer may not compel production of confidential communications between insured and its attorney. Rockwell Int'l Corp. v. Superior Court, 26 Cal. App. 4th 1255, 1266-1267, 32 Cal. Rptr. 2d 153, 159-160 (Ct. App. 1994).

Article 3.5. Lawyer Referral Service-Client Privilege

§ 965. Definitions. For purposes of this article, the following terms have the following meanings:

(a) "Client" means a person who, directly or through an authorized representative, consults a lawyer referral service for the purpose of retaining, or securing legal services or advice from, a lawyer in his or her professional capacity, and includes an incompetent who consults the lawyer referral service himself or herself or whose guardian or conservator consults the lawyer referral service on his or her behalf.

(b) "Confidential communication between client and lawyer referral service" means information transmitted between a client and a lawyer referral service in the course of that relationship and in confidence by a means that, so far as the client is aware, does not disclose the information to third persons other than those who are present to further the interests of the client in the consultation or those to whom disclosure is reasonably necessary for the transmission of the information or the accomplishment of the purpose for which the lawyer referral service is consulted.

(c) "Holder of the privilege" means any of the following:

(1) The client, if the client has no guardian or conservator.

(2) A guardian or conservator of the client, if the client has a guardian or conservator.

(3) The personal representative of the client if the client is dead, including a personal representative appointed pursuant to Section 12252 of the Probate Code.

(4) A successor, assign, trustee in dissolution, or any similar representative of a firm, association, organization, partnership, business trust, corporation, or public entity that is no longer in existence.

(d) "Lawyer referral service" means a lawyer referral service certified under, and operating in compliance with, Section 6155 of the Business and Professions Code or an enterprise reasonably believed by the client to be a lawyer referral service certified under, and operating in compliance with, Section 6155 of the Business and Professions Code.

§ 966. Lawyer referral service-client privilege.

(a) Subject to section 912 and except as otherwise provided in this article, the client, whether or not a party, has a privilege to refuse to disclose, and to prevent another from disclosing, a confidential communication between client and lawyer referral service if the privilege is claimed by any of the following:

(1) The holder of the privilege.

(2) A person who is authorized to claim the privilege by the holder of the privilege.

(3) The lawyer referral service or a staff person thereof, but the lawyer referral service or a staff person thereof may not claim the privilege if there is no holder of the privilege in existence or if the lawyer referral service or a staff person thereof is otherwise instructed by a person authorized to permit disclosure.

(b) The relationship of lawyer referral service and client shall exist between a lawyer referral service, as defined by 965, and the persons to whom it renders services, as well as between such persons and anyone employed by the lawyer referral service to render services to such persons. The word "persons" as used in this subdivision includes partnerships, corporations, limited liability companies, associations, and other groups and entities.

§ 967. Claiming of privilege. A lawyer referral service that has received or made a communication subject to the privilege under this article shall claim the privilege if the communication is sought to be disclosed and the client has not consented to the disclosure.

§ 968. Exceptions to privilege. There is no privilege under this article if either of the following applies:

(a) The services of the lawyer referral service were sought or obtained to enable or aid anyone to commit or plan to commit a crime or a fraud.

(b) A staff person of the lawyer referral service who receives a confidential communication in processing a request for legal assistance reasonably believes that disclosure of the confidential communication is necessary to prevent a criminal act that the staff person of the lawyer referral service reasonably believes is likely to result in the death of, or substantial bodily harm to, an individual.[*Added 2013.*]

Article 4. Privilege Not To Testify Against Spouse

§ 970. Privilege not to testify against spouse. Except as otherwise provided by statute, a married person has a privilege not to testify against his spouse in any proceeding.

Statutory Note

See Health & Safety Code § 120595 (privilege does not apply in proceedings relating to communicable disease prevention and control).

Case Note

The privilege of one spouse not to testify against the other depends upon a valid marriage being in existence when the witness is called to the stand. A witness whose divorce decree from the defendant was awarded days prior to taking the stand has no privilege not to testify. People v. Bradford, 70 Cal. 2d 333, 342-343, 74 Cal. Rptr. 726, 731, 450 P.2d 46, 51 (1969).

Law Revision Commission Comment

Under this article, a married person has two privileges: (1) a privilege not to testify against his spouse in any proceeding (Section 970) and (2) a privilege not to be called as a witness in any proceeding to which his spouse is a party (Section 971).

The privileges under this article are not as broad as the privilege provided by existing law. Under existing law, a married person has a privilege to prevent his spouse from testifying against him, but only the witness spouse has a privilege under this article. Under the existing law, a married person may refuse to testify for the other spouse, but no such privilege exists under this article. For a discussion of the reasons for these changes in existing law, see the Law Revision Commission's Comment to Code of Civil Procedure Section 1881 (superseded by the Evidence Code).

The rationale of the privilege provided by Section 970 not to testify against one's spouse is that such testimony would seriously disturb or disrupt the marital relationship. Society stands to lose more from such disruption than it stands to gain from the testimony which would be available if the privilege did not exist. The privilege is based in part on a previous recommendation and study of the California Law Revision Commission. See 1 Cal.Law Revision Comm'n, Rep., Rec. & Studies, Recommendation and Study Relating to the Marital "For and Against" Testimonial Privilege at F-1 (1957).

§ 971. Privilege not to be called as a witness against spouse. Except as otherwise provided by statute, a married person whose spouse is a party to a proceeding has a privilege not to be called as a witness by an adverse party to that proceeding without the prior express consent of the spouse having the privilege under this section unless the party calling the spouse does so in good faith without knowledge of the marital relationship.

Statutory Note

See Health & Safety Code § 120595 (privilege does not apply in proceedings relating to communicable disease prevention and control).

Law Revision Commission Comment

The privilege of a married person not to be called as a witness against his spouse is somewhat similar to the privilege given the defendant in a criminal case not to be called as a witness (Section 930). This privilege is necessary to avoid the prejudicial effect, for example, of the prosecution's calling the defendant's wife as a witness, thus forcing her to object before the jury. The privilege not to be called as a witness does not apply, however, in a proceeding where the other spouse is not a party. Thus, a married person may be called as a witness in a grand jury proceeding because his spouse is not a party to that proceeding, but the witness in the grand jury proceeding may claim the privilege under Section 970 to refuse to answer a question that would compel him to testify against his spouse.

§ 972. When privilege not applicable. A married person does not have a privilege under this article [§§ 970-973] in:

(a) A proceeding brought by or on behalf of one spouse against the other spouse.

(b) A proceeding to commit or otherwise place his or her spouse or his or her spouse's property, or both, under the control of another because of the spouse's alleged mental or physical condition.

(c) A proceeding brought by or on behalf of a spouse to establish his or her competence.

(d) A proceeding under the Juvenile Court Law, Chapter 2 (commencing with Section 200) of Part 1 of Division 2 of the Welfare and Institutions Code.

(e) A criminal proceeding in which one spouse is charged with:

(1) A crime against the person or property of the other spouse or of a child, parent, relative, or cohabitant of either, whether committed before or during marriage.

(2) A crime against the person or property of a third person committed in the course of committing a crime against the person or property of the other spouse, whether committed before or during marriage.

(3) Bigamy.

(4) A crime defined by Section 270 or 270a of the Penal Code.

(f) A proceeding resulting from a criminal act which occurred prior to legal marriage of the spouses to each other regarding knowledge acquired prior to that marriage if prior to the legal marriage the witness spouse was aware that his or her spouse had been arrested for or had been formally charged with the crime or crimes about which the spouse is called to testify.

(g) A proceeding brought against the spouse by a former spouse so long as the property and debts of the marriage have not been adjudicated, or in order to establish, modify, or enforce a child, family or spousal support obligation arising from the marriage to the former spouse; in a proceeding brought against a spouse by the other parent in order to establish, modify, or enforce a child support obligation for a child of a nonmarital relationship of the spouse; or in a proceeding brought against a spouse by the guardian of a child of that spouse in order to establish, modify, or enforce a child support obligation of the spouse. The married person does not have a privilege under this subdivision to refuse to provide information relating to the issues of income, expenses, assets, debts, and employment of either spouse, but may assert the privilege as otherwise provided in this article if other information is requested by the former spouse, guardian, or other parent of the child.

Any person demanding the otherwise privileged information made available by this subdivision, who also has an obligation to support the child for whom an order to establish, modify, or enforce child support is sought, waives his or her marital privilege to the same extent as the spouse as provided in this subdivision. [*Amended 1975, 1982, 1983, 1989.*]

Statutory Note

The 1983 Amendment added subdivision (f). The 1986 amendment added "parent, relative, or cohabitant" to subdivision (e)(1). The 1989 amendment added subdivision (g).

Case Note

Exception in subdivision (e)(2) for proceedings in which a spouse is charged with a crime against a third person committed in the course of committing a crime against the other spouse does not require that the crime against the other spouse be formally charged but only that the charged crime against the third person and the crime against the other spouse be logically related and be part of a continuous course of criminal conduct. People v. Sinohui, 28 Cal. 4th 205, 47 P.2d 629, 120 Cal. Rptr. 2d 783 (2002).

Law Revision Commission Comment

* * *[T]he exceptions in this section have been drafted so that they are consistent with those provided in Article 5 (commencing with Section 980) of this chapter (the privilege for confidential marital communications).* * *

§ 973. Waiver of privilege. (a) Unless erroneously compelled to do so, a married person who testifies in a proceeding to which his spouse is a party, or who testifies against his spouse in any proceeding, does not have a privilege under this article [§§ 970-973] in the proceeding in which such testimony is given.

(b) There is no privilege under this article [§§ 970-973] in a civil proceeding brought or defended by a married person for the immediate benefit of his spouse or of himself and his spouse.

Assembly Committee on Judiciary Comment

Section 973 contains special waiver provisions for the privileges provided by this article.

Subdivision (a). Under subdivision (a), a married person who testifies in a proceeding to which his spouse is a party waives both privileges provided for in this article. Thus, for example, a married person cannot call his spouse as a witness to give favorable testimony and have that spouse invoke the privilege provided in Section 970 to keep from testifying on cross-examination to unfavorable matters; nor can a married person testify for an adverse party as to particular matters and then invoke the privilege not to testify against his spouse as to other matters.

In any proceeding where a married person's spouse is not a party, the privilege not to be called as a witness is not available, and a married person may testify like any other witness without waiving the privilege provided under Section 970 so long as he does not testify against his spouse. However, under subdivision (a), the privilege not to testify against his spouse in that proceeding is waived as to all matters if he testifies against his spouse as to any matter.

The word "proceeding" is defined in Section 901 to include any action, civil or criminal. Hence, the privilege is waived for all purposes in an action if the spouse entitled to claim the privilege testifies at any time during the action. For example, if a civil action involves issues being separately tried, a wife whose husband is a party to the litigation may not testify for her husband at one trial and invoke and privilege in order to avoid testifying against him at a separate trial of a different issue. Nor may a wife testify against her husband at a preliminary hearing of a criminal action and refuse to testify against him at the trial.

Subdivision (b). This subdivision precludes married persons from taking unfair advantage of their marital status to escape their duty to give testimony under Section 776, which supersedes Code of Civil Procedure Section 2055. It recognizes a doctrine of waiver that has been developed in the California cases. Thus, for example, when suit is brought to set aside a conveyance from husband to wife allegedly in fraud of the husband's creditors, both spouses being named as defendants, it has been held that setting up the conveyance in the answer as a defense waives the privilege. Tobias v. Adams, 201 Cal. 689, 258 Pac. 588 (1927); Schwartz v. Brandon, 97 Cal.App. 30, 275 Pac. 448 (1929). But cf. Marple v. Jackson, 184 Cal. 411, 193 Pac. 940 (1920). Also, when husband and wife are joined as defendants in a quiet title action and assert a claim to the property, they have been held to have waived the privilege. Hagen v. Silva, 139 Cal.App.2d 199, 293 P.2d 143 (1956). And when both spouses joined as plaintiffs in an action to recover damages to one of them, each was held to have waived the privilege as to the testimony of the other. In re Strand, 123 Cal.App. 170, 11 P.2d 89 (1932). (It should be noted that, with respect to damages for personal injuries, Civil Code Section 163.5 (added by Cal.Stats.1957, Ch. 2334, § 1, p. 4066) provides that all damages awarded to a married person in a civil action for personal injuries are the separate property of such married person.) This principle of waiver has seemingly been developed by the case law to prevent a spouse from refusing to testify as to matters which affect his own interest on the ground that such testimony would also be "against" his spouse. It has been held, however, that a spouse does not waive the privilege by making the other spouse his agent, even as to transactions involving the agency. Ayres v. Wright, 103 Cal.App. 610, 284 Pac. 1077 (1930).

Article 5. Privilege for Confidential Marital Communications

§ 980. Privilege for confidential marital communications. Subject to Section 912 and except as otherwise provided in this article , a spouse, or the spouse's guardian or conservator if the spouse has a guardian or conservator, whether or not a party, has a privilege during the marital relationship and afterwards to refuse to disclose, and to prevent another from disclosing, a communication if the spouse claims the privilege and the communication was made in confidence between the spouse and the other spouse while they were married. [*Amended 2016.*]

Statutory Note

See Health & Safety Code § 120595 (privilege does not apply in proceedings relating to communicable disease prevention and control).

Case Note There is no privilege under this section for interspousal letters written from jail by prisoner who expects they will be intercepted. People v. Mickey, 54 Cal. 3d 612, 653-655, 286 Cal. Rptr. 801, 818-819, 818 P.2d 84, 101-102 (1991).

Physical facts pertaining to one spouse and observed by the other spouse are not confidential communications, which means "oral or written verbal expression from one spouse to the other." People v. Cleveland, 32 Cal. 4th 704, 11 Cal. Rptr. 3d 236, 86 P.3d 302 (2004).

Law Revision Commission Comment

Section 980 is the basic statement of the privilege for confidential marital communications. Exceptions to this privilege are stated in Sections 981-987.

Who can claim the privilege. Under Section 980, both spouses are the holders of the privilege and either spouse may claim it. Under existing law, the privilege may belong only to the nontestifying spouse inasmuch as Code of Civil Procedure Section 1881(1), superseded by the Evidence Code, provides: "[N]or can either . . . be, without the consent of the other, examined as to any communication made by one to the other during the marriage." (Emphasis added.) It is likely, however, that Section 1881(1) would be construed to grant the privilege to both spouses. See In re De Neef, 42 Cal.App.2d 691, 109 P.2d 741 (1941). But see People v. Keller, 165 Cal.App.2d 419, 423-424, 332 P.2d 174, 176 (1958) (dictum).

A guardian of an incompetent spouse may claim the privilege on behalf of that spouse. However, when a spouse is dead, no one can claim the privilege for him; the privilege, if it is to be claimed at all, can be claimed only by or on behalf of the surviving spouse.

Termination of marriage. The privilege may be claimed as to confidential communications made during a marriage even though the marriage has been terminated at the time the privilege is claimed. This states existing law. Code Civ.Proc. § 1881(1) (superseded by the Evidence Code; People v. Mullings, 83 Cal. 138, 23 Pac. 229 (1890). Free and open communication between spouses would be unduly inhibited if one of the spouses could be compelled to testify as to the nature of such communications after the termination of the marriage.

Eavesdroppers. The privilege may be asserted to prevent testimony by anyone, including eavesdroppers. To a limited extent, this constitutes a change in California law. See the Comment to Evidence Code § 954. See generally People v. Peak, 66 Cal.App.2d 894, 153 P.2d 464 (1944); People v. Morhar, 78 Cal.App. 380, 248 Pac. 975 (1926); People v. Mitchell, 61 Cal.App. 569, 215 Pac. 117 (1923). Section 980 also changes the existing law which permits a third party, to whom one of the spouses had revealed a confidential communication, to testify concerning it. People v. Swaile, 12 Cal.App. 192, 195-196, 107 Pac. 134, 137 (1909); People v. Chadwick, 4 Cal.App. 63, 72, 87 Pac. 384, 387, 388 (1906). See also Wolfle v. United States, 291 U.S. 7 (1934). Under Section 912, such conduct would constitute a waiver of the privilege only as to the spouse who makes the disclosure.

§ 981. Exception: Crime or fraud. There is no privilege under this article [§§ 980-987] if the communication was made, in whole or in part, to enable or aid anyone to commit or plan to commit a crime or a fraud.

Law Revision Commission Comment

California recognizes this as an exception to the lawyer-client privilege, but it does not appear to have been recognized in the California cases dealing with the confidential marital communications privilege. Nonetheless, the exception does not seem so broad that it would impair the values that the privilege is intended to preserve; in many cases, the evidence which would be admissible under this exception will be vital in order to do justice between the parties to a lawsuit. This exception would not, of course, infringe on the privileges accorded to a married person under Sections 970 and 971.

It is important to note that the exception provided by Section 981 is quite limited. It does not permit disclosure of communications that merely reveal a plan to commit a crime or fraud; it permits disclosure only of communications made to *enable* or *aid* anyone to commit or plan to commit a crime or fraud. Thus, unless the communication is for the purpose of obtaining assistance in the commission of the crime or fraud or in furtherance thereof, it is not made admissible by the exception provided in this section. Cf. People v. Pierce, 61 Cal.2d 879, 40 Cal.Rptr. 845, 395 P.2d 893 (1964) (husband and wife who conspire only between themselves against others cannot claim immunity from prosecution for conspiracy on the basis of their marital status).

§ 982. Exception: Commitment or similar proceedings. There is no privilege under this article [§§ 980-987] in a proceeding to commit either spouse or otherwise place him or his property, or both, under the control of another because of his alleged mental or physical condition.

Law Revision Commission Comment

* * * Commitment and competency proceedings are undertaken for the benefit of the subject person. Frequently, much or all of the evidence bearing on a spouse's competency or lack of competency will consist of communications to the other spouse. It would be undesirable to permit either spouse to invoke a privilege to prevent the presentation of this vital information inasmuch as these proceedings are of such vital importance both to society and to the spouse who is the subject of the proceedings.

§ 983. Exception: Proceeding to establish competence. There is no privilege under this article [§§ 980-987] in a proceeding brought by or on behalf of either spouse to establish his competence.

Law Revision Commission Comment

See the Comment to Section 982.

§ 984. Exception: Proceeding between spouses. There is no privilege under this article [§§ 980-987] in:

(a) A proceeding brought by or on behalf of one spouse against the other spouse.

(b) A proceeding between a surviving spouse and a person who claims through the deceased spouse, regardless of whether such claim is by testate or intestate succession or by inter vivos transaction.

Law Revision Commission Comment

The exception to the marital communications privilege for litigation between the spouses states existing law. Code Civ.Proc. § 1881(1) (superseded by the Evidence Code). Section 984 extends the principle to cases where one of the spouses is dead and the litigation is between his successor and the surviving spouse. See generally Estate of Gillett, 73 Cal.App.2d 588, 166 P.2d 870 (1946).

§ 985. Exception: Certain criminal proceedings. There is no privilege under this article [§§ 980-987] in a criminal proceeding in which one spouse is charged with:

(a) A crime committed at any time against the person or property of the other spouse or of a child of either.

(b) A crime committed at any time against the person or property of a third person committed in the course of committing a crime against the person or property of the other spouse.

(c) Bigamy.

(d) A crime defined by Section 270 or 270a of the Penal Code. [*Amended 1975.*]

§ 986. Exception: Juvenile court proceeding. There is no privilege under this article [§§ 980-987] in a proceeding under the Juvenile Court Law, Chapter 2 (commencing with Section 200) of Part 1 of Division 2 of the Welfare and Institutions Code. [*Amended 1982.*]

§ 987. Exception: Communication offered by spouse who is criminal defendant. There is no privilege under this article [§§ 980-987] in a criminal proceeding in which the communication is offered in evidence by a defendant who is one of the spouses between whom the communication was made.

Law Revision Commission Comment

This exception does not appear to have been recognized in any California case. Nonetheless, it is a desirable exception. When a married person is the defendant in a criminal proceeding and seeks to introduce evidence which is material to his defense, his spouse (or his former spouse) should not be privileged to withhold the information.

Article 6. Physician-Patient Privilege

§ 990. Physician. As used in this article [§§ 990-1007], "physician" means a person authorized, or reasonably believed by the patient to be authorized, to practice medicine in any state or nation.

Law Revision Commission Comment

Defining "physician" to include a person "reasonably believed by the patient to be authorized" to practice medicine changes the existing law which requires that the physician be licensed. See Code Civ.Proc. § 1881(4) (superseded by the Evidence Code). But, if this privilege is to be recognized, it should protect the patient from reasonable mistakes as to unlicensed practitioners. The privilege also should be applicable to communications made to a physician authorized to practice in any state or nation. When a California resident travels outside the State and has occasion to visit a physician during such travel, or when a physician from another state or nation participates in the treatment of a person in California, the patient should be entitled to assume that his communications will be given as much protection as they would be if he consulted a California physician in California. A patient should not be forced to inquire about the jurisdictions where the physician is authorized to practice medicine and whether such jurisdictions recognize the physician-patient privilege before he may safely communicate with the physician.

§ 991. Patient. As used in this article [§§ 990-1007], "patient" means a person who consults a physician or submits to an examination by a physician for the purpose of securing a diagnosis or preventive, palliative, or curative treatment of his physical or mental or emotional condition.

Senate Committee on Judiciary Comment

"Patient" means a person who consults a physician for the purpose of diagnosis or treatment. This definition modifies existing California law; under existing law, a person who consults a physician for diagnosis only has no physician-patient privilege. City & County of San Francisco v. Superior Court, 37 Cal.2d 227, 231, 231 P.2d 26, 28 (1951) (physician-patient privilege "cannot be invoked when no treatment is contemplated or given").

There seems to be little reason to perpetuate the distinction made between consultations for the purpose of diagnosis and consultations for the purpose of treatment. Persons do not ordinarily consult physicians from idle curiosity. They may be sent by their attorney to obtain a diagnosis in contemplation of some legal proceeding—in which case the attorney-client privilege will afford protection. See, e.g., City & County of San Francisco v. Superior Court, 37 Cal.2d 227, 231 P.2d 26 (1951). They may submit to an examination for insurance purposesCin which case the insurance contract will contain appropriate waiver provisions. They may seek diagnosis from one physician to check the diagnosis made by another. They may seek diagnosis from one physician in contemplation of seeking treatment from another. Communications made under such circumstances are as deserving of protection as are communications made to a treating physician.

§ 992. Confidential communication between patient and physician. As used in this article [§§ 990-1007], "confidential communication between patient and physician" means information, including information obtained by an examination of the patient, transmitted between a patient and his physician in the course of that relationship and in confidence by a means which, so far as the patient is aware, discloses the information to no third persons other than those who are present to further the interest of the patient in the consultation or those to whom disclosure is reasonably necessary for the transmission of the information or the accomplishment of the purpose for which the physician is consulted, and includes a diagnosis made and the advice given by the physician in the course of that relationship. [*Amended 1967.*]

Assembly Committee on Judiciary Comment

This section generally restates existing law, except that it is uncertain whether a doctor's statement to a patient giving his diagnosis is presently covered by the privilege. See Code Civ.Proc. § 1881(4) (superseded by the Evidence Code). See also the Comment to Evidence Code § 952.

The definition here is sufficiently broad to include matters that are not ordinarily thought of as "communications." It is the communications that are defined here, however, to which reference is made throughout the remainder of the article. Under Section 994, the privilege applies to the communications defined here. And the exceptions in Sections 996-1007 that relate to particular communications also apply to the communications defined here. Thus, there is no information protected by the privilege in Section 994 to which the exceptions cannot be applied in an appropriate case.

Law Revision Commission Comment - 1967 Amendment

The express inclusion of "a diagnosis" in the last clause will preclude a possible construction of this section that would leave an uncommunicated diagnosis unprotected by the privilege. Such a construction would virtually destroy the privilege. [8 Cal.L.Rev.Comm. Reports 101 (1967).]

§ 993. Holder of the privilege. As used in this article [§§ 990-1007], "holder of the privilege" means:

(a) The patient when he has no guardian or conservator.

(b) A guardian or conservator of the patient when the patient has a guardian or conservator.

(c) The personal representative of the patient if the patient is dead.

Law Revision Commission Comment

A guardian of the patient is the holder of the privilege if the patient has a guardian. If the patient has separate guardians of his estate and of his person, either guardian may claim the privilege. The provision making the personal representative of the patient the holder of the privilege when the patient is dead may change California law. The existing law may be that the privilege survives the death of the patient in some cases and that no one can waive it on behalf of the patient. See the discussion in Tentative Recommendation and a Study Relating to the Uniform Rules of Evidence (Article V. Privileges), 6 Cal.Law Revision Comm'n, Rep., Rec. & Studies 201, 408-410 (1964). Sections 993 and 994 enable the personal representative to protect the interest of the patient's estate in the confidentiality of these statements and to waive the privilege when the estate would benefit by waiver. When the patient's estate has no interest in preserving confidentiality, or when the estate has been distributed and the representative discharged, the importance of providing complete access to information relevant to a particular proceeding should prevail over whatever remaining interest the decedent may have had in secrecy.

§ 994. Physician-patient privilege. Subject to Section 912 and except as otherwise provided in this article [§§ 990-1007], the patient, whether or not a party, has a privilege to refuse to disclose, and to prevent another from disclosing, a confidential communication between patient and physician if the privilege is claimed by:

(a) The holder of the privilege;

(b) A person who is authorized to claim the privilege by the holder of the privilege; or

(c) The person who was the physician at the time of the confidential communication, but such person may not claim the privilege if there is no holder of the privilege in existence or if he or she is otherwise instructed by a person authorized to permit disclosure.

The relationship of a physician and patient shall exist between a medical or podiatry corporation as defined in the Medical Practice Act and the patient to whom it renders professional services, as well as between such patients and licensed physicians and surgeons employed by such corporation to render services to such patients. The word "persons" as used in this subdivision includes partnerships, corporations, limited liability companies, associations, and other groups and entities. [*Amended 1968, 1980, 1994.*]

Statutory Notes

The 1968 amendment added the last paragraph.

See Health & Safety Code § 120595 (privilege does not apply in proceedings relating to communicable disease prevention and control); Welfare & Inst. Code § 15637 (privilege does not apply to required reports of elder abuse); Govt. Code § 27491.8 (exception for use in coroner's inquest).

Law Revision Commission Comment

This section, like Section 954 (lawyer-client privilege), is based on the premise that the privilege must be claimed by a person who is authorized to claim the privilege. If there is no claim of privilege by a person with authority to make the claim, the evidence is admissible. See the Comments to Evidence Code §§ 993 and 954.

For the reasons indicated in the Comment to Section 954, an eavesdropper or other interceptor of a communication privileged under this section is not permitted to testify to the communication.

§ 995. When physician required to claim privilege. The physician who received or made a communication subject to the privilege under this article [§§ 990-1007] shall claim the privilege whenever he is present when the communication is sought to be disclosed and is authorized to claim the privilege under subdivision (c) of Section 994.

§ 996. Patient-litigant exception. There is no privilege under this article [§§ 990-1007] as to a communication relevant to an issue concerning the condition of the patient if such issue has been tendered by:

(a) The patient;

(b) Any party claiming through or under the patient;

(c) Any party claiming as a beneficiary of the patient through a contract to which the patient is or was a party; or

(d) The plaintiff in an action brought under Section 376 or 377 of the Code of Civil Procedure for damages for the injury or death of the patient.

Law Revision Commission Comment

Section 996 provides that the physician-patient privilege does not exist in any proceeding in which an issue concerning the condition of the patient has been tendered by the patient. If the patient himself tenders the issue of his condition, he should not be able to withhold relevant evidence from the opposing party by the exercise of the physician-patient privilege.

A limited form of this exception is recognized by Code of Civil Procedure Section 1881(4) (superseded by the Evidence Code) which makes the privilege inapplicable in personal injury actions. This exception is also recognized in various types of administrative proceedings where the patient tenders the issue of his condition. E.g., Labor Code §§ 4055, 5701, 5703, 6407, 6408 (proceedings before the Industrial Accident Commission). The exception provided by Section 996 applies not only to proceedings before the Industrial Accident Commission but also to any other proceeding where the patient tenders the issue of his condition. The exception in Section 996 also states existing law in applying the exception to other situations where the patient himself has raised the issue of his condition. In re Cathey, 55 Cal.2d 679, 690-692, 12 Cal.Rptr. 762, 768, 361 P.2d 426, 432 (1961) (prisoner in state medical facility waived physician-patient privilege by putting his mental condition in issue by application for habeas corpus); see also City & County of San Francisco v. Superior Court, 37 Cal.2d 227, 232, 231 P.2d 26, 28 (1951) (personal injury case).

Section 996 also provides that there is no privilege in an action brought under Section 377 of the Code of Civil Procedure (wrongful death). Under Code of Civil Procedure Section 1881(4) (superseded by the Evidence Code), a person authorized to bring the wrongful death action may consent to the testimony by the physician. As far as testimony by the physician is concerned, there is no reason why the rules of evidence should be different in a case where the patient brings the action and a case where someone else sues for the patient's wrongful death.

Section 996 also provides that there is no privilege in an action brought under Section 376 of the Code of Civil Procedure (parent's action for injury to child). In this case, as in a case under the wrongful death statute, the same rule of evidence should apply when the parent brings the action as applies when the child is the plaintiff.

§ 997. Exception: Crime or tort. There is no privilege under this article [§§ 990-1007] if the services of the physician were sought or obtained to enable or aid anyone to commit or plan to commit a crime or a tort or to escape detection or apprehension after the commission of a crime or a tort.

Law Revision Commission Comment

This section is considerably broader in scope than Section 956 which provides that the lawyer-client privilege does not apply when the communication was made to enable anyone to commit or plan to commit a crime or a fraud. Section 997 creates an exception to the physician-patient privilege where the services of the physician were sought or obtained to enable or aid anyone to commit or plan to commit a crime or a tort, or to escape detection or apprehension after commission of a crime or a tort. People seldom, if ever, consult their physicians in regard to matters which might subsequently be determined to be a tort, and there is no desirable end to be served by encouraging such communications. On the other hand, people often consult lawyers about matters which may later turn out to be torts and it is desirable to encourage discussion of such matters with lawyers. * * *

§ 998. Exception: Criminal or disciplinary proceeding. There is no privilege under this article [§§ 990-1007] in a criminal proceeding.

§ 999. Exception: Proceeding to recover damages for criminal conduct. There is no privilege under this article [§§ 990-1007] as to a communication relevant to an issue concerning the condition of the patient in a proceeding to recover damages on account of the conduct of the patient if good cause for disclosure of the communication is shown. [*Amended 1975.*]

Assembly Committee on Judiciary Comment - 1975 Amendment

tSection 999 is amended to provide an exception to the physician-patient privilege where good cause is shown for the disclosure of a relevant communication concerning the condition of a patient in a proceeding to recover damages on account of the conduct of the patient. Section 999 permits the disclosure of communications between patient and physician (see Section 992 broadly defining communication) where a need for such evidence is shown while at the same time protecting from disclosure the communications of persons whose conduct is not involved in the action for damages.

Section 999 permits disclosure not only in a case where the patient is a party to the action but also in a case where a party's liability is based on the conduct of the patient. An example of the latter situation is a personal injury action brought against an employer based on the negligent conduct of his employee who was killed in the accident. On the other hand, the section does not affect the privilege of nonparty patients in malpractice actions. See, e.g., Marcus v. Superior Court, 18 Cal.App.3d 22, 95 Cal.Rptr. 545 (1971). However, even in such malpractice actions, it sometimes may be possible to provide the necessary information without violating the privilege. See Rudnick v. Superior Court, 11 Cal.3d 924, 933 n. 13, 523 P.2d 643, 650-651 n. 13, 114 Cal.Rptr. 603, 610-611 n. 13 (1974).

The requirement that good cause be shown for the disclosure permits the court to protect the defendant against a "fishing expedition" into his medical records. Compare Evid. Code § 996 (patient-litigant exception). It should be noted that the exception provided by Section 999, like the other exceptions in this article, does not apply to the psychotherapist-patient privilege. That privilege is a separate and distinct privilege, and the exceptions to that privilege are much more narrowly drawn. See Evid. Code §§ 1010-1028.

Formerly, Section 999 provided an exception only in a proceeding to recover damages arising out of the criminal conduct of the patient. This "criminal conduct" exception has been eliminated as unnecessary in view of the "good cause" exception now provided by Section 999. Moreover, the "criminal conduct" exception was burdensome, difficult to administer, and ill designed to achieve the purpose of making needed evidence available. See Recommendation Relating to Evidence Code Section 999—"The Criminal Conduct" Exception to the Physician-Patient Privilege, 11 Cal.L. Revision Comm'n Reports 1147 (1973). [75 A.J. 1353]

§ 1000. Exception: Parties claiming through deceased patient. There is no privilege under this article [§§ 990-1007] as to a communication relevant to an issue between parties all of whom claim through a deceased patient, regardless of whether the claims are by testate or intestate succession or by inter vivos transaction.

Law Revision Commission Comment

See the Comment to Section 957.

§ 1001. Exception: Breach of duty arising out of physician-patient relationship. There is no privilege under this article [§§ 990-1007] as to a communication relevant to an issue of breach, by the physician or by the patient, of a duty arising out of the physician-patient relationship.

Law Revision Commission Comment

See the Comment to Section 958.

§ 1002. Exception: Intention of deceased patient concerning writing affecting property interest. There is no privilege under this article [§§ 990-1007] as to a communication relevant to an issue concerning the intention of a patient, now deceased, with respect to a deed of conveyance, will, or other writing, executed by the patient, purporting to affect an interest in property.

Law Revision Commission Comment

* * * See the Comment to Section 960.

§ 1003. Exception: Validity of writing affecting property interest. There is no privilege under this article [§§ 990-1007] as to a communication relevant to an issue concerning the validity of a deed of conveyance, will, or other writing, executed by a patient, now deceased, purporting to affect an interest in property.

§ 1004. Exception: Commitment or similar proceeding. There is no privilege under this article [§§ 990-1007] in a proceeding to commit the patient or otherwise place him or his property, or both, under the control of another because of his alleged mental or physical condition.

Law Revision Commission Comment

This exception covers not only commitments of mentally ill persons but also such cases as the appointment of a conservator under Probate Code Section 1751. In these cases, the proceedings are being conducted for the benefit of the patient and he should not have a privilege to withhold evidence that the court needs in order to act properly for his welfare. * * *

§ 1005. Exception: Proceeding to establish competence. There is no privilege under this article [§§ 990-1007] in a proceeding brought by or on behalf of the patient to establish his competence.

Law Revision Commission Comment

This exception is new to California law. When a patient has placed his mental condition in issue by instituting a proceeding to establish his competence, he should not be permitted to withhold the most vital evidence relating thereto.

§ 1006. Exception: Required report. There is no privilege under this article [§§ 990-1007] as to information that the physician or the patient is required to report to a public employee, or as to information required to be recorded in a public office, if such report or record is open to public inspection.

Law Revision Commission Comment

This exception is not recognized by existing law. However, no valid purpose is served by preventing the use of relevant information when the law requiring the information to be reported to a public office does not restrict disclosure.

§ 1007. Proceeding to terminate right, license or privilege. There is no privilege under this article [§§ 990-1007] in a proceeding brought by a public entity to determine whether a right, authority, license, or privilege (including the right or privilege to be employed by the public entity or to hold a public office) should be revoked, suspended, terminated, limited, or conditioned.

Assembly Committee on Judiciary Comment

Section 998 provides that the physician-patient privilege does not apply in criminal proceedings. Section 1007 provides that the physician-patient privilege may not be claimed in those administrative proceedings that are comparable to criminal proceedings, i.e., proceedings brought for the purpose of imposing discipline of some sort. Under existing law, the physician-patient privilege is available in all administrative proceedings conducted under the Administrative Procedure Act because it has been incorporated by reference in Government Code Section 11513 (c); but it is not specifically made available in administrative proceedings not conducted under the Administrative Procedure Act because the statute granting the privilege in terms applies only to civil actions. The Evidence Code sweeps away this distinction, which has no basis in reason, and conditions the availability of the privilege in administrative proceedings on the nature of the proceeding in which the privilege is invoked.

Article 7. Psychotherapist-Patient Privilege

§ 1010. Psychotherapist. As used in this article, "psychotherapist" means a person who is, or is reasonably believed by the patient to be:

(a) A person authorized to practice medicine in any state or nation who devotes, or is reasonably believed by the patient to devote, a substantial portion of his or her time to the practice of psychiatry.

(b) A person licensed as a psychologist under Chapter 6.6 (commencing with Section 2900) of Division 2 of the Business and Professions Code.

(c) A person licensed as a clinical social worker under Chapter 14 (commencing with Section 4991) of Division 2 of the Business and Professions Code, when he or she is engaged in applied psychotherapy of a nonmedical nature.

(d) A person who is serving as a school psychologist and holds a credential authorizing that service issued by the state.

(e) A person licensed as a marriage and family therapist under Chapter 13 (commencing with Section 4980) of Division 2 of the Business and Professions Code.

(f) A person registered as a psychological assistant who is under the supervision of a licensed psychologist or board certified psychiatrist as required by Section 2913 of the Business and Professions Code, or a person registered as an associate marriage and family therapist who is under the supervision of a licensed marriage and family therapist, a licensed clinical social worker, a licensed psychologist, or a licensed physician and surgeon certified in psychiatry, as specified in Section 4980.44 of the Business and Professions Code.

(g) A person registered as an associate clinical social worker who is under supervision as specified in Section 4996.23 of the Business and Professions Code.

(h) A person registered with the Board of Psychology as a registered psychologist who is under the supervision of a licensed psychologist or board certified psychiatrist.

(i) A psychological intern as defined in Section 2911 of the Business and Professions Code who is under the supervision of a licensed psychologist or board certified psychiatrist.

(j) A trainee, as defined in subdivision (c) of Section 4980.03 of the Business and Professions Code, who is fulfilling his or her supervised practicum required by subparagraph (B) of paragraph (1) of subdivision (d) of Section 4980.36 of, or subdivision (c) of Section 4980.37 of, the Business and Professions Code and is supervised by a licensed psychologist, a board certified psychiatrist, a licensed clinical social worker, a licensed marriage and family therapist, or a licensed professional clinical counselor.

(k) A person licensed as a registered nurse pursuant to Chapter 6 (commencing with Section 2700) of Division 2 of the Business and Professions Code, who possesses a master's degree in psychiatric-mental health nursing and is listed as a psychiatric-mental health nurse by the Board of Registered Nursing.

(l) An advanced practice registered nurse who is certified as a clinical nurse specialist pursuant to Article 9 (commencing with Section 2838) of Chapter 6 of Division 2 of the Business and Professions Code and who participates in expert clinical practice in the specialty of psychiatric-mental health nursing.

(m) A person rendering mental health treatment or counseling services as authorized pursuant to Section 6924 of the Family Code.

(n) A person licensed as a professional clinical counselor under Chapter 16 (commencing with Section 4999.10) of Division 2 of the Business and Professions Code.

(o) A person registered as an associate professional clinical counselor who is under the supervision of a licensed professional clinical counselor, a licensed marriage and family therapist, a licensed clinical social worker, a licensed psychologist, or a licensed physician and surgeon certified in psychiatry, as specified in Sections 4999.42 to 4999.48, inclusive, of the Business and Professions Code.

(p) A clinical counselor trainee, as defined in subdivision (g) of Section 4999.12 of the Business and Professions Code, who is fulfilling his or her supervised practicum required by paragraph (3) of subdivision (c) of Section 4999.32 of, or paragraph (3) of subdivision (c) of Section 4999.33 of, the Business and Professions Code, and is supervised by a licensed psychologist, a board-certified psychiatrist, a licensed clinical social worker, a licensed marriage and family therapist, or a licensed professional clinical counselor. [*Amended 1967, 1970, 1972, 1974, 1983, 1987, 1988, 1989. 1990, 1992, 1994, 2001, 2009, 2015, 2016, 2018.*]

Statutory Note

The 2001 amendment transferred from subdivision (a) to the opening clause the language, "a person who is, or is reasonably believed by the patient to be." Subdivisions (c) through (m) were added by successive amendments from 1970 through 2001.

Section 1 of Stats. 1992, c. 308 (A.B. 3035), which added subdivision (k), declared:

The Legislature finds and declares that registered nurses who have a master's of science degree in psychiatric mental health nursing are an important resource for providing psychotherapeutic services to individuals, groups, and families throughout California, and particularly to impoverished, minority, and other underserved populations. These master's-level psychiatric mental health nurses have been eligible for private insurance reimbursement since 1982. They are currently providing psychotherapeutic services in a wide range of clinical settings, including hospitals, clinics, and private practices. However, they are not included within the current legal definition of "psychotherapist" for purposes of the patient-psychotherapist evidentiary privilege. Because of this, their patients' communications are not privileged, and these patients are thus treated differently from patients served by other psychotherapists. This creates difficulties for these patients in accessing the care provided by these competent and duly licensed mental health professionals.

In order for patients served by master's-level psychiatric mental health nurses to be treated under the law on the same basis as other patients, it is necessary to identify these providers as "psychotherapists" for purposes of the patient-psychotherapist privilege.

Law Revision Commission Comment

A "psychotherapist" is defined to include only a person who is or who is reasonably believed to be a psychiatrist or who is a California certified psychologist (see Bus. & Prof.Code § 2900 et seq.). See the Comment to Section 990.

§ 1010.5. Privileged communication between patient and educational psychologist. A communication between a patient and an educational psychologist, licensed under Article 5 (commencing with Section 4986) of Chapter 13 of Division 2 of the Business and Professions Code, shall be privileged to the same extent, and subject to the same limitations, as a communication between a patient and a psychotherapist described in subdivisions (c), (d), and (e) of Section 1010. [*Added 1985.*]

§ 1011. Patient. As used in this article [§§ 1010-1027], "patient" means a person who consults a psychotherapist or submits to an examination by a psychotherapist for the purpose of securing a diagnosis or preventive, palliative, or curative treatment of his mental or emotional condition or who submits to an examination of his mental or emotional condition for the purpose of scientific research on mental or emotional problems.

Assembly Committee on Judiciary Comment

See the Comment to Section 991. Section 1011 is comparable to Section 991 (physician-patient privilege) except that the definition of "patient" in Section 1011 includes not only persons seeking diagnosis or treatment of a mental or emotional condition but also persons who submit to examination for purposes of psychiatric or psychological research. See the Comment to Section 1014.

§ 1012. Confidential communication between patient and psychotherapist. As used in this article [§§ 1010-1027], "confidential communication between patient and psychotherapist" means information, including information obtained by an examination of the patient, transmitted between a patient and his psychotherapist in the course of that relationship and in confidence by a means which, so far as the patient is aware, discloses the information to no third persons other than those who are present to further the interest of the patient in the consultation, or those to whom disclosure is reasonably necessary for the transmission of the information or the accomplishment of the purpose for which the psychotherapist is consulted, and includes a diagnosis made and the advice given by the psychotherapist in the course of that relationship. [*Amended 1967, 1970.*]

Case Notes

The participants' motives are largely immaterial in determining whether a communication satisfies the requirements of this section. Apart from the crime-tort exception (§ 1018), the dispositive fact is what the participants do, not why. Menendez v. Superior Court, 3 Cal. 4th 435, 454, 11 Cal. Rptr. 2d 92, 104, 834 P.2d 786, 798 (1992).

The presence of an eavesdropper, unknown to the patient, does not prevent a communication from being made "in confidence." Menendez v. Superior Court, 3 Cal. 4th 435, 447-450, 11 Cal. Rptr. 2d 92, 99-100, 834 P.2d 786, 793-794 (1992).

Law Revision Commission Comment

See the Comment to Section 992.

Law Revision Commission Comment - 1967 Amendment

The express inclusion of "a diagnosis" in the last clause will preclude a possible construction of this section that would leave an uncommunicated diagnosis unprotected by the privilege. Such a construction would virtually destroy the privilege. [8 Cal.L.Rev.Comm. Reports 101 (1967).]

Law Revision Commission Comment - 1970 Amendment

Section 1012 is amended to add "including other patients present at joint therapy" in order to foreclose the possibility that the section would be construed not to embrace marriage counseling, family counseling, and other forms of group therapy. However, it should be noted that communications made in the course of joint therapy are within the privilege only if they are made "in confidence" and "by a means which ... discloses the information to no third persons other than those ... to whom disclosure is reasonably necessary for ... the accomplishment of the purpose for which the psychotherapist is consulted." The making of a communication that meets these two requirements in the course of joint therapy would not amount to a waiver of the privilege. See Evidence Code Section 912(c) and (d). * * * [9 Cal.L.Rev.Comm. Reports 153 (1969).]

§ 1013. Holder of the privilege. As used in this article [§§ 1010-1027], "holder of the privilege" means:

(a) The patient when he has no guardian or conservator.

(b) A guardian or conservator of the patient when the patient has a guardian or conservator.

(c) The personal representative of the patient if the patient is dead.

Law Revision Commission Comment

See the Comment to Section 993.

§ 1014. Psychotherapist-patient privilege. Subject to Section 912 and except as otherwise provided in this article [§§ 1010-1027], the patient, whether or not a party, has a privilege to refuse to disclose, and to prevent another from disclosing, a confidential communication between patient and psychotherapist if the privilege is claimed by:

(a) The holder of the privilege.

(b) A person who is authorized to claim the privilege by the holder of the privilege.

(c) The person who was the psychotherapist at the time of the confidential communication, but the person may not claim the privilege if there is no holder of the privilege in existence or if he or she is otherwise instructed by a person authorized to permit disclosure.

The relationship of a psychotherapist and patient shall exist between a psychological corporation as defined in Article 9 (commencing with Section 2995) of Chapter 6.6 of Division 2 of the Business and Professions Code, a marriage and family therapy corporation as defined in Article 6 (commencing with Section 4987.5) of Chapter 13 of Division 2 of the Business and Professions Code, or a licensed clinical social workers corporation as defined in Article 5 (commencing with Section 4998) of Chapter 14 of Division 2 of the Business and Professions Code, and the patient to whom it renders professional services, as well as between those patients and psychotherapists employed by those corporations to render services to those patients. The word "persons" as used in this subdivision includes partnerships, corporations, limited liability companies, associations and other groups and entities. [*Amended 1969, 1972, 1989, 1990, 1994, 2002.*]

Statutory Notes

The 1969 amendment added the last paragraph, which was added to by the 1972, 1990, and 1994 amendments.

See Health & Safety Code § 120595 (privilege does not apply in proceedings relating to communicable disease prevention and control); Welfare & Inst. Code § 15637 (privilege does not apply to required reports of elder abuse); Govt. Code § 27491.8 (exception for use in coroner's inquest).

Case Note

Apart from statutory exceptions, the patient controls the privilege. The privilege to prevent disclosure by another survives broad disclosures of confidential communications as long as the disclosures were not made or authorized by the patient. These include unauthorized disclosures by the therapist as well as by third parties, such as eavesdroppers, interceptors, and finders. Despite such widespread disclosures, the patient may prevent further disclosures in legal proceedings. Menendez v. Superior Court, 3 Cal. 4th 435, 447-450, 11 Cal. Rptr. 2d 92, 99-100, 834 P.2d 786, 793-794 (1992).

Senate Committee on Judiciary Comment

This article creates a psychotherapist-patient privilege that provides much broader protection than the physician-patient privilege.

Psychiatrists now have only the physician-patient privilege which is enjoyed by physicians generally. On the other hand, persons who consult certified psychologists have a much broader privilege under Business and Professions Code Section 2904 (superseded by the Evidence Code). There is no rational basis for this distinction.

A broad privilege should apply to both psychiatrists and certified psychologists. Psychoanalysis and psychotherapy are dependent upon the fullest revelation of the most intimate and embarrassing details of the patient's life. Research on mental or emotional problems requires similar disclosure. Unless a patient or research subject is assured that such information can and will be held in utmost confidence, he will be reluctant to make the full disclosure upon which diagnosis and treatment or complete and accurate research depends.

The Law Revision Commission has received several reliable reports that persons in need of treatment sometimes refuse such treatment from psychiatrists because the confidentiality of their communications cannot be assured under existing law. Many of these persons are seriously disturbed and constitute threats to other persons in the community. Accordingly, this article establishes a new privilege that grants to patients of psychiatrists a privilege much broader in scope than the ordinary physician-patient privilege. Although it is recognized that the granting of the privilege may operate in particular cases to withhold relevant information, the interests of society will be better served if psychiatrists are able to assure patients that their confidences will be protected.

The Commission has also been informed that adequate research cannot be carried on in this field unless persons examined in connection therewith can be guaranteed that their disclosures will be kept confidential.

The privilege also applies to psychologists and supersedes the psychologist-patient privilege provided in Section 2904 of the Business and Professions Code. The new privilege is one for psychotherapists generally.

Generally, the privilege provided by this article follows the physician-patient privilege, and the Comments to Sections 990 through 1007 are pertinent. The following differences, however, should be noted:

(1) The psychotherapist-patient privilege applies in all proceedings. The physician-patient privilege does not apply in criminal proceedings. This difference in the scope of the two privileges is based on the fact that the Law Revision Commission has been advised that proper psychotherapy often is denied a patient solely because he will not walk freely to a psychotherapist for fear that the latter may be compelled in a criminal proceeding to reveal what he has been told. The Commission has also been advised that research in this field will be unduly hampered unless the privilege is available in criminal proceedings. Although the psychotherapist-patient privilege applies in a criminal proceeding, the privilege is not available to a defendant who puts his mental or emotional condition in issue, as, for example, by a plea of insanity or a claim of diminished responsibility. See Evidence Code §§ 1016 and 1023. In such a proceeding, the trier of fact should have available to it all information that can be obtained in regard to the defendant's mental or emotional condition. That evidence can often be furnished by the psychotherapist who examined or treated the patient-defendant.

(2) There is an exception in the physician-patient privilege for commitment or guardianship proceedings for the patient. Evidence Code § 1004. Section 1024 provides a considerably narrower exception in the psychotherapist-patient privilege.

(3) The physician-patient privilege does not apply in civil actions for damages arising out of the patient's criminal conduct. Evidence Code § 999. Nor does it apply in certain administrative proceedings. Evidence Code § 1007. No similar exceptions are provided in the psychotherapist-patient privilege. These exceptions appear in the physician-patient privilege because that privilege does not apply in criminal proceedings. See Evidence Code § 998. Therefore, an exception is also created for comparable civil and administrative cases. The psychotherapist-patient privilege, however, does apply in criminal cases; hence, there is no similar exception in administrative proceedings or civil actions involving the patient's criminal conduct.

§ 1015. When psychotherapist required to claim privilege. The psychotherapist who received or made a communication subject to the privilege under this article [§§ 1010-1027] shall claim the privilege whenever he is present when the communication is sought to be disclosed and is authorized to claim the privilege under subdivision (c) of Section 1014.

Law Revision Commission Comment

See the Comment to Section 995.

§ 1016. Exception: Patient-litigant exception. There is no privilege under this article [§§ 1010-1027] as to a communication relevant to an issue concerning the mental or emotional condition of the patient if such issue has been tendered by:

(a) The patient;

(b) Any party claiming through or under the patient;

(c) Any party claiming as a beneficiary of the patient through a contract to which the patient is or was a party; or

(d) The plaintiff in an action brought under Section 376 or 377 of the Code of Civil Procedure for damages for the injury or death of the patient.

Law Revision Commission Comment

See the Comment to Section 996.

§ 1017. Exception: Court-appointed psychotherapist. (a) There is no privilege under this article [§§ 1010-1027] if the psychotherapist is appointed by order of a court to examine the patient, but this exception does not apply where the psychotherapist is appointed by order of the court upon the request of the lawyer for the defendant in a criminal proceeding in order to provide the lawyer with information needed so that he or she may advise the defendant whether to enter or withdraw a plea based on insanity or to present a defense based on his or her mental or emotional condition.

(b) There is no privilege under this article [§§ 1010-1027] if the psychotherapist is appointed by the Board of Prison Terms to examine a patient pursuant to the provisions of Article 4 (commencing with Section 2960) of Chapter 7 of Title 1 of Part 3 of the Penal Code. [*Amended 1967, 1987.*]

Statutory Note

The power of courts to order mental examinations of *witnesses* in criminal cases (established in Ballard v. Superior Ct., 64 Cal. 2d 159, 49 Cal. Rptr.. 302, 410 P.2d 838 (1966)) is restricted by Penal Code § 1112, which provides:

Notwithstanding the provisions of subdivision (d) of Section 28 of Article I of the California Constitution, the trial court shall not order any prosecuting witness, complaining witness, or any other witness, or victim in any sexual assault prosecution to submit to a psychiatric or psychological examination for the purpose of assessing his or her credibility.

Mental examinations in civil cases are governed by Code Civ. Proc. § 2032.

Law Revision Commission Comment

Section 1017 provides an exception to the psychotherapist-patient privilege if the psychotherapist is appointed by order of a court to examine the patient. Generally, where the relationship of psychotherapist and patient is created by court order, there is not a sufficiently confidential relationship to warrant extending the privilege to communications made in the course of that relationship. Moreover, when the psychotherapist is appointed by the court, it is most often for the purpose of having the psychotherapist testify concerning his conclusions as to the patient's condition. It would be inappropriate to have the privilege apply in this situation. See generally 35 Ops.Cal.Atty.Gen. 226 (1960), regarding the unavailability of the present physician-patient privilege under these circumstances.

On the other hand, it is essential that the privilege apply where the psychotherapist is appointed by order of the court to provide the defendant's lawyer with information needed so that he may advise the defendant whether to enter a plea based on insanity or to present a defense based on his mental or emotional condition. If the defendant determines not to tender the issue of his mental or emotional condition, the privilege will protect the confidentiality of the communication between him and his court-appointed psychotherapist. If, however, the defendant determines to tender this issue—by a plea of not guilty by reason of insanity, by presenting a defense based on his mental or emotional condition, or by raising the question of his sanity at the time of the trial—the exceptions provided in Sections 1016 and 1023 make the privilege unavailable to prevent disclosure of the communications between the defendant and the psychotherapist.

Law Revision Commission Comment - 1967 Amendment

The words "or withdraw" are added to Section 1017 to make it clear that the psychotherapist-patient privilege applies in a case where the defendant in a criminal proceeding enters a plea based on insanity, submits to an examination by a court-appointed psychotherapist, and later withdraws the plea based on insanity prior to the trial on that issue. In such case, since the defendant does not tender an issue based on his mental or emotional condition at the trial, the privilege should remain applicable. Of course, if the defendant determines to go to trial on the plea based on insanity, the psychotherapist-patient privilege will not be applicable. See Section 1016.

It should be noted that violation of the constitutional right to counsel may require the exclusion of evidence that is not privileged under this article; and, even in cases where this constitutional right is not violated, the protection that this right affords may require certain procedural safeguards in the examination procedure and a limiting instruction if the psychotherapist's testimony is admitted. See In re Spencer, 63 Cal.2d 400, 46 Cal.Rptr. 753, 406 P.2d 33 (1965).

It is important to recognize that the attorney-client privilege may provide protection in some cases where an exception to the psychotherapist-patient privilege is applicable. See Section 952 and the Comment thereto. See also Sections 912(d) and 954 and the Comments thereto. [8 Cal.L.Rev.Comm. Reports 101 (1967).]

§ 1018. Exception: Crime or tort. There is no privilege under this article [§§ 1010-1027] if the services of the psychotherapist were sought or obtained to enable or aid anyone to commit or plan to commit a crime or a tort or to escape detection or apprehension after the commission of a crime or a tort.

Law Revision Commission Comment

See the Comment to Section 997.

§ 1019. Exception: Parties claiming through deceased patient. There is no privilege under this article [§§ 1010-1027] as to a communication relevant to an issue between parties all of whom claim through a deceased patient, regardless of whether the claims are by testate or intestate succession or by inter vivos transaction.

Law Revision Commission Comment

See the Comment to Section 957.

§ 1020. Exception: Breach of duty arising out of psychotherapist-patient relationship. There is no privilege under this article [§§ 1010-1027] as to a communication relevant to an issue of breach, by the psychotherapist or by the patient, of a duty arising out of the psychotherapist-patient relationship.

Law Revision Commission Comment

See the Comment to Section 958.

§ 1021. Exception: Intention of deceased patient concerning writing affecting property interest. There is no privilege under this article [§§ 1010-1027] as to a communication relevant to an issue concerning the intention of a patient, now deceased, with respect to a deed of conveyance, will, or other writing, executed by the patient, purporting to affect an interest in property.

Law Revision Commission Comment

See the Comment to Section 1002.

§ 1022. Exception: Validity of writing affecting property interest. There is no privilege under this article [§§ 1010-1027] as to a communication relevant to an issue concerning the validity of a deed of conveyance, will, or other writing, executed by a patient, now deceased, purporting to affect an interest in property.

Law Revision Commission Comment

See the Comment to Section 1002.

§ 1023. Exception: Proceeding to determine sanity of criminal defendant. There is no privilege under this article [§§ 1010-1027] in a proceeding under Chapter 6 (commencing with Section 1367) of Title 10 of Part 2 of the Penal Code initiated at the request of the defendant in a criminal action to determine his sanity.

Statutory Note

Penal Code § 1367 refers to "mental competence," not "sanity."

Law Revision Commission Comment

Section 1023 is included to make it clear that the psychotherapist-patient privilege does not apply when the defendant raises the issue of his sanity at the time of trial. The section probably is unnecessary because the exception provided by Section 1016 is broad enough to cover this situation.

§ 1024. Exception: Patient dangerous to himself or others. There is no privilege under this article [§§ 1010-1027] if the psychotherapist has reasonable cause to believe that the patient is in such mental or emotional condition as to be dangerous to himself or to the person or property of another and that disclosure of the communication is necessary to prevent the threatened danger.

Case Note

Section 1024 permits a psychotherapist not only to warn a potential victim but also in a later trial to reveal both the substance of the warning and the patient's statements that triggered the warning. Statements made in therapy that did not trigger the warning may not be revealed pursuant to this section. People v. Wharton, 53 Cal. 3d 522, 552-563, 280 Cal. Rptr. 631, 647-655, 809 P.2d 290, 307-314 (1991).

Law Revision Commission Comment

This section provides a narrower exception to the psychotherapist-patient privilege than the comparable exceptions provided by Section 982 (privilege for confidential marital communications) and Section 1004 (physician-patient privilege). Although this exception might inhibit the relationship between the patient and his psychotherapist to a limited extent, it is essential that appropriate action be taken if the psychotherapist becomes convinced during the course of treatment that the patient is a menace to himself or others and the patient refuses to permit the psychotherapist to make the disclosure necessary to prevent the threatened danger.

§ 1025. Exception: Proceeding to establish competence. There is no privilege under this article [§§ 1010-1027] in a proceeding brought by or on behalf of the patient to establish his competence.

Law Revision Commission Comment

See the Comment to Section 1005.

§ 1026. Exception: Required report. There is no privilege under this article [§§ 1010-1027] as to information that the psychotherapist or the patient is required to report to a public employee or as to information required to be recorded in a public office, if such report or record is open to public inspection.

Law Revision Commission Comment

See the Comment to Section 1006.

§ 1027. Exception: Child under 16 victim of crime. There is no privilege under this article [§§ 1010-1027] if all of the following circumstances exist:

(a) The patient is a child under the age of 16.

(b) The psychotherapist has reasonable cause to believe that the patient has been the victim of a crime and that disclosure of the communication is in the best interest of the child. [*Added 1970.*]

Law Revision Commission Comment - 1970 Addition

Section 1027 provides an exception to the psychotherapist-patient privilege that is analogous to the exception provided by Section 1024 (patient dangerous to himself or others). The exception provided by Section 1027 is necessary to permit court disclosure of communications to a psychotherapist by a child who has been the victim of a crime (such as child abuse) in a proceeding in which the commission of such crime is a subject of inquiry. Although the exception provided by Section 1027 might inhibit the relationship between the patient and his psychotherapist to a limited extent, it is essential that appropriate action be taken if the psychotherapist becomes convinced during the course of treatment that the patient is the victim of a crime and that disclosure of the communication would be in the best interest of the child. * * * [9 Cal.L.Rev.Comm. Reports 137 (1970).]

Article 8. Clergy-Penitent Privileges

§ 1030. Member of the Clergy. As used in this article [§§ 1030-1034], a "member of the clergy" means a priest, minister, religious practitioner, or similar functionary of a church or of a religious denomination or religious organization. [*Amended 2002.*]

Statutory Note

The 2002 amendments gender neutralized all of Article 8.

Law Revision Commission Comment

"Clergyman" is broadly defined in this section.

§ 1031. Penitent. As used in this article [§§ 1030-1034], "penitent" means a person who has made a penitential communication to a member of the clergy. [*Amended 2002.*]

Law Revision Commission Comment

This section defines "penitent" by incorporating the definitions in Sections 1030 and 1032.

§ 1032. Penitential communication. As used in this article [§§ 1030-1034], "penitential communication" means a communication made in confidence, in the presence of no third person so far as the penitent is aware, to a member of the clergy who, in the course of the discipline or practice of the clergy member's church, denomination, or organization, is authorized or accustomed to hear those communications and, under the discipline or tenets of his or her church, denomination, or organization, has a duty to keep those communications secret. [*Amended 2002.*]

Law Revision Commission Comment

Under existing law, the communication must be a "confession." Code Civ.Proc. § 1881(3) (superseded by the Evidence Code). Section 1032 extends the protection that traditionally has been provided only to those persons whose religious practice involves "confessions."

§ 1033. Privilege of penitent. Subject to Section 912, a penitent, whether or not a party, has a privilege to refuse to disclose, and to prevent another from disclosing, a penitential communication if he or she claims the privilege. [*Amended 2002.*]

Law Revision Commission Comment

This section provides the penitent with a privilege to refuse to disclose, and to prevent another from disclosing, a penitential communication. Because of the definition of "penitential communication," Section 1033 provides a broader privilege than the existing law.

Section 1033 differs from Code of Civil Procedure Section 1881(3) (superseded by the Evidence Code) in that Section 1881(3) gives a penitent a privilege only to prevent a clergyman from disclosing the communication. Literally, Section 1881(3) does not give the penitent himself the right to refuse disclosure. However, similar privilege statutes have been held to grant a privilege both to refuse to disclose and to prevent the other communicant from disclosing the privileged statement. See City & County of San Francisco v. Superior Court, 37 Cal.2d 227, 236, 231 P.2d 26, 31 (1951) (attorney-client privilege); Verdelli v. Gray's Harbor Commercial Co., 115 Cal. 517, 525-526, 47 Pac. 364, 366 (1897) ("a client cannot be compelled to disclose communications which his attorney cannot be permitted to disclose"). Hence, it is likely that Section 1881(3) would be similarly construed.

Section 1033 also protects against disclosure by eavesdroppers. In this respect, the section provides the same scope of protection that is provided by the other confidential communication privileges. See the Comment to Section 954.

§ 1034. Privilege of clergy. Subject to Section 912, a member of the clergy, whether or not a party, has a privilege to refuse to disclose a penitential communication if he or she claims the privilege. [*Amended 2002.*]

Law Revision Commission Comment

This section provides the clergyman with a privilege in his own right. Moreover, he may claim this privilege even if the penitent has waived the privilege granted him by Section 1033.

There may be several reasons for granting clergyman the traditional priest-penitent privilege. At least one underlying reason seems to be that the law will not compel a clergyman to violate—nor punish him for refusing to violate—the tenets of his church which require him to maintain secrecy as to confidential statements made to him in the course of his religious duties. See generally 8 Wigmore, Evidence §§ 2394-2396 (McNaughton rev. 1961).

The clergyman is under no legal compulsion to claim the privilege. Hence, a penitential communication will be admitted if the clergyman fails to claim the privilege and the penitent is deceased, incompetent, absent, or fails to claim the privilege. This probably changes existing law; but, if so, the change is desirable. For example, if a murderer had confessed the crime to a clergyman, the clergyman might under some circumstances (e.g., if the murderer has died) decline to claim the privilege and instead, give the evidence on behalf of an innocent third party who had been indicted for the crime. The extent to which a clergyman should keep secret or reveal penitential communications is not an appropriate subject for legislation; the matter is better left to the discretion of the individual clergyman involved and the discipline of the religious body of which he is a member.

Article 8.5. Sexual Assault Victim-Counselor Privilege

§ 1035. Victim. As used in this article [§§ 1035-1036.2], "victim" means a person who consults a sexual assault counselor for the purpose of securing advice or assistance concerning a mental, physical, or emotional condition caused by a sexual assault. [*Added 1980. Amended 2006.*]

§ 1035.2. Sexual assault counselor.

As used in this article, "sexual assault counselor" means any of the following:

(a) A person who is engaged in any office, hospital, institution, or center commonly known as a rape crisis center, whose primary purpose is the rendering of advice or assistance to victims of sexual assault and who has received a certificate evidencing completion of a training program in the counseling of sexual assault victims issued by a counseling center that meets the criteria for the award of a grant established pursuant to Section 13837 of the Penal Code and who meets one of the following requirements:

(1) Is a psychotherapist as defined in Section 1010; has a master's degree in counseling or a related field; or has one year of counseling experience, at least six months of which is in rape crisis counseling.

(2) Has 40 hours of training as described below and is supervised by an individual who qualifies as a counselor under paragraph (1). The training, supervised by a person qualified under paragraph (1), shall include, but not be limited to, the following areas:

(A) Law.
(B) Medicine.
(C) Societal attitudes.
(D) Crisis intervention and counseling techniques.
(E) Role playing.
(F) Referral services.
(G) Sexuality.

(b) A person who is employed by any organization providing the programs specified in Section 13835.2 of the Penal Code, whether financially compensated or not, for the purpose of counseling and assisting sexual assault victims, and who meets one of the following requirements:

(1) Is a psychotherapist as defined in Section 1010; has a master's degree in counseling or a related field; or has one year of counseling experience, at least six months of which is in rape assault counseling.

(2) Has the minimum training for sexual assault counseling required by guidelines established by the employing agency pursuant to subdivision (c) of Section 13835.10 of the Penal Code, and is supervised by an individual who qualifies as a counselor under paragraph (1). The training, supervised by a person qualified under paragraph (1), shall include, but not be limited to, the following areas:

(A) Law.
(B) Victimology.
(C) Counseling.
(D) Client and system advocacy.
(E) Referral services.

(c) A person who is employed by any organization providing the programs specified in Section 13835.2 of the Penal Code, whether financially compensated or not, for the purpose of counseling and assisting sexual assault victims, and who meets one of the following requirements:

(1) Is a psychotherapist as defined in Section 1010; has a master's degree in counseling or a related field; or has one year of counseling experience, at least six months of which is in rape assault counseling.

(2) Has the minimum training for sexual assault counseling required by guidelines established by the employing agency pursuant to subdivision (c) of Section 13835.10 of the Penal Code, and is supervised by an individual who qualifies as a counselor under paragraph (1). The training, supervised by a person qualified under paragraph (1), shall include, but not be limited to, the following areas:

(A) Law.
(B) Victimology.
(C) Counseling.
(D) Client and system advocacy.
(E) Referral services.

[Added 1980. Amended 1983, 1990, 2006, 2017.]

§ 1035.4. Confidential communication between the sexual assault counselor and the victim; disclosure. As used in this article [§§ 1035-1036.2], "confidential communication between the sexual assault counselor and the victim" means information transmitted between the victim and the sexual assault counselor in the course of their relationship and in confidence by a means which, so far as the victim is aware, discloses the information to no third persons other than those who are present to further the interests of the victim in the consultation or those to whom disclosures are reasonably necessary for the transmission of the information or an accomplishment of the purposes for which the sexual assault counselor is consulted. The term includes all information regarding the facts and circumstances involving the alleged sexual assault and also includes all information regarding the victim's prior or subsequent sexual conduct, and opinions regarding the victim's sexual conduct or reputation in sexual matters.

The court may compel disclosure of information received by the sexual assault counselor which constitutes relevant evidence of the facts and circumstances involving an alleged sexual assault about which the victim is complaining and which is the subject of a criminal proceeding if the court determines that the probative value outweighs the effect on the victim, the treatment relationship, and the treatment services if disclosure is compelled. The court may also compel disclosure in proceedings related to child abuse if the court determines the probative value outweighs the effect on the victim, the treatment relationship, and the treatment services if disclosure is compelled.

When a court is ruling on a claim of privilege under this article [§§ 1035-1036.2], the court may require the person from whom disclosure is sought or the person authorized to claim the privilege, or both, to disclose the information in chambers out of the presence and hearing of all persons except the person authorized to claim the privilege and such other persons as the person authorized to claim the privilege is willing to have present. If the judge determines that the information is privileged and must not be disclosed, neither he or she nor any other person may ever disclose, without the consent of a person authorized to permit disclosure, what was disclosed in the course of the proceedings in chambers.

If the court determines certain information shall be disclosed, the court shall so order and inform the defendant. If the court finds there is a reasonable likelihood that particular information is subject to disclosure pursuant to the balancing test provided in this section, the following procedure shall be followed:

(1) The court shall inform the defendant of the nature of the information which may be subject to disclosure.

(2) The court shall order a hearing out of the presence of the jury, if any, and at the hearing allow the questioning of the sexual assault counselor regarding the information which the court has determined may be subject to disclosure.

(3) At the conclusion of the hearing, the court shall rule which items of information, if any, shall be disclosed. The court may make an order stating what evidence may be introduced by the defendant and the nature of questions to be permitted. The defendant may then offer evidence pursuant to the order of the court. Admission of evidence concerning the sexual conduct of the complaining witness is subject to Sections 352, 782, and 1103. [*Added 1980. Amended 1983.*]

§ 1035.6. Holder of the privilege. As used in this article [§§ 1035-1036.2], "holder of the privilege" means:

(a) The victim when such person has no guardian or conservator.

(b) A guardian or conservator of the victim when the victim has a guardian or conservator.

(c) The personal representative of the victim if the victim is dead. [*Added 1980.*]

§ 1035.8. Sexual assault victim-counselor privilege. A victim of a sexual assault, whether or not a party, has a privilege to refuse to disclose, and to prevent another from disclosing, a confidential communication between the victim and a sexual assault counselor if the privilege is claimed by any of the following:

(a) The holder of the privilege;

(b) A person who is authorized to claim the privilege by the holder of the privilege; or

(c) The person who was the sexual assault counselor at the time of the confidential communication, but that person may not claim the privilege if there is no holder of the privilege in existence or if he or she is otherwise instructed by a person authorized to permit disclosure. [*Added 1980. Amended 2006.*]

§ 1036. Claim of privilege by sexual assault counselor. The sexual assault counselor who received or made a communication subject to the privilege under this article shall claim the privilege if he or she is present when the communication is sought to be disclosed and is authorized to claim the privilege under subdivision (c) of Section 1035.8. [*Added 1980. Amended 2006.*]

§ 1036.2. Sexual assault. As used in this article [§§ 1035-1036.2], "sexual assault" includes all of the following:

(a) Rape, as defined in Section 261 of the Penal Code.

(b) Unlawful sexual intercourse, as defined in Section 261.5 of the Penal Code.

(c) Rape in concert with force and violence, as defined in Section 264.1 of the Penal Code.

(d) Rape of a spouse, as defined in Section 262 of the Penal Code.

(e) Sodomy, as defined in Section 286 of the Penal Code, except a violation of subdivision (e) of that section.

(f) A violation of Section 288 of the Penal Code.

(g) Oral copulation, as defined in Section 287 of, or former Section 288a of,the Penal Code, except a violation of subdivision (e) of that section.

(h) Sexual penetration, as defined in Section 289 of the Penal Code.

(i) Annoying or molesting a child under 18, as defined in Section 647a of the Penal Code.

(j) Any attempt to commit any of the above acts. [*Added 1980. Amended 1988, 2001, 2018.*]

Statutory Note

The 1988 amendment added subdivisions (d) and (h). The 2001 amendment redefined "sexual penetration" in subdivision (h).

Article 8.7. Domestic Violence Victim-Counselor Privilege

§ 1037. Victim. As used in this article [§§ 1037-1037.7], "victim" means any person who suffers domestic violence, as defined in Section 1037.7. [*Added 1986.*]

§ 1037.1. Domestic violence counselor; qualifications; domestic violence victim service organization.

(a)(1) As used in this article, "domestic violence counselor" means a person who is employed by a domestic violence victim service organization, as defined in this article, whether financially compensated or not, for the purpose of rendering advice or assistance to victims of domestic violence and who has at least 40 hours of training as specified in paragraph (2).

(2) The 40 hours of training shall be supervised by an individual who qualifies as a counselor under paragraph (1), and who has at least one year of experience counseling domestic violence victims for the domestic violence victim service organization. The training shall include, but need not be limited to, the following areas: history of domestic violence, civil and criminal law as it relates to domestic violence, the domestic violence victim-counselor privilege and other laws that protect the confidentiality of victim records and information, societal attitudes towards domestic violence, peer counseling techniques, housing, public assistance and other financial resources available to meet the financial needs of domestic violence victims, and referral services available to domestic violence victims.

(3) A domestic violence counselor who has been employed by the domestic violence victim service organization for a period of less than six months shall be supervised by a domestic violence counselor who has at least one year of experience counseling domestic violence victims for the domestic violence victim service organization.

(b) As used in this article, "domestic violence victim service organization" means either of the following:

(1) A nongovernmental organization or entity that provides shelter, programs, or services to victims of domestic violence and their children, including, but not limited to, either of the following:

(A) Domestic violence shelter-based programs, as described in Section 18294 of the Welfare and Institutions Code.

(B) Other programs with the primary mission to provide services to victims of domestic violence whether or not that program exists in an agency that provides additional services.

(2) Programs on the campus of a public or private institution of higher education with the primary mission to provide support or advocacy services to victims of domestic violence. [*Added 1986. Amended 1990, 2008, 2017.*]

§ 1037.2. Confidential communication; compulsion of disclosure by court; claim of privilege.

(a) As used in this article [§§ 1037-1037.7], "confidential communication" means any information, including, but not limited to, written or oral communications, transmitted between the victim and the counselor in the course of their relationship and in confidence by a means which, so far as the victim is aware, discloses the information to no third persons other than those who are present to further the interests of the victim in the consultation or those to whom disclosures are reasonably necessary for the transmission of the information or an accomplishment of the purposes for which the domestic violence counselor is consulted. The term includes all information regarding the facts and circumstances involving all incidences of domestic violence, as well as all information about the children of the victim or abuser and the relationship of the victim with the abuser.

(b) The court may compel disclosure of information received by a domestic violence counselor which constitutes relevant evidence of the facts and circumstances involving a crime allegedly perpetrated against the victim or another household member and which is the subject of a criminal proceeding, if the court determines that the probative value of the information outweighs the effect of disclosure of the information on the victim, the counseling relationship, and the counseling services. The court may compel disclosure if the victim is either dead or not the complaining witness in a criminal action against the perpetrator. The court may also compel disclosure in proceedings related to child abuse if the court determines that the probative value of the evidence outweighs the effect of the disclosure on the victim, the counseling relationship, and the counseling services.

(c) When a court rules on a claim of privilege under this article [§§ 1037-1037.7], it may require the person from whom disclosure is sought or the person authorized to claim the privilege, or both, to disclose the information in chambers out of the presence and hearing of all persons except the person authorized to claim the privilege and such other persons as the person authorized to claim the privilege consents to have present. If the judge determines that the information is privileged and shall not be disclosed, neither he nor she nor any other person may disclose, without the consent of a person authorized to permit disclosure, any information disclosed in the course of the proceedings in chambers.

(d) If the court determines that information shall be disclosed, the court shall so order and inform the defendant in the criminal action. If the court finds there is a reasonable likelihood that any information is subject to disclosure pursuant to the balancing test provided in this section, the procedure specified in subdivisions (1), (2), and (3) of Section 1035.4 shall be followed. [*Added 1986; amended 2008.*]

§ 1037.3. Child abuse; reporting. Nothing in this article [§§ 1037-1037.7] shall be construed to limit any obligation to report instances of child abuse as required by Section 11166 of the Penal Code. [*Added 1986.*]

§ 1037.4. Holder of the privilege. As used in this article [§§ 1037-1037.7], "holder of the privilege" means:

(a) The victim when he or she has no guardian or conservator.

(b) A guardian or conservator of the victim when the victim has a guardian or conservator, unless the guardian or conservator is accused of perpetrating domestic violence against the victim. [*Added 1986; amended 2008.*]

§ 1037.5. Privilege of refusal to disclose communication; claimants. A victim of domestic violence, whether or not a party to the action, has a privilege to refuse to disclose, and to prevent another from disclosing, a confidential communication between the victim and a domestic violence counselor in any proceeding specified in Section 901 if the privilege is claimed by any of the following persons:

(a) The holder of the privilege.

(b) A person who is authorized to claim the privilege by the holder of the privilege.

(c) The person who was the domestic violence counselor at the time of the communication. However, that person may not claim the privilege if there is no holder of the privilege in existence or if he or she is otherwise instructed by a person authorized to permit disclosure. [*Added 1986; amended 2008.*]

§ 1037.6. Claim of privilege by counselor. The domestic violence counselor who received or made a communication subject to the privilege granted by this article [§§ 1037-1037.7] shall claim the privilege whenever he or she is present when the communication is sought to be disclosed and he or she is authorized to claim the privilege under subdivision (c) of Section 1037.5. [*Added 1986.*]

§ 1037.7. Domestic violence. As used in this article [§§ 1037-1037.7], "domestic violence" means "domestic violence" as defined in Section 6211 of the Family Code. [*Added 1993.*]

Law Revision Commission Comment - 1993 Addition

Section 1037.7 substitutes a reference to the Family Code provision defining "domestic violence" for the definitions of "abuse," "domestic violence," and "family or household member" in the former section. This is not a substantive change, since the Family Code definition of "domestic violence" continues the substance of the omitted definitions. See Fam. Code § 6211 ("domestic violence" defined) & Comment. See also Fam. Code §§ 6203 ("abuse" defined), 6209 ("cohabitant" and "former cohabitant" defined). [23 Cal.L.Rev.Comm. Reports 1 (1993).]

§ 1037.8. Notice; limitations on confidential communications. A domestic violence counselor shall inform a domestic violence victim of any applicable limitations on confidentiality of communications between the victim and the domestic violence counselor. This information may be given orally. [*Added 2002.*]

Article 8.8. Human Trafficking Caseworker-Victim Privilege

§ 1038. Privilege. (a) A trafficking victim, whether or not a party to the action, has a privilege to refuse to disclose, and to prevent another from disclosing, a confidential communication between the victim and a human trafficking caseworker if the privilege is claimed by any of the following persons:

(1) The holder of the privilege.

(2) A person who is authorized to claim the privilege by the holder of the privilege.

(3) The person who was the human trafficking caseworker at the time of the confidential communication or is presently the human trafficking caseworker for the victim. However, that person may not claim the privilege if there is no holder of the privilege in existence or if the person is otherwise instructed by the court or by another person authorized to permit disclosure.

(b) The human trafficking caseworker shall claim the privilege whenever the caseworker is present when the communication is sought to be disclosed and the caseworker is authorized to claim the privilege under this section.

(c) A human trafficking caseworker shall inform a trafficking victim of any applicable limitations on confidentiality of communications between the victim and the caseworker. This information may be given orally.

[*Added 2005. Amended 2019*]

§ 1038.1. Compulsion of disclosure by court.

(a) The court may compel disclosure of information received by a human trafficking caseworker that constitutes relevant evidence of the facts and circumstances involving a crime allegedly perpetrated against the victim and that is the subject of a criminal proceeding, if the court determines that the probative value of the information outweighs the effect of disclosure of the information on the victim, the counseling relationship, and the counseling services. (b) When a court rules on a claim of privilege under this article, it may require the person from whom disclosure is sought or the person authorized to claim the privilege, or both, to disclose the information in chambers out of the presence and hearing of all persons except the person authorized to claim the privilege and those other persons that the person authorized to claim the privilege consents to have present.

(c) If the judge determines that the information is privileged and shall not be disclosed, no person shall disclose, without the consent of a person authorized to permit disclosure, any information disclosed in the course of the proceedings in chambers. If the court determines that information shall be disclosed, the court shall so order and inform the defendant in the criminal action. If the court finds there is a reasonable likelihood that any information is subject to disclosure pursuant to the balancing test provided in this section, the procedure specified in paragraphs (1), (2), and (3) of Section 1035.4 shall be followed.

[*Added 2005. Amended 2019.*]

§ 1038.2. Definitions. As used in this article, the following terms have the following meanings:

(a) "Confidential communication" means all information, including but not limited to written and oral communication, transmitted between the victim and the human trafficking caseworker in the course of their relationship and in confidence by a means which, so far as the victim is aware, discloses the information to no third persons other than those who are present to further the interests of the victim in the consultation or those to whom disclosures are reasonably necessary for the transmission of the information or an accomplishment of the purposes for which the human trafficking caseworker is consulted and made with the victim's knowledge and consent. "Confidential communication" includes all information regarding the facts and circumstances relating to all incidences of human trafficking, as well as all information about the children of the victim and the relationship of the victim to the human trafficker.

(b) "Holder of the privilege" means:

(1) The victim if the victim has no guardian or conservator.

(2) A guardian or conservator of the victim if the victim has a guardian or conservator.

(3) The personal representative of the victim if the victim is deceased.

(c) "Human trafficking caseworker" means a person working for a human trafficking victim service organization, whether financially compensated or not, for the purpose of rendering advice or assistance to victims of human trafficking, who meets the requirements of paragraph (1) or (2) and who also meets the requirements of paragraph (3), if applicable:

(1) Has an advanced degree or license, such as a master's degree in counseling, social work, or a related field and at least one year of experience in a caseworker role working directly with victims of human trafficking.

(2) Has at least 40 hours of training as specified in this paragraph and is supervised by an individual who qualifies as a human trafficking caseworker under paragraph (1). The training, supervised by a person qualified under paragraph (1), shall include, but need not be limited to, the following areas:

(A) History of human trafficking.

(B) Civil and criminal law relating to human trafficking.

(C) Systems of oppression.

(D) Peer counseling techniques.

(E) Resources available to victims of human trafficking.

(F) Crisis intervention and counseling techniques.

(G) Role playing.

(H) Intersections of human trafficking and other crimes.

(I) Client and system advocacy.

(J) Referral services.

(K) Connecting to local, regional, and national human trafficking coalitions.

(L) Explaining privileged communications.

(3) If the caseworker has been employed by a human trafficking service organization for a period of less than six months, that caseworker is supervised by another human trafficking caseworker who has at least one year of experience working with human trafficking victims.

(d) "Human trafficking victim service organization" means a nongovernmental organization or entity that provides shelter, program, or other support services to victims of human trafficking and their children and that does all of the following:

(1) Employs staff that meet the requirements of a human trafficking caseworker as set forth in this section.

(2) Operates a telephone hotline, advertised to the public, for survivor crisis calls.

(3) Offers psychological support and peer counseling provided in accordance with this section.

(4) Makes staff available during normal business hours to assist victims of human trafficking who need shelter, programs, or other support services.

(e) "Victim" means a person who consults a human trafficking caseworker for the purpose of securing advice or assistance concerning a mental, physical, emotional, or other condition related to their experience as a victim of human trafficking.

[*Added 2005. Amended 2014, 2019.*]

§ 1038.3. No effect on reporting obligations. Nothing in this article shall be construed as limiting any obligation to report instances of child abuse as required by Section 11166 of the Penal Code. [*Added 2019.*]

Article 9. Official Information and Identity of Informer

§ 1040. Privilege for official information. (a) As used in this section, "official information" means information acquired in confidence by a public employee in the course of his or her duty and not open, or officially disclosed, to the public prior to the time the claim of privilege is made.

(b) A public entity has a privilege to refuse to disclose official information, and to prevent another from disclosing official information, if the privilege is claimed by a person authorized by the public entity to do so and either of the following apply:

(1) Disclosure is forbidden by an act of the Congress of the United States or a statute of this state.

(2) Disclosure of the information is against the public interest because there is a necessity for preserving the confidentiality of the information that outweighs the necessity for disclosure in the interest of justice; but no privilege may be claimed under this paragraph if any person authorized to do so has consented that the information be disclosed in the proceeding. In determining whether disclosure of the information is against the public interest, the interest of the public entity as a party in the outcome of the proceeding may not be considered.

(c) Notwithstanding any other law, the Employment Development Department shall disclose to law enforcement agencies, in accordance with subdivision (i) of Section 1095 of the Unemployment Insurance Code, information in its possession relating to any person if an arrest warrant has been issued for the person for commission of a felony. [*Amended 1984, 2015, 2016.*]

Statutory Note

See Bus. & Prof. Code § 19827 (privilege for communications in connection with the Gambling Control Act).

Case Note

Section 1040(b) protects draft report prepared by investigator for Department of Health Services, which relied substantially on hospital peer review committee records protected by hospital peer review privilege (§ 1157). Fox v. Kramer, 22 Cal. 4th 531, 542, 93 Cal. Rptr. 2d 497, 505, 994 P.2d 343, 350 (2000).

Assembly Committee on Judiciary Comment

Under existing law, official information is protected either by subdivision 5 of Code of Civil Procedure Section 1881 (which, like Section 1040, prohibits disclosure when the interest of the public would suffer thereby) or by specific statutes such as the provisions of the Revenue and Taxation Code prohibiting disclosure of information reported in tax returns. See, e.g., Rev. & Tax.Code §§ 19281-19289. Section 1881 is superseded by the Evidence Code, but the specific statutes protecting official information remain in effect. Evidence Code § 1040(b)(1).

Section 1040 permits the official information privilege to be invoked by the public entity or its authorized representative. Since the privilege is granted to enable the government to protect its secrets, no reason exists for permitting the privilege to be exercised by persons who are not concerned with the public interest. It should be noted, however, that another statute may provide a person with a privilege not to disclose a report he made to the government; the Evidence Code has no effect on that privilege. See the Comment to Evidence Code § 920. Where the government has received a report from an informant, the official information privilege may apply to that report. It does not apply, however, to the knowledge of the informant. The government does not acquire a privilege to prevent an informant from revealing his knowledge merely because that knowledge has been communicated to the government.

The official information privilege provided in Section 1040 does not extend to the identity of an informer. Section 1041 provides special rules for determining when the government has a privilege to keep secret the identity of an informer.

The privilege may be asserted to prevent testimony by anyone who has official information. This provides the public entity with more protection than existing law. See the Comment to Evidence Code § 954 (attorney-client privilege).

Official information is absolutely privileged if its disclosure is forbidden by either a federal or state statute. Other official information is subject to a conditional privilege: The judge must determine in each instance the consequences to the public of disclosure and the consequences to the litigant of nondisclosure and then decide which outweighs the other. He should, of course, be aware that the public has an interest in seeing that justice is done in the particular cause as well as an interest in the secrecy of the information.

§ 1041. Privilege for identity of informer. (a) Except as provided in this section, a public entity has a privilege to refuse to disclose the identity of a person who has furnished information as provided in subdivision (b) purporting to disclose a violation of a law of the United States or of this state or of a public entity in this state, and to prevent another from disclosing such identity, if the privilege is claimed by a person authorized by the public entity to do so and either of the following apply:

(1) Disclosure is forbidden by an act of the Congress of the United States or a statute of this state; or

(2) Disclosure of the identity of the informer is against the public interest because the necessity for preserving the confidentiality of his or her identity outweighs the necessity for disclosure in the interest of justice. The privilege shall not be claimed under this paragraph if a person authorized to do so has consented that the identity of the informer be disclosed in the proceeding. In determining whether disclosure of the identity of the informer is against the public interest, the interest of the public entity as a party in the outcome of the proceeding shall not be considered.

(b) The privilege described in this section applies only if the information is furnished in confidence by the informer to any of the following:

(1) A law enforcement officer;

(2) A representative of an administrative agency charged with the administration or enforcement of the law alleged to be violated; or

(3) Any person for the purpose of transmittal to a person listed in paragraph (1) or (2). As used in this paragraph, "person" includes a volunteer or employee of a crime stopper organization.

(c) The privilege described in this section shall not be construed to prevent the informer from disclosing his or her identity.

(d) As used in this section, "crime stopper organization" means a private, nonprofit organization that accepts and expends donations used to reward persons who report to the organization information concerning alleged criminal activity, and forwards the information to the appropriate law enforcement agency. [*Amended 2013.*]

On a motion attacking a search warrant, where disclosure of contents of sealed affidavit would disclose identity of confidential informant, court should conduct *in camera* hearing to determine need for confidentiality. Where confidentiality is upheld, procedures are prescribed for reviewing validity of the warrant. People v. Hobbs, 7 Cal. 4th 948, 30 Cal. Rptr. 2d 651, 873 P.2d 1246 (1994).

Law Revision Commission Comment

***Under existing law, the identity of an informer is protected by subdivision 5 of Code of Civil Procedure Section 1881 (which, like Section 1041, prohibits disclosure when the interest of the public would suffer thereby). Section 1881 is superseded by the Evidence Code.

* * * This privilege may be claimed under the same conditions as the official information privilege may be claimed, except that it does not apply if a person is called as a witness and asked if he is the informer.

§ 1042. Adverse order or finding in certain cases. (a) Except where disclosure is forbidden by an act of the Congress of the United States, if a claim of privilege under this article [§§ 1040-1047] by the state or a public entity in this state is sustained in a criminal proceeding, the presiding officer shall make such order or finding of fact adverse to the public entity bringing the proceeding as is required by law upon any issue in the proceeding to which the privileged information is material.

(b) Notwithstanding subdivision (a), where a search is made pursuant to a warrant valid on its face, the public entity bringing a criminal proceeding is not required to reveal to the defendant official information or the identity of an informer in order to establish the legality of the search or the admissibility of any evidence obtained as a result of it.

(c) Notwithstanding subdivision (a), in any preliminary hearing, criminal trial, or other criminal proceeding, any otherwise admissible evidence of information communicated to a peace officer by a confidential informant, who is not a material witness to the guilt or innocence of the accused of the offense charged, is admissible on the issue of reasonable cause to make an arrest or search without requiring that the name or identity of the informant be disclosed if the judge or magistrate is satisfied, based upon evidence produced in open court, out of the presence of the jury, that such information was received from a reliable informant and in his discretion does not require such disclosure.

(d) When, in any such criminal proceeding, a party demands disclosure of the identity of the informant on the ground the informant is a material witness on the issue of guilt, the court shall conduct a hearing at which all parties may present evidence on the issue of disclosure. Such hearing shall be conducted outside the presence of the jury, if any. During the hearing, if the privilege provided for in Section 1041 is claimed by a person authorized to do so or if a person who is authorized to claim such privilege refuses to answer any question on the ground that the answer would tend to disclose the identity of the informant, the prosecuting attorney may request that the court hold an in camera hearing. If such a request is made, the court shall hold such a hearing outside the presence of the defendant and his counsel. At the in camera hearing, the prosecution may offer evidence which would tend to disclose or which discloses the identity of the informant to aid the court in its determination whether there is a reasonable possibility that nondisclosure might deprive the defendant of a fair trial. A reporter shall be present at the in camera hearing. Any transcription of the proceedings at the in camera hearing, as well as any physical evidence presented at the hearing, shall be ordered sealed by the court, and only a court may have access to its contents. The court shall not order disclosure, nor strike the testimony of the witness who invokes the privilege, nor dismiss the criminal proceeding, if the party offering the witness refuses to disclose the identity of the informant, unless, based upon the evidence presented at the hearing held in the presence of the defendant and his counsel and the evidence presented at the in camera hearing, the court concludes that there is a reasonable possibility that nondisclosure might deprive the defendant of a fair trial. [*Amended 1965, 1969.*]

Assembly Committee on Judiciary Comment

Section 1042 provides special rules regarding the consequences of invocation of the privileges provided in this article by the prosecution in a criminal proceeding.

Subdivision (a). This subdivision recognizes the existing California rule in a criminal case. As was stated by the United States Supreme Court in United States v. Reynolds, 345 U.S. 1, 12 (1953), "since the Government which prosecutes an accused also has the duty to see that justice is done, it is unconscionable to allow it to undertake prosecution and then invoke its governmental privileges to deprive the accused of anything which might be material to his defense." This policy applies if either the official information privilege (Section 1040) or the informer privilege (Section 1041) is exercised in a criminal proceeding.

In some cases, the privileged information will be material to the issue of the defendant's guilt or innocence; in such cases, the law requires that the court dismiss the case if the public entity does not reveal the information. People v. McShann, 50 Cal.2d 802, 330 P.2d 33 (1958). In other cases, the privileged information will relate to narrower issues, such as the legality of a search without a warrant; in those cases, the law requires that the court strike the testimony of a particular witness or make some other order appropriate under the circumstances if the public entity insists upon its privilege. Priestly v. Superior Court, 50 Cal.2d 812, 330 P.2d 39 (1958).

In cases where the legality of an arrest is in issue, Section 1042 does not require disclosure of the privileged information if there was reasonable cause for the arrest aside from the privileged information, for in such a case the identity of the informer is immaterial. Cf. People v. Hunt, 216 Cal.App.2d 753, 756-757, 31 Cal.Rptr. 221, 223 (1963) ("The rule requiring disclosure of an informer's identity has no application in situations where reasonable cause for arrest and search exists aside from the informer's communication.")

Subdivision (a) applies only if the privilege is asserted by the State of California or a public entity in the State of California. Subdivision (a) does not require the imposition of its sanction if the privilege is invoked in an action prosecuted by the State and the information is withheld by the federal government or another state. Nor may the sanction be imposed where disclosure is forbidden by federal statute. In these respects, subdivision (a) states existing California law. People v. Parham, 60 Cal.2d 378, 33 Cal.Rptr. 497, 384 P.2d 1001 (1963) (prior statements of prosecution witnesses withheld by the Federal Bureau of Investigation; denial of motion to strike witnesses' testimony affirmed.

Subdivision (b). This subdivision codifies the rule declared in People v. Keener, 55 Cal.2d 714, 723, 12 Cal.Rptr. 859, 864, 361 P.2d 587, 592 (1961), in which the court held that "where a search is made pursuant to a warrant valid on its face, the prosecution is not required to reveal the identity of the informer in order to establish the legality of the search and the admissibility of the evidence obtained as a result of it." Subdivision (b), however, applies to all official information, not merely to the identity of an informer.

Subdivision (b) does not affect the rule that a defendant is entitled to know the identity of an informer in a case where the informer is a material witness with respect to facts directly relating to the defendant's guilt.

§ 1043. Peace or custodial officer personnel records; discovery or disclosure; procedure. (a) In any case in which discovery or disclosure is sought of peace or custodial officer personnel records or records maintained pursuant to Section 832.5 of the Penal Code or information from those records, the party seeking the discovery or disclosure shall file a written motion with the appropriate court or administrative body upon written notice to the governmental agency which has custody and control of the records, as follows:

(1) In a civil action, the written notice shall be given at the times prescribed by subdivision (b) of Section 1005 of the Code of Civil Procedure.

(2) In a criminal action, the written notice shall be served and filed at least 10 court days before the hearing. All papers opposing a motion so noticed shall be filed with the court at least five court days, and all reply papers at least two court days, before the hearing. Proof of service of the notice shall be filed no later than five court days before the hearing.

(b) The motion shall include all of the following:

(1) Identification of the proceeding in which discovery or disclosure is sought, the party seeking discovery or disclosure, the peace or custodial officer whose records are sought, the governmental agency which has custody and control of the records, and the time and place at which the motion for discovery or disclosure shall be heard.

(2) A description of the type of records or information sought.

(3) Affidavits showing good cause for the discovery or disclosure sought, setting forth the materiality thereof to the subject matter involved in the pending litigation and stating upon reasonable belief that the governmental agency identified has the records or information from the records.

(c) Upon receipt of a notice served pursuant to subdivision (a), the governmental agency shall immediately notify the individual whose records are sought.

(d) No hearing upon a motion for discovery or disclosure shall be held without full compliance with the notice provisions of this section except upon a showing by the moving party of good cause for noncompliance, or upon a waiver of the hearing by the governmental agency identified as having the records. [*Added 1978. Amended 1989, 2002, 2019.*]

Statutory Note

The 2002 amendment added custodial officers.

Case Note

To establish "good cause" for a *Pitchess* motion under § 1043(b)(3), affidavit must propose a defense, articulate how the claimed officer misconduct would be relevant to support that defense, and describe a plausible factual scenario supporting the claimed officer misconduct. To be plausible, a scenario must be one that "might or could have happened" and does not have to be probable or convincing. Warrick v. Superior Ct., 29 Cal. Rptr. 3d 2, 12 P.3d 2 (Cal. 2005).

§ 1044. Medical or psychological history records; right of access. Nothing in this article [§§ 1040-1047] shall be construed to affect the right of access to records of medical or psychological history where such access would otherwise be available under Section 996 or 1016. [*Added 1978. Amended 2012.*]

§ 1045. Peace or custodial officers; access to records of complaints, investigations of complaints, or discipline imposed; relevancy; protective orders. (a) Nothing in this article shall be construed to affect the right of access to records of complaints, or investigations of complaints, or discipline imposed as a result of those investigations, concerning an event or transaction in which the peace officer or custodial officer, as defined in Section 831.5 of the Penal Code, participated, or which he or she perceived, and pertaining to the manner in which he or she performed his or her duties, provided that information is relevant to the subject matter involved in the pending litigation.

(b) In determining relevance, the court shall examine the information in chambers in conformity with Section 915, and shall exclude from disclosure:

(1) Information consisting of complaints concerning conduct occurring more than five years before the event or transaction that is the subject of the litigation in aid of which discovery or disclosure is sought.

(2) In any criminal proceeding the conclusions of any officer investigating a complaint filed pursuant to Section 832.5 of the Penal Code.

(3) Facts sought to be disclosed that are so remote as to make disclosure of little or no practical benefit.

(c) In determining relevance where the issue in litigation concerns the policies or pattern of conduct of the employing agency, the court shall consider whether the information sought may be obtained from other records maintained by the employing agency in the regular course of agency business which would not necessitate the disclosure of individual personnel records.

(d) Upon motion seasonably made by the governmental agency which has custody or control of the records to be examined or by the officer whose records are sought, and upon good cause showing the necessity thereof, the court may make any order which justice requires to protect the officer or agency from unnecessary annoyance, embarrassment or oppression.

(e) The court shall, in any case or proceeding permitting the disclosure or discovery of any peace or custodial officer records requested pursuant to Section 1043, order that the records disclosed or discovered may not be used for any purpose other than a court proceeding pursuant to applicable law. [*Added 1978. Amended 1982, 2002.*]

Statutory Note

The 1982 amendment added subdivision (e). The 2002 amendment extended coverage to include custodial officers.

Case Note

This section applies in juvenile court wardship proceedings. City of San Jose v. Superior Court, 5 Cal. 4th 47, 53-54, 19 Cal. Rptr. 2d 73, 76, 850 P.2d 621, 624 (1993).

§ 1046. Allegation of excessive force by peace or custodial officer; copy of police or crime report. In any case, otherwise authorized by law, in which the party seeking disclosure is alleging excessive force by a peace officer or custodial officer, as defined in Section 831.5 of the Penal Code, in connection with the arrest of that party, or for conduct alleged to have occurred within a jail facility, the motion shall include a copy of the police report setting forth the circumstances under which the party was stopped and arrested, or a copy of the crime report setting forth the circumstances under which the conduct is alleged to have occurred within a jail facility. [*Added 1985. Amended 2002.*]

Statutory Note

The 2002 amendment added custodial officers.

§ 1047. Records of peace or custodial officers; exemption from disclosure. (a) Records of peace officers or custodial officers, as defined in Section 831.5 of the Penal Code, including supervisorial officers, who either were not present during the arrest or had no contact with the party seeking disclosure from the time of the arrest until the time of booking, or who were not present at the time the conduct is alleged to have occurred within a jail facility, shall not be subject to disclosure.

(b) Notwithstanding subdivision (a), if a supervisorial officer whose records are being sought had direct oversight of a peace officer or a custodial officer, as defined in Section 831.5 of the Penal Code and issued command directives or had command influence over the circumstances at issue, the supervisorial officer's records shall be subject to disclosure pursuant to Section 1045 if the peace officer or custodial officer under supervision was present during the arrest, had contact with the party seeking disclosure from the time of the arrest until the time of booking, or was present at the time the conduct at issue is alleged to have occurred within a jail facility. [*Added 1985. Amended 2002, 2019.*]

Statutory Note

The 2002 amendment added custodial officers.

Article 10. Political Vote

§ 1050. Privilege to protect secrecy of vote. If he claims the privilege, a person has a privilege to refuse to disclose the tenor of his vote at a public election where the voting is by secret ballot unless he voted illegally or he previously made an unprivileged disclosure of the tenor of his vote.

Law Revision Commission Comment

Section 1050 declares existing law. The California cases declaring such a privilege have relied upon the provision of the Constitution that "secrecy in voting be preserved." Cal.Const., Art. II, § 5. See Bush v. Head, 154 Cal. 277, 97 Pac. 512 (1908); Smith v. Thomas, 121 Cal. 533, 54 Pac. 71 (1898). Since the policy of ballot secrecy extends only to legally cast ballots, the California cases—as well as Section 1050—recognize that there is no privilege as to the tenor of an illegal vote. Patterson v. Hanley, 136 Cal. 265, 68 Pac. 821 (1902).

Article 11. Trade Secret

§ 1060. Privilege to protect trade secret. If he or his agent or employee claims the privilege, the owner of a trade secret has a privilege to refuse to disclose the secret, and to prevent another from disclosing it, if the allowance of the privilege will not tend to conceal fraud or otherwise work injustice.

Law Revision Commission Comment

This privilege is granted so that secret information essential to the continued operation of a business or industry may be afforded some measure of protection against unnecessary disclosure. Thus, the privilege prevents the use of the witness' duty to testify as the means for injuring an otherwise profitable business where more important interests will not be jeopardized. See generally 8 Wigmore, Evidence § 2212(3) (McNaughton rev. 1961). Nevertheless, there are dangers in the recognition of such a privilege. Copyright and patent laws provide adequate protection for many of the matters that might otherwise be classified as trade secrets. Recognizing the privilege as to such information would serve only to hinder the courts in determining the truth without providing the owner of the secret any needed protection. Again, disclosure of the matters protected by the privilege may be essential to disclose unfair competition or fraud or to reveal the improper use of dangerous materials by the party asserting the privilege. Recognizing the privilege in such cases would amount to a legally sanctioned license to commit the wrongs complained of, for the wrongdoer would be privileged to withhold his wrongful conduct from legal scrutiny.

Therefore, the privilege exists under this section only if its application will not tend to conceal fraud or otherwise work injustice. The limits of the privilege are necessarily uncertain and will have to be worked out through judicial decisions. * * *

§ 1061. Procedure for assertion of trade secret privilege. (a) For purposes of this section, and Sections 1062 and 1063:

(1) "Trade secret" means "trade secret," as defined in subdivision (d) of Section 3426.1 of the Civil Code, or paragraph (9) of subdivision (a) of Section 499c of the Penal Code.

(2) "Article" means "article," as defined in paragraph (2) of subdivision (a) of Section 499c of the Penal Code.

(b) In addition to Section 1062, the following procedure shall apply whenever the owner of a trade secret wishes to assert his or her trade secret privilege, as provided in Section 1060, during a criminal proceeding:

(1) The owner of the trade secret shall file a motion for a protective order, or the people may file the motion on the owner's behalf and with the owner's permission. The motion shall include an affidavit based upon personal knowledge listing the affiant's qualifications to give an opinion concerning the trade secret at issue, identifying, without revealing, the alleged trade secret and articles which disclose the secret, and presenting evidence that the secret qualifies as a trade secret under either subdivision (d) of Section 3426.1 of the Civil Code or paragraph (9) of subdivision (a) of Section 499c of the Penal Code. The motion and affidavit shall be served on all parties in the proceeding.

(2) Any party in the proceeding may oppose the request for the protective order by submitting affidavits based upon the affiant's personal knowledge. The affidavits shall be filed under seal, but shall be provided to the owner of the trade secret and to all parties in the proceeding. Neither the owner of the trade secret nor any party in the proceeding may disclose the affidavit to persons other than to counsel of record without prior court approval.

(3) The movant shall, by a preponderance of the evidence, show that the issuance of a protective order is proper. The court may rule on the request without holding an evidentiary hearing. However, in its discretion, the court may choose to hold an in camera evidentiary hearing concerning disputed articles with only the owner of the trade secret, the people's representative, the defendant, and defendant's counsel present. If the court holds such a hearing, the parties' right to examine witnesses shall not be used to obtain discovery, but shall be directed solely toward the question of whether the alleged trade secret qualifies for protection.

(4) If the court finds that a trade secret may be disclosed during any criminal proceeding unless a protective order is issued and that the issuance of a protective order would not conceal a fraud or work an injustice, the court shall issue a protective order limiting the use and dissemination of the trade secret, including, but not limited to, articles disclosing that secret. The protective order may, in the court's discretion, include the following provisions:

(A) That the trade secret may be disseminated only to counsel for the parties, including their associate attorneys, paralegals, and investigators, and to law enforcement officials or clerical officials.

(B) That the defendant may view the secret only in the presence of his or her counsel, or if not in the presence of his or her counsel, at counsel's offices.

(C) That any party seeking to show the trade secret, or articles containing the trade secret, to any person not designated by the protective order shall first obtain court approval to do so:

(i) The court may require that the person receiving the trade secret do so only in the presence of counsel for the party requesting approval.

(ii) The court may require the person receiving the trade secret to sign a copy of the protective order and to agree to be bound by its terms. The order may include a provision recognizing the owner of the trade secret to be a third-party beneficiary of that agreement.

(iii) The court may require a party seeking disclosure to an expert to provide that expert's name, employment history, and any other relevant information to the court for examination. The court shall accept that information under seal, and the information shall not be disclosed by any court except upon termination of the action and upon a showing of good cause to believe the secret has been disseminated by a court-approved expert. The court shall evaluate the expert and determine whether the expert poses a discernible risk of disclosure. The court shall withhold approval if the expert's economic interests place the expert in a competitive position with the victim, unless no other experts are available. The court may interview the expert in camera in aid of its ruling. If the court rejects the expert, it shall state its reasons for doing so on the record and a transcript of those reasons shall be prepared and sealed.

(D) That no articles disclosing the trade secret shall be filed or otherwise made a part of the court record available to the public without approval of the court and prior notice to the owner of the secret. The owner of the secret may give either party permission to accept the notice on the owner's behalf.

(E) Other orders as the court deems necessary to protect the integrity of the trade secret.

(c) A ruling granting or denying a motion for a protective order filed pursuant to subdivision (b) shall not be construed as a determination that the alleged trade secret is or is not a trade secret as defined by subdivision (d) of Section 3426.1 of the Civil Code or paragraph (9) of subdivision (a) of Section 499c of the Penal Code. Such a ruling shall not have any effect on any civil litigation.

(d) This section shall have prospective effect only and shall not operate to invalidate previously entered protective orders. [*Added 1990. Amended 2002.*]

Statutory Note

The 2002 amendment eliminated reference to protective orders entered by municipal courts.

§ 1062. Exclusion of public from criminal proceeding; motion; contents; hearing; determination. (a) Notwithstanding any other provision of law, in a criminal case, the court, upon motion of the owner of a trade secret, or upon motion by the People with the consent of the owner, may exclude the public from any portion of a criminal proceeding where the proponent of closure has demonstrated a substantial probability that the trade secret would otherwise be disclosed to the public during that proceeding and a substantial probability that the disclosure would cause serious harm to the owner of the secret, and where the court finds that there is no overriding public interest in an open proceeding. No evidence, however, shall be excluded during a criminal proceeding pursuant to this section if it would conceal a fraud, work an injustice, or deprive the People or the defendant of a fair trial.

(b) The motion made pursuant to subdivision (a) shall identify, without revealing, the trade secrets which would otherwise be disclosed to the public. A showing made pursuant to subdivision (a) shall be made during an in camera hearing with only the owner of the trade secret, the People's representative, the defendant, and defendant's counsel present. A court reporter shall be present during the hearing. Any transcription of the proceedings at the in camera hearing, as well as any articles presented at that hearing, shall be ordered sealed by the court and only a court may allow access to its contents upon a showing of good cause. The court, in ruling upon the motion made pursuant to subdivision (a), may consider testimony presented or affidavits filed in any proceeding held in that action.

(c) If, after the in camera hearing described in subdivision (b), the court determines that exclusion of trade secret information from the public is appropriate, the court shall close only that portion of the criminal proceeding necessary to prevent disclosure of the trade secret. Before granting the motion, however, the court shall find and state for the record that the moving party has met its burden pursuant to subdivision (b), and that the closure of that portion of the proceeding will not deprive the People or the defendant of a fair trial.

(d) The owner of the trade secret, the People, or the defendant may seek relief from a ruling denying or granting closure by petitioning a higher court for extraordinary relief.

(e) Whenever the court closes a portion of a criminal proceeding pursuant to this section, a transcript of that closed proceeding shall be made available to the public as soon as practicable. The court shall redact any information qualifying as a trade secret before making that transcript available.

(f) The court, subject to Section 867 of the Penal Code, may allow witnesses who are bound by a protective order entered in the criminal proceeding protecting trade secrets, pursuant to Section 1061, to remain within the courtroom during the closed portion of the proceeding. [*Added 1990.*]

§ 1063. Sealing of articles protected by protective order; procedures. The following provisions shall govern requests to seal articles which are protected by a protective order entered pursuant to Evidence Code Section 1060 or 1061:

(a) The People shall request sealing of articles reasonably expected to be filed or admitted into evidence as follows:

(1) No less than 10 court days before trial, and no less than five court days before any other criminal proceeding, the People shall file with the court a list of all articles which the People reasonably expect to file with the court, or admit into evidence, under seal at that proceeding. That list shall be available to the public. The People may be relieved from providing timely notice upon showing that exigent circumstances prevent that notice.

(2) The court shall not allow the listed articles to be filed, admitted into evidence, or in any way made a part of the court record otherwise open to the public before holding a hearing to consider any objections to the People's request to seal the articles. The court at that hearing shall allow those objecting to the sealing to state their objections.

(3) After hearing any objections to sealing, the court shall conduct an in camera hearing with only the owner of the trade secret contained within those articles, the People's representative, defendant, and defendant's counsel present. The court shall review the articles sought to be sealed, evaluate objections to sealing, and determine whether the People have satisfied the constitutional standards governing public access to articles which are part of the judicial record. The court may consider testimony presented or affidavits filed in any proceeding held in that action. The People, defendant, and the owner of the trade secret may file affidavits based on the affiant's personal knowledge to be considered at that hearing. Those affidavits are to be sealed and not released to the public, but shall be made available to the parties. The court may rule on the request to seal without taking testimony. If the court takes testimony, examination of witnesses shall not be used to obtain discovery, but shall be directed solely toward whether sealing is appropriate.

(4) If the court finds that the movant has satisfied appropriate constitutional standards with respect to sealing particular articles, the court shall seal those articles if and when they are filed, admitted into evidence, or in any way made a part of the court record otherwise open to the public. The articles shall not be unsealed absent an order of a court upon a showing of good cause. Failure to examine the court file for notice of a request to seal shall not constitute good cause to consider objections to sealing.

(b) The following procedure shall apply to other articles made a part of the court record:

(1) Where any articles protected by a protective order entered pursuant to Section 1060 or 1061 are filed, admitted into evidence, or in any way made a part of the court record in such a way as to be otherwise open to the public, the People, a defendant, or the owner of a trade secret contained within those articles may request the court to seal those articles.

(2) The request to seal shall be made by noticed motion filed with the court. It may also be made orally in court at the time the articles are made a part of the court record. Where the request is made orally, the movant must file within 24 hours a written description of that request, including a list of the articles which are the subject of that request. These motions and lists shall be available to the public.

(3) The court shall promptly conduct hearings as provided in paragraphs (2), (3), and (4) of subdivision (a). The court shall, pending the hearings, seal those articles which are the subject of the request. Where a request to seal is made orally, the court may conduct hearings at the time the articles are made a part of the court record, but shall reconsider its ruling in light of additional objections made by objectors within two court days after the written record of the request to seal is made available to the public.

(4) Any articles sealed pursuant to these hearings shall not be unsealed absent an order of a court upon a showing of good cause. Failure to examine the court file for notice of a request to seal shall not constitute good cause to consider objections to sealing. [*Added 1990.*]

Chapter 5. Immunity of Newsman from Citation for Contempt

§ 1070. Refusal to disclose news source. (a) A publisher, editor, reporter, or other person connected with or employed upon a newspaper, magazine, or other periodical publication, or by a press association or wire service, or any person who has been so connected or employed, cannot be adjudged in contempt by a judicial, legislative, administrative body, or any other body having the power to issue subpoenas, for refusing to disclose, in any proceeding as defined in Section 901, the source of any information procured while so connected or employed for publication in a newspaper, magazine or other periodical publication, or for refusing to disclose any unpublished information obtained or prepared in gathering, receiving or processing of information for communication to the public.

(b) Nor can a radio or television news reporter or other person connected with or employed by a radio or television station, or any person who has been so connected or employed, be so adjudged in contempt for refusing to disclose the source of any information procured while so connected or employed for news or news commentary purposes on radio or television, or for refusing to disclose any unpublished information obtained or prepared in gathering, receiving or processing of information for communication to the public.

(c) As used in this section, "unpublished information" includes information not disseminated to the public by the person from whom disclosure is sought, whether or not related information has been disseminated and includes, but is not limited to, all notes, outtakes, photographs, tapes or other data of whatever sort not itself disseminated to the public through a medium of communication, whether or not published information based upon or related to such material has been disseminated. [*Amended 1971, 1972, 1974.*]

Statutory Note

The 1971 amendment added protection for information procured by former employees. The 1974 amendment added protection for unpublished information.

Case Notes

Because this section and Cal. Const. art. I, § 2(b), are virtually identical, interpretation of the one applies to the other. Shield law's definition of "unpublished information" includes newsperson's unpublished, nonconfidential eyewitness observations of an occurrence in a public place. Shield law may be overcome by defendant's right to a fair trial in a criminal case. After defendant, seeking disclosure, shows reasonable possibility that the material is exonerating, court must balance (a) whether the unpublished information is confidential or sensitive, (b) interests sought to be protected by the shield law, (c) importance of the information to the defendant, and (d) alternative sources. Delaney v. Superior Court, 50 Cal. 3d 785, 268 Cal. Rptr. 753, 789 P.2d 934 (1990).

The rights of the press guaranteed by this section are not diminished by the People's right to "due process of law" in criminal cases. See Cal. Const. art. I, § 29. The more specific provisions of Cal. Const. art. I, § 28(d), p. 478, take precedence over § 29. Delaney, supra, which involved conflict between this section and defendant's federal constitutional right to a fair trial, does not apply to resolving state-law conflicts. Miller v. Superior Court, 21 Cal. 4th 883, 892-898, 89 Cal. Rptr. 2d 834, 840-844, 986 P.2d 170, 175-179 (1999).

Threshold showing of reasonable possibility that unpublished information would materially assist the defense is not made by speculation as to the probable contents of the information. People v. Sanchez, 12 Cal. 4th 1, 57, 47 Cal. Rptr. 2d 843, 879, 906 P.2d 1129, 1165 (1995).

Assembly Committee on Judiciary Comment

Section 1070 continues without change the provisions of subdivision 6 of Code of Civil Procedure Section 1881.

It should be noted that Section 1070, like the existing law, provides an immunity from being adjudged in contempt; it does not create a privilege. Thus, the section will not prevent the use of other sanctions for refusal of a newsman to make discovery when he is a party to a civil proceeding. See Code Civ.Proc. § 2034; Bramson v. Wilkerson, Civil No. 760973 (L.A.Super.Ct., January 4, 1962), as reported in 3 Cal.Disc.Proc. 72 (Metropolitan News Review Section, January 30, 1962) (memorandum opinion by Judge Philbrick McCoy).

DIVISION 9. EVIDENCE AFFECTED OR EXCLUDED BY EXTRINSIC POLICIES

Chapter 1. Evidence of Character, Habit, or Custom

§ 1100. Manner of proof of character. Except as otherwise provided by statute, any otherwise admissible evidence (including evidence in the form of an opinion, evidence of reputation, and evidence of specific instances of such person's conduct) is admissible to prove a person's character or a trait of his character.

Law Revision Commission Comment

Section 1100 states the kinds of evidence that may be used to prove a person's character or a trait of his character. The section makes it clear that reputation evidence, opinion evidence, and evidence of specific instances of conduct are admissible for this purpose.

Section 1100 is technically unnecessary because Section 351 declares that all relevant evidence is admissible. Hence, all of the evidence declared to be admissible by Section 1100 would be admissible anyway under the general provisions of Section 351. Section 1100 is included in the Evidence Code, however, to forestall the argument that Section 351 does not remove all judicially created restrictions on the kinds of evidence that may be used to prove character or a trait of character.

Subject to certain statutory restrictions, the character evidence described in Section 1100 is admissible under Section 351 whenever it is relevant. Evidence of a person's character or a trait of his character is relevant in three situations: (1) when offered on the issue of his credibility as a witness, (2) when offered as circumstantial evidence of his conduct in conformity with such character or trait of character, and (3) when his character or a trait of his character is an ultimate fact in dispute in the action.

Sections 786-790 establish restrictions that are applicable when character evidence is offered to attack or to support the credibility of a witness. See the Comments to Sections 787 and 788 for a discussion of the restrictions on the kinds of evidence admissible for this purpose.

Sections 1101-1104 substantially restrict the extent to which character evidence may be used as circumstantial evidence of conduct. See the Comments to those sections for a discussion of the kinds of evidence admissible for this purpose.

Section 1100 applies without restriction only when character or a trait of character is an ultimate fact in dispute in the action. As applied to this situation, Section 1100 is generally consistent with existing law, although the existing law is uncertain in some respects. Cases involving character as an ultimate issue have admitted opinion evidence (People v. Wade, 118 Cal. 672, 50 Pac. 841 (1897); People v. Samonset, 97 Cal. 448, 450, 32 Pac. 520, 521 (1893)), reputation evidence (Estate of Akers, 184 Cal. 514, 519-520, 194 Pac. 706, 708-709 (1920); People v. Samonset, supra), and evidence of specific acts (Guardianship of Wisdom, 146 Cal.App.2d 635, 304 P.2d 221 (1956); Currin v. Currin, 125 Cal.App.2d 644, 271 P.2d 61 (1954); Guardianship of Casad, 106 Cal.App.2d 134, 234 P.2d 647 (1951)). However, there are cases which exclude some kinds of evidence where particular traits are involved. For example, in cases involving the unfitness or incompetency of an employee, evidence of specific acts is admissible to prove such unfitness or incompetency, while evidence of reputation is not. E.g., Gier v. Los Angeles Consol. Elec. Ry., 108 Cal. 129, 41 Pac. 22 (1895). Section 1100 eliminates the uncertainties in existing law and makes admissible any evidence that is relevant to prove the character in issue.

§ 1101. Evidence of character to prove conduct. (a) General rule. Except as provided in this section and in Sections 1102, 1103, 1108, and 1109, evidence of a person's character or a trait of his or her character (whether in the form of an opinion, evidence of reputation, or evidence of specific instances of his or her conduct) is inadmissible when offered to prove his or her conduct on a specified occasion.

(b) Other acts. Nothing in this section prohibits the admission of evidence that a person committed a crime, civil wrong, or other act when relevant to prove some fact (such as motive, opportunity, intent, preparation, plan, knowledge, identity, absence of mistake or accident, or whether a defendant in a prosecution for an unlawful sexual act or attempted unlawful sexual act did not reasonably and in good faith believe that the victim consented) other than his or her disposition to commit such an act.

(c) Credibility of witness. Nothing in this section affects the admissibility of evidence offered to support or attack the credibility of a witness. [*Amended 1986, 1995, 1996.*]

Statutory Note

The 1986 amendment added to subdivision (b) "or whether a defendant in a prosecution for an unlawful sexual act or attempted unlawful sexual act did not reasonably and in good faith believe that the victim consented." In making the addition, the legislature declared:

It is the intent of the Legislature in enacting this act to clarify the holding in People v. Tassell, 36 Cal.3d 77, to the extent an inference can be drawn from that holding that evidence of another act is ipso facto inadmissible or irrelevant to the issue of a defendant's reasonable and good faith belief that the victim consented, by rejecting that inference and making it clear that that evidence can be relevant on that issue in a particular case, depending upon the circumstances there present.

Stats. 1986, c. 1432, §2.

The 1995 and 1996 amendments added to subdivision (a) the references to §§ 1108 and 1109.

Case Notes

Even if the 1982 adoption of Cal. Const. art. I, § 28 (d), abrogated § 1101, the legislature reenacted § 1101 in 1986 when it adopted an amendment to § 1101 by more than a two-thirds vote. People v. Ewoldt, 7 Cal. 4th 380, 390-394, 27 Cal. Rptr. 2d 646, 650-653, 867 P.2d 757, 761-764 (1994).

Evidence of another crime is not made inadmissible by the defendant's acquittal of that crime, but evidence of the acquittal is admissible to rebut the prosecution's evidence of guilt. People v. Griffin, 66 Cal. 2d 459, 464-466, 58 Cal. Rptr. 107, 110-111, 426 P.2d 507, 510-511 (1967).

Evidence of a "common scheme or plan" is admissible to prove not only identity or intent, but also to prove that the charged act was committed. The charged and uncharged acts need not be part of a single, continuing conception or plot. The plan need not be unusual if it supports an inference that the defendant used the same design to commit the charged and uncharged offenses. Probative value for this purpose must not be outweighed by danger of unfair prejudice (§ 352). People v. Ewoldt, 7 Cal. 4th 380, 393-407, 27 Cal. Rptr. 2d 646, 652-662, 867 P.2d 757, 763-773 (1994).

Law Revision Commission Comment

Section 1101 is concerned with evidence of a person's character (i.e., his propensity or disposition to engage in a certain type of conduct) that is offered as a basis for an inference that he behaved in conformity with that character on a particular occasion. Section 1101 is not concerned with evidence offered to prove a person's character when that character is itself in issue; the admissibility of character evidence offered for this purpose is determined under Sections 351 and 1100. Nor is Section 1101 concerned with evidence of character offered on the issue of the credibility of a witness; the admissibility of such evidence is determined under Section 786-790. See Evidence Code § 1101(c).

Civil cases. Section 1101 excludes evidence of character to prove conduct in a civil case for the following reasons. First, character evidence is of slight probative value and may be very prejudicial. Second, character evidence tends to distract the trier of fact from the main question of what actually happened on the particular occasion and permits the trier of fact to reward the good man and to punish the bad man because of their respective characters. Third, introduction of character evidence may result in confusion of issues and require extended collateral inquiry. * * *

Criminal cases. Section 1101 states the general rule that evidence of character to prove conduct is inadmissible in a criminal case. Sections 1102 and 1103 state exceptions to this general principle. See the Comment to Section 1102.

Evidence of misconduct to show fact other than character. Section 1101 does not prohibit the admission of evidence of misconduct when it is offered as evidence of some other fact in issue, such as motive, common scheme or plan, preparation, intent, knowledge, identity, or absence of mistake or accident. Subdivision (b) of Section 1101 makes this clear. * * *

§ 1102. Opinion and reputation evidence of character of criminal defendant to prove conduct. In a criminal action, evidence of the defendant's character or a trait of his character in the form of an opinion or evidence of his reputation is not made inadmissible by Section 1101 if such evidence is:

(a) Offered by the defendant to prove his conduct in conformity with such character or trait of character.

(b) Offered by the prosecution to rebut evidence adduced by the defendant under subdivision (a).

Case Note

That defendant is not a "sexual deviant" is a relevant character trait in prosecution for child molestation, which defendant may prove by expert testimony, by lay opinion testimony based on facts personally observed by the witness, or by the defendant's reputation for high moral character. People v. McAlpin, 53 Cal. 3d 1289, 1305-1311, 283 Cal. Rptr. 382, 391-396, 812 P.2d 563, 572-577 (1991).

Law Revision Commission Comment

Section 1102 and 1103 state exceptions (applicable only in criminal cases) to the general rule of Section 1101 that character evidence is not admissible to prove conduct in conformity with that character.

Sections 1102 and 1103 generally

Under Section 1102, the accused in a criminal case may introduce evidence of his good character to show his innocence of the alleged crime—provided that the character or trait of character to be shown is relevant to the charge made against him. This codifies existing law. People v. Chrisman, 135 Cal. 282, 67 Pac. 136 (1901). Sections 1101 and 1102 make it clear that the prosecution may not, on its own initiative, use character evidence to prove that the defendant had the disposition to commit the crime charged; but, if the defendant first introduces evidence of his good character to show the likelihood of innocence, the prosecution may meet his evidence by introducing evidence of the defendant's bad character to show the likelihood of guilt. This also codifies existing law. People v. Jones, 42 Cal.2d 219, 266 P.2d 38 (1954) (prosecution for sexual molestation of child; error to exclude expert psychiatric opinion that defendant was not a sexual psychopath); People v. Stewart, 28 Cal. 395 (1865) (murder prosecution; error to exclude evidence of defendant's good character for peace and quiet); People v. Hughes, 123 Cal.App.2d 767, 267 P.2d 376 (1954) (assault prosecution; evidence of defendant's violent nature held admissible after introduction of evidence showing his good character for peace and quiet). See California Criminal Law Practice 489-490 (Cal.Cont.Ed.Bar 1964).

Likewise, under Section 1103, the defendant may introduce evidence of the character of the victim of the crime where the conduct of the victim in conformity with his character would tend to exculpate the defendant; and, if the defendant introduces evidence of the bad character of the victim, the prosecution may introduce evidence of the victim's good character. This codifies existing law. People v. Hoffman, 195 Cal. 295, 311-312, 232 Pac. 974, 980 (1925) (murder prosecution; evidence of victim's good reputation for peace and quiet held inadmissible when defendant had not attacked reputation of victim); People v. Lamar, 148 Cal. 564, 83 Pac. 993 (1906) (murder prosecution; error to exclude evidence of victim's bad character for violence offered to prove victim was aggressor and defendant acted in self-defense); People v. Shea, 125 Cal. 151, 57 Pac. 885 (1899) (rape prosecution; error to exclude evidence of the prosecutrix's unchaste character offered to prove the likelihood of consent); People v. Fitch, 28 Cal.App.2d 31, 81 P.2d 1019 (1938) (murder prosecution; evidence of victim's good character for peace and quiet held admissible after defendant introduced evidence of victim's violent nature). See also Comment, 25 Cal.L.Rev. 459 (1937).

Thus, under Sections 1102 and 1103, the defendant in a criminal case is given the right to introduce character evidence that would be inadmissible in a civil case. However, evidence of the character of the defendant or the victim—though weak—may be enough to raise a reasonable doubt in the mind of the trier of fact concerning the defendant's guilt. And, since his life or liberty is at stake, the defendant should not be deprived of the right to introduce evidence even of such slight probative value.

Kinds of character evidence admissible to prove conduct under Sections 1102 and 1103.

The three kinds of evidence that might be offered to prove character as circumstantial evidence of conduct are: (1) evidence as to reputation, (2) opinion evidence as to character, and (3) evidence of specific acts indicating character. The admissibility of each of these kinds of evidence when character is sought to be proved as circumstantial evidence of conduct under Sections 1102 and 1103 is discussed below.

Reputation evidence. Reputation evidence is the ordinary means sanctioned by the cases for proving character as circumstantial evidence of conduct. Witkin, California Evidence § 125 (1958). See People v. Fair, 43 Cal. 137 (1872). Both Sections 1102 and 1103 codify the existing law permitting character to be proved by reputation.

Opinion evidence. There is recent authority for the admission of opinion evidence to prove character as circumstantial evidence of conduct. People v. Jones, 42 Cal.2d 219, 266 P.2d 38 (1954) (error to exclude expert psychiatric opinion that the defendant was not a sexual psychopath and, hence, unlikely to have violated Penal Code Section 288). However, opinion evidence generally has been held inadmissible. See People v. Spigno, 156 Cal.App.2d 279, 319 P.2d 458 (1957) (full discussion of the Jones case); California Criminal Law Practice 489-490 (Cal.Cont.Ed.Bar 1964).

The general rule under existing law excludes the most reliable form of character evidence and admits the least reliable. The opinions of those whose personal intimacy with a person gives them firsthand knowledge of that person's character are a far more reliable indication of that character than is reputation, which is little more than accumulated hearsay. See 7 Wigmore, Evidence § 1986 (3d ed. 1940). The danger of collateral issues seems no greater than that inherent in reputation evidence. Accordingly, both Section 1102 and Section 1103 permit character to be proved by opinion evidence.

Evidence of specific acts. Under existing law, the admissibility of evidence of specific acts to prove character as circumstantial evidence of conduct depends upon the nature of the conduct sought to be proved. Evidence of specific acts of the accused is excluded as a general rule in order to avoid the possibility of prejudice, undue confusion of the issues with collateral matters, unfair surprise, and the like. Thus, it is usually held that evidence of specific acts by the defendant is inadmissible to prove his guilt even though the defendant has opened the question by introducing evidence of his good character. See discussion in People v. Gin Shue, 58 Cal.App.2d 625, 634, 137 P.2d 742, 747-748 (1943). On the other hand, it is well settled that in a rape case the defendant may show the unchaste character of the prosecutrix by evidence of prior voluntary intercourse in order to indicate the unlikelihood of resistance on the occasion in question. People v. Shea, 125 Cal. 151, 57 Pac. 885 (1899); People v. Benson, 6 Cal. 221 (1856); People v. Battilana, 52 Cal.App.2d 685, 126 P.2d 923 (1942). However, in a homicide or assault case where the defense is self-defense, evidence of specific acts of violence by the victim is inadmissible to prove his violent nature (and, hence, that the victim was the aggressor) unless the prior acts were directed against the defendant himself. People v. Yokum, 145 Cal.App.2d 245, 302 P.2d 406 (1956); People v. Soules, 41 Cal.App.2d 298, 106 P.2d 639 (1940). But see People v. Carmichael, 198 Cal. 534, 548, 246 Pac. 62, 68 (1926) (if defendant had knowledge of victim's statement evidencing violent nature, the "statement was material and might have had an important bearing upon his plea of self-defense"); People v. Swigart, 80 Cal.App. 31, 251 Pac. 343 (1926). See also Comment, 25 Cal.L.Rev. 459, 466-469 (1937).

Section 1102 codifies the general rule under existing law which precludes evidence of specific acts of the defendant to prove character as circumstantial evidence of his innocence or of his disposition to commit the crime with which he is charged.

Section 1103 permits both the defendant and the prosecution to use evidence of specific acts of the victim of the crime to prove the victim's character as circumstantial evidence of his conduct. In this respect, the section harmonizes conflicting rules found in existing law.

§ 1103. Character of crime victim to prove conduct offered by defendant, or by prosecution to rebut; evidence of defendant's violent character after evidence of victim's violent character; complaining witness' sexual conduct and manner of dress. (a) In a criminal action, evidence of the character or a trait of character (in the form of an opinion, evidence of reputation, or evidence of specific instances of conduct) of the victim of the crime for which the defendant is being prosecuted is not made inadmissible by Section 1101 if the evidence is:

(1) Offered by the defendant to prove conduct of the victim in conformity with the character or trait of character.

(2) Offered by the prosecution to rebut evidence adduced by the defendant under paragraph (1).

(b) In a criminal action, evidence of the defendant's character for violence or trait of character for violence (in the form of an opinion, evidence of reputation, or evidence of specific instances of conduct) is not made inadmissible by Section 1101 if the evidence is offered by the prosecution to prove conduct of the defendant in conformity with the character or trait of character and is offered after evidence that the victim had a character for violence or a trait of character tending to show violence has been adduced by the defendant under paragraph (1) of subdivision (a).

(c) (1) Notwithstanding any other provision of this code to the contrary, and except as provided in this subdivision, in any prosecution under Section 261, 262, or 264.1 of the Penal Code, or under Section 286, 287, or 289 of, or former Section 288a of, the Penal Code, or for assault with intent to commit, attempt to commit, or conspiracy to commit a crime defined in any of those sections, except where the crime is alleged to have occurred in a local detention facility, as defined in Section 6031.4, or in a state prison, as defined in Section 4504, opinion evidence, reputation evidence, and evidence of specific instances of the complaining witness' sexual conduct, or any of that evidence, is not admissible by the defendant in order to prove consent by the complaining witness.

(2) Notwithstanding paragraph (3), evidence of the manner in which the victim was dressed at the time of the commission of the offense shall not be admissible when offered by either party on the issue of consent in any prosecution for an offense specified in paragraph (1), unless the evidence is determined by the court to be relevant and admissible in the interests of justice. The proponent of the evidence shall make an offer of proof outside the hearing of the jury. The court shall then make its determination and at that time, state the reasons for its ruling on the record. For the purposes of this paragraph, "manner of dress" does not include the condition of the victim's clothing before, during, or after the commission of the offense.

(3) Paragraph (1) shall not be applicable to evidence of the complaining witness' sexual conduct with the defendant.

(4) If the prosecutor introduces evidence, including testimony of a witness, or the complaining witness as a witness gives testimony, and that evidence or testimony relates to the complaining witness' sexual conduct, the defendant may cross-examine the witness who gives the testimony and offer relevant evidence limited specifically to the rebuttal of the evidence introduced by the prosecutor or given by the complaining witness.

(5) Nothing in this subdivision shall be construed to make inadmissible any evidence offered to attack the credibility of the complaining witness as provided in Section 782.

(6) As used in this section, "complaining witness" means the alleged victim of the crime charged, the prosecution of which is subject to this subdivision. [*Amended 1974, 1981, 1990, 1991, 1996, 1998, 2018.*]

Statutory Notes

The 1974 amendment added the "rape shield" provisions now in subdivision (c). The 1991 amendment added the provisions now in subdivision (b). The 1998 amendment added the provision now in paragraph (c)(2).

See Penal Code § 1127d (required instruction to jury when evidence of prior sexual conduct is received).

Law Revision Commission Comment

See the Comment to Section 1102.

§ 1104. Character trait for care or skill. Except as provided in Sections 1102 and 1103, evidence of a trait of a person's character with respect to care or skill is inadmissible to prove the quality of his conduct on a specified occasion.

Law Revision Commission Comment

Section 1104 places a further limitation on the use of character evidence. Under Section 1104, character evidence with respect to care or skill is inadmissible to prove that conduct on a specific occasion was either careless or careful, skilled or unskilled, except to the extent permitted by Sections 1102 and 1103.

* * * The purpose of the rule is to prevent collateral issues from consuming too much time and distracting the attention of the trier of fact from what was actually done on the particular occasion. Here, the slight probative value of the evidence balanced against the danger of confusion of issues, collateral inquiry, prejudice, and the like, warrants a fixed exclusionary rule.

§ 1105. Habit or custom to prove specific behavior. Any otherwise admissible evidence of habit or custom is admissible to prove conduct on a specified occasion in conformity with the habit or custom.

Law Revision Commission Comment

Section 1105, like Section 1100, declares that certain evidence is admissible. Hence, Section 1105 is technically unnecessary because Section 351 declares that all relevant evidence is admissible. Nonetheless, Section 1105 is desirable to assure that evidence of custom or habit (a regular response to a repeated specific situation) is admissible even where evidence of a person's character (his general disposition or propensity to engage in a certain type of conduct) is inadmissible.

The admissibility of habit evidence to prove conduct in conformity with the habit has long been established in California. Wallis v. Southern Pac. Co., 184 Cal. 662, 195 Pac. 408 (1921) (distinguishing cases holding character evidence as to care or skill inadmissible); Craven v. Central Pac. R.R., 72 Cal. 345, 13 Pac. 878 (1887). The admissibility of evidence of the custom of a business or occupation is also well established. Hughes v. Pacific Wharf & Storage Co., 188 Cal. 210, 205 Pac. 105 (1922) (mailing letter). However, under existing law, evidence of habit is admissible only if there are no eyewitnesses. Boone v. Bank of America, 220 Cal. 93, 29 P.2d 409 (1934). In earlier cases, the Supreme Court criticized the "no eyewitness" limitation:

> This limitation upon the introduction of such testimony seems rather illogical. If the fact of the existence of habits of caution in a given particular has any legitimate evidentiary weight, the party benefited ought to have the advantage of it for whatever it is worth, even against adverse eye-witnesses; and if the testimony of the eye-witnesses is in his favor, it would be at least a harmless cumulation of evidence to permit testimony of his custom or habit. [Wallis v. Southern Pac. Co., 184 Cal. 662, 665, 195 Pac. 408, 409 (1921).]

The "no eyewitness" limitation is undesirable. Eyewitnesses frequently are mistaken, and some are dishonest. The trier of fact should be entitled to weigh the habit evidence against the eyewitness testimony as well as all of the other evidence in the case. Hence, Section 1105 does not contain the "no eyewitness" limitation.

§ 1106. Sexual harassment, sexual assault, or sexual battery cases; opinion or reputation evidence of plaintiff's sexual conduct; inadmissibility; exception; cross-examination. (a) In any civil action alleging conduct which constitutes sexual harassment, sexual assault, or sexual battery, opinion evidence, reputation evidence, and evidence of specific instances of the plaintiff's sexual conduct, or any of that evidence, is not admissible by the defendant in order to prove consent by the plaintiff or the absence of injury to the plaintiff, unless the injury alleged by the plaintiff is in the nature of loss of consortium.

(b) Subdivision (a) does not apply to evidence of the plaintiff's sexual conduct with the alleged perpetrator.

c) Notwithstanding subdivision (b), in any civil action brought pursuant to Section 1708.5 of the Civil Code involving a minor and adult as described in Section 1708.5.5 of the Civil Code, evidence of the plaintiff minor's sexual conduct with the defendant adult shall not be admissible to prove consent by the plaintiff or the avsence of injury to the plaintiff. Such evidence of the plaintiff's sexual conduct may only be introduced to attack the credibility of the plaintiff in accordance with Section 783 or to prove something other than consent by the plaintiff if, upon a hearing of the court out of the presence of the jury, the defendant proves that the probative value of that evidence outweighs the prejudice to the plaintiff consistent with Section 352. [*Added 2014.*]

(d) If the plaintiff introduces evidence, including testimony of a witness, or the plaintiff as a witness gives testimony, and the evidence or testimony relates to the plaintiff's sexual conduct, the defendant may cross-examine the witness who gives the testimony and offer relevant evidence limited specifically to the rebuttal of the evidence introduced by the plaintiff or given by the plaintiff.

(e) This section shall not be construed to make inadmissible any evidence offered to attack the credibility of the plaintiff as provided in Section 783. [*Added 1985. Amended 2016.*]

§ 1107. Intimate partner battering and its effects; expert testimony in criminal actions; sufficiency of foundation; abuse and domestic violence; applicability to Penal Code; impact on decisional law. (a) In a criminal action, expert testimony is admissible by either the prosecution or the defense regarding intimate partner battering and its effects, including the nature and effect of physical, emotional, or mental abuse on the beliefs, perceptions, or behavior of victims of domestic violence, except when offered against a criminal defendant to prove the occurrence of the act or acts of abuse which form the basis of the criminal charge.

(b) The foundation shall be sufficient for admission of this expert testimony if the proponent of the evidence establishes its relevancy and the proper qualifications of the expert witness. Expert opinion testimony on intimate partner battering and its effects shall not be considered a new scientific technique whose reliability is unproven.

(c) For purposes of this section, "abuse" is defined in Section 6203 of the Family Code, and "domestic violence" is defined in Section 6211 of the Family Code and may include acts defined in Section 242, subdivision (e) of Section 243, Section 262, 273.5, 273.6, 422, or 653m of the Penal Code.

(d) This section is intended as a rule of evidence only and no substantive change affecting the Penal Code is intended.

(e) This section shall be known, and may be cited, as the Expert Witness Testimony on Intimate Partner Battering and Its Effects Section of the Evidence Code.

(f) The changes in this section that become effective on January 1, 2005, are not intended to impact any existing decisional law regarding this section, and that decisional law should apply equally to this section as it refers to "intimate partner battering and its effects" in place of "battered women's syndrome." [*Added 1991. Amended 1992, 1993, 2004.*]

Statutory Note

Section 2 of Stats. 1991, c. 812 (A.B. 785), which added § 1107, declared:

The Legislature does not intend Section 1107 of the Evidence Code to preclude the admissibility of evidence of battered women's syndrome under other statutory or case law.

The 2004 amendment changed "battered women's syndrome" to "intimate partner battering and its effects."

Case Note

Evidence of battered women's syndrome is relevant not only to whether the defendant actually believed it was necessary to kill in self-defense but also to whether her belief was reasonable. If the defendant testifies, the evidence also is relevant to her credibility. People v. Humphrey, 13 Cal. 4th 1073, 56 Ca. Rptr. 2d 142, 921 P.2d 1 (1996).

Expert testimony about the behavior of a victim of domestic violence may be admissible under § 801 even if it is not admissible under § 1107. People v. Brown, 33 Cal.4th 892, 16 Cal.Rptr.3d 447, 94 P.3d 574 (2004).

§ 1107.5. Expert testimony regarding effects of human trafficking on victims. (a) In a criminal action, expert testimony is admissible by either the prosecution or the defense regarding the effects of human trafficking on human trafficking victims, including the nature and effect of physical, emotional, or mental abuse on the beliefs, perceptions, or behavior of human trafficking victims.

(b) The foundation shall be sufficient for admission of this expert testimony if the proponent of the evidence establishes its relevancy and the proper qualifications of the expert witness.

(c) For purposes of this section, "human trafficking victim" is defined as a victim of an offense described in Section 236.1 of the Penal Code.

(d) This section is intended as a rule of evidence only and no substantive change affecting the Penal Code is intended. [*Added 2017.*]

§ 1108. Evidence of another sexual offense by defendant; disclosure; construction of section. (a) In a criminal action in which the defendant is accused of a sexual offense, evidence of the defendant's commission of another sexual offense or offenses is not made inadmissible by Section 1101, if the evidence is not inadmissible pursuant to Section 352.

(b) In an action in which evidence is to be offered under this section, the people shall disclose the evidence to the defendant, including statements of witnesses or a summary of the substance of any testimony that is expected to be offered in compliance with the requirements of Section 1054.7 of the Penal Code.

(c) This section does not limit the admission or consideration of evidence under any other section of this code.

(d) As used in this section, the following definitions shall apply:

(1) "Sexual offense" means a crime under the law of a state or of the United States that involved any of the following:

(A) Any conduct proscribed by subdivision (b) or (c) of Section 236.1, Section 243.4, 261, 261.5, 262, 264.1, 266c, 269, 286, 287, 288, 288.2, 288.5, or 289, or subdivision (b), (c), or (d) of Section 311.2 or Section 311.3, 311.4, 311.10, 311.11, 314, or 647.6, of the Penal Code.

(B) Any conduct proscribed by Section 220 of the Penal Code, except assault with intent to commit mayhem.

(C) Contact, without consent, between any part of the defendant's body or an object and the genitals or anus of another person.

(D) Contact, without consent, between the genitals or anus of the defendant and any part of another person's body.

(E) Deriving sexual pleasure or gratification from the infliction of death, bodily injury, or physical pain on another person.

(F) An attempt or conspiracy to engage in conduct described in this paragraph.

(2) "Consent" shall have the same meaning as provided in Section 261.6 of the Penal Code, except that it does not include consent which is legally ineffective because of the age, mental disorder, or developmental or physical disability of the victim. [*Added 1995. Amended 2001, 2002, 2017, 2018.*]

Statutory Notes

The 2001 amendment added in subdivision (d)(1)(A) reference to Penal Code § 269. The 2002 amendment replaced specific time limits in subdivision (b) with reference to Penal Code § 1054.7, and added subdivision (d)(1)(B), referring to Penal Code § 220.

The Assembly Journal for the 1995-96 Regular Session, p. 3277, contained the following letter from Assembly Member Rogan, dated Aug. 24, 1995, regarding A.B.882 (Stats.1995, c. 439):

This letter clarifies the intent of AB 882, which I authored. The bill concerns the admissibility in sexual offense cases of evidence that the defendant has committed another sexual offense or offenses.

AB 882 is modeled on Rules 413-15 of the Federal Rules of Evidence, and adapts the principle of these rules to the framework of California law. A number of statements were generated in the legislative history of the federal rules that can be consulted and relied on for explanation concerning the background, rationale, and effect of this reform. See 140 Cong.Rec. H8991-91 (daily ed. Aug. 21, 1994) (statement of Rep. Susan Molinari, principal House sponsor of Fed.R.Evid. 413-15): Karp, Evidence of Propensity and Probability in Sex Offense Cases and Other Cases, 70 Chicago-Kent L.Rev. 15 (1994) (text of address by author of Fed.R.Evid. 413-15): 137 Cong.Rec. S3238-42 (daily ed. March 13, 1991) (analysis statement accompanying proposal of Fed.R.Evid. 413-15 in § 635).

Specific explanation concerning AB 882, its relationship to prior California Law, and the need for its enactment in California, appears in an article by the legislation's sponsor, Attorney General Dan Lungren: Stopping Rapists and Child Molesters by Giving Juries All the Facts—Reforms in Federal and California Law (published in 1995 in Prosecutor's Brief, volume XVII, no. 2, at 13-14, 23).

During its consideration by the legislature, AB 882 was the subject of hearings before the Assembly Committee on Public Safety, the Senate Committee on Criminal Procedure, and the Senate Committee on Judiciary. Three amendments were adopted to the bill in connection with these hearings.

During the hearing before the Assembly Committee on Public Safety, the language of the new § 1108 of the Evidence Code was amended to provide explicitly that evidence of other offenses within the scope of the section is not subject to § 1101's prohibition of evidence of character or disposition. This makes it clear that § 1108 permits courts to admit such evidence on a common sense basis—without a precondition of finding a 'non-character' purpose for which it is relevant—and permits rational assessment by juries of evidence so admitted. This includes consideration of the other sexual offenses as evidence of the defendant's disposition to commit such crimes, and for its bearing on the probability or improbability that the defendant has been falsely or mistakenly accused of such an offense.

During the hearing before the Senate Committee on Criminal Procedure, the bill was amended to delete the direct application of the new § 1108 to civil actions. Nevertheless, the reform remains valuable to civil litigants who seek redress for sexual offenses. In cases where a criminal conviction for the underlying act is obtained with the help of new § 1108, normal collateral estoppel principles will generally foreclose the defendant from denying his commission of the offense in subsequent civil suit.

During the hearing before the Senate Committee on Judiciary, an amendment was adopted to provide explicitly that Evidence Code § 352 remains applicable to evidence offered under the new § 1108. While § 1108 explicitly supersedes § 1101's prohibition of evidence of character or disposition within its scope of application, it does not supersede other provisions of the Evidence Code, such as normal restrictions in hearsay and the court's authority to exclude evidence presenting an overriding likelihood of prejudice under § 352. Cf. People v. Ewoldt, 7 Cal. 4th 380, 404-08 (1994): People v. Balcom, 7 Cal. 4th 414, 426-27 (1994) (§ 352 balancing in relation to admission of evidence of other sexual offenses under § 1101).

The amendment adopted at the Judiciary Committee hearing simply makes this point explicit in relation to § 352. The reform does, however, affect the practical operation of § 352 balancing, because admission and consideration of evidence of other sexual offenses to show character or disposition would be no longer treated as intrinsically prejudicial or impermissible. Hence, evidence offered under § 1108 could not be excluded on the basis of § 352 unless 'the probability that its admission will ... create substantial danger of undue prejudice' (or other adverse effects identified in § 352) substantially outweighed its probative value concerning the defendant's disposition to commit the sexual offense or offenses with which he is charged and other matters relevant to the determination of the charge. As with other forms of relevant evidence that are not subject to any exclusionary principle, the presumption will be in favor of admission.

At the hearing before the Judiciary Committee, there was discussion whether more exacting requirements of similarity between the charged offense and the defendant's other offenses should be imposed. The decision was against making such a change, because doing so would tend to reintroduce the excessive requirements of specific similarity under prior law which AB 882 is designed to overcome, see Lungren, supra, at 14, and could often prevent the admission and consideration of evidence of other sexual offenses in circumstances where it is rationally probative. Many sex offenders are not 'specialists', and commit a variety of offenses which differ in specific character.

§ 1109. Evidence of defendant's other acts of domestic violence.

(a) (1) Except as provided in subdivision (e) or (f), in a criminal action in which the defendant is accused of an offense involving domestic violence, evidence of the defendant's commission of other domestic violence is not made inadmissible by Section 1101 if the evidence is not inadmissible pursuant to Section 352.

(2) Except as provided in subdivision (e) or (f), in a criminal action in which the defendant is accused of an offense involving abuse of an elder or dependent person, evidence of the defendant's commission of other abuse of an elder or dependent person is not made inadmissible by Section 1101 if the evidence is not inadmissible pursuant to Section 352.

(3) Except as provided in subdivision (e) or (f) and subject to a hearing conducted pursuant to Section 352, which shall include consideration of any corroboration and remoteness in time, in a criminal action in which the defendant is accused of an offense involving child abuse, evidence of the defendant's commission of child abuse is not made inadmissible by Section 1101 if the evidence is not inadmissible pursuant to Section 352. Nothing in this paragraph prohibits or limits the admission of evidence pursuant to subdivision (b) of Section 1101.

(b) In an action in which evidence is to be offered under this section, the people shall disclose the evidence to the defendant, including statements of witnesses or a summary of the substance of any testimony that is expected to be offered, in compliance with the provisions of Section 1054.7 of the Penal Code.

(c) This section shall not be construed to limit or preclude the admission or consideration of evidence under any other statute or case law.

(d) As used in this section:

(1) "Abuse of an elder or dependent person" means physical or sexual abuse, neglect, financial abuse, abandonment, isolation, abduction, or other treatment that results in physical harm, pain, or mental suffering, the deprivation of care by a caregiver, or other deprivation by a custodian or provider of goods or services that are necessary to avoid physical harm or mental suffering.

(2) "Child abuse" means an act proscribed by Section 273d of the Penal Code.

(3) "Domestic violence" has the meaning set forth in Section 13700 of the Penal Code. Subject to a hearing conducted pursuant to Section 352, which shall include consideration of any corroboration and remoteness in time, "domestic violence" has the further meaning as set forth in Section 6211 of the Family Code, if the act occurred no more than five years before the charged offense.

(e) Evidence of acts occurring more than 10 years before the charged offense is inadmissible under this section, unless the court determines that the admission of this evidence is in the interest of justice.

(f) Evidence of the findings and determinations of administrative agencies regulating the conduct of health facilities licensed under Section 1250 of the Health and Safety Code is inadmissible under this section. [*Added 1996. Amended 1998, 2000, 2004, 2005.*]

Statutory Note

The 2000 amendment expanded coverage to include "abuse of an elder or dependent adult." The 2004 and 2005 amendment revised the definitions in subd. (d).

Chapter 2. Mediation

Statutory Notes

See Bus. & Prof. Code § 467.5 (application of this chapter to dispute resolution programs funded by Department of Consumer Affairs); Govt. Code § 11420.30 (confidentiality of communications in alternative dispute resolution proceedings connected to administrative adjudication).

§ 1115. Definitions. For purposes of this chapter [§§ 1115-1128]:

(a) "Mediation" means a process in which a neutral person or persons facilitate communication between the disputants to assist them in reaching a mutually acceptable agreement.

(b) "Mediator" means a neutral person who conducts a mediation. "Mediator" includes any person designated by a mediator either to assist in the mediation or to communicate with the participants in preparation for a mediation.

(c) "Mediation consultation" means a communication between a person and a mediator for the purpose of initiating, considering, or reconvening a mediation or retaining the mediator. [*Added 1997.*]

Law Revision Commission Comment - 1997 Addition

Subdivision (a) of Section 1115 is drawn from Code of Civil Procedure Section 1775.1. To accommodate a wide range of mediation styles, the definition is broad, without specific limitations on format. For example, it would include a mediation conducted as a number of sessions, only some of which involve the mediator. The definition focuses on the nature of a proceeding, not its label. A proceeding may be a "mediation" for purposes of this chapter, even though it is denominated differently.

Under subdivision (b), a mediator must be neutral. The neutrality requirement is drawn from Code of Civil Procedure Section 1775.1. An attorney or other representative of a party is not neutral and so does not qualify as a "mediator" for purposes of this chapter.

A "mediator" may be an individual, group of individuals, or entity. See Section 175 ("person" defined). See also Section 10 (singular includes the plural). This definition of mediator encompasses not only the neutral person who takes the lead in conducting a mediation, but also any neutral who assists in the mediation, such as a case-developer, interpreter, or secretary. The definition focuses on a person's role, not the person's title. A person may be a "mediator" under this chapter even though the person has a different title, such as "ombudsperson." Any person who meets the definition of "mediator" must comply with Section 1121 (mediator reports and communications), which generally prohibits a mediator from reporting to a court or other tribunal concerning the mediated dispute.

Subdivision (c) is drawn from former Section 1152.5, which was amended in 1996 to explicitly protect mediation intake communications. See 1996 Cal. Stat. ch. 174, § 1. Subdivision (c) is not limited to communications to retain a mediator. It also encompasses contacts concerning whether to mediate, such as where a mediator contacts a disputant because another disputant desires to mediate, and contacts concerning initiation or recommencement of mediation, such as where a case-developer meets with a disputant before mediation. * * * [27 Cal.L.Rev.Comm. Reports App. 5 (1997).]

§ 1116. Effect of chapter. (a) Nothing in this chapter [§§ 1115-1128] expands or limits a court's authority to order participation in a dispute resolution proceeding. Nothing in this chapter authorizes or affects the enforceability of a contract clause in which parties agree to the use of mediation.

(b) Nothing in this chapter [§§ 1115-1128] makes admissible evidence that is inadmissible under Section 1152 or any other statute. [*Added 1997.*]

§ 1117. Application of chapter. (a) Except as provided in subdivision (b), this chapter [§1115-1128] applies to a mediation as defined in Section 1115.

(b) This chapter [§1115-1128] does not apply to either of the following:

(1) A proceeding under Part 1 (commencing with Section 1800) of Division 5 of the Family Code or Chapter 11 (commencing with Section 3160) of Part 2 of Division 8 of the Family Code.

(2) A settlement conference pursuant to Rule 3.1380 of the California Rules of Court. [*Added 1997; amended 2008.*]

Law Revision Commission Comments - 1997 Addition

Under subdivision (a) of Section 1117, mediation confidentiality and the other safeguards of this chapter apply to a broad range of mediations. See Section 1115 Comment.

Subdivision (b) sets forth two exceptions. Section 1117(b)(1) continues without substantive change former Section 1152.5(b). Special confidentiality rules apply to a proceeding in family conciliation court or a mediation of child custody or visitation issues. See Section 1040; Fam. Code §§ 1818, 3177.

Section 1117(b)(2) establishes that a court settlement conference is not a mediation within the scope of this chapter. A settlement conference is conducted under the aura of the court and is subject to special rules. [27 Cal.L.Rev.Comm. Reports App. 5 (1997).]

§ 1118. Oral agreements. An oral agreement "in accordance with Section 1118" means an oral agreement that satisfies all of the following conditions:

(a) The oral agreement is recorded by a court reporter or reliable means of audio recording.

(b) The terms of the oral agreement are recited on the record in the presence of the parties and the mediator, and the parties express on the record that they agree to the terms recited.

(c) The parties to the oral agreement expressly state on the record that the agreement is enforceable or binding, or words to that effect.

(d) The recording is reduced to writing and the writing is signed by the parties within 72 hours after it is recorded. [*Added 1997. Amended 2009.*]

Law Revision Commission Comments - 1997 Addition

Section 1118 establishes a procedure for orally memorializing an agreement, in the interest of efficiency. Provisions permitting use of that procedure for certain purposes include Sections 1121 (mediator reports and communications), 1122 (disclosure by agreement), 1123 (written settlement agreements reached through mediation), and 1124 (oral agreements reached through mediation). See also Section 1125 (when mediation ends). For guidance on authority to bind a litigant, see Williams v. Saunders, 55 Cal. App. 4th 1158, 64 Cal. Rptr. 2d 571 (1997) ("The litigants' direct participation tends to ensure that the settlement is the result of their mature reflection and deliberate assent.") [27 Cal.L.Rev.Comm. Reports App. 5 (1997).]

§ 1119. Written or oral communications during mediation process; admissibility. Except as otherwise provided in this chapter [§§ 1115-1128]:

(a) No evidence of anything said or any admission made for the purpose of, in the course of, or pursuant to, a mediation or a mediation consultation is admissible or subject to discovery, and disclosure of the evidence shall not be compelled, in any arbitration, administrative adjudication, civil action, or other noncriminal proceeding in which, pursuant to law, testimony can be compelled to be given.

(b) No writing, as defined in Section 250, that is prepared for the purpose of, in the course of, or pursuant to, a mediation or a mediation consultation, is admissible or subject to discovery, and disclosure of the writing shall not be compelled, in any arbitration, administrative adjudication, civil action, or other noncriminal proceeding in which, pursuant to law, testimony can be compelled to be given.

(c) All communications, negotiations, or settlement discussions by and between participants in the course of a mediation or a mediation consultation shall remain confidential. [*Added 1997.*]

Case Note

A showing of need in litigation does not overcome the protection of this section, which has no "good cause" exception. "Writings" protected by subdivision (b) should be broadly construed to include photographs, videotapes, witness statements, and raw test data prepared for the purpose of mediation. Rojas v. Superior Ct., 33 Cal. 4th 407, 15 Cal. Rptr. 3d 643, 93 P.3d 260 (2004)

Law Revision Commission Comments - 1997 Addition

* * * [Under S]ubdivision (c), [a] mediation is confidential notwithstanding the presence of an observer, such as a person evaluating or training the mediator or studying the mediation process. * * *

§ 1120. Evidence otherwise admissible. (a) Evidence otherwise admissible or subject to discovery outside of a mediation or a mediation consultation shall not be or become inadmissible or protected from disclosure solely by reason of its introduction or use in a mediation or a mediation consultation.

(b) This chapter does not limit any of the following:

(1) The admissibility of an agreement to mediate a dispute.

(2) The effect of an agreement not to take a default or an agreement to extend the time within which to act or refrain from acting in a pending civil action.

(3) Disclosure of the mere fact that a mediator has served, is serving, will serve, or was contacted about serving as a mediator in a dispute.

(4) The admissibility of declarations of disclosure required by Sections 2104 and 2105 of the Family Code, even if prepared for the purpose of, in the course of, or pursuant to, a mediation or a mediation consultation. [*Added 1997, Amended 2017.*]

Case Note

Section 2 of the enacting statute, SB-217, reads: It is the intent of the Legislature that this act codify the holding of Lappe v. Superior Court (2014) 232 Cal.App.4th 774.

§ 1121. Mediator's reports and findings. Neither a mediator nor anyone else may submit to a court or other adjudicative body, and a court or other adjudicative body may not consider, any report, assessment, evaluation, recommendation, or finding of any kind by the mediator concerning a mediation conducted by the mediator, other than a report that is mandated by court rule or other law and that states only whether an agreement was reached, unless all parties to the mediation expressly agree otherwise in writing, or orally in accordance with Section 1118. [*Added 1997.*]

Law Revision Commission Comments - 1997 Addition

Section 1121 * * * does not prohibit a mediator from providing a mediation participant with feedback on the dispute in the course of the mediation.

* * * Rather, the focus is on preventing coercion. As Section 1121 recognizes, a mediator should not be able to influence the result of a mediation or adjudication by reporting or threatening to report to the decisionmaker on the merits of the dispute or reasons why mediation failed to resolve it. Similarly, a mediator should not have authority to resolve or decide the mediated dispute, and should not have any function for the adjudicating tribunal with regard to the dispute, except as a non-decisionmaking neutral. * * *

§1122. Communications or writings; conditions to admissibility. (a) A communication or a writing, as defined in Section 250, that is made or prepared for the purpose of, or in the course of, or pursuant to, a mediation or a mediation consultation, is not made inadmissible, or protected from disclosure, by provisions of this chapter if any of the following conditions are satisfied:

(1) All persons who conduct or otherwise participate in the mediation expressly agree in writing, or orally in accordance with Section 1118, to disclosure of the communication, document, or writing.

(2) The communication, document, or writing was prepared by or on behalf of fewer than all the mediation participants, those participants expressly agree in writing, or orally in accordance with Section 1118, to its disclosure, and the communication, document, or writing does not disclose anything said or done or any admission made in the course of the mediation.

(3) The communication, document, or writing is related to an attorney's compliance with the requirements described in Section 1129 and does not disclose anything said or done or any admission made in the course of the mediation, in which case the communication, document, or writing may be used in an attorney disciplinary proceeding to determine whether the attorney has complied with Section 1129.

(b) For purposes of subdivision (a), if the neutral person who conducts a mediation expressly agrees to disclosure, that agreement also binds any other person described in subdivision (b) of Section 1115.

. [*Added 1997.Amended 2018.*]

Law Revision Commission Comments - 1997 Addition

* * * Subdivision (a)(1) states the general rule that mediation documents and communications may be admitted or disclosed only upon agreement of all participants, including not only parties but also the mediator and other nonparties attending the mediation (e.g., a disputant not involved in litigation, a spouse, an accountant, an insurance representative, or an employee of a corporate affiliate). Agreement must be express, not implied. For example, parties cannot be deemed to have agreed in advance to disclosure merely because they agreed to participate in a particular dispute resolution program.

Subdivision (a)(2) facilitates admissibility and disclosure of unilaterally prepared materials, but it only applies so long as those materials may be produced in a manner revealing nothing about the mediation discussion. Materials that necessarily disclose mediation communications may be admitted or disclosed only upon satisfying the general rule of subdivision (a)(1).

Mediation materials that satisfy the requirements of subdivisions (a)(1) or (a)(2) are not necessarily admissible or subject to disclosure. Although the provisions on mediation confidentiality do not bar admissibility or disclosure, there may be other bases for exclusion.

Subdivision (b) makes clear that if the person who takes the lead in conducting a mediation agrees to disclosure, it is unnecessary to seek out and obtain assent from each assistant to that person, such as a case developer, interpreter, or secretary. * * *

§ 1123. Written settlement agreements; conditions to admissibility. A written settlement agreement prepared in the course of, or pursuant to, a mediation, is not made inadmissible, or protected from disclosure, by provisions of this chapter [§§ 1115-1128] if the agreement is signed by the settling parties and any of the following conditions are satisfied:

(a) The agreement provides that it is admissible or subject to disclosure, or words to that effect.

(b) The agreement provides that it is enforceable or binding or words to that effect.

(c) All parties to the agreement expressly agree in writing, or orally in accordance with Section 1118, to its disclosure.

(d) The agreement is used to show fraud, duress, or illegality that is relevant to an issue in dispute. [*Added 1997.*]

Law Revision Commission Comments - 1997 Addition

Section 1123 consolidates and clarifies provisions governing written settlements reached through mediation. For guidance on binding a disputant to a written settlement agreement, see Williams v. Saunders, 55 Cal. App. 4th 1158, 64 Cal. Rptr. 2d 571 (1997) ("The litigants' direct participation tends to ensure that the settlement is the result of their mature reflection and deliberate assent.").

As to an executed written settlement agreement, subdivision (a) continues part of former Section 1152.5(a)(2). See also Ryan v. Garcia, 27 Cal. App. 4th 1006, 1012, 33 Cal. Rptr. 2d 158, 162 (1994) (Section 1152.5 "provides a simple means by which settlement agreements executed during mediation can be made admissible in later proceedings," i.e., the "parties may consent, as part of a writing, to subsequent admissibility of the agreement").

Subdivision (b) is new. It is added due to the likelihood that parties intending to be bound will use words to that effect, rather than saying their agreement is intended to be admissible or subject to disclosure.

As to fully executed written settlement agreements, subdivision (c) supersedes former Section 1152.5(a)(4). To facilitate enforceability of such agreements, disclosure pursuant to subdivision (c) requires only agreement of the parties. Agreement of the mediator and other mediation participants is not necessary. Subdivision (c) is thus an exception to the general rule governing disclosure of mediation communications by agreement. See Section 1122. * * *

A written settlement agreement that satisfies the requirements of subdivision (a), (b), (c), or (d) is not necessarily admissible or subject to disclosure. Although the provisions on mediation confidentiality do not bar admissibility or disclosure, there may be other bases for exclusion. * * * [27 Cal.L.Rev.Comm. Reports App. 5 (1997).]

§ 1124. Oral agreements; conditions to admissibility. An oral agreement made in the course of, or pursuant to, a mediation is not made inadmissible, or protected from disclosure, by the provisions of this chapter [§§ 1115-1128] if any of the following conditions are satisfied:

(a) The agreement is in accordance with Section 1118.

(b) The agreement is in accordance with subdivisions (a), (b), and (d) of Section 1118, and all parties to the agreement expressly agree, in writing or orally in accordance with Section 1118, to disclosure of the agreement.

(c) The agreement is in accordance with subdivisions (a), (b), and (d) of Section 1118, and the agreement is used to show fraud, duress, or illegality that is relevant to an issue in dispute. [*Added 1997.*]

Law Revision Commission Comments - 1997 Addition

Section 1124 sets forth specific circumstances under which mediation confidentiality is inapplicable to an oral agreement reached through mediation. Except in those circumstances, Sections 1119 (mediation confidentiality) and 1124 codify the rule of Ryan v. Garcia, 27 Cal. App. 4th 1006, 33 Cal. Rptr. 2d 158 (1994) (mediation confidentiality applies to oral statement of settlement terms), and reject the contrary approach of Regents of University of California v. Sumner, 42 Cal. App. 4th 1209, 50 Cal. Rptr. 2d 200 (1996) (mediation confidentiality does not protect oral statement of settlement terms). * * *

An oral agreement that satisfies the requirements of subdivision (a), (b), or (c) is not necessarily admissible or subject to disclosure. Although the provisions on mediation confidentiality do not bar admissibility or disclosure, there may be other bases for exclusion. * * * [27 Cal.L.Rev.Comm. Reports App. 5 (1997).]

§ 1125. End of mediation; satisfaction of conditions. (a) For purposes of confidentiality under this chapter [§§ 1115-1128], a mediation ends when any one of the following conditions is satisfied:

(1) The parties execute a written settlement agreement that fully resolves the dispute.

(2) An oral agreement that fully resolves the dispute is reached in accordance with Section 1118.

(3) The mediator provides the mediation participants with a writing signed by the mediator that states that the mediation is terminated, or words to that effect, which shall be consistent with Section 1121.

(4) A party provides the mediator and the other mediation participants with a writing stating that the mediation is terminated, or words to that effect, which shall be consistent with Section 1121. In a mediation involving more than two parties, the mediation may continue as to the remaining parties or be terminated in accordance with this section.

(5) For 10 calendar days, there is no communication between the mediator and any of the parties to the mediation relating to the dispute. The mediator and the parties may shorten or extend this time by agreement.

(b) For purposes of confidentiality under this chapter, if a mediation partially resolves a dispute, mediation ends when either of the following conditions is satisfied:

(1) The parties execute a written settlement agreement that partially resolves the dispute.

(2) An oral agreement that partially resolves the dispute is reached in accordance with Section 1118.

(c) This section does not preclude a party from ending a mediation without reaching an agreement. This section does not otherwise affect the extent to which a party may terminate a mediation. [*Added 1997.*]

Law Revision Commission Comments - 1997 Addition

By specifying when a mediation ends, Section 1125 provides guidance on which communications are protected by Section 1119 (mediation confidentiality).

Under subdivision (a)(1), if mediation participants reach an oral compromise and reduce it to a written settlement fully resolving their dispute, confidentiality extends until the agreement is signed by all the parties. * * *

Subdivision (a)(2) applies where mediation participants fully resolve their dispute by an oral agreement that is recorded and memorialized in writing in accordance with Section 1118. The mediation is over upon completion of that procedure, and the confidentiality protections of this chapter do not apply to any later proceedings, such as attempts to further refine the content of the agreement. See Section 1124 (oral agreements reached through mediation). Subdivisions (a)(3) and (a)(4) are drawn from Rule 14 of the American Arbitration Association's Commercial Mediation Rules (as amended, Jan. 1, 1992). Subdivision (a)(5) applies where an affirmative act terminating a mediation for purposes of this chapter does not occur.

Subdivision (b) applies where mediation partially resolves a dispute, such as when the disputants resolve only some of the issues (e.g., contract, but not tort, liability) or when only some of the disputants settle. * * * [27 Cal.L.Rev.Comm. Reports App. 5 (1997).]

§ 1126. Protections before and after mediation ends. Anything said, any admission made, or any writing that is inadmissible, protected from disclosure, and confidential under this chapter [§§ 1115-1128] before a mediation ends, shall remain inadmissible, protected from disclosure, and confidential to the same extent after the mediation ends. [*Added 1997.*]

§ 1127. Attorney's fees and costs. If a person subpoenas or otherwise seeks to compel a mediator to testify or produce a writing, as defined in Section 250, and the court or other adjudicative body determines that the testimony or writing is inadmissible under this chapter [§§ 1115-1128], or protected from disclosure under this chapter, the court or adjudicative body making the determination shall award reasonable attorney's fees and costs to the mediator against the person seeking the testimony or writing. [*Added 1997.*]

§ 1128. Subsequent trials; references to mediation. Any reference to a mediation during any subsequent trial is an irregularity in the proceedings of the trial for the purposes of Section 657 of the Code of Civil Procedure. Any reference to a mediation during any other subsequent noncriminal proceeding is grounds for vacating or modifying the decision in that proceeding, in whole or in part, and granting a new or further hearing on all or part of the issues, if the reference materially affected the substantial rights of the party requesting relief. [*Added 1997.*]

Law Revision Commission Comments - 1997 Addition

* * * An appropriate situation for invoking this section is where a party urges the trier of fact to draw an adverse inference from an adversary's refusal to disclose mediation communications. * * * [27 Cal.L.Rev.Comm. Reports App. 5 (1997).]

§ 1129. Mediation; confidentiality; disclosure. (a) Except in the case of a class or representative action, an attorney representing a client participating in a mediation or a mediation consultation shall, as soon as reasonably possible before the client agrees to participate in the mediation or mediation consultation, provide that client with a printed disclosure containing the confidentiality restrictions described in Section 1119 and obtain a printed acknowledgment signed by that client stating that he or she has read and understands the confidentiality restrictions.

b) An attorney who is retained after an individual agrees to participate in the mediation or mediation consultation shall, as soon as reasonably possible after being retained, comply with the printed disclosure and acknowledgment requirements described in subdivision (a).

(c) The printed disclosure required by subdivision (a) shall:

(1) Be printed in the preferred language of the client in at least 12-point font.

(2) Be printed on a single page that is not attached to any other document provided to the client.

(3) Include the names of the attorney and the client and be signed and dated by the attorney and the client.

(d) If the requirements in subdivision (c) are met, the following disclosure shall be deemed to comply with the requirements of subdivision (a):

Mediation Disclosure Notification and Acknowledgment

To promote communication in mediation, California law generally makes mediation a confidential process. California's mediation confidentiality laws are laid out in Sections 703.5 and 1115 to 1129, inclusive, of the Evidence Code. Those laws establish the confidentiality of mediation and limit the disclosure, admissibility, and a court's consideration of communications, writings, and conduct in connection with a mediation. In general, those laws mean the following:

• All communications, negotiations, or settlement offers in the course of a mediation must remain confidential.

• Statements made and writings prepared in connection with a mediation are not admissible or subject to discovery or compelled disclosure in noncriminal proceedings.

• A mediator's report, opinion, recommendation, or finding about what occurred in a mediation may not be submitted to or considered by a court or another adjudicative body.

• A mediator cannot testify in any subsequent civil proceeding about any communication or conduct occurring at, or in connection with, a mediation.

This means that all communications between you and your attorney made in preparation for a mediation, or during a mediation, are confidential and cannot be disclosed or used (except in extremely limited circumstances), even if you later decide to sue your attorney for malpractice because of something that happens during the mediation.

I, ________ [Name of Client], understand that, unless all participants agree otherwise, no oral or written communication made during a mediation, or in preparation for a mediation, including communications between me and my attorney, can be used as evidence in any subsequent noncriminal legal action including an action against my attorney for malpractice or an ethical violation.

NOTE: This disclosure and signed acknowledgment does not limit your attorney's potential liability to you for professional malpractice, or prevent you from (1) reporting any professional misconduct by your attorney to the State Bar of California or (2) cooperating with any disciplinary investigation or criminal prosecution of your attorney.

________ ________
[Name of Client] [Date signed]

________ ________
[Name of Attorney] [Date signed]

(e) Failure of an attorney to comply with this section is not a basis to set aside an agreement prepared in the course of, or pursuant to, a mediation. [*Added 2018.*]

Chapter 3. Other Evidence Affected or Excluded by Extrinsic Policies

§ 1150. Evidence to test a verdict. (a) Upon an inquiry as to the validity of a verdict, any otherwise admissible evidence may be received as to statements made, or conduct, conditions, or events occurring, either within or without the jury room, of such a character as is likely to have influenced the verdict improperly. No evidence is admissible to show the effect of such statement, conduct, condition, or event upon a juror either in influencing him to assent to or dissent from the verdict or concerning the mental processes by which it was determined.

(b) Nothing in this code affects the law relating to the competence of a juror to give evidence to impeach or support a verdict.

Case Notes

As to the standard for setting aside a verdict on the basis of juror misconduct in considering extraneous information, see People v. Nesler, 16 Cal. 4th 561, 66 Cal. Rptr. 2d 454, 941 P.2d 87 (1997); In re Carpenter, 9 Cal. 4th 634, 653, 38 Cal. Rptr. 2d 665, 677, 889 P.2d 985, 997 (1995).

As to the related problems of inquiring about jury misconduct during the course of a trial or during jury deliberations, and of replacing a juror who refuses to deliberate, see People v. Cleveland, 25 Cal. 4th 466, 106 Cal. Rptr. 2d 313, 21 P.3d 1225 (2001).

Assembly Committee on Judiciary Comment

Section 1150 codifies existing law which permits evidence of misconduct by a trial juror to be received but forbids the reception of evidence as to the effect of such misconduct on the minds of the jurors. People v. Stokes, 103 Cal. 193, 196-197, 37 Pac. 207, 208-209 (1894). Section 1150 makes no change in the rules concerning when testimony or affidavits of jurors may be received to impeach or support a verdict. Under existing law, a juror is incompetent to give evidence as to matters that might impeach his verdict. People v. Gray, 61 Cal. 164, 183 (1882). See also Siemsen v. Oakland, S.L., & H. Elec. Ry., 134 Cal. 494, 66 Pac. 672 (1901). He is competent, however, to give evidence that no misconduct was committed by the jury after independent evidence has been given that there was misconduct. People v. Deegan, 88 Cal. 602, 26 Pac. 500 (1891). By statute, a juror may give evidence by affidavit that a verdict was determined by chance. Code Civ.Proc. § 657(2). And the courts have held that affidavits of jurors may be used to prove that a juror concealed bias or other disqualification by false answers on voir dire or was mentally incompetent to serve as a juror. E.g., Williams v. Bridges, 140 Cal.App. 537, 35 P.2d 407 (1934) (false answer on voir dire); Noll v. Lee, 221 Cal.App.2d 81, 34 Cal.Rptr. 223 (1963) (hearing denied) (false answer on voir dire); Church v. Capital Freight Lines, 141 Cal.App.2d 246, 296 P.2d 563 (1956) (mental competence of juror).

Section 1150 also makes no change in the existing law concerning the *grounds* upon which a verdict may be set aside, i.e., what constitutes jury misconduct. See Code Civ.Proc. § 657 (civil case); Penal Code § 1181 (criminal case) [which provide, in pertinent part, as follows:

Code Civ. Proc. § 657:

The verdict may be vacated * * * and a new * * * trial granted * * * for any of the following causes, materially affecting the substantial rights of such party:

1. Irregularity in the proceedings of the court, jury or adverse party, or any order of the court or abuse of discretion by which either party was prevented from having a fair trial.

2. Misconduct of the jury; and whenever any one or more of the jurors have been induced to assent to any general or special verdict, or to a finding on any question submitted to them by the court, by a resort to the determination of chance, such misconduct may be proved by the affidavit of any one of the jurors. * * *

Penal Code § 1181:

When a verdict has been rendered or a finding made against the defendant, the court may, upon his application, grant a new trial, in the following cases only:

* * *

2. When the jury has received any evidence out of court, other than that resulting from a view of the premises, or of personal property;

3. When the jury has separated without leave of the court after retiring to deliberate upon their verdict, or been guilty of any misconduct by which a fair and due consideration of the case has been prevented;

4. When the verdict has been decided by lot, or by any means other than a fair expression of opinion on the part of all the jurors * * * .]

§ 1151. Subsequent remedial conduct. When, after the occurrence of an event, remedial or precautionary measures are taken, which, if taken previously, would have tended to make the event less likely to occur, evidence of such subsequent measures is inadmissible to prove negligence or culpable conduct in connection with the event.

Case Notes

This section does not apply to actions based on strict products liability. Ault v. International Harvester Co., 13 Cal. 3d 113, 117 Cal. Rptr. 812, 528 P.2d 1148 (1974, modified, 1975).

This section excludes only the subsequent actions taken to repair or correct a problem identified by an investigation, not the results of factual inquiries undertaken to determine whether such repair or correction was necessary. Fox v. Kramer, 22 Cal. 4th 531, 544, 93 Cal. Rptr. 2d 497, 506, 994 P.2d 343, 351 (2000) (dictum).

Law Revision Commission Comment

Section 1151 codifies well-settled law. Helling v. Schindler, 145 Cal. 303, 78 Pac. 710 (1904); Sappenfield v. Main Street etc. R.R., 91 Cal. 48, 27 Pac. 590 (1891). The admission of evidence of subsequent repairs to prove negligence would substantially discourage persons from making repairs after the occurrence of an accident.

Section 1151 does not prevent the use of evidence of subsequent remedial conduct for the purpose of impeachment in appropriate cases. This is in accord with Pierce v. J. C. Penney Co., 167 Cal.App.2d 3, 334 P.2d 117 (1959).

§ 1152. Offer to compromise and the like. (a) Evidence that a person has, in compromise or from humanitarian motives, furnished or offered or promised to furnish money or any other thing, act, or service to another who has sustained or will sustain or claims that he or she has sustained or will sustain loss or damage, as well as any conduct or statements made in negotiation thereof, is inadmissible to prove his or her liability for the loss or damage or any part of it.

(b) In the event that evidence of an offer to compromise is admitted in an action for breach of the covenant of good faith and fair dealing or violation of subdivision (h) of Section 790.03 of the Insurance Code, then at the request of the party against whom the evidence is admitted, or at the request of the party who made the offer to compromise that was admitted, evidence relating to any other offer or counteroffer to compromise the same or substantially the same claimed loss or damage shall also be admissible for the same purpose as the initial evidence regarding settlement. Other than as may be admitted in an action for breach of the covenant of good faith and fair dealing or violation of subdivision (h) of Section 790.03 of the Insurance Code, evidence of settlement offers shall not be admitted in a motion for a new trial, in any proceeding involving an additur or remittitur, or on appeal.

(c) This section does not affect the admissibility of evidence of any of the following:

(1) Partial satisfaction of an asserted claim or demand without questioning its validity when such evidence is offered to prove the validity of the claim.

(2) A debtor's payment or promise to pay all or a part of his or her preexisting debt when such evidence is offered to prove the creation of a new duty on his or her part or a revival of his or her preexisting duty. [*Amended 1967, 1987.*]

Statutory Note

The 1987 amendment added subdivision (b).

Law Revision Commission Comment

Section 1152, like Section 2078 of the Code of Civil Procedure which it supersedes, declares that compromise offers are inadmissible to prove liability. Because of the particular wording of Section 2078, an offer of compromise probably may not be considered as an admission even though admitted without objection. See Tentative Recommendation and a Study Relating to the Uniform Rules of Evidence (Article VI. Extrinsic Policies Affecting Admissibility), 6 Cal.Law Revision Comm'n, Rep., Rec. & Studies 601, 675-676 (1964). See also Scott v. Wood, 81 Cal. 398, 405-406, 22 Pac. 871, 873 (1889). Under Section 1152, however, nothing prohibits the consideration of an offer of settlement on the issue of liability if the evidence is received without objection. This modest change in the law is desirable. An offer of compromise, like other incompetent evidence, should be considered to the extent that it is relevant when it is presented to the trier of fact without objection.

The words "as well as any conduct or statements made in negotiation thereof" make it clear that statements made by parties during negotiations for the settlement of a claim may not be used as admissions in later litigation. This language will change the existing law under which certain statements made during settlement negotiations may be used as admissions. People v. Forster, 58 Cal.2d 257, 23 Cal.Rptr. 582, 373 P.2d 630 (1962). The rule excluding offers is based upon the public policy in favor of the settlement of disputes without litigation. The same public policy requires that admissions made during settlement negotiations also be excluded. The rule of the Forster case that permits such statements to be admitted places a premium on the form of the statement. The statement "Assuming, for the purposes of these negotiations, that I was negligent . . ." is inadmissible; but the statement "All right, I was negligent! Let's talk about damages . . ." may be admissible. See the discussion in People v. Glen Arms Estate, Inc., 230 Cal.App.2d 841, 863, 864, 41 Cal.Rptr. 303, 316 (1964). The rule of the Forster case is changed by Section 1152 because that rule prevents the complete candor between the parties that is most conducive to settlement.

Law Revision Commission Comment - 1967 Amendment

The amendment to Section 1152 is intended to clarify the meaning of the section without changing its substantive effect. The words "or will sustain" have been added to make it clear that the section applies to statements made in the course of negotiations concerning future loss or damage as well as past loss or damage. Such negotiations might occur as a result of an alleged anticipatory breach of contract or as an incident of an eminent domain proceeding. [8 Cal.L.Rev.Comm. Reports 101 (1967).]

§ 1153. Offer to plead guilty or withdrawn plea of guilty by criminal defendant. Evidence of a plea of guilty, later withdrawn, or of an offer to plead guilty to the crime charged or to any other crime, made by the defendant in a criminal action is inadmissible in any action or in any proceeding of any nature, including proceedings before agencies, commissions, boards, and tribunals.

§ 1153.5. Offer for civil resolution of crimes against property. Evidence of an offer for civil resolution of a criminal matter pursuant to the provisions of Section 33 of the Code of Civil Procedure, or admissions made in the course of or negotiations for the offer shall not be admissible in any action. [*Added 1982.*]

§ 1154. Offer to discount a claim. Evidence that a person has accepted or offered or promised to accept a sum of money or any other thing, act, or service in satisfaction of a claim, as well as any conduct or statements made in negotiation thereof, is inadmissible to prove the invalidity of the claim or any part of it.

Law Revision Commission Comment

Section 1154 stems from the same policy of encouraging settlement and compromise that is reflected in Section 1152. Except for the language "as well as any conduct or statements made in negotiation thereof," this section codifies existing law. Dennis v. Belt, 30 Cal. 247 (1866); Anderson v. Yousem, 177 Cal.App.2d 135, 1 Cal.Rptr. 889 (1960); Cramer v. Lee Wa Corp., 109 Cal.App.2d 691, 241 P.2d 550 (1952). The significance of the quoted language is indicated in the Comment to Section 1152.

§ 1155. Liability insurance. Evidence that a person was, at the time a harm was suffered by another, insured wholly or partially against loss arising from liability for that harm is inadmissible to prove negligence or other wrongdoing.

Law Revision Commission Comment

* * * Evidence of liability insurance might be inadmissible in the absence of Section 1155 because it is not relevant; Section 1155 assures its inadmissibility.

§ 1156. Records of medical or dental study of in-hospital staff committee. (a) In-hospital medical or medical-dental staff committees of a licensed hospital may engage in research and medical or dental study for the purpose of reducing morbidity or mortality, and may make findings and recommendations relating to such purpose. Except as provided in subdivision (b), the written records of interviews, reports, statements, or memoranda of such in-hospital medical or medical-dental staff committees relating to such medical or dental studies are subject to Title 4 (commencing with Section 2016.010) of Part 4 of the Code of Civil Procedure (relating to discovery proceedings) but, subject to subdivisions (c) and (d), shall not be admitted as evidence in any action or before any administrative body, agency, or person.

(b) The disclosure, with or without the consent of the patient, of information concerning him to such in-hospital medical or medical-dental staff committee does not make unprivileged any information that would otherwise be privileged under Section 994 or 1014; but, notwithstanding Sections 994 and 1014, such information is subject to discovery under subdivision (a) except that the identity of any patient may not be discovered under subdivision (a) unless the patient consents to such disclosure.

(c) This section does not affect the admissibility in evidence of the original medical or dental records of any patient.

(d) This section does not exclude evidence which is relevant evidence in a criminal action. [*Amended 1975, 2004.*]

Statutory Note

The 1975 amendment added "medical dental staff committees" and "dental studies."

Assembly Committee on Judiciary Comment

* * * [Subdivision (b)] makes it clear that the names of patients may not be disclosed without the consent of the patient. This limitation is necessary to preserve the physician-patient and psychotherapist-patient privileges.

§ 1156.1. Records of medical or psychiatric studies of quality assurance committees. (a) A committee established in compliance with Sections 4070 and 5624 of the Welfare and Institutions Code may engage in research and medical or psychiatric study for the purpose of reducing morbidity or mortality, and may make findings and recommendations to the county and state relating to such purpose. Except as provided in subdivision (b), the written records of interviews, reports, statements, or memoranda of such committees relating to such medical or psychiatric studies are subject to Title 4 (commencing with Section 2016.010) of Part 4 of the Code of Civil Procedure but, subject to subdivisions (c) and (d), shall not be admitted as evidence in any action or before any administrative body, agency, or person.

(b) The disclosure, with or without the consent of the patient, of information concerning him or her to such committee does not make unprivileged any information that would otherwise be privileged under Section 994 or 1014. However, notwithstanding Sections 994 and 1014, such information is subject to discovery under subdivision (a) except that the identity of any patient may not be discovered under subdivision (a) unless the patient consents to such disclosure.

(c) This section does not affect the admissibility in evidence of the original medical or psychiatric records of any patient.

(d) This section does not exclude evidence which is relevant evidence in a criminal action. [*Added 2002. Amended 2004.*]

§ 1157. Proceedings and records of organized committees having responsibility of evaluation and improvement of quality of care. (a) Neither the proceedings nor the records of organized committees of medical, medical-dental, podiatric, registered dietitian, psychological, marriage and family therapist, licensed clinical social worker, professional clinical counselor, pharmacist, or veterinary staffs in hospitals, or of a peer review body, as defined in Section 805 of the Business and Professions Code, having the responsibility of evaluation and improvement of the quality of care rendered in the hospital, or for that peer review body, or medical or dental review or dental hygienist review or chiropractic review or podiatric review or registered dietitian review or pharmacist review or veterinary review or acupuncturist review or licensed midwife review committees of local medical, dental, dental hygienist, podiatric, dietetic, pharmacist, veterinary, acupuncture, or chiropractic societies, marriage and family therapist, licensed clinical social worker, professional clinical counselor, or psychological review committees of state or local marriage and family therapist, state or local licensed clinical social worker, state or local licensed professional clinical counselor, or state or local psychological associations or licensed midwife associations or societies having the responsibility of evaluation and improvement of the quality of care, shall be subject to discovery.

(b) Except as hereinafter provided, a person in attendance at a meeting of any of the committees described in subdivision (a) shall not be required to testify as to what transpired at that meeting.

(c) The prohibition relating to discovery or testimony does not apply to the statements made by a person in attendance at a meeting of any of the committees described in subdivision (a) if that person is a party to an action or proceeding the subject matter of which was reviewed at that meeting, or to any person requesting hospital staff privileges, or in any action against an insurance carrier alleging bad faith by the carrier in refusing to accept a settlement offer within the policy limits.

(d) The prohibitions in this section do not apply to medical, dental, dental hygienist, podiatric, dietetic, psychological, marriage and family therapist, licensed clinical social worker, professional clinical counselor, pharmacist, veterinary, acupuncture, or chiropractic society committees that exceed 10 percent of the membership of the society, nor to any of those committees if any person serves upon the committee when his or her own conduct or practice is being reviewed.

(e) The amendments made to this section by Chapter 1081 of the Statutes of 1983, or at the 1985 portion of the 1985-86 Regular Session of the Legislature, or at the 1990 portion of the 1989-90 Regular Session of the Legislature, or at the 2000 portion of the 1999-2000 Regular Session of the Legislature, or at the 2011 portion of the 2011-12 Regular Session of the Legislature, or at the 2015 portion of the 2015-16 Regular Session of the Legislature, do not exclude the discovery or use of relevant evidence in a criminal action. [*Added 1968. Amended 1975, 1978, 1982, 1983, 1985, 1990, 1994, 2000, 2011, 2015, 2017.*]

Statutory Note

The amendments have expanded the occupations covered by this section.

Case Note

The hospital peer review privilege creates a privilege against discovery from medical staff committees and also bars compelled testimony, but it does not bar voluntary testimony. The privilege is not waived by hospital's submission of peer review committee records to Department of Health Services in connection with administrative investigation. Fox v. Kramer, 22 Cal. 4th 531, 539, 93 Cal. Rptr. 2d 497, 502, 994 P.2d 343, 347-348 (2000).

§ 1157.5. Organized committee of nonprofit medical care foundation or professional standards review organization. Except in actions involving a claim of a provider of health care services for payment for such services, the prohibition relating to discovery or testimony provided by Section 1157 shall be applicable to the proceedings or records of an organized committee of any nonprofit medical care foundation or professional standards review organization which is organized in a manner which makes available professional competence to review health care services with respect to medical necessity, quality of care, or economic justification of charges or level of care. [*Added 1973. Amended 1980.*]

§ 1157.6. Proceedings and records of quality assurance committees for county health facilities. Neither the proceedings nor the records of a committee established in compliance with Sections 4070 and 5624 of the Welfare and Institutions Code having the responsibility of evaluation and improvement of the quality of mental health care rendered in county operated and contracted mental health facilities shall be subject to discovery. Except as provided in this section, no person in attendance at a meeting of any such committee shall be required to testify as to what transpired thereat. The prohibition relating to discovery or testimony shall not apply to the statements made by any person in attendance at such a meeting who is a party to an action or proceeding the subject matter of which was reviewed at such meeting, or to any person requesting facility staff privileges. [*Added 1982.*]

§ 1157.7. Application of Section 1157 discovery or testimony prohibitions and of public records and meetings provisions. The prohibition relating to discovery or testimony provided in Section 1157 shall be applicable to proceedings and records of any committee established by a local governmental agency to monitor, evaluate, and report on the necessity, quality, and level of specialty health services, including, but not limited to, trauma care services, provided by a general acute care hospital which has been designated or recognized by that governmental agency as qualified to render specialty health care services. The provisions of Chapter 3.5 (commencing with Section 6250) of Division 7 of Title 1 of the Government Code and Chapter 9 (commencing with Section 54950) of Division 2 of Title 5 of the Government Code shall not be applicable to the committee records and proceedings. [*Added 1983.*]

§ 1158. Inspection and copying of patient's records. (a) For purposes of this section, "medical provider" means physician and surgeon, dentist, registered nurse, dispensing optician, registered physical therapist, podiatrist, licensed psychologist, osteopathic physician and surgeon, chiropractor, clinical laboratory bioanalyst, clinical laboratory technologist, or pharmacist or pharmacy, duly licensed as such under the laws of the state, or a licensed hospital.

(b) Before the filing of any action or the appearance of a defendant in an action, if an attorney at law or his or her representative presents a written authorization therefor signed by an adult patient, by the guardian or conservator of his or her person or estate, or, in the case of a minor, by a parent or guardian of the minor, or by the personal representative or an heir of a deceased patient, or a copy thereof, to a medical provider, the medical provider shall promptly make all of the patient's records under the medical provider's custody or control available for inspection and copying by the attorney at law or his or her representative.

(c) Copying of medical records shall not be performed by a medical provider, or by an agent thereof, when the requesting attorney has employed a professional photocopier or anyone identified in Section 22451 of the Business and Professions Code as his or her representative to obtain or review the records on his or her behalf. The presentation of the authorization by the agent on behalf of the attorney shall be sufficient proof that the agent is the attorney's representative.

(d) Failure to make the records available, during business hours, within five days after the presentation of the written authorization, may subject the medical provider having custody or control of the records to liability for all reasonable expenses, including attorney's fees, incurred in any proceeding to enforce this section.

(e) (1) All reasonable costs incurred by a medical provider in making patient records available pursuant to this section may be charged against the attorney who requested the records.

(2) "Reasonable cost," as used in this section, shall include, but not be limited to, the following specific costs: ten cents ($0.10) per page for standard reproduction of documents of a size 8 1/2 by 14 inches or less; twenty cents ($0.20) per page for copying of documents from microfilm; actual costs for the reproduction of oversize documents or the reproduction of documents requiring special processing which are made in response to an authorization; reasonable clerical costs incurred in locating and making the records available to be billed at the maximum rate of sixteen dollars ($16) per hour per person, computed on the basis of four dollars ($4) per quarter hour or fraction thereof; actual postage charges; and actual costs, if any, charged to the witness by a third person for the retrieval and return of records held by that third person.

(f) If the records are delivered to the attorney or the attorney's representative for inspection or photocopying at the record custodian's place of business, the only fee for complying with the authorization shall not exceed fifteen dollars ($15), plus actual costs, if any, charged to the record custodian by a third person for retrieval and return of records held offsite by the third person.

(g) If the records requested pursuant to subdivision (b) are maintained electronically and if the requesting party requests an electronic copy of such information, the medical provider shall provide the requested medical records in the electronic form and format requested by the requesting party, if it is readily producible in such form and format, or, if not, in a readable form and format as agreed to by the medical provider and the requesting party.

(h) A medical provider shall accept a signed and completed authorization form for the disclosure of health information if both of the following conditions are satisfied:

(1) The medical provider determines that the form is valid.

(2) The form is printed in a typeface no smaller than 14-point type and is in substantially the following form:

AUTHORIZATION FOR DISCLOSURE OF HEALTH INFORMATION PURSUANT TO EVIDENCE CODE SECTION 1158

The undersigned authorizes the medical provider designated below to disclose specified medical records to a designated recipient. The medical provider shall not condition treatment, payment, enrollment, or eligibility for benefits on the submission of this authorization.

Medical provider: ________________

Patient name: ________________

Medical record number: ________________

Date of birth: ________________

Address: ________________

Telephone number: ________________

Email: ________________

Recipient name: ________________

Recipient address: ________________

Recipient telephone number: ________________

Recipient email: ________________

Health information requested (check all that apply):

___Records dated from ______ to ______.

___Radiology records: ________ images or films ________ reports________digital/CD, if available.

___Laboratory results dated.

___Laboratory results regarding specific test(s) only (specify)________.

___All records.

___Records related to a specific injury, treatment, or other purpose (specify): ________.

Note: records may include information related to mental health, alcohol or drug use, and HIV or AIDS. However, treatment records from mental health and alcohol or drug departments and results of HIV tests will not be disclosed unless specifically requested (check all that apply):

___Mental health records.

___Alcohol or drug records.

___HIV test results.

Method of delivery of requested records:

___Mail

___Pick up

___Electronic delivery, recipient email: ________________

This authorization is effective for one year from the date of the signature unless a different date is specified here: ______________.

This authorization may be revoked upon written request, but any revocation will not apply to information disclosed before receipt of the written request.

A copy of this authorization is as valid as the original. The undersigned has the right to receive a copy of this authorization.

Notice: Once the requested health information is disclosed, any disclosure of the information by the recipient may no longer be protected under the federal Health Insurance Portability and Accountability Act of 1996 (HIPAA).

Patient signature*: ________________

Date: ________________

Print name: ________________

*If not signed by the patient, please indicate relationship to the patient (check one, if applicable):

___Parent or guardian of minor patient who could not have consented to health care.

___Guardian or conservator of an incompetent patient.

___Beneficiary or personal representative of deceased patient.

[*Added 1968. Amended 1970, 1974, 1975, 1978, 1980, 1986, 1987, 1993, 1997, 2015, 2016.*]

Statutory Note

The amendments have expanded the occupations covered by this section.

§ 1159. Animal experimentation in product liability actions. (a) No evidence pertaining to live animal experimentation, including, but not limited to, injury, impact, or crash experimentation, shall be admissible in any product liability action involving a motor vehicle or vehicles.

(b) This section shall apply to cases for which a trial has not actually commenced, as described in paragraph (6) of subdivision (a) of Section 581 of the Code of Civil Procedure, on January 1, 1993. [*Added 1992.*]

§ 1160. Admissibility of expressions of sympathy or benevolence; definitions. (a) The portion of statements, writings, or benevolent gestures expressing sympathy or a general sense of benevolence relating to the pain, suffering, or death of a person involved in an accident and made to that person or to the family of that person shall be inadmissible as evidence of an admission of liability in a civil action. A statement of fault, however, which is part of, or in addition to, any of the above shall not be inadmissible pursuant to this section.

(b) For purposes of this section:

(1) "Accident" means an occurrence resulting in injury or death to one or more persons which is not the result of willful action by a party.

(2) "Benevolent gestures" means actions which convey a sense of compassion or commiseration emanating from humane impulses.

(3) "Family" means the spouse, parent, grandparent, stepmother, stepfather, child, grandchild, brother, sister, half brother, half sister, adopted children of parent, or spouse's parents of an injured party. [*Added 2000.*]

Assembly Committee on Judiciary Comment

The author introduced this bill in an attempt to reduce lawsuits and encourage settlements by fostering the use of apologies in connection with accident-related injuries or death. The bill's sponsor, Judge Quentin Kopp, offers the following statement in support of the measure:

Assembly Bill 2804 adds a section to the Evidence Code rendering written, oral, or physical expressions of sympathy or gestures in the form of apology inadmissible in a trial or an action arising from an accident. Presently, apologies and similar expressions are admissible as purported exceptions to the hearsay rule in a trial by court or jury. Commentators and scholars and now courts and legislatures have observed that many lawsuits, although unquantifiable, result from anger which, in turn, results from a failure of another party to express regret or sympathy. Lawyers and insurers regularly advise parties to accidents not to express regret or convey an apology or statement of compassion, commiseration or contrition for fear it will be used against the parties and thereby cause them financial harm.

A number of commentators have recently opined that apology is underrated and underused as a tool in legal settings. For example, in a recent ABA Journal article on the topic, the author of the article stated that apology "is too often overlooked as a means for helping to resolve disputes, for serving as a lubricant to advance settlement talks, and for contributing to a solution that looks to the client's needs." (Steven Keeva, "Does Law Mean Never Having to Say You're Sorry?" ABA Journal at p. 64 (Dec. 1999).) The author of the article continued by noting that "[d]espite the distinctly human need to convey and receive expressions of regret and contrition, there are legal considerations, including the concern that an apology may be tantamount to an admission of guilt or liability." (Id., at p. 65.)

The Vermont Supreme Court recently ruled in a medical malpractice case that an apology by a physician for an "inadequate" operation is not an admission of liability. (Phinney v. Vinson (1992) 605 A.2d 849. The court similarly held that an apology for a serious mistake made during surgery does not establish an element of a malpractice claim. (Senesac v. Associates in Obstetrics and Gynecology (1982) 449 A.2d 900.) Case law in Georgia has also held that evidence of activity constituting a voluntary offer of assistance made on the impulse of benevolence or sympathy should be encouraged and should not be considered an admission of liability. (Deese v. Carroll City County Hospital (1992) 416 S.E.2d 127.)

In addition, at least two other states have adopted statutes that bar the admissibility of "benevolent gestures" or communications that express sympathy in connection with accident-related injuries. Massachusetts enacted a statute in 1986, upon which this bill is modeled, which provides that: "Statements, writings or benevolent gestures expressing sympathy or a general sense of benevolence relating to the pain, suffering or death of a person involved in an accident and made to such person or to the family of such person shall be inadmissible as evidence of an admission of liability in a civil action." (Mass. Annotated Laws, ch. 233, Section 23D (Lexis 1999).) Texas also recently enacted a statute providing that "[a] court in a civil action may not admit a communication that expresses sympathy or a general sense of benevolence relating to the pain, suffering, or death of an individual involved in an accident." (Texas Civil Practice and Remedies Code section 18.061 (West 2000).)

As noted above, this bill contains similar provisions barring the admissibility of an apology or other benevolent gestures in civil actions. It also contains clarifying language, which is not part of either the Massachusetts or Texas statutes, providing that only those portions of statements containing the apology would be rendered inadmissible. This is consistent with general evidentiary rules regarding declarations against interest. (See Evidence Code section 1230.)

The following hypothetical examples, which were offered by the sponsor, may be helpful to the Committee in understanding the parameters of the bill's proposed new evidence rule.

Hypothetical #1: An automobile accident occurs and one driver says to the other: "I'm sorry you were hurt."—or—"I'm sorry that your car was damaged." Under the bill, these statements would not be admissible in court.

Hypothetical #2: The same accident occurs, and one driver says to the other: "I'm sorry you were hurt, the accident was all my fault."—or—"I'm sorry you were hurt, I was using my cell phone and just didn't see you coming." Under the bill, only the portions of the statements containing the apology would be inadmissible; any other expression acknowledging or implying fault would continue to be admissible, consistent with present evidentiary standards.

§ 1161. Human trafficking; admissibility of evidence of engagement in commercial sexual act by victim or sexual history of victim. (a) Evidence that a victim of human trafficking, as defined in Section 236.1 of the Penal Code, has engaged in any commercial sexual act as a result of being a victim of human trafficking is inadmissible to prove the victim's criminal liability for the commercial sexual act.

(b) Evidence of sexual history or history of any commercial sexual act of a victim of human trafficking, as defined in Section 236.1 of the Penal Code, is inadmissible to attack the credibility or impeach the character of the victim in any civil or criminal proceeding. [*Amended 2013.*]

§ 1162. Admissibility of evidence of engagement in act of prostitution by victim of felony. Evidence that a victim of, or a witness to, a serious felony as defined in subdivision (c) of Section 1192.7 of, an assault in violation of subdivision (a) of Section 245 of, domestic violence in violation of Section 273.5 of, extortion in violation of Section 518 of, human trafficking in violation of Section 236.1 of, sexual battery in violation of subdivision (a) of Section 243.4 of, or stalking in violation of Section 646.9 of, the Penal Code, has engaged in an act of prostitution at or around the time they were the victim of or witness to the crime is inadmissible in a separate prosecution of that victim or witness to prove criminal liability for the act of prostitution. [*Added 2018. Amended 2019.*]

DIVISION 10. HEARSAY EVIDENCE

Chapter 1. General Provisions

§ 1200. The hearsay rule. (a) "Hearsay evidence" is evidence of a statement that was made other than by a witness while testifying at the hearing and that is offered to prove the truth of the matter stated.

(b) Except as provided by law, hearsay evidence is inadmissible.

(c) This section shall be known and may be cited as the hearsay rule.

Case Notes

Courts have the power to create new exceptions to the hearsay rule for classes of evidence for which there is substantial need and which possess inherent reliability. In re Cindy L., 17 Cal. 4th 15, 25-29, 69 Cal. Rptr. 2d 803, 809-812, 947 P.2d 1340, 1346-1349 (1997) (recognizing "child dependency" exception).

"Fresh complaint" doctrine re-examined. Evidence of victim's extrajudicial complaint may be relevant nonhearsay to prove commission of an offense by establishing the fact of, and circumstances surrounding, victim's disclosure of the offense to others. Promptness and spontaneity are relevant, but not prerequisite, to admissibility. Common law fresh complaint doctrine, which was applied in sexual assault cases, was based on false, yet widely assumed, behavioral stereotypes. Evidence of extrajudicial complaint addresses jury expectations based on those stereotypes. People v. Brown, 8 Cal. 4th 746, 35 Cal. Rptr. 2d 407, 883 P.2d 949 (1994).

Testimony as to the name by which a person or place is personally known to the witness is not hearsay because it does not recount out-of-court statements by others. People v. Kraft, 23 Cal. 4th 978, 1052, 99 Cal. Rptr. 2d 1, 50, 5 P.3d 68, 113 (2000).

Senate Committee on Judiciary Comment

Section 1200 states the hearsay rule. It defines hearsay evidence and provides that such evidence is inadmissible unless it meets the conditions of an exception established by law. Chapter 2 (commencing with Section 1220) of this division contains a series of exceptions to the hearsay rule. Other exceptions may be found in other statutes or in decisional law. But the fact that certain evidence meets the requirements of an exception to the hearsay rule does not necessarily make such evidence admissible. The exception merely provides that such evidence is not inadmissible under the hearsay rule. If there is some other rule of law—such as privilege or the best evidence rule—that makes the evidence inadmissible, the court is not authorized to admit the evidence merely because it falls within an exception to the hearsay rule. See also Evidence Code § 352.

Although the California courts have excluded hearsay evidence since the earliest days of the State (see, e.g., People v. Bob, 29 Cal.2d 321, 175 P.2d 12 (1946); Kilburn v. Ritchie, 2 Cal. 145 (1852)), the hearsay rule has never been clearly stated in statutory form. Code of Civil Procedure Section 1845 (superseded by Evidence Code Section 702) has at times been considered to be the statutory basis for the hearsay rule. People v. Spriggs, 60 Cal.2d 868, 872, 36 Cal.Rptr. 841, 844, 389 P.2d 377, 380 (1964). Analytically, however, Section 1845 does not deal with hearsay at all; it deals only with the requirement of personal knowledge. It is true that the section provides that there is an exception to the personal knowledge requirement "in those few express cases in which . . . the declarations of others, are admissible"; but "this section is inaccurate, so far as it refers to [this] exception. In such case the witness testifies merely to the making of the declaration, which he must have heard in order to be a competent witness to testify to it, and hence, the fact to which he testifies is a fact within his own knowledge, derived from his own perceptions." Sneed v. Marysville Gas etc. Co., 149 Cal. 704, 708, 87 Pac. 376, 378 (1906).

"Hearsay evidence" is defined in Section 1200 as "evidence of a statement that was made other than by a witness while testifying at the hearing and that is offered to prove the truth of the matter stated." Under this definition, as under existing case law, a statement that is offered for some purpose other than to prove the fact stated therein is not hearsay. Smith v. Whittier, 95 Cal. 279, 30 Pac. 529 (1892). See Witkin, California Evidence §§ 215-218 (1958).

The word "statement" used in the definition of "hearsay evidence" is defined in Section 225 as "oral or written verbal expression" or "nonverbal conduct . . . intended . . . as a substitute for oral or written verbal expression." Hence, evidence of a person's conduct out of court is not inadmissible under the hearsay rule expressed in Section 1200 unless that conduct is clearly assertive in character. Nonassertive conduct is not hearsay.

Some California cases have regarded evidence of nonassertive conduct as hearsay evidence if it is offered to prove the actor's belief in a particular fact as a basis for an inference that the fact believed is true. See, e.g., Estate of De Laveaga, 165 Cal. 607, 624, 133 Pac. 307, 314

(1913) ("the manner in which a person whose sanity is in question was treated by his family is not, taken alone, competent substantive evidence tending to prove insanity, for it is a mere extra-judicial expression of opinion on the part of the family"); People v. Mendez, 193 Cal. 39, 52, 223 Pac. 65, 70 (1924) ("circumstances of flight [of other persons from the scene of a crime] are in the nature of confessions . . . and are, therefore, in the nature of hearsay evidence") (overruled on other grounds in People v. McCaughan, 49 Cal.2d 409, 420, 317 P.2d 974, 981 (1957)).

Other California cases, however, have held that evidence of nonassertive conduct is not hearsay even though offered to prove that the belief giving rise to the conduct was based on fact. See, e.g., People v. Reifenstuhl, 37 Cal.App.2d 402, 99 P.2d 564 (1940) (hearing denied) (incoming telephone calls made for the purpose of placing bets admissible over hearsay objection to prove that place of reception was bookmaking establishment).11

Under the Evidence Code, nonassertive conduct is not regarded as hearsay for two reasons. First, one of the principal reasons for the hearsay rule—to exclude declarations where the veracity of the declarant cannot be tested by cross-examination—does not apply because such conduct, being nonassertive, does not involve the veracity of the declarant. Second, there is frequently a guarantee of the trustworthiness of the inference to be drawn from such nonassertive conduct because the actor has based his actions on the correctness of his belief, i.e., his actions speak louder than words.

Of course, if the probative value of evidence of nonassertive conduct is outweighed by the probability that such evidence will be unduly prejudicial, confuse the issues, mislead the jury, or consume too much time, the judge may exclude the evidence under Section 352.

Under Section 1200, exceptions to the hearsay rule may be found either in statutes or in decisional law. Under existing law, too, the courts have recognized exceptions to the exclusionary rule in addition to those exceptions expressed in the statutes. See People v. Spriggs, 60 Cal.2d 868, 874, 36 Cal.Rptr. 841, 844, 389 P.2d 377, 380 (1964).

§ 1201. Multiple hearsay. A statement within the scope of an exception to the hearsay rule is not inadmissible on the ground that the evidence of such statement is hearsay evidence if such hearsay evidence consists of one or more statements each of which meets the requirements of an exception to the hearsay rule. [*Amended 1967.*]

Law Revision Commission Comment

Section 1201 makes it possible to use admissible hearsay to prove another statement that is also admissible hearsay. For example, under Section 1201, an official reporter's transcript of the testimony at a previous trial may be used to prove the testimony previously given (Evidence Code § 1280); the former testimony may be used as evidence (Evidence Code § 1291) to prove that a party made a statement; and the party's statement is admissible against him as an admission (Evidence Code § 1220). Thus, under Section 1201, the evidence of the admission contained in the transcript is admissible because each of the hearsay statements involved is within an exception to the hearsay rule. * * *

§ 1202. Credibility of hearsay declarant. Evidence of a statement or other conduct by a declarant that is inconsistent with a statement by such declarant received in evidence as hearsay evidence is not inadmissible for the purpose of attacking the credibility of the declarant though he is not given and has not had an opportunity to explain or to deny such inconsistent statement or other conduct. Any other evidence offered to attack or support the credibility of the declarant is admissible if it would have been admissible had the declarant been a witness at the hearing. For the purposes of this section, the deponent of a deposition taken in the action in which it is offered shall be deemed to be a hearsay declarant.

Law Revision Commission Comment

Section 1202 deals with the impeachment of a declarant whose hearsay statement is in evidence as distinguished from the impeachment of a witness who has testified. It clarifies two points. *First*, evidence to impeach a hearsay declarant is not to be excluded on the ground that it is collateral. *Second*, the rule applying to the impeachment of a witness—that a witness may be impeached by an inconsistent statement only if he is provided with an opportunity to explain or deny it—does not apply to a hearsay declarant.

When hearsay evidence in the form of former testimony has been admitted, the California courts have permitted a party to impeach the hearsay declarant with evidence of an inconsistent statement made by the hearsay declarant *after* the former testimony was given, even though the declarant was never given an opportunity to explain or deny the inconsistency. People v. Collup, 27 Cal.2d 829, 167 P.2d 714 (1946). Apparently, however, former testimony may not be impeached by evidence of an inconsistent statement made *prior* to the former testimony unless the would-be impeacher either did not know of the inconsistent statement at the time the former testimony was given or unless he had provided the declarant with an opportunity to explain or deny the inconsistent statement. People v. Greenwell, 20 Cal.App.2d 266, 66 P.2d 674 (1937), as limited by People v. Collup, 27 Cal.2d 829, 167 P.2d 714 (1946). The courts permit dying declarations to be impeached by evidence of contradictory statements by the deceased despite the lack of any foundation, for only in very rare cases would it be possible to provide the declarant with an opportunity to explain or deny the inconsistency. People v. Lawrence, 21 Cal. 368 (1863).

Section 1202 substitutes for this case law a uniform rule permitting a hearsay declarant to be impeached by inconsistent statements in all cases, whether or not the declarant has been given an opportunity to explain or deny the inconsistency. If the hearsay declarant is unavailable as a witness, the party against whom the evidence is admitted should not be deprived of both his right to cross-examine and his right to impeach. Cf. People v. Lawrence, 21 Cal. 368, 372 (1863). If the hearsay declarant is available, the party electing to use the hearsay of such a declarant should have the burden of calling him to explain or deny any alleged inconsistencies.

Of course, the trial judge may curb efforts to impeach hearsay declarants if he determines that the inquiry is becoming too remote from the issues that are actually at stake in the litigation. Evidence Code § 352.

Section 1235 provides that evidence of inconsistent statements made by a trial witness may be admitted to prove the truth of the matter stated. No similar exception to the hearsay rule is applicable to a hearsay declarant's inconsistent statements that are admitted under Section 1202. Hence, the hearsay rule prohibits any such statement from being used to prove the truth of the matter stated. If the declarant is not a witness and is not subject to cross-examination upon the subject matter of his statements, there is no sufficient guarantee of the trustworthiness of the statements he has made out of court to warrant their reception as substantive evidence unless they fall within some recognized exception to the hearsay rule.

§ 1203. Cross-examination of hearsay declarant. (a) The declarant of a statement that is admitted as hearsay evidence may be called and examined by any adverse party as if under cross-examination concerning the statement.

(b) This section is not applicable if the declarant is (1) a party, (2) a person identified with a party within the meaning of subdivision (d) of Section 776, or (3) a witness who has testified in the action concerning the subject matter of the statement.

(c) This section is not applicable if the statement is one described in Article 1 (commencing with Section 1220), Article 3 (commencing with Section 1235), or Article 10 (commencing with Section 1300) of Chapter 2 of this division.

(d) A statement that is otherwise admissible as hearsay evidence is not made inadmissible by this section because the declarant who made the statement is unavailable for examination pursuant to this section.

Assembly Committee on Judiciary Comment

Hearsay evidence is generally excluded because the declarant was not in court and not subject to cross-examination before the trier of fact when he made the statement. People v. Bob, 29 Cal.2d 321, 325, 175 P.2d 12, 15 (1946).

In some situations, hearsay evidence is admitted because there is either some exceptional need for the evidence or some circumstantial probability of its trustworthiness, or both. People v. Brust, 47 Cal.2d 776, 785, 306 P.2d 480, 484 (1957); Turney v. Sousa, 146 Cal.App.2d 787, 791, 304 P.2d 1025, 1027-1028 (1956). Even though it may be necessary or desirable to permit certain hearsay evidence to be admitted despite the fact that the adverse party had no opportunity to cross-examine the declarant when the hearsay statement was made, there seems to be no reason to prohibit the adverse party from cross-examining the declarant concerning the statement. The policy in favor of cross-examination that underlies the hearsay rule, therefore, indicates that the adverse party should be accorded the right to call the declarant of a statement received in evidence and to cross-examine him concerning his statement.

Section 1203, therefore, reverses (insofar as a hearsay declarant is concerned) the traditional rule that a witness called by a party is a witness for that party and may not be cross-examined by him. Because a hearsay declarant is in practical effect a witness against the party against whom his hearsay statement is admitted, Section 1203 gives that party the right to call and cross-examine the hearsay declarant concerning the subject matter of the hearsay statement just as he has the right to cross-examine the witnesses who appear personally and testify against him at the trial.

Subdivisions (b) and (c) make Section 1203 inapplicable in certain situations where it would be inappropriate to permit a party to examine a hearsay declarant as if under cross-examination. Thus, for example, subdivision (b) does not permit counsel for a party to examine his own client as if under cross-examination merely because a hearsay statement of his client has been admitted; and, because a party should not have the right to cross-examine his own witness merely because the adverse party has introduced a hearsay statement of the witness, witnesses who have testified in the action concerning the subject matter of the statement are not subject to examination under Section 1203.

Subdivision (d) makes it clear that the unavailability of a hearsay declarant for examination under Section 1203 has no effect on the admissibility of his hearsay statements. The subdivision forestalls any argument that availability of the declarant for examination under Section 1203 is an additional condition of admissibility for hearsay evidence.

§ 1203.1. Hearsay offered at preliminary examination; application of § 1203. Section 1203 is not applicable if the hearsay statement is offered at a preliminary examination, as provided in Section 872 of the Penal Code. [*Added by Initiative (Prop. 115), 1990.*]

Statutory Note

Penal Code § 872(b) provides:

Notwithstanding Section 1200 of the Evidence Code, the finding of probable cause may be based in whole or in part upon the sworn testimony of a law enforcement officer or honorably retired law enforcement officer relating the statements of declarants made out of court offered for the truth of the matter asserted. An honorably retired law enforcement officer may only relate statements of declarants made out of court and offered for the truth of the matter asserted that were made when the honorably retired officer was an active law enforcement officer. Any law enforcement officer or honorably retired law enforcement officer testifying as to hearsay statements shall either have five years of law enforcement experience or have completed a training course certified by the Commission on Peace Officer Standards and Training that includes training in the investigation and reporting of cases and testifying at preliminary hearings.

Case Notes

Penal Code 872(b) is limited to investigating officers who have sufficient knowledge of the crime or circumstances under which the out-of-court statement was made to meaningfully assist the magistrate in assessing the reliability of the statement. Whitman v. Superior Court, 54 Cal. 3d 1063, 1072-1076, 2 Cal. Rptr. 2d 160, 164-167, 820 P.2d 262, 266-269 (1991). As so limited, it does not violate the Confrontation Clause because the hearsay is necessary and generally reliable, id. at 1077-1079 , 2 Cal. Rptr. 2d at 166-169, 820 P.2d at 269-271, and because the Confrontation Clause probably does not limit the admissibility of hearsay at a limited-purpose California preliminary hearing, id. at 1078-1083, 2 Cal. Rptr. 2d at 168-172 , 820 P.2d at 270-274.

Investigating officer's testimony as to nontestifying co-defendant's statement implicating defendant is admissible at preliminary hearing to support finding of probable cause, even though same statement would not be admissible at trial. People v. Miranda, 23 Cal. 4th 340, 96 Cal. Rptr. 2d 758, 1 P.3d 73 (2000).

§ 1204. Hearsay statement offered against criminal defendant. A statement that is otherwise admissible as hearsay evidence is inadmissible against the defendant in a criminal action if the statement was made, either by the defendant or by another, under such circumstances that it is inadmissible against the defendant under the Constitution of the United States or the State of California.

Assembly Committee on Judiciary Comment

Section 1204 is a statutory recognition that hearsay evidence that fits within an exception to the hearsay rule may nonetheless be inadmissible under the Constitution of the United States or the Constitution of California. Thus, Section 1220, which creates an exception for the statements of a party, is subject to the constitutional rule excluding evidence of involuntary confessions against a criminal defendant.

In People v. Underwood, 61 Cal.2d 113, 37 Cal.Rptr. 313, 389 P.2d 937 (1964), the California Supreme Court held that a prior inconsistent statement of a witness could not be introduced to impeach him in a criminal action when the statement would have been inadmissible as an involuntary confession if the witness had been the defendant. To the extent that the Underwood decision is based on constitutional principles, its effect is continued by Section 1204 and its principle is made applicable to all hearsay statements.

§ 1205. No implied repeal. Nothing in this division [§§ 1200-1380] shall be construed to repeal by implication any other statute relating to hearsay evidence.

Law Revision Commission Comment

Although some of the statutes providing for the admission of hearsay evidence will be repealed when the Evidence Code is enacted, a number of statutes will remain in the various codes. For the most part, these statutes are narrowly drawn to make a particular type of hearsay evidence admissible under specifically limited circumstances. To assure the continued validity of these provisions, Section 1205 states that they will not be impliedly repealed by the enactment of the Evidence Code.

Insofar as the Constitution of the United States is concerned, Section 1204 refers only to those rules required to be observed in state proceedings. It is not intended to make applicable in proceedings in California courts those rules the United States Constitution requires to be observed only in federal proceedings.

Chapter 2. Exceptions to the Hearsay Rule

Article 1. Confessions and Admissions

§ 1220. Admission of party. Evidence of a statement is not made inadmissible by the hearsay rule when offered against the declarant in an action to which he is a party in either his individual or representative capacity, regardless of whether the statement was made in his individual or representative capacity.

Note on Proposed Amendment

The Law Revision Commission tentatively decided in March 2003 to recommend no change to § 1220.

Law Revision Commission Comment

* * * The rationale underlying this exception is that the party cannot object to the lack of the right to cross-examine the declarant since the party himself made the statement. Moreover, the party can cross-examine the witness who testifies to the party's statement and can explain or deny the purported admission. The statement need not be one which would be admissible if made at the hearing. See Shields v. Oxnard Harbor Dist., 46 Cal.App.2d 477, 116 P.2d 121 (1941).

In a criminal action, a defendant's statement is not admissible under this section unless it was made voluntarily. Evidence Code § 1204.

§ 1221. Adoptive admission. Evidence of a statement offered against a party is not made inadmissible by the hearsay rule if the statement is one of which the party, with knowledge of the content thereof, has by words or other conduct manifested his adoption or his belief in its truth.

Note on Proposed Amendment

The Law Revision Commission tentatively decided in March 2003 to recommend no change to § 1221.

§ 1222. Authorized admission. Evidence of a statement offered against a party is not made inadmissible by the hearsay rule if:

(a) The statement was made by a person authorized by the party to make a statement or statements for him concerning the subject matter of the statement; and

(b) The evidence is offered either after admission of evidence sufficient to sustain a finding of such authority or, in the court's discretion as to the order of proof, subject to the admission of such evidence.

Note on Proposed Amendment

The Law Revision Commission tentatively decided in September 2004 to recommend no change in the sufficiency standard of § 1222(b).

Law Revision Commission Comment

Section 1222 provides a hearsay exception for authorized admissions. Under this exception, if a party authorized an agent to make statements on his behalf, such statements may be introduced against the party under the same conditions as if they had been made by the party himself. The authority of the declarant to make the statement need not be express; it may be implied. It is to be determined in each case under the substantive law of agency. Section 1222 restates an exception found in the first portion of subdivision 5 of Section 1870 of the Code of Civil Procedure. See Tentative Recommendation and a Study Relating to the Uniform Rules of Evidence (Article VIII. Hearsay Evidence), 6 Cal.Law Revision Comm'n, Rep., Rec. & Studies Appendix at 484-490 (1964).

§ 1223. Admission of co-conspirator. Evidence of a statement offered against a party is not made inadmissible by the hearsay rule if:

(a) The statement was made by the declarant while participating in a conspiracy to commit a crime or civil wrong and in furtherance of the objective of that conspiracy;

(b) The statement was made prior to or during the time that the party was participating in that conspiracy; and

(c) The evidence is offered either after admission of evidence sufficient to sustain a finding of the facts specified in subdivisions (a) and (b) or, in the court's discretion as to the order of proof, subject to the admission of such evidence.

Note on Proposed Amendment

The Law Revision Commission tentatively decided in March 2003 and September 2004 to recommend no change to § 1223, including the sufficiency standard of § 1223(c).

Law Revision Commission Comment

Section 1223 is a specific example of a kind of authorized admission that is admissible under Section 1222. The statement is admitted because it is an act of the conspiracy for which the party, as a co-conspirator, is legally responsible. People v. Lorraine, 90 Cal.App. 317, 327, 265 Pac. 893, 897 (1928). See California Criminal Law Practice 471-472 (Cal.Cont.Ed.Bar 1964). Section 1223 restates an exception found in subdivision 6 of Section 1870 of the Code of Civil Procedure.

§ 1224. Statement of declarant whose liability or breach of duty is in issue. When the liability, obligation, or duty of a party to a civil action is based in whole or in part upon the liability, obligation, or duty of the declarant, or when the claim or right asserted by a party to a civil action is barred or diminished by a breach of duty by the declarant, evidence of a statement made by the declarant is as admissible against the party as it would be if offered against the declarant in an action involving that liability, obligation, duty, or breach of duty.

Case Notes

As used in § 1224, "liability, obligation, [or] duty" does not include tort liabilities of employees that are imputed to their employers under the doctrine of *respondeat superior*. Markley v. Beagle, 66 Cal. 2d 951, 957-960, 59 Cal. Rptr. 809, 813-815, 429 P.2d 129, 133-135 (1967) (dictum as to § 1224) (employee made statement after termination of employment). Markley questioned and limited to its facts in Labis v. Stopper, 11 Cal. App. 3d 1003, 89 Cal. Rptr. 926 (1st Dist. Ct. App. 1970) (employee made statement while still employed).

Law Revision Commission Comment

Section 1224 restates in substance a hearsay exception found in Code of Civil Procedure Section 1851 (superseded by Evidence Code Sections 1224 and 1302). See Butte County v. Morgan, 76 Cal. 1, 18 Pac. 115 (1888); Ingram v. Bob Jaffe Co., 139 Cal.App.2d 193, 293 P.2d 132 (1956); Standard Oil Co. v. Houser, 101 Cal.App.2d 480, 225 P.2d 539 (1950). Section 1224, however, limits this hearsay exception to civil actions. Much of the evidence within this exception is also covered by Section 1230, which makes declarations against interest admissible. However, to be admissible under Section 1230, the statement must have been against the declarant's interest when made; this requirement is not stated in Section 1224.

Code of Civil Procedure Section 1851 provides for the admission of a declarant's statements in an action where the liability of the party against whom the statements are offered is based on the declarant's breach of duty. Butte County v. Morgan, 76 Cal. 1, 18 Pac. 115 (1888); Nye & Nissen v. Central etc. Ins. Corp., 71 Cal.App.2d 570, 163 P.2d 100 (1945). Section 1224 of the Evidence Code refers specifically to "breach of duty" in order to admit statements of a declarant whose breach of duty is in issue without regard to whether that breach gives rise to a liability of the party against whom the statements are offered or merely defeats a right being asserted by that party. For example, in Ingram v. Bob Jaffe Co., 139 Cal.App.2d 193, 293 P.2d 132 (1956), a statement of a person permitted to operate a vehicle was admitted against the owner of the vehicle in an action seeking to hold the owner liable on the derivative liability of vehicle owners established by Vehicle Code Section 17150. Under Section 1224, the statement of the declarant would also be admissible against the owner in an action brought by the owner to recover for damage to his vehicle where the defense is based on the contributory negligence of the declarant.

Section 1302 supplements the rule stated in Section 1224. Section 1302 creates an exception for judgments against a third person when one of the issues between the parties is the liability, obligation, or duty of the third person and the judgment determines that liability, obligation, or duty. Together, Sections 1224 and 1302 codify the holdings of the cases applying Code of Civil Procedure Section 1851. See Tentative Recommendation and a Study Relating to the Uniform Rules of Evidence (Article VIII. Hearsay Evidence), 6 Cal.Law Revision Comm'n, Rep., Rec. & Studies Appendix at 491-496 (1964). [7 Cal.L.Rev.Comm. Reports 1 (1965)].

§ 1225. Statement of declarant whose right or title is in issue. When a right, title, or interest in any property or claim asserted by a party to a civil action requires a determination that a right, title, or interest exists or existed in the declarant, evidence of a statement made by the declarant during the time the party now claims the declarant was the holder of the right, title, or interest is as admissible against the party as it would be if offered against the declarant in an action involving that right, title, or interest.

Law Revision Commission Comment

Section 1225 expresses a common law exception to the hearsay rule that is recognized in part in Section 1849 of the Code of Civil Procedure. Section 1849 (which is superseded by Section 1225) permits the statements of predecessors in interest of real property to be admitted against the successors; however, the California cases follow the general rule of permitting predecessors' statements to be admitted against successors of either real or personal property. Smith v. Goethe, 159 Cal. 628, 115 Pac. 223 (1911); 4 Wigmore, Evidence § 1082 et seq. (3d ed. 1940).

It should be noted that "statements made before title accrued in the declarant will not be receivable. On the other hand, the time of divestiture, after which no statements could be treated as admissions, is the time when the party against whom they are offered has by his own hypothesis acquired the title; thus, in a suit, for example, between A's heir and A's grantee, A's statements at any time before his death are receivable against the heir; but only his statements before the grant are receivable against the grantee." 4 Wigmore, Evidence § 1082 at 153 (3d ed. 1940).

Despite the limitations of Section 1225, some statements of a grantor made after divestiture of title will be admissible; but another theory of admissibility must be found. For example, later statement of his state of mind may be admissible on the issue of his intent. Evidence Code §§ 1950 and 1251. Where it is claimed that a conveyance was in fraud of creditors, the later statements of the grantor may be admissible not as hearsay but as evidence of the fraud itself (cf. Bush & Mallett Co. v. Helbing, 134 Cal. 676, 66 Pac. 967 (1901)) or as declarations of a co-conspirator in the fraud (cf. McGee v. Allen, 7 Cal.2d 468, 60 P.2d 1026 (1936)). See generally 4 Wigmore, Evidence § 1086 (3d ed. 1940).

Section 1225 supplements the rule provided in Section 1224. Under Section 1224, for example, a party suing an executor on an obligation incurred by the decedent prior to his death may introduce admissions of the decedent. Similarly, under Section 1225, a party sued by an executor on an obligation claimed to have been owed to the decedent may introduce admissions of the decedent.

§ 1226. Statement of minor child in parent's action for child's injury. Evidence of a statement by a minor child is not made inadmissible by the hearsay rule if offered against the plaintiff in an action brought under Section 376 of the Code of Civil Procedure for injury to such minor child.

Law Revision Commission Comment

See the Comment to Section 1227.

§ 1227. Statement of declarant in action for his wrongful death. Evidence of a statement by the deceased is not made inadmissible by the hearsay rule if offered against the plaintiff in an action for wrongful death brought under Section 377 of the Code of Civil Procedure.

Law Revision Commission Comment

Under existing law, an admission by a decedent is not admissible against his heirs or representatives in a wrongful death action brought by them. Marks v. Reissinger, 35 Cal.App. 44, 169 Pac. 243 (1917). Cf. Hedge v. Williams, 131 Cal. 455, 63 Pac. 721 (1901). The reason is that the action is a new action, not merely a survival of the decedent's action. This rule has been severely criticized and is contrary to the rule adopted by most American courts. Carr v. Duncan, 90 Cal.App.2d 282, 285, 202 P.2d 855, 856 (1949).

Under Section 1224, the admissions of a decedent are admissible to establish the liability of his executor. Similarly, when the executor brings an action for the decedent's death under Code of Civil Procedure Section 377, the defendant should be permitted to introduce the admissions of the decedent. Without Section 1227, in an action between two executors arising out of an accident which was fatal to both participants, the plaintiff executor would be able to introduce admissions of the defendant's decedent, but the defending executor would be unable to introduce admissions of the plaintiff's decedent.

Section 1227 changes the rule announced in the California cases and makes the admissions of the decedent admissible in wrongful death actions. Section 1226 provides a similar rule for the analogous cases arising under Code of Civil Procedure Section 376 (action by parent of injured child).

Section 1227 recognizes that, in an action brought under Code of Civil Procedure Section 377, the only reason for treating the admissions of a plaintiff's decedent differently from those of a defendant's decedent is a technical procedural rule. The plaintiff in a wrongful death action—and the parent of an injured child in an action under Code of Civil Procedure Section 376—stands in reality so completely on the right of the deceased or injured person that such person's admissions should be admitted against the plaintiff, even though (as a technical matter the plaintiff is asserting an independent right.

§ 1228. Admissibility of certain out-of-court statements of minors under the age of 12; establishing elements of certain sexually oriented crimes; notice to defendant. Notwithstanding any other provision of law, for the purpose of establishing the elements of the crime in order to admit as evidence the confession of a person accused of violating Section 261, 264.1, 285, 286, 287, 288, 289, or 647a of, or former Section 288a of, the Penal Code, a court, in its discretion, may determine that a statement of the complaining witness is not made inadmissible by the hearsay rule if it finds all of the following:

(a) The statement was made by a minor child under the age of 12, and the contents of the statement were included in a written report of a law enforcement official or an employee of a county welfare department.

(b) The statement describes the minor child as a victim of sexual abuse.

(c) The statement was made prior to the defendant's confession. The court shall view with caution the testimony of a person recounting hearsay where there is evidence of personal bias or prejudice.

(d) There are no circumstances, such as significant inconsistencies between the confession and the statement concerning material facts establishing any element of the crime or the identification of the defendant, that would render the statement unreliable.

(e) The minor child is found to be unavailable pursuant to paragraph (2) or (3) of subdivision (a) of Section 240 or refuses to testify.

(f) The confession was memorialized in a trustworthy fashion by a law enforcement official.

If the prosecution intends to offer a statement of the complaining witness pursuant to this section, the prosecution shall serve a written notice upon the defendant at least 10 days prior to the hearing or trial at which the prosecution intends to offer the statement.

If the statement is offered during trial, the court's determination shall be made out of the presence of the jury. If the statement is found to be admissible pursuant to this section, it shall be admitted out of the presence of the jury and solely for the purpose of determining the admissibility of the confession of the defendant. [*Added 1984. Amended 1985, 2018.*]

§ 1228.1. Signature of parent or guardian on child welfare services case plan; acceptance of services; use in court of law; failure to cooperate. (a) Except as provided in subdivision (b), neither the signature of any parent or legal guardian on a child welfare services case plan nor the acceptance of any services prescribed in the child welfare services case plan by any parent or legal guardian shall constitute an admission of guilt or be used as evidence against the parent or legal guardian in a court of law(b) A parent's or guardian's failure to cooperate, except for good cause, in the provision of services specified in the child welfare services case plan may be used as evidence, if relevant, in any hearing held pursuant to Section 366.21, 366.22, or 388 of the Welfare and Institutions Code and at any jurisdictional or dispositional hearing held on a petition filed pursuant to Section 300, 342, or 387 of the Welfare and Institutions Code. [*Added 1995. Amended 1997.*]

Article 2. Declarations Against Interest

§ 1230. Declaration against interest. Evidence of a statement by a declarant having sufficient knowledge of the subject is not made inadmissible by the hearsay rule if the declarant is unavailable as a witness and the statement, when made, was so far contrary to the declarant's pecuniary or proprietary interest, or so far subjected him to the risk of civil or criminal liability, or so far tended to render invalid a claim by him against another, or created such a risk of making him an object of hatred, ridicule, or social disgrace in the community, that a reasonable man in his position would not have made the statement unless he believed it to be true.

Note on Proposed Amendment

The Law Revision Commission tentatively decided in March 2005 to recommend no change to § 1230 except to strike "in the community" after "social disgrace."

Case Notes

Section 1230 does not apply to any portion of a statement that does not itself specifically disserve the interests of the declarant. People v. Leach, 15 Cal.3d 419, 441, 124 Cal. Rptr. 752, 767, 541 P.2d 296, 311 (1975).

No error to exclude declarant's claim to have committed a murder many years after the killing and after defendant had already been found guilty. Trial court could find that declarant wanted to aid his friend at little risk to himself. Trustworthiness is the focus of this exception. The court should consider not only the words but the circumstances in which they were spoken, declarant's possible motivation, and declarant's relationship to the defendant, and apply a broad and deep acquaintance with the ways human beings actually behave. Corroboration requirement of Fed. R. Evid. 804(b) (3) exemplifies the general suspicion with which the law looks upon such declarations. People v. Frierson, 53 Cal. 3d 730, 745-746, 280 Cal. Rptr. 440, 448, 808 P.2d 1197, 1205 (1991).

Assembly Committee on Judiciary Comment

Except for the requirement that the declarant be shown to be unavailable as a witness, Section 1230 codifies the hearsay exception for declarations against interest as that exception has been developed by the California courts (People v. Spriggs, 60 Cal.2d 868, 36 Cal.Rptr. 841, 389 P.2d 377 (1964)) and possibly expends the exception. It is not clear whether the existing exception for declarations against interest applies to statements that make the declarant an object of hatred, ridicule, or social disgrace in the community.

Under existing law, a declaration against interest is admissible regardless of the availability of the declarant to testify as a witness. People v. Spriggs, 60 Cal.2d 868, 36 Cal.Rptr. 841, 389 P.2d 377 (1964). Section 1230, however, conditions admissibility upon the unavailability of the declarant in order to require the proponent of the evidence to use the in-court testimony of the declarant if it is possible to do so. If the declarant disappoints the proponent and testifies inconsistently, the proponent may then show the prior inconsistent statement as substantive evidence of the facts stated. See Evidence Code § 1235 and the Comment thereto.

Section 1230 supersedes the partial and inaccurate statements of the exception for declarations against interest found in Code of Civil Procedure Sections 1853, 1870(4), and 1946(1). See People v. Spriggs, 60 Cal.2d 868, 871-872, 36 Cal.Rptr. 841, 844-845, 389 P.2d 377, 380-381 (1964). The requirement that the declarant have "sufficient knowledge of the subject" continues the similar common law requirement stated in Code of Civil Procedure Section 1853 that the declarant must have had some peculiar means—such as personal observation—for obtaining accurate knowledge of the matter stated. See 5 Wigmore, Evidence § 1471 (3d ed. 1940).

Article 2.5. Sworn Statements Regarding Gang-Related Crimes

§ 1231. Prior statements of deceased declarant; hearsay exception. Evidence of a prior statement made by a declarant is not made inadmissible by the hearsay rule if the declarant is deceased and the proponent of introducing the statement establishes each of the following:

(a) The statement relates to acts or events relevant to a criminal prosecution under provisions of the California Street Terrorism Enforcement and Prevention Act (Chapter 11 (commencing with Section 186.20) of Title 7 of Part 1 of the Penal Code).

(b) A verbatim transcript, copy, or record of the statement exists. A record may include a statement preserved by means of an audio or video recording or equivalent technology.

(c) The statement relates to acts or events within the personal knowledge of the declarant.

(d) The statement was made under oath or affirmation in an affidavit; or was made at a deposition, preliminary hearing, grand jury hearing, or other proceeding in compliance with law, and was made under penalty of perjury.

(e) The declarant died from other than natural causes.

(f) The statement was made under circumstances that would indicate its trustworthiness and render the declarant's statement particularly worthy of belief. For purposes of this subdivision, circumstances relevant to the issue of trustworthiness include, but are not limited to, all of the following:

(1) Whether the statement was made in contemplation of a pending or anticipated criminal or civil matter, in which the declarant had an interest, other than as a witness.

(2) Whether the declarant had a bias or motive for fabricating the statement, and the extent of any bias or motive.

(3) Whether the statement is corroborated by evidence other than statements that are admissible only pursuant to this section.

(4) Whether the statement was a statement against the declarant's interest. [*Added 1997.*]

Note on Proposed Amendment

The Law Revision Commission tentatively decided in March 2005 to recommend no change to §§ 1231-1231.4.

§ 1231.1. Statements made by deceased declarant; admissibility; notice of statement to adverse party. A statement is admissible pursuant to Section 1231 only if the proponent of the statement makes known to the adverse party the intention to offer the statement and the particulars of the statement sufficiently in advance of the proceedings to provide the adverse party with a fair opportunity to prepare to meet the statement. [*Added 1997.*]

§ 1231.2. Administer and certify oaths. A peace officer may administer and certify oaths for purposes of this article [§§ 1231-1231.4]. [*Added 1997. Amended 1998.*]

§ 1231.3. Testimony of law enforcement officer; hearsay. Any law enforcement officer testifying as to any hearsay statement pursuant to this article [§§ 1231-1231.4] shall either have five years of law enforcement experience or have completed a training course certified by the Commission on Peace Officer Standards and Training which includes training in the investigation and reporting of cases and testifying at preliminary hearings and trials. [*Added 1997.*]

§ 1231.4. Cause of death; deceased declarant. If evidence of a prior statement is introduced pursuant to this article [§§ 1231-1231.4], the jury may not be told that the declarant died from other than natural causes, but shall merely be told that the declarant is unavailable. [*Added 1997.*]

Article 3. Prior Statements of Witnesses

§ 1235. Inconsistent statement. Evidence of a statement made by a witness is not made inadmissible by the hearsay rule if the statement is inconsistent with his testimony at the hearing and is offered in compliance with Section 770.

Note on Proposed Amendment

The Law Revision Commission tentatively decided in March 2003 to recommend no change to § 1235.

Case Notes

When trial court concludes, on substantial evidence, that a witness's professed lapses of memory are false devices to avoid truthful answers, it may admit as inconsistent the witness's prior statements describing events that the witness now claims to have forgotten. People v. Arias, 13 Cal. 4th 92, 152, 51 Cal. Rptr. 2d 770, 809, 913 P.2d 980, 1018 (1996).

Finding based on substantial evidence that witness's memory lapses while testifying were genuine, not feigned, precluded finding of inconsistency between testimony and witness's prior statements describing his recollections of the event. People v. Price, 1 Cal. 4th 324, 413-414, 3 Cal. Rptr. 2d 106, 155, 821 P.2d 610, 659 (1992).

This section will support the admissibility of multiple hearsay as long as each declarant is called to the stand and testifies inconsistently with her prior statement. Extrinsic evidence of a prior inconsistent statement is admissible even though the witness denies having made the prior inconsistent statement. Thus, where A testifies and denies having made a certain statement to B, and B testifies and denies having told C that A made such a statement to B, C's testimony that B told C that A had made such a statement to B is admissible to prove the making of statements by both A to B and B to C. People v. Zapien, 4 Cal. 4th 929, 950-955, 17 Cal. Rptr. 2d 122, 130-134, 846 P.2d 704, 712-716 (1993).

Law Revision Commission Comment

Under existing law, when a prior statement of a witness that is inconsistent with his testimony at the trial is admitted in evidence, it may not be used as evidence of the truth of the matters stated. Because of the hearsay rule, a witness' prior inconsistent statement may be used only to discredit his testimony given at the trial. Albert v. McKay & Co., 174 Cal. 451, 456, 163 Pac. 666, 668 (1917).

Because a witness' inconsistent statement is not substantive evidence, the courts do not permit a party—even when surprised by the testimony—to impeach his own witness with inconsistent statements if the witness' testimony at the trial has not damaged the party's case in any way. Evidence tending only to discredit the witness is irrelevant and immaterial when the witness has not given damaging testimony. People v. Crespi, 115 Cal. 50, 46 Pac. 863 (1896); People v. Mitchell, 94 Cal. 550, 29 Pac. 1106 (1892); People v. Brown, 81 Cal.App. 226, 253 Pac. 735 (1927).

Section 1235 permits an inconsistent statement of a witness to be used as substantive evidence if the statement is otherwise admissible under the conditions specified in Section 770—which do not include surprise on the part of the party calling the witness if he is the party offering the inconsistent statement. Because Section 1235 permits a witness' inconsistent statements to be considered as evidence of the matters stated and not merely as evidence casting discredit on the witness, it follows that a party may introduce evidence of inconsistent statements of his own witness whether or not the witness gave damaging testimony and whether or not the party was surprised by the testimony, for such evidence is no longer irrelevant (and, hence, inadmissible).

Section 1235 admits inconsistent statements of witnesses because the dangers against which the hearsay rule is designed to protect are largely nonexistent. The declarant is in court and may be examined and cross-examined in regard to his statements and their subject matter. In many cases, the inconsistent statement is more likely to be true than the testimony of the witness at the trial because it was made nearer in time to the matter to which it relates and is less likely to be influenced by the controversy that gave rise to the litigation. The trier of fact has the declarant before it and can observe his demeanor and the nature of his testimony as he denies or tries to explain away the inconsistency. Hence, it is in as good a position to determine the truth or falsity of the prior statement as it is to determine the truth or falsity of the inconsistent testimony given in court. Moreover, Section 1235 will provide a party with desirable protection against the "turn-coat" witness who changes his story on the stand and deprives the party calling him of evidence essential to his case.

§ 1236. Prior consistent statement. Evidence of a statement previously made by a witness is not made inadmissible by the hearsay rule if the statement is consistent with his testimony at the hearing and is offered in compliance with Section 791.

Note on Proposed Amendment

The Law Revision Commission tentatively decided in March 2003 to recommend no change to § 1236.

Law Revision Commission Comment

Under existing law, a prior statement of a witness that is consistent with his testimony at the trial is admissible under certain conditions when the credibility of the witness has been attacked. The statement is admitted, however, only to rehabilitate the witness—to support his credibility—and not as evidence of the truth of the matter stated. People v. Kynette, 15 Cal.2d 731, 753-754, 104 P.2d 794, 805-806 (1940) (overruled on other grounds in People v. Snyder, 50 Cal.2d 190, 197, 324 P.2d 1, 6 (1958)).

Section 1236, however, permits a prior consistent statement of a witness to be used as substantive evidence if the statement is otherwise admissible under the rules relating to the rehabilitation of impeached witnesses. See Evidence Code § 791.

There is no reason to perpetuate the subtle distinction made in the cases. It is not realistic to expect a jury to understand that it cannot believe that a witness was telling the truth on a former occasion even though it believes that the same story given at the hearing is true.

§ 1237. Past recollection recorded. (a) Evidence of a statement previously made by a witness is not made inadmissible by the hearsay rule if the statement would have been admissible if made by him while testifying, the statement concerns a matter as to which the witness has insufficient present recollection to enable him to testify fully and accurately, and the statement is contained in a writing which:

(1) Was made at a time when the fact recorded in the writing actually occurred or was fresh in the witness' memory;

(2) Was made (i) by the witness himself or under his direction or (ii) by some other person for the purpose of recording the witness' statement at the time it was made;

(3) Is offered after the witness testifies that the statement he made was a true statement of such fact; and

(4) Is offered after the writing is authenticated as an accurate record of the statement.

(b) The writing may be read into evidence, but the writing itself may not be received in evidence unless offered by an adverse party.

Note on Proposed Amendment

The Law Revision Commission tentatively decided in September 2003 to recommend no change to § 1237.

Assembly Committee on Judiciary Comment

Section 1237 provides a hearsay exception for what is usually referred to as "past recollection recorded." Although the provisions of Section 1237 are taken largely from the provisions of Section 2047 of the Code of Civil Procedure, there are some substantive differences between Section 1237 and existing law.

The existing law requires that a foundation be laid for the admission of such evidence by showing (1) that the writing recording the statement was made by the witness or under his direction, (2) that the writing was made at the time when the fact recorded in the writing actually occurred or at another time when the fact was fresh in the witness' memory, and (3) that the witness "knew that the same was correctly stated in the writing." Under Section 1237, however, the writing may be made not only by the witness himself or under his direction but also by some other person for the purpose of recording the witness' statement at the time it was made. In addition, Section 1237 permits testimony of the person who recorded the statement to be used to establish that the writing is a correct record of the statement. Sufficient assurance of the trustworthiness of the statement is provided if the declarant is available to testify that he made a true statement and if the person who recorded the statement is available to testify that he accurately recorded the statement.

Under subdivision (b), as under existing law, the statement is read into evidence but may not itself be introduced in evidence by its proponent. See Anderson v. Souza, 38 Cal.2d 825, 243 P.2d 497 (1952). The adverse party, however, may introduce the writing as evidence. Cf. Horowitz v. Fitch, 216 Cal.App.2d 303, 30 Cal.Rptr. 882 (1963) (dictum).

§ 1238. Prior identification. Evidence of a statement previously made by a witness is not made inadmissible by the hearsay rule if the statement would have been admissible if made by him while testifying and:

(a) The statement is an identification of a party or another as a person who participated in a crime or other occurrence;

(b) The statement was made at a time when the crime or other occurrence was fresh in the witness' memory; and

(c) The evidence of the statement is offered after the witness testifies that he made the identification and that it was a true reflection of his opinion at that time.

Note on Proposed Amendment

The Law Revision Commission tentatively decided in March 2003 to recommend no change to § 1238.

Law Revision Commission Comment

Under Section 1235, evidence of a prior identification is admissible if the witness denies having made the prior identification or in any other way testifies inconsistently with the prior statement. Under Section 1238, evidence of a prior identification is admissible if the witness admits the prior identification and vouches for its accuracy.

Sections 1235 and 1238 codify exceptions to the hearsay rule similar to that which was recognized in People v. Gould, 54 Cal.2d 621, 7 Cal.Rptr. 273, 354 P.2d 865 (1960). In the Gould case, evidence of a prior identification made by a witness who could not repeat the identification at the trial was held admissible "because the earlier identification has greater probative value than an identification made in the courtroom after the suggestions of others and the circumstances of the trial may have intervened to create a fancied recognition in the witness' mind. [Citations omitted.] The failure of the witness to repeat the extrajudicial identification in court does not destroy its probative value, for such failure may be explained by loss of memory or other circumstances. [Moreover,] the principal danger of admitting hearsay evidence is not present since the witness is available at the trial for cross-examination." 54 Cal.2d at 626, 7 Cal.Rptr. at 275, 354 P.2d at 867.

As there was no discussion in the Gould opinion of the preliminary showing necessary to warrant admission of evidence of a prior identification, it cannot be determined whether Sections 1235 and 1238 modify the law as declared in that case.

Sections 1235 and 1238 deal only with the admissibility of evidence; they do not determine what constitutes evidence sufficient to sustain a verdict or finding. Hence, these sections have no effect on the holding of the Gould case that evidence of an extrajudicial identification that cannot be confirmed by an identification at the trial is insufficient to sustain a criminal conviction in the absence of other evidence tending to connect the defendant with the crime.

Article 4. Spontaneous, Contemporaneous, and Dying Declarations

§ 1240. Spontaneous statement. Evidence of a statement is not made inadmissible by the hearsay rule if the statement:

(a) Purports to narrate, describe, or explain an act, condition, or event perceived by the declarant; and

(b) Was made spontaneously while the declarant was under the stress of excitement caused by such perception.

Note on Proposed Amendment

The Law Revision Commission tentatively decided in September 2003 to recommend that "purports to narrate, describe, or explain" be changed to "relates to," as in FRE 803(2).

Case Note

The "event" described by a spontaneous statement may be another person's statement describing a relevant event. If the requirements for a spontaneous statement are met, admissibility depends on whether the other person's statement fits an exception to the hearsay rule. People v. Arias, 13 Cal. 4th 92, 150, 51 Cal. Rptr. 2d 770, 807-808, 913 P.2d 980, 1017 (1996) (witness described victim's spontaneous statement about defendant's boast regarding prior criminal exploit, which terrified victim).

Law Revision Commission Comment

Section 1240 is a codification of the existing exception to the hearsay rule for statements made spontaneously under the stress of excitement engendered by the event to which they relate. Showalter v. Western Pacific R.R., 16 Cal.2d 460, 106 P.2d 895 (1940). See Tentative Recommendation and a study relating to the Uniform Rules of Evidence, (Article, VIII. Hearsay Evidence), 6 Cal.Law Revision Comm'n, Rep., Rec. & Studies Appendix at 465-466 (1964). The rationale of this exception is that the spontaneity of such statements and the consequent lack of opportunity for reflection and deliberate fabrication provide an adequate guarantee of their trustworthiness.

§ 1241. Contemporaneous statement. Evidence of a statement is not made inadmissible by the hearsay rule if the statement:

(a) Is offered to explain, qualify, or make understandable conduct of the declarant; and

(b) Was made while the declarant was engaged in such conduct.

Note on Proposed Amendment

The Law Revision Commission tentatively decided in September 2003 to recommend the addition of a new § 1240.5, which would be an exception for present sense impressions as in FRE 803(1) and then to recommend repeal of § 1241 if it is made obsolete by the adoption of § 1240.5.

Case Note

California has no "present sense impression" exception to the hearsay rule. A statement is not admissible as a "contemporaneous statement" under § 1241 if the declarant's conduct is not in issue. People v. Hines, 15 Cal. 4th 997, 1034-1036, 64 Cal. Rptr. 2d 594, 621-622, 938 P.2d 388, 415-516 (1997).

Assembly Committee on Judiciary Comment

Under existing law, where a person's conduct or act is relevant but is equivocal or ambiguous, the statements accompanying it may be admitted to explain and make the conduct or act understandable. Code Civ.Proc. § 1850 (superseded by Evidence Code § 1241); Witkin, California Evidence § 216 (1958). Some writers do not regard evidence of this sort as hearsay evidence, but the definition in Section 1200 seems applicable to many of the statements received under this exception. Cf. 6 Wigmore, Evidence § 1772 et seq. (1940). Section 1241 removes any doubt that might otherwise exist concerning the admissibility of such evidence under the hearsay rule.

§ 1242. Dying declaration. Evidence of a statement made by a dying person respecting the cause and circumstances of his death is not made inadmissible by the hearsay rule if the statement was made upon his personal knowledge and under a sense of immediately impending death.

Note on Proposed Amendment

The Law Revision Commission tentatively decided in March 2005 to recommend no change in § 1242 as regards the type of cases in which a dying declaration may be used, but to amend § 1242 to make it applicable even if the declarant survives, so long as the declarant is unavailable.

Law Revision Commission Comment

Section 1242 is a broadened form of the well-established exception to the hearsay rule for dying declarations relating to the cause and circumstances of the declarant's death. The existing law—Code of Civil Procedure Section 1870(4) as interpreted by the courts—makes such declarations admissible only in criminal homicide actions. People v. Hall, 94 Cal. 595, 30 Pac. 7 (1892); Thrasher v. Board of Medical Examiners, 44 Cal.App. 26, 185 Pac. 1006 (1919). For the purpose of the admissibility of dying declarations, there is no rational basis for differentiating between civil and criminal actions or among various types of criminal actions. Hence, Section 1242 makes the exception applicable in all actions.

Under Section 1242, as under existing law, the dying declaration is admissible only if the declarant made the statement on personal knowledge. People v. Wasson, 65 Cal. 538, 4 Pac. 555 (1884); People v. Taylor, 59 Cal. 640 (1881).

Article 5. Statements of Mental or Physical State

§ 1250. Statement of declarant's then existing mental or physical state.(a) Subject to Section 1252, evidence of a statement of the declarant's then existing state of mind, emotion, or physical sensation (including a statement of intent, plan, motive, design, mental feeling, pain, or bodily health) is not made inadmissible by the hearsay rule when:

(1) The evidence is offered to prove the declarant's state of mind, emotion, or physical sensation at that time or at any other time when it is itself an issue in the action; or

(2) The evidence is offered to prove or explain acts or conduct of the declarant.

(b) This section does not make admissible evidence of a statement of memory or belief to prove the fact remembered or believed.

Note on Proposed Amendment

The Law Revision Commission tentatively decided in September 2003 to recommend that the following be added to § 1250(a)(2): "A declaration of intent to engage in conduct with another person may not be used to explain acts or conduct of the other person."

Case Note

Declarant's statement of intention to meet "people from Arizona" at his home to conduct a drug deal on the night declarant was killed was admissible to prove that declarant met those people that night for that purpose, given corroborating circumstances. People v. Majors, 18 Cal. 4th 385, 404-405, 75 Cal. Rptr. 2d 684, 697, 956 P.2d 1137, 1150 (1998).

Assembly Committee on Judiciary Comment

Section 1250 provides an exception to the hearsay rule for statements of the declarant's then existing mental or physical state. Under Section 1250, as under existing law, a statement of the declarant's state of mind at the time of the statement is admissible when the then existing state of mind is itself an issue in the case. Adkins v. Brett, 184 Cal. 252, 193 Pac. 251 (1920). A statement of the declarant's then existing state of mind is also admissible when relevant to show the declarant's state of mind at a time prior or subsequent to the statement. Watenpaugh v. State Teachers' Retirement System, 51 Cal.2d 675, 336 P.2d 165 (1959); Whitlow v. Durst, 20 Cal.2d 523, 127 P.2d 530 (1942); Estate of Anderson, 185 Cal. 700, 198 Pac. 407 (1921); Williams v. Kidd, 170 Cal. 631, 151 Pac. 1 (1915). Section 1250 also makes a statement of then existing state of mind admissible to "prove or explain acts or conduct of the declarant." Thus, a statement of the declarant's intent to do certain acts is admissible to prove that he did those acts. People v. Alcalde, 24 Cal.2d 177, 148 P.2d 627 (1944); Benjamin v. District Grand Lodge No. 4, 171 Cal. 260, 152 Pac. 731 (1915). Statements of then existing pain or other bodily condition also are admissible to prove the existence of such condition. Bloomberg v. Laventhal, 179 Cal. 616, 178 Pac. 496 (1919); People v. Wright, 167 Cal. 1, 138 Pac. 349 (1914).

A statement is not admissible under Section 1250 if the statement was made under circumstances indicating that the statement is not trustworthy. See Evidence Code § 1252 and the Comment thereto.

In light of the definition of "hearsay evidence" in Section 1200, a distinction should be noted between the use of a declarant's statements of his then existing mental state to prove such mental state and the use of a declarant's statements of other facts as circumstantial evidence of his mental state. Under the Evidence Code, no hearsay problem is involved if the declarant's statements are not being used to prove the truth of their contents but are being used as circumstantial evidence of the declarant's mental state. See the Comment to Section 1200.

Section 1250(b) does not permit a statement of memory or belief to be used to prove the fact remembered or believed. This limitation is necessary to preserve the hearsay rule. Any statement of a past event is, of course, a statement of the declarant's then existing state of mind—his memory or belief—concerning the past event. If the evidence of that state of mind—the statement of memory—were admissible to show that the fact remembered or believed actually occurred, any statement narrating a past event would be, by a process of circuitous reasoning, admissible to prove that the event occurred.

The limitation in Section 1250(b) is generally in accord with the law developed in the California cases. Thus, in Estate of Anderson, 185 Cal. 700, 198 Pac. 407 (1921), a testatrix, after the execution of a will, declared, in effect, that the will had been made at an aunt's request; this statement was held to be inadmissible hearsay "because it was merely a declaration as to a past event and was not indicative of the condition of mind of the testatrix at the time she made it." 185 Cal. at 720, 198 Pac. at 415 (1921).

A major exception to the principle expressed in Section 1250(b) was created in People v. Merkouris, 52 Cal.2d 672, 344 P.2d 1 (1959). That case held that certain murder victims' statements relating threats by the defendant were admissible to show the victims' mental stateCtheir fear of the defendant. Their fear was not itself an issue in the case, but the court held that the fear was relevant to show that the defendant had engaged in conduct engendering the fear, i.e., that the defendant had in fact threatened them. That the defendant had threatened them was, of course, relevant to show that the threats were carried out in the homicide. Thus, in effect, the court permitted the statements to be used to prove the truth of the matters stated in them. In People v. Purvis, 56 Cal.2d 93, 13 Cal.Rptr. 801, 362 P.2d 713 (1961), the doctrine of the Merkouris case was limited to cases where identity is an issue; however, at least one subsequent decision has applied the doctrine where identity was not in issue. See People v. Cooley, 211 Cal.App.2d 173, 27 Cal.Rptr. 543 (1962).

The doctrine of the Merkouris case is repudiated in Section 1250(b) because that doctrine undermines the hearsay rule itself. Other exceptions to the hearsay rule are based on some indicia of reliability peculiar to the evidence involved. People v. Brust, 47 Cal.2d 776, 785, 306 P.2d 480, 484 (1957). The exception created by Merkouris is not based on any probability of reliability; it is based on a rationale that destroys the very foundation of the hearsay rule.

To be distinguished from the Merkouris decision, however, are certain other cases in which the statements of a murder victim were used to prove or explain subsequent acts of the decedent, and not as a basis for inferring that the defendant did the acts charged in the statements. See, e.g., People v. Atchley, 53 Cal.2d 160, 172, 346 P.2d 764, 770 (1959); People v. Finch, 213 Cal.App.2d 752, 765, 29 Cal.Rptr. 420, 427 (1963). Statements of a decedent's then existing fear—i.e., his state of mind—may be offered under Section 1250, as under existing law, either to prove that fear when it is itself in issue or to prove or explain the decedent's subsequent conduct. Statements of a decedent narrating threats or brutal conduct by some other person may also be used as circumstantial evidence of the decedent's fearChis state of mindCwhen that fear is itself in issue or when it is relevant to prove or explain the decedent's subsequent conduct; and, for that purpose, the evidence is not subject to a hearsay objection because it is not offered to prove the truth of the matter stated. See the Comment to Section 1200. See also the Comment to Section 1252. But when such evidence is used as a basis for inferring that the alleged threatener must have made threats, the evidence falls within the language of Section 1250(b) and is inadmissible hearsay evidence.

§ 1251. Statement of declarant's previously existing mental or physical state. Subject to Section 1252, evidence of a statement of the declarant's state of mind, emotion, or physical sensation (including a statement of intent, plan, motive, design, mental feeling, pain, or bodily health) at a time prior to the statement is not made inadmissible by the hearsay rule if:

(a) The declarant is unavailable as a witness; and

(b) The evidence is offered to prove such prior state of mind, emotion, or physical sensation when it is itself an issue in the action and the evidence is not offered to prove any fact other than such state of mind, emotion, or physical sensation.

Note on Proposed Amendment

The Law Revision Commission tentatively decided in September 2003 to recommend no change to § 1251.

Law Revision Commission Comment

Section 1250 forbids the use of a statement of memory or belief to prove the fact remembered or believed. Section 1251, however, permits a statement of memory or belief of a past mental or physical state to be used to prove the previous mental or physical state when the previous mental or physical state is itself an issue in the case. If the past mental or physical state is to be used merely as circumstantial evidence of some other fact, the limitation in Section 1250 still applies and the statement of the past mental state is inadmissible hearsay.

The rule stated in Section 1251 is consistent with the California case law to the extent that it permits a statement of a prior mental state to be used as evidence of that mental state. See, e.g. People v. One 1948 Chevrolet Conv. Coupe, 45 Cal.2d 613, 290 P.2d 538 (1955) (statement of prior knowledge admitted to prove such knowledge); Kelly v. Bank of America, 112 Cal.App.2d 388, 246 P.2d 92 (1952) (statement of previous intent to retain title admitted to prove such intent). However, the California cases have held that statements of previous bodily conditions and symptoms are inadmissible to prove the existence of such conditions or symptoms, although they may be admitted as a basis for an expert's opinion. People v. Brown, 49 Cal.2d 577, 320 P.2d 5 (1958); Willoughby v. Zylstra, 5 Cal.App.2d 297, 42 P.2d 685 (1935). Section 1251 eliminates the distinction between statements of previous mental conditions and statements of previous physical sensations; it permits both to be admitted as evidence of the matters stated. Both kinds of statements are equally subjective, and there is no reason to believe that one kind is more unreliable than the other.

Section 1251 requires that the declarant be unavailable as a witness. Some California cases seem to indicate that the unavailability of the declarant is a necessary condition for the admission of his statements to prove a previous state of mind. See, e.g., Whitlow v. Durst, 20 Cal.2d 523, 524, 127 P.2d 530, 531 (1942) ("declarations of a decedent" admissible to show previous mental state); Kelly v. Bank of America, 112 Cal.App.2d 388, 246 P.2d 92 (1952). But other cases have admitted such statements without insisting on the declarant's unavailability. People v. One 1948 Chevrolet Conv. Coupe, 45 Cal.2d 613, 290 P.2d 538 (1955). Section 1251 requires a showing of the declarant's unavailability because the statements involved are narrations of past conditions. There is, therefore, a greater opportunity for the declarant to remember inaccurately or even to fabricate. Hence, Section 1251 permits such statements to be admitted only when the declarant's unavailability necessitates reliance upon his out-of-court statements.

A statement is not admissible under Section 1251 if the statement was made under circumstances indicating that the statement is not trustworthy. See Evidence Code 1252 and the Comment thereto.

§ 1252. Limitation on admissibility of statement of mental or physical state. Evidence of a statement is inadmissible under this article [§§ 1250-1253] if the statement was made under circumstances such as to indicate its lack of trustworthiness.

Law Revision Commission Comment

Section 1252 limits the admissibility of hearsay statements that would otherwise be admissible under Sections 1250 and 1251. If a statement of mental or physical state was made with a motive to misrepresent or to manufacture evidence, the statement is not sufficiently reliable to warrant its reception in evidence. The limitation expressed in Section 1252 has been held to be a condition of admissibility in some of the California cases. See, e.g., People v. Hamilton, 55 Cal.2d 881, 893, 895, 13 Cal.Rptr. 649, 656, 657, 362 P.2d 473, 480, 481 (1961); People v. Alcalde, 24 Cal.2d 177, 187, 148 P.2d 627, 632 (1944).

The Hamilton case mentions some additional limitations on the admissibility of statements offered in a criminal action to prove the declarant's mental statement. These additional limitations do not appear in the Evidence Code. In the Hamilton case, the court was concerned with a murder victim's statements that she was afraid of the accused, that the accused had threatened to kill her, and that the accused had beaten her. The statements were ostensibly offered to prove that the victim feared the accused and, therefore, to cast doubt on the accused's testimony that the victim had invited him to her house on the night of the murder. As the case was tried, however, the victim's declarations were used repeatedly in argument as a basis for the prosecution's claim that the beatings actually occurred, that the threats were actually made, and that the threats were carried out in the murder.

The court said that "testimony as to the 'state of mind' of the declarant . . . is admissible, but only when such testimony refers to threats as to future conduct on the part of the accused . . . and when [such declarations] show primarily the then state of mind of the declarant and not the state of mind of the accused. But . . . such testimony is not admissible if it refers solely to alleged past conduct on the part of the accused." 55 Cal.2d at 893-894, 13 Cal.Rptr. at 656, 362 P.2d at 480.

These additional limitations on the admissibility of state of mind evidence are not mentioned in the Evidence Code for two reasons. First, they are confusing and contradictory: The declarations are inadmissible if they refer to past conduct of the accused; nevertheless, they are admissible "only" when they refer to his past conduct, i.e., his threats. The declarations, to be admissible, must show primarily the state of mind of the declarant and not the state of mind of the accused; nevertheless, such declarations are admissible "only" if they refer to the accused's statements of his state of mind, i.e., his intent to do future harm to the victim.

Second, these additional limitations are unnecessary. Section 1200 makes it clear that statements of past events cannot be used to prove those events unless they fall within an exception to the hearsay rule; and Sections 1250 and 1251 make it clear that statements of a declarant's past state of mind may be used to prove only that state of mind and no other fact. The real problem in the Hamilton case was the fact that much of the evidence was offered ostensibly not as hearsay but as circumstantial evidence of the victim's fear (see Section 1200 and the Comment thereto); but the prosecution endeavored nevertheless to have the jury consider the evidence as hearsay evidence, i.e., as evidence that the events related actually occurred. Evidence Code Section 352 provides the judge with ample power to exclude evidence of this sort where its prejudicial effect outweighs its probative value. But, under Section 352, the judge must weigh the need for the evidence against the danger of its misuse in each case. The Evidence Code does not freeze the courts to the arbitrary and contradictory standards mentioned in the Hamilton case for determining when prejudicial effect outweighs probative value.

§ 1253. Statements for purposes of medical diagnosis or treatment; contents of statement; child abuse or neglect; age limitations. Subject to Section 1252, evidence of a statement is not made inadmissible by the hearsay rule if the statement was made for purposes of medical diagnosis or treatment and describes medical history, or past or present symptoms, pain, or sensations, or the inception or general character of the cause or external source thereof insofar as reasonably pertinent to diagnosis or treatment. This section applies only to a statement made by a victim who is a minor at the time of the proceedings, provided the statement was made when the victim was under the age of 12 describing any act, or attempted act, of child abuse or neglect. "Child abuse" and "child neglect," for purposes of this section, have the meanings provided in subdivision (c) of Section 1360. In addition, "child abuse" means any act proscribed by Chapter 5 (commencing with Section 281) of Title 9 of Part 1 of the Penal Code committed against a minor. [*Added 1995.*]

Note on Proposed Amendment

The Law Revision Commission tentatively decided in September 2003 to recommend no change to § 1253.

Article 6. Statements Relating to Wills and to Claims Against Estates

§ 1260. Statement concerning declarant's will. (a) Except as provided in subdivision (b), evidence of any of the following statements made by a declarant who is unavailable as a witness is not made inadmissible by the hearsay rule:

(1) That the declarant has or has not made a will or established or amended a revocable trust.

(2) That the declarant has or has not revoked his or her will, revocable trust, or an amendment to a revocable trust.

(3) That identifies the declarant's will, revocable trust, or an amendment to a revocable trust.

(b) Evidence of a statement is inadmissible under this section if the statement was made under circumstances that indicate its lack of trustworthiness. [*Amended 2009.*]

Law Revision Commission Comment

Section 1260 codifies an exception recognized in California case law. Estate of Morrison, 198 Cal. 1, 242 Pac. 939 (1926); Estate of Thompson, 44 Cal.App.2d 774, 112 P.2d 937 (1941). The section is, of course, subject to the provisions of Probate Code Sections 350 and 351 which relate to the establishment of a lost or destroyed will.

The limitation in subdivision (b) is not mentioned in the few court decisions involving this exception. The limitation is desirable, however, to assure the reliability of the hearsay that is admissible under this section.

§ 1261. Statement of decedent offered in action against his estate. (a) Evidence of a statement is not made inadmissible by the hearsay rule when offered in an action upon a claim or demand against the estate of the declarant if the statement was made upon the personal knowledge of the declarant at a time when the matter had been recently perceived by him and while his recollection was clear.

(b) Evidence of a statement is inadmissible under this section if the statement was made under circumstances such as to indicate its lack of trustworthiness.

Law Revision Commission Comment

The dead man statute (subdivision 3 of Section 1880 of the Code of Civil Procedure) prohibits a party who sues on a claim against a decedent's estate from testifying to any fact occurring prior to the decedent's death. The theory apparently underlying the statute is that it would be unfair to permit the surviving claimant to testify to such facts when the decedent is precluded by his death from doing so. To balance the positions of the parties, the living may not speak because the dead cannot.

The dead man statute operates unsatisfactorily. It prohibits testimony concerning matters of which the decedent had no knowledge and, hence, to which he could not have testified even if he had survived. It operates unevenly since it does not prohibit testimony relating to claims under, as distinguished from claims against, the decedent's estate even though the effect of such a claim may be to frustrate the decedent's plan for the disposition of his property. See the Law Revision Commission's Comment to Code of Civil Procedure Section 1880 and 1 Cal.Law Revision Comm'n, Rep., Rec. & Studies, Recommendation and Study Relating to the Dead Man Statute at D-1 (1957). The dead man statute excludes otherwise relevant and competent evidence—even if it is the only available evidence—and frequently this forces the courts to decide cases with a minimum of information concerning the actual facts. See the Supreme Court's complaint in Light v. Stevens, 159 Cal. 288, 292, 113 Pac. 659, 660 (1911) ("Owing to the fact that the lips of one of the parties to the transaction are closed by death and those of the other party by the law, the evidence on this question is somewhat unsatisfactory."). Hence, the dead man statute is not continued in the Evidence Code.

Under the Evidence Code, the positions of the parties are balanced by throwing more light, not less, on the actual facts. Repeal of the dead man statute permits the claimant to testify without restriction. To balance this advantage, Section 1261 permits hearsay evidence of the decedent's statements to be admitted. Certain safeguards—i.e., personal knowledge, recent perception, and circumstantial evidence of trustworthiness—are included in the section to provide some protection for the party against whom the statements are offered, for he has no opportunity to test the hearsay by cross-examination.

Article 7. Business Records

§ 1270. A business. As used in this article [§§ 1270-1272], "a business" includes every kind of business, governmental activity, profession, occupation, calling, or operation of institutions, whether carried on for profit or not.

Law Revision Commission Comment

This article restates and supersedes the Uniform Business Records as Evidence Act appearing in Sections 1953e through 1953h of the Code of Civil Procedure. The definition of "a business" in Section 1270 is substantially the same as that appearing in Code of Civil Procedure Section 1953e. A reference to "governmental activity" has been added to the Evidence Code definition to codify the decisions in cases holding the Uniform Act applicable to governmental records. See, e.g., Nichols v. McCoy, 38 Cal.2d 447, 240 P.2d 569 (1952); Fox v. San Francisco Unified School Dist., 111 Cal.App.2d 885, 245 P.2d 603 (1952).

The definition is sufficiently broad to encompass institutions not customarily thought of as businesses. For example, the baptismal and wedding records of a church would be admissible under the section to prove the events recorded. 5 Wigmore, Evidence § 1523 (3d ed. 1940). Cf. Evidence Code § 1315.

§ 1271. Business record. Evidence of a writing made as a record of an act, condition, or event is not made inadmissible by the hearsay rule when offered to prove the act, condition, or event if:

(a) The writing was made in the regular course of a business;

(b) The writing was made at or near the time of the act, condition, or event;

(c) The custodian or other qualified witness testifies to its identity and the mode of its preparation; and

(d) The sources of information and method and time of preparation were such as to indicate its trustworthiness.

Statutory Note

See Commercial Code § 1202 (admissibility of third-party documents authorized by contract in actions arising out of the contract).

Note on Proposed Amendment

The Law Revision Commission tentatively decided in November 2003 to recommend that the business duty rule and a requirement of personal knowledge be added to § 1271.

Case Note

Written record of psychiatric diagnosis is not admissible as a business record because diagnosis is an "opinion," not an "act, condition, or event." Diagnoses that simply record clinical observations (*e.g.*, a compound fracture) may qualify, but not diagnoses that summarize reasoning based on the consideration of many different factors. People v. Reyes, 12 Cal. 3d 486, 503, 116 Cal. Rptr. 217, 227, 526 P.2d 225, 235 (1974).

Law Revision Commission Comment

Section 1271 is the business records exception to the hearsay rule. It is stated in language taken from the Uniform Business Records as Evidence Act (Sections 1953e-1953h of the Code of Civil Procedure) and from Rule 63(13) of the Uniform Rules of Evidence.

Section 1271 requires the judge to find that the sources of information and the method and time of preparation of the record "were such as to indicate its trustworthiness." Under the language of Code of Civil Procedure Section 1953f, the judge must determine that the sources of information and method and time of preparation "were such as to justify its admission." The language of Section 1271 is more accurate, for the cases hold that admission of a business record is not justified when there is no preliminary showing that the record is reliable or trustworthy. E.g., People v. Grayson, 172 Cal.App.2d 372, 341 P.2d 820 (1959) (hotel register rejected because "not shown to be true and complete").

"The chief foundation of the special reliability of business records is the requirement that they must be based upon the first-hand observation of someone whose job it is to know the facts recorded. . . . But if the evidence in the particular case discloses that the record was not based upon the report of an informant having the business duty to observe and report, then the record is not admissible under this exception, to show the truth of the matter reported to the recorder." McCormick, Evidence § 286 at 602 (1954), as quoted in MacLean v. City & County of San Francisco, 151 Cal.App.2d 133, 143, 311 P.2d 158, 164 (1957).

Applying this standard, the cases have rejected a variety of business records on the ground that they were not based on the personal knowledge of the recorder or of someone with a business duty to report to the recorder. Police accident and arrest reports are usually held inadmissible because they are based on the narrations of persons who have no business duty to report to the police. MacLean v. City & County of San Francisco, 151 Cal.App.2d 133, 311 P.2d 158 (1957); Hoel v. City of Los Angeles, 136 Cal.App.2d 295, 288 P.2d 989 (1955). They are admissible, however, to prove the fact of the arrest. Harris v. Alcoholic Bev. Con. Appeals Bd., 212 Cal.App.2d 106, 23 Cal.Rptr. 74 (1963). Similar investigative reports on the origin of fires have been held inadmissible because they were not based on personal knowledge. Behr v. County of Santa Cruz, 172 Cal.App.2d 697, 342 P.2d 987 (1959); Harrigan v. Chaperon, 118 Cal.App.2d 167, 257 P.2d 716 (1953).

Section 1271 will continue the law developed in these cases that a business report is admissible only if the sources of information and the time and method of preparation are such as to indicate its trustworthiness.

§ 1272. Absence of entry in business records. Evidence of the absence from the records of a business of a record of an asserted act, condition, or event is not made inadmissible by the hearsay rule when offered to prove the nonoccurrence of the act or event, or the nonexistence of the condition, if:

(a) It was the regular course of that business to make records of all such acts, conditions, or events at or near the time of the act, condition, or event and to preserve them; and

(b) The sources of information and method and time of preparation of the records of that business were such that the absence of a record of an act, condition, or event is a trustworthy indication that the act or event did not occur or the condition did not exist.

Note on Proposed Amendment

The Law Revision Commission tentatively decided in November 2003 to recommend the same changes in § 1272 as it recommended for § 1271.

Law Revision Commission Comment

Technically, evidence of the absence of a record may not be hearsay. Section 1272 removes any doubt that might otherwise exist concerning the admissibility of such evidence under the hearsay rule. It codifies existing case law. People v. Torres, 201 Cal.App.2d 290, 20 Cal.Rptr. 315 (1962).

Article 8. Official Records and Other Official Writings

§ 1280. Record by public employee. Evidence of a writing made as a record of an act, condition, or event is not made inadmissible by the hearsay rule when offered in any civil or criminal proceeding to prove the act, condition, or event if all of the following applies:

(a) The writing was made by and within the scope of duty of a public employee.

(b) The writing was made at or near the time of the act, condition, or event.

(c) The sources of information and method and time of preparation were such as to indicate its trustworthiness. [*Amended 1996.*]

Statutory Note

The 1996 amendment added the phrases "in any civil or criminal proceeding" and "all of the following applies." It was enacted by the same bill that added § 452.5. See Statutory Note to § 452.5(b).

Note on Proposed Amendment

The Law Revision Commission tentatively decided in November 2003 to recommend that a personal knowledge requirement be added to § 1280.

Case Notes

A party offering a writing under this section may take advantage of the presumption "that official duty has been regularly performed" (§ 664), which shifts the burden of proof to the opponent of the evidence. People v. Martinez, 22 Cal. 4th 106, 125, 91 Cal. Rptr. 2d 687, 701, 900 P.2d 563, 576-577 (2000).

Timeliness should not be judged by arbitrary limits but, rather, by the nature of the information and the reliability of sources. Records that simply involve the transfer of information from one form of storage to another are less time-sensitive than records made from memory. People v. Martinez, 22 Cal. 4th 106, 128, 91 Cal. Rptr. 2d 687, 703, 900 P.2d 563, 578 (2000).

Law Revision Commission Comment

Section 1280 restates the substance of and supersedes Sections 1920 and 1926 of the Code of Civil Procedure. Although Sections 1920 and 1926 declare unequivocally that entries in public records are prima facie evidence of the facts stated, "it has been held repeatedly that those sections cannot have universal literal application." Chandler v. Hibberd, 165 Cal.App.2d 39, 65, 332 P.2d 133, 149 (1958). In fact, the cases require the same showing of trustworthiness in regard to an official record as is required under the business records exception. Behr v. County of Santa Cruz, 172 Cal.App.2d 697, 342 P.2d 987 (1959); Hoel v. City of Los Angeles, 136 Cal.App.2d 295, 288 P.2d 989 (1955). Section 1280 continues the law declared in these cases by explicitly requiring the same showing of trustworthiness that is required in Section 1271. See the Comment to Section 1271.

The evidence that is admissible under this section is also admissible under Section 1271, the business records exception. However, Section 1271 requires a witness to testify as to the identity of the record and its mode of preparation in every instance. In contrast, Section 1280, as does existing law, permits the court to admit an official record or report without necessarily requiring a witness to testify as to its identity and mode of preparation if the court takes judicial notice or if sufficient independent evidence shows that the record or report was prepared in such a manner as to assure its trustworthiness. See, e.g., People v. Williams, 64 Cal. 87, 27 Pac. 939 (1883) (census report admitted, the court judicially noticing the statutes prescribing the method of preparing the report); Vallejo etc. R.R. v. Reed Orchard Co., 169 Cal. 545, 571, 147 Pac. 238, 250 (1915) (statistical report of state agency admitted, the court judicially noticing the statutory duty to prepare the report).

§ 1281. Record of vital statistics. Evidence of a writing made as a record of a birth, fetal death, death, or marriage is not made inadmissible by the hearsay rule if the maker was required by law to file the writing in a designated public office and the writing was made and filed as required by law.

Law Revision Commission Comment

Section 1281 provides a hearsay exception for official reports concerning birth, death, and marriage. Official reports of such events occurring within California are now admissible under the provisions of Section 10577 of the Health and Safety Code. Section 1281 provides a broader exception which includes similar reports from other jurisdictions.

§ 1282. Finding of presumed death by authorized federal employee. A written finding of presumed death made by an employee of the United States authorized to make such finding pursuant to the Federal Missing Persons Act (56 Stats. 143, 1092, and P.L. 408, Ch. 371, 2d Sess. 78th Cong.; 50 U.S.C. App. 1001-1016), as enacted or as heretofore or hereafter amended, shall be received in any court, office, or other place in this state as evidence of the death of the person therein found to be dead and of the date, circumstances, and place of his disappearance.

Law Revision Commission Comment

Section 1282 restates and supersedes the provisions of Code of Civil Procedure Section 1928.1. The evidence made admissible under Section 1282 is limited to evidence of the fact of death and of the date, circumstances, and place of disappearance.

The determination by the federal employee of the date of the presumed death is a determination ordinarily made for the purpose of determining whether the pay of a missing person should be stopped and his name stricken from the payroll. The date so determined should not be given any consideration in the California courts since the issues involved in the California proceedings require determination of the date of death for a different purpose. Hence, Section 1282 does not make admissible the finding of the date of presumed death. On the other hand, the determination of the date, circumstances, and place of disappearance is reliable information that will assist the trier of fact in determining the date when the person died and is admissible under this section. Often the date of death may be inferred from the circumstances of the disappearance. See In re Thornburg's Estate, 186 Ore. 570, 208 P.2d 349 (1949); Lukens v. Camden Trust Co., 2 N.J.Super. 214, 62 A.2d 886 (Super.Ct.1948).

Section 1282 provides a convenient and reliable method of proof of death of persons covered by the Federal Missing Persons Act. See, e.g., In re Jacobsen's Estate, 208 Misc. 443, 143 N.Y.S.2d 432 (1955) (proof of death of 2-year-old dependent of serviceman where child was passenger on plane lost at sea).

§ 1283. Record by federal employee that person is missing, captured, or the like. An official written report or record that a person is missing, missing in action, interned in a foreign country, captured by a hostile force, beleaguered by a hostile force, besieged by a hostile force, or detained in a foreign country against his will, or is dead or is alive, made by an employee of the United States authorized by any law of the United States to make such report or record shall be received in any court, office, or other place in this state as evidence that such person is missing, missing in action, interned in a foreign country, captured by a hostile force, beleaguered by a hostile force, besieged by a hostile force, or detained in a foreign country against his will, or is dead or is alive.

§ 1284. Statement of absence of public record. Evidence of a writing made by the public employee who is the official custodian of the records in a public office, reciting diligent search and failure to find a record, is not made inadmissible by the hearsay rule when offered to prove the absence of a record in that office.

Note on Proposed Amendment

The Law Revision Commission tentatively decided in November 2003 to recommend that a statement of absence of public record under § 1284 be useable to prove not only absence of record but also the nonoccurrence or nonexistence of any matter of which a record is regularly made. This would conform to FRE 803(10).

Assembly Committee on Judiciary Comment

Just as the existence and content of a public record may be proved under Section 1530 by a copy accompanied by the attestation or certificate of the custodian reciting that it is a copy, the absence of such a record from a particular public office may be proved under Section 1284 by a writing made by the custodian of the records in that office stating that no such record was found after a diligent search. The writing must, of course, be properly authenticated. See Evidence Code §§ 1401, 1453. See also Code Civ.Proc. § 1893 (public official, on demand, must, furnish certificate or its equivalent that he did not find a designated writing after a diligent search). The exception is justified by the likelihood that such a statement made by the custodian of the records is accurate and by the necessity for providing a simple and inexpensive method of proving the absence of a public record.

Article 9. Former Testimony

§ 1290. Former testimony. As used in this article [§§ 1290-1294], "former testimony" means testimony given under oath in:

(a) Another action or in a former hearing or trial of the same action;

(b) A proceeding to determine a controversy conducted by or under the supervision of an agency that has the power to determine such a controversy and is an agency of the United States or a public entity in the United States;

(c) A deposition taken in compliance with law in another action; or

(d) An arbitration proceeding if the evidence of such former testimony is a verbatim transcript thereof.

Note on Proposed Amendment

The Law Revision Commission tentatively decided in March 2005 to recommend no change to § 1290.

Statutory Notes

See Code of Civ. Proc. § 2025(u) (admissibility of depositions taken in civil actions); Penal Code §§ 1345, 1362 (admissibility of depositions on conditional examination or taken under commission in criminal actions).

Case Note

Where requirements of former testimony exception are satisfied, the transcript of testimony is admissible as a public record, § 1280, and is prima facie evidence of the testimony and proceedings, Code. Civ. Proc. § 273. People v. Reed, 13 Cal. 4th 217, 225, 52 Cal. Rptr. 106, 111, 914 P.2d 184, 189 (1996).

Law Revision Commission Comment

The purpose of Section 1290 is to provide a convenient term for use in the substantive provisions in the remainder of this article. It should be noted that depositions taken in another action are considered former testimony under Section 1290, and their admissibility is determined by Sections 1291 and 1292. The use of a deposition taken in the same action, however, is not covered by this article. Code of Civil Procedure Sections 2016-2036 deal comprehensively with the conditions and circumstances under which a deposition taken in a civil action may be used at the trial of the action in which the deposition was taken, and Penal Code Sections 1345 and 1362 prescribe the conditions for admitting the deposition of a witness that has been taken in the same criminal action. These sections will continue to govern the use of depositions in the action in which they are taken.

§ 1291. Former testimony offered against party to former proceeding. (a) Evidence of former testimony is not made inadmissible by the hearsay rule if the declarant is unavailable as a witness and:

(1) The former testimony is offered against a person who offered it in evidence in his own behalf on the former occasion or against the successor in interest of such person; or

(2) The party against whom the former testimony is offered was a party to the action or proceeding in which the testimony was given and had the right and opportunity to cross-examine the declarant with an interest and motive similar to that which he has at the hearing.

(b) The admissibility of former testimony under this section is subject to the same limitations and objections as though the declarant were testifying at the hearing, except that former testimony offered under this section is not subject to:

(1) Objections to the form of the question which were not made at the time the former testimony was given.

(2) Objections based on competency or privilege which did not exist at the time the former testimony was given.

Note on Proposed Amendment

The Law Revision Commission tentatively decided in March 2005: (1) to recommend that a similar motive and interest requirement be added to § 1291(a)(1); (2) to recommend that § 1291(a)(2) be amended by codifying: (a) the rule of Simmons v. United States, 390 U.S. 377, 394 (1968), which prevents a defendant's testimony at the hearing on a motion to suppress from being used over objection at the defendant's trial; and (b) the rule of People v. Coleman, 13 Cal.3d 867 (1975), which prevents the testimony of a probationer at a probation revocation hearing from being used over objection in a subsequent criminal trial based on the same event; and (3) to recommend no change to § 1291(b)(1).

Case Note

Similarity between a party's interest and motive to cross-examine the declarant at the first trial of criminal charges and a retrial of the same charges following reversal is not affected by the fact that events occurring after the first trial may have led counsel at the second trial to alter the nature or scope of the cross-examination of the witness. People v. Alcala, 4 Cal. 4th 742, 784, 15 Cal. Rptr. 2d 432, 456, 842 P.2d 1192, 1216 (1992, modified, 1993).

Defense counsel's strategic decision not to vigorously cross-examine a prosecution witness at the preliminary hearing does not render the witness's preliminary hearing testimony inadmissible at the trial after the witness becomes unavailable. Because the witness's testimony had the same tendency to establish defendant's guilt, defendant's interest and motive in discrediting this testimony was identical. As long as defendant was given the opportunity for effective cross-examination, the requirements of this section are satisfied whether or not defendant availed himself fully of that opportunity. People v. Zapien, 4 Cal. 4th 929, 975-976, 17 Cal. Rptr. 2d 122, 147-148, 846 P.2d 704, 729-730 (1993).

Assembly Committee on Judiciary Comment

Section 1291 provides a hearsay exception for former testimony offered against a person who was a party to the proceeding in which the former testimony was given. For example, if a series of cases arises involving several plaintiffs and but one defendant, Section 1291 permits testimony given in the first trial to be used against the defendant in a later trial if the conditions of admissibility stated in the section are met.

Former testimony is admissible under Section 1291 only if the declarant is unavailable as a witness.

Paragraph (1) of subdivision (a) of Section 1291 provides for the admission of former testimony if it is offered against the party who offered it in the previous proceeding. Since the witness is no longer available to testify, the party's previous direct and redirect examination should be considered an adequate substitute for his present right to cross-examine the declarant.

Paragraph (2) of subdivision (a) of Section 1291 provides for the admissibility of former testimony where the party against whom it is now offered had the right and opportunity in the former proceeding to cross-examine the declarant with an interest and motive similar to that which he now has. Since the party has had his opportunity to cross-examine, the primary objection to hearsay evidence—lack of opportunity to cross-examine the declarant—is not applicable. On the other hand, paragraph (2) does not make the former testimony admissible where the party against whom it is offered did not have a similar interest and motive to cross-examine the declarant. The determination of similarity of interest and motive in cross-examination should be based on practical considerations and not merely on the similarity of the party's position in the two cases. For example, testimony contained in a deposition that was taken, but not offered in evidence at the trial, in a different action should be excluded if the judge determines that the deposition was taken for discovery purposes and that the party did not subject the witness to a thorough cross-examination because he sought to avoid a premature revelation of the weakness in the testimony of the witness or in the adverse party's case. In such a situation, the party's interest and motive for cross-examination on the previous occasion would have been substantially different from his present interest and motive.

Section 1291 supersedes Code of Civil Procedure Section 1870(8) which permits former testimony to be admitted in a civil case only if the former proceeding was an action between the same parties or their predecessors in interest, relating to the same matter, or was a former trial of the action in which the testimony is offered. Section 1291 will also permit a broader range of hearsay to be introduced against the defendant in a criminal action than has been permitted under Penal Code Section 686. Under that section, former testimony has been admissible against the defendant in a criminal action only if the former testimony was given in the same action—at the preliminary examination, in a deposition, or in a prior trial of the action. Likewise, Section 1291 will permit a broader range of hearsay to be introduced against the prosecution in a criminal action since the people of the State of California are a party to all criminal actions. See Penal Code § 684.

Subdivision (b) of Section 1291 makes it clear that objections based on the competence of the declarant or on privilege are to be determined by reference to the time the former testimony was given. Existing California law is not clear on this point; some California decisions indicate that competency and privilege are to be determined as of the time the former testimony was given, but others indicate that these matters are to be determined as of the time the former testimony is offered in evidence. See Tentative Recommendation and a Study Relating to the Uniform Rules of Evidence (Article VIII. Hearsay Evidence), 6 Cal.Law Revision Comm'n, Rep., Rec. & Studies Appendix at 581-585 (1964).

Subdivision (b) also provides that objections to the form of the question may not be used to exclude the former testimony. Where the former testimony is offered under paragraph (1) of subdivision (a), the party against whom the former testimony is now offered phrased the question himself; and where the former testimony is admitted under paragraph (2) of subdivision (a), the party against whom the testimony is now offered had the opportunity to object to the form of the question when it was asked on the former occasion. Hence, the party is not permitted to raise this technical objection when the former testimony is offered against him.

§ 1292. Former testimony offered against person not a party to former proceeding. (a) Evidence of former testimony is not made inadmissible by the hearsay rule if:

(1) The declarant is unavailable as a witness;

(2) The former testimony is offered in a civil action; and

(3) The issue is such that the party to the action or proceeding in which the former testimony was given had the right and opportunity to cross-examine the declarant with an interest and motive similar to that which the party against whom the testimony is offered has at the hearing.

(b) The admissibility of former testimony under this section is subject to the same limitations and objections as though the declarant were testifying at the hearing, except that former testimony offered under this section is not subject to objections based on competency or privilege which did not exist at the time the former testimony was given.

Note on Proposed Amendment

The Law Revision Commission tentatively decided in March 2005 to recommend no change to § 1292.

Assembly Committee on Judiciary Comment

Section 1292 provides a hearsay exception for former testimony given at the former proceeding by a person who is now unavailable as a witness when such former testimony is offered against a person who was not a party to the former proceeding but whose motive for cross-examination is similar to that of a person who had the right and opportunity to cross-examine the declarant when the former testimony was given. For example, if one occurrence gives rise to a series of cases involving one defendant and several plaintiffs, Section 1292 permits testimony given against the plaintiff in the first action to be used against a different plaintiff in a subsequent action if the conditions of admissibility stated in the section are met.

Code of Civil Procedure Section 1870(8) (which is superseded by this article) authorizes the admission of former testimony only if it was given in another action between the same parties and involving the same matter. Section 1292 substitutes for these restrictive requirements what is, in effect, a more flexible "trustworthiness" approach characteristic of other hearsay exceptions. The trustworthiness of the former testimony is sufficiently guaranteed because the former adverse party had the right and opportunity to cross-examine the declarant with an interest and motive similar to that of the present adverse party. Although the party against whom the former testimony is offered did not himself have an opportunity to cross-examine the witness on the former occasion, it can be generally assumed that most prior cross-examination is adequate if the same stakes are involved. If the same stakes are not involved, the difference in interest or motivation would justify exclusion. Even where the prior cross-examination was inadequate, there is better reason here for providing a hearsay exception than there is for many of the presently recognized exceptions to the hearsay rule. As Professor McCormick states:

> I suggest that if the witness is unavailable, then the need for the sworn, transcribed former testimony in the ascertainment of truth is so great, and its reliability so far superior to most, if not all the other types of oral hearsay coming in under the other exceptions, that the requirements of identity of parties and issues be dispensed with. This dispenses with the opportunity for cross-examination, that great characteristic weapon of our adversary system. But the other types of admissible oral hearsay, admissions, declarations against interest, statements about bodily symptoms, likewise dispense with cross-examination, for declarations having far less trustworthiness than the sworn testimony in open court, and with a far greater hazard of fabrication or mistake in the reporting of the declaration by the witness. [McCormick, Evidence § 238 at 501 (1954).]

Section 1292 does not make former testimony admissible in a criminal case. This limitation preserves the right of a person accused of crime to confront and cross-examine the witnesses against him. When a person's life or liberty is at stake—as it is in a criminal action—the defendant should not be compelled to rely on the fact that another person has had an opportunity to cross-examine the witness.

Subdivision (b) of Section 1292 makes it clear that objections based on competency or privilege are to be determined by reference to the time when the former testimony was given. Existing California law is not clear on this point; some California decisions indicate that competency and privilege are to be determined as of the time the former testimony was given, but others indicate that these matters are to be determined as of the time the former testimony is offered in evidence. See Tentative Recommendation and a Study Relating to the Uniform Rules of Evidence (Article VIII. Hearsay Evidence), 6 Cal.Law Revision Comm'n, Rep., Rec. & Studies Appendix, at 581-585 (1964).

§ 1293. Former testimony by minor child complaining witness at preliminary examination. (a) Evidence of former testimony made at a preliminary examination by a minor child who was the complaining witness is not made inadmissible by the hearsay rule if:

(1) The former testimony is offered in a proceeding to declare the minor a dependent child of the court pursuant to Section 300 of the Welfare and Institutions Code.

(2) The issues are such that a defendant in the preliminary examination in which the former testimony was given had the right and opportunity to cross-examine the minor child with an interest and motive similar to that which the parent or guardian against whom the testimony is offered has at the proceeding to declare the minor a dependent child of the court.

(b) The admissibility of former testimony under this section is subject to the same limitations and objections as though the minor child were testifying at the proceeding to declare him or her a dependent child of the court.

(c) The attorney for the parent or guardian against whom the former testimony is offered or, if none, the parent or guardian may make a motion to challenge the admissibility of the former testimony upon a showing that new substantially different issues are present in the proceeding to declare the minor a dependent child than were present in the preliminary examination.

(d) As used in this section, "complaining witness" means the alleged victim of the crime for which a preliminary examination was held.

(e) This section shall apply only to testimony made at a preliminary examination on and after January 1, 1990. [*Added 1989.*]

Note on Proposed Amendment

The Law Revision Commission tentatively decided in March 2005 to recommend no change to § 1293.

§ 1294. Unavailable witnesses; prior inconsistent statements; preliminary hearing or prior proceeding. (a) The following evidence of prior inconsistent statements of a witness properly admitted at a conditional examination, preliminary hearing, or trial of the same criminal matter pursuant to Section 1235 is not made inadmissible by the hearsay rule if the witness is unavailable and former testimony of the witness is admitted pursuant to Section 1291:

(1) A video recorded statement introduced at a preliminary hearing or prior proceeding concerning the same criminal matter.

(2) A transcript, containing the statements, of the preliminary hearing or prior proceeding concerning the same criminal matter.

(b) The party against whom the prior inconsistent statements are offered, at his or her option, may examine or cross-examine any person who testified at the preliminary hearing or prior proceeding as to the prior inconsistent statements of the witness.

(c) As used in this section, "conditional examination" has the same meaning as in Chapter 4 (commencing with Section 1335) of Title 10 of Part 2 of the Penal Code. [*Added 1996; amended 2006, 2018.*]

Article 10. Judgments

Statutory Note

See Penal Code § 2702 (admissibility of judgments establishing paternity or nonpaternity in prosecutions for abandonment and neglect of children).

§ 1300. Judgment of conviction of crime punishable as felony. Evidence of a final judgment adjudging a person guilty of a crime punishable as a felony is not made inadmissible by the hearsay rule when offered in a civil action to prove any fact essential to the judgment whether or not the judgment was based on a plea of nolo contendere. [*Amended 1982.*]

Statutory Note

The 1982 amendment removed the exclusion of judgments based on a plea of nolo contendere. See Penal Code § 1016, as amended.

Note on Proposed Amendment

The Law Revision Commission tentatively decided in June 2004 to recommend that § 1300 be expanded to allow a judgment of conviction of any crime to be used in a criminal action when offered by the accused, a judgment of conviction of a felony to be used in a criminal action when offered by the prosecution, and any such judgment to be useable whether or not based on a plea of nolo contendere.

Case Note

Evidence of acquittal is admissible to rebut prosecution evidence of guilt of another crime. People v. Griffin, 66 Cal. 2d 459, 464-466, 58 Cal. Rptr. 107, 110-111, 426 P.2d 507, 510-511 (1967).

Law Revision Commission Comment

Analytically, a judgment that is offered to prove the matters determined by the judgment is hearsay evidence. Uniform Rules of Evidence, Rule 63(20) Comment (1953); Tentative Recommendation and a Study Relating to the Uniform Rules of Evidence (Article VIII. Hearsay Evidence), 6 Cal.Law Revision Comm'n, Rep., Rec. & Studies Appendix at 539-541 (1964). It is in substance a statement of the court that determined the previous action ("a statement that was made other than by a witness while testifying at the hearing") that is offered "to prove the truth of the matter stated." Evidence Code § 1200. Therefore, unless an exception to the hearsay rule is provided, a judgment would be inadmissible if offered in a subsequent action to prove the matters determined.

Of course, a judgment may, as a matter of substantive law, conclusively establish certain facts insofar as a party is concerned. Teitlebaum Furs, Inc. v. Dominion Ins. Co., 58 Cal.2d 601, 25 Cal.Rptr. 559, 375 P.2d 439 (1962); Bernhard v. Bank of America, 19 Cal.2d 807, 122 P.2d 892 (1942). The sections of this article do not purport to deal with the doctrines of res judicata and estoppel by judgment. These sections deal only with the evidentiary use of judgments in those cases where the substantive law does not require that the judgments be given conclusive effect.

Section 1300 provides an exception to the hearsay rule for a final judgment adjudging a person guilty of a crime punishable as a felony. Hence, if a plaintiff sues to recover a reward offered by the defendant for the arrest and conviction of a person who committed a particular crime, Section 1300 permits the plaintiff to use a judgment of conviction as evidence that the person convicted committed the crime. The exception does not, however, apply in criminal actions. Thus, Section 1300 does not permit the judgment to be used in a criminal action as evidence of the identity of the person who committed the crime or as evidence that the crime was committed.

Section 1300 will change the California law. Under existing law, a conviction of a crime is inadmissible as evidence in a subsequent action. Marceau v. Travelers' Ins. Co., 101 Cal. 338, 35 Pac. 856 (1894) (evidence of a murder conviction held inadmissible to prove the insured was intentionally killed); Burke v. Wells, Fargo & Co., 34 Cal. 60 (1867) (evidence of a robbery conviction held inadmissible to prove the identity of robber in an action to recover reward). The change, however, is desirable, for the evidence involved is peculiarly reliable. The seriousness of the charge assures that the facts will be thoroughly litigated, and the fact that the judgment must be based upon a determination that there was no reasonable doubt concerning the defendant's guilt assures that the question of guilt will be thoroughly considered.

Section 1300 applies to any crime punishable as a felony. The fact that a misdemeanor sentence is imposed does not affect the admissibility of the judgment of a conviction under this section. Cf. Penal Code § 17. The exclusion of judgments based on a plea of nolo contendere from the exception in Section 1300 is a reflection of the policy expressed in Penal Code Section 1016.

§ 1301. Judgment against person entitled to indemnity. Evidence of a final judgment is not made inadmissible by the hearsay rule when offered by the judgment debtor to prove any fact which was essential to the judgment in an action in which he seeks to:

(a) Recover partial or total indemnity or exoneration for money paid or liability incurred because of the judgment;

(b) Enforce a warranty to protect the judgment debtor against the liability determined by the judgment; or

(c) Recover damages for breach of warranty substantially the same as the warranty determined by the judgment to have been breached.

Note on Proposed Amendment

The Law Revision Commission tentatively decided in June 2004 to recommend that § 1301 be repealed as superfluous.

Law Revision Commission Comment

If a person entitled to indemnity, or if the obligee under a warranty contract, complies with certain conditions relating to notice and defense, the indemnitor or warrantor is conclusively bound by any judgment recovered. Civil Code § 2778 (5); Code Civ.Proc. § 1912; McCormick v. Marcy, 165 Cal. 386, 132 Pac. 449 (1913).

Where a judgment against an indemnitee or person protected by a warranty is not made conclusive on the indemnitor or warrantor, Section 1301 permits the judgment to be used as hearsay evidence in an action to recover on the indemnity or warranty. * * *

§ 1302. Judgment determining liability of third person. When the liability, obligation, or duty of a third person is in issue in a civil action, evidence of a final judgment against that person is not made inadmissible by the hearsay rule when offered to prove such liability, obligation, or duty.

Note on Proposed Amendment

The Law Revision Commission tentatively decided in June 2004 to recommend that § 1302 be repealed as superfluous.

Article 11. Family History

§ 1310. Statement concerning declarant's own family history. (a) Subject to subdivision (b), evidence of a statement by a declarant who is unavailable as a witness concerning his own birth, marriage, divorce, a parent and child relationship, relationship by blood or marriage, race, ancestry, or other similar fact of his family history is not made inadmissible by the hearsay rule, even though the declarant had no means of acquiring personal knowledge of the matter declared.

(b) Evidence of a statement is inadmissible under this section if the statement was made under circumstances such as to indicate its lack of trustworthiness. [*Amended 1975.*]

Law Revision Commission Comment

Section 1310 provides a hearsay exception for a statement concerning the declarant's own family history. It restates in substance and supersedes Section 1870(4) of the Code of Civil Procedure. Section 1870(4), however, requires that the declarant be dead whereas unavailability of the declarant for any of the reasons specified in Section 240 makes the statement admissible under Section 1310.

The statement is not admissible if it was made under circumstances such as to indicate its lack of trustworthiness. The requirement is similar to the requirement of existing case law that the statement be made at a time when no controversy existed as to the matters stated. See, e.g., Estate of Walden, 166 Cal. 446, 137 Pac. 35 (1913); Estate of Nidever, 181 Cal.App.2d 367, 5 Cal.Rptr. 343 (1960). However, the language of Section 1310 permits the judge to consider the declarant's motives to tell the truth as well as his reasons to deviate therefrom in determining whether the statement is sufficiently trustworthy to be admitted as evidence.

§ 1311. Statement concerning family history of another. (a) Subject to subdivision (b), evidence of a statement concerning the birth, marriage, divorce, death, parent and child relationship, race, ancestry, relationship by blood or marriage, or other similar fact of the family history of a person other than the declarant is not made inadmissible by the hearsay rule if the declarant is unavailable as a witness and:

(1) The declarant was related to the other by blood or marriage; or

(2) The declarant was otherwise so intimately associated with the other's family as to be likely to have had accurate information concerning the matter declared and made the statement (i) upon information received from the other or from a person related by blood or marriage to the other or (ii) upon repute in the other's family.

(b) Evidence of a statement is inadmissible under this section if the statement was made under circumstances such as to indicate its lack of trustworthiness. [*Amended 1975.*]

Law Revision Commission Comment

Section 1311 provides a hearsay exception for a statement concerning the family history of another. Paragraph (1) of subdivision (a) restates in substance existing law as found in Section 1870(4) of the Code of Civil Procedure which it supersedes. Paragraph (2) is new to California law, but it is a sound extension of the present law to cover a situation where the declarant was a family housekeeper or doctor or so close a friend as to be included by the family in discussions of its family history.

There are two limitations on admissibility of a statement under Section 1311. First, a statement is admissible only if the declarant is unavailable as a witness within the meaning of Section 240. (Section 1870(4) requires that the declarant be deceased in order for his statement to be admissible.) Second, a statement is not admissible if it was made under circumstances such as to indicate its lack of trustworthiness. For a discussion of this requirement, see the Comment to Evidence Code § 1310.

§ 1312. Entries in family records and the like. Evidence of entries in family Bibles or other family books or charts, engravings on rings, family portraits, engravings on urns, crypts, or tombstones, and the like, is not made inadmissible by the hearsay rule when offered to prove the birth, marriage, divorce, death, parent and child relationship, race, ancestry, relationship by blood or marriage, or other similar fact of the family history of a member of the family by blood or marriage. [*Amended 1975.*]

§ 1313. Reputation in family concerning family history. Evidence of reputation among members of a family is not made inadmissible by the hearsay rule if the reputation concerns the birth, marriage, divorce, death, parent and child relationship, race, ancestry, relationship by blood or marriage, or other similar fact of the family history of a member of the family by blood or marriage. [*Amended 1975.*]

§ 1314. Reputation in community concerning family history. Evidence of reputation in a community concerning the date or fact of birth, marriage, divorce, or death of a person resident in the community at the time of the reputation is not made inadmissible by the hearsay rule.

Law Revision Commission Comment

Section 1314 restates what has been held to be existing law under Code of Civil Procedure Section 1963(30) with respect to proof of the fact of marriage. See People v. Vogel, 46 Cal.2d 798, 299 P.2d 850 (1956); Estate of Baldwin, 162 Cal. 471, 123 Pac. 267 (1912). However, Section 1314 has no counterpart in California law insofar as proof of the date or fact of birth, divorce, or death is concerned, since proof of such facts by reputation is presently limited to reputation in the family. See Estate of Heaton, 135 Cal. 385, 67 Pac. 321 (1902).

§ 1315. Church records concerning family history. Evidence of a statement concerning a person's birth, marriage, divorce, death, parent and child relationship, race, ancestry, relationship by blood or marriage, or other similar fact of family history which is contained in a writing made as a record of a church, religious denomination, or religious society is not made inadmissible by the hearsay rule if:

(a) The statement is contained in a writing made as a record of an act, condition, or event that would be admissible as evidence of such act, condition, or event under Section 1271; and

(b) The statement is of a kind customarily recorded in connection with the act, condition, or event recorded in the writing. [*Amended 1975.*]

Law Revision Commission Comment

Church records generally are admissible as business records under the provisions of Section 1271. Under Section 1271, such records would be admissible to prove the occurrence of the church activity—the baptism, confirmation, or marriage—recorded in the writing. However, it is unlikely that Section 1271 would permit such records to be used as evidence of the age or relationship of the participants, for the business records act has been held to authorize business records to be used to prove only facts known personally to the recorder of the information or to other employees of the business. Patek & Co. v. Vineberg, 210 Cal.App.2d 20, 23, 26 Cal.Rptr. 293, 294 (1962) (hearing denied); People v. Williams, 187 Cal.App.2d 355, 9 Cal.Rptr. 722 (1960); Gough v. Security Trust & Sav. Bank, 162 Cal.App.2d 90, 327 P.2d 555 (1958).

Section 1315 permits church records to be used to prove certain additional information. Facts of family history, such as birth dates, relationships, marital histories, etc., that are ordinarily reported to church authorities and recorded in connection with the church's baptismal, confirmation, marriage, and funeral records may be proved by such records under Section 1315.

Section 1315 continues in effect and supersedes the provisions of Code of Civil Procedure Section 1919a without, however, the special and cumbersome authentication procedure specified in Code of Civil Procedure Section 1919b. Under Section 1315, church records may be authenticated in the same manner that other business records are authenticated.

§ 1316. Marriage, baptismal and similar certificates. Evidence of a statement concerning a person's birth, marriage, divorce, death, parent and child relationship, race, ancestry, relationship by blood or marriage, or other similar fact of family history is not made inadmissible by the hearsay rule if the statement is contained in a certificate that the maker thereof performed a marriage or other ceremony or administered a sacrament and:

(a) The maker was a clergyman, civil officer, or other person authorized to perform the acts reported in the certificate by law or by the rules, regulations, or requirements of a church, religious denomination, or religious society; and

(b) The certificate was issued by the maker at the time and place of the ceremony or sacrament or within a reasonable time thereafter. [*Amended 1975.*]

Law Revision Commission Comment

Section 1316 provides a hearsay exception for marriage, baptismal, and similar certificates. This exception is somewhat broader than that found in Sections 1919a and 1919b of the Code of Civil Procedure (superseded by Evidence Code Sections 1315 and 1316). Sections 1919a and 1919b are limited to church records and, hence, with respect to marriages, to those performed by clergymen. Moreover, they establish an elaborate and detailed authentication procedure, whereas certificates made admissible by Section 1316 need meet only the general authentication requirement of Section 1401.

Article 12. Reputation and Statements Concerning Community History, Property Interests, and Character

§ 1320. Reputation concerning community history. Evidence of reputation in a community is not made inadmissible by the hearsay rule if the reputation concerns an event of general history of the community or of the state or nation of which the community is a part and the event was of importance to the community.

Statutory Note

See Health & Safety Code § 11575.5 (admissibility of reputation to prove the existence of a nuisance in action to abate nuisance under Controlled Substances Act).

Law Revision Commission Comment

Section 1320 provides a wider rule of admissibility than does Code of Civil Procedure Section 1870(11) which it supersedes in part. Section 1870 provides in relevant part that proof may be made of "common reputation existing previous to the controversy, respecting facts of a public or general interest more than thirty years old." The 30-year limitation is essentially arbitrary. The important question would seem to be whether a community reputation on the matter involved exists; its age would appear to go more to its venerability than to its truth. Nor is it necessary to include in Section 1320 the requirement that the reputation existed previous to controversy. It is unlikely that a community reputation respecting an event of general history would be influenced by the existence of a controversy.

§ 1321. Reputation concerning public interest in property. Evidence of reputation in a community is not made inadmissible by the hearsay rule if the reputation concerns the interest of the public in property in the community and the reputation arose before controversy.

Law Revision Commission Comment

Section 1321 preserves the rule in Simons v. Inyo Cerro Gordo Co., 48 Cal.App. 524, 192 Pac. 144 (1920). It does not require, however, that the reputation be more than 30 years old; it requires merely that the reputation arose before there was a controversy concerning the matter. See the Comment to Section 1320.

§ 1322. Reputation concerning boundary or custom affecting land. Evidence of reputation in a community is not made inadmissible by the hearsay rule if the reputation concerns boundaries of, or customs affecting, land in the community and the reputation arose before controversy.

§ 1323. Statement concerning boundary. Evidence of a statement concerning the boundary of land is not made inadmissible by the hearsay rule if the declarant is unavailable as a witness and had sufficient knowledge of the subject, but evidence of a statement is not admissible under this section if the statement was made under circumstances such as to indicate its lack of trustworthiness.

§ 1324. Reputation concerning character. Evidence of a person's general reputation with reference to his character or a trait of his character at a relevant time in the community in which he then resided or in a group with which he then habitually associated is not made inadmissible by the hearsay rule.

Law Revision Commission Comment

Section 1324 codifies a well-settled exception to the hearsay rule. See, e.g., People v. Cobb, 45 Cal.2d 158, 287 P.2d 752 (1955). Of course, character evidence is admissible only when the question of character is material to the matter being litigated. The only purpose of Section 1324 is to declare that reputation evidence as to character or a trait of character is not inadmissible under the hearsay rule.

Article 13. Dispositive Instruments and Ancient Writings

§ 1330. Recitals in writings affecting property. Evidence of a statement contained in a deed of conveyance or a will or other writing purporting to affect an interest in real or personal property is not made inadmissible by the hearsay rule if:

(a) The matter stated was relevant to the purpose of the writing;

(b) The matter stated would be relevant to an issue as to an interest in the property; and

(c) The dealings with the property since the statement was made have not been inconsistent with the truth of the statement.

Law Revision Commission Comment

Section 1330 restates the substance of existing California law relating to recitals in dispositive instruments. Although language in some cases appears to require that the dispositive instrument be ancient, cases may be found in which recitals in dispositive instruments have been admitted without regard to the age of the instrument. See Russell v. Langford, 135 Cal. 356, 67 Pac. 331 (1902) (recital in will); Pearson v. Pearson, 46 Cal. 609 (1873) (recital in will); Culver v. Newhart, 18 Cal.App. 614, 123 Pac. 975 (1912) (bill of sale). There is a sufficient likelihood that the statements made in a dispositive document, when related to the purpose of the document, will be true to warrant the admissibility of such documents without regard to their age.

§ 1331. Recitals in ancient writings. Evidence of a statement is not made inadmissible by the hearsay rule if the statement is contained in a writing more than 30 years old and the statement has been since generally acted upon as true by persons having an interest in the matter.

Law Revision Commission Comment

Section 1331 clarifies the existing law relating to the admissibility of recitals in ancient documents by providing that such recitals are admissible under an exception to the hearsay rule. Code of Civil Procedure Section 1963(34) (superseded by the Evidence Code) provides that a document more than 30 years old is presumed genuine if it has been generally acted upon as genuine by persons having an interest in the matter. The Supreme Court has held that a document meeting this section's requirements is presumed to be genuine—presumed to be what it purports to be—but that the genuineness of the document imports no verity to the recitals contained therein. Gwin v. Calegaris, 139 Cal. 384, 389, 73 Pac. 851, 853 (1903). Recent cases decided by district courts of appeal, however, have held that the recitals in such a document are admissible to prove the truth of the facts recited. Estate of Nidever, 181 Cal.App.2d 367, 5 Cal.Rptr. 343 (1960); Kirkpatrick v. Tapo Oil Co., 144 Cal.App.2d 404, 301 P.2d 274 (1956). In these latter cases, the courts have not insisted that the hearsay statement itself be acted upon as true by persons with an interest in the matter; the evidence has been admitted merely upon a showing that the document containing the statement is genuine. The age of a document alone is not a sufficient guarantee of the trustworthiness of a statement contained therein to warrant the admission of the statement into evidence. Accordingly, Section 1331 makes it clear that the statement itself must have been generally acted upon as true for at least 30 years by persons having an interest in the matter.

Article 14. Commercial, Scientific and Similar Publications

§ 1340. Commercial lists and the like. Evidence of a statement, other than an opinion, contained in a tabulation, list, directory, register, or other published compilation is not made inadmissible by the hearsay rule if the compilation is generally used and relied upon as accurate in the course of a business as defined in Section 1270.

§ 1341. Publications concerning facts of general notoriety and interest. Historical works, books of science or art, and published maps or charts, made by persons indifferent between the parties, are not made inadmissible by the hearsay rule when offered to prove facts of general notoriety and interest.

Article 15. Declarant Unavailable as Witness

§ 1350. Unavailable declarant; hearsay rule. (a) In a criminal proceeding charging a serious felony, evidence of a statement made by a declarant is not made inadmissible by the hearsay rule if the declarant is unavailable as a witness, and all of the following are true:

(1) There is clear and convincing evidence that the declarant's unavailability was knowingly caused by, aided by, or solicited by the party against whom the statement is offered for the purpose of preventing the arrest or prosecution of the party and is the result of the death by homicide or the kidnapping of the declarant.

(2) There is no evidence that the unavailability of the declarant was caused by, aided by, solicited by, or procured on behalf of, the party who is offering the statement.

(3) The statement has been memorialized in a tape recording made by a law enforcement official, or in a written statement prepared by a law enforcement official and signed by the declarant and notarized in the presence of the law enforcement official, prior to the death or kidnapping of the declarant.

(4) The statement was made under circumstances which indicate its trustworthiness and was not the result of promise, inducement, threat, or coercion.

(5) The statement is relevant to the issues to be tried.

(6) The statement is corroborated by other evidence which tends to connect the party against whom the statement is offered with the commission of the serious felony with which the party is charged. The corroboration is not sufficient if it merely shows the commission of the offense or the circumstances thereof.

(b) If the prosecution intends to offer a statement pursuant to this section, the prosecution shall serve a written notice upon the defendant at least 10 days prior to the hearing or trial at which the prosecution intends to offer the statement, unless the prosecution shows good cause for the failure to provide that notice. In the event that good cause is shown, the defendant shall be entitled to a reasonable continuance of the hearing or trial.

(c) If the statement is offered during trial, the court's determination shall be made out of the presence of the jury. If the defendant elects to testify at the hearing on a motion brought pursuant to this section, the court shall exclude from the examination every person except the clerk, the court reporter, the bailiff, the prosecutor, the investigating officer, the defendant and his or her counsel, an investigator for the defendant, and the officer having custody of the defendant. Notwithstanding any other provision of law, the defendant's testimony at the hearing shall not be admissible in any other proceeding except the hearing brought on the motion pursuant to this section. If a transcript is made of the defendant's testimony, it shall be sealed and transmitted to the clerk of the court in which the action is pending.

(d) As used in this section, "serious felony" means any of the felonies listed in subdivision (c) of Section 1192.7 of the Penal Code or any violation of Section 11351, 11352, 11378, or 11379 of the Health and Safety Code.

(e) If a statement to be admitted pursuant to this section includes hearsay statements made by anyone other than the declarant who is unavailable pursuant to subdivision (a), those hearsay statements are inadmissible unless they meet the requirements of an exception to the hearsay rule. [*Added 1985. Amended 2001.*]

Note on Proposed Amendment

The Law Revision Commission tentatively decided in March 2005 to recommend no change to § 1350, but to recommend the addition of a new § 1351, which would contain parallel provisions applicable to civil actions.

Article 16. Statements by Minors Describing Child Abuse or Neglect

§ 1360. Statements describing an act or attempted act of child abuse or neglect; criminal prosecutions; requirements. (a) In a criminal prosecution where the victim is a minor, a statement made by the victim when under the age of 12 describing any act of child abuse or neglect performed with or on the child by another, or describing any attempted act of child abuse or neglect with or on the child by another, is not made inadmissible by the hearsay rule if all of the following apply:

(1) The statement is not otherwise admissible by statute or court rule.

(2) The court finds, in a hearing conducted outside the presence of the jury, that the time, content, and circumstances of the statement provide sufficient indicia of reliability.

(3) The child either:

(A) Testifies at the proceedings.

(B) Is unavailable as a witness, in which case the statement may be admitted only if there is evidence of the child abuse or neglect that corroborates the statement made by the child.

(b) A statement may not be admitted under this section unless the proponent of the statement makes known to the adverse party the intention to offer the statement and the particulars of the statement sufficiently in advance of the proceedings in order to provide the adverse party with a fair opportunity to prepare to meet the statement.

(c) For purposes of this section, "child abuse" means an act proscribed by Section 273a, 273d, or 288.5 of the Penal Code, or any of the acts described in Section 11165.1 of the Penal Code, and "child neglect" means any of the acts described in Section 11165.2 of the Penal Code. [*Added 1995.*]

Note on Proposed Amendment

The Law Revision Commission tentatively decided in March 2005 to recommend no change to § 1360.

Case Note

Section 1360 does not apply in child dependency proceedings, but the provisions of this section were borrowed by the court in fashioning a judicially-created child dependency exception to the hearsay rule, see § 1200(b). In re Cindy L., 17 Cal. 4th 15, 29-31, 69 Cal. Rptr. 2d 803, 812-814, 947 P.2d 1340, 1349-1351 (1997).

Article 17. Physical Abuse

§ 1370. Threat of infliction of injury. (a) Evidence of a statement by a declarant is not made inadmissible by the hearsay rule if all of the following conditions are met:

(1) The statement purports to narrate, describe, or explain the infliction or threat of physical injury upon the declarant.

(2) The declarant is unavailable as a witness pursuant to Section 240.

(3) The statement was made at or near the time of the infliction or threat of physical injury. Evidence of statements made more than five years before the filing of the current action or proceeding shall be inadmissible under this section.

(4) The statement was made under circumstances that would indicate its trustworthiness.

(5) The statement was made in writing, was electronically recorded, or made to a physician, nurse, paramedic, or to a law enforcement official.

(b) For purposes of paragraph (4) of subdivision (a), circumstances relevant to the issue of trustworthiness include, but are not limited to, the following:

(1) Whether the statement was made in contemplation of pending or anticipated litigation in which the declarant was interested.

(2) Whether the declarant has a bias or motive for fabricating the statement, and the extent of any bias or motive.

(3) Whether the statement is corroborated by evidence other than statements that are admissible only pursuant to this section.

(c) A statement is admissible pursuant to this section only if the proponent of the statement makes known to the adverse party the intention to offer the statement and the particulars of the statement sufficiently in advance of the proceedings in order to provide the adverse party with a fair opportunity to prepare to meet the statement. [*Added 1996.*]

Statutory Note

Section 1 of Stats. 1996, c. 416 (A.B. 2068), which added § 1370, declared:

It is the intent of the Legislature that enactment of this statute shall not affect other evidentiary requirements, including, but not limited to, Sections 351 and 352, shall not impair a party's right to attack the credibility of the declarant pursuant to Section 1202, shall not affect the defendant's right to discovery for purposes of producing rebuttal evidence attacking the declarant's credibility, and shall not be used in a manner inconsistent with the defendant's right to due process and to confront witnesses under the United States or California Constitution.

§ 1380. Elder and dependent adults; statements by victims of abuse. (a) In a criminal proceeding charging a violation, or attempted violation, of Section 368 of the Penal Code, evidence of a statement made by a declarant is not made inadmissible by the hearsay rule if the declarant is unavailable as a witness, as defined in subdivisions (a) and (b) of Section 240, and all of the following are true:

(1) The party offering the statement has made a showing of particularized guarantees of trustworthiness regarding the statement, the statement was made under circumstances which indicate its trustworthiness, and the statement was not the result of promise, inducement, threat, or coercion. In making its determination, the court may consider only the circumstances that surround the making of the statement and that render the declarant particularly worthy of belief.

(2) There is no evidence that the unavailability of the declarant was caused by, aided by, solicited by, or procured on behalf of, the party who is offering the statement.

(3) The entire statement has been memorialized in a videotape recording made by a law enforcement official, prior to the death or disabling of the declarant.

(4) The statement was made by the victim of the alleged violation.

(5) The statement is supported by corroborative evidence.

(6) The victim of the alleged violation is an individual who meets both of the following requirements:

(A) Was 65 years of age or older or was a dependent adult when the alleged violation or attempted violation occurred.

(B) At the time of any criminal proceeding, including, but not limited to, a preliminary hearing or trial, regarding the alleged violation or attempted violation, is either deceased or suffers from the infirmities of aging as manifested by advanced age or organic brain damage, or other physical, mental, or emotional dysfunction, to the extent that the ability of the person to provide adequately for the person's own care or protection is impaired.

(b) If the prosecution intends to offer a statement pursuant to this section, the prosecution shall serve a written notice upon the defendant at least 10 days prior to the hearing or trial at which the prosecution intends to offer the statement, unless the prosecution shows good cause for the failure to provide that notice. In the event that good cause is shown, the defendant shall be entitled to a reasonable continuance of the hearing or trial.

(c) If the statement is offered during trial, the court's determination as to the availability of the victim as a witness shall be made out of the presence of the jury. If the defendant elects to testify at the hearing on a motion brought pursuant to this section, the court shall exclude from the examination every person except the clerk, the court reporter, the bailiff, the prosecutor, the investigating officer, the defendant and his or her counsel, an investigator for the defendant, and the officer having custody of the defendant. Notwithstanding any other provision of law, the defendant's testimony at the hearing shall not be admissible in any other proceeding except the hearing brought on the motion pursuant to this section. If a transcript is made of the defendant's testimony, it shall be sealed and transmitted to the clerk of the court in which the action is pending. [*Added 1999.*]

§ 1390. Statements against parties involved in causing unavailability of declarant as witness.

(a) Evidence of a statement is not made inadmissible by the hearsay rule if the statement is offered against a party that has engaged, or aided and abetted, in the wrongdoing that was intended to, and did, procure the unavailability of the declarant as a witness.

(b) (1) The party seeking to introduce a statement pursuant to subdivision (a) shall establish, by a preponderance of the evidence, that the elements of subdivision (a) have been met at a foundational hearing.

(2) The hearsay evidence that is the subject of the foundational hearing is admissible at the foundational hearing. However, a finding that the elements of subdivision (a) have been met shall not be based solely on the unconfronted hearsay statement of the unavailable declarant, and shall be supported by independent corroborative evidence.

(3) The foundational hearing shall be conducted outside the presence of the jury. However, if the hearing is conducted after a jury trial has begun, the judge presiding at the hearing may consider evidence already presented to the jury in deciding whether the elements of subdivision (a) have been met.

(4) In deciding whether or not to admit the statement, the judge may take into account whether it is trustworthy and reliable.

(c) This section shall apply to any civil, criminal, or juvenile case or proceeding initiated or pending as of January 1, 2011.

[*Added 2010; amended 2015, 2016.*]

DIVISION 11. WRITINGS

Chapter 1. Authentication and Proof of Writings

Article 1. Requirement of Authentication

§ 1400. Authentication defined. Authentication of a writing means (a) the introduction of evidence sufficient to sustain a finding that it is the writing that the proponent of the evidence claims it is or (b) the establishment of such facts by any other means provided by law.

Law Revision Commission Comment

Before any tangible object may be admitted into evidence, the party seeking to introduce the object must make a preliminary showing that the object is in some way relevant to the issues to be decided in the action. When the object sought to be introduced is a writing, this preliminary showing of relevancy usually entails some proof that the writing is authentic—i.e., that the writing was made or signed by its purported maker. Hence, this showing is normally referred to as "authentication" of the writing. But authentication, correctly understood, may involve a preliminary showing that the writing is a forgery or is a writing found in particular files regardless of its authorship. Cf. People v. Adamson, 118 Cal.App.2d 714, 258 P.2d 1020 (1953). When the requisite preliminary showing has been made, the judge admits the writing into evidence for consideration by the trier of fact. However, the fact that the judge permits the writing to be admitted in evidence does not necessarily establish the authenticity of the writing; all that the judge has determined is that there has been a sufficient showing of the authenticity of the writing to permit the trier of fact to find that it is authentic. The trier of fact independently determines the question of authenticity, and, if the trier of fact does not believe the evidence of authenticity, it may find that the writing is not authentic despite the fact that the judge has determined that it was "authenticated." See 7 Wigmore, Evidence §§ 2129-2135 (3d ed. 1940).

This chapter sets forth the rules governing this process of authentication. Sections 1400-1402 (Article 1) define and state the general requirement of authentication—either by evidence sufficient to sustain a finding of authenticity or by other means sanctioned by law. Sections 1410-1454 (Articles 2 and 3) set forth some of the means that may be used to authenticate certain kinds of writings. The operation and effect of these sections is explained in separate Comments relating to them.

Under Section 1400, as under existing law, a writing may be authenticated by the presentation of evidence sufficient to sustain a finding of its authenticity. See Verzan v. McGregor, 23 Cal. 339, 342-343 (1863). Under Section 1400, as under existing law, the authenticity of a particular writing also may be established by some means other than the introduction of evidence of authenticity. Thus, the authenticity of a writing may be established by stipulation or by the pleadings. See e.g., Code Civ.Proc. §§ 447 and 448. The requisite preliminary showing may also be supplied by a presumption. See, e.g., Evidence Code §§ 1450-1454, 1530. In some instances, a presumption of authenticity may also attach to a writing authenticated in a particular manner. See, e.g., Evidence Code § 643 (the ancient documents rule). Where a presumption applies, the trier of fact is required to find that the writing is authentic unless the requisite contrary showing is made. Evidence Code §§ 600, 604, 606.

§ 1401. Authentication required. (a) Authentication of a writing is required before it may be received in evidence.

(b) Authentication of a writing is required before secondary evidence of its content may be received in evidence.

Assembly Committee on Judiciary Comment

The requirement of authentication stated in subdivision (a) reflects existing law. Ten Winkel v. Anglo California Sec. Co., 11 Cal.2d 707, 81 P.2d 958 (1938). However, the requirement has never been stated in the California statutes.

Some cases have indicated that authentication is not necessary under certain circumstances, as, for example, when the execution of the writing is not in issue. See People v. Adamson, 118 Cal.App.2d 714, 258 P.2d 1020 (1953). This is true, however, only if "authentication" is construed narrowly to refer only to proof of due execution. The Evidence Code defines the term more broadly and requires all writings to be authenticated. The writing involved in the Adamson case was a letter that a witness claimed he had received and acted upon. Under the Evidence Code, the requirement of authentication would require a showing that the letter offered in evidence was in fact the one received and acted upon; and this is the preliminary showing that was found sufficient in the Adamson case.

The "writing" referred to in subdivision (a) is any writing offered in evidence; although it may be either an original or a copy, it must be authenticated before it may be received in evidence.

Authentication of a writing does not in and of itself authorize the writing to be admitted in evidence. The writing, of course, must be relevant and not be made inadmissible by any exclusionary rule—e.g., the hearsay rule, the best evidence rule, or the rule excluding a coerced confession. Thus, Section 1401 merely requires that an otherwise admissible writing be authenticated before it may be received in evidence.

Subdivision (b) of Section 1401 requires that a writing be authenticated even when it is not offered in evidence but is sought to be proved by a copy or by testimony as to its content under the circumstances permitted by Sections 1500-1510 (the best evidence rule). This is declarative of existing California law. Spottiswood v. Weir, 80 Cal. 448, 22 Pac. 289 (1889); Smith v. Brannan, 13 Cal. 107, 115 (1859); Forman v. Goldberg, 42 Cal.App.2d 308, 316-317, 108 P.2d 983, 988 (1941). Under Section 1401, therefore, if a person offers in evidence a copy of a writing, he must make a sufficient preliminary showing of the authenticity of both the copy and the original (i.e., the writing sought to be proved by the copy).

In some instances, however, authentication of a copy will provide the necessary evidence to authenticate the original writing at the same time. For example: If a copy of a recorded deed is offered in evidence, Section 1401 requires that the copy be authenticated—proved to be a copy of the official record. It also requires that the official record be authenticatedCproved to be the official record—because the official record is a writing of which secondary evidence of its content is being offered. Finally, Section 1401 requires the original deed itself to be authenticated—proved to have been executed by its purported maker—for it, too, is a writing of which secondary evidence of its content is being offered. The copy offered in evidence may be authenticated by the attestation or certification of the official custodian of the record as provided by Section 1530. Under Section 1530, the authenticated copy is prima facie evidence of the existence and content of the official record itself. Thus, the authenticated copy supplies the necessary authenticating evidence for the official record. Under Section 1600, the official record is prima facie evidence of the existence and content of the original deed and of its execution by its purported maker; hence, the official record is the requisite authenticating evidence for the original deed. Thus, the duly attested or certified copy of the record meets the requirement of authentication for the copy itself, for the official record, and for the original deed.

§ 1402. Authentication of altered writing. The party producing a writing as genuine which has been altered, or appears to have been altered, after its execution, in a part material to the question in dispute, must account for the alteration or appearance thereof. He may show that the alteration was made by another, without his concurrence, or was made with the consent of the parties affected by it, or otherwise properly or innocently made, or that the alteration did not change the meaning or language of the instrument. If he does that, he may give the writing in evidence, but not otherwise.

Article 2. Means of Authenticating and Proving Writings

§ 1410. Article not exclusive. Nothing in this article [§§ 1410-1421] shall be construed to limit the means by which a writing may be authenticated or proved.

Law Revision Commission Comment

This article (Sections 1410-1421) lists many of the evidentiary means for authenticating writings and supersedes the existing statutory expressions of such means.

Section 1410 is included in this article in recognition of the fact that it would be impossible to specify all of the varieties of circumstantial evidence that may be sufficient in particular cases to sustain a finding of the authenticity of a writing. Hence, Section 1410 ensures that the means of authentication listed in this article or stated elsewhere in the codes will not be considered the exclusive means of authenticating writings. Although Section 1410 has no counterpart in previous legislation, the California courts have never considered the listing of certain means of authentication in the various California statutes as precluding reliance upon other means of authentication. See, e.g., People v. Ramsey, 83 Cal.App.2d 707, 189 P.2d 802 (1948) (authentication by evidence of possession); Geary St. etc. R.R. v. Campbell, 39 Cal.App. 496, 179 Pac. 453 (1919) (corporate stock record book authenticated by age, appropriate custody, and unsuspicious appearance). See also the Comments to Sections 1420 and 1421.

§ 1410.5. Graffiti constitutes a writing; admissibility. (a) For purposes of this chapter [§§ 1400-1454], a writing shall include any graffiti consisting of written words, insignia, symbols, or any other markings which convey a particular meaning.

(b) Any writing described in subdivision (a), or any photograph thereof, may be admitted into evidence in an action for vandalism, for the purpose of proving that the writing was made by the defendant.

(c) The admissibility of any fact offered to prove that the writing was made by the defendant shall, upon motion of the defendant, be ruled upon outside the presence of the jury, and is subject to the requirements of Sections 1416, 1417, and 1418. [*Added 1989.*]

§ 1411. Subscribing witness' testimony unnecessary. Except as provided by statute, the testimony of a subscribing witness is not required to authenticate a writing.

Law Revision Commission Comment

When Section 1940 of the Code of Civil Procedure was enacted in 1872, it stated the common law rule that a subscribing witness to a witnessed writing must be produced to authenticate the writing or his absence must be satisfactorily accounted for. See Stevens v. Irwin, 12 Cal. 306 (1859). Section 1940 was amended by the Code Amendments of 1873-74 to remove the requirement that the subscribing witness be produced. Cal.Stats.1873-74, Ch. 383, § 231 (Code Amdts., p. 386). Instead, three alternative methods of authenticating a writing were listed.

Section 1411 states directly what the 1873-74 amendment to Code of Civil Procedure Section 1940 stated indirectlyCthat the common law rule requiring the production of a subscribing witness to a witnessed writing is not the law in California unless a statute specifically so requires.

§ 1412. Use of other evidence when subscribing witness' testimony required. If the testimony of a subscribing witness is required by statute to authenticate a writing and the subscribing witness denies or does not recollect the execution of the writing, the writing may be authenticated by other evidence.

Law Revision Commission Comment

When enacted in 1872, Code of Civil Procedure Section 1941 stated a limitation on the common law rule requiring proof of witnessed writings by a subscribing witness. Section 1941 provided, in effect, that this rule did not prohibit the authentication of a witnessed writing by other evidence if the subscribing witness denied or did not remember the execution of the writing. Evidence Code Section 1412, which supersedes Code of Civil Procedure Section 1941, retains this limitation on the subscribing witness rule in those few cases, such as those involving wills, where a statute requires the testimony of a subscribing witness to authenticate a writing.

§ 1413. Witness to the execution of a writing. A writing may be authenticated by anyone who saw the writing made or executed, including a subscribing witness.

§ 1414. Authentication by admission. A writing may be authenticated by evidence that:

(a) The party against whom it is offered has at any time admitted its authenticity; or

(b) The writing has been acted upon as authentic by the party against whom it is offered.

§ 1415. Authentication by handwriting evidence. A writing may be authenticated by evidence of the genuineness of the handwriting of the maker.

§ 1416. Proof of handwriting by person familiar therewith. A witness who is not otherwise qualified to testify as an expert may state his opinion whether a writing is in the handwriting of a supposed writer if the court finds that he has personal knowledge of the handwriting of the supposed writer. Such personal knowledge may be acquired from:

(a) Having seen the supposed writer write;

(b) Having seen a writing purporting to be in the handwriting of the supposed writer and upon which the supposed writer has acted or been charged;

(c) Having received letters in the due course of mail purporting to be from the supposed writer in response to letters duly addressed and mailed by him to the supposed writer; or

(d) Any other means of obtaining personal knowledge of the handwriting of the supposed writer.

§ 1417. Comparison of handwriting by trier of fact. The genuineness of handwriting, or the lack thereof, may be proved by a comparison made by the trier of fact with handwriting (a) which the court finds was admitted or treated as genuine by the party against whom the evidence is offered or (b) otherwise proved to be genuine to the satisfaction of the court.

§ 1418. Comparison of writing by expert witness. The genuineness of writing, or the lack thereof, may be proved by a comparison made by an expert witness with writing (a) which the court finds was admitted or treated as genuine by the party against whom the evidence is offered or (b) otherwise proved to be genuine to the satisfaction of the court.

Law Revision Commission Comment

Section 1418 is based on that portion of Code of Civil Procedure Section 1944 that permits a witness to compare questioned handwriting with handwriting the court has found to be genuine. However, Section 1418 applies to any form of writing, not just handwriting. This is in recognition of the fact that experts can now compare typewriting specimens and other forms of writing as accurately as they could compare handwriting specimens in 1872.

Although Code of Civil Procedure Section 1944 does not expressly require that the witness making the comparison be an expert witness (as Evidence Code Section 1418 does), the cases have nonetheless imposed this requirement. E.g., Spottiswood v. Weir, 80 Cal. 448, 22 Pac. 289 (1889). The witness' expertise may, of course, be derived from practical experience instead of from technical training. In re Newell's Estate, 75 Cal.App. 554, 243 Pac. 33 (1926) (experienced banker).

§ 1419. Exemplars when writing is 30 years old. Where a writing whose genuineness is sought to be proved is more than 30 years old, the comparison under Section 1417 or 1418 may be made with writing purporting to be genuine, and generally respected and acted upon as such, by persons having an interest in knowing whether it is genuine.

Law Revision Commission Comment

Section 1419 restates and supersedes the provisions of Code of Civil Procedure Section 1945. The apparent purpose of Section 1945, continued without substantive change in Evidence Code Section 1419, is to permit the judge to be satisfied with a lesser degree of proof of the authenticity of an exemplar when the writing offered in evidence is more than 30 years old.

§ 1420. Authentication by evidence of reply. A writing may be authenticated by evidence that the writing was received in response to a communication sent to the person who is claimed by the proponent of the evidence to be the author of the writing.

§ 1421. Authentication by content. A writing may be authenticated by evidence that the writing refers to or states matters that are unlikely to be known to anyone other than the person who is claimed by the proponent of the evidence to be the author of the writing.

Article 3. Presumptions Affecting Acknowledged Writings and Official Writings

§ 1450. Classification of presumptions in article. The presumptions established by this article [§§ 1450-1454] are presumptions affecting the burden of producing evidence.

Statutory Note

See Commercial Code § 1202 (presumption of authenticity of third-party documents authorized by contract in action arising out of the contract).

Law Revision Commission Comment

This article (Sections 1450-1454) lists several presumptions that may be used to authenticate particular kinds of writings. Section 1450 prescribes the effect of these presumptions. They require a finding of authenticity unless the adverse party produces evidence sufficient to sustain a finding that the writing in question is not authentic. See Evidence Code § 604 and the Comment thereto.

§ 1451. Acknowledged writings. A certificate of the acknowledgment of a writing other than a will, or a certificate of the proof of such a writing, is prima facie evidence of the facts recited in the certificate and the genuineness of the signature of each person by whom the writing purports to have been signed if the certificate meets the requirements of Article 3 (commencing with Section 1180) of Chapter 4, Title 4, Part 4, Division 2 of the Civil Code.

§ 1452. Official seals. A seal is presumed to be genuine and its use authorized if it purports to be the seal of:

(a) The United States or a department, agency, or public employee of the United States.

(b) A public entity in the United States or a department, agency, or public employee of such public entity.

(c) A nation recognized by the executive power of the United States or a department, agency, or officer of such nation.

(d) A public entity in a nation recognized by the executive power of the United States or a department, agency, or officer of such public entity.

(e) A court of admiralty or maritime jurisdiction.

(f) A notary public within any state of the United States.

Law Revision Commission Comment

Sections 1452 and 1453 eliminate the need for formal proof of the genuineness of certain official seals and signatures when such proof would otherwise be required by the general requirement of authentication.

Under existing law, formal proof of many of the signatures and seals mentioned in Sections 1452 and 1453 is not required because such signatures and seals are the subject of judicial notice. Code Civ.Proc. § 1875 (5), (6), (7), (8). (Section 1875 is superseded by Division 4 (Sections 450-460) of the Evidence Code.) The parties may not dispute a matter that has been judicially noticed. Code Civ.Proc. § 2102 (superseded by Evidence Code § 457). Hence, judicial notice of facts should be confined to matters concerning which there can be no reasonable dispute. The authenticity of writings purporting to be official writings should not be determined conclusively by the judge when there is serious dispute as to such authenticity. Therefore, Sections 1452 and 1453 provide that the official seals and signatures mentioned shall be presumed genuine and authorized until evidence is introduced sufficient to sustain a finding that they are not genuine or authorized. When there is such evidence disputing the authenticity of an official seal or signature, the trier of fact is required to determine the question of authenticity without regard to any presumption created by this section. See Evidence Code § 604 and the Comment thereto.

This procedure will dispense with the necessity for proof of authenticity when there is no real dispute as to such authenticity, but it will assure the parties the right to contest the authenticity of official writings when there is a real dispute as to such authenticity.

§ 1453. Domestic official signatures. A signature is presumed to be genuine and authorized if it purports to be the signature, affixed in his official capacity, of:

(a) A public employee of the United States.

(b) A public employee of any public entity in the United States.

(c) A notary public within any state of the United States.

§ 1454. Foreign official signatures. A signature is presumed to be genuine and authorized if it purports to be the signature, affixed in his official capacity, of an officer, or deputy of an officer, of a nation or public entity in a nation recognized by the executive power of the United States and the writing to which the signature is affixed is accompanied by a final statement certifying the genuineness of the signature and the official position of (a) the person who executed the writing or (b) any foreign official who has certified either the genuineness of the signature and official position of the person executing the writing or the genuineness of the signature and official position of another foreign official who has executed a similar certificate in a chain of such certificates beginning with a certificate of the genuineness of the signature and official position of the person executing the writing. The final statement may be made only by a secretary of an embassy or legation, consul general, consul, vice consul, consular agent, or other officer in the foreign service of the United States stationed in the nation, authenticated by the seal of his office.

Law Revision Commission Comment

Section 1454 supersedes the somewhat complex procedure for authenticating foreign official writings that is contained in subdivision 8 of Code of Civil Procedure Section 1918. Section 1454 is based on a proposed amendment to Rule 44 of the Federal Rules of Civil Procedure that has been prepared by the Advisory Committee on Civil Rules, the Commission and Advisory Committee on International Rules of Judicial Procedure, and the Columbia Law School Project on International Procedure. Proposed Amendments to Rules of Civil Procedure for the United States District Courts with Advisory Committee's Notes (mimeo., Feb. 25, 1964). Rule 44 and the proposed amendment, however, deal only with the question of authenticating copies of foreign official writings. Section 1454 relates to the authentication of any foreign official writing, whether it be an original or a copy.

The procedure set forth in Section 1454 is necessary for the reason that a United States foreign service officer may not be able to certify to the official position and signature of a particular foreign official. Accordingly, this section permits the original signature to be certified by a higher foreign official, whose signature can in turn be certified by a still higher official, and such certifications can be continued in a chain until a foreign official is reached as to whom the United States foreign service officer has adequate information upon which to base his final certification. See, e.g., New York Life Ins. Co. v. Aronson, 38 F.Supp. 687 (W.D.Pa.1941).

See also the Comment to Section 1452.

Chapter 2. Secondary Evidence of Writings

[Former Article 1. Best Evidence Rule. *Repealed 1998.*]

Article 1. Proof of the Content of a Writing

§ 1520. Content of writing; proof. The content of a writing may be proved by an otherwise admissible original. [*Added 1998.*]

Statutory Note

Stats. 1998, c. 100 (S.B. 177), which added §§ 1520-1523, also repealed former §§ 1500-1511 (the Best Evidence Rule).

Law Revision Commission Comments - 1998 Addition

Section 1520 continues former Section 1500 insofar as it permitted proof of the content of a writing by an original of the writing. See also Sections 1521 (Secondary Evidence Rule), 1522 (exclusion of secondary evidence in criminal action), 1523 (oral testimony of content of writing). [26 Cal.L.Rev.Comm. Reports 369 (1996).]

§ 1521. Secondary evidence rule. (a) The content of a writing may be proved by otherwise admissible secondary evidence. The court shall exclude secondary evidence of the content of writing if the court determines either of the following:

(1) A genuine dispute exists concerning material terms of the writing and justice requires the exclusion.

(2) Admission of the secondary evidence would be unfair.

(b) Nothing in this section makes admissible oral testimony to prove the content of a writing if the testimony is inadmissible under Section 1523 (oral testimony of the content of a writing).

(c) Nothing in this section excuses compliance with Section 1401 (authentication).

(d) This section shall be known as the "Secondary Evidence Rule." [*Added 1998.*]

Note on Proposed Amendment

The Law Revision Commission tentatively decided in September 2004 to recommend that § 1521(c) be amended to make clear that a dispute concerning authentication of a writing must be determined pursuant to § 1401, not § 1521.

Law Revision Commission Comments - 1998 Addition

Sections 1520 (proof of content of writing by original), 1521 (Secondary Evidence Rule), 1522 (exclusion of secondary evidence in criminal action), and 1523 (oral testimony of content of writing) replace the Best Evidence Rule and its exceptions. For background, see Best Evidence Rule, 26 Cal. L. Revision Comm'n Reports 369 (1996). Because of the breadth of the exceptions to the Best Evidence Rule, this reform is not a major departure from former law, but primarily a matter of clarification and simplification. Discovery principles remain unchanged.

Subdivision (a) makes secondary evidence generally admissible to prove the content of a writing. The nature of the evidence offered affects its weight, not its admissibility. The normal motivation of parties to support their cases with convincing evidence is a deterrent to introduction of unreliable secondary evidence. See also Section 412 (if party offers weaker and less satisfactory evidence despite ability to produce stronger and more satisfactory evidence, the evidence offered should be viewed with distrust).

The mandatory exceptions set forth in subdivisions (a)(1) and (a)(2) provide further protection against unreliable secondary evidence. Those exceptions are modeled on the exceptions to former Section 1511 and to Rule 1003 of the Federal Rules of Evidence. Cases interpreting those statutes provide guidance in applying subdivisions (a)(1) and (a)(2). See, e.g., United States v. Sinclair, 74 F.3d 753, 760-61 (7th Cir. 1996) (admitting copies of expense account reports was not unfair); Ruberto v. Commissioner of Internal Revenue, 774 F.2d 61, 64 (2d Cir. 1985) (tax court did not err in excluding photocopies of canceled checks, "since problems in matching the copies of the backs of the checks with copies of the fronts made them somewhat suspect"); Amoco Production Co. v. United States, 619 F.2d 1383, 1391 (10th Cir. 1980) (upholding trial court's determination that "admission of the file copy would be unfair because the most critical part of the original conformed copy is not completely reproduced in the 'duplicate'"); People v. Garcia, 201 Cal. App. 3d 324, 330, 247 Cal. Rptr. 94 (1988) (claim of unfairness "must be based on substance, not mere speculation that the original might contain some relevant difference"). Courts may consider a broad range of factors, for example: (1) whether the proponent attempts to use the writing in a manner that could not reasonably have been anticipated, (2) whether the original was suppressed in discovery, (3) whether discovery conducted in a reasonably diligent (as opposed to exhaustive) manner failed to result in production of the original, (4) whether there are dramatic differences between the original and the secondary evidence (e.g., the original but not the secondary evidence is in color and the colors provide significant clues to interpretation), (5) whether the original is unavailable and, if so, why, and (6) whether the writing is central to the case or collateral. A classic circumstance for exclusion pursuant to subdivision (a)(2) is if the proponent destroyed the original with fraudulent intent or the doctrine of spoliation of evidence otherwise applies.

Subdivision (b) explicitly establishes that Section 1523 (oral testimony of the content of writing), not Section 1521, governs the admissibility of oral testimony to prove the content of a writing.

Subdivision (c) makes clear that like other evidence, secondary evidence is admissible only if it is properly authenticated. Under Section 1401, the proponent must not only authenticate the original writing, but must also establish that the proffered evidence is secondary evidence of the original. See B. Jefferson, Jefferson's Synopsis of California Evidence Law, 30.1, at 470-71 (1985). [26 Cal.L.Rev.Comm. Reports 369 (1996).]

§ 1522. Additional grounds for exclusion of secondary evidence. (a) In addition to the grounds for exclusion authorized by Section 1521, in a criminal action the court shall exclude secondary evidence of the content of a writing if the court determines that the original is in the proponent's possession, custody, or control, and the proponent has not made the original reasonably available for inspection at or before trial. This section does not apply to any of the following:

(1) A duplicate as defined in Section 260.

(2) A writing that is not closely related to the controlling issues in the action.

(3) A copy of a writing in the custody of a public entity.

(4) A copy of a writing that is recorded in the public records, if the record or a certified copy of it is made evidence of the writing by statute.

(b) In a criminal action, a request to exclude secondary evidence of the content of a writing, under this section or any other law, shall not be made in the presence of the jury. [*Added 1998.*]

Law Revision Commission Comments - 1998 Addition

Subdivision (a) of Section 1522 sets forth a mandatory exception applicable only in criminal cases, which are governed by narrower discovery rules than civil cases. See Section 130 ("criminal action" includes criminal proceedings). See also Penal Code 1054-1054.7 (discovery in criminal cases). Section 1522 does not expand discovery obligations, it simply conditions use of secondary evidence on making the original reasonably available for inspection if the proponent has it. In determining whether the proponent of secondary evidence has made the original "reasonably available," the court should examine specific circumstances, such as the time, place, and manner of allowing inspection. The concept is fluid, not rigid. For example, making the original available moments before using secondary evidence may in general suffice if a defendant is rebutting a surprise contention, but not if the prosecution is presenting its case in chief. Similarly, what constitutes reasonable access to computer evidence may vary from system to system.

The exceptions in subdivisions (a)(1)-(a)(4) are drawn from exceptions to the former Best Evidence Rule (former Section 1500). Subdivision (a)(1) is drawn from former Section 1511. Subdivision (a)(2) is drawn from former Section 1504. Subdivision (a)(3) is drawn from former Section 1506. Subdivision (a)(4) is drawn from former Section 1507.

Subdivision (b) continues the requirement of the second sentence of former Section 1503(a), but applies it to all requests for exclusion of secondary evidence in a criminal trial.

See also Sections 1520 (proof of content of writing by original), 1521 (Secondary Evidence Rule), and 1523 (oral testimony of content of writing). [26 Cal.L.Rev.Comm. Reports 369 (1996).]

§ 1523. Oral testimony of the content of a writing; admissibility. (a) Except as otherwise provided by statute, oral testimony is not admissible to prove the content of a writing.

(b) Oral testimony of the content of a writing is not made inadmissible by subdivision (a) if the proponent does not have possession or control of a copy of the writing and the original is lost or has been destroyed without fraudulent intent on the part of the proponent of the evidence.

(c) Oral testimony of the content of a writing is not made inadmissible by subdivision (a) if the proponent does not have possession or control of the original or a copy of the writing and either of the following conditions is satisfied:

(1) Neither the writing nor a copy of the writing was reasonably procurable by the proponent by use of the court's process or by other available means.

(2) The writing is not closely related to the controlling issues and it would be inexpedient to require its production.

(d) Oral testimony of the content of a writing is not made inadmissible by subdivision (a) if the writing consists of numerous accounts or other writings that cannot be examined in court without great loss of time, and the evidence sought from them is only the general result of the whole. [*Added 1998.*]

Case Note

Where oral testimony is admissible to prove the contents of a lost document, the law does not require that the contents be proved verbatim. Dart Indus., Inc. v. Commercial Union Ins. Co., 28 Cal. 4th 1059, 1068-1069, 52 P.2d 79, 85-87 124 Cal. Rptr. 2d 142, 150-151 (2002).

Law Revision Commission Comments - 1998 Addition

Section 1523 preserves former law governing the admissibility of oral testimony to prove the content of a writing. See former Sections 1500, 1501-1509.

Subdivision (a) is based on an assumption that oral testimony as to the content of a writing is typically less reliable than other proof of the content of a writing. For background, see Best Evidence Rule, 26 Cal. L. Revision Comm'n Reports 369 (1996).

Subdivision (b) continues former Sections 1501 and 1505 without substantive change as to oral testimony of the content of a writing that is lost or has been destroyed.

Subdivision (c)(1) continues former Sections 1502 and 1505 without substantive change as to oral testimony of the content of a writing that was not reasonably procurable. In effect, subdivision (c)(1) also continues former Sections 1503 and 1505 without substantive change as to oral testimony of the content of a writing that the opponent has, but failed to produce at the hearing despite being expressly or impliedly notified that it would be needed. Under such circumstances, the writing was not reasonably procurable. Finally, subdivision (c)(1) continues former Sections 1506-1508 without substantive change as to oral testimony of the content of a writing where (1) the writing is in the custody of a public entity and the proponent could not have obtained it or a copy of it in the exercise of reasonable diligence, or (2) the writing has been recorded in the public records, the record or a certified copy of the writing is made evidence of the writing by statute, and the proponent could not have obtained it or a copy of it in the exercise of reasonable diligence. Subdivision (c)(2) continues former Sections 1504 and 1505 without substantive change as to oral testimony of the content of a collateral writing.

Subdivision (d) continues former Section 1509 without substantive change as to oral testimony of a voluminous writing.

See Sections 1520 (proof of content of writing by original), 1521 (Secondary Evidence Rule), and 1522 (exclusion of secondary evidence in criminal action). [26 Cal.L.Rev.Comm. Reports 369 (1996).]

Article 2. Official Writings and Recorded Writings

§ 1530. Copy of writing in official custody. (a) A purported copy of a writing in the custody of a public entity, or of an entry in such a writing, is prima facie evidence of the existence and content of such writing or entry if:

(1) The copy purports to be published by the authority of the nation or state, or public entity therein in which the writing is kept;

(2) The office in which the writing is kept is within the United States or within the Panama Canal Zone, the Trust Territory of the Pacific Islands, or the Ryukyu Islands, and the copy is attested or certified as a correct copy of the writing or entry by a public employee, or a deputy of a public employee, having the legal custody of the writing; or

(3) The office in which the writing is kept is not within the United States or any other place described in paragraph (2) and the copy is attested as a correct copy of the writing or entry by a person having authority to make attestation. The attestation must be accompanied by a final statement certifying the genuineness of the signature and the official position of (i) the person who attested the copy as a correct copy or (ii) any foreign official who has certified either the genuineness of the signature and official position of the person attesting the copy or the genuineness of the signature and official position of another foreign official who has executed a similar certificate in a chain of such certificates beginning with a certificate of the genuineness of the signature and official position of the person attesting the copy. Except as provided in the next sentence, the final statement may be made only by a secretary of an embassy or legation, consul general, consul, vice consul, or consular agent of the United States, or a diplomatic or consular official of the foreign country assigned or accredited to the United States. Prior to January 1, 1971, the final statement may also be made by a secretary of an embassy or legation, consul general, consul, vice consul, consular agent, or other officer in the foreign service of the United States stationed in the nation in which the writing is kept, authenticated by the seal of his office. If reasonable opportunity has been given to all parties to investigate the authenticity and accuracy of the documents, the court may, for good cause shown, (i) admit an attested copy without the final statement or (ii) permit the writing or entry in foreign custody to be evidenced by an attested summary with or without a final statement.

(b) The presumptions established by this section are presumptions affecting the burden of producing evidence. [*Amended 1970.*]

Law Revision Commission Comment

Section 1530 deals with three evidentiary problems. First, it is concerned with the problem of proving the content of an original writing by means of a copy, i.e., the best evidence rule. See Evidence Code § 1500. Second, it is concerned with authentication, for the copy must be authenticated as a copy of the original writing. Evidence Code § 1401. Finally, it is concerned with the hearsay rule, for a certification or attestation of authenticity is "a statement that was made other than by a witness while testifying at the hearing and that is offered to prove the truth of the matter stated." Evidence Code § 1200. Because this section is principally concerned with the use of a copy of a writing to prove the content of the original, it is located in the division relating to secondary evidence of writings.

Under existing California law, certain official records may be proved by copies purporting to have been published by official authority or by copies with attached certificates containing certain requisite seals and signatures. The rules are complex and detailed and appear for the most part in Article 2 (beginning with Section 1892) of Chapter 3, Title 2, Part IV of the Code of Civil Procedure.

Section 1530 substitutes for these rules a uniform rule that can be applied to all writings in official custody found within the United States and another rule applicable to all writings in official custody found outside the United States.

Subdivision (a)(1). Subdivision (a)(1) of Section 1530 provides that an official writing may be proved by a copy purporting to be published by official authority. Under Section 1918 of the Code of Civil Procedure, the acts and proceedings of the executive and legislature of any state, the United States, or a foreign government may be proved by documents and journals published by official authority. Subdivision (a)(1) in effect makes these provisions of Section 1918 applicable to all classes of official documents. This extension of the means of proving official documents will facilitate the proof of many official documents the authenticity of which is presumed (Evidence Code § 644) and is seldom subject to question.

Subdivision (a)(2) and (a)(3) generally. Paragraphs (2) and (3) of subdivision (a) of Section 1530 set forth the rules for proving the content of writings in official custody by attested or certified copies. A person who "attests" a writing merely affirms it to be true or genuine by his signature. Black, Law Dictionary (4th ed. 1951). Existing California statutes require certain writings to be "certified." Section 1923 of the Code of Civil Procedure (superseded by Evidence Code Section 1531) provides that the certificate affixed to a certified copy must state that the copy is a correct copy of the original, must be signed by the certifying officer, and must be under his seal of office, if he has one. Thus, the only difference between the words "attested" and "certified" is that the existing statutory definition of "certified" requires the use of a seal, if the authenticating officer has one, whereas the definition of "attested" does not. Section 1530 eliminates the requirement of the seal by the use of the word "attested." However, Section 1530 retains, in addition, the word "certified" because it is the more familiar term in California practice.

Subdivision (a)(2). Under existing law, copies of many records of the United States government and of the governments of sister states may be proved by a copy certified or attested by the custodian alone. See, e.g., Code Civ.Proc. §§ 1901 and 1918(1), (2), (3), (9); Corp.Code § 6600. Yet, other official writings must be certified or attested not only by the custodian but also by a higher official certifying the authority and signature of the custodian. In order to provide a uniform rule for the proof of all domestic official writings, subdivision (a)(2) extends the simpler and more expeditious procedure to all official writings within the United States.

Subdivision (a)(3). Under existing law, some foreign official records may be proved by a copy certified or attested by the custodian alone. See Code Civ.Proc. §§ 1901 and 1918(4). Yet, other copies of foreign official writings must be accompanied by three certificates: one executed by the custodian, another by a higher official certifying the authority and signature of the custodian, and a third by still another official certifying the signature and official position of the second official. See Code Civ.Proc. §§ 1906 and 1918(8).

For these complex rules, subdivision (a)(3) of Section 1530 substitutes a relatively simple and uniform procedure that is applicable to all classes of foreign official writings. Subdivision (a)(3) is based on a proposed amendment to Rule 44 of the Federal Rules of Civil Procedure that has been prepared by the Advisory Committee on Civil Rules, the Commission and Advisory Committee on International Rules of Judicial Procedure, and the Columbia Law School Project on International Procedure, Proposed Amendments to Rules of Civil Procedure for the United States District Courts with Advisory Committee's Notes (mimeo., Feb. 25, 1964).

Subdivision (a)(3) requires that the copy be attested as a correct copy by "a person having authority to make the attestation." In some foreign countries, the person with authority to attest a copy of an official writing is not necessarily the person with legal custody of the writing. See 2B Barron & Holtzoff, Federal Practice Procedure § 992 (Wright ed. 1961). In such a case, subdivision (a)(3) requires that the attester's signature and official position be certified by another official. If this is a United States foreign service officer stationed in the country, no further certificates are required. If a United States foreign service officer is not able to certify to the signature and official position of the attester, subdivision (a)(3) permits the attester's signature and official position to be certified by a higher foreign official, whose signature can in turn be certified by a still higher official. Such certifications can be continued in a chain until a foreign official is reached as to whom the United States foreign service officer has adequate information upon which to base his final certification. See, e.g., New York Life Ins. Co. v. Aronson, 38 F.Supp. 687 (W.D.Pa. 1941).

Subdivision (b). Where evidence is introduced that is sufficient to sustain a finding that the copy is not a correct copy, the trier of fact is required to determine whether the copy is a correct copy without regard to the presumptions created by this section. See Evidence Code § 604 and the Comment thereto.

Law Revision Commission Comment - 1970 Amendment

Section 1530 of the Evidence Code is concerned with the use of a copy of a writing in official custody to prove the content of the original. Section 1530 was deficient insofar as it prescribed, in subdivision (a) (3), the procedure for proof of foreign official writings. Subdivision (a) (3) requires that the copy of the foreign official record be attested as a correct copy by "a person having authority to make the attestation." The subdivision further requires that the first attester's signature and his official position be certified by a higher foreign official, whose signature can in turn be certified by a still higher official. Under the section as it formerly read, such certifications could be continued in a chain until a foreign official was reached as to whom a United States foreign service officer "stationed in the nation in which the writing is kept" had adequate information upon which to base his final certification. In other words, to prove a copy of a foreign official record, it was necessary to have a certificate of a United States foreign service officer stationed in the nation in which the writing was kept.

In some situations, it was impossible to satisfy the basic requirement of subdivision (a) (3) of Section 1530 because there were no United States foreign service officials in the particular foreign country (such as East Germany) and, hence, there was no one who could make the certificate required by subdivision (a) (3). As a result, in some situations, it was extremely difficult and expensive or even impossible to establish such matters as birth, legitimacy, marriage, death, or a will.

The problem described above was particularly troublesome in the case of a foreign will because Probate Code Section 361 was amended at the 1969 session to provide that a copy of a foreign will (and the related documents concerning the establishment of proof of the will in the foreign country) can be admitted in California "if such copy or other evidence satisfies the requirements of Article 2 (commencing with Section 1530) of Chapter 2 of Division 11 of the Evidence Code."

When Section 1530 of the Evidence Code was drafted in 1964, the Commission had the benefit of a proposed amendment to Rule 44 of the Federal Rules of Civil Procedure and based subdivision (a) (3) on that proposed amendment. After the Evidence Code was enacted in 1965, Rule 44 was revised (in 1966) to provide for proof of foreign official records. In the revision of Rule 44 in 1966, the defect pointed out above was discovered and provision was made in Rule 44 to cover the problem.

Rule 44 (as revised in 1966) includes the following provision to deal with the East Germany type of case:

> If reasonable opportunity has been given to all parties to investigate the authenticity and accuracy of the documents, the court may, for good cause shown, (i) admit an attested copy without final certification or (ii) permit the foreign official record to be evidenced by an attested summary with or without a final certification.

The Note of the Advisory Committee regarding revised Rule 44 states:

> Although the amended rule will generally facilitate proof of foreign official records, it is recognized that in some situations it may be difficult or even impossible to satisfy the basic requirements of the rule. There may be no United States consul in a particular foreign country; the foreign officials may not cooperate; peculiarities may exist or arise hereafter in the law or practice of a foreign country. See United States v. Grabina, 119 F.2d 863 (2d Cir.1941); and, generally, Jones, International Judicial Assistance: Procedural Chaos and a Program for Reform, 62 Yale L.J. 515, 548-49 (1953). Therefore the final sentence of subdivision (a) (2) provides the court with discretion to admit an attested copy of a record without a final certification, or an attested summary of a record with or without a final certification. See Rep. of Comm. on Comparative Civ.Proc. & Prac., Proc. A.B.A., Sec. Int'l & Comp. L. 123, 130-31 (1952); Model Code of Evidence ss 517, 519 (1942). This relaxation should be permitted only when it is shown that the party has been unable to satisfy the basic requirements of the amended rule despite his reasonable efforts. Moreover it is specially provided that the parties must be given a reasonable opportunity in these cases to examine into the authenticity and accuracy of the copy or summary.

Senate Bill No. 266 [Stats.1970, c. 41] adds the substance of the sentence of Rule 44 quoted above, making only those changes needed to conform the language of that sentence to the language used in Section 1530. The bill also adopts the language of Rule 44 which specifies the officers who can make the final certificate. The change made by adopting this language is to restrict the United States foreign service officers who can make the final certificate to certain specified responsible officers and to liberalize the provision by permitting "a diplomatic or consular official of the foreign country assigned or accredited to the United States" to make the final certificate. This latter conforming change achieves desirable conformity with Rule 44 and liberalizes the rule but at the same time assures that a responsible official will make the final certificate. [10 Cal.L.Rev.Comm. Reports 1022 (1970).]

§ 1531. Certification of copy for evidence. For the purpose of evidence, whenever a copy of a writing is attested or certified, the attestation or certificate must state in substance that the copy is a correct copy of the original, or of a specified part thereof, as the case may be.

Law Revision Commission Comment

Section 1531 is based on the provisions of Section 1923 of the Code of Civil Procedure. The language has been modified to define the process of attestation as well as the process of certification. Since Section 1530 permits a writing to be attested or certified for purposes of evidence without the attachment of an official seal, Section 1531 omits any requirement of a seal.

§ 1532. Official record of recorded writing. (a) The official record of a writing is prima facie evidence of the existence and content of the original recorded writing if:

(1) The record is in fact a record of an office of a public entity; and

(2) A statute authorized such a writing to be recorded in that office.

(b) The presumption established by this section is a presumption affecting the burden of producing evidence.

Law Revision Commission Comment

Section 1530 authorizes the use of a copy of a writing in official custody to prove the content of that writing. When a writing has been recorded, Section 1530 merely permits a certified copy of the record to be used to prove the record, not the original recorded writing. Section 1532 permits the official record to be used to prove the content of the original recorded writing. However, under the provisions of Section 1401, the original recorded writing must be authenticated before the copy can be introduced. If the writing was executed by a public official, or if a certificate of acknowledgment or proof was attached to the writing, the original writing is presumed to be authentic and no further evidence of authenticity is required. Evidence Code §§ 1450, 1451, and 1453.

Where evidence is introduced that is sufficient to sustain a finding that the original writing is not authentic, the trier of fact is required to determine the authenticity of the original writing without regard to the presumption created by this section. See Evidence Codes 604 and the Comment thereto.

Code of Civil Procedure Section 1951 (superseded by Evidence Code Section 1600) is similar to Section 1532, but the Code of Civil Procedure section relates only to writings affecting property. Section 1532 extends the principle of the Code of Civil Procedure section to all recorded writings. There is no comparable provision in existing law.

Article 3. Photographic Copies and Printed Representations of Writings

§ 1550. Types of evidence of a writing as admissible as the writing itself. (a) If made and preserved as a part of the records of a business, as defined in Section 1270, in the regular course of that business, the following types of evidence of a writing are as admissible as the writing itself:

(1) A nonerasable optical image reproduction or any other reproduction of a public record by a trusted system, as defined in Section 12168.7 of the Government Code, if additions, deletions, or changes to the original document are not permitted by the technology.

(2) A photostatic copy or reproduction.

(3) A microfilm, microcard, or miniature photographic copy, reprint, or enlargement.

(4) Any other photographic copy or reproduction, or an enlargement thereof.

(b) The introduction of evidence of a writing pursuant to subdivision (a) does not preclude admission of the original writing if it is still in existence. A court may require the introduction of a hard copy printout of the document. [*Amended 1992, 2002.*]

Statutory Note

The 2002 amendment completely rewrote this section. The enacting statute, § 2 of Stats. 2002, c. 124 (A.B. 2033), provides that the amendment "shall become operative on the date the Secretary of State adopts uniform standards for storing and recording permanent and nonpermanent documents in electronic media, as required by Section 12168.7 of the Government Code."

Law Revision Commission Comment

Section 1550 continues in effect those provisions of the Uniform Photographic Copies of Business and Public Records as Evidence Act that are now found in Code of Civil Procedure Section 1953i.

Section 1550 omits the requirement, contained in Section 1953i of the Code of Civil Procedure, that the original writing be a business record. As long as the original writing is admissible under any exception to the hearsay rule, its trustworthiness is sufficiently assured; and the requirement that the photographic copy be made in the regular course of business sufficiently assures the trustworthiness of the copy. If the original is admissible not as an exception to the hearsay rule but as evidence of an ultimate fact in the case (e.g., a will or a contract), a photographic copy, the trustworthiness of which is sufficiently assured by the fact that it was made in the regular course of business, should be as admissible as the original.

§ 1550.1. Admissibility of reproductions of files, records, writings, photographs, and fingerprints. Reproductions of files, records, writings, photographs, fingerprints or other instruments in the official custody of a criminal justice agency that were microphotographed or otherwise reproduced in a manner that conforms with the provisions of Section 11106.1, 11106.2, or 11106.3 of the Penal Code shall be admissible to the same extent and under the same circumstances as the original file, record, writing or other instrument would be admissible. [*Added 2004.*]

§ 1551. Photographic copies where original destroyed or lost. A print, whether enlarged or not, from a photographic film (including a photographic plate, microphotographic film, photostatic negative, or similar reproduction) of an original writing destroyed or lost after such film was taken or a reproduction from an electronic recording of video images on magnetic surfaces is admissible as the original writing itself if, at the time of the taking of such film or electronic recording, the person under whose direction and control it was taken attached thereto, or to the sealed container in which it was placed and has been kept, or incorporated in the film or electronic recording, a certification complying with the provisions of Section 1531 and stating the date on which, and the fact that, it was so taken under his direction and control. [*Amended 1969.*]

§ 1552. Printed representation of computer-generated information. (a) A printed representation of computer information or a computer program is presumed to be an accurate representation of the computer information or computer program that it purports to represent. This presumption is a presumption affecting the burden of producing evidence. If a party to an action introduces evidence that a printed representation of computer information or computer program is inaccurate or unreliable, the party introducing the printed representation into evidence has the burden of proving, by a preponderance of evidence, that the printed representation is an accurate representation of the existence and content of the computer information or computer program that it purports to represent.

(b) Subdivision (a) applies to the printed representation of computer-generated information stored by an automated traffic enforcement system. [*Added 1998, Amended 2012.*]

(c) Subdivision (a) shall not apply to computer-generated official records certified in accordance with Section 452.5 or 1530. [*Added 2012.*]

Law Revision Commission Comments - 1998 Addition

Subdivision (a) of Section 1552 continues former Section 1500.5(c) without substantive change, except that the reference to "best available evidence" is changed to "an accurate representation," due to the replacement of the Best Evidence Rule with the Secondary Evidence Rule. See Section 1521 Comment. See also Section 255 (accurate printout of computer data is an "original").

Subdivision (b) continues former Section 1500.5(d) without substantive change. [26 Cal.L.Rev.Comm. Reports 369 (1996).]

§ 1553. Printed representation of video or digital images.

(a) A printed representation of images stored on a video or digital medium is presumed to be an accurate representation of the images it purports to represent. This presumption is a presumption affecting the burden of producing evidence. If a party to an action introduces evidence that a printed representation of images stored on a video or digital medium is inaccurate or unreliable, the party introducing the printed representation into evidence has the burden of proving, by a preponderance of evidence, that the printed representation is an accurate representation of the existence and content of the images that it purports to represent. [*Added 1998, Amended 2012.*]

(b) Subdivision (a) applies to the printed representation of video or photographic images stored by an automated traffic enforcement system. [*Added 2012.*]

Law Revision Commission Comments - 1998 Addition

Section 1553 continues the last three sentences of the second paragraph of former Section 1500.6 without substantive change, except that the reference to "best available evidence" is changed to "an accurate representation," due to the replacement of the Best Evidence Rule with the Secondary Evidence Rule. See Section 1521 Comment. [26 Cal.L.Rev.Comm. Reports 369 (1996).]

Article 4. Production of Business Records

§ 1560. Compliance with subpoena duces tecum for business records. (a) As used in this article:

(1) "Business" includes every kind of business described in Section 1270.

(2) "Record" includes every kind of record maintained by a business.

(b) Except as provided in Section 1564, when a subpoena duces tecum is served upon the custodian of records or other qualified witness of a business in an action in which the business is neither a party nor the place where any cause of action is alleged to have arisen, and the subpoena requires the production of all or any part of the records of the business, it is sufficient compliance therewith if the custodian or other qualified witness delivers by mail or otherwise a true, legible, and durable copy of all of the records described in the subpoena to the clerk of the court or to another person described in subdivision (d) of Section 2026.010 of the Code of Civil Procedure, together with the affidavit described in Section 1561, within one of the following time periods:

(1) In any criminal action, five days after the receipt of the subpoena.

(2) In any civil action, within 15 days after the receipt of the subpoena.

(3) Within the time agreed upon by the party who served the subpoena and the custodian or other qualified witness.

(c) The copy of the records shall be separately enclosed in an inner envelope or wrapper, sealed, with the title and number of the action, name of witness, and date of subpoena clearly inscribed thereon; the sealed envelope or wrapper shall then be enclosed in an outer envelope or wrapper, sealed, and directed as follows:

(1) If the subpoena directs attendance in court, to the clerk of the court.

(2) If the subpoena directs attendance at a deposition, to the officer before whom the deposition is to be taken, at the place designated in the subpoena for the taking of the deposition or at the officer's place of business.

(3) In other cases, to the officer, body, or tribunal conducting the hearing, at a like address.

(d) Unless the parties to the proceeding otherwise agree, or unless the sealed envelope or wrapper is returned to a witness who is to appear personally, the copy of the records shall remain sealed and shall be opened only at the time of trial, deposition, or other hearing, upon the direction of the judge, officer, body, or tribunal conducting the proceeding, in the presence of all parties who have appeared in person or by counsel at the trial, deposition, or hearing. Records that are original documents and that are not introduced in evidence or required as part of the record shall be returned to the person or entity from whom received. Records that are copies may be destroyed.

(e) As an alternative to the procedures described in subdivisions (b), (c), and (d), the subpoenaing party in a civil action may direct the witness to make the records available for inspection or copying by the party's attorney, the attorney's representative, or deposition officer as described in Section 2020.420 of the Code of Civil Procedure, at the witness' business address under reasonable conditions during normal business hours. Normal business hours, as used in this subdivision, means those hours that the business of the witness is normally open for business to the public. When provided with at least five business days' advance notice by the party's attorney, attorney's representative, or deposition officer, the witness shall designate a time period of not less than six continuous hours on a date certain for copying of records subject to the subpoena by the party's attorney, attorney's representative, or deposition officer. It shall be the responsibility of the attorney's representative to deliver any copy of the records as directed in the subpoena. Disobedience to the deposition subpoena issued pursuant to this subdivision is punishable as provided in Section 2020.240 of the Code of Civil Procedure.

(f) If a search warrant for business records is served upon the custodian of records or other qualified witness of a business in compliance with Section 1524 of the Penal Code regarding a criminal investigation in which the business is neither a party nor the place where any crime is alleged to have occurred, and the search warrant provides that the warrant will be deemed executed if the business causes the delivery of records described in the warrant to the law enforcement agency ordered to execute the warrant, it is sufficient compliance therewith if the custodian or other qualified witness delivers by mail or otherwise a true, legible, and durable copy of all of the records described in the search warrant to the law enforcement agency ordered to execute the search warrant, together with the affidavit described in Section 1561, within five days after the receipt of the search warrant or within such other time as is set forth in the warrant. This subdivision does not abridge or limit the scope of search warrant procedures set forth in Chapter 3 (commencing with Section 1523) of Title 12 of Part 2 of the Penal Code or invalidate otherwise duly executed search warrants. [*Amended 1969, 1982, 1984, 1986, 1991, 1997, 1999. 2000, 2004, 2005, 2006, 2016.*]

Statutory Note

The 1986 amendment added the alternative procedures in subdivision (e).

Note on Proposed Amendment

The Law Revision Commission tentatively decided in November 2003 to recommend that the affidavit of the custodian or other qualified witness under § 1562 may be used to prove the absence of a record.

§ 1561. Affidavit accompanying records. (a) The records shall be accompanied by the affidavit of the custodian or other qualified witness, stating in substance each of the following:

(1) The affiant is the duly authorized custodian of the records or other qualified witness and has authority to certify the records.

(2) The copy is a true copy of all the records described in the subpoena duces tecum or search warrant, or pursuant to subdivision (e) of Section 1560 the records were delivered to the attorney, the attorney's representative, or deposition officer for copying at the custodian's or witness' place of business, as the case may be.

(3) The records were prepared by the personnel of the business in the ordinary course of business at or near the time of the act, condition, or event.

(4) The identity of the records.

(5) A description of the mode of preparation of the records.

(b) If the business has none of the records described, or only part thereof, the custodian or other qualified witness shall so state in the affidavit, and deliver the affidavit and those records that are available in one of the manners provided in Section 1560.

(c) If the records described in the subpoena were delivered to the attorney or his or her representative or deposition officer for copying at the custodian's or witness' place of business, in addition to the affidavit required by subdivision (a), the records shall be accompanied by an affidavit by the attorney or his or her representative or deposition officer stating that the copy is a true copy of all the records delivered to the attorney or his or her representative or deposition officer for copying. [*Amended 1969, 1986, 1987, 1996, 1999, 2016.*]

§ 1562. Admissibility of affidavit and copy of records. If the original records would be admissible in evidence if the custodian or other qualified witness had been present and testified to the matters stated in the affidavit, and if the requirements of Section 1271 have been met, the copy of the records is admissible in evidence. The affidavit is admissible as evidence of the matters stated therein pursuant to Section 1561 and the matters so stated are presumed true. When more than one person has knowledge of the facts, more than one affidavit may be made. The presumption established by this section is a presumption affecting the burden of producing evidence. [*Amended 1989, 1996.*]

§ 1563. One witness and mileage fee. (a) This article does not require tender or payment of more than one witness fee and one mileage fee or other charge, to a witness or witness' business, unless there is an agreement to the contrary between the witness and the requesting party.

(b) All reasonable costs incurred in a civil proceeding by a witness who is not a party with respect to the production of all or any part of business records requested pursuant to a subpoena duces tecum shall be charged against the party serving the subpoena duces tecum.

(1) "Reasonable costs," as used in this section, includes, but is not limited to, the following specific costs: ten cents ($0.10) per page for standard reproduction of documents of a size 8 1/2 by 14 inches or less; twenty cents ($0.20) per page for copying of documents from microfilm; actual costs for the reproduction of oversize documents or the reproduction of documents requiring special processing which are made in

response to a subpoena; reasonable clerical costs incurred in locating and making the records available to be billed at the maximum rate of twenty-four dollars ($24) per hour per person, computed on the basis of six dollars ($6) per quarter hour or fraction thereof; actual postage charges; and the actual cost, if any, charged to the witness by a third person for the retrieval and return of records held offsite by that third person.

(2) The requesting party, or the requesting party's deposition officer, shall not be required to pay the reasonablecosts or any estimate thereof before the records are available for delivery pursuant to the subpoena, but the witness may demand payment of costs pursuant to this section simultaneous with actual delivery of the subpoenaed records, and until payment is made, the witness is under no obligation to deliver the records.

(3) The witness shall submit an itemized statement for the costs to the requesting party, or the requesting party's deposition officer, setting forth the reproduction and clerical costs incurred by the witness. If the costs exceed those authorized in paragraph (1), or if the witness refuses to produce an itemized statement of costs as required by paragraph (3), upon demand by the requesting party, or the requesting party's deposition officer, the witness shall furnish a statement setting forth the actions taken by the witness in justification of the costs.

(4) The requesting party may petition the court in which the action is pending to recover from the witness all or a part of the costs paid to the witness, or to reduce all or a part of the costs charged by the witness, pursuant to this subdivision, on the grounds that those costs were excessive. Upon the filing of the petition the court shall issue an order to show cause and from the time the order is served on the witness the court has jurisdiction over the witness. The court may hear testimony on the order to show cause and if it finds that the costs demanded and collected, or charged but not collected, exceed the amount authorized by this subdivision, it shall order the witness to remit to the requesting party, or reduce its charge to the requesting party by an amount equal to, the amount of the excess. If the court finds the costs were excessive and charged in bad faith by the witness, the court shall order the witness to remit the full amount of the costs demanded and collected, or excuse the requesting party from any payment of costs charged but not collected, and the court shall also order the witness to pay the requesting party the amount of the reasonable expenses incurred in obtaining the order including attorney's fees. If the court finds the costs were not excessive, the court shall order the requesting party to pay the witness the amount of the reasonable expenses incurred in defending the petition, including attorney's fees.

(5) If a subpoena is served to compel the production of business records and is subsequently withdrawn, or is quashed, modified or limited on a motion made other than by the witness, the witness shall be entitled to reimbursement pursuant to paragraph (1) for all reasonable costs incurred in compliance with the subpoena to the time that the requesting party has notified the witness that the subpoena has been withdrawn or quashed, modified or limited. If the subpoena is withdrawn or quashed, if those costs are not paid within 30 days after demand therefor, the witness may file a motion in the court in which the action is pending for an order requiring payment, and the court shall award the payment of expenses and attorney's fees in the manner set forth in paragraph (4).

(6) If records requested to a subpoena duces tecum are delivered to the attorney, the attorney's representative, or the deposition officer for inspection or photocopying at the witness' place of business, the only fee for complying with the subpoena shall not exceed fifteen dollars ($15), plus the actual cost, if any, charged to the witness by a third person for retrieval and return of records held offsite by that third person. If the records are retrieved from microfilm, the reasonable costs, as defined in paragraph (1), applies.

(c) If the personal attendance of the custodian of a record or other qualified witness is required pursuant to Section 1564, in a civil proceeding, he or she shall be entitled to the same witness fees and mileage permitted in a case where the subpoena requires the witness to attend and testify before a court in which the action or proceeding is pending and to any additional costs incurred as provided by subdivision (b). [*Amended 1972, 1981, 1982, 1986, 1987, 1997, 1999, 2016.*]

§ 1564. Personal attendance of custodian and production of original records. The personal attendance of the custodian or other qualified witness and the production of the original records is not required unless, at the discretion of the requesting party, the subpoena duces tecum contains a clause which reads:

"The personal attendance of the custodian or other qualified witness and the production of the original records are required by this subpoena. The procedure authorized pursuant to subdivision (b) of Section 1560, and Sections 1561 and 1562, of the Evidence Code will not be deemed sufficient compliance with this subpoena." [*Amended 1984, 1986, 1987.*]

§ 1565. Service of more than one subpoena duces tecum. If more than one subpoena duces tecum is served upon the custodian of records or other qualified witness and the personal attendance of the custodian or other qualified witness is required pursuant to Section 1564, the witness shall be deemed to be the witness of the party serving the first such subpoena duces tecum. [*Amended 1969.*]

§ 1566. Applicability of article. This article [§§ 1560-1567] applies in any proceeding in which testimony can be compelled.

Law Revision Commission Comment

This section has no counterpart in the portion of the Code of Civil Procedure from which this article is taken. Section 1566 is intended to preserve the original effect of Code of Civil Procedure Sections 1998-1998.5 by removing Sections 1560-1565 from the limiting provisions of Section 300.

§ 1567. Employee income and benefit information; forms completed by employer; support modification or termination proceedings. A completed form described in Section 3664 of the Family Code for income and benefit information provided by the employer may be admissible in a proceeding for modification or termination of an order for child, family, or spousal support if both of the following requirements are met:

(a) The completed form complies with Sections 1561 and 1562.

(b) A copy of the completed form and notice was served on the employee named therein pursuant to Section 3664 of the Family Code. [*Added 1995.*]

Chapter 3. Official Writings Affecting Property

§ 1600. Record of document affecting property interest. (a) The record of an instrument or other document purporting to establish or affect an interest in property is prima facie evidence of the existence and content of the original recorded document and its execution and delivery by each person by whom it purports to have been executed if:

(1) The record is in fact a record of an office of a public entity; and

(2) A statute authorized such a document to be recorded in that office.

(b) The presumption established by this section is a presumption affecting the burden of proof. [*Amended 1967.*]

Law Revision Commission Comment

The sections in this chapter all relate to official writings affecting property. The provisions of some sections provide hearsay exceptions; other sections provide exceptions to the best evidence rule; still others provide authentication procedures.

Section 1600 is based on Code of Civil Procedure Section 1951, which it supersedes. It is similar to Section 1532 of the Evidence Code, which applies to all recorded writings, but it gives an added effect to the writings covered by its provisions. Under Section 1600, as under existing law, if an instrument purporting to affect an interest in property is recorded, a presumption of execution and delivery of the instrument arises. Thomas v. Peterson, 213 Cal. 672, 3 P.2d 306 (1931).

Law Revision Comment - 1967 Amendment

One effect of making the official record "prima facie evidence" is to create a rebuttable presumption. See Evidence Code § 602 ("A statute providing that a fact or group of facts is prima facie evidence of another fact establishes a rebuttable presumption."). The classification of this presumption as one affecting the burden of proof is consistent with the prior case law. See Thomas v. Peterson, 213 Cal. 672, 3 P.2d 306 (1931); DuBois v. Larke, 175 Cal.App.2d 737, 346 P.2d 830 (1959); Osterberg v. Osterberg, 68 Cal.App.2d 254, 156 P.2d 46 (1945). Such a classification tends to support the record title to property by requiring that the record title be sustained unless the party attacking it can actually prove its invalidity. See Evidence Code § 606 and Comment thereto. * * * [8 Cal.L.Rev.Comm. Reports 1 (1965).]

§ 1601. Proof of content of lost official record affecting property. (a) Subject to subdivisions (b) and (c), when in any action it is desired to prove the contents of the official record of any writing lost or destroyed by conflagration or other public calamity, after proof of such loss or destruction, the following may, without further proof, be admitted in evidence to prove the contents of such record:

(1) Any abstract of title made and issued and certified as correct prior to such loss or destruction, and purporting to have been prepared and made in the ordinary course of business by any person engaged in the business of preparing and making abstracts of title prior to such loss or destruction; or

(2) Any abstract of title, or of any instrument affecting title, made, issued, and certified as correct by any person engaged in the business of insuring titles or issuing abstracts of title to real estate, whether the same was made, issued, or certified before or after such loss or destruction and whether the same was made from the original records or from abstract and notes, or either, taken from such records in the preparation and upkeeping of its plant in the ordinary course of its business.

(b) No proof of the loss of the original writing is required other than the fact that the original is not known to the party desiring to prove its contents to be in existence.

(c) Any party desiring to use evidence admissible under this section shall give reasonable notice in writing to all other parties to the action who have appeared therein, of his intention to use such evidence at the trial of the action, and shall give all such other parties a reasonable opportunity to inspect the evidence, and also the abstracts, memoranda, or notes from which it was compiled, and to take copies thereof.

§ 1603. Deed by officer in pursuance of court process. A deed of conveyance of real property, purporting to have been executed by a proper officer in pursuance of legal process of any of the courts of record of this state, acknowledged and recorded in the office of the recorder of the county wherein the real property therein described is situated, or the record of such deed, or a certified copy of such record, is prima facie evidence that the property or interest therein described was thereby conveyed to the grantee named in such deed. The presumption established by this section is a presumption affecting the burden of proof. [*Amended 1967.*]

Law Revision Comment - 1967 Amendment

One effect of Section 1603 is to create a rebuttable presumption. See Evidence Code § 602 ("A statute providing that a fact or group of facts is prima facie evidence of another fact establishes a rebuttable presumption.").

Prior to the enactment in 1911 of Code of Civil Procedure Section 1928 (upon which Section 1603 of the Evidence Code is based), the recitals in a sheriff's deed, made pursuant to legal process, could not be used as evidence of the judgment, the execution, and the sale upon which the deed was based. The existence of the prior proceedings were required to be proved with independent evidence. Heyman v. Babcock, 30 Cal. 367, 370 (1866); Hihn v. Peck, 30 Cal. 280, 287-288 (1966). The enactment of the predecessor of Evidence Code Section 1603 had two effects. First, it obviated the need for such independent proof. See, e.g., Oakes v. Fernandez, 108 Cal.App.2d 168, 238 P.2d 641 (1951); Wagnor v. Blume, 71 Cal.App.2d 94, 161 P.2d 1001 (1945). See also Basye, Clearing Land Titles § 41 (1953). Second, it obviated the need for proof of a chain of title prior to the execution of the need. Krug v. Warden, 57 Cal.App. 563, 207 Pac. 696 (1922).

The classification of the presumption in Section 1603 as a presumption affecting the burden of proof is consistent with the classification of the similar and overlapping presumptions contained in Evidence Code Sections 664 (official duty regularly performed) and 1600 (official record of document affecting property). Like the presumption in Section 1600, the presumption in Section 1603 serves the purpose of supporting the record chain of title. [8 Cal.L.Rev.Comm. Reports 101 (1967).]

§ 1604. Certificate of purchase or of location of lands. A certificate of purchase, or of location, of any lands in this state, issued or made in pursuance of any law of the United States or of this state, is prima facie evidence that the holder or assignee of such certificate is the owner of the land described therein; but this evidence may be overcome by proof that, at the time of the location, or time of filing a preemption claim on which the certificate may have been issued, the land was in the adverse possession of the adverse party, or those under whom he claims, or that the adverse party is holding the land for mining purposes.

§ 1605. Authenticated Spanish title records. Duplicate copies and authenticated translations of original Spanish title papers relating to land claims in this state, derived from the Spanish or Mexican governments, prepared under the supervision of the Keeper of Archives, authenticated by the Surveyor-General or his successor and by the Keeper of Archives, and filed with a county recorder, in accordance with Chapter 281 of the Statutes of 1865-66, are admissible as evidence with like force and effect as the originals and without proving the execution of such originals. [*Amended 1967.*]

Law Revision Commission Comment - 1967 Amendment

Chapter 281 of the Statutes of 1865-66 required the California Secretary of State to cause copies to be made of all of the original Spanish title papers relating to land claims in this state derived from the Spanish and Mexican governments that were on file in the office of the United States Surveyor-General for California. These copies, authenticated by the Surveyor-General and the Keeper of Archives in his office, were then required to be recorded in the offices of the county recorders of the concerned counties.

Section 5 of the 1865-66 statute, which is now codified as Section 1605 of the Evidence Code, provided that the recorded copies would be admissible "as prima facie evidence" without proving the execution of the originals. It is apparent that the original purpose of the section was to provide an exception to the best evidence rule—which would have required production of the original or an excuse for its nonproduction before the recorded copy could be admitted—and an exception to the rule, now expressed in Evidence Code Section 1401(b), requiring the authentication of the original document as a condition of the admissibility of the copy. Section 1605, therefore, has been revised to reflect this original purpose [by substituting the words "are admissible as evidence" for "are receivable as prima facie evidence"]. [8 Cal.L.Rev.Comm. Reports 101 (1967).]

CONSTITUTION

Cal. Const. Art. I § 28(f)(2). Right to Truth-in-Evidence. Except as provided by statute hereafter enacted by a two-thirds vote of the membership in each house of the Legislature, relevant evidence shall not be excluded in any criminal proceeding, including pretrial and post conviction motions and hearings, or in any trial or hearing of a juvenile for a criminal offense, whether heard in juvenile or adult court. Nothing in this section shall affect any existing statutory rule of evidence relating to privilege or hearsay, or Evidence Code, Sections 352, 782 or 1103. Nothing in this section shall affect any existing statutory or constitutional right of the press. [*Added by initiative (Prop. 8), 1982.*]

Case Notes

This section, which exempts "any existing statutory or constitutional right of the press," preserves the newsperson's shield law (Cal. Const. art. I, § 2(b); Evid. Code § 1070) and, because of its specificity, takes precedence over provisions of Cal. Const. art. I, § 29, guaranteeing the People "due process of law" in criminal cases. Miller v. Superior Court, 21 Cal. 4th 883, 892-898, 89 Cal. Rptr. 2d 834, 840-844, 986 P.2d 170, 175-179 (1999).

For other cases interpreting Cal. Const. art. I, § 28(d), see Case Notes to §§ 786, 787, 788, 790, 1070, 1101(a).

Cal. Const. Art. I § 28(f)(4). Use of Prior Convictions. Any prior felony conviction of any person in any criminal proceeding, whether adult or juvenile, shall subsequently be used without limitation for purposes of impeachment or enhancement of sentence in any criminal proceeding. When a prior felony conviction is an element of any felony offense, it shall be proven to the trier of fact in open court. [*Added by initiative (Prop. 8), 1982.*]

Case Notes

Only felonies whose least adjudicated elements necessarily involve moral turpitude are admissible for impeachment purposes, and trial court has discretion under § 352 to exclude those that are unfairly prejudicial, see Cal. Const. art. I, § 28(d), *supra.* People v. Castro, 38 Cal. 3d 301, 211 Cal. Rptr. 719, 696 P.2d 111 (1985).

California follows Luce v. United States, 469 U.S. 38, 105 S.Ct. 460, 83 L.Ed. 2d 443 (1984), holding that denial of motion to exclude defendant's prior conviction for impeachment purposes is not reviewable on appeal if defendant fails to testify. People v. Collins, 42 Cal. 3d 378, 383-387, 228 Cal. Rptr. 899, 902-905, 722 P.2d 173, 176-179 (1986).